Comprehensive Natural Products Chemistry

Comprehensive Natural Products Chemistry

Editors-in-Chief

Sir Derek Barton†
Texas A&M University, USA

Koji Nakanishi
Columbia University, USA

Executive Editor

Otto Meth-Cohn
University of Sunderland, UK

Volume 9
CUMULATIVE INDEXES

1999

ELSEVIER

AMSTERDAM – LAUSANNE – NEW YORK – OXFORD – SHANNON – SINGAPORE – TOKYO

Elsevier Science Ltd., The Boulevard, Langford Lane, Kidlington, Oxford, OX5 1GB, UK

First edition 1999

Library of Congress Cataloging-in-Publication Data
Comprehensive natural products chemistry / editors-in-chief, Sir Derek Barton, Koji Nakanishi ; executive editor, Otto Meth-Cohn. -- 1st ed.
     p. cm.
   Includes index.
   Contents: v. 9. Cumulative indexes
   1. Natural products. I. Barton, Derek, Sir, 1918-1998. II. Nakanishi, Koji, 1925- . III. Meth-Cohn, Otto.
QD415.C63 1999
547.7--dc21   98-15249

British Library Cataloguing in Publication Data
Comprehensive natural products chemistry
   1. Organic compounds
   I. Barton, Sir Derek, 1918-1998 II. Nakanishi Koji III. Meth-Cohn Otto
   572.5

ISBN 0-08-042709-X (set : alk. paper)
ISBN 0-08-043161-5 (Volume 9 : alk. paper)

Typeset by BPC Digital Data Ltd., Glasgow, UK.
Printed and bound in Great Britain by BPC Wheatons Ltd., Exeter, UK.

Contents

Introduction   vii

Preface   ix

Sir Derek Barton (an obituary notice)   xi

Contributors to Volume 9   xiii

Abbreviations   xv

Contents of All Volumes   xix

An Historical Perspective of Natural Products Chemistry   xxi

Formula Index   1

Subject Index   71

Introduction

For many decades, Natural Products Chemistry has been the principal driving force for progress in Organic Chemistry.

In the past, the determination of structure was arduous and difficult. As soon as computing became easy, the application of X-ray crystallography to structural determination quickly surpassed all other methods. Supplemented by the equally remarkable progress made more recently by Nuclear Magnetic Resonance techniques, determination of structure has become a routine exercise. This is even true for enzymes and other molecules of a similar size. Not to be forgotten remains the progress in mass spectrometry which permits another approach to structure and, in particular, to the precise determination of molecular weight.

There have not been such revolutionary changes in the partial or total synthesis of Natural Products. This still requires effort, imagination and time. But remarkable syntheses have been accomplished and great progress has been made in stereoselective synthesis. However, the one hundred percent yield problem is only solved in certain steps in certain industrial processes. Thus there remains a great divide between the reactions carried out in living organisms and those that synthetic chemists attain in the laboratory. Of course Nature edits the accuracy of DNA, RNA, and protein synthesis in a way that does not apply to a multi-step Organic Synthesis.

Organic Synthesis has already a significant component that uses enzymes to carry out specific reactions. This applies particularly to lipases and to oxidation enzymes. We have therefore, given serious attention to enzymatic reactions.

No longer standing in the wings, but already on-stage, are the wonderful tools of Molecular Biology. It is now clear that multi-step syntheses can be carried out in one vessel using multiple cloned enzymes. Thus, Molecular Biology and Organic Synthesis will come together to make economically important Natural Products.

From these preliminary comments it is clear that Natural Products Chemistry continues to evolve in different directions interacting with physical methods, Biochemistry, and Molecular Biology all at the same time.

This new Comprehensive Series has been conceived with the common theme of "How does Nature make all these molecules of life?" The principal idea was to organize the multitude of facts in terms of Biosynthesis rather than structure. The work is not intended to be a comprehensive listing of natural products, nor is it intended that there should be any detail about biological activity. These kinds of information can be found elsewhere.

The work has been planned for eight volumes with one more volume for Indexes. As far as we are aware, a broad treatment of the whole of Natural Products Chemistry has never been attempted before. We trust that our efforts will be useful and informative to all scientific disciplines where Natural Products play a role.

D. H. R. Barton†   K. Nakanishi   O. Meth-Cohn

Preface

It is surprising indeed that this work is the first attempt to produce a "comprehensive" overview of Natural Products beyond the student text level. However, the awe-inspiring breadth of the topic, which in many respects is still only developing, is such as to make the job daunting to anyone in the field. Fools rush in where angels fear to tread and the particular fool in this case was myself, a lifelong enthusiast and reader of the subject but with no research base whatever in the field!

Having been involved in several of the *Comprehensive* works produced by Pergamon Press, this omission intrigued me and over a period of gestation I put together a rough outline of how such a work could be written and presented it to Pergamon. To my delight they agreed that the project was worthwhile and in short measure Derek Barton was approached and took on the challenge of fleshing out this framework with alacrity. He also brought his long-standing friend and outstanding contributor to the field, Koji Nakanishi, into the team. With Derek's knowledge of the whole field, the subject was broken down into eight volumes and an outstanding team of internationally recognised Volume Editors was appointed.

We used Derek's 80th birthday as a target for finalising the work. Sadly he died just a few months before reaching this milestone. This work therefore is dedicated to the memory of Sir Derek Barton, Natural Products being the area which he loved best of all.

OTTO METH-COHN
Executive Editor

SIR DEREK BARTON

Sir Derek Barton, who was Distinguished Professor of Chemistry at Texas A&M University and holder of the Dow Chair of Chemical Invention died on March 16, 1998 in College Station, Texas of heart failure. He was 79 years old and had been Chairman of the Executive Board of Editors for Tetrahedron Publications since 1979.

Barton was considered to be one of the greatest organic chemists of the twentieth century whose work continues to have a major influence on contemporary science and will continue to do so for future generations of chemists.

Derek Harold Richard Barton was born on September 8, 1918 in Gravesend, Kent, UK and graduated from Imperial College, London with the degrees of B.Sc. (1940) and Ph.D. (1942). He carried out work on military intelligence during World War II and after a brief period in industry, joined the faculty at Imperial College. It was an early indication of the breadth and depth of his chemical knowledge that his lectureship was in physical chemistry. This research led him into the mechanism of elimination reactions and to the concept of molecular rotation difference to correlate the configurations of steroid isomers. During a sabbatical leave at Harvard in 1949–1950 he published a paper on the "Conformation of the Steroid Nucleus" (*Experientia*, 1950, **6**, 316) which was to bring him the Nobel Prize in Chemistry in 1969, shared with the Norwegian chemist, Odd Hassel. This key paper (only four pages long) altered the way in which chemists thought about the shape and reactivity of molecules, since it showed how the reactivity of functional groups in steroids depends on their axial or equatorial positions in a given conformation. Returning to the UK he held Chairs of Chemistry at Birkbeck College and Glasgow University before returning to Imperial College in 1957, where he developed a remarkable synthesis of the steroid hormone, aldosterone, by a photochemical reaction known as the Barton Reaction (nitrite photolysis). In 1978 he retired from Imperial College and became Director of the Natural Products Institute (CNRS) at Gif-sur-Yvette in France where he studied the invention of new chemical reactions, especially the chemistry of radicals, which opened up a whole new area of organic synthesis involving Gif chemistry. In 1986 he moved to a third career at Texas A&M University as Distinguished Professor of Chemistry and continued to work on novel reactions involving radical chemistry and the oxidation of hydrocarbons, which has become of great industrial importance. In a research career spanning more than five decades, Barton's contributions to organic chemistry included major discoveries which have profoundly altered our way of thinking about chemical structure and reactivity. His chemistry has provided models for the biochemical synthesis of natural products including alkaloids, antibiotics, carbohydrates, and DNA. Most recently his discoveries led to models for enzymes which oxidize hydrocarbons, including methane monooxygenase.

The following are selected highlights from his published work:

The 1950 paper which launched Conformational Analysis was recognized by the Nobel Prize Committee as the key contribution whereby the third dimension was added to chemistry. This work alone transformed our thinking about the connection between stereochemistry and reactivity, and was later adapted from small molecules to macromolecules e.g., DNA, and to inorganic complexes.

Barton's breadth and influence is illustrated in "Biogenetic Aspects of Phenol Oxidation" (*Festschr. Arthur Stoll*, 1957, 117). This theoretical work led to many later experiments on alkaloid biosynthesis and to a set of rules for *ortho-para*-phenolic oxidative coupling which allowed the predication of new natural product systems before they were actually discovered and to the correction of several erroneous structures.

In 1960, his paper on the remarkably short synthesis of the steroid hormone aldosterone (*J. Am. Chem. Soc.*, 1960, **82**, 2641) disclosed the first of many inventions of new reactions—in this case nitrite photolysis—to achieve short, high yielding processes, many of which have been patented and are used worldwide in the pharmaceutical industry.

Moving to 1975, by which time some 500 papers had been published, yet another "Barton reaction" was born—"The Deoxygenation of Secondary Alcohols" (*J. Chem. Soc. Perkin Trans. 1*, 1975, 1574), which has been very widely applied due to its tolerance of quite hostile and complex local environments in carbohydrate and nucleoside chemistry. This reaction is the chemical counterpart to ribonucleotide® deoxyribonucleotide reductase in biochemistry and, until the arrival of the Barton reaction, was virtually impossible to achieve.

In 1985, "Invention of a New Radical Chain Reaction" involved the generation of carbon radicals from carboxylic acids (*Tetrahedron*, 1985, **41**, 3901). The method is of great synthetic utility and has been used many times by others in the burgeoning area of radicals in organic synthesis.

These recent advances in synthetic methodology were remarkable since his chemistry had virtually no precedent in the work of others. The radical methodology was especially timely in light of the significant recent increase in applications for fine chemical syntheses, and Barton gave the organic community an entrée into what will prove to be one of the most important methods of the twenty-first century. He often said how proud he was, at age 71, to receive the ACS Award for Creativity in Organic Synthesis for work published in the preceding five years.

Much of Barton's more recent work is summarized in the articles "The Invention of Chemical Reactions—The Last 5 Years" (*Tetrahedron*, 1992, **48**, 2529) and "Recent Developments in Gif Chemistry" (*Pure Appl. Chem.*, 1997, **69**, 1941).

Working 12 hours a day, Barton's stamina and creativity remained undiminished to the day of his death. The author of more than 1000 papers in chemical journals, Barton also held many successful patents. In addition to the Nobel Prize he received many honors and awards including the Davy, Copley, and Royal medals of the Royal Society of London, and the Roger Adams and Priestley Medals of the American Chemical Society. He held honorary degrees from 34 universities. He was a Fellow of the Royal Societies of London and Edinburgh, Foreign Associate of the National Academy of Sciences (USA), and Foreign Member of the Russian and Chinese Academies of Sciences. He was knighted by Queen Elizabeth in 1972, received the Légion d'Honneur (Chevalier 1972; Officier 1985) from France, and the Order of the Rising Sun from the Emperor of Japan. In his long career, Sir Derek trained over 300 students and postdoctoral fellows, many of whom now hold major positions throughout the world and include some of today's most distinguished organic chemists.

For those of us who were fortunate to know Sir Derek personally there is no doubt that his genius and work ethic were unique. He gave generously of his time to students and colleagues wherever he traveled and engendered such great respect and loyalty in his students and co-workers, that major symposia accompanied his birthdays every five years beginning with the 60th, ending this year with two celebrations just before his 80th birthday.

With the death of Sir Derek Barton, the world of science has lost a major figure, who together with Sir Robert Robinson and Robert B. Woodward, the cofounders of *Tetrahedron*, changed the face of organic chemistry in the twentieth century.

Professor Barton is survived by his wife, Judy, and by a son, William from his first marriage, and three grandchildren.

A. I. SCOTT
Texas A&M University

Reprinted from *Tetrahedron*, 1998, **54**, 8847

Photograph courtesy of Library and Information Centre, Royal Society of Chemistry. © The Nobel Foundation

Contributors to Volume 9

Mrs. L. Aslett
4 Orchard Road, Marlborough, Wiltshire, SN8 4AU, UK

Mr. P. Aslett
4 Orchard Road, Marlborough, Wiltshire, SN8 4AU, UK

Dr J. Newton
David John Services Ltd., 221 Wentworth Avenue, Farnham Royal, Slough, SL2 2AP, UK

Abbreviations

The most commonly used abbreviations in *Comprehensive Natural Products Chemistry* are listed below. Please note that in some instances these may differ from those used in other branches of chemistry

A	adenine
ABA	abscisic acid
Ac	acetyl
ACAC	acetylacetonate
ACTH	adrenocorticotropic hormone
ADP	adenosine 5'-diphosphate
AIBN	2,2'-azobisisobutyronitrile
Ala	alanine
AMP	adenosine 5'-monophosphate
APS	adenosine 5'-phosphosulfate
Ar	aryl
Arg	arginine
ATP	adenosine 5'-triphosphate
B	nucleoside base (adenine, cylosine, guanine, thymine or uracil)
9-BBN	9-borabicyclo[3.3.1]nonane
BOC	*t*-butoxycarbonyl (or carbo-*t*-butoxy)
BSA	*N,O*-bis(trimethylsilyl)acetamide
BSTFA	*N,O*-bis(trimethylsilyl)trifluoroacetamide
Bu	butyl
Bu^n	*n*-butyl
Bu^i	isobutyl
Bu^s	*s*-butyl
Bu^t	*t*-butyl
Bz	benzoyl
CAN	ceric ammonium nitrate
CD	cyclodextrin
CDP	cytidine 5'-diphosphate
CMP	cytidine 5'-monophosphate
CoA	coenzyme A
COD	cyclooctadiene
COT	cyclooctatetraene
Cp	h^5-cyclopentadiene
Cp*	pentamethylcyclopentadiene
12-Crown-4	1,4,7,10-tetraoxacyclododecane
15-Crown-5	1,4,7,10,13-pentaoxacyclopentadecane
18-Crown-6	1,4,7,10,13,16-hexaoxacyclooctadecane
CSA	camphorsulfonic acid
CSI	chlorosulfonyl isocyanate
CTP	cytidine 5'-triphosphate
cyclic AMP	adenosine 3',5'-cyclic monophosphoric acid
CySH	cysteine
DABCO	1,4-diazabicyclo[2.2.2]octane
DBA	dibenz[*a,h*]anthracene
DBN	1,5-diazabicyclo[4.3.0]non-5-ene

DBU	1,8-diazabicyclo[5.4.0]undec-7-ene
DCC	dicyclohexylcarbodiimide
DEAC	diethylaluminum chloride
DEAD	diethyl azodicarboxylate
DET	diethyl tartrate (+ or -)
DHET	dihydroergotoxine
DIBAH	diisobutylaluminum hydride
Diglyme	diethylene glycol dimethyl ether (or bis(2-methoxyethyl)ether)
DiHPhe	2,5-dihydroxyphenylalanine
Dimsyl Na	sodium methylsulfinylmethide
DIOP	2,3-*O*-isopropylidene-2,3-dihydroxy-1,4-bis(diphenylphosphino)butane
dipt	diisopropyl tartrate (+ or -)
DMA	dimethylacetamide
DMAD	dimethyl acetylenedicarboxylate
DMAP	4-dimethylaminopyridine
DME	1,2-dimethoxyethane (glyme)
DMF	dimethylformamide
DMF-DMA	dimethylformamide dimethyl acetal
DMI	1,3-dimethyl-2-imidazalidinone
DMSO	dimethyl sulfoxide
DMTSF	dimethyl(methylthio)sulfonium fluoroborate
DNA	deoxyribonucleic acid
DOCA	deoxycorticosterone acetate
EADC	ethylaluminum dichloride
EDTA	ethylenediaminetetraacetic acid
EEDQ	*N*-ethoxycarbonyl-2-ethoxy-1,2-dihydroquinoline
Et	ethyl
EVK	ethyl vinyl ketone
FAD	flavin adenine dinucleotide
Fl	flavin
FMN	flavin mononucleotide
G	guanine
GABA	4-aminobutyric acid
GDP	guanosine 5'-diphosphate
GLDH	glutamate dehydrogenase
gln	glutamine
Glu	glutamic acid
Gly	glycine
GMP	guanosine 5'-monophosphate
GOD	glucose oxidase
G-6-P	glucose-6-phosphate
GTP	guanosine 5'-triphosphate
Hb	hemoglobin
His	histidine
HMPA	hexamethylphosphoramide (or hexamethylphosphorous triamide)
Ile	isoleucine
INAH	isonicotinic acid hydrazide
IpcBH	isopinocampheylborane
Ipc$_2$BH	diisopinocampheylborane
KAPA	potassium 3-aminopropylamide
K-Slectride	potassium tri-*s*-butylborohydride

LAH	lithium aluminum hydride
LAP	leucine aminopeptidase
LDA	lithium diisopropylamide
LDH	lactic dehydrogenase
Leu	leucine
LICA	lithium isopropylcyclohexylamide
L-Selectride	lithium tri-*s*-butylborohydride
LTA	lead tetraacetate
Lys	lysine
MCPBA	*m*-chloroperoxybenzoic acid
Me	methyl
MEM	methoxyethoxymethyl
MEM-Cl	ß-methoxyethoxymethyl chloride
Met	methionine
MMA	methyl methacrylate
MMC	methyl magnesium carbonate
MOM	methoxymethyl
Ms	mesyl (or methanesulfonyl)
MSA	methanesulfonic acid
MsCl	methanesulfonyl chloride
MVK	methyl vinyl ketone
NAAD	nicotinic acid adenine dinucleotide
NAD	nicotinamide adenine dinucleotide
NADH	nicotinamide adenine dinucleotide phosphate, reduced
NBS	*N*-bromosuccinimider
NMO	*N*-methylmorpholine *N*-oxide monohydrate
NMP	*N*-methylpyrrolidone
PCBA	*p*-chlorobenzoic acid
PCBC	*p*-chlorobenzyl chloride
PCBN	*p*-chlorobenzonitrile
PCBTF	*p*-chlorobenzotrifluoride
PCC	pyridinium chlorochromate
PDC	pyridinium dichromate
PG	prostaglandin
Ph	phenyl
Phe	phenylalanine
Phth	phthaloyl
PPA	polyphosphoric acid
PPE	polyphosphate ester (or ethyl *m*-phosphate)
Pr	propyl
Pr^i	isopropyl
Pro	proline
Py	pyridine
RNA	ribonucleic acid
Rnase	ribonuclease
Ser	serine
Sia$_2$BH	disiamylborane
TAS	tris(diethylamino)sulfonium
TBAF	tetra-*n*-butylammonium fluoroborate
TBDMS	*t*-butyldimethylsilyl
TBDMS-Cl	*t*-butyldimethylsilyl chloride
TBDPS	*t*-butyldiphenylsilyl
TCNE	tetracyanoethene

TES	triethylsilyl
TFA	trifluoracetic acid
TFAA	trifluoroacetic anhydride
THF	tetrahydrofuran
THF	tetrahydrofolic acid
THP	tetrahydropyran (or tetrahydropyranyl)
Thr	threonine
TMEDA	*N,N,N',N'*,tetramethylethylenediamine[1,2-bis(dimethylamino)ethane]
TMS	trimethylsilyl
TMS-Cl	trimethylsilyl chloride
TMS-CN	trimethylsilyl cyanide
Tol	toluene
TosMIC	tosylmethyl isocyanide
TPP	tetraphenylporphyrin
Tr	trityl (or triphenylmethyl)
Trp	tryptophan
Ts	tosyl (or *p*-toluenesulfonyl)
TTFA	thallium trifluoroacetate
TTN	thallium(III) nitrate
Tyr	tyrosine
Tyr-OMe	tyrosine methyl ester
U	uridine
UDP	uridine 5'-diphosphate
UMP	uridine 5'-monophosphate

Contents of All Volumes

Volume 1   Polyketides and Other Secondary Metabolites Including Fatty Acids and Their Derivatives

Volume 2   Isoprenoids Including Carotenoids and Steroids

Volume 3   Carbohydrates and Their Derivatives Including Tannins, Cellulose, and Related Lignins

Volume 4   Amino Acids, Peptides, Porphyrins, and Alkaloids

Volume 5   Enzymes, Enzyme Mechanisms, Proteins, and Aspects of NO Chemistry

Volume 6   Prebiotic Chemistry, Molecular Fossils, Nucleosides, and RNA

Volume 7   DNA and Aspects of Molecular Biology

Volume 8   Miscellaneous Natural Products Including Marine Natural Products, Pheromones, Plant Hormones, and Aspects of Ecology

Volume 9   Cumulative Indexes

An Historical Perspective of Natural Products Chemistry

KOJI NAKANISHI

Columbia University, New York, USA

To give an account of the rich history of natural products chemistry in a short essay is a daunting task. This brief outline begins with a description of ancient folk medicine and continues with an outline of some of the major conceptual and experimental advances that have been made from the early nineteenth century through to about 1960, the start of the modern era of natural products chemistry. Achievements of living chemists are noted only minimally, usually in the context of related topics within the text. More recent developments are reviewed within the individual chapters of the present volumes, written by experts in each field. The subheadings follow, in part, the sequence of topics presented in Volumes 1–8.

1. ETHNOBOTANY AND "NATURAL PRODUCTS CHEMISTRY"

Except for minerals and synthetic materials our surroundings consist entirely of organic natural products, either of prebiotic organic origins or from microbial, plant, or animal sources. These materials include polyketides, terpenoids, amino acids, proteins, carbohydrates, lipids, nucleic acid bases, RNA and DNA, etc. Natural products chemistry can be thought of as originating from mankind's curiosity about odor, taste, color, and cures for diseases. Folk interest in treatments for pain, for food-poisoning and other maladies, and in hallucinogens appears to go back to the dawn of humanity

For centuries China has led the world in the use of natural products for healing. One of the earliest health science anthologies in China is the Nei Ching, whose authorship is attributed to the legendary Yellow Emperor (thirtieth century BC), although it is said that the dates were backdated from the third century by compilers. Excavation of a Han Dynasty (206 BC–AD 220) tomb in Hunan Province in 1974 unearthed decayed books, written on silk, bamboo, and wood, which filled a critical gap between the dawn of medicine up to the classic Nei Ching; Book 5 of these excavated documents lists 151 medical materials of plant origin. Generally regarded as the oldest compilation of Chinese herbs is Shen Nung Pen Ts'ao Ching (Catalog of Herbs by Shen Nung), which is believed to have been revised during the Han Dynasty; it lists 365 materials. Numerous revisions and enlargements of Pen Ts'ao were undertaken by physicians in subsequent dynasties, the ultimate being the Pen Ts'ao Kang Mu (General Catalog of Herbs) written by Li Shih-Chen over a period of 27 years during the Ming Dynasty (1573–1620), which records 1898 herbal drugs and 8160 prescriptions. This was circulated in Japan around 1620 and translated, and has made a huge impact on subsequent herbal studies in Japan; however, it has not been translated into English. The number of medicinal herbs used in 1979 in China numbered 5267. One of the most famous of the Chinese folk herbs is the ginseng root *Panax ginseng*, used for health maintenance and treatment of various diseases. The active principles were thought to be the saponins called ginsenosides but this is now doubtful; the effects could well be synergistic between saponins, flavonoids, etc. Another popular folk drug, the extract of the Ginkgo tree, *Ginkgo biloba* L., the only surviving species of the Paleozoic era (250 million years ago) family which became extinct during the last few million years, is mentioned in the Chinese Materia Medica to have an effect in improving memory and sharpening mental alertness. The main constituents responsible for this are now understood to be ginkgolides and flavonoids, but again not much else is known. Clarifying the active constituents and mode of (synergistic) bioactivity of Chinese herbs is a challenging task that has yet to be fully addressed.

The Assyrians left 660 clay tablets describing 1000 medicinal plants used around 1900–400 BC, but the best insight into ancient pharmacy is provided by the two scripts left by the ancient Egyptians, who

were masters of human anatomy and surgery because of their extensive mummification practices. The Edwin Smith Surgical Papyrus purchased by Smith in 1862 in Luxor (now in the New York Academy of Sciences collection), is one of the most important medicinal documents of the ancient Nile Valley, and describes the healer's involvement in surgery, prescription, and healing practices using plants, animals, and minerals. The Ebers Papyrus, also purchased by Edwin Smith in 1862, and then acquired by Egyptologist George Ebers in 1872, describes 800 remedies using plants, animals, minerals, and magic. Indian medicine also has a long history, possibly dating back to the second millennium BC. The Indian materia medica consisted mainly of vegetable drugs prepared from plants but also used animals, bones, and minerals such as sulfur, arsenic, lead, copper sulfate, and gold. Ancient Greece inherited much from Egypt, India, and China, and underwent a gradual transition from magic to science. Pythagoras (580–500 BC) influenced the medical thinkers of his time, including Aristotle (384–322 BC), who in turn affected the medical practices of another influential Greek physician Galen (129–216). The Iranian physician Avicenna (980–1037) is noted for his contributions to Aristotelian philosophy and medicine, while the German-Swiss physician and alchemist Paracelsus (1493–1541) was an early champion who established the role of chemistry in medicine.

The rainforests in Central and South America and Africa are known to be particularly abundant in various organisms of interest to our lives because of their rich biodiversity, intense competition, and the necessity for self-defense. However, since folk-treatments are transmitted verbally to the next generation via shamans who naturally have a tendency to keep their plant and animal sources confidential, the recipes tend to get lost, particularly with destruction of rainforests and the encroachment of "civilization." Studies on folk medicine, hallucinogens, and shamanism of the Central and South American Indians conducted by Richard Schultes (Harvard Botanical Museum, emeritus) have led to renewed activity by ethnobotanists, recording the knowledge of shamans, assembling herbaria, and transmitting the record of learning to the village.

Extracts of toxic plants and animals have been used throughout the world for thousands of years for hunting and murder. These include the various arrow poisons used all over the world. *Strychnos* and *Chondrodendron* (containing strychnine, etc.) were used in South America and called "curare," *Strophanthus* (strophantidine, etc.) was used in Africa, the latex of the upas tree *Antiaris toxicaria* (cardiac glycosides) was used in Java, while *Aconitum napellus*, which appears in Greek mythology (aconitine) was used in medieval Europe and Hokkaido (by the Ainus). The Colombian arrow poison is from frogs (batrachotoxins; 200 toxins have been isolated from frogs by B. Witkop and J. Daly at NIH). Extracts of *Hyoscyamus niger* and *Atropa belladonna* contain the toxic tropane alkaloids, for example hyoscyamine, belladonnine, and atropine. The belladonna berry juice (atropine) which dilates the eye pupils was used during the Renaissance by ladies to produce doe-like eyes (belladona means beautiful woman). The Efik people in Calabar, southeastern Nigeria, used extracts of the calabar bean known as esere (physostigmine) for unmasking witches. The ancient Egyptians and Chinese knew of the toxic effect of the puffer fish, fugu, which contains the neurotoxin tetrodotoxin (Y. Hirata, K. Tsuda, R. B. Woodward).

When rye is infected by the fungus *Claviceps purpurea*, the toxin ergotamine and a number of ergot alkaloids are produced. These cause ergotism or the "devil's curse," "St. Anthony's fire," which leads to convulsions, miscarriages, loss of arms and legs, dry gangrene, and death. Epidemics of ergotism occurred in medieval times in villages throughout Europe, killing tens of thousands of people and livestock; Julius Caesar's legions were destroyed by ergotism during a campaign in Gaul, while in AD 994 an estimated 50,000 people died in an epidemic in France. As recently as 1926, a total of 11,000 cases of ergotism were reported in a region close to the Urals. It has been suggested that the witch hysteria that occurred in Salem, Massachusetts, might have been due to a mild outbreak of ergotism. Lysergic acid diethylamide (LSD) was first prepared by A. Hofmann, Sandoz Laboratories, Basel, in 1943 during efforts to improve the physiological effects of the ergot alkaloids when he accidentally inhaled it. "On Friday afternoon, April 16, 1943," he wrote, "I was seized by a sensation of restlessness... ." He went home from the laboratory and "perceived an uninterrupted stream of fantastic dreams ... ." (*Helvetica Chimica Acta*).

Numerous psychedelic plants have been used since ancient times, producing visions, mystical fantasies (cats and tigers also seem to have fantasies?, see nepetalactone below), sensations of flying, glorious feelings in warriors before battle, etc. The ethnobotanists Wasson and Schultes identified "ololiqui," an important Aztec concoction, as the seeds of the morning glory *Rivea corymbosa* and gave the seeds to Hofmann who found that they contained lysergic acid amides similar to but less potent than LSD. Iboga, a powerful hallucinogen from the root of the African shrub *Tabernanthe iboga*, is used by the Bwiti cult in Central Africa who chew the roots to obtain relief from fatigue and hunger; it contains the alkaloid ibogamine. The powerful hallucinogen used for thousands of years by the American Indians, the peyote cactus, contains mescaline and other alkaloids. The Indian hemp plant, *Cannabis sativa*, has been used for making rope since 3000 BC, but when it is used for its pleasure-giving effects it is called

cannabis and has been known in central Asia, China, India, and the Near East since ancient times. Marijuana, hashish (named after the Persian founder of the Assassins of the eleventh century, Hasan-e Sabbah), charas, ghanja, bhang, kef, and dagga are names given to various preparations of the hemp plant. The constituent responsible for the mind-altering effect is 1-tetrahydrocannabinol (also referred to as 9-THC) contained in 1%. R. Mechoulam (1930–, Hebrew University) has been the principal worker in the cannabinoids, including structure determination and synthesis of 9-THC (1964 to present); the Israeli police have also made a contribution by providing Mechoulam with a constant supply of marijuana. Opium (morphine) is another ancient drug used for a variety of pain-relievers and it is documented that the Sumerians used poppy as early as 4000 BC; the narcotic effect is present only in seeds before they are fully formed. The irritating secretion of the blister beetles, for example *Mylabris* and the European species *Lytta vesicatoria*, commonly called Spanish fly, was used medically as a topical skin irritant to remove warts but was also a major ingredient in so-called love potions (constituent is cantharidin, stereospecific synthesis in 1951, G. Stork, 1921–; prep. scale high-pressure Diels–Alder synthesis in 1985, W. G. Dauben, 1919–1996).

Plants have been used for centuries for the treatment of heart problems, the most important being the foxgloves *Digitalis purpurea* and *D. lanata* (digitalin, diginin) and *Strophanthus gratus* (ouabain). The bark of cinchona *Cinchona officinalis* (called quina-quina by the Indians) has been used widely among the Indians in the Andes against malaria, which is still one of the major infectious diseases; its most important alkaloid is quinine. The British protected themselves against malaria during the occupation of India through gin and tonic (quinine!). The stimulant coca, used by the Incas around the tenth century, was introduced into Europe by the conquistadors; coca beans are also commonly chewed in West Africa. Wine making was already practiced in the Middle East 6000–8000 years ago; Moors made date wines, the Japanese rice wine, the Vikings honey mead, the Incas maize chicha. It is said that the Babylonians made beer using yeast 5000–6000 years ago. As shown above in parentheses, alkaloids are the major constituents of the herbal plants and extracts used for centuries, but it was not until the early nineteenth century that the active principles were isolated in pure form, for example morphine (1816), strychnine (1817), atropine (1819), quinine (1820), and colchicine (1820). It was a century later that the structures of these compounds were finally elucidated.

2. DAWN OF ORGANIC CHEMISTRY, EARLY STRUCTURAL STUDIES, MODERN METHODOLOGY

The term "organic compound" to define compounds made by and isolated from living organisms was coined in 1807 by the Swedish chemist Jons Jacob Berzelius (1779–1848), a founder of today's chemistry, who developed the modern system of symbols and formulas in chemistry, made a remarkably accurate table of atomic weights and analyzed many chemicals. At that time it was considered that organic compounds could not be synthesized from inorganic materials *in vitro*. However, Friedrich Wöhler (1800–1882), a medical doctor from Heidelberg who was starting his chemical career at a technical school in Berlin, attempted in 1828 to make "ammonium cyanate," which had been assigned a wrong structure, by heating the two inorganic salts potassium cyanate and ammonium sulfate; this led to the unexpected isolation of white crystals which were identical to the urea from urine, a typical organic compound. This well-known incident marked the beginning of organic chemistry. With the preparation of acetic acid from inorganic material in 1845 by Hermann Kolbe (1818–1884) at Leipzig, the myth surrounding organic compounds, in which they were associated with some vitalism was brought to an end and organic chemistry became the chemistry of carbon compounds. The same Kolbe was involved in the development of aspirin, one of the earliest and most important success stories in natural products chemistry. Salicylic acid from the leaf of the wintergreen plant had long been used as a pain reliever, especially in treating arthritis and gout. The inexpensive synthesis of salicylic acid from sodium phenolate and carbon dioxide by Kolbe in 1859 led to the industrial production in 1893 by the Bayer Company of acetylsalicylic acid "aspirin," still one of the most popular drugs. Aspirin is less acidic than salicylic acid and therefore causes less irritation in the mouth, throat, and stomach. The remarkable mechanism of the anti-inflammatory effect of aspirin was clarified in 1974 by John Vane (1927–) who showed that it inhibits the biosynthesis of prostaglandins by irreversibly acetylating a serine residue in prostaglandin synthase. Vane shared the 1982 Nobel Prize with Bergström and Samuelsson who determined the structure of prostaglandins (see below).

In the early days, natural products chemistry was focused on isolating the more readily available plant and animal constituents and determining their structures. The course of structure determination in the 1940s was a complex, indirect process, combining evidence from many types of experiments. The first

effort was to crystallize the unknown compound or make derivatives such as esters or 2,4-dinitrophenylhydrazones, and to repeat recrystallization until the highest and sharp melting point was reached, since prior to the advent of isolation and purification methods now taken for granted, there was no simple criterion for purity.   The only chromatography was through special grade alumina (first used by M. Tswett in 1906, then reintroduced by R. Willstätter). Molecular weight estimation by the Rast method which depended on melting point depression of a sample/camphor mixture, coupled with Pregl elemental microanalysis (see below) gave the molecular formula.   Functionalities such as hydroxyl, amino, and carbonyl groups were recognized on the basis of specific derivatization and crystallization, followed by redetermination of molecular formula; the change in molecular composition led to identification of the functionality.   Thus, sterically hindered carbonyls, for example the 11-keto group of cortisone, or tertiary hydroxyls, were very difficult to pinpoint, and often had to depend on more searching experiments.   Therefore, an entire paper describing the recognition of a single hydroxyl group in a complex natural product would occasionally appear in the literature.   An oxygen function suggested from the molecular formula but left unaccounted for would usually be assigned to an ether.

Determination of C-methyl groups depended on Kuhn–Roth oxidation which is performed by drastic oxidation with chromic acid/sulfuric acid, reduction of excess oxidant with hydrazine, neutralization with alkali, addition of phosphoric acid, distillation of the acetic acid originating from the C-methyls, and finally its titration with alkali.   However, the results were only approximate, since *gem*-dimethyl groups only yield one equivalent of acetic acid, while primary, secondary, and tertiary methyl groups all give different yields of acetic acid.   The skeletal structure of polycyclic compounds were frequently deduced on the basis of dehydrogenation reactions.   It is therefore not surprising that the original steroid skeleton put forth by Wieland and Windaus in 1928, which depended a great deal on the production of chrysene upon Pd/C dehydrogenation, had to be revised in 1932 after several discrepancies were found (they received the Nobel prizes in 1927 and 1928 for this "extraordinarily difficult structure determination," see below).

In the following are listed some of the Nobel prizes awarded for the development of methodologies which have contributed critically to the progress in isolation protocols and structure determination.   The year in which each prize was awarded is preceded by "Np."

Fritz Pregl, 1869–1930, Graz University, Np 1923. Invention of carbon and hydrogen microanalysis.   Improvement of Kuhlmann's microbalance enabled weighing at an accuracy of 1 µg over a 20 g range, and refinement of carbon and hydrogen analytical methods made it possible to perform analysis with 3–4 mg of sample.   His microbalance and the monograph *Quantitative Organic Microanalysis* (1916) profoundly influenced subsequent developments in practically all fields of chemistry and medicine.

The Svedberg, 1884–1971, Uppsala, Np 1926. Uppsala was a center for quantitative work on colloids for which the prize was awarded.   His extensive study on ultracentrifugation, the first paper of which was published in the year of the award, evolved from a spring visit in 1922 to the University of Wisconsin.   The ultracentrifuge together with the electrophoresis technique developed by his student Tiselius, have profoundly influenced subsequent progress in molecular biology and biochemistry.

Arne Tiselius, 1902–1971, Ph.D. Uppsala (T. Svedberg), Uppsala, Np 1948. Assisted by a grant from the Rockefeller Foundation, Tiselius was able to use his early electrophoresis instrument to show four bands in horse blood serum, alpha, beta and gamma globulins in addition to albumin; the first paper published in 1937 brought immediate positive responses.

Archer Martin, 1910–, Ph.D. Cambridge; Medical Research Council, Mill Hill, and Richard Synge, 1914–1994, Ph.D. Cambridge; Rowett Research Institute, Food Research Institute, Np 1952. They developed chromatography using two immiscible phases, gas–liquid, liquid–liquid, and paper chromatography, all of which have profoundly influenced all phases of chemistry.

Frederick Sanger, 1918–, Ph.D. Cambridge (A. Neuberger), Medical Research Council, Cambridge, Np 1958 and 1980. His confrontation with challenging structural problems in proteins and nucleic acids led to the development of two general analytical methods, 1,2,4-fluorodinitrobenzene (DNP) for tagging free amino groups (1945) in connection with insulin sequencing studies, and the dideoxynucleotide method for sequencing DNA (1977) in connection with recombinant DNA.   For the latter he received his second Np in chemistry in 1980, which was shared with Paul Berg (1926–, Stanford University) and Walter Gilbert (1932–, Harvard University) for their contributions, respectively, in recombinant DNA and chemical sequencing of DNA.   The studies of insulin involved usage of DNP for tagging disulfide bonds as cysteic acid residues (1949), and paper chromatography introduced by Martin and Synge 1944.   That it was the first elucidation of any protein structure lowered the barrier for future structure studies of proteins.

Stanford Moore, 1913–1982, Ph.D. Wisconsin (K. P. Link), Rockefeller, Np 1972; and William Stein, 1911–1980, Ph.D. Columbia (E. G. Miller); Rockefeller, Np 1972.   Moore and Stein cooperatively developed methods for the rapid quantification of protein hydrolysates by combining partition chroma-

tography, ninhydrin coloration, and drop-counting fraction collector, i.e., the basis for commercial amino acid analyzers, and applied them to analysis of the ribonuclease structure.

Bruce Merrifield, 1921–, Ph.D. UCLA (M. Dunn), Rockefeller, Np 1984. The concept of solid-phase peptide synthesis using porous beads, chromatographic columns, and sequential elongation of peptides and other chains revolutionized the synthesis of biopolymers.

High-performance liquid chromatography (HPLC), introduced around the mid-1960s and now coupled on-line to many analytical instruments, for example UV, FTIR, and MS, is an indispensable daily tool found in all natural products chemistry laboratories.

3. STRUCTURES OF ORGANIC COMPOUNDS, NINETEENTH CENTURY

The discoveries made from 1848 to 1874 by Pasteur, Kekulé, van't Hoff, Le Bel, and others led to a revolution in structural organic chemistry. Louis Pasteur (1822–1895) was puzzled about why the potassium salt of tartaric acid (deposited on wine casks during fermentation) was dextrorotatory while the sodium ammonium salt of racemic acid (also deposited on wine casks) was optically inactive although both tartaric acid and "racemic" acid had identical chemical compositions. In 1848, the 25 year old Pasteur examined the racemic acid salt under the microscope and found two kinds of crystals exhibiting a left- and right-hand relation. Upon separation of the left-handed and right-handed crystals, he found that they rotated the plane of polarized light in opposite directions. He had thus performed his famous resolution of a racemic mixture, and had demonstrated the phenomenon of chirality. Pasteur went on to show that the racemic acid formed two kinds of salts with optically active bases such as quinine; this was the first demonstration of diastereomeric resolution. From this work Pasteur concluded that tartaric acid must have an element of asymmetry within the molecule itself. However, a three-dimensional understanding of the enantiomeric pair was only solved 25 years later (see below). Pasteur's own interest shifted to microbiology where he made the crucial discovery of the involvement of "germs" or microorganisms in various processes and proved that yeast induces alcoholic fermentation, while other microorganisms lead to diseases; he thus saved the wine industries of France, originated the process known as "pasteurization," and later developed vaccines for rabies. He was a genius who made many fundamental discoveries in chemistry and in microbiology.

The structures of organic compounds were still totally mysterious. Although Wöhler had synthesized urea, an isomer of ammonium cyanate, in 1828, the structural difference between these isomers was not known. In 1858 August Kekulé (1829–1896; studied with André Dumas and C. A. Wurtz in Paris, taught at Ghent, Heidelberg, and Bonn) published his famous paper in Liebig's *Annalen der Chemie* on the structure of carbon, in which he proposed that carbon atoms could form C–C bonds with hydrogen and other atoms linked to them; his dream on the top deck of a London bus led him to this concept. It was Butlerov who introduced the term "structure theory" in 1861. Further, in 1865 Kekulé conceived the cyclo-hexa-1:3:5-triene structure for benzene (C_6H_6) from a dream of a snake biting its own tail. In 1874, two young chemists, van't Hoff (1852–1911, Np 1901) in Utrecht, and Le Bel (1847–1930) in Paris, who had met in 1874 as students of C. A. Wurtz, published the revolutionary three-dimensional (3D) structure of the tetrahedral carbon Cabcd to explain the enantiomeric behavior of Pasteur's salts. The model was welcomed by J. Wislicenus (1835–1902, Zürich, Würzburg, Leipzig) who in 1863 had demonstrated the enantiomeric nature of the two lactic acids found by Scheele in sour milk (1780) and by Berzelius in muscle tissue (1807). This model, however, was criticized by Hermann Kolbe (1818–1884, Leipzig) as an "ingenious but in reality trivial and senseless natural philosophy." After 10 years of heated controversy, the idea of tetrahedral carbon was fully accepted, Kolbe had died and Wislicenus succeeded him in Leipzig.

Emil Fischer (1852–1919, Np 1902) was the next to make a critical contribution to stereochemistry. From the work of van't Hoff and Le Bel he reasoned that glucose should have 16 stereoisomers. Fischer's doctorate work on hydrazines under Baeyer (1835–1917, Np 1905) at Strasbourg had led to studies of osazones which culminated in the brilliant establishment, including configurations, of the Fischer sugar tree starting from D-(+)-glyceraldehyde all the way up to the aldohexoses, allose, altrose, glucose, mannose, gulose, idose, galactose, and talose (from 1884 to 1890). Unfortunately Fischer suffered from the toxic effects of phenylhydrazine for 12 years. The arbitrarily but luckily chosen absolute configuration of D-(+)-glyceraldehyde was shown to be correct sixty years later in 1951 (Johannes-Martin Bijvoet, 1892–1980). Fischer's brilliant correlation of the sugars comprising the Fischer sugar tree was performed using the Kiliani (1855–1945)–Fischer method via cyanohydrin intermediates for elongating sugars. Fischer also made remarkable contributions to the chemistry of amino acids and to nucleic acid bases (see below).

4. STRUCTURES OF ORGANIC COMPOUNDS, TWENTIETH CENTURY

The early concept of covalent bonds was provided with a sound theoretical basis by Linus Pauling (1901–1994, Np 1954), one of the greatest intellects of the twentieth century. Pauling's totally interdisciplinary research interests, including proteins and DNA is responsible for our present understanding of molecular structures. His books *Introduction to Quantum Mechanics* (with graduate student E. B. Wilson, 1935) and *The Nature of the Chemical Bond* (1939) have had a profound effect on our understanding of all of chemistry.

The actual 3D shapes of organic molecules which were still unclear in the late 1940s were then brilliantly clarified by Odd Hassel (1897–1981, Oslo University, Np 1969) and Derek Barton (1918–1998, Np 1969). Hassel, an X-ray crystallographer and physical chemist, demonstrated by electron diffraction that cyclohexane adopted the chair form in the gas phase and that it had two kinds of bonds, "standing (axial)" and "reclining (equatorial)" (1943). Because of the German occupation of Norway in 1940, instead of publishing the result in German journals, he published it in a Norwegian journal which was not abstracted in English until 1945. During his 1949 stay at Harvard, Barton attended a seminar by Louis Fieser on steric effects in steroids and showed Fieser that interpretations could be simplified if the shapes ("conformations") of cyclohexane rings were taken into consideration; Barton made these comments because he was familiar with Hassel's study on *cis-* and *trans-*decalins. Following Fieser's suggestion Barton published these ideas in a four-page *Experientia* paper (1950). This led to the joint Nobel prize with Hassel (1969), and established the concept of conformational analysis, which has exerted a profound effect in every field involving organic molecules.

Using conformational analysis, Barton determined the structures of many key terpenoids such as ß-amyrin, cycloartenone, and cycloartenol (Birkbeck College). At Glasgow University (from 1955) he collaborated in a number of cases with Monteath Robertson (1900–1989) and established many challenging structures: limonin, glauconic acid, byssochlamic acid, and nonadrides. Barton was also associated with the Research Institute for Medicine and Chemistry (RIMAC), Cambridge, USA founded by the Schering company, where with J. M. Beaton, he produced 60 g of aldosterone at a time when the world supply of this important hormone was in mg quantities. Aldosterone synthesis ("a good problem") was achieved in 1961 by Beaton ("a good experimentalist") through a nitrite photolysis, which came to be known as the Barton reaction ("a good idea") (quotes from his 1991 autobiography published by the American Chemical Society). From Glasgow, Barton went on to Imperial College, and a year before retirement, in 1977 he moved to France to direct the research at ICSN at Gif-sur-Yvette where he explored the oxidation reaction selectivity for unactivated C–H. After retiring from ICSN he made a further move to Texas A&M University in 1986, and continued his energetic activities, including chairman of the *Tetrahedron* publications. He felt weak during work one evening and died soon after, on March 16, 1998. He was fond of the phrase "gap jumping" by which he meant seeking generalizations between facts that do not seem to be related: "In the conformational analysis story, one had to jump the gap between steroids and chemical physics" (from his autobiography). According to Barton, the three most important qualities for a scientist are "intelligence, motivation, and honesty." His routine at Texas A&M was to wake around 4 a.m., read the literature, go to the office at 7 a.m. and stay there until 7 p.m.; when asked in 1997 whether this was still the routine, his response was that he wanted to wake up earlier because sleep was a waste of time—a remark which characterized this active scientist approaching 80!

Robert B. Woodward (1917–1979, Np 1965), who died prematurely, is regarded by many as the preeminent organic chemist of the twentieth century. He made landmark achievements in spectroscopy, synthesis, structure determination, biogenesis, as well as in theory. His solo papers published in 1941–1942 on empirical rules for estimating the absorption maxima of enones and dienes made the general organic chemical community realize that UV could be used for structural studies, thus launching the beginning of the spectroscopic revolution which soon brought on the applications of IR, NMR, MS, etc. He determined the structures of the following compounds: penicillin in 1945 (through joint UK–USA collaboration, see Hodgkin), strychnine in 1948, patulin in 1949, terramycin, aureomycin, and ferrocene (with G. Wilkinson, Np 1973—shared with E. O. Fischer for sandwich compounds) in 1952, cevine in 1954 (with Barton Np 1966, Jeger and Prelog, Np 1975), magnamycin in 1956, gliotoxin in 1958, oleandomycin in 1960, streptonigrin in 1963, and tetrodotoxin in 1964. He synthesized patulin in 1950, cortisone and cholesterol in 1951, lanosterol, lysergic acid (with Eli Lilly), and strychnine in 1954, reserpine in 1956, chlorophyll in 1960, a tetracycline (with Pfizer) in 1962, cephalosporin in 1965, and vitamin B_{12} in 1972 (with A. Eschenmoser, 1925–, ETH Zürich). He derived biogenetic schemes for steroids in 1953 (with K. Bloch, see below), and for macrolides in 1956, while the Woodward–Hoffmann orbital symmetry rules in 1965 brought order to a large class of seemingly random cyclization reactions.

Another central figure in stereochemistry is Vladimir Prelog (1906–1998, Np 1975), who succeeded Leopold Ruzicka at the ETH Zürich, and continued to build this institution into one of the most active and lively research and discussion centers in the world. The core group of intellectual leaders consisted of P. Plattner (1904–1975), O. Jeger, A. Eschenmoser, J. Dunitz, D. Arigoni, and A. Dreiding (from Zürich University). After completing extensive research on alkaloids, Prelog determined the structures of nonactin, boromycin, ferrioxamins, and rifamycins. His seminal studies in the synthesis and properties of 8–12 membered rings led him into unexplored areas of stereochemisty and chirality. Together with Robert Cahn (1899–1981, London Chemical Society) and Christopher Ingold (1893–1970, University College, London; pioneering mechanistic interpretation of organic reactions), he developed the Cahn–Ingold–Prelog (CIP) sequence rules for the unambiguous specification of stereoisomers. Prelog was an excellent story teller, always had jokes to tell, and was respected and loved by all who knew him.

4.1 Polyketides and Fatty Acids

Arthur Birch (1915–1995) from Sydney University, Ph.D. with Robert Robinson (Oxford University), then professor at Manchester University and Australian National University, was one of the earliest chemists to perform biosynthetic studies using radiolabels; starting with polyketides he studied the biosynthesis of a variety of natural products such as the C_6–C_3–C_6 backbone of plant phenolics, polyene macrolides, terpenoids, and alkaloids. He is especially known for the Birch reduction of aromatic rings, metal–ammonia reductions leading to 19-norsteroid hormones and other important products (1942–) which were of industrial importance. Feodor Lynen (1911–1979, Np 1964) performed studies on the intermediary metabolism of the living cell that led him to the demonstration of the first step in a chain of reactions resulting in the biosynthesis of sterols and fatty acids.

Prostaglandins, a family of 20-carbon, lipid-derived acids discovered in seminal fluids and accessory genital glands of man and sheep by von Euler (1934), have attracted great interest because of their extremely diverse biological activities. They were isolated and their structures elucidated from 1963 by S. Bergström (1916–, Np 1982) and B. Samuelsson (1934–, Np 1982) at the Karolinska Institute, Stockholm. Many syntheses of the natural prostaglandins and their nonnatural analogues have been published.

Tetsuo Nozoe (1902–1996) who studied at Tohoku University, Sendai, with Riko Majima (1874–1962, see below) went to Taiwan where he stayed until 1948 before returning to Tohoku University. At National Taiwan University he isolated hinokitiol from the essential oil of *taiwanhinoki*. Remembering the resonance concept put forward by Pauling just before World War II, he arrived at the seven-membered nonbenzenoid aromatic structure for hinokitiol in 1941, the first of the troponoids. This highly original work remained unknown to the rest of the world until 1951. In the meantime, during 1945–1948, nonbenzenoid aromatic structures had been assigned to stipitatic acid (isolated by H. Raistrick) by Michael J. S. Dewar (1918–) and to the thujaplicins by Holger Erdtman (1902–1989); the term tropolones was coined by Dewar in 1945. Nozoe continued to work on and discuss troponoids, up to the night before his death, without knowing that he had cancer. He was a remarkably focused and warm scientist, working unremittingly. Erdtman (Royal Institute of Technology, Stockholm) was the central figure in Swedish natural products chemistry who, with his wife Gunhild Aulin Erdtman (dynamic General Secretary of the Swedish Chemistry Society), worked in the area of plant phenolics.

As mentioned in the following and in the concluding sections, classical biosynthetic studies using radioactive isotopes for determining the distribution of isotopes has now largely been replaced by the use of various stable isotopes coupled with NMR and MS. The main effort has now shifted to the identification and cloning of genes, or where possible the gene clusters, involved in the biosynthesis of the natural product. In the case of polyketides (acyclic, cyclic, and aromatic), the focus is on the polyketide synthases.

4.2 Isoprenoids, Steroids, and Carotenoids

During his time as an assistant to Kekulé at Bonn, Otto Wallach (1847–1931, Np 1910) had to familiarize himself with the essential oils from plants; many of the components of these oils were compounds for which no structure was known. In 1891 he clarified the relations between 12 different monoterpenes related to pinene. This was summarized together with other terpene chemistry in book form in 1909, and led him to propose the "isoprene rule." These achievements laid the foundation for the future development of terpenoid chemistry and brought order from chaos.

The next period up to around 1950 saw phenomenal advances in natural products chemistry centered on isoprenoids. Many of the best natural products chemists in Europe, including Wieland, Windaus, Karrer, Kuhn, Butenandt, and Ruzicka contributed to this breathtaking pace. Heinrich Wieland (1877–1957) worked on the bile acid structure, which had been studied over a period of 100 years and considered to be one of the most difficult to attack; he received the Nobel Prize in 1927 for these studies. His friend Adolph Windaus (1876–1959) worked on the structure of cholesterol for which he also received the Nobel Prize in 1928. Unfortunately, there were chemical discrepancies in the proposed steroidal skeletal structure, which had a five-membered ring B attached to C-7 and C-9. J. D. Bernal, Mineralogical Museums, Cambridge University, who was examining the X-ray patterns of ergosterol (1932) noted that the dimensions were inconsistent with the Wieland–Windaus formula. A reinterpretation of the production of chrysene from sterols by Pd/C dehydrogenation reported by Diels (see below) in 1927 eventually led Rosenheim and King and Wieland and Dane to deduce the correct structure in 1932. Wieland also worked on the structures of morphine/strychnine alkaloids, phalloidin/amanitin cyclopeptides of toxic mushroom *Amanita phalloides*, and pteridines, the important fluorescent pigments of butterfly wings. Windaus determined the structure of ergosterol and continued structural studies of its irradiation product which exhibited antirachitic activity "vitamin D." The mechanistically complex photochemistry of ergosterol leading to the vitamin D group has been investigated in detail by Egbert Havinga (1927–1988, Leiden University), a leading photochemist and excellent tennis player.

Paul Karrer (1889–1971, Np 1937), established the foundations of carotenoid chemistry through structural determinations of lycopene, carotene, vitamin A, etc. and the synthesis of squalene, carotenoids, and others. George Wald (1906–1997, Np 1967) showed that vitamin A was the key compound in vision during his stay in Karrer's laboratory. Vitamin K (K from "Koagulation"), discovered by Henrik Dam (1895–1976, Polytechnic Institute, Copenhagen, Np 1943) and structurally studied by Edward Doisy (1893–1986, St. Louis University, Np 1943), was also synthesized by Karrer. In addition, Karrer synthesized riboflavin (vitamin B$_2$) and determined the structure and role of nicotinamide adenine dinucleotide phosphate (NADP$^+$) with Otto Warburg. The research on carotenoids and vitamins of Karrer who was at Zürich University overlapped with that of Richard Kuhn (1900–1967, Np 1938) at the ETH Zürich, and the two were frequently rivals. Richard Kuhn, one of the pioneers in using UV-vis spectroscopy for structural studies, introduced the concept of "atropisomerism" in diphenyls, and studied the spectra of a series of diphenyl polyenes. He determined the structures of many natural carotenoids, proved the structure of riboflavin-5-phosphate (flavin-adenine-dinucleotide-5-phosphate) and showed that the combination of NAD-5-phosphate with the carrier protein yielded the yellow oxidation enzyme, thus providing an understanding of the role of a prosthetic group. He also determined the structures of vitamin B complexes, i.e., pyridoxine, *p*-aminobenzoic acid, pantothenic acid. After World War II he went on to structural studies of nitrogen-containing oligosaccharides in human milk that provide immunity for infants, and brain gangliosides. Carotenoid studies in Switzerland were later taken up by Otto Isler (1910–1993), a Ruzicka student at Hoffmann-La Roche, and Conrad Hans Eugster (1921–), a Karrer student at Zürich University.

Adolf Butenandt (1903–1998, Np 1939) initiated and essentially completed isolation and structural studies of the human sex hormones, the insect molting hormone (ecdysone), and the first pheromone, bombykol. With help from industry he was able to obtain large supplies of urine from pregnant women for estrone, sow ovaries for progesterone, and 4,000 gallons of male urine for androsterone (50 mg, crystals). He isolated and determined the structures of two female sex hormones, estrone and progesterone, and the male hormone androsterone all during the period 1934–1939 (!) and was awarded the Nobel prize in 1939. Keen intuition and use of UV data and Pregl's microanalysis all played important roles. He was appointed to a professorship in Danzig at the age of 30. With Peter Karlson he isolated from 500 kg of silkworm larvae 25 mg of a-ecdysone, the prohormone of insect and crustacean molting hormone, and determined its structure as a polyhydroxysteroid (1965); 20-hydroxylation gives the insect and crustacean molting hormone or ß-ecdysone (20-hydroxyecdysteroid). He was also the first to isolate an insect pheromone, bombykol, from female silkworm moths (with E. Hecker). As president of the Max Planck Foundation, he strongly influenced the postwar rebuilding of German science.

The successor to Kuhn, who left ETH Zürich for Heidelberg, was Leopold Ruzicka (1887–1967, Np 1939) who established a close relationship with the Swiss pharmaceutical industry. His synthesis of the 17- and 15-membered macrocyclic ketones, civetone and muscone (the constituents of musk) showed that contrary to Baeyer's prediction, large alicyclic rings could be strainless. He reintroduced and refined the isoprene rule proposed by Wallach (1887) and determined the basic structures of many sesqui-, di-, and triterpenes, as well as the structure of lanosterol, the key intermediate in cholesterol biosynthesis. The "biogenetic isoprene rule" of the ETH group, Albert Eschenmoser, Leopold Ruzicka, Oskar Jeger, and Duilio Arigoni, contributed to a concept of terpenoid cyclization (1955), which was consistent with the mechanistic considerations put forward by Stork as early as 1950. Besides making

the ETH group into a center of natural products chemistry, Ruzicka bought many seventeenth century Dutch paintings with royalties accumulated during the war from his Swiss and American patents, and donated them to the Zürich Kunsthaus.

Studies in the isolation, structures, and activities of the antiarthritic hormone, cortisone and related compounds from the adrenal cortex were performed in the mid- to late 1940s during World War II by Edward Kendall (1886–1972, Mayo Clinic, Rochester, Np 1950), Tadeus Reichstein (1897–1996, Basel University, Np 1950), Philip Hench (1896–1965, Mayo Clinic, Rochester, Np 1950), Oskar Wintersteiner (1898–1971, Columbia University, Squibb) and others initiated interest as an adjunct to military medicine as well as to supplement the meager supply from beef adrenal glands by synthesis. Lewis Sarett (1917–, Merck & Co., later president) and co-workers completed the cortisone synthesis in 28 steps, one of the first two totally stereocontrolled syntheses of a natural product; the other was cantharidin (Stork 1951) (see above). The multistep cortisone synthesis was put on the production line by Max Tishler (1906–1989, Merck & Co., later president) who made contributions to the synthesis of a number of drugs, including riboflavin. Besides working on steroid reactions/synthesis and antimalarial agents, Louis F. Fieser (1899–1977) and Mary Fieser (1909–1997) of Harvard University made huge contributions to the chemical community through their outstanding books *Natural Products related to Phenanthrene* (1949), *Steroids* (1959), *Advanced Organic Chemistry* (1961), and *Topics in Organic Chemistry* (1963), as well as their textbooks and an important series of books on Organic Reagents. Carl Djerassi (1923–, Stanford University), a prolific chemist, industrialist, and more recently a novelist, started to work at the Syntex laboratories in Mexico City where he directed the work leading to the first oral contraceptive ("the pill") for women.

Takashi Kubota (1909–, Osaka City University), with Teruo Matsuura (1924–, Kyoto University), determined the structure of the furanoid sesquiterpene, ipomeamarone, from the black rotted portion of spoiled sweet potatoes; this research constitutes the first characterization of a phytoallexin, defense substances produced by plants in response to attack by fungi or physical damage. Damaging a plant and characterizing the defense substances produced may lead to new bioactive compounds. The mechanism of induced biosynthesis of phytoallexins, which is not fully understood, is an interesting biological mechanistic topic that deserves further investigation. Another center of high activity in terpenoids and nucleic acids was headed by Frantisek Sorm (1913–1980, Institute of Organic and Biochemistry, Prague), who determined the structures of many sesquiterpenoids and other natural products; he was not only active scientifically but also was a central figure who helped to guide the careers of many Czech chemists.

The key compound in terpenoid biosynthesis is mevalonic acid (MVA) derived from acetyl-CoA, which was discovered fortuitously in 1957 by the Merck team in Rahway, NJ headed by Karl Folkers (1906–1998). They soon realized and proved that this C_6 acid was the precursor of the C_5 isoprenoid unit isopentenyl diphosphate (IPP) that ultimately leads to the biosynthesis of cholesterol. In 1952 Konrad Bloch (1912–, Harvard, Np 1964) with R. B. Woodward published a paper suggesting a mechanism of the cyclization of squalene to lanosterol and the subsequent steps to cholesterol, which turned out to be essentially correct. This biosynthetic path from MVA to cholesterol was experimentally clarified in stereochemical detail by John Cornforth (1917–, Np 1975) and George Popják. In 1932, Harold Urey (1893–1981, Np 1934) of Columbia University discovered heavy hydrogen. Urey showed, contrary to common expectation, that isotope separation could be achieved with deuterium in the form of deuterium oxide by fractional electrolysis of water. Urey's separation of the stable isotope deuterium led to the isotopic tracer methodology that revolutionized the protocols for elucidating biosynthetic processes and reaction mechanisms, as exemplified beautifully by the cholesterol studies. Using MVA labeled chirally with isotopes, including chiral methyl, i.e., -CHDT, Cornforth and Popják clarified the key steps in the intricate biosynthetic conversion of mevalonate to cholesterol in stereochemical detail. The chiral methyl group was also prepared independently by Duilio Arigoni (1928–, ETH, Zürich). Cornforth has had great difficulty in hearing and speech since childhood but has been helped expertly by his chemist wife Rita; he is an excellent tennis and chess player, and is renowned for his speed in composing occasional witty limericks.

Although MVA has long been assumed to be the only natural precursor for IPP, a non-MVA pathway in which IPP is formed via the glyceraldehyde phosphate-pyruvate pathway has been discovered (1995–1996) in the ancient bacteriohopanoids by Michel Rohmer, who started working on them with Guy Ourisson (1926–, University of Strasbourg, terpenoid studies, including prebiotic), and by Duilio Arigoni in the ginkgolides, which are present in the ancient *Ginkgo biloba* tree. It is possible that many other terpenoids are biosynthesized via the non-MVA route. In classical biosynthetic experiments, ^{14}C-labeled acetic acid was incorporated into the microbial or plant product, and location or distribution of the ^{14}C label was deduced by oxidation or degradation to specific fragments including acetic acid; therefore, it was not possible or extremely difficult to map the distribution of all radioactive carbons. The progress

in ^{13}C NMR made it possible to incorporate ^{13}C-labeled acetic acid and locate all labeled carbons. This led to the discovery of the nonmevalonate pathway leading to the IPP units. Similarly, NMR and MS have made it possible to use the stable isotopes, e.g., ^{18}O, ^{2}H, ^{15}N, etc., in biosynthetic studies. The current trend of biosynthesis has now shifted to genomic approaches for cloning the genes of various enzyme synthases involved in the biosynthesis.

4.3 Carbohydrates and Cellulose

The most important advance in carbohydrate structures following those made by Emil Fischer was the change from acyclic to the current cyclic structure introduced by Walter Haworth (1883–1937). He noticed the presence of a- and ß-anomers, and determined the structures of important disaccharides including cellobiose, maltose, and lactose. He also determined the basic structural aspects of starch, cellulose, inulin, and other polysaccharides, and accomplished the structure determination and synthesis of vitamin C, a sample of which he had received from Albert von Szent-Györgyi (1893–1986, Np 1937). This first synthesis of a vitamin was significant since it showed that a vitamin could be synthesized in the same way as any other organic compound. There was strong belief among leading scientists in the 1910s that cellulose, starch, protein, and rubber were colloidal aggregates of small molecules. However, Hermann Staudinger (1881–1965, Np 1953) who succeeded R. Willstätter and H. Wieland at the ETH Zürich and Freiburg, respectively, showed through viscosity measurements and various molecular weight measurements that macromolecules do exist, and developed the principles of macromolecular chemistry.

In more modern times, Raymond Lemieux (1920–, Universities of Ottawa and Alberta) has been a leader in carbohydrate research. He introduced the concept of *endo-* and *exo*-anomeric effects, accomplished the challenging synthesis of sucrose (1953), pioneered in the use of NMR coupling constants in configuration studies, and most importantly, starting with syntheses of oligosaccharides responsible for human blood group determinants, he prepared antibodies and clarified fundamental aspects of the binding of oligosaccharides by lectins and antibodies. The periodate–potassium permanganate cleavage of double bonds at room temperature (1955) is called the Lemieux reaction.

4.4 Amino Acids, Peptides, Porphyrins, and Alkaloids

It is fortunate that we have China's record and practice of herbal medicine over the centuries, which is providing us with an indispensable source of knowledge. China is rapidly catching up in terms of infrastructure and equipment in organic and bioorganic chemistry, and work on isolation, structure determination, and synthesis stemming from these valuable sources has picked up momentum. However, as mentioned above, clarification of the active principles and mode of action of these plant extracts will be quite a challenge since in many cases synergistic action is expected. Wang Yu (1910–1997) who headed the well-equipped Shanghai Institute of Organic Chemistry surprised the world with the total synthesis of bovine insulin performed by his group in 1965; the human insulin was synthesized around the same time by P. G. Katsoyannis, A. Tometsko, and C. Zaut of the Brookhaven National Laboratory (1966).

One of the giants in natural products chemistry during the first half of this century was Robert Robinson (1886–1975, Np 1947) at Oxford University. His synthesis of tropinone, a bicyclic amino ketone related to cocaine, from succindialdehyde, methylamine, and acetone dicarboxylic acid under Mannich reaction conditions was the first biomimetic synthesis (1917). It reduced Willstätter's 1903 13-step synthesis starting with suberone into a single step. This achievement demonstrated Robinson's analytical prowess. He was able to dissect complex molecular structures into simple biosynthetic building blocks, which allowed him to propose the biogenesis of all types of alkaloids and other natural products. His laboratory at Oxford, where he developed the well-known Robinson annulation reaction (1937) in connection with his work on the synthesis of steroids became a world center for natural products study. Robinson was a pioneer in the so-called electronic theory of organic reactions, and introduced the use of curly arrows to show the movements of electrons. His analytical power is exemplified in the structural studies of strychnine and brucine around 1946–1952. Barton clarified the biosynthetic route to the morphine alkaloids, which he saw as an extension of his biomimetic synthesis of usnic acid through a one-electron oxidation; this was later extended to a general phenolate coupling scheme. Morphine total synthesis was brilliantly achieved by Marshall Gates (1915–, University of Rochester) in 1952.

The yield of the Robinson tropinone synthesis was low but Clemens Schöpf (1899–1970) , Ph.D. Munich (Wieland), Universität Darmstadt, improved it to 90% by carrying out the reaction in buffer; he also worked on the stereochemistry of morphine and determined the structure of the steroidal alkaloid salamandarine (1961), the toxin secreted from glands behind the eyes of the salamander.

Roger Adams (1889–1971, University of Illinois), was the central figure in organic chemistry in the USA and is credited with contributing to the rapid development of its chemistry in the late 1930s and 1940s, including training of graduate students for both academe and industry. After earning a Ph.D. in 1912 at Harvard University he did postdoctoral studies with Otto Diels (see below) and Richard Willstätter (see below) in 1913; he once said that around those years in Germany he could cover all *Journal of the American Chemical Society* papers published in a year in a single night. His important work include determination of the structures of tetrahydrocannabinol in marijuana, the toxic gossypol in cottonseed oil, chaulmoogric acid used in treatment of leprosy, and the Senecio alkaloids with Nelson Leonard (1916–, University of Illinois, now at Caltech). He also contributed to many fundamental organic reactions and syntheses. The famous Adams platinum catalyst is not only important for reducing double bonds in industry and in the laboratory, but was central for determining the number of double bonds in a structure. He was also one of the founders of the *Organic Synthesis* (started in 1921) and the *Organic Reactions* series. Nelson Leonard switched interests to bioorganic chemistry and biochemistry, where he has worked with nucleic acid bases and nucleotides, coenzymes, dimensional probes, and fluorescent modifications such as ethenoguanine.

The complicated structures of the medieval plant poisons aconitine (from *Aconitum*) and delphinine (from *Delphinium*) were finally characterized in 1959–1960 by Karel Wiesner (1919–1986, University of New Brunswick), Leo Marion (1899–1979, National Research Council, Ottawa), George Büchi (1921–, mycotoxins, aflatoxin/DNA adduct, synthesis of terpenoids and nitrogen-containing bioactive compounds, photochemistry), and Maria Przybylska (1923–, X-ray).

The complex chlorophyll structure was elucidated by Richard Willstätter (1872–1942, Np 1915). Although he could not join Baeyer's group at Munich because the latter had ceased taking students, a close relation developed between the two. During his chlorophyll studies, Willstätter reintroduced the important technique of column chromatography published in Russian by Michael Tswett (1906). Willstätter further demonstrated that magnesium was an integral part of chlorophyll, clarified the relation between chlorophyll and the blood pigment hemin, and found the wide distribution of carotenoids in tomato, egg yolk, and bovine corpus luteum. Willstätter also synthesized cyclooctatetraene and showed its properties to be wholly unlike benzene but close to those of acyclic polyenes (around 1913). He succeeded Baeyer at Munich in 1915, synthesized the anesthetic cocaine, retired early in protest of anti-Semitism, but remained active until the Hitler era, and in 1938 emigrated to Switzerland.

The hemin structure was determined by another German chemist of the same era, Hans Fischer (1881–1945, Np 1930), who succeeded Windaus at Innsbruck and at Munich. He worked on the structure of hemin from the blood pigment hemoglobin, and completed its synthesis in 1929. He continued Willstätter's structural studies of chlorophyll, and further synthesized bilirubin in 1944. Destruction of his institute at Technische Hochschule München, during World War II led him to take his life in March 1945. The biosynthesis of hemin was elucidated largely by David Shemin (1911–1991).

In the mid 1930s the Department of Biochemistry at Columbia Medical School, which had accepted many refugees from the Third Reich, including Erwin Chargaff, Rudolf Schoenheimer, and others on the faculty, and Konrad Bloch (see above) and David Shemin as graduate students, was a great center of research activity. In 1940, Shemin ingested 66 g of ^{15}N-labeled glycine over a period of 66 hours in order to determine the half-life of erythrocytes. David Rittenberg's analysis of the heme moiety with his home-made mass spectrometer showed all four pyrrole nitrogens came from glycine. Using ^{14}C (that had just become available) as a second isotope (see next paragraph), doubly labeled glycine ^{15}NH$_2$^{14}CH$_2$COOH and other precursors, Shemin showed that glycine and succinic acid condensed to yield d-aminolevulinate, thus elegantly demonstrating the novel biosynthesis of the porphyrin ring (around 1950). At this time, Bloch was working on the other side of the bench.

Melvin Calvin (1911–1997, Np 1961) at University of California, Berkeley, elucidated the complex photosynthetic pathway in which plants reduce carbon dioxide to carbohydrates. The critical ^{14}CO$_2$ had just been made available at Berkeley Lawrence Radiation Laboratory as a result of the pioneering research of Martin Kamen (1913–), while paper chromatography also played crucial roles. Kamen produced ^{14}C with Sam Ruben (1940), used ^{18}O to show that oxygen in photosynthesis comes from water and not from carbon dioxide, participated in the *Manhattan* project, testified before the House UnAmerican Activities Committee (1947), won compensatory damages from the US Department of State, and helped build the University of California, La Jolla (1957). The entire structure of the photosynthetic reaction center (>10 000 atoms) from the purple bacterium *Rhodopseudomonas viridis* has been established by X-ray crystallography in the landmark studies performed by Johann Deisenhofer (1943–), Robert Huber (1937–), and Hartmut Michel (1948–) in 1989; this was the first membrane protein structure determined by X-ray, for which they shared the 1988 Nobel prize. The information gained from the full structure of this first membrane protein has been especially rewarding.

The studies on vitamin B$_{12}$, the structure of which was established by crystallographic studies performed by Dorothy Hodgkin (1910–1994, Np 1964), are fascinating. Hodgkin also determined the structure of penicillin (in a joint effort between UK and US scientists during World War II) and insulin. The formidable total synthesis of vitamin B$_{12}$ was completed in 1972 through collaborative efforts between Woodward and Eschenmoser, involving 100 postdoctoral fellows and extending over 10 years. The biosynthesis of fascinating complexity is almost completely solved through studies performed by Alan Battersby (1925–, Cambridge University), Duilio Arigoni, and Ian Scott (1928–, Texas A&M University) and collaborators where advanced NMR techniques and synthesis of labeled precursors is elegantly combined with cloning of enzymes controlling each biosynthetic step. This work provides a beautiful demonstration of the power of the combination of bioorganic chemistry, spectroscopy and molecular biology, a future direction which will become increasingly important for the creation of new "unnatural" natural products.

4.5 Enzymes and Proteins

In the early days of natural products chemistry, enzymes and viruses were very poorly understood. Thus, the 1926 paper by James Sumner (1887–1955) at Cornell University on crystalline urease was received with ignorance or skepticism, especially by Willstätter who believed that enzymes were small molecules and not proteins. John Northrop (1891–1987) and co-workers at the Rockefeller Institute went on to crystallize pepsin, trypsin, chymotrypsin, ribonuclease, deoyribonuclease, carboxypeptidase, and other enzymes between 1930 and 1935. Despite this, for many years biochemists did not recognize the significance of these findings, and considered enzymes as being low molecular weight compounds adsorbed onto proteins or colloids. Using Northrop's method for crystalline enzyme preparations, Wendell Stanley (1904–1971) at Princeton obtained tobacco mosaic virus as needles from one ton of tobacco leaves (1935). Sumner, Northrop, and Stanley shared the 1946 Nobel prize in chemistry. All these studies opened a new era for biochemistry.

Meanwhile, Linus Pauling, who in mid-1930 became interested in the magnetic properties of hemoglobin, investigated the configurations of proteins and the effects of hydrogen bonds. In 1949 he showed that sickle cell anemia was due to a mutation of a single amino acid in the hemoglobin molecule, the first correlation of a change in molecular structure with a genetic disease. Starting in 1951 he and colleagues published a series of papers describing the alpha helix structure of proteins; a paper published in the early 1950s with R. B. Corey on the structure of DNA played an important role in leading Francis Crick and James Watson to the double helix structure (Np 1962).

A further important achievement in the peptide field was that of Vincent Du Vigneaud (1901–1978, Np 1955), Cornell Medical School, who isolated and determined the structure of oxytocin, a posterior pituitary gland hormone, for which a structure involving a disulfide bond was proposed. He synthesized oxytocin in 1953, thereby completing the first synthesis of a natural peptide hormone.

Progress in isolation, purification, crystallization methods, computers, and instrumentation, including cyclotrons, have made X-ray crystallography the major tool in structural. Numerous structures including those of ligand/receptor complexes are being published at an extremely rapid rate. Some of the past major achievements in protein structures are the following. Max Perutz (1914, Np 1962) and John Kendrew (1914–1997, Np 1962), both at the Laboratory of Molecular Biology, Cambridge University, determined the structures of hemoglobin and myoglobin, respectively. William Lipscomb (1919–, Np 1976), Harvard University, who has trained many of the world's leaders in protein X-ray crystallography has been involved in the structure determination of many enzymes including carboxypeptidase A (1967); in 1965 he determined the structure of the anticancer bisindole alkaloid, vinblastine. Folding of proteins, an important but still enigmatic phenomenon, is attracting increasing attention. Christian Anfinsen (1916–1995, Np 1972), NIH, one of the pioneers in this area, showed that the amino acid residues in ribonuclease interact in an energetically most favorable manner to produce the unique 3D structure of the protein.

4.6 Nucleic Acid Bases, RNA, and DNA

The "Fischer indole synthesis" was first performed in 1886 by Emil Fischer. During the period 1881–1914, he determined the structures of and synthesized uric acid, caffeine, theobromine, xanthine, guanine, hypoxanthine, adenine, guanine, and made theophylline-D-glucoside phosphoric acid, the first synthetic nucleotide. In 1903, he made 5,5-diethylbarbituric acid or Barbital, Dorminal, Veronal, etc. (sedative), and in 1912, phenobarbital or Barbipil, Luminal, Phenobal, etc. (sedative). Many of his

syntheses formed the basis of German industrial production of purine bases. In 1912 he showed that tannins are gallates of sugars such as maltose and glucose. Starting in 1899, he synthesized many of the 13 a-amino acids known at that time, including the L- and D-forms, which were separated through fractional crystallization of their salts with optically active bases. He also developed a method for synthesizing fragments of proteins, namely peptides, and made an 18-amino acid peptide. He lost his two sons in World War I, lost his wealth due to postwar inflation, believed he had terminal cancer (a misdiagnosis), and killed himself in July 1919. Fischer was a skilled experimentalist, so that even today, many of the reactions performed by him and his students are so delicately controlled that they are not easy to reproduce. As a result of his suffering by inhaling diethylmercury, and of the poisonous effect of phenylhydrazine, he was one of the first to design fume hoods. He was a superb teacher and was also influential in establishing the Kaiser Wilhelm Institute, which later became the Max Planck Institute. The number and quality of his accomplishments and contributions are hard to believe; he was truly a genius.

Alexander Todd (1907–1997, Np 1957) made critical contributions to the basic chemistry and synthesis of nucleotides. His early experience consisted of an extremely fruitful stay at Oxford in the Robinson group, where he completed the syntheses of many representative anthocyanins, and then at Edinburgh where he worked on the synthesis of vitamin B_1. He also prepared the hexacarboxylate of vitamin B_{12} (1954), which was used by D. Hodgkin's group for their X-ray elucidation of this vitamin (1956). M. Wiewiorowski (1918–), Institute for Bioorganic Chemistry, in Poznan, has headed a famous group in nucleic acid chemistry, and his colleagues are now distributed worldwide.

4.7 Antibiotics, Pigments, and Marine Natural Products

The concept of one microorganism killing another was introduced by Pasteur who coined the term antibiosis in 1877, but it was much later that this concept was realized in the form of an actual antibiotic. The bacteriologist Alexander Fleming (1881–1955, University of London, Np 1945) noticed that an airborne mold, a *Penicillium* strain, contaminated cultures of *Staphylococci* left on the open bench and formed a transparent circle around its colony due to lysis of *Staphylococci*. He published these results in 1929. The discovery did not attract much interest but the work was continued by Fleming until it was taken up further at Oxford University by pathologist Howard Florey (1898–1968, Np 1945) and biochemist Ernst Chain (1906–1979, Np 1945). The bioactivities of purified "penicillin," the first antibiotic, attracted serious interest in the early 1940s in the midst of World War II. A UK/USA team was formed during the war between academe and industry with Oxford University, Harvard University, ICI, Glaxo, Burroughs Wellcome, Merck, Shell, Squibb, and Pfizer as members. This project resulted in the large scale production of penicillin and determination of its structure (finally by X-ray, D. Hodgkin). John Sheehan (1915–1992) at MIT synthesized 6-aminopenicillanic acid in 1959, which opened the route for the synthesis of a number of analogues. Besides being the first antibiotic to be discovered, penicillin is also the first member of a large number of important antibiotics containing the ß-lactam ring, for example cephalosporins, carbapenems, monobactams, and nocardicins. The strained ß-lactam ring of these antibiotics inactivates the transpeptidase by acylating its serine residue at the active site, thus preventing the enzyme from forming the link between the pentaglycine chain and the D-Ala-D-Ala peptide, the essential link in bacterial cell walls. The overuse of ß-lactam antibiotics, which has given rise to the disturbing appearance of microbial resistant strains, is leading to active research in the design of synthetic ß-lactam analogues to counteract these strains. The complex nature of the important penicillin biosynthesis is being elucidated through efforts combining genetic engineering, expression of biosynthetic genes as well as feeding of synthetic precursors, etc. by Jack Baldwin (1938–, Oxford University), José Luengo (Universidad de León, Spain) and many other groups from industry and academe.

Shortly after the penicillin discovery, Selman Waksman (1888–1973, Rutgers University, Np 1952) discovered streptomycin, the second antibiotic and the first active against the dreaded disease tuberculosis. The discovery and development of new antibiotics continued throughout the world at pharmaceutical companies in Europe, Japan, and the USA from soil and various odd sources: cephalosporin from sewage in Sardinia, cyclosporin from Wisconsin and Norway soil which was carried back to Switzerland, avermectin from the soil near a golf course in Shizuoka Prefecture. People involved in antibiotic discovery used to collect soil samples from various sources during their trips but this has now become severely restricted to protect a country's right to its soil. M. M. Shemyakin (1908–1970, Institute of Chemistry of Natural Products, Moscow) was a grand master of Russian natural products who worked on antibiotics, especially of the tetracycline class; he also worked on cyclic antibiotics composed of alternating sequences of amides and esters and coined the term depsipeptide for these in 1953. He died in 1970 of a sudden heart attack in the midst of the 7th IUPAC Natural Products

Symposium held in Riga, Latvia, which he had organized. The Institute he headed was renamed the Shemyakin Institute.

Indigo, an important vat dye known in ancient Asia, Egypt, Greece, Rome, Britain, and Peru, is probably the oldest known coloring material of plant origin, Indigofera and Isatis. The structure was determined in 1883 and a commercially feasible synthesis was performed in 1883 by Adolf von Baeyer (see above, 1835–1917, Np 1905), who founded the German Chemical Society in 1867 following the precedent of the Chemistry Society of London. In 1872 Baeyer was appointed a professor at Strasbourg where E. Fischer was his student, and in 1875 he succeeded J. Liebig in Munich. Tyrian (or Phoenician) purple, the dibromo derivative of indigo which is obtained from the purple snail Murex bundaris, was used as a royal emblem in connection with religious ceremonies because of its rarity; because of the availability of other cheaper dyes with similar color, it has no commercial value today. K. Venkataraman (1901–1981, University of Bombay then National Chemical Laboratory) who worked with R. Robinson on the synthesis of chromones in his early career, continued to study natural and synthetic coloring matters, including synthetic anthraquinone vat dyes, natural quinonoid pigments, etc. T. R. Seshadri (1900–1975) is another Indian natural products chemist who worked mainly in natural pigments, dyes, drugs, insecticides, and especially in polyphenols. He also studied with Robinson, and with Pregl at Graz, and taught at Delhi University. Seshadri and Venkataraman had a huge impact on Indian chemistry. After a 40 year involvement, Toshio Goto (1929–1990) finally succeeded in solving the mysterious identity of commelinin, the deep-blue flower petal pigment of the Commelina communis isolated by Kozo Hayashi (1958) and protocyanin, isolated from the blue cornflower Centaurea cyanus by E. Bayer (1957). His group elucidated the remarkable structure in its entirety which consisted of six unstable anthocyanins, six flavones and two metals, the molecular weight approaching 10 000; complex stacking and hydrogen bonds were also involved. Thus the pigmentation of petals turned out to be far more complex than the theories put forth by Willstätter (1913) and Robinson (1931). Goto suffered a fatal heart attack while inspecting the first X-ray structure of commelinin; commelinin represents a pinnacle of current natural products isolation and structure determination in terms of subtlety in isolation and complexity of structure.

The study of marine natural products is understandably far behind that of compounds of terrestrial origin due to the difficulty in collection and identification of marine organisms. However, it is an area which has great potentialities for new discoveries from every conceivable source. One pioneer in modern marine chemistry is Paul Scheuer (1915–, University of Hawaii) who started his work with quinones of marine origin and has since characterized a very large number of bioactive compounds from mollusks and other sources. Luigi Minale (1936–1997, Napoli) started a strong group working on marine natural products, concentrating mainly on complex saponins. He was a leading natural products chemist who died prematurely. A. Gonzalez Gonzalez (1917–) who headed the Organic Natural Products Institute at the University of La Laguna, Tenerife, was the first to isolate and study polyhalogenated sesquiterpenoids from marine sources. His group has also carried out extensive studies on terrestrial terpenoids from the Canary Islands and South America. Carotenoids are widely distributed in nature and are of importance as food coloring material and as antioxidants (the detailed mechanisms of which still have to be worked out); new carotenoids continue to be discovered from marine sources, for example by the group of Synnove Liaaen-Jensen, Norwegian Institute of Technology). Yoshimasa Hirata (1915–), who started research at Nagoya University, is a champion in the isolation of nontrivial natural products. He characterized the bioluminescent luciferin from the marine ostracod *Cypridina hilgendorfii* in 1966 (with his students, Toshio Goto, Yoshito Kishi, and Osamu Shimomura); tetrodotoxin from the fugu fish in 1964 (with Goto and Kishi and co-workers), the structure of which was announced simultaneously by the group of Kyosuke Tsuda (1907–, tetrodotoxin, matrine) and Woodward; and the very complex palytoxin, $C_{129}H_{223}N_3O_{54}$ in 1981–1987 (with Daisuke Uemura and Kishi). Richard E. Moore, University of Hawaii, also announced the structure of palytoxin independently. Jon Clardy (1943–, Cornell University) has determined the X-ray structures of many unique marine natural products, including brevetoxin B (1981), the first of the group of toxins with contiguous *trans*-fused ether rings constituting a stiff ladder-like skeleton. Maitotoxin, $C_{164}H_{256}O_{68}S_2Na_2$, MW 3422, produced by the dinoflagellate *Gambierdiscus toxicus* is the largest and most toxic of the nonbiopolymeric toxins known; it has 32 alicyclic 6- to 8-membered ethereal rings and acyclic chains. Its isolation (1994) and complete structure determination was accomplished jointly by the groups of Takeshi Yasumoto (Tohoku University), Kazuo Tachibana and Michio Murata (Tokyo University) in 1996. Kishi, Harvard University, also deduced the full structure in 1996.

The well-known excitatory agent for the cat family contained in the volatile oil of catnip, *Nepeta cataria*, is the monoterpene nepetalactone, isolated by S. M. McElvain (1943) and structure determined by Jerrold Meinwald (1954); cats, tigers, and lions start purring and roll on their backs in response to this lactone. Takeo Sakan (1912–1993) investigated the series of monoterpenes neomatatabiols, etc.

from Actinidia, some of which are male lacewing attractants. As little as 1 fg of neomatatabiol attracts lacewings.

The first insect pheromone to be isolated and characterized was bombykol, the sex attractant for the male silkworm, *Bombyx mori* (by Butenandt and co-workers, see above). Numerous pheromones have been isolated, characterized, synthesized, and are playing central roles in insect control and in chemical ecology. The group at Cornell University have long been active in this field: Tom Eisner (1929–, behavior), Jerrold Meinwald (1927–, chemistry), Wendell Roeloff (1939–, electrophysiology, chemistry). Since the available sample is usually minuscule, full structure determination of a pheromone often requires total synthesis; Kenji Mori (1935–, Tokyo University) has been particularly active in this field. Progress in the techniques for handling volatile compounds, including collection, isolation, GC/MS, etc., has started to disclose the extreme complexity of chemical ecology which plays an important role in the lives of all living organisms. In this context, natural products chemistry will be play an increasingly important role in our grasp of the significance of biodiversity.

5. SYNTHESIS

Synthesis has been mentioned often in the preceding sections of this essay. In the following, synthetic methods of more general nature are described. The Grignard reaction of Victor Grignard (1871–1935, Np 1912) and then the Diels–Alder reaction by Otto Diels (1876–1954, Np 1950) and Kurt Alder (1902–1956, Np 1950) are extremely versatile reactions. The Diels–Alder reaction can account for the biosynthesis of several natural products with complex structures, and now an enzyme, a Diels–Alderase involved in biosynthesis has been isolated by Akitami Ichihara, Hokkaido University (1997).

The hydroboration reactions of Herbert Brown (1912–, Purdue University, Np 1979) and the Wittig reactions of Georg Wittig (1897–1987, Np 1979) are extremely versatile synthetic reactions. William S. Johnson (1913–1995, University of Wisconsin, Stanford University) developed efficient methods for the cyclization of acyclic polyolefinic compounds for the synthesis of corticoid and other steroids, while Gilbert Stork (1921–, Columbia University) introduced enamine alkylation, regiospecific enolate formation from enones and their kinetic trapping (called "three component coupling" in some cases), and radical cyclization in regio- and stereospecific constructions. Elias J. Corey (1928–, Harvard University, Np 1990) introduced the concept of retrosynthetic analysis and developed many key synthetic reactions and reagents during his synthesis of bioactive compounds, including prostaglandins and gingkolides. A recent development is the ever-expanding supramolecular chemistry stemming from 1967 studies on crown ethers by Charles Pedersen (1904–1989), 1968 studies on cryptates by Jean-Marie Lehn (1939–), and 1973 studies on host–guest chemistry by Donald Cram (1919–); they shared the chemistry Nobel prize in 1987.

6. NATURAL PRODUCTS STUDIES IN JAPAN

Since the background of natural products study in Japan is quite different from that in other countries, a brief history is given here. Natural products is one of the strongest areas of chemical research in Japan with probably the world's largest number of chemists pursuing structural studies; these are joined by a healthy number of synthetic and bioorganic chemists. An important Symposium on Natural Products was held in 1957 in Nagoya as a joint event between the faculties of science, pharmacy, and agriculture. This was the beginning of a series of annual symposia held in various cities, which has grown into a three-day event with about 50 talks and numerous papers; practically all achievements in this area are presented at this symposium. Japan adopted the early twentieth century German or European academic system where continuity of research can be assured through a permanent staff in addition to the professor, a system which is suited for natural products research which involves isolation and assay, as well as structure determination, all steps requiring delicate skills and much expertise.

The history of Japanese chemistry is short because the country was closed to the outside world up to 1868. This is when the Tokugawa shogunate which had ruled Japan for 264 years was overthrown and the Meiji era (1868–1912) began. Two of the first Japanese organic chemists sent abroad were Shokei Shibata and Nagayoshi Nagai, who joined the laboratory of A. W. von Hoffmann in Berlin. Upon return to Japan, Shibata (Chinese herbs) started a line of distinguished chemists, Keita and Yuji Shibata (flavones) and Shoji Shibata (1915–, lichens, fungal bisanthraquinonoid pigments, ginsenosides); Nagai returned to Tokyo Science University in 1884, studied ephedrine, and left a big mark in the embryonic era of organic chemistry. Modern natural products chemistry really began when three extraordinary organic chemists returned from Europe in the 1910s and started teaching and research at their respective faculties:

Riko Majima, 1874–1962, C. D. Harries (Kiel University); R. Willstätter (Zürich): Faculty of Science, Tohoku University; studied urushiol, the catecholic mixture of poison ivy irritant.

Yasuhiko Asahina, 1881–1975, R. Willstätter: Faculty of pharmacy, Tokyo University; lichens and Chinese herb.

Umetaro Suzuki, 1874–1943, E. Fischer: Faculty of agriculture, Tokyo University; vitamin B_1(thiamine).

Because these three pioneers started research in three different faculties (i.e., science, pharmacy, and agriculture), and because little interfaculty personnel exchange occurred in subsequent years, natural products chemistry in Japan was pursued independently within these three academic domains; the situation has changed now. The three pioneers started lines of first-class successors, but the establishment of a strong infrastructure takes many years, and it was only after the mid-1960s that the general level of science became comparable to that in the rest of the world; the 3rd IUPAC Symposium on the Chemistry of Natural Products, presided over by Munio Kotake (1894–1976, bufotoxins, see below), held in 1964 in Kyoto, was a clear turning point in Japan's role in this area.

Some of the outstanding Japanese chemists not already quoted are the following. Shibasaburo Kitazato (1852–1931), worked with Robert Koch (Np 1905, tuberculosis) and von Behring, antitoxins of diphtheria and tetanus which opened the new field of serology, isolation of microorganism causing dysentery, founder of Kitazato Institute; Chika Kuroda (1884–1968), first female Ph.D., structure of the complex carthamin, important dye in safflower (1930) which was revised in 1979 by Obara *et al.*, although the absolute configuration is still unknown (1998); Munio Kotake (1894–1976), bufotoxins, tryptophan metabolites, nupharidine; Harusada Suginome (1892–1972), aconite alkaloids; Teijiro Yabuta (1888–1977), kojic acid, gibberelins; Eiji Ochiai (1898–1974), aconite alkaloids; Toshio Hoshino (1899–1979), abrine and other alkaloids; Yusuke Sumiki (1901–1974), gibberelins; Sankichi Takei (1896–1982), rotenone; Shiro Akabori (1900–1992), peptides, C-terminal hydrazinolysis of amino acid ; Hamao Umezawa (1914–1986), kanamycin, bleomycin, numerous antibiotics; Shojiro Uyeo (1909–1988), lycorine; Tsunematsu Takemoto (1913–1989), inokosterone, kainic acid, domoic acid, quisqualic acid; Tomihide Shimizu (1889–1958), bile acids; Kenichi Takeda (1907–1991), Chinese herbs, sesquiterpenes; Yoshio Ban (1921–1994), alkaloid synthesis; Wataru Nagata (1922–1993), stereocontrolled hydrocyanation.

7. CURRENT AND FUTURE TRENDS IN NATURAL PRODUCTS CHEMISTRY

Spectroscopy and X-ray crystallography has totally changed the process of structure determination, which used to generate the excitement of solving a mystery. The first introduction of spectroscopy to the general organic community was Woodward's 1942–1943 empirical rules for estimating the UV maxima of dienes, trienes, and enones, which were extended by Fieser (1959). However, Butenandt had used UV for correctly determining the structures of the sex hormones as early as the early 1930s, while Karrer and Kuhn also used UV very early in their structural studies of the carotenoids. The Beckman DU instruments were an important factor which made UV spectroscopy a common tool for organic chemists and biochemists. With the availability of commercial instruments in 1950, IR spectroscopy became the next physical tool, making the 1950 Colthup IR correlation chart and the 1954 Bellamy monograph indispensable. The IR fingerprint region was analyzed in detail in attempts to gain as much structural information as possible from the molecular stretching and bending vibrations. Introduction of NMR spectroscopy into organic chemistry, first for protons and then for carbons, has totally changed the picture of structure determination, so that now IR is used much less frequently; however, in biopolymer studies, the techniques of difference FTIR and resonance Raman spectroscopy are indispensable.

The dramatic and rapid advancements in mass spectrometry are now drastically changing the protocol of biomacromolecular structural studies performed in biochemistry and molecular biology. Herbert Hauptman (mathematician, 1917–, Medical Foundation, Buffalo, Np 1985) and Jerome Karle (1918–, US Naval Research Laboratory, Washington, DC, Np 1985) developed direct methods for the determination of crystal structures devoid of disproportionately heavy atoms. The direct method together with modern computers revolutionized the X-ray analysis of molecular structures, which has become routine for crystalline compounds, large as well as small. Fred McLafferty (1923–, Cornell University) and Klaus Biemann (1926–, MIT) have made important contributions in the development of organic and bioorganic mass spectrometry. The development of cyclotron-based facilities for crystallographic biology studies has led to further dramatic advances enabling some protein structures to be determined in a single day, while cryoscopic electron micrography developed in 1975 by Richard Henderson and Nigel Unwin has also become a powerful tool for 3D structural determinations of membrane proteins such as bacteriorhodopsin (25 kd) and the nicotinic acetylcholine receptor (270 kd).

Circular dichroism (c.d.), which was used by French scientists Jean B. Biot (1774–1862) and Aimé Cotton during the nineteenth century "deteriorated" into monochromatic measurements at 589 nm after R.W. Bunsen (1811–1899, Heidelberg) introduced the Bunsen burner into the laboratory which readily emitted a 589 nm light characteristic of sodium. The 589 nm $[a]_D$ values, remote from most chromophoric maxima, simply represent the summation of the low-intensity readings of the decreasing end of multiple Cotton effects. It is therefore very difficult or impossible to deduce structural information from $[a]_D$ readings. Chiroptical spectroscopy was reintroduced to organic chemistry in the 1950s by C. Djerassi at Wayne State University (and later at Stanford University) as optical rotatory dispersion (ORD) and by L. Velluz and M. Legrand at Roussel-Uclaf as c.d. Günther Snatzke (1928–1992, Bonn then Ruhr University Bochum) was a major force in developing the theory and application of organic chiroptical spectroscopy. He investigated the chiroptical properties of a wide variety of natural products, including constituents of indigenous plants collected throughout the world, and established semiempirical sector rules for absolute configurational studies. He also established close collaborations with scientists of the former Eastern bloc countries and had a major impact in increasing the interest in c.d. there.

   Chiroptical spectroscopy, nevertheless, remains one of the most underutilized physical measurements. Most organic chemists regard c.d. (more popular than ORD because interpretation is usually less ambiguous) simply as a tool for assigning absolute configurations, and since there are only two possibilities in absolute configurations, c.d. is apparently regarded as not as crucial compared to other spectroscopic methods. Moreover, many of the c.d. correlations with absolute configuration are empirical. For such reasons, chiroptical spectroscopy, with its immense potentialities, is grossly underused. However, c.d. curves can now be calculated nonempirically. Moreover, through-space coupling between the electric transition moments of two or more chromophores gives rise to intense Cotton effects split into opposite signs, exciton-coupled c.d.; fluorescence-detected c.d. further enhances the sensitivity by 50- to 100-fold. This leads to a highly versatile nonempirical microscale solution method for determining absolute configurations, etc.

   With the rapid advances in spectroscopy and isolation techniques, most structure determinations in natural products chemistry have become quite routine, shifting the trend gradually towards activity-monitored isolation and structural studies of biologically active principles available only in microgram or submicrogram quantities. This in turn has made it possible for organic chemists to direct their attention towards clarifying the mechanistic and structural aspects of the ligand/biopolymeric receptor interactions on a more well-defined molecular structural basis. Until the 1990s, it was inconceivable and impossible to perform such studies.

   Why does sugar taste sweet? This is an extremely challenging problem which at present cannot be answered even with major multidisciplinary efforts. Structural characterization of sweet compounds and elucidation of the amino acid sequences in the receptors are only the starting point. We are confronted with a long list of problems such as cloning of the receptors to produce them in sufficient quantities to investigate the physical fit between the active factor (sugar) and receptor by biophysical methods, and the time-resolved change in this physical contact and subsequent activation of G-protein and enzymes. This would then be followed by neurophysiological and ultimately physiological and psychological studies of sensation. How do the hundreds of taste receptors differ in their structures and their physical contact with molecules, and how do we differentiate the various taste sensations? The same applies to vision and to olfactory processes. What are the functions of the numerous glutamate receptor subtypes in our brain? We are at the starting point of a new field which is filled with exciting possibilities.

   Familiarity with molecular biology is becoming essential for natural products chemists to plan research directed towards an understanding of natural products biosynthesis, mechanisms of bioactivity triggered by ligand–receptor interactions, etc. Numerous genes encoding enzymes have been cloned and expressed by the cDNA and/or genomic DNA-polymerase chain reaction protocols. This then leads to the possible production of new molecules by gene shuffling and recombinant biosynthetic techniques. Monoclonal catalytic antibodies using haptens possessing a structure similar to a high-energy intermediate of a proposed reaction are also contributing to the elucidation of biochemical mechanisms and the design of efficient syntheses. The technique of photoaffinity labeling, brilliantly invented by Frank Westheimer (1912–, Harvard University), assisted especially by advances in mass spectrometry, will clearly be playing an increasingly important role in studies of ligand–receptor interactions including enzyme–substrate reactions. The combined and sophisticated use of various spectroscopic means, including difference spectroscopy and fast time-resolved spectroscopy, will also become increasingly central in future studies of ligand–receptor studies.

   Organic chemists, especially those involved in structural studies have the techniques, imagination, and knowledge to use these approaches. But it is difficult for organic chemists to identify an exciting and worthwhile topic. In contrast, the biochemists, biologists, and medical doctors are daily facing

exciting life-related phenomena, frequently without realizing that the phenomena could be understood or at least clarified on a chemical basis. Broad individual expertise and knowledge coupled with multidisciplinary research collaboration thus becomes essential to investigate many of the more important future targets successfully. This approach may be termed "dynamic," as opposed to a "static" approach, exemplified by isolation and structure determination of a single natural product. Fortunately for scientists, nature is extremely complex and hence all the more challenging. Natural products chemistry will be playing an absolutely indispensable role for the future. Conservation of the alarming number of disappearing species, utilization of biodiversity, and understanding of the intricacies of biodiversity are further difficult, but urgent, problems confronting us.

That natural medicines are attracting renewed attention is encouraging from both practical and scientific viewpoints; their efficacy has often been proven over the centuries. However, to understand the mode of action of folk herbs and related products from nature is even more complex than mechanistic clarification of a single bioactive factor. This is because unfractionated or partly fractionated extracts are used, often containing mixtures of materials, and in many cases synergism is most likely playing an important role. Clarification of the active constituents and their modes of action will be difficult. This is nevertheless a worthwhile subject for serious investigations.

Dedicated to Sir Derek Barton whose amazing insight helped tremendously in the planning of this series, but who passed away just before its completion. It is a pity that he was unable to write this introduction as originally envisaged, since he would have had a masterful overview of the content he wanted, based on his vast experience. I have tried to fulfill his task, but this introduction cannot do justice to his original intention.

ACKNOWLEDGMENT

I am grateful to current research group members for letting me take quite a time off in order to undertake this difficult writing assignment with hardly any preparation. I am grateful to Drs. Nina Berova, Reimar Bruening, Jerrold Meinwald, Yoko Naya, and Tetsuo Shiba for their many suggestions.

8. BIBLIOGRAPHY

"A 100 Year History of Japanese Chemistry," Chemical Society of Japan, Tokyo Kagaku Dojin, 1978.
K. Bloch, *FASEB J.*, 1996, **10**, 802.
"Britannica Online," 1994–1998.
Bull. Oriental Healing Arts Inst. USA, 1980, **5**(7).
L. F. Fieser and M. Fieser, "Advanced Organic Chemistry," Reinhold, New York, 1961.
L. F. Fieser and M. Fieser, "Natural Products Related to Phenanthrene," Reinhold, New York, 1949.
M. Goodman and F. Morehouse, "Organic Molecules in Action," Gordon & Breach, New York, 1973.
L. K. James (ed.), "Nobel Laureates in Chemistry," American Chemical Society and Chemistry Heritage Foundation, 1994.
J. Mann, "Murder, Magic and Medicine," Oxford University Press, New York, 1992.
R. M. Roberts, "Serendipity, Accidental Discoveries in Science," Wiley, New York, 1989.
D. S. Tarbell and T. Tarbell, "The History of Organic Chemistry in the United States, 1875–1955," Folio, Nashville, TN, 1986.

Formula Index

JOHN NEWTON
David John Services Ltd., Slough, UK

This index to the eight volumes of *Comprehensive Natural Products Chemistry* contains entries to significant specific compounds discussed in the text, equations, Table, Figures, or Schemes. Reagents or compounds mentioned only casually are not indexed. Significant compounds are indexed at the first reference in a section; subsequent references are not necessarily provided.

Most of the entries are to specific trivial chemical names, as given in the text, but some systematic names are also used and, on occasion, generic names such as 'sesquiterpene' or 'eudesmane.' Salts, such as 'cinnamate,' have been indexed as the acid. The reader is advised to search for related entries under the appropriate headings.

The element symbols within each formula are arranged according to the modified Hill system, in which the order is C, H, and then any remaining symbols arranged alphabetically.

AlCl₃, aluminum chloride, **7**, 126
Br₂, bromine, **7**, 96
Br₂Zn, zinc bromide, **7**, 126
CaCl₂, calcium chloride, **8**, 149
CCaO₃, calcium carbonate, **8**, 149
CeN₂H₄O₂, ceric ammonium nitrate, **7**, 126
CHN, cyanide, **3**, 378
CHN₆, 5-diazonium-1-*H*-tetrazole, **3**, 378
CHO, formyl, **7**, 120
CH₂ClF, chlorofluoromethane, **5**, 408
CH₂Cl₂, dichloromethane, **5**, 407
CH₂N₄, tetrazole, **6**, 82, **7**, 130, 137
CH₂O, formaldehyde, **3**, 381, 397, 398, 401, 408, 409, 411, 413, **5**, 408, **7**, 502
CH₂O₂, formic acid, **3**, 422, **5**, 166, 185, **8**, 209
CH₂O₃, carbonate, **1**, 3
CH₃, methyl, **7**, 130
CH₃ClO₂S, methanesulfonyl chloride, **7**, 118
CH₃NO, formamide, **6**, 253, **8**, 183
CH₃O₅P, phosphonoformic acid, **1**, 20, 869
CH₄, methane, **5**, 174, 218
CH₄N₂, formamidine, **7**, 124
CH₄N₂O, urea, **4**, 150, **6**, 253, **8**, 146
CH₄N₂O₂, hydroxyurea, **5**, 180
CH₄O, methanol, **5**, 186, **7**, 259, **8**, 209
CH₄S, methanethiol, **1**, 849, **7**, 259
CH₅N, methylamine, **3**, 411, 412, **4**, 67
CH₅NO, methoxyamine, **6**, 65, **7**, 93
CH₅NO₂P, methoxyphosphoramidite, **7**, 132
CH₅N₃O, semicarbazide, **6**, 65
CH₅O₄P, hydroxymethylphosphonic acid, **1**, 869
CH₆O₆P₂, methanediphosphonic acid, **5**, 158
CN₄O₈, tetranitromethane, **5**, 243, 353, **7**, 400
CO, carbon monoxide, **8**, 93
CO₂, carbon dioxide, **8**, 93, 209
CoH₁₈N₆, cobalt hexammine, **6**, 160
C₂Cl₄, tetrachloroethene, **5**, 410
C₂HCl₃, trichloroethene, **5**, 410
C₂HCl₃O₂, trichloroacetic acid, **7**, 126
C₂HF₃N₄, 5-trifluoromethyl-1*H*-tetrazole, **7**, 138
C₂H₂Br₃, 2,2,2-tribromoethyl, **7**, 130
C₂H₂Cl₂, 1,2-dichloroethene, **5**, 410
C₂H₂Cl₂O₂, dichloroacetic acid, **7**, 126
C₂H₂Cl₃, 2,2,2-trichloroethyl, **7**, 130
C₂H₂Cl₃OP, 2,2,2-trichloroethyl phosphorodichloridite, **7**, 108
C₂H₂F₂O₂, fluoroacetate, **8**, 148, 152
C₂H₂O₂, glyoxal, **7**, 95, 521
C₂H₂O₃, glyoxylate, **2**, 53, **3**, 381, 404, 413
C₂H₃Br, bromoethylene, **8**, 93
C₂H₃BrO, bromoacetaldehyde, **7**, 93
C₂H₃Cl, chloroethylene, **8**, 93
C₂H₃ClO, chloroacetaldehyde, **3**, 398, **7**, 93
C₂H₃FO₂, monofluoroacetic acid, **1**, 871
C₂H₃F₃O, 2,2,2-trifluoroethanol, **5**, 358
C₂H₃IO₂, iodoacetic acid, **3**, 394, **4**, 342, **5**, 156
C₂H₃NaO₂, sodium acetate, **1**, 294
C₂H₃O, acetyl, **1**, 120
C₂H₄, ethylene, **1**, 127, 128, 133, **3**, 9, **8**, 21, 22, 27, 91
C₂H₄Br₂, 1,2-dibromoethane, **5**, 403, 404, 405
C₂H₄Cl₂, 1,2-dichloroethane, **5**, 404, 405
C₂H₄INO, iodoacetamide, **1**, 358, **2**, 19, **3**, 398, **4**, 14, **5**, 353
C₂H₄NO₆P, phosphoglycolohydroxamate, **5**, 12
C₂H₄O, acetaldehyde, **3**, 373, 397, 409, 411, **5**, 189, 273
C₂H₄OPS, oxathiaphospholane, **7**, 133
C₂H₄O₂
    acetic acid, **1**, 298, **2**, 61, **3**, 422, **4**, 255, **8**, 209
    glycolaldehyde, **3**, 374, 386, 409, 425, 426, 429
C₂H₄O₂S, mercaptoacetic acid, **3**, 758
C₂H₄O₃, glycolic acid, **8**, 427
C₂H₄O₄S, sulfoacetaldehyde, **1**, 833

C₂H₅ClO
    2-chloroethanol, **5**, 191
    chloromethy methyl ether, **5**, 408
C₂H₅NO, ethanolamine, **3**, 403
C₂H₅NO₂, glycine, **1**, 838, **2**, 386, **3**, 246, 259, 264, 397, 398, 399, 401, 827, **4**, 62, 65, 140, **5**, 185, **8**, 209, 417
C₂H₅N₃O, 2-azidoethanol, **5**, 197
C₂H₅N₃O₂, *N*-methyl-*N*-nitrosourea, **1**, 783, **7**, 520
C₂H₅O₄P, phosphonoacetaldehyde, **1**, 869
C₂H₅O₅P
    acetyl phosphate, **3**, 392, 393, **5**, 144
    carboxymethanephosphonic acid, **5**, 158
C₂H₆, ethane, **5**, 221
C₂H₆NO₄P, phosphorylethanolamine, **3**, 402
C₂H₆NO₆P, phosphoglycolohydroxamate, **3**, 425, **5**, 36
C₂H₆O, ethanol, **1**, 295, **8**, 209, **3**, 422
C₂H₆OS
    dimethyl sulfoxide, **3**, 422
    mercaptoethanol, **3**, 392, 644, **4**, 14
    β-mercaptoethanol, **1**, 260, **3**, 394, **5**, 184, 199, 415, **7**, 376, 379
C₂H₆O₂
    1,2-ethanediol, **5**, 274
    ethylene glycol, **5**, 184, 188
    ethyl hydroperoxide, **5**, 246
C₂H₆O₃S₂, coenzyme M, **1**, 833
C₂H₆O₄S, dimethyl sulfate, **7**, 95, 253
C₂H₆S, DMS, **6**, 65
C₂H₆S₂, dimethyl disulfide, **8**, 161
C₂H₆S₃, dimethyl trisulfide, **8**, 161
C₂H₆S₄, dimethyl tetrasulfide, **8**, 161
C₂H₇N, dimethylamine, **3**, 411
C₂H₇NO, ethanolamine, **3**, 197, 296, **5**, 273
C₂H₇NS, cysteamine, **1**, 260
C₂H₇O₃P, ethanephosphonic acid, **5**, 158
C₂H₇O₄P, 2-hydroxyethylphosphonic acid, **1**, 869, 875
C₂H₈NOP, aminoethanolphosphate, **3**, 197
C₂H₈NO₃P, 2-aminoethylphosphonic acid, **1**, 865, 875
C₂H₈NO₄P, phosphoethanolamine, **3**, 296, 297, 300, **4**, 315
C₂I₄, tetraiodoethene, **5**, 410
C₂K₂O₄, potassium oxalate, **8**, 148
C₃H₂Cl₂N₂, 4,5-dichloroimidazole, **7**, 133
C₃H₂F₆O, 1,1,1,3,3,3-hexafluoro-2-propanol, **7**, 126
C₃H₃BrO₃
    bromopyruvate, **3**, 398, 423, **5**, 47
    3-bromopyruvate, **1**, 579, **5**, 44
C₃H₃ClO₂, chloroacrylic acid, **5**, 410
C₃H₃Cl₂O₂, 2,2-dichloropropionate, **5**, 405
C₃H₃N₃O₂, azomycin, **7**, 521
C₃H₃O₂, allyloxycarbonyl, **7**, 121
C₃H₄BrN, 3-bromopropionitrile, **6**, 93
C₃H₄Br₂O, 1,3-dibromopropan-2-one, **1**, 351
C₃H₄ClO₂
    chloropropionate, **5**, 405
    2-chloropropionate, **5**, 405, 406
C₃H₄FO₆P
    fluoro-PEP, **3**, 252
    3-fluoroPEP, **1**, 579, 594, 598
C₃H₄F₃NO₂, β,β,β-trifluoroalanine, **3**, 276
C₃H₄N, cyanoethyl, **7**, 119, 130
C₃H₄N₂, imidazole, **5**, 175
C₃H₄N₄O, 6-azacytosine, **7**, 322
C₃H₄O, acrolein, **7**, 502
C₃H₄O₂
    acrylic acid, **1**, 298
    malondialdehyde, **1**, 262, **5**, 189, **7**, 502
    methylglyoxal, **2**, 54, **5**, 37, 67
    2-oxetanone, **2**, 22
C₃H₄O₃
    enolpyruvate, **5**, 32, 33, 38
    malonate semialdehyde, **3**, 409, **5**, 410

pyruvic acid, **1**, 596, 610, **2**, 4, 53, 54, 55, 56, 376, **3**, 369, 373, 376, 377, 378, 380, 381, 391, 402, 405, 407, 408, 413, 414, 421, 422, 425, 426, 428, 429, 469, 470, 471, **5**, 38, 185, 217, 271

C₃H₄O₄
    hydroxypyruvate, **3**, 415
    tartronate semialdehyde, **3**, 402
C₃H₄O₆P, enediolate analogue, **5**, 12
C₃H₄O₆S, sulfopyruvate, **1**, 833
C₃H₄O₇P, 2-phosphoglycerate, **5**, 16
C₃H₅, 2-propenyl, **7**, 119
C₃H₅FO, fluoroacetone, **3**, 373
C₃H₅NO, cyanoethanol, **7**, 127
C₃H₅NO₂
    alanine enamine, **3**, 396
    dehydroalanine, **1**, 853, **4**, 7, 336
    2,3-dehydroalanine, **4**, 275,
C₃H₅N₂O₄P, 3′-phosphorimidazole, **6**, 134
C₃H₅O, propionyl, **7**, 120
C₃H₅O₂, methoxyacetyl, **7**, 120
C₃H₅O₆P , phosphenolpyruvate, **1**, 20, 346, 527, 574, 575, 577, 580, 593, 594, 833, 867, **3**, 251, 386, 387, 388, 390, 391, 393, **4**, 2, 10, 246, **5**, 16, 33, 38, 719
C₃H₆, propylene, **8**, 98
C₃H₆BrO₅P, bromohydroxyacetone phosphate, **5**, 36
C₃H₆ClNO₂, β-chloroalanine, **3**, 276
C₃H₆Cl₂, 1,3-dichloropropane, **3**, 408
C₃H₆Cl₂O, 1,3-dichloro-2-propanol, **5**, 409
C₃H₆N, aziridyl carbinyl radical, **5**, 210
C₃H₆N₂O₂, cycloserine, **3**, 277, **8**, 389
C₃H₆N₂O₄S, 3-aminomonobactamic acid, **4**, 187, 262
C₃H₆N₄S, thioethyltetrazole, **7**, 138
C₃H₆O
    acetone, **2**, 17, 21, **3**, 373, **5**, 198, 373
    propanal, **3**, 373, 394,
    propionaldehyde, **3**, 414
C₃H₆O₂
    hydroxyacetone, **2**, 54
    lactaldehyde, **3**, 414, 423
    propionic acid, **1**, 14, 298, **3**, 422, **5**, 271, **8**, 241, 422
C₃H₆O₂S, methyl thioglycolate, **7**, 560
C₃H₆O₃
    dihydroxyacetone, **1**, 144, **3**, 417, 419, 425
    glyceraldehyde, **2**, 55, **3**, 409, 419, 423
    3-hydroxypropionic acid, **1**, 298
    lactaldehyde, **3**, 424, 425, 426
    lactic acid, **3**, 6, 247, 272, 414, 422, 444, **5**, 80
C₃H₆O₆P
    phosphoenolpyruvate, **3**, 7
    phosphonopyruvate, **1**, 867
    PnPy, **1**, 868
C₃H₆O₆S, sulfolactic acid, **1**, 833
C₃H₇ClO, propane epichlorohydrin, **5**, 408
C₃H₇N
    dimethylaminomethylene, **6**, 87, **7**, 123
    dimethylformamidine, **6**, 87
    N-methylaziridine, **5**, 210
C₃H₇NO, dimethylformamide, **3**, 422
C₃H₇NO₂
    alanine, **1**, 537, **3**, 245, 248, 254, 259, 260, 272, 395, 405, 533, 826, **4**, 235, **5**, 185, **6**, 127, **8**, 427
    β-alanine, **4**, 339,
    D-alanine, **4**, 275
C₃H₇NO₂S, cysteine, **1**, 260, 840, 847, 848, **3**, 392, **4**, 162, 165, 227, 246, 354, **5**, 184, 186, **7**, 560, 565, **8**, 418
C₃H₇NO₂Se, selenocysteine, **4**, 354
C₃H₇NO₃
    β-aminooxypropionic acid, **3**, 634
    serine, **1**, 545, **2**, 386, **3**, 246, 259, 273, 397, 398, 400, 401, 422, **4**, 7, 227, 252, 354, 538, **6**, 127, **8**, 209

C₃H₇N₃O₂
    ENU, **6**, 67
    ethylnitrosourea, **7**, 253
C₃H₇O₃P, propenylphosphonic acid, **1**, 876
C₃H₇O₄P
    fosfomycin, **1**, 20, 593, 865, 875, **3**, 252, 275, **5**, 53, 62, 66
    phosphonomycin, **3**, 275
C₃H₇O₅P, glycidol phosphate, **5**, 36
C₃H₇O₆P
    dihydroxyacetone phosphate, **1**, 286, **2**, 52, 54, 375, **3**, 369, 408, 409, 414, 419, 424, 425, 426, 430, 431, 464, **5**, 36
    glyceraldehyde-3-phosphate, **2**, 3, 50, 50, 51, 52, 53, 54, 55, 56, 375, **3**, 373, 386, 390, 392, 393, 414, 417, 419, 421, 423, 428, 429, 430, 431, **4**, 69, **5**, 8, 36 **8**, 219
    3-phosphonolactic acid, **1**, 869
C₃H₇O₇P
    2-phosphoglycerate, **1**, 403, **5**, 27
    3-phosphoglycerate, **3**, 390
    3-phosphoglyceric acid, **3**, 390
C₃H₈BNO₄, alanine boronate, **3**, 276, 278
C₃H₈NO₄P, phosphinoalanine, **1**, 868
C₃H₈NO₅P
    alanine phosphonate, **3**, 276, 278
    glyphosate, **1**, 593, 596, **3**, 805, **4**, 4, 9, **5**, 349
C₃H₈NO₅PS, phosphocysteine, **5**, 144, 145
C₃H₈NO₆P, phosphoserine, **4**, 354, **5**, 144
C₃H₈N₂O₂, α,β-diaminopropionic acid, **8**, 434
C₃H₈O, 2-propanol, **5**, 186, **7**, 401, **8**, 209
C₃H₈O₂, 1,2-propanediol, **5**, 274
C₃H₈O₂S, thioglycerol, **3**, 392
C₃H₈O₃, glycerol, **1**, 141, **2**, 54, 282, **4**, 255, **8**, 427
C₃H₈O₃S₂, S-methyl coenzyme M, **1**, 833
C₃H₈O₇P₂
    FM monophosphate, **1**, 878
    isoprenyl pyrophosphate, **4**, 199
C₃H₈O₉P₂, dihydroxyacetone phosphate, **5**, 318
C₃H₈S₂, hydrodisulfide, **7**, 523
C₃H₉N, trimethylamine, **3**, 411, **8**, 418
C₃H₉NO
    isopropanolamine, **4**, 148
    trimethylamine oxide, **3**, 411, 412, **8**, 417
C₃H₉O₄P
    2-hydroxypropylphosphonic acid, **1**, 876
    trimethyl phosphate, **7**, 70
C₃H₉O₅P, 1,3-propanediol phosphate, **6**, 250
C₃H₉O₆P
    glycerol-P, **3**, 464
    3-PGA, **3**, 464, 470, 471, 472
    3-phosphoglycerate, **3**, 470
C₃H₉O₁₀P₂, 1,3-diphosphoglyceric acid, **4**, 69
C₃H₉O₁₀P₃, FM diphosphate, **1**, 878
C₃H₁₀N₂O₁₆P, N-aminoglyphosate, **1**, 597
C₃H₁₁NO₂, valine, **8**, 221
C₄H₃BrN₂O₂, 5-bromouridine, **7**, 316
C₄H₃FN₂O₂, 5-fluorouridine, **7**, 316
C₄H₃IN₂O₂, 5-iodouridine, **7**, 316
C₄H₃N₅O, 2-azahypoxanthine, **7**, 326
C₄H₄BrN₃, 5-bromodeoxycytosine, **7**, 78
C₄H₄BrN₃O, bromocytosine, **7**, 321
C₄H₄FN₃O, C-5-fluorocytosine, **7**, 322
C₄H₄N₂O
    2-pyrimidinone, **6**, 225, **7**, 254
    4-pyrimidinone, **7**, 254
C₄H₄N₂OS
    2-thiouracil, **7**, 314
    4-thiouridine, **7**, 315
C₄H₄N₂O₂
    maleic hydrazide, **8**, 34, 36
    pyrimidinedione, **7**, 261
    uracil, **5**, 182, **7**, 56

$C_4H_4N_2O_2S$, thiobarbituric acid, **7**, 385
$C_4H_4N_2S$
  2-thiopyrimidine, **7**, 260
  4-thiopyrimidine, **7**, 260
$C_4H_4N_2S_2$, 2,4-dithiopyrimidine, **7**, 260
$C_4H_4O_4$
  fumaric acid, **5**, 23
  maleic acid, **5**, 23
$C_4H_4O_5$, oxaloacetate, **2**, 53, **3**, 381, 391, 404, 413, **4**, 255, **5**, 25
$C_4H_5BrO_3$, bromoketobutyrate, **3**, 423
$C_4H_5NO_3$, N-hydroxysuccinimide, **6**, 77
C_4H_5NS, allyl isothiocyanate, **8**, 155, 173
$C_4H_5N_3$, 4'-iminopyrimidine, **3**, 417
$C_4H_5N_3O$
  cytosine, **7**, 56, 375
  pseudoisocytosine, **7**, 255
  pyrazineC-nucleoside, **7**, 256
$C_4H_5N_3O_2$
  5-aminouridine, **7**, 316
  6-azathymine, **7**, 319
  cytosine analogue, **7**, 256
  6-oxocytosine, **7**, 322
$C_4H_5O_2$, allyloxycarbonyl, **7**, 119, 136
$C_4H_5O_3$, acetoacetate, **2**, 17, 21, 24
$C_4H_5O_6P$, carboxyallenyl phosphate, **1**, 598
$C_4H_5O_7P$, CPEP, **1**, 871
$C_4H_6Cl_5O_2P$, 2,2,2-trichloro-1,1-dimethylethylphosphorodichloridite, **7**, 130
$C_4H_6N_2$, N-methylimidazole, **7**, 108
$C_4H_6N_2O_2$
  β-cyanoalanine, **8**, 145, 146
  piperazinedione, **1**, 546
$C_4H_6N_3OS$, methionine sulfoximine, **2**, 256
C_4H_6O
  crotonaldehyde, **7**, 502
  3,4-epoxy-1-butene, **5**, 52
$C_4H_6O_2$
  2,3-butanedione, **5**, 275, **7**, 503
  butyrolactone, **1**, 139
$C_4H_6O_2S_2$, asparagusic acid, **1**, 860
$C_4H_6O_3$
  acetoacetic acid, **1**, 295, **3**, 382
  succinic semialdehyde, **3**, 413
$C_4H_6O_4$
  4-hydroxy-2-ketobutyrate, **3**, 381, 382, 386
  succinic acid, **1**, 298, **2**, 53, **3**, 384, **4**, 92
$C_4H_6O_5$, malate, **2**, 53
$C_4H_6O_6$, tartaric acid, **5**, 155
$C_4H_7ClN_2$, N-methylimidazole hydrochloride, **7**, 138
$C_4H_7Cl_2O_4P$, dichlorovos, **1**, 447, 456
C_4H_7N, 3,4-dihydro-2H-pyrrole, **8**, 210
$C_4H_7NO_2$
  acetidine-2-carboxylic acid, **4**, 327
  1-aminocyclopropane-1-carboxylic acid, **1**, 133, **8**, 94, 104
  azetidine-2-carboxylic acid, **8**, 146
  2,3-dehydrobutyrine, **4**, 275,
  vinylglycine, **1**, 842, **4**, 168
$C_4H_7NO_2S$, γ-thioproline, **4**, 327
$C_4H_7NO_3$
  4-amino-3-ketobutyrate, **4**, 76
  aspartate 1-semialdehyde, **4**, 70
$C_4H_7NO_4$, aspartic acid, **3**, 248, 265, 404, 407, 632, **4**, 5, 165, 227
$C_4H_7NO_5$, 3-hydroxyaspartic acid, **3**, 404, 405, **4**, 280
$C_4H_7N_2$, dehydrobutyrin, **1**, 853
$C_4H_7N_3O$, 1-azido-4-hydroxy-2-butene, **5**, 52
C_4H_7O
  isobutyryl, **6**, 87
  2'-O-tetrahydrofuranyl, **6**, 84
$C_4H_7O_2$, butanoic acid, **8**, 165
$C_4H_7O_3$, β-hydroxybutyrate, **2**, 17, 18, 21

$C_4H_7O_5P$, deaminoketodemethylphosphinothricin, **1**, 872
$C_4H_7O_5PS$, methionine sulfoximine phosphate, **2**, 256
C_4H_8, 2-butene, **8**, 93
$C_4H_8N_2$, tetrahydropyrimidine, **7**, 460
$C_4H_8O_2$
  acetoin, **3**, 394
  butyric acid, **1**, 298
  ethyl acetate, **8**, 161, 209
  4-hydroxybutanal, **8**, 210
  isobutyric acid, **8**, 220
  2-methylpropanoic acid, **8**, 221
$C_4H_8O_2S$, 3-(methylthio)propanoic acid, **8**, 178
$C_4H_8O_3$
  acetic acid 2-hydroxyethyl ester, **5**, 192
  2-hydroperoxytetrahydrofuran, **7**, 95
  2-hydroxybutyric acid, **3**, 6, 272
  3-hydroxybutanoic acid, **1**, 295, **8**, 209
  4-hydroxybutyric acid, **1**, 298, **8**, 434
$C_4H_8O_4$, erythrose, **7**, 382
C_4H_9, isobutyl, **7**, 120
C_4H_9ClO, t-butyl hypochlorite, **5**, 173
C_4H_9N
  1-(dimethylamino)ethylidene, **7**, 123
  pyrrolidine, **4**, 30
C_4H_9NO, 2-methyl-2-nitrosopropane, **1**, 105
$C_4H_9NO_2$
  aminobutyric acid, **1**, 537, **4**, 252, 253
  2-aminobutyric acid, **1**, 533, 545, 842
  3-aminobutyrate, **1**, 538
  4-aminobutyrate, **1**, 538, **8**, 433
$C_4H_9NO_2S$
  homocysteine, **2**, 386, **5**, 263, 275
  3-methylcysteine, **4**, 252
  S-methylcysteine , **1**, 848, 849, **4**, 252
$C_4H_9NO_2Se$
  Se-methylselenocysteine, **4**, 357, **8**, 146
$C_4H_9NO_2S_2$, dithiohemiacetal, **1**, 848
$C_4H_9NO_3$
  allothreonine, **3**, 397, 398, 400, 401
  homoserine, **3**, 246, 249
  methylserine, **4**, 250
  O-methylserine, **1**, 842,
  threonine, **3**, 248, 382, 397, 398, 400, 401, **4**, 148, 327, 537
$C_4H_9NO_3S$, monothiohemiacetal, **1**, 848
$C_4H_9N_3O_2$, creatine, **8**, 457
$C_4H_9N_3O_3$, albizzine, **8**, 146
$C_4H_9O_2$, 2-methoxyethoxymethyl, **7**, 119
$C_4H_9O_4$, acetaldehyde dimethyl acetal, **7**, 378
$C_4H_9O_6P$, phosphonate, **1**, 579
$C_4H_9O_7P$
  erythrose 4-phosphate, **1**, 346, 527, 574, 575, 577, 578, 719, 850, **3**, 370, 386, 388, 391, 393, 414, 415, 417, 419, **4**, 2
  erythulose-1-phosphate, **3**, 408
C_4H_{10}, butane, **5**, 221
$C_4H_{10}AlCl$, chlorodiethylalane, **7**, 126
$C_4H_{10}B F_3O$, boron trifluoride etherate, **7**, 126
$C_4H_{10}NO_4P$, demethylphosphinothricin, **1**, 867
$C_4H_{10}NO_5P$, fosmidomycin, **1**, 865
$C_4H_{10}NO_6P$, O-phosphothreonine, **4**, 148
$C_4H_{10}N_2O_2$, 3,4-diaminobutyrate, **4**, 70
$C_4H_{10}N_2O_3$, canaline, **8**, 146
$C_4H_{10}N_2O_4$, 2,4-diaminobutyric acid, **3**, 247
$C_4H_{10}N_3O_5P$, creatine phosphate, **5**, 144
$C_4H_{10}O_2$
  butanediol, **5**, 147
  2,3-butanediol, **8**, 210
  t-butyl hydroperoxide, **5**, 232
$C_4H_{10}O_2S_2$, dithiothreitol, **1**, 260, 295, **3**, 376, 386, 644, **4**, 14, **5**, 184, 196, 198, 415, 417, **7**, 114, 163, 400, 405, 565, 666
$C_4H_{10}O_3$, glycoaldehyde dimethyl acetal, **7**, 402

C₄H₁₀O₄, erythritol, **3**, 393, 408, 544, **5**, 189
C₄H₁₁NO, 4-aminobutanol, **4**, 30
C₄H₁₁N₂O₂, α,τ-diaminobutyric acid, **8**, 146
C₄H₁₂N₂, putrescine, **3**, 721, **4**, 30
C₄H₁₃NO₇P₂, 2-(dimethylamino)ethyl diphosphate, **2**, 72,
    5, 335
C₄H₁₃N₃, diethylenetriamine, **7**, 162
C₄H₂₄Cl₄N₆Pt₂, tetramethylenediamine platinum
    complex, **7**, 169
C₄Cl₄O₂S, tetrachlorothiophene dioxide, **5**, 429
C₅H₃FN₄O, 2-fluorohypoxanthine, **7**, 326
C₅H₃F₃N₂O₂, trifluorothymine, **7**, 317
C₅H₃N₄S, C-6-thiopurine, **7**, 327
C₅H₄BrN₅
    8-bromoadenine, **7**, 325
    8-bromodeoxyguanine, **7**, 78
C₅H₄Br₂N₂O, 4,5-dibromopyrrole-2-carbamide, **8**, 440
C₅H₄NO₂, pyrrole-2-carboxylic acid, **8**, 221
C₅H₄N₄, purine, **3**, 397, **6**, 225
C₅H₄N₄O
    hypoxanthine, **5**, 80, 308, **6**, 225, **7**, 254, 325
    α-sarcin, **6**, 196
C₅H₄N₄O₂, xanthine, **7**, 326
C₅H₄N₄O₃, uric acid, **5**, 80, 238
C₅H₄N₄S, 6-thiopurine, **7**, 260
C₅H₄O₂
    furfural, **7**, 395
    2-methylene-3(2H)-furanone, **5**, 171, 182, 194
    3-methylene-3(2H)-furanone, **5**, 168
    α-pyrone, **1**, 11
    γ-pyrone, **1**, 11
C₅H₄O₃, 2-oxo-3-pentynoate, **5**, 45, 47
C₅H₅NO
    2-pyridinone, **6**, 225
    4-pyridinone, **6**, 225
C₅H₅N₅
    adenine, **5**, 74, **7**, 56
    2-aminopurine, **6**, 76, 163, 225, 227, 249, **7**, 254, 267
    3-isoadenine, **7**, 324
C₅H₅N₅O
    guanine, **7**, 56
    8-hydroxyadenine, **7**, 325
    N-6-hydroxyadenine, **7**, 324
    isoguanine, **6**, 225
    2-oxoadenine, **7**, 323
C₅H₅N₅O₂, 7-hydro-8-oxoguanine, **7**, 328
C₅H₅N₅S
    6-thioguanine, **3**, 79, **6**, 225
    C-6-thioguanine, **7**, 327
C₅H₆Cl₃O₂
    trichloro-t-butoxycarbonyl, **7**, 120
    trichloroisopropoxycarbonyl, **7**, 119
C₅H₆N₂, 2-aminopyridine, **7**, 254
C₅H₆N₂O
    N-acetylimidazole, **5**, 250
    3-deazacytosine, **7**, 254
C₅H₆N₂OS
    2-thiothymine, **7**, 314
    4-thiothymine, **5**, 391, **7**, 315
C₅H₆N₂O₂
    C-6-methyluridine, **7**, 319
    thymine, **5**, 373, **7**, 401
C₅H₆N₄, 3-deazaadenine, **7**, 268
C₅H₆N₆
    2-aminoadenine, **7**, 314, 323
    2,6-diaminopurine, **6**, 225, **7**, 267
C₅H₆O₂
    dihydropyrone, **1**, 752
    4-hydroxy-2-cyclopentenone, **1**, 178
C₅H₆O₃
    2-hydroxy-2,4-pentadienoate, **5**, 35, 43
    2-oxo-3-pentenoate, **5**, 35
    2-oxo-4-pentenoate, **5**, 35

siphonidin, **8**, 152
α,β-unsaturated ketone, **5**, 43
β,γ-unsaturated ketone, **5**, 43
C₅H₆O₄, 4,5-dioxovaleric acid, **4**, 70
C₅H₆O₅, 2-ketoglutarate, **1**, 69, 834, 843, 844, **3**, 382, 386,
    8, 94
C₅H₆O₆
    hydroxyketoglutarate, **3**, 382, 402, 421
    α-hydroxy-γ-ketoglutarate, **3**, 413
    4-hydroxy-2-ketoglutarate, **3**, 381, 385
C₅H₇ClO₃
    3-chlorolevulinic acid, **4**, 76
    5-chlorolevulinic acid, **4**, 76
C₅H₇F₃NO₃P, phosphoramidite, **7**, 154
C₅H₇F₃N₂O₃S, N-methylimidazolium trifluoromethane
    sulfonate , **7**, 138
C₅H₇NO₂, 3,4-dehydroproline, **4**, 327
C₅H₇NO₃, pyroglutamic acid, **4**, 30, **8**, 299
C₅H₇NO₅, α-ketoglutaric acid, **3**, 255
C₅H₇N₃, 5-methyldeoxycytosine, **7**, 78
C₅H₇N₃O
    methylcytosine, **7**, 321
    5-methylcytosine, **7**, 317
    C-5-methylcytosine, **7**, 325
    N-4-methylcytosine, **7**, 320, 324
C₅H₇N₃O₂
    6-aminothymine, **7**, 261
    N-4-methoxycytosine, **7**, 321
    C-5-methyl-6-oxocytosine, **7**, 322
C₅H₇N₃O₄, azaserine, **3**, 627
C₅H₇N₄OP, bistriazolylphosphite, **7**, 132
C₅H₇O
    4-pentenoyl, **7**, 120
    N-pent-4-enoyl, **7**, 121, 124
C₅H₇O₂
    levulinyl, **6**, 84
    4-oxovaleryl, **7**, 120
C₅H₈
    isoprene, **2**, 46, 62, 98
    1,4-pentadiene, **1**, 97
C₅H₈ClNO₄, 3-chloroglutamic acid, **3**, 255
C₅H₈Cl₂NO₂P, 2-cyano-1,1-dimethylethyl
    phosphorodichloridite, **7**, 130
C₅H₈O, allyl vinyl ether, **5**, 348, 349
C₅H₈O₂
    1-hydroperoxy-2,4-pentadiene, **1**, 97
    2,4-pentanedione, **5**, 440
C₅H₈O₂S₂
    1,2-dithiolan-3-one 1-oxide analogue, **7**, 524
    1,2-dithiolan-3-one 1-oxide, **7**, 523
    dithiolanone oxide, **7**, 523
C₅H₈O₃
    2-keto-3-methylbutanoate, **3**, 409
    2-ketovalerate, **3**, 382
    levulinic acid, **4**, 76
C₅H₈O₄
    acetolactate, **2**, 49
    2-′-deoxyribonolactone, **7**, 376
    glutaric acid, **1**, 298
    4-hydroxy-2-ketovalerate, **3**, 386, 413
    methylsuccinic acid, **1**, 679, **4**, 255
C₅H₈O₅
    keto-3-deoxyarabonate, **3**, 429
    2-keto-4,5-dihydroxyvalerate, **3**, 382
C₅H₈O₆
    2-keto-3-deoxyarabonate, **3**, 425
    2-keto-3-deoxyxylonate, **3**, 429
C₅H₉, 1-methylcyclopropylcarbinyl radical, **5**, 220
C₅H₉ClO, pivaloyl chloride, **7**, 139
C₅H₉FO₄, 2′-fluoro-2′-deoxyribose, **6**, 226
C₅H₉FO₅, 2-fluororibose, **6**, 76
C₅H₉F₃O₇P₂, 3-(trifluoromethyl)-2-butenyl diphosphate,
    2, 80, **5**, 320, 335

C₅H₉N, *N*-methylpyrrolidylidene, **7**, 123
C₅H₉NO, *N,N*-dimethylacrylamide, **5**, 430
C₅H₉NO₂
    allylglycine, **1**, 842, **4**, 168, 253
    proline, **4**, 30, 209, **8**, 210, 418
C₅H₉NO₃
    aminolevulinic acid, **4**, 140
    5-aminolevulinic acid, **4**, 62, 72, **8**, 62
    δ-aminolevulinic acid, **2**, 64
    5-amino-3,4,5,6-tetrahydro-6-hydroxy-2*H*-pyran-2-
        one, **4**, 69
    3,4-dihydroxy-5-hydroxymethyl-1-pyrroline, **3**, 130
    glutamate semialdehyde, **3**, 275
    glutamate 1-semialdehyde, **4**, 68, 69, **8**, 63
    hydroxyproline, **1**, 546, **3**, 382
    nectrisine, **3**, 134
C₅H₉NO₃S₂, methionine-*S*-sulfoximine, **3**, 627
C₅H₉NO₄, glutamic acid, **8**, 427
C₅H₉NO₄
    O-acetylserine, **4**, 165
    glutamic acid, **1**, 853, **3**, 245, 255, 259, 407, 627, **4**, 62,
        67, 227, 249, 355, **5**, 272, **8**, 40, 94
    methyl aspartate, **3**, 632
    N-methylaspartate, **6**, 103
    strombine, **8**, 417
    threo-β-methylaspartate, **5**, 272
C₅H₉NO₄S
    carboxymethylcysteine, **4**, 249
    S-carboxymethylcysteine, **1**, 842, **4**, 168
C₅H₉NO₅
    3-hydroxy-D-glutamic acid, **3**, 246
    β-methyl-3-hydroxyaspartate, **3**, 405
C₅H₉NO₅S₂, cysteine thiazolidine derivative, **1**, 833
C₅H₉O
    t-butylcarbonyl, **7**, 120
    tetrahydropyranyl, **6**, 84
C₅H₉OS, (butylthio)carbonyl, **7**, 119
C₅H₉O₂
    isobutoxycarbonyl, **7**, 120
    isopropoxyacetyl, **7**, 120
C₅H₉O₃S, 2-oxo-4-methylthiobutyrate, **8**, 94
C₅H₉O₇P, phosphinomethylmalic acid, **1**, 871
C₅H₁₀
    cyclopentane, **7**, 57
    1,1-dimethylcyclopropane, **5**, 220
    2-pentene, **1**, 214
C₅H₁₀F₂O₇P₂
    difluorodimethylallyl diphosphate, **5**, 331
    2,2-difluoroisopentenyl diphosphate, **2**, 81
C₅H₁₀N
    1-methyl-Δ-pyrrolinium cation, **4**, 30
    N-methyl-Δ-pyrrolinium salt, **4**, 27
C₅H₁₀NNaS₂, sodium diethyldithiocarbamate, **1**, 123
C₅H₁₀NO₄, 2-cyano-1,1-dimethylethyl phosphate, **7**, 130
C₅H₁₀N₂O
    3-amino-2-piperidone, **4**, 326
    proline amide, **5**, 44
C₅H₁₀N₂O₂S, *S*-aminovinyl-D-cysteine, **4**, 275, 279
C₅H₁₀N₂O₃, glutamine, **3**, 251, 838, **4**, 6, 355
C₅H₁₀N₂O₅S, arcamine, **8**, 417
C₅H₁₀O
    3-methyl-2-buten-1-ol, **8**, 220
    3-methyl-3-buten-1-ol, **8**, 220
    2-methyl-3-buten-2-ol, **8**, 200, 220
    2-methyl-1-buten-4-ol, **5**, 220
    1-methylcyclobutanol, **5**, 220
    3-pentanone, **8**, 210
    rose furan, **8**, 226
C₅H₁₀O₂
    3-hydroxy-3-methylbutan-2-one, **8**, 220
    isovaleric acid, **1**, 141, **8**, 220
    2-methylbutanoic acid, **8**, 221
    pentanoic acid, **8**, 210

    valeric acid, **1**, 298
C₅H₁₀O₂S, dimethyl-β-propiothetin, **8**, 459
C₅H₁₀O₃
    2-hydroperoxytetrahydropyran, **7**, 95
    hydroxyisovalerate, **1**, 545
    5-hydroxyvaleric acid, **1**, 298
C₅H₁₀O₄
    1,5-anhydropentitol, **3**, 544
    cordcepose, **3**, 312
    3-deoxy-D-*threo*-pentose, **3**, 312
    2-deoxyribose, **3**, 382, **5**, 191, **7**, 56
    2-deoxy-D-ribose, **3**, 312, 332
    deoxyribose, **3**, 372, **7**, 373
    deoxyxylulose, **2**, 168, 374
    1-deoxyxylulose, **1**, 838, 840, **2**, 55, 57
    1-deoxy-D-xylulose, **2**, 376
    deoxy-D-xylulose, **8**, 220
C₅H₁₀O₅
    apiose, **3**, 499
    arabinose, **1**, 331, **3**, 373, 424, 425, 426, 499, 601, 604,
        605
    pentulose, **1**, 839
    ribose, **3**, 392, **5**, 74, 184, 189, **7**, 56
    xylose, **3**, 169, 393, 429, 499, 604, 605
C₅H₁₀O₆, xylonate, **3**, 429
C₅H₁₀S
    2,2-dimethylthietane, **8**, 220
    2,3-dimethylthietane, **8**, 221
C₅H₁₀S₂
    3,3-dimethyl-1,2-dithiolane, **8**, 221
    3,4-dimethyl-1,2-dithiolane, **8**, 221
C₅H₁₁Cl₂N, mechlorethamine, **7**, 96
C₅H₁₁FO₇P₂
    allylic fluoride, **5**, 335
    fluorodimethylallyl diphosphate, **5**, 331
    2-fluoroisopentenyl diphosphate, **2**, 81
    3-(fluoromethyl)-3-butenyl diphosphate, **2**, 73
C₅H₁₁N
    N-methylpyrrolidine, **4**, 30
    piperidine, **7**, 380
C₅H₁₁NO₂
    δ-amino-*n*-valeric acid, **8**, 434
    betaine, **8**, 417
    CYB-3, **3**, 134
    2-hydroxymethyl-3-hydroxypyrrolidine, **3**, 130,
    norvaline, **1**, 842, **4**, 253, 327, 538
    valine, **1**, 840, **2**, 54, 55, 56, 58, 376, **4**, 162, 165, 179,
        209, 246, 327, 537, **7**, 639, **8**, 418
C₅H₁₁NO₂S
    3-amino-5-mercaptopentanoic acid, **8**, 538
    methionine, **1**, 847, **2**, 386, **3**, 397, 643, **4**, 165, 176, 354,
        5, 165, 185, 209, 217, 263, 275, **8**, 94, 458
    penicillamine, **5**, 184, 186
C₅H₁₁NO₂Se, selenomethionine, **4**, 354
C₅H₁₁NO₂S₂, *S*-(methylthiomethyl)cysteine, **1**, 847, 848
C₅H₁₁NO₃
    4-amino-5-hydroxyvaleric acid, **4**, 70
    D-AB1, **3**, 134, 141
    1,4-dideoxy-1,4-imino-D-arabinotol, **3**, 130
    1,4-dideoxy-1,4-imino-D-ribitol, **3**, 130, 134
    4-hydroxy-5-aminovaleric acid, **4**, 70
    N-hydroxyvaline, **4**, 253
    O-methylallothreonine, **4**, 253
C₅H₁₁NO₄
    2′-amino-2′-deoxyribose, **6**, 226
    Ara4N, **3**, 197
C₅H₁₁NO₅, 2-aminoribose, **6**, 76
C₅H₁₁NO₅S₂, *S*-(2-sulfoethyl)cysteine, **1**, 833
C₅H₁₁NS₂, diethyldithiocarbamate, **5**, 237
C₅H₁₁N₂O₂, 4,5-diaminovaleric acid, **4**, 70
C₅H₁₁O₆P
    homophosphonate, **1**, 579
    phosphonothrixin, **1**, 865

C₅H₁₁O₇P
  3-deoxyarabinose 5-phosphate, **1**, 581
  4-deoxyarabinose-5-phosphate, **3**, 389
  1-deoxypentulose phosphate, **2**, 55
  2-deoxyribose-5-phosphate, **3**, 373, 382
  deoxyxylulose 5-phosphate, **2**, 64
  1-deoxyxylulose 5-phosphate, **2**, 55
  1-deoxy-D-xylulose 5-phosphate, **2**, 4
  2-*C*-methylerythrose 4-phosphate, **2**, 4
C₅H₁₁O₈P
  arabinose 5-phosphate, **1**, 580, **3**, 387, 388, 389, 390, 391, 419, 509
  ribose monophosphate, **6**, 139
  ribose-5-phosphate, **3**, 387, 388, 391, 414, 416
  ribulose-5-phosphate, **3**, 414, 509
  xylulose-1-phosphate, **3**, 426
  xylulose-5-phosphate, **3**, 392, 393, 414, 416
C₅H₁₂NO₃PS₂, systemin, **8**, 119
C₅H₁₂NO₄P
  bialaphos, **1**, 20, **4**, 330
  phosphinothricin, **1**, 866, **2**, 257
C₅H₁₂NO₆P, FR33289, **1**, 865
C₅H₁₂N₂O₂
  ornithine, **3**, 246, 248, **4**, 30, 209, 326
C₅H₁₂N₂O₂S, 4-thialysine, **5**, 213
C₅H₁₂N₂O₃, β-hydroxyornithine, **8**, 588
C₅H₁₂N₄O₃, canavanine, **8**, 146
C₅H₁₂O
  2-methylbutanol, **8**, 220
  3-methylbutanol, **8**, 220
  1-pentanol, **1**, 209
C₅H₁₂O₄
  3-deoxy-L-*glycero*-tetronic acid, **3**, 195, 209
  2-methylerythritol, **2**, 56
  methylerythritol , **2**, 64
C₅H₁₂O₇P₂
  dimethylallyl diphosphate, **2**, 5, 7, 46, 62, 70, 98, 99, 102, 120, 340, 380, 392, **5**, 318, 331, 334
  isopentenyl diphosphate, **2**, 3, 45, 70, 98, 99, 102, 112, 118, 120, 168, 331, 340, 372, 374, 378, **3**, 262, **5**, 317, 318, 334, **8**, 272
  3-methyl-2-butenyl diphosphate, **8**, 219, 239
  3-methyl-3-butenyl diphosphate, **8**, 219, 220
C₅H₁₂O₈P₂, IPP epoxide, **5**, 335
C₅H₁₂O₁₁P₂, ribulose-1,5-bisphosphate, **3**, 397
C₅H₁₃NO, 4-methylaminobutanol, **4**, 27
C₅H₁₃NOS₂, *S*-(methylthiomethyl)cysteinol, **1**, 847
C₅H₁₃NO₂S₂, sparsomycin monooxodithioacetal moiety, **1**, 846
C₅H₁₃NO₉P₂, 1-amino-2-deoxy-3,5-diphosphateribofuranose, **7**, 400
C₅H₁₃O₇P
  erythritol derivative, **2**, 4
  2-methylerythritol 4-phosphate, **2**, 56
C₅H₁₃O₁₄P₂, 1-pyrophosphorylribose-5-phosphate, **3**, 476
C₅H₁₃O₁₄P₃, 5-phosphoribosyl pyrophosphate, **4**, 7
C₅H₁₃Si, (trimethylsilyl)ethyl, **7**, 119
C₅H₁₄NO, choline, **3**, 228
C₅H₁₄N₂
  cadaverine, **4**, 34, 165
  N-methylputrescine, **4**, 27, 30
C₅H₁₅ClNO₄P, phosphorylcholine, **3**, 228
C₅H₁₆N₂S, thiol, **7**, 417
C₆HCl₅O, pentachlorophenol, **5**, 411, 417, 418
C₆H₂Cl₄O₂, tetrachlorohydroquinone, **5**, 414, 418
C₆H₃ClN₂O₄, 1-chloro-2,4-dinitrobenzene, **1**, 260 , **5**, 63
C₆H₃Cl₂, dichlorophenyl, **7**, 119
C₆H₃Cl₂NO₂, 2,6-dichloroisonicotinic acid, **1**, 626
C₆H₃Cl₃O₂, trichlorohydroquinone, **5**, 414
C₆H₃N₃O₆, dinitrophenylthio, **7**, 119
C₆H₃N₃O₉S, 2,4,6-trinitrobenzenesulfonate, **5**, 353
C₆H₄, hex-1,5-diyne-3-ene, **7**, 557
C₆H₄Br₂O, 2,6-dibromophenol, **8**, 35

C₆H₄Br₂O₂, bromophenol oligomer, **8**, 461
C₆H₄Cl, chlorophenyl, **7**, 119, 130
C₆H₄Cl I, chloroiodobenzene, **5**, 72
C₆H₄ClNO₂, *p*-nitrochlorobenzene, **5**, 413
C₆H₄ClO₃P, 2-chloro-4*H*-1,3,2-benzodioxaphosphorin-4-one, **7**, 139
C₆H₄Cl₂O, 2,6-dichlorophenol, **8**, 230
C₆H₄Cl₂O₂, 2,6-dichlorohydroquinone, **5**, 414
C₆H₄Cl₄, 1,3,4,6-tetrachloro-1,4-cyclohexadiene, **5**, 409
C₆H₄NO, pyridylcarbonyl, **7**, 120
C₆H₄NO₂, nitrophenyl, **7**, 119
C₆H₄NO₂S, nitrophenylthio, **7**, 119
C₆H₄NO₄S, nitrophenylsulfonyl, **7**, 123
C₆H₄N₂O₆, 3,5-dinitrocatechol, **3**, 647
C₆H₄N₄, pteridine, **5**, 77
C₆H₄O₂, benzoquinone, **4**, 211
C₆H₄O₃, quinone, **7**, 536
C₆H₄O₄, 4-carboxymethylenebut-2-en-4-olide, **5**, 130
C₆H₅, phenyl, **7**, 119
C₆H₅BrN₂O₂, 5-(2-bromovinyl)uridine, **7**, 317
C₆H₅Cl, chlorobenzene, **5**, 72
C₆H₅ClHgO₃S , *p*-chloromercuribenzenesulfonic acid, **1**, 293, **2**, 283
C₆H₅ClO, *o*-chlorophenol, **3**, 408
C₆H₅Cl₂O₂P, dichlorophenylphosphate, **7**, 106
C₆H₅Cl₅, pentachlorocyclohexene, **5**, 409
C₆H₅FO₄, fluoromuconolactone, **5**, 132
C₆H₅I, iodobenzene, **5**, 72
C₆H₅NO₂
  nicotinic acid, **2**, 25
  nitrosocyclohexadienone, **5**, 244
C₆H₅NO₃
  nitrophenol, **8**, 212
  p-nitrophenol, **5**, 130, 150, 431
C₆H₅NO₅, 1,6-dihydroxy-2-oxoisonicotinic acid, **1**, 592
C₆H₅N₃
  7-deazapurine, **7**, 253
  deazapurine, **6**, 93
  1-hydroxybenzotriazole, **7**, 138
C₆H₅N₃, 3-deazapurine, **7**, 253
C₆H₅N₃O
  3-azidophenol, **3**, 408
  3,7-dihydroimidazo[1,2-a]pyrazin-3-one, **8**, 455
C₆H₅N₃O₂, 7-deazaxanthine, **7**, 326
C₆H₅N₅O, pterin, **1**, 837
C₆H₅N₅O₂, 4-triazolylpyrimidione, **6**, 93
C₆H₆ClN, β-chloroalanine, **3**, 100
C₆H₆Cl₆, lindane, **5**, 402, 403, 409
C₆H₆INO₄, *N*-(iodoacetoxy)succinimide, **7**, 159
C₆H₆NO, nicotinamide, **2**, 64
C₆H₆NO₆P, *p*-nitrophenyl phosphate, **5**, 142, 148
C₆H₆N₄
  1-aminobenzotriazole, **1**, 720
  6-methylpurine, **8**, 59
C₆H₆N₄O
  1-deazaguanine, **7**, 254
  3-deazaguanine, **7**, 254
  7-deazaguanine, **7**, 254
  pteridine hydrate, **5**, 77
C₆H₆O
  cyclohexadienone, **3**, 405
  phenol, **1**, 257, **3**, 384, 405, 407, **5**, 42, 246
C₆H₆OS, 4-hydroxythiophenol, **7**, 561
C₆H₆O₂
  catechol, **3**, 711, **8**, 173
  hydroquinone, **3**, 711, **8**, 186, 169, 171, 186
  pyrocatechol, **3**, 408
  resorcinol, **3**, 408, 755
C₆H₆O₃
  phloroglucinol, **1**, 715, 815, **3**, 624, 755, **8**, 460
  TAL, **1**, 416
  triacetic acid lactone, **1**, 3, 354, 412
  trihydroxybenzene, **7**, 536

$C_6H_6O_4$
muconate, **5**, 44
muconolactone, **5**, 132
3-oxoadipate enol-lactone, **3**, 384
$C_6H_6O_5$
2-hydroxymuconate, **5**, 32, 34, 41
maleyl acetate, **5**, 130
2-oxo-3-hexenediaote, **5**, 34, 41
2-oxo-4-hexenediioate, **5**, 34, 42
C_6H_6S, thiophenol, **7**, 132
C_6H_7N, 2-cyclopentenecarbonitrile, **1**, 70
C_6H_7NO
aminophenol, **3**, 412
aniline N-oxide, **3**, 412
$C_6H_7NO_2$, N-ethylmaleimide, **1**, 293, 491, **2**, 276, 283, 289,
    3, 80, **4**, 87, 335, **5**, 353, 407, 429
$C_6H_7NO_3$, 1-carbapen-2-em-3-carboxylic acid, **4**, 187
$C_6H_7NO_4$, clavam-2-carboxylate, **4**, 183
$C_6H_7N_3O_3$, carboxycytosine, **7**, 320
$C_6H_7N_5$
4-aminopteridine, **5**, 77
N-6-methyladenine, **7**, 324
N-6-methylaminopurine, **8**, 59
8-methyldeoxyguanine, **7**, 78
$C_6H_7N_5O$
8-methoxyadenine, **7**, 325
N-6-methoxyadenine, **7**, 324
C-6-O-methylguanine, **7**, 328
N-6-methyl-8-oxoadenine, **7**, 325
$C_6H_7N_5O_2$, 8-methoxyguanine, **7**, 325
$C_6H_7O_2$, furaneol, **8**, 165
$C_6H_7O_3PS$, aromatic thiol, **5**, 158
C_6H_8, cyclohexa-1,4-diene, **7**, 406
C_6H_8N, methylpyridyl, **7**, 119
$C_6H_8N_2$, p-phenylenediamine, **3**, 711
$C_6H_8N_2O_2$
C-4-O-methylthymine, **7**, 315
C-6-methylthymine, **7**, 319
O-2-methylthymine, **7**, 314
$C_6H_8N_2O_2S$, sulfanilamide, **5**, 349
$C_6H_8N_4$, 4-dimethylaminopyrimidine, **6**, 93
$C_6H_8N_6O$, 2-amino-6-methoxyaminopurine, **7**, 323
$C_6H_8O_2$
aleprolic acid, **1**, 69
6-hydroxycyclohexenone, **8**, 139
$C_6H_8O_3$
L-aculose, **3**, 312
3-oxo-4-hexenoic acid, **1**, 545
$C_6H_8O_5$
α-ketoadipate, **1**, 834
α-ketoglutarate, **3**, 425
2-oxo-1,6-hexanedioate, **5**, 44
$C_6H_8O_6$
ascorbate, **6**, 136
4-hydroxy-4-methyl-2-ketoglutarate, **3**, 385, 413
hydroxymethylketoglutarate, **3**, 385
2-keto-4-hydroxyglutarate, **3**, 425
2-keto-4-hydroxy-4-methylglutarate, **3**, 382
vitaminC, **4**, 211
$C_6H_8O_7$
citrate, **2**, 53, **3**, 386, 393, 454, 457, **4**, 255, **5**, 25
isocitrate, **2**, 53, **3**, 382
2-keto-3-deoxy-D-glucarate, **3**, 402
$C_6H_8O_8$, 5-keto-4-deoxyglucarate, **3**, 382
$C_6H_9BrO_4$, bromoconduritol, **3**, 20
C_6H_9N, cyclopentanecarbonitrile, **1**, 70
C_6H_9NOS, thiamine thiazole subunit, **1**, 837
$C_6H_9NO_2$, piperideine-6-carboxylic acid, **4**, 165
$C_6H_9NO_2S$
N-acetylhomocysteine thiolactone, **7**, 168
5-(1,2-dihydroxyethyl)-4-methylthiazole, **1**, 838
$C_6H_9NO_3$, 2-hydroxymethylclavam, **4**, 183
$C_6H_9NO_5$, 2-amino-3-ketoadipic acid, **4**, 66

$C_6H_9NS_2$, raphanusanin, **8**, 29
$C_6H_9N_2O_2$, 4-carboxy-1,3-dimethylimidazolium ion, **8**,
    442
$C_6H_9N_3O$, thiamine pyrimidine subunit, **1**, 837
$C_6H_9N_3O_2$
histidine, **3**, 369, 378, 393, 406, 632, **6**, 142, **8**, 209
N-4-methoxy-5-methylcytosine, **7**, 321
$C_6H_{10}F_2O_4$, 2-deoxy-2-fluoro-β-L-idosyl fluoride, **5**, 299
$C_6H_{10}F_2O_5$, 5-fluoro-α-D-glucosyl fluoride, **5**, 299
$C_6H_{10}N_2O_3$, 6-diazo-5-oxonorleucine, **7**, 542
$C_6H_{10}N_2O_6S$, SQ26180, **4**, 188
$C_6H_{10}O004$, L-cinerulose B, **3**, 312
$C_6H_{10}O$
2-hexenal, **1**, 84, 86, 89, **7**, 502, **8**, 152, 210
3-hexenal, **1**, 84, 87, 91
4-hexenal, **1**, 87, 5-hexenal, **1**, 86
leaf aldehyde, **1**, 87
$C_6H_{10}O_2$
cyclopentanecarboxylic acid, **1**, 70
4-hexanolide, **8**, 210
3-hexenoic acid, **4**, 254
4-hydroxyhex-2-enal, **8**, 147
5-methoxy allyl vinyl ether, **5**, 352
6-methoxy allyl vinyl ether, **5**, 350
4-oxo-2-hexenal, **8**, 210
$C_6H_{10}O_2S$, gonyauline, **8**, 457
$C_6H_{10}O_3$
D-cinerulose A, **3**, 312
L-cinerulose A, **3**, 312
ethyl acetoacetate, **2**, 17
2-ketohexanoic acid, **3**, 381
mevaldehyde, **2**, 32
$C_6H_{10}O_3S_2$, 1,2-dithiolan-3-one 1-oxide analogue, **7**, 524
$C_6H_{10}O_4$
adipic acid, **1**, 298, **4**, 181
2,6-dideoxy-D-*threo*-hexos-4-ulose, **3**, 312, 354
D-kerriose, **3**, 312
$C_6H_{10}O_5$
conduritol B-epoxide, **3**, 131
D-*ethyro*-3,6-dideoxy-2-hexulosonate, **3**, 423
diethyl pyrocarbonate, **1**, 588, **2**, 19, 33, 283, 311, 312,
    3, 378, 463, **6**, 65, **7**, 94, 253
4-keto-6-deoxyglucose, **3**, 351
streptose, **3**, 353
L-streptose, **3**, 312
$C_6H_{10}O_6$
aceric acid, **3**, 499, 503, 509
gluconolactone, **5**, 294
D-glucuno-1,5-lactone, **3**, 687
2-keto-3-deoxyfuconate, **3**, 425
2-keto-3-deoxygluconate, **3**, 423
$C_6H_{10}O_7$
galactonic acid, **3**, 429, 499,
glucuronic acid, **3**, 122, 161, 170, 499, 601
iduronic acid, **3**, 161, 171
2-keto-3-deoxygalactonate, **3**, 382, 425
2-keto-3-deoxygluconate, **3**, 425
$C_6H_{10}O_8$, 2-ketogluconate, **3**, 382
$C_6H_{11}FO_5$, α-glucosyl fluoride, **5**, 290, 301, 302, 303, 306
$C_6H_{11}NO_2$, pipecolic acid, **1**, 520
$C_6H_{11}NO_3$, aminoadipic acid semialdehyde, **4**, 243
$C_6H_{11}NO_4$
AAA, **4**, 182
Ala-Lac, **3**, 261, 272
aminoadipic acid, **1**, 840, 841, **4**, 162, 165, 174, 243,
    246
$C_6H_{11}NO_7S$, N-sulfonylglucosamine, **3**, 161
$C_6H_{11}N_2O_5$, β-D-glucoxyl azide, **5**, 290
$C_6H_{11}N_3O_5P$, phosphohistidine, **5**, 144, 145
$C_6H_{11}O_2$
hexanoic acid, **8**, 165
4-methoxytetrahydropyran-4-yl, **6**, 84
$C_6H_{11}O_2S$, 4-(methylthiomethoxy)butyryl, **7**, 127

C₆H₁₁O₉P
DKPG, **3**, 429
KDPG, **3**, 421
KDPGal, **3**, 429
5-keto-2-deoxygluconophosphate, **3**, 409
2-keto-3-deoxy-6-phosphogluconate, **3**, 414
C₆H₁₁O₁₀P
2-keto-3-deoxygalactonate 6-phosphate, **3**, 425
2-keto-3-deoxygluconate 6-phosphate, **3**, 425
C₆H₁₂NO₅, glucosamine, **1**, 150
C₆H₁₂NO₅P, *N*-acetyl DMPT, **1**, 871
C₆H₁₂N₂O₂, Ala-Ala, **3**, 260
C₆H₁₂N₂O₄S, lanthionine, **3**, 247, 259, 276, **4**, 275
C₆H₁₂N₂O₇S, *β*-2-thionylserine, **4**, 327
C₆H₁₂O
dimethyltetrahydrofuran, **5**, 186
hexanal, **1**, 84, 106, **8**, 210
2-hexenol, **1**, 84, 86
2-hexen-1-ol, **8**, 152
3-hexenol, **1**, 84, 85, 86, 89
5-hexenol, **1**, 86
leaf alcohol, **1**, 87
3-methyl-3-butenyl methyl ether, **8**, 220
C₆H₁₂O₂
capric acid, **1**, 298
hexanoic acid, **4**, 254, **8**, 210
3-hydroxy-2-hexanone, **8**, 210
propoin, **3**, 394
C₆H₁₂O₃
D-amicetose, **3**, 312
L-amicetose, **3**, 312
6-hydroxycapric acid, **1**, 298
D-rhodinose, **3**, 312
L-rhodinose, **3**, 312
C₆H₁₂O₄
abequose, **3**, 187, 192, 288, 312, 322, 346, 349
ascarylose, **3**, 312, 335, 346
D-boivinose, **3**, 312
D-canarose, **3**, 312
colitose, **3**, 186, 192, 312, 346, 348
2-deoxy-L-fucose, **3**, 312
D-digitoxose, **3**, 312
L-digitoxose, **3**, 312
3,5-dihydroxy-3-methylpentanoate, **8**, 219
kethoxal, **6**, 65
mevalonic acid, **2**, 3, 15, 46, 70, 263, 353, 363, 378, **4**, 51, **5**, 319, **8**, 69, 84
D-oliose, **3**, 312
olivose, **3**, 355
paratose, **3**, 187, 192, 312, 323, 346
tyvelose, **3**, 187, 192, 312, 323, 346
C₆H₁₂O₄S, 5′-methylthioribose, **8**, 96
C₆H₁₂O₅
D-allomethylose, **3**, 312
L-altromethylose, **3**, 312
D-antiarose, **3**, 312
6-deoxy-D-allose, **3**, 352
6-deoxy-*β*-L-altropyranose, **3**, 192
6-deoxyaltrose, **3**, 192
6-deoxy-L-altrose, **3**, 346
2-deoxyglucose, **1**, 585
2-deoxy-D-glucose, **3**, 312
2-deoxy-D-gulose, **3**, 312
4-deoxy-D-idose, **3**, 312
dihydrohydroxystreptose, **3**, 323
L-dihydrostreptose, **3**, 312
fucose, **1**, 331, **3**, 55, 71, 114, 116, 117, 146, 424, 425, 499, 604, 605, 611
D-fucose, **3**, 312
L-fucose, **3**, 312
2′-methoxy-2′-deoxyribose, **6**, 239
D-quinovose, **3**, 312
D-rhamnose, **3**, 312

L-rhamnose, **3**, 312
rhamnose, **3**, 288, 350, 499
D-talomethylose, **3**, 312
L-talomethylose, **3**, 312
C₆H₁₂O₆
fructose, **2**, 50, **3**, 414, 421, 431, 464, **8**, 162
galactose, **3**, 71, 109, 113, 146, 161, 170, 203, 414, 428, 429, 430, 499, 544, 604, 611, **6**, 206, **8**, 427
glucometasaccharinic acid, **3**, 429
glucose, **2**, 50, 52, 61, **3**, 112, 225, 392, 414, 417, 421, 422, 430, 444, 445, 464, 536, 604, 606, 810, **4**, 174, **8**, 162
inositol, **1**, 154, **3**, 410, 297
mannose, **3**, 288, 297, 499, 502, 544, **4**, 311, **8**, 162
myoinositol, **3**, 409, 506, 606
tagatose, **3**, 431
xylose, **3**, 417
C₆H₁₂O₆C₆H₁₂O₆
galactose, **3**, 430
glucose, **3**, 430
C₆H₁₂O₇, gluconate, **3**, 414, 423
C₆H₁₂P₆, galactose, **3**, 607
C₆H₁₂S, 3-methyl-3-butenyl methyl sulphide, **8**, 220
C₆H₁₃Cl, 1-chlorohexane, **5**, 405
C₆H₁₃NaO₂Si, sodium 3-trimethylsilylpropionate, **7**, 60
C₆H₁₃NO₂
alloisoleucine, **1**, 842, **4**, 169, 253
ε-amino-*n*-caproic acid, **8**, 434
6-deoxyfagomine, **3**, 130, 134
isoleucine, **1**, 853, **2**, 55, **4**, 165, 253, 327, 538, **8**, 221, 239
leucine, **2**, 49, 55, 376, **4**, 165, 209, 327, 545, **8**, 221, 239
norleucine, **4**, 327
C₆H₁₃NO₂S, homomethionine, **1**, 859
C₆H₁₃NO₃
4-amino-4,6-dideoxymannose, **3**, 207
6-deoxy-DMDP, **3**, 130, 134
3-*epi*-fagomine, **3**, 131, 134
fagomine, **3**, 130, 134, 143
C₆H₁₃NO₃S
mannostatin, **3**, 151, 156
mannostatin A, **3**, 27, 134
C₆H₁₃NO₄
deoxymannojirimycin, **3**, 148, 151
1-deoxymannojirimycin, **3**, 21, 22, 23, 24, 29, 31, 131, 134, 141, 154
deoxynojirimycin, **3**, 152
1-deoxynojirimycin, **3**, 18, 19, 31, 131, 134, 138, 139, 151, 152, 154, **5**, 302
2,5-dihydroxymethyl-3,4-dihydroxypyrrolidine, **3**, 130, 151
2,5-DM-3,4-DP, **8**, 152
DMDP, **3**, 134, 141, 152
DMJ, **3**, 155
madurosamine, **7**, 580
Rha4N, **3**, 209
C₆H₁₃NO₅
1,4-dideoxy-1,4-imino-D-mannitol, **3**, 154
galactostatin, **3**, 131, 134
glucosamine, **3**, 297, **4**, 69, 310
mannojirimycin, **3**, 134
mannosamine, **3**, 303
nojirimycin, **3**, 131, 134, 141, 142
nojirimycin B, **3**, 131
nojirimycin tetrazole, **5**, 305
C₆H₁₃O₈P
3-deoxy-6-phosphogalactose, **3**, 429
fuculose-1-phosphate, **3**, 424
rhamnulose-1-phosphate, **3**, 426
C₆H₁₃O₉
galactose-1-phosphate, **3**, 391
galactose-6-phosphate, **3**, 391
glucose-1-phosphate, **3**, 391
glucose-6-phosphate, **3**, 391

mannose-6-phosphate, **3**, 391
C$_6$H$_{13}$O$_9$P
  fructose-1-phosphate, **3**, 430
  fructose-6-phosphate, **3**, 204, 249, 391, 392, 393, 414,
    415, 417, 430, 464, 469, 470, 505
  Gal 1P, **3**, 203
  galactose-6-phosphate, **3**, 430
  glucose-1-phosphate, **3**, 7, 442, 444, 464, 471, 473, 475,
    476, 505, 506, 807, **5**, 304
  α-D-glucose-1-phosphate, **3**, 336, 349
  glucose 6-phosphate, **1**, 578, **3**, 204, 414, 464, 479, 482,
    483, 485, 807
  D-*arabino*-3-hexulose-6-phosphate, **3**, 413
  inositol-1-phosphate, **3**, 610
  Man 6P, **3**, 207
  mannose-6-phosphate, **3**, 29
  sorbose-1-phosphate, **3**, 426, 430
  tagatose-6-phosphate, **3**, 430
C$_6$H$_{13}$O$_{10}$P, 6-phosphogluconate, **2**, 52, **3**, 414
C$_6$H$_{14}$ClN, *N*,*N*-diethylaziridinium chloride, **3**, 575
C$_6$H$_{14}$FO$_3$P
  DFP, **3**, 303
  diisopropylfluorophosphate, **1**, 293
C$_6$H$_{14}$NO$_8$P
  glucosamine-1-phosphate, **3**, 251
  glucosamine-6-phosphate, **3**, 206, 251, 391
C$_6$H$_{14}$N$_2$O$_2$
  lysine, **3**, 245, 248, 259, 378, **4**, 162, 165, 176, 208, 243,
    4, 33, **5**, 206, **8**, 434
  β-lysine, **5**, 206
C$_6$H$_{14}$N$_2$O$_3$
  2,4-diamino-2,4,6-trideoxy-D-galactose, **3**, 192
  hydroxylysine, **3**, 247
C$_6$H$_{14}$N$_2$O$_4$, 2,3-diamino-2,3-dideoxy-D-glucose, **3**, 196
C$_6$H$_{14}$N$_4$O$_2$, arginine, **1**, 150, **8**, 417
C$_6$H$_{14}$O
  hexanol, **1**, 84
  1-hexanol, **8**, 210
C$_6$H$_{14}$O$_2$, 2,3-hexanediol, **8**, 211
C$_6$H$_{14}$O$_5$
  D-digitalose, **3**, 312
  D-thevetose, **3**, 312
C$_6$H$_{14}$O$_6$
  galactitol, **3**, 430
  mannitol, **1**, 131
  sorbitol, **1**, 131
C$_6$H$_{14}$O$_7$P$_2$
  3-ethyl-3-butenyl diphosphate, **2**, 72, 76
  homoisopentenyl pyrophosphate, **8**, 272
  3-methylenepentyl pyrophosphate, **8**, 236
  3-methyl-2-pentenyl diphosphate, **2**, 72, 76, **8**, 219,
    236
  3-methyl-3-pentenyl diphosphate, **2**, 72, 78, **8**, 236
C$_6$H$_{14}$O$_{10}$P$_2$, 5-pyrophosphomevalonate, **2**, 3
C$_6$H$_{14}$O$_{12}$P$_2$
  fructose diphosphate, **3**, 431
  fructose 1,6-diphosphate, **1**, 831, **2**, 52, **3**, 382, 386, 390,
    414, 419, 430, 431, 448, 464, 469, 470, 471, 473,
    474, 475, 476
  tagatose diphosphate, **3**, 431
  tagatose-1,6-diphosphate, **3**, 430, 431
C$_6$H$_{14}$O$_{12}$P$_2$, fructose-1,6-diphosphate, **3**, 470
C$_6$H$_{15}$ClSi, *tert*-butyldimethylsilyl chloride, **6**, 86
C$_6$H$_{15}$N, hexylamine, **8**, 161
C$_6$H$_{15}$N$_2$O$_5$P, phospholysine, **5**, 144
C$_6$H$_{15}$N$_4$O$_5$P
  *N*ε-*phosphate arginine*, **6**, 127
  phosphoarginine, **5**, 144
C$_6$H$_{15}$O$_9$
  inositol phosphate, **3**, 297
  phosphatidylinositol, **3**, 301
C$_6$H$_{15}$O$_{13}$P$_3$, 3-phospho-5-pyrophosphomevalonate, **2**, 3
C$_6$H$_{15}$O$_{15}$, glucose triphosphate, **4**, 311

C$_6$H$_{15}$Si
  2'-*t*-butyldimethylsilyl, **7**, 144
  O-*tert*-butyldimethylsilyl, **6**, 86
C$_6$H$_{16}$N$_2$
  hexamethylenediamine, **7**, 161
  tetramethylethylenediamine, **7**, 92
C$_6$Cl$_4$O$_2$, tetrachlorobenzoquinone, **5**, 419
C$_7$H$_2$F$_4$O$_3$, tetrafluoro-*p*-hydroxybenzoate, **5**, 418
C$_7$H$_2$K$_2$O$_6$, potassium chelidonate, **8**, 29
C$_7$H$_3$Cl$_2$N, 2,6-dichlorobenzonitrile, **3**, 610
C$_7$H$_3$Cl$_2$O, dichlorobenzoyl, **7**, 120
C$_7$H$_3$I$_3$O$_2$, 2,3,5-triiodobenzoic acid, **8**, 30, 34, 36, 68
C$_7$H$_4$ClO, chlorobenzoyl, **7**, 119, 120
C$_7$H$_4$Cl$_2$O$_2$
  2,4-dichlorobenzoate, **5**, 417
  3,4-dichlorobenzoic acid, **8**, 36
C$_7$H$_4$F$_2$O$_3$, 3,5-difluoro-*p*-hydroxybenzoate, **5**, 418
C$_7$H$_4$F$_5$NO, *O*-(2,3,4,5,6-
  pentafluorobenzyl)hydroxylamine, **1**, 632
C$_7$H$_4$NO$_3$, nitrobenzoyl, **7**, 120
C$_7$H$_4$N$_2$O$_6$, 3,4-dinitrobenzoic acid, **5**, 179
C$_7$H$_4$OSSe, 3*H*-1,2-benzothiaselenol-3-one, **7**, 293
C$_7$H$_4$O$_2$S, oxathiolanone, **7**, 523
C$_7$H$_4$O$_2$S$_2$
  3*H*-1,2-benzodithiol-3-one 1-oxide, **7**, 523
  1,2-dithiolan-3-one 1-oxide analogue, **7**, 524
  1,2-dithiolan-3-one 1-oxide, **7**, 523, 526
C$_7$H$_4$O$_3$S$_2$, 3*H*-1,2-benzodithiole-3-one 1,1-dioxide, **7**, 143
C$_7$H$_5$ClHgO$_2$, *p*-chloromercuribenzoate, **2**, 312, 359, 3,
    376, 378, **5**, 407
C$_7$H$_5$ClO$_2$
  2-chlorobenzoate, **5**, 417
  4-chlorobenzoate, **5**, 402, 411
  4-chlorobenzoic acid, **3**, 651
C$_7$H$_5$ClO$_3$
  chlorosalicylate, **3**, 378
  5-chlorosalicylic acid, **1**, 626
C$_7$H$_5$NaO$_7$S, polyclinal, **8**, 473
C$_7$H$_5$NO$_4$
  2,4-pyridinedicarboxylate, **1**, 725
  quinolinic acid, **3**, 395
C$_7$H$_5$NS, benzothiazole, **8**, 588
C$_7$H$_5$NS$_2$
  benzothiazole, **8**, 588
  2-mercaptobenzothiazole, **7**, 119, 131, 132
C$_7$H$_5$N$_3$O$_2$, *o*-nitrophenyldiazomethane, **6**, 85
C$_7$H$_5$N$_3$O$_2$S, *C*-5-thiazoleuridine, **7**, 317
C$_7$H$_5$N$_5$O$_2$, nitrophenyltetrazole, **7**, 138
C$_7$H$_5$N$_5$O$_3$, pterin-6-carboxylic acid, **1**, 837
C$_7$H$_5$O, benzoyl, **6**, 87, **7**, 119, 120
C$_7$H$_6$, 1,2,4-heptatriene-6-yne, **7**, 556
C$_7$H$_6$BrN$_2$O, *p*-azidophenacyl bromide, **7**, 169
C$_7$H$_6$Br$_2$O$_2$, bromophenol oligomer, **8**, 461
C$_7$H$_6$ClNO$_2$, *o*-nitrobenzyl chloride, **6**, 85
C$_7$H$_6$Cl$_2$O, 2,4-dichloroanisole, **8**, 34
C$_7$H$_6$HgO$_3$, *p*-hydroxymercuribenzoate, **3**, 393, 452
C$_7$H$_6$NO$_2$, *o*-nitrobenzyl, **6**, 85
C$_7$H$_6$NO$_2$S, nitrotolylthio, **7**, 119
C$_7$H$_6$N$_2$
  benzimidazole, **4**, 150
  C-5-propynylpyrimidine, **7**, 317
C$_7$H$_6$N$_2$O, 5-hydroxybenzimidazole, **4**, 150
C$_7$H$_6$N$_2$O$_2$, *C*-5-propynyluridine, **7**, 317
C$_7$H$_6$N$_4$, 4-triazolylpyridine, **6**, 93
C$_7$H$_6$N$_4$O, 1,1'-carbonyldiimidazole, **7**, 161
C$_7$H$_6$N$_4$O$_2$
  3-amino-1,2,4-benzotriazine 1,1-dioxide, **7**, 534
  C-5-(imidazol-2-yl)uridine, **7**, 318
C$_7$H$_6$O
  benzaldehyde, **3**, 377, 395, 396, 399, **8**, 165
C$_7$H$_6$O$_2$
  benzoic acid, **1**, 54, 74, 612, **3**, 649, **4**, 254
  p-hydroxybenzaldehyde, **3**, 622, 682, 696

salicylaldehyde, **3**, 376, 377, **8**, 139, 154
tropolone, **1**, 3
C₇H₆O₃
  hydroxybenzoic acid, **3**, 385, **8**, 169
  m-hydroxybenzoic acid, **1**, 74, 528, 610
  p-hydroxybenzoic acid, **1**, 574, 612, 815, **2**, 381, **3**, 640,
    696, 804, **5**, 348, 412, 418, **8**, 173
  protocatechualdehyde, **3**, 400,
  salicylic acid, **1**, 72, 129, 133, 294, 610, 612, 779, **5**, 24,
    8, 119, 169, 171
C₇H₆O₄
  2,3-dihydroxybenzoic acid, **1**, 610, 610, 700, **4**, 209
  2,5-dihydroxybenzoic acid, **1**, 700
  3,4-dihydroxybenzoic acid, **5**, 418, **8**, 173
  3,5-dihydroxybenzoic acid, **1**, 528
  gentisic acid, **1**, 411
  patulin, **1**, 2, 346, 411, 427
  protocatechuic acid, **1**, 585, 589, **3**, 385, 803, **8**, 171
  terreic acid, **1**, 411
C₇H₆O₅
  gallic acid, **3**, 10, 385, 800, 802, 803, 819, 820
  phloroglucinolcarboxylic acid, **1**, 815
C₇H₆S₅, 7-methylbenzopentathiapin, **7**, 527
C₇H₇, benzyl, **7**, 119, 130
C₇H₇FO₂S , phenylmethanesulfonyl fluoride, **1**, 293, 349
C₇H₇FO₅, 6-fluorodehydroshikimate, **1**, 592
C₇H₇NO
  phenylacetaldoxime, **1**, 130
  2-pyridyloxirane, **5**, 52, 53, 67
C₇H₇NO₂
  p-aminobenzoic acid, **1**, 72, 574, 611, 612, **4**, 4
  anthranilic acid, **1**, 574, 599, 611, 846, **3**, 395, 396, **4**, 6,
    8, 34
  homarine, **8**, 465
  p-hydroxyphenylacetaldehyde oxime, **1**, 858
  trigonelline, **8**, 29
C₇H₇NO₃
  3-amino-5-hydroxybenzoic acid, **1**, 527
  carbapen-2-em-3-carboxylic acid, **8**, 398
  p-nitrobenzyl alcohol, **5**, 431
  salicylhydroxamic acid, **1**, 123
C₇H₇N₂O, 4-(hydroxymethyl)benzenediazonium ion, **7**,
    543
C₇H₇N₃, 3-methylpyrazolo[4,3-*d*]pyrimidine, **8**, 68
C₇H₇N₃O, *C*-5-propynylcytosine, **7**, 322
C₇H₇N₃O₃, photoaffinity label, **1**, 588
C₇H₇N₃S , 2-methylthiopyrrolo[2,3-*d*]pyrimidine, **8**, 68
C₇H₈, toluene, **3**, 384, **5**, 42
C₇H₈FO₄P, fluorotolyl phosphate, **5**, 160
C₇H₈N₂, benzamidine, **1**, 349
C₇H₈N₂O₃, dephostatin, **7**, 521
C₇H₈N₄O₂, theobromine, **8**, 147
C₇H₈N₆O, *N*-6-carbamoylmethyladenine, **7**, 325
C₇H₈O
  cresol, **3**, 408
  m-cresol, **8**, 212
  p-cresol, **3**, 711, **8**, 161
C₇H₈O₂
  guaiacol, **8**, 150, 152
  p-hydroxybenzyl alcohol, **1**, 838
C₇H₈O₃, 4,5-dideoxydehydroshikimate, **1**, 592
C₇H₈O₄
  dehydroquinate 1,2-epoxy derivative, **1**, 588
  5-deoxydehydroshikimate, **1**, 592
C₇H₈O₅
  allyl vinyl ether 2,6-dicarboxylate, **5**, 366
  dehydroquinate derivative, **1**, 587
  dehydroshikimate, **1**, 585, 586, 589, 591, 591, 719
  3-dehydroshikimic acid, **3**, 804
  2-hydroxy-2,4-heptadiene-1,7-dioate, **5**, 35
  2-oxo-3-heptene-1,7-dioate, **5**, 35
  2-oxo-4-heptene-1,7-dioate, **5**, 35
C₇H₈O₆, 5-dehydroquinate, **4**, 2

C₇H₈O₈, 4-carboxy-4-hydroxy-2-ketoadipate, **3**, 385, 413
C₇H₈S, phenylmethanethiol, **3**, 758
C₇H₉FO₅, 6-fluoroshikimate, **1**, 592, 602
C₇H₉FO₆
  6-fluorodehydroquinate, **1**, 584
  6-fluoro-1-*epi*-dehydroquinate, **1**, 584
C₇H₉NO, *p*-anisidine, **3**, 709
C₇H₉NO₂
  gabaculine, **8**, 63
  methyl 4-methylpyrrole-2-carboxylate, **8**, 221
C₇H₉NO₃S, 5-(2-hydroxyethyl)-4-methylthiazole-2-
    carboxylic acid, **1**, 838
C₇H₉NO₄
  acyclic diene, **5**, 428
  aminoDHS, **1**, 527
  dehydroquinate imine derivative, **1**, 586, 587
  2-formyloxymethylclavam, **4**, 183
C₇H₉O₃, mesifuranone, **8**, 165
C₇H₁₀N₂, 4-(*N*,*N*-dimethylamino)pyridine, **7**, 163
C₇H₁₀N₂O₂
  N-3-ethylthymine, **7**, 315
  O-2-ethylthymine, **7**, 314
C₇H₁₀N₂O₄,
  α-amino-3-hydroxyl-5-methylisoxazole-4-propionate,
    6, 103
C₇H₁₀N₂O₅, heterocyclic DAP analogue, **3**, 277
C₇H₁₀O, 3-methylcyclohexenone, **8**, 211
C₇H₁₀O₂
  1-cyclohexenecarboxylic acid, **1**, 72
  2-cyclohexenecarboxylic acid, **1**, 72
  4-methyl-3,5-hexadienoic acid, **8**, 236
C₇H₁₀O₃
  4,5-dideoxyshikimate, **1**, 593
  5-hydroxycyclohex-1-enecarboxylic acid, **1**, 72
  δ-lactone, **1**, 508
C₇H₁₀O₄
  5-deoxyshikimate, **1**, 593
  4,5-dideoxydehydroquinate, **1**, 589
  2′-hydroxycyclopentylglyoxylate, **1**, 70
  α-ketopimelate semialdehyde, **1**, 69
C₇H₁₀O₅
  5-deoxydehydroquinate, **1**, 589
  diethyloxomalonate, **7**, 126,
  enol pyranose 2-deoxy analogue, **1**, 582
  6-fluoroshikimate, **1**, 593
  α-ketopimelate, **1**, 69, 834
  shikimic acid, **1**, 16, 72, 154, 574, 591, 592, 645, 719,
    850, **3**, 626, 804, **4**, 4
C₇H₁₀O₆
  1-*epi*-dehydroquinate, **1**, 584
  3-dehydroquinate, **1**, 586, **4**, 4
  dehydroquinate derivative, **1**, 587
  dehydroquinic acid, **1**, 581, 585, 589, 591, 719, **3**,
    804
  enolpyranose, **1**, 582, 583
  hydroxyketopimelate, **3**, 413
C₇H₁₀O₈
  DHA, **3**, 499, 503, 509
C₇H₁₁NO₂
  2-(2′-cyclopentenyl)glycine, **1**, 69
  hypoglycin, **8**, 146
C₇H₁₁NO₃, 2-hydroxyethylclavam, **4**, 182
C₇H₁₁NO₄, dehydroquinate derivative, **1**, 587
C₇H₁₁NO₅
  5-aminoshikimate, **1**, 593
  dehydroquinate imine derivative, **1**, 587
C₇H₁₁NS, 2-isobutyl-1,3-thiazole, **8**, 221
C₇H₁₁N₃O₄, misonidazole, **7**, 397, 417, 583
C₇H₁₁O₆P, 4,5-dideoxyshikimate 3-phosphate, **1**, 595
C₇H₁₁O₈P, shikimate 3-phosphate, **1**, 592, 593, 596, **4**, 4,
    10
C₇H₁₂FO₁₀P, 3-fluorodehydroquinate, **1**, 584
C₇H₁₂N₄O, *N*-4-(3-aminopropyl)cytosine, **7**, 320

$C_7H_{12}O$
  4-hepten-2-one, **8**, 208
  1-methyl-2-cyclohexen-1-ol, **8**, 211
  pheromone of *Dendroctonus pseudotsugae*, **8**, 40
  seudenol, **8**, 211
$C_7H_{12}O_2$
  cyclohexanecarboxylic acid, **1**, 72, 524
  2,6-heptanedione, **8**, 211
  2-methylhexanolide, **8**, 240
$C_7H_{12}O_3$, 3-hydroxycyclohexanecarboxylic acid, **1**, 72
$C_7H_{12}O_4$
  diethyl malonate, **1**, 3
  pimelic acid, **1**, 298, 826
$C_7H_{12}O_6$, quinic acid, **1**, 466, 585, 589
$C_7H_{12}O_7$
  3-deoxy-D-*arabino*-heptulosonate, **1**, 585
  homocitrate, **4**, 243
  4-*O*-methyl-D-glucuronic acid, **3**, 244, 601
$C_7H_{13}NO_3$
  calystegine A₃, **8**, 152
  calystegine A₃, **3**, 133, 134
  calystegine A₅, **3**, 133, 134
  calystegine A₆, **3**, 133, 134
  calystegine A₇, **3**, 133, 134
  theoleucine, **8**, 570
$C_7H_{13}NO_4$
  Ala-HBut, **3**, 272
  calystegine B₁, **3**, 133, 137, 139
  calystegine B₂, **3**, 133, 137, 139, 142
  calystegine B₃, **3**, 133, 137, 139
  calystegine B₄, **3**, 133, 137
  calystegine B₅, **3**, 133, 137
  calystegineV₂, **3**, 140
$C_7H_{13}NO_5$
  calystegineC₁, **3**, 133, 134, 137, 139, 140
  calystegineC₂, **3**, 133, 137
  L-decilonitrose, **3**, 312
  4,6-dideoxy-4-formamido-α-D-mannose, **3**, 192
$C_7H_{13}NS$, 4,5-dihydro-2-isobutyl-1,3-thiazole, **8**, 221
$C_7H_{13}O_8P$
  dehydroquinate derivative, **1**, 585
  2-deoxydehydroquinate, **1**, 585
$C_7H_{13}O_9P$
  2-deoxydehydroquinate, **1**, 585
  enolpyranose cyclic 2-deoxy analogue, **1**, 582
  phosphonate, **1**, 585
$C_7H_{13}O_{10}P$
  DAHP, **1**, 575, 581, 585, **3**, 387
  3-deoxy-D-*arabino*-heptulosonic acid 7-phosphate, **1**, 346, 527, 575, 719
  7-phospho-2-keto-3-deoxy-D-arabinoheptanoate, **3**, 386
$C_7H_{14}N$, FPP ammonium analogue, **5**, 338
$C_7H_{14}NO_9P$, aminoDAHP, **1**, 527
$C_7H_{14}N_2O_3$, calystegineN₁, **3**, 133
$C_7H_{14}N_2O_4$, diaminopimelic acid, **1**, 69, **3**, 245, 248, 256, 259
$C_7H_{14}N_2O_4S$, methyllanthionine, **4**, 275
$C_7H_{14}N_2O_4S_2$, kjenkolic acid, **1**, 848
$C_7H_{14}N_2O_5$
  2,6-diamino-3-hydroxypimelic acid, **3**, 247
  N-hydroxy-DAP, **3**, 276
$C_7H_{14}N_4$, diisopropyltetrazolide, **7**, 133
$C_7H_{14}N_4O_3$, α-ketoarginine, **8**, 568
$C_7H_{14}O$
  2-heptanone, **8**, 161, 169, 211
  4-heptanone, **8**, 211
  4-hepten-2-ol, **8**, 209
$C_7H_{14}OS$, *S*-methyl-*n*-thiolhexanoate, **1**, 849
$C_7H_{14}O_2$
  amyl acetate, **8**, 165
  ethyl 2-methylbutanoate, **8**, 165

  heptanoic acid, **1**, 298
  3-methyl-1-butyl acetate, **8**, 220
  methyl hexanoate, **8**, 210
$C_7H_{14}O_2S$, 7-mercaptoheptanoic acid, **1**, 834, 835
$C_7H_{14}O_3$
  2-hydroxyheptanoic acid, **1**, 162, 452
  2,3,6-trideoxy-4-*O*-methyl-D-*erythro*-hexose, **3**, 312
$C_7H_{14}O_3S$ 2,6-dideoxy-4-*S*-methyl-4-thio-D-*ribo*-hexose, **3**, 312
  gonyol, **8**, 458
$C_7H_{14}O_4$
  L-axenose, **3**, 312
  D-chalcose, **3**, 312
  chromose A, **3**, 313
  D-cymarose, **3**, 312
  L-cymarose, **3**, 312
  2,6-dideoxy-4-*O*-methyl-D-*arabino*-hexose, **3**, 312
  4,6-dideoxy-3-*O*-methyl-D-*ribo*-hexose, **3**, 312
  D-diginose, **3**, 312
  L-diginose, **3**, 312
  D-evermicose, **3**, 312, 342
  homomevalonic acid, **8**, 272
  D-mycarose, **3**, 312
  L-mycarose, **3**, 312
  mycarose, **3**, 342, 351, 352
  D-oleandrose, **3**, 312
  L-oleandrose, **3**, 312
  oleandrose, **3**, 355
  D-olivomose, **3**, 312
  D-sarmentose, **3**, 312
  L-sarmentose, **3**, 312
  D-variose, **3**, 312
$C_7H_{14}O_5$
  D-acofriose, **3**, 312
  L-acofriose, **3**, 312
  L-acovenose, **3**, 312
  D-curacose, **3**, 312
  6-deoxy-4-*O*-methyl-D-altrose, **3**, 312
  L-digitalose, **3**, 312
  D-evalose, **3**, 312
  methylfucose, **1**, 331
  L-vallarose, **3**, 312
  virenose, **3**, 323
  D-virenose , **3**, 312
  L-virenose, **3**, 312
$C_7H_{14}O_6$
  6-deoxy-D-*manno*-heptose, **3**, 192, 312
  1-methyl-β-D-glucopyranose, **3**, 810
  3-methyl-α-D-mannose, **3**, 186
  sequoyitol, **8**, 155
$C_7H_{14}O_7$
  heptenitol, **5**, 304
  L-*glycero*-D-*manno*-heptose, **3**, 187
$C_7H_{14}O_7P_2$, cyclopentylideneethyl diphosphate, **2**, 76
$C_7H_{15}N$, diisopropylaminomethylene, **7**, 123
$C_7H_{15}NO_2$, isoleucine methyl ester, **8**, 221, 223
$C_7H_{15}NO_3$
  carnitine, **1**, 49
  N-hydroxyethyl-2-hydroxymethyl-3-hydroxypyrrolidine, **3**, 130, 134
$C_7H_{15}NO_4$ 2,5-dideoxy-2,5-imino-DL-*glycero*-D-*manno*-D-heptitol, **3**, 130
  2,6-dideoxy-2-methylaminogalactose, **7**, 558
  homoDMDP, **3**, 134
  N-methyl-1-deoxynojirimycin, **3**, 19, 131
  N-methyl-DNJ, **3**, 134
$C_7H_{15}NO_5$, α-homonojirimycin, **3**, 131, 134, 141
$C_7H_{15}N_3O_2$, indospicine, **8**, 146
$C_7H_{15}O_{10}P$
  D-*glycero*-D-*manno*-heptose 7P, **3**, 222
  sedoheptulose 7-phosphate, **3**, 222, 414, 417
$C_7H_{16}ClNOS$, acetylthiocholine, **5**, 116
$C_7H_{16}ClNO_2$, acetylcholine, **1**, 297, **5**, 116

C₇H₁₆O
1-heptanol, **8**, 211
2-heptanol, **8**, 169, 208, 211
4-methyl-3-hexanol, **8**, 242
C₇H₁₆O₁₃P₂, sedoheptulose-1,7-diphosphate, **3**, 390
C₇H₁₇NO₂P, *N,N*-diisopropylphosphoramidite, **7**, 131
C₇H₁₇NO₈, neuraminate, **3**, 425
C₇H₁₇N₂OP, bisphosphoramidite, **7**, 133
C₇H₁₇N₃O₄P, anatoxin-a, **8**, 611, **4**, 30
C₇H₁₇O₈P, carbocyclic homophosphonate, **1**, 585
C₇H₁₉N₃, spermidine, **3**, 721, **4**, 30, **6**, 251
C₇H₅₈O₁₁, mosesin-1, **8**, 474
C₈H₁₁N, dimethylaniline, **3**, 412
C₈H₄O₃S₂, thiotropocin, **1**, 77, 849
C₈H₅NO₂, isatin, **8**, 429
C₈H₅NO₆, phosphoramidite, **7**, 158
C₈H₆BrN₃O, *p*-azidophenacyl bromide, **6**, 91
C₈H₆Br₂O, *p*-bromophenacylbromide, **1**, 293
C₈H₆ClO₂, chlorophenoxyacetyl, **7**, 120
C₈H₆Cl₂O₃, 2,4-dichlorophenoxyacetic acid, **5**, 411, **8**, 23, 34, 35
C₈H₆N₂O₂S, *C*-5-(thien-2-yl)uridine, **7**, 318
C₈H₆O₂
phenylacetic acid, **1**, 815
phenylglyoxal, **3**, 448, 451, 463, **5**, 275
C₈H₆O₃, carboxybenzaldehyde, **3**, 376, 377
C₈H₆O₄, terephthalate, **3**, 385
C₈H₆O₅, monoperphthalic acid, **6**, 65
C₈H₇Br₂NO₃, aeroplysinin-1 dienone, **8**, 468
C₈H₇ClO₂, 4-chlorophenylacetate, **5**, 417
C₈H₇F₃N₂O₃S, benzimidazole trifluoromethane sulfonate, **7**, 138
C₈H₇N
indole, **5**, 379, **8**, 34, 161
phenylacetonitrile, **8**, 26
C₈H₇NOS, *p*-methoxyphenyl isothiocyanate, **7**, 159
C₈H₇NO₂, benzoxazinones, **8**, 169
C₈H₇NO₃
desosamine, **3**, 335
N-formylanthranilic acid, **1**, 846
6-methoxy-2-benzoxazolinone, **8**, 29
C₈H₇NS, benzothiazole, **8**, 588
C₈H₇N₃O₂S
C-5-(4-methyl)thiazoleuridine, **7**, 318
C-5-(5-methyl)thiazoleuridine, **7**, 318
C₈H₇O
benzylcarbonyl, **7**, 120
toluoyl, **7**, 119, 120
C₈H₇O₂
benzyloxycarbonyl, **7**, 120
methoxybenzoyl, **7**, 119, 120
4-methoxybenzoyl, **7**, 120
phenoxyacetyl, **7**, 120, 121, 124
C₈H₇O₃, methyl salicylate, **8**, 165
C₈H₈, styrene, **5**, 173
C₈H₈Cl₂, 1,2-dichlorophenylethane, **5**, 173
C₈H₈Cl₂N₂O₂, dichloro(nitrophenethylamine), **8**, 431
C₈H₈Cl₃N, dichloro(chlorophenethylamine), **8**, 431
C₈H₈F₃NO₂, *N*-methylanilinium trifluoroacetate, **7**, 138
C₈H₈NO₂, nitrophenylethyl, **7**, 119, 130
C₈H₈NO₂S, nitrophenylthioethyl, **7**, 119
C₈H₈NO₄S, nitrophenylsulfonylethyl, **7**, 119
C₈H₈N₂, 5-methylbenzimidazole, **4**, 150
C₈H₈N₂O, 5-hydroxy-6-methylbenzimidazole, **4**, 150
C₈H₈N₂O₂, ricinine, **3**, 643
C₈H₈N₂O₃, pyrimidineacrylic acid, **1**, 847
C₈H₈N₂O₄, sparsomycin uracil acrylic acid moiety, **1**, 846
C₈H₈O, acetophenone, **5**, 373
C₈H₈O₂
p-hydroxyacetophenone, **3**, 640, **8**, 173, 190, 191
p-methoxybenzaldehyde, **3**, 395
methyl benzoate, **8**, 161
6-methylsalicylic aldehyde, **8**, 212

phenylacetic acid, **1**, 54, 77, 850, **4**, 174, 182, 244, 254, **8**, 26, 34
C₈H₈O₃
3,4-dihydroxyacetophenone, **8**, 190, 191
3-hydroxy-5-methylbenzoic acid, **1**, 401
2-hydroxyphenylacetic acid, **4**, 254
4-hydroxyphenylacetic acid, **3**, 413, **4**, 254, **5**, 46
p-hydroxyphenylacetic acid, **8**, 26
mandelic acid, **1**, 78, **5**, 16, 33
4-methoxytoluqinone, **1**, 411
methyl 4-hydroxybenzoate, **8**, 200
methyl salicylate, **8**, 150, 152, 156, 212
6-methylsalicylic acid, **1**, 2, 345, 410, 458, 849
phenoxyacetic acid, **4**, 254
vanillin, **3**, 622, 682, 696, **8**, 165
C₈H₈O₄
3,4-dihydroxyphenylacetic acid, **1**, 813
2,6-dimethoxybenzoquinone, **8**, 181
2,6-dimethoxy-*p*-benzoquinone, **8**, 175
homogentisic acid, **1**, 856
4-hydroxytropolone-3-carboxylic acid, **1**, 850
monoacetylphloroglucinol, **1**, 763
orsellinic acid, **1**, 2, 346, 410
vanillic acid, **3**, 696, 805, **8**, 169, 171
C₈H₈O₅, methyl gallate, **3**, 813, 820
C₈H₈O₇
5-(carboxymethyl)-2-hydroxymuconate, **5**, 34, 46
5-carboxymethyl-2-oxo-3-hexenedioate, **5**, 34
5-carboxymethyl-2-oxo-4-hexenedioate, **5**, 34
C₈H₉
p-tolylmethyl, **7**, 126
xylyl, **7**, 119
C₈H₉NO₂
acetaminophen, **5**, 184
methyl anthranilate, **8**, 161
C₈H₉NO₃, pyridoxal, **3**, 369, 371, 405, 407
C₈H₉NO₄, hematinic acid, **4**, 96
C₈H₉NO₅
clavulanic acid, **3**, 285, **4**, 173, 180, 182, 183, 185
C₈H₉NO₅S, *N*-succinimidyl-*S*-acetyl thioacetate, **7**, 168
C₈H₉O
benzyloxymethyl, **7**, 119
methoxybenzyl, **7**, 119
C₈H₉S, (phenylthio)ethyl, **7**, 119
C₈H₁₀NO₆P
pyridoxal phosphate, **1**, 826, 843, **2**, 56, **3**, 449, 469, 476, 545, **5**, 304
pyridoxal 5′-phosphate, **3**, 254, 448, 474, **4**, 65, 70, **5**, 207, 209, 211
C₈H₁₀N₂O₃S, 3-exomethylenecepham, **1**, 844
C₈H₁₀N₂O₃, theoalanine, **8**, 570
C₈H₁₀N₂O₃S, 7-aminodeacetoxycephalosporanic acid, **4**, 180
C₈H₁₀N₂O₄
clavaminic acid, **4**, 185
mimosine, **8**, 146
C₈H₁₀N₂O₄S, 7-aminodeacetoxycephalosporanic acid, **4**, 262
C₈H₁₀N₄O₂, caffeine, **4**, 26, **8**, 147, 167, 168, 169, 173
C₈H₁₀O₂, dimethoxybenzene, **5**, 379
C₈H₁₀O₄, penicillic acid, **1**, 2, 411, 427
C₈H₁₀O₅, endothall, **5**, 155, 158
C₈H₁₁ClO₂, 3-chloroacetylcyclohexanone, **1**, 588
C₈H₁₁N, dimethylaniline, **5**, 379
C₈H₁₁NO, dimethylaniline-*N*-oxide, **3**, 412
C₈H₁₁NO, tyramine, **8**, 430
C₈H₁₁NO₂, dopamine, **1**, 297
C₈H₁₁NO₃
noradrenalin, **8**, 432
noradreniline, **8**, 400
pyridoxine, **2**, 376
C₈H₁₁N₃O₃, *N*-4-(3-carboxypropyl)cytosine, **7**, 320
C₈H₁₁N₃O₆, dioxetane degradation product, **7**, 411

C$_8$H$_{12}$, fucoserratene, **8**, 420
C$_8$H$_{12}$ClN, *N,N*-dimethylaniline hydrochloride, **7**, 130
C$_8$H$_{12}$NO$_6$P, pyridoxol phosphate, **2**, 4
C$_8$H$_{12}$N$_2$
  diketopiperazine, **8**, 588
  N,N-dimethyl-*p*-phenylenediamine, **3**, 716
C$_8$H$_{12}$N$_2$O, 3-isopropyl-2-methoxypyrazine, **8**, 152
C$_8$H$_{12}$N$_2$O$_2$, 5-*tert*-butyluracil, **5**, 391
C$_8$H$_{12}$N$_2$O$_3$S, 6-aminopenicillanic acid, **3**, 283, **4**, 170, 181, 240
C$_8$H$_{12}$N$_2$O$_4$
  alanylclavam, **4**, 183
  dihydroclavaminic acid, **4**, 185
C$_8$H$_{12}$N$_2$O$_4$S
  3β-hydroxycepham, **1**, 844
  3β-methylenehydroxypenam β-sulfoxide, **1**, 844
  3β methylenehydroxypenam, **1**, 844
C$_8$H$_{12}$N$_2$O$_6$, kifunensine, **3**, 21, 25, 134, 148, 151, 155
C$_8$H$_{13}$O, 6-methyl-3,5-heptadien-2-one, **8**, 233
C$_8$H$_{12}$O$_2$
  2-ethyl-6-methyl-4*H*-2,3-dihydropyran-4-one, **8**, 211
  6-ethyl-2-methyl-4*H*-2,3-dihydropyran-4-one, **8**, 211
C$_8$H$_{12}$O$_3$, δ-lactone, **1**, 508
C$_8$H$_{12}$O$_4$, diethyl maleate, **7**, 665
C$_8$H$_{12}$O$_5$, α-ketosuberate, **1**, 834
C$_8$H$_{13}$NO
  supinidine, **4**, 31
  tropinone, **4**, 27, 30
C$_8$H$_{13}$NOS, hydroxylethylthiamine, **2**, 55
C$_8$H$_{13}$NO$_2$
  heliotridine, **4**, 31
  retronecine, **4**, 32, 33, **8**, 147, 152
C$_8$H$_{13}$NO$_3$, *N*-butyryl homoserine lactone, **8**, 398
C$_8$H$_{13}$NO$_4$,HAI-1, **8**, 395
C$_8$H$_{13}$NO$_4$S,NAG-thiazoline, **5**, 297
C$_8$H$_{13}$NO$_5$
  N-acetyl-Ala-Lac, **3**, 273
  7a-*epi*-alexaflorine, **3**, 131, 134
C$_8$H$_{13}$N$_2$O$_5$P, pyridoxamine 5′-phosphate, **4**, 70
C$_8$H$_{13}$N$_3$O, *N*-4-butylcytosine, **7**, 320
C$_8$H$_{13}$N$_3$O$_4$, 5-aminoimidazole β-D-ribofuranoside, **4**, 150
C$_8$H$_{13}$N$_5$O$_5$, deoxyguanosine degradation product, **7**, 411
C$_8$H$_{14}$ClN$_5$, atrazine, **5**, 411
C$_8$H$_{14}$N$_2$O$_4$
  aziridino-DAP, **3**, 276
  proclavaminic acid, **4**, 183
C$_8$H$_{14}$N$_3$O$_7$P, 5-aminoimidazole riboside, **1**, 838
C$_8$H$_{14}$N$_4$O, *N*-4-(4-aminobutyl)cytosine, **7**, 320
C$_8$H$_{14}$N$_4$O$_5$, deoxyguanosine degradation product, **7**, 411
C$_8$H$_{14}$N$_4$O$_6$, α-amino-β-oxalylaminopropionic acid, **8**, 146
C$_8$H$_{14}$O
  6-methyl-5-hepten-2-one, **8**, 232, 234
  6-methyl-6-hepten-2-one, **8**, 233
  1,5-octadien-3-ol, **1**, 239
  rillingol, **5**, 339
C$_8$H$_{14}$O$_2$
  brevicomin, **3**, 417
  2-butenyl butanoate, **8**, 210
  diketone, **8**, 242
  1,5-dimethyl-6,8-dioxabicyclo[3.2.1]octane, **8**, 233
  6,7-epoxy-6-methylheptan-2-one, **8**, 233
  frontalin, **8**, 41
  3-hydroxy-2,3-dimethylcyclohexanone, **8**, 270
  karahana lactone, **8**, 43
  lactone, **8**, 240
  1,3,3-trimethyl-2,7-dioxabicyclo[2.2.1]heptane, **8**, 232
C$_8$H$_{14}$O$_2$S$_2$, lipoic acid, **1**, 20, 832
C$_8$H$_{14}$O$_3$
  allyl ether of ethyl acetoacetate, **5**, 350
  2-ketooctanoic acid, **3**, 381
  δ-lactone, **1**, 508
C$_8$H$_{14}$O$_4$, suberic acid, **1**, 298
C$_8$H$_{14}$O$_5$ 2-*O*-acetyl-3,6-dideoxy-α-D-*xylo*- hexose, **3**, 187

D-chromose D, **3**, 312
3-(3-hydroxybutanoyloxy)butanoic acid, **8**, 209
L-pillarose, **3**, 312
trioxacarcinose B, **3**, 312
C$_8$H$_{14}$O$_6$, acetylfucose, **1**, 331
C$_8$H$_{14}$O$_7$
  N-acetylgalactose, **3**, 170
  N-acetylglucose, **3**, 170
C$_8$H$_{14}$O$_8$
  3-deoxy-D-*manno*-octulopyranosonic acid, **3**, 185
  KDO, **3**, 380, 387, 499, 503, 509
C$_8$H$_{15}$INO$_9$, *N*-acetylglucosamine-6-phosphate analogue, **3**, 275
C$_8$H$_{15}$N
  FPP ammonium analogue, **5**, 338
  tropane, **4**, 26
C$_8$H$_{15}$NO
  hygrine, **4**, 30, 30
  pseudotropine, **4**, 30
  trachelanthamine, **4**, 31
  tropine, **4**, 27, 30
  ψ-tropine, **4**, 30
C$_8$H$_{15}$NO$_2$, hastanecine, **4**, 31
C$_8$H$_{15}$NO$_3$
  platynecine, **4**, 31, 32
  rosmarinecine, **4**, 31
C$_8$H$_{15}$NO$_4$
  alexine, **3**, 131, 134
  australine, **3**, 20, 131, 134, 139, 140, 152
  1-*epi*-australine, **3**, 131, 134
  3-*epi*-australine, **3**, 131, 134
  7-*epi*-australine, **3**, 131, 134
  castanospermine, **3**, 20, 31, 381
  N-methylcalystegine B$_2$, **3**, 133, 137
C$_8$H$_{15}$NO$_5$
  2-acetamido-2,6-dideoxy-α-D-galactose, **3**, 194
  casuarine, **3**, 132, 134
  deoxy-*N*-acetylmannosamine, **3**, 380
  4-deoxy-*N*-acetylmannosamine, **3**, 391
  L-evernitrose, **3**, 312
  N-methylcalysteginC$_1$, **3**, 133, 137
  perosamine, **3**, 186, 195
  L-rubranitrose, **3**, 312
  tomosamine, **3**, 186
  viosamine, **3**, 186
C$_8$H$_{15}$NO$_6$
  N-acetyl-D-allosamine, **1**, 149, 150
  N-acetylgalactosamine, **3**, 70, 71, 111, 124, 146, 161, 305
  N-acetylglucosamine, **3**, 71, 111, 161, 229, 244, 275, 301, 380, **4**, 307
  N-acetylmannosamine, **3**, 378, 380, 390, 391
  N-acetyl-D-mannosamine, **3**, 378, 390
C$_8$H$_{15}$NO$_7$, *N*-glycolylmannosamine, **3**, 391
C$_8$H$_{15}$NS, 2-(2′-methylbutyl)-4,5-dihydrothiazole, **8**, 221
C$_8$H$_{15}$N$_3$O$_7$, streptozocin, **7**, 520
C$_8$H$_{15}$O$_7$P
  carbocyclic phosphonate, **1**, 585
  phosphonate, **1**, 582
C$_8$H$_{15}$O$_9$P, homophosphonate, **1**, 585
C$_8$H$_{15}$O$_{10}$P, 2-deoxy KDO-8P, **3**, 389
C$_8$H$_{15}$O$_{11}$P
  3-deoxy-D-*manno*-octulosonate 8-phosphate, **1**, 580
  KDO 8-phosphate, **3**, 387, 509
C$_8$H$_{16}$NO$_9$P
  N-acetylglycosamine-6-phosphate, **3**, 391
  N-acetyl-D-mannosamine-6-phosphate, **3**, 391
C$_8$H$_{16}$N$_2$O$_3$S , cysteinylvaline, **1**, 842, **4**, 250
C$_8$H$_{16}$N$_2$O$_7$, cycasin, **8**, 152
C$_8$H$_{16}$O
  4-methyl-3-heptanone, **8**, 242
  6-methyl-5-hepten-2-ol, **8**, 232
  methyl-2-hepten-4-ol, **8**, 245

2-octanone, **8**, 212
3-octanone, **8**, 150, 152, 211
2-octenal, **8**, 211
1-octen-3-ol, **8**, 211
pheromone of *Atta texana*, **8**, 45
sulcatol , **8**, 4, 46, 233
C₈H₁₆O₂
amyl propionate, **8**, 165
butyl butanoate, **8**, 210
3,3-dimethylbutyl acetate, **5**, 124,
1,7-dioxaspiro[5.5]decane, **8**, 212
ethyl hexanoate, **8**, 210
hexyl acetate, **8**, 210
2-(1-hydroxy-1-methylethyl)-5-
    methyltetrahydrofuran, **8**, 233
5-hydroxy-4-methyl-3-heptanone, **8**, 210, 242
3-hydroxy-2-octanone, **8**, 211
2-hydroxy-3-octanone, **8**, 211
isobutyroin, **3**, 394
octanoic acid , **1**, 832, **4**, 254
2,2,6-trimethyl-3-hydroxytetrahydropyran, **8**, 233
vittatol, **8**, 234
C₈H₁₆O₂S
6-mercaptooctanoic acid, **1**, 832
8-mercaptooctanoic acid, **1**, 832
C₈H₁₆O₃
8-hydroxycaprylic acid, **1**, 298
6-hydroxyoctanoic acid, **1**, 832
8-hydroxyoctanoic acid, **1**, 832
C₈H₁₆O₄
L-arcanose, **3**, 312
cladinose, **3**, 335, 342, 351
L-cladinose, **3**, 312
6,8-dihydroxyoctanoic acid, **1**, 832
C₈H₁₆O₅
D-labilose, **3**, 312
mycinose, **3**, 352
D-mycinose, **3**, 312
noviose, **3**, 342
L-noviose, **3**, 312
γ-octose, **3**, 317
vinelose, **3**, 342
L-vinelose, **3**, 312
yersiniose A, **3**, 312
yersiniose B, **3**, 312
C₈H₁₆O₇P₂, cyclohexylideneethyl diphosphate, **2**, 76
C₈H₁₆O₁₄P₂, 2,6-anhydro-3-deoxy-2β-phosphonylmethyl-
        8-phosphat e-D-*glycero*-D-*talo*-octonate, **3**, 389
C₈H₁₇N, coniine, **1**, 450
C₈H₁₇NO₃
8-amino-7-oxopelargonic acid, **1**, 826, 827
desosamine, **3**, 351
kedarosamine, **7**, 577
C₈H₁₇NO₄, mycaminose, **3**, 351, 352
C₈H₁₇NO₅
1-deoxynojirimycin, **3**, 143
N-hydroxyethyl-1-deoxynojirimycin, **3**, 143
C₈H₁₇O₉P, 7,8-dideoxy-4-octulose-1-phosphate, **3**, 414
C₈H₁₇O₁₁P, 3-deoxy-D-*manno*-2-octulosonate 8-
        phosphate, **1**, 76
C₈H₁₈, 2-methylheptadecane, **8**, 240
C₈H₁₈AlCl, chlorodiisobutylalane, **7**, 126
C₈H₁₈ClN₃, 1-(3-dimethylaminopropyl)-3-
        ethylcarbodiimide hydrochloride , **7**, 158
C₈H₁₈N₆O₄, streptidine, **3**, 353
C₈H₁₈O
4-methyl-3-heptanol, **8**, 242
2-methyl-4-heptanol, **8**, 245, 246
1-octanol, **8**, 162, 211
3-octanol, **8**, 49, 211
C₈H₁₈O₂, 2,3-octanediol, **8**, 211
C₈H₁₈PS, dibutylphosphinothioyl, **7**, 119
C₈H₂₀ClN, tetraethylammonium chloride, **8**, 434

C₈H₂₀N₂O₂, 7,8-diaminopelargonic acid, **1**, 826
C₈H₂₁N₃, homospermidine, **4**, 31
C₈H₂₂N₄, *N,N'*-bis(3-aminopropyl)ethylenediamine, **7**,
        159
C₈Cl₂N₂O₂, dichlorodicyanobenzoquinone, **5**, 376
C₉H₁₁NO₅, dihydroxyphenylserine, **3**, 400
C₉H₃N₉O₃P, tristriazolylphosphite, **7**, 139
C₉H₄O₆, stipitatonic acid, **1**, 3
C₉H₆I₂O₄, (diiodohydroxyphenyl)pyruvate, **5**, 47
C₉H₆N₂O₂
2,6-diisocyanatotoluene, **7**, 117
4-nitroquinoline, **7**, 96
C₉H₆N₂O₃, 4-nitroquinoline *N*-oxide, **7**, 522
C₉H₆N₂O₄, 2-carboxyquinoxaline di-*N*-oxide, **7**, 533
C₉H₆N₂S, brassilexin, **8**, 187
C₉H₆O₂, coumarin, **1**, 627, 628
C₉H₆O₃, umbelliferone, **1**, 19, 627, 628, **8**, 152
C₉H₆O₄, aesculetin, **1**, 628
C₉H₇BrO₄, bromoacetylsalicylic acid, **5**, 247, 248
C₉H₇Cl₂N, dichlorophenethyl isocyanide, **8**, 431
C₉H₇D₄O₃, 9-oxonona-5,7-dienoic acid, **8**, 425
C₉H₇NO, indole-3-carboxaldehyde, **8**, 26
C₉H₇NO₂S, 1,2-benzisothiazol-3-ylacetic acid, **8**, 35
C₉H₇NO₃S, 3-oxo-1,2-benzisothiazolin-2-ylacetic acid, **8**,
        36
C₉H₇N₂O₂S, nitrophenylthiopropiononitrile, **5**, 380
C₉H₇N₂O₆, 2,4-dinitrophenylethoxycarbonyl, **7**, 127
C₉H₇N₃O₂, *C*-5-(pyridin-2-yl)uridine, **7**, 318
C₉H₈BrNO₃, aeroplysinin-1, **8**, 468
C₉H₈ClHgNO, [(β-acryloylamino)phenyl]mercuric
        chloride, **6**, 138
C₉H₈ClO₄S, chlorophenylsulfonylethoxycarbonyl, **7**, 120
C₉H₈Cl₂O₃, 3-(2,4-dichlorophenoxy)propionic acid, **8**, 35
C₉H₈N, cyanophenethyl, **7**, 119
C₉H₈NO₄, nitrophenethyloxycarbonyl, **7**, 120
C₉H₈NO₆S, nitrophenylsulfonylethoxycarbonyl, **7**, 120
C₉H₈N₂O₂, nitrophenethyl isocyanide, **8**, 431
C₉H₈O, cinnamaldehyde, **8**, 161
C₉H₈O₂
cinnamic acid, **1**, 627, 635, 719, **3**, 2, 18, 624, 627, 681,
        804, 376, **8**, 169
p-coumaraldehyde, **3**, 655
hydroxycinnamaldehyde, **1**, 686
C₉H₈O₃
coumarate, **1**, 18, **3**, 602
m-coumaric acid, **3**, 640
o-coumaric acid, **3**, 640
p-coumaric acid , **1**, 627, 716, 719, 815, **3**, 620, 682, 696
hydroxycinnamic acid, **1**, 686, **3**, 9, 602
phenylpyruvic acid, **1**, 850, **4**, 5, **5**, 47, 344, 345
C₉H₈O₄
acetylsalicylic acid, **1**, 243
aspirin, **1**, 123, 257, **5** 193, 247, 248, 249
caffeic acid, **1**, 18, 645, 673, 716, 721, **3**, 651, 803, **8**,
        140, 141
p-hydroxyphenylpyruvate, **1**, 856, **4**, 5, **5**, 47, 344, 345
C₉H₈O₅
flavipin, **1**, 411
3,4-hydroxyphenylpyruvic acid, **4**, 39
3,4,5-trihydroxycinnamic acid, **3**, 641, 803
C₉H₉Br₂NO₂, aeroplysinin-I, **8**, 431
C₉H₉N, skatole, **8**, 161
C₉H₉NOS, benzothiazole, **8**, 588
C₉H₉NO₃
adrenochrome, **7**, 378
indole-3-methanesulfonic acid, **8**, 35
C₉H₉NO₄, *p*-nitrobenzyl acetate, **5**, 433
C₉H₉N₅O, *N*-4-(6-amino-2-pyridinyl)cytosine, **7**, 321
C₉H₉O
2,4-dimethylbenzoyl, **7**, 120
dimethylbenzoyl, **7**, 120
C₉H₉O₃, diimethoxybenzoyl, **7**, 120
C₉H₉O₄S, phenylsulfonylethoxycarbonyl, **7**, 119, 120

C₉H₁₀BrNO₃, bromotyrosine, **8**, 468
C₉H₁₀ClNO₂, chlorophenylalanine, **5**, 353
C₉H₁₀FNO₂, fluorophenylalanine, **5**, 353
C₉H₁₀F₂NO₅P, α-difluorophosphonate, **5**, 304
C₉H₁₀NO, dimethylaminobenzoyl, **7**, 120
C₉H₁₀NO₃, tyrosine, **5**, 344
C₉H₁₀N₂
    5,6-dimethylbenzimidazole, **4**, 149, **5**, 174
    dimethylbenzimidazole, **4**, 149
C₉H₁₀N₂O₂, p-aminophenylalanine, **5**, 347
C₉H₁₀N₂O₄, 4-nitrophenylalanine, **3**, 634
C₉H₁₀N₂O₅, nitrotyrosine, **5**, 244
C₉H₁₀N₄O₃, 2-azidotyrosine, **3**, 408
C₉H₁₀O
    p-hydroxyarylpropene, **1**, 645, 672
    p-hydroxyphenylpropene, **3**, 677
C₉H₁₀O₂
    p-coumaryl alcohol, **1**, 648, 654, 672, 685, **3**, 618, 676
    hydroxycinnamyl alcohol, **1**, 686
    phenylpropionic acid, **4**, 254
C₉H₁₀O₃
    atrolactic acid, **5**, 16
    dihydrocinnamic acid, **1**, 682
    methyl 6-methylsalicylate, **8**, 211
C₉H₁₀O₄
    2′,6′-dihydroxy-4′-methoxyacetophenone, **8**, 190
    jacaranone, **8**, 435
    methylorsellinic acid, **1**, 3
    α-pyrone, **1**, 401,
    veratric acid, **3**, 624, 703
C₉H₁₀O₄, ubiquinone-0, **8**, 436
C₉H₁₀O₅
    ethyl gallate, **3**, 813, 820
    syringic acid, **3**, 385, 696
C₉H₁₀O₈,
    2,8-dioxabicyclo[3.2.1]octane-3,4,5-tricarboxylic acid,
        2, 257
C₉H₁₀O₁₃P₂, shikimate 3-phosphate derivative, **1**, 598
C₉H₁₁, mesityl, **7**, 119
C₉H₁₁BrN₂O₅
    2′-bromo-2′-deoxyuridine, **7**, 382
    5-bromodeoxyuridine, **7**, 411, 419
C₉H₁₁BrN₂O₆, 5-bromouridine, **6**, 91, 228
C₉H₁₁ClO₂S, mesitylene sulfonyl chloride, **7**, 107
C₉H₁₁IN₂O₅
    2′-iodo-2′-deoxyuridine, **7**, 382
    5-iododeoxyuridine, **7**, 411
C₉H₁₁IN₂O₆, 5-iodouridine, **6**, 228
C₉H₁₁NO₂
    methyl N-methylanthranilate, **8**, 165
    β-phenylalanine, **2**, 222
    phenylalanine, **1**, 346, 574, 609, 716, 719, 840, 850, **3**,
        130, 261, 386, 405, 622, 677, 805, **4**, 2, 4, 16, 27,
        35, 209, 255, 325, 340, 342, 343, 345, **5**, 344, 345,
        346, 424, **6**, 127, 129, 165
C₉H₁₁NO₂S₅, lissoclinotoxin A, **7**, 527, **8**, 541
C₉H₁₁NO₂S₆, 3,4-desmethylvaracin, **8**, 542
C₉H₁₁NO₃
    2-aminooxy-3-phenylpropanoic acid, **3**, 627
    2-aminooxy-3-phenylpropionic acid, **3**, 804
    α-aminooxy-β-phenylpropionic acid, **1**, 808, **3**, 634
    hydroxyphenylalanine, **5**, 353
    phenylisoserine, **2**, 222
    β-phenylserine, **3**, 399
    threophenylserine, **4**, 327
    tyrosine, **1**, 16, 574, 609, 838, **3**, 261, 346, 378, 386, 405,
        408, 622, 640, **4**, 2, 4, 35, **5**, 345, 346, 424
    m-tyrosine, **3**, 634
C₉H₁₁NO₄
    dihydroxyphenylalanine, **4**, 39
    3,4-dihytdroxyphenylalanine, **8**, 432
    Dopa, **3**, 408, **8**, 146
    N-hydroxytyrosine, **1**, 858

    opsopyrroledicarboxylic acid, **4**, 86
C₉H₁₁NO₅
    dihydroxyphenylserine, **3**, 400
    N,N-dihydroxytyrosine, **1**, 858
C₉H₁₁NO₆, showdomycin, **8**, 390
C₉H₁₁NO₇, minimycin, **8**, 390
C₉H₁₁NO₇S, olivanic acid, **4**, 186
C₉H₁₁N₂O₅, uridine derivative, **7**, 376
C₉H₁₁N₂O₇, uridine derivative, **7**, 378
C₉H₁₁N₃O₃, alanine-4-nitroanilide, **1**, 279
C₉H₁₁N₅O₆, 5-azidouridine, **6**, 230
C₉H₁₁O₂, dimethoxybenzyl, **7**, 119
C₉H₁₂
    1-(1,3-butadienyl)-2-vinylcyclopropane, **8**, 424
    cumene, **3**, 384
    7-methylcyclooctatriene, **8**, 424
    1,3,5,7-nonatetraene, **8**, 424
C₉H₁₂BrNO₃S, dimethyl (2-hydroxy-5-
        nitrobenzyl)sulfonium bromide, **5**, 353
C₉H₁₂IN₃O₃, 5-[3-(iodoacetamido)propyl]uridine, **7**, 319
C₉H₁₂NO₅P, phosphonate, **5**, 304
C₉H₁₂N₂, nornicotine, **8**, 151
C₉H₁₂N₂O₃, nikkomycin, **3**, 423
C₉H₁₂N₂O₅
    2′-deoxyuridin-2′-yl, **7**, 382
    deoxyuridin-5-yl, **7**, 380
    2′-deoxyuridin-5-yl, **7**, 411
C₉H₁₂N₂O₅S
    2-thiouridine, **6**, 93
    4-thiouridine , **6**, 93, 225, 228
    6-thiouridine, **6**, 93
C₉H₁₂N₂O₆
    pseudoisocytidine, **7**, 262
    pseudouridine, **4**, 361
    uridine, **5**, 24
C₉H₁₂N₂O₁₃P₂, 2′-deoxy-3′-ketoUDP, **5**, 195
C₉H₁₂O₂
    cumene hydroperoxide, **5**, 232
    dihydro-p-coumaryl alcohol , **1**, 682, **3**, 677
    2-hydroxy-4,4,6-trimethyl-2,5-cyclohexadien-1-one, **8**,
        234
    2,6-nonadien-4-olide, **8**, 212
    oxoisophorone, **8**, 234
C₉H₁₂O₃
    nectriapyrone B, **8**, 600
    triketide lactone pyrone analogue, **1**, 515
    1,2,4-trimethoxybenzene, **8**, 161
C₉H₁₂O₄,
    2-hydroxy-5-methyl-7-methoxy-1-naphthoate, **7**, 558
C₉H₁₂O₆, 4-C-acetyl-6-deoxy-2,3-O-methylene-D-gala
        ctono-1,5-lactone, **3**, 312
C₉H₁₃ClN₂O₁₂P₂,ClUDP, **5**, 194
C₉H₁₃F₂O₁₁P₂, F₂CDP, **5**, 172
C₉H₁₃F₃N₂O₈P₂, 4-[2-diazotrifluoropropionyloxy]3-
        methyl-2-buten-1-ol, **2**, 126
C₉H₁₃NO, benzyldimethylamine oxide, **3**, 412
C₉H₁₃NO₂, dihydrophenylalanine, **8**, 178
C₉H₁₃NO₂S, 3-pentynoyl-N-acetylcysteamine, **1**, 354
C₉H₁₃NO₃
    adrenalin, **8**, 432
    epinephrine, **3**, 483, 485, 643, 644, **5**, 238, **7**, 378
C₉H₁₃NO₇S₂, [3-(methylthio)propyl]glucosinolate
        derivative, **1**, 859
C₉H₁₃N₂O₉P ,UMP, **6**, 97, 104, 139
C₉H₁₃N₃O₄
    2′-deoxycytidine, **7**, 272
    deoxycytidine, **7**, 375
C₉H₁₃N₃O₅
    C-nucleoside, **7**, 263
    cytidine, **5**, 24, **6**, 249,
    cytidine derivative, **7**, 117
C₉H₁₃N₃O₆, 4-amino-1-(β-D-ribofuranosyl)-2,6-[1H,3H] -
        pyrimidione, **7**, 272

C₉H₁₃N₄O₁₁P₂
2′-azido-2′-deoxyuridine diphosphate, **5**, 182
N₃UDP, **5**, 197
C₉H₁₃N₅O₄, dihydroneopterin, **3**, 374
C₉H₁₃N₅O₁₂P₂, 2′-azido-2′-deoxyruridine 5′-diphosphate, **3**, 330
C₉H₁₄ClN₅, 4-chloro-2-cyclobutylamino-6-ethylamino-*s*-triazine, **8**, 68
C₉H₁₄F₂O₁₄P₃, F₂CTP, **5**, 172
C₉H₁₄N₂O, 2-isobutyl-3-methoxypyrazine, **8**, 165
C₉H₁₄N₂O₆, zebularine 3,4-hydrate, **5**, 24
C₉H₁₄N₂O₁₁P₂S, 2′-deoxy-2′-mercaptouridine 5′-diphosphate, **3**, 330
C₉H₁₄N₂O₁₂P₂,UDP, **3**, 483
C₉H₁₄N₂O₁₅P₃,ClUTP, **5**, 195
C₉H₁₄N₄O₂, *N*-(3-acetamidopropyl)cytosine, **7**, 320
C₉H₁₄N₄O₄, *N*-9-amino-2′-deoxycytidine, **7**, 271
C₉H₁₄N₅O₁₅P₃, 5-azidodeoxyuridine triphosphate, **6**, 230
C₉H₁₄O
    botryococcenol, **5**, 338
    isophorone, **8**, 234
    2,6-nonadienal, **8**, 165
    γ-phorone, **8**, 234
C₉H₁₄O₂
    dehydrobrebicomin, **8**, 47
    3,4-dehydrobrevicomin, **8**, 213
    methylethylcyclohexanedione, **8**, 270
    4-methyl-2,6-octadienoic acid, **1**, 543
C₉H₁₄O₃
    cantharidin, **8**, 234
    triketide lactone ketone, **1**, 515
C₉H₁₄O₆
    D-aldgarose, **3**, 312
    aldgarose, **3**, 342; 6-deoxy-4-*C*-[1-hydroxyethyl]-2,3-*O*-methylene-D-galactono-1,5-lactone, **3**, 312
    4-*C*-[1-methoxyethyl]-2,3-*O*-methylene-L-ar abinono-1,5-lactone, **3**, 312
C₉H₁₅BrO₃S, diethyl (bromomethyl)methylthiomalonate, **5**, 271
C₉H₁₅NO₅
    N-acetyl-Ala-HBut, **3**, 273
    2-dehydropantoate, **3**, 409
C₉H₁₅NO₆
    1,6-anhydromuramic acid, **3**, 269
    muramic acid δ-lactam, **3**, 244
C₉H₁₅N₂O₁₅P₃,UTP, **3**, 479
C₉H₁₅N₂O₁₅P₃S, 5-sulfhydryluridine triphosphate, **6**, 230
C₉H₁₅N₃O₆, cytidine derivative, **5**, 24
C₉H₁₅N₆O₁₃P₃, 8-azido-ATP, **3**, 448
C₉H₁₅O₇P
    cis-vinyl homophosphonate, **1**, 582
    trans-vinyl homophosphonate, **1**, 582
C₉H₁₆, β-cyclogeraniolene, **8**, 234
C₉H₁₆NO₃, swainsonine, **3**, 25, 27, 28, 29, 151
C₉H₁₆N₂, 1,8-diazabicyclo[5,4,0]undec-7-ene, **7**, 114
C₉H₁₆N₂O₄, allosamizoline, **1**, 149
C₉H₁₆N₃O₅S, aminoadipylcysteine, **4**, 249
C₉H₁₆N₃O₁₂P₃, dideoxynucleotide, **7**, 664
C₉H₁₆N₃O₁₄P₃, cytidine triphosphate, **3**, 336
C₉H₁₆O
    3,5-dimethyl-3-hepten-2-one, **8**, 244
    3,6-nonadien-1-ol, **8**, 212
    6,8-nonadien-2-ol, **8**, 209, 212
    2-nonenal, **8**, 212
    3-nonenal, **1**, 235
    6-nonen-2-one, **8**, 212, 213
C₉H₁₆O₂
    brevicomin, **8**, 46, 213, 233
    dominicalure 1 1-methylethyl ester, **8**, 241
    2-ethyl-1,6-dioxaspiro[4.4]nonane, **8**, 199, 212
    4-hydroxy-2-nonenal, **1**, 234
    2-hydroxy-2,6,6-trimethylcyclohexanone, **8**, 234
    2-*epi*-lentiginosine, **3**, 132, 134

lentiginosine, **3**, 132, 134
7-methyl-1,6-dioxaspiro[4.5]decane, **8**, 212
4-methyl-6-octenoic acid, **1**, 543
τ-nonalactone, **8**, 165.
nonalactone, **8**, 389
olean, **8**, 41
C₉H₁₆O₃
    7-deoxy-6-*epi*-castanospermine, **3**, 132 , 134
    2,4-dimethyl-3,5-dihydroxy-*n*-heptanoic acid δ-lactone, **1**, 357, 361
    8-formyloctanoic acid, **1**, 91
    4-hydroperoxy-2-nonenal, **1**, 235
    3-hydroxy-4-methyl-6-octenoate, **1**, 534, 543
    2-ketononanoic acid, **3**, 381
    δ-lactone, **1**, 507
    δ-lactone triketide, **1**, 515
    9-oxononanoic acid, **1**, 235
    swainsonine, **3**, 130, 132, 134, 138, 140, 141, 142, 143, 144, 153, 155
    triketide lactone, **1**, 514
C₉H₁₆O₄
    azelaic acid, **1**, 298
    castanospermine, **3**, 130, 132, 134, 138, 139, 140, 141, 142, 143, 148, 151, 152, 155,
    6,7-*diepi*-castanospermine, **3**, 132, 134
    6-*epi*-castanospermine, **3**, 132, 134, 138
    2-(1′-hydroxybutyl)-3-hydroxymethyl-butyrolactone, **8**, 390
    IM-2, **1**, 140, **8**, 389
    1,5-pentanediol diacetate, **8**, 550
C₉H₁₆O₅, L-chromose B, **3**, 312
C₉H₁₆O₆, 2,3-epoxypropyl α-D-glucopyranoside, **5**, 303
C₉H₁₇N, azaFPP analogue, **5**, 330
C₉H₁₇NO, 4-[2-butenyl]-4-methylthreonine, **1**, 533
C₉H₁₇NO₃, β-cyclohexylserine, **1**, 538
C₉H₁₇NO₅
    N-acetyl-*N*-methylfucosamine, **3**, 229
    pantothenic acid, **3**, 409, **4**, 168, 342
C₉H₁₇NO₆, *N*-acetylmannosamine 6-*O*-methyl ether, **3**, 380
C₉H₁₇NO₆S, curacin A methyl sulfonate, **8**, 606
C₉H₁₇NO₈, neuraminic acid, **3**, 146
C₉H₁₇N₃O₆S, narain, **8**, 442
C₉H₁₇N₅O₃, deoxyguanidinoproclavaminic acid, **4**, 185
C₉H₁₇N₅O₄, guanidinoproclavaminic acid, **4**, 183
C₉H₁₇N₆O₆S, decarbamoyldeoxyneosaxitoxin sulfate, **8**, 485
C₉H₁₇N₆O₇S, decarbamoylneosaxitoxin sulfate, **8**, 485
C₉H₁₇N₁₁O₁₂, β-cyclohexylalanine, **1**, 538
C₉H₁₇O₈P, carbahomophosphonate, **1**, 582
C₉H₁₈ClN₂OP, 2-cyanoethyl-*N*,*N*-diisopropylchlorophosphoramidite, **6**, 85
C₉H₁₈N₃O, 4-amino-2,2,6,6-tetramethylpiperidine-*N*-oxyl, **7**, 162
C₉H₁₈N₂O₄
    methylserinylvaline, **4**, 250
    O-methylserylvaline, **1**, 842, **4**, 168
C₉H₁₈N₄O₄, octopine, **8**, 399
C₉H₁₈N₄O₄S, citrulline-cysteine, **6**, 142
C₉H₁₈N₆O₂, decarbamoyldeoxyneosaxitoxin, **8**, 485
C₉H₁₈N₆O₄, decarbamoylneosaxitoxin, **8**, 485
C₉H₁₈O
    2,6-dimethyl-5-hepten-1-ol, **8**, 233
    2,6-dimethyl-6-hepten-1-ol, **8**, 233
    3,4-dimethyl-6-hepten-1-ol, **8**, 507
    6-methyl-3-octanone, **8**, 244
    nonanal, **8**, 212
    2-nonanone, **8**, 212
    2-nonen-1-ol, **8**, 212
    3-nonen-1-ol, **8**, 212
    6-nonen-2-ol, **8**, 213
C₉H₁₈O₂
    5-methoxyoctan-2-one, **8**, 606

nonanoic acid, **8**, 212

C₉H₁₈O₃, 9-hydroxypelargonic acid, **1**, 298

C₉H₁₈O₅S, isopropyl β-thio-ᴅ-galactopyranoside, **7**, 647

C₉H₁₉N
dibutylmethylmethylene, **7**, 123
diisobutylaminomethylene, **7**, 123

C₉H₁₉NO, pinidinol, **8**, 176

C₉H₁₉N₃O₃, lysinoalanine, **4**, 280

C₉H₂₀N₂O₂, 7,8-diaminopelargonic acid, **1**, 827

C₉H₂₀N₂O₆, pseudaminic acid, **3**, 193

C₉H₂₀O
2-methyl-4-octanol, **8**, 245
3-methyl-4-octanol, **8**, 245
5-methyl-4-octanol, **8**, 245
1-nonanol, **8**, 212
2-nonanol, **8**, 212
5-nonanol, **8**, 212, 245

C₉H₂₀O₃Si₂, bis-TMS-enolpyruvate, **5**, 33

C₉H₂₀O₄S, dihydro-2,6-dimethyl-6-hepten-1-ol sulfate, **8**, 233

C₉H₂₀O₇P₂S
linalyl sulfonium ion analogue, **5**, 328
α-terpinyl sulfonium ion analogue, **5**, 328

C₉H₂₂O₄, maximowicziol, **1**, 686

C₉H₂₃NO₃Si, 3-aminopropyl triethoxysilane, **7**, 112

C₉H₂₄N₄, N,N'-bis(3-aminopropyl)-1,3-propanediamine, **7**, 159

C₁₀H₅Cl₄NO₂, ethylphthalimide, **5**, 429

C₁₀H₆O₃, juglone, **8**, 169, 170, 179

C₁₀H₆O₄, ayapin, **1**, 626, **8**, 189

C₁₀H₇Cl, chloronaphthalene, **3**, 378

C₁₀H₇Cl₂NO₂, 5,6-dichloroindole-3-acetic acid, **8**, 35

C₁₀H₇Cl₂NO₂, 5,6-dichloro-IAA, **8**, 34

C₁₀H₇NO₃, kynurenic acid, **3**, 395

C₁₀H₈, naphthalene, **1**, 414, **3**, 375, 384, **5**, 42

C₁₀H₈ClNO₂, 4-chloroindole-3-acetic acid, **8**, 26, 30

C₁₀H₈NO, indole-3-acetaldehyde, **8**, 26, 33

C₁₀H₈N₂, indole-3-acetonitrile, **8**, 26, 34

C₁₀H₈N₄O₄, hydroperoxyflavin, **5**, 418

C₁₀H₈O, 1-naphthol, **3**, 378, 716

C₁₀H₈O₂
benzalpyruvate, **3**, 377
DHN, **1**, 427
1,8-dihydroxynaphthalene, **1**, 415

C₁₀H₈O₃
2'-hydroxybenzalpyruvate, **3**, 377
5-hydroxy-2-methylchromone, **1**, 415
4-hydroxy-5-methylcoumarin, **1**, 625
1-oxoindan-4-carboxylic acid, **1**, 135
1,3,8-trihydroxynaphthalene, **1**, 427

C₁₀H₈O₃S, naphthalene sulfonate, **3**, 377

C₁₀H₈O₄
6,8-dihydroxy-3-methylisocoumarin, **1**, 415
furoin, **3**, 394
3,4-methylenedioxycinnamic acid, **8**, 169, 171
scopoletin, **1**, 626, 628, **8**, 189
T4HN, **1**, 414, 425, 427
tetrahydroxynaphthalene, **1**, 8
1,3,6,8-tetrahydroxynaphthalene, **1**, 414

C₁₀H₈O₅
2-carboxy-3-hydroxycinnamic acid, **8**, 179
m-carboxyphenylpyruvic acid, **1**, 610
dihydroxybenzalpyruvate, **3**, 376
isoochracinic acid, **8**, 179

C₁₀H₈O₈, EPSP synthase substrate, **1**, 598

C₁₀H₉BrNO₂S, 3-carbomethoxymethylbenzothiazolium bromide, **8**, 35

C₁₀H₉FO₆, 6-fluorochorismate, **1**, 602

C₁₀H₉NOS, brassicanal A, **8**, 187

C₁₀H₉NO₂
indoleacetic acid, **1**, 129, **3**, 520, **8**, 23
indole-3-acetic acid, **8**, 24, 26, 59
3-methylindole-2-carboxylic acid, **1**, 854

C₁₀H₉NO₃, 5-hydroxyindole-3-acetic acid, **8**, 26

C₁₀H₉NO₃S
brassicanalC, **8**, 187
ethyl 3-oxo-1,2-benzisothiazolin-2-ylcarboxylate, **8**, 35

C₁₀H₉NO₅, glycidyl-4-nitrobenzoate, **5**, 55

C₁₀H₉N₃O₆S, 5-thiocyanatouridine, **6**, 91

C₁₀H₉N₅O, kinetin, **4**, 27, **8**, 58

C₁₀H₉O₂, 2-(acetoxymethyl)benzoyl, **7**, 121

C₁₀H₁₀N₂, 2,2'-bipyridine, **7**, 92

C₁₀H₁₀N₂O
indoleacetaldoxime, **8**, 34
indole-3-acetaldoxime, **8**, 26
indoleacetamide, **8**, 34
indole-3-acetoamide, **8**, 26

C₁₀H₁₀N₂O₅, S-m-nitrobenzoylalanine, **3**, 396

C₁₀H₁₀N₂O₇, 5-carbonyluridine, **6**, 91

C₁₀H₁₀N₅O₆P, molybdenum cofactor form A, **1**, 835

C₁₀H₁₀N₅O₆PS, molybdenum cofactor form B, **1**, 835

C₁₀H₁₀N₅O₇P
compoundZ, **1**, 835
precursorZ, **1**, 835

C₁₀H₁₀O
benzalacetone, **1**, 752, 758, 761
benzylidene acetone, **3**, 376

C₁₀H₁₀O₂
2-(2,3-dihydroxyphenyl)cyclopropane-1-carboxylate, **5**, 221
safrole, **7**, 519

C₁₀H₁₀O₃
2-acetyl-6-methoxybenzaldehyde, **8**, 169
coniferaldehyde, **3**, 655
3,4-dihydro-4,8-dihydroxy-1(2H)-naphthalene, **1**, 429
mellein, **1**, 134, 416, **8**, 210, 213, 241
vermelone, **1**, 414, 427

C₁₀H₁₀O₄
ferulic acid, **1**, 18, 628, 733, **3**, 602, 620, 696, 502, **8**, 140, 169, 171
6-hydroxymellein, **1**, 416
isoferulic acid, **3**, 624
oxyconiferyl alcohol, **3**, 703
scytalone, **1**, 414, 427
2,4,8-trihydroxytetralone, **8**, 179

C₁₀H₁₀O₅
acetylorsellinic acid, **1**, 414
curvulinic acid, **1**, 414
2,4-diacetylphloroglucinol, **1**, 763
5-hydroxyferulic acid, **3**, 642, 644
3,4,6,8-tetrahydroxytetralone, **8**, 179

C₁₀H₁₀O₆
chorismic acid, **1**, 74, 346, 367, 574, 575, 585, 599, 600, 609, 719, 850, **4**, 2, 4, 6, 209, **5**, 344, 347, 348, 352, 354, 424, **8**, 428
endo-oxabicyclic diacid inhibitor, **5**, 358
hydroquinone-O,O'-diacetic acid, **7**, 114
isochorismate, **1**, 17, isochorismic acid, **1**, 609
isohemipinic acid, **3**, 703
prephenic acid, **1**, 17, 346, 367, 719, 850, **4**, 4, **5**, 344, 348, 354, 355, 359, 424

C₁₀H₁₁BrN₄O₄, 6-bromopurine riboside, **5**, 77

C₁₀H₁₁ClN₄O₄, 6-chloropurine riboside, **5**, 77

C₁₀H₁₁ClO₃
2-(3-chloro-4-methylphenoxy)propionic acid, **8**, 35
4-chlorophenoxyisobutyric acid, **8**, 36

C₁₀H₁₁FN₄O₄, 6-fluoropurine riboside, **5**, 77

C₁₀H₁₁IN₄O₄, 6-iodopurine riboside, **5**, 77

C₁₀H₁₁NO
indole-3-ethanol, **8**, 26
tryptophol, **8**, 178

C₁₀H₁₁NO₂S₄, lissoclinotoxin B, **8**, 541

C₁₀H₁₁NO₅
4-amino-4-deoxychorismic acid, **1**, 612, **5**, 347
4-amino-4-deoxyprephenate, **5**, 347

C₁₀H₁₁N₃O₃S, sulfamethoxazole, **5**, 349

$C_{10}H_{11}N_4O_5$, inosine, **7**, 626
$C_{10}H_{11}O_2S$, 2-(methylthiomethoxymethyl)benzoyl, **7**, 127
$C_{10}H_{11}O_4S$, tolylsulfonylethoxycarbonyl, **7**, 119
$C_{10}H_{12}$
  dimethylstyrene, **8**, 165
  2-phenylmethylcyclopropane, **5**, 220
$C_{10}H_{12}ClN_3O_7$, 2′-chloro-2′-deoxy-6′-nitrohomouridine, **5**, 193
$C_{10}H_{12}ClN_5O_3$, 2-chloro-2′-deoxyadenosine, **5**, 74
$C_{10}H_{12}FO_{10}P$
  6-fluoroEPSP, **1**, 600, 602
  9-fluoroEPSP, **1**, 595
$C_{10}H_{12}MoN_5O_8PS_2$, molybdenum cofactor, **1**, 835
$C_{10}H_{12}NO_6P_2$, aminophosphonophosphate analogue, **5**, 338
$C_{10}H_{12}N_2$, tryptamine, **4**, 46, 109, 110, 113, 114, 118, 121, 122, 124, 126, 127, 133, 135, **8**, 33, 430
$C_{10}H_{12}N_2O$, 6-hydroxytryptamine, **4**, 121
$C_{10}H_{12}N_2O_3$, kynurenine, **3**, 395
$C_{10}H_{12}N_2O_3S$, 7-aminocephalosporanic acid, **4**, 171, 262
$C_{10}H_{12}N_2O_6$, 5-formyldeoxyuridine, **7**, 407
$C_{10}H_{12}N_4O_4$
  deoxyinosine, **7**, 495
  2′-deoxyinosine, **5**, 73
  2′-deoxyisoinosine, **7**, 325,
  purine riboside, **5**, 76, 78, 79, **6**, 249
  thymine cyclobutane photodimer, **5**, 373
  thymine photodimer, **5**, 378
$C_{10}H_{12}N_4O_4S$
  deoxy-6-thioinosine, **7**, 279
  6-thioinosine, **6**, 229
$C_{10}H_{12}N_4O_5$, inosine, **5**, 73, 308, **6**, 76, 104, 249, **8**, 417
$C_{10}H_{12}N_4O_6$, xanthosine, **1**, 847
$C_{10}H_{12}N_5O_2$, 5′-deoxyadenosine-5′-yl, **5**, 208
$C_{10}H_{12}N_5O_3$, deoxyadenosine radical, **7**, 409
$C_{10}H_{12}N_5O_4$, deoxyguanosine radical, **7**, 409
$C_{10}H_{12}N_8O_4$, 8-azidoadenosine, **6**, 229
$C_{10}H_{12}N_8O_5$, 8-azidoguanosine, **6**, 229
$C_{10}H_{12}O$
  2-allyl-4-methyl phenol, **5**, 350
  allyl *p*-tolyl ether, **5**, 350
  estragole, **7**, 519
  methylchromane, **1**, 414
  nezukone, **2**, 107, 108
$C_{10}H_{12}O_2$
  2-acetyl-3,5-dimethylphenol, **1**, 401
  allylphenol, **1**, 686
  aroma component, **1**, 761
  p-cumate, **3**, 384
  epievodone, **8**, 169, 171
  eugenol, **1**, 645, 676, **8**, 165, **3**, 677, 717
  4-hydroxyphenylbutan-2-one, **1**, 761
  1-(*p*-hydroxyphenyl(-3-butanone, **8**, 165
  isoeugenol, **1**, 645, **3**, 677, 703, **8**, 161, 165,
  pentenylpyron-2-one, **8**, 213
  perillenal, **8**, 226
  2-phenylbutyric acid, **4**, 254
  4-phenylbutyric acid, **4**, 254
  γ-thujaplicin, **2**, 108
$C_{10}H_{12}O_3$
  coniferyl alcohol, **1**, 18, 647, 648, 652, 685, 688, **3**, 618, 676, 683, 699, 703, 717
  demethyl nectriapyrone A, **8**, 600
  iridotrial, **2**, 106, **4**, 112
$C_{10}H_{12}O_4$
  2′-hydroxy-4′,6′-dimethoxyacetophenone, **8**, 190
  PIBP, **1**, 760,
  syringaldehyde, **3**, 643, 682, 696
$C_{10}H_{12}O_5$
  3′,5′-dimethoxy-4′-hydroxy-(2-hydroxy)acetophenone, **8**, 190
  propyl gallate, **3**, 820
  N-propyl gallate, **1**, 123

$C_{10}H_{12}O_6$
  5,6-dihydrochorismic acid, **5**, 352
  oxabicyclic dicarboxylic acid, **5**, 425
$C_{10}H_{13}BrN_2O_4$, α-bromoporphobilinogen, **4**, 86
$C_{10}H_{13}BrN_5O_7P$, 8-bromoadenosine monophosphate, **5**, 82
$C_{10}H_{13}CrN_5O_{13}P_3$, chromium adenosine triphosphate, **3**, 448
$C_{10}H_{13}IN_2O$, *N*-(4-dimethylaminobenzene-4′)iodoacetamide, **7**, 168
$C_{10}H_{13}N$, actinidin, **8**, 227
$C_{10}H_{13}NO_2$, fusaric acid, **8**, 178
$C_{10}H_{13}NO_2S_5$, varacin, **7**, 527, **8**, 541
$C_{10}H_{13}NO_3$, 2-amino-4-hydroxy-4-phenylbutanoic acid, **3**, 395
$C_{10}H_{13}NO_5$
  arogenate, **3**, 626
  arogenic acid, **4**, 5, **5**, 344
$C_{10}H_{13}N_2O_8P$, thymidine phosphate, **7**, 401
$C_{10}H_{13}N_3O_4$, adenosine, **5**, 78
$C_{10}H_{13}N_3O_7$, cytosylglucuronic acid, **3**, 339
$C_{10}H_{13}N_4O_8P$, inosine 5′-monophosphate, **1**, 847, **8**, 417
$C_{10}H_{13}N_4O_9P$, xanthosine 5′-monophosphate, **1**, 847
$C_{10}H_{13}N_5$ N_6-(γ,γ-dimethylallylamino)p urine, **8**, 119
  ipA, **8**, 68
  isopentenyladenine, **2**, 1
$C_{10}H_{13}N_5O$, zeatin, **8**, 58, 60, 61, 69
$C_{10}H_{13}N_5O_2$
  3′-deoxyadenosine, **5**, 74
  2′,3′-dideoxyadenosine, **5**, 74
  2-hydroxyzeatin, **8**, 61
$C_{10}H_{13}N_5O_3$
  2-aminopurine-2′-deoxyriboside, **7**, 259
  cordycepin, **3**, 313, **4**, 200
  deoxyadenosine, **7**, 376, 409, 410, 122
  2′-deoxyadenosine, **5**, 73, 74, **7**, 625
  3′-deoxyadenosine, **6**, 206
  5′-deoxyadenosine, **5**, 74, 165, 170, 208, 217
  dideoxyguanosine, **6**, 163
$C_{10}H_{13}N_5O_4$
  adenosine, **5**, 73, 74, 81, **7**, 122, 625, **8**, 155
  2′-deoxyguanosine, **7**, 259, 279
  deoxyguanosine, **5**, 184, **6**, 163, **7**, 122, 398, 409, 410
  formycin, **5**, 74
  8-oxodeoxyadenosine, **7**, 410
  8-oxopurine, **7**, 409
$C_{10}H_{13}N_5O_4S$
  6-mercaptoguanosine, **3**, 117
  6-thioguanosine, **6**, 93, 228, 229
$C_{10}H_{13}N_5O_5$
  arabinosylguanine, **7**, 278
  araguanosine, **7**, 279
  guanine arabinoside, **5**, 74
  guanosine, **5**, 73, **6**, 160, 254, 257, 837, **7**, 122
  isoguanosine, **6**, 76, 93
  8-oxodeoxyguanosine, **7**, 410, 419
  8-oxopurine, **7**, 409
  xyloguanosine, **7**, 279
$C_{10}H_{13}N_5O_7$
  dioxetane, **7**, 411
  dioxetane degradation product, **7**, 411
$C_{10}H_{13}N_5O_8$, 5′-deoxyadenosine, **5**, 185
$C_{10}H_{13}O_2$, nepetalactone, **8**, 44
$C_{10}H_{13}O_{10}P$
  5-enolpyruvylshikimate 3-phosphate, **1**, 593
  EPSP, **1**, 575, 596, 600
  iso-EPSP, **1**, 600
  ketal, **1**, 596
$C_{10}H_{14}$
  p-cymene, **2**, 103, 136, 146
  4-methylene-6,6-dimethylbicyclo[3.3.1]hept-2-ene, **8**, 224
$C_{10}H_{14}FN_2O_{10}P_2$, 2′-fluoromethylene-2′-deoxycytidine 5′-diphosphate, **3**, 330

$C_{10}H_{14}F_2O_{14}P_2$, phosphate, **1**, 595
$C_{10}H_{14}MgN_5O_{13}P_3$, MgATP, **3**, 448
$C_{10}H_{14}NO_5PS$, parathion, **5**, 419
$C_{10}H_{14}NO_6P$, *O,O*-diethyl-4-nitrophenyl phosphate, **5**, 151
$C_{10}H_{14}N_2$
　nicotine, **3**, 643, **4**, 26, 30, **8**, 151, 162,
　N-phenylpiperazine, **5**, 380
$C_{10}H_{14}N_2O_3$, dihydrokynurenine, **3**, 396
$C_{10}H_{14}N_2O_4$
　porphobilinogen, **4**, 72, 141
　2-pyrimidinone-2′-deoxyriboside, **7**, 259
$C_{10}H_{14}N_2O_4S$, 4-thiothymidine, **6**, 228
$C_{10}H_{14}N_2O_5$
　hydroxyporphobilinogen, **4**, 86
　thymidine, **5**, 389, **7**, 56, 398, 401
$C_{10}H_{14}N_2O_6$, 5-hydroxymethyldeoxyuridine, **7**, 407
$C_{10}H_{14}N_2O_7$, 2-acetamido-3-acetimidoyl-2,3-dideoxy-*β*-D-m annuronic acid, **3**, 194
$C_{10}H_{14}N_4O_5$
　purine riboside hydrate, **5**, 78, 79
　purine riboside 1,6-hydrate, **5**, 76
$C_{10}H_{14}N_5O_6PS$, adenosine phosphorothioate, **6**, 249
$C_{10}H_{14}N_5O_6PS_2$, molybdopterin, **1**, 835
$C_{10}H_{14}N_5O_7P$
　adenosine-5′-monophosphate, **8**, 417
　AMP, **3**, 447, 470, 474, 476, 483, **5**, 80, **6**, 139
　5′-AMP, **2**, 39
$C_{10}H_{14}N_5O_7PS$
　guanosine monophosphorothioate, **6**, 138
　5′-guanosine monophosphorothioate, **6**, 129, 219
$C_{10}H_{14}N_5O_8$, 3′-guanosine monophosphate, **7**, 279
$C_{10}H_{14}N_5O_8P$
　5′-GMP, **6**, 160
　guanosine phosphate, **1**, 837
$C_{10}H_{14}N_5O_{17}P$, AMP, **3**, 469
$C_{10}H_{14}N_6O_3$, 2,6-diaminopurine-2′-deoxyriboside, **7**, 259
$C_{10}H_{14}O$
　carbone, **8**, 306
　car-3-en-5-one, **2**, 135
　carvacrol, **2**, 103, 146, **8**, 306
　carvone, **2**, 103, 110, 116, 144, 147, **8**, 142, 169
　chrysanthenone, **8**, 224
　eucarvone, **2**, 107, 108
　ipsdienone, **8**, 223
　isopiperitenone, **2**, 144
　isopiperitenone, **8**, 225
　menthofuran, **2**, 148, **8**, 169, 171, 226
　myrtenal, **8**, 224
　perillene, **8**, 226, 229
　pinocarbone, **8**, 224
　sabinone, **2**, 104, 147
　thymol, **2**, 62, 103, 146, **8**, 165, 306
　verbenone, **8**, 224
$C_{10}H_{14}OSi$, (hydroxystyryl)dimethylsilyl, **7**, 129
$C_{10}H_{14}O_2$
　β-acaridial, **8**, 225
　carvone oxide, **8**, 161
　decatrienone, **1**, 214
　dihydroconiferyl alcohol, **3**, 677
　1,5-dimethyl-6,8-dioxabicyclo[3.2.1]octane, **8**, 202
　dolichodial, **8**, 226
　elymnia furan, **8**, 226
　iridodial, **2**, 106, **4**, 112
　nepetalactone, **8**, 226
　nepetalactone lactol, **8**, 234
　10-oxogeranial, **4**, 110
$C_{10}H_{14}O_3$, dihydroconiferyl alcohol, **1**, 682
$C_{10}H_{14}O_4$
　2,7-dimethylocta-2,4-dienedioic acid, **8**, 87
　succinylacetone, **4**, 76
$C_{10}H_{15}ClN_5O_{13}P_3$, 2-chloro-ATP, **4**, 326

$C_{10}H_{15}NO$
　ephidrine, **4**, 26
　hordenine, **1**, 369
$C_{10}H_{15}NO_3$, 2-methoxycarbonyl-3-tropinone, **4**, 27
$C_{10}H_{15}NO_4$
　kainate, **6**, 103
　N-(3-oxohexanoyl)homoserine lactone, **4**, 187, **8**, 398
　VAI-1, **8**, 393
$C_{10}H_{15}N_2O_5$, 5,6-dihydrothymid-5-yl, **7**, 401, 403
$C_{10}H_{15}N_{2O8}P$, thymidilate, **3**, 397
$C_{10}H_{15}N_3O_4$
　2′-deoxy-5-methylcytidine, **7**, 259
　5-methyl-2′-deoxycytidine, **7**, 272
$C_{10}H_{15}N_3O_5$, 6-aminothymidine, **7**, 261
$C_{10}H_{15}N_3O_7$, 11-norTTX-6-ol, **8**, 481, 482, 484
$C_{10}H_{15}N_3O_8$, 11-norTTX-6,6-diol, **8**, 484
$C_{10}H_{15}N_4O_{13}P_3$, deoxyinosine triphosphate, **7**, 621
$C_{10}H_{15}N_5O$, dihydrozeatin, **8**, 61, 71
$C_{10}H_{15}N_5O_4$, formamidopyrimidine derivative, **7**, 409
$C_{10}H_{15}N_5O_5$, formamidopyrimidine derivative, **7**, 409
$C_{10}H_{15}N_5O_{10}P_2$, adenosine diphosphate, **1**, 592, **3**, 447, 452, 469, 470, 483, **4**, 326, **6**, 105, **7**, 106
$C_{10}H_{15}N_5O_{11}P_2$, 5′-GDP, **6**, 160
$C_{10}H_{15}N_5O_{13}P_2S$, 3′-phosphoadenosine 5′-phosphosulfate, **1**, 331, 859, **3**, 171
$C_{10}H_{15}N_5O_{14}$, 8-azidoguanosine triphosphate, **7**, 277
$C_{10}H_{15}O_2S$, adamantanesulfonate, **5**, 355
$C_{10}H_{15}O_3P$, adamantyl phosphate, **5**, 355
$C_{10}H_{15}O_3S$, adamantyl sulfate, **5**, 355
$C_{10}H_{16}$
　adamantane, **7**, 482
　camphene, **2**, 104, 107, 131, 139, 141, **8**, 169
　3-carene, **2**, 105, 135, **8**, 143, 165
　3,5-dimethyl-2,4,6-octatriene, **8**, 240
　limonene, **2**, 147, **8**, 142, 222, 225, 306
　myrcene, **2**, 98, 101, 102, 131, 141, **8**, 139, 143, 222, 306
　ocimene, **2**, 102, 132, **8**, 161, 222, 237
　β-ocimene, **8**, 150, 152, 207
　α-phellandrene, **2**, 103, 141
　β-phellandrene, **2**, 103, 137, 141
　pinene, **2**, 101, 131, **8**, 143
　α-pinene, **2**, 102, 104, 118, 134, 139, 141, **8**, 221, 224, 225
　β-pinene, **2**, 102, 104, 118, 131, 139, 141, **8**, 169, 221
　sabinene, **2**, 104, 136, 145
　santolinatriene, **2**, 108
　α-terpinene, **2**, 103, 146
　γ-terpinene, **2**, 103, 104, 136, 146
　terpinolene, **2**, 103, 105, 122, 131, 141
　α-thujene, **2**, 104, 136, **8**, 156
　verbenol, **2**, 104
$C_{10}H_{16}FeN_2O_8$
　Fe-EDTA, **7**, 397
　Fe(II)EDTA, **7**, 87
　ferrous ethylenediamine tetraacetate, **7**, 89
$C_{10}H_{16}FO_{11}P_2$, FMCDP, **5**, 172
$C_{10}H_{16}KNO_9S_2$, sinigrin, **1**, 858, **8**, 145, 152, 155
$C_{10}H_{16}N_2$
　diketopiperazine, **8**, 588
　tetramethylphenylenediamine, **5**, 237
$C_{10}H_{16}N_2O_2S$, cyclo-(proline-methionine), **8**, 590
$C_{10}H_{16}N_2O_3$, 5,6-dehydrodethiobiotin, **1**, 831
$C_{10}H_{16}N_2O_3S$, biotin, **1**, 826, **6**, 3, 20, 118, **7**, 116, 631
$C_{10}H_{16}N_2O_5$, 5,6-dihydrothymidine, **7**, 407
$C_{10}H_{16}N_2O_6$
　5,6-dihydro-5-hydroxythymidine, **7**, 401, 407
　thymidine hydrate, **7**, 408
$C_{10}H_{16}N_2O_7$
　2,3-diacetamido-2,3-dideoxygalacturonic acid, **3**, 229
　2,3-diacetamido-2,3-dideoxymannuronic acid, **3**, 229
　2,3-diacetamido-2,3-dideoxy-*β*-D-mannuronic acid, **3**, 194
　5,6-dihydro-5,6-dihydroxythymidine, **7**, 401, 407

thymidine glycol, **7**, 407, 417
C₁₀H₁₆N₂O₈,EDTA, **3**, 22, **6**, 200
C₁₀H₁₆N₃O₆, glutathione derivative, **7**, 417
C₁₀H₁₆N₄O₃, anserine, **3**, 643
C₁₀H₁₆N₄O₅, A19009, **3**, 275
C₁₀H₁₆N₄O₆, Sch37137, **3**, 275
C₁₀H₁₆N₅O₈P, 6-hydroxy-6-aminopurine ribose 5′-phosphate, **5**, 83
C₁₀H₁₆N₅O₁₁P₃, dideoxynucleotide, **7**, 664
C₁₀H₁₆N₅O₁₂, 2′,3′-dideoxyguanosine triphosphate, **7**, 279
C₁₀H₁₆N₅O₁₂P₃
  2′-deoxy-ATP, **4**, 326
  3-deoxy-ATP, **4**, 326
  dideoxynucleotide, **7**, 664
C₁₀H₁₆N₅O₁₂P₃S, ATP-γS, **6**, 127
C₁₀H₁₆N₅O₁₃, 2′-deoxyguanosine triphosphate, **7**, 279
C₁₀H₁₆N₅O₁₃P₃, adenosine triphosphate, **1**, 592, **3**, 393, 448, 449, 464, 471, 472, 473, 476, 483, **4**, 15, 315, 326, **5**, 80, **6**, 105, 121, 127, **7**, 106, 625, 631
C₁₀H₁₆N₅O₁₃P₃S, guanosine 5′-γ-thiotriphosphate, **6**, 219
C₁₀H₁₆N₅O₁₄P₃, guanosine triphosphate, **5**, 80, **6**, 160, 219
C₁₀H₁₆N₇O₈S, neosaxitoxin 11-*O*-sulfate, **8**, 485
C₁₀H₁₆N₇O₉S, neosaxitoxin 11-*N*-sulfate, **8**, 485
C₁₀H₁₆O
  1-adamantanol, **7**, 463
  amaitinol, **8**, 224
  artemisia ketone, **2**, 108
  camphor, **2**, 101, 129, 146, **8**, 142, 169
  carveol, **2**, 144, 147
  citral, **2**, 102, **8**, 161, 165, 222, 223
  cyclohexane derivative, **8**, 224
  dehydrocineol, **8**, 225
  diene, **1**, 396
  fenchone, **2**, 104, 107, **8**, 224, 306
  geranial, **2**, 98, **8**, 223, 232
  grandisal, **8**, 224
  ipsdienol, **2**, 101, **8**, 42, 223
  ipsenone, **8**, 223
  isocaranone, **2**, 135
  isopinocamphone, **2**, 146
  isopiperitenol, **2**, 144, 147
  isopulegone, **2**, 144, **8**, 306
  isothujone, **2**, 145
  3-isothujone, **2**, 146
  methanedienol, **8**, 225
  myrcenol, **8**, 224
  myrtenol, **2**, 146, **8**, 169, 224
  neral, **2**, 98, **8**, 223, 232
  perillyl alcohol, **2**, 102
  α-pinene, **8**, 4
  pinocamphone, **2**, 146
  pinocarveol, **2**, 146, **8**, 224
  pulegone, **2**, 62, 101, 103, 144, 147, **8**, 142, 306
  sabinol, **2**, 104, 145, 147
  thujone, **2**, 145
  3-thujone, **2**, 104, 146
  α-thujone, **8**, 167
  verbenol, **2**, 101, **8**, 224
C₁₀H₁₆O₂
  ascaridole, **2**, 146
  1,2-campholide, **2**, 114
  chrysanthemic acid, **2**, 108
  3,7-dimethyl-6-octen-4-olide, **8**, 226
  2,3-epoxyneral, **8**, 225
  geranic acid, **8**, 222, 223
  grandisoic acid, **8**, 224
  iridodial, **8**, 226
  iridomyrmecin, **8**, 226
  lineatin, **8**, 224
  3-methyl-2-butenyl 3-methyl-2-butenoate, **8**, 220
  nerolic acid, **8**, 222, 223
  10-oxogeraniol, **4**, 110
  phoracantholide I, **8**, 213

pyrethroid, **2**, 101
C₁₀H₁₆O₃
  α-campholonic acid, **2**, 114
  9-oxo-2-decenoic acid, **8**, 213
  10-oxo-8-decenoic acid, **1**, 211
C₁₀H₁₆O₄
  callosobruchusic acid, **8**, 225
  4,7-dihydroxy-3-methylheptanoic acid acetate lactone, **8**, 624
  2-hydroxycampholonic acid, **2**, 115
C₁₀H₁₆O₅, isoketocamphoric acid, **2**, 115
C₁₀H₁₆O₁₃P₂, phosphonate, **1**, 595
C₁₀H₁₇FO₁₄P₃, FMCTP, **5**, 172
C₁₀H₁₇N, polyzonimine, **8**, 234
C₁₀H₁₇NO₃, methylecgonine, **4**, 27
C₁₀H₁₇NO₆, linamarin 0003, **8**, 144, 152, 154, 183
C₁₀H₁₇NO₇S₃, [3-(methylthio)propyl]glucosinolate, **1**, 859
C₁₀H₁₇NO₈S₃, [3-(methylsulfinyl)propyl]glucosinolate, **1**, 859
C₁₀H₁₇NO₁₂P₂, shikimate 3-phosphate derivative, **1**, 597
C₁₀H₁₇N₂O₁₃P₃, dideoxynucleotide, **7**, 664
C₁₀H₁₇N₃O₆S
  glutamylcysteinylglycine, **7**, 560
  glutathione, **1**, 260, **3**, 392, **4**, 178, **5**, 53, 61, 67, 183, 186, 238, 408, 414, 275, 280, **7**, 393, 560
C₁₀H₁₇N₇O₄, saxitoxin, **8**, 485, 486
C₁₀H₁₇N₇O₅, neosaxitoxin, **8**, 485
C₁₀H₁₈
  bornane, **5**, 325
  camphane, **5**, 325
  dihydromyrcene, **2**, 138
  fenchane, **5**, 325
  isocamphane, **2**, 107
  pinane, **5**, 325
  sabinane, **5**, 322
  thujane, **5**, 325
C₁₀H₁₈Cl₂N₃OP, imidazole monoamidite, **7**, 133
C₁₀H₁₈N₂O₂
  cyclo-Ala-MeLeu, **1**, 542
  cycloalanyl-*N*-methylleucine, **1**, 545
C₁₀H₁₈N₂O₃, dethiobiotin, **1**, 826
C₁₀H₁₈N₂O₃S
  1-mercaptodethiobiotin, **1**, 830
  4-mercaptodethiobiotin, **1**, 830
C₁₀H₁₈N₂O₄
  acetaminodeoxycastanospermine, **3**, 29
  1-hydroxydethiobiotin, **1**, 830
  4-hydroxydethiobiotin, **1**, 830
C₁₀H₁₈N₂O₅, 1,4-dihydroxydethiobiotin, **1**, 830
C₁₀H₁₈N₃O₂, uridylate zwitterion, **7**, 319
C₁₀H₁₈N₃O₁₃P₃, 2′-methylene-2′-deoxycytidine triphosphate, **5**, 175
C₁₀H₁₈O
  artemisia alcohol, **2**, 109
  borneol, **2**, 104, 131, 146, **8**, 169
  camphor, **2**, 104, 113, 114
  chrysanthemyl alcohol, **2**, 109
  1,8-cineole, **2**, 103, 137 , **8**, 161, 169, 225
  cyclohexane derivative, **8**, 224
  3,7-dimethyl-2,7-octadien-1-ol, **8**, 222
  4,6-dimethyl-6-octen-3-one, **8**, 243
  4,6-dimethyl-4-octen-3-one, **8**, 243
  fenchol, **2**, 104, **2**, 137
  geraniol, **2**, 62, 70, 98, 102, 106, 113, 121, 310, **4**, 110, **8**, 161, 173, 222, 306
  γ-geraniol, **8**, 223
  gragranol, **8**, 224
  grandisol, **8**, 224
  ipsenol, **8**, 223,
  isoborneol, **2**, 104, 147
  4-isocaranol, **2**, 135
  isogeraniol, **8**, 223
  isomenthone, **2**, 144, **8**, 306

lavandulol, **2**, 108, **8**, 234
linalool, **2**, 102, 122, **8**, 150, 152, 156, 161, 162, 222,
    223, 306
menthone, **2**, 62, 114, 144, 147, **8**, 173, 306
7-methyl-3-methylene-7-octen-1-ol, **8**, 222
α-necrodol, **8**, 234
β-necrodol, **8**, 234
nerol, **2**, 98, 102, 113, 121, 310, **4**, 110, **8**, 161, 222,
    225
rose oxide, **8**, 225
sabinene hydrate, **2**, 136, 139
terpinen-4-ol, **2**, 103, **8**, 224
α-terpineol , **2**, 103, 122, 138, **8**, 224
terpineol, **8**, 306
thujyl alcohol, **2**, 104, 147

C₁₀H₁₈O₂
bicolorin, **8**, 234
3-decenoic acid, **8**, 213
2,4-dimethyl-5-ethyl-6,8-dioxabicyclo[3.2.1]octane, **8**,
    244
ethyl 3-octenoate, **8**, 211
hydroxycineole, **2**, 123
10-hydroxygeraniol, **2**, 106, **4**, 110
8-hydroxylinalool, **8**, 225
lactone, **1**, 511
linalool oxide, **8**, 225, 229, 234
3,4-menthone lactone, **2**, 114
2-octenyl acetate, **8**, 211
4-oxo-2-decenal, **8**, 213

C₁₀H₁₈O₃
9-hydroxy-2-decenoic acid, **8**, 199, 213
lactone, **1**, 511, 515
9-oxo-2-decenoic acid, **8**, 199

C₁₀H₁₈O₄, 2-(1′-hydroxyvaleryl)-3-hydroxymethyl-
    butyrolactone, **8**, 390

C₁₀H₁₈O₇P₂, 6-cyclopropylidene-3-methylhex-2-en-1-yl
    diphosphate, **2**, 127

C₁₀H₁₈S, 1-*p*-menthene-8-thiol, **8**, 165

C₁₀H₁₉FO₇P₂
2-fluorogeranyl diphosphate, **2**, 80, 126, **5**, 320, 327
2-fluorolinalyl diphosphate, **2**, 126, **5**, 327

C₁₀H₁₉N, keramaphidinC, **8**, 554

C₁₀H₁₉NO
epilupinine, **4**, 35
lupinine, **4**, 34, 35

C₁₀H₁₉NO₃S, *N*-acetylcysteamine thioester erythromycin
    analogue, **1**, 500

C₁₀H₁₉NO₈, neuraminic acid β-methyl glycoside, **3**, 378

C₁₀H₁₉N₂O₆P, demethylbialaphos, **1**, 867

C₁₀H₁₉N₄O, cytidylate zwitterion, **7**, 319

C₁₀H₂₀, *p*-menthane, **5**, 322, 325

C₁₀H₂₀N₂O₂Si₂, silylated pyrimidinedione, **7**, 260

C₁₀H₂₀N₂O₃, Ala-MeLeu, **1**, 548

C₁₀H₂₀N₂O₄, carbamate, **1**, 827

C₁₀H₂₀N₂S₄, tetraethylthiuram disulfide, **6**, 90

C₁₀H₂₀O
citronellol, **2**, 101, 121, **8**, 222
2-decanone, **8**, 181, 212
dihydrogeranol, **5**, 327
dihydrolinalool, **2**, 138, **5**, 327
dihydronerol, **5**, 327
4,6-dimethyl-3-octanone, **8**, 244, 243
isomenthol, **2**, 144
menthol, **2**, 114, 116, 144, **8**, 306
6-methylnonan-3-one, **8**, 244
neoisomenthol, **2**, 144
neomenthol, **2**, 114, 144
2,3,6-trimethyl-5-hepten-1-ol, **8**, 234

C₁₀H₂₀O₂
ethyl 4-methylheptanoate, **8**, 241
3-hydroxy-4-methyl-5-nonanone, **8**, 245
octyl acetate, **8**, 211
valeroin, **3**, 394

C₁₀H₂₀O₅, L-nogalose, **3**, 312

C₁₀H₂₀O₇P₂
bornyl diphosphate, **2**, 104, 119, 120, 129, 141
geranyl diphosphate, **2**, 7, 8, 46, 62, 70, 75, 125, 147,
    201, 380, 331, 340, **5**, 318, **8**, 219
linalyl diphosphate, **2**, 8, 99, 125, 130, 147, **5**, 325
neryl diphosphate, **2**, 98, 99, 125, 147

C₁₀H₂₁NO₄
N-butyldeoxynojirimycin, **3**, 143
N-butyl-1-deoxynojirimycin, **3**, 20

C₁₀H₂₂O
4-methyl-1-nonanol, **8**, 241
4-methyl-5-nonanol, **8**, 245

C₁₀H₂₂O₂
menthyl acetate, **2**, 114
sordidin, **8**, 40

C₁₀H₂₂O₇P₂
2,3-dihydrogeranyl diphosphate, **5**, 327
6,7-dihydrogeranyl diphosphate, **2**, 76, 138, **5**, 327
6,7-dihydrolinalyl diphosphate, **2**, 138

C₁₀H₂₂S₂, bis(3-methylbutyl) disulphide, **8**, 221

C₁₀H₂₆N₄, spermine, **3**, 721, **4**, 30, **7**, 159

C₁₀H₂₆O, 4-tridecenal, **8**, 241

C₁₁H₄F₄N₃O₄, *N*-hydroxysuccinimide ester of *p*-
    azidotetrafluorobenzoic acid, **7**, 161

C₁₁H₆Br₂N₂O, 7-bromoeudistomin D, **8**, 526

C₁₁H₆O₃
angelicin, **1**, 633
isopsoralen, **8**, 141
psoralen, **1**, 625, 631

C₁₁H₆O₄
bergaptol, **1**, 633
8-hydroxypsoralen, **1**, 634
xanthotoxol, **1**, 633

C₁₁H₆O₅, 5,8-dihydroxypsoralen, **1**, 633

C₁₁H₇BrN₂, eudestomin derivative, **8**, 525

C₁₁H₇BrN₂O, eudestomin derivative, **8**, 525

C₁₁H₇NO₄, 1,8-nitronaphthoic acid, **7**, 522

C₁₁H₇N₃O₂S, *C*-5-benzthiazoleuridine, **7**, 318

C₁₁H₇O, naphthoyl, **7**, 120, 123

C₁₁H₈O₂
menadione, **7**, 375, 398, **5**, 419
vitamin K₃, **8**, 436

C₁₁H₈O₃
dihydrofuranocoumarin, **1**, 630
1-hydroxy-2-naphthoic acid, **3**, 376

C₁₁H₈O₅, 2′-carboxybenzalpyruvate, **3**, 376

C₁₁H₉O₃, indolepyruvic acid, **8**, 33

C₁₁H₉O₄, acetoxymethylbenzoyl, **7**, 120

C₁₁H₁₀, methylnaphthalene, **3**, 378

C₁₁H₁₀N₃O
1-methoxyindole-3-acetonitrile, **8**, 26
4-methoxyindole-3-acetonitrile, **8**, 26

C₁₁H₁₀N₂OS₂
cyclobrassinin sulfoxide, **8**, 187
spirobrassinin, **8**, 187

C₁₁H₁₀N₂S₂, cyclobrassinin, **8**, 187

C₁₁H₁₀O₂, 1,4-dihydro-1-naphthoic acid, **8**, 35

C₁₁H₁₀O₄, lathodoratin, **8**, 189

C₁₁H₁₀O₅
sphagnum acid, **3**, 620
o-succinylbenzoic acid, **1**, 613

C₁₁H₁₁BrN₂O₃, 2-bromo-5-hydroxytryptophan, **8**, 570,
    573

C₁₁H₁₁FN₂O₂, fluorotryptophan, **5**, 331

C₁₁H₁₁NO
vitamin K, **2**, 376
vitamin K₅, **1**, 72

C₁₁H₁₁NO₂
3,4-dimethylindole-2-carboxylic acid, **1**, 854
indole-3-propionic acid, **4**, 51, **8**, 26

C₁₁H₁₁NO₃, 4-hydroxymethyl-3-methylindole-2-
    carboxylic acid, **1**, 854

C₁₁H₁₁NO₇, *p*-nitrophenyl riboside, **5**, 307

C₁₁H₁₁N₃O₄, nitrotryptophan, **5**, 331

C₁₁H₁₁N₇O₂, *N*-2-(3-imidazolepropionic acid, **7**, 327

C₁₁H₁₂Cl₂N₂O₅, chloramphenicol, **4**, 200, 227, **5**, 347, **7**, 664, 665

C₁₁H₁₂FN₅O₃, 2-fluoronaplanocin A, **5**, 74

C₁₁H₁₂N₂O, tambjamine A, **8**, 472

C₁₁H₁₂N₂O₂, tryptophan, **1**, 16, 257, 346, 574, 609, 846, 853, **3**, 386, 395, **4**, 2, 4, 5, 46, 109, 110, 123, 135, 227, **5**, 331, 346, 382, **7**, 639, **8**, 32, 418, 428

C₁₁H₁₂N₂O₂S₂, dioxybrassinin, **8**, 187

C₁₁H₁₂N₂O₃, 7-hydroxytryptophan, **1**, 846

C₁₁H₁₂N₂O₄, *N*-formylkynurenine, **1**, 846

C₁₁H₁₂N₂S₂, brassinin, **8**, 187

C₁₁H₁₂N₄O₄S
  1-(mesitylenesulfonyl)-3-nitro-1,2,4-triazole, **7**, 117
  1-(mesitylene-2-sulfonyl)-3-nitro-1,2,4-triazole, **6**, 82

C₁₁H₁₂O₂, ethyl cinnamate, **1**, 134

C₁₁H₁₂O₃
  3,4-dihydroisocoumarin, **8**, 241
  nakitriol, **8**, 609

C₁₁H₁₂O₄
  macrophomic acid, **1**, 16, 368, 388, 401
  methyl *p*-methoxycinnamate, **3**, 624
  pyrenocine A, **1**, 401
  sinapaldehyde, **3**, 651

C₁₁H₁₂O₅
  chorismate, **3**, 626
  raphanusol B, **8**, 29
  sinapate, **1**, 720, 733
  sinapic acid, **3**, 620, 696

C₁₁H₁₂O₆, chorismate methyl ether, **5**, 353

C₁₁H₁₃ClN₂O₃, 6-chloro-5-hydroxy-*N*-methyltryptophan, **8**, 573

C₁₁H₁₃F₃NO, *m*-(*N,N,N*-trimethylammonio)-trifluo-roacetophenone, **5**, 114

C₁₁H₁₃NO₃, vinylogous tyrosine, **8**, 568

C₁₁H₁₃N₅O₃, neplanocin A, **5**, 74

C₁₁H₁₃N₇O, guanine derivative, **7**, 328

C₁₁H₁₅O, *t*-butylbenzoyl, **7**, 120

C₁₁H₁₄
  6-(1,3-butadienyl)-1,4-cycloheptadiene, **8**, 420
  3-(1,3-butadienyl)-4-vinylcyclopentene, **8**, 420
  desmarestene, **8**, 424
  1-(1,3,5-hexatrienyl)-2-vinylcyclopropane, **8**, 424
  hormonsirene, **8**, 425

C₁₁H₁₄D₄, dihydrotetradeuterohormonsirene, **8**, 425

C₁₁H₁₄NO₆P, indole, **4**, 7

C₁₁H₁₄NO₇P, *p*-nitrophenyl carboxybutylphosphonate, **5**, 434

C₁₁H₁₄N₂
  gramine, **4**, 26
  7-methyltryptamine, **4**, 121
  N-methyltryptamine, **4**, 122

C₁₁H₁₄N₂O , cytisine, **4**, 34, **8**, 147, 152, 154, 167, 176

C₁₁H₁₄N₂O₄
  ethyl nitrophenethylcarbamate, **8**, 431
  Gly-Tyr, **5**, 184

C₁₁H₁₄N₂O₆, *N*-malonyl ACC, **8**, 96

C₁₁H₁₄N₄, 6-cyclobutylamino-2-methylpyrrolo[2,3-*d*]pyrimidine, **8**, 68

C₁₁H₁₄N₄O, peramine, **8**, 177

C₁₁H₁₄N₄O₄
  deazaadenosine, **6**, 76
  1-deazaadenosine, **5**, 77, 79
  7-*deazaadenosine*, **6**, 225
  N₇-deazaadenosine, **6**, 249
  tubericidin, **8**, 611

C₁₁H₁₄N₄O₅
  deazaguanosine, **6**, 76
  N₇-deazaguanosine, **6**, 249
  8-ketocoformycin, **5**, 76

C₁₁H₁₄N₅O₄, *O*-6-methyl-2′-deoxyguanosine, **7**, 626

C₁₁H₁₄O
  3-(1,2-epoxy)-3-butenyl-4-vinylcyclopentene, **8**, 420
  lamoxirene, **8**, 422

C₁₁H₁₄O₂
  decalindione, **5**, 440
  methyleugenol, **8**, 155
  5-phenyl-4-pentenylhydroperoxide, **5**, 237, 246

C₁₁H₁₄O₃
  1-benzyloxy-3,4-epoxy-2-butanol, **1**, 310
  methyleugenol, **3**, 677
  methyl *p*-2-hydroxyisopropyl benzoate, **2**, 136
  nakienone A, **8**, 609
  nakienone B, **8**, 609
  nakienoneC, **8**, 609
  nectriapyrone, **8**, 600

C₁₁H₁₄O₃S₂, pyrone, **1**, 396

C₁₁H₁₄O₄
  PIVP, **1**, 760
  sinapyl alcohol, **1**, 648, 654, 672, 685, **3**, 618, 676

C₁₁H₁₄O₅, pyrenocine B, **1**, 401

C₁₁H₁₅BrN₄O₄, thymine electrophile, **7**, 319

C₁₁H₁₅ClO, adamantanecarbonyl chloride, **7**, 139

C₁₁H₁₅NO₂, ethyl *N*-(2-phenethyl)carbamate, **8**, 431

C₁₁H₁₅NO₂S₄
  dimethoxy(methylthio)(aminoethyl)benzotrithiane, **8**, 542
  5-(methylthio)varacin, **8**, 542

C₁₁H₁₅NO₉P, nicotinic acid mononucleotide, **4**, 149

C₁₁H₁₅N₃O₇, 4,9-anhydroTTX, **8**, 481, 483

C₁₁H₁₅N₃O₁₁, TTX-11-carboxylic acid, **8**, 484

C₁₁H₁₅N₄O₃, 7-deaza-2′-deoxyadenosine, **7**, 626

C₁₁H₁₅N₄O₄, 7-deaza-adenosine, **7**, 626

C₁₁H₁₅N₅O₃
  aristeromycin, **1**, 152
  5′-deoxymethyladenosine, **5**, 271

C₁₁H₁₅N₅O₃S, 5′-methylthioadenosine, **8**, 96

C₁₁H₁₅N₅O₄, 1-methyladenosine, **4**, 361

C₁₁H₁₅N₅O₅
  2-amino-6-methoxypurine arabinoside, **5**, 74
  2-methylguanosine, **6**, 195
  2-*O*-methylguanosine, **7**, 279
  3′-*O*-methylguanosine, **7**, 279
  7-methylguanosine, **7**, 277
  N-1-methylguanosine, **6**, 225
  O₆-methylguanosine, **6**, 249, **7**, 277

C₁₁H₁₅N₅S, 2-methylthiozeatin, **8**, 62

C₁₁H₁₅O₂, adamantanecarboxylate, **5**, 355

C₁₁H₁₆
  3-(1-butenyl-4-vinylcyclopentene, **8**, 420
  divinylcyclopropane, **8**, 424
  ectocarpene, **8**, 420
  finavarrene, **8**, 422
  giffordene, **1**, 216, **8**, 423
  homosirene, **8**, 422
  3-methyl-7-methylene-1,3,8-nonatriene, **8**, 236
  1,3,5,8-undecatetraene, **8**, 423

C₁₁H₁₆Br₂N₂O, moloka′iamine, **8**, 440

C₁₁H₁₆FN₅O₁₀P₂, 2′-vinylfluoro-2′-deoxycytidine 5′-diphosphate, **5**, 182

C₁₁H₁₆NO₇P, InGP, **4**, 7

C₁₁H₁₆N₂O₄S , thienamycin, **3**, 285, **4**, 186

C₁₁H₁₆N₃O₈, 4-epiTTX, **8**, 481, 483

C₁₁H₁₆N₄O₄, 2′-deoxycoformycin, **5**, 74, 76, 78, 83

C₁₁H₁₆N₄O₅
  coformycin, **5**, 74, 79, 83
  p-nitrophenyl riboamidrazone, **5**, 307

C₁₁H₁₆N₄O₈P, 6-hydroxymethyl-5,6-dihydropurine ribonucleoside, **5**, 77

C₁₁H₁₆O, jasmone, **8**, 108

C₁₁H₁₆O₂
  butylated hydroxyanisole, **1**, 95
  2,4,6-decatrienoate, **8**, 213
  dihydroactinidiolide, **8**, 44, 234, 236

$C_{11}H_{16}O_3$
  cyclohexanedione, **5**, 440
  1,8-dimethyl-3-ethyl-2,9-dioxabicyclo[3.3.1]non-7-ene, **8**, 244
$C_{11}H_{16}O_4$, dihydrosinapyl alcohol, **3**, 677
$C_{11}H_{16}O_5$
  hypoxanthin base, **8**, 442
  trimethoxystyrene derivative, **8**, 442
$C_{11}H_{17}NO_2$, salsolidine, **4**, 40
$C_{11}H_{17}NO_2S_2$, lissoclinotoxinC, **8**, 541
$C_{11}H_{17}NO_3$
  isoproterenol, **1**, 294
  mescaline, **4**, 26
$C_{11}H_{17}NO_4$, N-(carboxyheptyl)maleimide, **5**, 250
$C_{11}H_{17}NO_8$
  2,7-anhydro-N-acetylneuraminic acid, **5**, 295
  2-deoxy-2,3-didehydro-N-acetylneuraminic acid, **3**, 378
$C_{11}H_{17}N_3O_5S$, 5-methylaminomethyl-2-thiouridine, **4**, 68
$C_{11}H_{17}N_3O_7$, 11-deoxyTTX, **8**, 481, 483
$C_{11}H_{17}N_3O_8$
  6-epi-TTX, **8**, 481, 483
  tetrodotoxin, **8**, 480, 486
$C_{11}H_{17}N_3O_9$, 11-oxoTTX, **8**, 481, 484
$C_{11}H_{17}N_4O_7P$, 2′-deoxycoformycin 5′-monophosphate, **5**, 83
$C_{11}H_{17}N_4O_8P$, coformycin 5′-phosphate, **5**, 80, 83, 84
$C_{11}H_{17}N_4O_{13}P_3$, 7-deaza-ATP, **4**, 326
$C_{11}H_{17}N_5O_{10}P_2$, 2′-C-methyladenosine diphosphate, **3**, 332
$C_{11}H_{18}$
  dictyotene, **8**, 420, 424
  4,8-dimethyl-1,3,7-nonatriene, **8**, 150, 152, 231
  homoocimene, **8**, 232, 236
  1,3,5-undecatriene, **8**, 420
$C_{11}H_{18}ClN_5$, 2-chloro-4-cyclohexylamino-6-ethylamino-s-triazine, **8**, 69
$C_{11}H_{18}FN_3O_6S$, fluoromethylglutathione, **5**, 408
$C_{11}H_{18}N_2$, diketopiperazine, **8**, 588
$C_{11}H_{18}N_2O_5$, hyrmidine hydrate isostere, **7**, 408
$C_{11}H_{18}N_3O_7$
  1-hydroxy-5,11-dideoxyTTX, **8**, 482
  11-norTTX-6-ol, **8**, 484
  5,6,11-trideoxyTTX, **8**, 482
$C_{11}H_{18}N_3O_8$, tetrodonic acid, **8**, 481, 483
$C_{11}H_{18}N_5O_{13}P_3$, 1-methyladenosine, **7**, 626
$C_{11}H_{18}O$
  epoxy alcohol, **1**, 310
  10-homonerol oxide, **8**, 237
$C_{11}H_{18}O_2$
  3-acetoxy-2,6-dimethyl-1,5-heptadiene, **8**, 235
  1,8-dimethyl-3-ethyl-2,9-dioxabicyclo[3.3.1]non-7-en-6-one, **8**, 244
  methyl 2,4-decadienoate, **8**, 199, 213
  neryl formate, **8**, 209, 222
  pheromone of *Periplaneta americana*, **8**, 46
$C_{11}H_{18}O_3P$, adamantyl methyl phosphate, **5**, 355
$C_{11}H_{19}FO_3S$, 2-fluorogeranyl methanesulfonate, **2**, 80
$C_{11}H_{19}NO_3$
  Garner's aldehyde, **8**, 551
  oxazolidine aldehyde, **8**, 551
$C_{11}H_{19}NO_6$, lotaustralin, **8**, 139, 144, 154
$C_{11}H_{19}NO_8$, N-acetylmuramic acid, **3**, 244, 275
$C_{11}H_{19}NO_9$
  acetylneuraminic acid, **3**, 378, 380
  N-acetylneuraminic acid, **3**, 101, 378, 381, 390, 391, **5**, 295
  N-glycolylmuramic acid, **3**, 244
  sialic acid, **3**, 3
$C_{11}H_{19}NO_{10}$
  glycolylneuraminic acid, **3**, 378
  N-glycolylneuraminic acid, **3**, 381
$C_{11}H_{19}N_3O_6S$, hydroxyglutathionylmethane, **5**, 408
$C_{11}H_{19}N_3O_7$, hydrazine DAP analogue, **3**, 277

$C_{11}H_{20}NO_{12}$,NeuAc9P, **3**, 391
$C_{11}H_{20}N_2O_6$, sacharopine, **4**, 243
$C_{11}H_{20}N_2O_8P$, plumbemycin, **1**, 865
$C_{11}H_{20}O$
  4,6-dimethyl-4-nonen-3-one, **8**, 243
  homogeraniol, **2**, 310
$C_{11}H_{20}O_2$
  2,8-dimethyl-1,7-dioxaspiro[5.5]undecane, **8**, 214
  dominacalure 1, **8**, 45, 241
  1-ethyl-3,5,7-trimethyl-2,8-dioxabicyclo[3.2.1]octane, **8**, 246
  lactone, **1**, 511, **8**, 240
  γ-undecalactone, **8**, 165
  5-undecenoic acid, **8**, 214
$C_{11}H_{20}O_3$
  4-acetylnonanoic acid, **8**, 114
  3-hexenyl 2-hydroxy-3-methylbutanoate, **8**, 221
  lactone, **1**, 511
  N-2, **1**, 147
$C_{11}H_{20}O_3S$, geranyl methanesulfonate, **2**, 80
$C_{11}H_{20}O_4$
  VBC, **8**, 385
  VBE, **1**, 140, **8**, 385
$C_{11}H_{20}O_5$, L-olivomycoseE, **3**, 312
$C_{11}H_{20}O_6$, 1,6-dioxadecalin derivative, **8**, 506
$C_{11}H_{20}O_7P_2$, diphosphate, **5**, 321
$C_{11}H_{20}S$, geranyl methyl sulphide, **8**, 223
$C_{11}H_{21}NO_4$, carbamate analogue, **1**, 827
$C_{11}H_{21}NO_4S$, N-(7-mercaptoheptanoyl)threonine, **1**, 835
$C_{11}H_{21}NO_8$, 2-deoxy-2,3-dihydro-N-acetylneuraminic acid, **5**, 295
$C_{11}H_{21}N_2O_6P$, bialaphos, **1**, 865
$C_{11}H_{22}$, 1-undecene, **1**, 91
$C_{11}H_{22}NO_7PS$
  7-mercaptoheptanoylthreonine phosphate, **1**, 835
  N-(7-mercaptoheptanoyl)threonine phosphate, **1**, 833, 834
$C_{11}H_{22}O$
  4,6-dimethylnonan-3-one, **8**, 244
  undecanal, **8**, 212
  2-undecanone, **8**, 214
  3-undecanone, **8**, 214
$C_{11}H_{22}O_2$
  ester, **8**, 241
  ethyl 4-methyloctanoate, **8**, 241
  1-methylethyl octanoate, **8**, 209, 211
  serricornin, **8**, 43
$C_{11}H_{22}O_3$
  (1,2-dihydroxy-4-methylpentyl)pyran, **8**, 507
  1-ethylpropyl 2-methyl-3-hydroxypentanoate, **8**, 241
$C_{11}H_{22}O_4$,VBC, **1**, 140
$C_{11}H_{22}O_7P_2$
  2,3-cyclopropylgeranyl diphosphate, **5**, 327
  homogeranyl diphosphate, **2**, 78
$C_{11}H_{23}N_2O_5PS$, bisphosphoramidite, **7**, 133
$C_{11}H_{23}N_2O_7PS$, 4′-phosphopantetheine, **1**, 27, 842, **4**, 209, 321, 339, 342, 343
$C_{11}H_{23}N_2O_7S$, 4-phosphopantetheine, **1**, 546
$C_{11}H_{23}O_5$, diethyl 5-oxo-1,9-nonanedioate, **8**, 213
$C_{11}H_{24}$, undecane, **8**, 204, 214
$C_{11}H_{24}N_3OP$, bisphosphoramidite, **7**, 133
$C_{11}H_{24}O$, 2-undecanol, **8**, 214
$C_{11}H_{24}O_{14}P_4$
  DMAPP bisubstrate analogue, **5**, 321
  IPP bisubstrate analogue, **5**, 321
$C_{11}H_{27}N_2O_3PS$, bisphosphoramidite, **7**, 133
$C_{11}H_{32}N_3O$, 4-aminohexylamino-2,2,6,6-tetramethylpiperidine-N-oxyl, **7**, 162
$C_{12}H_6O_2$, naphthylenedicarbonyl, **7**, 120
$C_{12}H_7Br_2NO$, 4,6-dibromo-3-hydroxycarbazole, **8**, 526
$C_{12}H_8Br_2N_2O$, 9-methyl-7-bromoeudistomin D, **8**, 526
$C_{12}H_8Cl_2N_2$, bauerine B, **8**, 529
$C_{12}H_8Cl_2N_2O$, bauerineC, **8**, 529

$C_{12}H_8N_2$
1,10-phenanthroline, **3**, 426, **6**, 88, 200
o-phenanthroline, **3**, 378
$C_{12}H_8N_2O_4$, myxin, **7**, 532
$C_{12}H_8O_4$
bergapten, **1**, 625, 626, 634, **8**, 168
xanthotoxin, **1**, 625, 626, 634, **8**, 141, 155, 167, 168
$C_{12}H_8O_5$, 5-hydroxyxanthotoxin, **1**, 633, 634
$C_{12}H_8S$, dibenzothiophene, **3**, 376
$C_{12}H_8S_3$, α-terthienyl, **8**, 169
$C_{12}H_9BrN_2$, brominated β-carboline, **8**, 529
$C_{12}H_9Cl\,F_3N_3O$
norflurazon, **2**, 341, 342, 347
SAN 9879, **2**, 338
$C_{12}H_9ClN_2$, bauerine A, **8**, 529
$C_{12}H_9NO_3$, 4-acetylquinoline-2-carboxylic acid, **1**, 855
$C_{12}H_9N_3O_2$, 5-azido-1-naphthaleneacetic acid, **8**, 35
$C_{12}H_{10}$, biphenyl, **3**, 384, 385
$C_{12}H_{10}ClO_3P$, diphenylchlorophosphate, **7**, 106, 139
$C_{12}H_{10}F_3NO_2$, *S*-4,4,4-trifluoro-3-(indole-3-yl)butyric acid, **8**, 36
$C_{12}H_{10}N_2O_3$, olefin, **5**, 428
$C_{12}H_{10}N_2S$, camalexin, **1**, 779, **8**, 187
$C_{12}H_{10}N_4$, benzylaminopurine, **8**, 119
$C_{12}H_{10}O_2$
eutypine, **8**, 180
naphthaleneacetic acid, **8**, 34
1-naphthaleneacetic acid, **4**, 27, **8**, 35, 68
naphthyl acetate, **3**, 820
$C_{12}H_{10}O_4$, 2-hydroxy-6-oxo-6-phenylhexa-2,4-dienoate, **3**, 376
$C_{12}H_{10}O_6$, diphlorethol, **8**, 441
$C_{12}H_{11}BrO_4$, 4-bromomethyl-6,7-dimethoxycoumarin, **1**, 543
$C_{12}H_{11}Cl_2NO_2$, 5,7-dichloroindole-3-isobutyric acid, **8**, 36
$C_{12}H_{11}F_3N_2O_2$, trifluoromethyltryptophan, **5**, 331
$C_{12}H_{11}N$, diphenylamine, **2**, 341
$C_{12}H_{11}NO_2$
carbaryl, **3**, 377
indole-3-carboxylic acid, **8**, 26
$C_{12}H_{11}NO_2S$, brassicanal B, **8**, 187
$C_{12}H_{11}NO_3$,
4-(1-hydroxyethyl)quinoline-2-carboxylic acid, **1**, 855
$C_{12}H_{11}NO_4$, *N*-(1-carboxypropyl)phthalimide, **8**, 35
$C_{12}H_{11}N_5$
benzyladenine, **8**, 59
cytokinin, **1**, 126
$C_{12}H_{11}O_{13}P$
EPSP synthase substrate, **1**, 598
hydroxymalonate, **1**, 598
$C_{12}H_{12}$, 2,6-dimethylnaphthalene, **3**, 378
$C_{12}H_{12}ClNO_2S$, dansyl chloride, **6**, 77
$C_{12}H_{12}N_4O_3$, 4-thiothymine photodimer, **5**, 391
$C_{12}H_{12}O_4$
1′-hydroxysafrole, **7**, 520
methylfuroin, **3**, 394
$C_{12}H_{12}O_5$
de-*O*-methyldiaporthin, **8**, 180
radicinin, **8**, 179
$C_{12}H_{13}ClN_2O_3$, 6-chloro-5-hydroxy-*N*-methyltryptophan, **8**, 573
$C_{12}H_{13}FN_2O_9$, 2′,4′-dinitrophenyl-2-deoxy-2-fluoro-β-D-glucopyranoside, **5**, 289
$C_{12}H_{13}F_3O$, thymyl trifluoroacetate, **8**, 306
$C_{12}H_{13}NO_2$
indolebutyric acid, **4**, 46, **8**, 30
indole-3-butyric acid, **8**, 26, 34
$C_{12}H_{13}N_2O_4S_2$, *N*-succinimidyl-3-(2-pyridyldithio)propionate, **7**, 168
$C_{12}H_{13}N_4O_3S$, photoexcited thiothymine, **5**, 391
$C_{12}H_{14}BrNO_2$,
2-methyl-3-bromo-(*N*-benzaldimino)alanine methyl ester, **5**, 210

$C_{12}H_{14}N_2OS_2$, methoxybrassinin, **8**, 187
$C_{12}H_{14}N_2O_2$
methyltryptophan, **5**, 331
2-methyltryptophan, **1**, 855
$C_{12}H_{14}N_2O_2S$, oxymethoxybrassinin, **8**, 187
$C_{12}H_{14}N_2O_3$, methoxytryptophan, **5**, 331
$C_{12}H_{14}N_2O_4S$, *S*-phenylacetylcysteinylglycine, **4**, 264, 265
$C_{12}H_{14}N_2O_5$
5-(1-propynyl)-2′-deoxyuridine, **7**, 272
5-(propynyl)-2′-deoxyuridine, **6**, 225
$C_{12}H_{14}N_2O_5S$, *S*-phenoxyacetylcysteinylglycine, **4**, 264, 265
$C_{12}H_{14}N_2O_{10}$, 2′,4′-dinitrophenyl-β-D-glucopyranoside, **5**, 290
$C_{12}H_{14}N_4$, 3,3-diaminobenzidine, **3**, 97
$C_{12}H_{14}N_4O_3S$, 4-thiothymine photodimer, **5**, 391
$C_{12}H_{14}O$, calaminthone, **8**, 169, 171
$C_{12}H_{14}O_2$, precocene I, **8**, 278
$C_{12}H_{14}O_3$
3,4-dihydroisocoumarin, **8**, 241
1′-hydroxyestragole, **7**, 520
$C_{12}H_{14}O_4$, deoxyradicinin, **8**, 179
$C_{12}H_{14}O_6$
dicarboxylic acid, **1**, 404
dimethyl chorismate, **5**, 352
$C_{12}H_{14}O_7$, phomazin, **8**, 179
$C_{12}H_{15}ClO_3$, clofibrate, **2**, 25
$C_{12}H_{15}FNO$, 1-[(2-fluorophenyl)]-4-methoxypiperidin-4-yl, **6**, 84
$C_{12}H_{15}IN_2O_6$, 2′,3′-isopropylidene-5-iodouridine, **6**, 91
$C_{12}H_{15}NO_2$, acetamidobenzylpropionaldehyde, **5**, 439
$C_{12}H_{15}NO_3S$, *N*-formylmethionine, **5**, 434
$C_{12}H_{15}NO_7$, *p*-nitrophenyl-α-D-glucopyranoside, **5**, 302
$C_{12}H_{15}NO_8$
p-nitrophenylgalactose, **5**, 438 1-*O*-(*p*-nitrophenyl)-β-D-glucose, **3**, 819
p-nitrophenyl-α-D-glucoside, **3**, 148
p-nitrophenyl-α-D-mannopyranoside, **3**, 154
p-nitrophenyl-α-D-mannoside, **3**, 24, 27
$C_{12}H_{15}N_3O_5S$, *S*-cyanoethyl-4-thiouridine, **6**, 93
$C_{12}H_{15}O$, *t*-butylbenzylcarbonyl, **7**, 120
$C_{12}H_{15}O_2$, *t*-butylphenoxyacetyl, **7**, 120, 121, 123
$C_{12}H_{15}O_2S$, 2-(isopropylthiomethoxymethyl)benzoyl, **7**, 127
$C_{12}H_{16}NO_9P$
carboxyphenylamino-1-deoxyribulose *S*-phosphate, **4**, 7
phosphoribosylanthranilate, **4**, 7
$C_{12}H_{16}N_2$, *N*,*N*-dimethyltryptamine, **1**, 369
$C_{12}H_{16}N_2O$
bufotenine, **8**, 155
N-methylcytisine, **8**, 176
methylcytisine, **8**, 154
$C_{12}H_{16}N_2O_5$, 3′-*O*-acetyl-2′-deoxythymidine, **7**, 185
$C_{12}H_{16}N_2O_8$, 5-methylcarboxymethyluridine, **4**, 360
$C_{12}H_{16}N_4$, 6-cyclopentylamino-2-methylpyrrolo[2,3-*d*]pyrimidine, **8**, 69
$C_{12}H_{16}O_2$
anastrephin, **8**, 236
elijopyrone D, **8**, 596
$C_{12}H_{16}O_3$
asarone, **8**, 155
cyercene 1, **8**, 462
elijopyrone B, **8**, 596
4′-hydroxy-3′-(3-methylbutanoyl)acetophenone, **8**, 189
jasmonic acid, **1**, 2, 7, 626
primin, **8**, 139
$C_{12}H_{16}O_4S$, gonyauline bis-α,β-unsaturated ester, **8**, 457
$C_{12}H_{16}O_5$, β-glucosyl benzene, **5**, 294
$C_{12}H_{16}O_6$
phenyl β-D-galactoside, **3**, 115
phenyl-β-D-glucopyranoside, **5**, 290
$C_{12}H_{16}O_7$, arbutin, **8**, 162, 186

$C_{12}H_{17}ClN_2O_4$, chlorotetain, **3**, 275
$C_{12}H_{17}ClN_4OS$, thiamine, **1**, 826, 837, **2**, 4, 55, 376, **3**, 369
$C_{12}H_{17}NO_3$, cerulenin, **1**, 29, 357, 491, 564, 752, **8**, 395
$C_{12}H_{17}N_2O_6$, 2′,3′-O-isopropylidene uridine, **7**, 405
$C_{12}H_{17}N_3O_3$, leucine-4-nitroanilide, **1**, 279
$C_{12}H_{17}N_3O_4S$, N-formidoylthienamycin, **4**, 186
$C_{12}H_{17}N_3O_6$, nagstatin, **3**, 134
$C_{12}H_{17}N_5O_4$, N6-dimethyladenosine, **6**, 195
$C_{12}H_{18}$, ectocarpene, **1**, 8
$C_{12}H_{18}ClNS$,CPTA, **2**, 338, 343
$C_{12}H_{18}FN_5O_{10}P_2$, GDP-2-deoxy-2-fluorofucose, **5**, 309
$C_{12}H_{18}N_2O_5$, bacilysin, **3**, 275
$C_{12}H_{18}O$
    5,7-dimethyl-2,6,8-decatrien-4-one, **8**, 244
    2-propyl-5-ethylbenzyl alcohol, **1**, 87
$C_{12}H_{18}O_2$
    adamantanylacetic acid, **5**, 355
    4,8-dimethyldecadien-10-olide, **8**, 236
    3,6-dodecadien-11-olide, **8**, 215
    3,6-dodecadien-12-olide, **8**, 215
    3,6,9-dodecatrienic acid, **8**, 423
    elijopyroneC, **8**, 596
    epicucurbic acid lactone, **1**, 118
    ferrulalactone I, **8**, 236
$C_{12}H_{18}O_3$
    elijopyrone A, **8**, 596
    epijasmonic acid, **1**, 121
    hydroxy acid, **1**, 220
    11-hydroxyjasmonic acid, **1**, 118
    12-hydroxyjasmonic acid, **1**, 118
    isojasmonic acid, **1**, 241
    7-isojasmonic acid, **1**, 231
    jasmonic acid, **1**, 117, 119, 228, 234, 240, **8**, 108, 151, 215
    miconidin, **8**, 139
    patuolide, **1**, 410
    tuberonic acid, **1**, 125
$C_{12}H_{18}O_4$
    buenolide, **1**, 145
    tuberonic acid, **8**, 117
$C_{12}H_{19}ClN_4O_7P_2S$
    thiamine diphosphate, **2**, 376
    thiamine pyrophosphate, **3**, 370
$C_{12}H_{19}NO_4$
    N-(carboxyheptyl)succinimide, **5**, 250
    conjugation factor, **8**, 399
$C_{12}H_{19}N_3O_6$, valclavam, **4**, 182
$C_{12}H_{19}N_3O_7S$, acetylglutathione, **2**, 19
$C_{12}H_{19}N_5O_3$, tetramethylguanidinium salt of 4-nitrobenzaldoxime, **7**, 117
$C_{12}H_{19}O_7P$, butenolide phosphate, **1**, 145
$C_{12}H_{20}$, 5-ethyl-3-methyl-2,4,6-nonatriene, **8**, 240
$C_{12}H_{20}N_4O_7P_2S$, thiamine pyrophosphate, **1**, 837
$C_{12}H_{20}N_4O_9S$, sulfazecin, **4**, 187, 188
$C_{12}H_{20}O$
    3,6,8-dodecatrien-1-ol, **8**, 214
    pheromone of *Biprorulus bibax*, **8**, 48
$C_{12}H_{20}O_2$
    1-acetoxymethyl-2,2-dimethyl-3-(1-methylvinyl)cyclobutane, **8**, 224
    3,4-bis(1′-butenyl)tetrahydro-2-furanol, **8**, 215
    bornyl acetate, **2**, 101, **8**, 306
    3,6-dodecadienoic acid, **8**, 423
    3-dodecen-11-olide, **8**, 215
    3-dodecen-12-olide, **8**, 215
    5-dodecen-4-olide, **8**, 215
    ethyl 2,4-decadienoate, **8**, 165
    geranyl acetate, **8**, 223, 306
    2-hexenyl 2-hexenoate, **8**, 210
    2-hexenyl 3-hexenoate, **8**, 210
    1-methylethyl 2,4-dimethyl-2,4-heptadienoate, **8**, 241
$C_{12}H_{20}O_3$
    cucurbic acid, **1**, 118, **8**, 114

dihydrojasmonic acid, **1**, 118
    9,10-dihydrojasmonic acid, **1**, 124, **8**, 116
    11-formyl-9-undecenoic acid, **1**, 91, 92
    11-formyl-10-undecenoic acid, **1**, 91
    8-oxocitronellyl acetate, **8**, 225
    12-oxo-9-dodecenoic acid, **1**, 103
    putaminoxin, **8**, 181
$C_{12}H_{20}O_4$
    6-dehydroVB A, **1**, 144, 145, **8**, 386
    9,10-dihydro-11-hydroxyjasmonic acid, **1**, 124, **8**, 116
    9,10-dihydro-12-hydroxyjasmonic acid, **8**, 116
    traumatic acid, **4**, 46
$C_{12}H_{20}O_5$
    butanolide ester derivative, **1**, 145
    dihydroxyacetone ester of 3-oxo-7-methyloctanoic acid, **8**, 385
$C_{12}H_{20}O_{10}$, anhydrocellobiose, **3**, 540
$C_{12}H_{21}FO_{10}$, β-cellobiosyl fluoride, **5**, 301
$C_{12}H_{21}NO_3$,VA1-2, **8**, 395
$C_{12}H_{21}O_7P$, 6-dehydroVB A phosphate, **1**, 145
$C_{12}H_{21}O_8P$, butenolide derivative, **1**, 145
$C_{12}H_{22}CaO_{14}$, D-glucal, **5**, 304
$C_{12}H_{22}N_3O_2P$, bis(2-cyanoethyl)diisopropylphosphoramidite, **7**, 168
$C_{12}H_{22}N_3O_6P$, N-acetyl DMBA, **1**, 871
$C_{12}H_{22}O$, 4,6-dimethyl-4-decen-3-one, **8**, 243
$C_{12}H_{22}O_2$
    3-acetoxy-7-methyl-6-nonene, **8**, 246
    C12:1, **1**, 340
    2-decenyl acetate, **8**, 213
    3,5-dimethyl-6-(1′-methylbutyl)tetrahydro-2*H*-pyran-2-one, **8**, 240
    4-dodecanolide, **8**, 215
    9-dodecenoic acid, **8**, 205
    11-dodecenoic acid, **8**, 205
    dominicalure 2, **8**, 46
    invictolide, **8**, 241, 244
    linalool derivative, **8**, 235
    1-methylbutyl 2,4-dimethyl-2-pentenoate, **8**, 241
    12-oxo-9-dodecenol, **1**, 106
    terpenoid, **8**, 235
$C_{12}H_{22}O_3$
    6-hydroxy-4-dodecanolide, **8**, 215
    lactone, **1**, 513
    N-4, **1**, 147
$C_{12}H_{22}O_4$
    butanolide A, **1**, 139
    N derivative, **1**, 147
    tetraketide, **1**, 508, 513, 515
    VB A, **1**, 140, **8**, 385
    VB B, **1**, 140, **8**, 385
    VB D, **1**, 140, **8**, 385
$C_{12}H_{22}O_9$, Glcα1,-(1,2-dideoxy)mannose, **3**, 20
$C_{12}H_{22}O_{10}$, β-2-deoxymaltose, **5**, 303
$C_{12}H_{22}O_{11}$
    cellobiose, **3**, 546, 570
    β-D-Fruf-(2→6)-β-D-Glcp, **3**, 195
    Galα1-3Gal, **3**, 81
    Glcα1,3Man, **3**, 20
    lactose, **3**, 43, 78, 112, 115, 430, **4**, 174
    maltose, **3**, 151, 444, 457, **5**, 302, 303
    nigerose, **3**, 148
    sucrose, **2**, 50, **3**, 9, 151, 421, 443, 444, 463, 505, 608, **8**, 162, 166
$C_{12}H_{23}N$, dodecadienamine, **8**, 545
$C_{12}H_{23}NO_8$, 2,5-dideoxy-2,5-imino-DL-*glycero*-D-*manno* D-*heptitol* 7-apioside, **3**, 130
$C_{12}H_{23}NO_9$
    1-deoxymannojirimycin 2-O-α-D-galactopyranoside, **3**, 131
    1-deoxymannojirimycin 6-O-α-D-galactopyranoside, **3**, 131
    1-deoxymannojirimycin 2-O-α-D-glucopyranoside, **3**, 131

1-deoxymannojirimycin 2-*O*-β-D-glucopyranoside, **3**, 131

1-deoxymannojirimycin 3-*O*-α-D-glucopyranoside, **3**, 131

1-deoxymannojirimycin 3-*O*-β-D-glucopyranoside, **3**, 131

1-deoxymannojirimycin 4-*O*-α-D-glucopyranoside, **3**, 131

1-deoxymannojirimycin 4-*O*-β-D-glucopyranoside, **3**, 131

1-deoxymannojirimycin 6-*O*-β-D-glucopyranoside, **3**, 131

2-*O*-α-D-galactopyranosyl-DNJ, **3**, 143

$C_{12}H_{24}NO_{13}P$, glucosamine phosphatidyl inositol, **3**, 300

$C_{12}H_{24}O$

4,8-dimethyldecanal, **8**, 40, 217, 236

tribolure, **8**, 246

$C_{12}H_{24}O_2$

decyl acetate, **8**, 162, 213

dodecanoic acid, **8**, 205

1,12,9-dodecenediol, **1**, 106

7-hydroxy-4,6-dimethyl-3-nonanone, **8**, 244

lauric acid, **3**, 220

$C_{12}H_{24}O_7P_2$, bishomogeranyl diphosphate, **2**, 78

$C_{12}H_{24}O_{15}$, GDP-fucose, **3**, 55

$C_{12}H_{24}O_{17}$, GDP-Man, **4**, 312

$C_{12}H_{24}O_{17}P_2$

GDP-mannose, **3**, 301

GDP-[3H]mannose, **3**, 300

$C_{12}H_{26}$, dodecane, **8**, 214

$C_{12}H_{26}NO_4P$, Ala-P-Ala, **3**, 277

$C_{12}H_{26}N_3OP$, bisphosphoramidite, **7**, 133

$C_{12}H_{26}N_4O_6$, neamine, **6**, 194

$C_{12}H_{26}O$, 1-dodecanol, **8**, 214

$C_{12}H_{26}O_7P_2$, 3-methyl-2-undecenyl diphosphate, **2**, 76

$C_{12}H_{27}P$, tributylphosphine, **7**, 130

$C_{12}H_{28}Cl_2OSi_2$, 1,3-dichloro-1,1,3,3-tetraisopropyldisiloxane, **6**, 85

$C_{13}H_6O_2$, 12,13-epoxy-2,4,6,8,10-tridecapentayne, **8**, 189

$C_{13}H_7NO$, acridone, **1**, 759

$C_{13}H_8$

phenylheptatriyne, **8**, 169

1-tridecan-3,5,7,9,11-pentayne, **8**, 189

$C_{13}H_8Br_4O_3$

3,5-dibromo-2-(3′,5′-dibromo-2′-methoxyphenoxy)phenol, **8**, 588

$C_{13}H_8Br_4O_4$, bromophenol oligomer, **8**, 461

$C_{13}H_8F_2O_3$, diflunisal, **1**, 294

$C_{13}H_8N_2$, diazo compound, **7**, 542

$C_{13}H_8O_3$, furanocoumarin, **1**, 19

$C_{13}H_8O_5$, xanthone, **1**, 760

$C_{13}H_8O_6$, hymenoquinone, **3**, 624

$C_{13}H_9N$, acridine, **7**, 116, 436

$C_{13}H_9N_2O$, phenylazobenzoyl, **7**, 120

$C_{13}H_9N_2O_2$, phenylazophenoxycarbonyl, **7**, 127

$C_{13}H_9O$, xanthenyl, **7**, 126

$C_{13}H_{10}Br_2N_2$, brominated β-carboline, **8**, 529

$C_{13}H_{10}NO$, diphenylformamido, **7**, 119

$C_{13}H_{10}N_2$, 9-aminoacridine, **7**, 444, 451, 467, 488

$C_{13}H_{10}N_2O_4$, iodonin, **7**, 532

$C_{13}H_{10}N_2S_3$, 2-pyridyl 3-isothiocyanotobenzyl disulfide, **6**, 227

$C_{13}H_{10}O$, benzophenone, **1**, 432, 760

$C_{13}H_{10}O_2$, dehydrosafynol, **8**, 189

$C_{13}H_{10}O_3$, mycosinol, **8**, 189, 190

$C_{13}H_{10}O_4$

2′-acetyl-2′,3′-dihydropsoralen, **1**, 632

bisnoryangonin, **1**, 19, 761, **3**, 624

$C_{13}H_{10}O_5$

hispidin, **1**, 761, **3**, 624

isopimpinellin, **1**, 633, 635

$C_{13}H_{10}O_6$, leucohymenoquinone, **3**, 624

$C_{13}H_{11}BrN_2$, brominated β-carboline, **8**, 529

$C_{13}H_{11}BrN_4O$, aplysinopsin derivative, **8**, 429

$C_{13}H_{11}N$

aminofluorene, **7**, 96

2-aminofluorene, **7**, 470, 522

$C_{13}H_{11}NO$

N-hydroxy-2-aminofluorene, **7**, 96

1-hydroxy-3-methylcarbazole, **4**, 54

$C_{13}H_{11}N_3$, proflavine, **7**, 435, 446

$C_{13}H_{12}BrN_4O$, dihydroaplysinopsin derivative, **8**, 429

$C_{13}H_{12}ClN_5$, tetcyclacis, **1**, 720

$C_{13}H_{12}N_2$, diaminofluorene, **3**, 713

$C_{13}H_{12}N_2O$

diphenylurea, **8**, 61

1-(1′-hydroxyethyl)-β-carboline, **8**, 529

$C_{13}H_{12}N_2O_5$, indole-3-acetylaspartic acid, **8**, 26

$C_{13}H_{12}N_2S$, methoxycamalexin, **8**, 187

$C_{13}H_{12}N_4O$, aplysinopsin derivative, **8**, 429

$C_{13}H_{12}O_2$, safynol, **8**, 189

$C_{13}H_{12}O_3$

methoxy-(2-naphthyl)acetic acid, **8**, 500

α-(2-naphthoxy)propionic acid, **8**, 36

$C_{13}H_{13}NO_3$, anthosamine A, **8**, 442

$C_{13}H_{13}N_4O$, dihydroaplysinopsin derivative, **8**, 429

$C_{13}H_{14}N_2O_3$, *N*-acetyltryptophan, **5**, 379

$C_{13}H_{14}O_4$, pyrenochaetic acid A, **1**, 401

$C_{13}H_{15}Br_2N_3O_2$, ceratinamine, **8**, 440

$C_{13}H_{16}N_2O$, tambjamineE, **8**, 472

$C_{13}H_{16}N_2O_8P$, nitrobenzyl phosphonate, **5**, 431

$C_{13}H_{16}N_4O_4$

thymine dimer, **5**, 375

thymine photodimer, **5**, 375

$C_{13}H_{16}N_4O_6$, 5-imidazolylmethyluridine, **6**, 225

$C_{13}H_{16}O_2$, 4′-hydroxy-3′-prenylacetophenone, **8**, 189, 190

$C_{13}H_{16}O_3$

4′-hydroxy-3′-(3-methylbutanoyl)acetophenone, **8**, 190

precocene II, **8**, 278

$C_{13}H_{16}O_4$

2-*tert*-butyl-2-methyl-1,3-benzodioxole-4-carboxylic acid, **8**, 503

dinor-ABA, **8**, 79

ethyl benzoate derivative, **1**, 401

pyrenochaetic acidC, **1**, 401

$C_{13}H_{16}O_5$, pyrenochaetic acid B, **1**, 401

$C_{13}H_{16}O_7$, 1-*O*-benzoylglucose, **3**, 810

$C_{13}H_{16}O_8$

2′-carboxyphenyl β-D-glucopyranoside, **5**, 290

4′-carboxyphenyl β-glucopyranoside, **5**, 290

1-*O*-*p*-hydroxybenzoylglucose, **3**, 807

1-*O*-hydroxybenzoyl-β-D-glucose, **3**, 806

$C_{13}H_{16}O_9$

1-*O*-protocatechuoylglucose, **3**, 807

1-*O*-protocatechuoyl-β-D-glucose, **3**, 806

tri-*O*-protocatechuoylglucose, **3**, 807

$C_{13}H_{16}O_{10}$

β-glucogallin, **3**, 10, 800, 802, 805, 807, 820, 821

4-*O*-β-D-glucosidogallic acid, **3**, 805

$C_{13}H_{16}O_{18}$, 6-galloylglucose, **3**, 809

$C_{13}H_{17}ClNO$, 1-[(2-chloro-4-methyl)phenyl]-4′-methoxypiperidin-4-yl, **6**, 84, **7**, 144

$C_{13}H_{17}NO_3$, phenyl *N*-formylnorleucine, **5**, 434

$C_{13}H_{17}N_4O_9$, chiriquitoxin 6,13-lactone, **8**, 482

$C_{13}H_{17}N_5O_8S_2$, aztreonam, **4**, 187

$C_{13}H_{18}N_2O_5S$, NS-398, **5**, 250, 252, 255

$C_{13}H_{18}N_4O_{10}$, chiriquitoxin, **8**, 482

$C_{13}H_{18}N_6O_3$, lupinic acid, **8**, 43, 61, 62, 483

$C_{13}H_{18}O_2$, ibuprofen, **1**, 123, 131, **5**, 248

$C_{13}H_{18}O_3$

dehydrovomifoliol, **8**, 88

methyl jasmonate, **1**, 7, 611, 626, **4**, 46

$C_{13}H_{18}O_6$, 1-benzyl-β-D-glucopyranose, **3**, 810

$C_{13}H_{18}O_7$, salicin, **8**, 139, 152, 154

$C_{13}H_{19}NO_2S_4$, 3,4-dimethoxy-6-(2′-*N*,*N*-dimethylaminoethyl)-5-(methylthio)benzotrithiane, **8**, 542

C$_{13}$H$_{19}$NO$_2$S$_6$, *N,N*-dimethyl-5-(methylthio)varacin, **8**, 542

C$_{13}$H$_{19}$NO$_3$
  7-angeloylheliotridine, **4**, 31
  pellotine, **4**, 26

C$_{13}$H$_{19}$N$_3$O$_5$S$_2$, sparsomycin, **1**, 845

C$_{13}$H$_{19}$N$_3$O$_6$S, 7-aminocephalosporanic acid, **4**, 180

C$_{13}$H$_{19}$N$_6$O$_8$P, alanyl adenylate, **7**, 628

C$_{13}$H$_{20}$, 3,5,7-trimethyl-2,4,6,8-decatetrene, **8**, 240

C$_{13}$H$_{20}$N$_2$O$_2$, procaine, **4**, 240

C$_{13}$H$_{20}$O
  2,5-epoxy-6,8-megastigmadiene, **8**, 45
  β-ionone, **8**, 234

C$_{13}$H$_{20}$O$_3$
  allenic ketone, **8**, 234
  1′-epistegobinone, **8**, 244
  methyl jasmonate, **1**, 117, 126, **8**, 108, 150, 215
  13-oxo-9,11-tridecadienoic acid, **1**, 209, 214
  stegobinone, **8**, 44, 244
  vomifoliol, **8**, 88

C$_{13}$H$_{20}$O$_4$
  drummondol, **8**, 88
  salonitenolide, **8**, 308

C$_{13}$H$_{20}$O$_6$, sylingolide, **1**, 148

C$_{13}$H$_{21}$NO, MPTA, **2**, 338, 343

C$_{13}$H$_{21}$NO$_{10}$
  O-acetyl-*N*-acetylneuraminic acid, **3**, 378
  N-acetyl-4-*O*-acetylneuraminic acid, **3**, 378

C$_{13}$H$_{21}$N$_2$O$_4$PS, cremat, **1**, 127

C$_{13}$H$_{21}$N$_3$O$_8$S, (*S*-D-lactoyl)glutathione, **5**, 67

C$_{13}$H$_{22}$F$_3$N$_2$O$_4$P, phosphoramidite, **7**, 171

C$_{13}$H$_{22}$N$_2$
  1,3-dicyclohexylcarbodiimide, **7**, 112
  dicyclohexylcarbodiimide, **6**, 82, **7**, 107

C$_{13}$H$_{22}$N$_2$O$_2$, pyrimidine photodimer model, **5**, 378

C$_{13}$H$_{22}$N$_2$O$_{10}$, trehazolin, **1**, 152, **3**, 134, 153

C$_{13}$H$_{22}$O
  geranylacetone, **8**, 161, 234
  5-(1-methylethyl)-8-methyl-6,8-nonadien-2-one, **8**, 235

C$_{13}$H$_{22}$O$_2$, geranyl propionate, **8**, 306

C$_{13}$H$_{22}$O$_3$
  dehydrodipropylguaiacol, **3**, 725
  2,3-dihydro-2,3,5-trimethyl-6-(2′-hydroxy-1′-methylbutyl)-4*H*-pyran-4-one, **8**, 244

C$_{13}$H$_{22}$O$_4$, A factor, **1**, 140, **8**, 380

C$_{13}$H$_{23}$F$_3$N$_3$O$_3$P, phosphoramidite, **7**, 154

C$_{13}$H$_{23}$NO$_5$S, 3-oxo-7-methyloctanoic acid *N*-acetylcysteamine thioester, **1**, 142

C$_{13}$H$_{24}$ClN$_2$O$_4$P, phosphoramidite, **7**, 171

C$_{13}$H$_{24}$N$_2$O
  cuscohygrine, **4**, 27, 30
  hygrinic acid, **4**, 30

C$_{13}$H$_{24}$N$_2$O$_5$S, acetylpantetheine, **2**, 19

C$_{13}$H$_{24}$O
  4-tridecenal, **8**, 219
  4,6,8-trimethyl-7,9-decadien-5-ol, **8**, 245

C$_{13}$H$_{24}$O$_2$, 8-tridecenoic acid, **8**, 207

C$_{13}$H$_{24}$O$_4$
  butanolide derivative, **1**, 140
  factor 1, **1**, 140
  2-(1-hydroxy-6-methylheptyl)-4-hydroxymethylbutanolide, **8**, 592

C$_{13}$H$_{24}$O$_5$, 6-*O*-butyrylcastanospermine, **3**, 143

C$_{13}$H$_{24}$O$_{11}$, methyl *β*-cellobioside, **3**, 546, 570

C$_{13}$H$_{25}$N, monomorine I, **8**, 216

C$_{13}$H$_{25}$NO$_8$, *N*-(3-deoxy-L-*glycero*-tetronyl)-D-p erosamine, **3**, 195

C$_{13}$H$_{25}$NO$_{10}$, -*α*-homonojirimycin 7-*O*-*β*-D-glucopyranoside, **3**, 131

C$_{13}$H$_{26}$
  4-tridecene, **8**, 214
  5-tridecene, **8**, 216

C$_{13}$H$_{26}$O, 2-tridecanone, **8**, 215, 216

C$_{13}$H$_{26}$O$_2$, 4,4,10*β*-trimethyldecal-3*β*-ol, **2**, 291

C$_{13}$H$_{26}$O$_3$, 10-propoxydecanoic acid, **4**, 316

C$_{13}$H$_{27}$NO
  1-aminotridec-5-en-2-ol, **8**, 545
  2-hydroxy-3-tridecenamine, **8**, 545
  2-hydroxy-4-tridecenamine, **8**, 545

C$_{13}$H$_{27}$N$_3$O$_{10}$, 2,6-diamino-2,6-imino-7-*O*-(*β*-D-gluco pyranosyl)-D-*glycero*-L-*gulo*-heptitol, **3**, 153

C$_{13}$H$_{28}$, tridecane, **8**, 214

C$_{13}$H$_{28}$N$_3$OP, bisphosphoramidite, **7**, 133

C$_{13}$H$_{31}$N$_2$OP, bis-amidite, **7**, 133

C$_{14}$H$_6$O$_8$, ellagic acid, **3**, 801, 817

C$_{14}$H$_8$N$_2$O$_8$S$_2$, 5,5′-dithiobis(2-nitrobenzoic acid), **1**, 293, 578, 601, **3**, 378, **5**, 353

C$_{14}$H$_8$O$_2$, anthraquinone, **1**, 432

C$_{14}$H$_8$O$_5$S, anthraquinone-2-sulfonate, **5**, 378

C$_{14}$H$_9$Cl$_5$, DDT, **5**, 401, 411

C$_{14}$I$_9$N$_2$O$_6$S, 2-(2,4-dinitrobenzenesulfenyloxymethyl)benzoyl, **7**, 127

C$_{14}$H$_{10}$
  anthracene, **7**, 436
  phenanthrene, **3**, 375, 377

C$_{14}$H$_{10}$ClNO$_4$, chloroaristolactam, **7**, 522

C$_{14}$H$_{10}$Cl$_2$O$_4$, mollisin, **1**, 3

C$_{14}$H$_{10}$F$_3$NO$_2$, flufenamic acid, **5**, 248

C$_{14}$H$_{10}$IN$_3$O, 5-iodoacetamido-1,10-phenanthroline, **6**, 76

C$_{14}$H$_{10}$O, phenanthrene 9,10-oxide, **5**, 62, 63

C$_{14}$H$_{10}$O$_4$, diphenic acid, **3**, 801

C$_{14}$H$_{10}$O$_6$, parasperone A, **1**, 417

C$_{14}$H$_{10}$O$_9$, digallic acid, **3**, 820

C$_{14}$H$_{10}$O$_{10}$
  dehydrodigallic acid, **3**, 801
  hexahydroxydiphenic acid, **3**, 10

C$_{14}$H$_{11}$Cl$_2$NO$_2$
  diclofenac, **5**, 248
  meclofenamate, **5**, 248

C$_{14}$H$_{11}$IO$_3$S, iodosuprofen, **5**, 232, 248

C$_{14}$H$_{11}$N, *N*-methylacridinium, **5**, 121

C$_{14}$H$_{11}$NO$_3$, 1,3-dihydroxy-*N*-methylacridone, **1**, 759

C$_{14}$H$_{11}$NO$_6$, dianthramine, **8**, 191

C$_{14}$H$_{11}$N$_3$O, 9-aminoacridine-4-carboxamide, **7**, 607

C$_{14}$H$_{11}$O, diphenylacetyl, **7**, 120

C$_{14}$H$_{11}$O$_3$
  methoxyphenoxybenzoyl, **7**, 120
  3-methoxy-4-phenoxybenzoyl, **7**, 123

C$_{14}$H$_{12}$, stilbene, **1**, 758

C$_{14}$H$_{12}$N$_4$O, 5-glycylamido-1,10-phenanthroline, **7**, 185

C$_{14}$H$_{12}$O$_2$
  benzoin, **3**, 395
  pinosylvin, **8**, 139

C$_{14}$H$_{12}$O$_3$
  resveratrol, **1**, 752, 757, **8**, 189, 190
  4,5′,8-trimethylpsoralen, **7**, 96

C$_{14}$H$_{12}$O$_4$
  eriobofuran, **8**, 187
  piceatannol, **8**, 189

C$_{14}$H$_{12}$O$_5$, 9-hydroxyeriobofuran, **8**, 187

C$_{14}$H$_{12}$O$_6$, YWA1, **1**, 419, 425

C$_{14}$H$_{13}$BrN$_4$O, aplysinopsin derivative, **8**, 429

C$_{14}$H$_{13}$ClN$_2$O$_5$, monomethyl 4-chloroindole-3-acetylaspartate, **8**, 26

C$_{14}$H$_{13}$ClN$_2$O, *N*-(2-hydroxyethyl)phenazinium chloride, **7**, 161

C$_{14}$H$_{13}$N$_3$O$_4$S$_2$, meloxicam, **5**, 252

C$_{14}$H$_{14}$N$_2$O, metyrapone, **5**, 419

C$_{14}$H$_{14}$N$_2$O$_2$, CC-1065 analogue, **7**, 505

C$_{14}$H$_{14}$N$_4$O, aplysinopsin derivative, **8**, 429

C$_{14}$H$_{14}$O$_2$, lunularin, **1**, 765

C$_{14}$H$_{14}$O$_3$
  aucuparin, **8**, 187
  demethylsuberosin, **1**, 628, 630
  isoaucuparin, **8**, 187
  naproxen, **5**, 248

osthenol, **1**, 628, 630, 631
   7-*O*-prenylumbelliferone, **1**, 630
   O-prenylumbelliferone, **1**, 635
$C_{14}H_{14}O_4$
   columbianetin, **1**, 628, 631, 633
   2'-hydroxyaucuparin, **8**, 187
   marmesin, **1**, 19, 628, 630, 631
   rhaphiolepsin, **8**, 187
$C_{14}H_{14}O_5$, 3'-hydroxymarmesin, **1**, 633
$C_{14}H_{14}O_6$, citreoisocoumarin, **1**, 419, 426
$C_{14}H_{15}BrClNO_6$, 5-bromo-4-chloro-3-indolyl-β-D-
   galactoside, **7**, 646
$C_{14}H_{15}BrN_4O$, dihydroaplysinopsin derivative, **8**, 429
$C_{14}H_{15}NO_3$, anthosamine B, **8**, 442
$C_{14}H_{15}NO_5$, methyl 1-acetylindole-3-glycerate, **8**, 35
$C_{14}H_{15}NO_8$, *o*-nitrobenzyl enolpyranose, **1**, 583
$C_{14}H_{15}N_3O$, dimethylaminoazobenzene-*N*-oxide, **3**, 412
$C_{14}H_{15}N_3O_2$, indolmycin, **1**, 150
$C_{14}H_{16}BrN_3OS$, eudestomin derivative, **8**, 525
$C_{14}H_{16}BrN_3O_2S$
   eudestomin derivative, **8**, 525
   eudistomin K sulfoxide, **8**, 527
$C_{14}H_{16}NO_3$, Belleau's reagent, **2**, 289
$C_{14}H_{16}N_2O_2$, phenylalanyl-prolyl-piperazinedione, **4**, 326
$C_{14}H_{16}N_2O_3$, oxetane, **5**, 387
$C_{14}H_{16}N_2O_8S_2$, dithiobis(*N*-succinimidyl)propionate, **7**, 168
$C_{14}H_{16}N_4O$, dihydroaplysinopsin derivative, **8**, 429
$C_{14}H_{17}NO_3$, fagaramide, **8**, 304
$C_{14}H_{17}NO_7$, dhurrin, **1**, 858
$C_{14}H_{17}N_3O_6$, *p*-nitrobenzylcarboxymethylglutamide, **5**, 432
$C_{14}H_{17}N_7$, berenil, **7**, 459
$C_{14}H_{18}N_2O_8$, 4-nitrophenyl β-*N*-acetylglucosaminide, **3**, 30
$C_{14}H_{18}N_4O_3$, trimethoprim, **5**, 349
$C_{14}H_{18}O_2$
   dienone, **7**, 508
   pterosin B, **7**, 508
$C_{14}H_{18}O_3$
   cyercene 2, **8**, 462
   cyercene 4, **8**, 462
   cyercene B, **8**, 462
   gyrinal, **8**, 234
$C_{14}H_{18}O_4$, nor-ABA, **8**, 79
$C_{14}H_{18}O_8$, phyllanthurinolactone, **8**, 41
$C_{14}H_{19}BrO_2$, deacetylkumausyne, **1**, 303
$C_{14}H_{19}NO_3$, ruspolinone, **4**, 30
$C_{14}H_{19}NO_4$, anisomycin, **4**, 30
$C_{14}H_{19}NO_6$, GalNAcα-phenyl, **3**, 71
$C_{14}H_{19}N_2NaO_4S$, penicillin F, **4**, 262, 267
$C_{14}H_{19}N_3O_5S$, *N*-hydroxysuccinimide, **7**, 154
$C_{14}H_{19}N_3O_6S$, deacetoxycephalosporin C, **1**, 840, 843, **4**, 164, 171
$C_{14}H_{19}N_3O_7S$
   deacetylcephalosporin, **4**, 172
   deacetylcephalosporin C, **1**, 840, 844, **4**, 164
$C_{14}H_{19}N_5O_6$, *N*-isobutyrylguanosine, **6**, 85
$C_{14}H_{20}ClNO_3$, 2-*N*,*N*-dimethylaminoethyl 4-
   chlorophenoxyacetate, **8**, 35
$C_{14}H_{20}Cl_5N_2OP$, bisphosphoramidite, **7**, 133
$C_{14}H_{20}F_5N_2OP$, bisphosphoramidite, **7**, 133
$C_{14}H_{20}N_2O_4S$, penicillin F, **4**, 162
$C_{14}H_{20}N_2O_5$, 5-(1-pentenyl)-2'-deoxyuridine, **7**, 636
$C_{14}H_{20}N_2O_6$, uridine derivative, **7**, 376
$C_{14}H_{20}N_4O_4$, 1,3-dimethylthymine dimer, **5**, 375
$C_{14}H_{20}N_6O_2$, discadenine, **8**, 62
$C_{14}H_{20}N_6O_5S$
   S-adenosylhomocysteine, **2**, 359, **5**, 215, **8**, 64
   S-adenosyl-L-homocysteine, **3**, 647
$C_{14}H_{20}O_3$
   gyrinidione, **8**, 234
   gyrinidone, **8**, 234

$C_{14}H_{20}O_{10}$, 2,3,4,6-tetra-*O*-acetyl-D-glucose, **3**, 821
$C_{14}H_{21}ClO_3$, chloriolin A, **8**, 601
$C_{14}H_{21}N_2NaO_4S$, penicillin DF, **4**, 262
$C_{14}H_{21}N_3O_6S$
   isopenicillin N, **1**, 840, **4**, 162, 169, 243
   penicillin N, **1**, 840, **4**, 164, 171
$C_{14}H_{22}$
   3,5-dimethyl-7-ethyl-2,4,6,8-decatetrene, **8**, 240
   3,5,7-trimethyl-2,4,6,8-undecatetraene, **8**, 240
$C_{14}H_{22}Cl_3N_2OP$, bisphosphoramidite, **7**, 133
$C_{14}H_{22}N_2O_6$
   piperidinol acetate, **8**, 551
   pseudodistomin C acetate, **8**, 550
   uridine derivative, **7**, 401
$C_{14}H_{22}N_2O_{16}P_2$
   UDP-apiose, **3**, 505
   UDP-D-apiose, **3**, 508, 517
   UDP-L-arabinose, **3**, 505
   UDP-xylose, **3**, 478, 480, 481, 507, 508, 510, 517, 604, 606, 608, 612
   UDP-D-xylose, **3**, 505, 507
$C_{14}H_{22}N_3O_7P$, lysine-pyridoxal 5'-phosphate, **4**, 65
$C_{14}H_{22}N_7O_8PS_2$, molybdenum cofactor
   bis(carboxamidomethyl) derivative, **1**, 835
$C_{14}H_{22}O$, hernandulcin, **8**, 41
$C_{14}H_{22}OSi$
   2-dimethylphenylsilylcyclohexanol, **2**, 317
   (hydroxystyryl)diisopropylsilyl, **7**, 129
$C_{14}H_{22}O_2$
   pheromone of *Cryptolestes turcicus*, **8**, 47
   rishitin, **2**, 183, 184
   sclerosporin, **8**, 408
   5,8-tetradecadien-13-olide, **8**, 216
$C_{14}H_{22}O_3$ 2,3-dihydro-2-ethyl-3,5-dimethyl-6-(1'-methyl-
   2'-oxobutyl)-4*H*-pyran-4-one, **8**, 244
   serricorone, **8**, 244
   α-serricorone, **8**, 207
$C_{14}H_{22}O_5$, triethoxy(dihydroxyphenyl)ethane, **8**, 442
$C_{14}H_{23}ClN_4O_8P_2S$, 2-hydroxyethylthiamine
   pyrophosphate, **3**, 370
$C_{14}H_{23}IN_4O_3S$, *N*-biotinyl-*N'*-iodoacetylethylenediamine, **7**, 632
$C_{14}H_{23}NO$, spilanthol, **8**, 303
$C_{14}H_{23}N_3O_{10}$, diethylenetriaminepentaacetic acid, **7**, 540
$C_{14}H_{24}$
   5-ethyl-7-methyl-3,5,7-undecatriene, **8**, 240
   sterpurene, **2**, 172
$C_{14}H_{24}$, germacrene B, **8**, 161
$C_{14}H_{24}BrN_2OP$, bisphosphoramidite, **7**, 133
$C_{14}H_{24}N_2O_7$, spectinomycin, **4**, 200
$C_{14}H_{24}N_3O_3P$, bisphosphoramidite, **7**, 133
$C_{14}H_{24}O_2$
   echinolone, **8**, 277
   geranyl butanoate, **8**, 223
   japonilure, **8**, 42, 49
   3,5-teradecadienoic acid, **8**, 216
   9,11-tetradecadienoic acid, **8**, 205
   tetradecan-4-olide, **8**, 216
   5-tetradecen-13-olide, **8**, 216
   5-tetradecen-4-olide, **8**, 216
$C_{14}H_{24}O_3$
   putaminoxin B, **8**, 181
   serricorole, **8**, 244
   undecadiene-1,2,3-triol 2,3-acetonide, **1**, 310
$C_{14}H_{24}O_4$
   blastmycinone, **3**, 312
   CTX-4B derivative, **8**, 502
$C_{14}H_{25}BrHgN_2O_2$, piperidine derivative, **8**, 551
$C_{14}H_{25}N$
   azaFPP analogue, **5**, 330
   tetradecatrienamine, **8**, 545
$C_{14}H_{25}NO$
   pellitorine, **1**, 333, **8**, 293

$C_{14}H_{25}NO_{10}$, casuarine 6-glucoside, **3**, 132

$C_{14}H_{25}NO_{11}$
  N-acetyllactosamine, **3**, 115, 119, 122
  Galβ1-3GlcNAc, **3**, 57
  Galβ1-4GlcNAc, **3**, 57
  lacto-*N*-biose, **3**, 115

$C_{14}H_{25}N_2OP$, bisphosphoramidite, **7**, 133

$C_{14}H_{25}N_3O_6S$
  ACV, **4**, 178, 226, 230, 235, 321
  ACV tripeptide, **1**, 840
  aminoadipylcysteinylvaline, **4**, 162, 167, 243, 246

$C_{14}H_{26}N$, sesquiterpene FPP analogue, **2**, 160

$C_{14}H_{26}NO_{14}P$, GlcNAc-PI, **3**, 301

$C_{14}H_{26}N_2O_2$, benzyl carbamate, **8**, 551

$C_{14}H_{26}N_2O_3$, piperidinol derivative, **8**, 551

$C_{14}H_{26}O$, 7-tetradecen-2-one, **8**, 216

$C_{14}H_{26}O_2$
  C14:1, **1**, 340
  7-dodecenyl acetate, **8**, 202
  9-dodecenyl acetate, **8**, 205
  11-dodecenyl acetate, **8**, 205
  9-tetradecenoic acid, **1**, 42, **8**, 207
  11-tetradecenoic acid, **8**, 205
  Δ-7-tetradecenoic acid, **3**, 197

$C_{14}H_{26}O_3$, 3-oxotetradecanoic acid, **3**, 196

$C_{14}H_{26}O_4$, butanolide derivative, **1**, 140

$C_{14}H_{26}O_7P_2$, FPP analogue, **5**, 332

$C_{14}H_{27}N$, tetradecadienamine, **8**, 545

$C_{14}H_{27}NO$, crucigasterin 225, **8**, 545

$C_{14}H_{27}NO_2$, 9-tetradecenyl nitrate, **8**, 207

$C_{14}H_{27}NO_8$, 2-*O*-methyl-*N*-(3-deoxy-L-*glycero*-te tronyl)-D-perosamine, **3**, 195

$C_{14}H_{27}N_5O_2$, 5-{4-[*N*,*N*-bis(3-aminopropyl)amino]butyl}-uridine, **7**, 319

$C_{14}H_{28}$, tetradecene, **8**, 216

$C_{14}H_{28}O$
  10-methyl-2-tridecanone, **8**, 244
  tetradecanal, **8**, 393
  5-tetradecen-1-ol, **8**, 219

$C_{14}H_{28}O_2$
  1,7-dimethylnonyl propanoate, **8**, 246
  myristic acid, **1**, 48, **3**, 220, 304, **8**, 205
  1,3,5,7-tetramethyldecyl formate, **8**, 244

$C_{14}H_{29}NO$
  N,*N*-dimethyldodecylamine *N*-oxide, **2**, 312
  dodecyldimethylamine *N*-oxide, **2**, 311

$C_{14}H_{30}$, tetradecane, **8**, 216

$C_{14}H_{30}Cl_3N_3OP$, bisphosphoramidite, **7**, 133

$C_{14}H_{31}N$, *N*,*N*-dimethyldodecylamine, **2**, 270

$C_{14}H_{36}N_3OP$, bisphosphoramidite, **7**, 133

$C_{15}H_2O$, euryfuran, **8**, 462

$C_{15}H_8O_5$, coumestrol, **1**, 722, 780, 781, 782, 786, 809, 810, 812, 815

$C_{15}H_8O_7$, allyl pyrophosphate, **2**, 38

$C_{15}H_{10}BrN_3$, eudistomin A, **8**, 525

$C_{15}H_{10}O_4$
  aloesaponarin II, **1**, 484
  chrysophanol, **1**, 429, 458
  daidzein, **1**, 19, 329, 774, 780, 781, 782, 783, 786, 791, 793, 795, 799, 800, 806, 810, 812, 815, **8**, 174
  6-deoxyemodin, **1**, 429
  7,4′-dihydroxyflavone, **1**, 794, **8**, 173
  pterocarp-6a-ene, **1**, 810
  rubiadin, **1**, 130

$C_{15}H_{10}O_5$
  apigenin, **1**, 724, **8**, 174
  emodin, **1**, 429, 458
  galangin, **1**, 726, 731
  genistein, **1**, 130, 329, 699, 774, 780, 781, 782, 783, 786, 791, 795, 799, 030.0195, 806, 814, **7**, 610, **8**, 174, 175
  2-hydroxydaidzein, **1**, 793
  2′-hydroxydaidzein, **1**, 796
  2′,4′,7-trihydroxyisoflavone, **1**, 810

6,7,4′-trihydroxyisoflavone, **1**, 815

$C_{15}H_{10}O_6$
  2′-hydroxygenistein, **1**, 795, 800, 806, 807
  kaempferol, **1**, 726, 728, 731, 733, **8**, 163, 174
  luteolin, **1**, 328, 685, 724, **3**, 644, **8**, 173, 174

$C_{15}H_{10}O_7$
  6-hydroxykaempferol, **1**, 733
  morin, **1**, 722
  quercetin, **1**, 726, 731, 733, **8**, 160

$C_{15}H_{10}O_8$
  gossypetin, **1**, 733, **8**, 160
  myricetin, **1**, 731
  quercetagetin, **1**, 733, **8**, 159

$C_{15}H_{12}O_5$, 2′-hydroxydihydrodaidzein, **1**, 796

$C_{15}H_{11}ClO_5$, pelargonidin, **1**, 728, 730, 731, **8**, 158

$C_{15}H_{11}ClO_6$
  cyanidin, **1**, 728, 730, 731, **8**, 158, 164
  cyanidin 3-glycoside, **8**, 164

$C_{15}H_{11}ClO_7$, delphinidin, **1**, 728, 730 , 731, **8**, 158, 164

$C_{15}H_{11}D_9O_4$, nonadeutero-ABA, **8**, 91

$C_{15}H_{11}I_4NO_4$, thyroxine, **5**, 47

$C_{15}H_{11}N$, 2-phenylquinoline, **7**, 468

$C_{15}H_{11}N_3$, eudestomin, **8**, 525

$C_{15}H_{11}O$
  diphenylacryloyl, **7**, 120
  α-phenylcinnamoyl, **7**, 120, 123

$C_{15}H_{11}O_2$
  fluorenylmethoxycarbonyl, **7**, 120, 123
  9-fluorenylmethyloxycarbonyl, **6**, 84

$C_{15}H_{11}O_3$, benzoyloxymethylbenzoyl, **7**, 120

$C_{15}H_{11}O_4NO_4$, thyroxine, **2**, 25

$C_{15}H_{11}O_9S$, 3,4-dihydroxylstyrene dimer, **8**, 442

$C_{15}H_{12}BrN_3$, eudestomin derivative, **8**, 525

$C_{15}H_{12}BrN_3O$
  eudestomin derivative, **8**, 525
  eudistomidin A, **8**, 527

$C_{15}H_{12}O$, chalcone, **1**, 758

$C_{15}H_{12}O_3$
  6′-deoxychalcone, **1**, 763, 764
  licodione, **1**, 739, 794

$C_{15}H_{12}O_4$
  chalcone, **1**, 764
  dihydrodaidzein, **1**, 810
  3,9-dihydroxypterocarpan, **1**, 797, 802, 804
  emodinanthrone, **1**, 431
  isoliquiritigenin, **1**, 732, 781
  liquiritigenin, **1**, 19, 725, 790, 791, 793, **3**, 778
  pinocembrin, **1**, 724, 725, **8**, 181
  pinocembrin chalcone, **1**, 722
  quinone methide, **3**, 754
  2′,4,4′-trihydroxychalcone, **1**, 790, 793, 799

$C_{15}H_{12}O_5$
  butein, **1**, 732
  dihydroemodin, **1**, 430
  2′-hydroxydihydrodaidzein, **1**, 797
  naringenin, **1**, 722, 724, 725, 728, 790, 791, 793, 795, **8**, 174
  naringenin chalcone, **1**, 721, 723, 790, 793, 814
  pinobanksin, **1**, 726, 728
  rubrofusarin, **1**, 4, 419
  2′,4,4′,6′-tetrahydroxychalcone, **1**, 789
  3,6a,9-trihydroxypterocarpan, **1**, 802, 804

$C_{15}H_{12}O_6$
  dihydrokaempferol, **1**, 724, 725, 726, 727, 728
  eriodictyol, **1**, 724, 725, 728, 752, **8**, 173, 174
  2-hydroxyflavanone, **1**, 795
  2-hydroxyisoflavanone, **1**, 792
  2-hydroxynaringenin, **1**, 725
  quinone methide, **3**, 758

$C_{15}H_{12}O_7$
  dihydroquercetin, **1**, 685, 725, 727, 728, 740, **3**, 750, 760
  3′,4′,5,5′,7-pentahydroxyflavanone, **1**, 724, 725
  7,8,3′,4′-tetrahydroxydihydroflavonol, **3**, 750

$C_{15}H_{12}O_8$, dihydromyricetin, **1**, 725, 726, 727, 728
$C_{15}H_{12}O_{14}$, 3,4-flavandiol, **3**, 756
$C_{15}H_{13}Cl_6NO_4$, hexachloronorbornene, **5**, 429
$C_{15}H_{13}FeNO_4$, *N*-hydroxysuccinimide ester of
　　ferrocenecarboxylic acid, **7**, 166
$C_{15}H_{13}FO_2$, flurbiprofen, **5**, 247, 248
$C_{15}H_{13}NO$, *N*-2-acetylaminofluorene, **3**, 116
$C_{15}H_{13}NO_3$, 2-methoxycarbazole-3-methylcarboxylate, **4**,
　　54
$C_{15}H_{13}N_3$, eudestomin derivative, **8**, 525
$C_{15}H_{13}N_3O$, eudestomin derivative, **8**, 525
$C_{15}H_{13}N_3O_4S$, piroxicam, **5**, 248, 252
$C_{15}H_{14}BrN_4$, lissoclinC, **8**, 541
$C_{15}H_{14}ClNO_3$, zomepirac, **5**, 252
$C_{15}H_{14}O_3$, equol, **1**, 699, 782, 783, 815
$C_{15}H_{14}O_4$
　　deoxyafzelechin, **1**, 730
　　guibourtacidin ion, **3**, 754
　　lunularic acid, **1**, 765, **8**, 73
　　wyerone, **8**, 189
$C_{15}H_{14}O_5$
　　afzelechin, **1**, 730
　　apiforol, **1**, 728
　　5-deoxyflavan-3,4-diol, **3**, 753
　　5,7-dihydroxyflavan-3,4-diol, **1**, 730
　　flavan-3,4-diol, **3**, 753
　　3,4-flavandiol, **3**, 755
　　guibourtacidin, **3**, 754
　　leucorobinetinidin carbocation, **3**, 754
　　7-methoxyeriobofuran, **8**, 187
　　mollisacacidin analogue, **3**, 754
$C_{15}H_{14}O_6$
　　aflatoxin B_3, **1**, 444
　　catechin, **1**, 717, 729, **3**, 748, 752, 756, 758
　　catechin carbocation, **3**, 758
　　catechol, **3**, 408
　　α-cotonefuran, **8**, 187
　　β-cotonefuran, **8**, 187
　　δ-cotonefuran, **8**, 187
　　ε-cotonefuran, **8**, 187
　　τ-cotonefuran, **8**, 187
　　5-deoxyflavan-3,4-diol, **3**, 753
　　2,8-dihydroxy-3,4,7-trimethoxydibenzofuran, **8**, 187
　　epicatechin, **1**, 730, **3**, 748, 752
　　flanan-3-ol, **3**, 758
　　fonsecin, **1**, 419
　　leucopelargonidin, **1**, 730, **3**, 753
　　leucorobinetinidin carbocation, **3**, 754
　　luteoforol, **1**, 728
　　mollisacacidin, **3**, 754, 755
　　parasiticol, **1**, 444
　　τ-pyrufuran, **8**, 187
　　α-pyrufuran, **8**, 187
　　β-pyrufuran, **8**, 187
　　teracacidin, **3**, 753, 755
$C_{15}H_{14}O_7$
　　catechin-4α-ol, **3**, 750
　　5-deoxyflavan-3,4-diol, **3**, 753
　　epigallocatechin, **1**, 730
　　flavan-3,4-diol, **3**, 753, 757, 758
　　gallocatechin, **1**, 729, **3**, 752
　　6-hydroxy-α-pyrufuran, **8**, 187
　　leucocyanidin, **1**, 727, 729, 730, **3**, 753, 755, 756, 760
　　leucorobinetinidin, **3**, 753, 754
　　leucorobinetinidin carbocation, **3**, 754
　　melacacidin, **3**, 753
$C_{15}H_{14}O_8$
　　flavan-3,4-diol, **3**, 753
　　leucodelphinidin, **1**, 727, 729, 730, **3**, 753
$C_{15}H_{15}ClN_2O_6$, 4-*O*-(4-chlorophenyl)uridine, **6**, 94
$C_{15}H_{15}NO$, navenone A, **8**, 465
$C_{15}H_{15}NO_2$, mefenamic acid, **5**, 248
$C_{15}H_{15}NO_3$, ismine, **4**, 44

$C_{15}H_{16}BrN_3O_2S$, eudistomidin C, **8**, 527
$C_{15}H_{16}NO_4S$, 2-danzylethoxycarbonyl, **7**, 127
$C_{15}H_{16}N_2O_6S_2$, ticarcillin, **4**, 268
$C_{15}H_{16}N_4O_2$, phenazine *N*-oxide, **7**, 533
$C_{15}H_{16}O_2S$, α-(2-naphthylmethylsulfido)isobutyric acid, **8**,
　　36
$C_{15}H_{16}O_3$, gerberacoumarin, **1**, 625
$C_{15}H_{16}O_4$
　　cyperine, **8**, 180
　　8-deoxylactucin, **8**, 142
　　2′-methoxyaucuparin, **8**, 187
　　4′-methoxyaucuparin, **8**, 187
$C_{15}H_{16}O_5$
　　lactucin, **8**, 142
　　pentalenolactone, **2**, 168, 171, 373
　　pentalenolactone A, **2**, 172
　　pentalenolactone B, **2**, 172
　　pentalenolactone P, **2**, 172
$C_{15}H_{16}O_9$, sinapoyl malonate, **3**, 642
$C_{15}H_{17}BrN_2$, arborescidine A, **8**, 528
$C_{15}H_{17}Br_2ClO_2$, obtusallene, **1**, 304
$C_{15}H_{17}F_3O_4$, 8′,8′,8′-trifluoro-ABA, **8**, 91
$C_{15}H_{17}NO_3$, norbelladine, **4**, 43
$C_{15}H_{17}NO_7$
　　4-*O*-(indole-3-acetyl)-glucopyranose, **8**, 26
　　6-*O*-(indole-3-acetyl)-glucopyranose, **8**, 26
　　2-*O*-(indole-3-acetyl)-*myo*-inositol, **8**, 26
　　1-(indole-3-acetyl)-*myo*-inositol, **8**, 26
$C_{15}H_{17}N_3O_6$
　　FR900482, **7**, 514, 518
　　5-pyridylmethyluridine, **6**, 225
$C_{15}H_{18}$, 1(14),2,5(15),6-germacratetraene, **8**, 228
$C_{15}H_{18}F_2O_4$
　　7′-difluoro-ABA, **8**, 79
　　8′,8′-difluoro-ABA, **8**, 91
$C_{15}H_{18}N_2O_6$, *C*-5-(1-propynyl)-2′-*O*-allyluridine, **7**, 317
$C_{15}H_{18}N_2O_9$, tri-*O*-acetyluridine, **7**, 117
$C_{15}H_{18}N_4O_4$
　　cyclopropyl thymine photodimer, **5**, 380
　　thymine photodimer, **5**, 380
$C_{15}H_{18}N_4O_5$, mitomycin C, **7**, 514, 529
$C_{15}H_{18}O_2$, 2,7-dihydroxycadalene, **2**, 186, 188
$C_{15}H_{18}O_2S$, 2-(acetoxyphenyl)hept-2-ynyl sulfide, **5**,
　　253
$C_{15}H_{18}O_3$
　　ABA γ-lactone, **8**, 74
　　acetylenic aldehyde, **8**, 77
　　8-epixanthatin, **1**, 375
　　lacinilene C, **2**, 186, 188
　　α-santonin, **8**, 308
　　xanthipungolide, **1**, 375
　　xerantholide, **8**, 308
$C_{15}H_{18}O_4$
　　bipolaroxin, **8**, 179
　　5′β,9′-cyclo-ABA, **8**, 81
　　grossheimin, **8**, 308
　　helenalin, **7**, 503
　　parthenin , **8**, 142
$C_{15}H_{18}O_5$
　　chrysartemin A, **8**, 308
　　zinnolide, **8**, 179
$C_{15}H_{18}O_6$, rifamycin analogue, **1**, 528
$C_{15}H_{18}O_7$
　　bilobalide, **8**, 310, 308
　　rifamycin analogue, **1**, 528
$C_{15}H_{18}O_8$
　　p-coumaric acid D-glucose, **3**, 640
　　2′-hydroxicinnamic acid 2′-*O*-glucoside, **1**, 627
$C_{15}H_{19}Br_2ClO$
　　dactylyne, **1**, 303
　　isodactylyne, **1**, 303
$C_{15}H_{19}Br_3O_3$, obtusin, **1**, 303
$C_{15}H_{19}FO_3$, 1′-deoxy-1′-fluoro-ABA, **8**, 77

C₁₅H₁₉FO₄
    3'-fluoro-ABA, **8**, 91
    8'-monofluoro-ABA, **8**, 90
C₁₅H₁₉FO₅
    3'-fluoro-8'-hydroxy-ABA, **8**, 91
    fluorophaseic acid, **8**, 91
C₁₅H₁₉NO, paliclavine, **4**, 53
C₁₅H₁₉NO₆, rifamycin B tetraketide intermediate, **1**, 527
C₁₅H₁₉N₃O₅, *C*-5-(1-propynyl)-2'-*O*-allylcytosine, **7**, 322
C₁₅H₁₉N₃O₆
    FR66969, **7**, 518
    FR66979, **7**, 514
C₁₅H₁₉N₄O₄
    cyclopropyl thymine photodimer, **5**, 380
    methylcyclopropyl thymine photodimer, **5**, 380
C₁₅H₁₉N₅O₃, cyclo-(Arg-dehydrotyrosine), **8**, 442
C₁₅H₂₀
    laurencenyne, **1**, 304
    1-pentadecene, **8**, 216
C₁₅H₂₀BrClO
    isolaurepinnacin, **1**, 303
    obtusenyne, **1**, 304
C₁₅H₂₀BrClO₂
    dactomelyne, **1**, 303
    notoryne, **1**, 312
C₁₅H₂₀Br₂O₂
    bromo allene, **1**, 314
    bromo oxolane, **1**, 314, 317
    isolaurallene, **1**, 304
    isolaureatin, **1**, 304
    isoprelaurefucin, **1**, 303
    kumausallene, **1**, 303
    laurallene, **1**, 304
    laureatin, **1**, 304
    laureepoxide, **1**, 303
    laureoxanyne, **1**, 303
C₁₅H₂₀ClN₅O₄, Ro 15-0216, **7**, 609
C₁₅H₂₀N₂O
    anagyrine, **8**, 147, 154, 176
    tambjamineC, **8**, 472
C₁₅H₂₀N₂O₄, fusarochromanone, **8**, 178
C₁₅H₂₀N₄O₈S, *O*-carbamoyl-DAC, **4**, 164, 172
C₁₅H₂₀O, pheromone of *Periplaneta americana*, **8**, 2
C₁₅H₂₀O₂
    alantolactone, **8**, 308
    isopreiplanone-A, **8**, 40
    periplanone A, **8**, 41, 49, 227
    pinguisone, **8**, 312
C₁₅H₂₀O₃
    ABA-aldehyde, **8**, 72, 86
    ABA 1'-aldehyde, **8**, 77
    cichoralexin, **8**, 189
    cyercene 3, **8**, 462
    cyercene 5, **8**, 462
    1'-deoxy-ABA, **8**, 77, 87
    muzigadial, **8**, 308
    periplanone B, **8**, 227
    quadrone, **2**, 174
    sporogen-AO 1, **2**, 177, **8**, 408
    terrecyclic acid, **2**, 174
C₁₅H₂₀O₄
    abscisic acid, **1**, 126, 133, 781, **2**, 62, 327, **4**, 46, **8**, 21, 22, 72, 119
    coronopilin, **8**, 308
    dehydroalliacolide, **2**, 177
    phomenone, **8**, 179
C₁₅H₂₀O₅
    7'-hydroxy-ABA, **8**, 90
    8'-hydroxy-ABA, **8**, 89
    phaseic acid, **8**, 73, 89
C₁₅H₂₀O₆, T-2 toxin, **2**, 203
C₁₅H₂₀O₇
    p-coumaryl alcohol glucoside, **3**, 676

nivalenol, **2**, 158
    phyllanthurinolactone, **8**, 37
C₁₅H₂₀O₈
    2'-acetylsalicin, **8**, 155
    anisatin, **8**, 167
C₁₅H₂₁BrO₂
    deacetyllaurencin, **1**, 303
    oxetane, **1**, 316
    oxolane, **1**, 316
    prelaureatin, **1**, 304, 317
C₁₅H₂₁BrO₃
    laurefucin, **1**, 303
    laureoxolane, **1**, 303
C₁₅H₂₁NO₃, acetamidobenzylhydroxyhexanone, **5**, 439
C₁₅H₂₁NO₃S, diketide, **1**, 517
C₁₅H₂₁NO₆, GalNAcα-benzyl, **3**, 71
C₁₅H₂₁N₃O, primaquine, **3**, 92
C₁₅H₂₁I₂N₃O₁₁, TTX-8-*O*-hemisuccinate, **8**, 484
C₁₅H₂₁N₄Ni, NiCR, **7**, 89
C₁₅H₂₁N₄O₁₆P₃, 5-imidazole uridine, **6**, 139
C₁₅H₂₁N₅O₄, ipA ribotide, **8**, 69
C₁₅H₂₁N₅O₅, 9-riboxylzeatin, **8**, 61
C₁₅H₂₁N₅O₇S, cylindrospermopsin , **8**, 611
C₁₅H₂₁O₃, periplanone-B, **8**, 2
C₁₅H₂₂
    cuparene, **2**, 163
    neolaurencenyne, **1**, 304
C₁₅H₂₂N₂O₂, 13α-hydroxymultiflorine, **4**, 35
C₁₅H₂₂N₂O₁₆P₂, UDP-4-keto-6-deoxy-D-glucose, **3**, 508
C₁₅H₂₂N₂O₁₈P₂
    UDP-galacturonic acid, **3**, 512
    UDP-D-galacturonic acid, **3**, 505, 507
    UDP-glucuronic acid, **3**, 468, 479, 507, 508, 518, 608, 610, 612
    UDP-D-glucuronic acid, **3**, 505, 506, 606
C₁₅H₂₂N₆O₅S
    adenosylmethionine, **5**, 165, 185
    S-adenosylmethionine, **1**, 62, 332, 423, 827, 831, 848, **2**, 359, **3**, 543, 643, **4**, 98, 335, **5**, 207, 217, 316, **8**, 94, 394
    S-adenosyl-L-methionine, **3**, 342
C₁₅H₂₂N₆O₁₁P, guanidine derivatives, **7**, 419
C₁₅H₂₂O
    dendrolasin, **8**, 229
    isolavetivone, **2**, 183
    isoperiplanol-A, **8**, 48
    nootkatone, **8**, 165
    periplanone D, **8**, 228
C₁₅H₂₂O₂
    ancistrofuran, **8**, 229, 234
    bakkenolide A, **8**, 308
    12,13-epoxytrichothec-9-ene, **2**, 164
    EPT, **2**, 164
    α-ionylideneacetic acid, **8**, 33
    laurediol, **1**, 304, 310, 316, 319
    polygodial, **8**, 308, 462, 466
C₁₅H₂₂O₃
    ABA-alcohol, **8**, 86
    ABA 1'-alcohol, **8**, 77
    9,10;12,13-diepoxytrichothecodiene, **2**, 164
    dihydroterrecyclic acid, **2**, 175
    1',2'-epoxy-β-ionylideneacetic acid, **8**, 86
    gemfibrozil, **2**, 259
    4'-hydroxy-α-ionylideneacetic acid, **8**, 87
    4'-hydroxy-β-ionylideneacetic acid, **8**, 86
    4'-hydroxy-γ-ionylideneacetic acid, **8**, 87
    ipomeamarone, **2**, 191
    pentalenic acid, **2**, 168, 171
    tricyclic sesquiterpene, **2**, 172
    warburganal, **8**, 308
    xanthoxin, **8**, 72
C₁₅H₂₂O₄
    ABA diol, **8**, 86, 87

alliacolide, **2**, 176
apo-9′-fucoxanthinone, **8**, 628
2′,3′-dihydro-ABA, **8**, 79
1′,4′-dihydroxy-γ-ionylideneacetic acid, **8**, 87
sambucinol, **2**, 203
xanthoxin acid, **8**, 87
C₁₅H₂₂O₅
dihydrophaseic acid, **8**, 74, 89
ovalicin, **2**, 165
C₁₅H₂₂O₆, 5′-hydroxydihydrophaseic acid, **8**, 89
C₁₅H₂₂O₉, aucubin , **8**, 152, 155, 307
C₁₅H₂₂O₁₀, catalpol, **8**, 155, 162, 307
C₁₅H₂₃ClO₂S, 2,4,6-triisopropylbenzenesulfonyl chloride, **7**, 107
C₁₅H₂₃N, polygodial pyrrole derivative, **8**, 466
C₁₅H₂₃NO₂, acetonide, **1**, 310
C₁₅H₂₃NO₃, castoramin, **8**, 229
C₁₅H₂₃NO₄, cycloheximide , **1**, 129, **8**, 97
C₁₅H₂₃N₃O, lysylphenylalanine, **7**, 464
C₁₅H₂₃N₃O₁₄P₂
CDP-3,6-dideoxy-D-*glycero*-D-*glycero*-4-hexulose, **3**, 336, 341
CDP-3,6-dideoxy-D-*glycero*-L-*glycero*-4-hexulose, **3**, 336
CDP-4-keto-3,6-dideoxyglucose, **3**, 208, 209
C₁₅H₂₃N₃O₁₅P₂
CDP-6-deoxy-L-*threo*-D-*glycero*-4-he xulose, **3**, 336, 349
CDP-4-keto-6-deoxyglucose, **3**, 336
C₁₅H₂₃N₃O₁₆P₂,CDP-D-glucose, **3**, 336
C₁₅H₂₃N₅O₄, N₆-isopentenyladenosine, **4**, 361
C₁₅H₂₃N₅O₄P, 9-riboxyl-ipA 5′-phosphate, **8**, 62
C₁₅H₂₃N₅O₁₁P₂, 9-riboxylzeatin 5′-phosphate, **8**, 61
C₁₅H₂₄
5-*epi*-aristolochene, **2**, 181
aristolochene, **2**, 5, 177, 194, 196, 202, 205
bergamotene, **2**, 165
bisabolene, **2**, 164
α-bisabolene, **2**, 162, **8**, 228
β-bisabolene, **2**, 162
α-bulnesene, **2**, 184
cadinene, **2**, 177
δ-cadinene, **2**, 186
caryophyllene, **2**, 167
α-cedrene, **2**, 191
cubenene, **2**, 191
α-cubebene, **8**, 228
cuprenene, **2**, 162
erythrodiene, **8**, 470
7-ethyl-3,5-dimethyl-2,4,6,8-undecatetraene, **8**, 240
eudesmane, **2**, 5
farnesene, **8**, 269
β-farnesene, **2**, 162, **8**, 144, 227
germacrene A, **2**, 5, 177, 179, 183, **2**, 186, 180, **8**, 227
α-guaiene, **2**, 184
humulene, **2**, 167, 196
β-humulene, **8**, 144
isochamigrene, **2**, 162
τ-muurolene, **8**, 144
patchoulene, **2**, 184
pentalenene, **2**, 168, 169
β-selinene, **2**, 185
terpenoid, **8**, 438
α-terrecyclene, **2**, 176
trichodiene, **2**, 158, 193, 202, 212
zingiberene, **8**, 142
C₁₅H₂₄N₂O
lupanine, **8**, 176
matrine, **4**, 33
C₁₅H₂₄N₂O₂, 13α-hydroxylupanine, **4**, 35
C₁₅H₂₄N₂O₄S, penicillinH, **4**, 262
C₁₅H₂₄N₂O₁₆P₂
UDP-rhamnose, **3**, 333
UDP-L-rhamnose, **3**, 505, 508

C₁₅H₂₄N₂O₁₇P₂
UDP-galactose, **3**, 174, 203, 288, 468, 478, 510, 515, 521
UDP-D-galactose, **3**, 505, 508
UDP-α-galactose, **3**, 109
UDP-glucose, **3**, 7, 174, 203, 225, 333, 444, 445, 452, 467, 468, 478, 479, 480, 482, 483, 487, 506, 508, 581, 603, 608, 612, 805
UDP-D-glucose, **3**, 508, **5**, 280
C₁₅H₂₄N₂O₁₇P₂,UDP-mannose, **3**, 478
C₁₅H₂₄N₃O₃
4′-demethylamphikuemin, **8**, 429
N-demethylamphikuemin, **8**, 429
C₁₅H₂₄N₃O₁₅P₂,CDP-fucose, **3**, 336
C₁₅H₂₄N₃O₁₆P₂,CDP-D-glucose, **3**, 337
C₁₅H₂₄N₆O₁₅P₂, 8-azido-ADPGlc, **3**, 448
C₁₅H₂₄O
acanthodoral, **2**, 192
caryophyllene epoxide, **8**, 142
caryophyllene α-oxide, **8**, 312
caryophyllene oxide, **8**, 228, 312
1-deoxycapsidiol, **2**, 182
farnesal, **8**, 227, 267
15-hydroxytrichodiene, **2**, 212, 213
α-ionylideneethanol, **8**, 87
isoacanthodoral, **2**, 192
nanimoal, **2**, 192
nomadone, **8**, 227
C₁₅H₂₄O₂
capsidiol, **2**, 1, 179, 182, 212
12,13-dihydrolaurediol, **1**, 304
12,13-epoxy-9,10-trichoene-2-ol, **2**, 164, 181
sesquiterpene, **8**, 466
sesquiterpene dialdehyde, **8**, 466
sesquiterpene peroxide, **8**, 439
supellapyrone, **8**, 241
2,4,5-tetradecatrienoate, **8**, 216
C₁₅H₂₄O₃
β-alkoxy aldehyde, **1**, 310
isotrichodiol, **2**, 164
phomodiol, **1**, 370
9β-trichodiol, **2**, 164
tricyclic sesquiterpene, **2**, 172
C₁₅H₂₄O₄, isotrichotriol, **2**, 164
C₁₅H₂₅
eudesmane cation, **2**, 183, 185
eudesmane intermediate, **2**, 181
helminthogermacradienyl cation, **2**, 187
C₁₅H₂₅F₃O₇P₂, trifluoro-FPP, **5**, 332
C₁₅H₂₅NS, sesquiterpene, **8**, 439
C₁₅N₂₅NO₅
echinatine, **4**, 31
rinderine, **4**, 31
C₁₅H₂₅N₃O₁₄P₂
CDP-abequose, **3**, 336
CDP-D-abequose, **3**, 347
CDP-ascarylose, **3**, 336
CDP-L-ascarylose, **3**, 336
CDP-paratose, **3**, 347
CDP-tyvelose, **3**, 347
C₁₅H₂₅N₃O₁₅P₂,
CDP-6-deoxy-D-glucose, **3**, 209
C₁₅H₂₅N₃O₁₆P₂,CDP-glucose, **3**, 452, 478, 481
C₁₅H₂₅N₄O₅P, bisphosphoramidite, **7**, 133
C₁₅H₂₆
betispiradiene, **2**, 183
δ-cadinene, **8**, 228
6,7-dihydrogermacrene, **2**, 180
2,6,10-trimethyldodecatriene, **2**, 355
vetispiradiene, **2**, 194
C₁₅H₂₆F₂O₇P₂, difluoro-FPP, **5**, 332
C₁₅H₂₆N₂, sparteine, **4**, 33
C₁₅H₂₆N₄O₈, Ala-Glu-*m*-DAP, **3**, 271

$C_{15}H_{26}O$
  α-bisabolene oxide, **8**, 228
  α-bisabolol, **2**, 355
  cadinol, **8**, 228,
  caparrapioxide, **8**, 229
  caparrapi oxide, **8**, 234
  drimenol, **8**, 308
  epicubenol, **2**, 189
  farnesol, **2**, 8, 156, 310, 355, **8**, 161, 227, 267
  lubimin, **2**, 179, 183
  nerolidol, **2**, 355, **8**, 227
  patchoulol, **2**, 184
  pheromone of *Matsucoccus feytaudi*, **8**, 47
  trichothecene, **2**, 163
  3,7,9-trimethyl-8,10-dodecadien-6-one, **8**, 244
$C_{15}H_{26}O_2$, hydroxylubimin, **2**, 183
$C_{15}H_{26}O_3$, trichothecolone, **2**, 164
$C_{15}H_{26}O_4$, dihydroxyfarnesoic acid, **8**, 274
$C_{15}H_{26}O_6$
  isotrichermol, **2**, 164
  tributyrin, **5**, 134
$C_{15}H_{27}BrO_3$
  hexahydrolaurefucin, **1**, 312
  laurediol, **1**, 312
$C_{15}H_{27}CoN_5O_4$,
  anilinomethylbis(dimethylglyoxime)cobalt, **5**, 266
$C_{15}H_{27}FO_7P_2$, fluoro-FPP, **2**, 160, **5**, 332
$C_{15}H_{27}N$, farnesylamine, **5**, 333
$C_{15}H_{27}NO_4$, viridiflorine, **4**, 31
$C_{15}H_{27}N_2OP$, bisphosphoramidite, **7**, 133
$C_{15}H_{28}N_2$, N-(1-n-dodecyl)-imidazole, **2**, 292
$C_{15}H_{28}N_2O_2$
  caprolactin A, **8**, 595
  caprolactin B, **8**, 595
$C_{15}H_{28}N_4O_6$,Ro 15-0216, **7**, 603
$C_{15}H_{28}N_8O$, sperminehypoxanthine, **7**, 326
$C_{15}H_{28}O$
  dihydrofarnesol, **2**, 161
  2,3-dihydrofarnesol, **8**, 227, 229
  dihydronerolidol, **2**, 161
  6,9-pentadecadienol, **1**, 101
$C_{15}H_{28}O_2$
  7-dodecenyl propanoate, **8**, 207
  1-methyl-9-dodecenyl acetate, **8**, 215
  2-methylethyl dodecenoate, **8**, 215
  moth sex pheromone, **8**, 209
  10-pentadecenoic acid, **8**, 207
  5-tetradecenoate, **8**, 216,
  8-tridecenyl acetate, **8**, 207
  3,7,11-trimethyl-2,10-dodecadien-1,7-diol, **8**, 227
$C_{15}H_{28}O_3$, 7-methoxytetradec-4enoic acid, **8**, 607
$C_{15}H_{28}O_7P_2$
  farnesyl diphosphate, **2**, 7, 8, 9, 38, 46, 62, 70, 74, 118,
    156, 196, 201, 246, 313, 331, 340, 358, 380, 389, 392,
    3, 262, **5**, 318
  nerolidyl diphosphate, **2**, 8, 157, 159, 187, 193, **5**, 329
$C_{15}H_{29}BrO_2$
  bromo ether, **1**, 308, 310
  oxolane, **1**, 318
$C_{15}H_{29}F_6N_2OP$, bisphosphoramidite, **7**, 133
$C_{15}H_{29}N$, monomorine III, **8**, 216
$C_{15}H_{30}$, 1-pentadecene, **8**, 217
$C_{15}H_{30}F_3N_2O_3P$, phosphoramidite, **7**, 154
$C_{15}H_{30}N_6O$, C-5-methyl-C-N-4-spermine cytosine, **7**, 322
$C_{15}H_{30}N_6O$, 2-pentadecanone, **8**, 216
$C_{15}H_{30}O_2$
  1-methyldodecyl acetate, **8**, 215
  10-methyldodecyl acetate, **8**, 246
  2-methylethyl dodecanoate, **8**, 215
  nerolidol derivative, **8**, 227
  pentadecanoic acid, **1**, 48
  9-pentadecene-6,7-diol, **1**, 307, 318
  12-pentadecene-6,7-diol, **1**, 308

pheromone of *Adoxophyes* sp., **8**, 48
$C_{15}H_{30}O_3$
  3-hydroxy-13-methyltetradecanoic acid, **4**, 208
  3,7,11-trimethyl-2-dodecen-1,7,11-triol, **8**, 227
$C_{15}H_{30}O_7P_2$
  6,7-dihydrofarnesyl diphosphate, **2**, 160, 180, **5**, 329
  6,7-dihydro-NPP, **2**, 161
$C_{15}H_{30}O_{10}$,
  3,6-dideoxy-4-C-(1,3-dimethoxy-4,5,6,7-
    tetrahydroxyheptyl)-D-xylo-hexose, **3**, 312
$C_{15}H_{32}$, pentadecane, **8**, 216
$C_{15}H_{32}N_3OP$, bisphosphoramidite, **7**, 133
$C_{15}H_{32}O$, 1,2,6-trimethyldodecanol, **8**, 247
$C_{15}H_{33}N_2OP$, bisphosphoramidite, **7**, 133
$C_{15}H_{33}N_8O_9PS$, phaseolotoxin, **4**, 203
$C_{15}H_{34}BrN$, dodecyltrimethylammonium bromide, **2**, 311
$C_{15}H_{35}N_2O_3PS$, bisphosphoramidite, **7**, 133
$C_{15}H_{40}O_2$, lardolure, **8**, 40, 209
$C_{15}H_{25}NS$, sesquiterpene, **8**, 439
$C_{15}O_{24}$, trichodiene, **2**, 203
$C_{16}C_{25}N$, sesquiterpene, **8**, 439
$C_{16}H_{10}$
  biphenyl, **6**, 118
  pyrene, **7**, 49
$C_{16}H_{10}N_2O_2$
  N-9-acridinylmaleimide, **7**, 167
  indigo, **4**, 211
$C_{16}H_{10}O_5$
  9-O-methylcoumestrol, **1**, 810
  pseudobaptigenin, **1**, 802
$C_{16}H_{10}O_5$, 5-hydroxy-6,7-methylenedioxyflavone, **8**, 175
$C_{16}H_{10}O_6$
  DMAC, **1**, 484
  hydroxypseudobaptigenin, **1**, 682
  2′-hydroxypseudobaptigenin, **1**, 665, 796
  5′-hydroxypseudobaptigenin, **1**, 802
$C_{16}H_{11}F_3O$, 2,2,2-trifluoro-1-(9-anthryl)ethanol, **8**, 270
$C_{16}H_{11}NO_4$, avenalumin, **8**, 189
$C_{16}H_{12}ClNO_3$, benoxaprofen, **1**, 294
$C_{16}H_{12}Cl_2O_7$, desmethyldihydrogeodin, **1**, 435
$C_{16}H_{12}N_4O$
  xestomanzamine A, **8**, 558
  xestomanzamine B, **8**, 558
$C_{16}H_{12}O_4$
  (dihydroxyphenyl)dihydroxynaphthalene, **8**, 442
  formononetin, **1**, 774, 780, 782, 786, 795, 799, 802, 808,
    809, 810, 812
  isoformononetin, **1**, 799
  7-methoxy-4′-hydroxyflavone, **8**, 17
$C_{16}H_{12}O_5$
  3-arylcoumarin, **1**, 786
  biochanin A, **1**, 780, 783, 791, 795, 799, 808, 813, **8**, 175
  calycosin, **1**, 795, 802
  7,4′-dihydroxy-3′-methoxyflavone, **8**, 173
  7,2′-dihydroxy-4′-methoxyisoflav-3-en-2-one, **1**, 810
  6,7-dihydroxy-4′-methoxyisoflavone, **1**, 809
  glycitein, **1**, 806, 815
  2′-hydroxyformononetin, **1**, 795, 796
  maackiain, **1**, 786, 795, 796, 797, 802, 803, 808, 814, **8**,
    192, 193
  5-O-methylgenistein, **1**, 800
  prunetin, **1**, 799, **8**, 175
  questin, **1**, 433
  vestitione, **1**, 795, 796
  vestitone, **1**, 797, 798
  xenognisin B, **8**, 175
$C_{16}H_{12}O_6$
  chrysoeriol, **3**, 644
  2′-hydroxybiochanin A, **1**, 795
  6a-hydroxymaackiain, **1**, 786, 800, 803, **8**, 192, 193
  1a-hydroxypterocarp-1,4-dien-3-one, **1**, 814
  kalafungin, **1**, 478
  pratensin, **1**, 795, 802, 809

sophorol, **1**, 665, 796, 803
$C_{16}H_{12}O_7$, tamarixetin, **1**, 740
$C_{16}H_{12}O_8$, patuletin, **1**, 740
$C_{16}H_{12}O_{12}S_2$, 3,4-dihydroxylstyrene dimer, **8**, 442
$C_{16}H_{13}ClO_6$, peonidin, **8**, 158
$C_{16}H_{13}ClO_7$, petunidin, **8**, 159, 164
$C_{16}H_{13}F_2NO_3S_2$, L-745,337, **5**, 252
$C_{16}H_{13}F_2NO_4S$, flosulide, **5**, 252
$C_{16}H_{13}NO_7$, 5-(3-carboxypropanamide)xanthotoxin, **3**, 647
$C_{16}H_{13}O_9P$, glucose-1-phosphate, **3**, 448
$C_{16}H_{14}ClN_3O_3$, dibenzoxazepine derivative, **1**, 192
$C_{16}H_{14}O_4$
  7,2′-dihydroxy-4′-methoxyisoflav-3-ene, **1**, 810
  isoflav-3-ene, **1**, 786
  medicarpin, **1**, 774, 777, 780, 786, 795, 796, 797, 798, 799, 802, 807, 808, 809, 812
$C_{16}H_{14}O_5$
  2′-hydroxyisoflavan, **1**, 814
  4-methoxychalcone, **1**, 385
  sakuranetin, **1**, 131, **8**, 181, 189
$C_{16}H_{14}O_6$
  hesperitin, **8**, 174
  mopanol, **3**, 754
  mutactin, **1**, 484
  peltogynol, **3**, 754
$C_{16}H_{14}O_7$
  desmethylsulochrin, **1**, 434, 435
  SEK4, **1**, 484, 488
  SEK4b, **1**, 484, 488
  SEK34, **1**, 484
$C_{16}H_{15}BrN_2O$, eudistalbin B, **8**, 528
$C_{16}H_{15}ClN_4O_5$, 6-*O*-(4-chlorophenyl)inosine, **6**, 94
$C_{16}H_{15}ClO_6$, griseofulvin, **1**, 437
$C_{16}H_{15}NO_4$, *N*-benzoylphenylisoserine, **2**, 222
$C_{16}H_{16}BrN_3OS$
  eudistomidin D, **8**, 527
  eudistomidin F, **8**, 527
$C_{16}H_{16}BrN_3O_2S$, eudistomidinE, **8**, 527
$C_{16}H_{16}N_3O_{11}P$, uridine 3′-(*p*-nitrophenyl phosphate), **6**, 95
$C_{16}H_{16}N_4O_4S$, 5-aminodansyluridine, **7**, 316
$C_{16}H_{16}O_3$, isopropyldihydrofuranocoumarin, **1**, 19
$C_{16}H_{16}O_3$, xenognisin A, **8**, 175
$C_{16}H_{16}O_4$
  anisoin, **3**, 395
  dimethoxybenzoin, **7**, 129
  vestitol, **1**, 774, 786, 812
$C_{16}H_{16}O_5$
  7,2′-dihydroxy-4′-methoxyisoflavanol, **1**, 797
  shikonin, **4**, 48
$C_{16}H_{16}O_7$, 6-methoxy-α-pyrufuran, **8**, 187
$C_{16}H_{16}O_8$, 7-hydroxy-6-methoxy-α-pyrufuran, **8**, 187
$C_{16}H_{17}BrN_2$, arborescidine B, **8**, 528
$C_{16}H_{17}KN_2O_4S$, penicillin, **1**, 466, **3**, 266, 283
$C_{16}H_{17}NO_3$
  crinine, **4**, 43
  norcoclaurine, **4**, 39, 41
$C_{16}H_{17}N_2NaO_4S$, penicillin, **4**, 197, 199, 200, 201
$C_{16}H_{17}N_3O_4$, anthramycin, **1**, 566, **7**, 497
$C_{16}H_{17}N_3O_4S$, cephalexin, **4**, 180
$C_{16}H_{17}N_3O_6$, *N*-benzoylcytidine, **6**, 85
$C_{16}H_{17}N_4$, lycorine, **4**, 43
$C_{16}H_{17}N_5$, DAPI, **7**, 456
$C_{16}H_{18}BrN_3$, eudistalbin A, **8**, 528
$C_{16}H_{18}BrN_3O_4S$, eudestomin, **8**, 525
$C_{16}H_{18}Cl_3N_3O_7S$, 2,3,5-trichloro-6-*S*-glutathionylhydroquinone, **5**, 415
$C_{16}H_{18}FN_3O_3$, norfloxacin, **7**, 462
$C_{16}H_{18}N_2$, agroclavine, **4**, 51
$C_{16}H_{18}N_2O$
  elymoclavine, **4**, 51
  lysergol, **8**, 148

$C_{16}H_{18}N_2O_4S$
  benzylpenicillin, **4**, 240, 243, 244
  penicillin G, **3**, 283, **4**, 164, 170, 182
$C_{16}H_{18}N_2O_5S$
  penicillin V, **4**, 164, 170, 180
  penicillin X, **4**, 264
$C_{16}H_{18}N_3O_5S$, phenoxymethylpenicillin, **4**, 254
$C_{16}H_{18}N_3O_7$, 5-pyridylmethylcarboxamidouridine, **6**, 92
$C_{16}H_{18}O_8$, 4-methylumb3elliferyl β-D-glucoside, **3**, 686
$C_{16}H_{18}O_8$, 1-caffeoyl-4-deoxyquinic acid, **8**, 140
$C_{16}H_{18}O_9$, chlorogenic acid, **1**, 786, **3**, 633, 805, 807, 820, **8**, 139, 140, 146, 155,
$C_{16}H_{19}BrN_2O$
  arborescidine C, **8**, 528
  arborescidine D, **8**, 528
$C_{16}H_{19}Br_2N_5O_4$, aerophobin-2, **8**, 468
$C_{16}H_{19}Cl_2N_3O_7S$, dichloro-*S*-glutathionylhydroquinone, **5**, 415
$C_{16}H_{19}IN_4O_6$
  thymine dimer, **5**, 376
  thymine photodimer, **5**, 376
$C_{16}H_{19}NO_3$, β-erythroidine, **4**, 43
$C_{16}H_{19}NO_4$, galanthine, **4**, 43
$C_{16}H_{19}N_2O_9S$, glucobrassicin, **8**, 155
$C_{16}H_{19}N_3O_4S$
  ampicillin, **3**, 285, **7**, 664, 665
  cephradine, **4**, 180
$C_{16}H_{19}N_3O_5S$, *p*-nitrophenyl ester of biotin, **7**, 154
$C_{16}H_{19}N_4O_6$, thymine dimer, **5**, 376
$C_{16}H_{20}N_2$, benzathine, **4**, 240
$C_{16}H_{20}N_2O$
  chanoclavine, **4**, 51
  isochrysohermidine, **7**, 503
$C_{16}H_{20}N_2O_2$, dimethylallyltryptophan, **4**, 52
$C_{16}H_{20}N_2O_3$, 4-[4′-hydroxy-3′-methylbut-2′-enyl]tryptophan, **4**, 52
$C_{16}H_{20}N_2O_4$, tomaymicin, **1**, 567
$C_{16}H_{20}N_2O_7S$, glucobrassin, **8**, 26
$C_{16}H_{20}N_2O_8$, *p*-nitrophenyl ester of *N,N*-bis(ethoxycarbonylmethyl)glycine, **7**, 164
$C_{16}H_{20}N_2O_8S$
  4-hydroxyglucobrassin, **8**, 26
  5-hydroxyglucobrassin, **8**, 26
$C_{16}H_{20}N_2O_{10}S_2$, 1-sulfoglucobrassin, **8**, 26
$C_{16}H_{20}N_4O_2$, tolypin, **1**, 534
$C_{16}H_{20}O_2$, cornexistin, **8**, 181
$C_{16}H_{20}O_3$
  ABA analogue, **8**, 77
  acetonide, **1**, 310
$C_{16}H_{20}O_3$, 14-hydroxycornexistin, **8**, 181
$C_{16}H_{20}O_5$
  curvularin, **8**, 601
  shikonin, **2**, 121
$C_{16}H_{21}BrO_3$, kumausyne, **1**, 303
$C_{16}H_{21}NO_6$, 13-*O*-acetyldicrotaline, **4**, 33
$C_{16}H_{21}N_3O_8S$
  cephalosporin, **2**, 208, **4**, 197, 200, 201
  cephalosporin C, **3**, 285, **4**, 160, 171, 172, 179, 240
$C_{16}H_{21}N_4O_{16}P_3$, 5-pyridylmethylcarboxamiduridine, **6**, 139
$C_{16}H_{22}N_2O_3S$, phenylacetylcysteinylvaline, **4**, 252
$C_{16}H_{22}N_3O_{15}P$, CMP-DHA, **3**, 505
$C_{16}H_{22}N_4O_9S$, cephamycin C, **4**, 164, 171, 173, 180
$C_{16}H_{22}O$
  7-methoxy-1,2-dihydrocadalenene, **2**, 188
  sporochnol A, **8**, 461
$C_{16}H_{22}O_2$
  sporochnol B, **8**, 461
  sporochnol C, **8**, 461
$C_{16}H_{22}O_3$
  cyercene A, **8**, 462
  versiol, **1**, 370

C$_{16}$H$_{22}$O$_4$
ABA methyl ester, **8**, 73
1′-*O*-methyl-ABA, **8**, 79
oncorhyncolide, **8**, 596

C$_{16}$H$_{22}$O$_5$
8′-methoxy-ABA, **8**, 89, 91
phaseic acid methyl ester, **8**, 75
14,15-secocurvularin, **8**, 601

C$_{16}$H$_{22}$O$_8$
coniferin, **3**, 676, 677, 703, 717
isoconiferin, **3**, 677, 683

C$_{16}$H$_{23}$NO, dehydroprenylhordenine, **1**, 369

C$_{16}$H$_{23}$NO$_4$, yamataimine, **4**, 33

C$_{16}$H$_{23}$NO$_6$, monocrotaline, **4**, 32, **7**, 518

C$_{16}$H$_{23}$N$_5$O$_5$
9-*β*-D-glucopyranosylzeatin, **8**, 62
O-*β*-D-glucopyranosylzeatin, **8**, 62
7-*β*-D-glucosylzeatin, **8**, 62

C$_{16}$H$_{23}$N$_5$O$_6$
7-glucosylzeatin, **8**, 61
9-glucosylzeatin, **8**, 61

C$_{16}$H$_{23}$N$_5$O$_{15}$P$_2$
GDP-4-keto-6-deoxy-L-galactose, **3**, 509
GDP-4-keto-6-deoxy-D-mannose, **3**, 208, 509

C$_{16}$H$_{24}$, germacrone, **8**, 142

C$_{16}$H$_{24}$N$_4$O$_3$S, 5-tris(2-aminoethyl)amino-1-naphthalenesulfonic acid, **7**, 178

C$_{16}$H$_{24}$O$_2$, hexadeca-4,7,10,13-tetraenoic acid, **1**, 304

C$_{16}$H$_{24}$O$_3$
dehydrojuvabione, **8**, 276
17-deoxysolanapyrone B, **1**, 396

C$_{16}$H$_{24}$O$_4$
brefeldin, **1**, 422
brefeldin A, **1**, 450, **3**, 88, 94, 96
cyclopentanoid, **1**, 231

C$_{16}$H$_{24}$O$_5$
dihydrophaseic acid methyl ester, **8**, 74
hymenovin, **7**, 503

C$_{16}$H$_{24}$O$_9$
7-deoxyloganic acid, **4**, 113
loganic acid, **2**, 106

C$_{16}$H$_{24}$O$_{10}$, loganic acid, **4**, 113

C$_{16}$H$_{25}$N
sesquiterpene, **8**, 439
sesquiterpene isocyanide, **8**, 439

C$_{16}$H$_{25}$NO, echinacein, **8**, 303

C$_{16}$H$_{25}$NS
sesquiterpene, **8**, 439
terpenoid, **8**, 438

C$_{16}$H$_{25}$N$_2$O$_4$S, penicillin K, **4**, 262, 264

C$_{16}$H$_{25}$N$_5$O$_{12}$P$_2$, 9-glucosylzeatin 6′-phosphate, **8**, 61

C$_{16}$H$_{25}$N$_5$O$_{14}$P$_2$, deoxy-ADP-glucose, **3**, 452

C$_{16}$H$_{25}$N$_5$O$_{15}$P$_2$
ADP-glucose, **3**, 7, 444, 445, 448, 452, 453, 454, 455, 457, 462, 465, 468, 470, 475, 481, 482
GDP-fucose, **3**, 207, 208, 333, 335, 516, 517
GDP-L-fucose, **3**, 505, 509
GDP-*β*-fucose, **3**, 114
GDP-Rha, **3**, 208

C$_{16}$H$_{25}$N$_5$O$_{16}$P$_2$
ADP-L-*glycero*-D-*manno*-heptose, **3**, 222
GDP-glucose, **3**, 452, 478, 481
GDP-D-glucose, **3**, 606
GDP-mannose, **3**, 207, 288, 333, 521, 612
GDP-D-mannose, **3**, 509, 606

C$_{16}$H$_{26}$
5,7-diethyl-3-methyl-2,4,6,8-undecatetraene, **8**, 240
homofarnesene, **8**, 269
1-methylcyclohexane, **8**, 237

C$_{16}$H$_{26}$K$_4$O$_6$P$_2$, bisphosphonate, **2**, 258

C$_{16}$H$_{26}$N$_2$O$_4$S, penicillin K, **4**, 162

C$_{16}$H$_{26}$N$_2$O$_{15}$P$_2$
dTDP-6-deoxy-L-altrose, **3**, 346

dTDP-6-deoxy-D-*xylo*-4-hexulose, **3**, 208
dTDP-6-deoxy-L-talose, **3**, 335
dTDP-dihydrostreptose, **3**, 353
dTDP-rhamnose, **3**, 208, 333, 335, 346

C$_{16}$H$_{26}$N$_2$O$_{16}$P$_2$
dTDP-glucose, **3**, 208, 333
TDP-glucose, **3**, 452, 478, 481

C$_{16}$H$_{26}$N$_3$O$_3$, amphikuemin, **8**, 429

C$_{16}$H$_{26}$O$_2$
apotrichothecene, **2**, 203
C16:3, **1**, 340
hexadeca-4,7,10-trienoic acid, **1**, 304
hexadeca-7,10,13-trienoic acid, **1**, 37, 41, 44
7,15-hexadecadien-4-olide, **8**, 217
7,10,13-hextrienoic acid, **1**, 231
8,11,14-hexatrienoic acid, **1**, 231
monoaic acid, **1**, 68

C$_{16}$H$_{26}$O$_3$
8,11,14-hexatrienoic acid, **1**, 231
juvabione, **8**, 276,
juvenile hormone III, **5**, 55, **8**, 43, 268
methyl 10,11-epoxyfarnesoate, **8**, 267

C$_{16}$H$_{26}$O$_4$, juvenile hormone III bisepoxide, **8**, 269

C$_{16}$H$_{27}$NO, terpenoid, **8**, 438

C$_{16}$H$_{27}$NO$_4$, PAI-1, **8**, 398

C$_{16}$H$_{28}$B$_{10}$N$_2$O$_7$, pyrimidine nucleoside, **7**, 221

C$_{16}$H$_{28}$N$_2$O$_{11}$
GlcNAcβ1-4GlcNAc, **3**, 58
N,*N*′-diacetylchitobiose, **3**, 143

C$_{16}$H$_{28}$O
farnesyl methyl ether, **8**, 267
homofarnesol, **2**, 310

C$_{16}$H$_{28}$O$_2$
C16:2, **1**, 340
geranyl hexanoate, **8**, 223
hexadeca-7,10-dienoic acid, **1**, 37, 41
10,12-hexadecadienoic acid, **8**, 205
hydnocarpic acid, **1**, 68
isoculmorin, **8**, 601
9,11-tetradecadienyl acetate, **8**, 205

C$_{16}$H$_{28}$O$_3$, silphiny-2α-yl mesylate, **2**, 176

C$_{16}$H$_{28}$O$_5$, cyclopentanoid, **1**, 231

C$_{16}$H$_{28}$O$_7$P$_2$, 12-methylidene-FPP, **2**, 181

C$_{16}$H$_{29}$NO, herculin, **8**, 303

C$_{16}$H$_{29}$NO$_2$Sn, stannoxane, **4**, 33

C$_{16}$H$_{29}$NO$_4$, *erythro*-monopivaloate, **8**, 551

C$_{16}$H$_{29}$N$_2$OP, bisphosphoramidite, **7**, 133

C$_{16}$H$_{29}$N$_3$O$_{14}$S$_2$
bulgecin, **5**, 297
bulgecin A , **3**, 270, 285

C$_{16}$H$_{30}$N$_7$O$_{13}$P$_3$, 8-(6-aminohexylamino)adenosine 5′-triphosphate, **7**, 198

C$_{16}$H$_{30}$O
bombykol, **8**, 3, 4, 205
9-hexadecenal, **8**, 205
11-hexadecenal, **8**, 205

C$_{16}$H$_{30}$O$_2$
C16:1, **1**, 340
ω-cycloheptylnonoate, **1**, 75
dihydrohydnocarpic acid, **1**, 68
3-dodecenyl 2-butenoate, **8**, 214
7-dodecenyl butyrate, **8**, 207
5-hexadecanolide, **8**, 217
hexadecanolide, **8**, 231
11-hexadecenoic acid, **8**, 205, 207
hexadec-3-enoic acid, **1**, 37
hexadec-6-enoic acid, **1**, 42
hexadec-7-enoic acid, **1**, 40
hexadec-9-enoic acid, **1**, 46
palmitoleic acid, **1**, 49
4-tetradecenyl acetate, **8**, 207
9-tetradecenyl acetate, **8**, 199, 207
11-tetradecenyl acetate, **8**, 205

C₁₆H₃₀O₅P₂, FPP analogue, **2**, 251, 254
C₁₆H₃₀O₆, neomenthyl β-D-glucoside, **2**, 114
C₁₆H₃₀O₆P₂, phosphonophosphate FPP analogue, **2**, 160
C₁₆H₃₁CoN₆O₄, bis(dimethylglyoximato)isopropyl(2-
    aminopyridine)Co(III), **5**, 267
C₁₆H₃₂, 1-hexadecene, **8**, 217
C₁₆H₃₂O
    9-hexadecenal, **8**, 217
    palmitaldehyde, **3**, 402
C₁₆H₃₂O₂
    7,11-hexadecadienyl acetate, **8**, 205
    hexadecanoic acid, **1**, 37, **3**, 219
    methyl 2,6,10-trimethyltridecanoate, **8**, 241
    palmitic acid, **1**, 24, 54, 297, 336, 358, **3**, 152, **4**, 13, 15,
        8, 203, 205
C₁₆H₃₂O₃, 8-hydroxyhexadecanoic acid, **1**, 228
C₁₆H₃₃ClO₂S, hexadecanesulfonyl chloride, **5**, 128
C₁₆H₃₄, hexadecane, **8**, 217
C₁₆H₃₄Cl₃N₂OP, bisphosphoramidite, **7**, 133
C₁₆H₃₄O₂
    11-hexadecenyl acetate, **8**, 200
    1,2,6-trimethyldecanol propanoate, **8**, 247
C₁₆H₃₆FN, tetra-*n*-butylammonium fluoride, **7**, 114
C₁₆H₃₈Br₂N₂, decamethonium, **5**, 116
C₁₇H₁₀O₆, demethylsterigmatocystin, **1**, 458, 462, 463
C₁₇H₁₁NO₇, aristolochic acid, **7**, 522, **8**, 152, 155
C₁₇H₁₂Br FO₂S₂, DuP 697, **5**, 250
C₁₇H₁₂Cl₂O₇, geodin, **1**, 413, 427, 431, 459
C₁₇H₁₂O₅, anhydropisatin, **1**, 775
C₁₇H₁₂O₆
    aflatoxin B₁, **1**, 410, 420, 444, 459, 443, 461, 467, **7**, 2,
        16, 511
    dihydrodemethylsterigmatocystin, **1**, 463
C₁₇H₁₂O₇
    aflatoxin B₁epoxide, **1**, 443
    aflatoxin 8,9-epoxide, **5**, 65
    aflatoxin G₁, **1**, 444
    aflatoxin M₁, **1**, 444
C₁₇H₁₄BrN₃OS, didemnolineC, **8**, 542
C₁₇H₁₄BrN₃S, didemnoline A, **8**, 542
C₁₇H₁₄Cl₂O₇, dihydrogeodin, **1**, 435
C₁₇H₁₄F₃N₃O₂S, celecoxib, **5**, 252
C₁₇H₁₄N₂, ellipticine, **7**, 603 , 605
C₁₇H₁₄N₂O, 9-hydroxyellipticine, **7**, 605
C₁₇H₁₄N₂O₂, 2-(4-methoxyphenyl)-3,3a-dihydro-8H-
        pyrazolo[5,1-a]isoindole-8-one, **8**, 36
C₁₇H₁₄N₂O₃, 2-[3-(4-methoxyphenyl)-5-pyrazoyl]benzoic
        acid, **8**, 36
C₁₇H₁₄O₄, chrysin dimethyl ether, **8**, 181
C₁₇H₁₄O₅, afrormosin, **1**, 775
C₁₇H₁₄O₆
    aflatoxin B₂, **1**, 444
    aflatoxin B₂a, **1**, 444
    pisatin, **1**, 665, 775, 779, 786, 796, 797, 800, 802, 803,
        813, **8**, 186, 189, 192
C₁₇H₁₄O₇
    aflatoxin G₂, **1**, 444
    aflatoxin G₂a, **1**, 444
    aflatoxin M₂, **1**, 444
    bisdechlorogeodin, **1**, 437
    cicerin, **1**, 808
    dermalactone, **1**, 410
    2-hydroxypisatin, **1**, 775
    ombuin, **1**, 740
    quercetin 7,3′-dimethyl ether, **8**, 181
    tricin, **8**, 169
C₁₇H₁₅BrN₃OS, didemnoline D, **8**, 542
C₁₇H₁₅ClO₇, malvidin, **8**, 158, 159, 164
C₁₇H₁₅NO₃, 2-*N,N*-acetoxyacetylaminofluorene, **7**, 96
C₁₇H₁₅N₃S, didemnoline B, **8**, 542
C₁₇H₁₅O₂, kinokiresinol, **1**, 705
C₁₇H₁₅O₃, oxyhinokiresinol, **1**, 705
C₁₇H₁₆N₂O₄, mitonafide, **7**, 606

C₁₇H₁₆O₃, lettucenin A, **1**, 130, **8**, 189
C₁₇H₁₆O₄
    coniferyl benzoate, **8**, 139
    cryptoresinol, **1**, 642, 686
C₁₇H₁₆O₆, homoferreirin, **1**, 808
C₁₇H₁₆O₇, sulochrin, **1**, 435
C₁₇H₁₇ClN₂O₃, chlorodibenzo[1,4]dioxin-1-carboxamide,
        7, 607
C₁₇H₁₇ClO₆, griseofulvin, **1**, 459, **4**, 198
C₁₇H₁₇NO₃, *p*-coumaroyl tyramine, **1**, 673
C₁₇H₁₇NO₄, caffeoyl tyramine, **1**, 673
C₁₇H₁₇N₅O₅, *N*-benzoyladenosine, **6**, 85
C₁₇H₁₇N₅O₅S, *N*-benzoyl-6-thioguanosine, **6**, 93
C₁₇H₁₇N₅O₁₆P₃S, 5-[(4-azidophenacyl)thio]uridine 5′-
        triphosphate, **7**, 216
C₁₇H₁₈FN₃O₃, ciptrofloxacin, **7**, 609
C₁₇H₁₈N₂O₂, amonafide, **7**, 606
C₁₇H₁₈N₂O₃, dibenzo[1,4]dioxin-1-carboxamide, **7**, 607
C₁₇H₁₈N₂O₆S, carboxypenicillin G, **4**, 252
C₁₇H₁₈N₆O₁₀, triazolo derivative, **7**, 117
C₁₇H₁₈N₆O₁₅P₃S, 5-[(4-azidophenacyl)thio]cytidine 5′-
        triphosphate, **7**, 216
C₁₇H₁₈O₄, sativan, **1**, 774
C₁₇H₁₈O₅, hydroxysugiresinol, **1**, 642
C₁₇H₁₈O₆
    5-*O*-(4-coumaroyl)shikimate, **3**, 640
    L-660,631, **1**, 208
C₁₇H₁₈O₇, 5-*O*-(4-coumaroyl)shikimate caffeic acid
        derivative, **3**, 640
C₁₇H₁₉ClN₂OS, chloropromazine-*N*-oxide, **3**, 412
C₁₇H₁₉NO₃
    coclaurine, **1**, 676
    dihydromorphinone, **4**, 40
    moiramide A, **8**, 594
    morphine, **4**, 26, 35
    piperine, **8**, 304
C₁₇H₁₉NO₄
    fenoxycarb, **8**, 275
    veprisin, **1**, 383
C₁₇H₁₉NO₅S, BM-13505, **1**, 189
C₁₇H₁₉NO₁₂, *N*-succinimidyl 4-*O*-β-D-glucosidogallate, **3**,
        805
C₁₇H₁₉N₂NaO₆S, methicillin, **3**, 274, 285
C₁₇H₁₉N₅O₅, 9-ribosyl-*N*₆-[*o*-hydroxybenzyl]adenine, **8**, 62
C₁₇H₁₉N₅O₈, tri-*O*-acetyluridine triazolo derivative, **7**,
        118
C₁₇H₁₉O₅, ceratiolin, **8**, 169
C₁₇H₂₀ClN₃, acridine orange, **7**, 428
C₁₇H₂₀N₄O₆, thymine dimer, **5**, 380
C₁₇H₂₀N₄O₇, thymine dimer, **5**, 376
C₁₇H₂₀N₄O₁₂P, dUpdU photodimer, **5**, 383
C₁₇H₂₀O₅, guaiacylglycerol-β-guaiacyl ether, **3**, 725
C₁₇H₂₀O₆, PR toxin, **2**, 177, 202, 205, 207
C₁₇H₂₁Br₄N₅O₂, pseudoceratidine, **8**, 440
C₁₇H₂₁NO₃
    6,7-dehydrohyoscyamine, **4**, 27
    galanthamine, **4**, 43
C₁₇H₂₁NO₄
    cocaine, **4**, 27
    hyoscine, **4**, 27
    scopolamine, **1**, 876, **4**, 26, 27, 30
C₁₇H₂₁NO₅
    anisodine, **4**, 26
    1,3-diketone, **5**, 438
C₁₇H₂₁N₄O₉P, riboflavin-5′-phosphate, **4**, 150
C₁₇H₂₁O₄, linalyl *p*-nitrobenzoate, **2**, 123
C₁₇H₂₂BrN₃, woodinine, **8**, 527
C₁₇H₂₂N₃O₇S, 5-methylglucobrassin, **8**, 26
C₁₇H₂₂N₃O₈S
    4-methoxyglucobrassin, **8**, 26
    neoglucobrassin, **8**, 26
C₁₇H₂₂N₄O₆, bispyrimidine, **5**, 380
C₁₇H₂₂N₄O₇, thymine dimer, **5**, 380

$C_{17}H_{22}O_5$
  ligulatin B, **8**, 308
  lipiferolide, **8**, 308
  xanthumin, **8**, 308
$C_{17}H_{22}O_6$
  tenulin, **8**, 308
  tetraneurin A, **8**, 308
  tetrodecamycin, **1**, 370
  tulipinolide diepoxide, **8**, 308
$C_{17}H_{22}O_7$
  3-acetyldeoxynivalenol, **2**, 164
  3-ADN, **2**, 164
$C_{17}H_{22}O_{10}$, 1-*O*-sinapoyl-*β*-D-glucose, **3**, 807
$C_{17}H_{23}BrO_3$, laurencin, **1**, 8, 303
$C_{17}H_{23}NO$, haminol A, **8**, 465
$C_{17}H_{23}NO_3$
  hyoscyamine, **4**, 26, 29, 30
  littorine, **4**, 29
$C_{17}H_{23}NO_3$
  atropine, **8**, 167
  hyoscyamine, **8**, 162
$C_{17}H_{23}NO_4$
  anisodamine, **4**, 26
  6α-hydroxyhyoscyamine, **1**, 878
  6β-hydroxyhyoscyamine, **4**, 27
$C_{17}H_{23}N_2O_2$, nitroalkane, **8**, 431
$C_{17}H_{23}N_4O_9P$, FMNH₁, **1**, 599
$C_{17}H_{24}O_2$, falcarindiol, **8**, 155
$C_{17}H_{24}O_4$
  isotrichodermin, **2**, 164
  trichodermin, **2**, 158
$C_{17}H_{24}O_5$
  cinnamodial, **8**, 308
  sambucinol, **2**, 164
$C_{17}H_{24}O_9$, syringin, **3**, 676
$C_{17}H_{24}O_{10}$
  secologanin, **2**, 106, **4**, 110, 113, 114, 118, 121, 122, 126, 127, 129, 133, 136
  verbenalin, **8**, 307
$C_{17}H_{25}NO_5$, senecionine, **8**, 147
$C_{17}H_{25}N_3O_4$, Ala-MeLeu-MeLeu, **1**, 548
$C_{17}H_{25}N_7O_5$, blasticidinS, **3**, 339
$C_{17}H_{26}N_3O_{15}P$, CMP-KDO, **3**, 505, 509
$C_{17}H_{26}N_8O_5$, blasticidinS, **4**, 200
$C_{17}H_{26}O_2$, heptadeca-6,9,12,14-tetraenoic acid, **1**, 39
$C_{17}H_{26}O_3$, olepupuane, **8**, 462
$C_{17}H_{26}O_4$
  diplodiatoxin, **1**, 388, 389
  [6]-gingerol, **1**, 766
$C_{17}H_{26}O_5$
  botrydial, **2**, 173
  sesquiterpene lactone, **2**, 173
$C_{17}H_{26}O_6$, pinolidoxin, **8**, 181
$C_{17}H_{26}O_{10}$, loganin, **2**, 106, **4**, 110, 113, **8**, 307
$C_{17}H_{26}O_{11}$, 10-hydroxyloganin, **4**, 113
$C_{17}H_{27}NO_6$, 3-acetylechinatine, **4**, 31
$C_{17}H_{27}N_3O_{16}P_2$, 3-deoxy-UDP-*N*-acetylglucosamine, **5**, 66
$C_{17}H_{27}N_3O_{17}P_2$
  UDP-*N*-acetyl-[3H]glucosamine, **3**, 300
  UDP-*N*-acetylglucosamine, **1**, 331, 593, **3**, 203, 206, 214, 219, 222, 249, 301, **5**, 66
$C_{17}H_{28}$
  bishomofarnesene, **8**, 269
  α-bishomofarnesene, **8**, 237
  homofarnesene, **8**, 237
$C_{17}H_{28}NO_5$, *N*-methyl-4-(neryloxy)pyridinium methyl sulfate , **2**, 123
$C_{17}H_{28}OS$, *S*-farnesylthioacetic acid, **2**, 359
$C_{17}H_{28}O_2$
  homofarnesylcarboxylate, **2**, 310
  Pl-201, **1**, 370
$C_{17}H_{28}O_3$
  HHT, 153.018

  12-hydroxy-5,8,10-heptadecatrienoic acid, **1**, 262
  juvenile hormone I, **8**, 4
  sesquiterpene, **8**, 466
$C_{17}H_{28}O_4$, shirimodiol 8-acetate, **8**, 312
$C_{17}H_{28}O_5$
  chrysartemin B, **8**, 308
  dihydrobotrydial, **2**, 173
$C_{17}H_{30}O$
  civetone, **8**, 231
  faranal, **2**, 78
  homofarnesyl methyl ether, **2**, 310
  4,6,10,12-tetramethyl-2,4-tridecadien-7-one, **8**, 245
$C_{17}H_{30}O_2$
  acetate, **8**, 235
  hydroprene, **8**, 275
  8,10-pentadecadienyl acetate, **8**, 207
  ZR-512, **8**, 436
$C_{17}H_{30}O_3$
  colneleic acid, **1**, 235
  12-hydroxy-8,10-heptadecadienoic acid, **1**, 261
$C_{17}H_{31}F_3N_3O_3P$, phosphoramidite, **7**, 154
$C_{17}H_{32}$, 6,9-heptadecadiene, **8**, 217
$C_{17}H_{32}B_{10}N_2O_7$, pyrimidine nucleoside, **7**, 221
$C_{17}H_{32}O$
  10-heptadecen-2-one, **8**, 217
  14-methyl-8-hexadecenal, **8**, 247
  oxylipin epoxide, **1**, 217
$C_{17}H_{32}O_2$
  ω-cycloheptyldecanoate, **1**, 75, 80
  ω-cyclohexylundecanoic acid, **1**, 71
  heptadec-9-enoic acid, **1**, 38
  heptadec-10-enoic acid, **1**, 46
  9,10-methylenehexadecanoic acid, **1**, 62
  1-methylethyl tetradecenoate, **8**, 216
  9-pentadecenyl acetate, **8**, 207
  10-pentadecenyl acetate, **8**, 207
$C_{17}H_{32}O_3$, 1,2,4-trihydroxyheptadec-16-yne, **8**, 181, 183
$C_{17}H_{32}O_6P_2$
  FPP analogue, **2**, 251, 254, 258
  FPP ether analogue, **2**, 160
$C_{17}H_{32}O_7P_2$
  bishomofarnesyl diphosphate, **2**, 78
  4,8-dimethylfarnesyl diphosphate, **2**, 78
$C_{17}H_{33}N_2O_3PS$, mercaptoalkylated phosphoramidite, **7**, 167
$C_{17}H_{33}N_2O_5PS$, mercaptoalkylated phosphoramidite, **7**, 167
$C_{17}H_{33}O_6P$, dioctanoyl phosphatidylmethanol, **5**, 109
$C_{17}H_{34}$, 1-heptadecene, **8**, 217
$C_{17}H_{34}N_4O_{10}$, ribostamycin, **4**, 200, **6**, 194
$C_{17}H_{34}O$, 6,12-dimethyl-2-pentadecanone, **8**, 244
$C_{17}H_{34}O_2$
  heptadecanoic acid, **1**, 39
  1-methylethyl tetradecanoate, **8**, 216
  methyl palmitate, **8**, 217,
  1-methyltetradecyl acetate, **8**, 216
  12-methyltetradecyl acetate, **8**, 247
  tetradecyl propanoate, **8**, 209, 216
$C_{17}H_{35}N_5O_6$, fortimicin A, **1**, 871
$C_{17}H_{36}$
  5,9-dimethylpentadecane, **8**, 247
  heptadecane, **8**, 217
$C_{17}H_{36}N_3OP$, bisphosphoramidite, **7**, 133
$C_{17}H_{36}O$, 6,10,13-trimethyltetradecan-1-ol, **8**, 241
$C_{17}H_{39}NO_4P$, dodecylphosphocholine, **5**, 110
$C_{18}H_{10}N_4O$, cystodamine, **8**, 539
$C_{18}H_{10}O_6$
  6-deoxyversicolorin A, **1**, 458
  saintopin, **7**, 600
$C_{18}H_{10}O_7$
  saintopin, **7**, 607
  versicolorin, **7**, 511
  versicolorin A, **1**, 447, 454, 457, 462

C₁₈H₁₀O₉, spirodienone, **1**, 459
C₁₈H₁₀O₉S, UCE1022, **7**, 600
C₁₈H₁₂
  benzanthracene, **7**, 436
  benzo[c]phenanthrene, **7**, 470
C₁₈H₁₂O₃, β-lapachone, **7**, 596
C₁₈H₁₂O₅, 2′,4,4′,6′-tetrahydroxychalcone, **1**, 786
C₁₈H₁₂O₆, sterigmatocystin, **1**, 1, 421, 444, 445, 458, 461,
    462, 467
C₁₈H₁₂O₇, versicolorin B, **1**, 457
C₁₈H₁₂O₈, versicolorin A hemiacetal, **1**, 457
C₁₈H₁₄BrN₃O₂S
  discorhabdin A, **7**, 501
  makaluvamine F, **7**, 501
C₁₈H₁₄N₄O₅S, sulfasalazine, **1**, 294
C₁₈H₁₄O₃, blechnic acid, **1**, 677
C₁₈H₁₄O₆
  dihydrosterigmatocystin, **1**, 463
  7-epiblechnic acid, **1**, 678
  sterigmatocystin, **7**, 511
C₁₈H₁₄O₇, megacerotonic acid, **1**, 645, 686
C₁₈H₁₄O₈
  aryldihydronaphthalene, **1**, 673
  blechnic acid, **1**, 647
  versiconal, **1**, 457
C₁₈H₁₄O₉, phloroglucinol oligomer, **8**, 460
C₁₈H₁₅O, o-anisyl-1-napahthylmethyl, **7**, 126
C₁₈H₁₆O₄, formononetin 7-ethyl ether, **1**, 795
C₁₈H₁₆O₆
  dihydroxytruxillic acid, **1**, 647
  fijiensin, **8**, 179
  nanaomycin, **1**, 478
C₁₈H₁₆O₈
  1′-hydroxyversicolorone, **1**, 454, 456, 457
  rosmarinic acid, **1**, 686
C₁₈H₁₇ClO₆, monorden, **1**, 534
C₁₈H₁₇F₄N₇O₁₄, phosphoramidite, **7**, 218
C₁₈H₁₇NO₅S₃, calicheamicinone, **7**, 569
C₁₈H₁₇N₂O, 9-hydroxy-2-methylellipticinium ion, **7**,
    605
C₁₈H₁₈FN₅O₇, 2-fluoro-6-O-(4-nitrophenethyl)inosine,
    6, 94
C₁₈H₁₈N₂O₆, tetramethoxyazo-p-methylene quinone, **3**,
    712
C₁₈H₁₈N₄O, furamidine, **7**, 457
C₁₈H₁₈N₄O₆S₄, 2,2′-azinobis-(3-ethylbenzothiazoline-6-
    sulfonate), **3**, 709
C₁₈H₁₈O₂
  anolignan B, **1**, 672, 704
  equilenin, **5**, 40
  magnolol, **1**, 691, 692, 693, **8**, 139, 140
C₁₈H₁₈O₃, lignan, **1**, 693
C₁₈H₁₈O₄
  enterolactone, **1**, 698
  ligballinol, **1**, 672
C₁₈H₁₈O₆
  3,3′-demethylarctigenin, **1**, 703
  samaderin A, **8**, 322
C₁₈H₁₈O₇, frenolicin, **1**, 14, 475, 478, **4**, 206
C₁₈H₁₈O₈, clerodane derivative, **2**, 226
C₁₈H₁₉NO₃
  codeinone, **4**, 37
  erysodienone, **4**, 43
  neopinone, **4**, 37
C₁₈H₁₉NO₄, feruloyl tyramine, **1**, 673, 685
C₁₈H₁₉NO₄S₃, calicheamicins, **3**, 313
C₁₈H₂₀BrN₃O₄, epinardin D, **7**, 501
C₁₈H₂₀N₂O, furamine, **7**, 458
C₁₈H₂₀N₂O₃, erymelanthine, **4**, 43
C₁₈H₂₀N₂O₅, duocarmycin analogue, **7**, 505
C₁₈H₂₀N₂O₆, syringaldazine, **3**, 712, 713
C₁₈H₂₀N₃O₇P, phosphonamidate, **5**, 436
C₁₈H₂₀N₆O₈S, 2′-O-tosyl-6′-nitrohomoadenosine, **5**, 194

C₁₈H₂₀O₂
  17β-dihydroequilenin, **5**, 40
  dihydroequilenin, **5**, 25
C₁₈H₂₀O₄
  ABA analogue, **8**, 77
  trimethoxyflavan, **3**, 752
C₁₈H₂₀O₅
  sorgolactone, **8**, 175
  4′,5,7-trimethoxy-2,4-flavan-4-ol, **3**, 756
C₁₈H₂₀O₆
  lignan, **3**, 677
  nagilactone D, **8**, 313
C₁₈H₂₁F₃N₂O₃, N-acetylleucylphenylalanyl
    trifluoromethyl ketone, **5**, 19
C₁₈H₂₁NO₃
  codeine, **4**, 35
  dihydrocodeinone, **4**, 40
  N-methylcoclaurine, **1**, 676
C₁₈H₂₁NO₄
  norprotosinomenine, **4**, 43
  norreticuline, **4**, 42
C₁₈H₂₂N₂, tubifoline, **4**, 51
C₁₈H₂₂N₂O₄, quinocarcin, **7**, 499, 500, 541
C₁₈H₂₂N₂O₄S₄, lissoclinotoxin D, **8**, 541
C₁₈H₂₂N₂O₈S, 1-acetylglucobrassin, **8**, 26
C₁₈H₂₂N₄O, phenylbenzimide, **7**, 607
C₁₈H₂₂N₄O₁₀S, uridylyl-(3′→5′)-(5′-thiouridine), **7**, 298
C₁₈H₂₂N₆O₁₂P₂
  adenosine diphosphopyridoxal, **3**, 453
  ADP-pyridoxal, **3**, 455
C₁₈H₂₂O₂
  4,6-estradiene-3,17-one, **5**, 34
  4,7-estradiene-3,17-one, **5**, 33
  5,7-estradiene-3,17-one, **5**, 33
  estrogen, **7**, 532
  3-hydroxy-3,5,7-estratrien-17-one, **5**, 32, 33
C₁₈H₂₂O₃, 1,5-octadien-3-ol, **1**, 211
C₁₈H₂₂O₄
  enterodiol, **1**, 698
  nordihydroguaiaretic acid, **1**, 95, 123, 221, 243, 291,
    690, 692, 695, **8**, 169
  prosolanapyrone III, **1**, 399
  solanapyrone A, **1**, 368, 388, 395
  solanapyrone D, **1**, 395
C₁₈H₂₃NO₆, dehydroretrorsine, **7**, 519
C₁₈H₂₃N₃O₇S, S-phenylacetylglutathione, **4**, 264
C₁₈H₂₃N₃O₈S, S-phenoxyacetylglutathione, **4**, 264, 265
C₁₈H₂₃N₄O₉S, thymine dimer, **5**, 380
C₁₈H₂₃N₄O₁₃PS, uridyl-(3′-5′)-(5′-thiouridine), **6**, 91
C₁₈H₂₄N₂, tubifolidine, **4**, 50
C₁₈H₂₄N₂O₄, isoxaben, **3**, 610
C₁₈H₂₄N₂O₁₇, 2,4-dinitrophenyl β-cellobioside, **5**, 301
C₁₈H₂₄N₄O₉S, thymine dimer, **5**, 380
C₁₈H₂₄N₅O₈P, dibutyryl-cAMP, **3**, 118
C₁₈H₂₄O₂
  estradiol, **1**, 699
  17β-estradiol, **1**, 782, **5**, 40
  oleic acid, **8**, 215
C₁₈H₂₄O₃, dicranenone A, **1**, 228
C₁₈H₂₄O₄
  prosolanapyrone II, **1**, 397
  solanapyrone B, **1**, 395
  solanapyrone E, **1**, 395
C₁₈H₂₅NO
  3-amino-1,3,5(10)-estratrien-17β-ol, **5**, 40
  anacyclin, **8**, 303
C₁₈H₂₅NO₄, coronatine, **1**, 122, 135
C₁₈H₂₅NO₅
  coronatine, **1**, 129
  intergerrimine, **4**, 33
  senecionine, **4**, 33, **8**, 176
C₁₈H₂₅NO₆
  retrorsine, **4**, 32, **7**, 518

usaramine, **4**, 33

C₁₈H₂₅NO₁₅, *p*-nitrophenyl-*β*-D-cellobioside, **5**, 291

C₁₈H₂₅N₃O₉P, 5-deazaFMNH₂, **1**, 600

C₁₈H₂₆Cl₄N₂O₅, mirabimideE, **8**, 611

C₁₈H₂₆N₂OS₂,PD164387, **5**, 252

C₁₈H₂₆N₂O₁₂, 5-methylcarboxymethyluridine-2′-*O*-methylribose, **4**, 360

C₁₈H₂₆N₁₀O₃, netropsin, **7**, 35, 452, 486, 505, 567

C₁₈H₂₆O₂, 19-nortestosterone, **5**, 40

C₁₈H₂₆O₃
  ecklonialactone A, **1**, 216
  egregiachloride olefin analogue, **1**, 216
  hydroxyoctadecanoic acid, **1**, 228

C₁₈H₂₆O₄, trisporic acid, **8**, 408

C₁₈H₂₆O₁₀, secologanin, **4**, 46

C₁₈H₂₇ClO₃, egregiachloride, **1**, 216

C₁₈H₂₇NO₅
  neoplatyphylline, **4**, 33
  platyphylline, **4**, 33

C₁₈H₂₇NO₆
  axillaridine, **4**, 33
  rosmarinine, **4**, 32

C₁₈H₂₇N₂O₃PS, phosphoramidite, **7**, 171

C₁₈H₂₈Br₂O₂Si
  oxolane, **1**, 316
  prelaureatin derivative, **1**, 317

C₁₈H₂₈O₂
  C18:4, **1**, 340
  kinoprene, **8**, 275
  octadeca-6,9,12,15-tetraenoic acid, **1**, 39, 42
  6,8,10,12-octadecatetraenoic acid, **1**, 224

C₁₈H₂₈O₃
  allene epoxide, **1**, 8
  auxin b lactone, **8**, 24
  colnelenic acid, **1**, 235
  12,13-EOD, **1**, 120
  12,13-epoxylinolenic acid, **1**, 119
  13-HPOT allene oxide, **1**, 231
  hydroxyoctadecadienoic acid, **1**, 220
  12-oxo-10,15-phytodienoic acid, **1**, 119
  12-oxophytodienoic acid, **1**, 123, 229, 231, 234, 241
  phytodienoic acid, **1**, 132, 240

C₁₈H₂₈O₄
  12,13-epoxylinolenic acid, **8**, 115
  12,13-epoxy-9-oxo-10,15-octadecadienoic acid, **1**, 214
  hydroxyformylheptadecatrienoic acid, **1**, 214
  hydroxyoxooctadecatrienoic acid, **1**, 214

C₁₈H₂₈O₆, botryaloic acid methyl ester, **2**, 173

C₁₈H₂₈O₈
  12-hydroxyjasmonic acid glucoside, **1**, 127
  tuberonic acid *β*-D-glucoside, **1**, 125

C₁₈H₂₈O₉
  11-hydroxyjasmonic acid *β*-D-glucoside, **1**, 125
  tuberonic acid glucoside, **8**, 108, 117

C₁₈H₂₉BrO₂Si
  laurencin derivative, **1**, 310
  oxetane, **1**, 312
  prelaureatin derivative, **1**, 317

C₁₈H₂₉N, piclavine, **8**, 546

C₁₈H₂₉NO, crucigasterin 275, **8**, 545

C₁₈H₂₉NO₄, *N*-jasmonoylisoleucine, **1**, 128, 135

C₁₈H₂₉NO₇, 7-acetyleuropine, **4**, 31

C₁₈H₂₉N₂O₂, AMO1618, **2**, 293

C₁₈H₂₉N₂O₅P, phosphoramidite, **7**, 185

C₁₈H₃₀, trishomofarnesene, **8**, 269

C₁₈H₃₀O, 9,12,15-octadecatrienal, **8**, 207

C₁₈H₃₀OS, *S*-farnesylthiopropionic acid, **2**, 359

C₁₈H₃₀O₂
  C18:3, **1**, 339, 340, 341
  11-deutero-6,9,12-octadecatrienoic acid, **1**, 221
  gorlic acid, **1**, 68
  10,12,14-hexadecatrienyl acetate, **8**, 207
  13-hexadecen-11-yn-1-yl acetate, **8**, 207

linolenic acid, **1**, 54, 123, 132, 134, 264, **8**, 2, 7, 115, 119, 204, 207, 215, 217

α-linolenic acid, **1**, 84, 87, 119, 128, 214

γ-linolenic acid, **1**, 215

9,11-octadecadien-13-olide, **8**, 218

octadeca-6,9,12-trienoic acid, **1**, 42

octadeca-9,12,15-trienoic acid, **1**, 35, 37, 40, 41, 44, 46

phytodienoic acid, **1**, 232

propanoate, **8**, 234

C₁₈H₃₀O₂Si
  laurencin derivative, **1**, 310
  trienyndiol, **1**, 316

C₁₈H₃₀O₃
  9-HOT*ω*6, **1**, 224
  13-HOT*ω*6, **1**, 224
  9-*α*-HOTE, **1**, 242
  13-hydroxylinolenic acid, **1**, 124
  9-hydroxy-10,12,15-octadecatrienoic acid, **1**, 209
  11-hydroxy-6,9,12-octadecatrienoic acid, **1**, 224
  10-hydroxyoctadecenynoic acid, **1**, 228
  insect juveline hormone, **8**, 265
  JK I, **8**, 236
  juvenile hormone I, **8**, 436
  ketodienoic acid, **1**, 220
  11-keto-9,12-octadecadienoic acid, **1**, 223
  9-KOTE, **1**, 243
  methyl 10,11-epoxy-3,11-dimethyl-7-ethyl-2,6-tridecadienoate, **8**, 267
  3-oxo-2-(2′-pentenyl)cyclopentaneoctanoic acid, **1**, 120, **8**, 115

C₁₈H₃₀O₄
  auxin b, **8**, 24
  auxin a lactone, **8**, 24
  10,11-diHOT, **1**, 221
  9,16-dihydroxy-10,12,14-octadecatrienoic acid, **1**, 236
  epoxyhydroxyoctadecadienoic acid, **1**, 214
  12,13-epoxy-9-hydroxy-10,15-octadecadienoic acid, **1**, 209
  13-HPLA, **1**, 123,
  9-*α*-HPOTE, **1**, 242
  13-hydroperoxylinolenic acid, **1**, 119, 124, 132, **4**, 46, **8**, 115, 119
  hydroperoxyoctatrienoic acid, **1**, 99
  13-hydroperoxyoctadecatrienoic acid, **1**, 230
  13-hydroperoxy-6,9,11-octadecatrienoic acid, **1**, 102
  13-hydroperoxy-9,11,15-octadecatrienoic acid, **1**, 95, 209
  13-hydroperoxyoctadeca-9,12,15-trienoic acid, **1**, 232
  12-ketohydroxylinoleic acid, **1**, 102
  α-ketol, **1**, 232
  γ-ketol, **1**, 232
  12-oxo-13-hydroxy-9,15-octadecadienoic acid, **8**, 115

C₁₈H₃₀O₉
  9,10-dihydro-11-hydroxyjasmonic acid glucopyranoside, **8**, 116
  9,10-dihydro-11-hydroxyjasmonic acid *β*-D-glucopyranoside, **1**, 124

C₁₈H₃₁FO₁₅, 4-deoxymaltotriosyl *α*-fluoride, **5**, 299

C₁₈H₃₁N, piclavine, **8**, 546

C₁₈H₃₁NO, crucigasterin, **8**, 545

C₁₈H₃₁NO₄
  N-(3-hydroxy-7-tetradecenoyl)-homoserine lactone, **8**, 400
  N-(7-isocurubinoyl)isoleucine, **1**, 128

C₁₈H₃₁N₃O₇S, *S*-octanoylglutathione, **4**, 264

C₁₈H₃₁N₅O₉, Ala-Glu-*m*-DAP-Ala, **3**, 271

C₁₈H₃₂N₂O₂, *β*-farnesyl amilanine, **5**, 333

C₁₈H₃₂O
  faranal, **8**, 237
  9,12-octadecadienal, **8**, 207

C₁₈H₃₂O₂
  C18:2, **1**, 340, 341
  chaulmoogric acid, **1**, 68

geranyl octanoate, **8**, 223
linoleic acid, **1**, 7, 34, 54, 84, 87, 98, 264, **8**, 119, 211, 215, 217
malvalic acid, **1**, 62
octadecadienoic acid, **1**, 98
octadeca-9,12-dienoic acid, **1**, 35, 37, 40, 45, 46, 98
octadecenolide, **8**, 218
propylure, **8**, 47

$C_{18}H_{32}O_3$
13-HOD, **1**, 234
13-hydroperoxy-α-linolenic acid, **1**, 102
8-hydroxylinoleic acid, **1**, 211, 212, **8**, 183
13-hydroxylinoleic acid, **1**, 102, **3**, 182, **8**, 181
15-hydroxylinoleic acid, **1**, 230
9-hydroxy-10,12-octadecadienoic acid, **1**, 209
13-hydroxyoctadecadienoic acid, **1**, 214
13-hydroxy-9,11-octadecadienoic acid, **1**, 111
laetisaric acid, **1**, 212

$C_{18}H_{32}O_4$
6-acetoxy-5-hexadecanolide, **8**, 217
7,8-dihydroxylinoleic acid, **1**, 211, 212
9-HPOD, **1**, 214, 233, 235
13-HPOD, **1**, 209, 214, 230, 233, 234
9-hydroperoxyoctadecadienoic acid, **1**, 235, 266
9-hydroperoxy-10,12-octadecadienoic acid, **1**, 95
10-hydroperoxyoctadeca-8,12-dienoic acid, **1**, 211
13-hydroperoxy-9,11-octadecadienoic acid, **1**, 95, 98, 102, 103, 105
hydroperoxyoctadecadienoic acid, **1**, 99
12-keto-13-hydroxy-9-octadecenoic acid, **1**, 119
plant growth hormone, **8**, 5

$C_{18}H_{32}O_5$
auxin a, **8**, 24
macrolide, **1**, 508
9,12,13-trihydroxy-10,15-octadecadienoic acid, **1**, 209

$C_{18}H_{32}O_{15}$, 2′-fucosyllactose, **3**, 55

$C_{18}H_{32}O_{16}$
cellotriose, **3**, 571, **5**, 301
maltotriose, **3**, 457, 481
raffinose, **8**, 162

$C_{18}H_{33}N$
piclavine, **8**, 546
tridecadienylpyridine, **8**, 549

$C_{18}H_{34}NO_{18}P$
Man1GlcN-PI, **3**, 305
Manα1-4GlcN1-6-inositol-phosphate, **3**, 295

$C_{18}H_{34}N_2O$
pseudodistomin A, **8**, 547
pseudodistomin B, **8**, 547

$C_{18}H_{34}O$
linoleyl alcohol, **1**, 98
3,13-octadecadien-1-ol, **8**, 207
1,5-octadien-3-ol, **1**, 211

$C_{18}H_{34}O_2$
C18:1, **1**, 340
ω-cycloheptylundecanoate, **1**, 75, 80
dihydrochaulmoogric acid, **1**, 68
dihydromalvalic acid, **1**, 62
octadecanolide, **8**, 218
octadec-6-enoic acid, **1**, 42
octadec-9-enoic acid, **1**, 37, 40 , 46
oleic acid, **1**, 7, 25, 49, 64, 210, **4**, 14, **8**, 217
vaccenic acid, **1**, 64, **2**, 50

$C_{18}H_{34}O_3$
ω-cycloheptyl-α-hydroxyundecanoate, **1**, 75, 80
9,10-epoxystearic acid, **1**, 210
gyptol, **8**, 45
13-hydroperoxyoctadecadienol, **1**, 106
ZR-515, **8**, 436

$C_{18}H_{34}O_4$
9-hydroperoxylinoleic acid, **1**, 109
13-hydroperoxylinoleic acid, **1**, 84, 106
linoleic acid 13-hydroperoxide, **1**, 95, 102

$C_{18}H_{36}N_4O_{11}$, kanamycin, **4**, 200, **6**, 194

$C_{18}H_{36}O$
7,8-epoxyoctadecane, **8**, 208
hexahydrofarnesylacetone, **8**, 234
6,10,14-trimethyl-5,9,13-pentadecan-2-one, **8**, 232

$C_{18}H_{36}O_2$
myristyl 2-methylpropanoate, **8**, 210
octadecanoic acid, **1**, 35, 37
stearic acid, **1**, 25, 297, **3**, 101, 304, **4**, 14, **8**, 181, 183, 203, 205, 213, 217

$C_{18}H_{36}O_3$, 9-HOD, **1**, 243

$C_{18}H_{36}O_6$, 9,10-dihydroxystearic acid, **1**, 210

$C_{18}H_{37}NO_2$
3-dehydrosphinganine, **3**, 89
sphingosine, **3**, 3, 88, 90, 99, 101

$C_{18}H_{38}$
9-methylgermacrene-B, **8**, 237
2-methylheptadecane, **8**, 249
7-methylheptadecane, **8**, 248

$C_{18}H_{38}NO_5P$
sphingosine phosphate, **3**, 99
sphingosine-1-phosphate, **3**, 88

$C_{18}H_{38}O_2$, hexadecyl acetate, **8**, 218

$C_{18}H_{39}NO_2$, sphinganine, **3**, 89, 90, 100

$C_{18}H_{40}NO_4P$, 1-desoxysphinganine-1-phosphonate, **3**, 403

$C_{18}H_{40}NO_5P$, sphinganine-1-phosphate, **3**, 403

$C_{18}H_{40}NO_6P$, 4-D-hydroxysphinganine-1-phosphate, **3**, 403

$C_{18}H_{42}O_2$, 2-butyl 7-tetradecenoate, **8**, 209

$C_{19}H_{11}NO_2$, N-(3-pyrenyl)maleimide, **7**, 168

$C_{19}H_{12}O_2$, anigorufone, **1**, 767

$C_{19}H_{12}O_3$, hydroxyanigorufone, **1**, 767

$C_{19}H_{12}O_4$, tetrangulol, **1**, 482

$C_{19}H_{12}O_7$, prostalidinC, **1**, 705

$C_{19}H_{13}BrN_2O$
eudistominR, **8**, 527
eudistominS, **8**, 527

$C_{19}H_{13}ClO_6$, austocystin, **7**, 511

$C_{19}H_{13}F_2NO_4$,CP-115,953, **7**, 603, 609

$C_{19}H_{13}N_3$, eudistominU, **8**, 528

$C_{19}H_{13}N_5O$, N-2-(anthracen-9-ylmethyl)guanine, **7**, 327

$C_{19}H_{13}O$, 9-phenylxanthen-9-yl, **6**, 83

$C_{19}H_{14}N_2$, 9-anilinoacridine, **7**, 606

$C_{19}H_{14}N_2O$, eudistomin T, **8**, 527

$C_{19}H_{14}N_4$, bilin, **1**, 274

$C_{19}H_{14}O_6$, O-methylsterigmatocystin, **1**, 445, 458, 459, 462, 467

$C_{19}H_{14}O_7$, 10-hydroxy-O-methylsterigmatocystin, **1**, 459

$C_{19}H_{15}$, trityl, **7**, 126

$C_{19}H_{15}N_3$, isoeudistominU, **8**, 528

$C_{19}H_{15}N_3O_2$, cystodytin J, **8**, 540

$C_{19}H_{15}S$, tritylthio, **7**, 119

$C_{19}H_{16}BrNO_4$, iodoindomethacin, **5**, 248

$C_{19}H_{16}ClNO_4$, indomethacin, **1**, 243, **5**, 10, 193, 243, 248, 252

$C_{19}H_{16}O_6$
dihydro-O-methylsterigmatocystin, **1**, 463
psorospermin, **7**, 511

$C_{19}H_{16}O_7$, urdamycin, **1**, 482

$C_{19}H_{17}Br_2NO_4$
botryllamide A, **8**, 539
botryllamideC, **8**, 539

$C_{19}H_{17}F_3N_4O_{13}P_3$, 2′,3′-dideoxy-5-[4-(3-trifluoromethyl-3H-diazirin-3-yl)s tyryl]UTP, **7**, 217

$C_{19}H_{17}F_4N_7O_{14}$, phoosphoramidite, **7**, 218

$C_{19}H_{17}NO_3$, rutacridone, **1**, 130

$C_{19}H_{18}BrNO_4$
botryllamide B, **8**, 539
botryllamide D, **8**, 539

$C_{19}H_{18}O_3$
formylphenylpentenylbenzoic acid, **5**, 426
1,5-hexadiene, **5**, 426

$C_{19}H_{18}O_4$, anolignan A, **1**, 704

C$_{19}$H$_{18}$O$_5$, coniferyl *p*-coumarate, **3**, 699
C$_{19}$H$_{18}$O$_7$, vernodalin, **8**, 308
C$_{19}$H$_{19}$N$_3$O$_6$
   naphthalimide, **7**, 407
   p-nitroanilide, **5**, 436
C$_{19}$H$_{19}$N$_3$O$_7$, cyclohexene, **5**, 428, 429
C$_{19}$H$_{19}$N$_7$O$_6$, folate, **3**, 375, 401
C$_{19}$H$_{20}$N$_2$O
   norfluorocurarine, **4**, 50
   tambjamine F, **8**, 472
C$_{19}$H$_{20}$N$_2$O$_2$, vincanidine, **4**, 121
C$_{19}$H$_{20}$O$_2$, lignan, **1**, 693
C$_{19}$H$_{20}$O$_3$
   cryptotanshinone, **2**, 228
   termilignan, **1**, 672, 691, **3**, 677
C$_{19}$H$_{20}$O$_4$, moracinC, **8**, 155
C$_{19}$H$_{20}$O$_5$
   GA$_{105}$, **8**, 56
   12-*epi*-teucvin, **8**, 318
   teucvin, **8**, 318
C$_{19}$H$_{20}$O$_6$, demethyldehydrodiconiferyl alcohol, **1**, 683
C$_{19}$H$_{20}$O$_7$, GA$_{59}$, **8**, 40
C$_{19}$H$_{21}$NO, quinuclidine derivative, **2**, 258
C$_{19}$H$_{21}$NO$_3$, thebaine, **4**, 35
C$_{19}$H$_{21}$NO$_4$
   naloxone, **4**, 40
   protoberberine, **4**, 40
   scoulerine, **4**, 41
C$_{19}$H$_{21}$NO$_5$, sinapoyl tyramine, **1**, 673
C$_{19}$H$_{22}$ClNS, SDZ 87-469, **2**, 276
C$_{19}$H$_{22}$N$_2$O$_2$, sarpagine, **4**, 118
C$_{19}$H$_{22}$O$_3$
   brombin II, **1**, 380
   brombin III, **1**, 380
C$_{19}$H$_{22}$O$_4$
   alnusdiol, **1**, 686
   12,15-cyclo-GA, **2**, 237
   ent-9,15-cyclo-20-norgibberell-16-ene, **8**, 56
   2,3-dehydro GA$_9$, **8**, 53
   9,11-dehydro-GA, **2**, 237
   diarylheptamoid, **1**, 686
   GA$_{73}$, **8**, 56, 57
   GA$_{103}$, **8**, 56, 57
C$_{19}$H$_{22}$O$_5$
   columbin, **8**, 167
   12,15-cyclo-GA, **2**, 237
   GA$_5$, **2**, 236, **8**, 43, 52, 53
   GA$_7$, **2**, 236, **8**, 45, 53
   GA$_{11}$, **8**, 37
   GA$_{31}$, **8**, 38
   GA$_{62}$, **8**, 40
   3-*epi*-GA$_{88}$, **8**, 56
   GA$_{95}$, **8**, 42
   GA$_{104}$, **8**, 56
   GA$_{106}$, **8**, 56
   GA$_{107}$, **8**, 56
   GA$_{108}$, **8**, 56
   GA$_{109}$, **8**, 56
   gibberellin A$_5$, **2**, 221
   3α-hydroxy-9,15-cyclo-GA$_9$, **8**, 56
   1β-hydroxy-9,15-cyclo-GA$_9$, **8**, 56
   thannilignan, **1**, 672, 691
C$_{19}$H$_{22}$O$_6$
   alectrol, **8**, 175
   antheridic acid, **2**, 237, **8**, 56
   cedrusin, **1**, 684, **3**, 677
   GA$_3$, **2**, 236, **8**, 45, 46, 50, 51, 54
   GA$_6$, **2**, 236, **8**, 43, 52, 53
   GA$_{22}$, **8**, 37
   GA$_{30}$, **8**, 38
   GA$_{68}$, **8**, 40
   GA$_{80}$, **8**, 41
   GA$_{92}$, **8**, 42

GA$_{94}$, **8**, 42
   gibberellic acid, **2**, 236, **8**, 40, 181
   gibberellin A$_3$, **2**, 221, **8**, 42
   20-norantherid-8(14),16-diene, **8**, 56
   strigol, **8**, 175
C$_{19}$H$_{22}$O$_7$
   GA$_{21}$, **8**, 38
   GA$_{26}$, **8**, 38
   GA$_{32}$, **8**, 44
   GA$_{33}$, **8**, 38
   GA$_{87}$, **8**, 41
   GA$_{93}$, **8**, 42
C$_{19}$H$_{23}$NO$_4$
   cocculine, **4**, 43
   orientaline, **4**, 40
   reticuline, **4**, 35, 41
C$_{19}$H$_{23}$NO$_{10}$,
   4-methylumbelliferyl-α-ᴅ-neuraminic acid, **5**, 295
C$_{19}$H$_{23}$N$_6$O$_8$P, phenylalanyl-AMP, **6**, 127
C$_{19}$H$_{23}$N$_6$O$_{12}$P, 3′-(thioinosylyl)-3′,5′)-uridine, **6**, 159
C$_{19}$H$_{23}$N$_7$O$_6$, tetrahydrofolic acid, **1**, 612, **2**, 386, **3**, 398, 401, **8**, 209
C$_{19}$H$_{24}$N$_4$O$_8$, thymine dimer, **5**, 378
C$_{19}$H$_{24}$O$_3$, centrolobol, **8**, 139
C$_{19}$H$_{24}$O$_4$
   GA$_9$, **2**, 234, **8**, 44, 45, 51, 52, 53, 55, 57
   gibberellin A$_9$, **8**, 57
   3′-*O*-methylnordihydroguaiaretic acid, **1**, 703
   ent-20-norgibberell-16-ene, **8**, 56
C$_{19}$H$_{24}$O$_5$
   GA$_4$, **2**, 236, **8**, 41, 45, 47, 52, 53
   GA$_{20}$, **2**, 234, **8**, 51, 52, 53, 54
   GA$_{40}$, **8**, 39
   GA$_{45}$, **8**, 39
   GA$_{51}$, **8**, 39
   GA$_{61}$, **8**, 40
   GA$_{69}$, **8**, 40
   GA$_{84}$, **8**, 41
   gibberellin A$_4$, **8**, 43
   montanin B, **8**, 319
   trichothecene, **1**, 466
   trichothecin, **2**, 1, 158
C$_{19}$H$_{24}$O$_6$
   C$_{29}$, **8**, 53
   GA$_1$, **2**, 236, **8**, 43, 45, 47, 52, 53, 54
   GA$_{29}$, **8**, 44, 45
   GA$_{34}$, **2**, 236, **8**, 45
   GA$_{35}$, **8**, 38
   GA$_{47}$, **8**, 38
   GA$_{54}$, **8**, 38
   GA$_{58}$, **8**, 39
   GA$_{60}$, **8**, 53
   3-*epi*-GA$_{63}$, **8**, 56
   GA$_{67}$, **8**, 39
   GA$_{71}$, **8**, 39
   GA$_{77}$, **8**, 39
   GA$_{81}$, **8**, 40
   GA$_{90}$, **8**, 40
   gibberellin A$_1$, **8**, 21, 40
   hydroxy-GA$_5$, **2**, 236
   onopordopicrin, **8**, 308
C$_{19}$H$_{24}$O$_7$
   C$_{76}$, **8**, 56
   GA$_8$, **2**, 236, **8**, 43, 45, 51
   GA$_{16}$, **8**, 37
   GA$_{48}$, **8**, 38
   GA$_{49}$, **8**, 38
   GA$_{50}$, **8**, 38
   GA$_{55}$, **8**, 39
   GA$_{56}$, **8**, 39
   GA$_{57}$, **8**, 39
   GA$_{72}$, **8**, 39
   GA$_{78}$, **8**, 40

GA$_{79}$, **8**, 40
GA$_{85}$, **8**, 40
GA$_{91}$, **8**, 41
lignan, **3**, 677
$C_{19}H_{24}O_8$
  GA$_{75}$, **8**, 40
  GA$_{86}$, **8**, 40
  GA$_{89}$, **8**, 40
$C_{19}H_{25}NO$, haminol B, **8**, 465
$C_{19}H_{25}NO_4$
  cocculidine, **4**, 43
  isococculidine, **4**, 43
  solanapyroneC, **1**, 395
  tetrahydroprotoberberine, **4**, 42
$C_{19}H_{25}N_4O_9P$, Ala-Ala analogue, **3**, 278
$C_{19}H_{26}N_2O$, geissoschizoline, **4**, 50
$C_{19}H_{26}N_2O_3S$, PD138387, **5**, 252
$C_{19}H_{26}O_2$
  4-androstene-3,17-dione, **5**, 33, 39, **8**, 230
  5-androstene-3,17-dione, **5**, 33, 39
  1,2-dehydrotestosterone, **8**, 230
  3-hydroxy-3,5-androstadiene-17-one, **5**, 33
$C_{19}H_{26}O_4$, laurediol acetate, **1**, 304
$C_{19}H_{26}O_5$, rubrosterone, **8**, 288, 292, 293
$C_{19}H_{26}O_6$
  CAL, **2**, 164
  calonectrin, **2**, 164
  GA$_{10}$, **8**, 36
  GA$_{82}$, **8**, 40
$C_{19}H_{26}O_7$, GA$_2$, **8**, 37
$C_{19}H_{27}Co$ IN$_4$O$_2$, benzylcobalamin iodide, **5**, 266
$C_{19}H_{27}NO_6$, emiline, **4**, 33
$C_{19}H_{27}N_3O_4$, Phe-Pro-Val, **4**, 345
$C_{19}H_{28}O$, 5α-androst-16-en-3-one, **8**, 230
$C_{19}H_{28}O_2$, testosterone, **1**, 699, **3**, 410, **8**, 230
$C_{19}H_{28}O_4$, VB A dibenzoate, **1**, 141
$C_{19}H_{28}O_5$, olepupuane, **8**, 462
$C_{19}H_{30}F_3N_4O_6P$, deoxyribonucleoside phosphoramidite, **7**, 233
$C_{19}H_{30}N_2O_2$, nitroalkane, **8**, 431
$C_{19}H_{30}N_2O_4$, pyridooxazole derivative, **8**, 549
$C_{19}H_{30}N_5O_6P$, phosphoramidite, **7**, 175
$C_{19}H_{30}O$, 5α-androst-16-en-3-ol, **8**, 230
$C_{19}H_{30}O_2$
  helifulvanic acid, **2**, 238
  nonadeca-6,9,12,16-tetraenoic acid, **1**, 39
  sterculynic acid, **1**, 62
$C_{19}H_{30}O_3$, 11α-hydroxyhelifulvanic acid, **2**, 238
$C_{19}H_{30}O_5$, shirimodiol diacetate, **8**, 312
$C_{19}H_{31}ClN_2O_2$
  AMO 1618, **2**, 305
  AMO 1619, **2**, 311
$C_{19}H_{32}$
  1,3,6,9-nonadecatetraene, **8**, 207
  3,6,9,18-nonadecatetraene, **1**, 218
$C_{19}H_{32}ClNO$
  cylindricine A, **8**, 546
  cylindricine B, **8**, 546
$C_{19}H_{32}N_2O_6$, pseudodistomin B tetraacetate, **8**, 549
$C_{19}H_{32}O_2$
  5-alkylresorcinol, **7**, 535
  methyl linolenate, **8**, 217
$C_{19}H_{32}O_3$
  JH 0, **8**, 236
  juvenile hormone 0, **8**, 269
  4-methyl-JH I, **2**, 78, **8**, 236, 237, 269
$C_{19}H_{32}O_5$, octalactin B, **8**, 590
$C_{19}H_{32}O_6$, octalactin A, **8**, 590
$C_{19}H_{33}Cl_2N_2OP$, bisphosphoramidite, **7**, 133
$C_{19}H_{33}NO_2S$, S-farnesylcysteine methyl ester, **2**, 353
$C_{19}H_{34}$
  1,3,6,9-nonadecatriene, **8**, 207
  3,6,9-nonadecatriene, **8**, 207, 208

6,9,18-nonadecatriene, **1**, 218
$C_{19}H_{34}ClN_2OP$, bisphosphoramidite, **7**, 133
$C_{19}H_{34}N_3O_3P$, bisphosphoramidite, **7**, 133
$C_{19}H_{34}O$
  9,10-epoxy-3,6-nonadecadiene, **8**, 207
  6,7-epoxy-3,9-nonadecadiene, **8**, 207
  3,4-epoxy-6,9-nonadecadiene, **8**, 207
  6,9-nonadecadien-3-one, **8**, 208
  pheromone of *Colotois pennaria*, **8**, 45
$C_{19}H_{34}O_2$
  hateramine, **8**, 431
  methyl linoleate, **1**, 98, **8**, 217
  oxylipin diepoxide, **1**, 217
  sterculic acid, **1**, 62
$C_{19}H_{34}O_3$
  2-hydroxysterculic acid, **1**, 62
  methoprene, **8**, 275
  rosaprostol, **1**, 196
$C_{19}H_{35}N$, diethylfarnesylamine, **8**, 267
$C_{19}H_{35}NO$, lepadiformine, **8**, 547
$C_{19}H_{36}O$
  10-nonadecenal, **8**, 219
  7-nonadecen-11-one, **8**, 208
$C_{19}H_{36}O_2$
  ω-cyclohexyltridecanoic acid, **1**, 71
  dihydrosterculic acid, **1**, 62
  lactobacillic acid, **1**, 62
  1-methylethyl 9-hexadecenoate, **8**, 217
  methyl oleate, **8**, 217
  nonadec-9-enoic acid, **1**, 38
  oxylipin vicinal diol, **1**, 217
$C_{19}H_{36}O_3$, methyl 3-hydroxy-2-pentylcyclopentane-1-octanoate, **1**, 121
$C_{19}H_{36}O_5$, betaenone B, **1**, 388
$C_{19}H_{36}O_6$, betaenone D, **1**, 388
$C_{19}H_{37}NaO_{10}S$, MTX derivative, **8**, 507
$C_{19}H_{38}$
  14-methyl-1-octadecene, **8**, 247
  2-methyl-7-octadecene, **8**, 242
$C_{19}H_{38}O$
  disparlure, **8**, 2, 41, 48, 208
  7,8-epoxy-2-methyloctadecane, **8**, 242
$C_{19}H_{38}O_2$
  diprionyl acetate, **8**, 247
  1-methylethyl 9-hexadecanoate, **8**, 217
  17-methyloctadecanoic acid, **8**, 240
  methyl stearate, **8**, 217
  nonadecanoic acid, **1**, 39
  pheromone of *Neodiprion pinetum*, **8**, 43
$C_{19}H_{40}$
  2,5-dimethylheptadecane, **8**, 248
  3,13-dimethylheptadecane, **8**, 248
  5,9-dimethylheptadecane, **8**, 247
  5,11-dimethylheptadecane, **8**, 248
  7,11-dimethylheptadecane, **8**, 248
  nonadecane, **8**, 217, 218
$C_{19}H_{41}NO_4P$, myristoyl-ACP, **5**, 130
$C_{19}H_{44}O_7$, 2-acetyl-14α-hydroxy-22-*epi*-pinnasterol, **8**, 280
$C_{19}H_{51}NO$, 2,3-dihydro-2-azasqualene *N*-oxide, **2**, 311
$C_{20}H_5Cl_4I_4K_2O_5$, Rose Bengal, **3**, 378
$C_{20}H_8Br_4Na_2O_{10}S_2$, sulfobromophthalein, **1**, 283
$C_{20}H_{10}O_5$, bulgarein, **7**, 600
$C_{20}H_{11}N_3O_4$, BE-13793C, **7**, 600
$C_{20}H_{12}$, benzo[a]pyrene, **5**, 58, **7**, 4, 470
$C_{20}H_{12}O$, benzo[a]pyrene-7,8-oxide, **5**, 58
$C_{20}H_{12}O_5$, fluorescein, **6**, 76, 229, **7**, 116
$C_{20}H_{12}O_7$, taiwaninE, **1**, 704
$C_{20}H_{14}NO_4$, sanguinarine, **1**, 131, **4**, 43
$C_{20}H_{14}N_2O_3$, rhodamine, **7**, 116
$C_{20}H_{14}O_2$, dihydrobenzo[a]pyrenediol, **5**, 58
$C_{20}H_{14}O_3$
  benzo[a]pyrenediol epoxide, **5**, 58
  benzo[a]pyrene-7,8-diol-9,10-epoxide, **5**, 58

7,8-dihydroxy-9,10-oxy-7,8,9,10-
     tetrahydrobenzo[a]pyrene, **5**, 64
C$_{20}$H$_{14}$O$_7$, tetracenomycin F1, **1**, 486
C$_{20}$H$_{14}$O$_8$
     prostalidin A, **1**, 705
     SEK15b, **1**, 486, 489
C$_{20}$H$_{15}$O$_2$
     9-*p*-methoxyphenylxanthen-9-yl, **6**, 83
     xanthenyl, **7**, 126
C$_{20}$H$_{16}$, 7,12-dimethylbenz[a]anthracene, **1**, 783
C$_{20}$H$_{16}$FN$_3$O$_4$, A62176, **7**, 462
C$_{20}$H$_{16}$NO$_2$
     fagaridine, **7**, 601
     isofagaridine, **7**, 601
C$_{20}$H$_{16}$N$_2$O$_4$
     camptothecin, **4**, 117, **7**, 544, 599
C$_{20}$H$_{16}$N$_4$OS, kuanoniamine D, **8**, 540
C$_{20}$H$_{16}$O$_7$
     averufin, **1**, 16, 447, 450, 453, 454, 457, 467
     PD116740, **1**, 482
C$_{20}$H$_{16}$O$_8$
     nidurufin, **1**, 455
     pseudonidurufin, **1**, 455
     RM80, **1**, 486
     SEK15, **1**, 486, 489
C$_{20}$H$_{16}$O$_9$, versiconal acetate, **1**, 447, 454, 456, 457, 467
C$_{20}$H$_{17}$, monomethyltrityl, **7**, 126
C$_{20}$H$_{17}$ClO, monomethoxytrityl chloride, **6**, 86
C$_{20}$H$_{17}$FN$_4$O$_4$, A-85226, **7**, 462
C$_{20}$H$_{17}$FO$_2$S$_2$, sulindac sulfide, **5**, 248
C$_{20}$H$_{17}$N$_3$O$_2$, aequorin derivative, **8**, 449
C$_{20}$H$_{17}$N$_3$O$_2$S, diplamine, **8**, 540
C$_{20}$H$_{17}$N$_3$O$_4$, 9-aminocamptothecin, **7**, 600
C$_{20}$H$_{18}$NO$_4$, berberine, **4**, 40 , 41
C$_{20}$H$_{18}$O$_4$, phaseollin, **1**, 775, 777, 785, 804, 812, 814
C$_{20}$H$_{18}$O$_5$
     glyceollin, **1**, 807
     glyceollin I, **1**, 775, 777, 779, 781, 802, 813, **8**, 189
     glyceollin II, **1**, 775, 777, 802
     glyceollin III, **1**, 775, 777, 802
     8-prenylgenistein, **1**, 800
     wighteone, **8**, 183
C$_{20}$H$_{18}$O$_6$
     averythrin, **1**, 453
     episesamin, **1**, 694
     kievitone, **1**, 722
     luteone, **1**, 815, **8**, 181, 183
     8-prenyl-2'-hydroxygenistein, **1**, 800
     sesamin, **1**, 658, 690, 694, 695, 698, **8**, 277
C$_{20}$H$_{18}$O$_7$
     averufanin, **1**, 453
     norsolorinic acid, **1**, 2, 420, 425, 447, 450, 454, 462, 467
     sesamolin, **1**, 658, 690, 694, **3**, 677, **8**, 277
C$_{20}$H$_{19}$NO$_3$, pyriproxyfen, **8**, 275
C$_{20}$H$_{19}$NO$_5$, protopine, **3**, 643
C$_{20}$H$_{19}$O$_2$, dimethoxytrityl, **6**, 83
C$_{20}$H$_{20}$O$_4$
     3,9-dihydroxy-10-dimethylallylpterocarpan, **1**, 804
     isobavachalcone, **1**, 130
     licarin B, **1**, 693
     phaseollidin, **1**, 814
C$_{20}$H$_{20}$O$_5$, 6-isopentenylnaringenin, **8**, 181
C$_{20}$H$_{20}$O$_6$
     α-conidendrin, **1**, 668, 691, 697
     conidendrin, **1**, 656
     keivitone, **1**, 814
     piperitol, **1**, 658
     sinapyl *p*-coumarate, **3**, 699
C$_{20}$H$_{20}$O$_6$, kievitone, **8**, 189
C$_{20}$H$_{20}$O$_7$
     averantin, **1**, 16, 447, 450, 452, 457, 462
     divanillyl tetrahydrofuran, **3**, 725, 731
     monoepoxylignanolide, **1**, 695

pungiolide A, **1**, 375
sesamolinol, **1**, 690
C$_{20}$H$_{20}$O$_8$
     6,8-di-*O*-methylhydroxyversicolorone, **1**, 455
     5'-hydroxyaverantin, **1**, 453
C$_{20}$H$_{20}$O$_{11}$, dihydroquercetin xyloside, **3**, 750
C$_{20}$H$_{20}$O$_{12}$, 1,6-diprotocatechuoylglucose, **3**, 809
C$_{20}$H$_{20}$O$_{14}$
     1,6-digalloylglucose, **3**, 809
     1,6-di-*O*-galloyl-*β*-D-glucose, **3**, 806, 822
     digalloylglucose, **3**, 807
C$_{20}$H$_{21}$ClO$_4$, fenofibrate, **2**, 259
C$_{20}$H$_{21}$NO$_4$
     canadine, **4**, 41
     papaverine, **4**, 35
C$_{20}$H$_{21}$N$_3$O$_4$, Trp-Tyr, **5**, 184
C$_{20}$H$_{21}$N$_4$, 7*H*-benzo[*e*]pyrido[4,3-*b*]indole, **7**, 608
C$_{20}$H$_{21}$N$_4$O, intoplicine, **7**, 607
C$_{20}$H$_{22}$N$_2$O$_2$
     akuammicine, **4**, 50
     benzoxazole derivative, **2**, 258
     gelsemine, **4**, 118
C$_{20}$H$_{22}$N$_2$O$_3$, cathenamine, **4**, 114
C$_{20}$H$_{22}$N$_3$O$_8$, tri-*O*-acetyluridine pyridinium derivative, **7**, 118
C$_{20}$H$_{22}$O$_4$
     dehydrodiisoeugenol, **1**, 693, **3**, 703
     dehydroguaiaretic acid, **3**, 703
     licarin A, **1**, 645, 678, 680, 693
C$_{20}$H$_{22}$O$_5$
     dehydrodiconiferyl alcohol, **3**, 651
     8'-hydroxy-3,3'-dimethoxy-7-oxo-8-*O*-4'-lignan, **1**, 692
C$_{20}$H$_{22}$O$_6$
     dehydrodiconiferyl alcohol, **1**, 641, 651, 652, 678, 680, 682, **3**, 677, 704
     dihydrodehydrodiconiferyl alcohol, **3**, 731
     o,*o*-dihydroxybiphenyl, **3**, 725
     dilignol, **3**, 705
     matairesinol, **1**, 647, 652, 661, 688, 691, 694, 698, 705
     pinoresinol, **1**, 640, 651, 652, 682, 705, **3**, 704, 708, 723
     syringaresinol, **3**, 717
C$_{20}$H$_{22}$O$_7$
     7'-hydroxymatairesinol, **1**, 668, 688, 691, 697
     nortrachelogenin, **1**, 642
C$_{20}$H$_{22}$O$_8$, picropodophyllone, **1**, 691
C$_{20}$H$_{22}$O$_9$
     astringin, **8**, 169
     dehydroginkgolide A, **2**, 395
     1-dehydroginkgolide A, **2**, 390, 394
     photodehydroginkgolide A, **2**, 390, 394, 395
     plicatic acid, **3**, 677
C$_{20}$H$_{22}$O$_{10}$, plicatic acid, **1**, 656, 668, 697, **3**, 651
C$_{20}$H$_{23}$Br$_4$N$_3$O$_6$, psammaplysin A, **8**, 440
C$_{20}$H$_{23}$Cl$_3$N$_2$O$_2$S, barbaramide, **8**, 608
C$_{20}$H$_{23}$NO$_4$
     cularine, **4**, 40
     naltrexone, **4**, 40
     tetrahydrocolumbamine, **4**, 41
C$_{20}$H$_{23}$N$_3$O$_5$, bioxalomycin α2, **7**, 500
C$_{20}$H$_{23}$N$_7$O$_6$
     5,10-methylene-tetrahydrofolate, **8**, 209
     methylenetetrahydrofolate, **3**, 397
C$_{20}$H$_{23}$N$_7$O$_7$, 10-formyltetrahydrofolate, **8**, 209
C$_{20}$H$_{24}$N$_2$O$_2$
     19,20-dihydroakuammicine, **4**, 51
     tubotaiwine, **4**, 50
C$_{20}$H$_{24}$N$_2$O$_3$
     3*β*-akuammigine, **4**, 118
     geissoschizine, **4**, 113
     11-hydroxypleiocarpamine, **4**, 121
C$_{20}$H$_{24}$O$_2$
     5,8,11,14-eicosatetraynoic acid, **1**, 221
     eicosatetraynoic acid, **1**, 243

C$_{20}$H$_{24}$O$_4$
    GA$_{73}$-Me, **8**, 57
    GA$_{73}$methyl ester, **8**, 56
    guaiaretic acid, **1**, 640, 676, **3**, 677
    ent-20-norgibberell-9(11),16-diene, **8**, 56
C$_{20}$H$_{24}$O$_5$
    GA$_{88}$-Me, **8**, 56, 57
    3-*epi*-GA$_{88}$-Me, **8**, 56, 57
    GA$_{96}$-Me, **8**, 56, 57
    myrocinC, **7**, 506
C$_{20}$H$_{24}$O$_6$
    dihydrodehydrodiconiferyl alcohol, **1**, 679, 680, 682,
        683, 688, **3**, 677
    lariciresinol, **1**, 662, 682
C$_{20}$H$_{24}$O$_7$
    1,7-dihydroxyisoginkgolide, **2**, 398
    dilignol, **3**, 705, 705
    ergochrome AA, **1**, 429
    guaiacylglycerol coniferyl alcohol ether, **3**, 704, 708
    guaiacylglycerol 8-*O*-4′-coniferyl alcohol ether, **1**, 652,
        641, 678, 680
    lignan, **3**, 677
    olivil, **1**, 688
C$_{20}$H$_{24}$O$_8$, vernodalol, **8**, 312
C$_{20}$H$_{24}$O$_8$S, podolactoneC, **8**, 313
C$_{20}$H$_{24}$O$_9$, ginkgolide A, **2**, 368, 377, 382, **8**, 313
C$_{20}$H$_{24}$O$_{10}$
    ginkgolide B, **2**, 368, 377, **8**, 313
    ginkgolide J, **2**, 368
    ginkgolide M, **2**, 368
    salicortin, **8**, 139
C$_{20}$H$_{24}$O$_{11}$, ginkgolideC, **2**, 368, **8**, 313
C$_{20}$H$_{24}$O$_{12}$, feruloylarabinofuranosylarabinose, **3**, 697
C$_{20}$H$_{25}$NO$_4$, norlaudanosoline, **4**, 37
C$_{20}$H$_{25}$NO$_{11}$, 5-*O*-arabinopyranosyl-2-*O*-(indole-3-
        acetyl)-*myo* D-inositol, **8**, 26
C$_{20}$H$_{25}$N$_7$O$_6$, methyltetrahydrofolate, **5**, 275
C$_{20}$H$_{26}$BrNO$_4$S,PGH$_2$analogue, **1**, 189
C$_{20}$H$_{26}$N$_2$O$_2$, ajmaline, **4**, 46, 110, 118, 122, 128
C$_{20}$H$_{26}$N$_2$O$_8$S$_3$, sirodesmin, **7**, 527
C$_{20}$H$_{26}$N$_{10}$O$_{12}$P, cyclic diguanylic acid, **3**, 581
C$_{20}$H$_{26}$O, juvocimene-1, **8**, 277
C$_{20}$H$_{26}$O$_2$, juvocimene-2, **8**, 277
C$_{20}$H$_{26}$O$_3$, halimedatrial, **8**, 462
C$_{20}$H$_{26}$O$_4$
    dibenzylbutane, **1**, 677
    GA$_9$-Me, **8**, 56
    GA$_{15}$, **8**, 51, 52
    momilactone, **1**, 131, **8**, 189
C$_{20}$H$_{26}$O$_5$
    GA$_{20}$-Me, **8**, 56, 57
    GA$_{24}$, **2**, 234
    GA$_{37}$, **8**, 52
    GA$_{44}$, **8**, 51
    GA$_{64}$, **8**, 39
    GA$_{70}$-Me, **8**, 56, 57
C$_{20}$H$_{26}$O$_6$
    eupatoriopicrin, **8**, 308
    GA$_{13}$, **8**, 45
    GA$_{19}$, **2**, 234, **8**, 43, 51, 54
    GA$_{24}$, **8**, 51
    GA$_{25}$, **2**, 234
    GA$_{27}$, **8**, 37
    GA$_{36}$, **8**, 37
    GA$_{38}$, **8**, 38
    GA$_{65}$, **8**, 40
    GA$_{98}$, **8**, 40
    GA$_{101}$, **8**, 40
    phenols, **1**, 679
    secoisolariciresinol, **1**, 651, 662, 688, 698
    shikodonin, **8**, 313
C$_{20}$H$_{26}$O$_7$
    cnicin, **8**, 169

GA$_{17}$, **2**, 234, **8**, 45, 51
GA$_{23}$, **8**, 37
GA$_{25}$, **8**, 44, 45, 51
GA$_{46}$, **8**, 38
GA$_{52}$, **8**, 38
GA$_{66}$, **8**, 39
GA$_{99}$, **8**, 41
GA$_{102}$, **8**, 41
guaiacylglycerol -8-*P*-4′-dihydroconiferyl alcohol
    ether, **1**, 682
lignan, **3**, 677
C$_{20}$H$_{26}$O$_8$
    GA$_{28}$, **8**, 37
    GA$_{39}$, **8**, 38
    GA$_{43}$, **8**, 38
C$_{20}$H$_{27}$NO$_1$, amygdalin, **8**, 167
C$_{20}$H$_{27}$NO$_3$, *N*-jasmonoyltyramine, **1**, 128
C$_{20}$H$_{27}$NO$_4$S, PGH$_2$analogue, **1**, 189
C$_{20}$H$_{27}$N$_4$O$_{12}$P, Dewar pyrimidinone, **5**, 389
C$_{20}$H$_{28}$O, retinal, **1**, 274, **2**, 327
C$_{20}$H$_{28}$O$_2$
    ferruginol orthoquinone, **2**, 397
    retinoic acid, **1**, 274, **2**, 327, **3**, 79, 118
    trachylobanoic acid, **8**, 142
C$_{20}$H$_{28}$O$_3$
    bacillariolide I, **1**, 227
    bacillariolide II, **1**, 227
    didemnilactone A, **8**, 543
    didemnilactone B, **8**, 543
    GA$_{12}$-aldehyde, **8**, 47, 50
    gibberellin A$_{12}$aldehyde, **2**, 232, 233
    hybridalactone, **1**, 219
    momililactone, **2**, 230
    phomactin B$_2$, **8**, 599
    phomactin C, **8**, 599
    phomactin D, **8**, 599
    phomactin E, **8**, 599
    phytocassane, **8**, 189
    pisiferic acid, **8**, 181
C$_{20}$H$_{28}$O$_4$
    agardhilactone, **1**, 221
    GA$_{12}$, **2**, 234, **8**, 44, 47, 51
    GA$_{53}$-aldehyde, **8**, 51
    PGA$_2$-1,15-lactone, **1**, 246
    PGA$_3$-1,15-lactone, **1**, 246
    PGE$_3$-1,15-lactone 11-acetate, **8**, 464
    PGE$_3$-1,15-lactone, **1**, 245
    prostaglandin A, **1**, 232
    ptilodene, **1**, 224
    sordaricin, **1**, 378
    transversial, **2**, 222
C$_{20}$H$_{28}$O$_5$
    cohumulone, **1**, 760
    GA$_{14}$, **2**, 236, **8**, 38
    GA$_{15}$, **2**, 234
    GA$_{53}$, **2**, 234, **8**, 47, 51, 54
    GA$_{110}$, **8**, 42
    GA$_{111}$, **8**, 42
    GA$_{112}$, **8**, 42
C$_{20}$H$_{28}$O$_6$
    C$_{74}$, **8**, 40
    GA$_{18}$, **8**, 36
    GA$_{44}$, **2**, 234
    GA$_{97}$, **8**, 41
    GA$_{100}$, **8**, 41
C$_{20}$H$_{28}$O$_8$, GA$_{41}$, **8**, 38
C$_{20}$H$_{28}$O$_{11}$, 2-*O*-[5-*O*-(*trans*-feruloyl)-β-L-
        arabinofuranosyl]-D-xylopyranose, **3**, 697
C$_{20}$H$_{29}$NO$_5$S, latrunculin B, **8**, 466
C$_{20}$H$_{29}$N$_3$O$_{19}$P$_2$,
    3-enolpyruvyl-1-UDP-*N*-acetylglucosamine, **3**, 251
C$_{20}$H$_{29}$N$_3$O$_{20}$P$_2$,
    UDP-*N*-acetylenolpyruvylglucosamine, **1**, 593

$C_{20}H_{30}Co IN_4O_2$, benzylcobalamin iodide, **5**, 266
$C_{20}H_{30}N_2O_3$, 3β-hydroxy-13α-tigloyloxylupanine, **4**, 35
$C_{20}H_{30}N_4O_6S$, biotinamidocaproic acid *N*-
    hydroxysuccinimide, **7**, 155
$C_{20}H_{30}O$
  annonene, **8**, 317
  ferruginol, **2**, 228, 379, 396
  ent-kaurenal, **8**, 50
  spatane-type diterpene, **8**, 459
$C_{20}H_{30}O_2$
  abietic acid, **2**, 228
  neo-abietic acid, **2**, 228
  16-deoxysarcophine, **8**, 617
  eicosanoid, **8**, 423
  5,7,9,14,17-eicosapentaenoic acid, **1**, 224
  5,8,10,12,14-eicosapentaenoic acid, **1**, 223
  eicosa-5,8,11,14,17-pentaenoic acid, **1**, 40
  eicosapentaenoic acid, **1**, 38, 161, 212
  ferruginol paraquinol, **2**, 397
  heteroscyphic acid A, **2**, 226
  9-hydroperoxyicosa-(5,7,11,14,17-pentaenoic acid, **8**, 423
  isopimaric acid, **2**, 228
  kaurenoic acid, **8**, 142
  ent-kaur-16-en-19-oic acid, **2**, 232, 238
  ent-kaurenoic acid, **8**, 50
  laevopimaric acid, **2**, 228
  oryzalexin, **2**, 230, **8**, 189
  rosenonolactone, **2**, 228
$C_{20}H_{30}O_3$
  ascidiatrienolide, **1**, 243
  8-HEPE, **1**, 246, 247
  11-HEPE, **1**, 248
  12-HEPE, **1**, 219, 237
  11-HETE, **1**, 243
  12-HETE, **1**, 237
  12-HPETE, **1**, 220
  13-hydroxyeicosapentaenoic acid, **1**, 222
  12-hydroxyeicosatetraenoic acid, **1**, 219
  ent-7α-hydroxykaur-16-en-19-oic acid, **2**, 232
  5,6-leukotriene A₄, **1**, 236
  leukotriene A₄, **1**, 263, 267, 279, 280, **5**, 52, 53, 54, 59,
    62, 65, 156, 168
  LTA₄methyl ester, **1**, 185
  neodidemnilactone, **8**, 543
  phomactin G, **8**, 599
  polyneuric acid, **1**, 221
  preclavulone-A, **1**, 241
$C_{20}H_{30}O_4$
  dihydroxyeicosadienoic acid, **1**, 220
  5,6-epoxy-15-hydroxyeicosa-7,9,11,13-tetraenoic acid,
    1, 239
  halicholactone, **1**, 243
  9-hydroperoxyeicosapentaenoic acid, **1**, 216
  8-hydroxy-13-keto-5,9,11,14-eicosatetraenoate, **1**, 222
  LTB₅, **1**, 237, 238
  neohalicholactone, **1**, 243
  15-PGA₂, **1**, 239, 240
  15-PGB₂, **1**, 240, 240
  PGE₂-1,15-lactone, **8**, 464
  PGJ₂, **1**, 163
  phomactin A, **8**, 599
  phomactin B, **8**, 599
  phomactin B₁, **8**, 599
  phomactin F, **8**, 599
  schizostatin, **2**, 257
$C_{20}H_{30}O_5$,PGE₃, **1**, 245, **8**, 464
$C_{20}H_{30}O_6$
  GA₄₂, **8**, 38
  GA₈₃, **8**, 40
  teumassilin, **8**, 319
$C_{20}H_{30}O_8$, ptaquiloside, **7**, 507
$C_{20}H_{31}F_3NO$, TBTFA, **5**, 122
$C_{20}H_{31}NO_3$, *p*-nitrophenyl myristate, **5**, 130

$C_{20}H_{31}NO_7$, heliosupine, **4**, 31
$C_{20}H_{31}N_3O_{19}P_2$,UDP-*N*-acetylmuramic acid, **3**, 251
$C_{20}H_{31}N_4O_{16}P$
  CMP-*N*-acetylneuraminic acid, **5**, 280
  cytidine 5′-monophosphate *N*-acetylneuraminic acid, **3**,
    228
$C_{20}H_{31}O_7S$, hymatoxin A, **8**, 179
$C_{20}H_{32}$
  abieta-7,13-diene, **2**, 218, 228, 230, 238
  8,12-abietadiene, **2**, 382, 383
  abietadiene, **2**, 381
  ent-atisir-15-ene, **2**, 230
  ent-atisir-16-ene, **2**, 230, 238
  ent-beyerene, **2**, 230
  casbene, **2**, 218, 219, 221
  cembrene, **8**, 222, 230
  1-cembrene, **2**, 220
  cembrene A, **2**, 220,
  cycloaraneosene, **1**, 378
  kaurene, **2**, 385
  kaur-16-ene, **2**, 218, 230, 231, 238, **8**, 7
  ent-kaurene, **8**, 47, 50
  levopimaradiene, **2**, 383
  neocembrene, **8**, 230
  phyllocladene, **2**, 237
  9β-pimara-7,15-diene, **2**, 229, 230
  pimara-8(14),15-diene, **2**, 228
  pimara-8,15-diene, **2**, 228
  pimaradiene, **2**, 228, 383
  ent-sandaracopimaradiene, **2**, 229
  sandaracopimaradiene, **2**, 226, 228
  ent-sclarene, **2**, 225
  sclarene, **2**, 225
  springene, **8**, 230
  stemar-16-ene, **2**, 238
  taxa-4,11-diene, **2**, 218, 220
  terpenoid, **8**, 438
  ent-trachylobane, **2**, 230
  transversadiene, **2**, 223
  1-verticillene, **2**, 221
  virescene, **2**, 226
$C_{20}H_{32}N_2O_3$,PGH₂analogue, **1**, 189
$C_{20}H_{32}N_6O_{12}S_2$, glutathione disulfide , **2**, 33, **5**, 417
$C_{20}H_{32}O$
  geranylcitronellal, **8**, 229
  geranylgeranial, **8**, 229
  oryzalexinS, **2**, 238
  spartane diterpene, **8**, 434
  spatane-type diterpene, **8**, 459
  taxa-4,11-dien-5-ol, **2**, 221
$C_{20}H_{32}O_2$
  arachidonic acid, **1**, 2, 10, 34, 98, 134, 209, 212, 255,
    273, 277, 291, 340, **5**, 105, 160, 226, 227, 233
  C20:4, **1**, 339
  cladocroic acid, **1**, 63
  eicosa-5,8,11,14-tetraenoic acid, **1**, 36, 40
  eicosa-8,11,14,17-tetraenoic acid, **1**, 40
  epofenonane, **8**, 275
  geranyl geranoate, **8**, 223
  2-ketoepimanool, **8**, 181, 181
  palustric acid, **2**, 228
  rosenonolactone, **2**, 228
  spatane-type diterpene, **8**, 459
  stemodinone, **2**, 238
  virescenol B, **2**, 228
$C_{20}H_{32}O_3$
  epoxyeicosatrienoic acid, **1**, 170
  5-HETE, **1**, 168, 176, 222, 230, 244, 245, 249
  8-HETE, **1**, 242, 246, 247
  9-HETE, **1**, 221, 246, 247
  11-HETE, **1**, 222, 223, 242, 248
  12-HETE, **1**, 176, 222, 230, 237, 238, 244, 245, 247, 248,
    249, 265

15-HETE, **1**, 222, 223, 230, 238, 247
13-hydroxyarachidonic acid, **1**, 222
15-hydroxyeicosatetraenoic acid, **5**, 249
5-hydroxyeicosatetraenoic acid, **1**, 291
5-hydroxy-7,9,11,14-eicosatetraenoic acid, **1**, 168
9-hydroxy-10,12-octadecadienoic acid, **1**, 223
13-hydroxy-9,11-octadecadienoic acid, **1**, 223
11-hydroxy-9,12-octadecadienoic acid, **1**, 223
12-KETE, **1**, 245

C₂₀H₃₂O₃S₂,PGH₂analogue, 1, 189

C₂₀H₃₂O₄
constanolactone, **1**, 243
constanolactone A, **1**, 219
8,15-diHETE, **1**, 237
5,12-dihydroxy-6,8,10,14-eicosatetraenoic acid, **1**, 249,
    5, 60, 61
8,9-epoxy-7-hydroxy-5,11,14-eicosatrienoic acid, **1**, 221
13,14-epoxy-15-hydroxy-5,8,11-eicosatrienoic acid, **1**,
    213
11,12-epoxy-15-hydroxy-5,8,13-eicosatrienoic acid, **1**,
    212
hepoxilin A₃, **1**, 245, 267
hepoxilin B₃, **1**, 267
5-HPETE, **1**, 184
8-HPETE, **1**, 240, 242, 247, 265
11-HPETE, **1**, 235
12-HPETE, **1**, 245, 264
15-HPETE, **1**, 264, 265, **5**, 239, 246
12-hydroperoxy-5,8,10,14-eicosatetraenoic acid, **1**, 263
15-hydroperoxy-5,8,11,13-eicosatetraenoic acid, **1**, 213,
    263
8-hydroperoxy-5,9,11,14-eicosatetraenoic acid, **1**, 263
5-hydroperoxyeicosatetraenoic acid, **1**, 291
5-hydroperoxy-6,8,11,14-eicosatetraenoic acid, **1**, 263
8-hydroperoxyeicosatetraenoic acid, **1**, 241
leukotriene B₄, **1**, 176, 184, 185, 237, 238, 249, 267, 279,
    281, 291, **5**, 54, 59, 61, 168

C₂₀H₃₂O₄S, PGI₂, 1, 189

C₂₀H₃₂O₅
hydroxyketo acid, **1**, 229
15-keto-PGF₂α, **1**, 242
levuglandin D₂, **1**, 165
levuglandinE₂, **1**, 165
lipoxin A₄, **1**, 170, 236, 237, 267, 281
lipoxin B₄, **1**, 267
LXA₄, **1**, 238
11-LXA₄, **1**, 237, 238
PGD₂, **1**, 163, 174, 193, 237, 242, 249, 260, 274, 276, 281
PGE, **1**, 281
PGE₂, **1**, 172, 236, 237, 242, 244, 245, 246, 249, 260, **8**,
    163, 464
PGH₂, **1**, 242, 257, **5**, 163, 182, 226, 234, 274, 276
PGI₂, **1**, 166
PGI₂, **1**, 249, 261, 277
prostacyclin, **1**, 10, **3**, 183
prostaglandinE₂, **1**, 283, **5**, 156, 226
PXA₂008., **1**, 261
thromboxane, **3**, 182
thromboxane A₂, **5**, 10, 176, 226
thromboxin A₂, **1**, 156, 281
10,11,12-trihydroxy-5,8,14,17-eicosatetraenoic acid, **1**,
    247
8,11,12-trihydroxy-5,9,14,17-eicosatetraenoic acid, **1**,
    237
trioxillin A₄, **1**, 247
TXA₂, **1**, 167, 183
TXB₂007, **1**, 246

C₂₀H₃₂O₆
8,15-dihydroperoxy-6,8,11,13-eicosatetraenoic acid, **1**,
    234
6-keto-PGE₁, **1**, 167
6-ketoPGF₁α, **1**, 237
PGG₂, **1**, 242, **5**, 163, 182, 226, 234

PGG₆, **1**, 257
platenolide, **1**, 526
rhodojaponin III, **8**, 313

C₂₀H₃₃NO₂, picatamine, 8, 546
C₂₀H₃₃NO₃, lepadin A, 8, 546
C₂₀H₃₃NO₃S, N-acetyl-S-farnesyl-cysteine, 2, 359, 361
C₂₀H₃₃NO₄, Aza-PGI₂, 1, 189
C₂₀H₃₄, dehydroabietane, 2, 384, 395
C₂₀H₃₄N₄O₆S₂, 1-mercaptodethiobiotin disulfide, 1, 830

C₂₀H₃₄O
abienol, **2**, 225
aphidicolin, **2**, 239
cembren-4-ol, **2**, 220
geranylcitronellol, **8**, 229
geranylgeraniol, **8**, 229
geranyllinalool, **8**, 229
kolavenol, **8**, 317
stemodin, **2**, 238

C₂₀H₃₄O₂
C20:3, **1**, 340
2,7,11-cembratriene-4,6-diol, **8**, 235
cembrene-4,6-diol, **2**, 220
cembrenediol, **2**, 220
C₂₀diunsaturated cyclopropanoid fatty acid, **1**, 63
dihomo-γ-linolenic acid, **1**, 161
α-4,8,13-duvatriene-1,3-diol, **8**, 181
11,14,17-eicosatrienoic acid, **1**, 218
eicosa-8,11,14-trienoic acid, **1**, 36, 40
stemarin, **2**, 238

C₂₀H₃₄O₃
12-oxo-10,15-phytodienoic acid, **8**, 115
12-oxophytodienoic acid, **8**, 119
thyrsiflorin, **2**, 239, 241

C₂₀H₃₄O₄
aphidicolin, **1**, 127, **2**, 239, **7**, 597, **8**, 179
betaenone E, **1**, 388
constanolactone, **1**, 244
5,12-diHETE, **1**, 236
PGA₂, **1**, 244

C₂₀H₃₄O₅
15-keto PGF₂α, **1**, 237
PGE₁, **1**, 160, 283
PGF, **1**, 281
PGF₂, **1**, 236, 237, 242, 245, 246, 249
PGF₂α, **1**, 163, 172, 261, 276, 283
11-*epi*-PGF₂α, **1**, 261, 276
PGI₁, **1**, 281
trioxilin, **1**, 170

C₂₀H₃₄O₆
13,14-dihydro-15-keto-PGF₂α, **1**, 196
6-keto-PGF₁α, **1**, 261, 261, 167
TXB₂, **1**, 176, 261

C₂₀H₃₅BrO₂, aplysin-20, 2, 225
C₂₀H₃₅NO, clavepictin B, 8, 546
C₂₀H₃₆, trinervitane, 8, 230
C₂₀H₃₆N₂OP, bisphosphoramidite, 7, 133
C₂₀H₃₆N₂O₂
pseudodistomin A acetate, **8**, 547
pseudodistomin B acetate, **8**, 547
C₂₀H₃₆N₃O₃P, bisphosphoramidite, 7, 133
C₂₀H₃₆O
episclareol, **8**, 181
sclareol, **8**, 181
C₂₀H₃₆O₂
11,14-eicosadienoic acid, **1**, 218
geranyl decanoate, **8**, 223
labdenediol, **2**, 225
sclareol, **2**, 225
C₂₀H₃₆O₅
dihydro-PGE, **1**, 162
13,14-dihydro-PGE₁, **1**, 162
C₂₀H₃₆O₇P₂
copalyl diphosphate, **2**, 5, 7, 8, 211, 218, 223, 226, 383,
    8, 47

C$_{20}$H$_{38}$

geranylgeranyl diphosphate, **2**, 5, 7, 10, 121, 201, 217, 331, 339, 340, 358, 381, **5**, 336, **8**, 47

labdadienyl diphosphate, **2**, 383

C$_{20}$H$_{38}$, 5,9-dimethyloctadecane, **8**, 248

C$_{20}$H$_{38}$N$_2$O$_4$, bicyclo[3.3.0]octane, **8**, 588

C$_{20}$H$_{38}$N$_6$O, stellettadine A, **8**, 443

C$_{20}$H$_{38}$O, 7-icosen-11-one, **8**, 208

C$_{20}$H$_{38}$O$_2$

ω-cycloheptyltridecanoate, **1**, 75

icosanolide, **8**, 218

11-octadecenyl acetate, **8**, 218

C$_{20}$H$_{38}$O$_3$, ω-cycloheptyl-α-hydroxytridecanoate, **1**, 75

C$_{20}$H$_{38}$O$_{11}$, octyl-β-D-maltoside, **3**, 481

C$_{20}$H$_{40}$, 10,14-dimethyl-1-octadecene, **8**, 247

C$_{20}$H$_{40}$O

11-icosen-1-ol, **8**, 218

phytol, **2**, 61, 63, **8**, 230, 234

C$_{20}$H$_{40}$O$_2$

arachidonic acid, **8**, 423

hexyl myristate, **8**, 210

9-octadecenyl acetate, **8**, 218

pheromone of *Diprion similis*, **8**, 44

C$_{20}$H$_{41}$N$_2$O$_2$P, phosphoramidite, **7**, 187

C$_{20}$H$_{42}$NO$_4$P, phosphoramidite, **7**, 170

C$_{20}$H$_{42}$NO$_6$P, 2-dodecanoylamino-1-hexanol phosphoglycol, **5**, 112

C$_{20}$H$_{42}$N$_7$O$_{19}$P$_3$S, caffeoyl-CoA, **3**, 639

C$_{20}$H$_{42}$O$_2$, octadecyl acetate, **8**, 218

C$_{20}$H$_{44}$NO$_8$P, 1-(*O*-octyl-2-(heptylphosphonyl))-glycero-3-phosphoethano lamine, **5**, 105

C$_{20}$H$_{50}$O, lanosterol, **2**, 12

C$_{17}$H$_{20}$BrN$_3$, ethidium bromide, **7**, 428

C$_{21}$G$_{39}$N$_7$O$_{12}$, streptomycin, **8**, 379

C$_{21}$H$_{12}$O$_7$, 5-carboxyfluorescein, **6**, 76

C$_{21}$H$_{14}$O$_7$

neojusticin A, **1**, 704

taiwaninE methyl ether, **1**, 704

C$_{21}$H$_{14}$O$_{15}$

nonahydroxytriphenic acid, **3**, 801

sanguisorbic acid, **3**, 801

valoneic acid, **3**, 801

C$_{21}$H$_{16}$O$_6$

justicidin B, **1**, 694, 704

retrojusticidin, **1**, 703

C$_{21}$H$_{16}$O$_8$

aklanonic acid, **1**, 487

4′-*O*-demethyldehydropodophyllotoxin, **1**, 691

prostalidin B, **1**, 705

C$_{21}$H$_{16}$O$_{10}$, theaflavic acid, **3**, 782

C$_{21}$H$_{18}$NO$_4$

chelerythrine, **7**, 601

nitidine, **7**, 601

C$_{21}$H$_{18}$N$_4$O$_2$

fumiquinazoline D, **8**, 603

fumiquinazolineE, **8**, 603

C$_{21}$H$_{18}$N$_4$O$_2$S, shermilamine B, **8**, 540

C$_{21}$H$_{18}$O$_5$, 5-*O*-methylderrone, **1**, 800

C$_{21}$H$_{18}$O$_7$

3,4-arylflavan-3-ol, **3**, 755

4-arylflavan-3-ol, **3**, 755

flavan-3,4-diol, **3**, 755

C$_{21}$H$_{18}$O$_8$

3,4-arylflavan-3-ol, **3**, 755

4-arylflavan-3-ol, **3**, 755, 756

flavan-3,4-diol, **3**, 755

C$_{21}$H$_{18}$O$_9$

3,4-arylflavan-3-ol, **3**, 755

4-arylflavan-3-ol, **3**, 756

flavan-3,4-diol, **3**, 755

C$_{21}$H$_{19}$, dimethyltrityl, **7**, 121, 126

C$_{21}$H$_{19}$N$_3$O$_3$S, amsacrine, **7**, 603, 606

C$_{21}$H$_{20}$BrN$_3$, ethidium bromide, **7**, 84, 432, 435, 446, 658

C$_{21}$H$_{20}$N$_2$O$_3$, serpentine, **4**, 46, 110, 135

C$_{21}$H$_{20}$O$_6$

curcumin, **1**, 766

7-methylluteone, **1**, 815

wailupemycin B, **8**, 597

C$_{21}$H$_{20}$O$_7$, wailupemycinC, **8**, 597

C$_{21}$H$_{20}$O$_8$, α-peltatin, **1**, 702

C$_{21}$H$_{20}$O$_{10}$

apigenin 7-glucoside, **8**, 173, 174

apigenin 7-*O*-β-glucoside, **1**, 809

galangin 3-*O*-glucoside, **1**, 731

genistin, **1**, 781

sulphurein, **8**, 159

C$_{21}$H$_{20}$O$_{11}$

kaempferol 3-*O*-glucoside, **1**, 731

luteolin 7-glucoside, **8**, 156

C$_{21}$H$_{20}$O$_{12}$, quercetin 3-*O*-glucoside, **1**, 731

C$_{21}$H$_{20}$O$_{13}$

gossypetin 7-*O*-glucoside, **1**, 733

myricetin 3-*O*-glucoside, **1**, 731

quercetin glucoside, **8**, 159

C$_{21}$H$_{21}$ClN$_2$O, welwitindolinone A isonitrile, **8**, 611

C$_{21}$H$_{21}$ClO$_5$ 1-chloro-2-deoxy-3,5-di-*O*-toluoyl-α-D-*erythro*-pentofuranose, **7**, 261

α-chloro-2-deoxyribose, **7**, 262

C$_{21}$H$_{21}$ClO$_{10}$, pelargonidin 3-*O*-glucoside, **1**, 731

C$_{21}$H$_{21}$ClO$_{11}$, cyanidin 3-*O*-glucoside, **1**, 731

C$_{21}$H$_{21}$ClO$_{12}$, delphinidin 3-*O*-glucoside, **1**, 731

C$_{21}$H$_{21}$FN$_2$O$_4$S, PGH$_2$analogue, **1**, 189

C$_{21}$H$_{21}$N, naftifine, **2**, 276

C$_{21}$H$_{22}$NO$_4$, coralyne, **7**, 467

C$_{21}$H$_{21}$NO$_6$, β-hydrastine, **4**, 42

C$_{21}$H$_{21}$N$_3$O$_7$, bicyclo[2.2.2]octene, **5**, 428

C$_{21}$H$_{21}$O$_5$, glycoside oxonium ion, **7**, 261

C$_{21}$H$_{21}$O$_{11}$, cyanidin 3-glucoside, **8**, 141

C$_{21}$H$_{22}$NO$_4$, coralyne, **7**, 601

C$_{21}$H$_{22}$N$_2$O$_2$ strychnine, **4**, 50, 110

C$_{21}$H$_{22}$N$_2$O$_7$, phenazine alkaloid esters, **8**, 592

C$_{21}$H$_{22}$O$_2$

endiandric acid A, **1**, 368

endiandric acid C, **1**, 368

C$_{21}$H$_{22}$O$_6$

bursehernin, **1**, 694

fargesin, **1**, 695, 704

kobusin, **1**, 661

C$_{21}$H$_{22}$O$_8$

plicatin, **1**, 697

wailupemycin A, **8**, 597

C$_{21}$H$_{22}$O$_9$, 2′,4,4′-trihydroxychalcone 4-*O*-glucoside, **1**, 791

C$_{21}$H$_{22}$O$_{10}$

coreopsin, **8**, 159

isosalipurposide, **1**, 722, 723, **8**, 159

naringenin 7-*O*-glucoside, **1**, 725

C$_{21}$H$_{22}$O$_{11}$, marein, **8**, 159

C$_{21}$H$_{22}$O$_{12}$, 2,3-dihydroquercetin 3-*O*-β-D-glucopyranoside, **1**, 750

C$_{21}$H$_{23}$Br$_4$N$_3$O$_7$, ceratinamide A, **8**, 440

C$_{21}$H$_{23}$NO$_9$, azicemicin B, **7**, 514

C$_{21}$H$_{23}$N$_3$O$_3$

brevianamide A, **1**, 386

brevianamide B, **1**, 386

C$_{21}$H$_{24}$BrN$_3$, eudistomidin B, **8**, 527

C$_{21}$H$_{24}$NO$_4$, 5,6-dihydrocoralyne, **7**, 601

C$_{21}$H$_{24}$N$_2$O$_2$

catharanthine, **4**, 46, 48

tabersonine, **4**, 46

C$_{21}$H$_{24}$N$_2$O$_3$

ajmalicine, **4**, 46, 110, 113, 116, 125, 135

diaboline, **4**, 50

19-epiajmalicine, **4**, 114, 125

geissoschizine, **4**, 49

11-hydroxytabersonine, **4**, 121

tetrahydroalstonine, **4**, 114, 125

$C_{21}H_{24}N_6O_4S_2$, dendroamide A, **8**, 610

$C_{21}H_{24}O_5$
  denudatin B, **1**, 677
  kadsurenone, **1**, 704
  lignan, **1**, 693
  5′-methoxydehydrodiisoeugenol, **1**, 693

$C_{21}H_{24}O_6$
  arctigenin, **1**, 645, 661, 703
  isoarctigenin, **1**, 667
  phylligenin, **1**, 662
  pinoresinol monomethyl ether, **1**, 661, 692

$C_{21}H_{24}O_7$
  medioresinol, **1**, 673, 688
  trachelogenin, **1**, 642, 690, 703

$C_{21}H_{24}O_9$
  isorhapontin, **8**, 169
  melampodin A, **8**, 308

$C_{21}H_{25}N$
  naftifine, **2**, 247
  terbinafine, **2**, 247, 270, 276

$C_{21}H_{25}N_3O_2$, deoxybrevianamide E, **1**, 386

$C_{21}H_{25}N_3O_5$, bioxalomycin β2, **7**, 500

$C_{21}H_{26}N_2O_3$
  preakuammicine, **4**, 49
  stemmadenine, **4**, 50
  β-yohimbine, **4**, 46
  yohimbine, **4**, 46, 110

$C_{21}H_{26}O_2$, probetaenone I, **1**, 389

$C_{21}H_{26}O_3$Si, 1,2-unsaturated sugar derivative, **7**, 263

$C_{21}H_{26}O_5$, *p*-coumaroyl-tetraketide lactone, **1**, 19

$C_{21}H_{26}O_6$, kobusinol A, **1**, 661

$C_{21}H_{26}O_7$, 5-methoxydihydrodehydrodiconiferyl alcohol, **1**, 688

$C_{21}H_{26}O_{12}$, plumieride, **8**, 307

$C_{21}H_{27}NO$, pulo′upone, **1**, 374

$C_{21}H_{27}NO_5$, *N*-jasmonoyltyrosine, **1**, 128

$C_{21}H_{27}NO_{12}$, 5-*O*-galactosyl-2-*O*-(indole-3-acetyl)-*myo*-inositol, **8**, 26

$C_{21}H_{27}N_3O_6$, naphthyridinomycin, **7**, 499

$C_{21}H_{27}N_7O$, oxyluciferin, **8**, 444

$C_{21}H_{27}N_7O_{14}P_2$, NAD, **2**, 28, 341, 342

$C_{21}H_{28}N_7O_{17}P_3$, NADP, **2**, 30, 341, 342

$C_{21}H_{28}O_2$
  isozonarone, **8**, 460
  zonarone, **8**, 460

$C_{21}H_{28}O_3$
  cybisterone, **8**, 230
  undecenyne, **1**, 310

$C_{21}H_{28}O_3S_2$
  polyketide triene, **1**, 396
  solanapyrone derivative, **1**, 396

$C_{21}H_{28}O_6$
  amphidinolide O, **8**, 622
  nigakilactone I, **8**, 322
  picrasin B, **8**, 322
  similikalactone B, **8**, 322

$C_{21}H_{28}O_9$, ABA ester with β-hydroxy-β-methylglutaric acid, **8**, 90

$C_{21}H_{29}BrO_4$, bromovulone, **1**, 241

$C_{21}H_{29}ClO$, chlorovulone I, **1**, 241

$C_{21}H_{29}IO_4$, iodovulone, **1**, 241

$C_{21}H_{29}NO_4$, equisetin, **1**, 370

$C_{21}H_{29}N_7O_{14}P_2$
  acetyl-3-dephospho-CoA, **2**, 19
  NADH, **3**, 393

$C_{21}H_{30}N_7O_{17}P_3$, NADPH, **1**, 591, 831, **2**, 16, 30, 32, 254, 268, **3**, 393, 414, 469, 474, 476, **5**, 336

$C_{21}H_{30}O_2$
  catechol derivative, **3**, 711
  chromazonarol, **8**, 460
  isozonarol, **8**, 460
  progesterone, **3**, 410
  zonarol, **8**, 460

$C_{21}H_{30}O_3$
  cortexone, **8**, 230
  17-hydroxyprogesterone, **3**, 637

$C_{21}H_{30}O_4$
  cortexolone, **3**, 637
  rapiculine, **1**, 370

$C_{21}H_{30}O_5$
  chlorovulone I epoxide, **1**, 241
  humulone, **1**, 760
  poststerone, **8**, 292, 293

$C_{21}H_{30}O_9$
  ABA glucoside, **8**, 90
  ABA glucosyl ester, **8**, 74, 90

$C_{21}H_{30}O_{10}$, phaseic acid glucoside, **8**, 90

$C_{21}H_{31}F_3N_5O_6P$, 5′-aminated deoxyribonucleoside phosphoramidite, **7**, 234

$C_{21}H_{31}NO_{10}$, 3-deoxyGalβ1-3Gal*N*Acα-benzyl, **3**, 79

$C_{21}H_{31}N_3O_{19}P_2$, enolbutyryl-UDP-*N*-acetylglucosamine, **3**, 254

$C_{21}H_{31}O_5$, 2α,3α-dihydroxy-B-homo-7-oxa-5 128a-pregnane-6,20-dione, **8**, 107

$C_{21}H_{32}N_4O_6$, HC-toxin, **4**, 226, 230, 235

$C_{21}H_{32}O_2$
  catechol derivative, **3**, 711
  pregnenolone, **1**, 630, 632

$C_{21}H_{32}O_3$
  17α,20β-dihydroxy-4-pregnen-3-one, **8**, 230
  17,20-dihydroxy-4-pregnen-3-one, **8**, 426

$C_{21}H_{32}O_4$ 2α,3α-dihydroxy-5α-pregnan e-6,10-dione, **8**, 107
  17,20,21-trihydroxy-4-pregnen-3-one, **8**, 230

$C_{21}H_{32}O_6$, isodomedin, **8**, 313

$C_{21}H_{32}O_{10}$, dihydrophaseic acid glucoside, **8**, 90

$C_{21}H_{33}N_2$
  arylalkylamine carbocation, **2**, 258
  geranyl derivative, **2**, 254

$C_{21}H_{33}N_2O_5P$, phenolic phosphoramidite, **7**, 177

$C_{21}H_{33}N_4O_2P$, phosphoramidite, **7**, 185

$C_{21}H_{33}N_5O_{10}$, *O*-glucosyl-9-riboxyldihydrozeatin, **8**, 61

$C_{21}H_{34}N_2O_2$, 10-formamidokalihinene, **8**, 437

$C_{21}H_{34}N_5O_6P$, phosphoramidite, **7**, 175

$C_{21}H_{34}O_2$, catechol derivative, **3**, 711

$C_{21}H_{34}O_2$Si, trimethylsilylpentadecatrienynediol acetonide, **1**, 310

$C_{21}H_{34}O_3S$, STA$_2$, **1**, 189

$C_{21}H_{34}O_3S_2$, U-46619 disulfide analogue, **1**, 188

$C_{21}H_{34}O_4$
  amphidinolide, **8**, 622
  carbacyclin, **1**, 190
  15-hydroperoxy-5,8,11,13-eicosatetraenoic acid, **1**, 102
  iloprost, **1**, 190
  isocarbacyclin, **1**, 190
  isocarbacyclin isomer, **1**, 190
  PGA$_1$, **1**, 162, 172
  PGB$_1$, **1**, 162, 172
  PGH$_2$ analogue, **1**, 188, 189
  PGI$_2$, **1**, 175, **1**, 181 2α,3α,6β-trihydroxy-5α-pregnan-20-one, **8**, 107
  U-46619, **1**, 188

$C_{21}H_{34}O_4S$, PGH$_2$ analogue, **1**, 189

$C_{21}H_{34}O_5$
  betaenone A, **1**, 388
  betaenone C, **1**, 388
  PGH$_2$ methyl ester, **1**, 182
  stemphyloxin I, **1**, 388

$C_{21}H_{34}O_6$
  9,11-epoxymethano-PGF$_{1\alpha}$, **1**, 261
  9,11-epoxymethano-PGF$_{2\alpha}$, **1**, 261, 262
  ornoprostil, **1**, 196

$C_{21}H_{34}O_7$, 10-methylplatenolide I, **1**, 526

$C_{21}H_{35}NO_3$, PGH$_2$ analogue, **1**, 189

$C_{21}H_{35}NO_5$, PGH$_2$ analogue, **1**, 189

$C_{21}H_{35}N_7O_{10}P_3$, Co-A thioanion, **2**, 34

C$_{21}$H$_{36}$, 1,3,6,9-henicosatetraene, **8**, 207

C$_{21}$H$_{36}$N$_7$O$_{10}$P$_3$, desthio-CoA, **2**, 34

C$_{21}$H$_{36}$N$_7$O$_{16}$P$_3$S, coenzyme A, **2**, 32, 34, **3**, 306, 409, **4**, 15, 222, **5**, 25, 185, 217

C$_{21}$H$_{36}$O
  9,10-epoxy-1,3,6-henicosatriene, **8**, 207
  9,10-epoxy-3,6-henicosatriene, **8**, 207

C$_{21}$H$_{36}$O$_2$
  catechol derivative, **3**, 711
  farnesyl hexanoate, **8**, 227
  5-pentadecylresorcinol, **8**, 181, 183

C$_{21}$H$_{36}$O$_5$, PGE$_1$, **1**, 172

C$_{21}$H$_{36}$O$_6$, 6-deoxyerythronolide B 5-keto analogue, **1**, 504

C$_{21}$H$_{37}$N$_2$O$_2$P, adamantylethyl phosphoramidite, **7**, 187

C$_{21}$H$_{38}$, 3,6,9-henicosatriene, **8**, 207

C$_{21}$H$_{38}$N$_2$O$_2$, cyclic amino alcohol, **2**, 257

C$_{21}$H$_{38}$N$_4$O$_5$P$_2$S, phosphoramidite, **7**, 168

C$_{21}$H$_{38}$O, 6,8-henicosadien-11-one, **8**, 208

C$_{21}$H$_{38}$O$_2$, 6,7-9,10-diepoxyhenicosadiene, **8**, 208

C$_{21}$H$_{38}$O$_5$
  5,6-dehydro-PGF$_{2\alpha}$ methyl ester, **1**, 182
  PGF$_{1\alpha}$, **1**, 160
  PGF$_{1\beta}$, **1**, 162

C$_{21}$H$_{38}$O$_6$, 6-deoxyerythronolide B, **1**, 497, 507, 515

C$_{21}$H$_{38}$O$_7$, erythronolide B, **1**, 498

C$_{21}$H$_{39}$N$_7$O$_{12}$, streptomycin, **1**, 140, **3**, 6, 350, 353, **4**, 200, **6**, 199, **7**, 433

C$_{21}$H$_{40}$O, 6-henicosen-11-one, **8**, 208

C$_{21}$H$_{40}$O$_2$, 1-methylethyl oleate, **8**, 218

C$_{21}$H$_{42}$
  7-henicosene, **8**, 218
  9-henicosene, **8**, 218

C$_{21}$H$_{42}$O$_2$, 10,14-dimethylpentadecyl 2-methylpropanoate, **8**, 241

C$_{21}$H$_{43}$N$_5$O$_7$, gentamycin, **6**, 194

C$_{21}$H$_{44}$
  3,7-dimethylnonadecane, **8**, 249
  henicosane, **8**, 217, 218

C$_{22}$H$_{14}$INO$_6$, 5-iodoacetamidofluorescein, **6**, 91

C$_{22}$H$_{18}$O$_6$, γ-indomycinone, **8**, 598

C$_{22}$H$_{18}$O$_7$, justicidin A, **1**, 694

C$_{22}$H$_{18}$O$_{11}$
  tetracenomycin, **1**, 432, 486, 490
  tetracenomycinC, **1**, 479

C$_{22}$H$_{19}$N$_3$O$_3$, cystodytin B, **1**, 381

C$_{22}$H$_{20}$N$_2$O$_5$, 7-ethyl-10-hydroxycamptothecin, **7**, 599

C$_{22}$H$_{20}$N$_3$O$_2$, cystodytin A, **8**, 540

C$_{22}$H$_{20}$O$_6$, phyllamycin B, **1**, 703

C$_{22}$H$_{20}$O$_6$S
  4α-benzyl thioether, **3**, 758
  4β-benzyl thioether, **3**, 758
  flanan-3-ol benzyl thioether, **3**, 760
  flavan-3-ol thioether, **3**, 758

C$_{22}$H$_{20}$O$_7$, 6,8-di-O-methylaverufin, **1**, 455

C$_{22}$H$_{20}$O$_8$, aklavinone, **1**, 14, 432, 482

C$_{22}$H$_{20}$O$_9$
  enterocin, **8**, 597
  enterocin derivative, **8**, 543
  3-pi-5-deoxyenterocin, **8**, 597

C$_{22}$H$_{20}$O$_{10}$
  5-deoxyenterocin, **8**, 597
  enterocin, **8**, 543
  granaticin, **1**, 478, **3**, 354, **4**, 206
  griseusin, **1**, 479
  tetracenomycin, **1**, 11

C$_{22}$H$_{21}$NO, Ro-43-6300, **2**, 292

C$_{22}$H$_{22}$IN$_3$, propidium iodide, **7**, 85

C$_{22}$H$_{22}$N$_4$O, furimidazoline, **7**, 460

C$_{22}$H$_{22}$N$_8$, bisanthrene, **7**, 440, 437, 606

C$_{22}$H$_{22}$O$_6$, ethyl pinoresinol, **1**, 692

C$_{22}$H$_{22}$O$_8$, podophyllotoxin, **1**, 671, 701, 702, **3**, 677, **7**, 609

C$_{22}$H$_{22}$O$_{13}$, patuletin 7-glucoside, **8**, 159

C$_{22}$H$_{23}$ClN$_2$O$_8$, aureomycin, **4**, 200

C$_{22}$H$_{23}$NO$_7$, narcotine, **4**, 35

C$_{22}$H$_{24}$Br$_2$N$_{10}$O$_2$
  bromopyrrole, **1**, 381
  dimeric bromopyrrole, **8**, 437

C$_{22}$H$_{24}$Br$_2$N$_{10}$O$_3$, dimeric bromopyrrole, **8**, 437

C$_{22}$H$_{24}$N$_2$O$_3$, icajine, **4**, 50

C$_{22}$H$_{24}$N$_2$O$_8$, tetracycline, **1**, 2, 446, **4**, 196, 200

C$_{22}$H$_{24}$N$_2$O$_9$, oxytetracycline, **1**, 11, 475, 481, 482, **4**, 206

C$_{22}$H$_{24}$N$_6$O$_2$S$_2$, polycarpine, **8**, 542

C$_{22}$H$_{24}$O$_7$, yatein, **1**, 694

C$_{22}$H$_{25}$ClO$_8$, tafricanin A, **8**, 316

C$_{22}$H$_{25}$F$_3$N$_7$O$_8$, (diazirino)trifluoroethylbenzoyl TTX, **8**, 488

C$_{22}$H$_{25}$NO$_4$, 7-demethyltylopharine, **8**, 155

C$_{22}$H$_{25}$NO$_6$, colchicine, **1**, 127, **4**, 26

C$_{22}$H$_{25}$NO$_9$, azecemicin A, **7**, 514

C$_{22}$H$_{25}$N$_6$O$_2$, coelenteramide benzofuran analogue, **8**, 457

C$_{22}$H$_{26}$Br$_2$O$_6$, bromogomisin J, **1**, 703

C$_{22}$H$_{26}$IN$_4$O$_{14}$P, thymine photodimer, **5**, 384

C$_{22}$H$_{26}$N$_2$O$_3$, 11-methoxytabersonine, **4**, 121

C$_{22}$H$_{26}$N$_2$O$_4$
  isoreserpiline, **4**, 118
  tetraphylline, **4**, 121

C$_{22}$H$_{26}$N$_2$O$_5$, horhammerinine, **4**, 121

C$_{22}$H$_{26}$N$_2$O$_5$S$_3$, S-deoxyleinamycin, **7**, 523

C$_{22}$H$_{26}$N$_2$O$_6$, dichotine, **4**, 50

C$_{22}$H$_{26}$N$_2$O$_6$S$_3$, leinamycin, **7**, 522

C$_{22}$H$_{26}$N$_4$O$_5$, cyanocycline A, **7**, 499

C$_{22}$H$_{26}$O$_4$
  denudatin B, **3**, 677
  lignan, **1**, 694
  machilusin, **1**, 693
  seratrodast, **1**, 198

C$_{22}$H$_{26}$O$_5$, calanolide A, **1**, 624

C$_{22}$H$_{26}$O$_6$
  burseran, **1**, 701
  epieudesmin, **1**, 694
  eudesmin, **1**, 661, 667, 692, 694, 695, 704

C$_{22}$H$_{26}$O$_8$
  lirioresinol A, **1**, 647
  lirioresinol B, **1**, 647
  syringaresinol, **1**, 649, 651, 673

C$_{22}$H$_{26}$O$_{12}$, catalposide, **8**, 307

C$_{22}$H$_{27}$N$_7$O
  luciferin, **8**, 444
  urochordamine A, **8**, 440
  urochordamine A', **8**, 441
  urochordamine B, **8**, 441
  urochordamine B', **8**, 441

C$_{22}$H$_{27}$N$_7$O$_2$, luciferinol, **8**, 444

C$_{22}$H$_{27}$N$_9$O$_4$, distamycin, **7**, 253, 486, 567, 505

C$_{22}$H$_{28}$Br$_2$Co$_2$O$_6$Si, enyne, **1**, 316

C$_{22}$H$_{28}$Br$_2$N$_{10}$O$_2$, sceptrin, **1**, 381

C$_{22}$H$_{28}$N$_2$O$_4$, vincine, **4**, 121

C$_{22}$H$_{28}$N$_2$O$_{11}$, terramycin, **4**, 200

C$_{22}$H$_{28}$N$_4$O$_6$, mitoxanthrone, **7**, 603, 606

C$_{22}$H$_{28}$O$_5$
  galbelgin, **1**, 692
  galgravin, **1**, 692
  veraguensin, **1**, 692

C$_{22}$H$_{28}$O$_6$
  gomisin J, **1**, 703
  pachypostaudin A, **1**, 642
  piperenone, **1**, 694
  quassin, **8**, 322

C$_{22}$H$_{28}$O$_7$
  cornutin B, **8**, 317
  kobusinol B, **1**, 661

C$_{22}$H$_{28}$O$_8$
  eucannabinolide, **8**, 308
  teumarin, **8**, 319

$C_{22}H_{28}O_{14}$, feruloylgalactopyranosylgalactose, **3**, 697
$C_{22}H_{29}ClO_9$, bisdeacetylsolenolide D, **8**, 431
$C_{22}H_{29}FO_5$
    dexamethasone, **1**, 248, **5**, 229
$C_{22}H_{29}NO_3$, pipercide, **8**, 304
$C_{22}H_{29}N_7O_5$, puromycin, **3**, 353, **4**, 200, 204
$C_{22}H_{30}N_2O_8$
    urauchimycin A, **8**, 589
    urauchimycin B, **8**, 589
$C_{22}H_{30}O_2$
    6,7-dehydroferruginol acetate, **2**, 397
    penostatin C, **8**, 603
$C_{22}H_{30}O_3$, spatane-type diterpene, **8**, 459
$C_{22}H_{30}O_5$
    amphidinolide P, **8**, 622
    PGE$_3$-1,15-lactone, **8**, 464
    PGE$_3$-1,15-lactone-11-acetate, **1**, 246
$C_{22}H_{30}O_6$
    laserolide, **8**, 308
    megaphone, **1**, 641, 677, **3**, 677
    neoquassin, **8**, 322
    picasin D, **8**, 322
$C_{22}H_{30}O_7$
    isomontanolide, **8**, 308
    picrasin E, **8**, 322
$C_{22}H_{30}O_8$, picrasin F, **8**, 322
$C_{22}H_{31}NO_4S$, PGH$_2$analogue, **1**, 189
$C_{22}H_{31}NO_5S$, latrunculin A, **8**, 466
$C_{22}H_{32}O_2$, docosahexaenoic acid, **1**, 291
$C_{22}H_{32}O_3$
    13-hydroxydocosahexaenoic acid, **1**, 237
    penostatin A, **8**, 603
    penostatin B, **8**, 603
$C_{22}H_{32}O_4$, iloprost, **1**, 196
$C_{22}H_{32}O_5$
    ajugarin V, **8**, 315
    methyl 15-acetoxy-PGA$_2$, **1**, 239
    PGE$_2$-1,15-lactone 11-acetate, **8**, 464
    prostaglandin-1,15-lactone, **8**, 464
$C_{22}H_{32}O_6$, ajugarin II, **8**, 315
$C_{22}H_{33}BrO_4$, bromo diterpene, **8**, 461
$C_{22}H_{33}BrO_5$, bromo diterpene, **8**, 461
$C_{22}H_{33}NO_2$, himgravin, **1**, 371
$C_{22}H_{33}NO_3$, ajaconine, **8**, 167
$C_{22}H_{33}NO_5$, PGH$_2$analogue, **1**, 189
$C_{22}H_{34}N$
    arylalkylamine carbocation, **2**, 258
    FPP ammonium ion analogue, **2**, 253 *N*-[5,9,13-trimethyl-4,8,12-tetradecatrien-1-yl]pyridinium cation, **2**, 291
$C_{22}H_{34}N_3O_2P$, phosphoramidite, **7**, 185
$C_{22}H_{34}N_5O_{15}P_3$, deoxycytidine triphosphate, **7**, 220
$C_{22}H_{34}O_3$
    dictyosphaerin, **1**, 215
    penostatin D, **8**, 603
    o-pentadecenylsalicylic acid, **8**, 139
    PGH$_2$analogue, **1**, 189
    pleuromutillin, **2**, 228
    spatane-type diterpene, **8**, 459
$C_{22}H_{34}O_5$
    prostaglandin-1,15-lactone, **8**, 464
    10,13,14-trihydroxy-4,7,11,16,19-docosapentaenoic acid, **1**, 237
$C_{22}H_{34}O_7$, forskolin, **3**, 53
$C_{22}H_{35}N_2O_3PS$, mercaptoalkylated phosphoramidite, **7**, 167
$C_{22}H_{36}ClNO$
    kalihinene X, **8**, 437
    kalihinene Y, **8**, 437
    kalihinene Z, **8**, 437
$C_{22}H_{36}O_2$, geranylgeranyl acetate, **8**, 229
$C_{22}H_{36}O_3$
    CTA$_2$, **1**, 189

PGH$_2$analogue, **1**, 189
$C_{22}H_{36}O_5$, limaprost, **1**, 196
$C_{22}H_{37}NaO_{15}S$, MTX derivative, **8**, 506
$C_{22}H_{37}NO_2$
    anadamide, **1**, 281
    clavepictin A, **8**, 546
$C_{22}H_{37}NO_9$, theopederin E, **8**, 581
$C_{22}H_{38}N_2O$, pseudodistomin C, **8**, 550
$C_{22}H_{38}O_4$
    amphidinin A, **8**, 622
    SQ29,535, **5**, 248
$C_{22}H_{38}O_5$
    carboprost, **1**, 194
    misoprostol, **1**, 196
$C_{22}H_{40}NO_5P$, didecanoyl phosphatidylethanolamine, **5**, 107
$C_{22}H_{40}O_2$
    docosenolide, **8**, 218
    dodec-13-enoic acid, **1**, 38
$C_{22}H_{42}N_4O_5$, decanoyl-Lys-Ala-Ala, **3**, 283
$C_{22}H_{42}O_2$
    docosanolide, **8**, 218
    dodec-7-enoic acid, **1**, 42
    11-icosenyl acetate, **8**, 218
    16-methyl-9-heptadecenyl 2-methylpropanoate, **8**, 241
$C_{22}H_{44}O_2$
    docosanoic acid, **1**, 48
    hexyl palmitate, **8**, 210
$C_{22}H_{46}O_2$, icosyl acetate, **8**, 218
$C_{23}H_{18}ClNOS_2$, SC58092, **5**, 252
$C_{23}H_{18}ClNO_3S_2$, SC58076, **5**, 252
$C_{23}H_{19}N_3O_3$
    isosegoline A, **1**, 381
    segoline A, **1**, 381
    segoline B, **1**, 381
$C_{23}H_{20}N_2O_8$, *N*-hydroxysuccinimide estere of 4′-[(3-carboxypropionamide)methyl]-4, 5′, 8-trimethylpsoralen, **7**, 161
$C_{23}H_{20}O_{11}$, elloramycin, **1**, 479, 480
$C_{23}H_{21}N_3O_2S$, lissoclin B, **8**, 541
$C_{23}H_{21}N_4NaO_5$, NC-190, **7**, 606
$C_{23}H_{21}N_4OS$, dehydrokuanoniamine B, **8**, 540
$C_{23}H_{22}O_6$
    deguelin, **1**, 806, 812
    rotenone, **1**, 810
$C_{23}H_{22}O_7$
    amorphigenin, **1**, 810
    α-toxicarol, **1**, 812
$C_{23}H_{22}O_9$, rhinacanthin E, **1**, 702
$C_{23}H_{22}O_{11}$, betavulgarin 2′-glucoside, **8**, 191
$C_{23}H_{23}N_3O_2S$
    benzo-1,3-oxathiazoline, **8**, 541
    lissoclin A, **8**, 541
$C_{23}H_{23}N_3O_5$
    SKF 104864, **7**, 599
    topotecan, **7**, 599
$C_{23}H_{24}N_4O_9$, nocardicin A, **4**, 188
$C_{23}H_{24}O_6$
    dipropyl pinoresinol, **1**, 692
    rot-2′-enoic acid, **1**, 805, 812
$C_{23}H_{24}O_7$
    steganacin, **3**, 677
    sumatrolic acid, **1**, 812
$C_{23}H_{24}O_8$
    5-methoxypodophyllotoxin, **1**, 671, 696
    podophyllotoxin, **1**, 696
$C_{23}H_{24}O_9$, rhinacanthin F, **1**, 702
$C_{23}H_{25}N_3$, naphthylquinoline, **7**, 468
$C_{23}H_{25}N_3O_2$, coelenteramide, **8**, 456
$C_{23}H_{25}N_3O_3$, coelenterazine amide, **8**, 452
$C_{23}H_{26}N_4O_{17}PS$, thymine photodimer, **5**, 384
$C_{23}H_{27}N$, butenafine, **2**, 276
$C_{23}H_{27}NO_4$, isocotylocrebine, **8**, 155

C$_{23}$H$_{27}$NO$_8$, narceine, **4**, 35
C$_{23}$H$_{28}$Cl$_3$N$_3$O, quinacrine mustard, **7**, 428, 470
C$_{23}$H$_{28}$N$_2$O$_4$, N-jasmonoyltryptophan, **1**, 128
C$_{23}$H$_{28}$N$_2$O$_5$, reserpiline, **4**, 118
C$_{23}$H$_{28}$N$_4$O, 8-propionate porphyrinogen, **4**, 97
C$_{23}$H$_{28}$O$_6$
  enprostil, **1**, 196
  gomisinN, **1**, 703
  magnolin, **1**, 661, 692
C$_{23}$H$_{28}$O$_7$
  epimagnolin A, **1**, 692, 693
  gomisin A, **1**, 676, 702, 703, **3**, 677
C$_{23}$H$_{28}$O$_{10}$, glaucolide A, **8**, 308
C$_{23}$H$_{28}$O$_{11}$, bruceine B, **8**, 322
C$_{23}$H$_{29}$ClN$_2$O, BIBX 79, **2**, 293
C$_{23}$H$_{29}$ClO$_4$, ascochlorine, **1**, 534
C$_{23}$H$_{29}$NO$_4$, N-methylcorydaline, **4**, 40
C$_{23}$H$_{29}$NO$_5$, N-(acetyl)jasmonylphenylalanine, **1**, 118
C$_{23}$H$_{29}$NO$_{12}$, hygromycin, **1**, 541
C$_{23}$H$_{29}$N$_4$O, manzamine C, **8**, 553
C$_{23}$H$_{29}$N$_5$O$_{10}$, 6-benzylamino-9[O-glucopyranosyl-(1→3)-ribofuranosyl]purine, **8**, 71
C$_{23}$H$_{30}$ClN$_3$O, quinacrine, **1**, 123, **7**, 428, 467
C$_{23}$H$_{30}$N$_2$O$_3$, cyclohexanol, **5**, 426
C$_{23}$H$_{30}$N$_2$O$_4$
  N-cucurbinoyltryptophan, **1**, 128
  geissovelline, **4**, 50
C$_{23}$H$_{31}$NO$_7$S, sulproston, **1**, 194
C$_{23}$H$_{32}$N$_2$O$_3$, vincaminoridine, **4**, 121
C$_{23}$H$_{32}$N$_6$O$_{14}$, polyoxin A, **3**, 286
C$_{23}$H$_{32}$O$_3$, polhovalide, **8**, 308
C$_{23}$H$_{33}$N$_3$, keramamineC, **8**, 554
C$_{23}$H$_{34}$O$_4$, spatane-type diterpene, **8**, 459
C$_{23}$H$_{34}$O$_5$
  compactin, **1**, 422, **2**, 378, 257, 353, 355, 363
  digoxigenin, **6**, 229
  mevastatin, **2**, 25
C$_{23}$H$_{34}$O$_6$, ajugarin IV, **8**, 315
C$_{23}$H$_{34}$O$_7$, picrasinC, **8**, 322
C$_{23}$H$_{35}$ClN$_2$O
  kalihinol A, **8**, 437
  terpenoid, **8**, 438
C$_{23}$H$_{35}$ClO$_6$, chloriolinC, **8**, 601
C$_{23}$H$_{35}$ClO$_7$, chloriolin B, **8**, 601
C$_{23}$H$_{35}$NaO$_7$, pravastatin, **1**, 422
C$_{23}$H$_{35}$NOS
  curacin A, **8**, 606, 608
  curacin B, **8**, 606
  curacinC, **8**, 606
C$_{23}$H$_{36}$N$_4$O$_5$, Ala-MeLeu-MeLeu-MeVal, **1**, 548
C$_{23}$H$_{36}$N$_6$O$_4$, Lys-Trp-Lys, **7**, 380
C$_{23}$H$_{36}$O$_2$, 5-alkylresorcinol, **7**, 535
C$_{23}$H$_{36}$O$_7$
  acetylandromedol, **8**, 162
  pravastatin, **2**, 246
  pravastin, **1**, 2
C$_{23}$H$_{37}$ClN$_2$O$_2$, terpenoid, **8**, 438
C$_{23}$H$_{37}$ClN$_2$O$_2$S, terpenoid, **8**, 438
C$_{23}$H$_{37}$ClN$_2$O$_3$, terpenoid, **8**, 438
C$_{23}$H$_{37}$NO$_4$, TX analogue, **1**, 189
C$_{23}$H$_{37}$N$_4$O$_6$PS, mercaptoalkylated phosphoramidite, **7**, 167
C$_{23}$H$_{38}$N$_3$O$_{19}$P$_3$,UDPMurNAc analogue, **3**, 278
C$_{23}$H$_{38}$N$_4$O$_{14}$
  allosamidin derivative, **1**, 149
  didemethylallosamidin, **1**, 151
C$_{23}$H$_{38}$N$_7$O$_{17}$P$_3$S, acetyl-CoA, **1**, 3, 25, 292, 294, 346, 718, **2**, 3, 12, 15, 46, 50, 51, 53, 376, **3**, 384, 393, 410, 649, **4**, 65, 227, 264, 543, **5**, 25, 185, 318, **8**, 203, 209
C$_{23}$H$_{38}$N$_7$O$_{18}$P$_3$S, S-carboxymethyl CoA, **5**, 26
C$_{23}$H$_{38}$O$_4$, arachidonylglycerol, **1**, 281

C$_{23}$H$_{38}$O$_5$
  gemeprost, **1**, 194
  tylactone, **1**, 525
C$_{23}$H$_{38}$O$_6$, betaenone F, **1**, 388
C$_{23}$H$_{39}$ClN$_2$O$_3$, 1-phenyl-2-decanoylamino-3-morpholino-1-propanol.HCl, **3**, 114
C$_{23}$H$_{39}$CoN$_5$O$_8$, anilino(2,2-dipropionatopropyl)bis(dimethylglyoximato)cobalt, **5**, 266
C$_{23}$H$_{40}$N$_2$O$_{16}$, GlcNAcβ1-6[GlcNAcβ1-2]Ma nα1-methyl, **3**, 55
C$_{23}$H$_{40}$N$_4$O$_{15}$, allosamidin derivative, **1**, 151
C$_{23}$H$_{41}$AlO, diisobutylaluminum-2,6-di-t-butyl-4-methylphenoxide, **1**, 177
C$_{23}$H$_{44}$O, 14-tricosen-10-one, **8**, 219
C$_{23}$H$_{44}$O$_2$
  octadecenyl isovalerate, **8**, 221
  octadecenyl 2-methylbutanoate, **8**, 221
C$_{23}$H$_{45}$NO$_3$,
  N-(1-oxododecyl)-4α,10-dimethyl-8-azadecal-3β-ol, **2**, 291
C$_{23}$H$_{45}$N$_5$O$_{14}$, paromomycin, **6**, 193
C$_{23}$H$_{46}$
  5-tricosene, **8**, 219
  7-tricosene, **8**, 218, 219
  9-tricosene, **8**, 200, 219
C$_{23}$H$_{46}$N$_6$O$_{13}$, neomycin, **6**, 194
C$_{23}$H$_{46}$O, 9,10-epoxytricosane, **8**, 219
C$_{23}$H$_{48}$NO$_6$P, 1-octyl-2-(N-dodecanoylamino)-2-deoxyglycero-3-phosphog lycol, **5**, 110
C$_{24}$H$_{12}$N$_4$, eilatin, **8**, 540
C$_{24}$H$_{15}$Br$_4$NO$_5$, polycitrin A, **8**, 539
C$_{24}$H$_{16}$CuN$_4$
  bis(1,10-phenanthroline)Cu, **7**, 253
  copper bis-phenanthroline complex, **7**, 373, 377, 380, 385, 397
  1,10-phenanthroline-cuprous ion complex, **7**, 86
C$_{24}$H$_{16}$O$_9$, sapurimycin, **7**, 510
C$_{24}$H$_{16}$O$_{12}$, phloroglucinol oligomer, **8**, 460
C$_{24}$H$_{17}$N$_3$O, trisindoline, **8**, 588
C$_{24}$H$_{18}$O$_8$, sinaiticin, **1**, 685, 687
C$_{24}$H$_{18}$O$_{13}$
  luteolin 7-(6″-malonylglucoside), **8**, 156
  luteolin 7-malonylglucoside, **8**, 155
C$_{24}$H$_{19}$O, p-anisyl-1-naphthylphenylmethyl, **7**, 126
C$_{24}$H$_{20}$N$_2$O$_{10}$, kinamycin, **7**, 541
C$_{24}$H$_{20}$O$_7$,UCE6, **7**, 600
C$_{24}$H$_{21}$N$_5$O$_4$
  fumiquinazoline F, **8**, 603
  fumiquinazoline G, **8**, 603
C$_{24}$H$_{22}$EuN$_4$O$_8$S, europium chelate of oligonucleotide, **7**, 201
C$_{24}$H$_{22}$N$_2$O$_8$, di-O-(indole-3-acetyl)-myo-inositol, **8**, 26
C$_{24}$H$_{23}$ClO$_{14}$, delphinidin 3-malonylglucoside, **8**, 159
C$_{24}$H$_{23}$N$_3$O$_7$, duocarmycinSA, **7**, 505
C$_{24}$H$_{23}$N$_3$O$_8$, duocarmycin A, **7**, 505
C$_{24}$H$_{23}$N$_4$O$_2$S, shermilamineC, **8**, 540
C$_{24}$H$_{23}$N$_5$O$_4$
  fumiquinazoline A, **8**, 603
  fumiquinazoline B, **8**, 603
C$_{24}$H$_{24}$N$_4$O$_4$S,CI-921, **7**, 606
C$_{24}$H$_{24}$O$_9$, steganacin, **1**, 676, 701
C$_{24}$H$_{25}$N$_3$O$_4$
  coelenteramide 1,2-dioxetanone, **8**, 456
  coelenterazine 5-hydroxyperoxide, **8**, 452
C$_{24}$H$_{25}$O$_2$Si, t-butyldiphenylsilyloxymethylbenzoyl, **7**, 120
C$_{24}$H$_{26}$FNO$_4$, fluvastatin, **2**, 246, 259
C$_{24}$H$_{26}$O$_6$
  dibutyl pinoresinol, **1**, 692
  egonol-2-methylbutanoate, **1**, 645
C$_{24}$H$_{26}$O$_7$, dihydroclerodin, **8**, 315
C$_{24}$H$_{27}$N$_3$O$_6$S, 9-(S-glutathionyl)-10-hydroxy-9,10-dihydrophenanthrene, **5**, 63

C$_{24}$H$_{27}$N$_4$O$_4$S, *N*-hydroxysuccinimide ester of 3-*N*-(4-carboxybutyl)methylamino-7-diimethylaminophenazathionium chloride, **7**, 159

C$_{24}$H$_{28}$F$_3$N$_3$O$_8$S$_2$, galactosidase inhibitor, **5**, 438

C$_{24}$H$_{28}$O$_8$, steganoate B, **1**, 701

C$_{24}$H$_{28}$O$_9$, erubin A, **3**, 756

C$_{24}$H$_{28}$O$_{11}$
  globularicisin, **8**, 307
  globularin, **8**, 307

C$_{24}$H$_{29}$ClO$_9$, tafricanin B, **8**, 316

C$_{24}$H$_{30}$O$_5$
  beraprost, **1**, 191, 196
  t-butylphenoxyacetic anhydride, **7**, 124

C$_{24}$H$_{30}$O$_6$
  diethyl pinoresinol, **1**, 692
  magnoshinin, **1**, 705
  yangambin, **1**, 661, 692
  yangambin A, **1**, 704

C$_{24}$H$_{30}$O$_6$S, compond 1737, **1**, 703

C$_{24}$H$_{30}$O$_7$, hypophyllanthin, **1**, 701

C$_{24}$H$_{30}$O$_8$
  cornutin A, **8**, 317
  margaspidin, **1**, 450

C$_{24}$H$_{32}$O$_5$, macrolactinE, **8**, 590

C$_{24}$H$_{32}$O$_6$
  acoradin, **1**, 647
  deoxyschizandrin, **1**, 703
  magnosalin, **1**, 705

C$_{24}$H$_{32}$O$_7$
  claculone I, **1**, 241
  inflexin, **8**, 313

C$_{24}$H$_{32}$O$_8$
  asatone, **1**, 379
  jodrellin A, **8**, 315

C$_{24}$H$_{32}$O$_{11}$, lignan, **3**, 677

C$_{24}$H$_{33}$ClN$_3$O$_3$P, acridinyl phosphoramidite, **7**, 181

C$_{24}$H$_{33}$NO$_3$, guineensine, **8**, 304

C$_{24}$H$_{34}$O$_4$, ferruginol ring-B-seco diacetate, **2**, 398

C$_{24}$H$_{34}$O$_5$
  beraprost analogue, **1**, 191
  macrolactin A, **8**, 590
  macrolactin F, **8**, 590

C$_{24}$H$_{34}$O$_6$
  okilactomycin, **1**, 370
  phyllanthin, **1**, 701

C$_{24}$H$_{34}$O$_7$
  ajugarin, **8**, 319
  ajugarin I, **8**, 315, 317
  clerodane, **8**, 314
  clerodin, **8**, 314, 315

C$_{24}$H$_{34}$O$_8$, 16,19-diacetylteumassilin, **8**, 319

C$_{24}$H$_{34}$O$_9$
  deoxynivalenol, **2**, 203
  simalikilactone D, **8**, 322

C$_{24}$H$_{34}$O$_{10}$, T-2 toxin, **2**, 164

C$_{24}$H$_{35}$BrO$_5$, bromo diterpene, **8**, 461

C$_{24}$H$_{35}$BrO$_6$, bromo diterpene, **8**, 461

C$_{24}$H$_{36}$O$_5$
  latanoprost, **1**, 196
  lovastatin, **1**, 410, **2**, 25, 246, 259, 261
  mevinolin, **1**, 384, **2**, 3, 60, 64, 355, 378

C$_{24}$H$_{36}$O$_6$, macrolactinic acid, **8**, 590

C$_{24}$H$_{36}$O$_8$, ajugarin III, **8**, 315

C$_{24}$H$_{37}$N$_5$O$_5$, Phe-Pro-Val-Orn, **4**, 326, 345

C$_{24}$H$_{38}$N$_7$O$_{19}$P$_3$S , malonyl-CoA, **1**, 25, 62, 147, 346, 716, 718, 732, 750, 759, 784, 789, **8**, 3, 203, 543

C$_{24}$H$_{38}$O$_2$, hexanorsqualene dialdehyde, **2**, 275

C$_{24}$H$_{38}$O$_4$
  amphidinoketide I, **8**, 633
  amphidinoketide II, **8**, 633
  amphidinolide J, **8**, 622
  LTB$_4$analogue, **1**, 192

C$_{24}$H$_{38}$O$_7$, trichoharzin, **8**, 600

C$_{24}$H$_{40}$N$_2$, conessine, **4**, 26

C$_{24}$H$_{40}$N$_2$O$_2$, pseudodistomin C acetate, **8**, 550

C$_{24}$H$_{40}$N$_4$O$_{14}$
  allosamidin derivative, **1**, 149
  demethylallosamidin, **1**, 149, 151

C$_{24}$H$_{40}$N$_7$O$_{17}$P$_3$S
  propanoyl-CoA, **8**, 203, 204, 209
  propionyl-CoA, **1**, 14, 356

C$_{24}$H$_{40}$O$_3$,PTA$_2$, **1**, 189

C$_{24}$H$_{41}$NO$_2$S, *S*-geranylgeranyl-cysteine α-carboxymethyl ester, **2**, 358

C$_{24}$H$_{41}$NO$_4$, mirabilene isonitrile A, **8**, 611

C$_{24}$H$_{41}$NO$_{10}$, mycalamide A, **8**, 581

C$_{24}$H$_{41}$N$_3$O$_{16}$, tri-*N*-acetylchitotriose, **3**, 30

C$_{24}$H$_{42}$N$_4$O$_{15}$, allosamidin derivative, **1**, 151

C$_{24}$H$_{42}$O$_6$, macrolide, **1**, 517

C$_{24}$H$_{42}$O$_{21}$, cellotetraose, **3**, 571, **5**, 301

C$_{24}$H$_{44}$NO$_{20}$, Manα1-6Manα1-4Glc*N*α1 -6*inositol*, **4**, 313

C$_{24}$H$_{44}$NO$_{23}$P, Man2-Glc*N*-PI, **3**, 304

C$_{24}$H$_{44}$N$_2$O$_4$, pseudodistomin B tetrahydroacetate, **8**, 548

C$_{24}$H$_{44}$O$_2$, neryl myristate, **8**, 222

C$_{24}$H$_{46}$N$_2$O$_{22}$P, Man*N*-Man-Glc*N*-PI, **3**, 303

C$_{24}$H$_{46}$O$_2$
  tetracosanolide, **8**, 218
  tetracos-19-enoic acid, **1**, 42

C$_{24}$H$_{46}$O$_{11}$, dodecyl-β-D-maltoside, **3**, 481

C$_{24}$H$_{48}$NO, 8-azadecaline, **2**, 304

C$_{24}$H$_{48}$O$_2$
  hexyl stearate, **8**, 210
  tetracosanoic acid, **1**, 49

C$_{24}$H$_{49}$NO$_2$,
  N-(1,5,9)-trimethyldecyl-4α,10-diimethyl-8-azadecal-3β-ol, **2**, 291

C$_{24}$H$_{50}$NO, *N*-alkylhydroxypiperidine, **2**, 304

C$_{24}$H$_{52}$N$_2$O$_5$P
  2-[*N*-palmitoylamino]propylphosphocholine, **1**, 293
  3-[*N*-palmitoylamino]propylphosphocholine, **1**, 293

C$_{24}$H$_{54}$OSn$_2$, bis(*n*-tributytin)-oxide, **8**, 431

C$_{25}$H$_{19}$N$_3$O$_2$, aequorin derivative, **8**, 449

C$_{25}$H$_{19}$N$_5$ORu, oxoruthenium complex, **7**, 374

C$_{25}$H$_{21}$NO$_4$,PGE$_2$agonist, **1**, 192

C$_{25}$H$_{21}$N$_3$O$_9$S$_2$, luciferin, **8**, 454

C$_{25}$H$_{22}$N$_4$O$_8$, streptonigrin, **7**, 529, 536

C$_{25}$H$_{22}$O$_{12}$, brainic acid, **1**, 647

C$_{25}$H$_{23}$ClN$_2$O$_5$, 5-carboxytetramethylrhodamine, **6**, 76

C$_{25}$H$_{23}$NO$_5$, jadomycin, **1**, 482

C$_{25}$H$_{24}$BrN$_3$O$_8$
  duocarmycin B$_1$, **7**, 505
  duocarmycin C$_1$, **7**, 505

C$_{25}$H$_{24}$ClN$_3$O$_8$
  duocarmycin B$_2$, **7**, 505
  duocarmycin C$_2$, **7**, 505

C$_{25}$H$_{24}$N$_2$O$_7$
  α-2'-deoxynucleoside, **7**, 261
  β-2'-deoxynucleoside, **7**, 261

C$_{25}$H$_{24}$O$_8$, maackoline, **1**, 685

C$_{25}$H$_{24}$O$_{12}$, formononetin 7-*O*-glucoside-6″-*O*-malonate, **1**, 780, 807

C$_{25}$H$_{24}$O$_{13}$, biochanin A 7-*O*-glucoside-6″-*O*-malonate, **1**, 809

C$_{25}$H$_{25}$N$_3$O$_2$, coelenterazine analogue, **8**, 448

C$_{25}$H$_{25}$N$_3$O$_8$, sibiromycin, **7**, 497

C$_{25}$H$_{25}$N$_4$O$_8$, streptonigrin, **7**, 528

C$_{25}$H$_{25}$N$_5$O$_5$, fumiquinazolineC, **8**, 603

C$_{25}$H$_{25}$N$_6$O,Hoechst dye 33258, **7**, 84, 252, 419, 595

C$_{25}$H$_{26}$BrN$_5$O$_{11}$, prosurugatoxin, **8**, 515

C$_{25}$H$_{26}$BrN$_5$O$_{13}$, surugatoxin, **8**, 515

C$_{25}$H$_{26}$N$_4$O$_3$S$_3$, leptosin, **8**, 527

C$_{25}$H$_{26}$O$_5$, shamixanthone, **1**, 434

C$_{25}$H$_{26}$O$_6$
  2'-hydroxylupalbigenin, **1**, 779
  tajixanthone, **1**, 434

$C_{25}H_{26}O_{12}$, medicarpin malonyl glucoside, **1**, 808
$C_{25}H_{28}O_6$, fumagillin, **2**, 165
$C_{25}H_{29}NO_7PDA$-I, **2**, 279
$C_{25}H_{30}O_5$
  heliocideH$_1$, **1**, 377
  heliocideH$_4$, **1**, 377
$C_{25}H_{30}O_6$, andibenin B, **1**, 378
$C_{25}H_{30}O_{11}$, lignan, **3**, 677
$C_{25}H_{30}O_{12}$, melampodinin, **8**, 308
$C_{25}H_{31}N_3O_5$, moiramide B, **8**, 594
$C_{25}H_{31}O_9$, renillafoulin A, **8**, 437
$C_{25}H_{32}N_2O_6$, vindoline, **4**, 46, 48, 121
$C_{25}H_{33}NO_{11}$
  deacetylipecoside, **4**, 123
  deacetylisoipecoside, **4**, 123
$C_{25}H_{32}O_9$
  platyphylloside, **8**, 139
  6α-senecioyloxychaparrinone, **8**, 322
$C_{25}H_{32}O_{10}$, lignan, **3**, 677
$C_{25}H_{32}O_{11}$, clemastanin A, **3**, 677
$C_{25}H_{34}N_3O_5P$, K-26, **1**, 865
$C_{25}H_{34}N_6O_2S_4$, tantazole B, **8**, 611
$C_{25}H_{34}O_7$, gradolide, **8**, 308
$C_{25}H_{34}O_9$, schkuhrin Ii, **8**, 308
$C_{25}H_{34}O_{12}$, lignan, **3**, 677
$C_{25}H_{35}O_7P_2$, geranylfarnesyl diphosphate, **5**, 325
$C_{25}H_{36}F_2O$, 29-difluoromethylidenehexanor-2,3-
    oxidosqualene, **2**, 287
$C_{25}H_{36}N_2O_2$, ircinal A, **1**, 381
$C_{25}H_{36}O_5$
  manoalide, **8**, 521
  spatane-type diterpene, **8**, 459
$C_{25}H_{36}O_7P_2$, geranylgeranyl diphosphate, **2**, 63
$C_{25}H_{37}NO_9$, 9,21-didehydroryanodine, **8**, 320
$C_{25}H_{38}F_3N_8O_5P$, 5′-aminated deoxyribonucleoside
    phosphoramidite, **7**, 234
$C_{25}H_{38}N_2O_2$, ircinal B, **1**, 381
$C_{25}H_{38}N_3O_5P$, phosphoramidite, **7**, 154
$C_{25}H_{38}O_2$, 12-deacetoxyscaradial, **8**, 467
$C_{25}H_{38}O_4$
  dysidiolide, **8**, 585
  fusarielin A, **1**, 370
  lintenolideC, **8**, 467
$C_{25}H_{38}O_5$
  isomacrolactinic acid, **8**, 590
  lintenolide D, **8**, 467
  lintenolide E, **8**, 467
  simvastatin, **2**, 25, 246
$C_{25}H_{40}N_2O_2$, ircinol A, **1**, 381
$C_{25}H_{40}N_2O_5S$, LTD$_4$
$C_{25}H_{40}N_2O_6S$, LTD$_4$, **1**, 168, 176, 249, 268
$C_{25}H_{40}N_7O_{17}P_3S$
  crotonoyl-CoA, **1**, 356, 544
  vinylacetyl-CoA, **1**, 74
$C_{25}H_{40}N_7O_{18}P_3S$, acetoacetyl-CoA, **1**, 356, **2**, 3, 16, 18,
    19, 22, 46, **4**, 65, **8**, 209, 544
$C_{25}H_{40}N_7O_{19}P_3S$
  methylmalonyl-CoA, **1**, 14, 361
  succinyl CoA, **1**, 827
$C_{25}H_{40}N_7O_{20}P_3S$, succinylCoA, **4**, 140
$C_{25}H_{41}NO_2$, U18666A, **2**, 292
$C_{25}H_{42}NO_3S$, N-acetyl-S-geranylgeranyl-cysteine, **2**, 359
$C_{25}H_{42}N_2$
  haliclonadiamine, **8**, 564
  papuamine, **8**, 564
$C_{25}H_{42}N_4O_{14}$
  allosamidin, **1**, 139, 149, 151, **5**, 297
  allosamidin derivative, **1**, 149
$C_{25}H_{42}N_7O_{17}P_3S$
  butyryl-CoA, **1**, 356, 544
  isobutyryl-CoA, **1**, 356, 761
$C_{25}H_{42}N_7O_{18}P_3S$
  3-hydroxybutanoyl-CoA, **8**, 209

  β-hydroxybutyryl-CoA, **1**, 356
$C_{25}H_{42}O_2$, 7,13,16,19-docosatetraenyl 2-
    methylpropanoate, **8**, 207
$C_{25}H_{43}NO_7$, methymycin, **1**, 500
$C_{25}H_{43}NO_{10}$, mycalamide B, **8**, 581
$C_{25}H_{43}NO_{18}$, acarbose, **5**, 299, 302, 303
$C_{25}H_{43}N_8O_{18}P_3S$, succinyl-CoA, **4**, 62, 65
$C_{25}H_{44}N_4O_{15}$, allosamidin derivative, **1**, 151
$C_{25}H_{44}O_5$, unoprostone, **1**, 196
$C_{25}H_{44}O_7P_2$, geranylfarnesyl diphosphate, **2**, 86
$C_{25}H_{44}O_{11}$, MTX derivative, **8**, 506
$C_{25}H_{45}NO_{18}$, dihydroacarbose, **5**, 302
$C_{25}H_{47}NO_5P$, didecanoyl phosphatidylcholine, **5**, 107
$C_{25}H_{48}N_6O_8$, desferrioxamine B, **7**, 540
$C_{25}H_{48}O_9$, 1-O-palmitoyl-3-O-β-D-galacto pyrano
    sylglycerol, **8**, 610
$C_{25}H_{50}$
  9-pentacosene, **8**, 219
  11-pentacosene, **8**, 219
$C_{26}H_{16}N_2$, bisacridine, **7**, 467
$C_{26}H_{19}N_3O_3$, dehydrocoelenterazine, **8**, 455
$C_{26}H_{21}N_3O_2$, aequorin derivative, **8**, 449
$C_{26}H_{21}N_3O_3$
  coelenteramide, **8**, 446
  coelenterazine, **8**, 446
$C_{26}H_{21}N_3O_4$, hydroxyaequorin, **8**, 450
$C_{26}H_{21}N_3O_9S_2$, oxyluciferin, **8**, 454
$C_{26}H_{22}N_4O_2$, coelenterazine analogue, **8**, 448
$C_{26}H_{22}O_7$, glycoside oxonium ion, **7**, 261
$C_{26}H_{23}N_3O_3$
  N-methyl coelenteramide, **8**, 452
  O-methyl coelenteramide, **8**, 452
$C_{26}H_{24}N_2O_4$,PGE$_2$agonist, **1**, 192
$C_{26}H_{24}O_{11}$, tuberculatin, **1**, 705
$C_{26}H_{25}Br_4N_3O_8$, psammaplysinE, **8**, 440
$C_{26}H_{26}FN_3O_2$, coelenterazine analogue, **8**, 449
$C_{26}H_{26}N_2$, yuehchukene, **1**, 369
$C_{26}H_{27}NO_9$, idarubicin, **4**, 200, **7**, 605
$C_{26}H_{27}N_3O_7$, 6-aminothymine glycoside, **7**, 261
$C_{26}H_{28}Cl_2N_4O_4$, ketoconazole, **1**, 720
$C_{26}H_{28}NO_{10}PS_2$, bis(methylsulfonylphenyl)
    glutamidobenzylphosphonate, **5**, 438
$C_{26}H_{28}O_9$, dihydrodehydrodiconiferyl alcohol triacetate,
    3, 677
$C_{26}H_{29}F_2N_7$, almitrine, **4**, 110
$C_{26}H_{29}NO$, tamoxifen, **1**, 783
$C_{26}H_{29}NOS_2$,NB-598, **2**, 277
$C_{26}H_{30}N_2O_8$
  strictosidine lactam, **4**, 116, 117
  vincoside lactam, **4**, 116
$C_{26}H_{30}O_8$
  FPL-55712, **1**, 191
  limonin, **8**, 321
$C_{26}H_{30}O_{11}$, 8-prenyldihydrokaempferol 7-glucoside, **8**, 156
$C_{26}H_{31}ClO_{10}$
  erythrolide A, **8**, 470
  erythrolide B, **8**, 470
$C_{26}H_{31}ClO_{11}$, erythrolide D, **8**, 470
$C_{26}H_{32}O_9$, harrisonin, **8**, 321
$C_{26}H_{32}O_{11}$
  dehydrodiconiferyl alcohol 4-O-β-D-glucoside, **3**,
    677
  dehydrodiconiferyl alcohol 4-O-glucoside, **1**, 696
  dehydrodiconiferyl alcohol 9-O-β-D-glucoside, **3**,
    677
$C_{26}H_{32}O_{12}$
  nortracheloside, **1**, 647
  wikstromol, **1**, 647, 701
$C_{26}H_{33}N_3O_4P$, phosphoramidite, **7**, 154
$C_{26}H_{33}O_9$, renillafoulin B, **8**, 437
$C_{26}H_{34}N_2O_6$, strychnosilidine, **4**, 50
$C_{26}H_{34}O_8$
  nigakilactone G, **8**, 322

picrasin A, **8**, 322

$C_{26}H_{34}O_{10}$, dihydrodehydrodiconiferyl alcohol 9-*O*-β-D-glucoside, **3**, 625

$C_{26}H_{34}O_{11}$
    dihydrodehydrodiconiferyl alcohol glucoside, **1**, 647, 680
    isobruceine A, **8**, 322
    lariciresinol 9-*O*-β-D-glucoside, **1**, 694, **3**, 625
    lariciresinol glucoside, **1**, 647

$C_{26}H_{35}N_2O_6P$, psoralen phosphoramidite, **7**, 184

$C_{26}H_{36}N_2O_5$, ypaoamide, **8**, 608

$C_{26}H_{36}N_2O_9$, blastmycin, **3**, 322

$C_{26}H_{36}O_8$, jodrellin B, **8**, 315

$C_{26}H_{36}O_9$, caryoptin, **8**, 314

$C_{26}H_{36}O_{12}$, lignan, **3**, 677

$C_{26}H_{37}ClN_3O_3P$, acridinyl phosphoramidite, **7**, 181

$C_{26}H_{38}F_3N_8O_5P$, 5′-aminated deoxyribonucleoside phosphoramidite, **7**, 234

$C_{26}H_{38}N_2$, keramaphidin, **1**, 381

$C_{26}H_{40}N_2O$, ingenamine, **1**, 381

$C_{26}H_{38}N_2O_2$
    ircinal A, **8**, 554
    ircinol A, **8**, 554

$C_{26}H_{38}O_4$, 5-alkylresorcinol, **7**, 535

$C_{26}H_{38}O_{10}$, clerodin hemiacetal, **8**, 314

$C_{26}H_{39}N_3O_2$, lyngbyatoxin, **8**, 603

$C_{26}H_{40}N_2$, keramaphidin B, **8**, 554, 555

$C_{26}H_{40}N_2O$
    ingenamine, **8**, 560
    xestocyclamine A, **8**, 560

$C_{26}H_{40}N_2O_2$
    ircinal alcohol, **8**, 556
    ircinal B, **8**, 554

$C_{26}H_{40}O_6$, erythromycin analogue, **1**, 517

$C_{26}H_{40}O_7$, trichoharzin, **1**, 370

$C_{26}H_{41}NO_{10}$, theopederin D, **8**, 581

$C_{26}H_{42}ClNO_5$, malyngamide I, **8**, 607

$C_{26}H_{42}N_2$, halicyclamine B, **8**, 566

$C_{26}H_{42}N_2O_2$
    ircinal B reduction product, **8**, 557
    ircinol B, **8**, 554

$C_{26}H_{42}N_7O_{18}P_3S$, 3-propionyl-CoA, **2**, 22

$C_{26}H_{43}N_5O_2S$, caldeonin, **8**, 538

$C_{26}H_{44}NNaO_7S$, sodium taurocholate, **3**, 116, 121

$C_{26}H_{44}N_2O_2$, ircinol B, **1**, 381

$C_{26}H_{44}N_4O_{14}$, allosamidin derivative, **1**, 149

$C_{26}H_{44}N_7O_{17}P_3S$
    isovaleryl-CoA, **1**, 147, 761
    valeryl-CoA, **1**, 356, **4**, 65, 262

$C_{26}H_{45}NO_{21}$, $Man_3GlcNAc$, **3**, 28

$C_{26}H_{46}N_2O_2$, dihydroxykeramaphidin, **8**, 555

$C_{26}H_{50}O_{11}$, tetradecyl-β-D-maltoside, **3**, 481

$C_{27}H_{22}O_{18}$, corilagin, **7**, 596

$C_{27}H_{23}Cl_2N_3O_5$, dichloronucleosides, **7**, 262

$C_{27}H_{23}N_3O_2$, aequorin derivative, **8**, 449

$C_{27}H_{23}N_5O_4$, pranlukast, **1**, 197

$C_{27}H_{24}N_2O_9$, vincoside, **4**, 129

$C_{27}H_{24}N_3O_5$, azatoxin, **7**, 610

$C_{27}H_{24}O_9$
    kapuramycin A3, **7**, 510
    kapurimycin A3, **7**, 510, 514

$C_{27}H_{24}O_{18}$
    trigalloylglucose, **3**, 807
    1,2,6-trigalloylglucose, **3**, 806, 809
    1,2,6-tri-*O*-galloyl-β-D-glucose, **3**, 822,
    1,3,6-trigalloylglucose, **3**, 809, 810

$C_{27}H_{25}Br_4NO_6$, theoneberine, **8**, 581

$C_{27}H_{26}O_9$, gilvocarcin V, **7**, 544, 545

$C_{27}H_{28}BrN_7O_5$, halocyamine A, **8**, 472

$C_{27}H_{28}N_6O$, Hoechst 33342, **7**, 595

$C_{27}H_{28}O_5$, 2,3-*O*-isopropylidene-5-*O*-trityl-D-ribofuranose, **7**, 262

$C_{27}H_{28}O_9$, steganangin, **1**, 701

$C_{27}H_{28}O_{11}$, tremulacin, **8**, 139

$C_{27}H_{29}NO_9$, 11-deoxydaunomycin, **7**, 530

$C_{27}H_{29}NO_{10}$
    daunomycin, **1**, 475, 487, **4**, 200, **7**, 438, 529, 544
    daunorubicin, **1**, 481, **3**, 324, 349, 353, **7**, 433, 527, 605

$C_{27}H_{29}NO_{11}$
    adriamycin, **4**, 200, **7**, 433, 438, 527, 528, 529, 530, 536, 568, 603
    doxorubicin, **1**, 481, 487, **3**, 324, 349, **4**, 200, **7**, 605
    epirubicin, **7**, 605

$C_{27}H_{30}N_2O_{10}$, 5-iminodaunomycin, **7**, 605

$C_{27}H_{30}O_7$, isorhamnetin 3-sophoroside, **8**, 163

$C_{27}H_{30}O_{15}$, vicenin-2, **8**, 155

$C_{27}H_{30}O_{16}$, rutin, **1**, 786

$C_{27}H_{30}O_{16}$
    quercetin 3-rutinoside, **8**, 156
    rutin, **8**, 139, 155

$C_{27}H_{31}ClO_{16}$, cyanine-3, **6**, 76

$C_{27}H_{31}ClO_{17}$, delphin, **8**, 159

$C_{27}H_{31}NOS_2$, NB-598, **2**, 270

$C_{27}H_{31}NO_4$, ilicicolin H, **1**, 370

$C_{27}H_{31}N_3O_2$, di-*t*-butylaequorin, **8**, 451

$C_{27}H_{31}N_3O_4$, aequorin butyl peroxide, **8**, 451

$C_{27}H_{32}ClNO_2$, tripanarol, **2**, 25

$C_{27}H_{32}NO_3PS$, mercaptoalkylated phosphoramidite, **7**, 167

$C_{27}H_{32}N_2O_6$, A-factor diphenylcarbanilate, **8**, 380

$C_{27}H_{32}N_2O_8$, raucaffricine, **1**, 130

$C_{27}H_{32}O_{13}$, narirutin, **8**, 155

$C_{27}H_{33}N_3O_6$, discodermide, **8**, 588

$C_{27}H_{33}N_3O_5$, andrimid, **8**, 594

$C_{27}H_{33}N_3O_6$, moiramide C, **8**, 594

$C_{27}H_{33}N_9O_{15}P_2$, FAD, **2**, 268, 272, 341

$C_{27}H_{34}BrN_4$, propidium bromide, **7**, 441

$C_{27}H_{34}F_3N_6O_5P$, 5′-aminated deoxyribonucleoside phosphoramidite, **7**, 234

$C_{27}H_{34}N_2O_9$
    strictosidine, **4**, 46, 48, 109
    vincoside, **4**, 113, 116, 117, 127

$C_{27}H_{34}N_2O_{10}$, 9-hydroxystrictosidine, **4**, 121

$C_{27}H_{34}O_5$
    gedunin, **8**, 321
    scopaducic acid B, **2**, 239
    scopalducic acid, **2**, 239

$C_{27}H_{34}O_7$, LTB_4 analogue, **1**, 192

$C_{27}H_{34}O_{11}$
    arctiin, **1**, 662, 695
    phyllirin, **1**, 662

$C_{27}H_{35}N_9O_{15}P_2$
    dihydroflavin, **5**, 383
    FADH, **5**, 375
    reduced flavin, **5**, 379

$C_{27}H_{35}O_9$, renillafoulin C, **8**, 437

$C_{27}H_{36}N_3O_4P$, phosphoramidite, **7**, 183

$C_{27}H_{36}O_5$, scopadulin, **2**, 239

$C_{27}H_{36}O_{11}$, teuflavoside, **8**, 319

$C_{27}H_{37}NO_8$, nargenicin A_1, **1**, 370, 384

$C_{27}H_{38}O_3$, δ-tocotrienol epoxide, **8**, 432, 442

$C_{27}H_{38}O_6$, pseudopterosin C, **8**, 521

$C_{27}H_{38}O_{10}$, trilobalide, **8**, 308

$C_{27}H_{40}N_6O_{17}P_3S$, biotinylated deoxyuridine triphosphate, **7**, 206

$C_{27}H_{40}N_7O_{17}P_3S_2$, 3-thiopheneacetyl-CoA, **4**, 266

$C_{27}H_{40}N_7O_{18}P_3S$, 3-furoylacetyl-CoA, **4**, 266

$C_{27}H_{40}O_3$, δ-tocotrienol epoxide, **8**, 432, 442

$C_{27}H_{40}O_4$, scalaradial, **8**, 467

$C_{27}H_{40}O_5$, amphidinolide K, **8**, 622

$C_{27}H_{40}O_6$
    lintenolide A, **8**, 467
    lintenolide B, **8**, 467

$C_{27}H_{42}FeN_4O_{12}$, ferrichrome, **4**, 199

$C_{27}H_{42}N_2O$, ingenamine B, **8**, 560

$C_{27}H_{42}N_5O_4PS$, phosphoramidite, **7**, 171

C$_{27}$H$_{42}$N$_7$O$_{18}$P$_3$S, 3-oxo-4-hexenoyl-CoA, **1**, 544
C$_{27}$H$_{42}$O$_5$, pinnasterol, **8**, 280
C$_{27}$H$_{42}$O$_6$, 3-dehydroecdysone, **8**, 279, 286
C$_{27}$H$_{42}$O$_7$, kaladasterone, **8**, 285
C$_{27}$H$_{43}$NO$_4$, malyngmideH, **8**, 606
C$_{27}$H$_{43}$NO$_{10}$, theopederinC, **8**, 581
C$_{27}$H$_{43}$N$_6$O$_{16}$P$_3$, deoxycytidine triphosphate, **7**, 220
C$_{27}$H$_{44}$F$_2$, TNS-difluoromethylidene, **2**, 275
C$_{27}$H$_{44}$N$_7$O$_{17}$P$_3$S, 3-hexenoyl-CoA, **4**, 262
C$_{27}$H$_{44}$N$_7$O$_{18}$P$_3$S, 3-oxohexanoyl-CoA , **8**, 394, **1**, 544
C$_{27}$H$_{44}$N$_7$O$_{19}$P$_3$S, mevaldyl-CoA, **2**, 32
C$_{27}$H$_{44}$N$_7$O$_{20}$P$_3$S
  HMG-CoA, **2**, 22, 24, 25, 28, 32
  3-hydroxy-3-methylglutaryl-CoA, **2**, 3
  hydroxymethylglutarylCoA, **2**, 46, 51
C$_{27}$H$_{44}$O
  5β-cholestan-3,24-dione, **8**, 230
  7-dehydrocholesterol, **2**, 258, **8**, 291
  TNS aldehyde, **2**, 275
C$_{27}$H$_{44}$O$_2$
  7-dehydro-25-hydroxycholesterol, **8**, 291
  24,25-epoxycholesterol, **2**, 270, 293
C$_{27}$H$_{44}$O$_4$, 2,25-deoxyecdysone, **8**, 288
C$_{27}$H$_{44}$O$_5$
  3-dehydroecdysone, **8**, 291
  2-deoxyecdysone, **8**, 288, 291, 293
C$_{27}$H$_{44}$O$_6$
  cheilanthone B, **8**, 285, 293
  2-deoxy-20-hydroxyecdysone, **8**, 293
  2-deoxy-3-*epi*-20-hydroxyecdysone, **8**, 288
  22-deoxy-20-hydroxyecdysone, **8**, 288, 293
  ecdysone, **8**, 279, 282
  β-ecdysone, **8**, 282
  2β,3β,14α,22,25-pentahydroxy-5β-cholest-7-en-6-one,
    8, 283
  ponasterone A, **8**, 279, 283, 288, 291, 293
C$_{27}$H$_{44}$O$_7$
  cheilanthone A, **8**, 285, 293
  crustedcysone, **8**, 283
  ecdysterone, **8**, 282
  20-hydroxyecdysone, **8**, 279, 282, 283, 291, 293
  22-*epi*-20-hydroxyecdysone, **8**, 293
C$_{27}$H$_{44}$O$_8$
  20,26-dihydroxyecdysone, **8**, 293
  polypodine B, **8**, 281, 291, 293
C$_{27}$H$_{44}$O$_9$, glycolipid, **8**, 618
C$_{27}$H$_{45}$NO$_{10}$, theopederin A, **8**, 581
C$_{27}$H$_{45}$O$_9$P, ecdysone 22-phosphate, **8**, 283
C$_{27}$H$_{46}$NO$_5$P$_2$, FPP analogue, **2**, 253
C$_{27}$H$_{46}$N$_2$O$_{17}$P$_3$S, hexanoyl-CoA, **1**, 356
C$_{27}$H$_{46}$N$_4$O$_{14}$, *N*-monoethyl allosamidin, **1**, 150
C$_{27}$H$_{46}$N$_7$O$_{17}$P$_3$S, hexanoyl-CoA, **4**, 262
C$_{27}$H$_{46}$O
  5β-cholestan-3-one, **8**, 230
  cholesterol, **1**, 53, **2**, 1, 11, 24, 27, 37, 74, 82, 246, 257,
    259, 263, 267, **3**, 98, 297, **7**, 116, **8**, 47, 230
C$_{27}$H$_{46}$O$_2$
  cholesterol 5,6-oxide, **5**, 54
  25-hydroxycholesterol, **2**, 259
  trisnorsqualene alcohol, **2**, 273
C$_{27}$H$_{47}$NaO$_9$S, polyhydroxysteroid, **8**, 471
C$_{27}$H$_{47}$O$_8$S, polyhydroxysteroid, **8**, 471
C$_{27}$H$_{47}$O$_9$S, polyhydroxysteroid, **8**, 471
C$_{27}$H$_{48}$O$_5$, polyhydroxysteroid, **8**, 471
C$_{27}$H$_{49}$N$_5$O$_6$, fellutamide B, **8**, 599
C$_{27}$H$_{49}$N$_5$O$_7$, fellutamide A, **8**, 599
C$_{27}$H$_{50}$O$_{16}$,
  Manα1-6(6-*O*-methylManα1-3) Manβ1-octyl, **3**, 50
C$_{27}$H$_{52}$
  7,11-heptacosadiene, **8**, 219
  7,13-heptacosadiene, **8**, 219
C$_{27}$H$_{54}$
  9-heptacosene, **8**, 219

13-heptacosene, **8**, 219
C$_{28}$H$_{20}$F$_3$N$_5$O$_2$, trifluoromethyldiazirinyl coelenterazine,
  8, 453
C$_{28}$H$_{23}$N$_3$O$_3$, *e*-aequorin, **8**, 447
C$_{28}$H$_{24}$O$_{12}$, proanthocyanidin A-2, **3**, 749
C$_{28}$H$_{25}$N$_3$O$_2$, aequorin derivative, **8**, 449
C$_{28}$H$_{26}$ClN$_3$O$_6$, β-chloro-2'-deoxynucleoside, **7**, 262
C$_{28}$H$_{26}$O$_{12}$, diphyllin acetyl apioside, **1**, 705
C$_{28}$H$_{28}$O$_{11}$, pillaromycin A, **3**, 322
C$_{28}$H$_{30}$N$_4$O$_8$, saframycin A, **7**, 497, 529
C$_{28}$H$_{30}$O$_8$, epistaganangin, **1**, 701
C$_{28}$H$_{31}$NO$_{10}$, menogaril, **7**, 606, 529
C$_{28}$H$_{31}$N$_5$O$_9$, dipyrimidine, **5**, 382
C$_{28}$H$_{32}$N$_4$O$_2$, communesin A, **8**, 601
C$_{28}$H$_{32}$O$_{10}$, lignan, **3**, 677
C$_{28}$H$_{32}$O$_{17}$, gossypetin 3'-methyl ether 3-rutinoside, **8**, 159
C$_{28}$H$_{33}$N$_3$O$_9$, saframycinC, **7**, 529
C$_{28}$H$_{34}$N$_2$O$_{11}$
  5-carboxystrictosidine, **4**, 118, 123
  5-carboxyvincoside, **4**, 118
C$_{28}$H$_{34}$N$_4$O$_9$P, bipyridinyl phosphotriester, **7**, 185
C$_{28}$H$_{34}$N$_8$O$_{15}$P$_2$, 5-deazaFAD, **1**, 600
C$_{28}$H$_{34}$O$_8$, desacetylnimbin, **8**, 329, 330
C$_{28}$H$_{34}$O$_9$
  gomisinE, **1**, 703
  nomilin, **8**, 321
C$_{28}$H$_{34}$O$_{10}$
  Cryptomeria japonica metabolite, **1**, 681
  gomisin D, **1**, 703
C$_{28}$H$_{36}$N$_2$O$_4$, psychotrine, **4**, 40
C$_{28}$H$_{36}$N$_2$O$_9$, *N*-methylstrictosidine, **4**, 122
C$_{28}$H$_{36}$O$_9$, 10-desacetylbaccatin III, **2**, 220, 222
C$_{28}$H$_{38}$ClN$_4$O$_3$P, acridinyl phosphoramidite, **7**, 181
C$_{28}$H$_{38}$KO$_8$P, bis(pivaloyloxy)methyl esters, **2**, 258
C$_{28}$H$_{38}$NO$_8$, nargenicin A, **1**, 374, 528
C$_{28}$H$_{38}$N$_4$O$_8$, pactamycin, **1**, 152
C$_{28}$H$_{38}$O$_9$, halimedatetraacetate, **8**, 462
C$_{28}$H$_{38}$O$_{14}$,
  feruloylarabinofuranosylxylopyranosylxylopyranose,
  3, 697
C$_{28}$H$_{39}$BrN$_7$O$_{17}$P$_3$S, 4-bromobenzoylCoA, **5**, 413
C$_{28}$H$_{39}$ClN$_7$O$_{17}$P$_3$S, 4-chlorobenzoylCoA, **5**, 411, 413
C$_{28}$H$_{39}$FN$_7$O$_{17}$P$_3$S, 4-fluorobenzoylCoA, **5**, 413
C$_{28}$H$_{40}$N$_2$O$_3$P, phosphoramidite, **7**, 154
C$_{28}$H$_{40}$N$_2$O$_4$, cephaeline, **4**, 40
C$_{28}$H$_{40}$N$_7$O$_{17}$P$_3$S, benzoyl-CoA, **1**, 760, **3**, 649, **4**, 264
C$_{28}$H$_{40}$N$_7$O$_{18}$P$_3$S
  2-hydroxybenzoyl-CoA, **1**, 760
  3-hydroxybenzoyl-CoA, **1**, 760
  4-hydroxybenzoyl-CoA, **1**, 760
C$_{28}$H$_{40}$N$_7$O$_{19}$P$_3$S, benzoyl-CoA, **1**, 755
C$_{28}$H$_{40}$N$_7$O$_{20}$P$_3$S, galloyl-CoA, **3**, 805
C$_{28}$H$_{40}$O$_4$, 5-alkylresorcinol, **7**, 535
C$_{28}$H$_{40}$O$_8$, taxuyunnanineC, **2**, 222
C$_{28}$H$_{41}$NO, U-106305, **1**, 63
C$_{28}$H$_{42}$N$_2$O, ingenamine D, **8**, 560
C$_{28}$H$_{42}$N$_7$O$_{17}$P$_3$S, penicillinV, **4**, 264
C$_{28}$H$_{43}$NO$_6$, hapalosin, **8**, 610
C$_{28}$H$_{43}$N$_7$O$_7$, nazumamide A, **8**, 576
C$_{28}$H$_{44}$ClNO$_6$
  malyngamide I acetate, **8**, 607
  stylocheilamide, **8**, 608
C$_{28}$H$_{44}$N$_2$O, xestocyclamine B, **8**, 560
C$_{28}$H$_{44}$N$_7$O$_{17}$P$_3$S, 2-cyclohexenylcarbonyl-CoA, **1**, 74
C$_{28}$H$_{44}$O, vitamin D, **1**, 368
C$_{28}$H$_{44}$O$_3$, ergosterol peroxide, **1**, 534
C$_{28}$H$_{44}$O$_8$, cyasterone, **8**, 282, 293
C$_{28}$H$_{46}$N$_7$O$_{18}$P$_3$S, 2-methyl-3-oxohexanoyl-CoA, **1**, 545
C$_{28}$H$_{46}$N$_7$O$_{19}$P$_3$S, pimeloylCoA, **1**, 826
C$_{28}$H$_{46}$O
  29,30-bisnoramyrin, **2**, 305
  1,1'-bisnor-2,3-oxidosqualene, **2**, 287
  10,15-didesmethyl-2,3-oxidosqualene, **2**, 286

C₂₈H₄₆O₂, 24,30-bisnor-2,3-oxidosqualene, **2**, 305

C₂₈H₄₆O₃
  cerevisterol, **1**, 534
  3-dehydro-6-deoxoteasterone, **8**, 105

C₂₈H₄₆O₄, 3-dehydroteasterone, **8**, 105

C₂₈H₄₆O₅, 3-dehydro-24-epicastasterone, **8**, 107

C₂₈H₄₆O₇, makisterone A, **8**, 279, 293

C₂₈H₄₇NaO₈S, polyhydroxysteroid, **8**, 471

C₂₈H₄₇NO, trisnorsqualene *N*-methyloxaziridine, **2**, 290

C₂₈H₄₇NO₁₁, theopederin B, **8**, 581

C₂₈H₄₈N₂O₁₇P₃S, heptanoyl-CoA, **1**, 356

C₂₈H₄₈N₄O₁₄, *N*-monopropyl allosamidin, **1**, 150

C₂₈H₄₈N₇O₁₇P₃S, heptanoyl-CoA, **4**, 262

C₂₈H₄₈O, campesterol, **2**, 303

C₂₈H₄₈O₂
  bisnorsqualene alcohol, **2**, 273
  geranylgeranyl octanoate, **8**, 229
  6-oxocampestanol, **8**, 105

C₂₈H₄₈O₃
  cathasterone, **8**, 105
  6-deoxoteasterone, **8**, 105
  6-deoxotyphasterol, **8**, 105

C₂₈H₄₈O₄
  6-deoxocastasterone, **8**, 107
  teasterone, **8**, 105
  typhasterol, **8**, 105

C₂₈H₄₈O₅
  castasterone, **8**, 99, 105
  3,24-diepicastasterone, **8**, 107

C₂₈H₄₈O₆
  brassinolide, **8**, 21, 99
  3,24-diepibrassinolide, **8**, 107
  3,24-diepi-25-hydroxycastasterone, **8**, 107
  24-epibrassinolide, **8**, 102
  20-hydroxy-3,24-diepicastasterone, **8**, 107

C₂₈H₄₈O₇
  3,24-diepi-25-hydroxybrassinolide, **8**, 107
  20-hydroxy-3,24-diepibrassinolide, **8**, 107

C₂₈H₄₈O₉, erythromycin analogue, **1**, 504

C₂₈H₄₉N, TNS-methylamine, **2**, 273

C₂₈H₄₉NaO₉S, polyhydroxysteroid, **8**, 471

C₂₈H₅₀N₂O₂
  araguspongine B, **8**, 560
  araguspongine D, **8**, 560
  araguspongineE, **8**, 560
  xestospongin A, **8**, 560
  xestosponginC, **8**, 560

C₂₈H₅₀N₂O₃
  demethylxzestospongin B, **8**, 562
  xestospongin D, **8**, 560

C₂₈H₅₀N₂O₄, araguspongineC, **8**, 560

C₂₈H₅₀O, campestanol, **8**, 105

C₂₈H₅₀O₂, 6α-hydroxycampestanol, **8**, 105

C₂₈H₅₁NO₁₅, GlcNAcβ1-2(6-deoxy)Manα1-6Glcβ1-octyl, **3**, 54

C₂₈H₅₁NO₁₆, GlcNAcβ1-2Manα1-3Manβ1-octyl, **3**, 52

C₂₈H₅₆O₃, 27-hydroxyoctacosanoic acid, **3**, 196, 222

C₂₉H₂₃NO₉, dynemicin M, **1**, 562

C₂₉H₂₄O₁₁, clecarmycin, **7**, 510

C₂₉H₂₅N₃O₄, dehydrocoelenterazine acetone adduct, **8**, 455

C₂₉H₂₆O₁₁, clecarmycin, **7**, 510

C₂₉H₂₈O₈, interiotherin A, **1**, 704

C₂₉H₃₀N₂O₃, PGE₂agonist, **1**, 192

C₂₉H₃₂BrN₇O₆, halocyamine B, **8**, 472

C₂₉H₃₂O₁₃, etoposide, **1**, 671, 701, **7**, 597, 603, 609, 610

C₂₉H₃₃O₁₆P, etoposide phosphate, **1**, 701

C₂₉H₃₅N₂O₂P, pyrenyl phosphoramidite, **7**, 178

C₂₉H₃₅O, 4-decyloxytrityl, **7**, 127

C₂₉H₃₆N₂O₄, emetamine, **4**, 40

C₂₉H₃₆O₉, nonadride, **2**, 257

C₂₉H₃₇NO₅, cytochalasin, **1**, 422

C₂₉H₃₇N₃O₆, A23187, **1**, 168, 289

C₂₉H₃₈NNaO₅, stawamycin, **1**, 374

C₂₉H₃₈NO₂PS, mercaptoalkylated phosphoramidite, **7**, 167

C₂₉H₃₈N₂O₄
  ikarugamycin, **1**, 374, **8**, 588
  O-methylpsychotrine, **4**, 40

C₂₉H₃₈N₂O₆
  alteramide A, **8**, 588
  bicyclo[3.3.0]octane hexacyclic compound, **8**, 588

C₂₉H₃₈O₈, roridinE, **2**, 202

C₂₉H₃₈O₁₁, toosendanin, **8**, 330

C₂₉H₃₈O₁₆, triphyllin B, **3**, 756

C₂₉H₄₀N₂O₄, emetine, **4**, 40

C₂₉H₄₀O₈, ajugalactone, **8**, 282

C₂₉H₄₀O₉, calotropin, **8**, 152

C₂₉H₄₀O₁₀, archangelolide, **8**, 308

C₂₉H₄₁N₂O₆P, psoralen phosphoramidite, **7**, 184

C₂₉H₄₂N₇O₁₇P₃S,PhAc-CoA, **4**, 244, 262

C₂₉H₄₂N₇O₁₇P₃S₂, thiophenoxyacetyl-CoA, **4**, 264

C₂₉H₄₂N₇O₁₈P₃S
  4-methoxybenzoylCoA, **5**, 414
  phenoxyacetyl-CoA, **4**, 264

C₂₉H₄₂O₁₀
  ajugapitin, **8**, 315
  clerodendron D, **8**, 152

C₂₉H₄₃N₈O₁₇P₃S, *N*-methylanthraniloyl-CoA, **1**, 759

C₂₉H₄₄N₂O₂, ingenamineC, **8**, 560

C₂₉H₄₄N₅O₅PS, phosphoramidite, **7**, 172

C₂₉H₄₄N₆O₇S₂, dansyl-*NH*-Cys-Val-Ile-Ala, **5**, 332

C₂₉H₄₄O₄, limatulone, **8**, 49

C₂₉H₄₄O₆
  2-acetylpinnasterol, **8**, 280
  polyporusteroneE, **8**, 280

C₂₉H₄₄O₇
  2-acetyl-14α-hydroxypinnasterol, **8**, 280
  3-acetyl-14α-hydroxypinnasterol, **8**, 280
  polyporusteroneC, **8**, 280

C₂₉H₄₄O₁₀, 4,15-dihydroajugapitin, **8**, 315

C₂₉H₄₅NO₈, 3-acetylzygadenine, **8**, 152

C₂₉H₄₆N₂O₃, TNSA-DZA, **2**, 279

C₂₉H₄₆O, 15-desmethyl-18,19-dihydro-2,3-oxidosqualene, **2**, 286

C₂₉H₄₆O₂, conicasterone, **1**, 379

C₂₉H₄₆O₃, perovscone, **1**, 377

C₂₉H₄₆O₅, polyporusterone D, **8**, 280

C₂₉H₄₆O₈, 3-acetyl-26-hydroxyecdysone, **8**, 292

C₂₉H₄₇NaO₄S, hymenosulfate, **8**, 618

C₂₉H₄₇N₃O₄, antillatoxin, **8**, 608

C₂₉H₄₈N₇O₁₇P₃S, 3-octenoyl-CoA, **4**, 262

C₂₉H₄₈O
  15-desmethyl-2,3-oxidosqualene, **2**, 286
  26-hydroxy-2,3-oxidosqualene, **2**, 286
  3β-hydroxyprotosta-17(20)[16,21-*cis*]-24-diene, **2**, 281
  6-normethyl-2,3-oxidosqualene, **2**, 7
  1′-nor-2,3-oxidosqualene, **2**, 287
  4-nor-2,3-oxidosqualene, **2**, 287
  stigmasterol, **2**, 303

C₂₉H₄₈O₂, 20-oxa-2,3-oxidosqualene, **2**, 280, 281, 284, 291

C₂₉H₄₈O₃, messagenin, **8**, 169

C₂₉H₄₈O₅, polyporusterone F, **8**, 280

C₂₉H₄₈O₆, polyporusterone A, **8**, 280

C₂₉H₄₈O₇
  makisteroneC, **8**, 293
  podecdysone B, **8**, 293

C₂₉H₄₉N, trisnorsqualene cyclopropylamine, **2**, 273

C₂₉H₄₉NO, TNS methyl hydroxylamine, **2**, 274

C₂₉H₅₀N₂O₂₁, GlcNAcβ1-6[GlcNAcβ1-2]Ma nα1-6Manβ1-methyl, **3**, 55

C₂₉H₅₀N₇O₁₇P₃S, octanoyl-CoA, **1**, 544, **4**, 262, 266

C₂₉H₅₀O
  phytosterol, **1**, 626
  β-sitosterol, **5**, 316

C$_{29}$H$_{50}$O$_2$
20-oxa-22,23-dihydro-2,3-oxidosqualene, **2**, 291
α-tocopherol, **1**, 95
vitaminE, **7**, 116
C$_{29}$H$_{50}$O$_6$
28-homobrassinolide, **8**, 102
25-methylbrassinolide, **8**, 104
C$_{29}$H$_{51}$ClN$_2$O$_2$, 1-phenyl-2-hexadecanoylamino-3-morpholino-1-propanol.HCl, **3**, 114
C$_{29}$H$_{51}$N
2-aza-2,3-dihydrosqualene, **2**, 304
2,3-dihydro-2-azasqualene, **2**, 311
C$_{29}$H$_{51}$NaO$_8$S, polyhydroxysteroid, **8**, 471
C$_{29}$H$_{51}$NO
2-aza-2,3-dihydrosqualene, **2**, 290
2-aza-2,3-dihydrosqualeneN-oxide, **2**, 304
19-aza-2,3-oxidosqualene, **2**, 290
C$_{29}$H$_{51}$NS$_2$, cholesterol derivative, **7**, 188
C$_{29}$H$_{52}$N$_2$O$_2$
araguaspongine A, **8**, 560
araguaspongine F, **8**, 560
araguaspongine G, **8**, 560
C$_{29}$H$_{52}$N$_2$O$_3$, xestospongin B, **8**, 560
C$_{29}$H$_{53}$NO, 10-aza-10,11-dihydro-2,3-oxidosqualene, **2**, 290
C$_{29}$H$_{56}$, 9,19-nonacosadiene, **8**, 219
C$_{29}$H$_{57}$O$_6$P , dimyristoylphosphatidylmethanol, **5**, 108, 109
C$_{29}$H$_{58}$
13-nonacosene, **8**, 219
14-nonacosene, **8**, 219
C$_{29}$H$_{58}$O
3,11-dimethylheptacosan-2-one, **8**, 240
3,7-dimethylheptacosan-2-one, **8**, 247
C$_{29}$H$_{63}$NO$_4$P, didodecanoyl-PC, **5**, 128
C$_{30}$H$_{16}$O$_8$, hypericin, **8**, 152
C$_{30}$H$_{17}$NO$_9$, dynemycin, **1**, 14
C$_{30}$H$_{18}$O$_8$
kudzuisoflavone A, **1**, 806
kudzuisoflavone B, **1**, 806
C$_{30}$H$_{18}$O$_{13}$, ascoquinone A, **1**, 417
C$_{30}$H$_{19}$, 4-(17-tetrabenzo[a,c,g,i]fluorenylmethyl, **7**, 127
C$_{30}$H$_{19}$NO$_8$, deoxydynemicin, **7**, 574
C$_{30}$H$_{19}$NO$_9$
dynemicin, **7**, 98
dynemicin A, **1**, 557, 559, **7**, 554, 574
C$_{30}$H$_{21}$NO$_9$, dynemycin A, **3**, 327
C$_{30}$H$_{22}$O$_8$, rugulosin, **1**, 431
C$_{30}$H$_{23}$NO$_{10}$, dynemicinH, **7**, 575
C$_{30}$H$_{23}$N$_3$O$_2$, coelenterazine analogue, **8**, 449
C$_{30}$H$_{24}$N$_2$O$_9$, β-ribonucleoside, **7**, 261
C$_{30}$H$_{24}$O, flavoskyrin, **1**, 374, 431
C$_{30}$H$_{26}$O$_2$, procyanidin B-1, **3**, 760
C$_{30}$H$_{26}$O$_{11}$
fisetinidol-(4α→8)-catechin, **3**, 758
fisetinidol-(4β→8)-catechin, **3**, 758
C$_{30}$H$_{26}$O$_{12}$
procyanidin, **3**, 758
procyanidin B-3, **3**, 756
procyanidin B-4, **3**, 756
procyanidin B-7, **3**, 748
procyanidin dimer B-1, **3**, 758
procyanidin dimer B-4, **3**, 758
C$_{30}$H$_{26}$O$_{13}$
epicatechin-(4α→8)-catechin, **3**, 749
prodelphinidin, **3**, 748
C$_{30}$H$_{26}$O$_{14}$, ergochrome, **1**, 458
C$_{30}$H$_{27}$BrN$_2$S$_2$,Stains-All, **7**, 85
C$_{30}$H$_{27}$NO$_{10}$
lamerarin A, **8**, 539
polycitrin B, **8**, 539
C$_{30}$H$_{27}$N$_3$O$_{15}$
enterobactin, **1**, 610, **4**, 199, 203, 209, 226, 235

C$_{30}$H$_{28}$O$_5$, thamnosin, **1**, 380
C$_{30}$H$_{28}$O$_6$
isothamnosin A, **1**, 380
isothamnosin B, **1**, 380
phebalin, **1**, 380
C$_{30}$H$_{29}$N$_3$O$_5$S$_2$, dehydrocoelenterazine dithiothreitol adduct, **8**, 455
C$_{30}$H$_{30}$N$_4$O$_4$, deuteroporphyrin IX, **6**, 137
C$_{30}$H$_{30}$O$_6$, gossypol, **2**, 186, 188
C$_{30}$H$_{30}$O$_8$, gossypol, **8**, 312
C$_{30}$H$_{30}$O$_9$, schisantherin D, **1**, 704
C$_{30}$H$_{30}$O$_{12}$
averantin, **1**, 452
procyanidin dimers, **3**, 758
C$_{30}$H$_{31}$N$_3$O$_2$, adamantylmethylcoelenterazine, **8**, 449
C$_{30}$H$_{31}$N$_3$O$_3$, adamantylmethylcoelenterazine, **8**, 449
C$_{30}$H$_{32}$O$_9$
dibenzodioxocin, **3**, 725
lappaol, **1**, 688
C$_{30}$H$_{34}$BrN$_5$O$_{15}$, neosurugatoxin, **8**, 515
C$_{30}$H$_{34}$O$_7$, ornativolide A, **1**, 375
C$_{30}$H$_{34}$O$_9$, oligolignol, **3**, 724
C$_{30}$H$_{34}$O$_{11}$, 7′-hydroxylappaolE, **1**, 688
C$_{30}$H$_{36}$O$_7$, dibenzodioxocin, **3**, 725
C$_{30}$H$_{36}$O$_9$, nimbin, **8**, 329, 330
C$_{30}$H$_{37}$NO$_2$, proxiphomin, **1**, 393
C$_{30}$H$_{38}$NO$_3$PS, mercaptoalkylated phosphoramidite, **7**, 167
C$_{30}$H$_{38}$NO$_9$, jacpaniculine, **1**, 685
C$_{30}$H$_{38}$N$_4$O$_2$S, virenamide B, **8**, 538
C$_{30}$H$_{38}$O$_6$, absinthin, **1**, 375
C$_{30}$H$_{38}$O$_{11}$, dihydrobuddlenol B, **1**, 688
C$_{30}$H$_{39}$N$_3$O$_4$Si, coelenterazine t-butyldimethylsilyl peroxide, **8**, 452
C$_{30}$H$_{40}$O$_{15}$, erubin B, **3**, 756
C$_{30}$H$_{40}$O$_{16}$, triphyllin A, **3**, 756
C$_{30}$H$_{41}$N$_2$O$_3$P, phosphoramidite, **7**, 154
C$_{30}$H$_{41}$N$_3$O$_4$P, phosphoramidite, **7**, 154
C$_{30}$H$_{41}$N$_9$O$_7$, cycloghdonamide analogue, **8**, 569
C$_{30}$H$_{42}$N$_2$O$_{15}$S$_2$, sinalbin, **8**, 145
C$_{30}$H$_{42}$N$_7$O$_{17}$P$_3$S, cinnamoyl-CoA, **1**, 752
C$_{30}$H$_{42}$N$_7$O$_{18}$P$_3$S , p-coumaroyl-CoA, **1**, 716, 732, 752, 757, 758, 784, 789, **3**, 625, 641, 649, 653
C$_{30}$H$_{42}$N$_7$O$_{19}$P$_3$S , caffeoyl-CoA , **1**, 716, 732, 752, **3**, 625, 649
C$_{30}$H$_{42}$N$_7$O$_{20}$P$_3$S, 3,4,5-trihydroxycinnamoyl-CoA, **1**, 721, **3**, 641
C$_{30}$H$_{42}$O$_2$, plagiospirolide E, **1**, 375
C$_{30}$H$_{42}$O$_7$
bienninC, **1**, 375
cucurbitacin I, **8**, 181
C$_{30}$H$_{43}$NO$_5$, halichomycin, **8**, 603
C$_{30}$H$_{43}$N$_2$O$_6$P, psoralen phosphoramidite, **7**, 184
C$_{30}$H$_{44}$N$_2$
ingamine B, **8**, 560
ingenamine F, **8**, 560
C$_{30}$H$_{44}$N$_2$O
ingamine A, **8**, 560
ingenamineE, **8**, 560
C$_{30}$H$_{44}$N$_7$O$_{17}$P$_3$S
dihydrocinnamoyl-CoA, **1**, 757, 758
methylphenylacetyl-CoA, **4**, 264
phenylpropionyl-CoA, **4**, 264
C$_{30}$H$_{44}$N$_7$O$_{18}$P$_3$S
dihydro-3-coumaroyl-CoA, **1**, 753
methoxyphenylacetyl-CoA, **4**, 264
C$_{30}$H$_{44}$O$_6$
amphidinolideE, **8**, 621, 620
cucurbitacin D, **8**, 152
C$_{30}$H$_{44}$O$_{10}$
debromoaplysiatoxin, **8**, 603
macrolactinC, **8**, 590
C$_{30}$H$_{46}$N$_2$O$_9$S, LTC$_4$, **1**, 176

C₃₀H₄₆N₃O₉S
  leukotrieneC₄, **1**, 168
  LTC₄, **1**, 184, 185
C₃₀H₄₇N₃O₈S
  5-hydroxy-6-glutathionyl-7,9,11,14-eicosatetraenoic
    acid, **1**, 168
  SRS-A, **1**, 168
C₃₀H₄₇N₃O₉S
  leukotrieneC₄, **1**, 280
  LTC₄, **1**, 268
C₃₀H₄₈
  dehydrosqualene, **5**, 338
  hop-22(29)-ene, **2**, 308, 310
C₃₀H₄₈N₂O
  isosarain 2, **8**, 562
  sarain 2, **8**, 562
C₃₀H₄₈N₆O₆, Phe-Pro-Val-Orn-Leu, **4**, 345
C₃₀H₄₈O, 20,21-dehydro-2,3-oxidosqualene, **2**, 281
C₃₀H₄₈O₂, theonellasterone, **1**, 379
C₃₀H₄₈O₃, ursolic acid, **8**, 169, 173
C₃₀H₄₈O₄, polyporusterone G, **8**, 280
C₃₀H₄₈O₅
  arjunolic acid, **8**, 191
  polyporusterone B, **8**, 280
C₃₀H₄₉, tertiary carbocation FPP analogue, **2**, 254
C₃₀H₄₉ClO, 6-chloromethyl-2,3-oxidosqualene, **2**, 7
C₃₀H₄₉NO, 24,25-iminolanosterol, **2**, 290
C₃₀H₅₀
  diploptene, **2**, 46, 47
  eupha-7,24-diene, **2**, 311, 312
  hopene, **2**, 5, 305, 307
  squalene, **2**, 5, 9, 38, 46, 47, 70, 108, 196, 246, 253,
    275, 300, 340, **5**, 319, 336, **8**, 161
C₃₀H₅₀MgO₇P₂, presqualene diphosphate, **2**, 246, 253
C₃₀H₅₀N₂O₂
  petrosin, **8**, 560
  petrosin A, **8**, 560
  petrosin B, **8**, 560
C₃₀H₅₀N₇O₁₈P₃S, 3-oxo-7-methyloctanoyl-CoA, **8**, 385
C₃₀H₅₀O
  achilleol A, **2**, 301
  α-amyrin, **2**, 305
  β-amyrin, **2**, 305
  bacchara-12,21-dienol, **2**, 301
  cycloartenol, **2**, 299, **5**, 316
  cyclopropylcarbinol, **2**, 254
  dammara-20,24-dienol, **2**, 301
  diplopterol, **2**, 307, 308, 310
  dipolypoda-8(26),13,17,21-tetraen-3-ol, **2**, 301
  euphol, **2**, 301
  fernenol, **2**, 301
  gorgosterol, **1**, 63
  hopan-3-ol, **2**, 308
  26-hydroxysqualene, **2**, 275
  lanosterol, **2**, 6, 38, 263, 279, 281, 303, **8**, 48
  3-*epi*-lanosterol, **2**, 287
  lupeol, **2**, 307
  malabarica-14(26),17,21-trien-3-ol, **2**, 301
  oxidosqualene, **2**, 282, 300
  2,3-oxidosqualene, **2**, 6, 268, 270, 275, 279, 280, 284,
    312
  6,7-oxidosqualene, **2**, 291
  10,11-oxidosqualene, **2**, 291
  rillingol, **2**, 254
  sitosterol, **2**, 64, 368, 377, 386
  squalene epoxide, **2**, 47, 275
  squalene oxide, **2**, 196
  squalenol, **5**, 338
C₃₀H₅₀O₂
  2,3:18,19-dioxidosqualene, **2**, 291
  2,3:22,23-dioxidosqualene, **2**, 270, 284
  dioxidosqualene, **2**, 275, 301
  24,25-epoxylanosterol, **2**, 293

21-hydroxylanosterol, **2**, 287
1-hydroxy-2,3-oxidosqualene, **2**, 287
29-hydroxy-2,3-oxidosqualene, **2**, 285, 287
a-onocerin, **2**, 301
2,3-oxidosqualene, **2**, 305
C₃₀H₅₀O₃, sayasapogenol A, **8**, 175
C₃₀H₅₀O₅, meliantriol, **8**, 325
C₃₀H₅₁, gammaceryl cation, **2**, 312
C₃₀H₅₁N
  2,3-dihydro-2,3-iminosqualene, **2**, 304, 311
  2,3-iminosqualene, **2**, 290, 312
  TNS *N*-methylcyclopropylamine, **2**, 273
C₃₀H₅₁O
  baccharanyl cation, **2**, 305
  cucurbita-5,24-dienol, **2**, 302
  cycloartenol, **2**, 302, 303
  dammarenyl cation, **2**, 303
  isoarborinol, **2**, 302
  lanosterol, **2**, 302
  lupenyl cation, **2**, 305
  oleanyl cation, **2**, 305
  parkeol, **2**, 302
  protosteryl cation, **2**, 302, 303
C₃₀H₅₂
  dammar-12-ene, **2**, 310
  dammar-13(17)-ene, **2**, 310
  2,3-dihydrosqualene, **2**, 310, 312
  euph-7-ene, **2**, 312
  hopane, **2**, 47
  lupane, **4**, 34
C₃₀H₅₂N, ammonium ion compound, **2**, 253
C₃₀H₅₂N₇O₁₇P₃S, nonaoyl-CoA, **4**, 262
C₃₀H₅₂O
  ambrein, **2**, 301
  10,11-dihydro-2,3-oxidosqualene, **2**, 286
  14,15-dihydro-2,3-oxidosqualene, **2**, 286
  18,19-dihydro-2,3-oxidosqualene, **2**, 286
  22,23-dihydro-2,3-oxidosqualene, **2**, 284
  diplopterol, **2**, 47, 312
  tetrahymanol, **2**, 305, 307, 312
C₃₀H₅₂O₇P₂, presqualene diphosphate, **2**, 10
C₃₀H₅₄N₂O₂
  araguspongineH, **8**, 560
  araguspongine J, **8**, 560
C₃₀H₅₆O₉, exophilin A, **8**, 601
C₃₀H₅₆O₁₁, halymecinE, **8**, 601
C₃₀H₆₀O, 3,7,15-trimethylheptacosan-2-one, **8**, 247
C₃₁H₂₂O₅, dracorubin, **3**, 752
C₃₁H₂₃O₂, 1,1-bis(4-methoxyphenyl)-1-pyrenylmethyl, **7**,
    127
C₃₁H₂₈F₂O, 29-difluoromethylidene-2,3-oxidosqualene, **2**,
    287
C₃₁H₃₀Br₆N₄O₁₁, isofistularin-3, **8**, 468
C₃₁H₃₁NO₆, toddacoumalone, **1**, 380
C₃₁H₃₁N₃O₅, isopropylideneC-nucleoside, **7**, 263
C₃₁H₃₂O₄, butenolide trityl derivative, **1**, 145
C₃₁H₃₃NO₉, ravidomycin, **7**, 545
C₃₁H₃₃N₃O₆S, zafirlukast, **1**, 197
C₃₁H₃₃N₃O₁₁
  azinomycin B, **7**, 513
  carzinophilin, **7**, 513
C₃₁H₃₄O₅, trityl butanolide derivative, **1**, 145
C₃₁H₃₄O₆
  isopropylidene trityl derivative, **7**, 262
  ribose derivative, **7**, 263
  shizukaol A, **1**, 377
C₃₁H₃₅ClO₁₃, cyanidin 3-succinylglucoside-5-glucoside, **8**,
    159
C₃₁H₃₆N₂O₁₁, novobiocin, **1**, 623, 625, **3**, 321, **7**, 596
C₃₁H₃₆O₁₁, hedyotolC, **1**, 688
C₃₁H₃₈N₄O₅, irenotecan, **7**, 599
C₃₁H₃₈O₈S, tetronothiodin, **1**, 370
C₃₁H₃₈O₉, toonacilin, **8**, 321

$C_{31}H_{39}NO_4$, phomopsichalasin, **1**, 374

$C_{31}H_{39}N_2O_2PS$, mercaptoalkylated phosphoramidite, **7**, 167

$C_{31}H_{39}N_5O_5$, ergocornine C, **1**, 534

$C_{31}H_{40}O_2$, menaquinone, **1**, 17

$C_{31}H_{40}O_8$, calbistrin A, **1**, 370

$C_{31}H_{41}NO_{10}$, digoxigenin ester with *N*-(*β*-carboxypropylsuccinimide), **7**, 160

$C_{31}H_{42}O_7$, aestivalin, **1**, 375

$C_{31}H_{42}O_{12}$, clerodendrin A, **8**, 314, 317, 319

$C_{31}H_{43}NO_4$, indanomycin, **1**, 374

$C_{31}H_{44}N_7O_{19}P_3S$, feruloyl-CoA, **1**, 18, 761, **3**, 625, 646, 653

$C_{31}H_{44}N_7O_{20}P_3S$, 5-hydroxyferuloyl-CoA, **3**, 642, 650

$C_{31}H_{44}O_4S_2$, methyl 6,10-bis(thiophenyl)-7,11-dihydroxyfarnesoate, **8**, 269

$C_{31}H_{45}Cl_3N_6O_{13}$, victorinC, **8**, 180

$C_{31}H_{45}N_{11}O_{18}P_3$, deoxycytidine triphosphate, **7**, 207

$C_{31}H_{46}N_4O_2S$, virenamide A, **8**, 538

$C_{31}H_{46}N_7O_{17}P_3S$, phenylbutyryl-CoA, **4**, 264

$C_{31}H_{46}O_2$, vitamin K₁, **4**, 4, **8**, 162, 436

$C_{31}H_{46}O_7$, amphidinolide A, **8**, 620

$C_{31}H_{46}O_9$, macrolactin B, **8**, 590

$C_{31}H_{47}NO_2$, squalene maleimide, **2**, 289

$C_{31}H_{48}N_6O_7S$, dansyl-NH-Cys-Val-Ile-Met-CO$_2$H, **5**, 332

$C_{31}H_{48}O_6$, fusidic acid, **2**, 281

$C_{31}H_{49}N_9O_{15}P_3S$, d(ATP) analogue, **7**, 206

$C_{31}H_{49}N_9O_{15}P_3S_3$, biotinylated deoxyuridine triphosphate, **7**, 206

$C_{31}H_{50}N_2O$
　　isosarain 1, **8**, 562
　　sarain 1, **8**, 562

$C_{31}H_{50}N_3$, madangamine A, **8**, 566

$C_{31}H_{50}O$
　　24-methylenecycloartenol, **2**, 304
　　21-methylidene lanosterol, **2**, 287
　　1-methylidene-2,3-oxidosqualene, **2**, 287
　　26-methylidene-2,3-oxidosqualene, **2**, 286
　　27-methylidene-2,3-oxidosqualene, **2**, 286
　　29-methylidene-2,3-oxidosqualene, **2**, 282, 285, 287

$C_{31}H_{50}O_2$, 29-methylene-2,3-oxidosqualene, **2**, 315

$C_{31}H_{51}N_7O_{16}P_3S$, biotinylated deoxyuridine triphosphate, **7**, 206

$C_{31}H_{52}N_2$, haliclamine B, **8**, 560

$C_{31}H_{52}N_2O_{11}S_2$, hypoxilin, **1**, 170

$C_{31}H_{52}O$
　　22,23-dihydro-22-methylene-2,3-oxidosqualene, **2**, 284, 304
　　homooxidosqualene, **2**, 287

$C_{31}H_{52}O_3$, tocopheryl acetate, **8**, 230

$C_{31}H_{53}NO_8$, mybutosine, **6**, 77

$C_{31}H_{53}N_3O_{19}P_2$, UDP-3-*O*-(3-hydroxymyristoyl)-Glc*N*Ac, **3**, 219

$C_{31}H_{54}N_2$, haliclamine A, **8**, 560

$C_{31}H_{54}N_2O_3$, pyridooxazole derivative, **8**, 551

$C_{31}H_{55}N$, *N,N*-diethyl-2,3-dihydro-2-azasqualene, **2**, 311

$C_{31}H_{55}NO_9$, o-mycaminosyl-tylactone, **3**, 352

$C_{31}H_{58}O_4$, tetrahydrofuran fatty acid, **1**, 217

$C_{31}H_{59}NO_7$, 1-[4,7-anhydro-4-*C*-(hydroxymethyl)-*β*-D-glucopyranosyloxy]-2-(dodecanoylamino)-4-dodecen-3-ol, **3**, 95

$C_{31}H_{60}$, 9,19-hentriacontadiene, **8**, 219

$C_{31}H_{62}$
　　11-hentriacontene, **8**, 219
　　9-hentriacontene, **8**, 219

$C_{31}H_{62}O$
　　3,11-dimethylnonacosan-2-one, **8**, 240
　　pheromone of *Blattella germanica*, **8**, 49

$C_{31}H_{62}O_2$, 3,11-dimethyl-29-hydroxynonacosan-2-one, **8**, 240 , 247

$C_{32}H_{19}N_6Na_5O_{15}S_5$, trypan red, **7**, 428

$C_{32}H_{26}O_{14}$, actinorhodin, **1**, 10, 337, 476, 484, 491, **4**, 179

$C_{32}H_{30}N_6O_6S_4$, leptosinC, **8**, 603

$C_{32}H_{30}N_6O_6S_6$, leptosin A, **8**, 603

$C_{32}H_{30}O_8$, vestitol-(4→5′)-vestitol, **1**, 775

$C_{32}H_{32}O_8$, toddasin, **1**, 380

$C_{32}H_{32}O_{13}S$, teniposide, **1**, 671, 701, **7**, 603, 609

$C_{32}H_{33}NaO_7$, guanidine salt, **7**, 263

$C_{32}H_{34}O_8$, cassumunarin A, **1**, 386

$C_{32}H_{35}NO_2$,PDA-II, **2**, 279

$C_{32}H_{36}N_2O_5$, chaetoglobosin A, **1**, 388, 391

$C_{32}H_{36}N_4O_2$, communesin B, **8**, 601

$C_{32}H_{37}NO_6$, cytochalasin K, **1**, 374

$C_{32}H_{38}N_2O_2$, prochaetoglobosin 1 derivative, **1**, 393

$C_{32}H_{38}O_{26}$, quercetin 3-(2$_G$-xylosylrutinoside), **8**, 156, 157

$C_{32}H_{40}N_4$
　　borreverine, **1**, 369
　　isoborreverine, **1**, 369

$C_{32}H_{40}N_4O_7P$, deoxyribonucleoside phosphoramidite, **7**, 233

$C_{32}H_{40}O_8$, handelin, **1**, 375

$C_{32}H_{40}O_{14}$
　　azadirachtin I, **8**, 327
　　celangulin, **8**, 312

$C_{32}H_{41}NO_3$, oteromycin, **1**, 370

$C_{32}H_{41}N_2O_5P$, phosphoramidite, **7**, 173

$C_{32}H_{42}N_3O_3P$, phosphoramidite, **7**, 154

$C_{32}H_{42}O_8$, desacetylsalannin, **8**, 329, 330

$C_{32}H_{42}O_{13}$, azadirachtin I, **8**, 325

$C_{32}H_{42}O_{17}$, hydroxypinoresinol 4′,4″-di-*O*-*β*-D-glucopyranoside, **1**, 705

$C_{32}H_{44}MgN_2O_8$, magnesidin A, **8**, 598

$C_{32}H_{44}N_8O_6S_5$, sulfosuccinimidyl 3-[2-[6-(biotinamido)-2-(*p*-azidobenzamide)hexanamido]ethyl]dithio]propionate, **7**, 159

$C_{32}H_{45}NO_4$, gymnodimine, **8**, 515

$C_{32}H_{46}N_7O_{20}P_3S$, sinapoyl-CoA, **3**, 625, 646, 649

$C_{32}H_{46}O_8$, cucurbitacin B, **8**, 320

$C_{32}H_{46}O_9$, cucurbitacin A, **8**, 320

$C_{32}H_{46}O_{16}$, secoisolariciresinol diglucoside, **1**, 668, 698

$C_{32}H_{48}N_2O_2$, culantraramine, **1**, 369

$C_{32}H_{48}N_2O_3$, saraine A, **8**, 562

$C_{32}H_{48}O_5$, lagunapyrone A, **8**, 596

$C_{32}H_{50}N_2$, halicyclamine A, **8**, 566

$C_{32}H_{50}N_2O_3$, culantraraminol, **1**, 369

$C_{32}H_{50}O_3$, hemibrevetoxin B, **8**, 511

$C_{32}H_{50}O_8$
　　amphidinolide B, **8**, 621
　　amphidinolide B₂, **8**, 629
　　amphidinolide B₃, **8**, 629
　　amphidinolide D, **8**, 622
　　amphidinolide G, **8**, 620, 622
　　amphidinolide H, **8**, 620, 622
　　amphidinolide L, **8**, 622

$C_{32}H_{52}N_2O$
　　isosarain 3, **8**, 562
　　sarain 3, **8**, 562

$C_{32}H_{52}N_8O_{17}P_3S$, deoxycytidine triphosphate, **7**, 207

$C_{32}H_{52}O_3$, 30-acetyl-2,3-oxidosqualene, **2**, 284

$C_{32}H_{54}O$, bishomofarnesyl ether, **2**, 310

$C_{32}H_{56}N_2$
　　haliclonacyclamine A, **8**, 566
　　haliclonacyclamine B, **8**, 566

$C_{32}H_{57}N_5O_5$, faAVIA, **5**, 333

$C_{32}H_{58}O_{10}$, halymecinC, **8**, 601

$C_{32}H_{60}N_2O_{31}P_2$, ethanolaminephosphate6Manα1-2Manα1-4Gl c*N*1-6phosphatidylinositol, **3**, 296

$C_{32}H_{60}N_4O_6S$, squalamine mimic, **8**, 475

$C_{32}H_{62}O_2$, phytyl dodecanoate, **8**, 230

$C_{32}H_{66}$, 17,21-dimethyltriacontane, **8**, 249

$C_{33}H_{21}N_7ORu$, oxoruthenium complex, **7**, 374

$C_{33}H_{22}N_{10}ORu$, oxoruthenium complex, **7**, 374

$C_{33}H_{25}NO_9$, d-*O*-methyldynemicin A methyl ester, **7**, 574

$C_{33}H_{26}O_{11}$, santarubin, **1**, 777

$C_{33}H_{27}NO_{11}S$, dynemicinS, **7**, 575

$C_{33}H_{27}N_3O_9$, tri-*O*-(indole-3-acetyl)-*myo*-inositol, **8**, 26

$C_{33}H_{34}N_4O_6$, biliverdin, **4**, 99

$C_{33}H_{34}O_{14}$, haedoxan A, **1**, 687, 693, 696

$C_{33}H_{35}ClO_{19}$, dimalonyldelphin, **8**, 159

$C_{33}H_{35}NO_{12}$, elsamycin, **7**, 529

$C_{33}H_{35}N_3O_6$, alkynyl nucleoside, **7**, 194

$C_{33}H_{36}N_4Na_2O_6$, luciferin air-oxidation product, **8**, 457

$C_{33}H_{36}N_4O_6$, bilirubin, **1**, 283

$C_{33}H_{37}N_3O_3$
    penochalasin A, **8**, 603
    penochalasin B, **8**, 603
    penochalasin C, **8**, 603

$C_{33}H_{38}N_2O_4$, chaetoglobosin J, **1**, 393

$C_{33}H_{38}N_4Na_2O_6$, dinoflagellate luciferin, **8**, 457

$C_{33}H_{38}N_4Na_2O_8$, Krill fluorescent substance F, **8**, 457

$C_{33}H_{38}N_4Na_2O_9$, oxy Krill fluorescent substance F, **8**, 457

$C_{33}H_{39}NO_{13}$, barminomycin I, **7**, 500

$C_{33}H_{40}N_2O_9$, reserpine, **4**, 46, 110

$C_{33}H_{40}O_{11}$, 6-acetyltoonacilin, **8**, 321

$C_{33}H_{42}N_4O_6$, phycoerythrobilin, **8**, 433

$C_{33}H_{42}O_{15}$
    azadirachtinH, **8**, 325
    3-tigloylazadirachtol, **8**, 325

$C_{33}H_{43}N_2O_5P$, phosphoramidite, **7**, 173

$C_{33}H_{44}O_9$, volkensin, **8**, 330

$C_{33}H_{46}N_2O_9$, viridiofungin, **2**, 257

$C_{33}H_{47}N_2O_4P$, phosphoramidite, **7**, 154

$C_{33}H_{47}N_9O_8$, cyclotheonamide D, **8**, 568

$C_{33}H_{52}O_{11}$, caribenolide I, **8**, 627

$C_{33}H_{54}O$
    26-cyclopropyl-2,3-oxidosqualene, **2**, 286, 287
    29-cyclopropyl-2,3-oxidosqualene, **2**, 286, 287

$C_{33}H_{54}O_{12}$, amphidinolideN, **8**, 622

$C_{33}H_{57}N_3O_9$
    enniatin, **4**, 235
    enniatin B, **4**, 226, 230

$C_{33}H_{58}N_7O_{17}P_3S$, dodecanoyl-CoA, **3**, 393, **8**, 204

$C_{33}H_{58}OSi$
    26-trimethylsilyl-2,3-oxidosqualene, **2**, 286
    29-trimethylsilyl-2,3-oxidosqualene, **2**, 285

$C_{33}H_{60}NO_6P_2$, FPP analogue, **2**, 253

$C_{33}H_{62}O_7$, PM-toxin, **1**, 424

$C_{33}H_{64}$
    5,27-tritriacontadiene, **8**, 219
    9,19-tritriacontadiene, **8**, 219

$C_{33}H_{66}$
    9-tritriacontene, **8**, 219
    11-tritriacontene, **8**, 219
    13-tritriacontene, **8**, 219

$C_{34}H_{24}O_{22}$, pedunculagin, **3**, 817

$C_{34}H_{26}O_{22}$, tellimagrandin I, **3**, 817, 818

$C_{34}H_{27}NO_9$, tri-*O*-methyldynemicin A methyl ester, **7**, 574

$C_{34}H_{28}O_{22}$
    1,2,3,6-tetragalloylglucose, **3**, 808
    1,2,4,6-tetragalloylglucose, **3**, 810
    1,2,3,6-tetra-*O*-galloyl-*β*-D-glucose, **3**, 822
    3-*O*-trigalloyl-1,2,4,6-tetra-*O*-galloyl-*β*-D-glucose, **3**, 816

$C_{34}H_{32}FeN_4O_4$, heme, **2**, 27, 74, 326, **4**, 62, 141

$C_{34}H_{32}FeN_4O_4S$, LPO haem, **1**, 307

$C_{34}H_{32}N_2O_8$, cannabisin B, **1**, 674, 695

$C_{34}H_{33}O_9$, trislevulinyloxytrityl, **7**, 126

$C_{34}H_{34}N_4O_4$, protoporphyrin IX, **2**, 326, 333, 346, **4**, 65, **6**, 137

$C_{34}H_{34}N_6O_6S_4$, leptosin K, **8**, 603

$C_{34}H_{35}N_3O_{10}$, alkynyl nucleoside, **7**, 194

$C_{34}H_{38}N_2O_8$, vepridimerine A, **1**, 383

$C_{34}H_{38}N_4O_2S$, virenamide C, **8**, 538

$C_{34}H_{38}N_4O_4$, mesoporphyrin IX, **6**, 137

$C_{34}H_{40}N_2O_7$, fluoresceinyl phosphoramidite, **7**, 177

$C_{34}H_{40}N_4O_4$
    protoporphyrinogen IX, **4**, 90, 94, 96, 98
    protoporphyrinogen XIII, **4**, 95, 98

$C_{34}H_{40}O_{16}$, azadirachtin K, **8**, 325

$C_{34}H_{42}N_2O_8$, arenastatin A, **8**, 613

$C_{34}H_{42}N_7O_5S_2$, cyclodidemnamide, **8**, 537

$C_{34}H_{42}O_{19}$, raphanusol A, **8**, 29

$C_{34}H_{43}ClO_{21}$, peonidin 3-sophoroside-5-glucoside, **8**, 159

$C_{34}H_{44}N_3O_3P$, phosphoramidite, **7**, 154

$C_{34}H_{44}N_4O_{11}$
    shimofuridin A, **8**, 532
    shimofuridin B, **8**, 532
    shimofuridin C, **8**, 532
    shimofuridin D, **8**, 532
    shimofuridin E, **8**, 532

$C_{34}H_{44}O_9$, salannin, **8**, 329, 330

$C_{34}H_{44}O_{14}$, azadirachtin D, **8**, 325

$C_{34}H_{45}N_2O_2PS$, mercaptoalkylated phosphoramidite, **7**, 167

$C_{34}H_{45}N_2O_5P$, phosphoramidite, **7**, 155, 173

$C_{34}H_{46}N_5O_8P$, anthraquinone phosphoramidite, **7**, 183

$C_{34}H_{46}O_{13}$
    angulatin A, **8**, 312
    trichilin A, **8**, 321

$C_{34}H_{46}O_{18}$
    syringaresinol di-*O*-*β*-D-glucopyranoside, **1**, 705
    syringaresinol di-*O*-*β*-D-glucoside, **1**, 705

$C_{34}H_{49}NO_4S_2$, 3-carboxy-4-nitrophenyldithio-1,1'2-trisnorsqualene, **2**, 289

$C_{34}H_{50}N_2O_3$, saraine B, **8**, 562

$C_{34}H_{50}N_7O_{25}P_3S$, 4-*O*-*β*-D-glucosidogalloyl-CoA, **3**, 805

$C_{34}H_{50}O_2$, plagiospirolide A, **1**, 375

$C_{34}H_{52}N_2O_3$, saraine C, **8**, 562

$C_{34}H_{57}O_5$, lagunapyrone B, **8**, 596

$C_{34}H_{58}N_2O_{26}$
    Man$_3$Glc*N*Ac$_2$, **3**, 15
    Man$_3$Glc*N*Ac$_{26}$, **3**, 24

$C_{34}H_{59}NO_{15}$, fumonisin B1, **3**, 101

$C_{34}H_{61}NO_{21}$, Manα1-6(Glc*N*Acβ1-2Manα1-3) Manβ1-octyl, **3**, 50, 52

$C_{34}H_{66}NO_6S$, flavocristamide A, **8**, 598

$C_{34}H_{67}N_3O_5S$, squalamine, **8**, 474

$C_{34}H_{68}NO_6S$, flavocristamide B, **8**, 598

$C_{34}H_{70}$, 15-methyltritriacontane, **8**, 249

$C_{35}H_{30}O_{12}$, hydnowightin, **1**, 685

$C_{35}H_{32}F_3N_3O_8$, alkynyl nucleoside, **7**, 194

$C_{35}H_{32}O_{13}$, pseudotsuganol, **1**, 685

$C_{35}H_{33}NO_{12}$
    neocarzinostatin, **1**, 557, 567, **7**, 98, 373, 380, 385, 394, 395, 418, 421
    neocarzinostatin chromophore, **7**, 482, 554, 558

$C_{35}H_{33}N_5O_8$, guanosine nucleoside derivative, **7**, 118

$C_{35}H_{34}N_2O_8$
    aryldihydronaphthalene lignanamide, **1**, 673
    demethylgrossamide, **1**, 674

$C_{35}H_{39}FeN_7O_8$, methidiumpropyl-ethylenediamine tetraacetate, **7**, 86

$C_{35}H_{42}N_2O_9$, rescinnamine, **4**, 46

$C_{35}H_{43}ClN_2O_7$, cryptophycin-3, **8**, 612

$C_{35}H_{43}ClN_2O_8$, cryptophycin-1, **8**, 612

$C_{35}H_{40}N_4O_4$, *N*-methylmesoporphyrin IX, **6**, 137

$C_{35}H_{43}N_4O_5P$, (pyrenylmethyl)thymidine phosphordiamidite, **7**, 234

$C_{35}H_{43}N_5O_9$, green fluorescent protein, **8**, 453

$C_{35}H_{44}N_4O$, manzamine A, **1**, 380

$C_{35}H_{44}O_{15}$, desepoxyazadirachtin, **8**, 325

$C_{35}H_{44}O_{16}$
    1-acetylazadirachtinH, **8**, 330
    azadirachtin, **8**, 143, 324
    marrangin, **8**, 330
    1-tigloyl-3-acetylazadirachtinin, **8**, 325

$C_{35}H_{45}N_2O_6P$, phosphoramidite, **7**, 173

$C_{35}H_{46}Br_2N_2O_4$, pseudodistomin 1-acetyl-4,5-bis(*p*-bromobenzoyl) derivative, **8**, 548

$C_{35}H_{46}N_4O$, manzamine B, **1**, 380

$C_{35}H_{47}O$, 4-hexadecyloxytrityl, **7**, 127

$C_{35}H_{48}ClNO_{10}$, callipeltoside A, **8**, 587

C$_{35}$H$_{48}$N$_2$O$_8$, ansatrienin A, **1**, 527

C$_{35}$H$_{48}$N$_3$O$_3$P, phosphoramidite, **7**, 154

C$_{35}$H$_{49}$Cl$_2$N$_2$O$_{15}$, aurantoside B, **8**, 580

C$_{35}$H$_{50}$N$_2$O$_7$, superstolide A, **1**, 371

C$_{35}$H$_{50}$O$_{12}$, macrolactin D, **8**, 590

C$_{35}$H$_{51}$Br$_4$N$_3$O$_7$, ceratinamide B, **8**, 440

C$_{35}$H$_{52}$O$_9$, amphidinolide F, **8**, 622, 620

C$_{35}$H$_{54}$O$_5$, lagunapyroneC, **8**, 596

C$_{35}$H$_{56}$O$_6$, papyriferic acid, **8**, 142

C$_{35}$H$_{56}$O$_{14}$, chalcomycin, **3**, 321

C$_{35}$H$_{58}$O$_{12}$, fungichromin, **1**, 451

C$_{35}$H$_{59}$ClO$_7$, blattellastanoside A, **8**, 230

C$_{35}$H$_{61}$ClO$_7$, blattellastanoside B, **8**, 230

C$_{35}$H$_{61}$NO$_{12}$, oleandomycin, **3**, 313, **4**, 198

C$_{35}$H$_{62}$N$_7$O$_{17}$P$_3$S, myristoyl-CoA, **3**, 305, **4**, 20

C$_{35}$H$_{62}$O$_4$, bacteriohopanetetrol, **2**, 47

C$_{35}$H$_{63}$NO$_3$, aminobacteriohopanetriol, **2**, 47

C$_{35}$H$_{66}$N$_4$O$_3$, lipogrammistin-A, **8**, 475

C$_{35}$H$_{68}$, 9,19-pentatriacontadiene, **8**, 219

C$_{35}$H$_{72}$, 15,19-dimethyltritriacontane, **8**, 249

C$_{36}$H$_{24}$N$_2$Ru, tris(1,10-phenanthroline)ruthenium, **7**, 88

C$_{36}$H$_{24}$N$_2$Zn, tris(1,10-phenanthroline)zinc, **7**, 88

C$_{36}$H$_{35}$N$_5$O$_{10}$S, guanosine nucleoside O-6-sulfonated derivative, **7**, 118

C$_{36}$H$_{36}$N$_2$O$_8$

  cannabisin D, **1**, 674, 695

  demethylgrossamide, **1**, 695

  grossamide, **1**, 674

C$_{36}$H$_{36}$N$_6$O$_9$S, dehydrocoelenterazine glutathione adduct, **8**, 455

C$_{36}$H$_{38}$N$_2$O$_9$, grossamide, **1**, 695

C$_{36}$H$_{40}$ClNO$_2$S, montelukast, **1**, 197

C$_{36}$H$_{40}$N$_2$O$_6$, berbamunine, **1**, 676

C$_{36}$H$_{42}$N$_4$O$_8$, dehydroisocoproporphyrinogen, **4**, 95

C$_{36}$H$_{43}$N$_9$O$_8$, cyclotheonamideC, **8**, 568

C$_{36}$H$_{44}$N$_4$O

  3,4-dihydromanzamine A, **8**, 557

  manzamine A, **8**, 553

C$_{36}$H$_{44}$N$_4$O$_2$

  6-deoxymanzamine X, **8**, 558

  6-hydroxymanzamine A, **8**, 557

  8-hydroxymanzamine A, **8**, 557

  manzamineE, **8**, 558

  manzamine oxide, **8**, 558

  manzamineY, **8**, 558

C$_{36}$H$_{44}$N$_4$O$_3$

  keramamine F, **8**, 554

  manzamine F, **8**, 557, 558

  manzamine X, **8**, 558

C$_{36}$H$_{44}$N$_4$O$_8$

  coproporphyrinogen I, **4**, 90

  coproporphyrinogen III, **4**, 65, 90

C$_{36}$H$_{45}$N$_3$O$_6$PS, biotinylated phosphoramidite, **7**, 171

C$_{36}$H$_{45}$N$_9$O$_8$, cyclotheonamide A, **8**, 568

C$_{36}$H$_{46}$Cl$_2$N$_2$O$_{15}$, aurantoside A, **8**, 580

C$_{36}$H$_{46}$N$_4$O

  manzamine B, **8**, 553

  manzamine J, **8**, 555

C$_{36}$H$_{46}$N$_4$O$_2$, manzamine oxide, **8**, 558

C$_{36}$H$_{47}$N$_9$O$_8$, cycloghdonamide analogue, **8**, 569

C$_{36}$H$_{48}$N$_2$O$_8$, ansatrienin A, **1**, 71

C$_{36}$H$_{48}$N$_2$O$_{12}$, rhodomycin, **3**, 313, 351, **4**, 200

C$_{36}$H$_{48}$N$_3$O$_6$P, benzophenanthridine phosphoramidite, **7**, 183

C$_{36}$H$_{48}$N$_3$O$_7$P, benzophenanthridine phosphoramidite, **7**, 183

C$_{36}$H$_{48}$N$_4$O, manzamine D, **8**, 553

C$_{36}$H$_{48}$N$_4$O$_2$, 1,2,3,4-tetrahydro-8-hydroxymanzamine A, **8**, 558

C$_{36}$H$_{48}$O$_{12}$

  heterotropatrione, **1**, 379

  isoheterotropatrione, **1**, 379

C$_{36}$H$_{48}$O$_{17}$

  22,23-dihydro-23-methoxyazadirachtin, **8**, 327

  isovepaol, **8**, 327

  vepaol, **8**, 327

C$_{36}$H$_{50}$N$_3$O$_4$P, phosphoramidite, **7**, 154

C$_{36}$H$_{50}$N$_3$O$_6$P

  benzophenanthridine phosphoramidite, **7**, 183

  phosphoramidite, **7**, 182

C$_{36}$H$_{50}$N$_4$O

  manzamineH, **8**, 555

  manzamine L, **8**, 557

C$_{36}$H$_{50}$O$_8$, 20-hydroxyecdysterone 2-cinnamate, **8**, 285

C$_{36}$H$_{52}$N$_7$O$_{23}$P$_3$S, p-coumaroyl-D-glucose, **3**, 641

C$_{36}$H$_{54}$N$_{11}$O$_{19}$, alterobactin B, **8**, 592

C$_{36}$H$_{56}$O$_6$, cylindrocyclophane A, **8**, 611

C$_{36}$H$_{56}$O$_8$, tetradecanoylphorbol acetate, **5**, 227

C$_{36}$H$_{56}$O$_{11}$, fusicoccin, **2**, 222, **8**, 178, 179

C$_{36}$H$_{56}$O$_{14}$, digitalin, **8**, 323

C$_{36}$H$_{58}$O$_{10}$, hederagenin 3-glucoside, **8**, 183

C$_{36}$H$_{59}$N$_7$O$_9$, cAM373, **8**, 408

C$_{36}$H$_{60}$O$_{30}$, α-cyclodextrin, **5**, 306

C$_{36}$H$_{62}$O$_{11}$, monensin, **3**, 88, 96, **4**, 200

C$_{36}$H$_{62}$O$_{31}$, maltohexaose, **5**, 305

C$_{36}$H$_{63}$NO$_{12}$, erythromycin analogue, **1**, 504

C$_{36}$H$_{63}$N$_3$O$_9$

  enniatin, **4**, 213, 335, **8**, 177

  enniatin A, **1**, 539, **4**, 321

C$_{36}$H$_{64}$N$_2$O$_{21}$, GlcNAcβ1-2Manα1-6(GlcNAc β1-2Manα1-3)Manβ1-octyl, **3**, 52

C$_{36}$H$_{65}$NO$_{12}$

  12-desmethylerythromycin, **1**, 509

  erythromycin D, **1**, 498

C$_{36}$H$_{65}$NO$_{13}$, erythromycin C, **1**, 498

C$_{36}$H$_{71}$NO$_3$, ceramide, **3**, 88, 90, 99, 101, 102

C$_{36}$H$_{71}$NO$_4$, symbioramide, **8**, 617

C$_{36}$H$_{73}$NO$_3$, dihydroceramide, **3**, 89, 90

C$_{36}$H$_{74}$, 21-methyl-8-pentatriacontene, **8**, 249

C$_{37}$H$_{33}$N$_7$O$_8$,CC-1065, **7**, 98, 492, 504

C$_{37}$H$_{44}$N$_2$O$_{14}$

  3α-pentaacetylstrictosidine, **4**, 116

  pentaacetylvincoside, **4**, 116

C$_{37}$H$_{45}$IN$_3$O$_8$P, 5-iododeoxyuridine phosphoramidite, **7**, 220

C$_{37}$H$_{46}$N$_4$O$_6$, aminoalkylated 4-thiodeoxyribonucleoside, **7**, 205

C$_{37}$H$_{47}$N$_9$O$_8$, cyclotheonamide B, **8**, 568

C$_{37}$H$_{48}$N$_4$O$_{11}$, shimofuridin F, **8**, 532

C$_{37}$H$_{49}$O$_2$, 9-(4-octadecyloxyphenyl)xanthen-9-yl, **7**, 127

C$_{37}$H$_{50}$N$_4$O$_2$, 1,2,3,4-tetrahydro-8-hydroxy-2-N-methylmanzamine A, **8**, 558

C$_{37}$H$_{50}$N$_4$O$_{11}$, shimofuridin G, **8**, 532

C$_{37}$H$_{54}$N$_{10}$O$_{18}$, alterobactin A, **8**, 592

C$_{37}$H$_{66}$N$_7$O$_{17}$P$_3$S

  hexadecanoyl-CoA, **8**, 204

  palmitoyl-CoA, **4**, 15, 20

C$_{37}$H$_{66}$O$_7$

  asimicin, **8**, 305

  squamosin, **8**, 305

C$_{37}$H$_{67}$NO$_{12}$

  10-desmethylerythromycin B, **1**, 509

  erythromycin B, **1**, 498

C$_{37}$H$_{67}$NO$_{13}$

  10-desmethylerythromycin A, **1**, 509

  erythromycin, **1**, 348, **3**, 351, 353, **4**, 1, 14, 200, 227

  erythromycin A, **1**, 495, **3**, 312

C$_{37}$H$_{72}$, 9,19-heptatriacontadiene, **8**, 219

C$_{37}$H$_{76}$

  15,23-dimethylpentatriacontane, **8**, 249

  pheromone of *Glossina pallidipes*, **8**, 42

C$_{38}$H$_{21}$Br$_8$NO$_7$, polycitone A, **8**, 539

C$_{38}$H$_{26}$N$_6$Rh, bis(phenanthroline)(9,10-phenanthrenequinone diimine)rhodium, **7**, 89

C$_{38}$H$_{37}$ClN$_2$O$_{11}$, maduropeptin chromophore, **7**, 580

C$_{38}$H$_{40}$N$_2$O$_{10}$, aryldihydronaphthalene lignanamide, **1**, 673

C$_{38}$H$_{40}$N$_2$P$_{10}$, lignan, **3**, 677

C$_{38}$H$_{41}$N$_3$O$_{11}$S, ecteinascidin 729, **8**, 531

C$_{38}$H$_{43}$N$_3$O$_{11}$S, ecteinascidin 743, **7**, 501

C$_{38}$H$_{44}$N$_{12}$O$_{23}$P$_2$, dinucleotide, **7**, 175

C$_{38}$H$_{45}$F$_3$N$_3$O$_8$P, trifluorothymidine phosphoramidite, **7**, 221

C$_{38}$H$_{45}$N$_4$O$_5$P, 5'-mercapto-2',5'-dideoxyribonucleoside-3'-*O*-phosphoram idite, **7**, 234

C$_{38}$H$_{47}$N$_4$O$_9$P, ribonucleoside phosphoramidite, **7**, 234

C$_{38}$H$_{48}$N$_2$O$_9$, kidamycin, **7**, 471

C$_{38}$H$_{48}$N$_8$O$_{12}$S, mureidomycin A, **3**, 280, 288

C$_{38}$H$_{54}$, 4,4'-diaponeurosporene, **2**, 341

C$_{38}$H$_{54}$F$_6$N$_2$O$_4$, cyclostellettamine A, **8**, 560

C$_{38}$H$_{57}$N$_5$O$_6$, motuporin, **8**, 576

C$_{38}$H$_{58}$, 4,4'-diaponeurosporene, **2**, 337, 323

C$_{38}$H$_{60}$, 4,4'-diapophytoene, **2**, 323, 324, 337, 341

C$_{38}$H$_{60}$O$_{18}$, stevioside, **8**, 166

C$_{38}$H$_{63}$NO$_{13}$, niddamycin, **1**, 525

C$_{38}$H$_{65}$NO$_{31}$, Man$_5$GlcNAc, **3**, 22

C$_{38}$H$_{66}$N$_2$O$_{23}$, GlcNAcβ1-6[GlcNAcβ1-2]Manα1-6Manβ1-methoxycarbonyloctyl, **3**, 55

C$_{38}$H$_{67}$N$_2$O$_7$P, tocopherol phosphoramidite, **7**, 189

C$_{38}$H$_{69}$NO$_{13}$, clarithromycin, **1**, 497

C$_{38}$H$_{72}$N$_2$O$_{12}$, azithromycin, **1**, 497

C$_{39}$H$_{34}$O$_4$, coenzyme Q6, **2**, 88

C$_{39}$H$_{37}$ClO$_{16}$, delphinidin 3-(*p*-coumarylglucoside)-5-malonylglucoside, **8**, 159

C$_{39}$H$_{38}$N$_5$O$_9$P, phosphoramidite, **7**, 175

C$_{39}$H$_{41}$ClN$_2$O$_{12}$, maduropeptin, **1**, 557

C$_{39}$H$_{42}$N$_4$O$_{14}$
harderoporphyrinogen, **4**, 95, 98
isoharderoporphyrinogen, **4**, 95, 98

C$_{39}$H$_{43}$N$_3$O$_{11}$S, ecteinascidin 743, **8**, 531

C$_{39}$H$_{43}$N$_3$O$_{12}$S, ecteinascidin 743 *N*(12)-oxide, **8**, 531

C$_{39}$H$_{46}$O$_{12}$, torreyanic acid, **1**, 378

C$_{39}$H$_{47}$N$_4$O$_8$, nitroxide-labeled nucleoside, **7**, 219

C$_{39}$H$_{48}$N$_5$O$_6$P, deoxyribonucleoside phosphoramidite, **7**, 233

C$_{39}$H$_{49}$NO$_{14}$, rifamycin B, **1**, 527

C$_{39}$H$_{49}$NO$_{16}$, nogalamycin, **1**, 482, **3**, 321, 349, 351, **7**, 351, 433, 437

C$_{39}$H$_{54}$N$_{10}$O$_{14}$S, α-amanitin, **6**, 178

C$_{39}$H$_{56}$F$_6$N$_2$O$_4$, cyclostellettamine B, **8**, 560

C$_{39}$H$_{56}$O$_4$, cyclodione, **1**, 377

C$_{39}$H$_{60}$O$_2$S$_2$, caldariellaquinone, **1**, 856

C$_{39}$H$_{61}$N$_5$O$_{12}$, onnamide A, **8**, 581

C$_{39}$H$_{64}$O$_{10}$, helminthosporoside A, **8**, 179

C$_{39}$H$_{66}$O$_{10}$, 23-macrolide, **8**, 579

C$_{39}$H$_{66}$O$_{11}$
21-macrolide, **8**, 579
swinholide derivative, **8**, 579

C$_{39}$H$_{72}$N$_8$O$_{11}$, iPD1, **8**, 408

C$_{39}$H$_{80}$
11,23-dimethylheptatriacontane, **8**, 249
13,25-dimethylheptatriacontane, **8**, 249

C$_{40}$H$_{27}$O$_6$, trisbenzoyloxytrityl, **7**, 123, 126

C$_{40}$H$_{36}$O$_{11}$, artonin, **1**, 385

C$_{40}$H$_{38}$N$_4$O$_{16}$, uroporphyrin III, **4**, 65

C$_{40}$H$_{38}$O$_{10}$, kuwanon J, **1**, 385

C$_{40}$H$_{42}$N$_2$O$_8$, cyclobutyldicarboxylic acid, **2**, 258

C$_{40}$H$_{43}$N$_3$O$_{12}$S, ecteinascidin 729 21-*O*-methyl-*N*(12)-formyl derivative, **8**, 531

C$_{40}$H$_{44}$N$_4$O$_8$, uroporphyrinogen III, **4**, 62, 72

C$_{40}$H$_{44}$N$_4$O$_{10}$, tolyporphin, **8**, 611

C$_{40}$H$_{44}$N$_4$O$_{16}$
uroporphyrinogen, **4**, 143
uroporphyrinogen I, **4**, 73, 86, 88, 90
uroporphyrinogen II, **4**, 86, 91
uroporphyrinogen III, **4**, 86
uroporphyrinogen IV, **4**, 86, 91

C$_{40}$H$_{44}$N$_{12}$O$_{10}$S$_2$, CI40622, **3**, 584

C$_{40}$H$_{44}$O$_{12}$, oligolignol, **3**, 724

C$_{40}$H$_{46}$ClN$_6$O$_6$P, halogenated deoxyribonucleoside phosphoramidite, **7**, 225

C$_{40}$H$_{46}$FN$_6$O$_7$P, halogenated deoxyribonucleoside phosphoramidite, **7**, 225

C$_{40}$H$_{46}$N$_4$O$_{16}$, precorrin 1, **4**, 143

C$_{40}$H$_{46}$N$_4$O$_{17}$
hydroxymethylbilane, **4**, 143
preuroporphyrinogen, **4**, 73, 80

C$_{40}$H$_{46}$N$_5$O$_8$PS, 5-thiocyanato-2'-deoxyuridine phosphoramidite, **7**, 202

C$_{40}$H$_{46}$O$_{14}$, cerberalignan, **1**, 688

C$_{40}$H$_{48}$F$_3$N$_4$O$_8$P, phosphoramidite, **7**, 156

C$_{40}$H$_{48}$N$_6$O$_{10}$, bouvardin, **4**, 202

C$_{40}$H$_{50}$N$_2$O$_{10}$, neopluramycin, **7**, 508

C$_{40}$H$_{50}$O$_2$, rhodoxanthin, **2**, 347, 323

C$_{40}$H$_{50}$O$_{14}$, zaragozic acidC, **2**, 251, 254, 255, 256, 257

C$_{40}$H$_{52}$O$_2$, canthaxanthin, **2**, 323, 337, 344, 347

C$_{40}$H$_{52}$O$_3$, phoenicoxanthin, **2**, 323

C$_{40}$H$_{52}$O$_4$, astaxanthin, **2**, 323, 335, 344, 347

C$_{40}$H$_{54}$O, echinenone, **2**, 323, 337, 344

C$_{40}$H$_{54}$O$_2$
3-hydroxyechinenone, **2**, 323
3'-hydroxyechinenone, **2**, 323

C$_{40}$H$_{54}$O$_3$, adonixanthin, **2**, 323, 335

C$_{40}$H$_{56}$
α-carotene, **2**, 323, 342
β-carotene, **2**, 5, 58, 60, 61, 323, 337, 342, 343, 344, 347, **8**, 164
γ-carotene, **2**, 323
β-isorenieratene, **2**, 323, 336
isorenieratene, **2**, 323, 336, 337
lycopene, **2**, 5, **8**, 164

C$_{40}$H$_{56}$O
β-cryptoxanthin, **2**, 344, 323
cryptoxanthin, **2**, 333

C$_{40}$H$_{56}$O$_2$
demethylspheroidenone, **2**, 323, 330
lutein, **2**, 61, 323, 342, 347, **8**, 87
zeaxanthin, **2**, 323, 325, 332, 333, 344, 347, **8**, 87, 469

C$_{40}$H$_{56}$O$_4$
neoxanthin, **8**, 87
violaxanthin, **8**, 72, 84, 87

C$_{40}$H$_{57}$N$_2$O$_3$PS$_2$, mercaptoalkylated phosphoramidite, **7**, 167

C$_{40}$H$_{58}$
dihydro-β-carotene, **2**, 323, 343, 344
neurosporene, **2**, 323, 324, 330, 334, 341, 343
β-zeacarotene, **2**, 323, 341, 344

C$_{40}$H$_{58}$F$_6$N$_2$O$_4$
cyclostellettamine C, **8**, 560
cyclostellettamine D, **8**, 560

C$_{40}$H$_{58}$O
demethylspheroidene, **2**, 323, 330
hydroxyneurosporene, **2**, 323, 330

C$_{40}$H$_{60}$
ζ-carotene, **2**, 323, 324, 331, 338, 341, 343
7,8,11,12-tetrahydrolycopene, **2**, 323, 324, 331

C$_{40}$H$_{60}$O$_2$, zeaxanthin, **2**, 337

C$_{40}$H$_{60}$O$_4$, maytenone, **1**, 377

C$_{40}$H$_{61}$BrN$_8$O$_9$, konbamide, **8**, 573

C$_{40}$H$_{62}$, phytofluene, **2**, 323

C$_{40}$H$_{63}$N$_5$O$_3$, adenosylhopane, **2**, 47

C$_{40}$H$_{64}$
15,15'-phytoene, **2**, 341
phytoene, **2**, 10, 108, 323, 324, 331, 334, 338, 340

C$_{40}$H$_{64}$O$_{12}$, nonactin, **1**, 451

C$_{40}$H$_{65}$NO$_9$, A83543A, **1**, 374

C$_{40}$H$_{66}$N$_8$O$_{10}$, cAD1, **8**, 408

C$_{40}$H$_{67}$N$_7$O$_9$, cCF10, **8**, 408

C$_{40}$H$_{74}$O$_{15}$, halymecin D, **8**, 601

C$_{40}$H$_{80}$NO$_8$P
dipalmitoylphosphatidylcholine, **3**, 198

lysopalmitoylphosphatidylcholine, **3**, 198

$C_{40}H_{89}N_{10}O_{13}P_3$, aminoalkylated adenosine triphosphate, **7**, 197

$C_{40}H_{89}N_{10}O_{14}P_3$, (6-aminohexyl)isoguanosine triphosphate, **7**, 199

$C_{41}H_{28}O_{24}$, casuarictin, **3**, 800, 802, 817

$C_{41}H_{28}O_{26}$, casuarinin, **3**, 783

$C_{41}H_{30}O_{25}$, tellimagrandin II, **3**, 800, 817, 818

$C_{41}H_{32}O_{26}$ 1,2,3,4,6-penta-*O*-galloyl-β-D-glucopyranose, **3**, 800

   penta-*O*-galloyl-β-D-glucopyranose, **3**, 10

   1,2,3,4,6-pentagalloylglucose, **3**, 809, 822

   1,2,3,4,6-pentagalloyl-β-D-glucose, **3**, 808

   1,2,3,4,6-penta-*O*-galloyl-β-D-glucose, **3**, 822

   pentagalloylglucose, **3**, 802, 806, 817, 820

$C_{41}H_{32}O_{28}$, chebulagic acid, **3**, 817, **7**, 596

$C_{41}H_{42}N_4O_{16}$, methylchlorin, **4**, 153

$C_{41}H_{46}N_4O_{16}$, dihydrosirohydrochlorin, **4**, 90

$C_{41}H_{47}F_3N_5O_9P$, ribonucleoside phosphoramidite, **7**, 230

$C_{41}H_{48}N_4O_{16}$, precorrin 2, **4**, 143

$C_{41}H_{48}N_5O_7P$, 3,*N*(4)-ethenodeoxyribocytidine phosphoramidite, **7**, 208

$C_{41}H_{48}N_7O_7P$, triazolo phosphoramidite, **7**, 193

$C_{41}H_{49}N_4O_{10}P$, deoxyuridine phosphoramidite, **7**, 198

$C_{41}H_{50}N_2O_{11}$, rubiflavin A, **7**, 510

$C_{41}H_{56}B_9N_4O_8P$, 5-(*o*-carboran-1-yl)-2′-deoxyuridine phosphoramidite, **7**, 221

$C_{41}H_{58}O_2$, spheroidenone, **2**, 323, 327, 345

$C_{41}H_{60}F_6N_2O_4$, cyclostellettamine E, **8**, 560

$C_{41}H_{60}O$

   methoxyneurosporene, **2**, 323, 330

   spheroidene, **2**, 323, 327, 345

$C_{41}H_{60}O_2$, hydroxyspheroidene, **2**, 323

$C_{41}H_{61}NO_9$, pinnatoxin A, **1**, 384, **8**, 520

$C_{41}H_{62}O_{10}$, amphidinolide C, **8**, 621

$C_{41}H_{64}N_2O_{13}S_5$, nemenamicin, **8**, 544

$C_{41}H_{65}N_9O_{28}P_2$, UDPMur*N*Ac-Ala-Glu-*m*-DAP-Ala-Ala, **3**, 258, 261

$C_{41}H_{66}O_{12}$, α-hederin, **8**, 323

$C_{41}H_{66}O_{12}$, α-hederin, **8**, 183

$C_{41}H_{66}O_{13}$, β-hederin, **8**, 183

$C_{41}H_{68}O_{13}$, T-toxin, **1**, 424

$C_{41}H_{69}BrO_{11}$, oscillariolide, **8**, 610

$C_{41}H_{73}NO_8$, bacteriohopane, **1**, 152

$C_{41}H_{84}$, 13,17-dimethylnonatriacontane, **8**, 249

$C_{41}H_{84}N_2O_6P$, sphingomyelin, **3**, 90, 97, 101

$C_{41}H_{86}N_2O_6P$, dihydrosphingomyelin, **3**, 90

$C_{42}H_{40}F_3N_5O_9P$, deoxyribonucleoside phosphoramidite, **7**, 233

$C_{42}H_{42}F_3N_4O_9P$, phosphoramidite, **7**, 197

$C_{42}H_{43}N_9O_{17}P_2$, BZDC-FAD, **2**, 279

$C_{42}H_{44}FeN_4O_{16}$, siroheme, **4**, 62, 90

$C_{42}H_{44}N_4O_{16}$, dimethylisobacteriochlorin, **4**, 153

$C_{42}H_{44}N_5O_9P$, phosphoramidite, **7**, 175

$C_{42}H_{44}N_5O_{10}P$, phosphoramidite, **7**, 175

$C_{42}H_{44}O_5$, longithorone, **1**, 378

$C_{42}H_{46}O_5$, longithorone A, **8**, 532

$C_{42}H_{48}N_4O_2$, Flexi-Di, **7**, 446

$C_{42}H_{48}N_7O_6P$, 1,*N*(6)-ethenodeoxyriboadenosine phosphoramidite, **7**, 208

$C_{42}H_{50}N_3O_9P$, non-nucleosidic phosphoramidite, **7**, 239

$C_{42}H_{50}N_4O_{16}$, precorrin 3, **4**, 143

$C_{42}H_{50}N_5O_7PS$, 4-thioated 2′-deoxyuridine phosphoramidite, **7**, 202

$C_{42}H_{50}N_5O_{11}P$, phosphoramidite, **7**, 229

$C_{42}H_{51}NiN_6O_{13}$, factor F_{430}, **4**, 62, 90

$C_{42}H_{51}NO_{15}$

   aclacinomycin B1, **3**, 321

   aclacinomycin B2, **3**, 321

$C_{42}H_{52}N_2O_{10}$

   hedamycin, **7**, 509

   pluramycin, **7**, 508

   pluramycin A, **7**, 508, 510

$C_{42}H_{53}F_3N_5O_8P$, aminoalkylated deoxyribonucleoside phosphoramidite, **7**, 191

$C_{42}H_{53}NO_{15}$

   aclacinomycin, **3**, 313, 351

   aclacinomycin A, **3**, 325, **4**, 200

$C_{42}H_{55}NO_7$, **8**, 177

$C_{42}H_{56}F_3N_4O_7P$, phosphoramidite, **7**, 155

$C_{42}H_{58}N_6O_9P$, deoxyribonucleoside phosphoramidite, **7**, 166

$C_{42}H_{58}O_{11}$, enterocin derivative, **8**, 543

$C_{42}H_{59}NO_{14}S_4$, namenamicin, **7**, 554, 581

$C_{42}H_{62}F_6N_2O_4$, cyclostellettamine F, **8**, 560

$C_{42}H_{62}O_6$, glycyrrhizin, **8**, 166

$C_{42}H_{63}NO_7$, spirolide B, **8**, 520

$C_{42}H_{63}NO_{10}$, pinnatoxin B, **8**, 520

$C_{42}H_{67}N_5O_{21}S$, liposidomycin B, **3**, 280

$C_{42}H_{67}O_{12}PS_4$, 1,2-bis[12-(lipoyloxy)-dodecanoyl]-glycero-3-phosphoglycerol, **5**, 110

$C_{42}H_{67}O_{13}$, maduralide, **8**, 592

$C_{42}H_{68}O_{14}$, polycavernoside B2, **8**, 516

$C_{42}H_{69}NO_{15}$, josamycin, **4**, 198

$C_{42}H_{70}N_8O_{10}$, iAD1, **8**, 408

$C_{42}H_{70}O_{35}$, β-cyclodextrin, **5**, 299, 306, **7**, 482

$C_{42}H_{71}N_7O_8$, niaraiamide A, **8**, 536

$C_{42}H_{72}O_{16}$, lankamycin, **3**, 321, 322

$C_{42}H_{72}O_{36}$, maltoheptaose, **5**, 302

$C_{42}H_{76}O_2$, geranylgeranyl docosanoate, **8**, 229

$C_{42}H_{76}O_{14}$, halymecin A, **8**, 601

$C_{42}H_{81}NO_8$

   GalCer, **3**, 91, 92, 102

   GlcCer, **3**, 91, 94, 101, 102

$C_{42}H_{81}NO_{11}S$, sulphatide, **3**, 102

$C_{42}H_{82}O_2$, octadecyl 9-tetracosenoate, **8**, 219

$C_{43}H_{18}Cl_6N_3O_6$, tris(4,5-dichlorophthalimido)trityl, **7**, 126

$C_{43}H_{44}CoN_4O_{16}$, cobalt-precorrin 3, **4**, 156

$C_{43}H_{46}N_4O_{16}$, trimethylisobacteriochlorin, **4**, 153

$C_{43}H_{49}N_7O_{10}$, virginiamycin, **1**, 140, **8**, 384

$C_{43}H_{49}N_7O_{20}S$, deoxycytidine triphosphate, **7**, 207

$C_{43}H_{50}N_4O_{17}$, precorrin 3 hydroxylactone, **4**, 143

$C_{43}H_{50}N_7O_7P$, deoxyluminarosine phosphoramidite, **7**, 208

$C_{43}H_{51}N_9O_8$, cycloghdonamide analogue, **8**, 569

$C_{43}H_{52}F_3N_5O_9P$, 4′-*C*-(aminomethyl)thymidine phosphoramidite, **7**, 232

$C_{43}H_{52}N_5O_7PS$, phosphoramidite, **7**, 202

$C_{43}H_{52}N_5O_{21}P_3S_2$, phosphoramidite, **7**, 209

$C_{43}H_{56}N_{10}O_{11}S$

   keramamide F, **8**, 572

   keramamide G, **8**, 572

$C_{43}H_{57}BrN_{10}O_{11}S$, keramamide H, **8**, 572

$C_{43}H_{58}N_5O_6PS$, biotinylated phosphoramidite, **7**, 171

$C_{43}H_{58}N_{10}O_9$, cyclotheonamide E, **8**, 568

$C_{43}H_{58}N_{10}O_{11}S$, keramamide J, **8**, 572

$C_{43}H_{59}NO_{14}S_4$, C-1027 chromophore, **7**, 578

$C_{43}H_{60}O_{12}$, goniodomin A, **8**, 614

$C_{43}H_{64}O_{11}$, gambierol, **8**, 503

$C_{43}H_{65}NO_7$, spirolide D, **8**, 520

$C_{43}H_{66}O_9$, amphidinolide M, **8**, 622

$C_{43}H_{68}O_{14}$, polycavernoside A2, **8**, 516

$C_{43}H_{68}O_{15}$, polycavernoside A, **8**, 515

$C_{43}H_{69}NO_{12}$

   ascomycin, **1**, 75

   FK520, **1**, 518

$C_{43}H_{73}N_7O_8$, nairaiamide B, **8**, 536

$C_{43}H_{74}N_2O_4$, spiramycin, **4**, 200

$C_{43}H_{74}N_2O_{14}$, spiramycin I, **1**, 525

$C_{43}H_{74}O_8$, 20-hydroxyecdysone 22-palmitate, **8**, 283

$C_{43}H_{76}N_3O_4P$, cholesteryl phosphoramidite, **7**, 187

$C_{44}H_{36}MnN_8$, tetrakis(*N*-methyl-4-pyridiniumyl)porphine manganese complex, **7**, 89

$C_{44}H_{43}F_3N_5O_9P$, phosphoramidite, **7**, 197

$C_{44}H_{44}ClN_3O_{12}$, C-1027, **1**, 557

$C_{44}H_{47}F_3N_5O_{10}P$, aminoalkylated deoxyribonucleoside phosphoramidite, **7**, 197

$C_{44}H_{49}CoN_4O_{16}$, factor 4, **4**, 154

$C_{44}H_{49}F_3N_5O_9P$, phosphoramidite, **7**, 194

$C_{44}H_{51}CoN_4O_{16}$, cobalt precorrin 4, **4**, 156

$C_{44}H_{53}CoN_4O_{16}$, cobalt precorrin 6, **4**, 156

$C_{44}H_{52}N_4O_{17}$, precorrin 4, **4**, 144

$C_{44}H_{52}N_{14}O_2$, biluciferyl, **8**, 445

$C_{44}H_{53}F_3N_5O_9P$, deoxyribonucleoside phosphoramidite, **7**, 195

$C_{44}H_{54}N_4O_{16}$, precorrin 6, **4**, 145

$C_{44}H_{56}N_4O_{16}$, dihydroprecorrin 6, **4**, 145

$C_{44}H_{57}N_4O_8PS_2$, mercaptoalkylated deoxyribonucleoside phosphoramidite, **7**, 203

$C_{44}H_{60}N_4O_8SSi$, 2-thiouridine phosphoramidite, **6**, 93

$C_{44}H_{62}N_8O_{11}$, viridogrisein, **1**, 546

$C_{44}H_{62}O_{11}$, enterocin derivative, **8**, 543

$C_{44}H_{65}BrN_{10}O_{14}$, perthamide B, **8**, 577

$C_{44}H_{68}O_{13}$
  dinophysistoxin 2, **8**, 490
  okadaic acid, **8**, 490
  okadaic acid 24-epimer, **8**, 492

$C_{44}H_{68}O_{13}S$, acanthifolicin, **8**, 491

$C_{44}H_{69}NO_{12}$, FK506, **1**, 75, 518, **4**, 2, 200, 541

$C_{44}H_{70}O_{15}$, polycavernoside B, **8**, 515

$C_{44}H_{74}O_7$, manzamenone A, **1**, 384

$C_{44}H_{75}NO_{11}$, scytophycin C, **8**, 579

$C_{44}H_{89}N_3O_4P$, polyalkyl phosphoramidite, **7**, 187

$C_{45}H_{35}N_7O_3Rh$, rhodium phenanthrenequinone diimine 5-glutaric acid monoamide 1, 10-phenanthroline, **7**, 165

$C_{45}H_{38}O_{16}$, angular triflavanoid, **3**, 758

$C_{45}H_{49}N_6O_{12}PS$, 5-[S-(2,4-dinitrophenyl)thio]-2′-deoxyuridine phosphoramidite, **7**, 203

$C_{45}H_{52}Cl_6N_3O_{10}P$, phosphoramidite, **7**, 178

$C_{45}H_{52}N_4O_{11}P$, deoxyribonucleoside phosphoramidite, **7**, 227

$C_{45}H_{52}N_5O_{12}P$, phosphoramidite, **7**, 166

$C_{45}H_{53}CoN_4O_{16}$, cobalt-precorrin 5, **4**, 156

$C_{45}H_{54}Cl_4N_3O_{10}P$, phosphoramidite, **7**, 178

$C_{45}H_{54}N_4O_{17}$, precorrin 5, **4**, 144

$C_{45}H_{56}N_8O_9$, pristinamycin I, **4**, 235

$C_{45}H_{57}N_4O_9PS$, phosphoramidite, **7**, 202

$C_{45}H_{57}N_4O_{11}P$, phosphoramidite, **7**, 194

$C_{45}H_{59}CoN_4O_{14}$, cobyrinic acid, **4**, 148, 154

$C_{45}H_{60}N_4O_{14}$
  hydrogenobyrinic acid, **4**, 141, 146, 153
  precorrin 8, **4**, 146

$C_{45}H_{62}N_5O_6PS$, phosphoramidite, **7**, 172

$C_{45}H_{62}N_6O_{12}$, hydrogenobyrinic acid diamide, **4**, 146

$C_{45}H_{64}N_4O_{22}P_3$, digoxigenin-labeled deoxyuridine triphosphate, **7**, 209

$C_{45}H_{66}NO_{10}$, pinnatoxin D, **8**, 520

$C_{45}H_{68}N_8O_{10}S$, cPD1, **8**, 408

$C_{45}H_{70}O_{10}$, glycolipid, **8**, 618

$C_{45}H_{70}O_{13}$, dinophysistoxin 1, **8**, 490, 492

$C_{45}H_{72}O_{14}$, polycavernoside A3, **8**, 516

$C_{45}H_{78}O_2$, cholesteryl oleate, **8**, 230, **5**, 134

$C_{46}H_{52}N_4O_2$, ditercalinium, **7**, 444

$C_{46}H_{53}NO_{12}$, cephalomannine, **2**, 220, 222

$C_{46}H_{53}N_4O_7PS$, phosphoramidite, **7**, 202

$C_{46}H_{54}N_5O_9PS$, deoxycytidine phosphoramidite, **7**, 193

$C_{46}H_{56}N_4O_{10}$, vincristine, **4**, 46, 110

$C_{46}H_{57}N_4O_7PS$, dansyl phosphoramidite, **7**, 178

$C_{46}H_{57}N_6O_8PS$, phosphoramidite, **7**, 202

$C_{46}H_{58}F_3N_5O_8P$, phosphoramidite, **7**, 191

$C_{46}H_{58}N_3O_8P$, phosphoramidite, **7**, 156

$C_{46}H_{58}N_3O_{10}P$, phosphoramidite, **7**, 178

$C_{46}H_{58}N_4O_9$
  vinblastine, **4**, 46
  vincaleucoblastine, **4**, 110

$C_{46}H_{60}N_5O_9PSSi$, uridine phosphoramidite, **7**, 202

$C_{46}H_{62}BrN_9O_{10}$, orbiculamide A, **8**, 570

$C_{46}H_{64}N_5O_6PS$, phosphoramidite, **7**, 172

$C_{46}H_{64}N_5O_8PS$, biotinyl phosphoramidite, **7**, 172

$C_{46}H_{64}O_7$, myxobactone, **2**, 323, 333, 346

$C_{46}H_{66}O_6$
  β-cryptoxanthin monoglucoside, **2**, 332
  myxobactin, **2**, 323, 334, 346

$C_{46}H_{66}O_7$
  β-cryptoxanthin monoglucoside, **2**, 323
  myxoxanthophyll, **2**, 323, 337
  zeaxanthin glucoside, **2**, 333
  zeaxanthin monoglucoside, **2**, 323, 332

$C_{46}H_{69}N_2O_5P$, polyalkyl phosphoramidite, **7**, 187

$C_{46}H_{71}NO_{15}$, glycookadaic acid, **8**, 491

$C_{46}H_{73}N_3O_3$, N-tryptophanyl aminobacteriohopanetriol, **2**, 47

$C_{46}H_{74}N_{14}O_{34}P_6S_2$
  methylmalonyl-CoA, **5**, 271, **8**, 240
  succinyl-CoA, **5**, 271

$C_{46}H_{75}NO_{13}$, tolytoxin, **8**, 610

$C_{46}H_{77}NO_{17}$, tylosine, **1**, 496, 500, 525, **3**, 352, **4**, 196

$C_{46}H_{78}N_2O_{86}$, Man₅GlcNAc₂, **3**, 24

$C_{46}H_{83}N_2O_4P$, tocopherol phosphoramidite, **7**, 189

$C_{47}H_{39}N_7O_2Ru$, N-hydroxysuccinimide ester of rhodium phenanthrenequinone diimine 4-butyric acid 4′-methylbipyridine, **7**, 165

$C_{47}H_{51}NO_{14}$, taxol, **2**, 213, 220, 222

$C_{47}H_{53}N_2O_4P$, phosphoramidite, **7**, 161

$C_{47}H_{54}N_5O_8P$, phosphoramidite, **7**, 199

$C_{47}H_{59}F_3N_5O_9P$, carbocyclic phosphoramidite, **7**, 235

$C_{47}H_{59}NO_{17}$
  altromycin B, **7**, 508, 509
  pluramycin, **7**, 508

$C_{47}H_{59}NO_{18}$, altromycin B, **7**, 471

$C_{47}H_{60}F_3N_5O_8P$, aminoalkylated deoxyribonucleoside phosphoramidite, **7**, 191

$C_{47}H_{63}N_5O_8P$, ribocytidine phosphoramidite, **7**, 208

$C_{47}H_{64}N_5O_8SSi$, 4-S-cyanoethyl-4-thiouridine phosphoramidite, **6**, 93

$C_{47}H_{65}N_4O_7PSi$, phosphoramidite, **7**, 231

$C_{47}H_{65}N_4O_9PSi$, 4′-C-(hydroxymethyl)thymidine phosphoramidite, **7**, 232

$C_{47}H_{66}N_5O_7PS$, biotin phosphoramidite, **7**, 172

$C_{47}H_{68}O_{15}$, PTX3, **8**, 498

$C_{47}H_{68}O_{17}$, bryostatin 1, **8**, 521

$C_{47}H_{70}O_{14}$
  avermectin B1, **1**, 523
  avermectin B1b, **1**, 496, 500
  PTX2, **8**, 498

$C_{47}H_{70}O_{15}$, PTZ1, **8**, 498

$C_{47}H_{74}NO_4$, lydicamycin, **1**, 370

$C_{47}H_{74}N_{12}O_{14}$, callipeltin B, **8**, 586

$C_{47}H_{76}IN_3O_{21}S_4$, calicheamicin γ1I, **7**, 568

$C_{47}H_{78}N_8O_8$, Ala-MeLeu-MeLeu-MeVal-MeBmt-Abu-MeGly-MeLeu, **1**, 548

$C_{48}H_{36}O_{30}$ 3-O-digalloyl-1,2,4,6-tetra-O-galloyl-β-D-glucose, **3**, 816
  1,2,3,6-tetra-O-galloyl-4-O-digalloyl-β-D-glucose, **3**, 813
  1,2,4,6-tetra-O-galloyl-3-O-digalloyl-β-D-glucose, **3**, 813
  1,3,4,6-tetra-O-galloyl-2-O-digalloyl-β-D-glucose, **3**, 813

$C_{48}H_{38}N_8$, TMPyP, **7**, 441

$C_{48}H_{48}N_6Ru$, tris(3,4,7,8-tetramethylphenanthroline)ruthenium, **7**, 88

$C_{48}H_{52}N_3O_6P$, phosphoramidite, **7**, 156

$C_{48}H_{52}N_5O_{12}P$, 2,4-dinitrophenyl deoxyribonucleoside phosphoramidite, **7**, 210

$C_{48}H_{53}N_3O_7P$, phosphoramidite, **7**, 155

$C_{48}H_{55}N_4O_{10}P$, deoxyribonucleoside phosphoramidite, **7**, 194

$C_{48}H_{55}N_8O_{13}P$, phosphoramidite, **7**, 175

$C_{48}H_{56}N_3O_6P$, phosphoramidite, **7**, 175

$C_{48}H_{57}N_4O_8P$, deoxyribonucleoside phosphoramidite, **7**, 192

$C_{48}H_{62}N_3O_9P$, phosphoramidite, **7**, 176

$C_{48}H_{62}N_7O_7PSe$, riboadenosine phosphoramidite, **7**, 208

$C_{48}H_{63}N_6O_{11}P$, phosphoramidite, **7**, 175

$C_{48}H_{64}F_3N_6O_9P$, deoxyribonucleoside phosphoramidite, **7**, 192

$C_{48}H_{64}N_5O_{12}P$, phosphoramidite, **7**, 175

$C_{48}H_{64}N_6O_8P$, nucleoside phosphoramidite, **7**, 219

$C_{48}H_{64}O_{21}$, chromocyclomycin, **3**, 313

$C_{48}H_{65}N_6O_9PS$, biotin phosphoramidite, **7**, 173

$C_{48}H_{73}N_2O_5P$, polyalkyl phosphoramidite, **7**, 187

$C_{48}H_{74}O_{14}$, Ivermectin, **1**, 523

$C_{48}H_{76}N_6O_{12}$, epididemnin A_1, **8**, 529

$C_{48}H_{80}O_{40}$, γ-cyclodextrin, **5**, 306

$C_{48}H_{85}N_5O_7$
  C6-NBD-Cer, **3**, 98
  C6-NBD-ceramide, **3**, 100

$C_{48}H_{86}O_{19}$, halymecin B, **8**, 601

$C_{48}H_{87}N_5O_7$, ((N-6-(7-nitro-2,1,3-benzoxadiazol-4-yl)aminohexanoyldi hydroceramide, **3**, 90

$C_{48}H_{91}NO_{13}$
  digalactosylceramide, **3**, 102
  LacCer, **3**, 94, 101, 102

$C_{49}H_{52}F_3N_5O_9P$, C-4′-amilkylated thymidine phosphoramidite, **7**, 232

$C_{49}H_{52}N_4O_6$, kapakahine B, **8**, 583

$C_{49}H_{56}N_3O_5P$, phosphoramidite, **7**, 161

$C_{49}H_{58}N_6S_2$, TOTO, **7**, 448

$C_{49}H_{59}N_5O_9P$, deoxyribonucleoside phosphoramidite, **7**, 219

$C_{49}H_{61}F_3N_9O_8P$, phosphoramidite, **7**, 191

$C_{49}H_{63}ClN_8O_8$, keramamide A, **8**, 573

$C_{49}H_{63}F_3N_5O_{10}P$, amilkylated phosphoramidite, **7**, 193

$C_{49}H_{63}N_6O_{22}P_3S_2$, phosphoramidite, **7**, 209

$C_{49}H_{64}N_3O_8P$, deoxyribonucleoside phosphoramidite, **7**, 239

$C_{49}H_{66}N_6O_8P$, nucleoside phosphoramidite, **7**, 219

$C_{49}H_{67}N_4O_{10}P$, levulinylated phosphoramidite, **7**, 204

$C_{49}H_{70}O_{13}$, bervetoxin A, **8**, 511

$C_{49}H_{70}O_{14}$, amphidinolideC tetraacetate, **8**, 621

$C_{49}H_{74}N_{10}O_{12}$, microcystin LR, **8**, 610

$C_{49}H_{74}O_4$
  ubiquinone, **2**, 51, 52
  ubiquinone-8, **8**, 436

$C_{49}H_{74}O_{14}$, avermectin, **4**, 200

$C_{49}H_{80}N_6O_{13}$, acylclodidemnin A, **8**, 529

$C_{49}H_{87}N_5O_7$, 1-O-methyl-C6-NBD-ceramide, **3**, 100

$C_{50}H_{54}O_{15}$, herpentol, **1**, 690

$C_{50}H_{56}N_5O_{10}P$, deoxyribonucleoside phosphoramidite, **7**, 195

$C_{50}H_{56}O_{16}$, oligolignol, **3**, 724

$C_{50}H_{58}N_4O_5$, Phe-Phe-Pro-Phe, **4**, 325

$C_{50}H_{60}N_5O_9P$, deoxyribonucleoside phosphoramidite, **7**, 205

$C_{50}H_{62}N_{12}O_{12}S_2$, triostin A, **7**, 352, 436, 444, 446, 488

$C_{50}H_{63}ClO_{16}$, chlorothricin, **1**, 370, 374, **3**, 355

$C_{50}H_{63}N_{10}O_7P$, deoxyribonucleoside phosphoramidite, **7**, 217

$C_{50}H_{65}N_4O_7PS$, phosphoramidite, **7**, 175

$C_{50}H_{69}N_5O_{10}P$, nucleoside phosphoramidite, **7**, 230

$C_{50}H_{70}O_{14}$, brevetoxin B, **8**, 511

$C_{50}H_{72}O_2$, okadaxanthin, **8**, 590

$C_{50}H_{72}O_{14}$, bervetoxin-3, **8**, 515

$C_{50}H_{74}O_{14}$, doramectin, **1**, 524

$C_{51}H_{14}N_{12}O_{12}S_2$, echinomycin, **7**, 444

$C_{51}H_{31}N_{15}O_{15}S$, berninamycin, **1**, 853

$C_{51}H_{43}N_{13}O_{12}S_6$, nosiheptide, **1**, 852

$C_{51}H_{50}N_4O_{21}$, rubradirin, **3**, 322

$C_{51}H_{56}F_3N_8O_8PS$, aminoalkylated deoxyribonucleoside phosphoramidite, **7**, 196

$C_{51}H_{58}N_4O_8P$, phosphoramidite, **7**, 157

$C_{51}H_{59}N_5O_9P$, deoxyribonucleoside phosphoramidite, **7**, 219

$C_{51}H_{59}N_6O_{10}PS$, dansylated deoxyribonucleoside phosphoramidite, **7**, 209

$C_{51}H_{60}ClN_4O_6P$, acridinyl phosphoramidite, **7**, 181

$C_{51}H_{62}N_5O_{10}P$, deoxyribonucleoside phosphoramidite, **7**, 205

$C_{51}H_{63}N_3O_5P$, phosphoramidite, **7**, 161

$C_{51}H_{64}N_{12}O_{12}S_2$, echinomycin, **7**, 436, 446, 488

$C_{51}H_{67}N_7O_{15}$, salinamide A, **8**, 593

$C_{51}H_{68}N_5O_{11}P$, phosphoramidite, **7**, 194

$C_{51}H_{70}ClN_7O_{15}$, salinamide B, **8**, 593

$C_{51}H_{72}O_2$, ubiquinone, **2**, 56

$C_{51}H_{74}O_2$
  dihydromenaquinone, **2**, 56
  menaquinone, **2**, 56

$C_{51}H_{78}O_{14}$, okadaic acid diol ester, **8**, 490

$C_{51}H_{78}O_{15}$, okadaic acid diol ester, **8**, 490

$C_{51}H_{79}NO_{13}$, rapamycin, **1**, 1, 75, 497, 518, 534, 541, **4**, 232

$C_{51}H_{80}O_{15}$, glycolipid, **8**, 618

$C_{51}H_{82}O_{23}$
  avenacoside A, **8**, 183
  avenacoside B, **8**, 183

$C_{51}H_{98}O$, 25,26-epoxyhenpentacontadiene, **8**, 219

$C_{51}J_{79}NO_{13}$, rapamycin, **1**, 2

$C_{52}H_{40}N_{10}O_6Ru$, ruthenium 5′-glutaric acid monoamide 1,10-phenanthroline dipyrido[3,2:a-2′,3′:c]phenazine, **7**, 165

$C_{52}H_{57}ClN_5O_7P$, acridinyl phosphoramidite, **7**, 181

$C_{52}H_{61}N_3O_7P$, phosphoramidite, **7**, 159

$C_{52}H_{65}N_8O_{11}P$, phosphoramidite, **7**, 205

$C_{52}H_{73}BrN_{10}O_{12}$, keramamide D, **8**, 572

$C_{52}H_{74}BrN_{15}O_{12}$, N-bromoacetylbradykinin, **6**, 138

$C_{52}H_{74}NNaO_{17}S$, brevetoxin B_1, **8**, 514

$C_{52}H_{76}O_{12}$, zeaxanthin diglucoside, **2**, 323, 332, 344

$C_{52}H_{76}O_{24}$, mithramycin, **1**, 480, **3**, 313, 322, 323

$C_{52}H_{78}N_{10}O_{28}P_2S$, UDPMurNAc-Ala-Glu-Lys(N_ε-dansyl)-Ala-Ala, **3**, 263

$C_{52}H_{80}O_{15}$, okadaic acid diol ester, **8**, 490

$C_{52}H_{88}N_2O_{91}$, Man₆GlcNAc₂, **3**, 24

$C_{52}H_{100}O_2$, meromycolic acid, **1**, 66

$C_{53}H_{52}N_7O_6P$, anthracenyl deoxyguanosine phosphoramidite, **7**, 222

$C_{53}H_{56}N_3O_6P$, pyrenyl phosphoramidite, **7**, 178

$C_{53}H_{57}N_4O_{10}P$, anthraquinonylmethyl deoxyribonucleoside phosphoramidite, **7**, 228

$C_{53}H_{58}N_2O_6P$, pyrenyl phosphoramidite, **7**, 178

$C_{53}H_{59}N_{12}O_{12}P$, deoxyribonucleoside phosphoramidite, **7**, 211

$C_{53}H_{60}ClN_3O_{15}$
  kedarcidin, **1**, 557
  kedarcidin chromophore, **7**, 575

$C_{53}H_{60}N_7O_9PS$, bipyridine deoxyribonucleoside phosphoramidite, **7**, 214

$C_{53}H_{65}N_3O_5P$, phosphoramidite, **7**, 161

$C_{53}H_{71}BrN_2O_{13}$
  phorboxazole A, **8**, 583
  phorboxazole B, **8**, 583

$C_{53}H_{75}BrN_{10}O_{12}$
  keramamideC, **8**, 572
  keramamideE, **8**, 572

$C_{53}H_{78}N_3O_8P$, deoxyribonucleoside phosphoramidite, **7**, 239

$C_{53}H_{80}O_2$, plastoquinone, **2**, 61

$C_{53}H_{80}O_{15}$, okadaic acid diol ester, **8**, 490

$C_{53}H_{93}N_7O_{13}$, surfactin, **4**, 198, 199, 202, 208, 283

$C_{53}H_{94}N_8O_{12}$, halobacillin, **8**, 594

$C_{53}H_{96}N_6O_{10}P$
  C6-NBD-SM, **3**, 98
  C6-NBD-sphingomyelin, **3**, 100
  NBD-sphingomyelin, **3**, 100

$C_{54}H_{55}N_7O_7P$, phosphoramidite, **7**, 223

$C_{54}H_{57}N_3O_7P$, phosphoramidite, **7**, 158

$C_{54}H_{57}N_4O_9P$, 2′-O-(2-anthracenemethyl)uridine phosphoramidite, **7**, 229

$C_{54}H_{60}N_4O_{10}P$, deoxyribonucleoside phosphoramidite, **7**, 236

$C_{54}H_{63}N_8O_{13}P$, 2,4-dinitrophenyl deoxyribonucleoside phosphoramidite, **7**, 210

$C_{54}H_{72}N_7O_9PS$, biotin phosphoramidite, **7**, 174

$C_{54}H_{74}N_2O_9$, ritterazine, **8**, 533

$C_{54}H_{74}N_2O_{10}$, cephalostatin, **8**, 533

$C_{54}H_{74}N_7O_{16}P$,EDTA deoxyribonucleoside phosphoramidite, **7**, 215

$C_{54}H_{76}N_2O_8$, ritterazine, **8**, 533

$C_{54}H_{76}N_2O_9$, ritterazine, **8**, 533

$C_{54}H_{76}N_2O_{10}$

   ritterazine, **8**, 533

   ritterazine A, **8**, 532

$C_{54}H_{76}N_2O_{11}$, ritterazine, **8**, 533

$C_{54}H_{77}BrN_{10}O_{12}$, keramamide B, **8**, 572

$C_{54}H_{78}N_2I_7$, ritterazine, **8**, 533

$C_{54}H_{78}N_2O_9$, ritterazine, **8**, 533

$C_{54}H_{80}N_2O_6$, ritterazine, **8**, 533

$C_{54}H_{82}O_4$, ubiquinone-9, **8**, 436

$C_{54}H_{90}N_6O_{18}$, valinomycin, **4**, 197

$C_{54}H_{91}N_3O_{41}$, GlcNAcMan$_5$GlcNAc$_2$, **3**, 25, 26

$C_{54}H_{95}NO_{46}$, Man$_8$GlcNAc, **3**, 22, 29

$C_{55}H_{40}O_{34}$ 1,2,4,6-tetra-*O*-galloyl-3-*O*-trigalloyl-β-D-glucose, **3**, 813

   1,4,6-tri-*O*-galloyl-2,3-di-*O*-digalloyl-β-D-glucose, **3**, 813

   1,3,6-tri-*O*-galloyl-2,4-di-*O*-digalloyl-β-D-glucose, **3**, 813

   1,2,6-tri-*O*-galloyl-3,4-di-*O*-digalloyl-β-D-glucose, **3**, 813

$C_{55}H_{59}N_4O_8P$, 2′-*O*-(1-pyrenylmethyl)uridine phosphodiamidite, **7**, 228

$C_{55}H_{59}N_5O_{10}P$, deoxyribonucleoside phosphoramidite, **7**, 195

$C_{55}H_{60}N_9O_8P$, deoxyguanosine phosphoramidite, **7**, 215

$C_{55}H_{68}CoN_9O_{16}$, adenoxyl cobyric acid, **4**, 148

$C_{55}H_{68}N_4O_6P$, phosphoramidite, **7**, 161

$C_{55}H_{68}O_7$, xuxuarine Aα, **1**, 378

$C_{55}H_{70}CoN_{11}O_{14}$, adenosyl cobyrinic acid diamide, **4**, 148

$C_{55}H_{72}MgN_4O_5$

   chlorophyll, **4**, 141

   chlorophyll a, **4**, 62

$C_{55}H_{73}IN_4O_{21}S_4$, calicheamicin γ1I, **3**, 326

$C_{55}H_{74}IN_3O_{21}S_4$, calicheamicin, **1**, 557

$C_{55}H_{74}N_2O_8$, ritterazine, **8**, 533

$C_{55}H_{74}N_7O_{23}P_3S_2$, phosphoramidite, **7**, 209

$C_{55}H_{76}N_2O_9$, ritterazine, **8**, 533

$C_{55}H_{80}Na_2O_{21}$, yessotoxin, **8**, 499

$C_{55}H_{80}Na_2O_{22}$, 45-hydroxyYTX, **8**, 500

$C_{55}H_{83}NO_{21}$

   avenacin A, **8**, 183

   avenacin B, **8**, 183

$C_{55}H_{84}N_{17}O_{21}S_3$

   bleomycin, **7**, 385, 387, 394, 397, 420, 544

   bleomycin A$_2$, **7**, 536

$C_{55}H_{86}O_{25}$

   camellidin I, **8**, 183

   camellidin II, **8**, 183

$C_{55}H_{91}O_4P$, undecaprenyl monophosphate, **3**, 214

$C_{55}H_{102}O_6$, 1,2-dioleyl-3-palmitylglycerol, **8**, 218

$C_{56}H_{62}N_7O_8P$, phosphoramidite, **7**, 223

$C_{56}H_{62}N_7O_9P$, phosphoramidite, **7**, 223

$C_{56}H_{65}ClN_5O_9P$, acridine deoxyribonucleoside phosphoramidite, **7**, 236

$C_{56}H_{73}N_4O_8P$, phosphoramidite, **7**, 175

$C_{56}H_{77}N_8O_{10}PS$, phosphoramidite, **7**, 205

$C_{56}H_{80}N_2O_{10}$, ritterazine, **8**, 533

$C_{56}H_{83}NO_{13}$, prorocentrolide, **8**, 496

$C_{56}H_{95}N_5O_{12}$,C6-NBD-GlcCer, **3**, 95, 100

$C_{56}H_{98}N_{16}O_{13}$

   polymyxin, **4**, 199, 200

   polymyxin B, **3**, 224

$C_{57}H_{58}N_7O_6P$, pyrenyl phosphoramidite, **7**, 224

$C_{57}H_{58}N_7O_7P$, pyrenyl phosphoramidite, **7**, 224

$C_{57}H_{63}ClN_7O_9P$, acridine derivative, **7**, 211

$C_{57}H_{65}ClO_{30}$, delphinidin 3-rutinoside-7-di(*p*-coumarylglucoside), **8**, 159

$C_{57}H_{67}N_2O_8P$, phosphoramidite, **7**, 156

$C_{57}H_{75}N_3O_{23}S_4$, esperamicin A$_{1c}$, **1**, 565

$C_{57}H_{82}O_{16}$, CTX3C, **8**, 503

$C_{57}H_{82}O_{26}$

   chromomycin, **4**, 198

   chromomycin A$_3$, **3**, 313, 323

$C_{57}H_{84}O_{18}$, CRX2A1, **8**, 503

$C_{57}H_{89}N_7O_{15}$, didemnin B, **8**, 521

$C_{57}H_{94}N_{10}O_{17}P_3$, alkynyl dideoxynucleotide triphosphate, **7**, 211

$C_{57}H_{94}O_{27}$, cyclamin, **8**, 183

$C_{57}H_{97}N_9O_{17}P_3$, alkynyl dideoxynucleotide triphosphate, **7**, 211

$C_{57}H_{104}O_6$, triolein, **5**, 134

$C_{58}H_{63}F_3N_9O_9P$, deoxyguanosine phosphoramidite, **7**, 200

$C_{58}H_{64}N_7O_{10}P$, phosphoramidite, **7**, 223

$C_{58}H_{67}N_{10}O_{10}P$, deoxyribonucleoside phosphoramidite, **7**, 214

$C_{58}H_{69}N_2O_8P$, non-nucleosidic phosphoramidite, **7**, 204

$C_{58}H_{70}N_4O_4P$, phosphoramidite, **7**, 178

$C_{58}H_{72}N_{10}O_9$, kapakahine A, **8**, 583

$C_{58}H_{72}N_{10}O_{10}$

   kapakahine C, **8**, 583

   kapakahine D, **8**, 583

$C_{58}H_{77}N_3O_{23}S_4$, esperamicin A$_{1b}$, **1**, 565

$C_{58}H_{79}N_8O_{16}P$, phosphoramidite, **7**, 215

$C_{58}H_{80}N_4O_{22}S_2$, esperamicinZ, **7**, 572

$C_{58}H_{82}N_2O_{11}$, ritterazine, **8**, 533

$C_{58}H_{83}CoN_{10}O_{12}$, adenoxyl cobinamide, **4**, 148

$C_{58}H_{84}CoN_{10}O_{15}P$, adenoxyl cobinamide phosphate, **4**, 149

$C_{58}H_{84}O_{26}$, olivomycin A, **3**, 313, 322, 323

$C_{58}H_{91}N_{13}O_{20}$, amphomycin, **3**, 281, 301

$C_{58}H_{98}O_{12}SSi_2$, okadaic acid 3-*O*-methylthiomethyl-1,24-olide, **8**, 492

$C_{59}H_{66}N_6O_{11}P$, deoxyribonucleoside phosphoramidite, **7**, 196

$C_{59}H_{66}N_9O_{10}PS$, phosphoramidite, **7**, 228

$C_{59}H_{78}N_2O_7$, ritterazine, **8**, 533

$C_{59}H_{79}N_3O_{23}S_4$

   esperamicin, **1**, 557, 14

   esperamicin A$_1$, **1**, 562, **3**, 326, **7**, 554, 571

$C_{59}H_{83}CoN_{14}O_{14}P$, 7-azabenzimidazolylcobamide, **4**, 150

$C_{59}H_{84}Cl_2O_{32}$, curamycin, **3**, 313

$C_{59}H_{84}N_2O_{18}$, candicidin, **1**, 612, **4**, 200

$C_{59}H_{88}N_2O_{17}$, perimycin, **1**, 612

$C_{59}H_{90}O_4$

   ubiquinone, **2**, 26, 27, 376, **4**, 4

   ubiquinone-10, **8**, 436

$C_{59}H_{92}O_{16}$, gambieric acid A, **8**, 509

$C_{59}H_{94}O_{21}$, hederasaponin B, **8**, 183

$C_{59}H_{94}O_{22}$, hederasaponinC, **8**, 183

$C_{59}H_{95}N_{11}O_{14}$, hormothamnin A, **8**, 609

$C_{59}H_{96}N_{10}O_{16}P_3$, alkynyl dideoxynucleotide triphosphate, **7**, 211

$C_{59}H_{100}N_8O_{18}P_3$, alkynyl dideoxynucleotide triphosphate, **7**, 211

$C_{59}H_{101}N_3O_{14}$, aplyronine A, **8**, 521

$C_{59}H_{108}N_2O_{21}$, GM3, **3**, 94, 101, 102

$C_{60}H_{62}N_7O_6P$, anthracenyl deoxyadenosine phosphoramidite, **7**, 223

$C_{60}H_{63}N_{12}O_{14}P$, deoxyguanosine phosphoramidite, **7**, 211

$C_{60}H_{65}N_4O_9PS$, nucleoside phosphoramidite, **7**, 231

$C_{60}H_{65}N_6O_{12}P$, 2′-deoxyuridine phosphoramidite, **7**, 226

$C_{60}H_{65}N_8O_{10}P$, ribonucleoside phosphoramidite, **7**, 231

$C_{60}H_{67}N_8O_9PS$, terpyridine deoxyribonucleoside phosphoramidite, **7**, 215

$C_{60}H_{72}N_4O_4P$, phosphoramidite, **7**, 178

$C_{60}H_{72}N_7O_{16}$, pyrimidine phosphoramidite, **7**, 211

$C_{60}H_{74}N_{14}O_{22}$, luzopeptinC, **7**, 488

$C_{60}H_{80}N_9O_{14}P$, deoxyribonucleoside phosphoramidite, **7**, 211

$C_{60}H_{84}CoN_{13}O_{15}P$, 5-hydroxybenzimidazolylcobamide, **4**, 150

$C_{60}H_{84}N_2O_{11}$, ritterazine, **8**, 533

$C_{60}H_{84}O_{16}$
    CTX4A, **8**, 503
    CTX4B, **8**, 501

$C_{60}H_{85}CoN_{11}O_{15}P$, *p*-cresolylcobamide, **4**, 150

$C_{60}H_{86}O_{19}$, ciguatoxin, **8**, 501

$C_{60}H_{92}N_{12}O_{10}$
    gramicidin, **4**, 283
    gramicidinS, **1**, 840, **4**, 196, 199, 202, 209, 213, 320, 321, 323, 344, 546

$C_{60}H_{92}N_{12}O_{18}$, gramicidin S, **4**, 208

$C_{60}H_{94}O_{16}$, gambieric acid B, **8**, 509

$C_{60}H_{98}O_{27}$, sakurasosaponin, **8**, 183

$C_{61}H_{86}CoN_{13}O_{15}P$, 5-methoxybenzimidazolylcobamide, **4**, 150

$C_{61}H_{86}N_{14}O_{21}$, aciculitin A, **8**, 584

$C_{61}H_{87}CoN_{14}O_{14}P$, 5,6-dimethyl-7-azabenzimidazolylcobamide, **4**, 150

$C_{61}H_{88}Cl_2O_{32}$, avilamycin, **1**, 414, **3**, 313

$C_{61}H_{100}O_{14}$, 7-*O*-palmitoyl DTX-1, **8**, 490

$C_{61}H_{111}N_{11}O_{12}$, 6 allylglycinecyclosporin A, **1**, 538

$C_{61}H_{111}N_{11}O_{13}$, cyclosporinO, **1**, 543

$C_{62}H_{60}N_9O_{10}P$, anthraquinonylmethyl deoxyribonucleoside phosphoramidite, **7**, 228

$C_{62}H_{68}N_9O_8P$
    2′-*O*-(bipyridinylalkyl)adenosine phosphoramidite, **7**, 229
    phosphoramidite, **7**, 198

$C_{62}H_{71}N_6O_9PS$, phosphoramidite, **7**, 205

$C_{62}H_{86}N_7O_9P$, phosphoramidite, **7**, 216

$C_{62}H_{86}N_{12}O_{16}$, actinomycin D, **7**, 432, 433, 436, 529, 607

$C_{62}H_{88}CoN_{13}O_{14}P$, cob(II)alamin, **5**, 171, 172, 176, 208, 266

$C_{62}H_{88}CoN_{13}O_{15}P$, 5-methoxy-6-methylbenzimidazolylcobamide, **4**, 150

$C_{62}H_{88}N_{14}O_{21}$, aciculitin B, **8**, 584

$C_{62}H_{89}CoN_{13}O_{14}P$
    cob(I)alamin, **5**, 266
    cob(III)alamin, **5**, 266

$C_{62}H_{89}CoN_{13}O_{15}P$, hydroxocobalamin, **5**, 265

$C_{62}H_{105}NO_{51}$, Man₉GlcNAc, **3**, 22

$C_{62}H_{111}N_{11}O_{11}$, 5*N*-methylcyclohexylalaninecyclosporin A, **1**, 538

$C_{62}H_{111}N_{11}O_{12}$
    cyclosporin, **4**, 199, 213, 217
    cyclosporin A, **1**, 16, **4**, 198, 226, 230, 234, 235, 321, 335, 534

$C_{62}H_{111}N_{11}O_{13}$, cyclosporineC, **1**, 534

$C_{63}H_{78}N_6O_{10}PSi$, ribonucleoside phosphoramidite, **7**, 201

$C_{63}H_{88}CoN_{14}O_{14}P$
    cobalamin, **4**, 140, 146, **5**, 263
    cyanocobalamin, **5**, 173, **7**, 638
    vitamin B₁₂, **4**, 62, 90, 140, **5**, 206

$C_{63}H_{88}N_{12}O_{16}$, actinomycin, **4**, 200, 232, 235

$C_{63}H_{90}N_{14}O_{21}$, aciculitin C, **8**, 584

$C_{63}H_{91}CoN_{13}O_{14}P$, methylcobalamin, **1**, 871, 876, **5**, 263, 265

$C_{63}H_{105}NO_{14}$, N-acetylglucosamine-pyrophosphate undecaprenol, **3**, 214

$C_{63}H_{113}N_{11}O_{12}$
    4 MeIle-cyclosporin A, **1**, 550
    cyclosporin D, **1**, 537
    cyclosporin G, **1**, 538, 549
    cyclosporin M, **1**, 538
    cyclosporinV, **1**, 550,
    N-methyl-₄-isoleucylcyclosporin, **1**, 538

$C_{64}H_{67}N_7O_{12}P$, PAH phosphoramidite, **7**, 225

$C_{64}H_{84}N_{12}O_{14}$, loloatin B, **8**, 595

$C_{64}H_{89}N_6O_9PS$, biotin phosphoramidite, **7**, 172

$C_{64}H_{89}N_8O_{13}P$, cholesteryl nucleoside phosphoramidite, **7**, 189

$C_{64}H_{92}N_3O_8P$, cholesteryl phosphoramidite, **7**, 188

$C_{64}H_{96}O_{17}$, BTXB₃, **8**, 514

$C_{64}H_{108}N_2O_{51}$, Man₈GlcNAc₂, **3**, 17, 20

$C_{65}H_{72}N_6O_{12}PSi$, uridine phosphoramidite, **7**, 200

$C_{65}H_{85}N_{13}O_{30}$, mycobacillin, **4**, 208, 216

$C_{65}H_{98}N_2O_{24}$, kijanimicin, **1**, 370

$C_{65}H_{100}O_{19}$, gambieric acid,C, **8**, 509

$C_{65}H_{101}NO_{28}S_2$, DTX-5a, **8**, 491

$C_{65}H_{116}N_{12}O_{13}$, 8-*β*-Ala-cyclosporin A, **1**, 550

$C_{66}H_{75}Cl_2N_9O_{24}$, vancomycin, **3**, 6, 261, 272, 281, 322, 327, **4**, 197, 217

$C_{66}H_{87}N_{13}O_{13}$, tyrocidine, **4**, 196, 202, 208, 213, 235, 320, 322, 323, 546

$C_{66}H_{92}N_{12}O_{10}$
    gramicidin B, **4**, 226
    gramicidinS, **4**, 235

$C_{66}H_{95}N_4O_9P$, cholesteryl phosphoramidite, **7**, 188

$C_{66}H_{97}ClO_{36}$, delphinidin 3-malonylglucoside-3′,5′-di(*p*-coumarylglucosyl)glucoside, **8**, 159

$C_{66}H_{102}O_{19}$, gambieric acid D, **8**, 509

$C_{66}H_{103}NO_{28}S_2$, DTX-5b, **8**, 491

$C_{66}H_{103}N_{17}O_{16}S$
    bacitracin, **4**, 196, 197, 199, 200, 202, 208, 217
    bacitracin A, **3**, 280

$C_{66}H_{104}O_{31}S_3$, DTX-4, **8**, 491, 493

$C_{66}H_{121}N_{18}O_{20}$, callipeltin A, **8**, 585

$C_{67}H_{75}N_7O_{17}P$, phosphoramidite, **7**, 236

$C_{67}H_{77}N_8O_{16}$, pyrimidine phosphoramidite, **7**, 211

$C_{67}H_{79}N_7O_{11}PS$, phosphoramidite, **7**, 216

$C_{67}H_{80}N_5O_{10}P$, deoxyribonucleoside phosphoramidite, **7**, 204

$C_{67}H_{99}CoN_{13}O_{14}P$, neopentylcobalamin, **5**, 173

$C_{67}H_{121}N_3O_{26}$, GM2, **3**, 100

$C_{68}H_{79}N_4O_{12}PS$, phosphoramidite, **7**, 178

$C_{68}H_{91}N_8O_{12}PS$, biotinylated deoxyribonucleoside phosphoramidite, **7**, 205

$C_{68}H_{96}CoN_{21}O_{21}P_2$, adenoxyl glucose diphosphate cobinamide, **4**, 149

$C_{68}H_{106}N_5O_{34}P$, moenomycin A, **3**, 281

$C_{68}H_{110}N_{22}O_{27}S_2$, tallysomycin A, **7**, 539

$C_{68}H_{116}N_5O_{34}P$, decahydromoenomycin, **3**, 281

$C_{68}H_{118}N_{18}O_{21}$, callipeltinC, **8**, 586

$C_{68}H_{123}N_{13}O_{14}$
    theonellapeptolide Ia, **8**, 573
    theonellapeptolide Ib, **8**, 573
    theonellapeptolide Ic, **8**, 573
    theonellapeptolide IId, **8**, 575

$C_{69}H_{73}ClO_{17}$, delphinidin 3-malonylglucoside-7-di(caffeylglucoside)-3′-caffeylglucoside, **8**, 159

$C_{69}H_{80}N_3O_{12}P$, 5-carboxyfluoresceinyl phosphoramidite, **7**, 178

$C_{69}H_{87}BrN_{16}O_{23}$
    theonellamide E, **8**, 575
    theonellamide F, **8**, 575

$C_{69}H_{125}N_{13}O_{14}$, theonellapeptolide Id, **8**, 573

$C_{70}H_{67}N_8O_{10}P$, phosphoramidite, **7**, 223

$C_{70}H_{89}BrN_{16}O_{23}$, theonellamide D, **8**, 575

$C_{70}H_{94}O_{17}$, YTX, **8**, 500

$C_{70}H_{106}N_3O_{11}P$, cholesteryl phosphoramidite, **7**, 188

$C_{70}H_{118}N_2O_{56}$, Man₉GlcNAc₂, **3**, 23, 24

$C_{70}H_{127}N_{13}O_{14}$, theonellapeptolide Ie, **8**, 573

$C_{71}H_{77}N_6O_{11}P$, phosphoramidite, **7**, 157

$C_{71}H_{101}CoN_{18}O_{17}P$, adenoxyl cobalamin, **4**, 149

$C_{71}H_{102}N_4O_{10}P$, deoxyribonucleoside phosphoramidite, **7**, 239

$C_{71}H_{122}O_{25}$, amphidinol 2, **8**, 617

$C_{71}H_{125}N_3O_{29}$, GD3, **3**, 101

$C_{72}H_{48}N_6Co$, Co(DIP)₃, **7**, 88

$C_{72}H_{48}N_6Rh$, Rh(DIP)₃, **7**, 88

$C_{72}H_{48}N_6Ru$, tris(4,7-diphenylphenanthroline)ruthenium, **7**, 88

$C_{72}H_{60}P_4Pd$, tetrakis(triphenylphosphino)palladium, **7**, 135

$C_{72}H_{85}N_{19}O_{18}S_5$, thiostrepton, **1**, 852, **6**, 195

$C_{72}H_{100}CoN_{18}O_{17}P$
  adenosylcobalamin, **4**, 140, **5**, 165, 170, 176, 206, 207, 218, 263
  adenosylcob(III)alamin, **5**, 266
  coenzyme B₁₂, **5**, 266,
  5′-deoxyadenosylcobinamide, **5**, 266

$C_{73}H_{83}Cl_2N_{10}O_{26}$, LY264826, **3**, 327

$C_{73}H_{99}CoN_{19}O_{17}P$, adenosylcobalamin, **3**, 330

$C_{73}H_{112}N_2O_{37}$, arugomycin, **3**, 313, 322, 324

$C_{73}H_{125}NaO_{27}S$, amphidinol, **8**, 615

$C_{73}H_{131}N_3O_{31}$, GM1, **3**, 100, 101

$C_{74}H_{59}N_8O_2PRu$, β-cyanoethyl-*N,N*-diisopropylphosphoramidite ruthenium complex, **7**, 185

$C_{74}H_{92}Br_2O_{26}$, theonellamide B, **8**, 575

$C_{74}H_{98}N_6O_3$, kauluamine, **8**, 560

$C_{74}H_{112}O_2$, botryoxanthin A, **8**, 618

$C_{75}H_{94}Br_2O_2$, theonellamideC, **8**, 575

$C_{75}H_{98}BrN_{16}O_{23}$, theonegramide, **8**, 576

$C_{76}H_{97}BrN_{16}O_{27}$, theonellamide A, **8**, 575

$C_{76}H_{106}CoN_{20}O_{17}P$, adenosylcobalamin-*N*-methylimidazole, **5**, 269

$C_{77}H_{67}NO_{13}$, erythromycin A, **3**, 322

$C_{77}H_{105}CoN_{19}O_{17}P$, adenosylcobalamin-pyridine, **5**, 269

$C_{78}H_{48}Al F_3O_3$, aluminum naphthoxide, **5**, 350

$C_{78}H_{130}O_{20}$, swinholide A, **8**, 579

$C_{78}H_{138}N_4O_{22}S_2$, theonezolide B, **8**, 581

$C_{78}H_{152}O_3$, mycolic acid, **1**, 66

$C_{79}H_{110}N_2O_{37}$, arugomycin, **7**, 351

$C_{79}H_{140}N_4O_{22}S_2$, theonezolide A, **8**, 581

$C_{80}H_{80}Cl_3NO_2$, *N*-methylanilinium trichloroacetate, **7**, 138

$C_{80}H_{93}Cl_3N_{10}O_{26}$, LY191145, **3**, 283

$C_{80}H_{124}N_{20}O_{22}S_5$, actagardine, **4**, 276, 280, 282

$C_{80}H_{142}N_4O_{22}S_2$, theonezolideC, **8**, 581

$C_{84}H_{148}N_4O_{39}$, GD1a, **3**, 100

$C_{85}H_{119}N_{23}O_{25}S_3$, ancovenin, **4**, 280

$C_{85}H_{128}N_{22}O_{23}S_5$, mersacidin, **3**, 281, **4**, 276, 280, 282, 289, 295

$C_{85}H_{145}N_7O_{29}$, C6-NBD-GM1, **3**, 100

$C_{88}H_{95}Cl_2N_9O_{33}$, teicoplanin, **3**, 281

$C_{88}H_{148}N_2O_{71}$
  Glc₃Man₉GlcNAc₂, **3**, 15, 18
  Glc₃Man₉GlcNAc₂, **3**, 41

$C_{89}H_{125}N_{25}O_{25}S_3$
  cinnamycin, **4**, 280, 282, 295
  duramycin, **4**, 280, 282

$C_{95}H_{57}ClO_{28}$, delphinidin 3-rutinoside 7-tetra(4-hydroxybenzoylglucosyl)glucoside, **8**, 159

$C_{95}H_{110}N_8O_{44}$, ristocetin A, **3**, 283

$C_{96}H_{136}Cl_3NO_{35}$, prymnesin-2, **8**, 518

$C_{98}H_{141}N_{25}O_{23}S_3$, epidermin, **4**, 279, 281, 286, 289, 290, 296, 298

$C_{99}H_{140}N_{20}O_{17}$
  gramicidin D, **4**, 323
  linear gramicidin, **4**, 320, 322

$C_{100}H_{100}N_{15}O_{26}P$, deoxyguanosine phosphoramidite, **7**, 208

$C_{100}H_{146}N_{24}O_{22}S_3$
  gallidermin, **4**, 279, 281, 283, 286, 300
  staphylococcin 1580, **4**, 279

$C_{119}H_{154}ClN_{22}O_{39}$, ramoplanin, **3**, 280

$C_{121}H_{203}N_{41}O_{38}S_6$, geographutoxin I, **8**, 476

$C_{122}H_{208}N_{42}O_{36}S_7$, geographutoxin II, **8**, 476

$C_{127}H_{220}N_3O_{53}$, ostereocin D, **8**, 510

$C_{129}H_{223}N_3O_{54}$, palytoxin, **8**, 509

$C_{131}H_{189}N_{37}O_{34}S_4$, streptococcin A-FF22, **4**, 279, 282, 292, 293

$C_{132}H_{184}N_{38}O_{37}S_5$
  lacticin 481, **4**, 279, 282, 292, 293
  lactococcin DR, **4**, 279

$C_{136}H_{227}N_{37}O_{34}S_3$, epilancin K7, **4**, 279, 284, 287

$C_{138}H_{228}NNaO_{56}S$, zooxanthellatoxin-B, **8**, 614

$C_{140}H_{232}NNaO_{57}S$, zooxanthellatoxin-A, **8**, 614

$C_{142}H_{249}N_{36}O_{46}$, pardaxinP-3, **8**, 473

$C_{143}H_{230}N_{42}O_{37}S_7$
  nisin, **4**, 199, 202, 276, 278, 281, 283, 291, 296, 299
  nisin A, **4**, 298

$C_{143}H_{251}N_{36}O_{46}$
  pardaxinP-1, **8**, 473
  pardaxinP-2-, **8**, 473

$C_{144}H_{231}N_{43}O_{38}S_7$, nisin Z, **4**, 279, 285

$C_{153}H_{235}N_{41}O_{40}S_6$, subtilin, **4**, 279, 281, 283, 286, 295, 296, 299

$C_{153}H_{256}N_{48}O_{38}S_3$, Pep5, **4**, 279, 281, 283, 286, 296, 299

$C_{163}H_{256}O_{68}S_2Na_2$, maitotoxin, **8**, 504

$C_{178}H_{274}N_{44}O_{43}S_4$, lactocinS, **4**, 279, 284, 294

$C_{218}H_{383}N_{62}O_{71}$, polytheonamide B, **8**, 577

Cl_2Cu,CuCl₂, **1**, 131

Cl_2Mg, magnesium chloride, **4**, 15

Cl_2NOP, dichlorophosphoramidite, **7**, 132

Cl_4Ti, titanium chloride, **7**, 126

HCl_2O_2P, phosphorodichloridous acid, **6**, 82

$HNaO_3S$, sodium bisulfite, **7**, 95

HNO_3, peroxynitrous acid, **5**, 236, 239

HN_3, hydrazoic acid, **5**, 197

HO, hydroxyl radical, **7**, 253

H_2MgO_2, magnesium hydroxide, **6**, 157

H_2O, water, **5**, 79

H_2O_2, hydrogen peroxide, **3**, 720, **7**, 540

H_2O_2Pb, lead hydroxide, **6**, 135, **6**, 157

H_2O_2Zn, zinc hydroxide, **5**, 79

H_3N, ammonia, **3**, 405, **5**, 80, 273

H_3NO, hydroxylamine, **2**, 33, **4**, 14, **5**, 406, 412, **7**, 93

H_3O_3PSe, selenophosphate, **4**, 355

H_3O_4P, *o*-phosphoric acid, **7**, 70

H_4BN, sodium borohydride, **4**, 14

H_4ClN, ammonium chloride, **5**, 350

H_4NO_3P, phosphoramidic acid, **6**, 82

$H_{15}ClCoN_5$, cobalt chloro pentaamine, **6**, 251

$H_{18}CoN_6$, cobalt hexaamine, **6**, 251

$H_{18}N_6Os$, osmium hexammine, **6**, 57

I_2, iodine, **6**, 73

K I, potassium iodide, **6**, 65

K MnO_4
  potassium manganate, **7**, 253
  potassium permanganate, **7**, 92

K_2O_3Te, potassium tellurate, **2**, 276

NO, nitric oxide, **3**, 183, 298, **5**, 239

OsO_4, osmium tetroxide, **7**, 92, 253

$TiCl_3$, titanium chloride, **6**, 65

Subject Index

PHILIP AND LESLEY ASLETT
Marlborough, Wiltshire, UK

Every effort has been made to index as comprehensively as possible, and to standardize the terms used in the index in line with the IUPAC Recommendations. In view of the diverse nature of the terminology employed by the different authors, the reader is advised to search for related entries under the appropriate headings.

The index entries are presented in letter-by-letter alphabetical sequence. Compounds are normally indexed under the parent compound name, with the substituent component separated by a comma of inversion. An entry with a prefix/locant is filed after the same entry without any attachments, and in alphanumerical sequence. For example, 'diazepines', '1,4-diazepines', and '2,3-dihydro-1,4-diazepines' will be filed as:-

    diazepines
    1,4-diazepines
    1,4-diazepines, 2,3-dihydro-

The Index is arranged in set-out style, with a maximum of three levels of heading. Location references refer to volume number (in bold) and page number (separated by a comma); major coverage of a subject is indicated by bold, elided page numbers; for example;

    triterpene cyclases, **299–320**
        amino acids, 315

See cross-references direct the user to the preferred term; for example,

    olefins *see* alkenes

See also cross-references provide the user with guideposts to terms of related interest, from the broader term to the narrower term, and appear at the end of the main heading to which they refer, for example,

    thiones
        see also thioketones

A

A19009, as glucosamine-6-phosphate synthase inhibitor, **3**, 275
A83094A, occurrence, **1**, 374
A83543A, structure, **1**, 374
AAA *see* L-α-aminoadipic acid (AAA)
aat genes *see pen* genes, *penDE*
ABA *see* abscisic acid
ABA-induced genes, expression, **8**, 83
abalones *see Haliotis* spp.
abasic site, formation, **7**, 493
ABC transporter-dependent pathway, homopolymeric chain biosynthesis, **3**, 212
ABC transporters, roles, **3**, 213
abequose
　in O-antigen, **3**, 345
　expression, **3**, 187
　occurrence, **3**, 312, 322
cis-abienol, biosynthesis, **2**, 225
Abies balsamea
　effects on *Pyrrhocoris apterus*, **8**, 276
　insect resistance, **8**, 177
　polysaccharides, **3**, 688
Abies excelsa, coniferin, **3**, 683
Abies grandis
　abietadiene synthases, **2**, 228, 384
　monoterpene biosynthesis studies, **2**, 114
Abies lisiocarpa, juvenoids, **8**, 276
Abies pectinata, coniferin, **3**, 683
Abies sachalinensis, juvabione, **8**, 276
abietadiene
　biosynthesis, **2**, 381
　as starting material, for dehydroabietane, **2**, 384
abieta-7,13-diene
　biosynthesis, **2**, 228
　isomers, **2**, 384
abieta-8,12-diene
　biosynthesis, **2**, 382
　as intermediate, **2**, 382
ent-abieta-7,13-diene
　formation, **2**, 230
　occurrence, **2**, 230
abietadiene synthases, **2**, 315
　catalysis, **2**, 384
　DDTA motif, **2**, 315
　functions, **2**, 217
　occurrence, **2**, 228
abietanes, as intermediates, **2**, 381
abietic acid, biosynthesis, **2**, 228
neo-abietic acid, biosynthesis, **2**, 228
ABP1 *see* auxin binding protein 1 (ABP1)
abrin, as seed toxin, **8**, 168
abscisic acid
　achiral analogue, biological activity, **8**, 81
　analogues, metabolism-resistant, **8**, 90
　analysis, via electron capture detector, **8**, 74
　binding, **8**, 81
　　sites, **8**, 82
　biological activity, **8**, 82
　biosynthesis, **8**, 84
　biosynthetic pathway, **8**, 87
　CD spectra, **8**, 76
　chemistry, **8**, 73
　chromatographic analysis, **8**, 74
　conformation
　　active, **8**, 79

　computer-aided analysis, **8**, 79
　conjugation, **8**, 90
　Cotton effect, **8**, 76
　1′,4′-*cis*-diol, Mill's rule, **8**, 72
　1′,4′-*trans*-diol, Mill's rule, **8**, 72
　discovery, **8**, 21
　effects, on root growth, **8**, 83
　enzyme-immunoassay, **8**, 74
　from
　　carotenoids, **8**, 87
　　violaxanthin, **8**, 72
　　xanthoxin, **8**, 86
　hexadeuteration, **8**, 74
　historical background, **8**, 72
　HPLC, **8**, 74
　isolation, **8**, 73
　and jasmonates
　　compared, **1**, 127
　　interactions, **1**, 133
　mass spectra, **8**, 84
　metabolism, **8**, 88
　and methyl jasmonate, compared, **1**, 126
　microinjection, **8**, 82
　as morphogen, **8**, 83
　NCI mass spectra, **8**, 77
　^{13}C NMR spectra, **8**, 76
　^{1}H NMR spectra, **8**, 76
　occurrence, **8**, 73
　optical resolution, **8**, 74
　optical rotatory dispersion, **8**, 76
　and osmotic stress, **8**, 83
　photoaffinity labeling, **8**, 82
　precursors, **2**, 327, **8**, 86
　properties, physicochemical, **8**, 74
　roles
　　in ethylene biosynthesis, **8**, 96
　　in gene expression, **8**, 97
　sink effect, **8**, 83
　soybean studies, **1**, 781
　specific optical rotation, **8**, 76
　as stress messenger, **8**, 82
　structure–activity relationship, **8**, 77
　UV spectra, **8**, 75
　x-ray analysis, **8**, 79
abscisic acid, 5′α,8′-cyclo-, biological activity, **8**, 81
abscisic acid, 5′β,9′-cyclo-, biological activity, **8**, 81
abscisic acid, 1′-deoxy-1′-fluoro-, biological activity, **8**, 77
abscisic acid, 7′-difluoro-, biological activity, **8**, 79
abscisic acid, 8′,8′-difluoro-, analogues, **8**, 91
abscisic acid, (1′S,2′R)-2′,3′-dihydro-, biological activity, **8**, 79
abscisic acid, (1′S,2′S)-2′,3′-dihydro-, biological activity, **8**, 79
abscisic acid, 8′,9′-dinor-, biological activity, **8**, 79
abscisic acid, 3′-fluoro-, analogues, **8**, 91
abscisic acid, 7′-hydroxy-, biosynthesis, **8**, 90
abscisic acid, 8′-hydroxy-
　biosynthesis, **8**, 89
　isomerization, **8**, 89
abscisic acid, 8′-methoxy-, activity, **8**, 89
abscisic acid, 1′-O-methyl-, biological activity, **8**, 77
abscisic acid, methyl ester
　EI mass spectra, **8**, 76
　GC-SIM, **8**, 77
　IR spectra, **8**, 75

occurrence, **8**, 73

abscisic acid, 8'-monofluoro-, activity, **8**, 89

abscisic acid, 7',7',7',8',8',8',9',9',9'-nonadeutero-, metabolism, **8**, 91

abscisic acid, 7'-nor-, biological activity, **8**, 79

abscisic acid, 8'-nor-, biological activity, **8**, 79

abscisic acid, 8',8',8'-trifluoro-, analogues, **8**, 91

(+)-abscisic acid
  analogues, alkylation, **8**, 79
  steric structures, **8**, 81

(−)-abscisic acid
  metabolism, **8**, 90
  pseudo-symmetry, **8**, 81
  steric structures, **8**, 81

2-(*E*)-abscisic acid
  activity, **8**, 77
  isomerization, **8**, 75

abscisic acid aldehyde, as intermediate, **8**, 72

abscisic acid-deficient mutants, studies, **8**, 86

abscisic acid, seed germination inhibition, **8**, 83

abscisin
  purification, **8**, 72
  use of term, **8**, 72

abscisin II
  structure, **8**, 72
  see also abscisic acid

abscission layer, effects of auxins on, **8**, 30

absinthin, occurrence, **1**, 375

AC6H, structure, **1**, 370

Acacia spp.
  isomelacacidin, **3**, 776
  melacacidin, **3**, 776
  proguibourtinidins, **3**, 775
  (*R*)-prunasin, **1**, 885
  (*S*)-sambunigrin, **1**, 885
  teracacidin, **3**, 776

Acacia caffra, proteracacinidins, dimeric, **3**, 776

Acacia galpinii
  epioritin-4α-ol, **3**, 776
  proteracacinidins, dimeric, **3**, 776

Acacia luederitzii, proguibourtinidins, **3**, 775

Acacia mearnsii, profisetinidins, **3**, 770, 772

Acacia melanoxylon
  promelacacinidin, **3**, 776
  (2*R*,3*S*)-7,8,3',4'-tetrahydroxydihydroflavonol, **3**, 750

acalyphin, biosynthesis, **1**, 887

Acanthamoeba castellani, UTP-glucose-1-phosphate uridylyltransferase, **3**, 478

Acanthella carvernosa
  antifouling agents, **8**, 438
  kalihinenes, **8**, 437

acanthifolicin, occurrence, **8**, 491

acanthodoral, occurrence, **2**, 192

Acanthodoris nanaimoensis
  acanthodoral, **2**, 192
  isoacanthodoral, **2**, 192
  nanaimoal, **2**, 192

Acanthopanax senticosus see Eleutherococcus senticosus

Acanthoscelides obtectus, methyl (*R*,2*E*)-2,4,5-tetradecatrienoate, **8**, 216

acarbose, structure, **5**, 299

α-acaridial, occurrence, **8**, 225

β-acaridial, occurrence, **8**, 225

Acarina
  pheromones, **8**, 222
  see also Aleuroglyphus ovatus; *Caloglyphus* spp.; *Lardoglyphus konoi*; *Tyrophagus similis*

ACC *see* cyclopropane-1-carboxylic acid, 1-amino- (ACC)

ACCase *see* acetyl-CoA carboxylase

ACC deaminase *see* 1-aminocyclopropane-1-carboxylate deaminase

accessible surface integrated field (ASIF), values, **6**, 65

ACC *N*-malonyltransferase, ethylene-induced, **8**, 96

AcCoAS *see* acetate-CoA ligase

ACC oxidase *see* 1-aminocyclopropane-1-carboxylate oxidase

ACC synthase *see* 1-aminocyclopropane-1-carboxylate synthase

aceric acid
  occurrence, **3**, 502
  precursors, **3**, 509

aceronosyltransferase(s)
  characterization, **3**, 518
  roles, in pectin biosynthesis, **3**, 511

Acer pseudoplatanus
  laccase, **3**, 712
  peroxidases, **3**, 718
  polygalacturonate 4-α-galacturonosyltransferase, **3**, 513

Acer rubrum, gramine, **8**, 336

Acer saccharinum, gramine, **8**, 336

Acer saccharum, laccase studies, **3**, 712

Acer tataricum, jasmonic acid, **8**, 118

acetal, ribo-, **7**, 257

acetaldehyde
  biosynthesis, **3**, 397
  as substrate, **3**, 373

acetaldehyde, bromo- (BAA), applications, DNA structure probes, **7**, 93

acetaldehyde, chloro- (CAA), applications, DNA structure probes, **7**, 93

acetaldehyde, phosphono-
  Baeyer–Villiger oxidation, **1**, 869
  as intermediate, **1**, 869

acetaldehyde oximes, *p*-hydroxyphenyl-, as intermediates, **1**, 889

acetaldehydes, halo-, applications, DNA structure probes, **7**, 93

acetals, bicyclic, occurrence, **8**, 213

acetamide, iodo-, **2**, 19
  effects, on mutases, **5**, 353

acetamides, as pheromones, **8**, 220

acetamidoyl groups, in *Legionella pneumophila*, **3**, 192

acetaminophen, oxidation, **5**, 183

acetate
  double labeled, **1**, 4
  as esperamicin A$_1$ precursor, **7**, 554
  metabolism, **2**, 52

acetate, 4-chlorophenyl-, dehalogenation, **5**, 417

acetate, cholesterylamino-, oligonucleotide attachment, **7**, 160

acetate, (2*E*)-2-decenyl, occurrence, **8**, 213

acetate, decyl, occurrence, **8**, 213

acetate, 2-*N*,*N*-dimethylaminoethyl 4-chlorophenoxy-, structure, **8**, 34

acetate, (1*S*,2*R*,6*R*)-diprionyl, occurrence, **8**, 247

acetate, (1*S*,2*S*,6*S*)-diprionyl, occurrence, **8**, 247

acetate, 11-dodecenyl
  biosynthesis, **8**, 205
  occurrence, **8**, 205

acetate, (*E*)-9-dodecenyl, occurrence, **8**, 205

acetate, (*Z*)-7-dodecenyl, occurrence, **8**, 202

acetate, (*Z*)-9-dodecenyl, occurrence, **8**, 205

acetate, ethyl, occurrence, **8**, 209

acetate, ethyl aceto-, synthesis, **2**, 17

acetate, geranyl
  fumigant activity, **8**, 306
  occurrence, **8**, 223

acetate, all-*trans*-geranylgeranyl, occurrence, **8**, 229

acetate, (10*E*,12*E*,14*Z*)-10,12,14-hexadecatrienyl, occurrence, **8**, 207

acetate, (*Z*)-11-hexadecenyl, as sex pheromone, **8**, 290

acetate, (*Z*)-13-hexadecen-11-yn-1-yl, occurrence, **8**, 207

acetate, hexadecyl, occurrence, **8**, 218

acetate, hexadecylamino-, oligonucleotide attachment, **7**, 160

acetate, hexyl, occurrence, **8**, 210
acetate, icosyl, occurrence, **8**, 218
acetate, *N*-methylanilinium trifluoro-, as coupling
    reaction activator, **7**, 138
acetate, methyl [2-¹³C]bromo-, coupling, **1**, 142
acetate, 3-methyl-1-butyl, occurrence, **8**, 220
acetate, (1*S*,9*E*)-1-methyl-9-dodecenyl, occurrence, **8**, 215
acetate, 10-methyldodecyl, occurrence, **8**, 246
acetate, (*S*)-1-methyldodecyl, occurrence, **8**, 215
acetate, 12-methyltetradecyl, occurrence, **8**, 246
acetate, (*S*)-1-methyltetradecyl, occurrence, **8**, 216
acetate, (*E*)-9-octadecenyl, occurrence, **8**, 218
acetate, (*Z*)-9-octadecenyl, occurrence, **8**, 218
acetate, (*Z*)-11-octadecenyl, occurrence, **8**, 218
acetate, octadecyl, occurrence, **8**, 218
acetate, (*E*)-2-octenyl, occurrence, **8**, 211
acetate, octyl, occurrence, **8**, 211
acetate, oxalo-
    β-decarboxylation, **3**, 381
    reactions, with glyoxylate, **3**, 413
acetate, (*E*)-8-oxocitronellyl, occurrence, **8**, 225
acetate, (8*E*,10*Z*)-8,10-pentadecadienyl, occurrence, **8**,
    207
acetate, (*E*)-9-pentadecenyl, occurrence, **8**, 207
acetate, (*Z*)-10-pentadecenyl, occurrence, **8**, 207
acetate, (9*E*,11*E*)-9,11-tetradecadienyl, biosynthesis, **8**,
    205
acetate, (*E*)-4-tetradecenyl, occurrence, **8**, 207
acetate, (*E*)-11-tetradecenyl, occurrence, **8**, 205
acetate, (*Z*)-9-tetradecenyl, occurrence, **8**, 199, 207
acetate, (*Z*)-11-tetradecenyl, occurrence, **8**, 205
acetate, (*Z*)-8-tridecenyl, occurrence, **8**, 207
[1,2-¹³C₂]acetate
    in brevetoxin studies, **8**, 511
    metabolism, via TCA cycle, **8**, 511
acetate-CoA ligase
    early studies, **4**, 256
    encoding, **4**, 255
    occurrence, **1**, 47, **4**, 256
    roles
        in penicillin biosynthesis, **4**, 267
        in penicillin G biosynthesis, **4**, 256
acetate:CoA ligase (AMP-forming) *see* acetate-CoA
    ligase
acetate hypothesis
    biochemical studies, **1**, 3
    biomimetic studies, **1**, 3
    concept of, **1**, 2
    verification, **1**, 3
acetate–propanoate sequences, roles, in ante-iso
    branching, **8**, 246
acetates
    as bacterial aromatic polyketide synthase primers, **1**,
        475
    conversion, to fatty acids, **1**, 24
    replacement, **8**, 237
acetates, (7*Z*,11*E*)-7,11-hexadecadienyl, occurrence, **8**,
    205
acetates, (7*Z*,11*Z*)-7,11-hexadecadienyl, occurrence, **8**,
    205
acetates, (*Z*)-9-hexadecenal, occurrence, **8**, 205
acetates, (*Z*)-11-hexadecenal, occurrence, **8**, 205
acetates, tocopheryl, occurrence, **8**, 230
acetate thiokinase *see* acetate-CoA ligase
acetic acid, in insects, **8**, 356
acetic acid, aceto-, effects, on platelet-activating factor, **1**,
    294
acetic acid, 5-azido-1-naphthalene-, structure, **8**, 34
acetic acid, dichloro-, effects, on purine bases, **7**, 121
acetic acid, 2,4-dichlorophenoxy- (2,4-D)
    auxin-like activity, **8**, 23, 34
    as environmental pollutant, **5**, 410
acetic acid, 3,4-dihydroxyphenyl-, biosynthesis, **1**, 813

acetic acid, 1′,2′-epoxy-*β*-ionylidene-, metabolism, **8**, 86
acetic acid, 4′-hydroxy-*β*-ionylidene-, metabolism, **8**, 86
acetic acid, *p*-hydroxyphenyl-, occurrence, **8**, 26
acetic acid, iodo-, labeling, **4**, 342
acetic acid, mercapto-, reactions, with flavan-4-ols, **3**, 758
acetic acid, monofluoro-, bialaphos biosynthesis
    inhibition, **1**, 871
acetic acid, 1-naphthalene-, structure, **8**, 34
acetic acid, phenyl- (PhAc)
    activation, **4**, 244
    biosynthesis, **1**, 54, 814, 850
    labeling, **4**, 254
    occurrence, **8**, 26
    in penicillin G biosynthesis, **4**, 244
    ring expansion, **1**, 77
acetic acid, trifluoro-, in profisetinidin cleavage, **3**, 771
acetic acids, phenoxy-, as herbicides, **8**, 34
acetoacetate carboxy-lyase *see* acetoacetate
    decarboxylase
acetoacetate decarboxylase, mimics, **5**, 440
acetoacetyl-ACP synthase, catalysis, **1**, 29
acetoacetyl-CoA
    biosynthesis, **2**, 3, 46
    in fatty acid biosynthesis, **8**, 209
acetoacetyl-CoA reductase(s), **2**, 18
acetoacetyl-CoA synthases *see* acetyl-CoA *C*-
    acetyltransferases
acetoacetyl-CoA thiolase *see* acetyl-CoA *C*-
    acetyltransferases
Acetobacter methanolicus
    lipopolysaccharides, **3**, 192
    lysogenic conversion, **3**, 216
    O-side chain expression, **3**, 192
Acetobacter pasteurianum, as substrate for hopene
    cyclases, **2**, 309
Acetobacter xylinum
    carboxymethyl cellulose, **3**, 584
    celluloses
        biosynthesis, **3**, 580
        cellulose I, **3**, 552
        studies, **3**, 562
        ultrastructural studies, **3**, 582
acetogenins
    biosynthesis, **8**, 202
    as pheromones, **8**, 203
    with unbranched carbon skeletons, **8**, 204
acetogenins, halogenated C15, isolation, **1**, 304
acetoin, biosynthesis, **3**, 394
acetolactate, metabolism, **2**, 49
acetone
    biosynthesis, **8**, 144
    as substrate, **3**, 373
acetone, dihydroxy-
    acylation, **1**, 144
    interconversion, **5**, 36
acetone, fluoro-, as substrate, **3**, 373
acetone, geranyl-
    biosynthesis, **8**, 234
    occurrence, **8**, 161, 232
acetone, hexahydrofarnesyl-, biosynthesis, **8**, 234
acetone phosphate, alkyldihydroxy-, biosynthesis, **1**, 286,
    286
acetone phosphate, dihydroxy- (DHAP)
    activation, **3**, 369
    activity, **3**, 464
    biosynthesis, **1**, 286, **3**, 409, 424, 430
    polarization, **5**, 12
    structure, **2**, 374
    transfer, **3**, 417
acetonitrile, *p*-hydroxyphenyl-, as intermediate, **1**, 889
acetonitrile, phenyl-, occurrence, **8**, 26
acetophenone, *m*-(*N*,*N*,*N*-trimethylammonio)trifluoro-
    (TMTFA)

binding, **5**, 122
complexation, with acetylcholinesterase, **5**, 117, 124
as transition state inhibitor, **5**, 114
acetophenones, as phytoalexins, **8**, 189
2-(acetoxymethyl)benzoyl, as protecting group, **7**, 121
acetyl-activating enzyme *see* acetate-CoA ligase
acetyl acyltransferase, sequencing, **1**, 412
acetylcholine, hydrolysis, **5**, 113
acetylcholine acetylhydrolase *see* acetylcholinesterase
acetylcholinesterase
    active site gorge, **5**, 123
    applications, **5**, 113
    catalysis, **5**, 113
        mechanisms, **5**, 117
        power, **5**, 118
    catalytic triad, functions, **5**, 119
    complexation, with *m*-(*N*,*N*,*N*-
        trimethylammonio)trifluoroacetophenone, **5**, 117,
        124
    electrostatic role, **5**, 120
    ligand binding, **5**, 120
    molecular recognition, structural bases, **5**, 123
    nucleophiles, **5**, 53
    occurrence, **5**, 112
    structure, **5**, 114
acetyl-CoA
    biosynthesis, **1**, 361, **2**, 376, **8**, 203
    carboxylation, **1**, 25
    condensation, **2**, 3, **8**, 210
    as energy source, **1**, 7
    K_m, **1**, 293
    occurrence, **8**, 209
    roles
        in fatty acid biosynthesis, **1**, 3, **8**, 204, 209
        in platelet-activating factor biosynthesis, **1**, 292
    as starting material
        for hydroxymethylglutaryl-CoA, **2**, 22
        for isoprenoids, **2**, 46
        for 6-methylsalicylic acid, **1**, 411
        for (*R*)-mevalonate, **2**, 16
        for mevalonic acid, **2**, **15–44**
    as substrate, **1**, 349
acetyl-CoA:acetyl-CoA *C*-acetyltransferases *see* acetyl-
    CoA *C*-acetyltransferases
acetyl-CoA *C*-acetyltransferases
    bacteria, **2**, 18
    biosynthesis, **2**, 18
    catalysis, **2**, 16, 17
    cleavage, **2**, 18
    cytosolic, encoding, **2**, 18
    human, **2**, 18
    occurrence, **2**, 18
    structure, **2**, 19
    substrate specificity, **2**, 18
acetyl-CoA *C*-acyltransferase(s)
    specificity, **2**, 18
    structure, **2**, 19
acetyl-CoA:1-alkyl-*sn*-glycero-3-phosphate
    acetyltransferase, activity, **1**, 296
acetyl-CoA:1-alkylglycerophosphocholine
    acetyltransferase
    activation, **1**, 295
    activity, increase, **1**, 294
    inhibition, **1**, 293
    phosphorylation, **1**, 294
    purification, **1**, 295
    sensitivity, **1**, 293
acetyl-CoA:carbon-dioxide ligase (ADP-forming) *see*
    acetyl-CoA carboxylase
acetyl-CoA carboxylase
    catalysis, **1**, 24, 25
    as flavonoid precursor, **1**, 718
    occurrence, **1**, 25

purification, **1**, 718
roles, in isoflavonoid biosynthesis, **1**, 786
structure, **1**, 25
acetyl-CoA:deacetylcephalosporin C acetyltransferase,
    catalysis, **4**, 172
acetyl-CoA:formate *C*-acetyltransferase *see* formate *C*-
    acetyltransferase
acetyl-CoA synthetase *see* acetate-CoA ligase
α-*N*-acetylgalactosaminide α-2,6-sialyltransferase, roles,
    in *O*-glycan synthesis, **3**, 80
acetylgalactosaminyl-*O*-glycosyl-glycoprotein β-1,3-*N*-
    acetylglucosaminyltransferase
    characterization, **3**, 76
    roles, in *O*-glycan synthesis, **3**, 76
acetylgalactosaminyl-*O*-glycosyl-glycoprotein β-1,6-*N*-
    acetylglucosaminyltransferase
    purification, **3**, 77
    roles, in *O*-glycan synthesis, **3**, 76
N-acetylgalactosaminyltransferases (Gal*N*AcTs)
    catalysis, **3**, 123
    characterization, **3**, 108
    Gal*N*AcT-1, catalysis, **3**, 123
    Gal*N*AcT-2, catalysis, **3**, 124
    Gal*N*AcT-3, catalysis, **3**, 124
β-*N*-acetylglucosamidase, occurrence, **5**, 297
N-acetylglucosamine-1-phosphate-uridyltransferase
    activity, **3**, 251
    catalysis, **3**, 206
N-acetylglucosamine-1-phosphodiester α-*N*-
    acetylglucosaminidase, roles, **3**, 29
N-acetylglucosamine phosphotransferase, catalysis, **3**, 29
α-*N*-acetylglucosaminidase, purification, **3**, 29
N-acetylglucosaminidases
    roles, **3**, 29
        in biosynthetic pathways, **3**, 14
β-*N*-acetylglucosaminidases, occurrence, **3**, 30
α-*N*-acetyl-D-glucosaminide *N*-
        acetylglucosaminohydrolase *see* α-*N*-
        acetylglucosaminidase
β-*N*-acetyl-D-glucosaminide β-1,4-galactosyltransferase
    see β-*N*-acetylglucosaminylglycopeptide β-1,4-
    galactosyltransferase
β-*N*-acetylglucosaminylglycopeptide β-1,4-
    galactosyltransferase
    activity, **3**, 43
    cDNA, isolation, **3**, 43
    domains
        catalytic, **3**, 43
        cystoplasmic, **3**, 43
        transmembrane, **3**, 43
    expression, **3**, 43, 44, 82
        regulatory mechanisms, **3**, 45
    gene
        localization, **3**, 43
        mutations, **3**, 45
        promoter control, **3**, 44
        transcription, **3**, 44
    hybrids, **3**, 45
    localization, **3**, 78
    murine studies, **3**, 44
    purification, **3**, 78
    roles
        fertilization mediation, **3**, 45
        in *N*-glycan synthesis, **3**, 43
    substrates, **3**, 81
    targeting, to Golgi apparatus, **3**, 45
N-acetylglucosaminyl-1-phosphate transferase, catalysis,
    3, 41
α-*N*-acetylglucosaminyl phosphodiesterase *see* *N*-
        acetylglucosamine-1-phosphodiester α-*N*-
        acetylglucosaminidase
N-acetylglucosaminyltransferase(s) (Glc*N*AcTs) *see* *N*-
    acetyllactosaminide β-1,6-*N*-
    acetylglucosaminyltransferase(s)

acetyl groups, in 2′-hydroxyl group protection, **6**, 84
N-acetyl groups, in *Legionella pneumophila*, **3**, 192
β-*N*-acetylhexosaminidase(s), occurrence, **5**, 296, 297
O-acetyl-L-homoserine acetate-lyase (adding
    methanethiol) *see O*-acetylhomoserine (thiol)-lyase
O-acetylhomoserine (thiol)-lyase
  catalysis, **5**, 275
  EPR studies, **5**, 175
  histidine side chains, **5**, 268
  structure, **5**, 269, 275
N-acetyllactosamine synthase *see* lactose synthase
N-acetyllactosaminide *β*-1,3-*N*-
    acetylglucosaminyltransferase
  occurrence, **3**, 77
  roles, in *O*-glycan synthesis, **3**, 77
N-acetyllactosaminide *β*-1,6-*N*-
    acetylglucosaminyltransferase(s)
  assays, **3**, 39
  catalysis, **3**, 122
  characterization, **3**, 108
  homologues, **3**, 225
  roles, in *N*-glycan synthesis, **3**, 50
  type I, **3**, 25
    catalysis, **3**, 122
    in *N*-glycan processing, **3**, 17
    and hereditary erythroblastic multinuclearity with a
      positive acidified serum, **3**, 27
    substrates, **3**, 149
N-acetyllactosaminide *α*-2,3-sialyltransferase (ST3Gal
    III)
  catalysis, **3**, 48
  roles, in *N*-glycan synthesis, **3**, 46
  sequences, **3**, 48
N-acetylmannosaminyltransferases, catalysis, **3**, 217
N-acetylmuramyl-L-alanine amidases, identification, **3**,
    271
N-acetylneuraminate lyase
  applications, **3**, 380
  biochemistry, **3**, 378
  catalysis, **3**, 378
  characterization, **3**, 378
  inhibition, **3**, 378
  isolation, **3**, 378
  occurrence, **3**, 379
  purification, **3**, 378
  structure, **3**, 379
  substrate specificity, **3**, 378
N-acetylneuraminate pyruvate-lyase *see N*-
    acetylneuraminate lyase
N-acetylneuraminate pyruvate-lyase (pyruvate-
    phosphorylating) *see N*-acetylneuraminate
    synthase
N-acetylneuraminate synthase
  biochemistry, **3**, 390
  catalysis, **3**, 390
  encoding, **3**, 390
  purification, **3**, 390
acetylsalicylic acid, acetyl-
  acetylation by, **5**, 250
  antiinflammatory activity, mechanisms, **1**, 10
  applications, early, **1**, 8
  effects
    on prostaglandin-endoperoxide synthases, **1**, 257, **5**,
      249
    on thromboxane A$_2$ biosynthesis, **5**, 226
  as lipoxygenase inhibitor, **1**, 243
  prostaglandin-endoperoxide synthase inhibition, **5**, 252
  as prostaglandin-endoperoxide synthase inhibitor, **1**,
    10, 123
acetyltransferases, **2**, 205
  activity, **1**, 292
  catalysis, **3**, 8
  inhibition, **1**, 293

  pathways, **2**, 207
  roles, in pectin biosynthesis, **3**, 518
  sensitivity, to detergents, **1**, 293
  substrates, **1**, 293
O-acetyltransferases, structure, **4**, 227
AChE *see* acetylcholinesterase
Achmeia (*Collisella*) *limatula*, limatulone, **8**, 7
Achroia innotata, nonanol, **8**, 212
Achyranthes aspera, fatty acids, **1**, 71
Aciculites orientalis, aciculitins, **8**, 584
aciculitins
  cytotoxicity, **8**, 584
  occurrence, **8**, 584
  structure, **8**, 584
acid:CoA ligase (AMP-forming) *see* long-chain-fatty-
    acid-CoA ligase
Acid Growth Theory, auxins, **8**, 31
acid lipases
  catalysis, **5**, 133
    mechanisms, **5**, 133
  evolution, **5**, 134
  gene structure, **5**, 133
  occurrence, **5**, 133
  roles, in ester hydrolysis, **5**, 103
  sequence similarities, **5**, 133
  x-ray crystal structure, **5**, 134
acid maltase *see* glucan 1,4-*α*-glucosidase
acid phosphatase
  classification, **5**, 140
  in honeybee venom, **8**, 355
acid phosphomonoesterase *see* acid phosphatase
acids, catalysis, **2**, 33
Acinetobacter spp.
  4-hydroxy-2-ketopimelate aldolase, **3**, 413
  4-hydroxy-2-ketovalerate aldolase, **3**, 384
  lipopolysaccharides, **3**, 190
Acinetobacter calcoaceticus, isoprenoid biosynthesis,
    mevalonate-independent pathway, **2**, 58
ACL *see* antigen-carrier lipid (ACL)
aclacinomycin, isolation, **4**, 200
aclacinomycins
  binding, **3**, 325
  biosynthesis, genetics, **3**, 351
  L-cinerulose B, **3**, 321
  2-deoxy-L-fucose, **3**, 313
aclavinone *see* aklavinone
AcMNPV vector, in strictosidine synthase expression, **4**,
    133
acn genes, *acnP*, encoding, **1**, 872
D-acofriose, occurrence, **3**, 312, 313
L-acofriose, occurrence, **3**, 312, 313
Acokanthera spp., cardenolides, **8**, 361
acoradin, occurrence, **1**, 647
Acorus calamus, acoradin, **1**, 647
ACP *see* acyl carrier protein (ACP)
ACPS *see* acyl carrier protein synthase (ACPS)
Acraea horta, larvae, cyanogenic plant feeding, **1**,
    883
Acremonium spp., in halymecins, **8**, 601
Acremonium chrysogenum
  cef genes, **4**, 172
    cefG, **4**, 172
  cephalosporin C biosynthesis, **4**, 164, 176
  isopenicillin N synthase, **4**, 169
  β-lactam biosynthesis, gene clusters, **4**, 173
  pcb genes, expression, **4**, 173
  penicillins, industrial production, **4**, 179
Acremonium coeniphialum, infection, **8**, 178
Acremonium luzulae
  cyclosporin C, **1**, 537
  cyclosporins, **1**, 534
acridine, 9-anilino-, applications, antineoplastic agents, **7**,
    606

acridine, 6-chloro-9-(*p*-chlorophenoxy)-2-methoxy-, synthesis, **7**, 237
acridine, 6-chloro-9-phenoxy-2-methoxy-, coupling, **7**, 211
acridine-4-carboxamide, 9-amino-, **7**, 607
acridine-4-carboxamides
　　2-1 analogues, cytotoxicity, **7**, 607
　　angular analogues, cytotoxicity, **7**, 607
　　cytotoxicity, **7**, 607
　　structural features, **7**, 606
acridine orange, applications, intercalating agents, **7**, 428
acridines, multi-
　　bisintercalation, **7**, 451
　　synthesis, **7**, 451
acridinones, imidazo-, structural features, **7**, 606
acridinones, triazolo-, structural features, **7**, 606
acridone, 1,3-dihydroxy-*N*-methyl-, biosynthesis, **1**, 759
acridone alkaloids, occurrence, **1**, 759
acridones, biosynthesis, **1**, 759
acridone synthase (ACS)
　　biosynthesis, **1**, 759
　　and chalcone synthase compared, **1**, 755
　　classification, **1**, 759
　　cloning, **1**, 19
Acrobasis vaccinii, (8*E*,10*Z*)-8,10-pentadecadienyl acetate, **8**, 207
Acrolepiopsis assectella
　　feeding, effect of saponins on, **8**, 144
　　henicosane, **8**, 218
　　heptadecane, **8**, 217
　　hexadecane, **8**, 217
　　nonadecane, **8**, 218
Acromyrmex octospinosus, antifeedant studies, **8**, 317
Acropora spp., *Synechocystis* spp. in, **8**, 609
Acrosiphonia coalita, oxylipins, **1**, 214
acrylamide, *N*,*N*-dimethyl-, cycloaddition, **5**, 430
acrylate, methyl, reactions, with 5-chloromercury-2'-deoxyuridine, **7**, 197
acrylic acid, chloro-, dehalogenation, **5**, 410
acryloylcholine, 3,3-dimethyl-, occurrence, **8**, 353
ACS *see* acridone synthase (ACS)
ACS genes
　　expression, **8**, 97
　　　auxin-induced, **8**, 97
　　　wound-induced, **8**, 97
*ACT*1 transcripts
　　accumulation, **6**, 209
　　stabilization, **6**, 209
actagardine
　　antibiotic activity, **4**, 276
　　biosynthesis, **4**, 280
　　cell wall biosynthesis inhibition, **4**, 282
　　structure, **4**, 280
act genes
　　biochemical analysis, **1**, 491
　　cloning, **1**, 476
　　combinatorial analysis, **1**, 487
　　deletion analysis, **1**, 484
　　expression, **1**, 484
　　sequencing, **1**, 476
　　translational coupling, **1**, 477
actinidine, occurrence, **8**, 226, 353
actinidiolide, dihydro-
　　enantiomeric purity, **8**, 7
　　homologues, **8**, 236
　　occurrence, **8**, 234
Actinomadura madurae, maduropeptin, **7**, 580
Actinomadura verrucosospora
　　esperamicin, **7**, 571
　　esperamicin A₁, **1**, 562
Actinomyces spp., actinomycin D, **7**, 608
Actinomycetales
　　antibiotics, **4**, 200

applications, **8**, 379
BE-13793C, **7**, 600
cephamycin biosynthesis, **4**, 172
eicosanoids, **1**, 208
future research, **8**, 392
genetics, **1**, 10
kedarcidin, **7**, 575
life cycle, **8**, 379
maduralide, **8**, 591
polyketides, **1**, 2
　　biosynthesis, **1**, 10
polyketide synthases, **1**, 10, 14
sesquiterpene synthases, **2**, 210
terpene synthase, future research, **2**, 210
UCE6, **7**, 600
actinomycin, applications, **4**, 199
actinomycin D
　　applications, **7**, 429
　　　antibiotics, **7**, 433, 529
　　　antineoplastic agents, **7**, 607
　　DNA damage, redox-dependent, **7**, 529
　　occurrence, **7**, 608
actinomycins, antineoplastic activity, **7**, 472
Actinoplannaceae, 2,6-diamino-3-hydroxypimelic acid, **3**, 246
actinorhodin
　　biochemical analysis, **1**, 491
　　biosynthesis, **1**, 10
　　deletion analysis, **1**, 484
　　genes, **1**, 11, **3**, 349
　　structure, **1**, 476
activator element (AE), use of term, **4**, 368
activator proteins
　　deficiency, sphingolipid storage disease induction, **3**, 100
　　roles
　　　in glycosphingolipid degradation, **3**, 3
　　　in lysosomal degradation of sphingolipids, **3**, 102
actomyosin ATPase, modulation induction, **8**, 614
L-aculose, occurrence, **3**, 312, 321
ACV *see* D-valine, δ-(L-α-aminoadipyl)-L-cysteinyl-(ACV)
acvA gene *see* *pcb* genes, *pcbAB*
ACVS *see* ACV synthetase
ACV synthetase
　　activity, **4**, 167
　　attachment sites, **4**, 168
　　catalysis, **4**, 167, 243
　　characteristics, **4**, 246
　　encoding, **4**, 168
　　isolation, **1**, 840
　　mechanistic studies, **4**, 246
　　multienzymes, **4**, 167
　　occurrence, **1**, 47, 840
　　purification, **1**, 840
　　reactions, **4**, 246
　　roles, in antibiotic biosynthesis, **4**, 201
　　sequencing, **1**, 546
　　substrate specificity, **4**, 168, 246
ACV tripeptides
　　biosynthesis, **1**, 840
　　　via non-ribosomal proteins, **4**, 167
　　cyclization, **1**, 842
acyclic linkers, in nucleoside analogues, **7**, 273
acyl-activating enzyme *see* acetate-CoA ligase; long-chain-fatty-acid-CoA ligase
acyl carrier protein (ACP)
　　in bacterial aromatic polyketide synthases, **1**, 475
　　catalysis, **1**, 348
　　conversion, **4**, 206
　　encoding, **1**, 356
　　Escherichia coli, **1**, 336
　　in fatty acid studies, **1**, 500

function, compared with NodF, **1**, 337
in gramicidin S synthetase, **4**, 331, 340
homologues, **1**, 332
4′-phosphopantetheine prosthetic group coupling, **1**, 334
roles, in acetogenin biosynthesis, **8**, 203
sequencing, **1**, 412
structure, three-dimensional, **1**, 363
structure–function relationship, **1**, 335
acyl carrier protein (ACP), 2-butanoyl-, roles, in acetogenin biosynthesis, **8**, 203
acyl carrier protein (ACP), (*R*)-3-hydroxybutanoyl-, roles, in acetogenin biosynthesis, **8**, 203
acyl carrier protein (ACP), 3-oxoacyl-, roles, in acetogenin biosynthesis, **8**, 203
acyl carrier protein (ACP), 3-oxobutanoyl-, roles, in acetogenin biosynthesis, **8**, 203
acyl carrier protein synthase (ACPS)
  identification, **4**, 206
  NodF activity, **1**, 336
  purification, **4**, 206
acyl-CoA
  derivatives, **4**, 244
  radiolabeling, **4**, 15
  transport, into mitochondrial matrix, **1**, 49
acyl-CoA:(acceptor) 2,3-oxidoreductase *see* acyl-CoA dehydrogenase
acyl-CoA:acetyl-CoA *C*-acyltransferase(s) *see* acetyl-CoA *C*-acyltransferase(s)
acyl-CoA:1-alkyl-*sn*-glycero-3-phosphate acyltransferase, fatty acid specificity, **1**, 288
acyl-CoA:6-aminopenicillanic acid acyltransferase
  identification, **4**, 243
  mechanistic studies, **4**, 259
  properties, **4**, 259
  substrate specificity, **4**, 259
acyl-CoA dehydrogenase, catalysis, **1**, 50
acyl-CoA desaturase(s) *see* stearoyl-CoA desaturase(s)
acyl-CoA:dihydroxyacetone phosphate acyltransferase
  localization, **1**, 286
  purification, **1**, 286
acyl-CoA:isopenicillin N acyltransferase (IAT)
  catalysis, **4**, 170
  purification, **4**, 170
acyl-CoA ligase, **4**, 331
acyl-CoA:malonyl-CoA *C*-acyltransferase (decarboxylating, oxoacyl- and enoyl-reducing and thioester hydrolyzing) *see* fatty acid synthase(s)
acyl-CoA oxidase
  catalysis, **1**, 50
  proteins, occurrence, **1**, 51
acyl-CoA:oxygen 2-oxidoreductase *see* acyl-CoA oxidase
acyl-CoA synthetase *see* long-chain-fatty-acid-CoA ligase
acyl-CoA thioesters, group-transfer potential, **3**, 807
acyl dehydrogenase *see* acyl-CoA dehydrogenase
acyl-enzyme intermediates, in acetyl-CoA *C*-acetyltransferase catalysis, **2**, 19
acyl-*S*-enzyme intermediates, formation, **2**, 22
acyl enzymes, reactivity, **3**, 267
1-acyl-glycerone-3-phosphate:long-chain-alcohol *O*-3-phospho-2-oxopropanyltransferase *see* alkylglycerone-phosphate synthase
acyl groups, α-oxidation, **8**, 204
acyl-lipid desaturases
  classification, **1**, 36
  occurrence, **1**, 36
N-acylneuraminate-9-phosphate pyruvate-lyase (pyruvate-phosphorylating) *see* *N*-acylneuraminate-9-phosphate synthase
N-acylneuraminate-9-phosphate synthase
  biochemistry, **3**, 391
  isolation, **3**, 391
  occurrence, **3**, 391

substrate specificity, **3**, 391
acylneuraminyl hydrolase *see* exo-α-sialidase(s)
acyl-4′-phosphopantetheine group, acyl transfer, **1**, 361
acyl-protein synthase, encoding, **8**, 394
acyl thioesters, as intermediates, **1**, 3
O-acyltransferases, encoding, **3**, 215
acyltransferases (ATs)
  acyl-CoA-dependent, **4**, 227
  in bacterial aromatic polyketide synthases, **1**, 475
  catalysis, **1**, 348
  domains, of peptide synthetases, **4**, 227
  domain swapping studies, **1**, 508
  encoding, **4**, 259, **8**, 394
  His motif, **4**, 227
  HygAT, **1**, 508
  immunoprecipitation analysis, **4**, 244
  late, Kdo-dependent, **3**, 223
  occurrence, **1**, 741
  RapAT, **1**, 508
  roles
    in fatty acid biosynthesis, **1**, 3
    in penicillin biosynthesis, **4**, 267
  substrate specificity, **4**, 261, 264
  superfamily, **4**, 227
  VenAT, **1**, 508
acyl transfer reactions
  catalysis, **4**, 340
    via peptide synthetases, **4**, 222
    via condensation domains, **4**, 232
Acyrthosiphon pisum, castanospermine toxicity, **3**, 141, **8**, 342
adaline, biosynthesis, **8**, 351
adamantane carbonyl chloride, as coupling reaction activators, **7**, 139
adamantanes, 1-substituted, as mutase mimics, **5**, 355
1-adamantanol, use as chemical switch, **7**, 463
ADARs
  activity, **6**, 101
  ADAR1
    catalysis, **6**, 101
    cloning, **6**, 101
    deamination specificity, **6**, 101
  ADAR2
    catalysis, **6**, 101
    characterization, **6**, 101
    deamination specificity, **6**, 102
  catalysis, **6**, 100
  specificity, **6**, 101
  substrates, **6**, 101
ADC *see* 4-deoxychorismate, 4-amino- (ADC)
ADD1/SREBP-1c, binding, **2**, 262
1,4-addition, in prostaglandin synthesis, **1**, 178
addition–elimination reactions, in nucleophilic aromatic substitution, **5**, 72
adenase *see* adenine deaminase
adenine, K_m, **5**, 74
adenine, 2-amino-, in oligodeoxynucleotides, **7**, 323
adenine, 8-bromo-, in oligodeoxynucleotides, **7**, 325
adenine, N^2-imidazolylpropyl-2-amino-, insertion, into oligonucleotides, **7**, 214
adenine, N^6-isopentyl- (ipA) *see* purine, N^6-(γ,γ-dimethylallylamino)-
adenine, N^6-methoxyl-, in oligodeoxynucleotides, **7**, 324
adenine, N^6-methyl-, **7**, 324
adenine, 2-oxo- (iso-G), hydrogen bonding pattern, **7**, 323
adenine, 9-ribosyl-N^6-(*o*-hydroxybenzyl)-, occurrence, **8**, 62
adenine aminase *see* adenine deaminase
adenine aminohydrolase *see* adenine deaminase
adenine deaminase
  biological functions, **5**, 85
  occurrence, **5**, 85
adenine nucleotides, concentration, **3**, 475

adenine phosphoribosyltransferase, **5**, 86
  interconversions, **8**, 70
adenines, cytokinin activity, **8**, 57
adenines, N^6-substituted, isolation, **8**, 61
adenocarcinomas, cultured, fucosyltransferases, **3**, 118
adenosine
  aptamer-binding ability, **7**, 625
  deamination, **5**, 73, **6**, 98
  depurination, **7**, 122
  K_m, **5**, 74
  as oviposition stimulant, **8**, 156
  as starting material, for ribonucleoside
      phosphoramidites, **7**, 231
adenosine, 8-azido-, applications, photoaffinity labeling,
    6, 229
adenosine, N^6-dimethyl-, effects on dimethyl A loop, **6**,
    195
adenosine, N^6-isopentenyl-, in Sec tRNA, **4**, 360
adenosine, 1-methyl-
  aptamer-binding ability, **7**, 625
  in Sec tRNA, **4**, 360
adenosine, 5′-thiomethyl-, phosphorolysis, **5**, 86
adenosine, 2′-O-tosyl-6′-nitrohomo-, in ribonucleotide
    reductase studies, **5**, 194
adenosine aminohydrolase *see* adenosine deaminase
adenosine deaminase
  biological functions, **5**, 73
  catalysis, **5**, 73
  catalytic site structure, **5**, 77
  chemical mechanisms, **5**, 79
  inhibitors, **5**, 74
    applications, **5**, 76
  interactions, with 1-deazaadenosine, **5**, 77
  kinetic isotope effects, **5**, 77
  leaving group specificity, **5**, 79
  mutation
    analysis, **5**, 78
    human, **5**, 79
  occurrence, **5**, 73
  properties, kinetic, **5**, 74
  protein structure, **5**, 77
  reaction mechanisms, **5**, 77
  solvent deuterium isotope effect, **5**, 77
  substrates, **5**, 74
  transition state inhibitors, **5**, 74
  transition state measures, **5**, 84
  transition state structure, **5**, 79
  x-ray crystal structure, **5**, 77
adenosine deaminase deficiency
  etiology, **5**, 73
  human
    mutational distribution, **5**, 79
    treatment, **5**, 76
adenosine deaminases that act on RNA (ADARs) *see*
    ADARs
adenosine diphosphate (ADP)
  binding folds, **2**, 341
  binding motifs, **2**, 341
  biosynthesis, **1**, 592
  glucose-1-phosphate adenylyltransferase inhibition, **3**,
      447
  as glucose-1-phosphate adenylyltransferase inhibitor,
      3, 470
adenosinediphosphoglucose, 8-azido-, as photoaffinity
    substrate, **3**, 448
adenosinediphosphoglucose (ADPGlc)
  biosynthesis, **3**, 8, 444
  Km values, **3**, 452
  roles, in starch biosynthesis, **3**, 444
  starch synthase activity, **3**, 445
  transporter, **3**, 465
adenosine diphosphopyridoxal (ADP-pyridoxal)
  applications, **3**, 453

modification, **3**, 453
adenosine kinase, interconversions, **8**, 70
8-Br-adenosine monophosphate, as substrate, **5**, 81
adenosine monophosphate (AMP)
  deamination, **5**, 80
  as glucose-1-phosphate adenylyltransferase inhibitor,
      3, 470
  inhibition, sensitivity, **3**, 474
adenosine nucleosidase, interconversions, **8**, 70
adenosine 5′-phosphate deaminase, characterization, **5**,
    80
adenosine-3′-phosphate 5′-phosphosulfate *see* 3′-
    phosphoadenosine 5′-phosphosulfate (PAPS)
adenosine phosphorylase, interconversions, **8**, 70
adenosine ribohydrolase *see* adenosine nucleosidase
adenosine 5′-β-thiodiphosphate, sulfur substitution
    studies, **6**, 224
adenosine 5′-γ-thiotriphosphate, in oligonucleotide
    synthesis, **6**, 223
adenosine 5′-triphosphatase (ATPase)
  activity, **7**, 603
  cation-pumping, **4**, 334
adenosine triphosphatase (potassium sodium), inhibition,
    8, 618
adenosine 5′-triphosphate, 2-azido-, labeling, **4**, 334
adenosine 5′-triphosphate, 8-azido-, as photoaffinity
    substrate, **3**, 448
adenosine 5′-triphosphate (ATP)
  activation, **4**, 246
  allosteric activator sites, **5**, 80
  amyloplastic, **3**, 464
  analogues, **4**, 326
  in dethiobiotin biosynthesis, **1**, 828
  and DNA topoisomerase II, **7**, 601
  in ethylene synthesis, **8**, 96
  intracellular, depletion, **4**, 282
  γ-phosphate transfer, **1**, 592
  in polyamine synthesis, **8**, 96
  in SELEX studies, **7**, 625
adenosylcobalamin (AdoCbl)
  biosynthesis, **4**, 149
  bond cleavage, in thiyl radical biosynthesis, **5**, 170
  bond dissociation energy, **5**, 208
  as cofactor, **5**, 165, 263
  edge shifts, **5**, 266
  homolysis, **5**, 269
  labilization, **5**, 268
  photolysis, **5**, 269
  as radical initiator, **5**, 218
  in ribonucleotide triphosphate reduction, **3**, 330
  roles, **5**, 206
    in enzymatic rearrangement, **5**, 208
    in hydrogen transfer mediation, **5**, 207
  thermolysis, **5**, 269
adenosylcobinamide, analogues, thermodynamic
    properties, **5**, 269
adenosyl cobyric acid synthase, roles, **4**, 148
adenosylhomocysteinase, homologues, **8**, 64
S-adenosyl-L-homocysteine, hydrolysis, **8**, 64
S-adenosyl-L-homocysteine hydrolase *see*
    adenosylhomocysteinase
adenosylhopane, occurrence, **2**, 47
S[5′-³H] adenosylmethionine, lysine 2,3-aminomutase
    activation, **5**, 208
S-adenosyl-L-methionine:caffeoyl-CoA 3-O-
    methyltransferase *see* caffeoyl-CoA O-
    methyltransferase
S-adenosyl-L-methionine:catechol O-methyltransferase
    see catechol O-methyltransferase
S-adenosyl-L-methionine:3,4-dihydroxy-*trans*-cinnamate
    3-O-methyltransferase *see* caffeate O-
    methyltransferase
S-adenosyl-L-methionine methylthioadenosine-lyase *see*
    1-aminocyclopropane-1-carboxylate synthase

S-adenosylmethionine methyl transferases, catalysis, **5**, 316
S-adenosyl-L-methionine:putrescine *N*-methyltransferase *see* putrescine *N*-methyltransferase
S-adenosyl-L-methionine (SAM)
  as amino donor, **1**, 827
  binding, **5**, 165, 185
    bi-bi mechanism, **3**, 647
  biosynthesis, **2**, 386
  cleavage, **5**, 209, 215, 217
    mechanisms, **5**, 215
  as cofactor, **3**, 643
  in cyclopropanation, **1**, 62
  enzyme catalysis, **2**, 343
  and enzyme radical formation, **5**, 217
  in *Escherichia coli*, **3**, 332
  in Gly-681 activation, **3**, 345
  hydrogen transfer mediation, **5**, 207, 208
  iron–sulfur clusters, in radical initiation, **5**, 213
  lysine 2,3-aminomutase activation, **5**, 207
  as methyl donor, **1**, 332, 739
  methyl group transfer, **1**, 423
  in neocarzinostatin chromophore, **7**, 554
  roles, in deoxysugar biosynthesis, **3**, 342
  as VAI-1 precursor, **8**, 394
adenovirus VA gene, localization, **4**, 362
adenylate, acyl, as intermediate, **3**, 651
adenylate cyclase, encoding, **3**, 478
adenylate cyclase toxin, mass spectra, **4**, 14
adenylate kinase, mass action ratio, **3**, 475
adenylation, aminoacyl, **4**, 321
adenylic acid deaminase *see* AMP deaminase
ADH *see* alcohol dehydrogenase (ADH)
Adhatoda vasica, vasicinol, **8**, 342
Adiantaceae, lignins, **3**, 625
adipate, 4-carboxy-4-hydroxy-2-keto-
  biosynthesis, **3**, 385
  cleavage, **3**, 385
adipate, α-keto-, as intermediate, **1**, 834
adipic acid, L-α-amino- (AAA)
  activation, **4**, 243
  catabolism, reduced, **4**, 179
  condensation, **1**, 840, **4**, 246
  in penicillin biosynthesis, **4**, 162, 165, 176
adipic acid, 2-amino-3-keto-
  in 5-aminolevulinate synthase biosynthesis, **4**, 66
  decarboxylation, **4**, 67
adipokinetic hormone (AKH)
  biochemistry, **8**, 299
  release, **8**, 302
adipose, glycogen synthase (mammalian), **3**, 479
AdoCbl *see* adenosylcobalamin (AdoCbl)
ado-cobinamide, biosynthesis, **4**, 148
ado-cobinamide phosphate, biosynthesis, **4**, 149
ado-cobyric acid, biosynthesis, **4**, 148
ado-cobyrinic acid *a,c*-diamide, encoding, **4**, 148
AdoMet *see* *S*-adenosyl-L-methionine (SAM)
adonixanthin, accumulation, **2**, 335
Adoxophyes spp.
  10-methyldodecylacetate, **8**, 246
  pheromones, **8**, 15
ADP *see* adenosine diphosphate (ADP)
ADPGlc *see* adenosinediphosphoglucose (ADPGlc)
ADPGlc PPase *see* glucose-1-phosphate adenylyltransferase
ADPglucose:1,4-α-D-glucan 4-α-D-glucosyltransferase *see* starch synthase(s)
ADPglucose:α-1,4-D-glucan-4-α-glucosyltransferase *see* glycogen synthase (bacterial)
ADP:α-D-glucose-1-phosphate adenylyltransferase *see* glucose-1-phosphate adenylyltransferase
ADPglucose pyrophosphorylase *see* glucose-1-phosphate adenylyltransferase

ADP-L-*glycero*-D-*manno*-heptose, biosynthesis, **3**, 224
ADP-D-*glycero*-D-*manno*-heptose-6-epimerase, **3**, 226
ADP-heptose-synthase, roles, **3**, 224
adrenoceptors, classification, **1**, 198
adrenodoxin, iron centers, **3**, 337
adrenodoxin reductase *see* ferredoxin-NADP$^+$ reductase
Adriamycin *see* doxorubicin
adult T-cell leukemia (ATL), mechanisms, **3**, 58
adynerin, insect sequestration, **8**, 363
AE *see* activator element (AE)
Aedes aegypti
  activity against, **1**, 693
  prostaglandins, **1**, 248
Aegilops ovata, monoepoxylignanolides, **1**, 695
ae mutants, of rice, **3**, 467
Aenictus rotundatus, 1,3,3-trimethyl-2,7-dioxabicyclo[2.2.1]heptane, **8**, 232
AEP *see* phosphonic acid, 2-aminoethyl- (AEP)
Aequorea spp., cDNA library, **8**, 446
Aequorea aequorea, aequorin, **8**, 446
Aequorea victoria
  aequorin, **8**, 446
  green fluorescent protein, **8**, 453
aequorin
  blue fluorescent protein in, **8**, 446
  luminescence activity, **8**, 447
  occurrence, **8**, 446
  recombinant, and natural aequorin compared, **8**, 448
  reduction, **8**, 450
  separation, via HPLC, **8**, 447
  use of photoaffinity labeling, **8**, 453
Aerobacter aerogenes *see* *Klebsiella pneumoniae*
Aeromonas hydrophila, glucose-1-phosphate adenylyltransferase, **3**, 447
Aeromonas salmonicida, ABC polysaccharide transport system, **3**, 213
aeroplysinin-1
  cytotoxicity, **8**, 469
  isolation, **8**, 431
  occurrence, **8**, 468
aesculetin
  biosynthesis, **1**, 628
  as intermediate, **1**, 628
aesculitannin G, structure, **3**, 779
Aesculus hippocastanum, proanthocyanidins, **3**, 779
aestivalin, occurrence, **1**, 375
A-factor
  AphD protein production, **8**, 383
  biosynthesis, **1**, 8
  discovery, **8**, 380
  from *S*-(−)-paraconic acid, **8**, 381
  isolation, **1**, 140
  occurrence, **8**, 379
  StrR protein production, **8**, 383
  structure, **8**, 380
  synthesis, **8**, 380
  see also butyrolactone, 2*S*-isocaproyloyl-4*S*-hydroxymethyl-
A-FF22 *see* streptococcin A-FF22
affinin *see* spilanthol
affinity reagents, phosphatase inhibition, **5**, 160
afl-2 genes *see* *afl* genes, *aflR*
aflatoxin B$_1$
  antifungal activity, **1**, 2
  biosynthesis, molecular biological approaches, **1**, 461
  carcinogenicity, **1**, 443
  folding patterns, **1**, 448
  from, *O*-methylsterigmatocystin, **1**, 459
  metabolic activation, **7**, 512
  occurrence, **1**, 443
  sequence specificity, **7**, 513
  structure, **1**, 410, 444
  synthesis, **1**, 459, **7**, 512

aflatoxin B₂, structure, **1**, 444
aflatoxin G₁, structure, **1**, 444
aflatoxin G₂, structure, **1**, 444
aflatoxins
    biosynthesis, **1**, 411, **443–471**
        pathways, **1**, 16
        polyketide synthases in, **1**, 420
        regulatory mechanisms, **1**, 467
        via Diels–Alder reaction, **1**, 16
    biosynthetic gene clusters, **1**, 421
    blocked mutants, **1**, 446
    common polyketide folding pattern, **1**, 448
    DNA damage induction, **7**, 511
    fluorescence, **8**, 176
    from, *Aspergillus* spp., **7**, 470
    intermediates, synthesis, **1**, 450
    ¹³C NMR spectra, **1**, 448
    occurrence, **1**, 420
    studies, **7**, 492
    toxicity, **8**, 176
afl genes
    aflR
        cloning, **1**, 462
        identification, **1**, 467
African elephant *see Loxodonta africana*
African palm weevils *see Rhynchophorus* spp.
afrormosin, occurrence, **1**, 775
afs genes, *afsA*, occurrence, **1**, 147, **8**, 382
afzelechin, **3**, 771
Agardhiella subulata, agardhilactone, **1**, 221
agardhilactone, occurrence, **1**, 221
Agaricus campestris, catechol oxidases, **3**, 709
Agelas conifera
    bromopyrroles, **1**, 381, **8**, 437
    sceptrin, **1**, 381
Ageratum houstonianum
    precocene I, **8**, 278
    precocene II, **8**, 278
Ageratum scoridonoides, encecalin, **8**, 337
aggrecan
    binding, **3**, 164
    localization, **3**, 164
    promoters, **3**, 167
aggregation pheromones
    assassin bugs, **8**, 221
    bark beetles, **8**, 198
    bees, **8**, 223
    Ips spp., **8**, 223
    lineatin, **8**, 224
    Pissodes spp., **8**, 224
    Pityogenes spp., **8**, 224
    cis-verbenol, **8**, 224
    trans-verbenol, **8**, 224
aggregation substance (AS), use of term, **8**, 408
aging, and DNA damage, **7**, 372
Agkistrodon piscivorus piscivorus, venom, phospholipase
    A₂, **5**, 110
Aglaia elliptica, rocaglamide, **8**, 340
Aglaia odorata, rocaglamide, **8**, 340
Aglaophenia pluma, β-carbolines, **8**, 529
aglycones
    biosynthesis, **1**, 668
    classification, **1**, 774
    degradation, **1**, 881
    enantiomeric purity, **1**, 679
    glycosylation, **1**, 737
    optical activity, **1**, 680
    as substrates, **1**, 733
    synthesis, **7**, 558
aglycones, cyclopentenoid, occurrence, **1**, 70
aglycones, isoflavonoid, accumulation, **1**, 808
AGPs *see* arabinogalactan proteins (AGPs)
agricultural crops, viroids, **6**, 171

Agriopis aurantiaria, (6*Z*,9*Z*)-(3*S*,4*R*)-3,4-epoxy-6,9-
    nonadecadiene, **8**, 207
Agriopis marginaria
    (3*Z*,9*Z*)-(6*S*,7*R*)-6,7-epoxy-3,9-nonadecadiene, **8**, 207
    (3*Z*,6*Z*,9*Z*)-3,6,9-nonadecatriene, **8**, 207
Agriotes spp., sex pheromones, **8**, 223
Agrobacterium spp., β-glucosidase, **5**, 289
Agrobacterium aurantiacum
    carotenoid biosynthesis, **2**, 335
    crt genes, **2**, 335
    in vivo functional assays, **2**, 344
Agrobacterium faecalis, β-glucosidases, **3**, 686
Agrobacterium rhizogenes
    rol genes, **8**, 72
    root transformation, **3**, 142
Agrobacterium tumefaciens
    autoinducers, **8**, 399
    conjugation factor, **8**, 399
    crown gall induction, **8**, 69, 399
    glucose-1-phosphate adenylyltransferase, **3**, 469
    indoleacetamide, **8**, 34
    as plant pathogen, **8**, 392
    T-DNA, **1**, 41
agrocin 84, 3-deoxy-D-*threo*-pentose, **3**, 313
agroclavine, biosynthesis, **4**, 53
Agromyza frontella, 3,7-dimethylnonadecane, **8**, 249
Agrostis ipsilon, insecticidal activity against, **8**, 322
AGV *see* Australian grapevine viroid (AGV)
AHBA *see* benzoic acid, 3-amino-5-hydroxy- (AHBA)
AICA *see* imidazole-4-carboxamide, 5-amino- (AICA)
ain genes, *ainS*, discovery, **8**, 395
Aiptasia pulchella, dinoflagellates, symbiotic, **8**, 428
ajaconine, as seed toxin, **8**, 168
ajmalicine
    biosynthesis, **4**, 46, 113, 125
    from, 3β-vincoside, **4**, 116
    pharmacological activity, **4**, 110
ajmaline
    antiarrhythmic activity, **4**, 110
    biosynthesis, **4**, 46
    early studies, **4**, 47
    strictosidine studies, **4**, 118
Ajuga spp., antifeedant studies, **8**, 316
Ajuga chamaepitys, ajugapitin, **8**, 315
Ajuga iva, antifeedant studies, **8**, 316
ajugalactone, structure, **8**, 282
ajugapitin, antifeedant activity, **8**, 315
ajugapitin, 4,15-dihydro-, occurrence, **8**, 315
Ajuga pseudoiva, 4,15-dihydroajugapitin, **8**, 315
Ajuga remota, ajugarins, **8**, 315
Ajuga reptans
    antifeedant activity, **8**, 316
    hydroxycinnamoyltransferases, **1**, 741
    malonyltransferases, **1**, 741
ajugarin, antifeedant activity, **8**, 319
ajugarin I, antifeedant activity, **8**, 315
(±)-ajugarin I, synthesis, **8**, 317
ajugarin II, antifeedant activity, **8**, 315
ajugarin III, antifeedant activity, **8**, 315
ajugarin IV, antifeedant activity, **8**, 315
ajugarin V, antifeedant activity, **8**, 315
ajugarins, occurrence, **8**, 315
AKH *see* adipokinetic hormone (AKH)
aklanonic acid, biosynthesis, **1**, 487
aklavinone
    biosynthesis, **1**, 482
    cloning, **1**, 11
akuammicine, 19,20-dihydro-, biosynthesis, **4**, 50
3β-akuammigine, strictosidine studies, **4**, 118
ALA *see* levulinic acid, amino- (ALA)
L-Ala adding enzyme *see* UDP-*N*-acetylmuramate–
    alanine ligase
D-Ala-D-Ala adding enzyme, catalysis, **3**, 261

ALA dehydratase *see* porphobilinogen synthase
alamethicin, occurrence, **1**, 539
alanine, in pelargonic acid biosynthesis, **1**, 826
alanine, β-chloro-, alanine racemase inhibition, **3**, 275
alanine, β-cyano-
    effects, on herbivores, **8**, 146
    neurotoxicity, **8**, 144
alanine, L-β-farnesyl amino- (faA)
    analogues, **5**, 333
    inhibitory activity, **5**, 333
alanine, phosphino-, analogues, **1**, 868
alanine, phosphinothricylalanyl-, isolation, **1**, 865
alanine, β,β,β-trifluoro-, alanine racemase inhibition, **3**, 275
D-alanine
    biosynthesis, **3**, 254
    cross-links, **3**, 248
    in cyclosporin studies, **1**, 538
    removal, **3**, 245
    as starting material, for cyclosporins, **1**, 543
L-alanine
    biosynthesis, **3**, 395
    in cyclosporin studies, **1**, 538
    occurrence, **3**, 246
    reactions, with benzaldehyde, **3**, 395
β-alanine
    biosynthesis, **5**, 87
    in peptide fragments, **4**, 338
D-alanine-D-alanine adding enzyme, inhibition, **3**, 278
D-alanine–D-alanine ligase
    D-cycloserine activity, **3**, 277
    encoding, **3**, 260
alanine:alanine ligase (ADP-forming) *see* D-alanine–D-alanine ligase
D-alanine-D-alanine peptidase, **3**, 274
alanine boronate, as slow-binding inhibitor, **3**, 276
β-alaninecyclosporins, synthesis, **1**, 549
D-alanine dehydrogenase, encoding, **3**, 254
D-alanine:D-lactate ligase, specificity, **3**, 261
alanine methyl ester, 2-methyl-3-bromo(*N*-benzaldimino)-, rearrangement, **5**, 210
alanine phosphonate, as slow-binding inhibitor, **3**, 276
alanine racemase(s)
    homologues, **4**, 342
    purification, **3**, 254
    roles, in cyclosporin biosynthesis, **1**, 545
alantolactone, antifeedant activity, **8**, 308
alanyl adenylate (alanyl-AMP), synthesis, **7**, 628
alanylalanine synthetase *see* D-alanine–D-alanine ligase
alanyl-AMP *see* alanyl adenylate (alanyl-AMP)
Albery–Knowles analysis, triose-phosphate isomerase, **5**, 8
Albizzia lophanta, djenkolic acid, **1**, 848
albizziine, effects, on herbivores, **8**, 146
albumin mRNA
    degradation, **6**, 213
    murine, **6**, 214
Alcaligenes PC-1
    carotenoid biosynthesis, **2**, 335
    crt genes, **2**, 335
alcohol, coniferyl
    accumulation, **3**, 629
    coupling, **3**, 618
    isomers, occurrence, **3**, 683
    in lignins, **3**, 620
    metabolic pool size, **3**, 629
    occurrence, **3**, 625
    oxidation, **3**, 703
    studies, **3**, 649
alcohol, *E*-coniferyl
    biosynthesis, **1**, 18
    dimers, **1**, 647
    oxidation, **1**, 648

    radical coupling, **1**, 652
    stereoselective coupling, **1**, 680
alcohol, *p*-coumaryl
    accumulation, **3**, 629
    coupling, **1**, 685, **3**, 618
    in lignins, **3**, 620
    metabolic pool size, **3**, 629
    occurrence, **3**, 625
    oxidation, **1**, 648
alcohol, dihydro-*p*-coumaryl, reduction, **1**, 682
alcohol, dihydrodehydrodiconiferyl, biosynthesis, **3**, 731
alcohol, ($-$)-dihydrodehydrodiconiferyl, occurrence, **1**, 647
alcohol, *p*-hydroxybenzyl, release, **1**, 838
alcohol, perillyl, applications, **2**, 102
alcohol, 2-propyl-5-ethylbenzyl, identification, **1**, 87
alcohol, sinapyl
    coupling, **3**, 618
    in lignins, **3**, 620
    oxidation, **1**, 648
alcohol, trisnorsqualene (TNSA), as non-competitive inhibitor, **2**, 273
alcohol dehydrogenase (ADH)
    in green odor production, **1**, 92
    homology, **1**, 261
alcohol dehydrogenases, short-chain, catalysis, **8**, 407
alcohol ethers, ($\pm$)-guaiacylglycerol 8-*O*-4′-coniferyl, biosynthesis, **3**, 704
alcohol ethers, guaiacylglycerol 8-*O*-4′-coniferyl
    biosynthesis, **3**, 714
    coupling, **1**, 640
    glycosylation, **3**, 684
    metabolism, **1**, 680
    reduction, **1**, 682
alcohol glucoside, *p*-coumaryl
    biosynthesis, **3**, 676
    occurrence, **3**, 677
alcohol 9-*O*-β-D-glucoside, dihydrodehydrodiconiferyl, occurrence, **3**, 625
alcohol 4-*O*-glucosides, ($\pm$)-dehydrodiconiferyl, cell division stimulation, **1**, 695
alcohol:NAD$^+$ oxidoreductase *see* alcohol dehydrogenase (ADH)
alcohols, cyclic amino, synthesis, **2**, 257
alcohols, dehydrodiconiferyl
    biosynthesis, **3**, 710, 714
    coupling, **1**, 640
    enantiomers, **1**, 679
    metabolism, **1**, 680, 683
    occurrence, **1**, 680, 698
    structure, **1**, 681
alcohols, ($\pm$)-dehydrodiconiferyl, biosynthesis, **3**, 704
alcohols, dihydrocinnamyl, biosynthesis, **3**, 677
alcohols, dihydroconiferyl, reduction, **1**, 682
alcohols, dihydrodehydrodiconiferyl
    biosynthesis, **1**, 688
    enantiomers, **1**, 651
    reduction, **1**, 682
C$_6$-alcohols, unsaturated
    in green odor, **1**, 84
    isomers, biosynthesis, **1**, 85
aldecalmycin, biosynthesis, **1**, 370
aldehyde reductase *see* alcohol dehydrogenase (ADH)
aldehydes
    DNA adducts of, **7**, 502
    DNA damage induction, **7**, 502
aldehydes, 3-keto-, occurrence, **8**, 204
aldehydes, α,β-unsaturated, DNA adduct formation by, **7**, 502
C$_6$-aldehydes, unsaturated
    biosynthesis, pathways, **1**, 89
    in green odor, **1**, 84
    seasonal variations, **1**, 107

isomers, biosynthesis, **1**, 85
aldgamycin E, D-aldgarose, **3**, 322
D-aldgarose
   occurrence, **3**, 312, 322
   tracer studies, **3**, 342
alditols, oligoglycosyl, biosynthesis, **3**, 499
aldo–keto reductase family, molecular phylogeny, **1**, 276
aldol additions, in antibody catalysis, **5**, 439
aldolase antibodies, mechanisms, **5**, 438
aldolases
   biochemistry, **3**, 2, 7, **367–440**
   identified, **3**, 372
   mechanisms, undetermined, **3**, 408
   nucleophile activation, **3**, 369
   overview, **3**, 368
   phospho*enol*pyruvate utilization, **3**, 386
   Schiff base-forming, **3**, 372
   see also fructose-bisphosphate aldolase
aldolases, divalent metal-catalyzed, biochemistry, **3**, 385
aldolases, pyridoxal-dependent, biochemistry, **3**, 395
aldolases, thiamine-dependent, biochemistry, **3**, 392
aldol condensation
   in antibody catalysis, **5**, 437, 439
   in butyrolactone biosynthesis, **1**, **139–158**
   in cyclopentanoid biosynthesis, **1**, **139–158**
   intramolecular, **1**, 144
aldol reaction
   enzymatic, mechanisms, **3**, 368, 7
   nucleophile activation
      via Schiff base/enamine formation, **3**, 369
      via zinc, **3**, 369
   stereospecificity, **3**, 396
   via preformed enolate nucleophiles, **3**, 370
   via pyridoxal, **3**, 371
   via thiamine diphosphate, **3**, 370
Aleochara curtula
   (*Z*)-7-henicosene, **8**, 218
   (*Z*)-7-tricosene, **8**, 218
aleprolic acid, roles, **1**, 68
Aleuroglyphus ovatus, neryl myristate, **8**, 222
aleurone cells
   abscisic acid receptors, **8**, 83
   enzyme activity, **8**, 45
alexine, structure, **3**, 131
alfalfa *see Medicago sativa*
alfalfa aphid *see Therioaphis maculata*
algae
   celluloses, studies, **3**, 554
   chemical defense, **8**, 459
   cyclic bromoethers, functions, **1**, 322
   isoprenoid biosynthesis, mevalonate-independent
      pathway, **2**, 60
   and lignin evolution, **3**, 622
   oxylipins, reviews, **1**, 213
   sex attractants, **8**, 420
   starch biosynthesis, **3**, 445
   and vascular plant evolution, **3**, 622
   see also Charophyceae; Chlorophyta; cyanobacteria;
      Ectocarpus siliculosus; marine algae;
      microalgae; Phaeophyta; Rhodophyta;
      Scytonema pseudohofmanni
alg genes, *algC*, **3**, 204, 207
Alicyclobacillus acidocaldarius
   hopanes, **1**, 71
   hopene cyclase, purification, **2**, 308
   isolation, **1**, 71
   mutants, **1**, 71
Alicyclobacillus acidoterrestris
   fatty acids, **1**, 71
   hopanoids, **2**, 56
   hopene cyclase, gene cloning, **2**, 313
   isoprenoids, **2**, 52
      biosynthesis, **2**, 377

Alicyclobacillus cycloheptanicus, fatty acids, **1**, 71, 75
6,9-alkadienes, as pheromones, **8**, 207
(9*Z*,13*Z*)-9,13-alkadienes, occurrence, **8**, 219
alkaline phosphatase
   binding, **5**, 158
   biochemistry, **5**, 153
   classification, **5**, 140
alkaline phosphomonoesterase *see* alkaline phosphatase
alkaline protease, occurrence, **8**, 398
alkaloids
   as ant venoms, **8**, 357
   applications, **4**, 25
   biosynthesis, **3**, 10, **4**, 2, **25–59**, **5**, 47
      overview, **4**, **1–11**
      studies, **4**, 26
   classification, **4**, 26
   definitions, **8**, 342
   from
      amino acids, **4**, 26
      histidine, **4**, 54
      lysine, **4**, 33
      ornithine, **4**, 26
      phenylalanine, **4**, 35
      tryptophan, **4**, 46
      tyrosine, **4**, 35
   future research, **4**, 54
   insecticidal activity, **8**, 342
   marine, discovery, **1**, 380
   in nectars, **8**, 162
   occurrence, **3**, 4, **4**, 25, **8**, 164
   plant, ecological significance, **8**, 146
   semi-parasite uptake, **8**, 175
      selective, **8**, 176
   toxicity, **8**, 144
   see also acridone alkaloids; Amaryllidaceae alkaloids;
      benzylisoquinoline alkaloids; carbazole alkaloids; *β*-
      carboline alkaloids; clavine alkaloids; decacyclic
      alkaloids; ergot alkaloids; erythrina alkaloids;
      glucoalkaloids; heteroyohimbine alkaloids;
      imidazole alkaloids; indole alkaloids; indolizidine
      alkaloids; isoquinoline alkaloids; monoterpenoid
      indole alkaloids; morphine alkaloids; nicotine
      alkaloids; peptide ergot alkaloids; phenanthrene
      alkaloids; phthalideisoquinoline alkaloids;
      piperidine alkaloids; polyhydroxy alkaloids;
      pyridoacridine alkaloids; pyrrolidine alkaloids;
      pyrroline alkaloids; pyrrolizidine alkaloids (PAs);
      quinolizidine alkaloids (QAs); *Rauwolfia*
      alkaloids; strychnos alkaloids; tobacco alkaloids;
      tropane alkaloids; *Vinca* alkaloids; wilfordine
      alkaloids
alkanes, on insect cuticles, **8**, 204
alkanes, nitro-, isolation, **8**, 431
1-alkanols, oxidation, **8**, 204
2-alkanols, biosynthesis, **8**, 204
3-alkanols, biosynthesis, **8**, 204
2-alkanones, biosynthesis, **8**, 204
3-alkanones, biosynthesis, **8**, 204
3,6,9-alkatrienes, as pheromones, **8**, 207
alkenes
   alkylation, **2**, 4
   on insect cuticles, **8**, 204
1-alkenes, biosynthesis, **8**, 204
1-alken-3-ones, as pheromones, **8**, 202
alk genes, *alkK*, occurrence, **1**, 47
alkoxyl radicals
   DNA damage induction, **7**, 510
   from vinyl epoxides, **7**, 510
1-alkyl-2-acetylglycerol cholinephosphotransferase *see*
      diacylglycerol cholinephosphotransferase
alkylacylglycerol cholinephosphotransferase *see*
      diacylglycerol cholinephosphotransferase
alkylating agents

biotin-based, **7**, 632
DNA damage induction, **7**, 372
as probes, **6**, 63
alkylation
electrophilic, **5**, **315–341**
chain elongation, **5**, 318
alkyldihydroxyacetonephosphate synthase *see*
alkylglycerone-phosphate synthase
alkyl disulfide tethers, **6**, 227
alkyl-enzyme intermediates
hydrolysis, **5**, 57
in microsomal epoxide hydrolases, **5**, 55
in soluble epoxide hydrolases, **5**, 55
synthesis, **5**, 56
alkylglycerone-phosphate synthase
catalysis, **1**, 288
localization, **1**, 288
1-alkyl-*sn*-glycero-3-phosphoethanolamine
ethanolaminehydrolase *see*
alkylglycerophosphoethanolamine
phosphodiesterase
alkylglycerophosphoethanolamine phosphodiesterase,
activity, **1**, 288
allatostatins
biochemistry, **8**, 301
occurrence, **8**, 301
allatotropins
biochemistry, **8**, 301
occurrence, **8**, 301
allelochemicals
allomone, **8**, 198
definition, **8**, 2
kairomone, **8**, 198
synomone, **8**, 198
allelopathic agents
monoterpenes, **2**, 101
phenolic constituents, **8**, 169
allelopathy
plants, **8**, 169
reviews, **8**, 169
allene epoxide, as intermediate, **1**, 7
allene-oxide cyclase
discovery, **1**, 120
in jasmonic acid biosynthesis, **8**, 115
allene oxide pathway, mechanisms, **1**, 232, 240
allene oxides
biosynthesis, **1**, 119
as intermediates, **1**, 226
allene oxide synthase *see* hydroperoxide dehydratase
Allescheria boydii, activity against, **1**, 691
alliacolide, occurrence, **2**, 176
Allium cepa
bulb development, **1**, 127
4′-*O*-glucosyltransferases, **1**, 738
allograft rejection, prevention, **1**, 540
D-alloisoleucine, replacement, **4**, 253
D-allomethylose
biosynthesis, **3**, 352
occurrence, **3**, 312
allomones
definition, **8**, 2
development, **2**, 101
as repellents, **8**, 198
roles, **8**, 198
defense, **8**, 202, 465
allopurinol, as synthon, **7**, 332
allosamidin(s)
analogues, conversion studies, **1**, 151
binding inhibition, **5**, 297
biological activity, **1**, 139, 149
biosynthesis, **1**, 149
carbon atoms, **1**, 150
isolation, **1**, 149

nitrogen atoms, **1**, 150
structure, **1**, 149
D-allosamine, biosynthesis, **1**, 150
D-allosamine, *N*-acetyl-, occurrence, **1**, 149
allosamizoline
cyclopentane ring formation, mechanisms, **1**, 152
structure, **1**, 149
allosterism, **2**, 113
allothreonine, *O*-methyl-, replacement, **4**, 253
Alloxysta victrix, 6-methyl-5-hepten-2-one, **8**, 232
allylic cations, energy barriers to rotation, **2**, 122
allylic systems, tertiary, stabilization, **2**, 122
alnusdiol, occurrence, **1**, 686
Alsophila pometaria
1,3,6,9-nonadecatetraene, **8**, 207
1,3,6,9-nonadecatriene, **8**, 207
alstonine, tetrahydro-, biosynthesis, **4**, 113, 125
altenolide, occurrence, **1**, 375
alteramide A
occurrence, **8**, 588
structure, **8**, 588
Alternaria alternata
melanin, **1**, 427
protection from, **8**, 183
Alternaria kikuchina, activity against, **1**, 534
Alternaria solani, solanapyrones, **1**, 395
alterobactins, occurrence, **8**, 592
Alteromonas spp., alteramide A, **8**, 588
Alteromonas luteoviolacea, alterobactins, **8**, 592
Altocid *see* methoprene
altromycin B
applications, antibiotics, **7**, 471
DNA damage induction, **7**, 508
intercalation, **7**, 471
NMR studies, **7**, 471
aluminum naphthoxide, applications, in Claisen
rearrangements, **5**, 350
α-amanitin, viroid inhibition, **6**, 178
Amaranthus caudatus, betacyanins, **8**, 69
Amaryllidaceae alkaloids
biosynthesis, **4**, 43
occurrence, **4**, 43
Amauris spp., linalool oxide, **8**, 225
Amblyomma variegatum, pheromones, **8**, 212
ambrosia beetles
3-hydroxy-3-methylbutan-2-one, **8**, 220
lineatin, **8**, 224
see also Gnathotrichus spp.; *Platypus flavicornis*;
Trypodendron spp.
American cockroach *see Periplaneta americana*
American palm weevil *see Rhynchophorus palmarum*
Ametabola, lifecycle, **8**, 265
D-amicetose, occurrence, **3**, 312, 321
L-amicetose, occurrence, **3**, 312
amidates, synthesis, **7**, 109
amide, (2*S*,3*R*)-2,3-epox-4-oxo-7,10-dodecadienoyl- *see*
cerulenin
amides
antisense oligonucleotide linkages, **7**, 300
bond formation
catalysis, **4**, **221–238**
condensation domains, **4**, 230
via ribozymes, **6**, 128
cleavage, **5**, 437
amide synthases
catalysis, **6**, 141
comparisons, **6**, 142
evolution, **6**, 139
selection, **6**, 138
amidolyase, activity, **4**, 259
amine oxidases, occurrence, **3**, 721
amines
antisense oligonucleotide linkages, **7**, 301

long-chain, occurrence, **8**, 545
D-amino acid aminotransferase
   purification, **3**, 256
   x-ray crystal structure, **3**, 256
amino acid ligases, ATP-dependent, inhibition, **3**, 277
amino-acid racemase(s), homologues, **4**, 342
amino acids
   biosynthesis, **4**, 2
      overview, **4**, 1–11
   conjugation, **6**, 138
   as cyanogenic glycoside precursors, **1**, 885
   as feeding attractants and stimulants, **8**, 417
   host factor activity, **8**, 428
   motifs, common, **2**, 315
   nonprotein, **1**, 69
      effects on herbivores, **8**, 146
      toxicity, **8**, 146
   peptide cross-link attachment, **3**, 264
   in proteins, **4**, 354
   residues, *N*-methylation, **4**, 335
   sequons, **3**, 74
   as starting materials
      for alkaloids, **4**, 26
      for cephalosporins, **4**, 165
      for cephamycins, **4**, 165
      for penicillins, **4**, 165
   see also aromatic amino acids; protein amino acids
amino acids, *m*-carboxy-, biosynthesis, **1**, 619
amino acids, dehydro-, removal, **4**, 283
amino acids, mycosporine-like, absorbance, **8**, 428
D-amino acids
   biosynthesis
      inhibition, **3**, 275
      in peptidoglycan, **3**, 254
L-amino acids
   activation, **1**, 546
   biosynthesis, **1**, 546
aminoacrylyl-tRNA, as intermediate, **4**, 355
aminoacyl synthetase, interactions, with tRNA^{Ser}, **6**, 222
aminoacyl-tRNA synthetase(s)
   activity increase, cytokinin-induced, **8**, 59
   catalysis, **7**, 628
L-α-aminoadipic acid reductase, activity, **4**, 176
δ-(L-α-aminoadipyl)-L-cysteinyl-D-valine synthetase
      (ACVS) *see* ACV synthetase
p-aminobenzoate synthase, regulatory mechanisms, **5**, 344
γ-aminobutyric acid transferases, inhibition, **1**, 616
1-aminocyclopropane-1-carboxylate deaminase, bacterial
      genes, **8**, 98
1-aminocyclopropane-1-carboxylate oxidase
   activity, **1**, 133
   antisense genes, **8**, 98
   induction, regulatory mechanisms, **8**, 98
   isozyme genes, expression, **8**, 98
1-aminocyclopropane-1-carboxylate synthase
   antisense genes, **8**, 98
   auxin activation, **8**, 31
   cDNA cloning, **8**, 97
   induction, **8**, 97
   isozyme genes, expression, **8**, 98
   roles, **8**, 95
amino groups, exocyclic, protection, **6**, 87
2-amino-4-hydroxy-6-(D-*erythro*-1,2,3-
      trihydroxypropyl)-7,8-dihydropteridine
      glycolaldehyde-lyase *see* dihydroneopterin
      aldolase
aminolevulinate dehydratase *see* porphobilinogen
      synthase(s)
5-aminolevulinate hydro-lyase (adding 5-aminolevulinate
      and cyclizing) *see* porphobilinogen synthase(s)
5-aminolevulinate synthase
   ALAS1, **4**, 65
   ALAS2, **4**, 65

catalysis, **4**, 62
early studies, **4**, 67
encoding, **4**, 65
kinetics, **4**, 65
mechanisms, **4**, 65
occurrence, **4**, 65
structure, **4**, 67
substrate specificity, **4**, 65
5-aminolevulinic acid dehydratase *see* porphobilinogen
      synthase(s)
5-aminolevulinic acid synthase *see* 5-aminolevulinate
      synthase
aminomutases, adenosylcobalamin-dependent,
      coenzymes, **5**, 209
6-aminopenicillanic acid acyltransferase, activity, **4**, 259
aminopeptidase(s), molecular phylogeny, **1**, 279
amino sugar, **7**, 554
aminotransferase(s), genetic encoding, **4**, 5
Amitermes spp., caparrapioxide, **8**, 229
amitinol
   biosynthesis, **8**, 224
   occurrence, **8**, 224
Ammi majus
   caffeoyl-CoA *O*-methyltransferase, **3**, 672
   coumarins, **1**, 623
      accumulation, **1**, 626
Ammi visnaga, pyranocoumarins, **1**, 628
ammodendrine
   occurrence, **8**, 344
   structure, **8**, 344
Ammodendron conollyii, ammodendrine, **8**, 344
ammonia
   production, in muscle, **5**, 80
   roles, in L-tyrosine biosynthesis, **3**, 405
ammonium bromide, dodecyltrimethyl-, as inhibitor, **2**,
      311
ammonium chloride, tetraethyl-, larval settlement
      inhibition, **8**, 434
ammonium ion compounds, reactions, with inorganic
      diphosphate, **2**, 253
ammonium ions
   analogues, **5**, 337
   in phenylpropanoid metabolism, **3**, 627
amnesic shellfish poisoning (ASP), etiology, **1**, 227
AMO 1618
   as cycloartenol cyclase inhibitor, **2**, 305
   as hopene cyclase inhibitor, **2**, 311
amonafide, **7**, 609
   inhibition, **7**, 606
Amorpha fruticosa
   amorphigenin, **1**, 810
   rotenoid biosynthesis, **8**, 342
   rotenone, **1**, 810
amorphigenin
   from 7-hydroxy-2′,4,5′-trimethoxyisoflavone, **8**, 342
   occurrence, **1**, 810
AMP *see* adenosine monophosphate (AMP)
AMPA *see* isoxazole-4-propionate, α-amino-3-hydroxyl-
      5-methyl- (AMPA)
AMP-activated protein kinase (AMPK)
   nomenclature, **2**, 39
   purification, **2**, 39
AMP aminase *see* AMP deaminase
AMP aminohydrolase *see* AMP deaminase
AMP deaminase
   biological functions, **5**, 80
   catalytic site structure, **5**, 81
   chemical mechanisms, **5**, 81
   cooperative kinetics, **5**, 81
   isozymes, **5**, 81
   kinetic isotope effects, **5**, 81
   kinetic properties, **5**, 80
   localization, **5**, 81

molecular electrostatic potential surfaces, **5**, 84
regulatory mechanisms, allosteric, **5**, 80
transition state inhibitors, **5**, 83
slow-onset, **5**, 83
transition state measures, **5**, 84
transition state structure, **5**, 82
AMP deaminase deficiency
and muscle weakness, **5**, 81
prevalence, **5**, 80
Amphibia, oxylipins, **1**, 248
amphidinin A, structure, **8**, 627
Amphidinium spp.
amphidinoketides, **8**, 633
amphidinolides, **8**, 615, 619
caribenolide I, **8**, 627
studies, **8**, 619
Amphidinium klebsii, amphidinol, **8**, 615
amphidinoketides, occurrence, **8**, 633
amphidinol
antifungal activity, **8**, 615
occurrence, **8**, 615
structure, **8**, 615
amphidinolide A, structure, **8**, 620
amphidinolide B
absolute configuration, **8**, 629
structure, **8**, 621
amphidinolide B₁, structure, **8**, 629
amphidinolide B₂, structure, **8**, 629
amphidinolide B₃, structure, **8**, 629
amphidinolide C
stereochemistry, **8**, 630
structure, **8**, 621
amphidinolide D, structure, **8**, 622
amphidinolide E, structure, **8**, 621
amphidinolide F, structure, **8**, 622
amphidinolide G, structure, **8**, 621
amphidinolide H, structure, **8**, 621
amphidinolide J
biosynthesis, **8**, 632
pathways, **8**, 633
¹³C NMR spectra, **8**, 631
structure, **8**, 622
amphidinolide K, structure, **8**, 626
amphidinolide L, structure, **8**, 626
amphidinolide M, structure, **8**, 627
amphidinolide N
cytotoxicity, **8**, 627
structure, **8**, 627
amphidinolide O, structure, **8**, 628
amphidinolide P, structure, **8**, 628
amphidinolide Q, structure, **8**, 629
amphidinolides
biosynthesis, **8**, 631
cytotoxicity, **8**, 633
occurrence, **8**, 615, 619
structure, **8**, 619, 620
amphikeumin, structure, **8**, 429
Amphimedon spp.
ircinol A, **1**, 380
ircinol B, **1**, 380
keramaphidins, **8**, 554
manzamines, **8**, 557
Amphiprion clarkii, symbiosis, **8**, 429
Amphiprion ocellaris, symbiosis, **8**, 430
Amphiprion perideraion, symbiosis, **8**, 429
Amphiscolops spp.
Amphidinium spp. in, studies, **8**, 619
Symbiodinium spp. in, **8**, 614
see also flatworms
amphomycin, polyprenyl phosphate chelation, **3**, 281
ampicillin, biosynthesis, **3**, 283
AMPK *see* AMP-activated protein kinase (AMPK)
AMP:pyrophosphate phospho-D-ribosyltransferase *see*
adenine phosphoribosyltransferase

AMP pyrophosphorylase *see* adenine
phosphoribosyltransferase
m-AMSA *see* amsacrine
amsacrine, **7**, 609
as DNA topoisomerase II inhibitor, **7**, 603
hepatotoxicity, **7**, 606
Amsonia tabernaemontana, strictosidine studies, **4**, 117
Amycolatopsis mediterranei, rifamycin, **1**, 527
Amycolatopsis orientalis, quartromicin A₁, **1**, 374
amygdalin, degradation, **1**, 890
as seed toxin, **8**, 168
(*R*)-amygdalin, occurrence, **1**, 886
amygdalin hydrolase, in amygdalin degradation, **1**, 890
α-amylase
amino acid residues, **3**, 462
$(\beta/\alpha)_8$-barrel structural domains, **3**, 459
and branching enzymes, **3**, 459
sequences, **3**, 459, **5**, 298
substrate distortion, **5**, 299
superfamily, **5**, 298
suppression, **8**, 83
synthesis, *de novo*, **8**, 46
β-amylase, occurrence, **5**, 301
γ-amylase *see* glucan 1,4-α-glucosidase
amylases, degradative mechanisms, **3**, 442
amyloglucosidase *see* glucan 1,4-α-glucosidase
amyloid precursor protein (APP), and Alzheimer's
disease, **7**, 372
amylolytic enzymes, catalytic regions, **3**, 459
amylomaltase *see* 4-α-glucanotransferase
amylopectin
biosynthesis, **3**, 445, 458
in vivo, **3**, 466
in starch synthase activity measurement, **3**, 454
structure, **3**, 442
cluster model, **3**, 466
amylopectin II, deficiency, **3**, 455
amylopectin 6-glucanohydrolase *see* α-dextrin endo-1,6-
α-glucosidase
amylophosphorylase *see* glycogen phosphorylase;
maltodextrin phosphorylase
amyloplasts
interactions, with cytosol, **3**, 466
occurrence, **3**, 464
structure, **3**, 463
amylose
biosynthesis, **3**, 445
structure, **3**, 442
studies, **3**, 546
amylose extender
alleles, **3**, 461
mutants, **3**, 461, 462
amylosucrase, occurrence, **3**, 445
α-amyrin cyclase, inhibitors, **2**, 305
β-amyrin cyclase
inhibitors, **2**, 305
Rabdosia japonica, purification, **2**, 305
amyrin cyclases
biochemistry, **2**, 305
synthesis, **2**, 305
An-1 gene, cloning, **8**, 47
Anabaena spp.
carotenoid biosynthesis, **2**, 337
glucose-1-phosphate adenylyltransferase, **3**, 449
Anabaena flos-aquae f. *flos-aquae*
9*R*-hydroxy-10*E*,12*Z*-octadecadienoic acid, **1**, 209
9*R*-hydroxy-10*E*,12*Z*,15*Z*-octadecatrienoic acid, **1**, 209
Anabaena PCC7120, desaturases, **1**, 42
Anabaena thaliana
desaturases, **1**, 40
*FAD*7 gene, mutation, **1**, 44
Anabaena variabilis
desaturases, **1**, 40

3-phosphoshikimate 1-carboxyvinyltransferase, glyphosate tolerance, **1**, 598
anabaseine, occurrence, **8**, 347, 358
anabasine
   biosynthesis, **8**, 348
   occurrence, **8**, 347, 358
anabasine, *N*-methyl-, occurrence, **8**, 358
anabasine sulfate, toxicity, **8**, 348
Anabasis aphylla
   anabasine, **8**, 347
   aphylline, **8**, 344
   lupinine, **8**, 344
anacardic acids, occurrence, **8**, 303
Anacridium melanorhoda, feeding, and phenolics, **8**, 141
anacyclin, occurrence, **8**, 303
Anacyclus pyrethrum
   anacyclin, **8**, 303
   pellitorine, **1**, 333, **8**, 303
anadamide, occurrence, **1**, 281
Anadyomene stellata, 5*Z*,8*Z*,10*E*,12*E*,14*Z*-eicosapentaenoic acid, **1**, 223
anaerobic ribonucleotide reductase activating enzyme (ARR-AE), catalysis, **5**, 218
anaerobic ribonucleotide reductase (ARR)
   activation, **1**, 831, **5**, 217
   glycyl radicals, **5**, 218
Anaglyptus subfasciatus
   (*R*)-3-hydroxy-2-hexanone, **8**, 210, 211
   (*R*)-3-hydroxy-2-octanone, **8**, 211
anagyrine
   host–parasite chemical transfer, **8**, 176
   insect sequestration, **8**, 154
   toxicity, **8**, 147
anaphylaxis, mediation, **1**, 286
Anastrepha suspensa
   (3*Z*,6*Z*)-3,6-nonadien-1-ol, **8**, 212
   (*Z*)-3-nonen-1-ol, **8**, 212
   suspensolide, **8**, 236
anastrephin
   biosynthesis, **8**, 236
   occurrence, **8**, 236
anatabine, occurrence, **8**, 347
anatomical distribution, drimane sesquiterpenoids, **8**, 462
(+)-anatoxin-a, biosynthesis, **4**, 30
anatoxin-a(s), structure, **8**, 610
anboina *see Conus geographus*
AnCF *see Aspergillus nidulans* CCAAT binding factor (AnCF)
ancistrofuran
   occurrence, **8**, 229
   structure, **8**, 234
Ancistrotermes spp., ancistrofuran, **8**, 229
Ancistrotermes cavithorax, β-cyclogeraniolene, **8**, 234
ancovenin
   biosynthesis, **4**, 202
   structure, **4**, 280
Ancylobacter aquaticus, haloalkane dehalogenases, **5**, 403
andibenin B, occurrence, **1**, 378
Andira inermis, antibiotics, **8**, 167
Andrena spp.
   Dufour's gland secretions, **8**, 223, 227
   geranylgeranyl octanoate, **8**, 229
Andrena wilkella, (2*S*,6*R*,8*S*)-2,8-dimethyl-1,7-dioxaspiro[5.5]undecane, **8**, 214
andrimid
   methicillin-resistant *Staphylococcus aureus* inhibition, **8**, 594
   occurrence, **8**, 594
andromedol, acetyl-, in nectars, **8**, 162
3,5-androstadien-17-one, 3-hydroxy-, isolation, **5**, 33
4-androstene-3,17-dione
   from, 5-androstene-3,17-dione, **5**, 33
   occurrence, **8**, 230

5-androstene-3,17-dione, as starting material, for 4-androstene-3,17-dione, **5**, 33
5α-androst-16-en-3-ol, as pheromone, **8**, 230
androstenone, structure, **8**, 230
5α-androst-16-en-3-one, as pheromone, **8**, 230
androst-5-en-17-one, 3β-[2-(diethylamino)ethoxy]-, as inhibitor of sterol biogenesis, **2**, 292
Anemarrhena asphodeloides
   cis-hinokiresinol, **1**, 704
   oxy-*cis*-hinokiresinol, **1**, 704
Anemia flexuosa, antheridiogens, **8**, 55
Anemia phyllitidis
   antheridic acid, **8**, 56
      biosynthesis, **8**, 57
   antheridiogens, **8**, 55
Anemia rotundifolia, antheridiogens, **8**, 56
anemone fish *see Amphiprion ocellaris*
Anethum graveolens, dillapiole, **8**, 336
Angelica archangelica, coumarins, **1**, 625
angelicin, from, (−)-columbianetin, **1**, 633
Angiospermae
   alkaloids, **4**, 25
   β-glucosidases, **3**, 683
   herbaceous, monoterpene synthases, **2**, 127, 142
   lignans, **1**, 647
   lignins, **3**, 620
      cell wall deposition, **3**, 690
      evolution, **3**, 625
      heterogeneity, **3**, 692
angucyclines, structure, **1**, 482
Anguilla anguilla, prostaglandins, **1**, 236
Anguilla japonica, feeding attractants and stimulants, **8**, 417
Anguina agrostis, *Lolium rigidum* infection by, **8**, 177
angulatin, insecticidal activity, **8**, 344
angulatin A
   antifeedant activity, **8**, 308, 312
   occurrence, **8**, 312
Angulatus celastris
   angulatin A, **8**, 312
   celangulin, **8**, 312
Aniba megaphylla, (−)-megaphone, **1**, 677
anigorufone
   incorporation experiments, **1**, 404
   occurrence, **1**, 766
anigorufone, hydroxy-, occurrence, **1**, 766
Anigozanthos preissii, anigorufone, **1**, 404
aniline, 2,4-dinitro-, as intramolecular fluorescence quencher, **7**, 208
aniline hydrochloride, *N*,*N*-dimethyl-, as activator, **7**, 130
anilinium trichloroacetate, *N*-methyl-, as coupling reaction activator, **7**, 138
anilinoacridines
   applications, intercalating agents, **7**, 606
   as DNA topoisomerase II inhibitors, **7**, 606
animals
   desaturation in, **1**, 35
   fatty acid synthases, **1**, 30
   glycogen, **3**, 443
      structure, **3**, 442
   health, effects of isoflavonoids on, **1**, 782
   hydroxymethylglutaryl-CoA reductases, **2**, 27
   metal requirements, **4**, 75
   trans-methylation studies, **3**, 643
   non-mammalian, oxylipins, **1**, 236
   stearoyl-CoA desaturases, **1**, 39
anisatin, as seed toxin, **8**, 168
p-anisidine, staining, **3**, 709
anisoin, cleavage, **3**, 395
anisole, 2,4-dichloro-, as antiauxin, **8**, 34
anisole, 3,4-dichloro-, structure, **8**, 34
(−)-anisomycin, biosynthesis, **4**, 30
p-anisyldiphenylmethyl groups, in oligonucleotide synthesis, **7**, 107

o-anisyl-1-naphthylmethyl, as trityl protecting groups, **7**, 126

p-anisyl-1-naphthylphenylmethyl, as trityl protecting groups, **7**, 126

Annelida, oxylipins, **1**, 249.

Annona muricata, squamosin, **8**, 305

Annona squamosa, squamosin, **8**, 305

annonene, synthesis, **8**, 317

annonin I *see* squamosin

annonins, insecticidal activity, **8**, 305

Anobium punctatum, pheromones, **8**, 244

Anogeissus acuminata, anolignans, **1**, 703

anolignan A, HIV-1 reverse transcriptase inhibition, **1**, 703

anolignan B
   HIV-1 reverse transcriptase inhibition, **1**, 703
   structure, **1**, 672

Anomala spp.
   (4*R*,5*Z*)-5-dodecen-4-olide, **8**, 215
   pheromones, **8**, 212

Anomala actiescostata, pheromones, **8**, 216

Anomala albopilosa
   (4*R*,5*Z*)-5-dodecen-4-olide, **8**, 215
   (*E*)-2-nonenal, **8**, 212
   (*E*)-2-nonen-1-ol, **8**, 212

Anomala cuprea, (*R*)-4-dodecanolide, **8**, 215

Anomala orientalis
   (*E*)-7-tetradecen-2-one, **8**, 216
   (*Z*)-7-tetradecen-2-one, **8**, 216

Anomala osakana
   pheromones, **8**, 12
   (*S*)-5-tetradecen-4-olide, **8**, 216

Anomala rufocuprea, methyl (*Z*)-5-tetradecenoate, **8**, 216

Anopheles spp., diuretic hormone, **8**, 300

ANS *see* anthocyanidin synthase (ANS)

ansamycins, structure, **1**, 527

ansatrienin A
   occurrence, **1**, 71
   structure, **1**, 527

anserine, methyl group, **3**, 643

Antelaea azadirachta see Azadirachta indica

antelopes
   2-isobutyl-1,3-thiazole, occurrence, **8**, 220
   3-methyl-2-buten-1-ol, **8**, 220
   see also springbok antelopes

antheridial formation, studies, **8**, 56

antheridic acid
   activity, **8**, 56
   biosynthesis, **2**, 237, **8**, 57
   use of term, **8**, 55

antheridiogens
   biosynthesis, **8**, 55, 57
   definition, **8**, 22
   occurrence, **8**, 55

Anthocerotae
   evolution, **1**, 645
   lignans, **1**, 645
   and lignin evolution, **3**, 624

anthocyanidins
   biosynthesis, **1**, 717
   from, flavan-3,4-diols, **1**, 718
   and pollination, **8**, 158

anthocyanidin synthase (ANS)
   biochemistry, **1**, 730
   cDNA clones, isolation, **1**, 730
   genetics, **1**, 730
   molecular biology, **1**, 730

anthocyanins
   antioxidant activity, **3**, 792
   biological activity, **1**, 19
   biosynthesis, **1**, 732, 737
   early studies, **1**, 715
   occurrence

blue-flowered plant species, **8**, 158
   blue fruits, **8**, 164
   fruits, **8**, 164
   sinapoylation, **1**, 741
   structure, **1**, 715
   as substrates, **1**, 809
   vacuolar uptake, **1**, 809

Anthonomus grandis, phagostimulants, **8**, 229

Anthophoridae
   geranic acid, **8**, 223
   nerolic acid, **8**, 223

anthosamines, occurrence, **8**, 442

Anthosigmella aff. *raromicrosclera*, anthosamines, **8**, 442

anthracenediones
   applications, intercalating agents, **7**, 606
   as DNA topoisomerase II inhibitors, **7**, 606

anthracenes, as DNA topoisomerase II inhibitors, **7**, 606

anthracycline, biosynthesis, **1**, 432

anthracycline antibiotics
   applications, antitumor agents, **3**, 324
   biological activity, **3**, 324
   biosynthesis, genetics, **3**, 349

anthracyclines
   applications, **7**, 428
   as DNA topoisomerase II inhibitors, **7**, 605
   formaldehyde-mediated covalent attachment to DNA, **7**, 530
   intercalation, **7**, 446
   isolation, **4**, 200
   use in pyrimidine triplex stabilization, **7**, 467
   x-ray crystal structure, **7**, 436

anthracyclinones, applications, antineoplastic agents, **1**, 2

anthramycin
   applications, antibiotics, **7**, 497
   cardiotoxicity, **7**, 497
   occurrence, **1**, 566

anthranilate
   biosynthesis, via shikimate pathway, **1**, 574
   N-labeled, **8**, 34

anthranilate, *N*-(2-methoxyacrylyl), intercalation, **7**, 574

anthranilate, phosphoribosyl- (PRA), biosynthesis, **4**, 7

anthranilate synthase(s)
   functions, **4**, 5
   regulatory mechanisms, **5**, 344

anthranilic acid, biosynthesis, **1**, 611, **3**, 395

anthranilic acid, 6-hydroxy-, as starting material, for sarubicin A, **1**, 617

anthrapyrazoles, structural features, **7**, 606

anthraquinoids, biosynthesis, **1**, 429

anthraquinone, 9-amino-1,4,6-trihydroxy-, in dynemicin A, **7**, 574

anthraquinone, 1,3,6,8-tetrahydroxy-, metabolites, **1**, 446

anthraquinones
   biosynthesis, **1**, 617, **7**, 554
   DNA binding studies, **7**, 468
   from, anthrones, **1**, 420
   migration, **1**, 455
   photochemical DNA damage, **7**, 544
   as starting materials, for benzophenones, **1**, 432
   threading intercalating agents, **7**, 451

Anthrenus spp., female sex pheromones, **8**, 213

Anthrenus flavipes, (*Z*)-3-decenoic acid, **8**, 213

Anthrenus sarnicus, pheromones, **8**, 214

Anthrenus verbasci
   (*E*)-5-undecenoic acid, **8**, 214
   (*Z*)-5-undecenoic acid, **8**, 214

Anthrobacter globiformis, 1,4-α-glucan branching enzymes, **3**, 444

anthrone oxygenase(s), mechanisms, **1**, 432, 11

anthrones, as starting materials, for anthraquinones, **1**, 420

D-antiarose, occurrence, **3**, 312, 313

antiasthmatic agents

leukotrienes, **1**, 197
lignans, **1**, 704
montelukast, **1**, 197
pranlukast, **1**, 197
seratrodast, **1**, 198
zafirlukast, **1**, 197
antiauxins
structure, **8**, 26
synthetic, **8**, 34
antibiotic resistance, mechanisms, **4**, 197
antibiotics
actinomycin D, **7**, 433, 529
altromycin B, **7**, 471
aminoglycosides, **6**, 193
anthramycin, **7**, 497
applications, DNA structure probes, **7**, 98
arugamycin, **7**, 351
autogenous, modification, **4**, 198
azinomycin B, **7**, 513
bacterial
biological activity, **3**, 323
deoxysugars, **3**, 312
bacterial resistance, **3**, 271, 5
barminomycin I, **7**, 500
benzoisochromanequinones, **3**, 354
biosynthesis, **1**, 840
genetics, **4**, 327
bioxalomycins, **7**, 499
C-1027, **7**, 554
calicheamicins, **7**, 554
carzinophilin, **7**, 513
CC-1065, **7**, 504
chalcomycin, **3**, 321
chromoproteins, **7**, 554
chrysomycin A, **7**, 545
clecarmycins, **7**, 510
cleomycin, **7**, 539
commercial, development, **4**, 200
cyanocyclines, **7**, 499
cyclopropane-containing, **7**, 504, 506
daunomycin, **7**, 527
definition, **8**, 2
deoxysugars, genetics, **3**, 349
discorhabdin A, **7**, 501
doxorubicin, **7**, 433, 527, 528
duocarmycin A, **7**, 505
duocarmycin SA, **7**, 505
dynemicins, **7**, 554, 574
early studies, **4**, 160
ecteinascidin 743, **7**, 501
elsamicin, **7**, 529
epinardin D, **7**, 501
erythromycins, **1**, 496
esperamicins, **7**, 554, 571
fosfomycin, **5**, 53, 62, 66
gilvocarcin V, **7**, 544, 545
hedamycin, **7**, 509
kapurimycin A3, **7**, 510
kedarcidin, **7**, 554, 575
kinamycins, **7**, 541
lankamycin, **3**, 321, 322
leptosins, **7**, 527
lissoclinotoxin A, **7**, 527
maduropeptin, **7**, 554, 580
makaluvamine F, **7**, 501
mitomycin C, **7**, 529
myrocin C, **7**, 506
namenamicin, **7**, 554, 581
naphthyridinomycin, **7**, 499
neocarzinostatin, **7**, 554
neomycin, mechanisms, **7**, 433
nogalamycin, **7**, 351, 433, 437
ovalicin, **2**, 165

oxazolidine, DNA adduct formation, **7**, 499
paromomycin, **6**, 193
phleomycin, **7**, 539
platomycins, **7**, 539
pluramycins, **7**, 471, 508
protein, **7**, 558
quinocarcin, **7**, 500
ravidomycin, **7**, 545
renieramycins, **7**, 497
safracins, **7**, 497
saframycin A, **7**, 529
saframycins, **7**, 497
secretion
extracellular, **4**, 198
intracellular, **4**, 198
self-resistance, **4**, 196
sequential screening, **4**, 211
sibiromycin, **7**, 497
sirodesmins, **7**, 527
streptomycin, mechanisms, **7**, 433
streptonigrin, **7**, 528
tallysomycin, **7**, 539
tetrazomine, **7**, 500
varacin, **7**, 527
victomycin, **7**, 539
YA-56, **7**, 539
zorbamycin, **7**, 539
zorbonamycins, **7**, 539
see also anthracycline antibiotics; antitumor
antibiotics; enediyne antibiotics; β-lactam
antibiotics; orthosomycin antibiotics; penicillins;
peptide antibiotics; quinoxaline antibiotics
antibodies
active, **5**, 442
aldolase, mechanisms, **5**, 438
antiphosphonamidate, **5**, 430
antiphosphonate, **5**, 430
binding affinities, **5**, 441
as entropy traps, **5**, 423
and enzymes compared, **5**, 441
esterolytic, **5**, 430
monoclonal, **7**, 570
phosphonates, **5**, 442
progesterone-binding, **5**, 442
see also catalytic antibodies; Diels–Alderase antibodies
antibodies, anti-idiotype, isolation, **8**, 64
antibody 1E9
catalysis, **5**, 429
sequencing, **5**, 429
antibody 1F7
Fab' binding pocket, **5**, 364
structure, **5**, 364
studies, **5**, 425
antibody 13G5, functions, **5**, 430
antibody 17E8
active site residues, **5**, 436
catalysis, **5**, 434
characterization, **5**, 434
mechanisms, **5**, 436
mutants, **5**, 436
antibody 33F12
catalysis, **5**, 439
crystal structure, **5**, 440
antibody 38C2, catalysis, **5**, 439
antibody 39A11
binding, **5**, 428
sequencing, **5**, 429
structure, **5**, 428
antibody 43C9
active site residues, **5**, 436
amide cleavage, **5**, 437
mechanisms, **5**, 436
antibody 48G7

characterization, **5**, 434
efficiency
 catalytic, **5**, 434
 chemical, **5**, 434
antibody catalysis
 applications, **5**, 423
 characterization, **5**, 424
 development, **5**, 423
 efficiency, **5**, 423, 441
 future research, **5**, 441, 443
 mechanisms, **5**, **423–445**
  aldol condensations, **5**, 437
  Claisen rearrangements, **5**, 424
  cycloaddition reactions, **5**, 428
  Diels–Alder reactions, **5**, 428
  hydrolytic reactions, **5**, 430
  oxy-Cope rearrangement, **5**, 426
  pericyclic reactions, **5**, 424
 and product inhibition, **5**, 428
 rate enhancements, **5**, 423
antibody catalysts
 design, strategies, **5**, 425
 esterases, **5**, 431
 future research, **5**, 442
 mechanisms, **5**, 423
 phosphodiester linkage cleavage, **6**, 95
 selectivity, **5**, 423
 see also catalytic antibodies
antibody CNJ206
 catalytic efficiency, **5**, 434
 characterization, **5**, 434
antibody D2.3
 catalysis, **5**, 432
 complexation, **5**, 432
 efficiency, chemical, **5**, 434
 generation, **5**, 431
 substrates, **5**, 433
 x-ray crystal structure, **5**, 431
antibody D2.4, catalysis, **5**, 433
antibody D2.5, catalysis, **5**, 433
antibody DB3, sequencing, **5**, 429
antibody–DNA interactions, disulfide hairpin, **7**, 363
anticytokinins
 development, **8**, 67
 flowering induction, **8**, 69
 lateral bud studies, **8**, 68
 see also cytokinins
antidepressant agents, lignans, **1**, 704
antidiabetic drugs, nojirimycins, **3**, 143
antifeedants
 activity, in marine organisms, **8**, 459
 insects, mechanisms, **8**, 303
 lignans, **1**, 694
 marine algae, **8**, 459
 in octocorals, **8**, 470
 polygodial, **8**, 462
 polyhydroxysteroids, **8**, 471
 in Porifera, **8**, 465
 red alga, **8**, 461
 seasonal variations, **8**, 316
antifouling agents
 occurrence, **8**, 438
 organotins, **8**, 431
 toxicity, **8**, 431
antifungal agents
 arbutin, **8**, 186
 avenacin A, **8**, 183
 avenacin B, **8**, 183
 avenacoside A, **8**, 183
 avenacoside B, **8**, 183
 blasticidin S, **3**, 339
 camellidin I, **8**, 183
 camellidin II, **8**, 183

episclareol, **8**, 181
α-hederin, **8**, 183
β-hederin, **8**, 183
hydroquinone, **8**, 186
2-ketoepimanool, **8**, 181
lipophilic, in plants, **8**, 181
long-chain fatty acids, **8**, 183
naftifine, **2**, 247, 276
sakurasosaponin, **8**, 183
sclareol, **8**, 181
in symbiosis, **8**, 429
terbinafine, **2**, 247
antigen-carrier lipid (ACL), identification, **3**, 209
antigene strategy, **7**, 466
O-antigen ligase complexes, structure, **3**, 227
O-antigen polymerase, catalysis, **3**, 211
antigens, *O*-glycans, **3**, 71, 78
O-antigen(s)
 deoxysugars, genetics, **3**, 345
 lipopolysaccharides, **3**, 180, 322
antiinfective agents
 azicemicins, **7**, 514
 azomycin, **7**, 521
 myxin, **7**, 532
 norfloxacin, **7**, 462
 pluramycins, **7**, 508
 quinolones, **7**, 462
antiinflammatory agents
 development, **1**, 257
 lignans, **1**, 704
 manoalide, **8**, 521
 pseudopterosin C, **8**, 521
antijuvenile hormones
 applications, **8**, 303
 occurrence, **8**, 278
antillatoxin
 occurrence, **8**, 608
 structure, **8**, 608
antimalarial agents, quinacrine, **7**, 428
anti-Markovnikov addition, in oxidosqualene cyclization, **2**, 280
anti-Markovnikov cyclization, in (−)-camphene biosynthesis, **2**, 141
antimicrobial activity, eudistomins, **8**, 525
antimicrobial defense, constitutive, **8**, 181
antimitotic agents, curacin A, **8**, 608
antineoplastic agents
 actinomycin D, **7**, 429, 607
 9-anilinoacridine, **7**, 606
 anthracyclinones, **1**, 2
 aplyronine A, **8**, 521
 bisanthracycline, **7**, 451
 bisantrene, **7**, 440, 606
 bleomycin, **7**, 536
 bryostatin I, clinical trials, **8**, 521
 camptothecin, **7**, 594
 daunomycin, **7**, 527
 didemnin B, clinical trials, **8**, 521
 ditercalinium, **7**, 444
 doxorubicin, **7**, 594, 527
 dual inhibitors, **7**, 607
 ecteinascidins, **8**, 521
 etoposide, **7**, 594
 intoplicine, **7**, 607
 lignans, **1**, 698
 mitomycin C, **7**, 514
 myrocin C, **7**, 506
 pluramycins, **7**, 508
 quinobenzoxazines, **7**, 462
 quinocarcin, **7**, 500
 saintopin, **7**, 607
 taxol, **2**, 220
 tetrazomine, **7**, 500

varacin, **7**, 527
antioxidant activity, and chemoprotection, **1**, 700
antiphytoalexins, occurrence, **8**, 191
Antirrhinum majus
  chalcone synthase, **1**, 758
    genes, **1**, 755
  flavone synthases, **1**, 724
  6′-hydroxychalcones, **1**, 736
antisense genes
  1-aminocyclopropane-1-carboxylate oxidase, **8**, 98
  1-aminocyclopropane-1-carboxylate synthase, **8**, 98
  peptide nucleic acids, **6**, 95
antisense mRNA, expression, **2**, 212, **3**, 457
antisense oligonucleotides, **7**, 142
  with altered DNA backbones, **7**, **285–311**
    design issues, **7**, 306
    early studies, **7**, 289
    future research, **7**, 307
  amide linkages, **7**, 300
  amine linkages, **7**, 301
  applications, **7**, 286
  binding, with mRNA, **7**, 286
  binding affinity, assessment, **7**, 288
  carbamate linkages, **7**, 301
  carbon linkages, **7**, 305
  cellular uptake, **7**, 289
  chimeric, **7**, 287, 294
  classification, **7**, 289
  definitions, **7**, 286
  dephosphono linkages, **7**, 298
  ether linkages, **7**, 305
  formacetal linkages, **7**, 305
  guanidine linkages, **7**, 300
  hydroxylamine linkages, **7**, 302
  melting temperature, **7**, 288
  MMI linkages, **7**, 302
  nitrogen-containing linkages, **7**, 299
  non-phosphate backbone linkages, properties, **7**, 299
  non-phosphate sugar linkages, **7**, 306
  oxygen-containing linkages, **7**, 304
  phosphate-modified linkages, **7**, 290
    anionic, **7**, 291
    cationic, **7**, 294
    neutral, **7**, 294
  phosphodiester linkages, **7**, 287
  silicon-containing linkages, **7**, 303
  sulfide linkages, **7**, 304
  sulfonamide linkages, **7**, 304
  sulfonate linkages, **7**, 304
  sulfone linkages, **7**, 304
  sulfur-containing linkages, **7**, 304
  synthesis
    automated, **7**, 285
    economic factors, **7**, 289
    large-scale, **7**, 289
  Tm values, **7**, 288
  urea linkages, **7**, 301
  use of term, **7**, 286
antisense RNA, studies, **3**, 455, **6**, 75
antisense strand *see* noncoding strand
Anti-Shine–Dalgarno (ASD) sequence, **6**, 202
antitrypanosomal agents, berenil, **7**, 452, 459
antitumor agents
  anthracycline antibiotics, **3**, 324
  bleomycin, **7**, 186
  calicheamicin γ_1^I, **3**, 326
  camptothecins, **7**, 594
  coumarins, **1**, 624
  cucurbitacins, **8**, 320
  daunomycin, **3**, 324
  doxorubicin, **3**, 324, **7**, 594
  ecteinascidins, **8**, 521
  enediyne antibiotics, **1**, 14, 557

etoposide, **7**, 594
  leptosins, **8**, 603
  lignans, **1**, 701
  myrocin C, **7**, 506
  theopederins, **8**, 581
antitumor antibiotics, DNA strand breakage induction, **7**, 420
ant lions
  nerol oxide, **8**, 225
  see also Grocus bore
ants
  caryophyllene oxide, **8**, 228
  (*S*)-2,3-dihydrofarnesol, **8**, 227
  2,6-dimethyl-5-hepten-1-ol, **8**, 233
  Dufour's gland secretions, **8**, 237
  formic acid, **8**, 209
  10-formyltetrahydrofolate, **8**, 209
  geranic acid, **8**, 223
  lactones, **8**, 226
  mellein, **8**, 210, 213
  5,10-methylenetetrahydrofolate, **8**, 209
  6-methyl-5-hepten-2-one, **8**, 232
  methyl 6-methylsalicylate, **8**, 211
  monoterpenes, **8**, 222
  nerolic acid, **8**, 223
  perillene, **8**, 226
  polyketides, **8**, 211
  protein venoms, **8**, 359
  sex pheromones, **8**, 214
  trail pheromones, **8**, 198, 210
  tridecane, **8**, 214
  (*Z*)-4-tridecene, **8**, 214
  undecane, **8**, 214
  venoms, **8**, 356
    alkaloids, **8**, 357
  see also Aenictus rotundatus; *Bothroponera soror*;
    Camponotus spp.; *Crematogaster scutellaris*;
    Ectatomma ruidum; *Formica* spp.; *Iridomyrmex*
    spp.; *Iridomyrmex humilis*; *Labidus praedator*;
    Lasius spp.; leaf-cutting ants; *Leptogenys*
    diminuta; *Monomorium* spp.; *Myrmica* spp.;
    Myrmicaria eumenoides; *Oecophylla longinoda*;
    Pharaoh's ants; *Tapinoma* spp.
Aonidiella aurantii, sex pheromones, **8**, 235
Aonidiella citrina, pheromones, **8**, 234
AOP *see* propanoic acid, β-aminooxy- (AOP)
AOPP *see* propanoic acid, L-2-aminooxy-3-
    phenylpropanoic acid (AOPP)
AOS *see* allene-oxide cyclase
6-APA *see* penicillanic acid, 6-amino- (6-APA)
apa-2 genes, cloning, **1**, 462
apamine
  in honeybee venom, **8**, 355
  neurotoxicity, **8**, 355
Apex *see* methoprene
Aphaenogaster spp.
  anabaseine, **8**, 347
  venoms, **8**, 358
Aphaenogaster fulva
  anabaseine, **8**, 358
  anabasine, **8**, 358
Aphaenogaster tennesseensis
  anabaseine, **8**, 358
  anabasine, **8**, 358
aphanorphine, biosynthesis, **4**, 30
aphidicolin
  biosynthesis, **2**, 239
  DNA polymerase α inhibition, **7**, 597
  as DNA polymerase-α inhibitor, **1**, 127
  occurrence, **2**, 239
  phytotoxicity, **8**, 179
aphids
  alarm pheromones, **8**, 221

(*E*)-*β*-farnesene, **8**, 227
resistance, and tannins, **8**, 142
rotenone toxicity, **8**, 341
sex pheromones, **8**, 226
see also *Alloxysta victrix*; *Megoura viciae*;
   Rhopalosiphum padi
Aphis gossypii, activity against, **8**, 305
Aphis nerii, sequestration, **8**, 363
Aphis rumicis, anabasine sulfate toxicity, **8**, 348
Aphomia gularis, aphrodisiac of, **8**, 212
Aphomia sociella, pheromones, **8**, 213
Aph proteins, AphD, occurrence, **8**, 383
aphylline, occurrence, **8**, 344
Apiaceae, coumarins, **1**, 623
apical dominance, effect of cytokinins on, **8**, 59
apical dormancy, effects of auxin on, **8**, 30
apigenin 6-*C*-glucoside see isovitexin
apigenin 7-glucoside
   roles
      in legume–*Rhizobium* symbiosis, **8**, 173
      in node gene expression, **8**, 173
apigenin 7-*O*-glucoside, NMR analysis, **1**, 741
apigenin 7-*O*-*β*-glucoside, as substrate, **1**, 809
apigenin 8-*C*-glucoside see vitexin
apiogalacturonans, occurrence, **3**, 499
apiole, occurrence, **8**, 336
apioside, diphyllin acetyl, antiinflammatory activity, **1**, 705
apiosyltransferase(s)
   characterization, **3**, 517
   roles, in pectin biosynthesis, **3**, 511
Apis cerana, melittin, **8**, 355
Apis dorsata
   (2*E*)-2-decenyl acetate, **8**, 213
   melittin, structure, **8**, 355
Apis florea
   (2*E*)-2-decenyl acetate, **8**, 213
   melittin, structure, **8**, 355
Apis mellifera
   (*Z*)-11-icosen-1-ol, **8**, 218
   makisterone A, **8**, 279
   melittin, **8**, 355
   venom, **8**, 354
      characterization, **8**, 355
      constituents, **8**, 355
      phospholipase A₂, **5**, 105
Apium graveolens, coumarins, **1**, 625
Aplidium albicans, didemnins, **8**, 530
Aplidium longithorax
   longithorone, **1**, 377
   longithorone A, **3**, 532
Aplidium multiplicatum, shimofuridin A, **8**, 532
aplydilactone, biosynthesis, **1**, 244
aplyronine A
   applications, antineoplastic agents, **8**, 521
   enantioselective total synthesis, **8**, 521
   occurrence, **8**, 521
Aplysia spp., aplysiatoxins, **8**, 603
Aplysia californica
   halogenated monoterpenes, **2**, 106
   hepoxillin A₃, **1**, 245
   prostaglandins, **1**, 245
   signal transduction, studies, **1**, 245
Aplysia dactylomela
   dactomelynes, **1**, 303
   dactylyne, **1**, 303
   isodactylyne, **1**, 303
Aplysia juliana, feeding stimulants, **8**, 419
Aplysia kurodai
   aplydilactone, **1**, 244
   aplyronine A, **8**, 521
   aplysin-20, **2**, 225
aplysiatoxins, occurrence, **8**, 603

aplysin-20, occurrence, **2**, 225
apoaequorin, occurrence, **8**, 447
APOBEC-1
   catalysis, mechanisms, **6**, 100
   cloning, **5**, 94
   mRNA editing, **6**, 98
   substrates, **6**, 98
apoB editing catalytic subunit see APOBEC-1
Apocynaceae
   indole alkaloid studies, **4**, 113, 119
   isoflavonoids, **1**, 774
   strychnos alkaloids, **4**, 49
Apogon endekataenia, *Penicillium fellutanum* in, **8**, 599
apoII mRNA
   in chicken, **6**, 214
   degradation, **6**, 213
apolipoprotein B
   mRNA editing
      localization, **6**, 99
      occurrence, **6**, 99
      studies, **5**, 94, **6**, 98
apolipoprotein B-48 protein, roles, in lipoprotein
      metabolism, **6**, 99
apolipoprotein B-100 protein, roles, in lipoprotein
      metabolism, **5**, 94, **6**, 99
apolipoproteins, roles, in mammals, **6**, 99
aponeocarzinostatin, proteolytic activity, **7**, 559
apoprotein, **7**, 558
   proteolytic activity, **7**, 582
   roles, in enediyne antibiotics, **7**, 582
apoptosis
   bcl-2 and, **7**, 597
   and enediyne antibiotics, **7**, 582
   p53 and, **7**, 597
   topoisomerase-directed agents and, **7**, 597
aporphines, biosynthesis, **4**, 40
apotrichothecenes, occurrence, **2**, 203
APP see amyloid precursor protein (APP)
apple moth see *Epiphyas postvittana*
APS kinase, activity, **1**, 331
aptamers
   applications
      in diagnostics, **6**, 226
      pharmaceutical, **7**, 640
      in therapeutics, **6**, 226
   characterization, **7**, 638
   footprinting experiments, **7**, 634
   in vitro selection, **6**, 225
   isolation, **6**, 226
   nucleic acid-binding, **7**, 629
   nucleic acid vs. protein, **7**, 638
   protein-binding, **7**, 626
   selection, **6**, 118
   SELEX studies, **7**, 624
   structure, **7**, 627
      guanine–quadruplex, **7**, 627
   synthesis, **7**, 625
   targets, **6**, 226
   use of term, **7**, 617
aquacob(I)alamin adenosyltransferase see cob(I)alamin
      adenosyltransferase
aquatic organisms, prostaglandins, reviews, **1**, 208
aquatic toad see *Xenopus laevis*
aqueous ethanol
   antibacterial properties, **8**, 470
   occurrence, **8**, 470
   protein phosphorylation modulation, **8**, 470
Arabidopsis spp.
   cytokinin-resistant mutants, **8**, 65
   desaturases, **1**, 40
   expressed sequence tag databases, **3**, 611
   ferulate 5-hydroxylase, **3**, 671
   *GA*4 genes, **8**, 53

gai genes, **8**, 54
gibberellin 20-oxidase, cDNA cloning, **8**, 52
isopentenyl diphosphate isomerases, cDNA cloning, **2**, 73
lignin studies, **3**, 659
mutants, **1**, 779
NADPH reductase, **1**, 817
Arabidopsis thaliana
brassinosteroid biosynthesis, **8**, 105
caffeoyl-CoA *O*-methyltransferase, **3**, 671
cDNA cloning, **2**, 250
cDNA expression, **1**, 742
cellulose biosynthesis, **3**, 581
chalcone synthase
chemically induced mutant, **1**, 759
genes, **1**, 755
genetics, **1**, 789
chorismate mutase, **5**, 347
trans-cinnamate 4-monooxygenase, localization, **3**, 669
cinnamyl-alcohol dehydrogenases, **3**, 676
4-coumarate-CoA ligase, **3**, 674
cycloartenol cyclase, cDNA cloning, **2**, 305
*fah*1 mutant, **3**, 642
flavonol synthase, **1**, 727
gene cloning, **2**, 224
and characterization, **2**, 307
geranylgeranyl diphosphate synthase, gene cloning, **2**, 87
geranyl*trans*transferase, **2**, 82
gibberellin-deficient mutants, **8**, 47
gibberellin 20-oxidases, **2**, 236
glucose-1-phosphate adenylyltransferase, **3**, 451
glutamyl-tRNA reductase, **4**, 68
hydroxymethylglutaryl-CoA reductases, isozymes, **2**, 39
kaurene synthase A, **2**, 211
lupeol cyclase, cDNA cloning, **2**, 307
mutants, **3**, 472
oxidosqualene-cycloartenol cyclase, **2**, 282
phenylalanine ammonia-lyase, **3**, 659
gene promoter expression, **3**, 667
sequence homology, **1**, 654
stomatal aperture regulation, **8**, 82
thiohydroximate *β*-D-glucosyltransferase, **1**, 859
arabinans, structure, **3**, 499
D-arabinitol, 1,4-dideoxy-1,4-imino- (D-AB1)
insecticidal activity, **3**, 141
structure, **3**, 130
arabinogalactan proteins (AGPs)
characterization, **3**, 610
localization, **3**, 502
arabinogalactans
structure, **3**, 499
Type I, **3**, 502
Type II, **3**, 502
arabinose, coupling, **1**, 331
D-arabinose, reactions, with pyruvate, **3**, 373
L-arabinose, 3-*O*-(3-*O*-feruloyl-*α*-L-arabinofuranosyl)-, occurrence, **3**, 697
arabinose 5-phosphate, reactions, with phospho*enol*pyruvate, **1**, 580, **3**, 387
arabinosyltransferase(s)
activity, reduction, **3**, 520
characterization, **3**, 515, 605
inhibition, **3**, 520
roles, in pectin biosynthesis, **3**, 511
arabis mosaic virus (ArMV), satellite RNA, hairpin ribozymes, **6**, 247
Araceae, 2,5-dihydroxymethyl-3,4-dihydroxypyrrolidine, **3**, 134
arachidonate cascade, mechanisms, **1**, 8, 255
arachidonate 5-lipoxygenase
catalysis, **1**, 263

mutation studies, **1**, 264
arachidonate 8-lipoxygenase, catalysis, **1**, 265
arachidonate 12-lipoxygenase, catalysis, **1**, 264
arachidonate 15-lipoxygenase
activity, **1**, 265
catalysis, **1**, 265
arachidonate:oxygen 5-oxidoreductase *see* arachidonate 5-lipoxygenase
arachidonate:oxygen 8-oxidoreductase *see* arachidonate 8-lipoxygenase
arachidonate:oxygen 12-oxidoreductase *see* arachidonate 12-lipoxygenase
arachidonate:oxygen 15-oxidoreductase *see* arachidonate 15-lipoxygenase
arachidonic acid
in 1-alkyl-2-acylglycerophosphocholine, **1**, 291
binding, **5**, 247
biosynthesis, **1**, 255
metabolism, **1**, 249, 256
occurrence, **1**, 209, 212, **8**, 423, 479
oxidation, **1**, 160
oxygenation, **5**, 233, 240, 244
pools, **5**, 256
roles
in eicosanoid biosynthesis, **1**, 160
in jasmonic acid biosynthesis, **1**, 2
in prostaglandin biosynthesis, **1**, 163
slow reacting substance of anaphylaxis stimulation, **1**, 168
as starting material, for leukotrienes, **1**, 10
structure, **1**, 160
arachidonic acid, 13-hydroxy- (13-HAA), occurrence, **1**, 222
arachidonic acid cascade
future research, **1**, 283
molecular evolution of proteins in, **1**, **273–284**
use of term, **1**, 160
arachidonyl-CoA synthase *see* long-chain-fatty-acid-CoA ligase
Arachis hypogaea
germination inhibition, **1**, 695
stilbene synthase, **1**, 752, 753
Arachnida, oxylipins, **1**, 249
Aralia cordata, cinnamyl-alcohol dehydrogenases, **3**, 656, 676
arborescidines, occurrence, **8**, 528
arbutin, applications, antifungal agents, **8**, 186
L-arcanose, occurrence, **3**, 312, 322
Archaea
hydroxymethylglutaryl-CoA reductases, biosynthesis, **2**, 24
isoprenoid biosynthesis, **2**, 23
membrane phospholipids, **2**, 23
archangelolide, antifeedant activity, **8**, 308
archegonial formation, inhibition, **8**, 57
Arctia caja, 3,3-dimethylacryloylcholine, **8**, 353
(+)-arctigenin
biosynthesis, **1**, 667
occurrence, **1**, 645
(−)-arctigenin
biosynthesis, **1**, 662, 667
HIV-1 virus inhibition, **1**, 703
occurrence, **1**, 645, 662
Arctiidae
2-methylheptadecane, **8**, 249
pheromones, **8**, 207
sex pheromones, **8**, 247
see also Holomelinea spp.
(−)-arctiin
biosynthesis, **1**, 662
germination inhibitory activity, **1**, 695
occurrence, **1**, 662
Arctium lappa

(−)-arctiin, **1**, 695
lappaols, **1**, 688
secoisolariciresinol biosynthesis, **1**, 671
ardacin, biosynthesis, **1**, 483
ard genes, cloning, **1**, 483
arenastatin A
cytotoxicity, **8**, 613
occurrence, **8**, 613
structure, **8**, 613
arene-oxide hydratase(s) *see* epoxide hydrolase(s)
arene oxides, biosynthesis, **1**, 620
AREs *see* AU rich elements (AREs)
Arg-7, mutagenesis, **5**, 367
Arg-39
as general acid catalyst, **5**, 43
p*Ka*, **5**, 44
Arg-61, binding, **5**, 45
Arg-90, mutagenesis, **5**, 367
Arg-120, mutagenesis, **5**, 247
Arg-439, roles, in glycine carboxyl group binding, **4**, 67
arginine
deprotonation, **1**, 589
residues, **3**, 463
roles
in saxitoxin biosynthesis, **8**, 486
in tetrodotoxin biosynthesis, **8**, 482
L-[guanidino-^{13}C,^{15}N$_2$]arginine, structure, **1**, 150
arginine codons
AGA
editing, **6**, 103
in plant genes, **2**, 211
AGG, in plant genes, **2**, 211
Argyrotaenia velutinana
9-dodecenyl acetate, **8**, 205
11-dodecenyl acetate, **8**, 205
11-tetradecenyl acetate, **8**, 205
Ariflorae, cyclobutane lignans, **1**, 686
Ariocarpus kolschoubeyanus, hordenine, **8**, 336
Ariocarpus scapharostrus, hordenine, **8**, 336
Arisarum vulgare, irnine, **4**, 30
aristeromycin, structure, **1**, 152
aristolochene
from, farnesyl diphosphate, **2**, 179
occurrence, **2**, 177
as starting material, for PR-toxin, **2**, 178
(−)-aristolochene, occurrence, **2**, 177
epi-aristolochene
biosynthesis, **2**, 5, 181
from, farnesyl diphosphate, **2**, 181
5-*epi*-aristolochene synthase
from tobacco, **2**, 209
purification, **5**, 330
aristolochene synthase(s), **2**, 205
genes, isolation, **2**, 206
occurrence, **2**, 177, 205
purification, **5**, 330
epi-aristolochene synthase(s)
crystal structures, **2**, 5, 181, 196
occurrence, **2**, 181
presteady-state kinetics, **2**, 181, 194
Aristolochia spp., aristolochic acid, **7**, 522, **8**, 363
Aristolochia indica, (−)-aristolochene, **2**, 177
aristolochic acid
DNA adducts with, **7**, 522
insect sequestration, **8**, 152, 363
occurrence, **7**, 522
reductive activation, **7**, 522
arjunolic acid, as phytoalexin, **8**, 190
Armoracia spp., peroxidase, Compound I, **5**, 236
Armoracia lapathifolia
hydrogen peroxide biosynthesis, **3**, 721
sinigrin studies, **1**, 859
Armoracia rusticana, hairy roots, cytokinin-induced, **8**, 68

ArMV *see* arabis mosaic virus (ArMV)
arogenate
biosynthesis, **5**, 344
metabolic pool size, **3**, 627
arogenate dehydratase *see* carboxycyclohexadienyl
dehydratase
arogenate dehydrogenase *see* cyclohexadienyl
dehydrogenase
L-arogenate hydro-lyase (decarboxylating) *see*
carboxycyclohexadienyl dehydratase
L-arogenate:NAD$^+$ oxidoreductase *see* cyclohexadienyl
dehydrogenase
aro genes
*aro*1, encoding, **1**, 598
aroA
encoding, **1**, 593
mutation, **1**, 598
aroB, encoding, **1**, 593
aroC
cloning, **1**, 599
aroE, cloning, **1**, 591
aroL, cloning, **1**, 592
encoding, **1**, 575
aroid odors, analysis, **8**, 161
aromatases (AROs)
in bacterial aromatic polyketide synthases, **1**, 475
combinatorial analysis, **1**, 489
aromatic-L-amino-acid carboxy-lyase *see* aromatic-L-
amino-acid decarboxylase
aromatic-L-amino-acid decarboxylase
activity, **4**, 54, 135
in auxin biosynthesis, **8**, 33
as cytoplasmic enzyme, **4**, 125
localization, **4**, 124
regulatory mechanisms, **4**, 135
aromatic amino acids
biosynthesis, **4**, 2, **5**, 344
and herbicide developments, **4**, 9
overview, **4**, 1–11
regulatory mechanisms, **4**, 7
via shikimate pathway, **1**, 345, **4**, 2
in triterpene cyclases, **2**, 316
aromatic compounds, chlorinated, as environmental
pollutants, **5**, 410
aromatic compounds, nitro-, DNA damage induction, **7**,
521
aromatic compounds, planar, in water, dimerization, **7**,
432
aromatic compounds, unfused
binding to calf thymus DNA, **7**, 452
dichroism, **7**, 455
NMR spectra, **7**, 455
synthesis, **7**, 452
viscosity, **7**, 455
aromatic polyketides, unreduced, structure, **1**, 479
aromatic sensitizers, nitro-, misonidazole, **7**, 583
aromatic substitution, and deamination, **5**, 72
aromatic systems
small, partial intercalation, **7**, 463
unfused, base-pair propeller twist, **7**, 452
arom complex
3-dehydroquinate synthase functional domain, **1**,
582
functions, **1**, 575
occurrence, **1**, 575
overexpression, **1**, 598
arom genes
aromA, overexpression, **1**, 598
clusters, occurrence, **1**, 589
arom multifunctional enzyme
overexpression, **1**, 593
shikimate 5-dehydrogenase, **1**, 591
arom pentafunctional enzyme

catalysis, **1**, 598
occurrence, **1**, 598
arom pentafunctional protein, expression, **1**, 598
arom protein
overproduction, **1**, 591
sequencing, **1**, 590
AROs *see* aromatases (AROs)
Arothron nigropunctatus, tetrodotoxins, **8**, 482
Arp proteins, ArpA, occurrence, **8**, 382
ARR *see* anaerobic ribonucleotide reductase (ARR)
ARR-AE *see* anaerobic ribonucleotide reductase
activating enzyme (ARR-AE)
Arrhenius activation energy, nucleic acids, **7**, 41
arsenate, phosphatase inhibition, **5**, 158
artecanin, antifeedant activity, **8**, 308
Artemisia spp., cichoriin, **8**, 337
Artemisia absinthium
absinthin, **1**, 375
(+)-sabinene-3-hydroxylases, **2**, 145
Artemisia campestris, antifeedants, **8**, 338
Artemisia herba-alba, eudesmanolide adducts, **1**, 377
artemisia ketone, biosynthesis, **2**, 108
Arthrinium phaeosperumum, *threo*-3-hydroxyaspartic
acid, **3**, 405
Arthrobacter spp.
chlorobenzoyl CoA dehalogenase, **5**, 411
haloalcohol dehalogenases, **5**, 408
Arthrobacter viscosus
glucose-1-phosphate adenylyltransferase, **3**, 469
glycogen synthase, activity, **3**, 452
Arthropoda
chemical defense, **8**, 201
ecdysteroids, biosynthesis, **8**, 290
oxylipins, **1**, 246
see also *Balanus balanoides*; *Carcinus maenas*; *Elminius
modestus*; *Limulus polyphemus*; *Rhithropanopeus
harrisii*
arthropodin, occurrence, **8**, 435
artonin, structure, **1**, 385
arugamycin
applications, antibiotics, **7**, 351
structure, **7**, 351
arugomycin
binding, **3**, 324
2-deoxy-L-fucose, **3**, 313
L-diginose, **3**, 313
trideoxysugars, **3**, 322
Arum maculatum, volatiles, **8**, 161
Arundo donax, gramine, **8**, 336
arylalkylamines, as farnesyl-diphosphate
farnesyltransferase inhibitors, **2**, 258
arylamine synthase
catalysis, **5**, 347
regulatory mechanisms, **5**, 344
arylpyrone synthase, characterization, **1**, 765
AS *see* aggregation substance (AS)
asarone, as oviposition stimulant, **8**, 156
Asarum teitonense, asatone, **1**, 379
asatone, occurrence, **1**, 379
ASBV *see* avocado sunblotch viroid (ASBV)
ascaridole, biosynthesis, **2**, 146
ascarylose
biosynthesis, **3**, 335
pathways, **3**, 348
isolation, **3**, 346
occurrence, **3**, 192, 312, 313
asc genes
in 3,6-deoxysugar biosynthesis, **3**, 342
G+C content, **3**, 349
Ascidiacea
blood cells
homogenate, **8**, 524
sulfate accumulation, **8**, 524

β-carbolines, **8**, 525
chemical defense, mechanisms, **8**, 472
eudistomins, **8**, 525
symbiosis, **8**, 428
vanadium accumulation, **8**, 521
ESR studies, **8**, 523
in morula cells, **8**, 523
neutron-activation analysis, **8**, 522
in signet ring cells, **8**, 523
vanadocytes, **8**, 523
Ascidia gemmata
blood cells, vanadium accumulation, **8**, 524
vanadium concentrations, **8**, 523
ascidians *see* Ascidiacea
ascidiatrienolides, occurrence, **1**, 243
Asclepias spp., cardiac glycosides, **8**, 154
Asclepias curassavica
cardiac glycosides, **8**, 362
insect oviposition stimulants, **8**, 156
Asclepias syriaca, nicotine, **8**, 347
Ascochyta rabiei
effects on (−)-maackiain, **1**, 814
elicitors, **1**, 808
resistance, **1**, 795
solanapyrone A, **1**, 395
solanapyrone C, **1**, 395
Ascogaster reticulatus, (*Z*)-9-hexadecenal, **8**, 217
ascoglossan mollusk *see* *Cyerce cristallina*
Ascomycetes, polyketides, **1**, 410
ascomycin
biosynthesis, **1**, 75, 518
immunosuppressant activity, **1**, 518
ascoquinone A, occurrence, **1**, 417
ascorbate, superoxide production by, **7**, 540
ascorbate oxidase
homology, **1**, 435
x-ray crystal structure, **3**, 714
ASD sequence *see* Anti-Shine–Dalgarno (ASD) sequence
AsgA protein, phosphorelays, **8**, 406
asg genes, encoding, **8**, 406
asialofetuin, **3**, 119
Asian elephant *see* *Elephas maximus*
ASIF *see* accessible surface integrated field (ASIF)
A-signal, functions, **8**, 406
asimicin, occurrence, **8**, 305
Asimina triloba, asimicin, **8**, 305
ASP *see* amnesic shellfish poisoning (ASP)
Asp-38, identification, **5**, 39
Asp-84, in hydroxymethylbilane synthase, **4**, 82
Asp-84-Ala, properties, **4**, 84
Asp-84-Asn, properties, **4**, 84
Asp-84-Glu, x-ray crystal structure, **4**, 84
Asp-99
mutagenesis, **5**, 41
roles, in dienol stabilization, **5**, 41
Asp-279, mutagenesis, **4**, 67
asparagusic acid, biosynthesis, **1**, 860
Asparagus officinalis, seedlings, anticytokinin-induced
flowering, **8**, 69
aspartase *see* aspartate ammonia-lyase
aspartate
deamination, **3**, 632
in hydroxymethylglutaryl-CoA reductase catalysis, **2**,
34
aspartate, β-methyl-, deamination, **3**, 632
aspartate, β-methyl-3-hydroxy-, as substrate, **3**, 404
D-aspartate
biosynthesis, **3**, 265
residues, **3**, 248
D-aspartate, *N*-methyl- (NMDA)
blocking, by conantokins, **8**, 478
receptors, **6**, 103
L-aspartate, *erythro*-3-hydroxy-, as substrate, **3**, 404

aspartate ammonia-lyase, x-ray crystal structure, **3**, 634
aspartate racemase, occurrence, **3**, 257
aspartate 1-semialdehyde, as transaminating substrate, **4**, 70
aspartic acid, *erythro*-3-hydroxy-, structure, **4**, 280
aspartic acid, *threo*-3-hydroxy-, isolation, **3**, 405
aspen *see Populus* spp.
Aspergillus spp.
  β-amylase, **5**, 301
  averufanin, **1**, 453
  genes, structural, **1**, 466
  glucan 1,4-α-glucosidase, **5**, 301
  mutants, complementation, **1**, 461
  polyketides, **1**, 410
  tannin degradation, **3**, 819
Aspergillus flavus
  aflatoxin B$_1$, **1**, 443
  aflatoxins, **1**, 420
  anthraquinone metabolites, **1**, 446
  and turkey X disease, **1**, 444
Aspergillus fonsecaeus, fonsecin, **1**, 419
Aspergillus fumigatus
  fumagillin, **2**, 165
  fumiquinazolines, **8**, 603
Aspergillus methanolica
  dehydroquinase, **1**, 591
    type II, **1**, 588
Aspergillus nidulans
  acetate-CoA ligase, **4**, 256
  ACV synthetase, **1**, 840
  arom gene cluster, **1**, 589
  arom genes, **1**, 598
  arom pentafunctional enzyme, **1**, 598
  arom pentafunctional protein, **1**, 598
  ascoquinone A, **1**, 417
  dehydroquinase, **1**, 586, 589, 591
    type II, **1**, 588
  3-dehydroquinate synthase, **1**, 582
  dehydroshikimate dehydratase, **1**, 590
  gene homologues, **1**, 467
  genetics, **1**, 14
  β-lactam biosynthesis, gene clusters, **4**, 173
  mutations, **4**, 178
  pcb genes
    expression, **4**, 173, 177
    overexpression, **4**, 180
  penDE genes, **4**, 170
  penicillin biosynthesis, **4**, 267
  qut gene cluster, **1**, 589
  shikimate 5-dehydrogenase, **1**, 591
  shikimate kinase, **1**, 592
  shikimate pathway, **1**, 575
  stcP genes, disruptions, **1**, 463
  sterigmatocystin, **1**, 421
  trpC gene, **1**, 541
  wA gene, **1**, 417
Aspergillus nidulans CCAAT binding factor (AnCF), use of term, **4**, 177
Aspergillus niger
  β-*N*-acetylglucosamidase, **5**, 297
  activity against, **1**, 534, 691, 779
  biotin biosynthesis, **1**, 829
  (±)-eudesmin incubation, **1**, 692
  tannase, **3**, 819
Aspergillus nomius
  aflatoxin B$_1$, **1**, 443
  aflatoxins, **1**, 420
Aspergillus ochraceus, **8**, 213
Aspergillus oryzae
  adenosine deaminase, **5**, 74
  α-amylase, **5**, 298
  and α-amylase promoter, **1**, 414
  genetics, **1**, 14

sporogen-AO 1, **8**, 408
Aspergillus parasiticus
  aflatoxin B$_1$, **1**, 443
  aflatoxins, **1**, 420
  aflR genes, **1**, 467
  cell-free extracts, **1**, 457
  mutants, **1**, 446, 453
  norA genes, **1**, 467
  parasperone A, **1**, 417
Aspergillus saitoi, α1,2-mannosidases, **3**, 24
Aspergillus sojae, applications, **1**, 461
Aspergillus terreus
  aristolochene, **2**, 177
  aristolochene synthases, **2**, 205
  quadrone, **2**, 174
  seco-anthraquinones, **1**, 431
  terrecyclic acid, **2**, 174
Aspergillus terreus ATCC 20542, lovastatin, **1**, 422
Aspergillus variecolor, andibenin B, **1**, 378
Aspergillus versicolor, sterigmatocystin, **1**, 445
Aspidiotus nerii, sequestration, **8**, 363
aspirin *see* acetylsalicylic acid
Asp residues, DDTA motif, mutation, **2**, 315
assassin bug *see Pristhesancus plagipennis*
astaxanthin
  accumulation, **2**, 335
  in bacteria, **2**, 344
  biosynthesis, **2**, 344
  chemical synthesis, **2**, 347
asthma
  mediation, **1**, 160, 168
  role of platelet-activating factor in, **1**, 298
Astilbe chinensis, phenylalanine ammonia-lyase, localization, **3**, 662
Astragalus spp.
  selenium concentrations, **4**, 357
  swainsonine, **3**, 140
Astragalus lentiginosus, swainsonine, excretion, **3**, 141
Astragalus oxyphysus, swainsonine, **3**, 134
astringency, development, **3**, 791
astringin, as allelopathic agent, **8**, 169
Atapozoa spp.
  chemical defense, **8**, 472
  larvae, bacterial symbionts, **8**, 472
Atelops chiriquiensis, chiriquitoxin, **8**, 482
Athalia rosae, feeding stimulation, **8**, 317
atherosclerosis
  etiology, **3**, 195
  and high fat diet, **3**, 792
  and lipoprotein overproduction, **5**, 94
  phosphatidylcholine roles in, **1**, 298
A,T-hook peptides, **7**, 486
ent-atisir-15-ene, biosynthesis, **2**, 230
ent-atisir-16-ene, biosynthesis, **2**, 230
ATL *see* adult T-cell leukemia (ATL)
ATP *see* adenosine 5′-triphosphate (ATP)
ATP:adenosine 5′-phosphotransferase *see* adenosine kinase
ATP:AMP phosphotransferase *see* adenylate kinase
ATPase *see* adenosine 5′-triphosphatase (ATPase)
H$^+$-ATPase, effects of auxins on, **8**, 31
ATP-binding consensus motifs, A and B sites, **3**, 213
ATP:cob(I)alamin *Co*β-adenosyltransferase *see* cob(I)alamin adenosyltransferase
ATP:phosphorylase-*b* phosphotransferase *see* phosphorylase kinase
ATP pyrophosphate-lyase (cyclizing) *see* adenylate cyclase
ATP:pyruvate 2-*O*-phosphotransferase *see* pyruvate kinase
ATP:shikimate 3-phosphotransferase(s) *see* shikimate kinase(s)
ATP:sulfate adenylyltransferase *see* sulfate adenylyltransferase

ATP-sulfurylase *see* sulfate adenylyltransferase
ATP:undecaprenol phosphotransferase *see* undecaprenol kinase(s)
ATPβS *see* adenosine 5′-β-thiodiphosphate
ATPγS *see* adenosine 5′-γ-thiotriphosphate
atrazine chlorohydrolase(s), characterization, **5**, 414
Atropa belladonna, nicotine, **8**, 347
atropine, as seed toxin, **8**, 168
atrovenetinone, occurrence, **1**, 379
ATs *see* acyltransferases (ATs)
Atta cepholotes, antifeedant studies, **3**, 317
Attagenus elongatulus, (Z,Z)-3,5-tetradecadienoic acid, **8**, 216
Attagenus megatoma, (E,Z)-3,5-tetradecadienoic acid, **8**, 216
Atta texana
    ketones, **8**, 242
    pheromones, bioactivity, **8**, 12
atX genes, cloning, **1**, 414
AUBF protein, mRNA decay promotion, **6**, 208
Aucuba japonica
    aucubin, **8**, 307
    iridoid glycosides, **8**, 307
aucubin
    insect sequestration, **8**, 152
    occurrence, **8**, 307
    as oviposition stimulant, **8**, 156
aucuparin synthase, occurrence, **1**, 765
AUG
    initiation codon, **6**, 202
    roles
        methionine codon, **4**, 358
        protein synthesis codon, **4**, 358
        in universal genetic code, **4**, 358
Aulacophora foveicollis, antifeedant activity against, **8**, 342
aurantosides
    cytoxicity, **8**, 580
    NMR spectra, **8**, 580
    occurrence, **8**, 580
Aureobacterium barkerei, 3-deoxy-D-*manno*-octulosonate aldolase, **3**, 373
aureolic acids, biological activity, **3**, 323
aureomycin, discovery, **4**, 200
AU rich elements (AREs)
    characterization, **6**, 208
    localization, **6**, 206
    roles, in mRNA decay, **6**, 208
aurones
    precursors, **1**, 716
    structure, **1**, 715
austocystins, DNA damage induction, **7**, 511
Australian grapevine viroid (AGV), sequencing, **6**, 175
australine
    as α-glucosidase I inhibitor, **3**, 19, 152
    occurrence, **3**, 134
    structure, **3**, 131
    structure–activity relationships, **3**, 139
    toxicity, **3**, 140
Austrovenus stutchburyi, brevetoxin B$_1$, **8**, 514
autoinducers
    with *N*-acyl homoserine lactone skeleton, **8**, 392
    of *Agrobacterium tumefaciens*, **8**, 399
    of *Erwinia carotovora*, **8**, 398
    of LuxR-LuxI family, **8**, 397
    of *Pseudomonas aeruginosa*, **8**, 398
    of *Rhizobium leguminosarum*, **8**, 400
    use of term, **8**, 392
    of *Vibrio fischeri*, **8**, 393
    of *Vibrio harveyi*, **8**, 395
autoinduction, use of term, **8**, 393
autointoxication, prevention, mechanisms, **4**, 197
autolytic enzymes, inhibition, **3**, 285

autoregulating factor *see* A-Factor
autoregulators, use of term, **8**, 380
autotomy
    mechanisms, **8**, 462
    in *Tethys fimbria*, **8**, 464
autotoxicity, **8**, 169
    and predator-induced defenses, **8**, 462
auxin a, purification, **8**, 24
auxin agonists, synthetic, **8**, 34
auxin antagonists *see* antiauxins
auxin b, purification, **8**, 24
auxin binding protein 1 (ABP1), purification, **8**, 32
auxin binding proteins
    purification
        via affinity chromatography, **8**, 32
        via photoaffinity labeling, **8**, 32
auxin a lactone, purification, **8**, 24
auxins
    Acid Growth Theory, **8**, 31
    analysis, **8**, 25
        Avena curvature test, **8**, 24, 25
        GLC, **8**, 25
        LC–MS, **8**, 26
        single ion monitoring, **8**, 25
    biological activity, **8**, 26
    biosynthesis
        via tryptophan-independent pathway, **8**, 34
        via tryptophan pathway, **8**, 32
    chemistry, **8**, 24
    depolarization, **8**, 32
    discovery, **8**, 21
    effects, on plants, **8**, 26
    functions, **8**, 22
    Gene Theory, **8**, 31
    historical background, **8**, 23
    jasmonic acid responsive gene expression inhibition, **1**, 132
    natural, **8**, 26
    phototropism studies, **8**, 23
    polar transport, **8**, 30
    purification, **8**, 24
        HPLC, **8**, 25
    roles, in ethylene biosynthesis, **8**, 96
    sink function, **8**, 30
    structure, **8**, 26
    synthetic, **8**, 34
    two-point attachment theory, **8**, 32
auxins, azido-, applications, photoaffinity labeling, **8**, 32
AVE *see* vinyl ether, allyl (AVE)
ave genes
    aveAI, encoding, **1**, 523
    aveAII, encoding, **1**, 523
    aveD, **1**, 524
    aveF, **1**, 524
Avena spp., phototropism studies, **8**, 23
avenacin A, applications, antifungal agents, **8**, 183
avenacin B, applications, antifungal agents, **8**, 183
avenacoside A, applications, antifungal agents, **8**, 183
avenacoside B, applications, antifungal agents, **8**, 183
Avena curvature test, development, **8**, 24
Avena sativa
    amine oxidases, **3**, 721
    15R-hydroxylinoleic acid, **1**, 230
    linoleic acids, metabolic pathways, **1**, 230
    oxylipins, **1**, 229
averantin
    configuration, **1**, 457
    determination, **1**, 446
    as intermediate, **1**, 16
    synthesis, **1**, 450, 452
avermectin B1b, structure, **1**, 496
avermectin(s)
    analogues, mutasynthesis, **1**, 524

biosynthesis, **1**, 522, 14
   genetics, **1**, 523, **3**, 355
isolation, **4**, 200
occurrence, **1**, 522
precursor studies, **1**, 523
averufanin, isolation, **1**, 453
averufin
   configuration, **1**, 457
   determination, **1**, 446
   folding patterns, **1**, 448
   hexanoate incorporation, **1**, 451
   as intermediate, **1**, 16
   synthesis, **1**, 453
avian liver, isopentenyl diphosphate isomerase, **2**, 71
avicel plates, in *Haliotis discus* studies, **8**, 419
avidin
   binding affinity, with biotin, **7**, 620
   interactions, with biotin, **7**, 154
avilamycin
   D-curacose, **3**, 313
   occurrence, **1**, 414
avocado sunblotch viroid (ASBV)
   double hammerhead structure, **6**, 180
   hammerhead self-cleavage structure, **6**, 180
      sequences, **6**, 183
   hosts, **6**, 171, 182
   localization, **6**, 178
   pathogenicity, **6**, 185
axenomycins, L-axenose, **3**, 322
L-axenose, occurrence, **3**, 312, 322
axillaridine, biosynthesis, **4**, 33
axillary, 5α-androst-16-en-3-ol, **8**, 230
ayapin, accumulation, **1**, 625
AZ-28
   binding, **5**, 426
   characterization, **5**, 426
   structure, **5**, 427
AZA *see* azaserine (AZA)
azaatrovenetin, occurrence, **1**, 379
5-azacytidine, antineoplastic activity, **5**, 88
6-azacytosine, in oligodeoxynucleotides, **7**, 322
8-azadecalins, as cycloartenol cyclase inhibitor, **2**, 291, 304
Azadirachta excelsa, neem triterpenoids, **8**, 330
Azadirachta indica
   gedunin, **8**, 321
   growth requirements, **8**, 333
   limonoids, **8**, 321
   tissue culture, **8**, 329
Azadirachta siamensis, neem triterpenoids, **8**, 330
azadirachtin
   absolute configuration, **8**, 327
   antifeedant activity, **8**, 324, 331
   applications, growth inhibitors, **8**, 322
   biosynthesis, **8**, 329
   ecdysteroid antagonistic activity, **8**, 331
   effects, on insect reproduction, **8**, 331
   growth inhibitory activity, **8**, 331
   hydrogenation, **8**, 332
   insecticidal activity, **8**, 143
      prospects, **8**, 332
   isolation, **8**, 324, 327
   localization, **8**, 325

NMR spectra, **8**, 327
occurrence, **8**, 324
properties, **8**, 314
   chemical, **8**, 328
   physiological, **8**, 331
reactions, reviews, **8**, 328
resistance, **8**, 333
structure, **8**, 327
structure–activity relationships, **8**, 332
systemic action, **8**, 333
toxicity, mammalian, **8**, 332
azadirachtin, 3-desacetyl-, isolation, **8**, 327
azadirachtin, 11-methoxy-, antifeedant activity, **8**, 332
azadirachtin, 1-tigloyl-3-acetyl-, isolation, **8**, 325
azadirachtin B, structure, **8**, 325
azadirachtin D, isolation, **8**, 325
azadirachtin H, isolation, **8**, 325
azadirachtin H, 1-acetyl- *see* marrangin
azadirachtin I
   biosynthesis, **8**, 329
   isolation, **8**, 325, 327
azadirachtin K, isolation, **8**, 325
azadirachtins, 22,23-dihydro-23-methoxy-, isolation, **8**, 327
azadirachtol, structure, **8**, 327
azadirachtol, 3-tigloyl-, isolation, **8**, 325
azadirachtols, isolation, **8**, 327
azafulvenes, as intermediates, **4**, 85
8-azaguanine, applications, guanine deaminase inhibitors, **5**, 86
azaserine (AZA), as glutamine 2-oxoketoglutarate amino transferase inhibitor, **3**, 627
2-azasqualene, 2,3-dihydro-, as inhibitor, **2**, 311
azasqualenes, analogues, **2**, 290
aza sugars, inhibitory activity, **5**, 308
6-azathymine, in oligodeoxynucleotides, **7**, 319
azatoxin(s)
   as DNA topoisomerase II inhibitors, **7**, 610
   as dual inhibitors, **7**, 610
   as tubulin polymerization inhibitors, **7**, 610
azatyrosyl, chloro-, in kedarcidin chromophore, **7**, 575
azetidine-2-carboxylic acid, effects, on herbivores, **8**, 146
azicemicins
   applications, antiinfective agents, **7**, 514
   possible DNA reactions of, **7**, 514
azinomycin B
   applications, antibiotics, **7**, 513
   DNA reactions of, **7**, 513
   occurrence, **7**, 513
   sequence specificity, **7**, 513
aziridines, DNA alkylation, **7**, 513
azithromycin, structure, **1**, 497
azomycin
   applications, antiinfective agents, **7**, 521
   DNA reactions with, **7**, 521
   glyoxal formation from, **7**, 521
   oxygen radical production by, **7**, 521
   reductive activation of, **7**, 521
Azospirillum amazonense, 2-dehydro-3-deoxyphosphogluconate aldolase, **3**, 421
Azotobacter vinelandii, pyruvate dehydrogenase multienzyme complex, **4**, 342
azuki bean weevil *see Callosobruchus chinensis*

B

BA *see* benzyladenine (BA); bialaphos (BA)
BAA *see* acetaldehyde, bromo- (BAA)
Babylonia japonica, surugatoxin, **8**, 515
Baccharis spp.
  clerodanes, **8**, 316
  trichothecenes, **2**, 202
bac genes, occurrence, **3**, 281
bacillariolides, occurrence, **1**, 227
Bacillariophyta
  fresh water, algal pheromones, **8**, 425
  oxylipins, **1**, 226
Bacillus spp.
  D-amino acid aminotransferase, **3**, 256
  carotenoid biosynthesis, **2**, 323
  chitinases, **5**, 297
  halobacillin, **8**, 594
  mersacidin biosynthesis, **4**, 280
  metabolite biosynthesis, **4**, 197
  suicide-avoiding mechanisms, **4**, 198
Bacillus acidocaldarius see Alicyclobacillus acidocaldarius
Bacillus brevis
  bialaphos, **4**, 330
  gramicidin S, **4**, 321
  gramicidin S synthetase 1, **1**, 47
  grs genes, **4**, 328
  mutations, **4**, 323, 334
  peptide antibiotics, **4**, 321
  peptide synthetases, **4**, 321
  spores, defective, **4**, 323
  tyrothricin biosynthesis, **4**, 320
Bacillus brevis ATCC 8185 *see Bacillus parabrevis*
Bacillus cereus, sporogen, **8**, 402
Bacillus circulans
  cyclomaltodextrin glucanotransferase, **5**, 306
  xylan endo-1,3-β-xylosidase, **5**, 290, 292
Bacillus licheniformis
  bacitracin, **4**, 199
  bcr genes, **4**, 199
Bacillus macerans amylase *see* cyclomaltodextrin
  glucanotransferase(s)
Bacillus megaterium, cyanocobalamin biosynthesis, **4**, 150
Bacillus parabrevis, tyrocidine biosynthesis, **4**, 208, 322
Bacillus polymyxa, β-glucosidase A, **3**, 687
Bacillus rhamnosifermentans, rhamnulose-1-phosphate
  aldolase, **3**, 426
Bacillus sphaericus
  biotin biosynthesis, **1**, 826, 830
  endotoxin biosynthesis, **4**, 198
  laccase, **3**, 711
Bacillus stearothermophilus
  branching enzymes, **3**, 480
  geranyl*trans*transferase, **2**, 74, 82
    Cys residues, **2**, 85
    purification, **2**, 83
  geranyl*trans*transferase gene, mutagenesis, **2**, 85
  1,4-α-glucan branching enzymes, **3**, 444
  prenyltransferase II, **2**, 90
Bacillus subtilis
  adenine deaminase, **5**, 85
  chorismate mutase, **1**, 367, **5**, 358, 425
  competence, **8**, 401
  competence pheromones, **8**, 401
  competence stimulating factor, **8**, 402
  dCTP deaminase, **5**, 94
  2-dehydro-3-deoxyphosphoheptonate aldolase, **1**, 577
  endospores, **8**, 401
  extracellular differentiation factor A, **8**, 402
  farnesyl diphosphate isomerase, cloning, **2**, 74
  ferrochelatase, **4**, 101
    structure, **4**, 101
  heptaprenyl diphosphate synthases, GerC proteins, **2**,
    90
  hexaprenyl diphosphate synthases, **2**, 88
  inhibition, **1**, 692
  isopentenyl diphosphate, **2**, 46
  morphological differentiation, **8**, 401
  physical differentiation, **8**, 401
  shikimate kinase, **1**, 592
  shikimate pathway, **1**, 575
  spo genes, **8**, 402
  sporulation factors, **8**, 402
  subtilin biosynthesis, **4**, 279
  surfactin
    biosynthesis, **4**, 208
    secretion, **4**, 198
  transketolase, **3**, 416
  UGA in, **4**, 357
  uroporphyrinogen-III synthase, **4**, 90
Bacillus thuringiensis, endotoxin biosynthesis, **4**, 198
bacilysin, as glucosamine-6-phosphate synthase inhibitor,
  3, 275
bacitracin
  bioactive properties, **4**, 197
  biosynthesis, **4**, 196, 202, 208
  isopentenyl diphosphate binding, **4**, 199
  peptidoglycan biosynthesis inhibition, **3**, 280
bacitracin A, complexation, **3**, 280
bacteria
  acetyl-CoA *C*-acetyltransferases, **2**, 18
  anoxygenic photosynthetic, carotenoid biosynthesis, **2**,
    327, 344
  antibiotic-resistant, peptidoglycan biosynthesis, **3**, 271,
    5
  bioactive metabolites, **8**, 587
  branching enzymes, **3**, 458
  crtE genes, **2**, 348
  dimethylallyl*trans*transferases, **2**, 73
  eicosanoids, **1**, 208
  fatty acids, biosynthesis, **1**, 29, 334
  glucose-1-phosphate adenylyltransferase, regulatory
    mechanisms, **3**, 473
  glycogen biosynthesis, **3**, **441–495**
  isoprenoid biosynthesis, mevalonate-independent
    pathway, **2**, 58
  metabolism, role of isochorismic acid in, **1**, **609–622**
  methanogenic, nickel cofactors, **4**, 72
  methanotropic, **5**, 218
  nonphotosynthetic, carotenoid biosynthesis, **2**, 331, 345
  ruminal, tannin degradation, **3**, 819
  serotyping, **3**, 185
  tannin degradation, **3**, 819
bacterial alkaline phosphatase (BAP), applications, in
  dephosphorylation, **7**, 661
bacterial aromatic polyketides
  occurrence, **1**, 474
  use of term, **1**, 474
bacterial aromatic polyketide synthases
  act genes, **1**, 477
  biochemical analysis, **1**, 490
  biosynthesis, combinatorial, **1**, 491

definitions, **1**, 474
encoding
  gene characteristics, **1**, 476
  methods, **1**, 475
engineering, **1**, **473–494**
  rational design, **1**, 491
enzymatic activity, **1**, 475
function, **1**, **473–494**
future research, **1**, 492
gene clusters, **1**, 476
  combinatorial analysis, **1**, 487
  deletion analysis, **1**, 484
  domain analysis, **1**, 490
primer units, **1**, 475
protein engineering, **1**, 491
recombinant
  chemical analysis, **1**, 483
  genetic construction, **1**, 483
structure, **1**, **473–494**
bacterial cell walls
  composition, **3**, 242
  Gram-negative, **3**, 242
  Gram-positive, **3**, 242
  peptidoglycan layer, **3**, 242
  peptidoglycan structure, **3**, 242
bacterial dioxygenases, **5**, 62
Bacterial Polysaccharide Gene Nomenclature (BPGN),
    proposals, **3**, 203
bacteriochlorophyll *a* (Bchl *a*)
  accumulation, **2**, 327
  biosynthesis genes, **2**, 330
  pigment levels, **2**, 344
bacteriochlorophyll (Bchl)
  accumulation, **2**, 344
  biosynthesis, **4**, 72
  carotenoid protection, **2**, 326
  pigments, **2**, 322
bacteriohopane, structure, **1**, 152
bacteriohopanetetrol, **2**, 47
bacteriohopanetriol, amino-, **2**, 47
bacteriophages
  filamentous, **7**, 637
  R17 coat protein, cross-linking, **6**, 229
  RNA enzymes, **6**, 110
  T4 lysozyme, **5**, 298
bacteriophage T7 promoters, terpene synthase expression,
    2, 210
bacteriophage λ, as expression vector, **7**, 649
Bacteroides fragilis, lipid A, phosphate-free structure, **3**,
    197
bacteroids, formation, **8**, 400
Bactrian camel, ketones, **8**, 230
Bactrocera oleae
  olean, **8**, 15
  pheromones, **8**, 15
baculovirus
  and Class 1 α1,2-mannosidase, **3**, 24
  and lepidopteran insect Sf9 cells, **3**, 24
Baikiaea plurijuga, profisetinidins, **3**, 772
baker's yeast
  catalysis, **1**, 368
  isopentenyl diphosphate isomerase, **2**, 71
bakkenolide A, antifeedant activity, **8**, 308
Balanus spp., biofouling, **8**, 435
Balanus amphitrite
  cyprid larvae, attachment inhibition, **8**, 472
  pheromones, larval settlement-inducing, **8**, 435
Balanus balanoides
  arthropodin, **8**, 435
  oxylipins, **1**, 247
balsam fir *see Abies balsamea*
bamboo *see Bambusa oldhami* Munro; *Phyllostachys* spp.
Bambusa oldhami Munro, phenylalanine ammonia-lyase,
    3, 659

banana weevil *see Cosmopolites sordidus*
BAP *see* bacterial alkaline phosphatase (BAP)
Baphia nitida, isoflavenes, **1**, 775
BarA *see* butyrolactone autoregulator receptor A
barbaramide
  molluscicidal activity, **8**, 608
  occurrence, **8**, 608
  structure, **8**, 608
bar genes, *barA*, helix-turn-helix motifs, **8**, 387
bark beetles
  aggregation pheromones, **8**, 198, 200, 220
  attractants, α-cubebene, **8**, 228
  brevicomin, **8**, 213
  caryophyllene oxide, **8**, 228
  chemical ecology, **8**, 224
  chrysanthenone, **8**, 224
  defenses against, **2**, 111
  enantiomeric composition, **8**, 199
  interactions, with conifers, **2**, 101
  larvae, predation, **8**, 224
  monoterpenes, **8**, 221
    roles, **8**, 223
  pheromones, **8**, 223
  spiroacetals, **8**, 212
  tree resistance to, **8**, 223
  verbenone, **8**, 224
  see also Conophthorus spp.; *Dendroctonus* spp.;
    Dryocoetes spp.; *Gnathotrichus* spp.; *Ips* spp.;
    Leperisinus varius; *Pityogenes* spp.; *Pityophthorus*
    spp.; *Polygraphus poligraphus*; *Pteleobius vittatus*;
    Scolytus spp.; *Taphrorychus bicolor*
barley
  aleurone layers, **8**, 83
  leaves, cytokinin-binding proteins, **8**, 64
  soluble starch synthases, **3**, 455
  waxy locus, DNA sequence, **3**, 454
  see also Hordeum vulgare
barley seeds, tillering promotion, **8**, 68
barley yellow dwarf virus (BYDV)
  hammerhead ribozymes, **6**, 121
  satellite RNA, cleavage, **6**, 237
barminomycin I, **7**, 531
  applications, antibiotics, **7**, 500
  DNA adduct formation, **7**, 500
barnacles
  biofouling, **8**, 435
  cyprid larvae, **8**, 437
  hatching factor, **1**, 247
  see also Balanus balanoides; *Elminius modestus*
Bar proteins, BarA, purification, **8**, 387
Bartlett pears, aroma, **8**, 199
BAS *see* benzalactone synthase (BAS)
BAS 110, as cytochromes P450 inhibitors, **1**, 795
BAS 111, as cytochromes P450 inhibitors, **1**, 795
base excision repair, pathways, **5**, 393
bases
  active site, **2**, 19
  analogues, **6**, 224
  catalysis, **2**, 33
basic-helix-loop-helix peptides, **7**, 480
  IEB E47, **7**, 480
  MyoD, expression, **7**, 481
  USF, **7**, 480
  see also helix-turn-helix peptides
basic-leucine zipper proteins *see* bZip
basic zipper proteins *see* bZip
bauerines, occurrence, **8**, 529
BBE *see* reticuline oxidase
BCCP *see* biotin-carboxyl-carrier protein (BCCP)
B-cells *see* B-lymphocytes
bch genes, **2**, 330
  in *Rhodobacter* spp., **2**, 344
Bchl *see* bacteriochlorophyll (Bchl)

Bchl *a see* bacteriochlorophyll (Bchl *a*)
bcr genes, roles, **4**, 199
BE-13793C, occurrence, **7**, 600
bean leaves, endopolyploidy, **8**, 59
BED *see* eudistomin D, 7-bromo- (BED)
beech bark beetle *see Taphrorychus bicolor*
bees
    2,3-dihydropyrans, **8**, 211
    2,6-dimethyl-5-hepten-1-ol, **8**, 233
    Dufour's gland secretions, **8**, 220, 223, 227, 229
    geranyl geranoate, **8**, 223
    6-methyl-5-hepten-2-one, **8**, 232
    monoterpenes, **8**, 222
    venoms, **8**, 355
    see also Andrena wilkella; Anthophoridae; *Apis
        dorsata*; bumblebees; *Centris* spp.; *Colletes* spp.;
        Euglossa spp.; *Holcopasites calliopsidis*;
        honeybees; *Lasioglossum malachurum*; *Lestrimelitta
        limao*; *Nomada* spp.; *Panurginus* spp.;
        Tetragonisca angustula; *Xylocopa hirsutissima*
beetles
    m-cresol, **8**, 211
    (*Z,E*)-α-farnesene, **8**, 227
    lactones, **8**, 226
    6-methyl-5-hepten-2-one, **8**, 232
    see also Agriotes spp.; *Aleochara curtula*; ambrosia
        beetles; *Anobium punctatum*; *Anomala* spp.; bark
        beetles; canthariphilous beetles; carpet beetles;
        Carpophilus spp.; *Cathartus quadricollis*; *Cryptolestes*
        spp.; cucujiid beetles; *Cyclas formicarius*;
        Dineutes spp.; drugstore beetles; Dytiscidae;
        Epilachna borealis; *Gyrinus* spp.; *Kheper* spp.; leaf
        beetles; *Limonius californicus*; *Limonius canus*; *Lytta
        vesicatoria*; *Necrodes surinamensis*; Nitidulidae;
        Oryctes rhinoceros; *Oryzaephilus* spp.;
        Rhizophagus grandis; rove beetles; scarab beetles;
        Tenebrionid spp.; *Tribolium* spp.; *Trogoderma* spp.;
        water beetles; whirligig beetles; *Xylotrechus* spp.
BEI *see* branching enzyme I (BEI)
BEIIa *see* branching enzyme IIa (BEIIa)
BEIIb *see* branching enzyme IIb (BEIIb)
Bembix spp., rose oxide, **8**, 225
benoxaprofen, acetyl-CoA:1-
        alkylglycerophosphocholine acetyltransferase
        inhibition, **1**, 293
benzalactone synthase (BAS)
    condensation, **1**, 761
    evolution, **1**, 762
benzaldehyde, reactions, with L-alanine, **3**, 395
benzaldehyde, *o*-carboxy-
    biosynthesis, **3**, 375
    as metabolite, **3**, 377
benzaldehyde, *p*-hydroxy-
    biosynthesis, **3**, 622
    occurrence, **3**, 696
benzaldoxime, *syn*-4-nitro-, in oligonucleotide synthesis,
        7, 117
benzamide, *N*,2-dihydroxy- *see* salicylhydroxamic acid
benzamide, *o*-hydroxy-, **7**, 580
benz[*a*]anthracene, 7,12-dimethyl-, carcinogenicity, **1**, 783
benzathine, solubility, **4**, 240
benzene, chloro-, from, iodobenzene, **5**, 72
benzene, 1-chloro-2,4-dinitro-, enzyme studies, **5**, 63
benzene, chloroiodo-, as intermediate, **5**, 72
benzene, β-glucosyl, binding, **5**, 294
benzene, iodo-, as starting material, for chlorobenzene, **5**,
        72
benzene, *p*-nitrochloro-, rate constants, **5**, 413
benzeneacetic acid, α-methyl-4-(2-methylpropyl)- *see*
        ibuprofen
benzenediazonium ion, 4-(hydroxymethyl)-, DNA
    reactions of, **7**, 543
benzenediazonium ions, occurrence, **7**, 543

1,2-benzenediol:oxygen oxidoreductase(s) *see* catechol
        oxidase(s)
benzenediol:oxygen oxidoreductase(s) *see* laccase(s)
benzenemethanamine, (*E*)-*N*-ethyl-*N*-(6,6-dimethyl-2-
        hepten-4-ynyl)-3-[(3,3′-bithiophen-5-yl)methoxy]-, as
        potent inhibitor of vertebrate squalene epoxidase,
        2, 277
benzenes, alkenyl-
    DNA adducts with, **7**, 519
    metabolic activation of, **7**, 519
benzenes, trihydroxy-, DNA cleavage, mechanisms, **7**, 535
benzenes, 1,2,4-trihydroxy-, DNA damage induction, **7**,
        535
benzeneseleninic anhydride, reactions, with ferruginol, **2**,
        397
benzene sulfonate, 2,4,6-trinitro-, mutase inactivation, **5**,
        353
1,4-benzenoid biradical
    discovery, **7**, 556
    reactivity, **7**, 578
benzimidazole, 5,6-dimethyl- (DBI)
    in adenosylcobalamin, **5**, 174
    biosynthesis, **4**, 149
        anoxic, **4**, 150
        via oxygen-dependent pathway, **4**, 150
benzimidazole, 5-hydroxy-, as starting material, for 5-
        hydroxy-6-methylbenzimidazole, **4**, 150
benzimidazole, 5-hydroxy-6-methyl-, from, 5-
        hydroxybenzimidazole, **4**, 150
benzimidazole trifluoromethane sulfonate, as coupling
        reaction activator, **7**, 138
benzimidazolylcobamide, 5-hydroxy-, occurrence, **4**, 150
benzimidazolylcobamide, 5-methoxy-6-methyl-,
        occurrence, **4**, 150
benzimides, phenyl-, cytotoxicity, **7**, 607
1,2-benzisothiazolin-2-ylacetic acid, 3-oxo-, structure, **8**,
        34
1,2-benzisothiazolin-2-ylcarboxylate, ethyl 3-oxo-,
        structure, **8**, 34
1,2-benzisothiazol-3-ylacetic acid, structure, **8**, 34
benzoate, *p*-amino-, biosynthesis, via shikimate pathway,
        1, 574
benzoate, coniferyl, effects, on herbivores, **8**, 139
benzoate, 2,4-dichloro-, dehalogenation, **5**, 417
benzoate, glycidyl-4-nitro-
    enantiomers
        kinetic mechanisms, **5**, 55
        presteady-state kinetics, **5**, 55
benzoate, 2-halo-, dehalogenation, **5**, 417
benzoate, hydroxy-, metabolism, **3**, 385
benzoate, *p*-hydroxy-, biosynthesis, via shikimate
        pathway, **1**, 574
benzoate, methyl 4-hydroxy-, occurrence, **8**, 200
benzoate, methyl-*p*-2-hydroxyisopropyl, biosynthesis, **2**,
        136
benzodiazepine, receptors, **2**, 345
benzodihydropentalene, formation, **7**, 578
4*H*-1,3,2-benzodioxaphosphorin-4-one, 2-chloro-, in *H*-
        phosphonate synthesis, **7**, 139
3*H*-1,2-benzodithiol-3-one 1,1-dioxide, in oligonucleotide
        synthesis, **7**, 142
3*H*-1,2-benzodithiol-3-one 1-oxide
    DNA cleavage by, **7**, 524
    oxygen radical production, **7**, 524
    reactions
        with nitrogen nucleophiles, **7**, 526
        with thiol, **7**, 523
benzoic acid
    biosynthesis, **1**, 54
    oxidation, **1**, 612
benzoic acid, 4-acetyl-3-methoxy-5-methyl- *see*
        macrophomic acid
benzoic acid, *p*-amino-, biosynthesis, **1**, 611, 612

benzoic acid, 3-amino-5-hydroxy- (AHBA)
  biosynthesis, **1**, 527
  feeding studies, **1**, 528
benzoic acid, 3,4-dichloro-, structure, **8**, 34
benzoic acid, 2,3-dihydro-2,3-dihydroxy-, biosynthesis, **1**, 616
benzoic acid, 2,3-dihydroxy-, biosynthesis, **1**, 610, 611, 615, 616
benzoic acid, 4-hydroxy-, biosynthesis, **3**, 804
benzoic acid, *p*-hydroxy-
  biosynthesis, **1**, 814
  occurrence, **3**, 696
  polyprenylation, **2**, 381
benzoic acid, *o*-malonyl-, **1**, 615
benzoic acid, 2-[3-(4-methoxyphenyl)-5-pyrazoyl]-, structure, **8**, 34
benzoic acid, *o*-succinyl- (OSB)
  biosynthesis, **1**, 613
  coenzyme A esters, **1**, 615
  from, 2-oxoglutaric acid, **1**, 614, 617
  metabolism, **1**, 615
  as starting material
    for 1,4-dihydroxy-2-naphthoic acid, **1**, 615
    for menaquinones, **1**, 617
    for phylloquinone, **1**, 617
benzoic acid, 3,4,5-trihydroxy- *see* gallic acid
benzoic acid, 2,3,5-triiodo- (TIBA)
  as antiauxin, **8**, 34
  as auxin transport inhibitor, **8**, 30
  structure, **8**, 34
benzoic acid esters, *p*-azidotetrafluoro-, reactions, with oligodeoxyribonucleotides, **7**, 161
benzoic acids, biosynthesis, **3**, 803
benzoin, cleavage, **3**, 395
benzoin aldolase
  biochemistry, **3**, 394
  isolation, **3**, 394
  substrate specificity, **3**, 395
benzoisochromanequinones
  applications, antibiotics, **3**, 354
  structure, **1**, 476
benzoisoquinolinediones
  applications, intercalating agents, **7**, 606
  as DNA topoisomerase II inhibitors, **7**, 606
benzopentathiepins, isolation, **8**, 541
benzophenanthridine phosphoramidites, synthesis, **7**, 183
benzo[*c*]phenanthridines, as DNA topoisomerase I inhibitors, **7**, 601
benzophenazines
  applications, intercalating agents, **7**, 606
  as DNA topoisomerase II inhibitors, **7**, 606
benzophenone photophores, **2**, 279
benzophenones
  biosynthesis, **1**, 759
    via Baeyer–Villiger type reaction, **1**, 433
    from, anthraquinones, **1**, 432
benzophenone synthase, biosynthesis, **1**, 759
1-benzopyran-2-ones *see* coumarins
2*H*-benzopyrans, 2-flavanyl-4-aryl-3,4-dihydro-, biosynthesis, **3**, 774
benzo[*a*]pyrene
  genotoxicity, **7**, 225
  as starting material, for diolepoxides, **5**, 58
benzo[*a*]pyrene, (7*R*,8*S*,9*S*,10*R*)-7,8-dihydroxy-9,10-oxy-7,8,9,10-tetrahydro-, structure, **5**, 63
7*H*-benzo[*e*]pyrido[4,3-*b*]indoles, as DNA topoisomerase I inhibitor, **7**, 608
11*H*-benzo[*g*]pyrido[4,3-*b*]indoles, hydroxy-, as DNA topoisomerase II inhibitor, **7**, 608
p-benzoquinone, 2,6-dimethoxy-, as haustorial inducer, **8**, 175
benzothiazole, 2-mercapto-, for methyl phosphotriester deprotection, **7**, 119

benzothiazolium bromide, 3-carbomethoxymethyl-, structure, **8**, 34
benzothiopyranoindazoles, structural features, **7**, 606
1,2,4-benzotriazine 1,4-dioxide, 3-amino, **7**, 534
  DNA damage induction, **7**, 534
  hydroxyl radical production by, **7**, 534
benzotriazole, 1-hydroxy-, as coupling reaction activator, **7**, 138
2*H*-1,4-benzoxazine 5-carboxylate, 3,4-dihydro-7-methoxy-2-methylene-3-oxo-, in C-1027 chromophore, **7**, 578
2-benzoxazolinone, 6-methoxy- (MBOA), occurrence, **8**, 26
benzoyl, 2-(2,4-dinitrobenzene sulfenyloxymethyl)- (DNBSB), as 5′-hydroxyl protecting group, **7**, 127
benzoyl, 2-hydroxy-3,6-dimethyl-, in maduropeptin chromophore, **7**, 580
benzoyl, 2-(isopropylthiomethoxymethyl)- (PTMT), as 5′-hydroxyl protecting group, **7**, 127
benzoyl, 4-methoxy-, use in phosphodiester chemistry, **7**, 120
benzoyl, 3-methoxy-4-phenoxy-, deoxyadenosine protection, **7**, 123
benzoyl, 2-(methylthiomethoxymethyl)- (MTMT), as 5′-hydroxyl protecting group, **7**, 127
benzoyl-CoA, non-recognition, **4**, 264
benzyl, as phosphate protecting groups, **7**, 130
benzyladenine (BA)
  effects on greening, **8**, 59
  RNA incorporation, **8**, 59
benzyl groups, *o*-nitro-, in 2′-hydroxyl group protection, **6**, 85
benzylisoquinoline alkaloids
  biosynthesis, **4**, 39
  occurrence, **4**, 35
benzylpenicillin *see* penicillin G
beraprost
  applications, **1**, 196
    pharmaceutical, **1**, 196
  biological activity, **1**, 190
(*R,S*)-berbamunine, biosynthesis, **1**, 676
(*R,S*)-*nor*-berbamunine, biosynthesis, **1**, 676
berberine, tetrahydro- *see* (−)-canadine
berberine-bridge-forming enzyme (BBE) *see* reticuline oxidase
berberines
  biosynthesis, **4**, 40
  enzymes, **4**, 41
Berberis stolonifera, *N*-methylcoclaurines, **1**, 676
berenil
  applications, antitrypanosomal agents, **7**, 452, 459
  calorimetric studies, **7**, 459
  hydrodynamic studies, **7**, 459
  structure, **7**, 452
bergamotene
  biosynthesis, **2**, 165
  ²H NMR spectra, **2**, 166
(−)-β-*trans*-bergamotene, absolute configuration, **2**, 166
bergamotene synthases
  as membrane-bound protein, **2**, 167
  occurrence, **2**, 165
bergapten
  accumulation, **1**, 634
  levels, seasonal, **1**, 625
  occurrence, **8**, 338
  phototoxicity, **8**, 338
  as seed toxin, **8**, 168
bergaptol, biosynthesis, **1**, 633
Bergman reaction, **7**, 554
  σ,σ-biradical, **7**, 556
  and Myers reaction, compared, **7**, 556
Bergman rearrangement
  activation parameters, **7**, 556

molecular calculations, **7**, 556
thermodynamics, **7**, 556
betacyanins, formation, cytokinin-induced, **8**, 69
betaenone A
occurrence, **1**, 388
x-ray spectra, **1**, 388
betaenone B, structure, **1**, 388
betaenone C
occurrence, **1**, 388
total synthesis, **1**, 389
(−)-betaenone C, total synthesis, **1**, 389
betaenone F, occurrence, **1**, 388
betaenones, ^{13}C NMR spectra, **1**, 389
betaglycan, localization, **3**, 164
betavulgarin 2′-glucoside, as phytoalexin, **8**, 191
Beta vulgaris
cinnamoyl-CoA, **3**, 650
4-coumarate 3-hydroxylase, **3**, 640
polysaccharides, esterification, **3**, 502
Betula maximowicziana
alnusdiol, **1**, 686
maximowicziol, **1**, 686
Betula papyrifera, lignins, **3**, 692
Betula platyphylla, and feeding inhibition, **8**, 139
Betula verrucosa, polysaccharides, **3**, 688
ent-beyerene, biosynthesis, **2**, 230
Bhat *see Clerodendron infortunatum*
Biacore system, nucleic acid kinetic studies, **7**, 40
bialaphos (BA)
biosynthesis, **1**, 20, **865–880**
inhibition, **1**, 871
biosynthetic genes, molecular cloning, **1**, 873
isolation, **1**, 865
^{31}P NMR spectra, **1**, 867
occurrence, **1**, 866, **4**, 330
bibenzyl synthases
biosynthesis, **1**, 758
use of term, **1**, 753
bi-bi mechanisms
binding, **3**, 647
ordered, **3**, 336, 448, 478
BIBX 79, applications, **2**, 293
bicolorin, occurrence, **8**, 234
bicyclodeoxynucleosides
effects, of DNA triplex formation, **7**, 273
synthesis, **7**, 257
bicyclo[7.3.1]diynene, biosynthesis, **7**, 554
bicyclo[7.3.0]dodecadienediyne, in neocarzinostatin
chromophore, **7**, 554
bicyclo[7.3.0]dodecadiynene, synthesis, **7**, 554
bicyclo[7.3.0]dodeca-4,10,12-trien-2,6-diyne, in C-1027
chromophore, **7**, 578
bicyclo[7.3.0]enediyne, occurrence, **1**, 557
bicyclo[7.3.1]enediyne, occurrence, **1**, 557
bicyclo[3.3.1]hept-2-ene, 4-methylene-6,6-dimethyl- *see*
verbenene
bicyclo[3.2.1]octane, 1,5-dimethyl-6,8-dioxo- *see*
frontalin
bicyclo[2.2.2]octanes, as haptens, **5**, 428
bicyclo[7.3.1]tridec-4-ene-2,6-diyne *see* calicheamicinone
bicyclo[7.3.1]tridec-3-ene-1,5-diyne-8,9-epoxide, in
dynemicin A, **7**, 574
biennin C, occurrence, **1**, 375
biflavonoids, definitions, **3**, 748
biglycan
localization, **3**, 164
structure, **3**, 166
bilobalide
antifeedant activity, **8**, 308
biosynthesis, **2**, 61
occurrence, **8**, 308
BINAL-H *see* diisobutylaluminum-2,6-di-*t*-butyl-4-
methyl phenoxide (BINAL-H)

binding sites
metal, probing, **7**, 258, 259
SELEX studies, **7**, 619
binding substance (BS), use of term, **8**, 408
bioactive natural products
absolute configuration
assignment of, **8**, 6
chiroptical methods, **8**, 6
determination, **8**, 6
NMR methods, **8**, 6
via GC, **8**, 6
via HPLC, **8**, 6
applications, **8**, 3
chirality, **8**, 6
classification, **8**, 2
developmental stages, **8**, 2
enantioselective synthesis, **8**, 6
future research, **8**, 16
overview, **8**, 1–18
structure
determination, **8**, 6
false, **8**, 4
studies, **8**, 2
trends, **8**, 3
synthesis, importance of, **8**, 3
biochanin A
biosynthesis, **1**, 791, 799
as hyphal growth inhibitor, **8**, 175
occurrence, **1**, 808
spore germination stimulation, **1**, 780
biochanin A, 2′-hydroxy-, biosynthesis, **1**, 795
biochanin A, 3′-hydroxy- *see* pratensin
biochemical assays, interpretation, **7**, 265
biochemical processes
effect of nucleoside analogues on, **7**, 265
nucleoside analogue probes, **7**, **251–284**
biochemistry, computational, and future research, **5**, 134
biofilm, formation, **8**, 430
biofouling
barnacles, **8**, 435
Hydrozoa, **8**, 431
macro-fouling, **8**, 430
mechanisms, **8**, 430
micro-fouling, **8**, 430
microorganisms, **8**, 430
Mollusca, **8**, 432
Polychaeta, **8**, 432
ships, **8**, 431
Urochordata, **8**, 440
bio genes
bioC, encoding, **1**, 826
bioH, encoding, **1**, 826
biogenetic isoprene rule, **2**, 3, 98
in eremophilene sesquiterpenes, **2**, 178
formulation, **2**, 98
reformulation, **2**, 156
biological isoprene unit *see* isopentenyl diphosphate
(IDP)
bioluminescence
genes, **8**, 393
in jellyfish, **8**, 446
in luminous squid, **8**, 454
in marine organisms, **8**, 444
mechanisms, **8**, 444, 447
microalgae, **8**, 457
structure–function relationships, **8**, 447
biosphere, cellulose biosynthesis, **3**, 579
biosurfactants, rhamnolipids, **8**, 398
biosynthetic pathways, **4**, 1
future research, **4**, 10
mixed, **1**, 381
substrate-level controls, **3**, 43
biotechnology, and gene cloning, **2**, 72

biotin
   binding affinity, with avidin, **7**, 620
   biosynthesis, **1**, 826
   incorporation, into oligonucleotides, **7**, 171
   interactions
      with avidin, **7**, 154
      with streptavidin, **7**, 154
   roles, in fatty acid biosynthesis, **1**, 3
biotin carboxylase
   in acetyl-CoA carboxylase, **1**, 25
   sequencing, **1**, 26
biotin-carboxyl-carrier protein (BCCP)
   in acetyl-CoA carboxylase, **1**, 25
   sequencing, **1**, 26
biotin-carboxyl-carrier-protein:carbon-dioxide ligase *see*
      biotin carboxylase
biotin phosphoramidites
   applications, **7**, 173
   availability, **6**, 229
biotin–streptavidin complexes, applications, **7**, 174
biotin synthase, catalysis, **1**, 829
bioxalomycins
   applications, antibiotics, **7**, 499
   NMR spectra, **7**, 500
   occurrence, **7**, 499
   relationship, with naphthyridinomycin, **7**, 500
biphenyls
   degradation, **3**, 384
   as phytoalexins, **8**, 187
bipindogenin, occurrence, **8**, 361
bipolaroxin, phytotoxicity, **8**, 179
Biprorulus bibax
   (3*R*,4*S*,1′*E*)-3,4-bis(1′-butenyl)tetrahydro-2-furanol, **8**,
      215
   pheromones, **8**, 3, 14
σ,π-biradical, in Myers reaction, **7**, 556
σ,σ-biradical, in Bergman reaction, **7**, 556
Birch, A. J., acetate hypothesis, **1**, 2
birds
   frugivorous, and seed dispersal, **8**, 167
   UDP-*N*-acetylglucosamine:R₁(R₂)Manα1-
      6R₃[GlcNAc to Manα1-6] β-1,4-*N*-
      acetylglucosaminyltransferase VI, **3**, 55
bisabolene, biosynthesis, **2**, 164
(*Z*)-α-bisabolene, biosynthesis, **2**, 162
α-bisabolene, occurrence, **8**, 228
β-bisabolene
   biosynthesis, **2**, 162
   occurrence, **2**, 164
(*Z*)-α-bisabolene oxide, occurrence, **8**, 228
bisanthracycline
   applications, antineoplastic agents, **7**, 451
   high antineoplastic activity, **7**, 451
bisantrene
   antineoplastic activity, **7**, 440, 606
   applications, antineoplastic agents, **7**, 440, 606
   use in the synthesis of threading intercalating agents, **7**,
      440
(4α→8)-bis-catechin *see* procyanidin B₃
(+)-bisdechlorogeodin, occurrence, **1**, 437
(−)-bisdechlorogeodin, occurrence, **1**, 437
bisfurans, synthesis, **1**, 457
bisfurans, dihydro-
   structure, **1**, 443
   synthesis, **1**, 450
(*Z*,*E*)-α-bishomofarnesene, occurrence, **8**, 237
bishomomanicone, occurrence, **8**, 243
bisintercalators
   affinity, increase in, **7**, 444
   echinomycin, **7**, 448
   Flexi-Di, **7**, 446
   and neighbor exclusion, **7**, 444
   rigid, neighbor exclusion, **7**, 449

specificity in binding, concerted interactions, **7**, 448
   threading, **7**, 449
   TOTO, **7**, 448
   triostin, **7**, 448
   YOYO, **7**, 448
(4α→6)-bismesquitol, occurrence, **3**, 783
(5→6)-bismesquitol, occurrence, **3**, 783
1,1-bis(4-methoxyphenyl)-1-pyrenyl methyl, as 5′-
      hydroxyl protecting group, **7**, 127
bisnoryangonin, biosynthesis, **1**, 761, **3**, 624
bisphosphates, in DNA damage studies, **7**, 390
bisphosphonates, as farnesyl-diphosphate
      farnesyltransferase inhibitors, **2**, 256, 258
bis(pivaloyloxy)methyl esters, bioreversible, **2**, 258
bissesquiterpene lactone, occurrence, **1**, 375
bistheonellasterone, occurrence, **1**, 379
bistricarbonyl, DNA cross-linking by, **7**, 503
bivalves, symbiosis, **8**, 426
Bixa orellana, (−)-aristolochene, **2**, 177
black cherry *see Prunus serotina*
black pine *see Pinus thunbergii*
black spot disease *see Alternaria alternata*
black spruce *see Picea mariana*
black swallowtail butterfly *see Papilio polyxenes*
black tea
   (*Z*)-3-hexenol, **1**, 87
   theaflavins, **3**, 782
   thearubigins, **3**, 782
Blakeslea trispora, trisporic acid, **8**, 408
blasticidin S
   applications, **4**, 199
   antifungal agents, **3**, 339
   biosynthesis, **3**, 339
blastmycinone, occurrence, **3**, 312, 321
Blattaria, venoms, **8**, 360
Blattella craniifer
   aggregation pheromones, **8**, 211
   4-heptanone, **8**, 211
   tetradecane, **8**, 216
   undecane, **8**, 214
Blattella germanica
   aggregation pheromones, **8**, 230
   antifeedant activity against, **8**, 338
   branched hydrocarbons, **8**, 240
   haplophytine toxicity, **8**, 345
   pheromones, **8**, 14, 247
blattellastanosides, occurrence, **8**, 230
Blechnaceae, lignans, **1**, 647
(−)-blechnic acid
   biosynthesis, **1**, 678
   occurrence, **1**, 647, 677
Blechnum orientale
   (−)-blechnic acid, **1**, 677
   lignans, **1**, 647
bleomycin
   antitumor activity, **7**, 186
   applications
      antineoplastic agents, **7**, 536
      antitumor agents, **7**, 186
      DNA structure probes, **7**, 98
   DNA binding, **7**, 536, 538
   DNA cleavage by, **7**, 536
   DNA damage induction, **7**, 384, 394
   DNA strand breakage induction, **7**, 420
   metal binding, **7**, 537
   sequence specificity, **7**, 539
Bletilla striata, stilbene synthases, **1**, 753
blood clotting, cascade, **7**, 626, 640
blood clotting factor 10a, inhibition, **3**, 1
blood group A, *O*-glycans, **3**, 81
blood group B
   galactosyltransferases, **3**, 39
   O-glycans, **3**, 81

blood group Cad antigen, synthesis, **3**, 82
blood group H α-2-fucosyltransferase *see* galactoside 2-α-
    L-fucosyltransferase
blood group i antigen, regulatory mechanisms, **3**, 77
blood groups, fucosyltransferases, **3**, 55
blood group Sd^a antigen, synthesis, **3**, 82
bluebell *see Hyacinthoides non-scripta*
blue fluorescent proteins (BFP)
    luminescence studies, **8**, 452
    occurrence, **8**, 446
blue-green algae *see* cyanobacteria
blue mold disease, resistance to, **8**, 181
B-lymphocytes
    CD22β adhesion, **3**, 46
    development, **5**, 73
    lipopolysaccharide activation, **3**, 182
BM-13505, as thromboxane antagonist, **1**, 189
BME *see* ethanol, 2-mercapto- (BME)
BMS-188494, as cholesterol lowering agent, phase I
    clinical trials, **2**, 258
Bmt *see* L-threonine, (4*R*)-4-[(*E*)-2-butenyl]-4-methyl-
BNCT *see* boron neutron capture therapy (BNCT)
boar-taint steroid *see* 5α-androst-16-en-3-one
D-boivinose, occurrence, **3**, 312, 313
bolas spiders *see Mastophora cornigera*
boll weevils
    sex pheromones, **8**, 224
    see also Anthonomus grandis
bollworm *see Spodoptera littoralis*
Bombay phenotypes, **3**, 55
Bombus spp.
    geranylcitronellol, **8**, 229
    geranylgeraniol, **8**, 229
Bombus hypnorum, geranylcitronellyl esters, **8**, 229
Bombus terrestris, geranylcitronellyl esters, **8**, 229
bombykol
    biosynthesis, **8**, 205
    occurrence, **8**, 3, 205
    structure, **8**, 3
Bombyx spp.
    eclosion hormone, **8**, 301
    pheromone biosynthesis activating neuropeptide, **8**, 300
bombyxin
    biochemistry, **8**, 301
    occurrence, **8**, 301
    use of term, **8**, 295
Bombyx mori
    activity against, **1**, 693
        antifeedant, **8**, 337, 342
    bombykol, **8**, 3, 205
    bombyxin, **8**, 301
    diapause hormone, **8**, 300
    ecdysone, **8**, 279, 282
    ecdysone 22-phosphate, **8**, 283
    lignan studies, **8**, 339
    pheromones, **8**, 3
    pilocarpine toxicity, **8**, 342
    prothoracicotropic hormone, **8**, 295
    rotenone toxicity, **8**, 341
boranophosphates, synthesis, **7**, 293
Bordetella pertussis
    lipopolysaccharide biosynthesis, **3**, 228
    lipopolysaccharides, **3**, 185
bornanes, characterizations, **2**, 104
borneol
    as allelopathic agent, **8**, 171
    structure, **2**, 104
(+)-borneol, oxidation, **2**, 146
bornyl acetate
    occurrence, **8**, 139
    structure, **2**, 101
(+)-bornyl diphosphate cyclase, substrate studies, **5**, 327
bornyl diphosphate synthases, cyclization, **2**, 133

(+)-(1*R*,4*R*)-bornyl diphosphate synthases, catalysis, **2**,
    128
(−)-(1*S*,4*S*)-bornyl diphosphate synthases, catalysis, **2**,
    128
borohydride, as cofactor, **7**, 558
boron neutron capture therapy (BNCT)
    applications, **7**, 221
        cancer treatment, **7**, 293
borreverine, biosynthesis, **1**, 369
Bossiella orbigiana, 5*Z*,8*Z*,10*E*,12*E*,14*Z*-
    eicosapentaenoic acid, **1**, 223
bostrychid beetle *see Prostephanus truncatus*
Bothroponera soror
    2-undecanol, **8**, 214
    2-undecanone, **8**, 214
botryaloic acid methyl ester, ^{2}H NMR spectra, **2**, 173
botrydial, dihydro-, occurrence, **2**, 173
botrydials
    biosynthesis, **2**, 173
    occurrence, **2**, 173
botryllamides
    occurrence, **8**, 539
    structure, **8**, 539
Botryllus spp., botryllamides, **8**, 539
botryococcenol, biosynthesis, **5**, 338
Botryococcus braunii Berkeley, botryoxanthin A, **8**, 618
Botryodiplodia theobromae see Lasiodiplodia theobromae
botryoxanthin A
    occurrence, **8**, 618
    structure, **8**, 618
Botrytis spp., abscisic acid, **8**, 73
Botrytis cinerea
    abscisic acid biosynthetic pathway, **8**, 87
    activity against, **1**, 534
    botrydial, **2**, 173
    dihydrobotrydial, **2**, 173
    7-methyl luteone, **1**, 815
bouvardin, occurrence, **4**, 202
Bovidae, porphobilinogen synthase, **4**, 75
bovine colostrum, polypeptide *N*-
    acetylgalactosaminyltransferase, **3**, 74
bovine pancreas
    phospholipase A$_2$, **5**, 105, 110
    sterol esterase, **5**, 125
bovine pituitary 20 S proteasome, inhibition, **3**, 325
BPGN *see* Bacterial Polysaccharide Gene Nomenclature
    (BPGN)
BPO *see* bromoperoxidase (BPO)
BPS *see* benzophenone synthase
Brachynus spp., chemical defenses, **8**, 364
bracken fern, carcinogenicity, **7**, 507
bradykinin, *N*-bromoacetyl-, in ribozyme studies, **6**, 138
Bradyrhizobium spp., symbiosis, **1**, 780
Bradyrhizobium japonicum
    adenosylhopane, **2**, 47
    chemoattractants, **1**, 781
    hopene cyclase gene
        cloning, **2**, 313
        open reading frames, **2**, 313
    nod genes, **1**, 329
brain
    embryonic, nerve cell adhesion molecules, **3**, 50
    fucosyltransferases, **3**, 115
Brainea insignis, lignans, **1**, 647
brain hormone
    use of term, **8**, 294, 295
    see also prothoracicotropic hormone (PTTH)
(−)-brainic acid, occurrence, **1**, 647
brain tissue, fucosyltransferases, **3**, 117
branched chains, formation, **8**, 237
branching, ante-iso, **8**, 246
branching enzyme I (BEI)
    activity, **3**, 460

long-chain transfers, **3**, 466
structure, **3**, 461
branching enzyme IIa (BEIIa)
  activity, **3**, 460
  structure, **3**, 461
branching enzyme IIb (BEIIb)
  activity, **3**, 460
  small-chain transfers, **3**, 462, 466
  structure, **3**, 461
branching enzymes
  α-amylase catalytic sites, **3**, 459
  assays, **3**, 458
    branch linkage, **3**, 458
    iodine, **3**, 458
    phosphorylase stimulation, **3**, 458
  bacteria, **3**, 458
  catalysis, amino acid residues, **3**, 462
  deficiency, in mutants, **3**, 461
  genes
    allelic forms, **3**, 460
    cDNA clones, **3**, 462
    isoforms, **3**, 459
    tissue-specific, **3**, 461
  localization, **3**, 468
  molecular weight, **3**, 480
  overexpression, **3**, 486
  plants, **3**, 458
    isoforms, **3**, 459
  properties, **3**, 479
  proteolysis, **3**, 460
  roles, in human glycogen storage disease (type IV), **3**, 480
  see also 1,4-α-glucan branching enzyme
Brassicacae, indoleglucosinolates, **8**, 26, 34
Brassica juncea, enzymes, **1**, 859
brassicanals, as phytoalexins, **8**, 187
Brassica napus
  desaturases, **1**, 40, 41
  enoyl reductase, **1**, 363
  3-indolylmethyl glucosinolate, **1**, 130
  1-methoxy-3-indolylmethyl glucosinolate, **1**, 130
  thiohydroximate β-D-glucosyltransferase, **1**, 859
brassilexin, as phytoalexin, **8**, 187
brassinin, as phytoalexin, **8**, 187
brassinin, dioxy-, as phytoalexin, **8**, 187
brassinin, methoxy-, as phytoalexin, **8**, 187
brassinin, oxymethoxy-, as phytoalexin, **8**, 187
brassinolide
  discovery, **8**, 21
  isolation, **8**, 99
  metabolism, **8**, 107
  25-methylation, **8**, 107
  synthesis, **8**, 100
brassinosteroids (BRs)
  analysis, **8**, 100
  applications, stress alleviation, **8**, 105
  bioassays, **8**, 104
  biochemistry, **8**, 99
  biological activity, **8**, 104
  biosynthesis, **8**, 105
    inhibitors, **8**, 107
    mutants, **8**, 105
  chemistry, **8**, 99
  classification, **8**, 100
  detection
    via HPLC, **8**, 100
    via LC–MS, **8**, 100
  fluorescent boronates, **8**, 100
  historical background, **8**, 99
  metabolism, **8**, 107
  ^{13}C NMR spectra, **8**, 100
  ^{1}H NMR spectra, **8**, 100
  occurrence, **8**, 99

physiology, **8**, 104
purification
  via column chromatography, **8**, 100
  via GC-MS, **8**, 100
response mutants, **8**, 105
reviews, **8**, 99
separation, via HPLC, **8**, 100
structure, **8**, 99
structure-activity relationship, **8**, 104
studies, **2**, 303
synthesis, **8**, 100
brassins, discovery, **8**, 99
breast cancer
  β-1,3-galactosyl-*O*-glycosyl-glycoprotein β-1,6-*N*-acetylglucosaminyltransferase activity, **3**, 76
  protective agents, lignans, **1**, 698
  and soy-rich diets, **1**, 782
brefeldin, biosynthesis, **1**, 422
brefeldin A
  cellular transport inhibition, **3**, 88
  effects, on sphingomyelin biosynthesis, **3**, 98
  protein secretion inhibition, **3**, 96
B-related factor (BRF)
  gene encoding, isolation, **4**, 368
  in yeast, **4**, 367
brevetoxin A (BTX-A), x-ray crystal structure, **8**, 511
brevetoxin B (BTX-B)
  2D INADEQUATE experiments, **8**, 511
  applications, **8**, 512
  total synthesis, **8**, 511
  x-ray crystal structure, **8**, 511
brevetoxin B$_1$ (BTX-B$_1$), occurrence, **8**, 514
brevetoxin B$_3$ (BTX-B$_3$), occurrence, **8**, 514
brevetoxins (BTX)
  occurrence, **8**, 511
  pore formation, mechanisms, **8**, 512
brevianamide A, biosynthesis, **1**, 386
brevianamide B, biosynthesis, **1**, 386
Brevibacterium ammoniagenes
  fatty acid synthase, **1**, 32
    catalytic domains, **1**, 33
    products, **1**, 33
Brevibacterium epidermidis, glycitein, demethylation, **1**, 815
Brevibacterium lactofermentum, glutamic acid, **1**, 872
brevican
  binding, **3**, 164
  promoters, **3**, 167
brevicomin
  as aggregation pheromone, **8**, 233
  occurrence, **8**, 213
endo-brevicomin, occurrence, **8**, 213
(+)-*endo*-brevicomin, occurrence, **8**, 213
exo-brevicomin, synthesis, **3**, 417
(+)-*exo*-brevicomin, occurrence, **8**, 213
(±)-*exo*-brevicomin, occurrence, **8**, 12
exo-brevicomin, 3,4-dehydro-, occurrence, **8**, 213
BRF *see* B-related factor (BRF)
BRM genes, *BRM2*, **1**, 428
broad bean *see* Vicia faba
brombin II, occurrence, **1**, 380
brombin III, occurrence, **1**, 380
Brombya platynema
  brombin II, **1**, 380
  brombin III, **1**, 380
brominated organic compounds, occurrence, **5**, 402
bromine atoms
  electron affinity, **1**, 323
  ionization potential, **1**, 323
  negative, **1**, 304
  positive, **1**, 304
bromo-etherification, biosynthetic, **1**, 310
bromoethers, cyclization, **1**, 322

bromoethers, cyclic, precursors, **1**, 8
bromoperoxidase (BPO)
　in cyclic bromoether biosynthesis, **1**, 318
　mechanisms, **1**, 304
　purification, **1**, 317
bronchoconstrictors, leukotrienes, **1**, 176
bronchospasm, prostaglandin-induced, **1**, 174
Bronze-2 genes, cloning, **1**, 742
Brookhaven Protein Data Bank, **5**, 119, 129
brook trout *see Salvelinus fontinalis*
brosimonin A, occurrence, **1**, 385
Brosimopsis oblongifolia, brosimonin A, **1**, 385
brown algae *see* Phaeophyta
brown-banded cockroach *see Supella longipalpa*
brown tailed moth *see Euproctis similis*
brp genes
　brpA
　　cloning, **1**, 873
　　localization, **1**, 873
Brucea amarissima, bruceine B, **8**, 322
bruceine B, occurrence, **8**, 322
bruchid beetle *see Caryedes brasiliensis*
Bryonia dioica, α-linolenic acid, **1**, 128
Bryophyta
　and lignin evolution, **3**, 624
　see also Hepaticae; Musci
bryostatin I
　applications, antineoplastic agents, **8**, 521
　occurrence, **8**, 521
BS *see* binding substance (BS)
BsgI, DNA cleavage protection, **7**, 629
B-signal, functions, **8**, 406
Bt2 protein, occurrence, **3**, 465
Bt genes
　Bt 1, products, **3**, 466
　Bt 2, mutation, **3**, 447
BTX *see* brevetoxins (BTX)
BU4514N, biosynthesis, **1**, 370
Bucculatrix thurberiella, tetradecenyl nitrates, **8**, 207
BuChE *see* cholinesterase
buckwheat *see Fagopyrum esculentum*
Buddlea globosa, catalpol, **8**, 307
Buddlea variabilis, catalpol, **8**, 307
buddlenol B, dihydro-, occurrence, **1**, 688
budworm *see Heliothis virescens*
buffers, in RNA structural probing, **6**, 69
bufotenine, as oviposition stimulant, **8**, 156
bugs
　1,8-cineole, **8**, 225
　(2*S*,6*R*,8*S*)-2,8-dimethyl-1,7-dioxaspiro[5.5]undecane,
　　8, 214
　limonene, **8**, 225
　monoterpenes, **8**, 222
　(*E*)-4-oxo-2-hexenal, **8**, 210
　α-pinene, **8**, 225
　see also Biprorulus bibax; *Nezara viridula*; *Oechalia*
　　schellenbergii; *Riptortus clavatus*
Bugula neritina, bryostatin I, **8**, 521
bulgarein
　as DNA topoisomerase I inhibitor, **7**, 600
　DNA winding activity, **7**, 600
　occurrence, **7**, 600
bulgecins, biological activity, **3**, 285
bullfrog *see Rana catesbiana*
α-bulnesene, biosynthesis, **2**, 184
bumblebees
　(*S*)-2,3-dihydrofarnesol, **8**, 227
　(*E*,*E*)-farnesol, **8**, 227
　venom, constituents, **8**, 355
　see also Bombus spp.; *Psithyrus* spp.; *Pyrobombus* spp.
Buprestidae
　β-D-glucose, **8**, 221
　pyrrole-2-carboxylic acid, **8**, 221

Burkholderia caryophylli, isoprenoid biosynthesis,
　mevalonate-independent pathway, **2**, 58
Burkholderia gladioli, isoprenoid biosynthesis,
　mevalonate-independent pathway, **2**, 58
Burkholderia spp., lipopolysaccharides, **3**, 190
Burmese lacquer tree *see Malanorrhea usitata*
burnet moth *see Zygaena trifolii*
Bursatella leachii, cyclopropenoid fatty acids, **1**, 63
(−)-bursehernin, growth inhibitory activity, **1**, 694
Bursera microphylla, (−)-burseran, **1**, 701
(−)-burseran, antitumor activity, **1**, 701
bursicon
　biochemistry, **8**, 301
　distribution, in insects, **8**, 301
　occurrence, **8**, 301
butanal, 4-hydroxy-, in sex pheromones, **8**, 210
[1-²H₁,1-³H]butane, oxygenation, **5**, 221
(2*RS*,3*RS*)-2,3-butanediol, occurrence, **8**, 210
2,3-butanedione, possible DNA damage induction, **7**, 503
butanoate, (*E*)-2-butenyl, occurrence, **8**, 210
butanoate, butyl, occurrence, **8**, 210
butanoate, egonol-2-methyl-, occurrence, **1**, 645
butanoate, (*Z*)-3-hexenyl (*R*)-2-hydroxy-3-methyl-, **8**, 221
butanoic acid, 2-amino-4-hydroxy-4-phenyl-,
　biosynthesis, **3**, 395
butanoic acid, (3*R*)-3-hydroxy-, occurrence, **8**, 209
butanoic acid, (3*R*,3*R*)-3-(3-hydroxybutanoyloxy)-,
　occurrence, **8**, 209
butanoic acid, 2-methyl-, occurrence, **8**, 221
butanol, 2-methyl-, biosynthesis, **8**, 220
butanol, 3-methyl-, biosynthesis, **8**, 220
butanolide phosphates, conversion, to virginiae
　butanolide A, **1**, 146
butanolides, occurrence, **8**, 384
butan-2-one, 3-hydroxy-3-methyl-, occurrence, **8**, 220
butan-2-one, 4-hydroxyphenyl- (pHPB)
　characterization, **1**, 761
　occurrence, **1**, 761
　purification, **1**, 761
2-butene, biological activity, **8**, 93
2-butenoate, 3-methyl-2-butenyl 3-methyl-, occurrence, **8**,
　220
(*E*)-2-butenoate, (*Z*)-3-dodecenyl, occurrence, **8**, 214
buten-4-ol, 2-methyl-, biosynthesis, **5**, 220
2-buten-1-ol, (*E*)-4-[2-diazotrifluoropropionyloxy]-3-
　methyl- (DATFP-DMAPP), uncompetitive
　inhibition patterns, **2**, 126
2-buten-1-ol, 3-methyl-, occurrence, **8**, 220
3-buten-1-ol, 3-methyl-, occurrence, **8**, 220
3-buten-2-ol, 2-methyl-
　effects, on mice, **8**, 200
　occurrence, **8**, 200, 220
2-butenyl diphosphate, 3-trifluoro-, as substrate, **5**, 320
3-butenyl diphosphate, 3-ethyl-, as substrate homologues,
　for isopentenyl diphosphate isomerase, **2**, 72
3-butenyl diphosphate, 3-(fluoromethyl)-, use in gene
　cloning, **2**, 72
2-butenyl diphosphates, (*Z*)-3-(trifluoromethyl)-
　as substrate analogues, **2**, 80
　synthesis, **5**, 335
butterflies
　6-methyl-5-hepten-2-one, **8**, 232
　see also Amauris spp.; Danainae; *Danaus plexippus*;
　　Elymnias thryallis; *Euploea* spp.; *Heliconius pachinus*;
　　Idea spp.; Ithomiidae; Lycaenidae; monarch
　　butterflies; *Papilio memnon*; *Parnassius phoebus*;
　　Pieris spp.; swallowtail butterflies
butyrate, as bacterial aromatic polyketide synthase
　primer, **1**, 475
butyrate, 4-amino-3-keto-, synthesis, **4**, 76
butyrate, D-2-hydroxy-, as substrate, **3**, 272
butyrate, 4-hydroxy-2-keto-, cleavage, **3**, 381
butyrates, D-amino-, substitution, **1**, 549

butyric acid, D-amino-, replacement, **4**, 253
butyric acid, L-amino-, replacement, **4**, 252
butyric acid, 4-amino- (GABA), larval settlement
    induction, **8**, 433
butyric acid, 2,4-diamino-, occurrence, **3**, 246
butyric acid, α,τ-diamino-, effects, on herbivores, **8**, 146
butyric acid, β-hydroxy-, effects, on platelet-activating
    factor, **1**, 294
butyrolactone, 2-(1′-hydroxyalkyl)-3-hydroxymethyl-,
    structure, **8**, 389
butyrolactone, 2*R*-isocapryloyl-4*R*-hydroxymethyl-,
    structure, **8**, 381
butyrolactone, 2*S*-isocapryloyl-4*S*-hydroxymethyl-
    structure, **8**, 380
    see also A-factor
butyrolactone autoregulator receptor A, purification, **8**,
    387

butyrolactones
    biosynthesis, **1**, **139–158**
    skeleton, **1**, 144
    in *Streptomyces* spp., **8**, 378
butyryl, 4-(methylthiomethoxy)- (MTMB), as 5′-
    hydroxyl protecting group, **7**, 127
butyrylcholinesterase (BuChE) *see* cholinesterase
BW5147PHA^{R}2.7, mutation, **3**, 19
BYDV *see* barley yellow dwarf virus (BYDV)
bZip
    DNA binding motif, **7**, 482
    motif, truncation, **7**, 482
    peptides, **7**, 482
        isolation by *in vitro* selection, **7**, 482

C

C4H *see trans*-cinnamate 4-monooxygenase
C6-NBD-ceramide, 1-*O*-methyl-, labeling, **3**, 100
C6-NBD-GM1, transport, **3**, 100
C-1027
  activation, **7**, 578
  applications, **7**, 578
  DNA damage, **7**, 579
    inhibition, **7**, 580
  kinetic solvent isotope effect, **7**, 578
  occurrence, **7**, 578
  structure, **7**, 554, 578
  tRNA cleavage, anticodon region, **7**, 580
CAA *see* acetaldehyde, chloro- (CAA)
cabbage, lipoxygenase activity, **1**, 93
cabbage moth *see Mamestra brassicae*
cacodylate, applications, in RNA structural probing, **6**,
    69
Cacospongia cf. *linteiformis*, sesterterpenes, **8**, 467
cadalene, 2,7-dihydroxy-
  biosynthesis, **2**, 188
  occurrence, **2**, 186
cadalenene, (1*S*)-7-methoxy-1,2-dihydro-
  ^{13}C NMR spectra, **2**, 188
  ^{2}H NMR spectra, **2**, 188
  occurrence, **2**, 188
CADD *see* computer-aided drug design (CADD)
caddis flies
  endo-brevicomin, **8**, 213
  (4*S*,6*S*)-4,6-dimethyloctan-3-one, **8**, 242
  ketones, **8**, 242
  (2*S*,6*Z*)-6-nonen-2-ol, **8**, 213
  (*Z*)-6-nonen-2-one, **8**, 213
  see also Hesperophylax occidentalis; *Rhyacophila
      fasciata*
cadinanyl cation, 1,2-hydride shift, **2**, 191
δ-cadinene
  biosynthesis, **2**, 187
  occurrence, **2**, 186, **8**, 228
cadinenes, biosynthesis, **2**, 177, 186
cadinene synthases
  occurrence, **2**, 210
  purification, **2**, 186
δ-cadinene synthases
  biosynthesis, **2**, 186
  cDNA cloning, **2**, 187
cadinol, occurrence, **8**, 228
CADs *see* cinnamyl-alcohol dehydrogenase(s)
Caenorhabditis elegans
  ω³-desaturases, **1**, 40
  isopentenyl diphosphate isomerases, cDNA cloning, **2**,
      73
  α-1,3-mannosyl-glycoprotein β-1,2-*N*-
      acetylglucosaminyltransferase, genes, **3**, 50
  Sec tRNA$^{[Ser]Sec}$ gene, **4**, 361
Caenorhabditis reinhardtii, desaturases, **1**, 40
Caesalpinia coriaria, tannase, **3**, 820
caffeate *O*-methyltransferase, catalysis, **3**, 643
caffeic acid
  biosynthesis, **1**, 18, **3**, 640
  in gallic acid biosynthetic pathway, **3**, 803
  metabolic pool size, **3**, 629
  methylation, **3**, 624, 646
  O-methylation, **3**, 644
  occurrence, **1**, 645
(*Z*)-caffeic acid, insecticidal activity, **8**, 337

caffeic acid esters, occurrence, **8**, 140, 175
caffeic acid 3-*O*-methyltransferase (COMT), activity, **1**,
    799
caffeine
  as allelopathic agent, **8**, 171
  occurrence, **8**, 147
  as seed toxin, **8**, 168
caffeoyl-CoA, as starter unit, **1**, 752
caffeoyl-CoA *O*-methyltransferase
  catalysis, **3**, 643
  genetics, **3**, 671
  localization, **3**, 672
  occurrence, **3**, 672
1-caffeoyl-4-deoxyquinic acid, occurrence, **8**, 140
3-caffeoylquinate *see* chlorogenic acid
calaminthone, as allelopathic agent, **8**, 171
calanolide A
  chemical synthesis, **1**, 624
  as HIV-1-specific reverse transcriptase inhibitor, **1**, 624
calanolides, applications, **1**, 624
calbistrin A, biosynthesis, **1**, 370
Calceolaria spp., *ent*-stemarenes, **2**, 241
Calceolaria thyrsiflora, thyrsiflorins, **2**, 239
calcineurin
  binding, **1**, 541
  inhibitors, **5**, 154
  isotope effects, **5**, 151
  mutants, cyclosporin A-resistant, **1**, 541
  structure, **5**, 157
calcium carbonate, effects, on herbivores, **8**, 149
calcium chloride, effects, on herbivores, **8**, 149
calcium ions, effects of abscisic acid on, **8**, 82
calcium release, from sarcoplasmic reticulum, **8**, 526
Caldariella acidophila, caldariellaquinone biosynthesis, **1**,
    856
caldariellaquinone
  biosynthesis, **1**, 856
  occurrence, **1**, 856
caledonin
  occurrence, **8**, 538
  structure, **8**, 538
calf intestine alkaline phosphatase (CIP), applications, in
    dephosphorylation, **7**, 661
calf liver, UTP-glucose-1-phosphate uridylyltransferase,
    3, 478
calf spleen, phosphorylase, **5**, 306, 308
calf thymus, DNA, **7**, 452
calicheamicin γ$_1^I$
  affinity cleavage, **7**, 571
  antitumor activity, **3**, 326
  applications, antitumor agents, **3**, 326
  DNA damage, DS lesions, **7**, 570
  efficacy, **7**, 568
  solubility, **7**, 569
  structure, **7**, 568
  tetrasaccharide domain, **7**, 571
calicheamicin–glutathione disulfide, formation, **7**, 570
calicheamicin–glutathione trisulfide, formation, **7**, 570
calicheamicinone
  in calicheamicin γ$_1^I$, **7**, 569
  stereochemistry, **7**, 569
calicheamicin(s)
  L-acofriose, **3**, 313
  activation, **7**, 569
    trisulfide chemistry, **7**, 570

applications, antibiotics, **7**, 554
  DNA damage, **7**, 570
    induction, **7**, 385
  DNA strand breakage induction, **7**, 421
  in enediyne antibiotics, **1**, 557
  enediyne moiety, **7**, 554
  occurrence, **7**, 568
  role of oligosaccharide amino group, **7**, 570
  structure, **7**, 568
calicheamicin ε, formation, **7**, 570
California red scale *see Aonidiella aurantii*
callatostatins, occurrence, **8**, 301
Callipelta spp.
  callipeltin A, **8**, 585
  callipeltoside A, **8**, 587
callipeltin A
  antiviral activity, **8**, 585
  occurrence, **8**, 585
  structure, **8**, 585
callipeltin B, isolation, **8**, 586
callipeltins
  antifungal activity, **8**, 586
  cytotoxicity, **8**, 586
callipeltoside A
  cytotoxicity, **8**, 587
  occurrence, **8**, 587
  structure, **8**, 587
Calliphora spp.
  ecdysone, **8**, 282
  ecdysteroids, **8**, 280
Calliphora vomitoria, callatostatins, **8**, 301
Callistephus chinensis
  anthocyanidin synthase, **1**, 730
  chalcone isomerases, **1**, 723
  malonyltransferases, **1**, 741
Callosamia spp., feeding, and toxin tolerance, **8**, 140
callose synthetase *see* 1,3-β-glucan synthase
Callosobruchus chinensis, callosobruchusic acid, **8**, 225
callosobruchusic acid, occurrence, **8**, 225
Callosobruchus maculatus, α-glucosidase sensitivity, **3**, 141
callus
  formation, **8**, 59
  Lerix leptolepis, α-cedrene, **2**, 191
calmodulin inhibitors, eudistomidin A, **8**, 527
calnexin
  functions, **3**, 147
  and glycoproteins, **3**, 31
Caloglyphus spp., 8-hydroxylinalool, **8**, 225
Caloglyphus polyphyllae, β-acaridial, **8**, 225
Caloglyphus rodriguezi, undecane, **8**, 214
Caloncoba echinata
  fatty acids, **1**, 68
  feeding experiments, **1**, 69
calonectrin, biosynthesis, **2**, 164
Calophyllum inophyllum, calanolide A, **1**, 624
Calophyllum lanigerum, calanolides, **1**, 624
Calophyllum teysmannii, calanolide A, **1**, 624
calorimetry
  differential scanning, **7**, 28
  isothermal titration, **7**, 31
  in nucleic acid hybridization reactions, **7**, 21
  in RNA structural transition analyses, **6**, 26
  see also differential scanning calorimetry (DSC);
    isothermal titration calorimetry (ITC)
Calospilos miranda, antifeedant activity against, **8**, 345
calotropin, insect sequestration, **8**, 152
calreticulin
  and glycoproteins, **3**, 31
  localization, **3**, 20
calycosin, biosynthesis, **1**, 795, 802
Calystegia sepium, calystegines, **3**, 132, 134, 142
calystegine A$_3$
  insect sequestration, **8**, 152

structure, **3**, 133
calystegine A$_5$, structure, **3**, 133
calystegine A$_6$, structure, **3**, 133
calystegine A$_7$, structure, **3**, 133
calystegine B$_1$
  structure, **3**, 133
  structure–activity relationships, **3**, 139
calystegine B$_2$
  occurrence, **3**, 140, 142
  plant growth inhibition, **3**, 142
  structure, **3**, 133
  structure–activity relationships, **3**, 139
calystegine B$_2$, *N*-methyl-, isolation, **3**, 133
calystegine B$_3$
  structure, **3**, 133
  structure–activity relationships, **3**, 139
calystegine B$_4$, structure, **3**, 133
calystegine B$_5$, structure, **3**, 133
calystegine C$_1$
  occurrence, **3**, 140
  structure, **3**, 133
  structure–activity relationships, **3**, 139
calystegine C$_1$, *N*-methyl-, isolation, **3**, 133
calystegine C$_2$, structure, **3**, 133
calystegines
  antimicrobial activity, **3**, 142
  biological activity, **3**, 140
  from, pseudotropine, **4**, 29
  occurrence, **3**, 132, 134, 140
  structure, **3**, 133
  structure–activity relationships, **3**, 139
  toxicity, **3**, 140
camalexin, as phytoalexin, **8**, 187
camalexin, methoxy-, as phytoalexin, **8**, 187
cambium cells
  monolignols
    accumulation, **3**, 676
    conversion, **3**, 676
    early studies, **3**, 676
cambium sap, lignins, **3**, 677
Camellia japonica, green odor studies, **1**, 84
Camellia sinensis
  enzyme activity, **1**, 108
  green odor studies, **1**, 84
  jasmonic acid, **1**, 128
camelliatannins, structure, **3**, 785
camellidin I, applications, antifungal agents, **8**, 183
camellidin II, applications, antifungal agents, **8**,
    183
Campanulaceae, 2,5-dihydroxymethyl-3,4-
    dihydroxypyrrolidine, **3**, 134
campestanol, synthesis, **8**, 105
campestanol, 6α-hydroxy-, synthesis, **8**, 105
campestanol, 6-oxo-, synthesis, **8**, 105
campesterol, in brassinosteroid biosynthesis, **8**, 105
camphanes, characterizations, **2**, 104
camphene
  rearrangement, **2**, 107
  structure, **2**, 104
(−)-camphene, biosynthesis, **2**, 141
1,2-campholide, biosynthesis, **2**, 114
campholonic acid, 2-hydroxy-, biosynthesis, **2**, 114
α-campholonic acid, biosynthesis, **2**, 114
camphor
  applications, **2**, 101
  catabolism, **2**, 114
  effects, on herbivores, **8**, 142
  structure, **2**, 104
camphor, 6-oxo-, biosynthesis, **2**, 114
(+)-camphor, biosynthesis, **2**, 146
camphoric acid, isoketo-, biosynthesis, **2**, 114
Camponotus spp.
  3,4-dihydroisocoumarin, **8**, 241

propanoate, **8**, 240
Camponotus herculaneus, invictolide, **8**, 240
Camponotus pennsylvanicus, undecane, **8**, 214
Camponotus rufipes, 3,4-dihydroisocoumarin, **8**, 241
cAMP receptor protein (CRP), encoding, **3**, 478
Camptotheca acuminata, camptothecin, **4**, 117, **7**, 599
camptothecin, applications, antineoplastic agents, **7**, 594
camptothecin, 9-amino-, water solubility, **7**, 600
camptothecin(s)
 antitumor agents, **7**, 594
 as DNA topoisomerase I inhibitors, **7**, 599
 from, strictosamide, **4**, 117
 irenotecan, **7**, 599
 occurrence, **7**, 599
 photochemical DNA damage, **7**, 544
 topotecan, **7**, 599
Campylobacter jejuni
 lipid A, structure, **3**, 200
 3-phosphoshikimate 1-carboxyvinyltransferase, **1**, 593
Campyloma verbasci
 (*E*)-2-butenyl butanoate, **8**, 210
 butyl butanoate, **8**, 210
CaMV 35S promoters, in gene expression regulation, **2**, 211
Canadian beaver *see Castor fiber*
(−)-canadine, occurrence, **8**, 344
canadine synthase, substrate specificity, **4**, 42
canadinic acid, as intermediate, **4**, 42
D-canarose *see* 2,6-dideoxy-D-*arabino*-hexose
Canavalia ensiformis
 β-N-acetylhexosaminidase, **5**, 297
 canavanine, **8**, 346
 fungal infection, **1**, 799
canavanine
 effects, on herbivores, **8**, 146
 occurrence, **8**, 346
cancer
 boron neutron capture therapy, **7**, 293
 and DNA damage, **7**, 372
 and *N*-glycosylation, **3**, 14
 treatment, polyhydroxy alkaloids, **3**, 142
 see also breast cancer; colon cancer; lung cancer;
  prostate cancer; skin cancer
candicidin
 antifungal activity, **4**, 200
 biosynthesis, **1**, 612
Candida 107, phosphoketolase, **3**, 393
Candida albicans
 demethylallosamidin studies, **1**, 149
 genetic code, **4**, 360
 lanosterol synthase, **2**, 282
 squalene epoxidase, **2**, 270
Candida humicola, threonine aldolase, **3**, 400
Candida lipolytica, desaturation activity, **1**, 45
Candida pseudotropicalis, UDPglucose 4-epimerase, **3**, 508
Candida rugosa, lipases, **5**, 128, 129
Candida tropicalis
 2-enoyl-CoA hydratase, **1**, 52
 3*R*-hydroxyacyl-CoA dehydrogenase, **1**, 52
Candida utilis, transaldolase, **3**, 419
canellal, antifeedant activity, **8**, 308
canin, antifeedant activity, **8**, 308
cannabinoids
 receptors, **1**, 281
  molecular phylogeny, **1**, 281
(−)-cannabisin B
 antifeedant activity, **1**, 695
 occurrence, **1**, 674
(−)-cannabisin D
 antifeedant activity, **1**, 695
 occurrence, **1**, 674
Cannabis sativa, lignan amides, **1**, 676

cantharidin
 biosynthesis, **8**, 350, 351
 insecticidal activity, **8**, 350
 insect sequestration, **8**, 363
 occurrence, **8**, 234, 350
 toxicity, **8**, 350
canthariphilous beetles, cantharidin sequestration, **8**, 350
canthariphilous flies, cantharidin sequestration, **8**, 350
canthaxanthin
 accumulation, **2**, 337
 in astaxanthin biosynthesis, **2**, 344
 chemical synthesis, **2**, 347
caparrapi oxide
 occurrence, **8**, 229
 structure, **8**, 234
caproic acid, *N*-biotinyl-6-amino-, conjugation, **7**, 197
caproic acid, digoxigenin-*O*-succinyl-ε-amino-,
  conjugation, **7**, 197
caprolactins
 antiviral activity, **8**, 595
 cytotoxicity, **8**, 595
 occurrence, **8**, 595
Capsicum annuum
 capsidiol, **2**, 181
 chloroplast stroma, phytoene synthases, **5**, 339
 geranylgeranyl diphosphate synthase, **8**, 50
  gene cloning, **2**, 87
 geranyl*trans*transferase, cloning, **2**, 74
 grossamides, **1**, 676
 hydroperoxide lyase activity, **1**, 95
 isopentenyl diphosphate isomerase, purification, **2**, 71
Capsicum chinense, 5-hydroxyferulic acid, **3**, 671
capsidiol
 biosynthesis, **2**, 181, 182
 and 15-hydroxytrichodiene levels, compared, **2**, 212
 ^{13}C NMR spectra, **2**, 182
 ^{2}H NMR spectra, **2**, 182
 occurrence, **2**, 181
carane monoterpenes, characterization, **2**, 105
Carassius auratus
 17α,20β-dihydroxy-4-pregnen-3-one, **8**, 230
 prostaglandin F$_{2α}$, **1**, 237
 prostaglandins, **1**, 237
 sex pheromones, **8**, 426
Carausius spp., diuretic hormone, **8**, 300
carbacyclin, biological activity, **1**, 190
carbamate, ethyl *N*-(2-phenethyl)-, isolation, **8**, 431
carbamate, methoxy-, in esperamicin, **7**, 573
1-carbamate, *trans*-1,3-butadiene-, cycloaddition, **5**, 430
carbamates
 antisense oligonucleotide linkages, **7**, 301
 ring-closure, mechanisms, **1**, 828
carbamoylaspartic dehydrase *see* dihydroorotase
O-carbamoyl deacetylcephalosporin C hydroxylase,
  hydroxylation, **4**, 172
carbanilates, diphenyl-, occurrence, **8**, 380
carbanions
 generation, **5**, 6
 as intermediates, **5**, 6
CarBank data bank, **3**, 40
(5*R*)-carbapen-2-em-3-carboxylic acid, occurrence, **8**, 398
1-carbapen-2-em-3-carboxylic acid, biosynthesis, **4**, 187
carbapenems
 antibiotic activity, **4**, 186
 biochemistry, **4**, 186
 biosynthesis, **4**, 187
 characterization, **4**, 240
 genetics, **4**, 187
 occurrence, **8**, 398
carbaryl, catabolic routes, **3**, 377
carbazole, 4,6-dibromo-3-hydroxy- (DBHC), binding, **8**, 526
carbazole alkaloids

biosynthesis, **4**, 54
occurrence, **4**, 54
carbenium ions, as intermediates, **5**, 6
carbinols, tertiary cyclopropyl-, rillingol, **2**, 254
carbinyl cations, cyclopropyl-, rearrangement, **5**, 337
carbinyl cations, tertiary cyclopropyl-
as intermediates, **2**, 254
as starting materials, **5**, 339
carbinyl radicals, aziridyl, reactions, **5**, 210
carbinyl radicals, azocyclopropyl-
as intermediates, **5**, 209
rearrangement, **5**, 209
chemical models, **5**, 210
carbinyl radicals, cyclopropyl-, rearrangement, **5**, 210
carbinyl radicals, 1-methylcyclopropyl-, rearrangement,
5, 220
carbocation, and the S_N1 process, **5**, 52
carbocationic intermediates, in presqualene diphosphate
conversion to squalene, **2**, 253
carbocations
biochemistry, **2**, 4
biosynthesis
via allylic diphosphate ionization, **2**, 7
via epoxide protonation, **2**, 6
via protonation–alkene alkylation, **2**, 5
via protonation–deprotonation, **2**, 5
reactions, **2**, 11
carbocyclic analogues, **7**, 256
carbodiimide, use in formation of dumb-bell DNAs, **7**,
366
carbodiimide, 1,3-dicyclohexyl-, **7**, 111
carbodiimide, dicyclohexyl- (DCC), in oligonucleotide
synthesis, **6**, 82, **7**, 107
carbodiimide hydrochloride, 1-(3-dimethylaminopropyl)-
3-ethyl (EDC), in oligonucleotide coupling, **7**,
158
carbohydrate-deficient glycoprotein syndrome (CDGS)
and *N*-glycosylation, **3**, 14
α-1,6-mannosyl-glycoprotein β-1,2-*N*-
acetylglucosaminyltransferase role in, **3**, 52
type I, etiology, **3**, 59
type II, etiology, **3**, 59
carbohydrate epitopes, localization, **3**, 504
carbohydrates
biosynthesis, pathways, **3**, 2
chains, *O*-linkages, **3**, 70
mass spectra, **3**, 1
metabolism, **5**, 157, 316
Entner–Doudoroff pathway, **3**, 421
nanoprobe studies, **3**, 1
NMR spectra, **3**, 1
overview, **3**, **1–11**
structural diversity, **3**, 1
structure, CarBank data bank, **3**, 40
x-ray crystallography, **3**, 1
β-carboline alkaloids
biosynthesis, **4**, 54
occurrence, **8**, 553
β-carbolines
occurrence, **8**, 525, 529
structure, **8**, 529
carbon acids
enolization, **5**, 6, 7, 11
enol tautomers, pK_a, **5**, 7
carbonate, roles, in fatty acid biosynthesis, **1**, 3
carbonate, cyclic, functionality, in natural products, **1**,
208
carbonate dehydratase, zeatin-induced, **8**, 66
carbonate hydro-lyase *see* carbonate dehydratase
carbon–carbon bond formation, **3**, 7
and farnesyl-diphosphate farnesyltransferase, **2**, 246
ribozyme-catalyzed, **6**, 139
carbon–cobalt bonds

cleavage
acceleration, **5**, 173
catalysis, **5**, 172
homolysis
catalysis, **5**, 172
entropy-driven, **5**, 176
reformation, **5**, 177
strength, **5**, 173
carbon dioxide
biological activity, **8**, 93
receptors for, **8**, 209
carbon fixation, in photosynthesis, **3**, 443
carbonic anhydrase *see* carbonate dehydratase
carbonium ions, in isopentenyl diphosphate isomerase
reaction, **2**, 72
carbon monoxide, biological activity, **8**, 93
carbon–phosphorus bonds, formation reactions, **1**, 868
carbon phosphorus–carbon bonds, in bialaphos, **1**, 866
carbon–phosphorus compounds, natural, biosynthesis, **1**,
865–880
carbon–sulfur bonds, natural products containing,
biosynthesis, **1**, 20
carbonyl, 2,4-dinitrophenylethoxy- (DNPEoc), as 5'-
hydroxyl protecting group, **7**, 127
carbonyl, fluorenylmethoxy (FMOC)
applications, 5'-hydroxyl group protection, **7**, 127
deoxyadenosine protection, **7**, 123
carbonyl, *p*-phenylazophenyloxy- (PAPoc), as 5'-
hydroxyl protecting group, **7**, 127
carbonyl compounds
isomers, **5**, 31
nucleophilic substitution, **5**, 7
2'-carboxybenzalpyruvate aldolase *see* 4-(2-
carboxyphenyl)-2-oxobut-3-enoate aldolase
carboxycyclohexadienyl dehydratase, catalysis, **5**, 344
carboxylic acid, (2*R*)-cyclopent-2-enyl- *see* aleprolic acid
carboxylic acid, (1*R*,3*R*,4*R*)-3,4-dihydro-, **1**, 75
carboxylic acids, as bacterial aromatic polyketide
synthase primers, **1**, 475
carboxylic acids, hydroxy-, detection, **1**, 297
carboxyl transferase(s)
in acetyl-CoA carboxylase, **1**, 25
sequencing, **1**, 27
types of, **1**, 27
carboxymethylenebutenolidase
catalysis, **5**, 130
mechanisms, **5**, 132
nucleophiles, **5**, 53
occurrence, **5**, 112
structure, **5**, 130
4-carboxymethylenebut-2-en-4-olide lactonohydrolase
see carboxymethylenebutenolidase
5-carboxymethyl-2-hydroxymuconate isomerase
catalysis, **5**, 46
crystal structure, **5**, 47
evolutionary relationships, **5**, 46
kinetic barriers, **5**, 35
5-(carboxymethyl)-2-oxo-3-hexene-1,6-dioate (COHED)
decarboxylase, catalysis, **5**, 38
carboxypeptidase II, occurrence, **5**, 112
carboxypeptidase catalytic triad, occurrence, **1**, 893
D,D-carboxypeptidases, roles, in peptidoglycan
biosynthesis, **3**, 267
carboxypeptidase Y mutants, occurrence, **3**, 31
4-(2-carboxyphenyl)-2-oxobut-3-enoate aldolase
biochemistry, **3**, 375
purification, **3**, 376
(3*E*)-4-(2-carboxyphenyl)-2-oxobut-3-enoate 2-
carboxybenzaldehyde-lyase *see* 4-(2-carboxyphenyl)-
2-oxobut-3-enoate aldolase
carboxyphosphono*enol*pyruvate phosphonomutase
C-P bond formation, **1**, 870
genetics, **1**, 874

homogeneity, **1**, 870
homology, **1**, 877
carboxyphosphono*enol*pyruvate synthase, encoding, **1**, 874
5-*O*-(1-carboxyvinyl)-3-phoshoshikimate phosphate-lyase *see* chorismate synthase
carcinogenesis, and DNA damage, **7**, 582
carcinogens
  aflatoxins, **7**, 470
  2-aminofluorene, **7**, 470
  covalent, **7**, 470
  nitrosamines, **7**, 521
  polycyclic aromatic hydrocarbons, **7**, 470
carcinostatic agents, deamination, **5**, 86
Carcinus maenas
  8*R*-hydroxyeicosapentaenoic acid, **1**, 246
  8*R*-hydroxyeicosatetraenoic acid, **1**, 246
  thromboxane B₂, **1**, 246
cardenolides
  insect sequestration, **8**, 361, 362, 363
  occurrence, **8**, 361
cardioaccelerating substances, use of term, **8**, 299
cardioaccelerators, structure, **8**, 300
Cardiochiles nigriceps, (7*Z*,13*Z*)-7,13-heptacosadiene, **8**, 219
cardiotonic agents, striatoxin, **8**, 478
cardiovascular system, peripheral circulation, prostaglandin studies, **1**, 196
car-3-ene
  biosynthesis, **2**, 135
  occurrence, **8**, 143
(+)-car-3-ene synthases, incubation, **2**, 135
car-3-en-5-one, biosynthesis, **2**, 135
car genes
  carA, encoding, **4**, 187
  carC, encoding, **4**, 187
  carI
    encoding, **4**, 187
    mutations, **8**, 399
  carR, **4**, 187
    isolation, **8**, 399
  cloning, **4**, 187
  mutants, **2**, 334
  nomenclature, **2**, 327
Caribbean fruit flies
  sex pheromones, **8**, 236
  see also Anastrepha suspensa
caribenolide I
  cytotoxicity, **8**, 627
  occurrence, **8**, 627
  structure, **8**, 627
carnitine, roles, in acyl-CoA transport, **1**, 49
carnitine acyltransferases, histidines, catalysis, **4**, 227
carnocin, structure, **4**, 277
α-carotene, biosynthesis, **2**, 342
β-carotene
  accumulation, **2**, 335
  in foods, **2**, 347
  biosynthesis, **2**, 5, 58
  chemical synthesis, **2**, 347
  in fruit pigment, **8**, 164
  hydroxylation, **2**, 344
  structure, **2**, 327
  as substrate, **2**, 344
β-carotene, dihydro-, biosynthesis, **2**, 343
β,β-carotene, (3*R*,3′*R*)-3,3′-bis(β-D-glucosyloxy)- *see* zeaxanthin diglucoside
β,β-carotene, (3*R*)-3-(β-D-glucosyloxy)- *see* β-cryptoxanthin monoglucoside
β,φ-carotene *see* β-isorenieratene
β,ψ-carotene, 7′,8′-dihydro- *see* β-zeacarotene
β,ψ-carotene, 1′-glucosyloxy-3,4,3′,4′-tetrahydro-1′,2′-dihydro- *see* myxobactin

ζ-carotene
  biosynthesis, **2**, 324, 338
  functions, **2**, 340
  as intermediate, **2**, 331
  structure, **2**, 324
  as substrate, **2**, 341, 343
φ,φ-carotene *see* isorenieratene
ψ,ψ-carotene *see* lycopene
ψ,ψ-carotene, 7,8-dihydro- *see* neurosporene
ψ,ψ-carotene, 1-methoxy-3,4-didehydro-1,2,7′,8′-tetrahydro- *see* spheroidene
ψ,ψ-carotene, 1-methoxy-1,2,7′,8′-tetrahydro- *see* methoxyneurosporene
ψ,ψ-carotene, 7,8,11,12,7′,8′,11′,12′-octahydro- *see* phytoene
ψ,ψ-carotene, 7,8,7′,8′-tetrahydro- *see* ζ-carotene
ψ,ψ-carotene, 7,8,11,12-tetrahydro- *see* lycopene, 7,8,11,12-tetrahydro-
ζ-carotene desaturase, discovery, **2**, 341
(3*R*,3′*R*)-β,β-carotene-3,3′-diol *see* zeaxanthin
β,ψ-carotene-3,1′-diol, 2′-(β-L-rhamnopyranosyloxy)-3,4′-didehydro-1′,2′-dihydro- *see* myxoxanthophyll
β,β-carotene-4,4′-dione *see* canthaxanthin
β,β-carotene-4,4′-dione, 3,3′-dihydroxy- *see* astaxanthin
β-carotene hydroxylase, homologues, **2**, 343
carotene oxidase(s) *see* lipoxygenase(s)
carotenes
  accumulation, **2**, 336
  biosynthesis, **2**, 377
  carbon dioxide activity, **2**, 377
  use of term, **2**, 323
carotenogenesis
  blue light-induced, **2**, 333, 346
  in *Streptomyces* spp., **2**, 346
carotenoid desaturases
  CrtI-type, **2**, 341, 348
  CrtP-type, **2**, 341
  definition, **2**, 340
carotenoids
  in abscisic acid biosynthesis, **8**, 84
  applications, **2**, 347
    coloring agents, **2**, 347
  binding, **2**, 325
  biosynthesis, **2**, 26, **321–352**
    in bacteria, **2**, 327
    biochemical pathway, **2**, 324
    enzymes, **2**, 338
    evolutionary conservation, **2**, 339
    gene nomenclature, **2**, 327
    genes, **2**, 327
    genetic engineering, **2**, 347
    inhibitors, **2**, 324, 333, 338
    issues, **2**, 348
    light-induced, **2**, 345
    overview, **2**, 322
    regulatory mechanisms, **2**, 344
  C₃₀, biosynthesis, **2**, 331, 337
  C₄₀, biosynthesis, **2**, 331, 337
  C₄₅, biosynthesis, **2**, 331
  C₅₀, biosynthesis, **2**, 331
  chemical synthesis, **2**, 347
  classification, **2**, 323
  color range, **2**, 322
  degradation products, **8**, 234
  functions, **2**, 326
  localization, **2**, 325
  nomenclature, **2**, 322
  occurrence, **2**, 322
    fruits, **8**, 164
    pollen, **8**, 163
    Porifera, **8**, 469, 589
    yellow flower pigmentation, **8**, 160
  overproduction, **2**, 336

photooxidative damage mediation, **2**, 326
pigment–protein complexes, **2**, 325
semisystematic names, **2**, 322
as starting materials, for abscisic acid, **8**, 87
structure, **2**, 322
trivial names, **2**, 322
underproduction, **2**, 336
use of term, **2**, 323
see also carotenes; xanthophylls
(3*R*)-*β*,*β*-caroten-3-ol *see β*-cryptoxanthin
β,*β*-caroten-3-ol, (3*R*,3′*R*)-3′-(*β*-D-glucosyloxy)- *see*
        zeaxanthin monoglucoside
ψ,*ψ*-caroten-1-ol, 3,4-didehydro-1,2,7′,8′-tetrahydro- *see*
        demethylspheroidene
ψ,*ψ*-caroten-1-ol, 1,2,7′,8′-tetrahydro- *see*
        hydroxyneurosporene
β,*β*-caroten-4-one *see* echinenone
β,*β*-caroten-4-one, (3*S*,3′*R*)-3,3′-dihydroxy- *see*
        adonixanthin
β,*ψ*-caroten-4-one, 1′-glucosyloxy-3′,4′-didehydro-1′,2′-
        dihydro- *see* myxobactone
ψ,*ψ*-caroten-2-one, 1-hydroxy-3,4-didehydro-1,2,7′,8′-
        tetrahydro- *see* demethylspheroidenone
ψ,*ψ*-caroten-2-one, 1-methoxy-3,4-didehydro-1,2,7′,8′-
        tetrahydro- *see* spheroidenone
carpacin, occurrence, **8**, 336
carpenter bees *see Xylocopa hirsutissima*
carpet beetles
    sex pheromones, **8**, 214
    see also Anthrenus spp.
Carpoglyphus lactis, pheromones, **8**, 13
Carpophilus spp., aggregation pheromones, **8**, 240
Carpophilus brachypterus, (2*E*,4*E*,6*E*,8*E*)-3,5,7-trimethyl-
        2,4,6,8-decatetrene, **8**, 240
Carpophilus davidsoni
    (2*E*,4*E*,6*E*)-3,5-dimethyl-2,4,6-octatriene, **8**, 240
    (2*E*,4*E*,6*E*)-5-ethyl-3-methyl-2,4,6-nonatriene, **8**, 240
    pheromones, **8**, 240
Carpophilus freemani, (2*E*,4*E*,6*E*)-5-ethyl-3-methyl-2,4,6-
        nonatriene, **8**, 240
Carpophilus mutilatus, pheromones, **8**, 240
Carposina spp.
    (*Z*)-7-icosen-11-one, **8**, 208
    (*Z*)-7-nonadecen-11-one, **8**, 208
carquinostatin B, source of, **2**, 59
carrion beetle *see Necrodes surinamensis*
carrot *see Daucus carota*
CarR protein, functions, **8**, 399
Cartharmus tinctorius
    caffeoyl-CoA *O*-methyltransferase, **3**, 672
    microsomes, desaturation, **1**, 38
carvacrol
    biosynthesis, **2**, 103
    ovicidal activity, **8**, 306
(−)-*trans*-carveol
    biosynthesis, **2**, 144
    as substrate, **2**, 147
carvone
    antifeedant activity, **8**, 306
    effects, on herbivores, **8**, 142
    structure, **2**, 103
(−)-carvone, biosynthesis, **2**, 144
Carya illinoensis, juglone, **8**, 339
Carya ovata, juglone, **8**, 339
Caryedes spp., canavanine metabolism, **8**, 346
Caryedes brasiliensis, canavanine detoxification, **8**, 146
β-caryophyllene, biosynthesis, **2**, 167
caryophyllene epoxide, effects, on herbivores, **8**, 142
caryophyllene oxide
    occurrence, **8**, 228
    toxicity, **8**, 312
caryophyllene *α*-oxide, antifeedant activity, **8**, 308
β-caryophyllene synthase, activity, **2**, 167

Caryoptera divaricata
    caryoptin, **8**, 314
    caryoptin hemiacetal, **8**, 314
    clerodin hemiacetal, **8**, 314
caryoptin, occurrence, **8**, 314
caryoptin hemiacetal, occurrence, **8**, 314
carzinophilin
    applications, antibiotics, **7**, 513
    DNA reactions of, **7**, 513
    occurrence, **7**, 513
casbene synthase(s)
    cDNA clone, **2**, 220
    functions, **2**, 217
    and limonene synthases compared, **2**, 183
    occurrence, **2**, 219
        castor beans, **2**, 209
casein kinase II
    in rephosphorylation, **3**, 483
    synergism, **3**, 484
cassava *see Manihot esculenta*
cassettes, use of term, **1**, 504
Cassia fistula, propelargonidins, **3**, 769
cassiaflavan-(4*β*→8)-epiafzelechin-(4*β*→8)-epiafzelechin,
        structure, **3**, 777
cassiaflavan-(4*α*→8)-epiafzelechins, structure, **3**, 777
cassiaflavan-(4*β*→8)-epiafzelechins, structure, **3**, 777
Cassiopeia xamachana, streptomycetes in, **8**, 593
cassumunarin A, occurrence, **1**, 385
castanospermine
    analogues, **3**, 381
    antimetastatic activity, **3**, 142
    antiviral activity, **3**, 143
    applications
        cerebral malaria prevention, **3**, 143
        α-glucosidase inhibitors, **3**, 19, 31, 151
        immunosuppressive agents, **3**, 143
    discovery, **3**, 130
    insecticidal activity, **3**, 141
    occurrence, **3**, 134, **8**, 342
    plant growth inhibition, **3**, 141
    structure, **3**, 132
    structure–activity relationships, **3**, 138, 139
    toxicity, **3**, 140
castanospermine, 6-*O*-butyryl-, applications, in AIDS
        therapy, **3**, 143
Castanospermum australe
    australine, **3**, 134, 140
    castanospermine, **3**, 140, **3**, 151, **8**, 342
    seed growth inhibition, **3**, 141
castasterone
    isolation, **8**, 99
    metabolism, **8**, 107
    synthesis, **8**, 100
castasterone, 6-deoxo-, as intermediate, **8**, 107
(−)-castoramin, occurrence, **8**, 229
castor beans *see Ricinus communis*
Castor fiber, (−)-castoramin, **8**, 229
casuarictin
    biosynthesis, **3**, 800
    inhibitory effects, **3**, 802
Casuarinaceae, casuarine, **3**, 134
casuarine
    occurrence, **3**, 134
    structure, **3**, 132
casuarinin, condensation, **3**, 783
CAT *see* chloramphenicol acetyltransferase (CAT)
catalase, homology, **8**, 66
Catalpa spp.
    catalposide, **8**, 307
    globularicisin, **8**, 307
    globularin, **8**, 307
catalpalactone, biosynthesis, **1**, 618, 620
Catalpa ovata, catalponol biosynthesis, **1**, 618

catalpol
  in nectars, **8**, 162
  occurrence, **8**, 307
  as oviposition stimulant, **8**, 156
catalponol, biosynthesis, **1**, 618, 620
catalponon, biosynthesis, **1**, 618
catalposide, occurrence, **8**, 307
catalysis
  amide bond formation, **4**, 221–238
  antibodies, mechanisms, **5**, 423–445
  chorismate mutases, **5**, 343–370
  ester bond formation, **4**, 221–238
  evolution, **6**, 127
catalytic antibodies, **2**, 124, **5**, 354, 358
  future research, **2**, 317
  kinetic parameters, **1**, 399
  synthesis, **6**, 95
  see also antibody catalysts
catalytic elution, use of term, **7**, 632
catalytic RNA *see* ribozymes
catechin, epigallo-, oxidative coupling, **3**, 782
catechin, epigallocatechin-(4*β*→6)-gallo-, nomenclature, **3**, 748
catechin, gallo-
  rearrangement, **3**, 784
  stereochemistry, **3**, 752
catechin, tetra-*O*-methyl-
  biosynthesis, **3**, 772
  conformation, **3**, 789
ent-catechin, chemical synthesis, **3**, 765
catechin-(4*α*→8)-epicatechin *see* procyanidin B$_4$
catechin-3-gallate, epigallo-
  antineoplastic activity, **3**, 792
  antioxidant activity, **3**, 792
  occurrence, **3**, 792
(+)-catechinic acid, biosynthesis, **3**, 765
catechin-4*α*-ol *see* leucocyanidin
catechin-4*β*-ol, biosynthesis, **3**, 750
catechin(s)
  biosynthesis, **1**, 717, 727
  nomenclature, **3**, 748
  oxidative coupling, **3**, 783
catechol, oxidation, **3**, 711
catecholamines, in wasp venom, **8**, 356
catechol *O*-methyltransferase
  purification, **3**, 644
  x-ray crystal structure, **3**, 647
catechol oxidase(s)
  in induced plant defense, **8**, 150
  occurrence, **3**, 709
  roles, in lignin biosynthesis, **3**, 709
catenane(s)
  kinetoplastid, **7**, 343
  structure, **7**, 361
  synthesis, **7**, 361
catfish *see* Ictalusus punctatus
cat fleas *see* Ctenocephalides felis
catharanthine
  biosynthesis, **4**, 46, 48
  occurrence, **4**, 46
Catharanthus spp., catharanthine biosynthesis, **4**, 46
Catharanthus roseus
  aromatic-L-amino-acid decarboxylase, **4**, 135
  classification, **4**, 113
  2,3-dihydroxybenzoic acid, **1**, 611
  glucoalkaloids, **4**, 113
  isochorismate synthases, **1**, 618
  loganic acid methyltransferase studies, **4**, 112
  NADPH-cytochrome P450 reductase, **3**, 639
  strictosidine synthase
    purification, **4**, 118
    substrate specificity, **4**, 121
  see also Vinca rosea

Cathartus quadricollis, quadrilure, **8**, 246
cathasterone, synthesis, **8**, 105
cathenamine, biosynthesis, **4**, 114
cationic acids, pK_a, **5**, 7
cationic species, enzymatic stabilization, **2**, 123
cation-π interactions
  in dimethylallyl*trans*transferase reaction, **2**, 84
  in monoterpene synthase studies, **2**, 123
  in oxidosqualene cyclase mechanisms, **2**, 281
catnip, nepetalactone in, **8**, 226
cauliflower buds, plastids, **3**, 464
Caulobacter crescentus, 2-dehydro-3-deoxy-6-phosphogalactonate aldolase, **3**, 429
CBD *see* cellulose binding domain (CBD)
CBF-1 *see* cytokinin-binding factor-1 (CBF-1)
CBHI *see* cellobiohydrolase I (CBHI)
CBHII *see* cellobiohydrolase II (CBHII)
cbi genes
  homologues, **4**, 152
  occurrence, **4**, 153
CC-1065
  analogues
    with altered reactivity, **7**, 506
    sequence selectivity, **7**, 505
  applications, DNA structure probes, **7**, 98
  conjugation, **7**, 169
  cytotoxicity, mechanisms, **7**, 506
  DNA reactions with, **7**, 504
  occurrence, **7**, 504
  studies, **7**, 492
CCAAT box
  characterization, **4**, 177
  in human squalene synthase, **2**, 261
  in *β*-lactam biosynthesis, **4**, 177
CCCV *see* coconut cadang cadang viroid (CCCV)
CChMV *see* chrysanthemum chlorotic mottle viroid (CChMV)
CCR genes
  *CCR*1, expression **3**, 674
  *CCR*2, expression, **3**, 676
CD11c/CD18, as endotoxin transmembrane signaling receptor, **3**, 181
CD14, as lipopolysaccharide receptor, **3**, 181
CD22*β*, B-lymphocyte adhesion, **3**, 46
CD44
  O-glycans, **3**, 71
  as hyaluronan receptor, **3**, 174
CD45, T-lymphocyte adhesion, **3**, 46
CD62P antigen *see* PADGEM protein
CDGS *see* carbohydrate-deficient glycoprotein syndrome (CDGS)
cDNA
  cloning, 1-aminocyclopropane-1-carboxylate synthase, **8**, 97
  for farnesyl-diphosphate farnesyltransferase, **2**, 250
  α-glucosidase I encoding, **3**, 18
  human, cloning, **2**, 73
  libraries
    in cloning, **7**, 654
    probing, **1**, 656
  photodamage, **7**, 164
  for prostaglandin I synthase, **1**, 261
  for squalene epoxidase, **2**, 270
  for thromboxane-A synthase, **1**, 262
cDNA subtractive hybridization, use in gene isolation, **2**, 208
CDPabequose-synthase, encoding, **3**, 208
CDPcholine, in platelet-activating factor biosynthesis, **1**, 295
CDPcholine:1-alkyl-2-acetyl-*sn*-glycerol cholinephosphotransferase, activity, **1**, 295
CDPcholine:1,2-diacylglycerol cholinephosphotransferase *see* diacylglycerol cholinephosphotransferase

CDP-6-deoxy-Δ3,4-glucoseen-reductase, coding, **3**, 208
CDP-6-deoxy-L-*threo*-D-*glycero*-4-hexulose-3-dehydrase
    catalysis, **3**, 338
    roles, in 3,6-dideoxyhexose biosynthesis, **3**, 337
CDP-6-deoxy-L-*threo*-D-*glycero*-4-hexulose-3-dehydrase
    reductase, roles, in 3,6-dideoxyhexose
    biosynthesis, **3**, 339
CDP-6-deoxy-D-*xylo*-4-hexulose-3-dehydratase, coding,
    3, 208
CDP-3,6-dideoxy-D-*glycero*-D-*glycero*-4-hexulose-5-
    epimerase, roles, in 3,6-dideoxyhexose biosynthesis,
    3, 341
CDP-3,6-dideoxy-D-*glycero*-L-*glycero*-4-hexulose-4-
    reductase, roles, in 3,6-dideoxyhexose biosynthesis, **3**,
    341
CDPethanolamine:1,2-diacylglycerol
    ethanolaminephosphotransferase *see*
    ethanolaminephosphotransferase
CDPglucose
    glycogen synthase activity, **3**, 452
    pyrophosphorolysis, **3**, 478
CDP-D-glucose, biosynthesis, **3**, 335
CDP-D-glucose-4,6-dehydratase
    coding, **3**, 208
    occurrence, **3**, 334
    roles, in 3,6-dideoxyhexose biosynthesis, **3**, 336
CDP-6-Δ-3,4-glucoseen reductase, catalysis, **1**, 156
CDPglucose pyrophosphorylase *see* glucose-1-phosphate
    cytidylyltransferase
CDPparatose synthase, encoding, **3**, 208
CDPtyvelose-2-epimerase, encoding, **3**, 209
CDRP *see* 1-deoxy ribulose *S*-phosphate,
    carboxyphenylamino- (CDRP)
CDS *see* copalyl diphosphate synthase (CDS)
CEase *see* sterol esterase
Cedrela odorata, gedunin, **8**, 321
α-cedrene, occurrence, **2**, 191
(±)-cedrusins, biosynthesis, **1**, 683
cef genes
    cefD
        encoding, **4**, 171
        localization, **4**, 171
    cefE
        encoding, **4**, 172
        transcription, **4**, 179
    cefEF, expression, **4**, 172
    cefF
        encoding, **4**, 172
        transcription, **4**, 179
    cefG, **4**, 172
        cloning, **4**, 172
celabenzine, occurrence, **8**, 344
celangulin
    antifeedant activity, **8**, 308, 312
    insecticidal activity, **8**, 344
    occurrence, **8**, 312
celecoxib, prostaglandin-endoperoxide synthase
    inhibition, **5**, 252
celery, ketones, **8**, 230
cell cultures
    in biochemical studies, advantages, **1**, 784
    elicitor responses, **1**, 784
    gene-for-gene resistance, expression, **1**, 784
cell death
    lantibiotic-induced, **4**, 280
    topoisomerase-directed, cellular pharmacology, **7**, 596
    see also apoptosis
cell differentiation, ST6Gal I expression, **3**, 46
cell division, and cytokinins, **8**, 57
cell enlargement, cytokinin-induced, **8**, 58
cell fractionation studies, protease localization, **2**, 359
cell lysis *see* cytolysis
cell membranes

interactions, with lipopolysaccharides, **3**, 201
    permeability, alteration, **4**, 199
cellobiase(s) *see* β-glucosidase(s)
cellobiohydrolase I (CBHI), occurrence, **3**, 593
cellobiohydrolase II (CBHII)
    occurrence, **3**, 593, **5**, 300
    structure, **5**, 301
cellobiohydrolase(s), activity, **3**, 566
cellobiose, computational modeling, **3**, 570
cellobiose, anhydro-, homopolymers, **3**, 530
cellobioside, β-methyl-, structure, **3**, 576
cell regulation, hormonal effects, **3**, 443
cells
    activation, mechanisms, **3**, 201
    competent, in transformation, **7**, 662
cell suspension cultures, terpene synthase expression
    studies, **2**, 211
cellulase(s)
    in *Erwinia carotovora*, **8**, 398
    occurrence, **3**, 593
    as sesquiterpenoid phytoalexin elicitor, **2**, 212
Cellulomonas fimi
    endoglucanase A, **5**, 300
    exoglycanase, **5**, 289, 292
    exo-β-1,4-glycanase, **5**, 290
cellulose, carboxymethyl (CMC), occurrence, **3**, 584
cellulose binding domain (CBD), functions, **3**, 593
cellulose(s)
    aggregation, **3**, 531, 585
        lateral, **3**, 537
        regulatory mechanisms, **3**, 586
    applications, **3**, 532
        industrial, **3**, 8, 533
    biochemistry, **3**, **529–598**
    biodegradation, **3**, 592
    biogenesis, **3**, 579, 580
    biological aspects, **3**, 579
    biosynthesis, **3**, 2, 8, 531, 580
    chain polarity, **3**, 536
    characterization, **3**, 529, 530, 588
        early studies, **3**, 532
        methods, **3**, 576
    computational modeling, **3**, 570
    constituents, **3**, 533
    crystalline lattices
        I$_\alpha$ form, **3**, 533, 540, 554
        I$_\beta$ form, **3**, 533, 554
    crystallography
        problems, **3**, 536
        studies, **3**, 535, 535
    definitions, **3**, 530
    diversity, **3**, 530
    early studies, **3**, 530
    electron microscopy, **3**, 566, 578
    future research, **3**, 532, 594
    historical background, **3**, 531, 532
        1840–1920 period, **3**, 533
        1920–1975 period, **3**, 535
        1975–present, **3**, 539
    hydrolysis, studies, **3**, 554
    IR spectra, **3**, 539, 543, 555
    lineshape analysis, **3**, 560
    molecular dynamics simulation, **3**, 571
    molecular mechanics studies, **3**, 571
    native
        aggregation, **3**, 586
        compound, **3**, 589
        ^{13}C NMR spectra, **3**, 591
        pure, **3**, 587
        structure, **3**, 586
    ^{13}C NMR spectra, **3**, 540, 549, 559, 578
        mathematical analyses, **3**, 564
        non-linear least-squares analysis, **3**, 565

principal components analysis, **3**, 564
proton spin-relaxation edited, **3**, 562
resolution enhancement protocols, **3**, 562
occurrence, **3**, 531
oligomers, **3**, 573
polymorphy, **3**, 572
Raman spectra, **3**, 539, **3**, 541, 542, 555, 578
roles, early studies, **3**, 535
solid supports derived from, **7**, 110
solubility, **3**, 531
spectroscopy, **3**, 542
structure, **3**, 531, 540
  chemical implications, **3**, 575
  early studies, **3**, 532
  at microscale level, **3**, 574
  models, **3**, 538
  at nanoscale level, **3**, 573
  polymer hypothesis, **3**, 532
  summary, **3**, 577
  symmetry, **3**, 536
as substrates, **3**, 530
supramolecular organization, **3**, 574
type I
  conformation, **3**, 536, 539, 545
  ^{13}C NMR spectra, **3**, 552
  Raman spectra, **3**, 545
type II
  analyses, **3**, 572
  conformation, **3**, 536, 539, 545
  Raman spectra, **3**, 545
type III
  analyses, **3**, 572
  synthesis, **3**, 537
type IV
  analyses, **3**, 572
  Raman spectra, **3**, 573
  synthesis, **3**, 537, 572
  x-ray diffraction, **3**, 573
ulstrastructural organization, **3**, 582
use of term, **3**, 530
x-ray crystal structure, early studies, **3**, 535
cellulosomes, occurrence, **3**, 593
cell wall
  analysis, **3**, 601
  biosynthesis, inhibition, **4**, 282
  constituents, **3**, 590
  early studies, **3**, 534
  hemicelluloses, **3**, 600
  lignins
    biosynthesis, **3**, 618
    configuration, **3**, 687
    deposition, **3**, 690
    heterogeneity, **3**, 691
  models, **3**, 589
  polysaccharides, **3**, 688
  primary, **3**, 498
    composition, **3**, 498
    structure, **3**, 498
2,7,11-cembratriene-4,6-diol *see* duvatriendiol
1*S*-cembrene, **2**, 220
neo-cembrene, **2**, 220
cembrene A, occurrence, **8**, 230
cembrenediols, **2**, 220
cembrene 4,6-diols, biosynthesis, **2**, 220
cembrene 4-ols, biosynthesis, **2**, 220
cembrenes, occurrence, **2**, 220
Centaurea spp., cichoriin, **8**, 337
Centaurea cyanus, malonyltransferases, **1**, 741
Centris spp., monoterpenes, **8**, 223
centrolobol, applications, feeding inhibitors, **8**, 139
Cephaelis ipecacuanha, isoquinoline alkaloids, **4**, 40
cephalaspidean mollusk *see Haminoea navicula*
Cephalocereus senilis

chalcone isomerases, **1**, 723
4-coumarate-CoA ligase, **1**, 721
cephalomannine, biosynthesis, **2**, 221
cephalosporin, bioactive properties, **4**, 197
cephalosporin, 7-methoxy-, biosynthesis, **4**, 173
cephalosporinase(s) *see* β-lactamase(s)
cephalosporin C
  biosynthesis, **4**, 164, 240
    in fungi, **4**, 172
    regulation, **4**, 181
    industrial production, effects of D,L-methionine on, **4**, 176
  β-lactamase resistance, **3**, 285
  resistance, **4**, 160
cephalosporin C, deacetyl, biosynthesis, **1**, 840
cephalosporins
  biochemistry, **4**, 160
  biosynthesis, **1**, 840
    genetics, **4**, 173
    overview, **4**, 162
  characterization, **4**, 240
  from, amino acids, **4**, 165
  industrial production, **4**, 173, 179
  β-lactamase resistance, **3**, 285
Cephalosporium acremonium
  ACV synthetase, **1**, 840
  isopenicillin N synthase, **1**, 842
Cephalosporium aphidicola, aphidicolin, **2**, 239
Cephalosporium caerulens
  cerulenin, **1**, 357
  3β-hydroxyprotosta-17(20)[16,21-*cis*],24-diene, **2**, 281
cephalostatin 1, structure, **8**, 533
cephamycin C
  biosynthesis, **4**, 164
  β-lactamase resistance, **3**, 285
cephamycin C synthetase, catalysis, **4**, 173
cephamycins
  biochemistry, **4**, 160
  biosynthesis
    in Actinomycetales, **4**, 172
    genetics, **4**, 173
    overview, **4**, 162
    regulation, **4**, 179
  characterization, **4**, 240
  from, amino acids, **4**, 165
ceph-3-ems, structure, **4**, 160
Cerambycidae
  pheromones, **8**, 210, 211, 213
  see also Phoracantha synonyma
Ceramiaceae, cyclic bromoethers, **1**, 303
ceramide
  biosynthesis, **3**, 88
  galactosylation, **3**, 92
  roles, in signal transduction, **3**, 3
  transport, **3**, 91
ceramide, dihydro-
  biosynthesis, in endoplasmic reticulum, **3**, 89
  signaling inactivity, **3**, 90
ceramide, *N*-6(7-nitro-2,1,3-benzoxadiazol-4-yl)aminohexanoyldihydro-, as starting material, for sphingolipids, **3**, 90
ceramide-1-sulfonic acids, occurrence, **8**, 598
ceratiolin, as allelopathic agent, **8**, 169
Ceratitis capitata
  3,4-dihydro-2*H*-pyrrol, **8**, 210
  ethyl acetate, **8**, 209
  ethyl (*E*)-3-octenoate, **8**, 211
  (*E,E*)-α-farnesene, **8**, 227
  geranyl acetate, **8**, 223
Ceratocystis ulmi, ceratoulmin, **8**, 181
ceratoulmin
  occurrence, **8**, 181
  phytotoxicity, **8**, 181

cerberalignans, occurrence, **1**, 688
Cerbera manghas, cerberalignans, **1**, 688
Cerbera odollam, cerberalignans, **1**, 688
Cercidiphyllum japonicum, lignans, **1**, 691
Cercospora spp., abscisic acid, **8**, 73
Cercospora cruenta, abscisic acid biosynthetic pathway, **8**, 87
Cercospora pini-densiflorae, abscisic acid biosynthetic pathway, **8**, 87
Cercospora rosicola, abscisic acid biosynthetic pathway, **8**, 87
Cercospora transversiana, transversial, **2**, 222
cercosporin, phototoxicity, **8**, 176
cereals, aleurone cells, enzyme activity, **8**, 45
cerebroside, fruiting-inducing, occurrence, **8**, 408
ceric ammonium nitrate, trityl group removal, **7**, 126
cerulenin
    antifungal activity, **1**, 564
    6-methylsalicylic acid inactivation, **1**, 357
    occurrence, **1**, 357
Cestoda, arachidonic acid metabolism, **1**, 249
CEV *see* citrus exocortis viroid (CEV)
cevadine, toxicity, **8**, 349
CF *see* conjugation factor (CF)
Cfa genes
    encoding, **1**, 65
    occurrence, **1**, 66
CFA synthase *see* cyclopropane fatty acid (CFA) synthase
c-fos mRNA
    AU rich elements, **6**, 208
    cis-acting sequences, **6**, 208
    deadenylation studies, **6**, 206
    poly(A) shortening, **6**, 206
CGTases *see* cyclomaltodextrin glucanotransferase(s)
chaetoglobosin A
    biosynthesis, **1**, 392
    ^{2}H NMR spectra, **1**, 393
    occurrence, **1**, 391
chaetoglobosin J, synthesis, **1**, 393
chaetoglobosin O, occurrence, **1**, 371
chaetoglobosins
    biological activity, **1**, 391
    occurrence, **1**, 391
    endo-selective Diels–Alder reaction, **1**, 392
Chaetomium spp., chaetoglobosins, **1**, 391
Chaetomium subaffine, chaetoglobosin A, **1**, 392
Chagas' disease, etiology, **3**, 143
Chain, Sir Ernst Boris (1906–79), antibiotic studies, **4**, 200
chain-termination method
    applications, in cloning, **7**, 664
    for DNA sequencing, **7**, 620
chalcomoracin, labeling studies, **2**, 64
chalcomycin
    applications, antibiotics, **3**, 321
    4,6-dideoxy-3-*O*-methyl-D-*ribo*-hexose, **3**, 321
    4,6-dideoxy-3-*O*-methyl-D-*xylo*-hexose, **3**, 321
chalcone, 2′,4,4′,6′-tetrahydroxy- *see* naringenin chalcone
chalcone, 4,2′,4′,6′-tetrahydroxy-, structure, **3**, 780
chalcone, 2′,4,4′-trihydroxy-, as isoflavonoid precursor, **1**, 799
chalcone 3-hydroxylase, biochemistry, **1**, 736
chalcone isomerase(s)
    biochemistry, **1**, 722
    catalysis, **1**, 790
    cDNA clones, isolation, **1**, 724
    gene expression, **1**, 724
    genetics, **1**, 723
    inhibitors, **1**, 722
    molecular biology, **1**, 723
    occurrence, **1**, 724
    purification, **1**, 723
    roles, in isoflavonoid biosynthesis, **1**, 790
    types of, **1**, 717

chalcone ketide reductase (CHKR)
    biochemistry, **1**, 732
    cDNA clones, isolation, **1**, 732
    genetics, **1**, 732
    molecular biology, **1**, 732
    nomenclature, **1**, 732
    purification, **1**, 732
chalcone 2′-*O*-methyltransferase (ChalOMT)
    cDNA clones, isolation, **1**, 740
    genetics, **1**, 800
chalcone reductase (CHR)
    catalysis, **1**, 790
    characterization, **1**, 790
    encoding, **1**, 790
    expression, **1**, 790
    interactions, with chalcone synthase, **1**, 790
    occurrence, **1**, 790
chalcones
    biosynthesis, **1**, 721, 750
        via phenylpropanoid pathway, **1**, 750
    co-occurrence, with flavans, **3**, 752
    as intermediates, **1**, 715, 716
    isomerization, non-enzymatic, **1**, 752
    reduction, **1**, 789
    roles, in ultraviolet patterning, **8**, 160
    stability, **1**, 722
    as starting materials, for flavanones, **1**, 717
    structure, **1**, 715
chalcones, 6′-hydroxy-
    biosynthesis, **1**, 790
    occurrence, **1**, 736
chalcone synthase (CHS), **1**, **749–771**
    and acridone synthase compared, **1**, 755
    activity
        after heterologous expression, **1**, 754
        studies, **1**, 758
    biochemistry, **1**, 721, 734
    byproducts, **1**, 750
    catalysis, **1**, 412, **1**, 19, 716, 789, 790
    cDNA clones, isolation, **1**, 721
    characterization, **1**, 789
    cloning, **1**, 19
    condensation, **1**, 756
    consensus sequences, **1**, 754, 756
    conversions to stilbene synthase, via mutagenesis, **1**, 758
    cysteine
        active site environment, **1**, 756
        conserved, **1**, 756
    definitions, **1**, 750
    dimers, **1**, 752
    evolution, **1**, 762
    excision, of transposable element, **1**, 758
    function, **1**, 756
    future research, **1**, 765
    gene families, **1**, 755
    genetics, **1**, 721, 789
    interactions, with chalcone reductase, **1**, 790
    intermediates, modification, **1**, 763
    intron, conserved, **1**, 753
    molecular biology, **1**, 721
    mutant proteins, **1**, 756, 758
    occurrence, **1**, 750
    properties, **1**, 752
    purification, **1**, 732
    reactions, **1**, 750
    regulatory mechanisms, **1**, 789
    relationship tree, **1**, 753
    ring folding, **1**, 751
    sequencing, **1**, 753
    and stilbene synthase compared, **1**, 754
    structure, **1**, 756
    substrate specificity, **1**, 752

subunit interactions, **1**, 757
superfamily, **1**, 759
ChalOMT *see* chalcone 2′-*O*-methyltransferase (ChalOMT)
chanoclavine, as starting material, for lysergic acid, **4**, 52
chaperones, use of term, **3**, 31
chaperonins, roles, in protein folding, **7**, 645
Charophyceae, evolution, **3**, 622
Chauliognathus lecontei, (8*Z*)-dihydromatricaria acid, **8**, 351
chaulmoogric acid, occurrence, **1**, 68
chaulmoogric acid, dihydro-, occurrence, **1**, 68
chebulagic acid, applications, direct protein binding agents, **7**, 595
cheese mite *see Tyrophagus putrescentiae*
cheilanthones
    activity, **8**, 293
    Cotton effect, **8**, 285
    IR spectra, **8**, 285
Cheiranthus spp., cardiac glycosides, **8**, 156
chelatases, isolation, **7**, 632, 634
chelerythrine, occurrence, **7**, 601
Chelidonium majus, labeling studies, **2**, 62
chemical biology, use of term, **7**, 6
chemical channels, roles, **8**, 198
chemical cleavage method
    applications, in cloning, **7**, 664
    DNA sequencing, **7**, 620
    modified, in DNA structure probing, **7**, 82
chemical communication
    isoprenoids in, **8**, 219
    studies, **8**, 202
chemical defense
    algae, **8**, 459
    applications, **8**, 198
    in ascidians, **8**, 472
    in corals, **1**, 240
    evolution, **8**, 201
    in fish, **8**, 473
    marine organisms, reviews, **8**, 459
    in Mollusca, **8**, 462
    in plants, tannin–tannase system, **3**, 821
    in Porifera, **8**, 465
chemical ecology
    insect, biochemistry, **8**, **263–375**
    microbial, and microbial hormones, **8**, **377–413**
    use of term, **8**, 2, 202
    see also marine chemical ecology; plant chemical ecology
chemically initiated electron exchange luminescence (CIEEL), mechanisms, **8**, 444
chemical messages
    selectivity, **8**, 200
    sensitivity, **8**, 200
    signal-to-noise ratio, **8**, 199
chemical shifts
    differences, **6**, 5
    mechanisms, **6**, 5
    units, **6**, 5
chemical signals
    applications, **8**, 198
    evolution, **8**, 198
    see also semiochemicals
chemiluminescence, imidazopyrazines, **8**, 452
chemistry
    encoded combinatorial, SELEX studies, **7**, 619
    and molecular biology, relevance, **7**, 6
chemoprotection
    and antioxidant activity, **1**, 700
    via lignans, **1**, 699
chemoreception, mechanisms, **8**, 417
chemotaxis, definitions, **8**, 198
chemotherapy

combinational, topoisomerase agents in, **7**, 597
DNA topoisomerases in, **7**, 594
Chenopodium ambrosioides, α-terpinene synthases, **2**, 136
cherry fly *see Rhagoletis cerasi*
cherry-oat aphid *see Rhopalosiphum padi*
chicken
    apoII mRNA, **6**, 214
    fatty acid synthase, **1**, 348
    α-1,3-mannosyl-glycoprotein β-1,2-*N*-acetylglucosaminyltransferase, genes, **3**, 50
chicken liver
    apoII mRNA, **6**, 214
    fatty acid synthase, **1**, 32
    geranyl*trans*transferase, **2**, 70
    gene cloning, **2**, 74
chicken retina, platelet-activating factor, **1**, 297
chickpeas
    2′-hydroxyformononetin, **1**, 795
    isoflavone reductase, **1**, 796
    isoflavones, **1**, 795
    isoflavonoid glycosides, **1**, 808
    pterocarpan synthase, **1**, 797
    roots, β-glucosidases, **1**, 809
    see also Cicer arietinum
chicks, neural retinal cells, galactosyltransferases, **3**, 111
chicory yellow mottle virus (ChYMV), satellite RNA, hairpin ribozymes, **6**, 247
Chilo auricilius
    (*Z*)-10-pentadecenyl acetate, **8**, 207
    (*Z*)-9-tetradecenyl acetate, **8**, 207
    (*Z*)-8-tridecenyl acetate, **8**, 207
Chilorcorus cacti, coccinellines, **8**, 351
Chilo suppressalis, ecdysteroids, **8**, 280
chimeric transcripts, analysis, **6**, 206
chimpanzees, diet, **8**, 165
Chinese cobra *see Naja naja atra*
Chinese hamster ovary (CHO)
    cells, **3**, 169
        fucosyltransferases, **3**, 119
        mutants, **3**, 170
Chinese hamsters, α-1,3-mannosyl-glycoprotein β-1,2-*N*-acetylglucosaminyltransferase, genes, **3**, 50
Chinese rhubarb *see Rheum officinale*
Chinese yew *see Taxus chinensis*
chiral amplification, applications, **8**, 202
chiral compounds, enantiomeric composition, **8**, 199
chirality
    early studies, **8**, 6
    significance of, **8**, 6
chiriquitoxin
    occurrence, **8**, 482
    voltage-gated sodium channel blocking, **8**, 482
Chironomus fusciceps, inhibition, **8**, 275
CHIs *see* chalcone isomerase(s)
chitin
    roles, **1**, 149
    structure, **3**, 286
chitinase(s)
    activity, **1**, 149
    inhibitors, **1**, 149
    occurrence, **5**, 296, 297
    reviews, **8**, 186
    in systemic acquired resistance, **1**, 133
chitinovorins, structure, **4**, 160
chitin synthase(s), **1**, 329
    roles, **1**, 149
    substrates, **3**, 286
chitin-UDP *N*-acetylglucosaminyltransferase(s) *see* chitin synthase(s)
chitobiase(s) *see* β-*N*-acetylhexosaminidase(s)
chitobiose, distortion, **5**, 297
chitodextrinase(s) *see* chitinase(s)
chitoheptaose, *N*-acetyl-, as phytoalexin elicitor, **1**, 131

CHKR *see* chalcone ketide reductase (CHKR)
Chl *see* chlorophyll (Chl)
Chl *a see* chlorophyll *a* (Chl *a*)
Chlamydia spp.
  epitopes, genus-specific, **3**, 195
  lipopolysaccharides, **3**, 195
Chlamydia pneumoniae, infections, **3**, 195
Chlamydia psittaci, infections, **3**, 195
Chlamydia trachomatis
  3-deoxy-D-*manno*-octulosonate transferase, **3**, 518
  infections, **3**, 195
Chlamydomonas reinhardtii
  desaturases, **1**, 45
  glucose-1-phosphate adenylyltransferase, **3**, 470
  glutamyl-tRNA^Glu reductase, **4**, 68
  isoprenoid biosynthesis, mevalonate-independent
    pathway, **2**, 61
  mutations, **3**, 455, 466, 473
    in starch synthesis, **3**, 458
  starch synthase, **3**, 445
Chl *b see* chlorophyll *b* (Chl *b*)
chlorambucil–oligonucleotide conjugates, synthesis, **7**, 197
chloramphenicol
  biosynthesis, **5**, 347
  discovery, **4**, 200
chloramphenicol acetyltransferase (CAT)
  activity, **3**, 52
  His motif, **4**, 227
  RNA transcription, **6**, 183
chloramphenicol acyltransferases, acyl transfer reactions, **4**, 332
Chloranthus japonicus, shizukaol A, **1**, 377
chlordecone-alcohol:NADP⁺ 2-oxidoreductase *see* chlordecone reductase
chlordecone reductase, catalysis, **1**, 276
Chlorella spp., jasmonic acid, **8**, 108
Chlorella fusca, isoprenoid biosynthesis, mevalonate-independent pathway, **2**, 61
Chlorella pyrenoidosa
  glucose-1-phosphate adenylyltransferase, **3**, 470
  9-hydroperoxyoctadecadienoic acid, **1**, 214
  13-hydroperoxyoctadecadienoic acid, **1**, 214
  jasmonic acid pathway enzymes, **1**, 121
  oxylipin metabolism, **1**, 209
Chlorella vulgaris
  fatty acids, desaturation, **1**, 38
  glucose-1-phosphate adenylyltransferase, **3**, 470
  stearate desaturation, **1**, 38
chlorinated organic compounds
  applications, **5**, 401
  biodegradation, **5**, 401
  mineralization, **5**, 401
  occurrence, **5**, 402
  problems, **5**, 401
chloriolins, occurrence, **8**, 601
4-chlorobenzoate chlorohydrolase *see* 4-chlorobenzoate dehalogenase(s)
4-chlorobenzoate:CoA ligase, studies, **3**, 651
3-chlorobenzoate dehalogenase(s), occurrence, **5**, 417, 420
4-chlorobenzoate dehalogenase(s), occurrence, **5**, 411
chlorobenzoyl CoA dehalogenase
  aryl-enzyme intermediates, mechanisms, **5**, 412
  catalysis, **5**, 13, 413
    strategies, **5**, 414
  crystal structure, **5**, 413
  mechanisms, **5**, 412
  mutagenesis, site-directed, **5**, 413
  occurrence, **5**, 411
  pre-steady state kinetic studies, **5**, 413
  rate-limiting step, **5**, 413
Chlorobiaceae, glucose-1-phosphate adenylyltransferase, **3**, 469

chlorogenic acid
  antifeedant activity, **8**, 140
  biosynthesis, **3**, 805, 807
  as insect attractant, **8**, 156
  occurrence, **8**, 337
  as oviposition stimulant, **8**, 156
1-chlorohexane halidohydrolase *see* haloalkane dehalogenase(s)
chloroperoxidase, isolation, problems, **1**, 323
4-chlorophenylacetate dioxygenase, occurrence, **5**, 417
chlorophyll *a* (Chl *a*), accumulation, **2**, 347
chlorophyll *b* (Chl *b*), accumulation, **2**, 347
chlorophyll (Chl)
  biosynthesis, **4**, 68, 72
    promotion, **8**, 59
  and carotenoid biosynthesis, **2**, 322
  carotenoid protection, **2**, 326
  depletion, effect of kinetin on, **8**, 58
  leaf content, and hydroperoxide lyase activity, **1**, 93
Chlorophyta
  jasmonic acid pathway, **1**, 121
  α-linolenic acid, **1**, 214
  stearidonic acid, **1**, 214
chloroplasts
  desaturases, **1**, 40
  DNA synthesis, cytokinin-stimulated, **8**, 59
  isopentenyl diphosphate incorporation, **2**, 377
  occurrence, **3**, 464
  replication, cytokinin-stimulated, **8**, 59
  in starch synthesis, **3**, 463
  transit sequences, **2**, 211
chlorosis, coronatine-induced, **1**, 135
chlorotetain, as glucosamine-6-phosphate synthase inhibitor, **3**, 275
chlorothricin
  analogues, **1**, 374
  biosynthesis, **1**, 370
  deoxygenation, **3**, 354
  structure, **1**, 370
chlorovulones, occurrence, **1**, 241
chlorphenotane, as environmental pollutant, **5**, 410
CHMI *see* 5-carboxymethyl-2-hydroxymuconate isomerase
CHO *see* Chinese hamster ovary (CHO)
5β-cholestan-3-one, occurrence, **8**, 230
5β-cholest-7-en-6-one, 2β,3β,14α,22R,25S-pentahydroxy-, structure, **8**, 282
cholesterol
  biosynthesis
    early studies, **2**, 3
    farnesyl-diphosphate farnesyltransferase in, **2**, 246
  in brassinosteroid biosynthesis, **8**, 105
  enantiomeric purity, **8**, 7
  homeostasis, **2**, 24
    transcriptional control, **2**, 37
  occurrence, **8**, 230
  as starting material, for 20-hydroxyecdysone, **8**, 291
  supplies, for insects, **8**, 290
cholesterol, 7-dehydro-25-hydroxy-, as intermediate, **8**, 291
cholesterol, 25-hydroxy-, in human squalene synthase regulation, **2**, 259
cholesterol, 24-methylene-, in brassinosteroid biosynthesis, **8**, 105
cholesterol, 24-methylene-25-methyl-, in brassinosteroid biosynthesis, **8**, 105
cholesterol esterase *see* sterol esterase
cholesterol-lowering agents *see* hypocholesterolemic agents
cholesterol–oligonucleotide conjugates, carcinoma cell studies, **7**, 188
cholesterol 5,6-oxide, specific microsomal enzyme, **5**, 54
cholesteryl ester synthase *see* sterol esterase

cholic acid, esters, **7**, 159
choline acyltransferases, histidines, catalysis, **4**, 227
cholinephosphotransferase *see* diacylglycerol
          cholinephosphotransferase
cholinesterase
    activity, **5**, 113
    catalysis, **5**, 113
    structure, **5**, 114
    see also acetylcholinesterase
cholinesterase I *see* acetylcholinesterase
cholinesterase II (unspecific) *see* cholinesterase
Cholodony–Went theory, of phototropism, **8**, 26
Chondrococcus spp., halogenated monoterpenes, **2**, 106
Chondrococcus hornemanni, 1,5Z-octadien-3S-ol, **1**, 211
chondroitin sulfate (CS)
    binding, **3**, 4
    biosynthesis, **3**, 171
    substitution, **3**, 161
Chordariales, sexual reproduction, **8**, 422
chorismate
    activation parameters, **5**, 348
    biosynthesis, **1**, 74
    dissociation, **1**, 602
    from
        erythrose-4-phosphate, **1**, 574
        phospho*enol*pyruvate, **1**, 574
    pseudo-diaxial forms, **5**, 348
    rearrangement, **5**, 348, 424
chorismate, 6-fluoro, biosynthesis, **1**, 602
(−)-chorismate, as starting material, for prephenate, **1**,
        367
chorismate monoesters, studies, **5**, 352
chorismate mutase(s)
    activation, **4**, 5
        parameters, **5**, 354
    applications
        commercial, **5**, 349
        therapeutic, **5**, 349
    catalysis, **5**, **343–370**
        QM/MM studies, **5**, 366
        structural requirements, **5**, 352
    catalytic efficiency, **5**, 425
    characterization, **5**, 346
    CHARMM studies, **5**, 366
    in Claisen rearrangement, **5**, 424
    electrostatic effects, **5**, 363
    entropy traps, **5**, 354
    four-helix bundle, **5**, 363
    GAMESS studies, **5**, 366
    gene fusion, **5**, 346
    gene replication, **5**, 346
    genetics, **5**, 346
    hydrogen bonds, **5**, 363
    inhibition, studies, **5**, 355
    interactions
        coiled-coil, **5**, 361
        helix-helix, **5**, 361
        hydrophobic, **5**, 365
    IR spectra, **5**, 355
        Fourier transform, **5**, 356
    isotope effects, **5**, 355
    kinetic parameters, **1**, 399
    mechanisms, **5**, 365
    MINDO studies, **5**, 366
    molecular mechanics studies, **5**, 366
    mutagenesis
        site-specific, **5**, 367
        studies, **5**, 366
    NMR spectra, **5**, 355
    occurrence, **1**, 367, **5**, 345
    pH dependency, **5**, 356
    properties, kinetic, **5**, 354, 356, 365
    regulatory mechanisms, **5**, 344, 346
    roles
        in prephenate biosynthesis, **1**, 367
        in shikimate pathway, **5**, 344
    structure
        parameters, **5**, 353
        studies, **5**, 358
    x-ray crystal structure, **5**, 358
chorismate pyruvate-lyase (amino-accepting) *see*
        anthranilate synthase(s)
chorismate pyruvatemutase(s) *see* chorismate mutase(s)
chorismate synthase
    catalysis, **1**, 599
    and flavin mononucleotides, **1**, 599
    flavin reductase activity, **1**, 599
    mechanism, **1**, 599
    occurrence, **1**, 599
    purification, **1**, 599
chorismic acid
    biosynthesis, **1**, 612, **4**, 2
    Claisen rearrangement, **1**, 619
    as intermediate, **1**, 345, **4**, 4
    roles, in shikimate pathway, **5**, 344
    as starting material, for isochorismic acid, **1**, 619
    stereochemistry, **1**, 610
    structure, **1**, 609
chorismic acid, 5,6-dihydro-, rearrangement, **5**, 352
Choristoneura fumiferana
    antifeedant activity against, **8**, 345
    infestations, and plant resistance, **8**, 177
Chou–Fasman algorithm, in polyketide synthase studies,
        1, 426
CHR *see* chalcone reductase (CHR)
Chromatiaceae, glucose-1-phosphate
        adenylyltransferase, **3**, 469
chromatin, **7**, 582
    structure, **7**, 8
chromatography, ion-exchange, in oligonucleotide
        purification, **7**, 144
chromazonarol, isolation, **8**, 460
chromium adenosine triphosphate (CrATP), as enzyme
        inhibitor, **3**, 448
Chromobacterium violaceum, lipid A, structure, **3**, 200
chromomycin
    antineoplastic activity, **4**, 198
    DNA binding, **7**, 9
chromomycins
    biological activity, **3**, 323
    2,6-dideoxy-D-*arabino*-hexose, **3**, 313
    D-olivomose, **3**, 313
    structure, **3**, 324
chromone, 5-hydroxy-2-methyl-, occurrence, **1**, 415
chromoproteins
    applications, antibiotics, **7**, 554
    endocytosis model, **7**, 582
    structure, **7**, 554
D-chromose A *see* D-olivomose
L-chromose B, occurrence, **3**, 312, 321
D-chromose C *see* 2,6-dideoxy-D-*arabino*-hexose
D-chromose D, occurrence, **3**, 312, 313
chromosomal mapping
    of human squalene synthase genes, **2**, 262
    of mouse *Fdft1* gene, **2**, 262
chromosome 1, prostaglandin-endoperoxide synthase-2
        gene mapping, **5**, 228
chromosome 8, mapping, **2**, 262
chromosome 9, prostaglandin-endoperoxide synthase-1
        gene mapping, **5**, 228
chromosome 14, mapping, **2**, 262
chromosome 2p12-p13, human, α-glucosidase I gene, **3**,
        18
chromosome 3F2, murine, **3**, 23
chromosome 4A13, murine, **3**, 23
chromosome 9p13-21, β4GalT localization, **3**, 43

chrysanthemic acid, biosynthesis, **2**, 108
chrysanthemum chlorotic mottle viroid (CChMV)
    characterization, **6**, 182
    hammerhead self-cleavage structure, **6**, 180
    hosts, **6**, 171, 186
    localization, **6**, 178
Chrysanthemum cinerariaefolium, pyrethrins, **8**, 333
Chrysanthemum coccineum, pyrethrins, **8**, 333
Chrysanthemum segetum, flavonol hydroxylation, **1**, 733
chrysanthemum stunt viroid (CSV)
    hosts, **6**, 171
    sequencing, **6**, 175
chrysanthemyl system, studies, **5**, 337
chrysanthenone, biosynthesis, **8**, 224
chrysartemin A, antifeedant activity, **8**, 308
chrysartemin B, antifeedant activity, **8**, 308
chrysin dimethyl ether, antifungal activity, **8**, 181
Chrysochloa spp., cardenolides, **8**, 361
Chrysolina spp., cardenolides, **8**, 361
Chrysolina coerulans
    bipindogenin, **8**, 361
    periplogenin, **8**, 361
    sarmentiogenin, **8**, 361
Chrysolina herbacea
    bipindogenin, **8**, 361
    periplogenin, **8**, 361
    sarmentiogenin, **8**, 361
Chrysomela spp., 8-hydroxylinalool, **8**, 225
Chrysomela lapponica
    2-methylbutanoic acid, **8**, 221
    2-methylpropanoic acid, **8**, 221
Chrysomelidae, defensive sterols, **8**, 361
chrysomycin A, applications, antibiotics, **7**, 545
chrysophanol, biosynthesis, **1**, 429
Chrysophyrys major, feeding attractants and stimulants, **8**, 418
Chrysosplenium americanum
    flavonol glycoside pathway, **1**, 739
    glucosyltransferases, **1**, 738
    5-hydroxyferulic acid, **3**, 671
    proteins, **1**, 739
CHS *see* chalcone synthase (CHS)
CHS genes
    promoters, **1**, 817
    transcription, **1**, 817
chymotrypsin
    active sites, **5**, 19
    branching enzyme proteolysis, **3**, 460
    catalysis, **5**, 18
        mechanisms, **5**, 19
    catalytic triad, **5**, 24
α-chymotrypsin
    low barrier hydrogen bonds, **5**, 119
    substrates, **7**, 637
ChYMV *see* chicory yellow mottle virus (ChYMV)
CI-921, water solubility, **7**, 606
Cibacron Blue 3GA, in SELEX processes, **7**, 624
cicadas, eicosanoids, **1**, 248
Cicer arietinum
    amine oxidases, **3**, 721
    β-glucosidases, **3**, 686
    7-*O*-glucoside malonylation, **1**, 741
cicerin, occurrence, **1**, 808
cichoriin, occurrence, **8**, 337
Cichorium intybus
    aesculetin biosynthesis, **1**, 628
    cichoriin, **8**, 337
cider manufacture, apple spoilage, **1**, 346
CIEEL *see* chemically initiated electron exchange luminescence (CIEEL)
cigarette beetle *see Lasioderma serricorne*
ciguatera
    causes, **8**, 501

clinical symptoms, **8**, 501
    gambieric acid-induced, **8**, 508
ciguatoxins (CTX)
    Caribbean, occurrence, **8**, 503
    CD spectra, **8**, 503
    ciguatera induction, **8**, 501
    NMR spectra, **8**, 502
    occurrence, **8**, 501
    structure, **8**, 501, 503
cimicidine, insecticidal activity, **8**, 345
Cinchona pubescens, strictosidine studies, **4**, 117
1,8-cineole
    mass spectra, **2**, 137
    occurrence, **8**, 225
    structure, **2**, 103
cinerin I, isolation, **8**, 333
cinerin II, isolation, **8**, 333
cineroctine, isolation, **4**, 33
cinerulose A, occurrence, **3**, 321
D-cinerulose A, occurrence, **3**, 312, 321
L-cinerulose A, occurrence, **3**, 312, 321
L-cinerulose B, occurrence, **3**, 312, 321
cineverine, isolation, **4**, 33
cin genes, *cinA*, cloning, **4**, 295
cinnabarone, occurrence, **3**, 781
cinnamaldehyde:NADP$^+$ oxidoreductase (CoA-cinnamoylating) *see* cinnamoyl-CoA reductase
cinnamaldehydes, *p*-hydroxy-, biosynthesis, **3**, 651
cinnamate, hydroxylation, **1**, 627, 719
cinnamate, methyl *p*-methoxy-, biosynthesis, **3**, 624
cinnamate 4-hydroxylase (C4H) *see trans*-cinnamate 4-monooxygenase
trans-cinnamate 4-monooxygenase
    biochemistry, **1**, 719
    catalysis, **3**, 635
    cDNA clones, isolation, **1**, 720
    cloning, **3**, 637
    early studies, **3**, 635
    as flavonoid precursor, **1**, 719
    genetics, **1**, 720
    localization, **3**, 669
    molecular biology, **1**, 720
    purification, **1**, 720, **3**, 637
    roles
        in isoflavonoid biosynthesis, **1**, 784
        in monolignol biosynthesis, **3**, 635
trans-cinnamate,NADPH:oxygen oxidoreductase (4-hydroxylating) *see trans*-cinnamate 4-monooxygenase
cinnamic acid, 4-hydroxy-3-methoxy- *see* ferulic acid
cinnamic acid, 3,4-methylenedioxy-, toxicity, **8**, 171
cinnamic acid, 3,4,5-trihydroxy-, β-oxidation, **3**, 803
trans-cinnamic acid
    identification, **3**, 632
    as starting material, for coumarins, **1**, 626
cinnamic acid esters, hydroxy-, biosynthesis, **1**, 786
cinnamic acid 4-hydroxylase *see trans*-cinnamate 4-monooxygenase
cinnamic acid(s)
    biosynthesis, **1**, 2, 3, 624, 631
    cyclization, **1**, 625
    degradation, **3**, 803
    as flavonoid precursors, **1**, 719
    metabolism, **3**, 681
    methoxylation, **1**, 733
    as substrates, **3**, 637, 670
cinnamic acids, dihydro-, **1**, 682
cinnamic acids, hydroxy-
    antioxidant activity, **1**, 817
    binding, **3**, 697
cinnamic acids, 4-hydroxy-, lactonization, **1**, 627
cinnamic acids, *p*-hydroxy-, occurrence, **3**, 620
cinnamodial

antifeedant activity, **8**, 308
  occurrence, **8**, 308
Cinnamomum spp., carpacin, **8**, 336
Cinnamomum camphora, apiole, **8**, 336
Cinnamosa fragrans, cinnamodial, **8**, 308
cinnamoyl, α-phenyl-, deoxyadenosine protection, **7**, 123
cinnamoyl-CoA
  biosynthesis, **3**, 650
  β-oxidation, **3**, 803
  as starter unit, **1**, 752
cinnamoyl-CoA esters, hydroxy-, as intermediates, **3**, 649, 651
cinnamoyl-CoA:NADP(H)-dependent oxidoreductases, localization, **3**, 6245
cinnamoyl-CoA:NADP oxidoreductase *see* cinnamoyl-CoA reductase
cinnamoyl-CoA reductase, roles, in monolignol biosynthesis, **3**, 651
cinnamycin
  activity, **4**, 282
  binding, **4**, 282
  biosynthesis, **4**, 202
  structure, **4**, 280
cinnamycin–lysophosphatidylethanolamine complex, structure, **4**, 282
cinnamyl-alcohol dehydrogenase(s)
  catalysis, **3**, 653
  cloning, **3**, 655, 676
  detection, **3**, 655
  encoding, **3**, 656
  genetics, **3**, 676
  isoforms, **3**, 676
  K_m, **3**, 658
  localization, **3**, 676
  occurrence, **3**, 655
  purification, **3**, 656
  roles, in monolignol biosynthesis, **3**, 656
  structure, **3**, 656
  substrate specificity, **3**, 655
cinnamyl-alcohol:NADP$^+$ oxidoreductase(s) *see* cinnamyl-alcohol dehydrogenase(s)
Ciona savignyi, urochordamines, **8**, 440
CIP *see* calf intestine alkaline phosphatase (CIP)
circadian rhythms, microalgae studies, **8**, 457
Circe effect, mechanism, **5**, 76
circular DNA
  double-stranded
    enzymatic closure **7**, 354
    nonenzymatic closure **7**, 354
  occurrence, **7**, 343
  polymerase recognition, rolling circles, **7**, 363
  single-stranded
    closure, **7**, 366
    enzymatic closure, **7**, 366
    ligation, **7**, 366
    nonenzymatic closure, **7**, 366
circular RNA
  occurrence, **7**, 344
  products, synthesis, **7**, 367
citral
  as intermediate, **2**, 102
  occurrence, **8**, 222, 223
  as starting material, for iridoids, **8**, 234
citrate, in starch synthase activity measurement, **3**, 454
citrate synthase, catalysis, **5**, 25
(*R*)-citrate synthase, occurrence, **1**, 872
citreoisocoumarin, structure, **1**, 419
Citrobacter spp., lipopolysaccharides, **3**, 321
Citrobacter freundii
  glucose-1-phosphate adenylyltransferase, **3**, 469
  isoprenoid biosynthesis, mevalonate-independent pathway, **2**, 58
  tyrosine phenol-lyase, **3**, 407

Citrobacter intermedius, tyrosine phenol-lyase, **3**, 405
Citrofortunella mitis, β-selinene, **2**, 185
citronellal, geranyl-, occurrence, **8**, 229
citronellol
  occurrence, **8**, 222
  structure, **2**, 101
citronellol, geranyl-, occurrence, **8**, 229
citronellyl esters, geranyl-, occurrence, **8**, 229
citrulline, δ-amino groups, **6**, 142
Citrus chinensis, chalcone isomerases, **1**, 722
citrus exocortis viroid (CEV)
  cDNA clones, **6**, 184
  characterization, **6**, 171
  D-92 variant, sequence duplication, **6**, 175
  hosts, **6**, 171, 186
  pathogenicity, **6**, 185
  replication, **6**, 175
    inhibition, **6**, 178
  sequencing, **6**, 174
citrus fruit, peel, as source of monoterpenes, **2**, 102
citrus fruits, 2-methyl-3-buten-2-ol, **8**, 200
Citrus paradisi, flavonone 7-*O*-glucosyltransferases, **1**, 737
civetone, structure, **8**, 230
*CKI*1 genes, encoding, **8**, 65
ckr genes, mutations, **8**, 65
4CL *see* 4-coumarate-CoA ligase
L-cladinose
  in erythromycin, **3**, 351
  genetics, **3**, 335
  occurrence, **3**, 312, 322
  tracer studies, **3**, 342
Cladocroce incurvata, cladocroic acid, **1**, 63
cladocroic acid, occurrence, **1**, 63
Cladophora spp., celluloses, NMR spectra, **3**, 565
Cladosporium cucumerinum, activity against, **1**, 779
Claisen condensation
  in ethyl acetoacetate synthesis, **2**, 17
  in isoprenoid biosynthesis, **2**, 16
Claisen rearrangements, **5**, 349
  in antibody catalysis, **5**, 424
  catalysis, **5**, 350
  in chorismate mutase catalysis, **5**, 344
  Monte Carlo simulations, **5**, 351
  rates, factors affecting, **5**, 349
  solvent effects, **5**, 350
  substituent effects, **5**, 352
clarithromycin, structure, **1**, 497
Clarkia spp., linalool synthases, **2**, 113
Clarkia breweri
  5-hydroxyferulic acid, **3**, 671
  isopentenyl diphosphate isomerases, cDNA cloning, **2**, 73
  linalool synthases, **2**, 102
Clarkia xantiana, mutants, **3**, 473
Clausena excavata, carbazole alkaloids, **4**, 54
Clausena heptaphylla, carbazole alkaloids, **4**, 54
clavaminate synthase (CS)
  enzymatic activity, **4**, 185
  isolation, **4**, 185
clavams
  biochemistry, **4**, 182
  biosynthesis, **4**, 183
  gene clusters, **4**, 185
  genetics, **4**, 183
Clavelina cylindrica
  clavepictines, **8**, 546
  cylindricines, **8**, 546
  piclavines, **8**, 546
  pictamine, **8**, 546
Clavelina lepadiformis, lepadiformine, **8**, 547
clavepictines, occurrence, **8**, 546
Claviceps spp.
  epoxides, **1**, 210

isopentenyl diphosphate isomerases
    inhibition, **5**, 335
    purification, **2**, 71
Claviceps purpurea
    dimethylallyltryptophan synthases, **5**, 331
    ergochromes, **1**, 429
    ergopeptines, **4**, 53
    ergot alkaloids, **4**, 51, **8**, 178
clavicipitic acid, biosynthesis, **4**, 53
clavine alkaloids
    biosynthesis, **4**, 51
    occurrence, **4**, 51
claviridenone-a, occurrence, **1**, 241
clavulanic acid
    biosynthesis, **4**, 183
    characterization, **4**, 240
    detection, **4**, 182
    gene clusters, **4**, 185
    β-lactamase inhibition, **3**, 285, **4**, 182
Clavularia viridis
    allene oxide pathway, **1**, 232, 240
    chlorovulones, **1**, 241
    claviridenone-a, **1**, 241
    clavulones, **1**, 241
clavulones
    activity, **1**, 242
    biosynthetic pathways, proposed, **1**, 240
    occurrence, **1**, 241
cleavable complexes
    and cytotoxic potency, correlation, **7**, 596
    topoisomerase inhibition, **7**, 594
cleavable complex mediators, **7**, 596
    classes, **7**, 599, 603
    intercalating agents, **7**, 604
        minimal, **7**, 607
    topoisomerase poisons, **7**, 594
cleavage–ligation reactions, hairpin ribozyme-mediated, **6**, 251
cleavage mechanisms, hepatitis delta virus ribozyme-mediated, **6**, 253
clecarmycins
    applications, antibiotics, **7**, 510
    possible DNA damage induction, **7**, 510
Clematis stans, monosaccharides, **1**, 684
cleomycin
    applications, antibiotics, **7**, 539
    structure, **7**, 539
clerodane diterpenes, biosynthesis, **8**, 318
clerodanes
    antifeedant activity, **8**, 317, 318
        bioassays, **8**, 317
    biological activity, **8**, 315
    biosynthesis, **2**, 225, **8**, 317
    as feeding stimulants, **8**, 317
    insecticidal activity, **8**, 312, 314
    neurophysiological properties, **8**, 318
    structure, **8**, 318
    synthesis, **8**, 317
cis-clerodanes, biosynthesis, **2**, 225
neo-clerodanes, use of term, **8**, 314
trans-clerodanes, biosynthesis, **2**, 225
clerodendrin, insect sequestration, **8**, 363
clerodendrin A
    antifeedant activity, **8**, 319
    occurrence, **8**, 314, 317
clerodendron A, structure, **8**, 319
clerodendron B, occurrence, **8**, 319
clerodendron C, occurrence, **8**, 319
clerodendron D, insect sequestration, **8**, 152
Clerodendron inerme
    clerodendron B, **8**, 319
    clerodendron C, **8**, 319
Clerodendron infortunatum, clerodin, **8**, 314

Clerodendron myricoides, myricoside, **8**, 336
Clerodendron trichotomum, clerodendrin A, **8**, 314, 317
clerodin
    antifeedant activity, **8**, 315
    antifeedant index, **8**, 315
    occurrence, **8**, 314
    x-ray crystal structure, **8**, 314
clerodin, dihydro-, antifeedant activity, **8**, 315
clerodin hemiacetal, occurrence, **8**, 314
ent-neo-clerodins, use of term, **8**, 314
click beetles *see Agriotes* spp.
climate, effects on ethylene biosynthesis, **8**, 96
cloning
    background colonies, **7**, 664
    case studies, **7**, 667
    cDNA libraries, **7**, 654
    for chemists, **7**, **643–674**
    dephosphorylation in, **7**, 661
    full length proteins, **7**, 645
    historical background, **7**, 643
    homology mapping in, **7**, 646
    insert identity
        chain-termination method, **7**, 664
        chemical cleavage method, **7**, 664
        verification, **7**, 664
    insert screening, **7**, 664
    ligation in, **7**, 661
    overview, **7**, 644
    processes, **7**, 644
        bulk oligonucleotide production, **7**, 652
        expression system selection, **7**, 646
        target DNA sequence selection, **7**, 645
        vector selection, **7**, 647
    strategies
        bacterial aromatic polyketide synthases, **1**, 475
        developments, **7**, 644
        homology-based, **1**, 476
        triterpene cyclase genes, **2**, 313
    subdomains, **7**, 645
    see also molecular cloning
Clostridium spp.
    cellulosomes, **3**, 593
    diol dehydrase, **5**, 274
    glycogen, **3**, 443
Clostridium acidi–urici, (*R*)-citrate synthase, **1**, 872
Clostridium barkeri
    cyanocobalamin, **4**, 150
    nicotinic acid hydroxylase, **4**, 375
Clostridium formicoaceticum, 5-methoxy-6-methylbenzimidazolylcobamide, **4**, 150
Clostridium pasteurianum
    glucose-1-phosphate adenylyltransferase, **3**, 470
    threonine aldolase, **3**, 400
Clostridium propionicum, lactoyl-CoA dehydratase, **1**, 601
Clostridium subterminale, lysine 2,3-aminomutase, **5**, 206
Clostridium tetanomorphum, methylaspartate mutase, **5**, 272
Clostridium thermoaceticum, cyanocobalamin biosynthesis, **4**, 140
Clostridium thermocellum, endocellulase D, **5**, 300
CLV *see* columnea latent viroid (CLV)
*cma*1 gene, identification, **1**, 66
*cma*2 gene, identification, **1**, 66
CMAS-1 *see* cyclopropane mycolic acid synthase (CMAS-1)
CMC *see* cellulose, carboxymethyl (CMC)
cmc genes
    cmcH, encoding, **4**, 172
    cmcI, localization, **4**, 172
    cmcJ, cloning, **4**, 173
CMCT *see p*-toluene sulfonate, 1-cyclohexyl-3-(2-morpholinoethyl)carbodiimide methyl-(CMCT)

CMP-*N*-acetylneuraminate:β-D-galactoside α-2,3-*N*-acetylneuraminyltransferase *see* β-galactoside α-2,3-sialyltransferase

CMP-*N*-acetylneuraminate:β-D-galactosyl-1,4-*N*-acetyl-β-D-glucosamine α-2,6-*N*-acetylneuraminyltransferase *see* β-galactoside α-2,6-sialyltransferase (ST6Gal I)

CMP-*N*-acetylneuraminate:β-D-galactosyl-1,4-*N*-acetyl-D-glucosaminylglycoprotein α-2,3-*N*-acetylneuraminyltransferase *see* *N*-acetyllactosaminide α-2,3-sialyltransferase (ST3Gal III)

CMP-*N*-acetylneuraminate:glycano-1,3-(*N*-acetyl-α-D-galactosaminyl)-glycoprotein α-2,6-*N*-acetylneuraminyltransferase *see* α-*N*-acetylgalactosaminide α-2,6-sialyltransferase

CMP-*N*-acetylneuraminic acid, structure, **5**, 280

CMP-3-deoxy-D-*manno*-octulopyranosonate, **3**, 220

CMP-KDO, biosynthesis, **3**, 509

CMP-Kdo-synthase, roles, **3**, 221

CMP-sialic acid, binding, **3**, 79, 80

CMP-sialic acid:Galβ1-4GlcNAc-R/Galβ1-3GalNAc-R α2-3-sialyltransferase (ST3Gal IV)
  cloning, **3**, 49
  gene, localization, **3**, 49

CMP-sialic acid:Galβ1-3/4GlcNAc-R α2-3-sialyltransferase *see* *N*-acetyllactosaminide α-2,3-sialyltransferase (ST3Gal III)

CMP-sialic acid:Galβ1-4GlcNAc-R α-2,6-sialyltransferase *see* β-galactoside α-2,6-sialyltransferase (ST6Gal I)

CMP-sialic acid:Galβ1-3/4GlcNAc-R α2-3-sialyltransferase II (ST3N II), encoding, **3**, 48

CMP-sialic acid:sialylα2-3Galβ1-4GlcNAc-R α2-8-sialyltransferase (ST8Sia III), encoding, **3**, 49

CMP-sialic acid:[sialylα2-8]*ₙ*sialylα2-3Galβ1-3/4GlcNAc-R α2-8-sialyltransferase (ST8Sia II)
  expression, **3**, 49
  roles, in brain development, **3**, 50

CMP-sialic acid:[sialylα2-8]*ₙ*sialylα2-3Galβ1-3/4GlcNAc-R α2-8-sialyltransferase (ST8Sia IV)
  autopolysialylation, **3**, 50
  expression, **3**, 49
  roles, in brain development, **3**, 50

c-myc mRNA
  AU rich elements, **6**, 208
  deadenylation, **6**, 208

cnicin, as allelopathic agent, **8**, 171

Cnidaria
  prostaglandins, **1**, 239
  see also *Clavularia viridis*; *Gersemia fruticosa*; *Hydractinia echinata*; *Hydra vulgaris*; *Plexaura homomalla*; *Pseudoplexaura porosa*

CoA *see* coenzyme A (CoA)

CoA-independent transacylase
  catalysis, **1**, 292
  roles, **1**, 292

CoASAc *see* acetyl-CoA

cob(I)alamin adenosyltransferase, coupling, **4**, 148

cob(II)alamin
  biosynthesis, **3**, 330, **5**, 170
    kinetics, **5**, 176
  as cofactor, **5**, 410

cobalamin
  biochemistry, **5**, 265
  biosynthesis, **5**, 263
  as cofactor, **5**, 263
  enzymes, structure, **5**, 174
  from, hydrogenobyrinic acid, **4**, 146
  occurrence, **5**, 263
  protein role, **5**, 268
  reactivity, **5**, 265
  structure, **5**, 265

  studies, **5**, 173
  x-ray crystal structure, **5**, 266

cobalamin, cyano-
  analogues, benzimidazole bases, **4**, 150
  auxotrophic mutants, **1**, 868
  biosynthesis, **4**, 149, 90
    anoxic pathway, **4**, 150, 154
    cobalt insertion, **4**, 146, 153
    early studies, **4**, 140
    enzymatically controlled steps, **4**, **139–158**
    genes, **4**, 152
    oxygen-requiring pathway, **4**, 140
    ring contraction, **4**, 144, 154
  RNA binders, **7**, 638

cobalamin, methyl-
  as cofactor, **5**, 263
  edge shifts, **5**, 266
  in *P*-methylation, **1**, 871
  as methyl donor, **1**, 876

cobalamin, neopentyl-, carbon–cobalt bond cleavage, **5**, 173

cobalamin-dependent enzymes
  biochemistry, **5**, **263–278**
  classification, **5**, 270
  enzymology, **5**, **263–278**
  future research, **5**, 276
  negative catalysis, **5**, 269
  reaction mechanisms, **5**, 270

cobalamins, alkyl-
  dealkylation, **5**, 172
  reactivity, **5**, 266

cobalamin synthase, roles, **4**, 149

cobaloxime, analogues, **5**, 266

cobalt(III), *trans*-bis(dimethylglyoximato)isopropyl(2-aminopyridine)-, structure, **5**, 267

cobalt(III)-bleomycin complexes, structure, **7**, 539

cobalt–carbon bonds
  in cobalamins, **5**, 266
  dissociation energies, **5**, 267
  homolysis, **5**, 267
  lability, **5**, 266
  thermolysis, **5**, 267

cobaltochelatase, roles, **4**, 148

cobalt–precorrin 3, biosynthesis, **4**, 156

cobalt–precorrin 4, biosynthesis, **4**, 156

cobamide, 7-azabenzimidazolyl-, biosynthesis, **4**, 150

cobamide, *p*-cresolyl-, biosynthesis, **4**, 150

cob genes
  characterization, **4**, 152
  cobA, encoding, **4**, 143
  cobB, encoding, **4**, 146
  cobC, encoding, **4**, 148
  cobD, encoding, **4**, 148
  cobF, encoding, **4**, 145
  cobG, encoding, **4**, 143
  cobH, encoding, **4**, 146
  cobI, encoding, **4**, 143
  cobJ, encoding, **4**, 144
  cobK, encoding, **4**, 145
  cobL, encoding, **4**, 146
  cobM, encoding, **4**, 144
  cobN, encoding, **4**, 148
  cobO, encoding, **4**, 148
  cobP, encoding, **4**, 149
  cobQ, encoding, **4**, 148
  cobS, encoding, **4**, 148
  cobT, encoding, **4**, 148
  cobU, encoding, **4**, 149
  cobV, encoding, **4**, 149
  homologues, **4**, 152

cobinamide kinase, roles, **4**, 149

cobinamide synthase, roles, **4**, 148

cobra venom, slow reacting substance studies, **1**, 160

cob[II]yrinic acid *a,c*-diamide adenosyltransferase, roles, **4**, 148

cob[II]yrinic acid *a,c*-diamide reductase, roles, **4**, 148

cob[II]yrinic acid *a,c*-diamide synthase *see* cobaltochelatase

cocaine
  biosynthesis, pathways, **4**, 27
  occurrence, **8**, 344

cocarboxylase *see* thiamine diphosphate

Coccidae
  pheromones, **8**, 234
  propanoates, **8**, 209
  see also Israeli pine scale; *Matsucoccus* spp.

Coccinella spp., coccinelline, **8**, 351

Coccinella septempunctata, sequestration, **8**, 351

Coccinella unidecimpunctata, sequestration, **8**, 363

Coccinellidae, reflex bleeding, **8**, 351

coccinelline, occurrence, **8**, 351

coccinellines, insecticidal activity, **8**, 351

cocculidine, biosynthesis, **4**, 43

cocculine, biosynthesis, **4**, 43

Cochliobolus heterostrophus, T-toxins, **1**, 424

Cochliobolus miyabeanus, melanin, **1**, 427

cockroaches
  1-dodecanol, **8**, 214
  pheromones, **8**, 214
  sex pheromones, **8**, 210
  venoms, **8**, 360
  see also Blattella spp.; *Eublaberus distanti*; *Eurycotis floridana*; *Nauphoeta cinerea*; *Periplaneta* spp.

coclaurines, *N*-methyl-, occurrence, **1**, 676

coconut cadang cadang viroid (CCCV)
  effects, **6**, 169
  hosts, **6**, 171, 186
  localization, **6**, 178
  pathogenicity, **6**, 185
  replication, **6**, 175
  sequence duplication, **6**, 175
  sequencing, **6**, 175

coconut rhinoceros beetle *see Oryctes rhinoceros*

coconut tinangaja viroid (CTiV), hosts, **6**, 171

codeinone, biosynthesis, **4**, 40

codling moth *see Laspeyresia pomonella*

codon–anticodon complexes, recognition, **6**, 194

coelenterazines
  roles, in bioluminescence, **8**, 452
  structure, **8**, 446

coenzyme A (CoA)
  in catalysis, **2**, 34
  discovery, **4**, 222
  release, **2**, 19

coenzyme A thioanions, protonation, **2**, 39

coenzyme A thioesters, identification, **1**, 544

coenzyme M (CoM)
  biosynthesis, **1**, 833
  structure, **1**, 833

cofactors
  diferric, **5**, 164, 166, 177
    reduction, **5**, 184
  non-hydrolyzable, **7**, 603

Coffea arabica, alkaloids, **8**, 147

coffee leaf miner *see Perileucoptera coffeella*

coffee plant *see Coffea arabica*

coformycin, 8-keto-, binding, **5**, 76

(*R*)-coformycin 5′-phosphate, transition state inhibition, **5**, 84

coformycin(s)
  adenosine deaminase inhibition, **5**, 74
  transition state structure, **5**, 79

(*R*)-coformycin(s)
  AMP deaminase inhibition, **5**, 83
  binding energy, **5**, 76

COHED decarboxylase *see* 5-(carboxymethyl)-2-oxo-3-hexene-1,6-dioate (COHED) decarboxylase

cohumulone, isomerization, **1**, 760

colanic acid, occurrence, **3**, 207

colchicine, binding inhibition, **8**, 606

Coleochaete spp., evolution, **3**, 622

Coleomegilla maculata, ochtodenols, **8**, 224

Coleoptera, venoms, **8**, 354

Colias eurytheme, 1-hexanol, **8**, 210

colicins, biosynthesis, **4**, 202

colitose
  biosynthesis, **3**, 348
  isolation, **3**, 345
  occurrence, **3**, 186, 312

collared peccary *see Tayassu tajacu*

Collembola, chemical defense, **8**, 361

Colletes spp., aggregation pheromones, **8**, 223

Colletotrichum lagenarium
  melanin biosynthesis studies, **1**, 414
  *PKS*1 gene, **1**, 414

Colletotrichum lindemuthianum, melanin, **1**, 427

Collie, J.N., ketene studies, **1**, 2

colloid chemistry, developments, **3**, 534

colneleic acid, occurrence, **1**, 235

colnelenic acid, occurrence, **1**, 235

COLO 205
  occurrence, **3**, 118
  sialyltransferases, **3**, 120

colon cancer
  chemoprevention, **1**, 700
  nonsteroid antiinflammatory agent-mediated, **5**, 226
  prostaglandin-endoperoxide synthase studies, **1**, 258

colon mucosa, platelet-activating factor, **1**, 297

Colophospermum mopane
  mopanane-(4β→6)-fisetinidol, **3**, 777
  profisetinidins, **3**, 772
  proguibourtinidins, **3**, 775

Colorado potato beetle *see Leptinotarsa decemlineata*

coloring agents, carotenoids, **2**, 347

Colotois pennaria, pheromones, **8**, 14, 207

Colpomenia bullosa, volatiles, **8**, 422

(±)-columbianetin, assays, **1**, 633

(−)-columbianetin
  biosynthesis, **1**, 628
  from, osthenol, **1**, 628
  as starting material, for angelicin, **1**, 633

columbin, as seed toxin, **8**, 168

Columnea hybrida, flavanone 4-reductase, **1**, 728

columnea latent viroid (CLV), sequence homology, **6**, 175

CoM *see* Coenzyme M (CoM)

com genes, encoding, **4**, 208

commensalism, definition, **8**, 426

common spruce *see Picea abies*

communesins
  cytotoxicity, **8**, 601
  occurrence, **8**, 601

compactin
  effects, on fibroblasts, **2**, 353
  as hydroxymethylglutaryl-CoA reductase inhibitor, **2**, 378
  as sterol biosynthesis inhibitor, **2**, 257
  structure, **1**, 422

comparative sequence analysis, rRNA secondary structure studies, **6**, 190

compartmentation, cyanogenic glucosides, **1**, 884

competence, in *Bacillus subtilis*, **8**, 401

competence pheromones, in *Bacillus subtilis*, **8**, 401

competence stimulating factor (CSF), occurrence, **8**, 402

complementary DNA (cDNA) *see* cDNA

complementation, studies, **3**, 480

Compositae
  acetophenones, **8**, 189
  alkaloids, **8**, 146
  isoflavonoids, **1**, 774
  phytoalexins, **8**, 189

sesquiterpene lactones, **8**, 189
Compound I
　biosynthesis, **5**, 234
　roles, in prostaglandin-endoperoxide synthase
　　　activation, **5**, 246
Compound II, roles, in prostaglandin-endoperoxide
　　synthase activation, **5**, 246
compound Z, structure, **1**, 835
compression wood
　formation, **3**, 693
　　microgravity studies, **3**, 694
computational modeling
　biochemistry, **5**, 134
　cellulose studies, **3**, 570
computer-aided drug design (CADD), effectiveness, **4**,
　　216
Comstock mealy bug *see Pseudococcus comstocki*
COMT *see* caffeic acid 3-*O*-methyltransferase (COMT)
con A *see* concanavalin A (con A)
conantokins
　NMDA blocking, **8**, 478
　occurrence, **8**, 478
concanavalin A (con A), thrombin immobilization, **7**, 627
condensation domains
　acyl transfer reactions, **4**, 232
　evidence for existence of, **4**, 233
　peptide synthetases, **4**, 227
　　waiting position, **4**, 232
　roles, in bond formation, **4**, 230
condensed tannins *see* proanthocyanidins
conduritol, bromo-, as α-glucosidase II inhibitor, **3**, 20
conduritol epoxides, applications, **5**, 287
cone beetles *see Conophthorus* spp.
cone shells
　classification, **8**, 476
　ecological studies, **8**, 476
　feeding, **8**, 476
　marine toxins, **8**, 476
　peptide toxins, **8**, 476
conformation, switching, **7**, 359
confused flour beetle *see Tribolium confusum*
congenital dyserythropoietic anemia type II, etiology, **3**,
　　59
conicasterone, occurrence, **1**, 379
Conidae, distribution, **8**, 476
α-conidendrin
　biosynthesis, **1**, 668
　induction, **1**, 691
　occurrence, **1**, 668, 697
coniferaldehyde, as intermediate, **3**, 629
coniferin
　biosynthesis, **3**, 676
　hydrolysis, **3**, 686
　occurrence, **3**, 677, 683
　polymerization, **3**, 703
(*E*)-coniferin, as substrate, **3**, 686
conifer resins
　applications, **2**, 101
　composition, **2**, 101
conifers
　interactions, with bark beetles, **2**, 101
　terpentines, applications, **2**, 102
coniferyl-alcohol glucosyltransferase, catalysis, **3**, 683
coniferyl alcohol oxidase
　characterization, **3**, 710
　occurrence, **3**, 709
　properties, **3**, 710
　purification, **3**, 710
　roles, in lignin biosynthesis, **3**, 709
conjugal transfer, of Ti plasmids, **8**, 399
conjugate acids, pK_a, **5**, 8
conjugate groups, attachment to DNA, **7**, **153–249**
conjugation factor (CF)

characterization, **8**, 399
　see also L-homoserine lactone, *N*-(3-oxooctanoyl)-
Conoderus vespertinus, nicotine metabolism, **8**, 348
conodipine-M, occurrence, **8**, 479
Conophthorus spp., **8**, 212
　(2*R*,5*S*)-pityol, **8**, 233
conotoxin GIIIA
　disulfide bridges, **8**, 478
　NOE, **8**, 478
　structure, three-dimensional, **8**, 478
μ-conotoxin GIIIA *see* geographutoxin I (GTX I)
μO-conotoxin MrVIA/B, occurrence, **8**, 480
conotoxin NgVIA, occurrence, **8**, 480
αA-conotoxin PIVA, occurrence, **8**, 480
conotoxins, occurrence, **8**, 477
α-conotoxins
　ImI, **8**, 480
　structure, **8**, 477
μ-conotoxins, structure, **8**, 477
ω-conotoxins
　calcium channel blocking, **8**, 477
　photoaffinity labeling, **8**, 477
Conotrachelus nenuphar, (+)-grandisoic acid, **8**, 224
constanolactone A, occurrence, **1**, 219
constanolactones, structure, **1**, 243, 244
Constantinea simplex
　constanolactone A, **1**, 244
　12*S*-hydroxyeicosatetraenoic acid, **1**, 219
controlled-pore glass (CPG), in automated
　　oligonucleotide synthesis, **7**, 112, 156
Conus eburneus, eburnetoxin, **8**, 479
Conus geographus
　conantokins, **8**, 478
　conotoxins, **8**, 477
　geographutoxin I, **8**, 476
　geographutoxin II, **8**, 476
　occurrence, **8**, 476
　toxicity, **8**, 476
　　to humans, **8**, 476
Conus imperialis, α-conotoxin ImI, **8**, 480
Conus magus
　conodipine-M, **8**, 479
　myotoxins, MgTX, **8**, 479
　phospholipase A₂, **8**, 479
Conus marmoreus, μO-conotoxin MrVIA/B, **8**, 480
Conus nigropunctatus, conotoxin NgVIA, **8**, 480
Conus purpurascens, αA-conotoxin PIVA, **8**, 480
Conus striatus, striatoxin, **8**, 478
Conus tessulatus, tessulatoxin, **8**, 479
Conus textile, arachidonic acid, **8**, 479
convergent evolutionary pathways, and glutathione
　　transferases, **5**, 61
convergine, occurrence, **8**, 351
Convolvulaceae, calystegines, **3**, 134
Convolvulus arvensis, alkaloid biosynthesis, **4**, 29
copalyl diphosphate, **2**, 211
　as intermediate, **2**, 382
　as starting material, for tricyclic diterpenes, **2**, 226
copalyl diphosphate, 8-carbonium ion, conformation, **2**,
　　223
ent-copalyl diphosphate
　biosynthesis, **2**, 5
　cyclization, **2**, 8
　as starting material
　　for *ent*-kaur-16-ene, **2**, 231
　　for tricyclic diterpenes, **2**, 229
　as substrate, **2**, 7
ent-copalyl diphosphate, 8-carbonium ion, biosynthesis,
　　2, 223
syn-copalyl diphosphate, as starting material, for tricyclic
　　diterpenes, **2**, 229
copalyl diphosphate synthase (CDS)
　in *ent*-kaurene biosynthesis, **8**, 47

occurrence, **8**, 47
ent-copalyl diphosphate synthases
  functions, **2**, 217
  occurrence, **2**, 224
copalyl pyrophosphate (CPP) *see* copalyl diphosphate
copper(II) chloride, as abiotic elicitor, **1**, 131
copper metalloenzymes, studies, **1**, 577
copper phenanthroline, applications, DNA structure
    probes, **7**, 86
copper TMPyP(4), Watson–Crick base pair disruption, **7**,
    443
Coprinus cinereus, laccase, **3**, 714
coproporphyrinogen-III, biosynthesis, **4**, 90
coproporphyrinogenase(s) *see* coproporphyrinogen
    oxidase(s)
coproporphyrinogen oxidase(s)
  aerobic, **4**, 95
  anaerobic, **4**, 95
  catalysis, **4**, 94
  genetic encoding, **4**, 95
  mechanisms, **4**, 96
  side chain oxidation, **4**, 95
  steric course studies, **4**, 96
coproporphyrinogen:oxygen oxidoreductase
    (decarboxylating) *see* coproporphyrinogen
    oxidase(s)
coral reefs, metabolites, **8**, 465
corals
  chemical defense, **1**, 240
  oxylipins, **1**, 239
  see also Clavularia viridis; Cnidaria; *Gersemia*
     fruticosa; Gorgonacea; *Plexaura homomalla*;
     Pseudoplexaura porosa; *Sarcophyton glaucum*
coralyne, 5,6-dihydro-, inhibition, **7**, 601
coralyne(s)
  as DNA topoisomerase I inhibitors, **7**, 601
  inhibition, **7**, 601
  use in pyrimidine triplex stabilization, **7**, 467
corazonin, structure, **8**, 300
Corcyra cephalonica, hexahydrofarnesylacetone, **8**, 234
cordycepin
  cordycepose, **3**, 313
  discovery, **4**, 200
  inhibition, **8**, 97
  in mRNA studies, **6**, 206
cordycepin, 5′-cholesteryl-, as HIV-1 inhibitor, **7**, 189
cordycepose, occurrence, **3**, 312, 313
core 1 β3-Gal-T *see* glycoprotein-*N*-acetylgalactosamine
core 2 β6-GlcNAc-T *see* β-1,3-galactosyl-*O*-glycosyl-
    glycoprotein β-1,6-*N*-acetylglucosaminyltransferase
core 3 β3-GlcNAc-T *see* acetylgalactosaminyl-*O*-glycosyl-
    glycoprotein β-1,3-*N*-
    acetylglucosaminyltransferase
core 4 β6-GlcNAc-T *see* acetylgalactosaminyl-*O*-glycosyl-
    glycoprotein β-1,6-*N*-
    acetylglucosaminyltransferase
coreopsin, roles, in ultraviolet patterning, **8**, 160
Coreopsis grandiflora, 6′-deoxychalcones, **1**, 736
Corey's lactone
  in prostaglandin synthesis, **1**, 177
  synthesis, **1**, 177
corilagin, applications, direct protein binding agents, **7**,
    595
corn *see Zea mays*
corn borer *see Ostrinia nubilalis*
corn earworm *see Helicoverpa zea*
cornexistin, phytotoxicity, **8**, 181
corn rootworms, 1,7-dimethylnonylpropanoate, **8**, 246
corn seeds, desiccation, and dehydrin expression, **8**, 83
Cornus florida, verbenalin, **8**, 307
Cornutia grandifolia
  cornutin A, **8**, 317
  cornutin B, **8**, 317

cornutin A, occurrence, **8**, 317
cornutin B, occurrence, **8**, 317
coronatine
  biosynthesis, **1**, 122
  effects on plants, **1**, 135
  jasmonate-inducible glycosyltransferase mRNA
    induction, **1**, 129
  occurrence, **1**, 135
  structure, **1**, 135
  synthesis, total, **1**, 122
coronopilin, antifeedant activity, **8**, 308
corpora allata
  acylglycerols, **8**, 274
  juvenile hormone biosynthesis, **8**, 266, 271, 301
corpus allatum *see* corpora allata
corpus cardiacum
  neural factors, **8**, 299
  prothoracicotropic hormone, **8**, 279
corrinoids, biosynthesis, **4**, 72
Cortaderia selloana, ferulic acid biosynthesis, **3**, 644
cortexone, occurrence, **8**, 230, 361
corticosteroids, occurrence, **8**, 361
Corydalis bulbosa, (−)-canadine, **8**, 344
Corydalis sempervirens, 3-phosphoshikimate 1-
    carboxyvinyltransferase, glyphosate tolerance,
    1, 598
Corylus sieboldiana
  8–5′ linked lignans, **1**, 684
  8–8′ linked lignans, **1**, 684
Corynebacterium spp.
  carotenoid biosynthesis, **2**, 323
  haloalcohol dehalogenases, **5**, 408
  haloalkane dehalogenases, **5**, 403
  L-homoserine, **3**, 249
Corynebacterium ammoniagenes, 2-*C*-methyl-D-
    erythritol, **2**, 56
Corynebacterium diphtheriae, stearate desaturation, **1**, 38
Corynebacterium fascians, effects on apial dominance, **8**,
    59
Corynebacterium rathayi, *Lolium rigidum* infection by, **8**,
    177
Corynebacterium sepedonicum, 2,4-dichlorobenzoyl CoA
    dehalogenase, **5**, 417
Corynebacterium tritici, 2,4-diaminobutyric acid, **3**, 246
corynetoxins, toxicity, to grazing sheep, **8**, 177
Coryne uchidai, biofouling, **8**, 431
COS M9 cells, overexpression, **3**, 486
cosmid library, construction, **1**, 414
Cosmopolites sordidus
  pheromones, **8**, 7
  sordidin, **8**, 7, 245
Costa Rican fruit bats, and seed dispersal, **8**, 167
Costaticella hastata, β-carbolines, **8**, 529
cotinine, in nicotine metabolism, **8**, 348
cotinine *N*-oxide, insect excretion, **8**, 348
cotton
  cadinene synthases, **2**, 210
  celluloses, **3**, 530
    NMR spectra, **3**, 565
  microfibrils, **3**, 587
  ^{13}C NMR spectra, **3**, 550
  sesquiterpenoid phytoalexins, **2**, 212
  see also Gossypium spp.
cotton bollworm *see Helicoverpa armigera*
Cotton effects, ecdysteroids, **8**, 285
Cottoniella filamentosa, hepoxillin B$_3$, **1**, 219
p-coumaraldehyde, as intermediate, **3**, 629
coumaran 7-glucoside, 6,7-dihydroxy- *see* cichoriin
coumarans, phenyl-, ring reduction, **1**, 681
3-*p*-coumarate, IR spectra, **8**, 285
4-coumarate
  biosynthesis, **1**, 627, 814
  as starting material, for flavonoids, **1**, 733

p-coumarate, coniferyl, linking, **3**, 698
4-coumarate-CoA ligase
　biochemistry, **1**, 720
　catalysis, **3**, 648
　cloning, **3**, 650
　as flavonoid precursor, **1**, 720
　genetics, **1**, 721
　isoforms, **3**, 651, 676
　molecular biology, **1**, 721
　occurrence, **1**, 47, **3**, 674
　promoter expression studies, **3**, 675
　purification, **1**, 720, **3**, 650
　regulatory mechanisms, **1**, 785
　roles
　　in isoflavonoid biosynthesis, **1**, 784
　　in monolignol biosynthesis, **3**, 648
4-coumarate:CoA ligase (AMP-forming) *see* 4-
　　coumarate-CoA ligase
4-coumarate 3-hydroxylase
　catalysis, **3**, 640
　roles, in monolignol biosynthesis, **3**, 639
p-coumarate 3-hydroxylase
　expression, **3**, 671
　K_m, **3**, 658
coumaric acid, cyclization, **1**, 627
m-coumaric acid, insecticidal activity, **8**, 337
o-coumaric acid, insecticidal activity, **8**, 337
p-coumaric acid
　biosynthesis, **1**, 18, **3**, 624, 631, 638
　esterification, **3**, 698
　insecticidal activity, **8**, 337
　isolation, **3**, 696
　occurrence, **3**, 620
coumarin, 4-hydroxy-5-methyl-, biosynthesis, **1**, 625
coumarin phosphoramidites, synthesis, **7**, 182
coumarins
　accumulation, modulation, **1**, 625
　antiinflammatory activity, **1**, 624
　antitumor activity, **1**, 624
　applications
　　antitumor agents, **1**, 624
　　biotechnological, **1**, 624
　　medicinal, **1**, 624
　biosynthesis, **1**, 2, 18, **623–637**
　　future research, **1**, 635
　　mechanisms, **1**, 626
　classification, **1**, 623
　　biosynthetic, **1**, 625
　from, *trans*-cinnamic acid, **1**, 626
　localization, **1**, 625
　occurrence, **1**, 623, 625
　ontogenesis, **1**, 625
　physiological activity, **1**, 625
　platelet inhibitory activity, **1**, 624
　structure, **1**, 623
coumarins, 3-aryl-, as intermediates, **1**, 786, 810
coumarins, 4-hydroxy-
　applications, **1**, 624
　biosynthesis, **1**, 625
　structure, **1**, 623
coumarin systems, dimeric, **1**, 380
4-coumaroyl-CoA
　biosynthesis, **1**, 716
　condensation, **1**, 789
　pathways, **1**, 716
　roles, in isoflavonoid biosynthesis, **1**, 784
　as starter unit, **1**, 752
p-coumaroyl-CoA hydroxylases, occurrence, **3**, 641
4-coumaroyl-CoA synthetase *see* 4-coumarate-CoA ligase
p-coumaroyl-D-glucose hydroxylase, purification, **3**, 641
3-*O*-(4-coumaroyl)rutinosido-5-*O*-glucosides,
　　methylation, **1**, 739
p-coumaroyl-tetraketide lactone (CTAL), biosynthesis, **1**,
　19

coumermycin, applications, direct protein binding agents,
　7, 596
coumestans, biosynthesis, **1**, 786, 810
coumestrol
　biosynthesis, **1**, 810
　as chalcone isomerase inhibitor, **1**, 722
　half-life, **1**, 812
　and quail population control, **1**, 782
counterion condensation effect, nucleic acids, **7**, 20
coupling reaction
　activators, **7**, 138
　internucleotidic, mechanisms, **7**, 137
　in RNA synthesis, **6**, 81
cowpea trypsin inhibitors, encoding, **8**, 150
COX *see* prostaglandin-endoperoxide synthase(●)
COX-1 *see* prostaglandin-endoperoxide synthase-1
COX-2 *see* prostaglandin-endoperoxide synthase-2
CP-67,804, DNA studies, **7**, 603
CP-115,953
　DNA studies, **7**, 603
　as DNA topoisomerase II inhibitor, **7**, 603
　structure, **7**, 609
CPG *see* controlled-pore glass (CPG)
CPP *see* copalyl diphosphate
CPTA *see* triethylamine, 2-(4-chlorophenylthio)- (CPTA)
Crassostrea gigas, prostaglandins, **1**, 244
Crassostrea virginica, larval settlement induction, **8**, 432
Crataegus oxyacantha
　mistletoe lignin studies, **3**, 702
　oligomeric leucocyanidins, **3**, 757
CrATP *see* chromium adenosine triphosphate (CrATP)
creatine, isolation, **8**, 457
cre genes, *creA*, roles, **4**, 255
Crematogaster spp.
　cross-conjugated polyenones, **8**, 359
　6-methyl-3-octanone, **8**, 244
　(*S*)-3-octanol, **8**, 211
　3-octanone, **8**, 211
Crematogaster scutellaris, acetyl-CoA, **8**, 209
creosote bush *see Larrea tridentata*
m-cresol, occurrence, **8**, 211
p-cresol
　occurrence, **8**, 161
　oxidation, **3**, 711
Cribrochalina olemda, kapakahines, **8**, 583
Crick, Francis Harry Compton (1916–), DNA structure
　　studies, **7**, 81
crickets, prostaglandin E$_2$, **1**, 248
Criegée rearrangement, in DNA damage, **7**, 387, 394
crinine, biosynthesis, **4**, 43
Cristaria plicata, flavocristamides, **8**, 598
Crithidia fasciculata, inosine-uridine nucleoside
　　hydrolase, **5**, 306
Crithmum maritimum, dillapiole, **8**, 336
critical aggregate concentration (CAC),
　　lipopolysaccharides, **3**, 198
croalbinecine, biosynthesis, **4**, 31
Cro protein, helix-turn-helix motifs, **7**, 478
cross-linking, terminal, **6**, 230
cross-links
　chemical, **6**, 227
　involving psoralens, **7**, 545
Crotalaria axillaris, axillaridine biosynthesis, **4**, 33
Crotolaria spp., monocrotaline, **8**, 361
Crotolaria cobalticola, isobavachalcone, **1**, 130
crotonase(s)
　active sites, **5**, 14
　catalysis, **5**, 13
　structure, **5**, 13
crown ethers, synthesis, **5**, 357
crown galls
　causes, **8**, 399
　and cytokinins, **8**, 69

nopaline, **8**, 399
octopine, **8**, 399
opine, **8**, 399
crp genes, encoding, **3**, 478
crt genes
    in *Agrobacterium aurantiacum*, **2**, 335
    in *Alicaligenes* PC-1, **2**, 335
    crtB
        enzyme, **2**, 340
        homologues, **2**, 340
        mutations, **2**, 330, 333
        structural conservation, **2**, 339
        see also phytoene synthases
    crtD, mutations, **2**, 330
    crtE
        in bacteria, **2**, 348
        in *Erwinia herbicola*, **2**, 87
        mutations, **2**, 330, 333
        shared motifs, **2**, 339
        structural conservation, **2**, 339
        see also geranylgeranyl diphosphate synthase(s)
    crtF, mutations, **2**, 330
    crtI
        mutations, **2**, 330
        structural conservation, **2**, 339
        see also phytoene desaturases
    cryptic, **2**, 346
    in *Erwinia* spp., **2**, 332
    in *Flavobacterium* spp., **2**, 337
    in *Myxococcus xanthus*, **2**, 334, 346
    nomenclature, **2**, 327
    in *Rhodobacter* spp., **2**, 327
    in *Staphylococcus aureus*, **2**, 337
    in *Streptomyces griseus*, **2**, 336
    in *Synechococcus* spp., **2**, 337
    in *Thermus thermophilus*, **2**, 335
    transcriptional operons, **2**, 348
Cruciferae, indole phytoalexins, **8**, 187
crucigasterins
    occurrence, **8**, 545
    structure, **8**, 545
cruentol, occurrence, **8**, 245
crustecdysone *see* ecdysone, 20-hydroxy-
cryptands, synthesis, **5**, 357
Cryptocercus punctulatus, (4*R*,5*R*,6*S*,7*E*,9*E*)-4,6,8-trimethyl-7,9-decadien-5-ol, **8**, 245
Cryptococcus albidus, ethylene, **8**, 93
Cryptolestes spp., (*Z*)-5-tetradecen-13-olide, **8**, 216
Cryptolestes ferrugineus
    (11*S*,3*Z*)-3-dodecen-11-olide, **8**, 215
    ferrulactone, **8**, 236
Cryptolestes pusillus, (*Z*)-3-dodecen-12-olide, **8**, 215
Cryptolestes turcicus
    pheromones, **8**, 14
    (5*Z*,8*Z*)-5,8-tetradecadien-13-olide, **8**, 216
Cryptomeria japonica
    (−)-cryptoresinol, **1**, 686
    leucoanthocyanidin 4-reductase, **1**, 729
    lignification, **3**, 691
    8–5′ linked lignans, **1**, 681, 684
    8–8′ linked lignans, **1**, 684
    polysaccharides, **3**, 690
    xylem cells, **3**, 682
cryptophycin-1
    occurrence, **8**, 611
    structure, **8**, 612
(−)-cryptoresinol
    biosynthesis, **1**, 686
    occurrence, **1**, 686
cryptotanshinone, biosynthesis, **2**, 228
β-cryptoxanthin
    as intermediate, **2**, 344
    as substrate, **2**, 344

cryptoxanthin glucosides, biosynthesis, **2**, 333
β-cryptoxanthin monoglucoside, biosynthesis, **2**, 332
ε-crystallin, homology, **1**, 261
crystal structures
    properties, **6**, 11
    and solution structures compared, **6**, 11, 12
CS *see* chondroitin sulfate (CS); clavaminate synthase (CS)
CSF *see* competence stimulating factor (CSF)
cs genes
    cs1, cloning, **4**, 185
    cs2
        cloning, **4**, 185
        localization, **4**, 185
C-signal, functions, **8**, 406
CSV *see* chrysanthemum stunt viroid (CSV)
CTAL *see* *p*-coumaroyl-tetraketide lactone (CTAL)
Ctenocephalides felis, activity against, **8**, 306
Ctenochaetus striatus, maitotoxin, **8**, 504
Ctenocolum tuberculatum, feedant activity, **3**, 141
CTiV *see* coconut tinangaja viroid (CTiV)
Ctmp *see* piperidin-4-yl, 1-[(2-chloro-4-methyl)phenyl]-4′-methoxy- (Ctmp)
CTP:D-glucose-1-phosphate cytidylyltransferase *see* glucose-1-phosphate cytidylyltransferase
CTP:phosphocholine cytidyltransferase, activation, **1**, 296
CTX *see* ciguatoxins (CTX)
α-cubebene, as bark beetle attractant, **8**, 228
(+)-cubenene, synthesis, **2**, 191
Cubitermes umbratus, cembrene A, **8**, 230
cucujiid beetles
    cucujolides, **8**, 236
    macrocyclic lactones, **8**, 215
cucujolides, occurrence, **8**, 236
cucumbers
    cotyledons, etiolated, **8**, 66
    hypocotyl assays
        activity, **8**, 45
        gibberellin activity, **8**, 57
Cucumis melo, phenylalanine ammonia-lyase, localization, **3**, 662
Cucumis sativus, *trans*-cinnamate 4-monooxygenase, localization, **3**, 669
cucurbic acid
    occurrence, **1**, 118
    synthesis, **8**, 114
Cucurbitaceae, cucurbitacins, **8**, 320
cucurbitacin A, structure, **8**, 320
cucurbitacin B, detection, by insects, **8**, 320
[14]C-cucurbitacin B, as starting material, for 23,24-dihydrocucurbitacin D, **8**, 362
cucurbitacin D, insect sequestration, **8**, 152
cucurbitacin D, 23,24-dihydro-, from, ^{14}C-cucurbitacin B, **8**, 362
cucurbitacin I, antifungal activity, **8**, 181
cucurbitacins
    antitumor activity, **8**, 320
    applications, antitumor agents, **8**, 320
    insecticidal activity, **8**, 320
    insect sequestration, **8**, 362
    occurrence, **8**, 320
Cucurbita maxima
    ACS genes, **8**, 97
    1-aminocyclopropane-1-carboxylate synthase studies, **8**, 97
    ent-kaurene synthase, **8**, 47
    ent-kaur-16-ene synthase, **2**, 231
Cucurbita pepo, cucurbic acid, **1**, 118
culantraramine, occurrence, **1**, 369
culantraraminol, occurrence, **1**, 369
cularines, biosynthesis, **4**, 40
Culex spp., pheromones, **8**, 217

Culex pipiens, (5*R*,6*S*)-6-acetoxy-5-hexadecanolide, **8**, 217
Culex quinquefasciatus, egg dispersion pheromones, **8**, 217
p-cumate, degradation, **3**, 384
cumene, degradation, **3**, 384
cuparene, biosynthesis, **2**, 163
cuprenene, biosynthesis, **2**, 162
curacin A
    antiproliferative activity, **8**, 606
    applications, antimitotic agents, **8**, 608
    brine shrimp toxicity, **8**, 606
    colchicine binding inhibition, **8**, 606
    enantioselective synthesis, **8**, 606
    microtubule assembly inhibition, **8**, 606
    occurrence, **8**, 606
D-curacose, occurrence, **3**, 312, 313
curamycin, D-curacose, **3**, 313
Curculio caryae, grandisol, **8**, 224
Curculionidae
    pheromones, **8**, 212, 241
    see also *Metamasius hemipterus*
curcumin, biosynthesis, **1**, 766
cur genes, functions, **1**, 480
Curtobacterium pusillum, fatty acids, **1**, 71
Curvularia lunata, activity against, **1**, 691
curvularin, occurrence, **8**, 601
cuscohygrine, occurrence, **4**, 30
Cutleria multifida, 7-methylcyclooctatriene, **8**, 424
CV-1 cells, SV40 DNA replication inhibition, **7**, 169
cwh genes
    *cwh*41
        cloning, **3**, 18
        α-glucosidase I activity, **3**, 18
    *cwh*41 mutant
        β1,6-glucans reduction, **3**, 18
        K1 killer toxin resistance, **3**, 18
cya genes, encoding, **3**, 478
Cyamopsis tetragonoloba
    galactomannan biosynthesis, **3**, 521
    mannosyltransferase, **3**, 521
cyanide, biosynthesis, **8**, 144
cyanidin
    in bird pollinated plants, **8**, 158
    methylation, **1**, 739
cyanidin-3-glucoside, larval growth inhibition, **8**, 141
cyanidins, in fruit pigment, **8**, 164
Cyanidium caldarium, labeling studies, **2**, 61
cyanine phosphoramidites, synthesis, **7**, 177
β-cyanoalanine synthase
    biosynthesis, **1**, 884
    cyanide detoxification, **8**, 144
cyanobacteria
    arogenate pathway, **4**, 5
    bioactive natural products, **8**, 603
    carotenoid biosynthesis, **2**, 337
        regulatory mechanisms, **2**, 347
    Δ^{12}-desaturases, **1**, 40
    ω^3-desaturases, **1**, 41
    ω^6-desaturases, **1**, 40
    desaturation in, **1**, 36
    eicosanoids, **1**, 209
    glg genes, **3**, 462
    1,4-α-glucan branching enzyme, **3**, 444
    glucose-1-phosphate adenylyltransferase, **3**, 449
    metabolites, multi-drug resistance reversal activity, **8**, 610
    mutants, **2**, 338
    occurrence, **8**, 428
    phytoene desaturases, **2**, 341
    proteins, carotenoid-binding, **2**, 325
    stearoyl-CoA desaturases, **1**, 40
    symbiosis, **8**, 426

symbiotic, **8**, 580
see also *Scytonema pseudohofmanni*
cyanocyclines
    applications, antibiotics, **7**, 499
    occurrence, **7**, 499
cyanogen bromide, use in the formation of dumb-bell DNAs, **7**, 366
cyanogenesis
    definitions, **1**, 881
    level variations, **1**, 882
    mechanisms, **1**, 20, 881
    and metabolism, **1**, 884
    phylogenic distribution, in plants, **1**, 882
    plant–animal interactions, **1**, 882
    plant–microbe interactions, **1**, 882
    plants, **8**, 145
    and polymorphism, **1**, 882
cyanogens, effects, on seed dispersal, **8**, 167
cyanohydrin
    biosynthesis, **1**, 887
    degradation, **1**, 881
cyanophytes see cyanobacteria
cyasterone
    moulting hormone activity, **8**, 293
    structure, **8**, 282
Cyatheaceae, lignins, **3**, 625
Cyathea dealbata, cellulose, **3**, 591
CYB3 see pyrrolidine, 2-hydroxymethyl-3-hydroxy-(CYB3)
cybisterone, occurrence, **8**, 230
*CYC*1 transcripts, accumulation, **6**, 209
Cycas spp, cycasin, **8**, 362
cycasin, insect sequestration, **8**, 152, 362
Cyclamen persicum, flavonol synthase, **1**, 727
cyclases (CYCs)
    in bacterial aromatic polyketide synthases, **1**, 475
    combinatorial analysis, **1**, 489
Cyclas formicarius, (*Z*)-3-dodecenyl (*E*)-2-butenoate, **8**, 214
cyclitols, amino-, biosynthesis, **3**, 6
cyclization
    Type A, diterpenes, **2**, 219
    Type A–Type B, diterpenes, **2**, 226
    Type B, diterpenes, **2**, 223
cyclization products, groups, **2**, 300
cycloaddition reactions, in antibody catalysis, **5**, 428
cycloalkylamines, as farnesyl-diphosphate farnesyltransferase inhibitors, **2**, 258
cycloaraneosene, occurrence, **1**, 378
cycloaromatization
    of enediyne compounds, **7**, 557
    transition-metal mediated, **7**, 557
cycloartenol
    from, all-*trans* (*S*)-2,3-oxidosqualene, **2**, 303
    occurrence, **2**, 303
cycloartenol cyclases, **2**, **299–319**
    Arabidopsis thaliana, **2**, 303
    biochemistry, **2**, 303
    genetics, **2**, 305
    inhibitors, **2**, 304
    pea seedlings, **2**, 303
    purification, **2**, 303
    Rabdosia japonica, **2**, 303
    reaction mechanisms, **2**, 304
    substrate specificity, **2**, 304
cyclobrassinin, as phytoalexin, **8**, 187
cyclobrassinin sulfoxide, as phytoalexin, **8**, 187
cyclobutane, (1*R*-*cis*)-(+)-1-acetoxymethyl-2,2-dimethyl-3-(1-methylvinyl)-, occurrence, **8**, 224
cyclobutane, (+)-*cis*-1-(2-hydroxyethyl)-1-methyl-2-isopropenyl- see grandisol
cyclobutaneacetic acid, (1*R*,2*S*)-1-methyl-2-(1-methylethenyl)- see (+)-grandisoic acid

cyclobutane lignans, occurrence, **1**, 686
cyclobutane photodimers
    base excision repair pathway, **5**, 393
    isomeric, **5**, 373
    mutagenesis induction, **5**, 394
    translesion synthesis, **5**, 394
cyclobutane pyrimidine photodimer radical anions
    cleavage, antibody-catalyzed, **5**, 382
    detection, via EPR, **5**, 380
    electronic structure calculations, via AM1 UHF
        method, **5**, 382
    formation, **5**, 379
    fragmentation
        intermediate trapping, **5**, 380
        isotope effects on, **5**, 381, 383
        mechanisms, **5**, 379
    β-isotope effects on, **5**, 381
    photo-CIDNP spectra, **5**, 379, 384
cyclobutane pyrimidine photodimer radical cations
    alkene extrusion, **5**, 378
    electronic structure calculations, via AM1 UHF
        method, **5**, 378
    formation, **5**, 376
    fragmentation
        intermediate trapping, **5**, 376
        isotope effects on, **5**, 378
        mechanisms, **5**, 376
    photo-CIDNP spectra, **5**, 378, 384
    stability, **5**, 376
cyclobutane pyrimidine photodimers
    formation, mechanisms, **5**, 372
    photoreactivation, **5**, 375
    repair pathways, **5**, 372
cyclobutanol, 1-methyl-, biosynthesis, **5**, 220
cyclobutyl cations, as source of natural products, **2**, 109
cyclodecapeptides, biosynthesis, **4**, 325
β-cyclodextrin, hydrolysis, **5**, 299
cyclodextrins
    applications, **8**, 202
    in GC, **8**, 202
cyclodextrins, anthryl(alkylamino)-, **7**, 463
cyclodidemnamide
    occurrence, **8**, 537
    structure, **8**, 537
cyclodione, occurrence, **1**, 377
cyclodipeptides, biosynthesis, **1**, 548
β-cyclogeraniolene, occurrence, **8**, 234
9,15-cyclogibberellins, nomenclature, **8**, 56
cyclohepta-amylose, structure, studies, **3**, 546
1,4-cycloheptadiene, (+)-(6S)-(1Z-butadienyl)- *see*
        ectocarpene
cyclohepta-1,4-dienes, biosynthesis, **8**, 424
cycloheptanecarboxylic acids, biosynthesis, **1**, 76
cyclohexa-amylose, structure, studies, **3**, 546
cyclohexadiene, **7**, 557
    biosynthesis, **5**, 321
cyclohexa-1,3-diene, (3S)-(−)-1-methyl-5(1-hydroxy-1-
        methylethyl)- *see* m-methandienol
1,4-cyclohexadiene, 1,3,4,6-tetrachloro-, biosynthesis, **5**,
        409
2,4-cyclohexadiene-1-carboxylate, 2-succinyl-6-hydroxy-
        (SHCHC), as intermediate, **1**, 615, 618
cyclohexa-1,5-dienecarboxylic acid, (−)-trans-(3R,4R)-
        3,4-dihydroxy-, biosynthesis, **1**, 619
cyclohexa-4,6-dienecarboxylic acid, (+)-trans-(3S,4S)-
        2,3-dihydroxy-, biosynthesis, **1**, 619
4,6-cyclohexadiene-1-carboxylic acid, trans-3-[(1-
        carboxyethenyl)oxy]-2-hydroxy- *see* isochorismic
        acid
2,5-cyclohexadien-1-one, 2-hydroxy-4,4,6-trimethyl- *see*
        lanierone
cyclohexadienyl dehydrogenase, catalysis, **5**, 344
cyclohexane, (4Z,4′E)-4-(1,5′-dimethyl-4-heptenylidene)-
        1-methyl- *see* homo-γ-bisabolene

cyclohexane, γ-hexachloro- *see* lindane
cyclohexanecarboxylic acid, trans-dihydro- (DHCHC),
        biosynthesis, **1**, 519
cyclohexanecarboxylic acids, from, shikimic acid, **1**, 72
cyclohexanedione, dimethyl-, as starting material, for
        juvenile hormone III, **8**, 270
cyclohexanedione, methylethyl-, reduction, **8**, 270
cyclohexanes, dihydro-, from, shikimic acid, **1**, 75
cyclohexanoids, ring-expansion, **2**, 107
cyclohexanone, (S)-3-hydroxy-2,3-dimethyl-, as
        intermediate, **8**, 270
cyclohexanone, 2-hydroxy-2,6,6-trimethyl-, occurrence,
        8, 234
cyclohexene, γ-pentachloro-, biosynthesis, **5**, 409
cyclohex-1-enecarboxylic acid, 5-hydroxy-, reduction, **1**,
        72
cyclohexenes, in antibody catalyst design, **5**, 428
2-cyclohexen-1-ol, 1-methyl-, occurrence, **8**, 211
cyclohexenone, 6-hydroxy-, toxicity, **8**, 139
cyclohexenone, 3-methyl- *see* seudenone
1-cyclohexenylcarbonyl-CoA reductase, purification, **1**,
        74
cyclohexenyl diphosphates, biosynthesis, **5**, 321
cycloheximide, in plant gene expression, **8**, 97
cyclomaltodextrin glucanotransferase(s)
    occurrence, **5**, 306
    sequences, **3**, 459, **5**, 298
cyclonerodiol, occurrence, **2**, 205
cyclooctatriene, 7-methyl-, biosynthesis, **8**, 424
cyclooxygenase–peroxidase integration, kinetic models, **5**,
        244
cyclooxygenase(s) *see* prostaglandin-endoperoxide
        synthase(s)
cyclopentaneoctanoic acid, 3-oxo-2-(2-pentenyl)-,
        biosynthesis, **1**, 120
cyclopentanoids, biosynthesis, **1**, **139–158**
cyclophanes, cationic, partial intercalation, **7**, 466
cyclophanes, polyaromatic, as hosts, **2**, 123
cyclophilins
    biosynthesis, **1**, 540
    genes, cloning, **1**, 541
    immunosuppressive activity, **1**, 540
    occurrence, **1**, 541
cyclopropanation, mechanisms, **1**, 62, 64
cyclopropane, 1,1-dimethyl-, oxygenation, **5**, 220
cyclopropane, D,L-trans-2-phenylmethyl-, oxygenation, **5**,
        220
cyclopropane, trans-2-phenylmethyl-, oxygenation, **5**, 220
cyclopropane-1-carboxylate, 2-(2,3-dihydroxyphenyl)-,
        oxygenation, **5**, 220
cyclopropane-1-carboxylic acid, 1-amino- (ACC)
    biosynthesis, **1**, 133
    as intermediate, **8**, 94
cyclopropane-1-carboxylic acid, N-malonyl-1-amino-,
        biosynthesis, **8**, 96
cyclopropane fatty acid (CFA) synthase, discovery, **1**, 65
cyclopropane mycolic acid synthase (CMAS-1), structure,
        1, 66
cyclopropanes
    Cope rearrangement, **8**, 424
    DNA damage induction, **7**, 504
D-cycloserine
    activity, **3**, 277
    occurrence, **8**, 389
cyclospirolactone, formation, **7**, 564
cyclosporin, N-methylisoleucyl-
    anti-HIV1 activity, **1**, 550
    biosynthesis, **1**, 538
cyclosporin A
    applications
        immunosuppressive agents, **1**, 16
        in transplantation, **1**, 540
    biological activity, **1**, 534

peptide bonds, **4**, 226
protein binding, **1**, 541
secretion, **4**, 198
cyclosporin B, biosynthesis, **1**, 538
cyclosporin C
  biosynthesis, suppression, **1**, 537
  occurrence, **1**, 537
cyclosporin–cyclophilin complexes
  phosphatase inhibitory activity, **1**, 541
  regulatory mechanism, **1**, 541
cyclosporin D, biosynthesis, **1**, 538
cyclosporin G, pharmaceutical activity, **1**, 550
cyclosporin M, constituents, **1**, 538
cyclosporin metabolites, antifungal activity, **1**, 534
cyclosporin production associated element, use of term, **1**, 543
cyclosporin(s)
  analogues, **1**, 549
    future research, **1**, 550
  antifungal activity, **1**, 534, 541
  applications, **4**, 199
    future trends, **1**, 550
    in transplantation, **1**, 550
  biosynthesis, **1**, 538, **4**, 321
    directed, **1**, 538
    enhancement, **1**, 537
  discovery, **1**, 534
  environmental implications, **1**, 534
  enzyme characterization, **1**, 543
  feeding studies, **1**, 538
  fermentation improvement, **1**, 536
  from
    D-alanine, **1**, 543
    (4*R*)-4-[(*E*)-2-butenyl]-4-methyl-L-threonine, **1**, 543
  function, ecological, **1**, 533
  genetics, **1**, 538
  insecticidal activity, **1**, 534
  occurrence, **1**, 533
  producer identification, **1**, 543
  production levels, **1**, 535
  production strains, **1**, 534
  roles, in lipopeptide biosynthesis, **1**, **533–555**
  strain improvement, **1**, 536
  structural analogs, **1**, 535
  structure, **1**, 533
    effectiveness, **1**, 550
  synthesis
    in vitro, **1**, 546
    preparative enzymatic, **1**, 550
cyclosporin synthetase
  catalysis, **1**, 533
  characterization, **1**, 539, 546
  functional analysis, **1**, 548
  gene
    disruption, **1**, 542
    manipulation, **1**, 541
    structure, **1**, 547
  genes, isolation, **1**, 539
  genetics, **1**, 547
  molecular weight, **1**, 546
  roles, in cyclosporin biosynthesis, **1**, 546
  structure, **1**, 547
    interpretation, **1**, 548
  substrate specificity, **1**, 550
cyclostellettamines, occurrence, **8**, 560
cyclotheonamides
  occurrence, **8**, 568
  structure, **8**, 569
  thrombin inhibiting activity, **8**, 568
  total synthesis, **8**, 569
CYCs *see* cyclases (CYCs)
Cyerce cristallina
  chemical defense, **8**, 462

mucous secretion, ichthyotoxicity, **8**, 464
cyercenes, isolation, **8**, 462
Cyl enzymes
  CylM, functions, **4**, 294
  CylT, functions, **4**, 294
cyl genes
  *cylA*1, encoding, **4**, 293
  *cylA*2, encoding, **4**, 293
cylindricines
  occurrence, **8**, 546
  structures, **8**, 546
Cylindrocarpum lucidum, cyclosporins, **1**, 534
Cylindrocladium floriidanum, chaetoglobosin O, **1**, 371
cylindrocyclophane A, structure, **8**, 610
cylindrospermopsin, structure, **8**, 610
D-cymarose, occurrence, **3**, 312, 313
L-cymarose, occurrence, **3**, 312, 313
p-cymene, biosynthesis, **2**, 103, 136
Cynoglossum officinale, pyrrolizidine alkaloids, **4**, 31
cypemycin, structure, **4**, 277
Cyperaceae, oxylipins, **1**, 229
cyperine, phytotoxicity, **8**, 179
Cyperus iria, juvenile hormone III, **8**, 276
Cypridina hilgendorfii see Vargula hilgendorfii
cyprids
  larval attachment inhibition, **8**, 437
  larval settlement inhibition, **8**, 436
Cyprinus carpio, lipoxins, **1**, 238
Cys-61, mutagenesis, **1**, 578
Cys-234, modification, **4**, 76
Cys-242, mutants, **4**, 85
Cys-328, mutagenesis, **1**, 578
CysAliAliXaa tetrapeptides, prenylation, **2**, 358
cys genes, *cysG*, occurrence, **4**, 141
cysteamine, *N*-acetyl- (NAC), thioesters, **1**, 142, 421, 451, 498
cysteamine, hexanoyl-*N*-acetyl, isotopic incorporation, **1**, 451
cysteine
  biosynthesis, **4**, 165
  conserved, **1**, 756
  DNA damage, **7**, 560
  functionalities, **7**, 616
  p*K*, **7**, 616
  in sesquiterpene synthase, **2**, 193
  structure, **4**, 354
cysteine, *N*-acetyl-*S*-farnesyl-, as prenylated protein methylation inhibitor, **2**, 361
cysteine, 3-methyl-, as substrate, **4**, 252
cysteine, *S*-methyl-
  biosynthesis, **1**, 848
  as intermediate, **1**, 849
  replacement, **4**, 252
cysteine, *S*-(methylthiomethyl)-
  biosynthesis, **1**, 848
  as intermediate, **1**, 849
cysteine, *S*-(2-sulfonyl)-, as intermediate, **1**, 833
D-cysteine, *S*-aminovinyl-, **4**, 284
L-cysteine
  in coenzyme M biosynthesis, **1**, 833
  condensation, **1**, 840
  as esperamicin A₁ sulfur source, **7**, 554
  in penicillin biosynthesis, **4**, 162, 165
  as sparsomycin precursor, **1**, 847
cysteine methyl ester, *S*-farnesyl-, source of, **2**, 353
cysteine phosphatases
  homology, **5**, 144
  rate-limiting steps, **5**, 148
cysteines
  active site, **2**, 19, 22
  derivatization, **2**, 33
  hydroxymethylglutaryl-CoA reductase inhibition, **2**, 33
cysteine thiols, hydrogen abstraction, **5**, 199

cysteinol, *S*-(methylthiomethyl)-, as intermediate, **1**, 849
cysteyl-tRNA synthetase, in selenocysteine
    aminoacylation, **4**, 357
cystisine, *N*-methyl-, insect sequestration, **8**, 154
cystodamine
    occurrence, **8**, 539
    structure, **8**, 539
Cystodytes spp.
    cystodytin A, **8**, 540
    pyridoacridines, **8**, 540
Cystodytes dellechiajei
    cystodamine, **8**, 539
    cystodytins, **1**, 381
cystodytin A, occurrence, **8**, 540
cystodytin B, biosynthesis, **1**, 381
cystodytin J, occurrence, **8**, 540
cystodytins, occurrence, **1**, 381
Cystoseira barbata, lignins, erroneous reports, **3**, 622
cytidine
    deamination, **6**, 98
    hydrolysis, **5**, 24
    transamination, **5**, 96
    transglycosylation, **5**, 96
cytidine, N^6-amino-2′-deoxy-, synthesis, **7**, 271
cytidine, 2′-deoxy-5-methyl-, synthesis, **7**, 259
cytidine, 5,6-dihydro-, deamination, **5**, 88
cytidine, 4-*N*-methyl-, as substrate, **5**, 91
cytidine aminohydrolase *see* cytidine deaminase
cytidine deaminase
    biological functions, **5**, 87
    bound inhibitors, structure, **5**, 91
    catalysis, **5**, 24
    catalytic site structure, **5**, 91
    inhibitors, **5**, 88
    kinetic properties, **5**, 87
    mechanisms, **5**, 92
    occurrence, **5**, 87
    protein structure, **5**, 90
    transition state inhibitors, **5**, 89
    transition state similarity measures, **5**, 92
cytidine 5′-diphosphates, 2′-fluoromethylene, reactions,
    with ribonucleotide reductases, **5**, 172
cytidine 5′-monophosphate *N*-acetylneuraminic acid, as
    sugar nucleotide donor, **3**, 229
cytidine-5′-triphosphate, 5-[(4-azidophenacyl)thio]-,
    synthesis, **7**, 216
cytidine 5′-triphosphates, 2′-fluoromethylene, reactions,
    with ribonucleotide reductases, **5**, 172
cytidyl 5′-diphosphate sugars
    CDPabequose, biosynthesis, **3**, 208
    CDPparatose, biosynthesis, **3**, 208
    CDPtyvelose, biosynthesis, **3**, 208
cytisine
    host–parasite chemical transfer, **8**, 176
    insect sequestration, **8**, 152
    toxicity, **8**, 147
    to seeds, **8**, 168
cytisine, *N*-methyl-, host–parasite chemical transfer, **8**,
    176
cytochalasin K, structure, **1**, 374
cytochalasin(s)
    biosynthesis, **1**, 422
    structure, **1**, 371
cytochrome-*c* oxidase, roles, in lignin biosynthesis, **3**, 716
cytochrome oxidase subunit II gene, sequencing, **5**, 96
cytochrome P450$_{TYR}$, isolation, **1**, 889
cytochrome P450 enzymes
    biological activity, inhibition, **1**, 255
    early studies, **3**, 637
    in gibberellin biosynthesis, **8**, 47
cytochrome P450 monooxygenases
    coding, **1**, 467
    encoding, **2**, 205, **8**, 50

roles, in furanocoumarin biosynthesis, **1**, 630
cytochrome P450 oxygenases, occurrence, **2**, 116
cytochrome P450 reductases, occurrence, **3**, 670
cytochromes P450
    activation, **1**, 443
    and aflatoxin epoxide, **7**, 470
    applications, in fungal natural products, **2**, 207
    catalysis, **1**, 628, **3**, 638
    enantioselectivity, **5**, 58
    and the endoplasmic reticulum, **5**, 54
    gene transcription, **1**, 129
    inhibitors, **1**, 389, 795
        studies, **2**, 384
    and *ent*-kaurenoic acid 7β-hydroxylase, **8**, 50
    occurrence, **1**, 210
    purification, **3**, 637
    regioselectivity, **5**, 58
    roles
        in eicosanoid biosynthesis, **1**, 160
        in eicosanoid metabolism, **1**, 268
        in 2-hydroxyisoflavanone synthase reactions, **1**, 793
        in hydroxylation, **3**, 637
        in jasmonic acid studies, **1**, 130
        in monoterpene biosynthesis, **2**, 145
        in ring cleavage, **2**, 390
        in unsaturated fatty acid precursor oxidation, **1**, 210
cytokines, biosynthesis, **3**, 183
cytokinin
    discovery, **8**, 57
    in senescence studies, **1**, 126
cytokinin autonomous tissue, studies, **8**, 67
cytokinin-binding factor-1 (CBF-1), characterization, **8**,
    63
cytokinin-binding proteins
    characterization, **8**, 63
        problems, **8**, 65
    effects, on transcriptional regulation, **8**, 64
cytokinin-7-glucosyl transferase, glucose donors, **8**, 71
cytokinin hydroxylase, in *trans*-zeatin biosynthesis, **8**, 70
cytokinin oxidase
    occurrence, **8**, 71
    roles, in cytokinin degradation, **8**, 71
cytokinins
    alternative (cyanide-resistant) electron transport
        inhibition, **8**, 64
    attraction centers, **8**, 59
    availability, regulatory mechanisms, **8**, 70
    bioassays, **8**, 59
    biochemistry, **8**, 57
    biological activity, **8**, 62
    biosynthesis, **8**, 69
    chemistry, **8**, 60
    degradation, **8**, 71
    discovery, **8**, 21
    effects on greening, mechanisms, **8**, 62
    extraction, **8**, 60
    gene expression, regulatory mechanisms, **8**, 66
    historical background, **8**, 57
    isolation
        chromatography, **8**, 60
        solvent partitioning, **8**, 60
    and light, **8**, 65
    metabolism, **8**, 69
        enzymes in, **8**, 72
        regulatory mechanisms, **8**, 71
    nucleotides, **8**, 69
    organ formation induction, **8**, 59
    purification, **8**, 60
    roles
        in ethylene biosynthesis, **8**, 96
        in gene expression, **8**, 97
    signal transduction, analysis, **8**, 65
    structure, **8**, 61

synthesis, **8**, 62
transformation, with *ipt* genes, **8**, 63
transpiration stimulation, **8**, 59
tRNA-derived, **8**, 69
use of term, **8**, 57
cytolysin
  characterization, **4**, 276
  gene clusters, **4**, 292
  peptides, **4**, 279
  structure, **4**, 279
  toxicity, **4**, 276
cytolysis, mechanisms, **7**, 667
cytoplasm, isopentenyl diphosphate biosynthesis, **2**, 60
cytosine
  bromination, **7**, 96
  exocyclic amino group, protection groups, **7**, 120
  iodination, **7**, 96

cytosine, N^4-alkyl-, in oligodeoxynucleotides, **7**, 320
cytosine, 5-fluoro-, as starting material, for 5-fluorouracil, **5**, 93
cytosine, 2′-fluoro-5-iodo-1-β-D-arabinofuranosyl- (FIAC), antineoplastic activity, **5**, 88
cytosine, N^4-methoxy-, in oligodeoxynucleotides, **7**, 321
cytosine, C^5-propynyl-, in oligodeoxynucleotides, **7**, 322
cytosine aminohydrolase *see* cytosine deaminase
cytosine arabinoside, antineoplastic activity, **5**, 88
cytosine deaminase
  biological functions, **5**, 93
  occurrence, **5**, 93
cytosol, interactions, with amyloplasts, **3**, 466
cytosylglucuronic acid, conversion, to blasticidin S, **3**, 339
cytotoxic potency, and cleavable complex, correlation, **7**, 596

D

2,4-D *see* acetic acid, 2,4-dichlorophenoxy- (2,4-D)
D-AB1 *see* D-arabinitol, 1,4-dideoxy-1,4-imino- (D-AB1)
DAC *see* deacetylcephalosporin (DAC)
Dacrydium intermedium
   3-*p*-coumarate, **8**, 285
   20-hydroxyecdysterone 2-cinnamate, **8**, 285
   sclarene, **2**, 225
   ent-sclarene, **2**, 225
DAC synthase, catalysis, **1**, 840
dactomelynes, occurrence, **1**, 303
dactylyne, occurrence, **1**, 303
Dacus oleae
   diethyl 5-oxo-1,9-nonanedioate, **8**, 212
   (*R*)-1,7-dioxaspiro[5.5]decane, **8**, 212
'daddy-long-legs' *see* Tipulidae
dad genes
   dadB, expression, **3**, 254
   occurrence, **3**, 254
daffodil chromoplasts, isopentenyl diphosphate
     isomerase, **2**, 71
Dahlia variabilis
   6′-deoxychalcones, **1**, 736
   dihydrokaempferol 4-reductase, **1**, 727, 728
DAHP *see* 3-deoxy-D-*arabino*-(2-)heptulosonate 7-
     phosphate (DAHP)
DAHP synthase *see* 2-dehydro-3-
     deoxyphosphoheptonate aldolase
DAHP synthetase *see* 2-dehydro-3-
     deoxyphosphoheptonate aldolase
daidzein
   biosynthesis, **1**, 791
     via isoflavone synthase reaction, **1**, 786
   as chemoattractant, **1**, 780
   half-life, **1**, 812
   as nodulating gene expression inhibitor, **8**, 174
   occurrence, **1**, 774
   precursors, **1**, 799
   and quail population control, **1**, 782
daidzein, 2′-hydroxydihydro-, biosynthesis, **1**, 796
Dalbergia monetaria, epiguibourtinidol-(4β→8)-
     epicatechin, **3**, 775
Dalbergia odorifera, vestitol, **1**, 775
Daldinia concentrica
   1,8-dihydroxynaphthalene, **1**, 415
   5-hydroxy-2-methylchromone, **1**, 415
damalachawin, occurrence, **3**, 781
dammarenyl cation, conformation, **2**, 301
DANA *see* neuraminic acid, 2-deoxy-2,3-dihydro-*N*-
     acetyl- (DANA)
Danainae
   edulanes, **8**, 234
   hexahydrofarnesylacetone, **8**, 234
   isophorones, **8**, 234
   nerolidol, **8**, 227
   see also Euploea sylvester; *Idea* spp.
Danaus spp., terpenoids, **8**, 235
Danaus plexippus
   edulanes, **8**, 234
   milkweed plant feeding adaptation, **8**, 149
   oviposition, plant choice, **8**, 156
   plant toxin sequestration, **8**, 152
   sequestration, **8**, 362
dangling ends, definition, **6**, 31
2-dansylethoxycarbonyl (Dnseoc), as 5′-hydroxyl
     protecting group, **7**, 127

DAOC *see* deacetoxycephalosporin C (DAOC)
DAP dehydrogenase *see* diaminopimelate dehydrogenase
daphnane, biosynthesis, **2**, 223
Daphne mezereum, linalool, **8**, 161
Daphne tangutica, (−)-pinoresinol, **1**, 645
daphnodorin A, structure, **3**, 780
daphnodorin B
   rearrangement, **3**, 780
   structure, **3**, 780
daphnodorin D-1, rearrangement, **3**, 780
daphnodorins, biochemistry, **3**, 780
DAPI *see* indole, 4′,6-diamino-2-phenyl- (DAPI)
dark spore germination, studies, **8**, 56
Darwin, Charles Robert (1809–82)
   Ginkgo biloba studies, **2**, 367
   The Power of Movement in Plants (1880), **8**, 23
Dasymutilla klugii, venom, **8**, 354
Dasymutilla occidentalis, dihydromanicone, **8**, 244
DATFP-DMAPP *see* 2-buten-1-ol, (*E*)-4-[2-
     diazotrifluoropropionyloxy]-3-methyl- (DATFP-
     DMAPP)
dATP *see* deoxyadenosine triphosphate
Datura spp., hyoscyamine biosynthesis, **4**, 27
Datura stramonium
   capsidiol, **2**, 181
   hyoscyamine studies, **4**, 27
   putrescine *N*-methyltransferase activity, **4**, 27
Daucus carota
   anthocyanin sinapoylation, **1**, 741
   caffeoyl-CoA *O*-methyltransferase, **3**, 672
   cell adhesion, **3**, 520
   6-hydroxymellein synthase, **1**, 416
   labeling studies, **2**, 61
   root, geranylgeranyl diphosphate synthase, **2**, 86
   transferases, **1**, 742
dau genes
   in daunosamine biosynthesis, **3**, 342
   mutants, **1**, 487
daunomycin
   anticancer activity, **1**, 481
   applications
     antibiotics, **7**, 527
     antineoplastic agents, **7**, 527
     antitumor agents, **3**, 324
   biosynthesis, **1**, 475, 481
     genetics, **3**, 349
   deletion analysis, **1**, 487
   formaldehyde-mediated covalent attachment to DNA,
     7, 530
   isolation, **4**, 200
   occurrence, **7**, 605
   photochemical DNA damage, **7**, 544
   quinone methide, UV-vis spectra, **7**, 529
daunomycin, 5-imino-, inhibitor, **7**, 605
daunorubicin *see* daunomycin
daunosamine, biosynthesis, genetics, **3**, 342
DBHC *see* carbazole, 4,6-dibromo-3-hydroxy- (DBHC)
DBI *see* benzimidazole, 5,6-dimethyl- (DBI)
DCC *see* carbodiimide, dicyclohexyl- (DCC)
DCHQ *see* quinone, 2,6-dichlorohydro- (DCHQ)
dCMP aminohydrolase *see* dCMP deaminase
dCMP deaminase
   binding, **5**, 94
   biological functions, **5**, 93
   isolation, **5**, 93

roles, in deoxyribonucleotide biosynthesis, **5**, 93
*DCP*1 gene
  deletion, **6**, 212
  encoding, **6**, 209, 210
DCTAEA motif, **2**, 283
DCTA motif
  in hopene cyclases, **2**, 315
  in lanosterol cyclase, **2**, 315
dCTP aminohydrolase *see* dCTP deaminase
dCTP deaminase
  biological functions, **5**, 94
  occurrence, **5**, 94
ddl genes
  ddlA, cloning, **3**, 260
  ddlB, localization, **3**, 260
  occurrence, **3**, 260
DDN *see* 1(2*H*)-naphthalene, 3,4-dihydro-4,8-dihydroxy-
  (DDN)
DDT *see* chlorphenotane
DDTA motif
  in abietadiene synthase, **2**, 315
  Asp residues, mutation, **2**, 315
  in hopene cyclases, **2**, 315
  in kaurene synthase A, **2**, 315
DDXXD motifs, occurrence, **5**, 331
deacetoxycephalosporin C/deacetylcephalosporin
  synthase, catalysis, **1**, 840
deacetoxycephalosporin C (DAOC), biosynthesis, **1**, 840,
  4, 171
deacetoxycephalosporin C expandase, ring expansion, **4**,
  171
deacetoxycephalosporin C synthase
  catalysis, **1**, 840
  ring expansion, **4**, 171
deacetylases, roles, in proteoglycan biosynthesis, **3**, 162
N-deacetylation, in lipid A biosynthesis, **3**, 220
deacetylcephalosporin C hydroxylase, ring expansion, **4**,
  171
deacetylcephalosporin (DAC), biosynthesis, **4**, 172
deadenylation
  cis-acting sequences, **6**, 208
  cytoplasmic, enzymology, **6**, 208
  and 3′ to 5′ degradation, **6**, 212
  genetics, **6**, 207
  roles, in eukaryotic mRNA decay, **6**, 206, 207
deamination
  chemical, **5**, 80
  enzymatic, **5**, 73
  nucleosides, **5**, 71–100
  nucleotides, **5**, 71–100
  purines, **5**, 73
    overview, **5**, 72
  pyrimidines, **5**, 87
    overview, **5**, 72
deaminoketodemethylphosphinothricin (DKDPT),
  biosynthesis, **1**, 872
7-deazaadenine, in oligodeoxynucleotides, **7**, 330
1-deazaadenosine
  binding, **5**, 77
  interactions, with adenosine deaminase, **5**, 77
7-deazaadenosine
  aptamer-binding ability, **7**, 625
  incorporation studies, **6**, 225
7-deaza-8-azapurines, in oligodeoxynucleotides, **7**, 331
3-deazacytidine, cytidine deaminase inhibition, **5**, 91
7-deaza-2′-deoxyadenosine, in aptamer synthesis, **7**, 626
1-deazaguanine, **7**, 254
3-deazaguanine, in oligodeoxynucleotides, **7**, 330
7-deazaguanine, **7**, 513
  pK_a, **7**, 331
3-deazapurines, **7**, 253
7-deazapurines, **7**, 253
debranching enzyme *see* α-dextrin endo-1,6-α-
  glucosidase; isoamylase

debromoaplysiatoxin, occurrence, **8**, 603
DEBS *see* 6-deoxyerythronolide B synthase (DEBS)
DEBS proteins
  DEBS1
    cleavage, **1**, 514
    structure, **1**, 504
  DEBS1 1+TE, **1**, 507
    isolation, **1**, 515
  DEBS1 1-TE
    isolation, **1**, 515
    occurrence, **1**, 507
  DEBS3, structure, **1**, 504
  fusion, **1**, 513
  in vitro studies, **1**, 514
  overexpression, **1**, 504
  proteolysis, **1**, 506
  sequencing, **1**, 501
decacyclic alkaloids, occurrence, **8**, 358
(2*E*,4*Z*)-2,4-decadienoate, methyl, occurrence, **8**, 199, 213
7,9-decadien-5-ol, (4*R*,5*R*,6*S*,7*E*,9*E*)-4,6,8-trimethyl-,
  occurrence, **8**, 245
decadien-10-olide, (3*E*,8*E*)-4,8-dimethyl- *see* suspensolide
2*E*,4*E*-decadienylamide, *N*-isobutyl- *see* pellitorine
decaketides, biosynthesis, **1**, 417
decalin polyketides, 1,2-dialkyl-, structure, **1**, 370
decanal, (4*R*,8*R*)-4,8-dimethyl-, occurrence, **8**, 236
decanal, 4,8-dimethyl-, occurrence, **8**, 217
decanoic acid, occurrence, **8**, 209
2-decanoic acid, (*E*)-9-hydroxy-, occurrence, **8**, 213
9-decanolide *see* phoracantholide I
2-decanone, occurrence, **8**, 212
decapping enzymes, encoding, **6**, 209
decaprenyl diphosphate synthases, occurrence, **2**, 91
di-trans,poly-cis-decaprenyl*cis*transferase(s), occurrence,
  2, 92
decarboxylation, mechanisms, **4**, 91, 92
2,4,6,8-decatetrene, (2*E*,4*E*,6*E*,8*E*)-3,5,7-trimethyl-,
  occurrence, **8**, 240
(2*E*,4*E*,6*Z*)-2,4,6-decatrienoate, methyl, occurrence, **8**,
  213
2,6,8-decatrien-4-one, (2*E*,5*R*,6*E*,8*E*)-5,7-dimethyl-,
  occurrence, **8**, 244
2*E*,6*Z*,8*E*-decatrienylamide, *N*-isobutyl- *see* spilanthol
2-decenal, (*E*)-4-oxo-, occurrence, **8**, 213
8*E*-decenoic acid, 10-oxo-, occurrence, **1**, 211
(*E*)-2-decenoic acid, 9-hydroxy-, occurrence, **8**, 199
(*E*)-2-decenoic acid, 9-oxo-
  biosynthesis, **8**, 213
  occurrence, **8**, 199, 213
(*Z*)-3-decenoic acid, occurrence, **8**, 213
4-decen-3-one, (*E*)-4,6-dimethyl-, occurrence, **8**, 243
L-decilonitrose
  occurrence, **3**, 312
  structure, **3**, 322
decilorubicin
  L-diginose, **3**, 313
  trideoxysugars, **3**, 322
decorin
  localization, **3**, 164
  structure, **3**, 166
Dectomax *see* doramectin
defensive glands, toxins, **8**, 361
degenerate primers
  design, **2**, 210
  use in taxadiene synthase isolation, **2**, 209
deguelin
  isolation, **8**, 341
  occurrence, **1**, 812
deguelin cyclase, isolation, **1**, 812
DegU protein, functions, **8**, 402
dehalogenases
  catalysis, mechanisms, **5**, 14
  characterization, **5**, 410

complexation, **5**, 14
evolutionary origin, **5**, 402
occurrence, **5**, 409
poor catalytic abilities, **5**, 403
reductive, roles, **5**, 414
sequence homology analysis, **5**, 402
structure, **5**, 13
see also microbial dehalogenases
dehalogenases, aliphatic, biochemistry, **5**, 403
dehalogenases, aromatic
  biochemistry, **5**, 410
  hydrolytic, **5**, 411
  O₂-dependent, **5**, 417
Dehalospirillum multivorans
  dehalogenase, **5**, 410
  tetrachloroethene dehalogenase, **5**, 420
dehydratase, in fatty acid studies, **1**, 500
dehydrin, expression, and desiccation, **8**, 83
dehydroabietane
  from, abietadiene, **2**, 384
  isolation, **2**, 395
(+)-dehydroabietane
  roles, **2**, 384
    in ginkgolide biosynthesis, **2**, 384
2,3-dehydroalanine (Dha)
  in lantibiotics, **4**, 275
  residues, **4**, 283
dehydroalliacolide, ²H NMR spectra, **2**, 176
9,10-dehydroanthracene biradical, **7**, 579
  retro-Bergman reaction, **7**, 579
dehydroazasirosterol, occurrence, **1**, 379
1,4-dehydrobenzene biradicals, structure, **7**, 572
trans-1,2-dehydrobenzene-1,2-diol dehydrogenase,
    catalysis, **1**, 276
(1*R*,5*S*,7*R*)-dehydro-*exo*-brevicomin, occurrence, **8**, 12
(*Z*)-2,3-dehydrobutyrine (Dhb)
  in lantibiotics, **4**, 275
  residues, **4**, 283
7-dehydrocholesterol, biosynthesis, **8**, 291
dehydrocineol, occurrence, **8**, 225
dehydrocoelenterazine, isolation, **8**, 454
dehydro *iso*-coproporphyrinogen, as intermediate, **4**, 95
3-dehydro-6-deoxoteasterone, as intermediate, **8**, 105
2-dehydro-3-deoxyglucarate aldolase
  biochemistry, **3**, 402
  mechanisms, **3**, 402
  purification, **3**, 402
2-dehydro-3-deoxy-D-glucarate tartronate-semialdehyde-
    lyase *see* 2-dehydro-3-deoxyglucarate aldolase
2-dehydro-3-deoxy-D-gluconate-6-phosphate D-
    glyceraldehyde-3-phosphate-lyase *see* 2-dehydro-3-
    deoxyphosphogluconate aldolase
2-dehydro-3-deoxy-D-*arabino*-heptonate-7-phosphate D-
    erythrose-4-phosphate-lyase (pyruvate-
    phosphorylating) *see* 2-dehydro-3-
    deoxyphosphoheptonate aldolase
2-dehydro-3-deoxy-D-octonate-8-phosphate D-arabinose-
    5-phosphate-lyase (pyruvate-phosphorylating)
    see 2-dehydro-3-deoxyphosphooctonate aldolase
2-dehydro-3-deoxy-D-pentonate aldolase, biochemistry,
    3, 429
2-dehydro-3-deoxy-L-pentonate aldolase
  activity, **3**, 425
  biochemistry, **3**, 425
  occurrence, **3**, 426
2-dehydro-3-deoxy-6-phosphogalactonate aldolase
  biochemistry, **3**, 428
  catalysis, **3**, 428
  isolation, **3**, 429
  mechanisms, **3**, 429
  purification, **3**, 429
  substrate specificity, **3**, 429
2-dehydro-3-deoxyphosphogluconate aldolase

applications, reagents, **3**, 423
biochemistry, **3**, 421
catalysis, **3**, 421
expression, **3**, 422
kinetics, **3**, 423
mechanisms, **3**, 423
occurrence, **3**, 421
purification, **3**, 421
sequences, **3**, 422
stability, **3**, 422
structure, **3**, 422
5-dehydro-2-deoxyphosphogluconate aldolase
  biochemistry, **3**, 409
  catalysis, **3**, 409
  isolation, **3**, 410
2-dehydro-3-deoxyphosphoheptonate aldolase
  active sites, studies, **1**, 578
  applications, **3**, 387
  assays, **1**, 578
  biochemistry, **3**, 386
  catalysis, **3**, 386, **5**, 345
  encoding, **4**, 2
  expression, **3**, 386
  genetics, **1**, 577
  isolation, **3**, 386
  isozymes, **1**, 575
  mechanisms, **1**, 577, 594
  metal dependence, **1**, 577
  occurrence, **3**, 386
  in shikimate pathway, **1**, 575
  substrates, **1**, 578
  substrate specificity, **3**, 509
2-dehydro-3-deoxyphosphooctonate aldolase
  biochemistry, **3**, 387
  catalysis, **1**, 580, **3**, 221, 387, 509
  cloning, **3**, 388
  mechanisms, **1**, 577, **3**, 389
  mutations, **3**, 389
  purification, **3**, 388
  stereochemistry, **3**, 390
  substrate specificity, **3**, 390
cis-dehydro-4,4′-diapophytoene, biosynthesis, **5**, 338
dehydrodigallic acid, linkages, **3**, 801
dehydrodiisoeugenol
  biosynthesis, **3**, 703
  structure, **3**, 703
dehydrodiisoeugenol, 5′-methoxy-, antibacterial activity,
    1, 692
dehydrodipropylguaiacol, biosynthesis, **3**, 725
3-dehydroecdysone
  biosynthesis, **8**, 291
  IR spectra, **8**, 285
  release, **8**, 279
3-dehydro-24-epicastasterone, 3-epimerization, **8**, 107
9(11)-dehydroergosterol, occurrence, **1**, 379
dehydrogenation, monolignols, early *in vitro* studies, **3**,
    703
1-dehydroginkgolide A
  daylight exposure, **2**, 390
  photocyclization, **2**, 394
dehydroguaiaretic acid, biosynthesis, **3**, 703
2,6-dehydroindacene biradical
  conformation change, **7**, 564
  formation, **7**, 562
(+)-dehydrojuvabione, isolation, **8**, 276
dehydrokuanoniamaine B, occurrence, **8**, 540
dehydrolipoamide acyltransferase, **4**, 332
2-dehydropantoate formaldehyde-lyase *see*
    ketopantoaldolase
dehydropolymerisates (DHPs)
  biosynthesis, **3**, 711
  molecular weight distributions, **3**, 730
dehydroprenylhordenine, Diels–Alder adducts, **1**, 369

dehydroquinase(s)
　catalysis, **1**, 589
　genetics, **1**, 590
　inhibition, **1**, 588
　K_m, **1**, 591
　occurrence, **1**, 589, 590
　qut genes, **1**, 590
　type I, **1**, 591
　　catalysis, **1**, 586
　　mechanism, **1**, 586
　type II, **1**, 591
　　catalysis, **1**, 588
　　mechanism, **1**, 588
　　substrate specificity, **1**, 589
dehydroquinate
　common pool, **1**, 591
　dehydration, **1**, 585, 589
　from, 3-deoxy-D-*arabino*-(2-)heptulosonate 7-
　　phosphate, **1**, 581
　as intermediate, **1**, 589
dehydroquinate, (3*S*)-3-fluoro-
　as starting material
　　for (6*S*)-6-fluorodehydroquinate, **1**, 584
　　for (6*S*)-6-fluoro-1-*epi*dehydroquinate, **1**, 584
dehydroquinate, (6*R*)-6-fluoro-, from, 3(*R*)-3-fluoro3-
　　deoxy-D-arabinoheptulosonate 7-phosphate, **1**, 584
dehydroquinate, (6*S*)-6-fluoro-, from, (3*S*)-3-
　　fluorodehydroquinate, **1**, 584
1-*epi*dehydroquinate, biosynthesis, **1**, 583
1-*epi*dehydroquinate, (6*S*)-6-fluoro-, from, (3*S*)-3-
　　fluorodehydroquinate, **1**, 584
(2*R*)-[2-³H]dehydroquinate, kinetic isotope effects, **1**, 587
3-dehydroquinate, as starting material, for
　　dehydroshikimate, **1**, 586
3-dehydroquinate dehydratase(s)
　catalysis, **1**, 585, **4**, 4
　type I, **1**, 585
　type II, **1**, 585
3-dehydroquinate hydro-lyase(s) *see* 3-dehydroquinate
　　dehydratase(s)
3-dehydroquinate synthase
　binding, **1**, 593
　catalysis, **1**, 581
　inhibitors, **1**, 582, 585
　mechanism, **1**, 582
　purification, **1**, 581
　substrates, **1**, 585
dehydroquinate synthase(s)
　catalysis, **4**, 2
　K_{NAD}, **3**, 337
dehydroshikimate
　biosynthesis, **1**, 585, 589
　common pool, **1**, 591
　from, 3-dehydroquinate, **1**, 586
　as intermediate, **1**, 589
　reduction, **1**, 591
dehydroshikimate, (6*R*)-6-fluoro-, as starting material, for
　　6-fluoroshikimate, **1**, 592
dehydroshikimate, (6*S*)-6-fluoro-, as starting material, for
　　6-fluoroshikimate, **1**, 592
[2-³H]dehydroshikimate, biosynthesis, **1**, 587
dehydroshikimate dehydratase
　catalysis, **1**, 589
　genetics, **1**, 590
　K_m, **1**, 591
　occurrence, **1**, 590
　qut genes, **1**, 590
3-dehydroshikimic acid
　aromatization, **3**, 803
　degradation, **3**, 804
dehydrosqualene *see* 4,4′-diapophytoene
3-dehydroteasterone, mediation, **8**, 105
1,2-dehydrotestosterone, occurrence, **8**, 230

α,2-dehydrotoluene biradical, formation, **7**, 566
α,3-dehydrotoluene biradical, **7**, 556
6-dehydrovirginiae butanolide A
　enzymatic resolution, **1**, 145
　as precursor, **1**, 145
　synthesis, **1**, 145
dehydrovomifoliol, metabolism, **8**, 88
deiodinases
　Type 1, catalytic activity, **4**, 374
　Type 3, catalytic activity, **4**, 374
delaminomycin A, biosynthesis, **1**, 370
deletion analysis, bacterial aromatic polyketide synthase
　　gene clusters, **1**, 484
DeLey–Doudoroff pathway, in glycolysis, **3**, 414
delphinidin
　in bee pollinated plants, **8**, 158
　in fruit pigment, **8**, 164
demethylallosamidin
　biosynthesis, **1**, 151
　chitinase inhibition, **1**, 149
demethylation, in oligonucleotide synthesis, **7**, 130
demethylbialaphos, structure, **1**, 867
demethylbialaphos, *N*-acetyl-, accumulation, **1**, 871
(±)-demethylgrossamide
　antifeedant activity, **1**, 695
　occurrence, **1**, 674
demethyl nectriapyrone A, occurrence, **8**, 600
demethylphosphinothricin, structure, **1**, 867
demethylphosphinothricin, *N*-acetyl-, accumulation, **1**,
　　871
demethylspheroidene, accumulation, **2**, 330
demethylspheroidenone, accumulation, **2**, 330
7-demethyltylopharine, as oviposition stimulant, **8**, 156
Dendranthema grandiflora, anthocyanidin synthase, **1**, 730
Dendranthema morifolium, malonyltransferases, **1**, 741
dendroamide A, structure, **8**, 610
Dendrobium pierardii, shihunine biosynthesis, **1**, 618
Dendroctonus spp.
　(+)-*exo*-brevicomin, **8**, 213
　frontalin, **8**, 202, 233
Dendroctonus brevicomis
　exo-brevicomin, **8**, 12
　feeding habits, **8**, 143
　pheromones, **8**, 12
Dendroctonus frontalis
　frontalin, **8**, 14
　pheromones, **8**, 14
Dendroctonus jeffreyi, heptanol, **8**, 211
Dendroctonus pseudotsugae, pheromones, **8**, 14, 211
Dendroctonus rufipennis, verbenene, **8**, 224
Dendroctonus simplex
　frontalin, **8**, 233
　6-methyl-6-hepten-2-one, **8**, 233
Dendroctonus vitei, heptanol, **8**, 211
Dendrodoris spp.
　chemical defense, **8**, 462
　mucous secretion, **8**, 462
dendrolasin, occurrence, **8**, 229
Dennstaedtia bipinnata, lignins, **3**, 625
Dennstaedtiaceae, lignins, **3**, 625
(+)-denudatin B
　biosynthesis, **1**, 678
　occurrence, **1**, 677
6-deoxoteasterone, synthesis, **8**, 105
(+)-1′-deoxyabscisic acid, biological activity, **8**, 77
deoxyadenosine, 8-bromo-, reactions, with
　　aminoalkylthiolate salts, **7**, 198
2′-deoxyadenosine
　aptamer-binding ability, **7**, 625
　deamination, **5**, 73
　K_m, **5**, 74
2′-deoxyadenosine, 2-mercapto-, as starting material, for
　　aminoalkylated deoxyribonucleoside
　　phosphoramidites, **7**, 196

2-*Cl*-2'-deoxyadenosine, adenosine deaminase resistance, **5**, 74

3'-deoxyadenosine, K_m, **5**, 74

5'-deoxyadenosine
biosynthesis, **5**, 165, 170, 185, 208, 209, 217
K_m, **5**, 74

deoxyadenosinediphosphoglucose, activity, **3**, 452

deoxyadenosines
depurination, **7**, 122
fluorescent, synthesis, **7**, 208

deoxyadenosine triphosphate, accumulation, **5**, 73

5'-deoxyadenosine-5'-yl, biosynthesis, **5**, 208

5-deoxyadenosylcobalamin, homolysis, **5**, 273

5'-deoxyadenosyl radicals
biosynthesis, **3**, 330, **5**, 208, 215
stability, **5**, 212

7-deoxyaglycone, tautomerization, **7**, 529

6-deoxy-D-allose *see* D-allomethylose

6-deoxy-β-L-altropyranose, O-specific chains, **3**, 192

6-deoxy-L-altrose, occurrence, **3**, 312

3-deoxyanthocyanidins, biosynthesis, **1**, 728

3-deoxyarabinose 5-phosphate, inhibitory activity, **1**, 580

3-deoxy-L-arabonate, 2-keto-, biosynthesis, **3**, 425

deoxybrevianamide E, feeding experiments, **1**, 386

deoxycastanospermine, acetamino-, inhibitory activity, **3**, 29

6'-deoxychalcones
biosynthesis, **1**, 716, 732, 763, 790
as intermediates, **1**, 732
occurrence, **1**, 736

6'-deoxychalcone synthase *see* chalcone synthase (CHS)

4-deoxychorismate, 4-amino- (ADC)
biosynthesis, **5**, 347
catalysis, **1**, 612

2'-deoxycoformycin
AMP deaminase inhibition, **5**, 83
binding, **5**, 76
resistance, **5**, 78
transition state inhibition, **5**, 74

11-deoxycorticosterone *see* cortexone

deoxycytidine, photoionization, **7**, 375

2'-deoxycytidine, 5-(1-propynyl)-, DNA triplex
destabilization, **7**, 272

2'-deoxycytidine 5'-diphosphate, 2'-vinylfluoro-
(VFCDP), interactions, **5**, 181

deoxycytidine phosphoramidites, incorporation, into
oligodeoxyribonucleotides, **7**, 193

2'-deoxycytidines
spin-labeled, **7**, 219
as substrates, **5**, 88, 91

deoxycytidine triphosphates
spin-labeled, as substrates, **7**, 220
synthesis, **7**, 207

11-deoxydaunomycin, quinone methide, NMR spectra, **7**, 529

2'-deoxy-3-deazaadenosine, in oligodeoxynucleotides, **7**, 329

5-deoxydehydroquinate, as substrate, **1**, 589

5-deoxydehydroshikimate, binding, **1**, 592

6-deoxy-2,3-di-O-methyl-D-allose *see* D-mycinose

4-deoxy-4-N-dimethylamino-5,5-dimethyl-β-D-
ribopyranoside, in C-1027 chromophore, **7**, 578

6-deoxy-2,4-di-O-methyl-D-galactose, occurrence, **3**, 312

deoxydynemicin, occurrence, **7**, 574

2-deoxyecdysone
biosynthesis, **8**, 291
moulting hormone activity, **8**, 293
synthesis, **8**, 288

2,25-deoxyecdysone, synthesis, **8**, 288

5-deoxyenterocin, occurrence, **8**, 543, 597

6-deoxyerythronolide B, as intermediate, **1**, 497

6-deoxyerythronolide B synthase (DEBS)
catalysis, **1**, 348

cleavage sites, **1**, 350
occurrence, **1**, 425
roles, in triketide lactone biosynthesis, **1**, 357
structure, **1**, 14

6-deoxyfagomine, structure, **3**, 130

5-deoxyflavan-3-ols, regioselectivity, **3**, 789

5-deoxyflavanones, as intermediates, **1**, 717

5-deoxyflavones, roles, in legume–*Rhizobium* symbiosis, **8**, 173

5-deoxyflavonoids, biosynthesis, **1**, 732

2'-deoxyformycin, **7**, 333

5-deoxy-3-C-formyl-L-lyxose *see* L-streptose

2-deoxy-L-fucose
in esperamicins, **3**, 313, **7**, 571
occurrence, **3**, 312

deoxyfucose-anthranilate, **7**, 572

6-deoxy-D-galactose *see* D-fucose

6-deoxy-L-galactose *see* L-fucose

3-deoxy-D-glucarate, 2-keto-, biosynthesis, **3**, 402

3-deoxygluconate, 2-keto-, biosynthesis, **3**, 423

2-deoxygluconophosphate, 5-keto-, cleavage, **3**, 409

2-deoxy-β-D-glucopyranosides, 2-acetamido-, cleavage, **5**, 297

2-deoxy-D-glucose
isolation, **3**, 313
occurrence, **3**, 312

6-deoxy-D-glucose *see* D-quinovose

deoxyguanosine, depurination, **7**, 122

deoxyguanosine, 8-oxo-
mutagenicity, **7**, 410
oxidative stress, **7**, 411

2'-deoxyguanosine, O^6-methyl-, in aptamer synthesis, **7**, 626

5'-deoxyguanosine, **7**, 571

2-deoxy-D-gulose
isolation, **3**, 313
occurrence, **3**, 312

6-deoxy-D-gulose *see* D-antiarose

3-deoxy-D-*arabino*-heptanoate, 7-phospho-2-keto-,
biosynthesis, **3**, 386

6-deoxy-D-*manno*-heptose, occurrence, **3**, 312

3-deoxy-D-*lyxo*-2-heptulopyranosylaric acid
occurrence, **3**, 502
precursors, **3**, 509

3-deoxy-D-*arabino*-heptulosonate, accumulation, **1**, 585

3-deoxy-D-*arabino*-(2-)heptulosonate 7-phosphate, 3(R)-
3-fluoro, as starting material, for (6R)-6-
fluorodehydroquinate, **1**, 584

3-deoxy-D-*arabino*-(2-)heptulosonate 7-phosphate
(DAHP)
analogues, as dehydroquinase inhibitor, **1**, 585
in shikimic acid pathway, **1**, 527
as starting material, for dehydroquinate, **1**, 581

3-deoxy-D-*arabino*-2-heptulosonic-7-phosphate
synthetase *see* 2-dehydro-3-deoxyphosphoheptonate
aldolase

deoxyhexose, biosynthesis, mechanisms, **3**, 332

2-deoxy-D-*arabino*-hexose *see* 2-deoxy-D-glucose

2-deoxy-D-*xylo*-hexose *see* 2-deoxy-D-gulose

4-deoxy-D-*arabino*-hexose *see* 4-deoxy-D-idose

6-deoxyhexoses
biosynthesis, **3**, 332, 333
genetics, **3**, 346
in *Serratia marcescens*, **3**, 190

3-deoxyhopanoids, in bacteria, **2**, 47

6-deoxy-4-C-[1-(S)-hydroxyethyl]-2,3-O-methylene-D-
galactono-1,5-lactone, occurrence, **3**, 312

5-deoxy-3-C-(hydroxymethyl)-L-lyxose *see* L-
dihydrostreptose

4-deoxy-D-idose, occurrence, **3**, 312

deoxyinosine, covalent DNA adduct structure
determination, **7**, 495

2'-deoxyinosine, biosynthesis, **5**, 73

deoxyinosine triphosphate (dITP), in DNA mutation, **7**, 621

2'-deoxyisoinosine, synthesis, **7**, 325

8-deoxylactucin, effects, on herbivores, **8**, 142

deoxylapachol, occurrence, **8**, 339

5-deoxyleucocyanidins, stability, **3**, 753

5-deoxyleucodelphinidins, stability, **3**, 753

5-deoxyleucopelargonidins, stability, **3**, 753

deoxyluminarosine phosphoramidites, synthesis, **7**, 208

4-deoxymaltotriosyl α-fluoride, as substrate, **5**, 299

1-deoxymannojirimycin (DMJ)
    inhibition, **3**, 24
    α-mannosidase inhibition, broad-specificity, **3**, 28
    α1,2-mannosidase inhibition, **3**, 22
    α1,2-mannosidase sensitivity, **3**, 23
    structure, **3**, 130
    as yeast α1,2-mannosidase inhibitor, **3**, 21

6-deoxy-D-mannose *see* D-rhamnose

6-deoxy-L-mannose *see* L-rhamnose

6-deoxy-3-*O*-methyl-L-altrose, occurrence, **3**, 312

6-deoxy-4-*O*-methyl-D-altrose, occurrence, **3**, 312

6-deoxy-2-*O*-methyl-D-galactose, occurrence, **3**, 312

6-deoxy-2-*O*-methyl-L-galactose, occurrence, **3**, 312

6-deoxy-3-*O*-methyl-D-galactose *see* D-digitalose

6-deoxy-3-*O*-methyl-L-galactose *see* L-digitalose

6-deoxy-4-*O*-methyl-D-galactose *see* D-curacose

6-deoxy-3-*O*-methyl-D-glucose *see* D-thevetose

6-deoxy-3-*C*-methyl-D-gulose *see* D-virenose

6-deoxy-3-*C*-methyl-L-gulose *see* L-virenose

6-deoxy-3-*C*-methyl-D-mannose *see* D-evalose

6-deoxy-3-*O*-methyl-D-mannose *see* D-acofriose

6-deoxy-3-*O*-methyl-L-mannose *see* L-acofriose

6-deoxy-5-*C*-methyl-4-*O*-methyl-L-*lyxo*-hexose *see* L-noviose

6-deoxy-3-*C*-methyl-2-*O*-methyl-L-talose *see* L-vinelose

6-deoxy-3-*O*-methyl-D-talose, occurrence, **3**, 312

6-deoxy-3-*C*-methyl-2,3,4-*O*-trimethyl-L-mannose *see* L-nogalose

deoxynivalenol, source, **2**, 203

deoxynivalenol, 3-acetyl-, biosynthesis, **2**, 164

deoxynojirimycin, *N*-butyl-, applications, in AIDS therapy, **3**, 143

1-deoxynojirimycin, *N*-butyl-, as α-glucosidase inhibitor, **3**, 19

1-deoxynojirimycin, *N*-hydroxyethyl-, applications, antidiabetic drugs, **3**, 143

1-deoxynojirimycin, *N*-methyl-, as α-glucosidase inhibitor, **3**, 19

1-deoxynojirimycin (DNJ)
    antiviral activity, **3**, 143
    complexation, **5**, 302
    as α-glucosidase inhibitor, **3**, 19, 31, 151
    as α-mannosidase inhibitor, **3**, 154
    roles, **3**, 18
    structure, **3**, 130
    structure–activity relationships, **3**, 138

2'-deoxynucleosides, 2'-mercapto-, incorporation, **6**, 226

deoxynucleoside-triphosphate:DNA deoxynucleotidyltransferase (DNA-directed) *see* DNA-directed DNA polymerase

deoxynucleoside triphosphates, incorporation, **6**, 222

2'-deoxynucleoside triphosphates, 2'-amino-, as substrates, **6**, 219

2'-deoxynucleoside triphosphates, 2'-fluoro-, as substrates, **6**, 219

2'-deoxynucleotide radicals, 3'-keto-
    biosynthesis, **5**, 166, 194
    reduction, **5**, 168, 196, 197

deoxynucleotides, from, nucleotides, **5**, 164

deoxynucleotides, 3'-keto-
    biosynthesis, **5**, 168
    as intermediates, **5**, 191

2'-deoxynucleotides, reactions, with ribonucleotide reductases, **5**, 172

2'-deoxynucleotides, 2'-fluoro-, as substrates, **5**, 195

2'-deoxynucleotides, 3'-keto-
    enolate anions, **5**, 196
    reduction, **5**, 198

(−)-7-*epi*-deoxynupharidine, occurrence, **8**, 344

3-deoxy-D-*manno*-octulosonate D-arabinose-lyase *see* 3-deoxy-D-*manno*-octulosonate (KDO) aldolase

3-deoxy-D-*manno*-octulosonate (KDO)
    attachment, **3**, 221
    occurrence, **3**, 502
    oligosaccharides, **3**, 185
    precursors, **3**, 509

3-deoxy-D-*manno*-octulosonate (KDO) aldolase
    biochemistry, **3**, 373
    occurrence, **3**, 373
    substrate specificity, **3**, 373

3-deoxy-D-*manno*-octulosonate (KDO) transferase
    catalysis, **3**, 222
    characterization, **3**, 518
    roles, in pectin biosynthesis, **3**, 511

3-deoxy-D-*manno*-octulosonate 8-phosphate (KDO8P), biosynthesis, **1**, 580

3-deoxy-D-*manno*-2-octulosonic acid 8-phosphate synthase *see* 2-dehydro-3-deoxyphosphooctonate aldolase

2-deoxy-D-*erythro*-pentose *see* 2-deoxy-D-ribose

3-deoxy-D-*erythro*-pentose *see* cordycepose

3-deoxy-D-*threo*-pentose, occurrence, **3**, 312, 313

4-deoxyprephenate, 4-amino-, biosynthesis, **5**, 347

2'-deoxypyrimidine nucleosides, 2'-amino-, substitution, **6**, 226

2'-deoxypyrimidine nucleosides, 2'-fluoro-, substitution, **6**, 226

2-deoxy-D-rhamnose *see* 2,6-dideoxy-D-*arabino*-hexose

deoxyribocyclobutadipyrimidine pyrimidine-lyase(s) *see* deoxyribodipyrimidine photo-lyase(s)

deoxyribodipyrimidine photo-lyase(s)
    action spectra, **5**, 376
    catalysis, **5**, 375
    cofactors, **5**, 375
    crystal structure, **5**, 376
    mechanisms, **5**, 385
    occurrence, **5**, 375
    photoreactivation mechanisms, **5**, 375
    in transient absorption spectroscopy, **5**, 384

2-deoxyribonolactone, formation, **7**, 567

2'-deoxyribonolactone
    in DNA damage, **7**, 373
    lesion formation, **7**, 376
    mechanisms, **7**, 377

deoxyribonuclease, activity, effects of cytokinins on, **8**, 59

deoxyribonuclease I (DNase I)
    in DNA fragmentation, **7**, 621
    footprinting, **7**, 252
    disadvantages, **7**, 252

2'-deoxyribonucleoside-diphosphate:oxidized-thioredoxin 2'-oxidoreductase *see* ribonucleoside-diphosphate reductase

deoxyribonucleoside phosphoramidites
    development, **7**, 130
    EDTA-functionalized, **7**, 215
    from
        adenosine, **7**, 231
        5-iododeoxyuridine, **7**, 194
    synthesis, **7**, 166, 192

deoxyribonucleoside phosphoramidites, 5'-aminated, synthesis, **7**, 234

deoxyribonucleoside phosphoramidites, aminoalkylated
    from, 2-mercapto-2'-deoxyadenosine, **7**, 196
    synthesis, **7**, 195

deoxyribonucleoside phosphoramidites, amthraquinonylmethyl, insertion, into oligodeoxyribonucleotides, **7**, 228

deoxyribonucleoside phosphoramidites, biotinylated, synthesis, **7**, 205
deoxyribonucleoside phosphoramidites, bipyridine, synthesis, **7**, 214
deoxyribonucleoside phosphoramidites, dansylated, incorporation, into oligodeoxyribonucleotides, **7**, 209
deoxyribonucleoside phosphoramidites, 2,4-dinitrophenyl-, insertion, into oligonucleotides, **7**, 210
deoxyribonucleoside phosphoramidites, mercaptoalkylated, synthesis, **7**, 203
deoxyribonucleoside phosphoramidites, terpyridine, synthesis, **7**, 215
2′,5′-deoxyribonucleoside-3′-*O*-phosphoramidites, 5′-mercapto-, synthesis, **7**, 234
4′-deoxyribonucleosides, synthesis, **7**, 264
2′-deoxyribonucleoside-triphosphate:oxidized-thioredoxin 2′-oxidoreductase *see* ribonucleoside-triphosphate reductase
deoxyribonucleotides
  biosynthesis, **5**, 93
    genetics, **3**, 342
    pathways, **3**, 328
  2-deoxy-D-gulose, **3**, 313
deoxyribose, biosynthesis, mechanisms, **3**, 328
2′-deoxyribose, conformation, **7**, 67
2′-deoxyribose, 2′-fluoro-, hydrogen bonding, **6**, 226
2-deoxy-D-ribose
  biosynthesis, **3**, 332
  monodeoxygenation, **3**, 313
  occurrence, **3**, 312
2-deoxy-D-ribose-5-phosphate acetaldehyde-lyase *see* deoxyribose-phosphate aldolase (DERA)
deoxyribose-phosphate aldolase (DERA)
  biochemistry, **3**, 372
  early studies, **3**, 373
  expression, **3**, 372
  occurrence, **3**, 373
  substrate specificity, **3**, 373
2′-β-D-deoxyribosepyrimidin-2-one 5′-phosphate, deaminase inhibition, **5**, 94
deoxyribosyl radicals, oxidation, **7**, 415
deoxyribozymes
  catalysis, **6**, 129
  catalytic efficiency, **7**, 635
  DNA ligation, **6**, 134
  DNA substrate cleavage, **6**, 136
  inhibition, **7**, 634
  isolation, **6**, 141
  RNA cleavage, **6**, 137
  search for, **7**, 632
  selection, **6**, 136
  SELEX studies, **7**, 619
  see also DNA enzymes
2′-deoxyribozymes, **7**, 278
1-deoxy ribulose *S*-phosphate, carboxyphenylamino-(CDRP)
  biosynthesis, **4**, 7
  decarboxylation, **4**, 7
16-deoxysarcophine
  calcium antagonistic activity, **8**, 617
  occurrence, **8**, 617
  structure, **8**, 617
5-deoxyshikimate, phosphorylation, **1**, 593
deoxysugars
  in antibiotics, genetics, **3**, 7, 349
  in O-antigen, genetics, **3**, 345
  biochemistry, **3**, 2, 7, **311–365**
  biological activity, **3**, 322
  biosynthesis
    genetics, **3**, 342
    mechanisms, **3**, 328
    pathways, **3**, 328

deoxygenation, **3**, 313
DNA footprinting, **3**, 323
future research, **3**, 356
gene clusters, **3**, 346
genetic studies, importance of, **3**, 356
localization, **3**, 322
nomenclature, **3**, 312
occurrence, **37**, 312
roles, **3**, 356
  in cell–cell interactions, **3**, 312
  structure–activity relationships, **3**, 312
deoxysugars, branched-chain, **3**, 312
  biosynthesis, **3**, 342
  occurrence, **3**, 321
2,6-deoxysugars, biosynthesis, **3**, 354
3,6-deoxysugars, biosynthesis, genetics, **3**, 342
6-deoxy-D-talose *see* D-talomethylose
6-deoxy-L-talose *see* L-talomethylose
3-deoxy-L-*glycero*-tetronic acid, in *Vibrio cholerae*, **3**, 195
5′-deoxythymine, 5′-amino-, **7**, 233
deoxyuridine, 6-amino-, incorporation, into oligodeoxyribonucleotides, **7**, 199
deoxyuridine, 5-bromo-
  DNA-containing, sensitization, **7**, 416
  in DNA damage, **7**, 411
deoxyuridine, 5-formyl-, synthesis, **7**, 407
deoxyuridine, 5-hydroxymethyl-, synthesis, **7**, 407
deoxyuridine, 5-iodo-
  in DNA damage, **7**, 411
  as starting material, for deoxyribonucleoside phosphoramidites, **7**, 194
2′-deoxyuridine, 2′-iodo-, photolysis, **7**, 382
2′-deoxyuridine, 5-(1-pentenyl)-, SELEX studies, **7**, 636
2′-deoxyuridine, 5-(propynyl)-, incorporation into thrombin aptamer, **6**, 225
2′-deoxyuridine, 5-(1-propynyl)-, DNA triplex stabilization, **7**, 272
2′-deoxyuridine, 5-thiocyanato-, synthesis, **7**, 202
2′-deoxyuridine diphosphate, 2′-azido- (N₃UDP)
  inhibition studies, **5**, 182
  kinetic isotope effects, **5**, 187
deoxyuridine monophosphate, tetrahydro-, deaminase inhibition, **5**, 94
deoxyuridine monophosphate (dUMP), biosynthesis, **5**, 93
deoxyuridine phosphoramidites, 5-iodo-, synthesis, **7**, 220
2′-deoxyuridine phosphoramidites, 5-[*S*-(2,4-dinitrophenyl)thio]-, synthesis, **7**, 203
2′-deoxyuridin-2′-yl, synthesis, **7**, 382
2′-deoxyuridin-5-yl, roles, in DNA strand breakage, **7**, 411
6-deoxyversicolorin A, synthesis, **1**, 458
3-deoxyxylonate, 2-keto-, biosynthesis, **3**, 429
5-deoxy-L-xylose, 3-*C*-carboxy- *see* aceric acid
1-deoxy-D-xylulose
  biosynthesis, **2**, 55, 376
  identification, **1**, 838
  as starting material
    for pyridoxine, **2**, 376
    for thiamine, **2**, 376
deoxy-D-xylulose, as intermediate, **8**, 219
1-deoxy-D-xylulose 5-phosphate
  biosynthesis, **2**, 4, 55
  as starting material, for isoprenoids, **2**, 64
deoxyxylulose phosphate synthase, encoding, **2**, 377
1-deoxyxyluloside, methyl, deuterium-labeled, **2**, 62
DEPC *see* pyrocarbonate, diethyl (DEPC)
dephosphophosphorylase kinase *see* phosphorylase kinase
dephosphorylation, in cloning, **7**, 661
dephostatin
  occurrence, **7**, 521
  possible DNA reactions with, **7**, 521

depolarization, auxins, **8**, 32
Depressaria pastinacella, seed predation, inhibition, **8**, 168
meta-depside bonds, structure, **3**, 800
depsides, structure, **1**, 2
depsidones, structure, **1**, 2
depsipeptides, **7**, 352
    biosynthesis, **4**, 199
    structure, **7**, 352
depurination, in oligonucleotide chain, **7**, 122
DERA *see* deoxyribose-phosphate aldolase (DERA)
Dermacentor variabilis, cholesteryl oleate, **8**, 230
(+)-dermalactone, structure, **1**, 410
dermatan sulfate (DS)
    binding, **3**, 4
    biosynthesis, **3**, 171
    substitution, **3**, 161
Dermestes maculatus
    1-methylethyl (*Z*)-9-hexadecenoate, **8**, 217
    pheromones, **8**, 218
    2-propanol, **8**, 209
    sex pheromones, **8**, 215
    tetradecanoic acid, **8**, 216
    (9*Z*)-tetradecenoic acid, 1-methylethyl esters, **8**, 216
Derris spp., rotenone, **8**, 340
Derris chinensis, rotenone, **8**, 340
Derris elliptica
    2,5-dihydroxymethyl-3,4-dihydroxypyrrolidine, **8**, 342
    malaccol, **8**, 341
    rotenoid biosynthesis, **8**, 342
    rotenone, **8**, 340
Derris malaccensis, malaccol, **8**, 341
derrone, 5-*O*-methyl-, accumulation, **1**, 800
10-desacetylbaccatin III, biosynthesis, **2**, 221
10,12-desaturase, **8**, 205
Δ^6-desaturase *see* linoleoyl-CoA desaturase
desaturase(s)
    classification, **1**, 35
    hydrophobicity, **1**, 36
    mechanisms, **1**, 38
    membrane-bound, **1**, 43
    occurrence, **8**, 205, 207
    purification, **1**, 39
    reaction centers, **1**, 42
    roles, **1**, 54
    unusual, **1**, 42
Δ^9-desaturase(s) *see* stearoyl-CoA desaturase(s)
Δ^{11}-desaturases
    occurrence, **8**, 205
    roles in pheromone biosynthesis, **8**, 205
Δ^{12}-desaturase(s), occurrence, **1**, 40
ω^3-desaturase(s), occurrence, **1**, 40, 41
ω^6-desaturase(s)
    occurrence, **1**, 40
    purification, **1**, 43
desaturation
    in animals, **1**, 35
    in cyanobacteria, **1**, 36
    hydrogen removal, stereospecificity, **1**, 38
    in marine bacteria, **1**, 38
    in plants, **1**, 36
    unsaturated fatty acids, **1**, 35
        physiological significance, **1**, 44
desepoxyazadirachtin, isolation, **8**, 325
desert locusts *see Schistocerca gregaria*
12-desmethylerythromycin, biosynthesis, **1**, 508
10-desmethylerythromycin A, biosynthesis, **1**, 508
10-desmethylerythromycin B, biosynthesis, **1**, 508
desmethylsulochrin, biosynthesis, **1**, 434, 435
desmethylsulochrin *O*-methyltransferase, catalysis, **1**, 435
D-desosamine
    biosynthesis, genetics, **3**, 342, 351
    in erythromycin, **3**, 351
    genetics, **3**, 335

occurrence, **3**, 321
desoxyxylulose, in terpene biosynthesis, **8**, 305
desthio-CoA, in catalysis, **2**, 34
destruxin synthetase, genetics, **1**, 540
Desulfomonile tiedjei, 3-chlorobenzoate dehalogenase, **5**, 417, 420
Desulfovibrio desulfuricans, 2-*C*-methyl-D-erythritol, **2**, 56
Desulfovibrio gigas, protoporphyrinogen oxidase, **4**, 100
Desulfovibrio vulgaris, heme c, studies, **4**, 103
Detarium microcarpum, antifeedant studies, **8**, 317
det genes, mutants, **8**, 66
dethiobiotin, biosynthesis, **1**, 826
dethiobiotin:sulfur sulfurtransferase *see* biotin synthase
dethiobiotin synthetase, NMR analysis, **1**, 827
dethiobiotin synthetase complexes, crystal structures, **1**, 827   ′
deuteration, and DNA damage, **7**, 567
deuterium isotopes
    effects
        on cyclobutane pyrimidine photodimer radical anion fragmentation, **5**, 381
        on cyclobutane pyrimidine photodimer radical cation fragmentation, **5**, 378
deuteromycetes, phomactins, **8**, 599
deutero-6,9,12-octadecatrienoic acids, occurrence, **1**, 221
DEVH proteins, mutations, **6**, 213
Devonian, fossil plants, **1**, 645
Dewar pyrimidinone
    formation, **5**, 389
    lability, **5**, 389
    mutagenesis induction, **5**, 394
    repair pathways, **5**, 372
dexamethasone, as inhibitor, **1**, 248
α-dextrin endo-1,6-α-glucosidase
    identity, **3**, 468
    roles, **3**, 446
    sequences, **3**, 459
α-dextrin 6-glucanohydrolase *see* α-dextrin endo-1,6-α-glucosidase
DFP, as GPI anchor biosynthesis inhibitor, **3**, 303
DFR *see* dihydrokaempferol 4-reductase
DGDG *see* glycerol, digalactosyldiacyl- (DGDG)
Dha *see* 2,3-dehydroalanine (Dha)
DHA *see* 3-deoxy-D-*lyxo*-2-heptulopyranosylaric acid
DHAP *see* acetone phosphate, dihydroxy- (DHAP)
DHA-transferase
    characterization, **3**, 518
    roles, in pectin biosynthesis, **3**, 511
Dhb *see* (*Z*)-2,3-dehydrobutyrine (Dhb)
DHCHC *see* cyclohexanecarboxylic acid, *trans*-dihydro- (DHCHC)
DHGO *see* dihydrogeodin oxidase (DHGO)
DHPs *see* dehydropolymerisates (DHPs)
dhurrin, biosynthesis, **1**, 858
(*S*)-dhurrin, structure, **1**, 887
Diabrotica spp., propanoates, **8**, 209
Diabrotica balteata, (6*R*,10*R*)-6,12-dimethyl-2-pentadecanone, **8**, 244
Diabrotica speciosa, sequestration, **8**, 362
Diabrotica undecimpunctata, (*R*)-10-methyl-2-tridecanone, **8**, 244
Diabrotica vergifera, activity against, **8**, 306
2,3-diacetamido-2,3-dideoxygalacturonic acid, biosynthesis, **3**, 229
2,3-diacetamido-2,3-dideoxymannuronic acid, assembly, **3**, 229
diacetyl, possible DNA damage induction, **7**, 503
diacylglycerol cholinephosphotransferase, catalysis, **1**, 289
Diadasia rinconis rinconis, venom, **8**, 354
dialdehydes, biosynthesis, **2**, 106
dialkylpyrrolidines, occurrence, **8**, 357
dialkylpyrrolines, occurrence, **8**, 357

diamine, *N*-biotinyl-*N*′-iodoacetylethylene-, applications, **7**, 632

L,L-2,6-diaminoheptanedioate 2-epimerase *see* diaminopimelate epimerase

meso-2,6-diaminoheptanedioate:NADP⁺ oxidoreductase (deaminating) *see* diaminopimelate dehydrogenase

(3*S*)-3,6-diaminohexanoate 5,6-aminomutase *see* β-lysine 5,6-aminomutase

diaminopimelate dehydrogenase, inhibition, **3**, 277

diaminopimelate epimerase, purification, **3**, 257

dianthramine, as antiphytoalexin, **8**, 191

Dianthus caryophyllus
anthocyanidin synthase, **1**, 730
caffeoyl-CoA *O*-methyltransferase, **3**, 672
chalcone isomerases, **1**, 723
flavonoid 3′-monooxygenase, **1**, 736
naringenin 3-dioxygenase, **1**, 726

diapause, control of, **8**, 265

diapause hormone, biochemistry, **8**, 300

diaphorase *see* dihydrolipoamide dehydrogenase

4,4′-diapocarotene, 7,8-dihydro- *see* 4,4′-diaponeurosporene

4,4′-diapocarotene, 7,8,11,12,7′,8′,11′,12′-octahydro- *see* 4,4′-diapophytoene

4,4′-diaponeurosporene
accumulation, **2**, 337
biosynthesis, **2**, 337

all-*trans*-4,4′-diaponeurosporene, biosynthesis, **2**, 341

4,4′-diapophytoene
biosynthesis, **2**, 324
desaturation, **2**, 337

diapophytoene desaturases, definition, **2**, 340

diaporthin, de-*O*-methyl-, phytotoxicity, **8**, 180

diarrhetic shellfish poisoning (DSP)
Japan (1976), **8**, 489
role of dinophysistoxin 1 in, **8**, 490
role of okadaic acid in, **8**, 490
role of pectenotoxins in, **8**, 497
role of yessotoxins in, **8**, 497

diatoms *see* Bacillariophyta

1,8-diazabicyclo[5,4,0]undec-7-ene (DBU), in oligonucleotide synthesis, **7**, 114

1,3-diazepin-2-one nucleoside, cytidine deaminase inhibition, **5**, 89

diazo compounds, DNA damage induction, **7**, 541

diazoic acid, methyl-, as intermediate, **7**, 520

diazonium compounds, DNA damage induction, **7**, 541

diazonium ions, **7**, 543

dibenzo[1,4]dioxin-1-carboxamide, cytotoxicity, **7**, 607

dibenzodioxocins
biosynthesis, **3**, 725
cleavage, **3**, 725
in lignins, **3**, 725

dibenzofurans, as phytoalexins, **8**, 187

dicarbonyl, DNA damage induction, **7**, 503

1,3-dicarbonyl compounds, as pheromones, **8**, 202

dicarboxylic acids
detection, **1**, 297
roles
in antibody catalysis, **5**, 425
in okadaic acid biosynthesis, **8**, 493

dicarboxylic acids, cyclobutyl-, as farnesyl-diphosphate farnesyltransferase inhibitors, **2**, 258

dicarboxylyl residues, detection, **1**, 298

Dicentra spp., protopine, **3**, 643

Dichelobacter nodosus, 3-phosphoshikimate 1-carboxyvinyltransferase, **1**, 593

2,4-dichlorobenzoate dioxygenase, occurrence, **5**, 417

2,4-dichlorobenzoyl CoA dehalogenase(s), occurrence, **5**, 417

2,6-dichlorohydroquinone dehalogenase, occurrence, **5**, 414

dichloromethane chloride-lyase(s) (chloride-hydrolyzing) *see* dichloromethane dehalogenase(s)

dichloromethane dehalogenase(s)
catalysis, **5**, 408
mechanisms, **5**, 408
occurrence, **5**, 407
purification, **5**, 407

dichlorovos *see* phosphate, dimethyl 2,2-dichlorovinyl-

Dichothrix baueriana, bauerines, **8**, 529

dichroism
flow, **7**, 432, 455
linear, in furamidine DNA binding studies, **7**, 458

Dicksonia squarrosa, lignins, **3**, 625

diclausenan, occurrence, **1**, 384

Dicotyledonae
cell walls, **3**, 498
lignin heterogeneity, **3**, 692

dicranenone A
antifungal activity, **1**, 228
occurrence, **1**, 228

dicranenone B, antifungal activity, **1**, 228

Dicranum elongatum, oxylipins, **1**, 228

Dicranum scoporium, dicranenone A, **1**, 228

Dictyopteris spp., feeding deterrents, **8**, 460

Dictyosphaeria sericea, dictyosphaerin, **1**, 215

dictyosphaerin
occurrence, **1**, 215
structure, **1**, 215

Dictyostelium discoideum
lysosomal α-mannosidase, **3**, 28
α-mannosidase, **3**, 150
Ras proteins, **2**, 360

dictyotene, biosynthesis, **8**, 423

9,21-didehydroryanodine, occurrence, **8**, 319

didemethylallosamidin, biosynthesis, **1**, 151

didemnilactone, occurrence, **1**, 243

didemnilactones, occurrence, **8**, 543

didemnin B
applications, antineoplastic agents, **8**, 521
occurrence, **8**, 521

didemnins
antiviral activity, **8**, 530
cytotoxicity, **8**, 530
immunosuppressive activity, **8**, 530
occurrence, **8**, 529
structure, **8**, 529

didemnolines, occurrence, **8**, 542

Didemnum spp.
(*R*)-(*E*)-1-aminotridec-5-en-2-ol, **8**, 545
didemnolines, **8**, 542
enterocins, **8**, 543

Didemnum candidum, ascidiatrienolides, **1**, 243

Didemnum molle
cyclodidemnamide, **8**, 537
kakelokelose, **8**, 544

Didemnum moseleyi, didemnilactones, **1**, 243, **8**, 543

Didemnum rodriguesi, caledonin, **8**, 538

2′,3′-dideoxyadenosine, *K*ₘ, **5**, 74

2′,3′-dideoxycytidine, degradation, **5**, 88

4,5-dideoxydehydroquinate, as substrate, **1**, 589

4,5-dideoxydehydroshikimate, binding, **1**, 592

3,6-dideoxy-4-*C*-(1,3-dimethoxy-4,5,6,7-tetrahydroxyheptyl)-D-*xylo*-hexose, occurrence, **3**, 312

2,4-dideoxy-4-*N*-(dimethylamino)-L-fucopyranoside, in kedarcidin chromophore, **7**, 575

2,4-dideoxy-4-(*N*-ethylamino)-3-*O*-methyl-α-L-xylopyranoside, in calicheamicin γ₁^I, **7**, 569

4,6-dideoxy-4-formamido-α-D-mannose, repeating units, **3**, 192

2,6-dideoxy-α-D-galactose, 2-acetamido-, in *Pseudomonas aeruginosa*, **3**, 194

2,3-dideoxy-D-glucose, 2,3-diamino-, in lipid A, **3**, 196

2,6-dideoxy-D-*arabino*-hexose
  deoxygenation, **3**, 354
  nomenclature, **3**, 313
  occurrence, **3**, 312
2,6-dideoxy-D-*lyxo*-hexose *see* D-oliose
2,6-dideoxy-D-*lyxo*-hexose, 4-*O*-acetyl- *see* D-chromose D
2,6-dideoxy-D-*ribo*-hexose *see* D-digitoxose
2,6-dideoxy-D-*xylo*-hexose *see* D-boivinose
2,6-dideoxy-L-*lyxo*-hexose *see* 2-deoxy-L-fucose
2,6-dideoxy-L-*ribo*-hexose *see* L-digitoxose
2,6-dideoxy-L-*xylo*-hexose, 4-*C*-acetyl- *see*
        trioxacarcinose B
3,6-dideoxy-D-*arabino*-hexose *see* tyvelose
3,6-dideoxy-D-*ribo*-hexose *see* paratose
3,6-dideoxy-D-*xylo*-hexose *see* abequose
3,6-dideoxy-L-*arabino*-hexose *see* ascarylose
3,6-dideoxy-L-*xylo*-hexose *see* colitose
3,6-dideoxyhexoses
  as antigenic determinants, **3**, 208
  biosynthesis, **3**, 332, 335
    genetics, **3**, 347
  occurrence, **3**, 187
2,6-dideoxy-D-*erythro*-hexos-3-ulose *see* D-kerriose
2,6-dideoxy-D-*threo*-hexos-4-ulose, occurrence, **3**, 312
3,6-dideoxy-L-*glycero*-hexos-4-ulose *see* L-cinerulose B
D-*erythro*-3,6-dideoxy-2-hexulosonate, biosynthesis, **3**,
        423
4,6-dideoxy-4-(hydroxyamino)-β-D-glucopyranoside
  in calicheamicin γ_1^1, **7**, 569
  in esperamicin, **7**, 572
2,6-dideoxy-4-*C*-[1-(*S*)-hydroxyethyl]-L-*xylo*-hexose *see*
        γ-octose
3,6-dideoxy-4-*C*-[1-(*R*)-hydroxyethyl]-D-*xylo*-hexose *see*
        yersiniose B
3,6-dideoxy-4-*C*-[1-(*S*)-hydroxyethyl]-D-*xylo*-hexose *see*
        yersiniose A
4,6-dideoxy-3-*C*-[1-(*S*)-hydroxyethyl]-D-*ribo*-hexose 3,1′-
        carbonate *see* D-aldgarose
1,4-dideoxy-1,4-imino-D-mannitol, cytosolic α-
        mannosidase inhibition, **3**, 27
2,3-dideoxy-β-D-mannuronic acid, 2-acetamido-3-
        acetimidoyl-, in *Pseudomonas aeruginosa*, **3**, 194
2,3-dideoxy-β-D-mannuronic acid, 2,3-diacetamido-, in
        Pseudomonas aeruginosa, **3**, 194
2,6-dideoxy-2-methylaminogalactose, **7**, 558
2,6-dideoxy-3-*C*-methyl-D-*arabino*-hexose *see* D-
        evermicose
2,6-dideoxy-3-*C*-methyl-D-*ribo*-hexose *see* D-mycarose
2,6-dideoxy-3-*C*-methyl-L-*arabino*-hexose, 4-*O*-acetyl-
        see L-chromose B
2,6-dideoxy-3-*C*-methyl-L-*ribo*-hexose *see* L-mycarose
2,6-dideoxy-3-*C*-methyl-L-*xylo*-hexose *see* L-axenose
2,6-dideoxy-3-*O*-methyl-D-*arabino*-hexose *see* D-
        oleandrose
2,6-dideoxy-3-*O*-methyl-D-*lyxo*-hexose *see* D-diginose
2,6-dideoxy-3-*O*-methyl-D-*ribo*-hexose *see* D-cymarose
2,6-dideoxy-3-*O*-methyl-D-*xylo*-hexose *see* D-sarmentose
2,6-dideoxy-3-*O*-methyl-L-*arabino*-hexose *see* L-
        oleandrose
2,6-dideoxy-3-*O*-methyl-L-*lyxo*-hexose *see* L-diginose
2,6-dideoxy-3-*O*-methyl-L-*ribo*-hexose *see* L-cymarose
2,6-dideoxy-3-*O*-methyl-L-*xylo*-hexose *see* L-sarmentose
2,6-dideoxy-4-*O*-methyl-D-*arabino*-hexose, occurrence, **3**,
        312
2,6-dideoxy-4-*O*-methyl-D-*lyxo*-hexose *see* D-olivomose
2,6-dideoxy-4-*O*-methyl-L-*ribo*-hexose, occurrence, **3**, 312
4,6-dideoxy-3-*O*-methyl-D-*ribo*-hexose, occurrence, **3**,
        312, 321
4,6-dideoxy-3-*O*-methyl-D-*xylo*-hexose, occurrence, **3**,
        312, 321
2,6-dideoxy-3-*C*-methyl-3-*O*-methyl-L-*ribo*-hexose *see* L-
        cladinose
2,6-dideoxy-3-*C*-methyl-3-*O*-methyl-L-*xylo*-hexose *see* L-
        arcanose

2,6-dideoxy-4-*S*-methyl-4-thio-D-*ribo*-hexose,
        occurrence, **3**, 312
2,6-dideoxy-4-*S*-methylthio-β-D-ribohexopyranoside, in
        esperamicin, **7**, 572
2,4-dideoxy-4-(*N*-isopropylamino)-3-*O*-methyl-α-L-
        xylopyranoside, in esperamicin, **7**, 572
7,8-dideoxy-4-octulose-1-phosphate, biosynthesis, **3**, 413
4,5-dideoxyshikimate, phosphorylation, **1**, 593
4,5-dideoxyshikimate-3-phosphate, reactions, with
        phospho*enol*pyruvate, **1**, 595
2,6-dideoxysugars, biosynthesis, **3**, 351
3,6-dideoxysugars
  biosynthesis, **3**, 351
  localization, **3**, 322
4,6-dideoxysugars, biosynthesis, **3**, 351
2,6-dideoxy-4-*S*-thio-β-D-ribohexopyranoside, in
        calicheamicin γ_1^1, **7**, 569
DIECA *see* sodium diethyldithiocarbamate
Diels–Alderase antibodies
  catalysis, **5**, 429
  future research, **5**, 442
Diels–Alderases
  catalysis, **1**, 367
  future research, **1**, 405
Diels–Alder reaction
  in aflatoxin biosynthesis, **1**, 16
  in antibody catalysis, **5**, 428
  biological, **1**, 370
  inverse-electron demand, **1**, 377
  in lovastatin biosynthesis, **1**, 422
  mechanisms, **1**, 367
  in polyketide phytotoxin biosynthesis, **1**, 367–408
  endo-selective, **1**, 392
Diels–Alder synthases, selections, **6**, 142
Diels–Alder type steroids, occurrence, **1**, 379
dienediyne, **7**, 582
dienelactone hydrolase (DLH) *see*
        carboxymethylenebutenolidase
dienes
  conformation, steric hindrance, **5**, 33
  as sex pheromones, **8**, 207
E,*E*-dienes, occurrence, **1**, 370
dienoic acids, biosynthesis, **1**, 39
dienolates
  as intermediates, stability, **5**, 39
  metal-stabilized, **5**, 38
dienols
  isolation, **5**, 32
  stability, **5**, 32
dienones, cytotoxicity, **8**, 469
E-dienophiles, occurrence, **1**, 370
3,24-diepibrassinolide, occurrence, **8**, 107
2,3-diepicastasterone, metabolism, **8**, 107
3,24-diepicastasterone, occurrence, **8**, 107
(3*Z*)-*cis*-6,7-*cis*-9,10-diepoxyhenicosadiene, occurrence,
        8, 207
diesters, synthesis, **7**, 109
diet
  high fat, and atherosclerosis, **3**, 792
  human, protective factors, **1**, 698, **3**, 791
differential gene expression, use in gene isolation, **2**,
        208
differential scanning calorimetry (DSC)
  disadvantages, **6**, 26
  in RNA structural transition analyses, **6**, 26
diflunisal, acetyl-CoA:1-alkylglycerophosphocholine
        acetyltransferase inhibition, **1**, 293
digestive system, cytoprotection, **1**, 196
digest maps, proteolytic, **3**, 461
digging wasps *see* *Bembix* spp.
D-diginose, occurrence, **3**, 312, 313
L-diginose, occurrence, **3**, 312, 313
digitalin

insect sequestration, **8**, 361
occurrence, **8**, 323
Digitalis purpurea, digitalin, **8**, 323
D-digitalose, occurrence, **3**, 312, 313
L-digitalose, occurrence, **3**, 312, 313
digitonin, as tetrahymanol cyclase inactivator, **2**, 312
D-digitoxose, occurrence, **3**, 312, 313
L-digitoxose, occurrence, **3**, 312
diglucosides, occurrence, **1**, 882
diglucosides, cyanogenic, translocation, **1**, 884
digoxigenins
    oligonucleotide conjugation, **7**, 160
    oligonucleotide labeling, **6**, 229, **7**, 209
diguanilate cyclase, roles, in cellulose biosynthesis, **3**, 581
8*R*,15*S*-diHETE *see* eicosatetraenoic acid, 8*R*,15*S*-
    dihydroxy- (8*R*,15*S*-diHETE)
5,12-diHETE *see* eicosatetraenoic acid, 5,12-dihydroxy
    (5,12-diHETE)
10*R*,11*S*-diHOT, biosynthesis, **1**, 221
dihydro-3-coumaroyl-CoA, as substrate, **1**, 753
2,3-dihydro-2,3-dihydroxybenzoate dehydrogenases,
    encoding, **1**, 616
2,3-dihydro-2,3-dihydroxybenzoate:NAD$^+$
    oxidoreductase(s) *see* 2,3-dihydro-2,3-
    dihydroxybenzoate dehydrogenase(s)
2,3-dihydro-2,3-dihydroxybenzoate synthase(s) *see*
    isochorismatase(s)
dihydroflavanol reductase, sequencing, comparisons, **1**,
    797
dihydroflavonol 4-reductase (DFR) *see*
    dihydrokaempferol 4-reductase
dihydrogeodin oxidase (DHGO), catalysis, **1**, 435
dihydrokaempferol 4-reductase
    biochemistry, **1**, 727
    genetics, **1**, 729
    molecular biology, **1**, 729
    occurrence, **1**, 729
    purification, **1**, 727
dihydrolipoamide dehydrogenase, catalysis, **3**, 338
dihydrolipoamide:NAD$^+$ oxidoreductase *see*
    dihydrolipoamide dehydrogenase
dihydroneopterin aldolase
    biochemistry, **3**, 374
    isolation, **3**, 374
dihydroorotase, sequencing, **5**, 86
dihydroprecorrin 6 methyltransferase, roles, **4**, 146
L-dihydrostreptose
    localization, **3**, 323
    occurrence, **3**, 312, 321
dihydroxyacetonetransferase *see* transaldolase
2,3-dihydroxybiphenyl-1,2-dioxygenase, **5**, 67
7,2′-dihydroxy-4′-methoxyisoflavanol (DMI)
    dehydratase, catalysis, **1**, 797
(5*Z*,13*E*)-(15*S*)-11α,15-dihydroxy-9-oxoprost-13-
    enoate:NAD$^+$ 15-oxidoreductase *see* 15-
    hydroxyprostaglandin dehydrogenase (NAD$^+$)
dihydrozeatin:NADP$^+$ oxidoreductase *see* zeatin
    reductase
diimidazole, 1,1′-carbonyl-, reactions, with
    oligodeoxyribonucleotides, **7**, 162
diisobutylaluminum-2,6-di-*t*-butyl-4-methyl phenoxide
    (BINAL-H), in prostaglandin synthesis, **1**, 177
diketides, as intermediates, **1**, 765
diketones, occurrence, **8**, 242
1,3-diketones, aldolase antibodies, **5**, 438
diLewis X, sialyl-, roles, **3**, 120
dillapiole, occurrence, **8**, 336
Dilophus okamurai
    feeding deterrents, **8**, 459
    methanol extracts, **8**, 434
DIM *see* D-mannitol, 1,4-dideoxy-1,4-imino- (DIM)
dimerization domain, DNA binding, **7**, 482
dimethylallyl cations, lifetime, **5**, 320, 332

dimethylallyltransferase(s) *see*
    dimethylallyl*trans*transferase(s)
dimethylallyl*trans*transferase(s), **2**, **69–96**
    activity, monitoring, **2**, 119
    analogues, synthesis, **2**, 70
    avian, substrate binding experiments, **2**, 80
    catalysis, **5**, 316
    cation-π interaction, **2**, 84
    chain length determination, mechanisms, **2**, 87
    characterization, **2**, 73
    classification, **2**, 74, 93
    cloning, **1**, 806
    1-4′ condensation, **2**, 80
    mechanistic studies, **2**, 80
    and monoterpenes, **2**, 88
    occurrence, **1**, 742, **2**, 88, 121
    pig liver, **8**, 272
    purification, **2**, 70
    studies, **1**, 628, **2**, 120
    use of term, **2**, 69
dimethylallyltryptophan synthase(s)
    catalysis, **5**, 331
    genetic studies, **5**, 331
    Hammett plots, **5**, 331
    kinetic constants, **5**, 331
    linear free energy correlations, **5**, 331
    mechanistic studies, **5**, 331
    purification, **5**, 331
dimethyl A loops, in 16S rRNA, **6**, 195
dimethylamine *N*-oxide, dodecyl-
    as inhibitor, **2**, 311
    as tetrahymanol cyclase inhibitor, **2**, 312
dimethylaniline-*N*-oxide aldolase
    activity, **3**, 412
    biochemistry, **3**, 411
dimyristoyllecithin bilayers, interactions, with gramicidin
    S, **4**, 322
Dineutes spp., gyrinal, **8**, 234
2,4-dinitrophenyl (DNP) groups, addition, to
    oligonucleotides, **7**, 174
dinoflagellates *see* Dinoflagellida
Dinoflagellida
    bioluminescence, **8**, 457
    epiphytic, ciguatera induction, **8**, 501
    goniodomin, **8**, 613
    luciferin, isolation, **8**, 457
    symbiosis, **8**, 426
    see also zooxanthellae
Dinophysis spp., okadaic acid, **8**, 490
dinophysistoxin 1 (DTX-1), occurrence, **8**, 490
dinophysistoxin 4 (DTX-4)
    Baeyer–Villiger reaction, **8**, 496
    biosynthesis, **8**, 493
Dinoponera grandis, venom, **8**, 354
dinucleotide-binding motif, **2**, 272
dinucleotide-binding sites, intercalation, **7**, 436
dinucleotide phosphoramidites, in oligonucleotide
    synthesis, **7**, 135
dinucleotides, crystallization, **7**, 435
diol dehydrase
    amino acid residues, **5**, 275
    catalysis, **5**, 274
    occurrence, **5**, 274
    reactions, **5**, 264
diol epoxide derivatives, and polycyclic aromatic
    hydrocarbons, **7**, 470
diolepoxides, from, benzo[a]pyrene, **5**, 58
diols, chiral vicinal, and epoxide hydrolases, **5**, 59
Dioscorea spp., stilbene synthases, **1**, 753
Dioscorea batatas, jasmonic acid, **1**, 127
Dioscoreophyllum cumminsii, sweet proteins, **8**, 166
Diospyros kaki, astringency, **8**, 167
2,7-dioxabicyclo[2.2.1]heptane, 1,3,3-trimethyl-,
    biosynthesis, **8**, 232

2,9-dioxabicyclo[3.3.1]non-7-ene, (2*R*,3*S*,5*S*)-1,8-dimethyl-3-ethyl-, occurrence, **8**, 244

2,9-dioxabicyclo[3.3.1]non-7-en-6-one, (1*R*,3*S*,5*S*)-1,8-dimethyl-3-ethyl-, occurrence, **8**, 244

2,8-dioxabicyclo[3.2.1]octane, (1*S*,2*R*,5*R*,7*S*)-1-ethyl-3,5,7-trimethyl- *see* sordidin

6,8-dioxabicyclo[3.2.1]octane, 1,5-dimethyl- *see* frontalin

6,8-dioxabicyclo[3.2.1]octane, (1*S*,2*R*,4*S*,5*R*)-2,4-dimethyl-5-ethyl- *see* α-multistriatin

6,8-dioxabicyclo[3.2.1]octane, (1*S*,2*R*,5*R*)-2-ethyl-1,5-dimethyl- *see* bicolorin

1,6-dioxaspiro[4.5]decane, (5*R*,7*S*)-7-methyl-, occurrence, **8**, 212

(*R*)-1,7-dioxaspiro[5.5]decane, occurrence, **8**, 212

1,6-dioxaspiro[4.4]nonane, 2-ethyl-, occurrence, **8**, 199

1,6-dioxaspiro[4.4]nonane, (2*S*,5*R*)-2-ethyl-, occurrence, **8**, 212, 213

1,7-dioxaspiro[5.5]undecane, (2*S*,6*R*,8*S*)-2,8-dimethyl-, occurrence, **8**, 214

1,2-dioxetanone, as luminescence intermediate, **8**, 456

dioxins, as environmental pollutants, **5**, 410

dioxygen, roles, in DNA damage, **7**, 583

dioxygenase(s)
  occurrence, **1**, 211, **5**, 417
  2-oxoglutarate-dependent
    in gibberellin biosynthesis, **8**, 47
    properties, **8**, 52
    reviews, **8**, 50

o-diphenolase(s) *see* catechol oxidase(s)

diphenol oxidase(s) *see* catechol oxidase(s)

diphenylamine, CrtI enzyme sensitivity, **2**, 341

diphlorethol, occurrence, **8**, 441

diphosphate
  inorganic, as inhibitor of trichodiene synthase, **2**, 160, **5**, 333
  reactions, with ammonium ion compounds, **2**, 253
  synergistic binding, **5**, 338

diphosphate, bornyl, hydrolysis, **2**, 104

diphosphate, 6-cyclopropylidene-3*E*-methylhex-2-en-1-yl, isomerization, **2**, 127

diphosphate, dimethylallyl (DMAPP)
  analogues, **5**, 331
  biosynthesis, **2**, 5, 70
  condensation, **2**, 98
  interconversion, **2**, 392
  roles, in farnesyl diphosphate, **5**, 318
  as substrate, **2**, 7, 379, **5**, 321

diphosphate, 2-(dimethylamino)ethyl, as isopentenyl diphosphate isomerase inhibitor, **2**, 72

diphosphate, homoisopentenyl, as intermediate, **8**, 272

diphosphate, 3-methyl-2-butenyl
  equilibrium, **8**, 219
  in terminal branching, **8**, 239

diphosphate, 3-methyl-3-butenyl, biosynthesis, **8**, 219

diphosphate, 3-methylenepentyl, isomerization, **8**, 236

diphosphate, 3-methyl-2-pentenyl, biosynthesis, **8**, 219, 236

diphosphate, 3-methyl-3-pentenyl, biosynthesis, **8**, 236

diphosphate anions, coupling, with carbocations, **2**, 133

diphosphate esters, allylic, ionization, **2**, 7

diphosphates, allylic
  ionization, **2**, 7
  in terpenoid metabolism, **2**, 98

diphosphohydrolases, activity, **2**, 98

diphosphonate, dimethylallyl methylene (DMAPCP), K_m, **2**, 81

diphosphonate, isopentenyl methylene (IPCP), V_{max}, **2**, 81

Diplococcus pneumoniae, 4-α-glucanotransferase induction, **3**, 445

Diplodia maydis, diplodiatoxin, **1**, 388

diplodiatoxin, occurrence, **1**, 388

(+)-diplodiatoxin, total synthesis, **1**, 389

Diploptera punctata, allatostatins, **8**, 301

diplopterol, **2**, 308
  as by-product, **2**, 307
  synthesis, **2**, 309, 310

Diplosoma virens, virenamides, **8**, 538

Diprion spp., pheromones, **8**, 247

Diprionidae
  diprionol, **8**, 247
  propanoic acid esters, **8**, 241

diprionol, occurrence, **8**, 247

Diprion pini, (1*S*,2*R*,6*R*)-1,2,6-trimethyldodecanol, **8**, 247

Diprion similis
  (1*S*,2*R*,6*R*)-diprionyl acetate, **8**, 247
  pheromones, **8**, 14

Diptera
  bursicon, **8**, 301
  juvenile hormone III bisepoxides, biosynthesis, **8**, 272

dipyrromethane
  as cofactor, **4**, 81
    mechanisms, **4**, 84

o-diquinone, biosynthesis, **3**, 709

direct protein binding agents
  chebulagic acid, **7**, 595
  corilagin, **7**, 595
  coumermycin, **7**, 596
  DNA topoisomerase inhibitors, **7**, 595
  β-lapachone, **7**, 595
  novobiocin, **7**, 596

dirigent proteins
  active sites, **3**, 732
  cloning, **1**, 654
  coupling modes, **1**, 677
  free radical capture mechanisms, **3**, 723
  genetics, **1**, 654
  homology, **1**, 654
  kinetic parameters, **1**, 658
  roles
    in lignin biosynthesis, **3**, 722
    in 8–8′ phenoxy radical coupling, **1**, 672
    in pinoresinol biosynthesis, **1**, 652
    in (+)-pinoresinol biosynthesis, **1**, 657

Dirofilaria immitis, prostaglandin D₂, **1**, 249

Dirphia spp., histamine, **8**, 360

disaccharides
  hydrolysis, **1**, 890
  ¹³C NMR spectra, **3**, 560

discadenine
  applications, **8**, 61
  synthesis, **8**, 62

Discodermia dissoluta, discodermide, **8**, 588

discodermide, occurrence, **8**, 588

discorhabdin A
  applications, antibiotics, **7**, 501
  occurrence, **7**, 501
  possible DNA reactions of, **7**, 501

disease resistance, in plants, **1**, 132

diseases
  congenital, and glycan synthesis defects, **3**, 59
  effects, on *O*-glycan structure, **3**, 70

disparlure, occurrence, **8**, 4, 12

(+)-disparlure, occurrence, **8**, 207

distamycin
  DNA binding, **7**, 567
    minor groove, **7**, 486

c-d distance rule, in monocyclic enediynes, **7**, 557

Distilium racemosum, brassinosteroids, **8**, 99

disulfide, bis(3-methylbutyl), occurrence, **8**, 220

disulfide, 2-pyridyl 3-isothiocyanatobenzyl, reactions, with 2′-aminonucleotides, **6**, 227

disulfide bonds, formation, **6**, 89

disulfides
  in bicyclic oligonucleotide synthesis, **7**, 360
  cross-links, **6**, 227
  hairpin, antibody–DNA interactions, **7**, 363

ditercalinium
  applications, antineoplastic agents, **7**, 444
  intercalation, **7**, 446
  x-ray crystal structure, **7**, 444
diterpene cyclases, occurrence, **2**, 384
diterpenes
  biosynthesis, **2**, 60, **217–243**
    genetic engineering, **2**, 241
  cembrenes, **2**, 220
  future research, **2**, 241
  insecticidal activity, **8**, 312
  occurrence, **8**, 230
  as pheromones, **8**, 229
  Type A cyclization, **2**, 219, 220
    definition, **2**, 219
  Type A–Type B cyclization, **2**, 220
  Type B cyclization, **2**, 223
    definition, **2**, 219
  Type B–Type A cyclization, **2**, 226
diterpenes, pentacyclic, biosynthesis, **2**, 230
diterpenes, tetracyclic, biosynthesis, **2**, 230
diterpenes, tricyclic
  from
    copalyl diphosphate, **2**, 226
    ent-copalyl diphosphate, **2**, 229
    syn-copalyl diphosphate, **2**, 229
diterpene synthases, GC-MS analysis, **2**, 211
diterpenoids, applications, **8**, 35
5,5′-dithiobis(2-nitrobenzoic acid)
  in chorismate synthase studies, **1**, 601
  reactions, **5**, 353
1,2-dithiolane, 3,3-dimethyl-, occurrence, **8**, 220
1,2-dithiolane, 3,4-dimethyl-, occurrence, **8**, 220
1,2-dithiolane-4-carboxylic acid *see* asparagusic acid
1,2-dithiolan-3-one 1-oxides, DNA damage induction, **7**,
    522
1,2-dithiole-3-thiones
  DNA damage induction, **7**, 526
  oxygen radicals from, **7**, 526
dithiole-3-thiones/thiol mixtures, superoxide production
    by, **7**, 540
2,4-dithiopyrimidines, synthesis, **7**, 260
dithiothreitol (DTT), **7**, 565
dithymidylyl phosphorothioate, reactions, with *N*-(1-
    pyrene)maleimide, **7**, 240
dITP *see* deoxyinosine triphosphate (dITP)
diuretic hormones
  biochemistry, **8**, 300
  release, **8**, 302
divalent metal ions, in dimethylallyl*trans*transferase
    reaction, chain length distribution, **2**, 92
1,5-diyne-3-ene system, reactivity, **7**, 557
diynene *see* enediyne
djenkolic acid
  biosynthesis, **1**, 848
  as intermediate, **1**, 849
  occurrence, **1**, 848
DKDPT *see* deaminoketodemethylphosphinothricin
    (DKDPT)
DLH *see* carboxymethylenebutenolidase
Dlochrysa spp., cardenolides, **8**, 361
DMAPCP *see* diphosphonate, dimethylallyl methylene
    (DMAPCP)
DMAPP *see* diphosphate, dimethylallyl (DMAPP)
DMAT *see* tryptophan, dimethylallyl- (DMAT)
DMAT synthase(s) *see* dimethylallyltryptophan
    synthase(s)
DMDP *see* pyrrolidine, 2,5-dihydroxymethyl-3,4-
    dihydroxy- (DMDP)
DMI *see* isoflavanol, 7,2′-dihydroxy-4′-methoxy- (DMI)
DMJ *see* 1-deoxymannonojirimycin (DMJ)
DMS *see* sulfate, dimethyl (DMS)
DMTr *see* trityl, dimethoxy- (DMTr)

DNA
  adenine derivatives, **7**, 323
  with altered bases, **7**, **313–339**
    future research, **7**, 335
  applications, **7**, 2, 7
    catalysts, **7**, 11
    computation, **7**, 11
    diagnostic tools, **7**, 9
    therapeutic agents, **7**, 9
  azoles, **7**, 333
  B-form double helix, **7**, 432
  branched, **7**, 356
    synthesis, **7**, 204
  bulged, as catalyst, **7**, 564
  C1′-position, and DNA damage, **7**, 373
  C2′-position, and DNA damage, **7**, 380
  C3′-position, and DNA damage, **7**, 383
  C4′-position, and DNA damage, **7**, 384
  C5′-position, and DNA damage, **7**, 394
  catalysts
    selection, **7**, 630
    SELEX studies, **7**, 619
  chemiluminescent detection, **7**, 161
  chemistry, **7**, 7
    future research, **7**, 8
    and medicine, **7**, 4
  classical intercalation model, features, **7**, 432
  C-linked nucleosides, **7**, 332
  closed circular superhelical, and intercalation
    unwinding angle, **7**, 433
  conjugate group attachment, **7**, **153–249**
  cyclization, **7**, 366
  cytosine derivatives, **7**, 320
  disulfide bond formation, **7**, 366
  folding, complex, **7**, 617
  3′-formylphosphate-ended, **7**, 583
  groove shape, RNA compared, **7**, 452
  guanine derivatives, **7**, 327
  heterocyclic bases, **7**, 616
  historical perceptions, **7**, 615
  hydrodynamic properties, **7**, 630
  imine formation, **7**, 366
  interactions, with natural products, **7**, 5, 9
  ionizing radiation, targeting, **7**, 375
  kinetics
    determination, **7**, 37
    relaxation, **7**, 37
  knotted, **7**, 347
  as ligand, **7**, 10
  linear, viscosity, **7**, 433
  linker, damage, **7**, 567
  loops
    hairpin, **7**, 629
    internal, **7**, 629
  major groove, α-helices in, **7**, 477
  maxicircles, **7**, 343
  methylation, **7**, 646
  microheterogeneity, **7**, 567
  minicircles, **7**, 343, 630
  minor groove binders
    distamycin, **7**, 567
    netropsin, **7**, 567
  and molecular biology, overview, **7**, **1–13**
  as molecular scaffold, **7**, 10
  mutagenesis, **7**, 621
  nucleosome, cleavage, **7**, 567
  as organic natural product, **7**, 1
  photochemistry, **5**, 372
  physical properties, **7**, 7
  plasmid, **7**, 570
    in cloning, **7**, 647
  preorganization, **7**, 360
  protons

exchangeable, **7**, 60
  non-exchangeable, **7**, 60
purine analogues, **7**, 329
pyrimidines, adjacent, **5**, 372
γ-radiolysis, **7**, 375, 398, 417
reactions, with intercalating agents, **7**, 470
relaxation, DNA topoisomerase I-mediated, **7**, 597
reporter group attachment, **7**, **153–249**
scission, *in vitro* studies, **7**, 567
selection, **7**, **615–641**
  in vitro, **7**, 617
SELEX studies, **7**, 617
shuffling, **7**, 621
single-stranded, from double helices, **7**, 620
supercoiled, catalytic relaxation mechanism, **7**, 598
T4
  binding of pyrrolo[1,4]benzodiazepines to, **7**, 495
  CC-1065 binding to, **7**, 505
as tapes, **7**, 615
telomeres, **7**, 346
thymine derivatives, **7**, 314
topologically modified
  future research, **7**, 367
  synthesis, **7**, 363
transformation, into *Escherichia coli*, **7**, 662
ultraviolet radiation, **5**, 372
  mutations, **5**, 396
viral, probe for bulge sites, **7**, 565
see also cDNA; circular DNA; dsDNA; Dumb-bell
  DNA; ssDNA
DNA adducts
  with aflatoxins, **7**, 511
  with aldehydes, **7**, 502
  with alkenylbenzenes, **7**, 519
  with barminomycin I, **7**, 500
  with bioxalomycins, **7**, 499
  with CC-1065, **7**, 504
  with cyanocyclines, **7**, 499
  with duocarmycins, **7**, 504
  with epoxides, **7**, 508
  with leinamycin, **7**, 522
  with mitomycin C, **7**, 514
  with naphthyridinomycin, **7**, 499
  with quinocarcin, **7**, 499
  reactions, with pyrrolo[1,4]benzodiazepines, **7**, 495
  with renieramycins, **7**, 497
  with safracins, **7**, 497
  with saframycins, **7**, 497
  with tetrazomine, **7**, 499
DNA alkylation
  5′-aminoalkylation, **7**, 165
  by pluramycins, sequence specificity, **7**, 508
  by quinones, **7**, 531
DNA amplification *see* gene amplification
DNA backbone
  altered, **7**, 287
    in antisense applications, **7**, **285–311**
  religation, **7**, 599
DNA bending
  by CC-1065, **7**, 506
  circular permutation, **7**, 354
  sequence motifs, **7**, 630
DNA binding
  dimerization domain, **7**, 482
  groove-binding agents, **7**, 435, 595
  helix-type-dependent, **7**, 460
  intercalation, **7**, 428, 7
  minor-groove, **7**, 428
    by CC-1065, **7**, 505
  molecular, **7**, 7
  negative cooperation, neighbor exclusion, **7**, 446
  SELEX studies, **7**, 619
DNA binding modes

sequence-dependent, **7**, 456
  unfused aromatic compounds, **7**, 455
DNA binding peptides, **7**, 352, **477–490**
  based on protein motifs, **7**, 477
DNA binding proteins, sequences, **7**, 622
DNA cleavage
  affinity, **7**, 253
  by 5-alkyl resorcinols, **7**, 536
  by bleomycin, **7**, 536
  by CC-1065, **7**, 504
  by diazo and diazonium compounds, **7**, 541
  by diazo ketones, **7**, 542
  by 6-diazo-5-oxo-L-norleucine, DNA damage
    induction, **7**, 542
  by duocarmycins, **7**, 504
  by epoxides, **7**, 508
  by kinamycin, **7**, 541
  by leinamycin, **7**, 522
  by resorcinols, **7**, 535
  pattern, **7**, 596
  ribozyme-catalyzed, **6**, 126
  with α,β-unsaturated aldehydes, **7**, 502
DNA cloning *see* molecular cloning
DNA conformation
  determination, **7**, 75
    computational methods, **7**, 75
  molecular dynamics simulations, **7**, 76
  structural parameters, **7**, 76
DNA cross-linking
  agents, pyrrole-derived, **7**, 514
  by azinomycin B, **7**, 513
  by formaldehyde, **7**, 502
  by FR 66979, **7**, 518
  by FR 900482, **7**, 518
  by isochrysohermidine, **7**, 503
  by mitomycin C, **7**, 514
  by pyrrolizidine alkaloids, **7**, 518
  and DNA structure probes, **7**, 96
DNA damage
  adduct formation, **7**, 585
  and aging, **7**, 372
  alkaline labile lesion formation, mechanisms, **7**,
    387
  amplification, **7**, 401, 419
  attack sites, **7**, 583
  biological consequences, **7**, 494
  C1′-position reactions, **7**, 373
  C2′-position reactions, **7**, 380
  C3′-position reactions, **7**, 383
  C4′-position reactions, **7**, 384
  C5′-position reactions, **7**, 394
  and cancer, **7**, 372
  and carcinogenesis, **7**, 582
  chemistry, **7**, **371–425**, 554, 582
  covalent drug–DNA adducts, **7**, 492, 582
  and deuteration, **7**, 567
  deuterium isotope effect, **7**, 560
  dioxygen in, **7**, 583
  effects, **7**, 34
  enediyne compound-induced, **7**, **553–592**
  from ultraviolet radiation, **7**, 561
  interstrand transfer, **7**, 419
  mechanisms, **7**, 558, 582
  modes, **7**, 372
  and mutation, **7**, 372
  natural product-induced, **7**, 495
  natural products classification, **7**, 492
  and nitroimidazoles, **7**, 583
  oxidative, **7**, 582
  oxidizing agent-induced, **7**, 384
  and 3′-phosphoglycolate, **7**, 583
  and 3′-phosphopentenaldehyde, **7**, 583
  and 3′-phosphopyridazine, **7**, 583

prevalence, **7**, 372
protection agents, **7**, 417
of pyrrolizidine alkaloids, by oxidative activation, **7**, 518
radiosensitization, **7**, 583
rate-determining step, **7**, 560
sensitization, **7**, 417
sequence-specificity, **7**, 560
and sugar peroxyradical, **7**, 582
via oxidation, **7**, 376
DNA deoxyribophosphodiesterase, catalysis, **5**, 393
DNA-directed DNA polymerase
functions, **5**, 393
inhibition by aphidicolin, **7**, 597
DNA-directed RNA polymerase(s)
applications, in oligoribonucleotide synthesis, **6**, 218
characteristics, **4**, 367
gene transcription, **4**, 362
binding factors, **4**, 368
TATA-dependent, **4**, 366
substrates, **6**, 219, 226
transcription, **4**, 323
DNA–DNA duplexes, T_m values, **7**, 288
DNA drug complexes, structure, **7**, 351
DNA duplexes
^{13}C HMQC spectra, **7**, 73
^{15}N HMQC spectra, **7**, 72
base pairs
identification, **7**, 66
lifetimes, **7**, 76
twist, **7**, 76
bent, **7**, 630
B-form, non-exchangeable proton distances, **7**, 66
formation, **7**, 43
glycosidic angles, determination, **7**, 76
HETCOR studies, **7**, 71
hydration, **7**, 34
^{1}H NMR spectra, **7**, 60
^{31}P NMR spectra
limitations, **7**, 72
proton-decoupled, **7**, 70
NOESY spectra, **7**, 65
fingerprint region, **7**, 65
DNA enzymes
artificial, **6**, 262
characteristics, **6**, 262
discovery, **6**, 237
isolation, **6**, 262
selection, **6**, 136
see also deoxyribozymes
DNA footprinting
deoxysugar studies, **3**, 323
interference, **7**, 252, 253
protection, **7**, 252
DNA function, **7**, 342
effects of purines on, **7**, 410
effects of pyrimidines on, **7**, 407
overview, **7**, 2
DNA β-glucosyltransferase, catalysis, **3**, 684
DNA helicase II, catalysis, **5**, 393
DNA intercalators, **7**, **427–476**
applications, DNA structure probes, **7**, 83
structure, **7**, 433
topological changes, **7**, 446
DNA ligase (ATP)
applications, **7**, 363
in oligoribonucleotide synthesis, **6**, 218
functions, **5**, 393
DNA modification
covalent
by natural products, **7**, **491–552**
mechanisms, **7**, 493
purine, **7**, 323

pyrimidine, **7**, 314
polycyclic heterocycles, **7**, 334
topological, **7**, **341–369**
DNA nucleotidyltransferase (DNA-directed) *see* DNA-directed DNA polymerase
DNA photolyase *see* deoxyribodipyrimidine photolyase(s)
DNA polymerase I *see* DNA-directed DNA polymerase
DNA polymerase II *see* DNA-directed DNA polymerase
DNA polymerase III *see* DNA-directed DNA polymerase
DNA polymerase III
mechanisms, **7**, 349
sliding clamp, **7**, 350
DNA polymerases
activity, **7**, 194
mutagenesis, **7**, 621
DNA polymerase α *see* DNA-directed DNA polymerase
DNA polymerase β *see* DNA-directed DNA polymerase
DNA polymerase γ *see* DNA-directed DNA polymerase
DNA processing enzymes, cytotoxic response depression, **7**, 597
DNA–proflavine complex, intercalation sites, **7**, 435
DNA–protein binding *see* protein–DNA binding
DNA recognition, by topoisomerase I, **7**, 598
DNA recombination
in vitro, **7**, 621
junctions, **7**, 346
DNA repair enzyme *see* DNA ligase (ATP)
DNA replication
problems, **7**, 346
rolling circles, **7**, 346
topology and, **7**, 346
DNA–RNA damage, chemistry, **7**, 582
DNA–RNA duplexes
in hammerhead ribozymes, **6**, 242
Tm values, **7**, 288
DNA–RNA hybrids, **7**, 567
damage, **7**, 566
duplexes, **7**, 34
DNase I *see* deoxyribonuclease I (DNase I)
DNA sequences
conformation switching, **7**, 359
consensus double-stranded, **7**, 628
diversity, **7**, 621
nucleoside analogue incorporation, **7**, 259
random, **7**, 622
sequestration, **7**, 620
viral, detection, **7**, 205
DNA sequencing
automated, **7**, 620
chemical cleavage method, **7**, 620
modified, **7**, 82
techniques, **7**, 620
DNA strand breakage, **1**, 557
antitumor antibiotic-induced, **7**, 420
2′-deoxyuridin-5-yl in, **7**, 411
direct, **7**, 380
mechanisms, **7**, 387
dsDNA, **7**, 418
mechanisms, **7**, 418
DNA structure, **7**, 342
A-form, **7**, 76, 82
B-form, **7**, 76, 82
branched, applications, **7**, 352
circular, **7**, 354
cuboid, **7**, 354
determination
via NMR spectroscopy, **7**, **55–80**
via x-ray crystallography, **7**, 55
early studies, **7**, 81
effects of purines on, **7**, 410
effects of pyrimidines on, **7**, 407
elements, **7**, 56

eukaryotic, **7**, 82
knotted, research, **7**, 353
man-made
  applications, **7**, 352
  non-linear topology, **7**, 352
modifications, **7**, 3
molecular probes of, **7**, **81–103**
nomenclature, **7**, 56
non-B, **7**, 82
overview, **7**, 1
parameters, helical, **7**, 58
probes
  DNA intercalators, **7**, 83
  metal complexes, **7**, 85
  selection, **7**, 83
  transition metals, **7**, 85
Watson–Crick base pair alignments, **7**, 58, 66
Z-form, **7**, 77, 82
  assays, **7**, 96
  double-stranded RNA adenosine deaminase affinity,
    5, 86
  ^{1}H NMR spectra, **7**, 78
DNA surveillance, mechanisms, **7**, 597
DNA synthesis
  automated, **7**, 617, 619
  chemical, **7**, 619
  importance of, **7**, 2
  inhibition, **7**, 554
  large-scale, **7**, 142
  mechanisms, **7**, 2
  phosphoramidite methodology, **7**, 130, 292
  ultrafast, **7**, 120
DNA topoisomerase I
  as cancer chemotherapeutic target, **7**, 594
  cleavage/religation equilibrium, **7**, 599
  DNA binding, **7**, 598
  DNA cleavage sites, **7**, 598
  DNA recognition, **7**, 598
  enzyme turnover, **7**, 599
  mechanisms, **7**, 594
    catalytic, **7**, 598
  post-strand passage cleavage/religation equilibrium, **7**,
    599
  pre-strand passage cleavage/religation equilibrium, **7**,
    598
  strand passage, **7**, 599
DNA topoisomerase I inhibitors, **7**, 597
  benzo[c]phenanthridines, **7**, 601
  bulgarein, **7**, 600
  coralynes, **7**, 601
  indolocarbazoles, **7**, 600
  naphthacenequinones, **7**, 600
DNA topoisomerase II
  adenosine 5′-triphosphatase activity, inhibition, **7**, 603
  and adenosine 5′-triphosphate, **7**, 601
  ATP hydrolysis and enzyme turnover, **7**, 603
  as cancer chemotherapeutic target, **7**, 594
  cleavable complex mediators, non-intercalating agents,
    7, 609
  composite pharmacophore, **7**, 610
  double strand passage, **7**, 603
  inhibition, **3**, 324, 462
  mechanisms, **7**, 594
    catalytic, **7**, 602
  post strand passage cleavage/religation equilibrium, **7**,
    603
  pre-strand passage/religation equilibrium, **7**, 602
  recognition of binding site, **7**, 602
DNA topoisomerase II inhibitors, **7**, 601
DNA topoisomerase IIα
  molecular mass, **7**, 601
  and topoisomerase IIβ compared, **7**, 601
DNA topoisomerase IIβ, molecular mass, **7**, 601

DNA topoisomerase inhibitors, **7**, **593–614**
  applications, direct protein binding agents, **7**, 595
  intercalation, **7**, 595
  mechanisms, **7**, 595
  minor groove binding, **7**, 595
  overview, **7**, 594
DNA topoisomerase(s)
  in chemotherapy, **7**, 594
  cytotoxicity, **7**, 596
  future research, **7**, 611
  inhibition, **1**, 783
    cleavable complex, **7**, 594
    modes, **7**, 595
  overview, **7**, 347
  physiological roles, **7**, 594
  poisons, cleavable complex mediators, **7**, 594
DNA triplexes, **7**, 270
  applications, **7**, 142
  canonical base triplets, **7**, 629
  formation, **7**, 366
  5-halogenated pyrimidines, **7**, 316
  pH-independent, **7**, 271
  'purine motif', **7**, 629
  pyrimidine–purine–pyrimidine, **7**, 270
    stability, **7**, 271
  SELEX studies, **7**, 629
  stability, **7**, 47
    studies, **7**, 273
  structure, **7**, 77
DNAzymes *see* deoxyribozymes
DNBSB *see* benzoyl, 2-(2,4-dinitrobenzene
  sulfenyloxymethyl)- (DNBSB)
DNJ *see* 1-deoxynojirimycin (DNJ)
DNP groups *see* 2,4-dinitrophenyl (DNP) groups
dnr genes, in daunosamine biosynthesis, **3**, 342, 350
dNTPs *see* deoxynucleoside triphosphates
docosahexaenoic acid, in platelet-activating factor
  studies, **1**, 291
docosahexaenoic acid, 13-hydroxy-, occurrence, **1**, 237
docosanoate, geranylgeranyl, occurrence, **8**, 229
docosanolide, occurrence, **8**, 218
4Z,7Z,11E,16Z,19Z-docosapentaenoic acid, 10,13,14-
  trihydroxy-, occurrence, **1**, 237
docosenolide, occurrence, **8**, 218
DODC *see* oxadicarbocyanine, 3,3′-diethyl- (DODC)
2,10-dodecadien-1,7-diol, 3,7,11-trimethyl-, occurrence,
  8, 227
(3Z,6Z)-3,6-dodecadien-12-olide, occurrence, **8**, 215
(11R,3Z,6Z)-3,6-dodecadien-11-olide, occurrence, **8**, 215
8,10-dodecadien-6-one, (3S,7R,8E,10E)-3,7,9-trimethyl-,
  occurrence, **8**, 244
dodecane, occurrence, **8**, 214
dodecanoate, phytyl, occurrence, **8**, 229
dodecanoic acids, occurrence, **8**, 209, 215
dodecanol, (1S,2R,6R)-1,2,6-trimethyl-, occurrence, **8**,
  247
1-dodecanol, occurrence, **8**, 214
4-dodecanolide, (4S,6S)-6-hydroxy-, occurrence, **8**, 215
(R)-4-dodecanolide, occurrence, **8**, 215
dodecanoyl-CoA, decarboxylation, **8**, 204
dodecanucleotides, synthesis, **7**, 317
dodecatriene, all-*trans*-2,6,10-trimethyl-
  in lamin B, **2**, 355
  structure, **2**, 355
(3Z,6Z,8E)-3,6,8-dodecatrien-1-ol, occurrence, **8**, 214
(5Z)-dodecenoic acid, 2-methylethyl esters, occurrence,
  8, 215
(7Z)-dodecenoic acid, 2-methylethyl esters, occurrence,
  8, 215
9-dodecenoic acid, biosynthesis, **8**, 205
(9Z)-dodecenoic acid, 2-methylethyl esters, occurrence,
  8, 215
11-dodecenoic acid, biosynthesis, **8**, 205

4-dodecen-3-ol, (2*S*,3*R*,4*E*)-1-[4,7-anhydro-4-*C*-(hydroxymethyl)-*β*-D-glucopyranosyloxy]-2-(dodecanoylamino)-, studies, **3**, 95

(4*R*,5*Z*)-5-dodecen-4-olide, occurrence, **8**, 215

(11*S*,3*Z*)-3-dodecen-11-olide, occurrence, **8**, 215

(*Z*)-3-dodecen-12-olide, occurrence, **8**, 215

2-dodecen-1,7,11-triol, 3,7,11-trimethyl-, occurrence, **8**, 227

dogs, sex pheromones, methyl 4-hydroxybenzoate, **8**, 200

dolichodial, occurrence, **8**, 226

dolichol, oligosaccharide linkage, **3**, 15

dolichol diphosphate *N*-acetylglucosamine (Dol-PP-GlcNAc), biosynthesis, **3**, 41

dolichol diphosphate (Dol-PP), structure, **3**, 41

dolichol diphosphate oligosaccharide, biosynthesis, **3**, 41

dolicholide, 25-methylation, **8**, 107

dolichol phosphate, monosaccharide linkage, **3**, 15, 3

dolichol phosphate D-mannose (Dol-P-Man)
    functions, **4**, 306
    as mannose donor, **3**, 301

dolichol phosphate sugars, biosynthesis, **5**, 280

dolichols, synthesis, **2**, 247

dolichyl diphosphate, dephosphorylation, **3**, 288

dolichyl phosphate, roles, in glycoprotein biosynthesis, **3**, 286

dolichyl-phosphate-mannose synthase *see* dolichyl-phosphate *β*-D-mannosyltransferase

dolichyl-phosphate-mannose synthase (Dol-P-Man synthase) *see* dolichyl-phosphate *β*-D-mannosyltransferase

dolichyl-phosphate *β*-D-mannosyltransferase
    catalysis, **3**, 301
    cloning, **4**, 311
    gene, **4**, 307

Dol-P-Man *see* dolichol phosphate D-mannose (Dol-P-Man)

Dol-P-Man synthase *see* dolichyl-phosphate *β*-D-mannosyltransferase

Dol-PP *see* dolichol diphosphate (Dol-PP)

Dol-PP-GlcNAc *see* dolichol diphosphate *N*-acetylglucosamine (Dol-PP-GlcNAc)

dominicalure 1, occurrence, **8**, 14, 241

dominicalure 2, occurrence, **8**, 14, 241

donor:hydrogen-peroxide oxidoreductase(s) *see* peroxidase(s)

L-DOPA *see* phenylalanine, L-3,4-dihydroxy- (L-DOPA)

dopa decarboxylase *see* aromatic-L-amino-acid decarboxylase

dopamine, in honeybee venom, **8**, 355

doramectin, isolation, **1**, 524

dormancy
    breakage initiation, **1**, 128
    and dormin, **8**, 72
    role of abscisic acid in, **1**, 133
    role of jasmonates in, **1**, 128

dormin
    use of term, **8**, 72
    see also abscisic acid

double-stranded DNA *see* dsDNA

double-stranded RNA *see* dsRNA

Douglas-fir beetle *see* Dendroctonus pseudotsugae

Douglas-fir tussock moth *see* Orgyia pseudotsugata

doxorubicin, **7**, 528, 536
    anticancer activity, **1**, 481
    applications
        antibiotics, **7**, 433, 527, 528
        antineoplastic agents, **7**, 527, 594
        antitumor agents, **3**, 324, **7**, 594
    biosynthesis, **1**, 481
        genetics, **3**, 349
    deletion analysis, **1**, 487
    as DNA topoisomerase II inhibitor, **7**, 603
    isolation, **4**, 200

occurrence, **7**, 605

oxidative generation of formaldehyde by, **7**, 530

DPM1 *see* dolichyl-phosphate-mannose synthase (Dol-P-Man synthase)

dps genes, deletion analysis, **1**, 487

Dracaena cinnabari
    cinnabarone, **3**, 781
    damalachawin, **3**, 781

dracorubin, biosynthesis, **3**, 752

Drechslera nodulosum, tryptophol, **8**, 178

drimane esters, localization, **8**, 462

drimane sesquiterpenoids, anatomical distribution, **8**, 462

drimenol
    antifeedant activity, **8**, 308
    occurrence, **8**, 308

Drosophila spp.
    aggregation pheromones, **8**, 218
    (*Z*)-10-heptadecen-2-one, **8**, 217
    (*Z*)-11-octadecenyl acetate, **8**, 218
    Sec tRNA[Ser]Sec gene, **4**, 361

Drosophila americana, (*Z*)-9-henicosene, **8**, 218

Drosophila buschkii
    (*S*)-1-methyltetradecyl acetate, **8**, 216
    2-pentadecanone, **8**, 216

Drosophila hydei
    2-pentadecanone, **8**, 216
    2-tridecanone, **8**, 215

Drosophila lummei, (*Z*)-9-henicosene, **8**, 218

Drosophila melanogaster
    Class 1 α1,2-mannosidases, **3**, 24
    dirigent proteins, **1**, 654
    ecdysteroids, **8**, 280
    GmII homologue, **3**, 27
    growth inhibition, **1**, 693
    insecticidal activity against, **8**, 344
    juvenile hormones, **8**, 269
    makisterone A, **8**, 279
    mas genes, **3**, 24
    (6-4) photoproduct lyase, **5**, 386
    prothoracicotropic hormone, **8**, 295
    Ras proteins, **2**, 360
    (*Z*)-7-tricosene, **8**, 219

Drosophila mulleri, (*S*)-1-methyldodecyl acetate, **8**, 215

Drosophila novamexicana, (*Z*)-9-henicosene, **8**, 218

Drosophila virilis
    ethyl hexanoate, **8**, 210
    (*Z*)-10-henicosene, **8**, 218
    methyl hexanoate, **8**, 210

drought, effects on ethylene biosynthesis, **8**, 96

drug design, strategies, **4**, 216

drugs
    from marine natural products, **8**, 521
    inactivation, **4**, 198
    intercalating agents, discovery, **7**, 428

drugstore beetles
    stegobinone, **8**, 244
    see also Stegobium paniceum

drug transport, problems, **7**, 607

drummondol, metabolism, **8**, 88

Drymis lanceolata, polygodial, **8**, 308

Drymis winteri, drimenol, **8**, 308

Dryocoetes spp., aggregation pheromones, **8**, 213

Dryocoetes affaber, (+)-*endo*-brevicomin, **8**, 213

Dryocoetes confusus, (+)-*endo*-brevicomin, **8**, 213

DS *see* dermatan sulfate (DS)

DSC *see* differential scanning calorimetry (DSC)

dsDNA
    breakage, **7**, 418
    detection, **7**, 166

D-signal, functions, **8**, 407

DSP *see* diarrhetic shellfish poisoning (DSP)

dsRNA
    binding proteins, **5**, 86, **6**, 101

and ribonuclease L activation, **6**, 214
    unwinding protein, **5**, 86
dTDP-6-deoxy-L-altrose
    biosynthesis, genetics, **3**, 342
    homology, **3**, 346
dTDP-6-deoxy-D-*xylo*-4-hexulose-3,5-epimerase,
    catalysis, **3**, 208
dTDP-6-deoxy-L-talose, biosynthesis, **3**, 334
dTDP-dihydrostreptose, biosynthesis, **3**, 353
dTDP-dihydrostreptose synthase, consensus pattern, **3**,
    337
dTDP-D-glucose-4,6-dehydratase, mediation, **3**, 208
dTDP-rhamnose
    biosynthesis, **3**, 334, 346
        genetics, **3**, 342
    pathway, **3**, 208
dTpdT dinucleotide photodimers, formation, **5**, 375
dTTP:α-D-glucose-1-phosphate thymidylyltransferase
        see glucose-1-phosphate thymidylyltransferase
DTX-1 *see* dinophysistoxin 1 (DTX-1)
Duboisia hopwoodii, nicotine, **8**, 347
Dubos, René Jules (1901–82), tyrothricin studies, **4**, 320
duckweed *see Lemna* spp.
Dufour's gland secretions
    ants, **8**, 237
    bees, **8**, 220, 223, 227, 229
    ponerine ants, **8**, 229
dumb-bell DNA
    as decoys, **7**, 362
    use of carbodiimide in, **7**, 366
    use of cyanogen bromide in, **7**, 366
dumb-bell RNA, as decoys, **7**, 362
dUMP *see* deoxyuridine monophosphate (dUMP)
Dunaliella spp.
    jasmonic acid, **8**, 108
    phenylalanine ammonia-lyase, **3**, 622
Dunaliella marina, phenylalanine ammonia-lyase,
    localization, **3**, 662
dung beetles *see Kheper* spp.
duocarmycin
    analogues
        with altered reactivity, **7**, 506
        sequence selectivity, **7**, 505
duocarmycin A
    applications, antibiotics, **7**, 505
    properties, **7**, 505
duocarmycin B₁, properties, **7**, 505
duocarmycin B₂, properties, **7**, 505
duocarmycin C₁, properties, **7**, 505
duocarmycin C₂, properties, **7**, 505
duocarmycins
    cytotoxicity, mechanisms, **7**, 506
    DNA reactions with, **7**, 504
    occurrence, **7**, 505
duocarmycin SA
    applications, antibiotics, **7**, 505
    properties, **7**, 505
dUpdU photodimers, cleavage, **5**, 383

duramycin, structure, **4**, 280
duramycin B, structure, **4**, 280
duramycin C, structure, **4**, 280
duramycins, biosynthesis, **4**, 202
durian fruit *see Duria zibethium*
Duria zibethium, odor principles, **8**, 165
duvatriendiol, occurrence, **8**, 235
α-4,8,13-duvatriene-1,3-diol, antifungal activity, **8**, 181
dwarf-1 genes, mutation, **8**, 53
Dwarf-3 genes, maize, **8**, 50
Dwarf-8 maize, **8**, 54
dwarf maize *see Zea mays*
dwarf mutants
    gibberellin-insensitive, **8**, 54
    single gene, **8**, 36
dwarf rice *see Oryza sativa*
dwarf rice assay, antheridic acid activity, **8**, 57
dyes
    aromatic, DNA binding, **7**, 83
    heterocyclic, in SELEX processes, **7**, 624
    intercalating agents, discovery, **7**, 428
    organic, in SELEX processes, **7**, 624
dynemicin A
    activation, **7**, 575
    anthracycline features, **7**, 574
    binding motif, **7**, 575
    biosynthesis, **1**, 559
        studies, **1**, 559
    DNA B-Z junction cleavage, **7**, 575
    DNA damage, **7**, 575
    in enediyne antibiotics, **1**, 557
    ¹³C NMR spectra, **1**, 559
    occurrence, **1**, 559, **7**, 574
    reduced nicotinamide adenine dinucleotide phosphate
        activation, **7**, 575
    sequence specificity, **3**, 327
    structure, **1**, 570, **7**, 574
dynemicin A methyl ester, tri-*O*-methyl-, synthesis, **7**, 574
dynemicin H, synthesis, **7**, 575
dynemicin N, synthesis, **7**, 575
dynemicin(s)
    antibiotic activity, **1**, 14
    applications
        antibiotics, **7**, 554, 574
        DNA structure probes, **7**, 98
    structure, **7**, 554
dynemicin S, synthesis, **7**, 575
Dysidea spp.
    sesquiterpenes, **8**, 466
    Vibrio spp. in, **8**, 588
Dysidea arenaria, arenastatin A, **8**, 613
Dysidea etheria, dysidiolide, **8**, 585
dysidiolide
    occurrence, **8**, 585
    structure, **8**, 585
Dytiscidae
    defensive sterols, **8**, 361
    steroids, **8**, 230
    testosterone, **8**, 230

E

E$_1$ *see* CDP-6-deoxy-L-*threo*-D-*glycero*-4-hexulose-3-
   dehydrase
E$_3$ *see* CDP-6-deoxy-L-*threo*-D-*glycero*-4-hexulose-3-
   dehydrase reductase
E$_p$ *see* α-D-glucose-1-phosphate cytidylyltransferase
9E3 mRNA
   degradation, **6**, 213
   polyadenylation, **6**, 214
E358A mutant, activity, **5**, 290
EAC *see* epoxy allylic carbocations (EAC)
EAL *see* ethanolamine ammonia-lyase
early nonsense codons, localization, **6**, 210
earthworms, platelet-activating factor, **1**, 286, 297
eastern cottonwood *see* Populus deltoides
EB *see* ethidium bromide (EB)
ebg genes, occurrence, **5**, 289
eburnetoxin (ETX), occurrence, **8**, 479
EC *see* adenosine nucleosidase
EC 1.1.1.1 *see* alcohol dehydrogenase (ADH)
EC 1.1.1.22 *see* UDPglucose 6-dehydrogenase
EC 1.1.1.25 *see* shikimate 5-dehydrogenase
EC 1.1.1.34 *see* hydroxymethylglutaryl-CoA reductase(s)
EC 1.1.1.35 *see* 3-hydroxyacyl-CoA dehydrogenase
EC 1.1.1.36 *see* acetoacetyl-CoA reductase(s)
EC 1.1.1.81 *see* hydroxypyruvate reductase
EC 1.1.1.88 *see* hydroxymethylglutaryl-CoA reductase(s)
EC 1.1.1.141 *see* 15-hydroxyprostaglandin
   dehydrogenase (NAD$^+$)
EC 1.1.1.188 *see* prostaglandin F synthase
EC 1.1.1.195 *see* cinnamyl-alcohol dehydrogenase(s)
EC 1.1.1.219 *see* dihydrokaempferol 4-reductase
EC 1.1.1.225 *see* chlordecone reductase
EC 1.1.1.234 *see* flavanone 4-reductase (FNR)
EC 1.1.1.242 *see* zeatin reductase
EC 1.1.3.22 *see* xanthine oxidase
EC 1.2.1.44 *see* cinnamoyl-CoA reductase
EC 1.3.1.12 *see* prephenate dehydrogenase(s)
EC 1.3.1.28 *see* 2,3-dihydro-2,3-dihydroxybenzoate
   dehydrogenase(s)
EC 1.3.1.42 *see* 12-oxophytodienoate reductase
EC 1.3.1.43 *see* cyclohexadienyl dehydrogenase
EC 1.3.1.50 *see* tetrahydroxynaphthalene reductase
EC 1.3.3.3 *see* coproporphyrinogen oxidase
EC 1.3.3.4 *see* protoporphyrinogen oxidase(s)
EC 1.3.3.6 *see* acyl-CoA oxidase
EC 1.3.99.3 *see* acyl-CoA dehydrogenase
EC 1.3.99.13 *see* long-chain-acyl-CoA dehydrogenase
   (LCADH)
EC 1.4.1.2 *see* glutamate dehydrogenase
EC 1.4.1.16 *see* diaminopimelate dehydrogenase
EC 1.5.3.9 *see* reticuline oxidase
EC 1.8.1.4 *see* dihydrolipoamide dehydrogenase
EC 1.9.3.1 *see* cytochrome-*c* oxidase
EC 1.10.3.1 *see* catechol oxidase(s)
EC 1.10.3.2 *see* laccase(s)
EC 1.11.1.6 *see* catalase
EC 1.11.1.7 *see* peroxidase(s)
EC 1.11.1.9 *see* glutathione peroxidase
EC 1.13.11.12 *see* lipoxygenase(s)
EC 1.13.11.31 *see* arachidonate 12-lipoxygenase
EC 1.13.11.33 *see* arachidonate 15-lipoxygenase
EC 1.13.11.34 *see* arachidonate 5-lipoxygenase
EC 1.13.11.40 *see* arachidonate 8-lipoxygenase
EC 1.14.11.9 *see* naringenin 3-dioxygenase
EC 1.14.11.11 *see* hyoscyamine 6*S*-hydroxylase

EC 1.14.11.13 *see* gibberellin 2β-dioxygenase(s)
EC 1.14.11.15 *see* gibberellin 3β-dioxygenase(s)
EC 1.14.13.11 *see* *trans*-cinnamate 4-monooxygenase
EC 1.14.13.21 *see* flavonoid 3′-monooxygenase
EC 1.14.13.25 *see* methane monooxygenase
EC 1.14.13.53 *see* isoflavone, 2′-hydroxylase
EC 1.14.99.1 *see* prostaglandin-endoperoxide synthase(s)
EC 1.14.99.5 *see* stearoyl-CoA desaturase(s)
EC 1.14.99.7 *see* squalene epoxidase (SE)
EC 1.14.99.25 *see* linoleoyl-CoA desaturase
EC 1.17.4.1 *see* ribonucleoside-diphosphate reductase
EC 1.17.4.2 *see* ribonucleoside-triphosphate reductase
EC 1.18.1.2 *see* ferredoxin-NADP$^+$ reductase
EC 2.1.1.6 *see* catechol *O*-methyltransferase
EC 2.1.1.53 *see* putrescine *N*-methyltransferase
EC 2.1.1.68 *see* caffeate *O*-methyltransferase
EC 2.1.1.104 *see* caffeoyl-CoA *O*-methyltransferase
EC 2.1.2.1 *see* threonine aldolase
EC 2.2.1.1 *see* transketolase
EC 2.2.1.2 *see* transaldolase
EC 2.3.1.9 *see* acetyl-CoA *C*-acetyltransferases
EC 2.3.1.16 *see* acetyl-CoA *C*-acyltransferase(s)
EC 2.3.1.37 *see* 5-aminolevulinate synthase
EC 2.3.1.54 *see* formate *C*-acetyltransferase
EC 2.3.1.74 *see* chalcone synthase (CHS)
EC 2.3.1.85 *see* fatty acid synthase(s)
EC 2.3.1.90 *see* β-glucogallin *O*-galloyltransferase
EC 2.3.1.151 *see* benzophenone synthase
EC 2.3.2.12 *see* peptidyltransferase
EC 2.4.1.1 *see* glycogen phosphorylase; maltodextrin
   phosphorylase; phosphorylase(s)
EC 2.4.1.3 *see* 4-α-glucanotransferase
EC 2.4.1.4 *see* amylosucrase
EC 2.4.1.11 *see* glycogen(starch) synthase
EC 2.4.1.16 *see* chitin synthase(s)
EC 2.4.1.17 *see* glucuronosyltransferase(s)
EC 2.4.1.18 *see* 1,4-α-glucan branching enzyme
EC 2.4.1.19 *see* cyclomaltodextrin glucanotransferase(s)
EC 2.4.1.21 *see* starch synthase(s)
EC 2.4.1.22 *see* lactose synthase
EC 2.4.1.25 *see* 4-α-glucanotransferase
EC 2.4.1.27 *see* DNA β-glucosyltransferase
EC 2.4.1.34 *see* 1,3-β-glucan synthase
EC 2.4.1.38 *see* β-*N*-acetylglucosaminylglycopeptide β-
   1,4-galactosyltransferase
EC 2.4.1.41 *see* polypeptide *N*-
   acetylgalactosaminyltransferase
EC 2.4.1.43 *see* polygalacturonate 4-α-
   galacturonosyltransferase
EC 2.4.1.65 *see* galactoside 3(4)-L-fucosyltransferase
EC 2.4.1.69 *see* galactoside 2-α-L-fucosyltransferase
EC 2.4.1.83 *see* dolichyl-phosphate β-D-
   mannosyltransferase
EC 2.4.1.91 *see* flavonol 3-*O*-glucosyltransferase (FGT)
EC 2.4.1.101 *see* α-1,3-mannosyl-glycoprotein β-1,2-*N*-
   acetylglucosaminyltransferase
EC 2.4.1.102 *see* β-1,3-galactosyl-*O*-glycosyl-
   glycoprotein β-1,6-*N*-acetylglucosaminyltransferase
EC 2.4.1.111 *see* coniferyl-alcohol glucosyltransferase
EC 2.4.1.122 *see* glycoprotein-*N*-acetylgalactosamine
EC 2.4.1.143 *see* α-1,6-mannosyl-glycoprotein β-1,2-*N*-
   acetylglucosaminyltransferase
EC 2.4.1.144 *see* β-1,4-mannosyl-glycoprotein β-1,4-*N*-
   acetylglucosaminyltransferase
EC 2.4.1.145 *see* α-1,3-mannosyl-glycoprotein β-1,4-*N*-
   acetylglucosaminyltransferase

EC 2.4.1.146 *see* β-1,3-galactosyl-*O*-glycosyl-
    glycoprotein β-1,3-*N*-acetylglucosaminyltransferase
EC 2.4.1.147 *see* acetylgalactosaminyl-*O*-glycosyl-
    glycoprotein β-1,3-*N*-acetylglucosaminyltransferase
EC 2.4.1.148 *see* acetylgalactosaminyl-*O*-glycosyl-
    glycoprotein β-1,6-*N*-acetylglucosaminyltransferase
EC 2.4.1.149 *see* *N*-acetyllactosaminide β-1,3-*N*-
    acetylglucosaminyltransferase
EC 2.4.1.150 *see* *N*-acetyllactosaminide β-1,6-*N*-
    acetylglucosaminyltransferase(s)
EC 2.4.1.155 *see* α-1,3(6)-mannosyl-glycoprotein β-1,6-*N*-
    acetylglucosaminyltransferase
EC 2.4.1.182 *see* lipid-A-disaccharide synthase
EC 2.4.1.186 *see* glycogenin glucosyltransferase
EC 2.4.1.204 *see* zeatin *O*-β-D-xylosyl transferase(s)
EC 2.4.2.1 *see* purine-nucleoside phosphorylase
EC 2.4.2.7 *see* adenine phosphoribosyltransferase
EC 2.4.99.1 *see* β-galactoside α-2,6-sialyltransferase
    (ST6Gal I)
EC 2.4.99.3 *see* α-*N*-acetylgalactosaminide α-2,6-
    sialyltransferase
EC 2.4.99.4 *see* β-galactoside α-2,3-sialyltransferase
EC 2.4.99.6 *see* *N*-acetyllactosaminide α-2,3-
    sialyltransferase (ST3Gal III)
EC 2.5.1.1 *see* dimethylallyl*trans*transferase(s)
EC 2.5.1.8 *see* tRNA isopentenyltransferase
EC 2.5.1.10 *see* geranyl*trans*transferase(s)
EC 2.5.1.11 *see* *trans*-octaprenyl*trans*transferase(s)
EC 2.5.1.17 *see* cob(I)alamin adenosyltransferase
EC 2.5.1.18 *see* glutathione transferase(s)
EC 2.5.1.19 *see* 3-phosphoshikimate 1-
    carboxyvinyltransferase
EC 2.5.1.21 *see* farnesyl-diphosphate farnesyltransferase
EC 2.5.1.26 *see* alkylglycerone-phosphate synthase
EC 2.5.1.29 *see* geranylgeranyl diphosphate synthase(s)
EC 2.5.1.30 *see* *trans*-hexaprenyl*trans*transferase
EC 2.5.1.31 *see* *di-trans,poly-cis*-
    decaprenyl*cis*transferase(s)
EC 2.5.1.32 *see* geranylgeranyl-diphosphate
    geranylgeranyltransferase
EC 2.5.1.37 *see* leukotriene C$_4$ synthase
EC 2.5.1.40 *see* aristolochene synthase(s)
EC 2.7.1.20 *see* adenosine kinase
EC 2.7.1.37 *see* protein kinase(s)
EC 2.7.1.38 *see* phosphorylase kinase
EC 2.7.1.40 *see* pyruvate kinase
EC 2.7.1.66 *see* undecaprenol kinase(s)
EC 2.7.1.71 *see* shikimate kinase(s)
EC 2.7.4.3 *see* adenylate kinase
EC 2.7.7.4 *see* sulfate adenylyltransferase
EC 2.7.7.6 *see* DNA-directed RNA polymerase(s)
EC 2.7.7.7 *see* DNA-directed DNA polymerase
EC 2.7.7.9 *see* UTP-glucose-1-phosphate
    uridylyltransferase
EC 2.7.7.12 *see* UDPglucose-hexose-1-phosphate
    uridylyltransferase
EC 2.7.7.24 *see* glucose-1-phosphate
    thymidylyltransferase
EC 2.7.7.27 *see* glucose-1-phosphate adenylyltransferase
EC 2.7.7.33 *see* glucose-1-phosphate cytidylyltransferase
EC 2.7.7.52 *see* RNA uridylyltransferase
EC 2.7.8.1 *see* ethanolaminephosphotransferase
EC 2.7.8.2 *see* diacylglycerol cholinephosphotransferase
EC 2.8.1.6 *see* biotin synthase
EC 3.1.1.3 *see* triacylglycerol lipase(s)
EC 3.1.1.4 *see* phospholipase A$_2$
EC 3.1.1.5 *see* lysophospholipase
EC 3.1.1.7 *see* acetylcholinesterase
EC 3.1.1.8 *see* cholinesterase
EC 3.1.1.11 *see* pectinesterase
EC 3.1.1.13 *see* sterol esterase
EC 3.1.1.20 *see* tannase
EC 3.1.1.45 *see* carboxymethylenebutenolidase

EC 3.1.2.4 *see* 3-hydroxyisobutyryl-CoA hydrolase
EC 3.1.2.22 *see* palmitoyl-protein thioesterase(s)
EC 3.1.3.1 *see* alkaline phosphatase
EC 3.1.3.2 *see* acid phosphatase
EC 3.1.3.5 *see* 5'-nucleotidase
EC 3.1.3.9 *see* glucose-6-phosphatase
EC 3.1.3.16 *see* phosphoprotein phosphatase(s)
EC 3.1.3.48 *see* protein-tyrosine-phosphatase(s)
EC 3.1.4.3 *see* phospholipase C
EC 3.1.4.45 *see* *N*-acetylglucosamine-1-phosphodiester α-
    N-acetylglucosaminidase
EC 3.1.21.1 *see* deoxyribonuclease I (DNase I)
EC 3.1.26.5 *see* ribonuclease P
EC 3.2.1.1 *see* α-amylase
EC 3.2.1.2 *see* β-amylase
EC 3.2.1.3 *see* glucan 1,4-α-glucosidase
EC 3.2.1.4 *see* cellulase(s)
EC 3.2.1.14 *see* chitinase(s)
EC 3.2.1.15 *see* polygalacturonase
EC 3.2.1.17 *see* lysozyme(s)
EC 3.2.1.18 *see* exo-α-sialidase(s)
EC 3.2.1.20 *see* α-glucosidase(s)
EC 3.2.1.21 *see* β-glucosidase(s)
EC 3.2.1.23 *see* β-galactosidase(s)
EC 3.2.1.24 *see* α-mannosidase(s)
EC 3.2.1.29 *see* β-*N*-acetylhexosaminidase(s)
EC 3.2.1.30 *see* β-*N*-acetylhexosaminidase(s)
EC 3.2.1.32 *see* xylan endo-1,3-β-xylosidase
EC 3.2.1.41 *see* α-dextrin endo-1,6-α-glucosidase
EC 3.2.1.50 *see* α-*N*-acetylglucosaminidase
EC 3.2.1.52 *see* β-*N*-acetylhexosaminidase(s)
EC 3.2.1.68 *see* isoamylase
EC 3.2.3.1 *see* thioglucosidase(s)
EC 3.3.1.1 *see* adenosylhomocysteinase
EC 3.3.2.1 *see* isochorismatase(s)
EC 3.3.2.3 *see* epoxide hydrolase(s)
EC 3.3.2.6 *see* leukotriene-A$_4$ hydrolase
EC 3.4.21.1 *see* chymotrypsin
EC 3.4.21.9 *see* enteropeptidase
EC 3.4.21.12 *see* lytic endopeptidase(s)
EC 3.4.21.37 *see* leukocyte elastase
EC 3.5.1.11 *see* penicillin amidase
EC 3.5.2.3 *see* dihydroorotase
EC 3.5.2.6 *see* β-lactamase(s)
EC 3.5.4.1 *see* cytosine deaminase
EC 3.5.4.2 *see* adenine deaminase
EC 3.5.4.3 *see* guanine deaminase
EC 3.5.4.4 *see* adenosine deaminase
EC 3.5.4.5 *see* cytidine deaminase
EC 3.5.4.6 *see* AMP deaminase
EC 3.5.4.12 *see* dCMP deaminase
EC 3.5.4.13 *see* dCTP deaminase
EC 3.7.1.3 *see* kynureninase
EC 3.8.1.3 *see* haloacetate dehalogenase(s)
EC 3.8.1.5 *see* haloalkane dehalogenase(s)
EC 3.8.1.6 *see* 4-chlorobenzoate dehalogenase(s)
EC 4.1.1.4 *see* acetoacetate decarboxylase
EC 4.1.1.9 *see* malonyl-CoA decarboxylase
EC 4.1.1.37 *see* uroporphyrinogen decarboxylase(s)
EC 4.1.1.39 *see* ribulose-bisphosphate carboxylase
EC 4.1.1.47 *see* tartronate-semialdehyde synthase
EC 4.1.2.2 *see* ketotetrose-phosphate aldolase
EC 4.1.2.4 *see* deoxyribose-phosphate aldolase (DERA)
EC 4.1.2.5 *see* threonine aldolase
EC 4.1.2.9 *see* phosphoketolase
EC 4.1.2.10 *see* mandelonitrile lyase
EC 4.1.2.12 *see* ketopantoaldolase
EC 4.1.2.13 *see* fructose-bisphosphate aldolase
EC 4.1.2.14 *see* 2-dehydro-3-deoxyphosphogluconate
    aldolase
EC 4.1.2.15 *see* 2-dehydro-3-deoxyphosphoheptonate
    aldolase
EC 4.1.2.16 *see* 2-dehydro-3-deoxyphosphooctonate
    aldolase

EC 4.1.2.17 *see* L-fuculose-phosphate aldolase
EC 4.1.2.18 *see* 2-dehydro-3-deoxy-L-pentonate aldolase
EC 4.1.2.19 *see* rhamnulose-1-phosphate aldolase
EC 4.1.2.20 *see* 2-dehydro-3-deoxyglucarate aldolase
EC 4.1.2.21 *see* 2-dehydro-3-deoxy-6-phosphogalactonate aldolase
EC 4.1.2.22 *see* fructose-6-phosphate phosphoketolase
EC 4.1.2.23 *see* 3-deoxy-D-*manno*-octulosonate (KDO) aldolase
EC 4.1.2.24 *see* dimethylaniline-*N*-oxide aldolase
EC 4.1.2.25 *see* dihydroneopterin aldolase
EC 4.1.2.26 *see* phenylserine aldolase
EC 4.1.2.27 *see* sphinganine-1-phosphate aldolase
EC 4.1.2.28 *see* 2-dehydro-3-deoxy-D-pentonate aldolase
EC 4.1.2.29 *see* 5-dehydro-2-deoxyphosphogluconate aldolase
EC 4.1.2.30 *see* 17α-hydroxyprogesterone aldolase
EC 4.1.2.32 *see* trimethylamine-oxide aldolase
EC 4.1.2.34 *see* 4-(2-carboxyphenyl)-2-oxobut-3-enoate aldolase
EC 4.1.2.35 *see* propioin synthase
EC 4.1.2.38 *see* benzoin aldolase
EC 4.1.3.3 *see* *N*-acetylneuraminate lyase
EC 4.1.3.4 *see* hydroxymethylglutaryl-CoA lyase(s)
EC 4.1.3.5 *see* hydroxymethylglutaryl-CoA synthase(s)
EC 4.1.3.13 *see* oxalomalate lyase
EC 4.1.3.14 *see* 3-hydroxyaspartate aldolase
EC 4.1.3.16 *see* 4-hydroxy-2-oxoglutarate aldolase
EC 4.1.3.17 *see* 4-hydroxy-4-methyl-2-oxoglutarate aldolase
EC 4.1.3.19 *see* *N*-acetylneuraminate synthase
EC 4.1.3.20 *see* *N*-acylneuraminate-9-phosphate synthase
EC 4.1.3.21 *see* homocitrate synthase (HS)
EC 4.1.3.27 *see* anthranilate synthase(s)
EC 4.1.3.36 *see* naphthoate synthase(s)
EC 4.1.99.2 *see* tyrosine phenol-lyase
EC 4.1.99.3 *see* deoxyribodipyrimidine photo-lyase(s)
EC 4.1.99.4 *see* 1-aminocyclopropane-1-carboxylate deaminase
EC 4.1.99.6 *see* trichodiene synthase(s)
EC 4.2.1.1 *see* carbonate dehydratase
EC 4.2.1.10 *see* 3-dehydroquinate dehydratase(s)
EC 4.2.1.11 *see* phosphopyruvate hydratase
EC 4.2.1.18 *see* methylglutaconyl-CoA hydratase
EC 4.2.1.20 *see* tryptophan synthase(s)
EC 4.2.1.24 *see* porphobilinogen synthase(s)
EC 4.2.1.51 *see* prephenate dehydratase(s)
EC 4.2.1.54 *see* lactoyl-CoA dehydratase
EC 4.2.1.75 *see* uroporphyrinogen-III synthase(s)
EC 4.2.1.76 *see* UDPglucose 4,6-dehydratase
EC 4.2.1.91 *see* carboxycyclohexadienyl dehydratase
EC 4.2.1.92 *see* hydroperoxide dehydratase
EC 4.2.1.94 *see* scytalone dehydratase
EC 4.2.2.2 *see* pectate lyase
EC 4.2.2.10 *see* pectin lyase
EC 4.2.99.10 *see* *O*-acetylhomoserine (thiol)-lyase
EC 4.3.1.1 *see* aspartate ammonia-lyase
EC 4.3.1.3 *see* histidine ammonia-lyase
EC 4.3.1.5 *see* phenylalanine ammonia-lyase
EC 4.3.1.7 *see* ethanolamine ammonia-lyase
EC 4.3.1.8 *see* hydroxymethylbilane synthase(s)
EC 4.3.2.2 *see* strictosidine synthase
EC 4.4.1.14 *see* 1-aminocyclopropane-1-carboxylate synthase
EC 4.5.1.3 *see* dichloromethane dehalogenase(s)
EC 4.6.1.1 *see* adenylate cyclase
EC 4.6.1.3 *see* 3-dehydroquinate synthase
EC 4.6.1.4 *see* chorismate synthase
EC 4.6.1.5 *see* pentalenene synthase(s)
EC 4.6.1.7 *see* casbene synthase(s)
EC 4.99.1.1 *see* ferrochelatase(s)
EC 5.1.1.1 *see* alanine racemase(s)
EC 5.1.1.3 *see* glutamate racemase

EC 5.1.1.7 *see* diaminopimelate epimerase
EC 5.1.1.10 *see* amino-acid racemase(s)
EC 5.1.1.13 *see* aspartate racemase
EC 5.1.2.2 *see* mandelate racemase
EC 5.1.3.2 *see* UDPglucose 4-epimerase
EC 5.1.3.5 *see* UDParabinose 4-epimerase
EC 5.1.3.6 *see* UDPglucuronate 4-epimerase
EC 5.3.1.1 *see* triose-phosphate isomerase (TIM)
EC 5.3.1.24 *see* phosphoribosylanthranilate isomerase(s)
EC 5.3.2.1 *see* phenylpyruvate tautomerase
EC 5.3.3.2 *see* isopentenyl-diphosphate Δ-isomerase
EC 5.3.99.2 *see* prostaglandin D synthase
EC 5.3.99.3 *see* prostaglandin E synthase
EC 5.3.99.4 *see* prostaglandin I synthase
EC 5.3.99.5 *see* thromboxane-A synthase
EC 5.3.99.6 *see* allene-oxide cyclase
EC 5.4.2.2 *see* phosphoglucomutase
EC 5.4.2.8 *see* phosphomannomutase
EC 5.4.3.2 *see* lysine 2,3-aminomutase
EC 5.4.3.3 *see* β-lysine 5,6-aminomutase
EC 5.4.3.5 *see* D-ornithine 4,5-aminomutase
EC 5.4.99.1 *see* methylaspartate mutase
EC 5.4.99.2 *see* methylmalonyl-CoA mutase
EC 5.4.99.4 *see* 2-methyleneglutarate mutase
EC 5.4.99.5 *see* chorismate mutase(s)
EC 5.4.99.6 *see* isochorismate synthase(s)
EC 5.4.99.7 *see* lanosterol synthase
EC 5.4.99.9 *see* UDPgalactopyranose mutase(s)
EC 5.5.1.6 *see* chalcone isomerase(s)
EC 6.1.1.1 *see* tyrosine-tRNA ligase
EC 6.1.1.11 *see* serine-tRNA ligase
EC 6.1.1.17 *see* glutamate-tRNA ligase(s)
EC 6.2.1.1 *see* acetate-CoA ligase
EC 6.2.1.3 *see* long-chain-fatty-acid-CoA ligase
EC 6.2.1.12 *see* 4-coumarate-CoA ligase
EC 6.3.1.2 *see* glutamate-ammonia ligase
EC 6.3.2.4 *see* D-alanine–D-alanine ligase
EC 6.3.2.8 *see* UDP-*N*-acetylmuramate–alanine ligase
EC 6.3.4.14 *see* biotin carboxylase
EC 6.4.1.2 *see* acetyl-CoA carboxylase
EC 6.5.1.1 *see* DNA ligase (ATP)
ECA *see* enterobacterial common antigen (ECA)
ECB *see* embryonic chicken brain (ECB)
Ecballium elaterium, ligballinol, **1**, 672
ECCDA *see* *Escherichia coli*, cytidine deaminase
ecdysis
  definition, **8**, 265
  and juvenile hormones, **8**, 265
  mediation, **8**, 279
ecdysis-triggering hormone (ETH)
  biochemistry, **8**, 301
  occurrence, **8**, 301
ecdysone
  isolation, **8**, 279, 282
  NMR spectra, **8**, 287
  occurrence, **8**, 280
  structure, **8**, 282
  synthesis, **8**, 287
  transport, **8**, 279
ecdysone, 3-acetyl-26-hydroxy-, biosynthesis, **8**, 292
ecdysone, 2-deoxy-3-epi-20-hydroxy-, synthesis, **8**, 288
ecdysone, 2-deoxy-20-hydroxy-, moulting hormone activity, **8**, 293
ecdysone, 22-deoxy-20-hydroxy-
  moulting hormone activity, **8**, 293
  synthesis, **8**, 288
ecdysone, 20,26-dihydroxy-, biosynthesis, **8**, 293
ecdysone, 22-*epi*-20-hydroxy-, moulting hormone activity, **8**, 293
ecdysone, 20-hydroxy-, **8**, 282
  activity, **8**, 293
  biosynthesis, **8**, 279, 291
  from cholesterol, **8**, 291

mass spectra, **8**, 286
moulting hormone activity, **8**, 293
NMR spectra, **8**, 287
occurrence, **8**, 280
synthesis, **8**, 288
β-ecdysone *see* ecdysone, 20-hydroxy-
ecdysone 22-palmitate, 20-hydroxy-, occurrence, **8**, 283
ecdysone 22-phosphate, occurrence, **8**, 283
ecdysonoic acids
  biosynthesis, **8**, 293
  ecdysone 22-phosphate, **8**, 283
ecdysteroids
  bioassays, **8**, 280
  biochemistry, **8**, 279
  biosynthesis, **8**, 290
  capillary electrophoresis, **8**, 290
  CD spectra, **8**, 285
  chemical analysis, **8**, 289
  column liquid chromatography, **8**, 289
  Cotton effects, **8**, 285
  EI spectra, **8**, 286
  fluorescence, **8**, 285
  GLC, **8**, 289
  IR spectra, **8**, 285
  isolation, **8**, 282
  mass spectra, **8**, 286
  metabolism, **8**, 292
  ^{13}C NMR spectra, **8**, 287
  ^{1}H NMR spectra, **8**, 287
  NMR spectra, **8**, 287
  occurrence, **8**, 279, 280
  optical activity, **8**, 285
  optical rotatory dispersion, **8**, 285
  plants, biosynthesis, **8**, 291
  radioimmunoassays, **8**, 290
  roles, in ecdysis mediation, **8**, 279
  structure, **8**, 282, 284
  structure–activity relationships, **8**, 280, 292
  studies, **8**, 290
  synthesis, **8**, 287
  TLC, **8**, 289
  UV spectra, **8**, 284
ecdysterone *see* ecdysone, 20-hydroxy-
ecdysterone 2-cinnamate, 20-hydroxy-, IR spectra, **8**, 285
Echinacea angustifolia
  echinacein, **8**, 303
  echinolone, **8**, 277
Echinacea pallida, echinacein, **8**, 303
echinacein, occurrence, **8**, 303
echinatine, biosynthesis, **4**, 32
echinenone
  accumulation, **2**, 337
  in astaxanthin biosynthesis, **2**, 344
Echinochloa crusgalli, root inhibition, **3**, 141
Echinodermata
  oxylipins, **1**, 247
  see also sea urchins; starfish
echinolone, occurrence, **8**, 277
echinomycin
  applications, quinoxaline antibiotics, **7**, 444
  bisintercalation, **7**, 488
    with neighbor exclusion, **7**, 446
  specificity, **7**, 448
Eciton burchelli, venom, **8**, 354
ecklonialactone A, isolation, **1**, 216
ecklonialactone B, isolation, **1**, 216
Ecklonia stolonifera, eicosanoids, **1**, 216
eclosion hormone (EH)
  biochemistry, **8**, 301
  occurrence, **8**, 301
ecology
  chemical
    monoterpenes in, **2**, 101
  plants, **8**, **137–196**
  see also chemical ecology
Ectatomma quadridens, venom, **8**, 354
Ectatomma ruidum
  Dufour's gland secretions, **8**, 229
  pheromones, **8**, 229
Ecteinascidia turbinata, ecteinascidins, **8**, 531
ecteinascidin 743
  applications, antibiotics, **7**, 501
  DNA adducts of, **7**, 501
  occurrence, **7**, 501
ecteinascidins
  antitumor activity, **8**, 521
  applications
    antineoplastic agents, **8**, 521
    antitumor agents, **8**, 521
  occurrence, **8**, 531
  structure, **8**, 531
ectocarpene
  biosynthesis, **1**, 8
  roles, **1**, 8
  structure, **8**, 420
Ectocarpus siliculosus
  gametes, **8**, 423
  sex attractants, **8**, 420
  sex pheromones, identification, **8**, 421
ectoenzyme, role in sperm–egg interactions, **3**, 29
ED-110, synthesis, **7**, 600
EDC *see* carbodiimide hydrochloride, 1-(3-
    dimethylaminopropyl)-3-ethyl (EDC)
EDF-A *see* extracellular differentiation factor A (EDF-
    A)
Edman degradation, automated, **4**, 336
edulanes, occurrence, **8**, 234
Edwardsiella tarda, glucose-1-phosphate
    adenylyltransferase, **3**, 469
EFE *see* ethylene-forming enzyme (EFE)
H^{+}-efflux, effects of auxins on, **8**, 31
EF-G, binding, **6**, 202
EF-hand proteins
  occurrence, **8**, 446
  structure, **8**, 446
EF-Tu, binding, **6**, 202
EGF *see* epidermal growth factor (EGF)
egregiachlorides, occurrence, **1**, 216
Egregia menziesii
  egregiachlorides, **1**, 216
  eicosanoids, **1**, 216
E-HODMAT *see* L-tryptophan, 4-[(E)-4′-hydroxy-3′-
    methylbut-2′-enyl]- (E-HODMAT)
11Z,14Z-eicosadienoic acid, occurrence, **1**, 218
eicosanoid receptors, **1**, 280
  classification, **1**, 198
  molecular biology, **1**, 200
  structure, **1**, 198
eicosanoids
  agonists, synthesis, **1**, 186
  antagonists, synthesis, **1**, 186
  applications, pharmaceutical, **1**, 193
  biochemistry, **1**, 161
  biological activity, **1**, 160
    in mammals, **1**, 172
  biosynthesis, **1**, 160, 161, **255–271**
    via arachidonate cascade, **1**, 255
    via free radical pathway, **1**, 171
    via lipoxygenase pathways, **1**, 168
    via P450 pathways, **1**, 168
  definitions, **1**, 160, 207
  early studies, **1**, 8, 160
  from, fatty acids, **1**, 24
  functionalization, **8**, 423
  future research, **1**, 200
  historical background, **1**, 160

metabolism, **1**, **255–271**
  cytochromes P450 in, **1**, 268
  occurrence, **1**, 207
    Actinomycetales, **1**, 208
    bacteria, **1**, 208
    cyanobacteria, **1**, 209
    fungi, **1**, 209
    mammals, **1**, **159–206**
    microorganisms, **1**, 208
    nonmammals, **1**, **207–254**
    plants, **1**, 209
  structure, **1**, 161
  synthesis, **1**, 177
  use of term, **1**, 160
eicosapentaenoic acid, 9-hydroperoxy- (9-HPEPE), biosynthesis, **1**, 216
eicosapentaenoic acid, 8*R*-hydroxy- (8*R*-HEPE), occurrence, **1**, 246, 247
eicosapentaenoic acid, 11*R*-hydroxy- (11*R*-HEPE), occurrence, **1**, 248
eicosapentaenoic acid, 12*R*-hydroxy- (12*R*-HEPE), occurrence, **1**, 248
eicosapentaenoic acid, 12*S*-hydroxy- (12*S*-HEPE), occurrence, **1**, 219, 237
eicosapentaenoic acid, 13-hydroxy-, occurrence, **1**, 222
5*Z*,7*E*,9*E*,14*Z*,17*Z*-eicosapentaenoic acid, occurrence, **1**, 224
5*Z*,8*Z*,10*E*,12*E*,14*Z*-eicosapentaenoic acid, occurrence, **1**, 223
eicosapentaenoic acid (EPA)
  occurrence, **1**, 38, 212
  structure, **8**, 423
5*Z*,9*E*,11*E*,14*E*-eicosatetraenoate, 8-hydroxy-13-keto-, occurrence, **1**, 222
eicosatetraenoic acid, 5,12-dihydroxy- (5,12-diHETE), occurrence, **1**, 236
eicosatetraenoic acid, 8*R*,15*S*-dihydroxy- (8*R*,15*S*-diHETE), occurrence, **1**, 237
eicosatetraenoic acid, 5-hydroperoxy- (5-HPETE) occurrence, **1**, 235
  in platelet-activating factor studies, **1**, 291
eicosatetraenoic acid, 8*R*-hydroperoxy- (8*R*-HPETE), occurrence, **1**, 240, 241, 247
eicosatetraenoic acid, 11-hydroperoxy- (11-HPETE), occurrence, **1**, 235
eicosatetraenoic acid, 12-hydroperoxy- (12-HPETE), occurrence, **1**, 245
eicosatetraenoic acid, 12*S*-hydroperoxy- (12*S*-HPETE), occurrence, **1**, 220
eicosatetraenoic acid, 15-hydroperoxy- (15-HPETE), as substrate, **1**, 170
eicosatetraenoic acid, 5-hydroxy- (5-HETE)
  occurrence, **1**, 222, 230, 244, 245, 249
  in platelet-activating factor studies, **1**, 291
eicosatetraenoic acid, 8-hydroxy- (8-HETE), occurrence, **1**, 242, 247
eicosatetraenoic acid, 8*R*-hydroxy- (8*R*-HETE), occurrence, **1**, 246, 247
eicosatetraenoic acid, 9-hydroxy- (9-HETE), occurrence, **1**, 247
eicosatetraenoic acid, 9*S*-hydroxy- (9*S*-HETE), occurrence, **1**, 221
eicosatetraenoic acid, 11-hydroxy- (11-HETE), occurrence, **1**, 222, 223
eicosatetraenoic acid, 11*R*-hydroxy- (11*R*-HETE), occurrence, **1**, 242, 243, 248
eicosatetraenoic acid, 12-hydroxy- (12-HETE)
  biosynthesis, **1**, 169
  occurrence, **1**, 222, 230, 238, 244, 245, 247
eicosatetraenoic acid, 12*R*-hydroxy- (12*R*-HETE), occurrence, **1**, 248
eicosatetraenoic acid, 12*S*-hydroxy- (12*S*-HETE)
  isolation, **1**, 219

occurrence, **1**, 237
eicosatetraenoic acid, 15-hydroxy- (15-HETE), occurrence, **1**, 222, 223, 230, 238, 247
5*Z*,9*E*,14*Z*,17*Z*-eicosatetraenoic acid, 8,11,12-trihydroxy-, occurrence, **1**, 237
5*Z*,9*E*,14*Z*,17*Z*-eicosatetraenoic acid, (8*R*,11*S*,12*R*)-trihydroxy- *see* trioxilin A₄
6*E*,8*Z*,11*Z*,13*E*-eicosatetraenoic acid, 8*S*,15*S*-dihydroperoxy-, occurrence, **1**, 234
7*E*,9*E*,11*Z*,13*E*-eicosatetraenoic acid, 5,6-epoxy-15-hydroxy-, as intermediate, **1**, 238
6,10-*trans*-8,14-*cis*-eicosatetraenoic acid, 5*S*,12*R*-dihydroxy-, occurrence, **1**, 248
6,10-*trans*-8,14-*cis*-eicosatetraenoic acid, (5*S*,12*R*)-5,12-dihydroxy-, biosynthesis, **5**, 61
6,8,10-*trans*-14-*cis*-eicosatetraenoic acid, (5*S*,12*R*)-5,12-dihydroxy-, biosynthesis, **5**, 60
6,8,10-*trans*-14-*cis*-eicosatetraenoic acid, (5*S*,12*S*)-5,12-dihydroxy-, biosynthesis, **5**, 60
5,8,11,13-eicosatetraenoic acid, 15*S*-hydroperoxy-, as intermediate, **1**, 212
5,8,14,17-eicosatetraenoic acid, 10,11,12-trihydroxy-, occurrence, **1**, 247
7,9,11,14-eicosatetraenoic acid, 5-hydroxy-, structure, **1**, 168
7,9,11,14-eicosatetraenoic acid, 5-hydroxy-6-*S*-glutathionyl- *see* slow reacting substance of anaphylaxis (SRS-A)
eicosatetraenoic acids, dihydroperoxy-, biosynthesis, **1**, 264
eicosatetraenoic acids, hydroperoxy-, biosynthesis, **1**, 263
eicosatetraenoic acids, hydroxy-, biosynthesis, **1**, 263
5,8,11,14-eicosatetraynoic acid (ETYA), as lipoxygenase inhibitor, **1**, 221, 243
5*Z*,8*Z*,11*Z*-eicosatrienoic acid, 13*R*,14*R*-epoxy-15*S*-hydroxy-, structure, **1**, 212
5*Z*,8*Z*,13*E*-eicosatrienoic acid, 11*S*,12*R*-epoxy-15*S*-hydroxy-, structure, **1**, 212
11*Z*,14*Z*,17*Z*-eicosatrienoic acid, occurrence, **1**, 218
(11*Z*)-eicosen-1-ol, occurrence, **8**, 355
eIF-4G, association, **6**, 210
eilatin, occurrence, **8**, 540
ELAM-1 *see* endothelial leukocyte adhesion molecule-1 (ELAM-1)
elastolytic proteases, occurrence, **8**, 398
Eldana saccharina
  eldanolide, **8**, 226
  hexahydrofarnesylacetone, **8**, 234
eldanolide, occurrence, **8**, 226
electron affinic agents, DNA damage sensitization, **7**, 417
electron density maps
  interpretation, **6**, 11
  resolution, **6**, 11
electron microscopy
  cellulose studies, **3**, 566, 578
  immunogold, **3**, 468
electron spin, and J-coupling, **6**, 5
electron spin echo envelope modulation (ESEEM), in lysine 2,3-aminomutase studies, **5**, 211
electron transfer
  involving photoexcited states, **7**, 544
  proton-coupled, studies, **5**, 179
electrophilic assistance, in epoxide ring openings, **5**, 63
electrophilic reactions
  with DNA, **7**, 493
  enzymes, **5**, **315–341**
  studies, methods, **5**, 317
electrophoresis, capillary, **8**, 269
Electrophorus electricus, acetylcholinesterase, **5**, 117, 120
electroporation, mechanisms, **7**, 663
electrostatic interactions, intermediate stabilization, **5**, 27
Eleocharis microcarpa, oxylipins, **1**, 229
elephants

musth temporal gland secretion, **8**, 202
see also Elephas maximus; *Loxodonta africana*
Elephas maximus, sex pheromones, (*Z*)-7-dodecenyl
    acetate, **8**, 202
Eleusine indica, pathogens, **8**, 178
Eleutherococcus senticosus, (+)-syringaresinol di-*O*-β-D-
    glucoside, **1**, 705
elicitors
    cell culture responses, **1**, 784
    in isoflavonoid studies, **1**, 784
elijopyrones
    occurrence, **8**, 596
    structure, **8**, 596
Elk enzymes, ElkP, sequencing, **4**, 291
ellagic acid, biosynthesis, **3**, 817
ellagitannins
    applications, chemotherapeutic agents, **3**, 817
    biological activity, **3**, 817
    biosynthesis, **3**, 800, 817
        problems, **3**, 817
    chemical synthesis, **3**, 817
    dimerization, **3**, 801
    occurrence, **3**, 817
    oligomerization, **3**, 801
    structure, diversity, **3**, 817
ellipticine
    as DNA topoisomerase II inhibitor, **7**, 603
    occurrence, **7**, 605
ellipticine, 9-hydroxy-, toxicity, **7**, 605
ellipticines
    applications, intercalating agents, **7**, 605
    as DNA topoisomerase II inhibitors, **7**, 605
ellipticinium ion, 9-hydroxy-2-methyl-, water solubility,
    7, 605
elliptone, isolation, **8**, 341
elloramycin, biosynthesis, **1**, 480
elm bark beetles *see Scolytus* spp.
elm genes, isolation, **1**, 480
Elminius modestus, oxylipins, **1**, 247
elongation factors
    bacterial, **4**, 370
    binding sites, **6**, 195
    interactions, with sarcin–ricin loop, **6**, 196
    specific, **4**, 369
elongation β3-GlcNAc-T *see* β-1,3-galactosyl-*O*-glycosyl-
        glycoprotein β-1,3-*N*-acetylglucosaminyltransferase
elsamicin
    applications, antibiotics, **7**, 529
    DNA damage, redox-dependent, **7**, 529
elymnia furan, occurrence, **8**, 226
Elymnias thryallis, elymnia furan, **8**, 226
Embden–Meyerhof–Parnas pathway
    of glucose, **3**, 419
    in glycolysis, **3**, 414
    isoprenoid studies, **2**, 52
embryo development, and glycan recognition, **3**, 14
embryogenesis, *N*-glycan roles in, **3**, 52
embryonal carcinoma, cells, fucosyltransferases, **3**, 118
embryonic chicken brain (ECB)
    galactosyltransferases, **3**, 111
    membranes, Golgi-rich, **3**, 111
emerald shiner *see Notropis atherinoides*
emodin
    methylation, **1**, 432
    reduction, **1**, 458
emodin, dihydro-, occurrence, **1**, 430
emodinanthrone, activity, **1**, 431
emodinanthrone oxygenase
    catalysis, **1**, 431
    reaction mechanism, **1**, 432
emodin deoxygenase, nomenclature, **1**, 430
emodin *O*-methyltransferase, catalysis, **1**, 432
enamines, in aldol reaction, **3**, 369

enantioselective synthesis, in bioactive natural products,
    8, 6
encecalin, occurrence, **8**, 337
Encelia californica, encecalin, **8**, 337
endiandric acid A, biosynthesis, **1**, 367
endiandric acid C, biosynthesis, **1**, 367
endocellulase D, occurrence, **5**, 300
endocellulase E2
    occurrence, **5**, 300, 300
    structure, **5**, 301
endocytosis
    chromoprotein model, **7**, 582
    topology, **3**, 98, 3
endo-1,4-β-glucanase *see* cellulase(s)
endoglucanase A, occurrence, **5**, 300
endoglucanase(s), occurrence, **3**, 593
endoglucanase V, occurrence, **5**, 300
endoglycosidases, roles, **3**, 14
endo-α-mannosidases
    alternate processing pathways, **3**, 20
    in Golgi apparatus, **3**, 17
    purification, **3**, 20
endomembrane system
    N-glycan biosynthesis, **3**, 38
    glycosyltransferases binding, **3**, 39
endonucleolytic cleavage, and eukaryotic mRNA decay,
    6, 213
endo-oxabicyclic diacids, biosynthesis, **5**, 355
endoperoxide isomerase *see* prostaglandin E synthase
endophytes, fungal, **8**, 178
endoplasmic reticulum (ER)
    cell fractionation studies, **2**, 359
    and cytochromes P450, **5**, 54
    cytosolic α-mannosidase, **3**, 27
    dihydroceramide biosynthesis, **3**, 89
    gibberellin processing, **2**, 385
    α-glucosidase I, **3**, 18
        activity, **3**, 18
    α-glucosidase II activity, **3**, 19
    N-glycan biosynthesis, **3**, 38, 3
    and *N*-glycan processing, **3**, 17
    glycosphingolipid biosynthesis, **3**, 88, 3
    glycosylation, **3**, 4
    mammalian, α1,2-mannosidases, **3**, 22
    α-mannosidase immunolocalization, **3**, 28
    α1,2-mannosidases, **3**, 17, 148
    and microsomal epoxide hydrolase, **5**, 54
    oligosaccharide biosynthesis, **3**, 145
    oligosaccharide linkage, **3**, 15
    protein folding, **3**, 31
    rat squalene synthase, **2**, 263
endoplasmic reticulum–Golgi complex, glycosphingolipid
        biosynthesis, **3**, 88
endoplasmic reticulum–Golgi–plasma membrane,
        transport pathways, **3**, 98
endopolyploidy, benzyladenine-induced, **8**, 59
endoproteinase, prenyl protein-specific, **2**, 359
endosomal membranes, glycosphingolipids, **3**, 87
endosomes, α-mannosidase immunolocalization, **3**, 28
endospores, in *Bacillus subtilis*, **8**, 401
endothall, calcineurin inhibition, **5**, 154
endothelial leukocyte adhesion molecule-1 (ELAM-1)
    functions, **3**, 57
    O-glycan binding, **3**, 71
    ligands, **3**, 57
endothelium cells
    leukocyte homing, **3**, 57
    surface markers, upregulation, **3**, 298
endotoxin-neutralizing protein (ENP), occurrence, **3**, 181
endotoxins
    biology, **34**, 180
    biosynthesis, **4**, 198
    conformation, **3**, 199

effects, on immune system, **3**, 198
future research, **3**, 229
host cell interactions
 receptor-dependent, **3**, 198
 receptor-independent, **3**, 198
lipopolysaccharides, **3**, 180
supramolecular structure, **3**, 199
synchroton small-angle x-ray diffraction spectra, **3**, 199
see also lipopolysaccharides (LPS)
endo-1,3-β-xylanase *see* xylan endo-1,3-β-xylosidase
endoxyloglucan transferases
 cloning, **3**, 612
 effects, on xyloglucans, **3**, 609
enediolates, as intermediates, stabilization, **5**, 38
enediols
 as intermediates, **3**, 335, 342
 cis configuration, **5**, 36
enediyne antibiotics
 with apoprotein, **7**, 582
 and apoptosis, **7**, 582
 applications, antitumor agents, **1**, 14, 557
 biological activity, **3**, 326
 biosynthesis, **1**, **557–571**, **7**, 554
 classes, **7**, 554, 582
 classification, **7**, 582
 DNA/RNA damage mechanisms, **7**, 582
 DNA damage induction, **7**, 544
 mechanisms, **7**, 556
 molecular modeling, **7**, 557
 structure, **1**, 557, **7**, 556
enediyne core, biosynthesis, analysis, **1**, 570
enediyne(s)
 aromatization, **7**, 556
 cycloaromatization, **7**, 557
 ab initio calculations, **7**, 557
 definition, **7**, 554
 DNA damage induction, **7**, 385, 394, **553–592**
 ionic intermediates, **7**, 557
 nomenclature, **7**, 554
 radical anion, **7**, 557
 radical cation, **7**, 557
 reactivity, **7**, 557
 reviews, **7**, 554
 in vivo/in vitro DNA damage activity, **7**, 554
enediyne(s), monocyclic, c-d distance rule, **7**, 557
energy charge, definition, **3**, 474
energy of maintenance, definition, **3**, 443
ene–yne metabolites, occurrence, **1**, 228
enniatin
 biosynthesis, **4**, 321
 in cyclosporin biosynthesis, **4**, 213
 occurrence, **1**, 538
enniatin B
 biosynthesis, **4**, 235
 cyclization, **4**, 231
 ester bonds, **4**, 226
enniatin synthetase
 sequencing, **1**, 547
 substrate binding, **1**, 538
 substrate specificity, **1**, 550
enod genes, expression, **1**, 328
enolase *see* phosphopyruvate hydratase
enolate anions
 generation, **5**, 6
 stabilization, **5**, 12, 13, 16
enolate intermediates, **5**, 32
 metal-stabilized, **5**, 38
 unstable, **5**, 36
enolate nucleophiles, preformed, in aldol reaction, **3**, 370
enolates, stereospecific protonation, **5**, 39
enolization
 carbon acids, **5**, 7
 mechanisms, **5**, 6

enolpyranose intermediates, biosynthesis, **1**, 583
enolpyranoses, biosynthesis, **1**, 582
(6*R*)-[6²H]-5-enolpyruvyl-shikimate 3-phosphate, as
 substrate, **1**, 601
5-enolpyruvyl-shikimate 3-phosphate, (6*R*)-6-fluoro-
 in flavin semiquinone, **1**, 600
 as substrate, **1**, 600
 synthesis, **1**, 602
5-enolpyruvyl-shikimate 3-phosphate, (6*S*)-6-fluoro-,
 synthesis, **1**, 602
5-enolpyruvyl-shikimate 3-phosphate, 9-fluoro-,
 biosynthesis, **1**, 594
iso-5-enolpyruvyl-shikimate 3-phosphate, biosynthesis, **1**,
 600
5-enolpyruvyl-shikimate 3-phosphate (EPSP),
 biosynthesis, **1**, 593
5-*enol*pyruvylshikimate-3-phosphate synthase *see* 3-
 phosphoshikimate 1-carboxyvinyltransferase
enolpyruvyl-UDP-*N*-acetylglucosamine, conversion, **3**,
 252
enols
 isolation, **5**, 32
 ketonization, **5**, 33
 pK_a, **5**, 33
 stability, **5**, 32
 stabilization, **5**, 36
enone–dienol tautomerization
 occurrence, **5**, 32
 partitioning factors, **5**, 33
 in solution, **5**, 33
2-enoyl-CoA hydratase
 activity, **1**, 51
 occurrence, **1**, 52
enoyl reductase
 catalysis, **1**, 348
 disruption, **1**, 504
 in fatty acid studies, **1**, 500
 homology, **1**, 423
 inactivity, **1**, 337
 occurrence, **1**, 363
ENP *see* endotoxin-neutralizing protein (ENP)
enprostil, biological activity, **1**, 196
Enstar *see* kinoprene
EntB isochorismatase, roles, **4**, 209
Enterobacter aerogenes
 glucose-1-phosphate adenylyltransferase, **3**, 469
 glycogen, **3**, 443
 see also *Klebsiella pneumoniae*
Enterobacter cloacae, glucose-1-phosphate
 adenylyltransferase, **3**, 469
Enterobacter hafniae, glucose-1-phosphate
 adenylyltransferase, **3**, 470
Enterobacteriaceae
 LeLoir pathway, **3**, 203
 lipopolysaccharides, **3**, 185
enterobacterial common antigen (ECA), **3**, 206
 precursors, **3**, 206
enterobactin
 amide bonds, **4**, 226
 applications, **4**, 199
 biosynthesis, **1**, 610, 611, 615, 620, **4**, 209, 235, **5**, 344
 ester bonds, **4**, 226
 occurrence, **4**, 203
enterocins, occurrence, **8**, 543, 597
Enterococcus spp.
 D-lactate, **3**, 247
 vancomycin resistance, **3**, 272, 5
 inhibition, **8**, 595
Enterococcus faecalis
 aspartate racemase, **3**, 257
 cytolysin biosynthesis, **4**, 279
 peroxidases, **3**, 722
 plasmid transfer, **8**, 408

sex pheromones
  conjugation control, **8**, 407
  inhibitors, **8**, 408
  structures, **8**, 408
Enterococcus faecium, van genes, **3**, 272
Enterococcus gallinarum, D-serine, **3**, 247
enterodiol, metabolism, **1**, 698
enterokinase *see* enteropeptidase
enterolactone
  metabolism, **1**, 698
  sex hormone binding globulin studies, **1**, 699
Enteromorpha intestinalis, *Penicillium* spp. in, **8**, 601, 603, 603
enteropeptidase, applications, proteolytic cleavage, **7**, 648
ent genes
  encoding, **4**, 209
  entC
    homologues, **1**, 611
    mutation, **1**, 613
    occurrence, **1**, 610
    roles, in enterobactin biosynthesis, **1**, 615
Entner–Doudoroff pathway, **2**, 50
  of carbohydrate metabolism, **3**, 421
  in glycolysis, **3**, 414
entropy traps, chorismate mutases, **5**, 354
ENU *see* urea, *N*-ethyl-*N*-nitroso- (ENU)
envelope (conformation), definition, **7**, 56
enyne-allene, nomenclature, **7**, 554
enyne-cumulene
  half-life, **7**, 560
  nomenclature, **7**, 554
enzymatic radical mechanisms, studies, **5**, 205
enzymatic reactions, keto–enol tautomerism in, **5**, **31–50**
enzyme-catalyzed reactions
  intermediates in, **5**, 6
  mechanisms, **5**, 6
enzyme cofactors
  biosynthesis, **1**, 826
  oxygen-linked manganese centers, **3**, 345
enzyme–inhibitor complexes, NMR spectra, **5**, 24
enzyme inhibitors, mechanism-based, **5**, 438
enzyme–nitroaromatic systems, superoxide production by, **7**, 540
enzyme purification, in gene isolation, **2**, 206
enzymes
  activating, **5**, 206
  active sites
    reactive intermediate stabilization, **5**, **5–29**
    structure, **5**, 12
  acyl, reactivity, **3**, 267
  amylolytic, catalytic regions, **3**, 459
  and antibodies compared, **5**, 441
  autolytic, inhibition, **3**, 285
  catalysis, promiscuous reactions, **3**, 39
  catalytic efficiency, **5**, 437
    evolution, **5**, 8
    and natural selection, **5**, 442
  components, **6**, 109
  covalent glycosyl, as intermediates, **5**, 284
  decapping, encoding, **6**, 209
  DNA processing, cytotoxic response depression, **7**, 597
  effect of gibberellins on, **8**, 45
  electrophilic reactions, **5**, **315–341**
  Elk, sequencing, **4**, 291
  evolution, **6**, 127
  exoenzymes, occurrence, **8**, 398
  ferrous, as intermediates, **5**, 246
  flavin adenine dinucleotide-dependent, occurrence, **3**, 640
  flavoenzymes, binding, **2**, 272
  O-glycan-specific, **3**, 70
  hydrolytic, **5**, 430

effect of gibberellins on, **8**, 45
3-hydroxy-5-ketohexanoyl, as intermediate, **1**, 354
isoprenoid, **5**, 318
Las, functions, **4**, 295
methylation, DNA modification by, **7**, 546
microsomal, **5**, 62
  mechanisms, **5**, 65
  structure, **5**, 65
  in xenobiotic metabolism, **5**, 65
in organic synthesis, **5**, 59
in penicillin biosynthesis, localization, **4**, 244
polyenzymes, early studies, **4**, 320
proficient, **5**, 368
reaction mechanisms, **5**, 205
restriction, DNA modification by, **7**, 546
selenoenzymes, structure-based catalytic mechanism, **4**, 375
serine, bond lengths, **5**, 119
single-turnover, **6**, 150
slow-binding, inhibition, **3**, 277
steady-state kinetics, studies, **2**, 250
structural features, **7**, 616
transgenic, **3**, 462
see also branching enzymes; cobalamin-dependent enzymes; Cyl enzymes; cytochrome P450 enzymes; debranching enzymes; DNA enzymes; Epi enzymes; Gdm enzymes; Lan enzymes; Lct enzymes; mammalian enzymes; metalloenzymes; oxidosqualene cyclase enzymes; Pep enzymes; plant enzymes; protein enzymes; RNA enzymes; yeast enzymes
enzyme therapy, severe combined immunodeficiency disease, **5**, 73
enzyme–transition state complexes, transition state binding energy, **5**, 76
Eohostimella spp., lignins, **3**, 622
eosinophils, 1-alkyl-2-acylglycerophosphocholine, **1**, 291
EPA *see* eicosapentaenoic acid (EPA)
Ephestia elutella, (*E*)-phytol, **8**, 230
ent-epiafzelechin-(4α→8)-epiafzelechin, occurrence, **3**, 769
19-epiajmalicine, biosynthesis, **4**, 113, 125
7a-epialexaflorine, structure, **3**, 131
7-epiblechnic acid, biosynthesis, **1**, 678
24-epibrassinolide
  12β-hydroxylation, **8**, 107
  25-hydroxylation, **8**, 107
  26-hydroxylation, **8**, 107
  metabolism, **8**, 107
  synthesis, **8**, 100
24-epicampesterol, in brassinosteroid biosynthesis, **8**, 105
2-epicastasterone, metabolism, **8**, 107
3-epicastasterone, metabolism, **8**, 107
24-epicastasterone
  12β-hydroxylation, **8**, 107
  metabolism, **8**, 107
epicatechin
  epimerization, to *ent*-catechin, **3**, 765
  nomenclature, **3**, 748
  oxidative coupling, **3**, 782
epicatechin, 3-*O*-gallo-, condensation, **3**, 783
ent-epicatechin
  chemical synthesis, **3**, 766
  epimerization, to catechin, **3**, 765
epicatechin-(4β→6)-catechin
  nomenclature, **3**, 748
  trapping, **3**, 765
ent-epicatechin-(4α→8)-*ent*-catechin, nomenclature, **3**, 748
epicatechin-(4α→8)-*ent*-epiafzelechin, structure, **3**, 764
ent-epicatechin-(4α→8)-epiafzelechin, structure, **3**, 764
epicatechin-(2β→7,4β→8)-epicatechin
  biosynthesis, **3**, 779

nomenclature, **3**, 749
ent-epicatechin-(4α→8)-*ent*-epicatechin, structure, **3**, 764
epicatechin-(4β→8)-3-*O*-galloyl-*ent*-epicatechin-(4α→8)-
    ent-epicatechin, 3-*O*-galloyl-, structure, **3**, 764
epicubenol
   biosynthesis, **2**, 189
   occurrence, **2**, 189
   synthesis, **2**, 191
epidermal cell layers, effects of auxins on, **8**, 30
epidermal cells, vacuoles, cyanogenic glucoside
    sequestration, **1**, 884
epidermal growth factor (EGF), expression, **3**, 53
epidermin
   biosynthesis, **4**, 202, 279
   expression system, **4**, 298
   gene clusters, localization, **4**, 286
   structure, **4**, 279
Epidermophyton floccosum, activity against, **1**, 691
(5*Z*,13*E*)-(15*S*)-9α,11α-epidioxy-15-hydroxyprosta-5,13-
    dienoate E-isomerase *see* prostaglandin E synthase
(5*Z*,13*E*)-(15*S*)-9α,11α-epidioxy-15-hydroxyprosta-5,13-
    dienoate 6-isomerase *see* prostaglandin I synthase
(5,13)-(15*S*)-9α,11α-epidioxy-15-hydroxyprosta-5,13-
    dienoate D-isomerase *see* prostaglandin D synthase
(5*Z*,13*E*)-(15*S*)-9α,11α-epidioxy-15-hydroxyprosta-5,13-
    dienoate thromboxane-A$_2$-isomerase *see*
    thromboxane-A synthase
epidistenin-(4β→8)-epidistenins, structure, **3**, 777
Epi enzymes
   EpiB 990, encoding, **4**, 288
   EpiC 455, encoding, **4**, 288
   EpiD
     characterization, **4**, 289
     substrate specificity, **4**, 290
   EpiH, encoding, **4**, 290
   EpiP, isolation, **4**, 291
   EpiQ
     functions, **4**, 296
     operator sites, **4**, 296
(+)-epieudesmin, antifeedant activity, **1**, 694
epievodone, as allelopathic agent, **8**, 171
ent-epifisetinidol, **3**, 771
   conformation, **3**, 789
   structure, **3**, 761
epi genes
   epiD, encoding, **4**, 289
   epiE, localization, **4**, 298
   epiF, localization, **4**, 298
   epiG, localization, **4**, 298
epiguibourtinidol-(4β→8)-epicatechin, occurrence, **3**, 775
(*R*)-epiheterodendrin, biosynthesis, **1**, 886
epijasmonate, methyl, chemical synthesis, **8**, 112
(+)-epijasmonate, methyl
   isomerization, **1**, 134
   occurrence, **1**, 134
(+)-epijasmonic acid, configuration, **1**, 134
Epilachna spp., azadirachtin studies, **8**, 331
Epilachna borealis, tocopheryl acetates, **8**, 230
Epilachna varivestis
   antifeedant activity against, **8**, 321
   epilachnine, **8**, 351
   feeding inhibition, **8**, 322
   growth inhibition, **8**, 321, 326
Epilachna vijintioctopunctata, antifeedant activity against,
    8, 342
epilachnine
   biosynthesis, **8**, 351
   occurrence, **8**, 351
epilancin K7
   biosynthesis, **4**, 279
   gene clusters, localization, **4**, 287
(*S*)-epilotaustralin, structure, **1**, 885
(+)-epimagnolin A

demethylation, **1**, 692
   growth inhibitory activity, **1**, 693
epimanool, 2-keto-, applications, antifungal agents, **8**, 181
epimerases, roles, in proteoglycan biosynthesis, **3**, 4, 162
epimerization
   in-chain, mechanisms, **1**, 546
   via peptide synthetases, mechanisms, **4**, 235
epimesquitol-4α-ol *see* melacacidin
ent-epimopanone, coupling, **3**, 777
epinardin D
   applications, antibiotics, **7**, 501
   occurrence, **7**, 501
   possible DNA adduct reactions of, **7**, 501
epinephrine
   effects, on phosphorylation, **3**, 485
   methyl group, **3**, 643
epioritin-(4β→6)-epioritin-4α-ol, isolation, **3**, 776
epioritin-4α-ol, occurrence, **3**, 776
Epipactis palustris, stilbene synthases, **1**, 753
Epiphyas postvittana, (*E*)-11-hexadecenoic acid, **8**, 205
epipodophyllotoxins
   as DNA topoisomerase II inhibitors, **7**, 609
   etoposide, **7**, 609
   teniposide, **7**, 609
Epirrita autumnata, (3*Z*,6*Z*,9*Z*)-1,3,6,9-henicosatetraene,
    8, 207
epirubicin, cardiotoxicity, **7**, 605
episclareol, applications, antifungal agents, **8**, 181
episteganangin, antitumor activity, **1**, 701
episulfonium, from, leinamycin, **7**, 524
(−)-episyringaresinol *see* (−)-lirioresinol A
12-epiteucvin, antifeedant activity, **8**, 318
epithienamycins, occurrence, **4**, 186
epitopes
   genus-specific, **3**, 195
   phase-variable lipopolysaccharide, **3**, 229
2*Z*-8-epixanthatin, occurrence, **1**, 375
epofenonane, structure, **8**, 275
epoxidation, squalene epoxidase, equation, **2**, 269
epoxide–DNA, and intercalation, **7**, 470
epoxide formation, by dehydrogenation of secondary
    alcohol, **1**, 878
epoxide hydratase(s) *see* epoxide hydrolase(s)
epoxide hydrolase(s), **5**, 53
   classes, **5**, 54
   enantioselectivity, **5**, 58
   families, **5**, 53
     α/β-hydrolase-fold superfamily, **5**, 53
   leukotriene-A$_4$ hydrolase, **5**, 54
   mechanisms, kinetic, **5**, 55
   possible stereospecific synthesis, of epoxides, **5**, 59
   regioselectivity, **5**, 58
   roles
     in lipoxin biosynthesis, **1**, 267
     in metabolism, **5**, 58
     in organic synthesis, **5**, 59
   use in chiral vicinal diol production, **5**, 59
epoxides
   absolute configuration, and biological activity, **8**, 207
   DNA damage induction, **7**, 508
   nucleophilic additions to, mechanisms, **5**, 52
   nucleophilic openings, **5**, 51–70
   occurrence, **1**, 210
   protonation, **2**, 6
   ring-opening
     electrophilic assistance, **5**, 63
     enzyme-catalyzed, **5**, 53
     and phenanthrene 9,10-oxide, **5**, 62
   S$_N$1 processes, **5**, 52
   S$_N$2 processes, **5**, 52
   as substrates, **5**, 62
epoxyalcohol, formation, **1**, 232
epoxy allylic carbocations (EAC), in oxylipin biosynthetic
    pathways, **1**, 213

8,9-epoxybicyclo[7.3.0]dodecadienediyne, in kedarcidin chromophore, **7**, 575
3,4-epoxy-1-butene, conjugate addition, **5**, 52
epoxyeicosatrienoic acids, biosynthesis, **1**, 170
10,11-epoxyfarnesoate, methyl, juvenile hormone activity, **8**, 267
(3Z,6Z)-(9S,10R)-9,10-epoxy-3,6-henicosatriene, occurrence, **8**, 207
(3Z,6Z)-9,10-epoxy-1,3,6-henicosatriene, occurrence, **8**, 207
25,26-epoxyhenpentacontadienes, occurrence, **8**, 219
epoxyhydroxyacids, occurrence, **1**, 219
(7E,9E,11Z,14Z)-(5S,6S)-5,6-epoxyicosa-7,9,11,14-tetraenoate:glutathione leukotriene-transferase (epoxide-ring-opening) *see* leukotriene C₄ synthase
(7E,9E,11Z,14Z)-(5S,6S)-5,6-epoxyicosa-7,9,11,14-tetraenoate hydrolase *see* leukotriene-A₄ hydrolase
(24S)-24,25-epoxylanosterol, biosynthesis, **2**, 293
2,5-epoxy-6,8-megastigmadiene, enantiomeric purity, **8**, 7
2S,3S-epoxyneral, occurrence, **8**, 225
2,3-epoxyneral, occurrence, **8**, 225
(3Z,6Z)-9,10-epoxy-3,6-nonadecadiene, as sex pheromone, **8**, 207
(6Z,9Z)-(3S,4R)-3,4-epoxy-6,9-nonadecadiene, occurrence, **8**, 207
(7R,8S)-7,8-epoxyoctadecane *see* monachalure
(9Z)-(13S)-12,13-epoxyoctadeca-9,11,15-trienoate isomerase (cyclizing) *see* allene-oxide cyclase
2,3-epoxysqualene lanosterol-cyclase *see* lanosterol synthase
2,3-epoxysqualene mutase (cyclizing, lanosterol-forming) *see* lanosterol synthase
(−)-cis-9,10-epoxystearic acid, biosynthesis, **1**, 210
12,13-epoxy-9,10-trichoene-2-ol, biosynthesis, **2**, 164
12,13-epoxy-trichothec-9-ene, biosynthesis, **2**, 164
EPSP *see* 5-enolpyruvyl-shikimate 3-phosphate (EPSP)
EPSP synthase *see* 3-phosphoshikimate 1-carboxyvinyltransferase
Epstein–Barr virus, gene, promoters, **4**, 362
equilenin, spectral characteristics, **5**, 39
equilenin, 17β-dihydro-, spectral characteristics, **5**, 40
equilibrium constant, determination, **6**, 23
equisetin, biosynthesis, **1**, 370
Equisetum arvense
  nicotine, **8**, 347
  styrylpyrones, **1**, 761
equol
  biosynthesis, **1**, 815
  sex hormone binding globulin studies, **1**, 699
ER *see* endoplasmic reticulum (ER)
Erannis defoliaria
  (3Z,9Z)-(6S,7R)-6,7-epoxy-3,9-nonadecadiene, **8**, 207
  pheromones, **8**, 14
eremomycin, dimerization, **3**, 282
eremophilenes, biosynthesis, **2**, 5
ergobalansinine, isolation, **4**, 53
ergochromes, biosynthesis, **1**, 429, 458
ergocornine C, isolation, **1**, 534
ergolenes, biosynthesis, **4**, 52
ergopeptines, biosynthesis, **4**, 53
ergophilone A, occurrence, **1**, 384
ergosterol, occurrence, **1**, 379
ergot alkaloids
  biosynthesis, **4**, 51, **5**, 331
  as feeding deterrents, **8**, 148
  occurrence, **4**, 51, **8**, 178
Erhlich, Paul
  dye research, **7**, 428
  magic bullet hypothesis, **7**, 428
Erigon affinis, spilanthol, **8**, 303
Eriocrania cicatricella, **8**, 211

(R)-2-heptanol, **8**, 208
(4Z,2R)-4-hepten-2-ol, **8**, 208
(Z)-4-hepten-2-one, **8**, 208
eriodictyol
  roles
    in legume–*Rhizobium* symbiosis, **8**, 173
    in node gene expression, **8**, 173
  synthesis, **1**, 752
eriodictyol 4′-methyl ether *see* hesperetin
Eriodictyon spp., antifeedants, **8**, 338
erm genes, *ermE*, **1**, 14, 501
erubin A, stereochemistry, **3**, 756
erubin B, stereochemistry, **3**, 756
Erwinia spp.
  carotenoid biosynthesis, **2**, 332, 345
  crt genes, **2**, 332
Erwinia amylovora, S-dihydrophenylalanine, **8**, 178
Erwinia carotovora
  autoinducers, **8**, 398
  carbapenems, **8**, 398
  cellulase, **8**, 398
  exoenzymes, **8**, 398
  exp genes, **8**, 398
  isoprenoid biosynthesis, mevalonate-independent pathway, **2**, 58
  soft rot induction, **8**, 398
  virulence factors, **8**, 398
Erwinia chrysanthemi, shikimate kinase, **1**, 592
Erwinia herbicola
  carotenoid biosynthesis, **2**, 332, 345
  carotenoid biosynthesis gene, **2**, 87
  crt genes, **2**, 333
    crtE, **2**, 87
  CrtY enzyme, activity, **2**, 342
  glucose, **2**, 345
  pigment, accumulation, **2**, 345
  tyrosine phenol-lyase, **3**, 405
Erwinia uredovora
  carotenoid biosynthesis, **2**, 332
  crt genes, **2**, 333
  geranylgeranyl diphosphate synthase, **2**, 85
  in vivo functional assays, **2**, 344
ERYF1 *see* GATA-1
ery genes
  in D-desosamine biosynthesis, **3**, 342
  eryAI, encoding, **1**, 501
  eryAII, encoding, **1**, 501
  eryAIII, encoding, **1**, 501
  in D-mycarose, **3**, 351
  in mycarose biosynthesis, **3**, 342
erymelanthine, biosynthesis, **4**, 43
Erysimum spp., cardiac glycosides, **8**, 156
erythraline, biosynthesis, **4**, 43
Erythrina spp., erythrina alkaloids, **4**, 42
erythrina alkaloids
  biosynthesis, **4**, 42
  occurrence, **4**, 42
erythritol
  biosynthesis, **3**, 393
  in cellulose studies, **3**, 544
erythritol, methyl-, deuterium labeling studies, **2**, 57
D-erythritol, 2-C-methyl-, biosynthesis, **2**, 56
D-erythritol 4-phosphate, 2-C-methyl-, biosynthesis, **2**, 56
erythrocytes
  5-aminolevulinate synthase, **4**, 65
  glycoprotein-N-acetylgalactosamine, **3**, 75
  human, uroporphyrinogen decarboxylase, **4**, 92
  UTP-glucose-1-phosphate uridylyltransferase, **3**, 478
erythromycin A
  applications, pharmaceutical, **1**, 497
  L-cladinose, **3**, 322
  D-desosamine, **3**, 321
  isolation, **1**, 497

structural, **1**, 496
erythromycin B
  biosynthesis, **1**, 498
  free acid incorporation, **1**, 498
erythromycin C, biosynthesis, **1**, 498
erythromycin D, as intermediate, **1**, 498
erythromycin polyketide synthase
  catalysis, **1**, 497
  domains, **1**, 503
  function, **1**, 503
  genetic engineering, **1**, 506
  genetics, **1**, 501
  inactivation, **1**, 517
  isolation, **1**, 504
  organization, **1**, 503
  structural studies, **1**, 504
erythromycin(s)
  analogues, mutasynthesis, **1**, 517
  antibacterial activity, **4**, 200
  applications, antibiotics, **1**, 2, 496
  biosynthesis, **1**, 1, 14, 24, **495–532**
    genetics, **3**, 351
    macrolide core assembly, **1**, 498
    pathways, **1**, 497
  discovery, **4**, 200
  structure, **1**, 497
erythronolide, 6-deoxy-, polyketide synthase studies, **1**,
    14
erythronolide B, biosynthesis, **1**, 498
Erythropodium caribaeorum, chemical defense, **8**, 470
erythrose, 2-C-methyl-, **2**, 4
erythrose-4-phosphate
  analogues, **1**, 579
  biosynthesis, **3**, 417
  catalysis, **1**, 575
  reactions
    with phospho*enol*pyruvate, **1**, 575, **4**, 2
    with pyruvate, **3**, 370
  as starting material, for chorismate, **1**, 574
  synthesis, **1**, 578
D-erythrose-4-phosphate
  biosynthesis, **3**, 393
  reactions, with phospho*enol*pyruvate, **3**, 386
Erythroxylon coca, cocaine, **8**, 344
Erythroxylum coca, cocaine biosynthesis, **4**, 27
erythrulose-1-phosphate formaldehyde-lyase *see*
    ketotetrose-phosphate aldolase
erythrulose-1-phosphate synthetase *see* ketotetrose-
    phosphate aldolase
Escherichia aurescens, glucose-1-phosphate
    adenylyltransferase, **3**, 469
Escherichia coli
  acetoacetyl-ACP synthase, **1**, 29
  acetyl-CoA carboxylase, **1**, 25
  N-acetylneuraminate lyase, **2**, 378
    substrate specificity, **3**, 381
  acyl carrier protein, **1**, 336
  S-adenosyl-L-methionine, **3**, 332
  anaerobic ribonucleotide reductases, **3**, 332, **5**, 217
  apoaequorin, **8**, 447
  aro genes, **1**, 593, 599
  aromatic amino acid biosynthesis, **4**, 2
    regulatory mechanisms, **4**, 7
  aspartate ammonia-lyase, **3**, 634
  base excision repair pathway, **5**, 393
  bio genes, **1**, 826
    mutants, **1**, 830
  biotin biosynthesis, **1**, 826
  branching enzymes, **3**, 480
    overexpression, **3**, 462
  cell lines, **7**, 646
    availability, **7**, 646
    mutations, **7**, 646

chorismate mutase, **4**, 5, **5**, 345, 360, 425
  in cloning techniques, **7**, 646
    disadvantages, **7**, 647
cyclopropane fatty acids, **1**, 63
cytidine deaminase, **5**, 87
  catalytic mechanisms, **6**, 100
cytosine deaminase, **5**, 93
dCTP deaminase, **5**, 94
ddl genes, **3**, 260
2-dehydro-3-deoxy-6-phosphogalactonate aldolase, **3**,
    429
2-dehydro-3-deoxyphosphoheptonate aldolase, **1**, 575
2-dehydro-3-deoxyphosphooctonate aldolase, **3**, 388
dehydroquinases, **1**, 586, 590
dehydroquinate synthase, **1**, 599
dehydroshikimate dehydratase, **1**, 590
3-dehydroshikimic acid degradation, **3**, 804
3-deoxy-D-*manno*-octulosonate transferase, **3**, 518
deoxyribodipyrimidine photo-lyases, **5**, 375
deoxysugar biosynthesis, genetics, **3**, 345
deoxyxylulose phosphate synthase, encoding, **2**, 377
diaminopimelate epimerase, **3**, 257
DNA transformation into, **7**, 662
ebg genes, **5**, 289
enterobactin, **4**, 209
ent genes, **4**, 209
enzyme condensation studies, **1**, 758
  in expression systems, **7**, 646
  expression vectors, **7**, 648
fadD gene, **1**, 47
formate C-acetyltransferase, **5**, 217
formate dehydrogenase H, **4**, 357
fructose-1,6-bisphosphate, concentration, **3**, 476
geranyl*trans*transferase, **2**, 82, **5**, 323
  mutants, **5**, 323
  purification, **2**, 83
glg genes, **3**, 449, 453
  cloning, **3**, 477
1,4-α-glucan branching enzyme, **3**, 444
4-α-glucanotransferase induction, **3**, 445
glucose-1-phosphate adenylyltransferase, **3**, 447, 469
glutamyl-tRNA reductase, **4**, 68
glycogen, **3**, 443
glycogen-branching enzymes, **3**, 462
glycogen synthase, expression, **3**, 485
4-hydroxy-2-ketovalerate aldolase, **3**, 384
hydroxymethylbilane synthase, **4**, 81
4-hydroxy-2-oxoglutarate aldolase, **3**, 382
intestinal infections, classification, **3**, 185
isochorismate synthases, **1**, 611
isopentenyl diphosphate, **2**, 46
  biosynthesis, **2**, 376
isopentenyl diphosphate isomerases, **2**, 71, **5**, 336
  cDNA cloning, **2**, 73
isoprenoids, **2**, 52
  biosynthesis, **2**, 377
ketopantoaldolase, **3**, 409
lacZ gene, β-galactosidase, **5**, 289, 290
lip genes, **1**, 832
lipid A
  chemical synthesis, **3**, 197
  structure, **3**, 200
lipopolysaccharide biosynthesis, **3**, 202
lipopolysaccharides, **3**, 185
  core types, **3**, 187
maltodextrin phosphorylase, **5**, 305
menaquinones, **2**, 54
5-methylaminomethyl-2-thiouridine, **4**, 68
moe genes, **1**, 835
mur genes, **3**, 258
mutagenesis, **5**, 394
mutants, **3**, 445, 473
  distribution, **5**, 396

octaprenyl diphosphate synthase, **2**, 91
  gene cloning, **2**, 92
penicillin-binding proteins, **3**, 266
pentalene synthase, **5**, 330
peptidoglycan, **3**, 249
phospho-Mur*N*Ac-pentapeptide translocase, gene
  encoding, **3**, 263
3-phosphoshikimate 1-carboxyvinyltransferase, **1**, 593,
  599
photoproducts, thymine-derived, **5**, 373
pKSS1 vector, **4**, 133
O-polysaccharides, assembly, **3**, 212
porphobilinogen synthase, **4**, 76
  active site, **4**, 77
  x-ray crystal structure, **4**, 76
prephenate dehydratase, **4**, 5
protein expression, **4**, 289
protein farnesyltransferase overproduction, **5**, 334
proteins, bulk production, **7**, 665
recombinant proteins, **1**, 889
rhamnulose-1-phosphate aldolase, **3**, 426
ribonuclease P, **6**, 153
ribonucleoside-diphosphate reductase, **5**, 171
ribonucleotide reductases, **3**, 329, **5**, 164
  inactivation, **5**, 168
  subunits, **5**, 185
  thiyl radicals, **5**, 177
RNA, sense/antisense, **6**, 75
rRNA
  5S, **6**, 13, 58, 192
  S8 binding sites, **6**, 72
selenocysteine biosynthesis, **4**, 355
serotyping, **3**, 185
shikimate 5-dehydrogenase, **1**, 590, 591
shikimate kinase, **1**, 590, 592
shikimate pathway, **1**, 575
stearoyl-ACP desaturase overexpression, **1**, 42
strictosidine synthase gene expression, **4**, 133
tagatose-1,6-diphosphate aldolase, **3**, 431
terpene synthase, **2**, 202
terpene synthase genes
  expression, **2**, 210
  site-directed mutagenesis, **2**, 202
thioredoxin, **4**, 357
thiyl radical biosynthesis, **5**, 185
threonine aldolase, **3**, 400
transaminases, **4**, 5
transketolase, **3**, 416
tRNA^{Asp}, **6**, 223
tRNA^{Ser}, **6**, 222
tryptophan synthase, **4**, 7
tyrosyl radicals, **5**, 240
TyrR protein, **4**, 9
ubiquinone, **2**, 51, 56
  biosynthesis, **2**, 49
uroporphyrinogen-III synthase, **4**, 90
vetispiradiene synthase, **5**, 330
zeaxanthin biosynthesis, **2**, 337
Escherichia coli B
  glycogen synthases, **3**, 452
  mutants, **3**, 473
Escherichia coli K-12
  characteristics, **3**, 186
  cores, **3**, 187
  3-dehydroquinate synthase, **1**, 581
  glg genes, **3**, 477
  glycogen synthases, **3**, 452
  mutants, **3**, 473
  transaldolase, **3**, 419
Eschscholtzia californica
  berberine bridge enzyme, **4**, 41
  jasmonic acid, **1**, 125
ESEEM *see* electron spin echo envelope modulation
  (ESEEM)

E-selectin *see* endothelial leukocyte adhesion molecule-1
  (ELAM-1)
E-signal, functions, **8**, 407
ESP A$_1$ *see* esperamicin A$_1$ (ESP A$_1$)
esperamicin
  antibiotic activity, **1**, 14
  DNA damage induction, **7**, 385
  in enediyne antibiotics, **1**, 557
esperamicin A, biosynthesis, studies, **1**, 559
esperamicin A$_1$ (ESP A$_1$)
  antitumor activity, **3**, 326
  biosynthesis, **1**, 562
  biosynthetic studies, **7**, 554
  carbamate moiety, **7**, 554
  enediyne core, biosynthesis, **1**, 564
  intercalative binding model, **7**, 574
  K_a, **7**, 574
  methyl groups, biosynthetic origin, **1**, 566
  minor-major groove binding model, **7**, 574
  ^{13}C NMR spectra, **1**, 565
  nucleosome linker damage, **7**, 574
  occurrence, **1**, 562
  radioactive precursor labeling studies, **1**, 562
  sulfur atoms, biosynthetic origin, **1**, 565
esperamicin C, DNA damage, **7**, 573
esperamicins
  activation, **7**, 572
  applications, antibiotics, **7**, 554, 571
  2-deoxy-L-fucose, **3**, 313, **7**, 571
  DNA damage, **7**, 571, 573
  DNA strand breakage induction, **7**, 421
  enediyne moiety, **7**, 554
  occurrence, **7**, 571
  structure, **7**, 571
esperamicin X, x-ray crystal structure, **7**, 569, 571
esperamicin Z, **7**, 572
essential oils
  applications, **2**, 102
  composition, factors affecting, **2**, 147
  occurrence, **2**, 102
esterases
  as antibody catalysts, **5**, 431
  catalytic power, **5**, 104
  future research, **5**, 134
  of α/β hydrolase fold family, **5**, 112
    in esterase hydrolysis, **5**, 103
    functional diversity, **5**, 113
  Michaelis–Menten mechanism, **5**, 103
  structure, **5**, 430
  substrates, **5**, 103
ester–ether linkages, lignins, **3**, 696
esters
  bond formation
    catalysis, **4**, **221–238**
    condensation domains, **4**, 230
  hydrolysis, **5**, **101–137**
    enzyme families, **5**, 103
    homogeneous vs. heterogeneous catalysis, **5**, 103
    mechanistic diversity, **5**, 102
    occurrence, **5**, 101
ESTHER database, access, **5**, 112
Estigmene acrea
  (3*Z*,6*Z*,9*Z*)-3,6,9-henicosatriene, **8**, 207
  linolenic acid, **8**, 207
  pheromones, **8**, 207
4,6-estradien-3,17-one, isolation, **5**, 34
4,7-estradien-3,17-one, from, 5,7-estradien-3,17-one, **5**, 33
5,7-estradien-3,17-one, as starting material, for 4,7-
  estradien-3,17-one, **5**, 33
17β-estradiol, spectral characteristics, **5**, 40
estragole
  carcinogenic action, **7**, 519
  DNA damage induction, **7**, 519

1,3,5(10)-estratrien-17β-ol, 3-amino-, spectral
 characteristics, **5**, 39
3,5,7-estratrien-17-one, 3-hydroxy-, isolation, **5**, 32, 33
estrogens, metabolic activation of DNA adduct
 formation, **7**, 532
ESTs *see* expressed sequence tags (ESTs)
ethane, 1,2-dibromo-, K_m, **5**, 403
ethane, 1,2-dichloro-, interactions, **5**, 404
[1-²H,³H]ethane
 stereochemical studies, **5**, 221
 as substrate, **5**, 219
ethanol, occurrence, **8**, 209
ethanol, amino-, occurrence, **3**, 197
ethanol, 2-chloro-, oxidation, **5**, 192
ethanol, β-cyano-, in oligonucleotide synthesis, **7**, 127
ethanol, 2-mercapto- (BME), **7**, 565
ethanol, 2,2,2-trifluoro-, mutase studies, **5**, 357
ethanol, (*R*)-(−)-2,2,2-trifluoro-1-(9-anthryl)-, in juvenile
 hormone synthesis, **8**, 270
ethanolamine ammonia-lyase
 catalysis, **5**, 273
 occurrence, **5**, 273
 reactions, **5**, 264
 stopped-flow kinetic studies, **5**, 273
ethanolamine phosphate (EtNP)
 in GPI anchor biosynthesis, **3**, 302
 transfer, **4**, 315
ethanolamine phosphate (EtNP)-Man3-Glc*N*-PI,
 biosynthesis, **4**, 315
ethanolaminephosphotransferase, catalysis, **1**, 289
ethene, *cis*-1,2-dichloro-, biosynthesis, **5**, 410
ethene, tetrachloro-, as terminal electron receptor, **5**, 410
ethene, trichloro-, as terminal electron receptor, **5**, 410
β-etherase, catalysis, **5**, 417
ethers, antisense oligonucleotide linkages, **7**, 305
ethers, cyclic bromo-
 biogenesis, **1**, 304
 biosynthesis
 from Rhodophyta, **1**, **303–324**
 via bromoperoxidase, **1**, 318
 via lactoperoxidase, **1**, 307
 functions, in algae, **1**, 322
ethidium
 DNA binding, **7**, 457, 460
 intercalation, **7**, 446
 unwinding angle, **7**, 432
 RNA binding, bulged bases, **7**, 469
ethidium bromide (EB)
 applications
 DNA quantitation, **7**, 661
 DNA structure probes, **7**, 84
 intercalating agents, **7**, 428
 in polymerase chain reaction evaluation, **7**, 658
 use with electrophoresis gels, **7**, 428
ethidium–RNA complex
 major and minor grooves, **7**, 435
 phosphate groups, **7**, 435
 steric clash, **7**, 435
ethyl, β-cyano-, as phosphate protecting groups, **7**, 130
ethyl, *p*-nitrophenyl-, as phosphate protecting groups, **7**,
 130
ethyl, 2,2,2-trichloro-, as phosphate protecting groups, **7**,
 130
ethyl *trans*-cinnamate, occurrence, **1**, 134
ethyl diphosphate, 2-(dimethylamino)-, inhibitory
 activity, **5**, 335
ethylene
 biochemistry, **8**, 91
 biological activity, **8**, 91
 structural requirements, **8**, 93
 biosynthesis, **1**, 128, 133, **8**, 93
 coronatine-induced, **1**, 135
 factors affecting, **8**, 96

induction, **1**, 133
 regulatory mechanisms, **8**, 96
 stimulation, **1**, 127
 via ACC pathway, **8**, 94
 via 2-oxoglutarate-dependent pathway, **8**, 94
 via 2-oxo-4-methylthiobutyrate-dependent pathway,
 8, 94
 discovery, **8**, 21
 genetic engineering, **8**, 98
 and jasmonates, interactions, **1**, 133
 occurrence, **8**, 93
 roles, physiological, **8**, 91
ethylene, bromo-, biological activity, **8**, 93
ethylene, chloro-, biological activity, **8**, 93
ethylene-forming enzyme (EFE)
 identification, **8**, 95
 occurrence, **8**, 94
ethylene glycol
 dehydration, **5**, 188
 oxidation, **5**, 188
ethyl groups, mercapto-, attachment, **6**, 227
ethyl radicals, 1,2-dihydroxy-
 biosynthesis, **5**, 189
 dehydration, **5**, 189
EtNP *see* ethanolamine phosphate (EtNP)
etoposide
 applications
 antineoplastic agents, **7**, 594
 antitumor agents, **7**, 594
 pharmaceutical, **1**, 701
 as DNA topoisomerase II inhibitor, **7**, 603, 609
etoposide phosphate, applications, pharmaceutical, **1**, 701
ETX *see* eburnetoxin (ETX)
ETYA *see* 5,8,11,14-eicosatetraynoic acid (ETYA)
eubacteria
 eicosanoids, **1**, 208
 isoprenoid biosynthesis, mevalonate-independent
 pathway, **2**, 58
Eubacterium limosum
 cyanocobalamin, **4**, 150
 5,6-dimethylbenzimidazole biosynthesis, **4**, 150
Eublaberus distanti
 4-heptanone, **8**, 211
 1-octanol, **8**, 211
 undecane, **8**, 214
Eucalyptus spp., terpenes, **8**, 144
Eucalyptus elaeophora, lignin studies, **3**, 690
Eucalyptus gunnii
 caffeoyl-CoA *O*-methyltransferase, **3**, 671
 cinnamoyl-CoA:NADP(H)-dependent
 oxidoreductases, **3**, 624
 cinnamoyl-CoA reductase, **3**, 653
 cinnamyl-alcohol dehydrogenases, **3**, 656
eucannabinolide, antifeedant activity, **8**, 308
eucarvone, biosynthesis, **2**, 107
Eucommia ulmoides
 hedyotol C, **1**, 688
 (+)-hydroxpinoresinol 4′,4′′-di-*O*-β-D-
 glucopyranoside, **1**, 704
 lignans, **1**, 651
 medioresinol, **1**, 673
 (+)-syringaresinoldi-*O*-β-D-glucopyranoside, **1**, 704
eudesmane, biosynthesis, **2**, 5
eudesmanolides, adducts, occurrence, **1**, 377
(+)-eudesmin
 antifeedant activity, **1**, 694
 occurrence, **1**, 661
(±)-eudesmins
 antiinflammatory activity, **1**, 704
 metabolism, **1**, 692
eudistalbins, occurrence, **8**, 528
Eudistoma album, eudistalbins, **8**, 528
Eudistoma fragum, woodinine, **8**, 527

Eudistoma glaucus, eudistomidin A, **8**, 527
Eudistoma olivaceum
    eudistomin H, **8**, 528
    eudistomins, **8**, 525, 527
eudistomidin A
    calmodulin inhibition, **8**, 527
    occurrence, **8**, 527
eudistomidins, properties, **8**, 527
eudistomin D, 7-bromo- (BED), calcium release
        induction, **8**, 526
eudistomin D, 9-methyl-7-bromo- (MBED)
    calcium release induction, **8**, 526
    ³H-labeled, binding, **8**, 526
eudistomin H, biosynthesis, studies, **8**, 528
eudistomin K
    occurrence, **8**, 527
    structure, **8**, 527
eudistomins
    antimicrobial activity, **8**, 525
    antiviral activity, **8**, 525, 527
    calcium release induction, **8**, 526
    cAMP phosphodiesterase inhibition, **8**, 527
    isolation, **8**, 525
    occurrence, **8**, 525
eudistomin U
    occurrence, **8**, 528
    structure, **8**, 528
eugenigrandin A, in psiguavin biosynthesis, **3**, 784
eugenol
    insecticidal activity, **8**, 337
    stereoselective coupling, **1**, 680
eugenol, methyl-, as oviposition stimulant, **8**, 156
Euglena spp.
    arom pentafunctional enzyme, **1**, 598
    jasmonic acid, **8**, 108
Euglena gracilis
    dehydroquinases, **1**, 586
    glutamyl-tRNA reductase, recognition problems, **4**, 68
    3-phosphoshikimate 1-carboxyvinyltransferase, **1**, 593
    shikimate pathway, **1**, 575
    threonine aldolase, **3**, 400
Euglossa spp., orchid pollination, **8**, 224
eukaryotes
    glycosylphosphatidylinositol biosynthesis, **3**, 6, **295–309**
    isoprenoid biosynthesis, mevalonate-independent
        pathway, **2**, 60
    porphobilinogen synthase, **4**, 76
    RNA enzymes, **6**, 110
    RNA–protein complexes, **6**, 112
    selenocysteine metabolism, **4**, 354
    shikimate pathway, **4**, 2
eukaryotic cells
    acetyl-CoA carboxylase, **1**, 26
    ferrochelatase, **4**, 101
    mRNA turnover, **6**, **205–216**
    studies, **2**, 353
eukaryotic mRNA
    decay
        deadenylation in, **6**, 206
        intermediates, **6**, 206, 210
        via endonucleolytic cleavage, **6**, 213
    degradation, **6**, 205
        via deadenylation, **6**, 209
    3′ to 5′ degradation, and deadenylation, **6**, 212
    poly(A) tails, shortening, **6**, 206
    translation, effects on poly(A) tail shortening, **6**, 208
    turnover, **6**, **205–216**
Euonymus alatus f. ciliato-dentatus
    flavonol 3-*O*-xylosyltransferases, **1**, 737
    flavonone 7-*O*-glucosyltransferases, **1**, 737
eupatoriopicrin, antifeedant activity, **8**, 308
Eupatorium glandulosum, encecalin, **8**, 337

eupha-7,24-diene, GC, **2**, 311
Euphausia pacifica, krill fluorescent substance F, **8**, 457
euph-7-ene, from, 2,3-dihydrosqualene, **2**, 312
Euphorbiaceae, 2,5-dihydroxymethyl-3,4-
        dihydroxypyrrolidine, **3**, 134
Euploea spp., edulanes, **8**, 234
Euploea sylvester, linalools, **8**, 235
Euplotes octocarinatus, UGA in, **4**, 357
Eupomatia laurina, (−)-licarin A, **1**, 679
Euproctis chrysorrhoea
    (7*Z*,13*Z*,16*Z*,19*Z*)-7,13,16,19-docosatetraenyl 2-
        methylpropanoate, **8**, 207
    pheromones, **8**, 241
Euproctis pseudoconspera, (*R*)-10,14-dimethylpentadecyl
        2-methylpropanoate, **8**, 241
Euproctis similis, sex pheromones, **8**, 221, 241
Euproctis taiwana, (*Z*)-16-methyl-9-heptadecenyl 2-
        methylpropanoate, **8**, 241
European eel *see Anguilla anguilla*
European hornet *see Vespa crabro*
European roe deer, farnesyl hexanoate, **8**, 227
europine, 7-acetyl-, isolation, **4**, 31
europium(III)–texaphyrin–oligodeoxyribonucleotide
        conjugate, synthesis, **7**, 163
Eurycotis floridana, (2*RS*,3*RS*)-2,3-butanediol, **8**, 210
Eurygaster integriceps, homo-γ-bisabolene, **8**, 237
Euschistus spp.
    methyl (2*E*,4*Z*)-2,4-decadienoate, **8**, 213
    methyl 2,6,10-trimethyltridecanoate, **8**, 241
    secretions, **8**, 199
eutypine, phytotoxicity, **8**, 179
D-evalose, occurrence, **3**, 312, 321
Evasterias troschelii, 8*R*-hydroperoxyeicosatetraenoic
        acid, **1**, 247
D-evermicose, occurrence, **3**, 312, 321
everninomicin, D-curacose, **3**, 313
everninomicins, trideoxysugars, **3**, 322
L-evernitrose
    occurrence, **3**, 312, 321
    structure, **3**, 322
evolution
    molecular, early studies, **7**, 617
    and point mutation, **6**, 140
    'RNA World' hypothesis, **6**, 146, **7**, 617, 630
exaltolide, structure, **8**, 230
excision repair pathways, mechanisms, **5**, 372
exercise, lactate formation, **3**, 444
Exochomus quadripustulus, coccinellines, **8**, 351
exocytosis, mechanisms, **3**, 98
exoenzymes, occurrence, **8**, 398
exo-1,4-α-glucosidase *see* glucan 1,4-α-glucosidase
exoglycanase, occurrence, **5**, 289, 292
exo-β-1,4-glycanase, occurrence, **5**, 290
exoglycosidases, roles, **3**, 14
exohydrolases, roles, in glycosphingolipid degradation, **3**, 102
Exomala orientalis
    (*E*)-7-tetradecen-2-one, **8**, 216
    (*Z*)-7-tetradecen-2-one, **8**, 216
exo-α-mannosidases, roles, **3**, 21
exons
    binding sites, **6**, 152
    ligation, **6**, 150
    α-1,3-mannosyl-glycoprotein β-1,2-*N*-
        acetylglucosaminyltransferase localization, **3**, 50
exonuclease III, catalysis, **5**, 393
exonucleases
    activity, **6**, 105, 207
    purification, **6**, 208
exonucleolytic decay
    3′-poly(A) tail protection, **6**, 207
    via decapping reactions, **6**, 209
exophilin A

absolute chemical structure, **8**, 601
antimicrobial activity, against Gram-positive bacteria,
    8, 601
occurrence, **8**, 601
Exopiala pisciphila, exophilin A, **8**, 601
exopolysaccharide (EPS), biosynthesis, **3**, 203
exo-α-sialidase(s)
    Brønsted constants, **5**, 294
    inhibitors, **5**, 296
    mutagenesis studies, **5**, 296
    occurrence, **5**, 294
    roles, **5**, 294
exosomes
    roles, in 3′ to 5′ degradation, **6**, 213
    use of term, **6**, 213
exotoxin A, occurrence, **8**, 398
expandase, purification, **1**, 843
expandase–hydroxylase, biosynthesis, **1**, 843
expansins

effects, on xyloglucans, **3**, 609
isolation, **8**, 30
exp genes
    expI, encoding, **8**, 398
    expR, localization, **8**, 398
expressed sequence tags (ESTs)
    databases, hemicelluloses, **3**, 611
    screening, **3**, 58
expression system
    components, **7**, 646
    selection, for cloning, **7**, 646
expression vectors
    for *Escherichia coli*, **7**, 648
    promoter regions, **7**, 647
    types of, **7**, 648
extracellular differentiation factor A (EDF-A),
    occurrence, **8**, 402
Eyring transition state enthalpy, nucleic acids, **7**, 41

F

F3′5′H *see* flavonoid 3′,5′-hydroxylase
F3′H *see* flavonoid 3′-monooxygenase
F5H *see* ferulate 5-hydroxylase
faA *see* alanine, L-*β*-farnesyl amino- (faA)
FAA genes, occurrence, **1**, 47
faAVIA, inhibitory activity, **5**, 333
Fab fragments
  abequose binding, **3**, 322
  catalysis, **5**, 438
fab genes
  fabF, encoding, **1**, 362
  fabH, homologues, **1**, 481
  fabZ, mutations, **3**, 221
Fabry's disease, etiology, **3**, 140
factor-1, isolation, **1**, 140
factor-2
  isolation, **8**, 398
  see also L-homoserine lactone, *N*-butyryl-
factor IV
  isolation, **4**, 154
  structure, **4**, 154
factor F$_{430}$, biosynthesis, **4**, 90
factor X$_a$, applications, proteolytic cleavage, **7**, 648
FAD *see* flavin adenine dinucleotide (FAD)
fad genes
  FAD7, mutation, **1**, 44
  FAD2-1, encoding, **1**, 44
  FAD2-2, encoding, **1**, 44
  fadD
    encoding, **1**, 47
    mutation, **1**, 49
FADH *see* flavin adenine dinucleotide (reduced) (FADH)
fagaramide
  insecticidal activity, **8**, 337
  occurrence, **8**, 304
Fagara xanthoxyloides see *Zanthoxylum senegalense*
fagaridine, occurrence, **7**, 601
fagaronine chloride, reverse transcriptase activity, **7**, 182
fagomine, antihypoglycemic activity, **3**, 143
Fagopyrum esculentum
  glucosyltransferases, **1**, 738
  phenylalanine ammonia-lyase, localization, **3**, 662
  rutin, **8**, 338
Fagus grandifolia
  coniferyl alcohols, **3**, 683
  UDPglucose:glucosyltransferases, **3**, 683
*fah*1 mutants, occurrence, **3**, 642
false hemlock looper *see Nepytia freemani*
Fannia canicularis, (*Z*)-9-pentacosene, **8**, 219
fao genes
  faoA, encoding, **1**, 53
  faoAB, formation, **1**, 53
  faoB, encoding, **1**, 53
  faoC, cloning, **1**, 49
  faoD, **1**, 49
faranal
  absolute structure determination, **2**, 78
  asymmetric synthesis, **2**, 78
  occurrence, **2**, 78, **8**, 237
Farfugium japonicum, green odor components, **1**, 91
fargesin
  antiinflammatory activity, **1**, 704
  germination inhibitory activity, **1**, 695
farnesal
  juvenile hormone activity, **8**, 267

  as starting material, for norsesquiterpenes, **8**, 234
(*E,E*)-farnesal, occurrence, **8**, 227
farnesene, occurrence, **8**, 269
(*E,E*)-*α*-farnesene, occurrence, **8**, 227
(*E*)-*β*-farnesene
  homologues, **8**, 230
  occurrence, **8**, 227
  toxicity, **8**, 144
trans-*α*-farnesene, in plant odor, **8**, 156
(*Z,E*)-*α*-farnesene, occurrence, **8**, 227
β-farnesene, biosynthesis, **2**, 162
farnesoate, methyl
  as juvenile hormone III precursor, **8**, 276
  reactions, with hydrogen chloride, **8**, 267
farnesoate, methyl 6,10-bis(thiophenyl)-7,11-dihydroxy-,
    biosynthesis, **8**, 269
farnesoic acids, dihydroxy-, biosynthesis, **8**, 274
farnesol
  degradation, **8**, 236
  early studies, **2**, 156
  in hydroxymethylglutaryl-CoA reductase degradation,
    2, 38
  ionization, **2**, 8
  juvenile hormone activity, **8**, 267
  as starting material, for sesquiterpenes, **2**, 156
farnesol, (*S*)-2,3-dihydro-, occurrence, **8**, 227
(*E,E*)-farnesol, occurrence, **8**, 227
farnesylamine, inhibitory activity, **5**, 333
farnesylamine, diethyl, juvenile hormone activity, **8**, 267
farnesylation, of proteins, **2**, 354
farnesyl diphosphate
  activity, **2**, 38
  analogues, as substrates, **5**, 332
  binding sites, **2**, 250
  biosynthesis, **2**, 70, **2**, 392, **5**, 318
  in carotenoid biosynthesis, **2**, 331
  coupling, **2**, 9
  cyclization, **2**, 169
    by trichodiene synthase, **2**, 158
    to epicubenol, **2**, 189
  Cys-Aaa-Aaa-Xxx tetrapeptide sequence, **5**, 332
  deprotonation, **2**, 170
  deprotonation–reprotonation, **2**, 170
  diphosphate moiety, replacements for, **2**, 257
  farnesyl group transfer, **2**, 358
  folding, in sesquiterpene biosynthesis, **2**, 157
  ionization, **2**, 8, 157, 193, 194
    by terpenoid cyclases, **2**, 162
  isomerization, to nerolidyl diphosphate, **2**, 156
  localization, **2**, 379
  motifs, **2**, 339
  as starting material
    for aristolochene, **2**, 179
    for *epi*-aristolochene, **2**, 181
    for pentalenenes, **2**, 168
    for squalene, **2**, 108
    for trichodiene, **2**, 158
    for vetispiradiene, **2**, 183
  as substrate, **2**, 7
    for farnesyl-diphosphate farnesyltransferase, **2**, 247
  S$_{0.5}$ value, **2**, 252
  in trichothecanes, **2**, 158
  vinyl analogue, as mechanism-based inhibitor, **2**, 180
farnesyl diphosphate, 6,7-dihydro-, **5**, 329
farnesyl diphosphate, 4,8-dimethyl-, biosynthesis, **2**, 78

[1-^{3}H,12,13-^{14}C]farnesyl diphosphate, cyclization, **2**, 158
cis,trans-farnesyl diphosphate, steady-state kinetic
    parameters, **2**, 159
trans,trans-farnesyl diphosphate
    isomerization, **2**, 8
    steady-state kinetic parameters, **2**, 159
farnesyl-diphosphate farnesyltransferase, **2, 245–266**
    ammonium ion analogues, **5**, 337
    in carbon–carbon bond formation, **2**, 246
    cDNAs for, **2**, 250
    effects of reduced nicotinamide adenine dinucleotide
        phosphate on, **2**, 254
    encoding, aspartate-rich motif, **2**, 250
    enzymology, **5**, 339
    inhibition, **5**, 333
    mechanisms, **2**, 253
    mechanistic studies, **5**, 336
    nonrecombinant, purification, **2**, 248
    product studies, **5**, 338
    purification, **2**, 248, **5**, 339
    recombinant, purification, **2**, 249
    regulatory mechanisms, **1**, 628, **2**, 248, 259
    roles, in abscisic acid regulation, **8**, 83
    solubilization, **5**, 339
    structure, **2**, 253
    substrate, farnesyl diphosphate, **2**, 247
farnesyl-diphosphate farnesyltransferase inhibitors, **2**,
    256
    crtB structural conservation, **2**, 340
    enzyme studies, **2**, 38
    motifs, **2**, 340
    natural products
        compactin, **2**, 257
        function, **2**, 257
        nonadrides, **2**, 257
        phosphinothricin, **2**, 257
        schizostatin, **2**, 257
        structure, **2**, 257
        taboxinine-*β*-lactam, **2**, 257
        viridiofungins, **2**, 257
    steady-state kinetic values, **2**, 252
    synthetic, **2**, 257
        arylalkylamines, **2**, 258
        bisphosphonates, **2**, 258
        cycloalkylamines, **2**, 258
        cyclobutyldicarboxylic acids, **2**, 258
        phosphonates, **2**, 258
        α-phosphonosulfonates, **2**, 258
        3-substituted quinuclidines, **2**, 258
trans,trans-farnesyl-diphosphate farnesyltransferase(s)
    (bicyclizing) *see* aristolochene synthase(s)
trans,trans-farnesyl-diphosphate:isopentenyl-
    diphosphate farnesyl*trans*transferase *see*
    geranylgeranyl diphosphate synthase(s)
2-*trans*,6-*trans*-farnesyldiphosphate pyrophosphate-lyase
    (cyclizing, pentalene-forming) *see* pentalenene
    synthase(s)
trans,trans-farnesyl-diphosphate sesquiterpenoid-lyase(s)
    see trichodiene synthase(s)
farnesyl-diphosphate synthase(s) *see*
    geranyl*trans*transferase(s)
farnesyl group, in proteins, **2**, 354
farnesyl methyl ether, juvenile hormone activity, **8**, 267
farnesyl pyrophosphate (FPP) *see* farnesyl diphosphate
farnesyltransferase *see* farnesyl-diphosphate
    farnesyltransferase
farnesyl*trans*transferase(s) *see* geranylgeranyl
    diphosphate synthase(s)
Far proteins, FarA, binding property, **8**, 390
FAS *see* fatty acid synthase(s)
fas-1A, insertional activation, **1**, 465
FAS2 *see* fasciculin-2 (FAS2)
fasciculin-2 (FAS2), binding, **5**, 114

fas genes
    FAS 1, encoding, **1**, 33
    FAS 2, encoding, **1**, 33
    occurrence, **1**, 33
fatty acid cyclooxygenase(s) *see* prostaglandin-
    endoperoxide synthase(s)
fatty acid desaturase(s) *see* stearoyl-CoA desaturase(s)
fatty acid epoxides, metabolism, **5**, 58
fatty acid reductase, encoding, **8**, 394
fatty acids
    acyl carrier protein, **4**, 340
    biochemistry, **1, 1–22**
    biomethylation, **1**, 65
    biosynthesis, **1**, 2, 5, **23–59**, **4**, 344, **5**, 87, **8**, 203
        in bacteria, **1**, 334
        mechanisms, **1**, 25, 34
        and 6-methylsalicylic acid biosynthesis, **1**, 354
        pathways, **1**, 34, 54
        and peptide synthesis, **4**, 232
        and polyketide biosynthesis, **1**, 500
    biosynthetic interrelationships, **1**, 80
    C16:1, occurrence, **1**, 340
    C16:2, occurrence, **1**, 340
    C16:3, occurrence, **1**, 340
    C18:1, occurrence, **1**, 340
    C18:2
        occurrence, **1**, 339
        synthesis, **1**, 341
    C18:3
        occurrence, **1**, 339
        synthesis, **1**, 341
    C18:4
        occurrence, **1**, 340
        synthesis, **1**, 341
    C20, metabolites, **1**, 160
    C20:3, occurrence, **1**, 339
    C20:4, occurrence, **1**, 339
    carbon atoms, **1**, 24
    degradation, **1, 23–59**
        mechanisms, **1**, 47
    as eicosanoid precursors, **1**, 24
    elongation, microsomal vs. mitochondrial, **1**, 34
    essential, **1**, 24
    fluorination, **1**, 65
    free, in nectars, **8**, 162
    as fuel molecules, **1**, 24
    isolation, **1**, 384
    in lipo-chitin oligosaccharides, **1**, 326
    metabolism, **8**, 204
    occurrence
        fungi, **1**, 450
        marine algae, **8**, 422
    oxidation, **1**, 24, **2**, 18
        early studies, **1**, 54
    β-oxidation, **8**, 204
    oxygenation, **5**, 233
    in palmitoylated proteins, **4**, 15
    as primary metabolites, **1**, 1
    properties, **1**, 334
    remodeling, **3**, 296, 301
    roles
        in acetogenin biosynthesis, **8**, 203
        physiological, **1**, 24
    as source of pheromones, **8**, 203
    structure, **1**, 24
    and tea leaf blending, **1**, 87
    transfer, **1**, 340
fatty acids, carbocyclic, occurrence, **1**, 61
fatty acids, cyclic, biosynthesis, **1, 61–82**
fatty acids, ω-cycloheptyl
    biosynthesis, **1**, 62, 76
    distribution, **1**, 75
    function, **1**, 75

fatty acids, ω-cyclohexyl
  biosynthesis, **1**, 62, 72
  distribution, **1**, 71
  function, **1**, 71
fatty acids, ω-cyclopentenyl
  biosynthesis, **1**, 62, 68
  distribution, **1**, 68
fatty acids, ω-cyclopent-2-enyl
  biosynthesis, **1**, 68
  occurrence, **1**, 68
fatty acids, ω-cyclopentyl
  biosynthesis, **1**, 68, 70
  distribution, **1**, 68
fatty acids, cyclopropane, occurrence, **1**, 62
fatty acids, cyclopropenoid, occurrence, **1**, 62
fatty acids, cyclopropenyl
  biosynthesis, **1**, 64
  distribution, **1**, 62
  function, **1**, 62
fatty acids, cyclopropyl
  biosynthesis, **1**, 64
  distribution, **1**, 62
  function, **1**, 62
  structure, **1**, 62
fatty acids, furan, occurrence, **1**, 226
fatty acids, (*R*)-3-hydroxy, lipid A backbone acylation, **3**, 195
fatty acids, long-chain, applications, antifungal agents, **8**, 183
fatty acids, medium-chain, **4**, 256
fatty acids, polyunsaturated
  biosynthesis, model, **1**, 337
  in mammals, **1**, 161
fatty acids, saturated
  biosynthesis, **1**, 24
  chain elongation, **1**, 34
  degradation, **1**, 7
fatty acids, straight-chain, occurrence, **1**, 2
fatty acids, unsaturated
  biosynthesis, **1**, 7, 34
  cyclization, bromocation-induced, **1**, 8
  desaturation
    characterization, **1**, 35
    physiological significance, **1**, 44
  nutritional adaptation, **1**, 46
  oxygenation, **1**, 8
  temperature adaptation, **1**, 45
fatty acids, α,β-unsaturated
  in plants, **1**, 333
  synthesis, **1**, 332
fatty acid synthase(s), **1**, 451
  biosynthesis, **1**, 464
  catalysis, **1**, 24, 27
  classes, **1**, 29
  constituent proteins, **1**, 501
  enzymology, **1**, 3
  fatty acid studies, **1**, 500
  genes, **1**, 465
  inactivation, **1**, 357
  as models for polyketide synthases, **1**, 347
  molecular weights, **1**, 30
  NADPH specificity, **1**, 28
  occurrence, **1**, 5
  roles, in acetogenin biosynthesis, **8**, 203
  sequencing, **1**, 348, 363, 412
  structure, **1**, 29
  Type I
    active centers, **1**, 32
    activities, **1**, 348
    domains, **1**, 32
    genetics, **1**, 7
    models, **1**, 30
    occurrence, **1**, 5

    subclasses, **1**, 29
    substrate specificity, **1**, 347
  Type II
    binding, **1**, 29
    genetics, **1**, 7
    isolation, **1**, 29
    occurrence, **1**, 29, 5
    substrate specificity, **1**, 347
fatty acid thiokinase (long-chain) *see* long-chain-fatty-acid-CoA ligase
fatty acyl chains, in palmitoylated proteins, **4**, 15
fatty acyl groups
  cleavage, **4**, 14
  release, from palmitoylated proteins, **4**, 14
fava beans, amyloplasts, **3**, 464
FBA 28, applications, **3**, 583
FBAs *see* fluorescent brightening agents (FBAs)
*Fdft*1 gene, chromosomal mapping, **2**, 262
Fe^{II}EDTA *see* ferrous ethylenediamine tetraacetate (Fe^{II}EDTA)
feedback regulation, gibberellin 20-oxidase, **8**, 54
feeding attractants
  fish, **8**, 417
  marine animals, **8**, 417
  Mollusca, **8**, 418
feeding deterrents *see* antifeedants
feeding stimulants
  fish, **8**, 417
  marine animals, **8**, 417
  Mollusca, **8**, 418
fellutamides
  cytotoxicity, **8**, 600
  nerve growth factor synthesis stimulation, **8**, 600
  occurrence, **8**, 599
  structure, **8**, 599
fem genes, mutations, **3**, 264
fenchanes, characterizations, **2**, 104
(−)-*endo*-fenchol, mass spectra, **2**, 137
(−)-*endo*-fenchol synthases, studies, **2**, 130
fenchone
  fumigant activity, **8**, 306
  rearrangement, **2**, 107
  structure, **2**, 104
(−)-fenchone, occurrence, **8**, 224
fenoxycarb, applications, in horticulture, **8**, 275
Fenton chemistry, in RNA metal binding site mapping, **6**, 157
Fenton reaction, **7**, 540
  metal ions in, **7**, 417
fenugreek *see* Trigonella foenum-graecum
fep genes, roles, **4**, 209
Fe^{3+}-PGH synthase, water ligands, **5**, 236
ferns *see* Pteridophyta
ferredoxin-NADP$^+$ reductase
  family, **3**, 339
  hydroquinone, reduction, **3**, 339
ferrichrome, applications, **4**, 199
ferric uptake regulatory protein (Fur)
  regulatory mechanisms, **1**, 616
  roles, **1**, 611
ferrocene–oligonucleotide conjugates, synthesis, **7**, 166
ferrocenes, binding, **5**, 430
ferrochelatase(s)
  catalysis, **4**, 100
  inhibition, **4**, 103
  mechanisms, **4**, 103
  metal specificity, **4**, 101
  molecular biology, **4**, 101
  mutagenesis, site-directed, **4**, 101
  occurrence, **4**, 101
  in porphyrin metallation, **7**, 634
  properties, **4**, 101
  sequencing, **4**, 101

structure, **4**, 101
ferrocytochrome-*c*:oxygen oxidoreductase *see*
cytochrome-*c* oxidase
ferroheme *see* heme
ferroprotoporphyrin *see* heme
ferrous enzymes, as intermediates, **5**, 246
ferrous ethylenediamine tetraacetate (Fe^{II}EDTA)
applications
DNA structure probes, **7**, 89
intron structure probes, **6**, 151
in rRNA studies, **6**, 200
footprinting, **6**, 157
in sarcin–ricin loop cleavage, **6**, 196
ferruginol
biosynthesis, **2**, 228
isolation, **2**, 396
occurrence, **2**, 379, **8**, 245
reactions, with benzeneseleninic anhydride, **2**, 397
ferrulactone, occurrence, **8**, 236
fertilization, mediation, **3**, 45
ferulate, as starting material, for flavonoids, **1**, 733
ferulate 5-hydroxylase
detection, **3**, 642
localization, **3**, 671
roles, in monolignol biosynthesis, **3**, 641
ferulic acid
as allelopathic agent, **8**, 171
antifeedant activity, **8**, 140
biosynthesis, **1**, 18, **3**, 624, 644
bonding, **3**, 697
etherification, **3**, 698
as intermediate, **3**, 629
occurrence, **3**, 620, 696
ferulic acid, 5-hydroxy-
methylation, **3**, 644, 646
occurrence, **3**, 642, 671
feruloyl-CoA, 5-hydroxy-, as methylation substrate, **3**,
650
fescue grass *see* Festuca arundinacea
fes genes, roles, **4**, 209
Festuca arundinacea, ergot alkaloids, **8**, 178
fetuin, **3**, 119
FGM *see* formononetin 7-*O*-glucoside-6″-*O*-malonate
(FGM)FGT *see* flavonol 3-*O*-
glucosyltransferase (FGT)
FHT *see* naringenin 3-dioxygenase
FIAC *see* cytosine, 2′-fluoro-5-iodo-1-β-D-
arabinofuranosyl- (FIAC)
Fibrobacter spp., classification, **7**, 158
fibroblasts
growth factor, **6**, 226
multivesicular storage bodies, **3**, 100
fibromodulin, localization, **3**, 164
figs, seed dispersal, **8**, 165
filter-feeders, chemical defense, **8**, 465
fire ants *see* Solenopsis invicta
fire bee *see* Trigona mellicolor
fire-blight *see* Erwinia amylovora
fireflies
luciferase, **4**, 331, 348
see also Lampyridae
fischerin, biosynthesis, **1**, 370
fisetinidol, **3**, 760
as profisetinidin precursor, **3**, 771
structure, **3**, 761
fisetinidol, tri-*O*-methyl-, biosynthesis, **3**, 772
fisetinidol-(4α→6)-catechin-(8→4β)-fisetinidol,
isomerization, **3**, 774
fisetinidol-(4→6)-catechins, conformation, **3**, 790
fisetinidol-(4→8)-catechins
cleavage, **3**, 773
conformation, **3**, 790
as starting materials, for tetrahydropyrano[2,3-
f]chromenes, **3**, 772

fisetinidol-(4α→6)-catechins, conformation, **3**, 790
fisetinidol-(4α→8)-catechins
conformation, **3**, 790
as intermediates, **3**, 758
fisetinidol-(4β→8)-catechins, as intermediates, **3**, 758
fisetinidol-(4α→6′)-peltogynan-4α-ol, biosynthesis, **3**, 777
fisetinidol-(4α→2′)-robinetinidol, as profisetinidin
precursor, **3**, 771
fisetinidol-(4α→6)-robinetinidol, as profisetinidin
precursor, **3**, 771
fisetinidol-(4β→6)-robinetinidol, synthesis, **3**, 771
fish
chemical defense, **8**, 473
chemoreception, **8**, 417
feeding attractants, **8**, 417
feeding stimulants, **8**, 417
lipoxins, **1**, 237
odorous compounds, **1**, 239
oxylipins, **1**, 236
pheromones, **8**, 230
prostaglandin E$_2$, **1**, 236
prostaglandin F$_{2α}$, **1**, 236
prostaglandins
in non-reproductive tissues, **1**, 236
in reproduction, **1**, 237
taste sensitivity, **8**, 417
trioxilins, **1**, 237
UDP-*N*-acetylglucosamine:R$_1$(R$_2$)Manα1-
6R$_3$[Glc*N*Ac to Manα1-6] β-1,4-*N*-
acetylglucosaminyltransferase VI, **3**, 55
see also Amphiprion ocellaris; *Carassius auratus*;
Ictalusus punctatus; *Oncorhynchus mykiss*; puffer fish;
Salmo gairdneri; *Salvelinus fontinalis*; starfish
FK506
applications, immunosuppressive agents, **1**, 518, 2
biosynthesis, **1**, 75, 518
genetics, **1**, 14
immunosuppressant activity, **1**, 518
occurrence, **1**, 520
FK520 *see* ascomycin
Flacourtiaceae
fatty acids, **1**, 68
metabolites, **1**, 70
flambamycin, D-curacose, **3**, 313
FLAP *see* 5-lipoxygenase activating protein (FLAP)
flatworms
symbiosis, **8**, 426
see also Amphiscolops spp.
flavan, 2*S*-7,3′-dihydroxy-4′-methoxy-, biosynthesis, **3**,
781
flavan, trimethoxy-, structure, **3**, 752
(2*R*,3*S*,4*S*)-flavan-2,3-*trans*-3,4-*cis*-diols, reduction, **1**,
729
flavan-3,4-diols
as A-ring quinone methide electrophiles, **3**, 753
biosynthesis, **1**, 715, 717
co-occurrence, with flavans, **3**, 752
definitions, **3**, 748
as flavan-4-carbocation precursors, **3**, 753
from, dihydroflavonols, **1**, 727
as incipient electrophiles, **3**, 758
as intermediates, **3**, 750
roles, in proanthocyanidin biosynthesis, **3**, 750, 753
as starting materials, for anthocyanidins, **1**, 718
substitution, **3**, 755
2,4-*trans*-flavan-4-ol, 4′,5,7-trimethoxy-, isolation, **3**, 756
(2*S*)-flavan-4-ol:NADP$^+$ 4-oxidoreductase *see* flavanone
4-reductase (FNR)
(2*R*,3*S*)-flavan-2,3-*trans*-3-ols, biosynthesis, **1**, 729
flavan-3-ols
4α-benzyl thioethers, biosynthesis, **3**, 758
4β-benzyl thioethers, biosynthesis, **3**, 758
biosynthesis, **1**, 715

C-4 thioethers, as incipient electrophiles, **3**, 758
cleavage, **3**, 752
  as intermediates, **3**, 750
  nucleophilicity, **3**, 752
  oligomers, **3**, 782
  phenol oxidative coupling, **3**, 752
  rearrangement, base-catalyzed, **3**, 765
  roles, in proanthocyanidin biosynthesis, **3**, 750, 752
flavan-3-ols, 4-aryl-
  aromatic quadrant rule, **3**, 764
  CD spectra, **3**, 763
flavan-3-ols, 2,3-*cis*-3,4-*trans*-4-aryl-, biosynthesis, **3**, 755
flavan-3-ols, 8-[1-(2-hydroxyethylsulfanyl)ethyl]-,
    biosynthesis, **3**, 791
flavan-4-ols
  biosynthesis, **3**, 756
  reactions, with mercaptoacetic acid, **3**, 758
  reduction, **3**, 750
  roles, in proanthocyanidin biosynthesis, **3**, 750
6-flavan-3-ols, 4α-(2-hydroxymethylsulfanyl)-,
    biosynthesis, **3**, 791
flavanone, as starting material, for isoflavone, **1**, 791
2*S*-flavanone, reduction, **3**, 777
flavanone 2-hydroxylase, purification, **1**, 793
flavanone 3-hydroxylase (FHT) *see* naringenin 3-
    dioxygenase
flavanone lyase(s) (decyclizing) *see* chalcone isomerase(s)
flavanone 4-reductase (FNR)
  activity, **1**, 728
  biochemistry, **1**, 727
  genetics, **1**, 729
  molecular biology, **1**, 729
flavanones
  biosynthesis, **1**, 715, 752
  co-occurrence, with flavans, **3**, 752
  from, chalcones, **1**, 717
  hydroxylation, **1**, 717
  as intermediates, **1**, 717
  as substrates, **1**, 793
  toxicity, **8**, 141
(2*S*)-flavanones
  biosynthesis, **1**, 722
  reduction, **1**, 728
(−)-(2*S*)-flavanones, as substrates, **1**, 790
flavans
  co-occurrence, **3**, 752
  roles, in proanthocyanidin biosynthesis, **3**, 750, 752
  as starting materials, for quinone methides, **3**, 752
flavans, deoxotetrahydrochalcone-, biosynthesis, **3**, 781
flavan-4-thioethers, as incipient electrophiles, **3**, 758
Flaveria bidentis, 7-*O*-sulfotransferases, **1**, 740
Flaveria chloraefolia
  flavonol 3-*O*-sulfotransferase, **1**, 740
  flavonol sulfotransferases, **1**, 741
flavin
  oxidized, photodimer cleavage sensitization, **5**, 384
  reduced, photodimer cleavage sensitization, **5**, 384
flavin adenine dinucleotide-dependent enzymes,
    occurrence, **3**, 640
flavin adenine dinucleotide (FAD)
  in carotenoid biosynthesis, **2**, 341
  occurrence, **3**, 339
flavin adenine dinucleotide (FAD), 5-deaza-, substitution,
    1, 599
flavin adenine dinucleotide (reduced) (FADH), as
    cofactor, **5**, 375
flavin mononucleotides
  binding, **1**, 600
  and chorismate synthase, **1**, 599
  release, **4**, 289
flavin oxidoreductases, **1**, 464
flavin semiquinone(s)
  biosynthesis, **1**, 600, **3**, 339

characterization, **5**, 385
flavipin, structure, **1**, 411
Flavobacterium spp.
  ACV synthetase, encoding, **1**, 840
  carotenoid biosynthesis, **2**, 323
  crt genes, **2**, 337
  haloalcohol dehalogenases, **5**, 408
  isochorismate synthases, **1**, 611
flavocristamides
  DNA polymerase α inhibition, **8**, 598
  occurrence, **8**, 598
  structure, **8**, 598
flavodoxin
  binding, **5**, 185
  in biotin biosynthesis, **1**, 831
flavodoxin reductase
  binding, **5**, 185
  in biotin biosynthesis, **1**, 831
flavoenzymes, binding, **2**, 272
flavone, 7,4′-dihydroxy-, biosynthesis, **1**, 795
flavone, 5-hydroxy-6,7-methylenedioxy-, as zoospore
    attractant, **8**, 175
flavones, biosynthesis, **1**, 715, 717
flavones, 2′-hydroxy-, chelating activity, **1**, 736
flavone synthases (FNSs)
  biochemistry, **1**, 724
  FNS I
    catalytic mechanisms, **1**, 725
    occurrence, **1**, 724
    purification, **1**, 724
  FNS II
    activity, **1**, 724
    catalytic mechanisms, **1**, 725
    occurrence, **1**, 724
  genetics, **1**, 725
  molecular biology, **1**, 725
  occurrence, **1**, 724
flavonoid carboxylic esters
  biochemistry, **1**, 741
  biosynthesis, **1**, 741
  genetics, **1**, 742
  molecular biology, **1**, 742
flavonoid 3′,5′-hydroxylase
  activity, **1**, 735
  cDNA clones, isolation, **1**, 736
flavonoid 3′-hydroxylase (F3′H) *see* flavonoid 3′-
    monooxygenase
flavonoid 3′-*O*-methyltransferase, occurrence, **1**, 739
flavonoid methyltransferases, classification, **1**, 739
flavonoid 3′-monooxygenase, activity, **1**, 735, 736
flavonoid, NADPH:oxygen oxidoreductase (3′-
    hydroxylating) *see* flavonoid 3′-monooxygenase
flavonoid pigments, roles, in ultraviolet patterning, **8**, 160
flavonoids
  acylation, **1**, 740
  antifungal activity, **8**, 181
  antioxidant activity, **1**, 817
  applications, **1**, 714
  A-ring hydroxylation, **1**, 733
  biosynthesis, **1**, 2, 19, **713–748**, **3**, 750
    theories, **1**, 715
  B-ring hydroxylation, **1**, 733
    biochemistry, **1**, 734
    genetics, **1**, 736
    molecular biology, **1**, 736
  classes, biosynthesis, **1**, 721
  classification, **1**, 714
  cloning, **1**, 19
  diversity, **1**, 733
  early studies, **1**, 715
  effects, on seed dispersal, **8**, 167
  from
    4-coumarate, **1**, 733

dihydroflavonols, **3**, 750
  ferulate, **1**, 733
  sinapate, **1**, 733
future research, **1**, 742
glutathione transfer
  biochemistry, **1**, 742
  genetics, **1**, 742
  molecular biology, **1**, 742
glycosylation
  biochemistry, **1**, 737
  genetics, **1**, 738
  molecular biology, **1**, 738
insecticidal activity, **8**, 338
methylation
  biochemistry, **1**, 739
  genetics, **1**, 740
  molecular biology, **1**, 740
modification, **1**, 733
nucleophilicity, **3**, 760
oxidative coupling, **3**, 782
pathways, **1**, 715
precursors
  biosynthesis, **1**, 718
  enzymes, **1**, 716
prenylation, **1**, 742
reduced nucleophilicity, **3**, 761
roles, **1**, 714
  defensive, **8**, 141
  in legume–*Rhizobium* symbiosis, **8**, 173
  in node gene expression, **8**, 173
secretion, **1**, 326
structure, **1**, **2**, 714, 774
toxicity, **8**, 141
flavonoid sulfate esters
  biochemistry, **1**, 740
  biosynthesis, **1**, 740
  genetics, **1**, 741
  molecular biology, **1**, 741
flavonol, 5,7,3′,4′-tetrahydroxy- *see* quercetin
flavonol, (2*R*,3*S*)-7,8,3′,4′-tetrahydroxydihydro-,
    occurrence, **3**, 750
flavonol 3-*O*-glucosides, occurrence, **1**, 741
flavonol 3-*O*-glucosyltransferase (FGT)
  in anthocyanin biosynthesis, **1**, 737
  biochemistry, **1**, 731
  cDNA clones, isolation, **1**, 732
  genetics, **1**, 731
  molecular biology, **1**, 731
  occurrence, **1**, 731
flavonol 6-hydroxylase, nomenclature, **1**, 733
flavonols
  biosynthesis, **1**, 715
  co-occurrence, with flavans, **3**, 752
  6-hydroxylation, **1**, 733
  8-hydroxylation, **1**, 733
  yellow, roles in ultraviolet patterning, **8**, 160
flavonols, dihydro-
  biosynthesis, **1**, 715
  as starting materials
    for flavan-3,4-diols, **1**, 727
    for flavonoids, **3**, 750
flavonols, 2,3-*cis*-dihydro-, isolation, **3**, 750
flavonols, 2′-hydroxy-, chelating activity, **1**, 736
flavonol 3-*O*-sulfotransferase, characterization, **1**, 740
flavonol sulfotransferases
  cDNA clones, **1**, 741
    isolation, **1**, 741
flavonol synthase (FLS)
  activity, **1**, 726
  biochemistry, **1**, 726
  cDNA clones, isolation, **1**, 727
  genetics, **1**, 727
  molecular biology, **1**, 727

occurrence, **1**, 726
flavonol 3-*O*-xylosyltransferases, purification, **1**, 737
flavonone 7-*O*-glucosyltransferases, occurrence, **1**, 737
flavorings, terpenoids, **2**, 212
flavoskyrin
  biosynthesis, **1**, 431
  occurrence, **1**, 374
flax *see Linum usitatissimum*
flea beetle *see Phyllotetra cruciferae*
Fleming, Sir Alexander (1881–1955), penicillin discovery,
    4, 160, 200, 319
Flexi-Di, x-ray crystal structure, **7**, 446
flies
  peripheral nervous system, development, **3**, 24
  spiroacetals, **8**, 212
  see also caddis flies; canthariphilous flies; *Fannia
    canicularis*; fruit flies; *Lycoriella mali*; *Musca
    domestica*; sawflies; Sciaridae; tsetse flies
'flippase' protein, model, **3**, 265
flooding, effect on ethylene biosynthesis, **8**, 96
floral volatiles
  and headspace analysis, **8**, 161
  roles, in pollination, **8**, 161
Florey, Sir Howard Walter, Baron Florey (1898–1968),
    antibiotic studies, **4**, 200
florigen, identification problems, **8**, 22
flosulide, prostaglandin-endoperoxide synthase
    inhibition, **5**, 252
flowers
  flavonoid studies, **1**, 715
  pigments, **8**, 157
    blue, **8**, 159
  senescence, **1**, 133
  ultraviolet patterning, **8**, 160
  yellow coloration, **1**, 736
FLS *see* flavonol synthase (FLS)
fluidity, and lipid A, **3**, 198
fluorene, 2-*N*,*N*-acetoxyacetylamino- (N-AcO-AAF),
    applications, DNA structure probes, **7**, 96
fluorene, *N*-2-acetylamino-, carcinogenicity, **3**, 116
fluorene, 2-amino-, 2D-NMR, **7**, 470
fluorene, *N*-(2′-deoxyguanosin-8-yl)-2-(acetylamino)-,
    roles, in mutagenesis, **7**, 223
fluorene, diazo-, occurrence, **7**, 541
fluorescein, oligonucleotide labeling, **6**, 229
fluorescein isothiocyanate, reactions, with
    aminoalkylated oligonucleotides, **7**, 193
fluorescence, guanosine-specific, **6**, 227
fluorescent brightening agents (FBAs), applications, in
    cellulose studies, **3**, 583
fluorescent dyes, interactions, with phosphorothioates, **6**,
    223
fluorescent labels, for oligoribonucleotides, **6**, 227
fluorides, allylic, synthesis, **5**, 335
fluorides, 5-fluoroglycosyl, as reagents, **5**, 287
fluoroacetate
  insect sequestration, **8**, 152
  toxicity, **8**, 148
fluoroacetate dehalogenase(s), expression, **5**, 407
fluorophores
  chemical insertion, in RNA, **6**, 76
  groove-binding, **7**, 238
fluvastatin
  applications, clinical, **2**, 246
  in rat squalene synthase activity, **2**, 259
FM *see* fosfomycin (FM)
FMOC *see* carbonyl, fluorenylmethoxy (FMOC)
FNR *see* ferredoxin-NADP⁺ reductase; flavanone 4-
    reductase (FNR)
Foeniculum vulgare, (−)-*endo*-fenchol synthases, **2**, 130
folate, 10-formyltetrahydro-, occurrence, **8**, 209
folate, methylenetetrahydro-, biosynthesis, **3**, 397
folate, 5,10-methylenetetrahydro-, occurrence, **8**, 209

folate coenzymes, biosynthesis, **5**, 344
folic acid, tetrahydro- (THF)
  in ginkgolide biosynthesis, **2**, 386
  structure, **1**, 612
Fomes spp., tannin degradation, **3**, 819
Fomes annosus, infection, **1**, 691
fom genes
  *fom*1
    cloning, **1**, 877
    homology, **1**, 877
  *fom*3, cloning, **1**, 877
  *fom*4, cloning, **1**, 877
fonsecin, occurrence, **1**, 419
food additives, galactomannans, **3**, 8
formacetals, antisense oligonucleotide linkages, **7**, 305
formaldehyde
  biosynthesis, **3**, 381, **5**, 408
  DNA cross-linking by, **7**, 502
  from, trimethylamine, **3**, 411
formamide, biosynthesis, **8**, 183
formamidine, in oligonucleotide synthesis, **7**, 123
formamidine, dimethyl-, applications, group protection, **6**, 87
formate, neryl, occurrence, **8**, 209, 222
formate, (1*R*,3*R*,5*R*,7*R*)-1,3,5,7-tetramethyldecyl *see* lardolure
formate *C*-acetyltransferase, **3**, 332
  activating enzyme, **5**, 217
  activation, **1**, 831, **5**, 217
  catalysis, **5**, 185
  glycyl radicals in, **5**, 185
  homology, **3**, 345
  protein radical generation, **5**, 206
formate dehydrogenase H, TGA codon, **4**, 357
Formica spp.
  geranylgeraniol, **8**, 229
  mellein, **8**, 241
formic acid
  as ant venom, **8**, 356
  biosynthesis, **8**, 356
  occurrence, **8**, 209, 359
formic acid, phosphono-
  formation, **1**, 869
  as metabolite, **1**, 869
Formica lugubris, undecane, **8**, 214
Formica rufa, mellein, **8**, 241
formononetin
  effects on infertility, **1**, 782
  half-life, **1**, 812
  3'-hydroxylation, **1**, 802
  as isoflavonoid precursors, **1**, 799
  mammary gland proliferation stimulation, **1**, 782
  occurrence, **1**, 774
formononetin, 2'-hydroxy-
  biosynthesis, **1**, 795
  reduction, **1**, 795
formononetin, 3'-hydroxy- *see* calycosin
formononetin 7-*O*-glucoside-6''-*O*-malonate (FGM), occurrence, **1**, 780, 806
formononetin,NADPH:oxygen oxidoreductase (2'-hydroxylating) *see* isoflavone, 2'-hydroxylase
formycin
  isolation, **5**, 74
  as substrate, **5**, 74
forskolin, effects, on hepatoma cells, **3**, 53
Forssman hapten, biosynthesis, **3**, 124
Forsythia spp.
  cDNA encoding, **1**, 654
  lignans, **1**, 704
    biosynthetic pathways, **1**, 662
Forsythia europaea, (+)-pinoresinol, **1**, 645
Forsythia intermedia
  (−)-arctigenin, **1**, 645

laccase, **3**, 714
lignans, **1**, 662
  optical purity, **1**, 651
lignins, **3**, 733
matairesinol *O*-methyltransferase, **1**, 667
(+)-pinoresinol/(+)-lariciresinol reductase, **1**, 663
xylem cells, **3**, 733
Forsythia koreana, (+)-pinoresinol/(+)-lariciresinol reductase, **1**, 665
Forsythia suspensa
  dirigent proteins, **3**, 733
  hydrogen peroxide biosynthesis, **3**, 721
  lignans, **1**, 662
fortimicin A, *C*-methylation, **1**, 871
FosA
  mechanisms, **5**, 67
  sequence similarity, **5**, 67
  structure, **5**, 67
FosB
  sequence similarity, **5**, 67
  structure, **5**, 67
fosfazinomycin, isolation, **1**, 865
fosfomycin diphosphate, biosynthesis, **1**, 878
fosfomycin diphosphate phosphotransferase, encoding, **1**, 878
fosfomycin (FM)
  alkylation, **3**, 252
  applications, antibiotics, **5**, 53, 62, 66
  biosynthesis, **1**, 20, **865–880**
    pathways, **1**, 867, 875
  biosynthetic genes, molecular cloning, **1**, 876
  complexation, **1**, 593
  as enzyme inhibitor, **3**, 275
  irreversible inactivation, **1**, 878
  isolation, **1**, 865
  mechanisms, **5**, 66
  occurrence, **1**, 869, 875, 876, **5**, 66
  oxirane ring, **5**, 53
  structure, **5**, 62
  see also phosphonic acid, (1*R*,2*S*)-1,2-epoxypropyl-
fosfomycin monophosphate, biosynthesis, **1**, 878
fosfomycin monophosphate phosphotransferase, encoding, **1**, 878
fosfomycin resistance proteins, **5**, 61
  mechanisms, **5**, 66
  relationships, with other metalloenzymes, **5**, 67
  structure, **5**, 66
fosmidomycin, isolation, **1**, 865
fossils, plants, **1**, 645
Fpg protein, in DNA repair, **7**, 410
FPL-55712, as slow reacting substance of anaphylaxis antagonist, **1**, 191
Fpmp *see* piperidin-4-yl, 1-[(2-fluoro)phenyl]-4-methoxy-(Fpmp)
FPP *see* farnesyl diphosphate
FPPases *see* geranyl*trans*transferase(s)
FR 31564 *see* fosmidomycin
FR 33289
  biosynthesis, **1**, 869
    pathways, **1**, 867
  isolation, **1**, 865
FR 66979
  DNA damage induction, **7**, 518
  reduction-dependent DNA reaction, **7**, 518
FR 900482
  DNA damage induction, **7**, 518
  reduction-dependent DNA reaction, **7**, 518
Fractogel, in oligonucleotide synthesis, **7**, 113
Fractogel TMAE-650, high resolution anion exchange fast liquid chromatography, **4**, 327
Fragaria ananassa Duch, phenylalanine ammonia-lyase, **3**, 659
fragrances, terpenoids, **2**, 212

fragranol, occurrence, **8**, 224
Franklin, Rosalind Elsie (1920–58), DNA structure
    studies, **7**, 81
Frankliniella occidentalis
    decyl acetate, **8**, 213
    pheromones, **8**, 214
Fraxinus mandschurica, dirigent proteins, genes, **1**, 656
free radicals
    biosynthesis, **3**, 339
    random coupling hypothesis, limitations, **1**, 647
French beans *see Phaseolus vulgaris*
French Paradox, **3**, 792
fren genes
    cloning, **1**, 478
    combinatorial analysis, **1**, 489
    sequencing, **1**, 478
frenolicin
    biosynthesis, **1**, 478, **4**, 206
    cloning, **1**, 11
fresh green odor *see* green odor
Freudenberg, peroxidase studies, **3**, 717
frogs, Costa Rican *see Atelops chiriquiensis*
frogs
    α-1,3-mannosyl-glycoprotein β-1,2-*N*-
        acetylglucosaminyltransferase, genes, **3**, 50
    sequestration, **8**, 363
frontalin
    biosynthesis, **8**, 233
    occurrence, **8**, 14, 202
fructose-1,6-bisphosphate
    concentrations, **3**, 475
    as electrophile, **3**, 390
    glucose-1-phosphate adenylyltransferase activation, **3**,
        469, 470
    occurrence, **3**, 476
fructose-bisphosphate aldolase
    biochemistry, **3**, 419
    catalysis, **3**, 419
    isolation, **3**, 419
D-fructose-1,6-bisphosphate D-glyceraldehyde-3-
    phosphate-lyase *see* fructose-bisphosphate aldolase
fructose-1,6-diphosphatase, roles, in carbohydrate
    metabolism, **5**, 157
fructose-2,6-diphosphatase, structure, **5**, 157
fructose-1,6-diphosphate *see* fructose-1,6-bisphosphate
fructose-1,6-diphosphate aldolase *see* fructose-
    bisphosphate aldolase
fructose-6-phosphate
    biosynthesis, **3**, 414, 417
    cleavage, **3**, 393
    glucose-1-phosphate adenylyltransferase activation, **3**,
        469, 470
D-fructose-6-phosphate D-erythrose-4-phosphate-lyase
    (phosphate-acetylating) *see* fructose-6-phosphate
    phosphoketolase
fructose-6-phosphate phosphoketolase
    biochemistry, **3**, 393
    catalysis, **3**, 393
    purification, **3**, 393
    substrate specificity, **3**, 393
fruit flies
    (2*S*,6*R*,8*S*)-2,8-dimethyl-1,7-dioxaspiro[5.5]undecane,
        8, 214
    see also Anastrepha suspensa; Caribbean fruit flies;
        Drosophila spp.; Mexican fruit flies
fruiting bodies, in *Myxococcus xanthus*, **8**, 404
fruit rot, etiology, **1**, 534
fruits
    astringency, **8**, 167
    chemical attractants, **8**, 164
    odors, **8**, 165
        principles, **8**, 165
    parthenocarpic, **8**, 46

pigments, **8**, 164
    color preferences, **8**, 164
    iridosome structure, **8**, 164
    rejection, and high tannin levels, **8**, 167
    ripening, **1**, 133
        and starch degradation, **3**, 443
    sourness, **8**, 167
    sucrose-rich, bird digestion, **8**, 166
    sweet proteins, **8**, 166
fruticolide, occurrence, **1**, 375
*FSTri*5 gene, isolation, **2**, 203
fucogangliosides, biosynthesis, **3**, 116
fucosamine, *N*-acetyl-*N*-methyl-, assembly, **3**, 229
fucosamine, *N*-methyl- *see* 2,6-dideoxy-2-
    methylaminogalactose
fucose, 2-*O*-methyl, biosynthesis, **3**, 519
D-fucose, occurrence, **3**, 312
L-fucose, occurrence, **3**, 312, 313
α1,6-fucose, residues, **3**, 49
fucoserratene, structure, **8**, 421
fucoses, coupling, **1**, 331
fucosidases, inhibition, **5**, 308
fucosylglycolipids, biosynthesis, **3**, 114
fucosyltransferases (FucTs)
    catalysis, **3**, 114
    characterization, **3**, 108, 516. 605
    FucT-2
        binding, **3**, 115
        in brain, **3**, 115
        catalysis, **3**, 114
        in hepatomas, **3**, 116
        in rat bone marrow, **3**, 116
        in serum, **3**, 115
        in spleen, **3**, 115
    FucT-3
        in adenocarcinomas, **3**, 118
        in brain tissue, **3**, 117
        catalysis, **3**, 116
        in Chinese hamster ovary cells, **3**, 119
        in embryonic carcinoma cells, **3**, 118
        in human amniotic fluid, **3**, 118
        in neuroblastomas, **3**, 117
        oncofetal activity, **3**, 117
    isolation, **3**, 605
    linkage, **3**, 38
    occurrence, **5**, 308
    roles
        in *N*-glycan synthesis, **3**, 55
        in pectin biosynthesis, **3**, 511
α2-FucT *see* GDPfucose:Galβ-R α-1,2-fucosyltransferase
    (α2-FucT)
FucT III *see* galactoside 3(4)-L-fucosyltransferase
FucT IV *see* GDPfucose:Galβ1-4GlcNAc (Fuc to
    GlcNAc) α-1,3-fucosyltransferase IV (FucT IV)
FucTs *see* fucosyltransferases (FucTs)
L-fuculose-phosphate aldolase
    biochemistry, **3**, 424
    genes, localization, **3**, 425
    isolation, **3**, 425
    occurrence, **3**, 424
    substrate specificity, **3**, 425
Fucus spp., sex pheromones, **8**, 421
Fucus vesiculosus, lignins, erroneous reports, **3**, 622
Fugu rubripes, tetrodotoxins, **8**, 481
fukinanolide, antifeedant activity, **8**, 308
fullerene–oligonucleotide conjugates
    applications, **7**, 167
    synthesis, **7**, 167
fullerenes, reactions, with 5'-mercaptoalkylated
    oligonucleotides, **7**, 167
fumagillin
    occurrence, **2**, 165
    structure, **2**, 165

fumaric acids, *cis-trans* equilibria, **5**, 23
fumaric aminase *see* aspartate ammonia-lyase
fumiquinazolines
　cytotoxicity, **8**, 603
　occurrence, **8**, 603
　structure, **8**, 603
fumonisin B1, ceramide synthase inhibition, **3**, 101
fungal lipids, biological activity, **1**, 209
fungal transformants, gene expression, **4**, 268
fungi
　abscisic acid, **8**, 73, 87
　bioactive metabolites, **8**, 599
　cephalosporin C biosynthesis, **4**, 172
　curvularin, **8**, 601
　cyclosporins, **1**, 533
　eicosanoids, **1**, 209
　fatty acids, **1**, 450
　filamentous
　　genome complexity, **1**, 411
　　polyketide biosynthesis, **1**, **409–441**
　gene disruption, **2**, 208
　gibberellins, **8**, 38
　glycosidase processing, **3**, 14
　imperfect, **1**, 410
　β-lactam biosynthesis, regulation, **4**, 173
　and lignin evolution, **3**, 624
　mycotoxin-producing, **8**, 177
　phytopathogenic
　　melanin biosynthesis, **1**, 414
　　metabolism, **1**, 813
　polyketides, biosynthesis, **1**, 10, 14
　polypeptides, biosynthesis, **1**, 14
　secondary metabolites, **1**, 409
　stearoyl-CoA desaturases, **1**, 39
　terpenoids, **2**, 202
Fur *see* ferric uptake regulatory protein (Fur)
furamidine
　DNA binding, **7**, 457, 460
　DNA complexes, molecular modeling comparisons, **7**, 458
　structure, **7**, 452
furamine
　applications, intercalating agents, **7**, 458
　DNA complexes, molecular modeling comparisons, **7**, 458
　structure, **7**, 452
furan, 2-hydroperoxytetrahydro- (THF-OOH), applications, DNA structure probes, **7**, 95
furan, 2-(1-hydroxy-1-methylethyl)-5-methyltetrahydro- *see* pityol
furaneol, as odor principle, **8**, 165
furanoclerodanes, occurrence, **2**, 226
furanocoumarin, isopropyldihydro-, biosynthesis, **1**, 19
furanocoumarins
　accumulation, **1**, 625
　biosynthesis, **1**, 19
　in induced chemical defense, **8**, 151
　localization, **1**, 625
　occurrence, **1**, 628
　phototoxicity, **8**, 141
　as seed toxins, **8**, 168
　toxicity, **1**, 623, **8**, 141, 338
　see also psoralens
furanocoumarins, dihydro-
　biosynthesis, **1**, 628

cytochrome P450 enzymatic activity, **1**, 630
2-furanol, (3*R*,4*S*,1′*E*)-3,4-bis(1′-butenyl)tetrahydro-, occurrence, **8**, 215
furanone, lesion formation, mechanisms, **7**, 377
3-(2*H*)-furanone, 3-methylene-, biosynthesis, **5**, 168, 194
3-(2*H*)-furanones, 4-hydroxy-5-methyl-, superoxide production by, **7**, 540
furans, diphenyl-
　DNA minor-groove vs. intercalation features, **7**, 457
　structure, **7**, 457
furans, divanillyl tetrahydro-, biosynthesis, **3**, 731
furan-3-spiro-4′-cyclohexadienone, tetrahydro-, in lignins, **3**, 727
furaquinocins, **2**, 59
furniture beetle *see Anobium punctatum*
furoin, biosynthesis, **3**, 394
furoin, methyl-, biosynthesis, **3**, 394
3-furoylacetyl-CoA, as substrate, **4**, 266
fusaric acid, phytotoxicity, **8**, 178
fusarielin A, biosynthesis, **1**, 370
Fusarium spp.
　apotrichothecenes, **2**, 203
　cyclonerodiol, **2**, 205
　deoxynivalenol, **2**, 203
　enniatin, **1**, 538
　gibberellins, **2**, 205
　halymecins, **8**, 601
　sambucinol, **2**, 203
　trichodiene synthase, **2**, 203
　　activity, **2**, 206
　T-2 toxin, **2**, 203
Fusarium culmorum, rubrofusarin, **1**, 419
Fusarium diseases, in wheat and maize, **2**, 203
Fusarium graminearum, terpenoid production loss, **2**, 206
Fusarium moniliforme, rice infection, **8**, 38
Fusarium oxysporum
　cytochromes P450, **1**, 210
　lipoxygenase, **1**, 210
　P450oxy, **1**, 211
　phosphoketolase, **3**, 393
Fusarium sambucinum, trichodiene synthase, **2**, 158
Fusarium solani
　kievitone, detoxification, **1**, 814
　lignan conversion, **1**, 692
　phaseollidin, detoxification, **1**, 814
　phaseollin, metabolism, **1**, 814
　spore germination, **1**, 780
Fusarium sporotrichioides
　gene expression changes, **2**, 208
　trichodiene synthase, **2**, 158, 161
　　coding, **5**, 330
　　purification, **2**, 203
　Tri4 gene, **2**, 164
fusicoccin
　occurrence, **2**, 222, **8**, 179
　phytotoxicity, **8**, 178
Fusicoccum amygdali, fusicoccin, **2**, 222, **8**, 179
fusion proteins
　applications, **7**, 647
　bulk production
　　isolation, **7**, 666
　　purification, **7**, 666
　cleavage, **7**, 667
　isolation, **7**, 648
Fusobacterium nucleatum, lanthionine, **3**, 246
Fyn proteins, acylation, **4**, 20

G

*GA*1 locus, cloning, via genomic subtraction, **8**, 47
GA1 protein, amino acids, **8**, 50
*GA*4 genes, occurrence, **8**, 53
*ga*1-3 gene, occurrence, **8**, 54
gaa genes
    *gaa*1, **4**, 316
      mutation, **3**, 303
gabaculine
    biosynthesis, **1**, 616, 620
    inhibitory activity, **8**, 63
Gaeumannomyces graminis
    dioxygenase, **1**, 211
    omega hydroxylase, **1**, 211
GAGs *see* glycans, glycosamino- (GAGs)
Gaillardia aestivalis, aestivalin, **1**, 375
*GAL*1 promoter, transcription studies, **6**, 206
*GAL*10 mRNA, stabilization, **6**, 209
galactan I
    O-acetylation, **3**, 189
    structure, **3**, 188
galactan II, structure, **3**, 189
galactans, structure, **3**, 499
galactocerebroside, synthesis, **3**, 109
galactofuranosyl-transferase, activity, **3**, 212
galactolipids, linolenic acid in, **1**, 119
galactomannans
    applications, food additives, **3**, 8
    biosynthesis, **3**, 2, 8, **497–527**
      future research, **3**, 522
    functions, **3**, 521
    localization, **3**, 521
    occurrence, **3**, 498
    research, **3**, 522
    structure, **3**, 521, 607
    substitution, **3**, 521
galactopyranosyl-transferase, activity, **3**, 212
galactosamine, *N*-acetyl-, GalT-3 activity, **3**, 111
D-galactose, 2,4-diamino-2,4,6-trideoxy-, occurrence, **3**, 190
D-galactose, 4-*O*-(6-*O*-feruloyl-*β*-D-galactopyranosyl)-, occurrence, **3**, 697
β-galactose, *p*-nitrophenyl-, hydrolysis, **5**, 438
β-galactosidase-fusion protein, expression, **1**, 428
β-galactosidase(s), occurrence, **5**, 289, 290
β-D-galactoside, 5-bromo-4-chloro-3-indolyl-, structure, **7**, 646
galactoside 2-*α*-L-fucosyltransferase, encoding, **3**, 55
galactoside 3(4)-L-fucosyltransferase
    genes, cloning, **3**, 57
    roles, in *N*-glycan synthesis, **3**, 57
β-D-galactoside galactohydrolase(s) *see* *β*-galactosidase(s)
β-galactoside *α*-2,3-sialyltransferase
    encoding, **3**, 80
    N-glycosylation, **3**, 79
    regulatory mechanisms, **3**, 79
    roles, in *O*-glycan synthesis, **3**, 79
    substrate specificity, **3**, 79
β-galactoside *α*-2,6-sialyltransferase (ST6Gal I)
    catalysis, **3**, 46
    expression
      and gene transcription, **3**, 46
      variations, **3**, 46
    Golgi apparatus targeting, **3**, 48
    roles, in *N*-glycan synthesis, **3**, 46
    sequences, **3**, 48

galactostatin, structure, **3**, 130
galactosylceramide (GalCer)
    biosynthesis, **3**, 91, 92
    localization, **3**, 92
galactosyldiglyceride, synthesis, **3**, 109
β-1,3-galactosyl-*O*-glycosyl-glycoprotein *β*-1,3-*N*-acetylglucosaminyltransferase
    occurrence, **3**, 77
    roles, in *O*-glycan elongation, **3**, 77
β-1,3-galactosyl-*O*-glycosyl-glycoprotein *β*-1,6-*N*-acetylglucosaminyltransferase
    activity, **3**, 76
    genes, localization, **3**, 78
    occurrence, **3**, 76
    roles, in *O*-glycan synthesis, **3**, 76
galactosyl-1-phosphate-transferase, activity, **3**, 210
galactosyl-pyrophosphoryl-undecaprenol-synthetase, encoding, **3**, 210
galactosyltransferases (GalTs)
    activity, **3**, 521
    characterization, **3**, 108, 515, 604
    GalT-1, catalysis, **3**, 109
    GalT-2
      activity, **3**, 94
      biosynthesis, **3**, 110
      catalysis, **3**, 110
      topology, **3**, 94
    GalT-3
      activity, **3**, 111
      catalysis, **3**, 111
      kinetic properties, **3**, 112
    GalT-4
      activity, **3**, 111
      catalysis, **3**, 112
      categorization, **3**, 112
      kinetic properties, **3**, 112
      purified, **3**, 111
    GalT-5, cloning, **3**, 113
    human blood group B, **3**, 39
    roles, in pectin biosynthesis, **3**, 511
galacturonosyltransferases
    activity, reduction, **3**, 520
    characterization, **3**, 512
    roles, in pectin biosynthesis, **3**, 511
    solubilization, **3**, 514
galacturonosyltransferase-V, roles, in pectin biosynthesis, **3**, 511
galanthamine, biosynthesis, **4**, 43
galanthine, biosynthesis, **4**, 43
(+)-galbelgin, demethylation, **1**, 692
Galbulimima baccata, himgravin, **1**, 371
GalCer *see* galactosylceramide (GalCer)
GalE *see* UDPglucose 4-epimerase
Galerita janus, formic acid, **8**, 356
gal genes
    galE, **3**, 203
    galF, **3**, 204
    galT, **3**, 203
    galU, **3**, 203, 204
galgravin, demethylation, **1**, 692
Galium mollugo, isochorismate synthases, **1**, 611, 618
gallate, *N*-propyl, as prostaglandin-endoperoxide synthase inhibitor, **1**, 123
Galleria melonella, pheromone biosynthesis, studies, **8**, 212

Galleria wax assay, development, **8**, 266
gallic acid
  biosynthesis, **3**, 10
  degradation, **3**, 385
  in esterification processes, **3**, 800
  occurrence, **3**, 803
  reactions, with uridinediphosphoglucose, **3**, 805
[^{14}C]gallic acid, esterification, **3**, 821
gallidermin
  antibacterial activity, **4**, 300
  biosynthesis, **4**, 202, 279
  mutagenesis, site-directed, **4**, 300
  structure, **4**, 279
gallotannin(s)
  biosynthesis, **3**, 10, 811
  Chinese, **3**, 800
  purification, **3**, 822
  Turkish, **3**, 800
    occurrence, **3**, 813
galloyl-CoA, in β-glucogallin biosynthesis, **3**, 805
1-*O*-galloyl-β-D-glucose:1-*O*-galloyl-β-D-glucose *O*-
    galloyltransferase *see* β-glucogallin *O*-
    galloyltransferase
galloyltransferase C, purification, **3**, 816
Gal*N*Ac 6-*O*-sulfotransferase
  catalysis, **3**, 174
  cloning, **3**, 171
α3-Gal*N*Ac-transferase, blood group A-dependent, roles,
    3, 81
Gal*N*AcTs *see* *N*-acetylgalactosaminyltransferases
    (Gal*N*AcTs)
Gal*N*Acα-benzyl, in *O*-glycan studies, **3**, 71
Gal*N*Acα-serine/threonine, occurrence, **3**, 71
Gal 6-*O*-sulfotransferase, catalysis, **3**, 174
α3-GalT *see* UDPgalactose:Gal-R α1,3-Gal-transferase
β3-GalT *see* UDPgalactose:Glc*N*Ac-R β-1,3-
    galactosyltransferase (β3-GalT)
β4-GalT *see* β-*N*-acetylglucosaminylglycopeptide β-1,4-
    galactosyltransferase
GalT-1 *see* galactosyltransferases (GalTs), GalT-1
GalT-2 *see* galactosyltransferases (GalTs), GalT-2
GalT-3 *see* galactosyltransferases (GalTs), GalT-3
GalT-4 *see* galactosyltransferases (GalTs), GalT-4
GalT-5 *see* galactosyltransferases (GalTs), GalT-5
α3-Gal-transferase, blood group B-dependent, roles, **3**, 81
GalTs *see* galactosyltransferases (GalTs)
Gambierdiscus toxicus
  ciguatoxins, **8**, 501
  gambieric acids, **8**, 508
  maitotoxin, **8**, 501, 504
gambieric acids
  antifungal properties, **8**, 508
  isolation, **8**, 509
  occurrence, **8**, 508
gambiriin A-1, biosynthesis, **3**, 781
gambiriins, biosynthesis, **3**, 781
gammacerane-3α,21α-diol, biosynthesis, **2**, 312
gammacerane-3β,21α-diol, biosynthesis, **2**, 312
gangliosides
  biosynthesis, **3**, 95
  structure, **3**, 87
gangliosidosis, and multivesicular storage bodies, **3**, 100
gangrene, of hooves, **8**, 178
GAP *see* glyceraldehyde 3-phosphate (GAP)
garcilivin A, occurrence, **1**, 384
gardimycin *see* actagardine
gas chromatography (GC), applications, **8**, 6
gas chromatography–mass spectrometry (GC-MS)
  diterpene synthase studies, **2**, 211
  gibberellins, **8**, 44
    studies, **8**, 43
  monoterpene synthase studies, **2**, 211
  in plant hormone studies, **8**, 23

gastropods
  chemical defense, **8**, 465
  chemoreception, **8**, 418
  feeding stimulants, **8**, 420
GATA-1, cloning, **7**, 670
Gaucher's disease
  characterization, **3**, 102
  etiology, **3**, 140
GAUSSIAN 94, applications, **5**, 119
GBSSs *see* granule-bound starch synthases (GBSSs)
GC *see* gas chromatography (GC)
GC boxes, in promoters, **3**, 44
GC-MS *see* gas chromatography–mass spectrometry
    (GC-MS)
gdh genes, in mycarose biosynthesis, **3**, 342
Gdm enzymes
  GdmH, encoding, **4**, 290
  GdmT, encoding, **4**, 290
GDP *see* geranyl diphosphate (GDP)
GDP-Col, pathway, **3**, 207
GDP-2-deoxy-2-fluorofucose, inhibitory activity, **5**, 308
GDPfucose
  biosynthesis, **3**, 334
  pathway, **3**, 207
GDP-L-fucose
  biosynthesis, **3**, 509
  occurrence, **3**, 509
GDPfucose:β-*N*-acetylglucosaminide (Fuc to Asn-linked
    Glc*N*Ac) α-1,3-fucosyltransferases, roles, in *N*-glycan
    synthesis, **3**, 58
GDPfucose:β-*N*-acetylglucosaminide (Fuc to Asn-linked
    Glc*N*Ac) α-1,6-fucosyltransferases, roles, in *N*-glycan
    synthesis, **3**, 58
GDP-L-fucose:β-D-galactosyl-*N*-acetyl-D-glucosaminyl-
    R 4-L-fucosyltransferase *see* galactoside 3(4)-L-
    fucosyltransferase
GDPfucose:Galβ-R α-1,2-fucosyltransferase (α2-FucT)
  encoding, **3**, 55
  overexpression, **3**, 81
GDPfucose:Galβ1-4/3Glc*N*Ac (Fuc to Glc*N*Ac) α-1,3/4-
    fucosyltransferase III (FucT III) *see* galactoside 3(4)-
    L-fucosyltransferase
GDPfucose:Galβ1-4Glc*N*Ac (Fuc to Glc*N*Ac) α-1,3-
    fucosyltransferase IV (FucT IV), roles, in *N*-
    glycan synthesis, **3**, 57
GDPfucose:Galβ1-4Glc*N*Ac (Fuc to Glc*N*Ac) α-1,3-
    fucosyltransferase V (FucT V), roles, in *N*-
    glycan synthesis, **3**, 57
GDPfucose:Galβ1-4Glc*N*Ac (Fuc to Glc*N*Ac) α-1,3-
    fucosyltransferase VI (FucT VI), roles, in *N*-
    glycan synthesis, **3**, 57
GDPfucose:Galβ1-4Glc*N*Ac (Fuc to Glc*N*Ac) α-1,3-
    fucosyltransferase VII (FucT VII), roles, in *N*-
    glycan synthesis, **3**, 58
GDPglucose
  glycogen synthase activity, **3**, 452
  pyrophosphorolysis, **3**, 478
GDPMan *see* guanosinediphosphomannose (GDPMan)
GDP-D-mannose, as substrate, **3**, 509
GDPmannose pyrophosphorylase, catalysis, **3**, 207
gedunin, occurrence, **3**, 321
Gelidium spp., jasmonic acid, **8**, 108
gel retardation, analyses, **3**, 478
gelsemine, strictosidine studies, **4**, 118
gemacranolides, antifeedant activity, **8**, 308
gene amplification, **7**, **615–641**
gene clusters
  bacterial aromatic polyketide synthases, **1**, 476
  cloning, **1**, 475
  expression, host–vector system, **1**, 484
  fungal terpenoid pathways, **2**, 205
  RfaH-regulated, **3**, 228
gene disruption

in gene characterization, **2**, 208
gene replacement, **2**, 208
integrative gene disruption, **2**, 208
gene expression
auxin studies, **8**, 31
differential, **2**, 208
inhibition, **7**, 286
and mRNA turnover, **6**, 205
gene families, and gene identification, **2**, 211
general acid–base catalysts
anion competition, **5**, 290
applications, **5**, 32
in RNA structural probing, **6**, 68
glycosidases, **5**, 286
identification, **5**, 39, 43
intermediate stabilization, **5**, 37
leaving group dependence, **5**, 290
mechanisms, **5**, 36
pH-rate dependence, **5**, 290
pK_a cycling, **5**, 293
positional requirements, **5**, 293
roles, **5**, 37
gene replacement, techniques, **1**, 869
gene replacement therapy, severe combined
immunodeficiency disease, **5**, 73
genes
class III
classification, **4**, 362
TATA box, **4**, 366
transcription, **4**, 366
cloning, **7**, **643–674**
defensive, **1**, 132
housekeeping, regulation, **1**, 135
pathway, clustering, **1**, 465
regulation, **1**, 135
TATA-containing, transcription, **4**, 368
wound-responsive, **1**, 130
Gene Theory, auxins, **8**, 31
genetic code
universal
almost, **4**, 358
AUG in, **4**, 358
UGA in, **4**, 357
genetic engineering
of diterpene biosynthesis, **2**, 241
ethylene, **8**, 98
penicillins, **4**, 240
genetic mutations, random nature of, **5**, 79
genetics
early studies, **1**, 715
penicillin biosynthesis, **4**, 244
gene transcription, and ST6Gal I expression, **3**, 46
gene transference, horizontal, **4**, 245
genistein
antineoplastic activity, **1**, 783
biosynthesis, **1**, 791
as chemoattractant, **1**, 780
chemoprotective activity, **1**, 783
as DNA topoisomerase II inhibitor, **7**, 603, 610
DNA topoisomerase inhibition, **1**, 783
glucose uptake inhibition, **1**, 783
as hyphal growth inhibitor, **8**, 175
as isoflavonoid precursor, **1**, 786
as nodulating gene expression inhibitor, **8**, 174
prenylation, **1**, 806
and quail population control, **1**, 782
sex hormone binding globulin studies, **1**, 699
genistein, 2′-hydroxy-
occurrence, **1**, 795
prenylation, **1**, 806
as substrate, **1**, 800
genistein, 5-*O*-methyl-, accumulation, **1**, 800
genistein, 8-prenyl-2′-hydroxy-, as substrate, **1**, 800

genisteine, occurrence, **1**, 130
genkwanol B, structure, **3**, 780
genkwanols, biochemistry, **3**, 780
genotoxic agents, ultraviolet radiation, **5**, 372
gentamycin, resistance, **6**, 194
gentiobiase(s) *see* β-glucosidase(s)
gentisic acid, structure, **1**, 411
geodin, analogues, **1**, 459
geodin, desmethyldihydro-, as substrate, **1**, 435
geodin, dihydro-, biosynthesis, **1**, 435
(+)-geodin
biosynthesis, **1**, 431, 432, 435
occurrence, **1**, 412
geographutoxin I (GTX I)
occurrence, **8**, 476
SS linkages, **8**, 478
structure, **8**, 476
synthesis, via solid phase method, **8**, 477
geographutoxin II (GTX II)
effect on sodium channels, in skeletal muscle, **8**, 477
nerve and muscle sodium channel discrimination, **8**, 477
occurrence, **8**, 476
structure, **8**, 476
geography cone *see Conus geographus*
Geometridae
(6*Z*,9*Z*)-6,9-heptadecadiene, **8**, 217
pheromones, **8**, 207
sex pheromones, **8**, 217, 247
Geotrichum candidum
demethylallosamidin studies, **1**, 149
triacylglycerol lipase, **5**, 112, 129
geranial, occurrence, **8**, 223, 232
geranic acid, occurrence, **8**, 222, 223
geraniin, as protoxin, **3**, 821
geraniol
biosynthesis, **2**, 62, 102
cyclization inhibition, **2**, 98
occurrence, **8**, 222
ovicidal activity, **8**, 306
as starting material
for juvenile hormone III bisepoxide, **8**, 271
for loganin, **4**, 110
geraniol, 10-hydroxy-, biosynthesis, **2**, 106
γ-geraniol, occurrence, **8**, 222
geranyl cation–diphosphate ion pair, collapse, **2**, 99
geranyl diphosphate, 2,3-cyclopropyl-, as substrate, **5**, 327
geranyl diphosphate, [1-³H]-2,3-cyclopropyl(methano)-, as substrate, **2**, 138
geranyl diphosphate, 2,3-dihydro-, as substrate, **5**, 327
geranyl diphosphate, 6,7-dihydro-, as substrate, **2**, 138, **5**, 327
geranyl diphosphate, 2-fluoro-, as substrate, **2**, 80, 126, **5**, 320, 327
geranyl diphosphate (GDP), **8**, 219
biosynthesis, **2**, 120
in carotenoid biosynthesis, **2**, 331
cyclization, **2**, 8
as intermediate, **2**, 70, 98
isomerization–cyclization sequence, **2**, 99
K_m, **2**, 125
roles, in farnesyl diphosphate, **5**, 318
as starting material, for cyclic monoterpenes, **2**, 99
as substrate, **2**, 7, 379
geranyl-diphosphate:isopentenyl-diphosphate
geranyl*trans*transferase(s) *see*
geranyl*trans*transferase(s)
geranyl diphosphate synthase(s) *see*
dimethylallyl*trans*transferase(s)
geranylfarnesyl diphosphate (GFDP), synthesis, **2**, 86, **5**, 325
geranylfarnesyl diphosphate synthase, occurrence, **2**, 88
geranyl geranial, occurrence, **8**, 229

geranyl geraniol, occurrence, **8**, 229, 230
geranyl geranoate, occurrence, **8**, 223
S-geranylgeranyl-cysteine α-carboxylmethyl ester, in
    geranylgeranylated proteins, **2**, 358
geranylgeranyl-diphosphate geranylgeranyltransferase,
    homology, **2**, 250
geranylgeranyl diphosphate (GGDP)
    biosynthesis, **2**, 372, 379
    in carotenoid biosynthesis, **2**, 331
    condensation, **5**, 336
    cyclization, **2**, 5, 217, 381, 382
        to taxa-4,11-diene, **2**, 220, 220
        all-trans cyclization, **2**, 237
    folding, **8**, 320
    geranylgeranyl group transfer, **2**, 358
    in phytoene biosynthesis, **2**, 10
    as starting material, for phytoene, **2**, 108
    as substrate, **2**, 7
geranylgeranyl-diphosphate pyrophosphate-lyase
    (cyclizing) *see* casbene synthase(s)
geranylgeranyl diphosphate synthase(s)
    in carotenoid biosynthesis, **2**, 339
    enzymology, **2**, 86
    gene cloning, **2**, 87
    genes, identification, **2**, 70
    homology, **2**, 250
    localization, **8**, 50
    mammalian, purification, **2**, 87
    occurrence, **2**, 85, 86, 87
    product chain length determination, **2**, 88
    sequences, **5**, 323
    structural conservation, **2**, 339, 348
geranylgeranyl group, in proteins, **2**, 354
geranylgeranyl pyrophosphate (GGPP) *see*
    geranylgeranyl diphosphate (GGDP)
geranylgeranyltransferases, regulatory mechanisms, **1**,
    628
geranyl methylene diphosphonate (GPCP), K_m, **2**, 81
geranyl octanoate, occurrence, **8**, 223
geranyl propionate, ovicidal activity, **8**, 306
geranyl*trans*transferase(s)
    ancestry, **5**, 318
    applications, **2**, 78
    aspartate in, **2**, 162
    aspartate-rich regions, **5**, 322, 324
    asymmetric synthesis, **2**, 78
    avian, x-ray analyses, **2**, 86
    bisubstrate analogues, **5**, 321
    catalysis, **5**, 316
    catalytic motifs, **2**, 84
    comparative primary structures, **2**, 83
    conversion to geranylgeranyl diphosphate synthase, **2**,
        85
    crystallization, **2**, 70
    crystal structure, **2**, 83
        data, **2**, 162
        studies, **5**, 324
    C-terminal region, **2**, 85
    enzymology, **2**, 74, **5**, 323
    gene cloning, **2**, 82
    homology, **2**, 250
    interconvertible forms, **2**, 74
        Cys residue oxidation, **2**, 85
    linear free energy, **5**, 320
    mechanisms, **2**, 79
    mechanistic studies, **5**, 318
    mutagenesis
        random chemical, **2**, 85
        site-directed, **2**, 84, **5**, 323
    occurrence, **2**, 74, 82
    overproduction, **2**, 82
    phylogenetic relationships, **5**, 323
    product chain length determination, **2**, 86

    production, **5**, 323
    purification, **2**, 70
    reactions, with substrate homologues, **2**, 76
    sequences, **5**, 324
    silkworms, substrate specificities, **2**, 76
    stereochemistry of reaction, **2**, 75
    x-ray crystal structure, **5**, 324
Gerbera hybrida, flavone synthases, **1**, 725
GerC proteins, *Bacillus subtilis*, heptaprenyl diphosphate
    synthases, **2**, 90
cis-germacradienyl cation, **2**, 191
(2*Z*,6*E*,8*S*)-1(14),2,5(15),6-germacratetraene *see*
    periplanene-Br
germacrene, dihydro-, biosynthesis, **2**, 180
germacrene, 6,7-dihydro-, biosynthesis, **2**, 180
germacrene A
    as intermediate of aristolochene, **2**, 179
    protonation, **2**, 5
(−)-germacrene A, occurrence, **8**, 227
germacrene B
    as floral volatile, **8**, 161
    occurrence, **8**, 161
germacrene B, 9-methyl-, structure, **8**, 237
germacrone, effects, on herbivores, **8**, 142
German cockroach *see Blattella germanica*
germination
    and starch degradation, **3**, 443
    seeds, gibberellin-induced, **8**, 46
Gersemia fruticosa, prostaglandin biosynthesis, **1**, 242
GF-1 *see* GATA-1
GFDP *see* geranylfarnesyl diphosphate (GFDP)
GFDP synthase *see* geranylfarnesyl diphosphate synthase
GFPP *see* geranylfarnesyl diphosphate (GFDP)
GGDP *see* geranylgeranyl diphosphate (GGDP)
GGDP synthase(s) *see* geranylgeranyl diphosphate
    synthase(s)
GGPP *see* geranylgeranyl diphosphate (GGDP)
giant silk moth *see Hyalophora cecropia*
Giardia lamblia, prenylation, **2**, 363
Gibberella fujikuroi
    ent-copalyl diphosphate, **2**, 224
    dihydrojasmonic acid, **1**, 118
    gibberellins, **2**, 233, **8**, 36, 38
    jasmonic acid conjugate, **1**, 117
    jasmonoids, **1**, 121
    (−)-kaur-16-ene, **8**, 7
Gibberella fujikuroi Sawada et Wollenweber, rice
    infection, **8**, 2
ent-gibberellane, modifications, **8**, 36
Gibberella pulcaus, trichodiene synthases, cloning, **5**, 330
Gibberella pulicaris, enzyme, purification, **2**, 203
gibberellic acid, biosynthesis, **2**, 236
(gibberellin-1),2-oxoglutarate:oxygen oxidoreductase
    (2β-hydroxylating) *see* gibberellin 2β-dioxygenase(s)
(gibberellin-20),2-oxoglutarate:oxygen oxidoreductase
    (3β-hydroxylating) *see* gibberellin 3β-
    dioxygenase(s)
gibberellin A$_1$, isolation, **8**, 39
gibberellin A$_3$
    applications, **8**, 3
    isolation, **8**, 39
    structure, **8**, 2
gibberellin A$_4$
    isolation, **8**, 41
    synthesis, **8**, 2
gibberellin A$_{19}$, occurrence, **8**, 43
gibberellin A$_{12}$-aldehyde
    activity, **8**, 51
    biosynthesis, **2**, 232, **8**, 47
    oxidation, **2**, 234
gibberellin A$_{73}$ methyl ester
    activity, **8**, 57
    biosynthesis, **8**, 57

occurrence, **8**, 56
gibberellin-deficient mutants, from *Arabidopsis thaliana*, **8**, 47
gibberellin 2β-dioxygenase(s), occurrence, **8**, 53
gibberellin 3β-dioxygenase(s), functions, **8**, 52
gibberellin glucosides, activity, **8**, 45
gibberellin glucosyl esters, hydrolysis, **8**, 45
gibberellin glycosyl esters (GA-GEs), extraction, **8**, 43
gibberellin glycosyl ether (GA-GEt), extraction, **8**, 43
gibberellin 3β-hydroxylase(s) *see* gibberellin 3β-dioxygenase(s)
gibberellin 13-hydroxylase(s), occurrence, **8**, 51
gibberellin 7-oxidase, occurrence, **8**, 51
gibberellin 20-oxidase(s)
  catalysis, **8**, 51
  cDNA cloning
    from *Arabidopsis*, **8**, 52
    from pumpkin, **8**, 51
  cloning, **2**, 236
  feedback regulation, **8**, 54
  purification, **2**, 236
gibberellins (GAs)
  active, **8**, 22
  applications, **8**, 35
  biological activity, **8**, 44
  biosynthesis, **2**, 233, 385, **8**, 47
    pathways, **8**, 22
  biosynthesis regulation, **8**, 54
    by light, **8**, 54
    by temperature, **8**, 55
    feedback, **8**, 54
  characterization, reviews, **8**, 43
  chemistry, **8**, 43
  conjugated, **8**, 43
  deficiency, single gene mutants, **8**, 45
  discovery, **8**, 21
  early-13-hydroxylation pathway, **8**, 47, 51
  early-non-hydroxylation pathway, **8**, 47, 51
  effects, on enzymes, **8**, 45
  free, **8**, 43
  fungal, **8**, 38
  gas chromatography–mass spectrometry, **8**, 43, 44
  high performance liquid chromatography, **8**, 44
  historical background, **8**, 38
  isolation, reviews, **8**, 43
  isotope labeled, **8**, 44
  occurrence, **2**, 205, 233, **8**, 36, 38
  overview, **8**, 35
  physiologically activity, **8**, 44
  plants, **8**, 42
    male sex expression, **8**, 46
  research, **8**, 2
  structure, **8**, 36
  structure–activity relationships, **8**, 45
  via solid-phase extraction, **8**, 44
  via solvent fractionation, **8**, 43
  seed germination induction, **8**, 46
Gibbonsia elegans, limpet predation, **8**, 7
giffordene, biosynthesis, **1**, 216, **8**, 423
Giffordia mitchellae, giffordene, **1**, 216
gilvocarcin V
  applications, antibiotics, **7**, 544, 545
  photochemical DNA damage, **7**, 544
[6]-gingerol, biosynthesis, **1**, 766
Ginkgoaceae, ecdysteroids, lack of, **8**, 280
Ginkgo biloba
  anacardic acids, **8**, 303
  applications, therapeutic, **2**, 367
  bilobalide, **8**, 308
  dehydroabietane, **2**, 395
  (+)-dehydroabietane, **2**, 384
  embryos, **2**, 370
    [U-^{13}C]-D-glucose incorporation, **2**, 372, 374

  incubation, **2**, 384, 386
  isopentenyl diphosphate biosynthesis, **2**, 373
  isoprenoid biosynthesis, **2**, 61
  ginkgolides, **8**, 303, 313
  historical interest in, **2**, 367
  insect immunity, **8**, 303
  isopentenyl diphosphate biosynthesis, **2**, 373, 374, 381
  leucoanthocyanidin 4-reductase, **1**, 729
  lignification, **3**, 691
  myths, **2**, 367
  odor principles, **8**, 165
  resistance, **2**, 367
ginkgolide A
  biosynthesis, **2**, 381
  labeling patterns, **2**, 377
  NMR spectra, **2**, 382, 384, 391
  oxidation, **2**, 390
  radioactive specimens, **2**, 388
ginkgolide B
  biosynthesis, **2**, 368, 381
  radioactive specimens, **2**, 388
ginkgolide C, radioactive specimens, **2**, 388
ginkgolides
  applications, platelet activating factor antagonists, **2**, 367
  biological system, **2**, 369
  biosynthesis, **2**, 61, **367–400**
    early stages, **2**, 381
    early studies, **2**, 368
    from tricyclic intermediates, **2**, 386
    late stages, **2**, 381
    via acetate–mevalonate pathway, **2**, 374
    via deoxyxylulose pathway, **2**, 374, 384
  t-butyl groups, **2**, 386
  discovery, **2**, 368
  INADEQUATE spectra, **2**, 372
  incorporation rates, **2**, 371
  ^{13}C NMR spectra, **2**, 371, 374
  ^{1}H NMR spectra, **2**, 371
  occurrence, **8**, 303, 313
  structure, **2**, 368
  toxicity, **8**, 308
  tricyclic intermediates, configuration, **2**, 393
ginseng, cardiovascular activity, **1**, 705
GIPLs *see* glycosylinositol phospholipids (GIPLs)
glandular trichomes
  enzyme isolation, **2**, 118
  monoterpenes in, **2**, 110
glaucolide A, antifeedant activity, **8**, 308
GlcATs *see* glucuronyltransferases (GlcATs)
GlcCer *see* glucosylceramide (GlcCer)
Glc$_3$Man$_9$GlcNAc$_2$
  processing, **3**, 17
  as starting material, for *N*-glycans, **3**, 15
GlcNAc *see* glucosamine, *N*-acetyl- (GlcNAc)
GlcNAc-PI *see* inositol, *N*-acetylglucosaminylphosphatidyl- (GlcNAc-PI)
GlcNAcTs *see* *N*-acetyllactosaminide β-1,6-*N*-acetylglucosaminyltransferase(s)
GlcN-acyl PI *see* inositol, acylglucosaminylphosphatidyl- (GlcN-acyl PI)
GlcN-PI *see* inositol, glucosaminylphosphatidyl- (GlcN-PI)
GlcTs *see* glucosyltransferases (GlcTs)
Gleditsia triacanthos, oligomeric leucocyanidins, **3**, 757
glg genes
  cloning, **3**, 477
  Glg1p, coding, **3**, 481
  Glg2p, coding, **3**, 481
  glgA, **3**, 477
    cloning, **3**, 453
    expression, **3**, 478
  glgB, **3**, 477

cloning, **3**, 459
 expression, **3**, 478
 sequence, **3**, 462
glgBX operon, **3**, 478
glgC, **3**, 477
 expression, **3**, 478
 occurrence, **3**, 449
glgCAP operon, **3**, 478
glgP, **3**, 477
glgX, **3**, 477
 occurrence, **3**, 477
Gliomastix luzulae see Acremonium luzulae
glm genes
 glmM, coding, **3**, 206
 glmS, coding, **3**, 206
 glmU, **3**, 206
global alignments, in terpene synthase enzymes, **2**, 209
β-globin mRNA
 AU rich element effects, **6**, 208
 deadenylation studies, **6**, 206
 nonsense mutation, **6**, 211
Globodera pallida, growth inhibition, **1**, 694
Globodera rostochiensis, growth inhibition, **1**, 694
globularicisin, occurrence, **8**, 307
globularin, occurrence, **8**, 307
Glomus spp., vesicular arbuscular mycorrhizal (VAM)
 association, **1**, 780
Glossina spp.
 diuretic hormone, **8**, 300
 female contact pheromones, **8**, 249
Glossina morsitans
 dodecane, **8**, 214
 pentadecane, **8**, 216
Glossina morsitans morsitans, sex stimulants, **8**, 249
Glossina pallidipes
 15,23-dimethylpentatriacontane, **8**, 249
 pheromones, **8**, 16
gls genes
 glsI mutant, **3**, 18
 isolation, **3**, 147
GLTs *see* glycosyltransferases (GLTs)
Glu-165, roles, **5**, 36
Glu-198, identification, **1**, 891
Glu-524, roles, in arachidonic acid binding, **5**, 247
D-Glu adding enzyme
 inhibition, **3**, 278
 purification, **3**, 259
glucagon
 effects, on phosphorylation, **3**, 485
 regulatory mechanisms, **3**, 444
α-1,4-glucan
 biosynthesis, regulatory mechanisms, **3**, 472
 genes, cloning, **3**, 477
β-1,6-glucan, biosynthesis, **3**, 18
glucanase(s), in systemic acquired resistance, **1**, 133
1,4-α-glucan branching enzyme, catalysis, **3**, 444, 446
1,4-α-D-glucan:1,4-α-D-glucan 6-α-D-(1,4-α-D-glucano)-
 transferase *see* 1,4-α-glucan branching enzyme
1,4-α-D-glucan glucanohydrolase *see* α-amylase
1,4-(1,3;1,4)-β-D-glucan 4-glucanohydrolase *see*
 cellulase(s)
1,4-α-D-glucan 4-α-D-(1,4-α-D-glucano)-transferase
 (cyclizing) *see* cyclomaltodextrin
 glucanotransferase(s)
1,4-α-D-glucan glucohydrolase *see* glucan 1,4-α-
 glucosidase
glucan 1,4-α-glucosidase
 occurrence, **5**, 301
 structure, **3**, 139
glucan–iodine complexes
 in branching enzyme assays, **3**, 458
 $\lambda_{\max}$ increase, **3**, 455
1,4-α-D-glucan maltohydrolase *see* β-amylase

1,4-α-D-glucan:orthophosphate α-D-glucosyltransferase
 see glycogen phosphorylase; maltodextrin
 phosphorylase; phosphorylase(s)
4-α-glucanotransferase, induction, **3**, 445
glucans
 endogenous, in starch synthase activity measurement,
  3, 454
 from
  maltose, **3**, 444
  sucrose, **3**, 444
α-glucans, as glycogen synthase primers, **3**, 452
1,3-β-glucan synthase, transcription, inhibition, **1**, 550
β-glucan synthase, activity, **8**, 31
glucan synthases, characterization, **3**, 606
1,3-β-D-glucan-UDP glucosyltransferase *see* 1,3-β-glucan
 synthase
glucoalkaloids, occurrence, **4**, 113
glucoamylase *see* glucan 1,4-α-glucosidase
glucobrassicin, as oviposition stimulant, **8**, 156
glucocorticoids
 antiinflammatory, **5**, 229
 prostaglandin-endoperoxide synthase-2 inhibition, **1**,
  257, **5**, 256
 regulatory mechanisms, **3**, 444
glucodextrinase *see* glucan 1,4-α-glucosidase
β-glucogallin
 biosynthesis, **3**, 805
 exchange reactions, with D-glucose, **3**, 810
 group-transfer potential, **3**, 807
 isolation, **3**, 805
 roles, **3**, 821
 substitution, **3**, 800
β-glucogallin, [^{14}C-glucosyl]-, synthesis, **3**, 821
β-glucogallin *O*-galloyltransferase, occurrence, **3**, 808
glucoinvertase(s) *see* a-glucosidase(s)
glucomannans
 cellulose studies, **3**, 585
 occurrence, **3**, 601
glucomannan synthases, characterization, **3**, 606
gluconeogenesis, glucose formation, **3**, 444
gluconolactone, binding, **5**, 294
β-D-glucopyranose, 1-*O*-galloyl- *see* β-glucogallin
β-D-glucopyranose, 1,2,3,4,6-penta-*O*-galloyl-,
 biosynthesis, **3**, 800
6-*O*-glucopyranoside, structure, **3**, 132
7-*O*-β-D-glucopyranoside, structure, **3**, 130
D-glucopyranoside, 1,1-difluoro-, hydrolysis, **5**, 302
α-D-glucopyranoside, 2,3-epoxypropyl, as inactivator, **5**,
 303
β-D-glucopyranoside, 2′,4′-dinitrophenyl-2-deoxy-2-
 fluoro-, applications, **5**, 289
β-D-glucopyranoside, *p*-nitrophenyl-, cleavage, **3**, 819
β-D-glucopyranoside, *N*-octyl-, applications, **5**, 339
2-*O*-glucopyranosides, structure, **3**, 130
glucosamine, *N*-acetyl- (GlcNAc)
 bisecting, **3**, 43
 deacetylation, **4**, 310
 in glycoprotein biosynthesis, **3**, 275
 in peptidoglycan, **3**, 244
glucosamine, nonacylated, occurrence, **3**, 297
[1-^{13}C,2-^{15}N]-D-glucosamine, feeding experiments, **1**, 150
[3-^{2}H]glucosamine, biosynthesis, **1**, 154
[4-^{2}H]glucosamine, biosynthesis, **1**, 154
[5-^{2}H]glucosamine, biosynthesis, **1**, 154
[6-^{2}H$_2$]-D-glucosamine, biosynthesis, **1**, 154
glucosamine-1-phosphate, biosynthesis, **3**, 251
glucosamine-1-phosphate, *N*-acetyl-, accumulation, **3**,
 251
glucosamine-6-phosphate, biosynthesis, **3**, 251
glucosamine-1-phosphate acyltransferase
 activity, **3**, 251
 catalysis, **3**, 206
glucosamine-6-phosphate synthase

inhibition, **3**, 275
overexpression, **3**, 251
glucosamine-pyrophosphorylundecaprenol, *N*-acetyl-,
   biosynthesis, **3**, 214
glucosamines, β-1,4-linked *N*-acetyl-
   oligomers, **1**, 329
   residues, **1**, 329
glucosamines, UDP-*N*-acetyl-, synthesis, **1**, 331
glucosaminides, solvolysis, **5**, 298
glucose
   donor, **3**, 442
   in *Erwinia herbicola*, **2**, 345
   incorporation, into isoprenoids, **2**, 50
   metabolism, **2**, 50
     via Embden–Meyerhof–Parnas pathway, **2**, 52
   in penicillin production, **4**, 174
glucose, digalloyl-, biosynthesis, **3**, 806
glucose, 6-*O*-galloyl-, studies, **3**, 809
glucose, 1-*O*-*p*-hydroxybenzoyl-, as acyl donor, **3**, 807
glucose, pentagalloyl-
   inhibitory effects, **3**, 802
   oxidation, **3**, 817
glucose, 1,2,3,4,6-pentagalloyl-
   biosynthesis, **3**, 809
     pathways, **3**, 810
   galloylation, **3**, 812
glucose, [U-^{14}C]pentagalloyl-, as substrate, **3**, 817
glucose, 1-*O*-protocatechuoyl-, as acyl donor, **3**, 807
glucose, 1,2,3,6-tetragalloyl-, biosynthesis, **3**, 808
glucose, 1,2,4,6-tetragalloyl-, biosynthesis, **3**, 809, 811
glucose, trigalloyl-, biosynthesis, **3**, 806
glucose, 1,2,6-trigalloyl-, biosynthesis, **3**, 807, 809
glucose, 1,3,6-trigalloyl-, biosynthesis, **3**, 809, 811
D-glucose
   conformation, **3**, 800
   as esperamicin A$_1$ precursor, **7**, 554
   exchange reactions, with β-glucogallin, **3**, 810
   labeled, as ginkgolide precursor, **2**, 371
[U-^{13}C]-D-glucose, incorporation, **2**, 372, 374
β-D-glucose, occurrence, **8**, 221
β-D-glucose, 1,6-di-*O*-galloyl-
   biosynthesis, **3**, 806
   isolation, **3**, 822
   synthesis, **3**, 822
β-D-glucose, 1-*O*-hydroxybenzoyl-, as substrate, **3**, 806
β-D-glucose, 1,2,3,4,6-penta-*O*-galloyl-, occurrence, **3**,
   822
β-D-glucose, 1-*O*-protocatechuoyl-, as substrate, **3**, 806
β-D-glucose, 1-*O*-sinapoyl-, group-transfer potential, **3**,
   807
β-D-glucose, 1,2,3,6-tetra-*O*-galloyl-, occurrence, **3**, 822
β-D-glucose, 1,2,3,6-tetra-*O*-galloyl-4-*O*-digalloyl-,
   identification, **3**, 813
β-D-glucose, 1,2,4,6-tetra-*O*-galloyl-3-*O*-digalloyl-,
   identification, **3**, 813
β-D-glucose, 1,3,4,6-tetra-*O*-galloyl-2-*O*-digalloyl-,
   identification, **3**, 813
β-D-glucose, 1,2,4,6-tetra-*O*-galloyl-3-*O*-trigalloyl-,
   identification, **3**, 813
β-D-glucose, 1,2,6-tri-*O*-galloyl-, synthesis, **3**, 822
β-D-glucose, 1,2,6-tri-*O*-galloyl-3,4-di-*O*-digalloyl-,
   biosynthesis, **3**, 813
β-D-glucose, 1,3,6-tri-*O*-galloyl-2,4-di-*O*-digalloyl-,
   identification, **3**, 813
β-D-glucose, 1,4,6-tri-*O*-galloyl-2,3-di-*O*-digalloyl-,
   identification, **3**, 813
glucoseens, as intermediates, **3**, 338
glucose esters, galloyl-, biosynthesis, **3**, 806
glucose-6-phosphatase, roles, in carbohydrate
   metabolism, **5**, 157
glucose-1-phosphate
   apparent affinities, **3**, 476
   group-transfer potential, **3**, 807

glucose-6-phosphate
   activation, **3**, 483
   activity ratio, **3**, 485
   group-transfer potential, **3**, 807
   in starch synthesis, **3**, 464
   translocator, **3**, 464
   transporter, **3**, 464
glucose-1-phosphate adenylyltransferase
   activators, **3**, 469
     overlapping specificity, **3**, 470
   activity, **3**, 464
   binding sites, specificity, **3**, 470
   catalysis, **3**, 444
   chemical modification studies, **3**, 448
   CL1136
     activity, **3**, 474
     sensitivity, **3**, 474
   effector sites, **3**, 448
   equilibrium dialysis, **3**, 448
   functions, **3**, 451
   as homotetramer, **3**, 452
   inhibition, **3**, 447
   inhibitors, **3**, 469, 470
   isoforms, **3**, 464
   kinetic studies, **3**, 471
   molecular weight, **3**, 447
   occurrence, **3**, 469
   properties, **3**, 447
     allosteric, **3**, 472
   reaction mechanisms, **3**, 448
   roles, in α-1,4-glucan biosynthesis, **3**, 472
   sensitivity, **3**, 476
   sequences, evolution, **3**, 451
   SG5
     activity, **3**, 474
     sensitivity, **3**, 474
   SG14, glycogen accumulation, **3**, 476
   structure, **3**, 447
     subunits, **3**, 447
   substrates, **3**, 448
glucose-1-phosphate cytidylyltransferase, coding, **3**, 208
α-D-glucose-1-phosphate cytidylyltransferase
   mechanisms, **3**, 336
   roles, in 3,6-dideoxyhexose biosynthesis, **3**, 336
glucose-6-phosphate phosphatase, phosphohistidine in, **5**,
   144
D-glucose-6-phosphate phosphohydrolase *see* glucose-6-
   phosphatase
glucose-1-phosphate thymidylyltransferase, catalysis, **3**,
   208
glucose-1-phosphate uridylyltransferase *see* UTP-
   glucose-1-phosphate uridylyltransferase
glucose phosphomutase *see* phosphoglucomutase
α-D-glucose 1,6-phosphomutase *see* phosphoglucomutase
glucoses, 1-*O*-acyl-, donor potential, **3**, 810
glucoses, galloyl-
   biosynthesis, **3**, 821
     pathways, **3**, 810
   tanning capacity, **3**, 802
glucoses, hexagalloyl-, identification, **3**, 813
glucose transferase, purification, **8**, 90
glucosidase, in free cytokinin release, **8**, 71
α-D-glucosidase, in honeybee venom, **8**, 355
α-glucosidase I
   catalysis, **3**, 18
   cDNA encoding, **3**, 18
   characterization, **3**, 18
   gene, localization, **3**, 18
   in *N*-glycan processing, **3**, 17
   inactivation, **3**, 18
   occurrence, **3**, 18, 147
   processing, **3**, 42, 147
   purification, **3**, 147

α-glucosidase I inhibitors, **3**, 19
α-glucosidase II
  binding sites, **3**, 20
  functions, **3**, 147
  gene, localization, **3**, 19
  in *N*-glycan processing, **3**, 17
  immunolocalization, **3**, 19
  and lymphoma cell mutant, **3**, 19
  mammalian, **3**, 19
  occurrence, **3**, 19
  processing, **3**, 42
  properties, **3**, 148
  roles, **3**, 19
α-glucosidase II inhibitors, **3**, 20
glucosidase inhibitors
  biochemistry, **3**, 151
  reviews, **3**, 19
  roles, **3**, 19
α-glucosidase inhibitors
  effects, on glycoproteins, **3**, 31
  roles, **3**, 20
α-glucosidase(s)
  assays, **3**, 148
  roles, **3**, 18
    in biosynthetic pathways, **3**, 14
  sequences, **5**, 298
β-glucosidase(s)
  active site titration, **5**, 289
  catalysis, **3**, 685
    mechanisms, **3**, 686
  inhibition, **3**, 802
  occurrence, **1**, 809, 884, 891, **3**, 683, 685, **5**, 289
  purification, **3**, 686
  roles
    in lignification, **3**, 686
    in lignin biosynthesis, **3**, 676, 686
  substrate specificity, **1**, 809
23-*O*-glucoside, metabolism, **8**, 107
β-D-glucoside, neomenthyl-, biosynthesis, **2**, 114
α-D-glucoside glucohydrolase *see* a-glucosidase(s)
β-D-glucoside glucohydrolase *see* β-glucosidase(s)
glucosides
  biosynthesis, **8**, 90
  in lignans, **3**, 684
glucosides, cyano-, insect sequestration, **8**, 362
glucosides, cyanogenic, compartmentation, **1**, 884
β-D-glucosides, occurrence, **2**, 106
β-D-glucosides, thioacetamido, NAG-thiazoline
    biosynthesis, **5**, 297
4-*O*-β-D-glucosidogallate, *N*-succinimidyl, biosynthesis,
    3, 805
4-*O*-β-D-glucosidogallic acid, biosynthesis, **3**, 805
4-*O*-β-D-glucosidogalloyl-CoA, biosynthesis, **3**, 805
glucosidosucrase(s) *see* a-glucosidase(s)
glucosinolate, allyl *see* sinigrin
glucosinolate, desulfobenzyl-, sulfation, **1**, 859
glucosinolate, *p*-hydroxybenzyl- *see* sinalbin
glucosinolates
  biosynthesis, **1**, 858
  as insect attractants, **8**, 156
  roles, **1**, 130
  structure, **5**, 290
  toxicity, **8**, 145
glucosinolates, aliphatic, in induced chemical defense, **8**,
    151
glucosinolates, 3-indolylmethyl
  accumulation, **1**, 130
  occurrence, **1**, 130
glucosinolates, 1-methoxy-3-indolylmethyl, occurrence,
    1, 130
β-D-glucosylamine, *N*-bromoacetyl-, labeling, **1**, 891
glucosylated 38kd protein
  as primer, **3**, 467

roles, **3**, 463
glucosylceramide, C6-NBD-, as substrate, **3**, 94
glucosylceramide (GlcCer)
  biosynthesis, **3**, 91, 94
  galactosylation, **3**, 94
glucosyl esters, biosynthesis, **8**, 90
α-D-glucosyl fluoride, 5-fluoro-, α-glucosidase
    inactivation, **5**, 299
4′-*O*-glucosyltransferases, occurrence, **1**, 738
5-*O*-glucosyltransferases, characterization, **1**, 738
glucosyltransferases (GlcTs)
  characterization, **1**, 738, **3**, 108, 604
  GlcT-1, sequences, **3**, 113
  roles
    with glycoproteins, **3**, 31
    in lignin biosynthesis, **3**, 676
  sequences, **3**, 459
glucuronoarabinoxylans
  characterization, **3**, 600
  cross-linking, **3**, 601
  structure, **3**, 606
glucuronoarabinoxylan synthases, characterization, **3**,
    606
glucuronosyltransferase(s)
  characterization, **3**, 518
  occurrence, **1**, 738
  roles, in pectin biosynthesis, **3**, 511
7-*O*-glucuronosyltransferases, occurrence, **1**, 737
glucuronyltransferases (GlcATs)
  catalysis, **3**, 122
  characterization, **3**, 108
Glu-Glu-Phe α-tubulin epitopes, localization, **5**, 323
glutamate
  roles
    in 5-aminolevulinic acid biosynthesis, **4**, 67
    in hydroxymethylglutaryl-CoA reductase catalysis,
      2, 34
    in thiostrepton biosynthesis, **1**, 853
glutamate-165, as general base catalyst, **5**, 36
glutamate-406, roles, **4**, 70
glutamate-ammonia ligase, inhibitors, **2**, 257, **3**, 627
L-glutamate:ammonia ligase (ADP-forming) *see*
    glutamate-ammonia ligase
glutamate dehydrogenase, substrates, **1**, 873
glutamate mutase *see* methylaspartate mutase
L-glutamate:NAD⁺ oxidoreductase (deaminating) *see*
    glutamate dehydrogenase
glutamate oxaloacetate transaminase, substrates, **1**,
    873
glutamate pyruvate transaminase, substrates, **1**, 873
glutamate racemase
  encoding, **3**, 255
  overexpression, **3**, 255
  roles, in peptidoglycan biosynthesis, **3**, 255
glutamate receptors
  blocking, **8**, 478
  classification, **6**, 103
  mRNA, **6**, 103
  subunits, **5**, 87
glutamate-γ-semialdehyde, as glucosamine-6-phosphate
    synthase inhibitor, **3**, 275
glutamate 1-semialdehyde aminotransferase(s)
  activity, **8**, 63
  catalysis, **4**, 69
  isolation, **4**, 67
  mechanisms, **4**, 70
  occurrence, **4**, 70
  structure, **4**, 70
  suicide inactivation, **4**, 70
glutamate 1-semialdehyde (GSA)
  analogues, **4**, 70
  roles, in tetrapyrrole biosynthesis, **4**, 69
  transamination, **8**, 63

glutamate-tRNA ligase(s)
  activity, **8**, 63
  biosynthesis, **4**, 68
  isolation, **4**, 67
  occurrence, **4**, 68
D-glutamic acid
  biosynthesis, **3**, 254
  in peptides, **3**, 245
  in peptidoglycan, **3**, 246
D-glutamic acid, *threo*-3-hydroxy-, occurrence, **3**, 246
(*S*)-glutamic acid, taste, **8**, 10
glutamic dehydrogenase *see* glutamate dehydrogenase
L-glutamine:D-fructose-6-phosphateamidotransferase,
  coding, **3**, 206
glutamine 2-oxoketoglutarate amino transferase
  (GOGAT), inhibitors, **3**, 627
glutamine synthetase (GS) *see* glutamate-ammonia ligase
glutamyl-tRNA reductase(s), **8**, 63
  activity, **8**, 63
  catalysis, **4**, 68
  inhibition, **4**, 68
  isolation, **4**, 67
  mechanisms, **4**, 69
  recognition, **4**, 68
  substrate specificity, **4**, 68
glutamyl-tRNA synthetase(s) *see* glutamate-tRNA
  ligase(s)
glutarate, hydroxyketo-, inhibitory activity, **3**, 421
glutarate, 4-hydroxy-2-keto-
  cleavage, **3**, 381
  equilibrium constants, **3**, 385
glutarate, α-hydroxy-γ-keto-, biosynthesis, **3**, 413
glutarate, hydroxymethylketo-, cleavage, **3**, 385
glutarate, 4-hydroxy-4-methyl-2-keto-
  biosynthesis, **3**, 385
  equilibrium constants, **3**, 385
glutarate, α-keto-
  in amphidinolide J biosynthesis, **8**, 632
  chain elongation, **1**, 69
  as intermediate, **1**, 834
glutarate, 2-oxo-
  as starting material, for succinsemialdehyde, **1**, 614
  as substrate, **8**, 93
glutaredoxin
  in *Escherichia coli*, **3**, 330
  structure, **5**, 62
glutaric acid, β-hydroxy-β-methyl-, conjugation, **8**, 90
glutaric acid, 2-oxo-, as starting material, for *o*-
  succinylbenzoic acid, **1**, 614, 617
glutathione *S*-alkyltransferase(s) *see* glutathione
  transferase(s)
glutathione *S*-aralkyltransferase(s) *see* glutathione
  transferase(s)
glutathione *S*-aryltransferase(s) *see* glutathione
  transferase(s)
glutathione disulfide, hydroxymethylglutaryl-CoA
  reductase inhibition, **2**, 33
glutathione (GSH), **7**, 559
  addition, to epoxides, **5**, 61
  binding, **4**, 264
  binding domain, **5**, 62
  in dichloromethane dehalogenase catalysis, **5**, 408
  DNA damage, **7**, 560
  in nucleophilic epoxide opening, **5**, 53
  prostaglandin-endoperoxide synthase inhibition, **5**, 245
glutathione:hydrogen-peroxide oxidoreductase *see*
  glutathione peroxidase
glutathione peroxidase, **5**, 62
  GPX1, applications, **4**, 371
  GPX2, activity, **4**, 371
  GPX3, mRNA levels, **4**, 371
  GPX4, activity, **4**, 371
  prostaglandin-endoperoxide synthase inhibition, **5**, 245

  selenocysteine in, **4**, 357
  termination codons, **4**, 371
glutathione transferase(s)
  activity, **1**, 742
  catalysis, **4**, 264, **5**, 53
  families, **5**, 61
    classification, **1**, 274, 275
    molecular phylogeny, **1**, 275
  membrane-bound, structure, **5**, 65
  microsomal
    chemical modification, **5**, 65
    mechanism, **5**, 65
    trimeric structure, **5**, 65
  occurrence, **8**, 31, 32
  regioselectivity, **5**, 63, 64
  soluble, **5**, 61
    catalytic mechanisms, **5**, 63
    structure, **5**, 62
  stereoselectivity, **5**, 63, 64
  superfamily, **5**, 408, 414
glutathione *S*-transferase(s) (GST) *see* glutathione
  transferase(s)
glycan, recognition, **3**, 14
glycan chains, roles, in biological processes, **3**, 2
glycans, glycosamino- (GAGs)
  biosynthesis, **3**, 4, 169
  chemical synthesis, **3**, 169
  structure, **3**, 4, 161
  types of, **3**, 161
glycans, lactosamino-, use of term, **3**, 173
glycans, lipophospho- (LPGs)
  biosynthesis, **3**, 307
  structure, **3**, 307, 6
N-glycans
  biosynthesis, **3**, 3, 5, 15
    factors affecting, **3**, 3, 38
    glycosyltransferases in, **3**, **37–67**
    overview, **3**, 40
  classification, **3**, 15
  complex, **3**, 15, 17, 75
    antennae, **3**, 40
    conformation, **3**, 53
    formation, **3**, 20
  from
    $Glc_3Man_9GlcNAc_2$, **3**, 15
    oligosaccharides, **3**, 15
  future research, **3**, 60
  and *O*-glycans compared, **3**, 70
  high mannose, **3**, 15
  hybrid, **3**, 15
    accumulation, **3**, 27
    formation, **3**, 27
    use of term, **3**, 41
  in lepidopteran insect Sf9 cells, **3**, 24
  processing, **3**, 14, 17, 28, 42
    glycosidases in, **3**, 18
    α1,2-mannosidases in, **3**, 21
  roles, in embryogenesis, **3**, 52
  structure, **3**, 3, 15, 38
    overview, **3**, 40
  synthesis, **3**, 69
    defects, **3**, 59
O-glycans
  acidity, **3**, 71
  antigens on, **3**, 71
  as antigens, **3**, 78
  biological significance, **3**, 71
  biosynthesis
    factors affecting, **3**, 70, 72
    initiation, **3**, 73
  branching, **3**, 77
  core structure, **3**, 71
    synthesis, **3**, 75

elongation, **3**, 77
endothelial leukocyte adhesion molecule-1 binding, **3**, 71
fucosylation, **3**, 81
functions, **3**, 71
and *N*-glycans compared, **3**, 70
on glycoproteins, **3**, 69
on mucins, **3**, 70, 3
occurrence, **3**, 70
processing, **3**, 73
roles, **3**, 69, 70
sialic acid residues, **3**, 79
structure, **3**, 71, 3
sulfation, **3**, 80
synthesis
glycosyltransferases in, **3**, **69–85**
termination reactions, **3**, 78
O-glycan sulfate esters, roles, in glycosylation, **3**, 81
glyceollin I
level increase, **1**, 781
as phytoalexin, **8**, 189
glyceollin(s)
accumulation, **1**, 807
half-life, **1**, 812
6a-hydroxylation, **1**, 802
tolerance, **1**, 782
glyceraldehyde phosphate, biosynthesis, **2**, 52
D-glyceraldehyde 3-phosphate
biosynthesis, **3**, 430
reactions
with acetyl phosphate, **3**, 392
with pyruvate, **3**, 421
glyceraldehyde 3-phosphate (GAP)
coupling reactions, **2**, 4
dihydroxyacetone phosphate transfer, **3**, 417
as electrophile, **3**, 390
from, pyruvate, **2**, 50
interconversion, **5**, 36
as starting material, **8**, 219
for isopentenyl diphosphate, **2**, 54
structure, **2**, 374
as substrate, **3**, 386
D-glyceraldehyde-3-phosphate ketol-isomerase *see* triose-phosphate isomerase (TIM)
glycerate, 2-phospho- (2-PGA), as substrate, **5**, 27
D-glycerate:NADP$^+$ 2-oxidoreductase *see* hydroxypyruvate reductase
glyceric acid, 3-phospho-, as phospho*enol*pyruvate substitute, **3**, 390
glycerol
as carbon source, **2**, 54
oxidation, **1**, 144
glycerol, digalactosyldiacyl- (DGDG), as substrate, **1**, 37
glycerol, 1,2-dioleyl-3-palmityl-, occurrence, **8**, 217
glycerol, monogalactosyldiacyl- (MGDG), as substrate, **1**, 37
glycerol, (2*S*)-1-*O*-palmitoyl-3-*O*-β-D-galactopyranosyl-occurrence, **8**, 610
structure, **8**, 610
glycerol, sulfoquinobosyldiacyl- (SQDG), as substrate, **1**, 37
[1,3-^{13}C$_2$]glycerol, in virginiae butanolide A studies, **1**, 141
sn-glycerol, 1-alkyl-, phosphorylation, **1**, 288
sn-glycerol, 1-alkyl-2-acetyl-, in platelet-activating factor biosynthesis, **1**, 295, 297
sn-glycerol, 1-alkyl-2-acyl-, biosynthesis, **1**, 288
glycerol dehydrase, reactions, **5**, 264
glycerolipids
biosynthesis, **1**, 144, 147
feeding stimulant activity, **8**, 419, 420
glycerols, acyl-, biosynthesis, **8**, 274
glycerols, alkylacyl-, occurrence, **4**, 307
glycerols, diacyl-, occurrence, **4**, 307, **8**, 441

glycerols, triacyl-, occurrence, **8**, 207
glycerophosphatase *see* acid phosphatase; alkaline phosphatase
glycerophosphocholine, 1-acyl-, as substrate, **1**, 293
glycerophosphocholine, 1-acyl-2-(5-oxovaleroyl)-, neutrophil activation, **1**, 298
glycerophosphocholine, 1-alkyl-
biosynthesis, **1**, 289, 292
roles, in platelet-activating factor biosynthesis, **1**, 292
as substrate, **1**, 293
glycerophosphocholine, 1-alkyl-2-acyl-
accumulation, **1**, 289
biosynthesis, **1**, 289
hydrolysis, **1**, 289, 291
via CoA-independent transacylase, **1**, 292
localization, **1**, 291
glycerophosphoethanolamine, 1-alkenyl-2-acetyl-, biosynthesis, **1**, 293
glycerophosphoethanolamine, 1-alkenyl-2-acyl-
accumulation, **1**, 289
biosynthesis, **1**, 289
glycerophosphoethanolamine, 1-alkyl-2-acyl-
biosynthesis, **1**, 289
metabolism, **1**, 289
glycerophospholipids, **3**, 220
glycine
biosynthesis, **3**, 397
reactions, with succinyl-CoA, **4**, 65
glycine, D-allyl-, replacement, **4**, 253
glycine, 2-(2'-cyclopentenyl)-, occurrence, **1**, 69
glycine, (2-cyclopentyl)-, as cyanogenic glycoside precursor, **1**, 885, 887
glycine, γ-L-glutamyl-D,L-cysteinyl-, **7**, 560
glycine, (*S*-phenoxyacetyl)cysteinyl-, as substrate, **4**, 264
glycine, (*S*-phenylacetyl)cysteinyl-, as substrate, **4**, 264
glycine, *N*-(phosphonomethyl)- *see* glyphosate
Glycine max
β-amylase, **5**, 301
cells, adenosinediphosphoglucose, **3**, 463
chalcone isomerases, **1**, 722
chalcone ketide reductase, **1**, 732
chalcone synthase, **1**, 732
trans-cinnamate 4-monooxygenase, **1**, 720
cinnamoyl-CoA reductase, **3**, 652
coproporphyrinogen oxidase, **4**, 95
4-coumarate-CoA ligase, **1**, 720
desaturases, **1**, 40, 41
8*S*,15*S*-dihydroperoxy-6*E*,8*Z*,11*Z*,13*E*-eicosatetraenoic acid, **1**, 234
3,9-dihydroxypterocarpan, **1**, 802
flavone synthases, **1**, 724
flavonoid 3'-*O*-methyltransferase, **1**, 739
genisteine, **1**, 130
hybridization, **4**, 134
9*S*-hydroperoxyoctadecadienoic acid, **1**, 233
13*S*-hydroperoxyoctadecadienoic acid, **1**, 233
2'-hydroxygenistein, **1**, 795
2'-hydroxylase activity, **1**, 795
infection, **1**, 807
isoflavone glycosides, **1**, 806
isoflavone reductase, **1**, 796
isoflavones, **1**, 815
metabolism, **1**, 815
isoflavone synthase, **1**, 793
jasmonic acid, **1**, 124
lipoxygenase, metabolism, **1**, 232
lipoxygenase-1, **1**, 99
O-methyltransferases, **3**, 644
nodulation, **1**, 781
proline-rich proteins, **3**, 732
pterocarpan synthase, **1**, 797
roots, abscisic acid studies, **1**, 781
glycine reductase, selenocysteine in, **4**, 357

glycine reductase selenoprotein A, interactions, **4**, 374
glycine-rich proteins (GRPs), occurrence, cell walls, **3**, 732
glycitein, demethylation, **1**, 815
glycobiology, field of study, **3**, 1
glycochemistry, field of study, **3**, 1
glycoconjugates
  occurrence, **3**, 333
  polysaccharides, **3**, 313
glycoforms, definitions, **3**, 41
glycogen
  accumulation, **3**, 443
    rates, **3**, 475
    in stationary phase, **3**, 476
  bacterial
    biosynthesis, **3**, 444
    structure, **3**, 442
  biosynthesis, **3**, 2, 7, **441–495**
    enzyme properties, **3**, 447
    genetic regulation, **3**, 477
    in mammals, **3**, 446, 478
    regulatory mechanisms, **3**, 468
  fungal, structure, **3**, 442
  hepatic, **3**, 444
  mammalian
    structure, **3**, 442
    studies, **3**, 443
  occurrence, **3**, 443
  roles
    in animals, **3**, 443
    in bacteria, **3**, 443
  structure, **3**, 442
  synthesis, primers, **3**, 480
glycogenase *see* α-amylase; β-amylase
glycogen debranching enzyme
  occurrence, **5**, 306
  sequences, **5**, 298
glycogen 6-glucanohydrolase *see* isoamylase
glycogenin *see* glycogenin glucosyltransferase
glycogenin glucosyltransferase
  catalysis, **3**, 481
  overexpression, **3**, 486
  as primer, for glycogen synthesis, **3**, 480
  properties, **3**, 480
  in rabbit muscle, **3**, 446
  roles, in glycogen biosynthesis, **3**, 481
  x-ray crystal structure, **3**, 481
glycogenolysis, lactate formation, **3**, 444
glycogen phosphorylase
  activated, **5**, 304
  occurrence, **5**, 303
  synergistic inhibition, **5**, 304
glycogen(starch) synthase, catalysis, **3**, 446
glycogen synthase (bacterial)
  catalytic sites, **3**, 453
  conserved regions, **3**, 455
  genes, structural, **3**, 453
  and glycogen synthase (mammalian) compared, **3**, 452
  occurrence, **3**, 444
  primers, **3**, 452
  properties, **3**, 452
  reactions, reversibility, **3**, 453
  structure, **3**, 452
    via site-directed mutagenesis, **3**, 453
  substrates, **3**, 453
glycogen synthase kinase-3 (GSK-3)
  activation, **3**, 488
  inactivation, **3**, 488
  phosphorylation sites, **3**, 484
glycogen synthase kinase-5 (GSK-5), phosphorylation
  sites, **3**, 484
glycogen synthase (mammalian)
  activity, phosphorylation, **3**, 485
  and glycogen synthase (bacterial) compared, **3**, 452

occurrence, **3**, 479
overexpression, **3**, 486
phosphorylation
  in vitro studies, **3**, 485
  in vivo studies, **3**, 485
properties, **3**, 479
purification, **3**, 479
regulation, via phosphorylation–dephosphorylation, **3**,
  482
regulatory mechanisms, **3**, 482
skeletal muscle stimulation, insulin-induced, **3**, 487
subunits, **3**, 479
types of, **3**, 479
glycolaldehyde, as substrate, **3**, 386
glycolaldehydetransferase *see* transketolase
glycolipid:galactosyltransferases (GSL:GalTs)
  characterization, **3**, 108
  nomenclature, **3**, 109
glycolipid:glycosyltransferases (GSL:GLTs),
  characterization, **3**, 108
glycolipids
  adenosine triphosphatase (potassium sodium)
    inhibition, **8**, 618
  biosynthesis, **3**, 2
    regulation, **3**, 124
  catalysis, **3**, 109
  deoxysugars, **3**, 312
  fatty acids in, **1**, 24
  occurrence, **3**, 295
  sialylated, **3**, 49
glycolysis
  enzymes of, **3**, 414
  Ginkgo biloba embryo metabolism, **2**, 372
  lactate formation, **3**, 444
  pathways
    DeLey–Doudoroff, **3**, 414
    Embden–Myerhof–Parnas, **3**, 414
    Entner–Doudoroff, **3**, 414
glycopeptides
  effects, on Gram-positive bacteria, **3**, 281
  peptidoglycan assembly inhibition, **3**, 272
  semi-synthetic, **3**, 282
P-glycoprotein, and *Vinca* alkaloids, **8**, 613
glycoprotein-*N*-acetylgalactosamine
  localization, **3**, 75
  occurrence, **3**, 75
  roles, in *O*-glycan synthesis, **3**, 75
glycoprotein-*N*-acetyl-D-glucosaminyl-phospho-D-
    mannose *N*-acetyl-D-glucosaminylphosphohydrolase
    see N-acetylglucosamine-1-phosphodiester α-*N*-
    acetylglucosaminidase
glycoprotein 4-β-galactosyl-transferase *see* β-*N*-
    acetylglucosaminylglycopeptide β-1,4-
    galactosyltransferase
glycoprotein(s), **3**, 109
  biosynthesis, **3**, 2, 288
    glycosidases in, **3**, 17
    glycosyltransferases in, **3**, 17
    and peptidoglycan biosynthesis, **3**, 286
  catabolism, **3**, 28
  characterization, **3**, 600
  deoxysugars, **3**, 312
  folding
    role of α-glucosidases in, **3**, 31
    role of glucosyltransferase in, **3**, 31
  O-glycans in, **3**, 69
    structures, **3**, 71
  malfolded, proteolytic degradation, **3**, 31
  occurrence, **3**, 143
    cell walls, **3**, 732
  polylactosamine-containing, **3**, 118
  processing inhibitors, **3**, 150
  sialylated, **3**, 49

studies, **1**, 890
transport, **3**, 31
viral
  early studies, **4**, 13
  palmitoylation, **4**, 15
viral envelope, structure, **4**, 14
in yeasts, **3**, 22
glycosidase inhibitors, **3**, 18
  antimicrobial activity, **3**, 142
  biochemistry, **3**, **129–160**
  biological activity, **3**, 140
  biosynthesis, **3**, 2, 4
  early studies, **3**, 130
  insecticidal activity, **3**, 141
  isolation, **3**, 134
  mammalian toxicity, **3**, 140
  occurrence, **3**, 134
  plant growth inhibitory activity, **3**, 141
  structure, **3**, 130
  structure–activity relationships, **3**, 138
  therapeutic activity, **3**, 142
glycosidases
  catalysis, **3**, 2, 17
  cell mutants, **3**, 18
  characterization, **3**, 18
  classification, **3**, 14, **5**, 281
  effects, on oligosaccharides, **3**, 38
  endo mode of action, **5**, 282
  exo mode of action, **5**, 282
  functions, **3**, 14
  N-glycan processing, **3**, 18
  Hammett relationships, **5**, 288
  inhibition, **3**, 138, **5**, 308
  inversion, **3**, 14
  inverting, **5**, 281, 284, 300
    catalytic flexibility, **5**, 290
    transfers to water, **5**, 300
    transglycosylation, **5**, 290, 301
  kinetic isotope effects, **5**, 288
  of oligosaccharide processing pathway, asparagine-
    linked, **3**, **13–35**
  processing, **3**, 14, 18
    cDNAs, **3**, 18
    genes, **3**, 18
    and quality control, **3**, 31
  reaction mechanisms, **5**, 284
  recombinant, **3**, 18
  retaining, **5**, 281, 284
    deglycosylation, **5**, 289
    general acid–base catalysts, **5**, 286, 290
    glycosylation, **5**, 289
    intermediate trapping, **5**, 286
    non-covalent interactions, **5**, 292
    nucleophiles, **5**, 286
    substrate-assisted catalysis, **5**, 286
    transfers to water, **5**, 289
    trapped intermediates, **5**, 292
    trapping, **5**, 286
  roles
    complex carbohydrate turnover, **3**, 14
    in *N*-glycan processing, **3**, 14
    in glycoprotein biosynthesis, **3**, 17
    polysaccharide catabolism, **3**, 14
  sequence similarities, **5**, 281
  stereochemistry, **5**, 288
  structure, **5**, 282
  use of term, **5**, 280
β-glycosidases
  crystal structure, **1**, 891
  in cyanogenic glycoside hydrolysis, **1**, 881
  degradation, **1**, 890
N-glycoside, activity, **8**, 71
glycosides

fluorination, **5**, 287
occurrence, **1**, 737
glycosides, amino-
  applications, antibiotics, **6**, 193
  binding, **6**, 193
  biosynthesis, **3**, 6, **4**, 196
glycosides, cardiac, **8**, 152, 154
  L-aculose, **3**, 321
  biological activity, **3**, 328
  4,6-dideoxy-3-*O*-methyl-D-*ribo*-hexose, **3**, 321
  and insect oviposition, **8**, 156
  insect sequestration, **8**, 362, 363
  occurrence, **8**, 360
  roles, in oviposition deterrence, **8**, 156
glycosides, cyanogenic
  biosynthesis, **1**, **881–895**
  chemical properties, **1**, 885
  cyclopentenoid aglycone-containing, biosynthesis, **1**, 70
  degradation, **1**, **881–895**
  hydrogen cyanide release, **1**, 20
  occurrence, **1**, 882
  pathways, channeled, **1**, 887
  precursors, **1**, 885
  toxicity, **8**, 144, 183
glycosides, 2-deoxy-2-fluoro-, as reagents, **5**, 287
glycosides, flavonoid, malonylation, **1**, 741
glycosides, flavonol
  as insect oviposition stimulants, **8**, 156
  in pollen, **8**, 163
glycosides, fluoro-, development, **5**, 287
glycosides, iridoid, occurrence, **8**, 307
glycosides, isoflavonoid, occurrence, **1**, 808
glycosides, steroid, and hemolytic saponins compared, **8**, 474
glycosides, trinitrophenyl 2-deoxy-2,2-difluoro-, as reagents, **5**, 287
glycosidic bonds, formation, **3**, 209
Glycosmis pentaphylla, carbazole alkaloids, **4**, 54
glycosphingolipids (GSLs), **3**, 49
  biosynthesis, **3**, 2, 3, **107–128**
    in endoplasmic reticulum–Golgi complex, **3**, 88
    in vitro, **3**, 115
    pathways, **3**, 100
    regulation, **3**, 4, **107–128**
  classification, **3**, 87
  degradation, **3**, 3, 102
  endocytic pathways, **3**, 3, 104
  metabolism, catabolic product recycling, **3**, 3, 100
  occurrence, **3**, 87
  oligosaccharide chains, **3**, 88
  oligosaccharide mimicry, **3**, 228
  reviews, **3**, 108
  structure, **3**, 87
glycosylamines, *N*-bromoacetyl-, applications, **5**, 287
glycosylation
  acid-catalyzed
    for the synthesis of purine nucleosides, **7**, 260
    for the synthesis of pyrimidine nucleosides, **7**, 260
  importance, in biological systems, **3**, 14
  localization, **1**, 809
N-glycosylation, and cancer, **3**, 14
O-glycosylation, mediation, **3**, 75
glycosyl enzymes, covalent, as intermediates, **5**, 284
glycosyl epoxides, applications, **5**, 287
glycosyl hydrolases
  classification, **5**, 281
  Family 1, **1**, 890
    x-ray crystal structure, **3**, 687
glycosylinositol phospholipids (GIPLs)
  biosynthesis, **3**, 307
  moieties, **3**, 307
  structure, **3**, 6, 295
glycosylphosphatidylinositol anchor *see* GPI anchor

glycosyl transfer, in carbohydrate metabolism, **5**, 316
glycosyltransferases (GLTs)
  activity
    divalent metal ion effects, **3**, 73
    and membrane composition, **3**, 73
  binding, to endomembrane system, **3**, 39
  catalysis, **3**, 2, 17, 209, 510
  cDNA encoding, **3**, 75
  characterization, **3**, 604
  clans, **5**, 282
  classification, **5**, 281
  domain structure, **3**, 44, 70
  effects, on oligosaccharides, **3**, 38
  encoding, **3**, 351
  evolution, **3**, 59
  exons, **3**, 73
  expression, mechanisms, **3**, 59
  future research, **5**, 310
  gene families, **3**, 59
  genetics, **3**, 3, 73
  as glycoproteins, **3**, 73
  in Golgi apparatus, **3**, 17, 70
  homo-oligomerization, **3**, 45
  inhibition, **1**, 738
  Internet resources, **3**, 38
  localization, **3**, 70, 73
    sub-Golgi, **3**, 95
  mechanisms, **5**, **279–314**
  membrane-bound, cleavage, **3**, 70
  occurrence, **1**, 129
  overexpression, **3**, 59
  purification, **3**, 58, 604
  roles
    in *N*-glycan biosynthesis, **3**, 3, **37–67**
    in *O*-glycan biosynthesis, 33, 70
    in glycoprotein biosynthesis, **3**, 17
    in glycosphingolipid biosynthesis, **3**, 108, 4
    in pectin biosynthesis, **3**, 511
    in polysaccharide biosynthesis, **3**, 510
    in serine/threonine-GalNAc *O*-glycan synthesis, **3**, **69–85**
  specificity, **3**, 95, 109
    substrate, **3**, 73
  substrates, nucleoside diphosphate sugars, **3**, 505
  topology, **3**, 95
  transgene, **3**, 59
  use of term, **5**, 280
glycyl radicals
  Gly-681, activation, **3**, 345
  localization, **5**, 217
  in pyruvate formate lyase, **5**, 185
  roles, in thiyl radical biosynthesis, **5**, 185
Glycyrrhiza echinata
  chalcone reductase, **1**, 790
  chalcone synthase, **1**, 732
  licodione, **1**, 794
  liquiritigenin, **1**, 790
  naringenin, **1**, 790
Glycyrrhiza glabra, glycyrrhizin, **8**, 166
glycyrrhizin, occurrence, **8**, 166
glyoxal
  applications, DNA structure probes, **7**, 95
  formation, **7**, 521
glyoxal, methyl-, **5**, 67
  biosynthesis, **2**, 54
  occurrence, **5**, 37
glyoxal, phenyl-
  in branching enzyme studies, **3**, 463
  labeling, **3**, 451
  as photoaffinity substrate, **3**, 448
glyoxalase I, **5**, 62, 67
glyoxylate
  biosynthesis, **3**, 381

reactions, with oxaloacetate, **3**, 413
glyoxylate carbo-ligase *see* tartronate-semialdehyde synthase
glyoxylate carboxy-lyase (dimerizing) *see* tartronate-semialdehyde synthase
glyoxylate cycles, in acetate metabolism, **2**, 52, 58
glyoxylic acid cycle, inhibition, **4**, 255
glyoxysomes, phenylalanine ammonia-lyase, **3**, 662
Glyphodes pyloalis, (10*E*,12*E*,14*Z*)-10,12,14-hexadecatrienyl acetate, **8**, 207
glyphosate
  as competitive inhibitor, **1**, 597
  complexation, **1**, 597
  herbicidal activity, **1**, 593, 4, 9, **5**, 349
  inhibitory activity, **3**, 804
  as mixed inhibitor, **1**, 597
  NMR spectra, **1**, 597
  3-phosphoshikimate 1-carboxyvinyltransferase inhibition, **1**, 596
  targets, **1**, 593
  tolerance, **1**, 598
  as transition state analogue, **1**, 597
  as uncompetitive inhibitor, **1**, 597
glyphosate, *N*-amino-, inhibitory activity, **1**, 597
glypicans, localization, **3**, 164
GM1 ganglioside, biosynthesis, **3**, 111
GM2 activator protein, encoding, **3**, 102
GM2 ganglioside
  biosynthesis, **3**, 111
  occurrence, **3**, 123
GM2 ganglioside, acetyl-, synthesis, **3**, 111
GM2 ganglioside, lyso-, deacylation, **3**, 111
GM3 ganglioside, as acceptor, **3**, 123
GM-CSF mRNA, AU rich elements, **6**, 208
GmII homologue, isolation, **3**, 27
GMP-140 *see* PADGEM protein
Gnathotrichus spp., sulcatol, **8**, 232
Gnathotrichus sulcatus
  pheromones, **8**, 14
  sulcatol, **8**, 3, 14
gnd genes, recombination, **3**, 217
GnT I *see* α-1,3-mannosyl-glycoprotein β-1,2-*N*-acetylglucosaminyltransferase
GnT II *see* α-1,6-mannosyl-glycoprotein β-1,2-*N*-acetylglucosaminyltransferase
GnT III *see* β-1,4-mannosyl-glycoprotein β-1,4-*N*-acetylglucosaminyltransferase
GnT IV *see* α-1,3-mannosyl-glycoprotein β-1,4-*N*-acetylglucosaminyltransferase
GnT V *see* α-1,3(6)-mannosyl-glycoprotein β-1,6-*N*-acetylglucosaminyltransferase
GnT VI *see* UDP-*N*-acetylglucosamine:R$_1$(R$_2$)Manα1-6R$_3$[GlcNAc to Manα1-6] β-1,4-*N*-acetylglucosaminyltransferase VI
goat liver, UTP-glucose-1-phosphate uridylyltransferase, **3**, 478
GOGAT *see* glutamine 2-oxoketoglutarate amino transferase (GOGAT)
goldfish *see Carassius auratus*
Golgi apparatus
  β-*N*-acetylglucosaminylglycopeptide β-1,4-galactosyltransferase targeting, **3**, 45
  effects of auxins on, **8**, 31
  endo α-mannosidase, **3**, 19, 20
  N-glycan biosynthesis, **3**, 3, 38
  O-glycan biosynthesis, **3**, 72
  and *N*-glycan processing, **3**, 17
  glycosphingolipids, **3**, 87
    biosynthesis, **3**, 88, 3
  glycosylation, **3**, 4
  glycosyltransferases, **3**, 17, 70, 95
    compartmentalization, **3**, 96
  mammalian

α-mannosidase IA, **3**, 22
α-mannosidase IB, **3**, 22
α1,2-mannosidases, **3**, 22
α1,2-mannosidase IA, **3**, 148
α-mannosidase II, **3**, 17, 25
α-mannosidases
   and hereditary erythroblastic multinuclearity with a
     positive acidified serum, **3**, 27
   immunolocalization, **3**, 28
   α1,2-mannosidases, **3**, 17, 148
   rat liver, **3**, 23
mannosyltransferases, **3**, 17
murine, α1,2-mannosidase IA, **3**, 23
nucleoside diphosphate sugars, **3**, 509
polysaccharide biosynthesis, **3**, 504, 601
   sites, **3**, 602
protein retention, mechanisms, **3**, 45
targeting, ST6Gal I, **3**, 48
Golgi body *see* Golgi apparatus
Golgi complex *see* Golgi apparatus
(+)-gomisin A
   biosynthesis, **1**, 676
   hepatotoxicity prevention, **1**, 702
   occurrence, **1**, 676
(−)-gomisin J, anti-HIV activity, **1**, 703
Gomphonema parvulum, pheromones, **8**, 425
Goniodoma spp., goniodomin, **8**, 613
Goniodoma pseudogoniaulax, goniodomin A, **8**, 613
goniodomin, occurrence, **8**, 613
goniodomin A
   actomyosin ATPase modulation induction, **8**, 614
   antifungal activity, **8**, 614
   occurrence, **8**, 613
   structure, **8**, 613
Gonyaulax polyedra
   gonyauline, **8**, 457
   gonyol, **8**, 458
   methionine feeding experiments, **8**, 458
gonyauline
   from, methionine, **8**, 458
   occurrence, **8**, 457
   structure, **8**, 458
gonyol, occurrence, **8**, 458
goose grass *see Eleusine indica*
Gorgonacea, (−)-germacrene A, **8**, 227
gorgonian octocoral *see Erythropodium caribaeorum*
gorlic acid, occurrence, **1**, 68
Gosling, Raymond G., DNA structure studies, **7**, 81
gossypetin, roles, in ultraviolet patterning, **8**, 160
Gossypium spp.
   heliocides H₁, **1**, 377
   heliocides H₄, **1**, 377
Gossypium arboreum, cadinene synthase, **2**, 186
Gossypium hirsutum
   cadinene, **2**, 186
   gossypol, **8**, 312
   β-1,4-linkage formation, **3**, 581
gossyplure, occurrence, **8**, 4
gossypol
   antifeedant activity, **8**, 308
   biosynthesis, **2**, 186, 188
   occurrence, **2**, 186, **8**, 312
gout, etiology, **5**, 80
gpal genes
   *gpal*2
      cloning, **3**, 667
      expression, **3**, 667
   *gpal*3, cloning, **3**, 667
GPI *see* inositol, glycosylphosphatidyl- (GPI)
GPI1 protein, roles, in *N*-
   acetylglucosaminylphosphatidylinositol biosynthesis,
   4, 309
GPI anchored protein, **3**, 296, **4**, 305

deficiency, **4**, 306
structure, **4**, 307
GPI anchor(s)
   biosynthesis, **3**, 2, **4**, **305–318**
     of core structure, **3**, 300
     genetics, **3**, 296, 299, **4**, 307
     inhibitors, **3**, 303
     intermediates, **4**, 307
     orientation, **4**, 306
     protein complexes, **4**, 309
     species differences, **3**, 304
     topology, **3**, 303, 6
   definitions, **3**, 296
   discovery, **3**, 296
   functions, **3**, 296
   occurrence, **3**, 295, 6
   roles
     in protein transport, **3**, 297
     in signal transduction, **3**, 6, 297
     as second messengers, **3**, 297
   species differences, **3**, 297
   structure, **3**, 6, 296
GPI genes
   *GPI*1
     characterization, **4**, 309
     cloning, **4**, 309
     homology, **3**, 301
   *GPI*2
     encoding, **4**, 309
     homology, **3**, 301
   *GPI*3, homology, **3**, 301
   *GPI*8, **4**, 316
     cloning, **3**, 303
   *GPI*10, cloning, **3**, 301
GPI:protein transamidase
   in GPI anchor biosynthesis, **4**, 315
   reactions, **4**, 316
GPP *see* geranyl diphosphate (GDP)
G-proteins
   coupled receptors, **1**, 280
   G₍Qα₎, palmitoylation, **4**, 21
   G₍Sα₎
     depalmitoylation, **4**, 20
     palmitoylation, **4**, 20
   heterotrimeric, in signal transduction, **4**, 20
   palmitoylation, **4**, 20
   α-subunits, **4**, 20
Gracilaria spp., food poisoning, **8**, 518
Gracilaria edulis see *Polycavernosa tsudai*
Gracilariopsis lemaneiformis
   hydroperoxides, rearrangement, **1**, 212
   12S-hydroxyeicosatetraenoic acid, **1**, 219
   oxylipins, **1**, 220
   vicinal diol biosynthesis, **1**, 220
gradolide, antifeedant activity, **8**, 308
Gräfe's factors
   functions, **8**, 391
   structure, **8**, 391
gra genes
   cloning, **1**, 478
   in deoxysugar biosynthesis, **3**, 342
   sequencing, **1**, 478
grain beetle *see Cryptolestes turcicus*
gramicidin, biosynthesis, **1**, 520
gramicidin B, peptide bonds, **4**, 226
gramicidin D, RNA synthesis inhibition, **4**, 323
gramicidin S
   amphiphilicity, **4**, 322
   antibiotic activity, **4**, 322
   biosynthesis, **4**, 196, 202, 208, 209, 323, 342, 235
     genetics, **4**, 327
     grs gene encoding, **4**, 328
   clinical trials, **4**, 199

occurrence, **4**, 321
ornithine residues, **4**, 322
structure, three-dimensional, **4**, 321
structure–activity relationships, **4**, 322
gramicidins, linear
discovery, **4**, 320
membrane activity, **4**, 323
gramicidin S synthetase
acyl carrier protein, **4**, 340
aminoacyl adenylation domain, **4**, 331, 334
aminoacyl thiolation domain, **4**, 335
biochemistry, **4**, **319–352**
elongation domain, **4**, 340
future research, **4**, 348
Grs proteins, **4**, 328
peptidyl carrier protein, **4**, 340
4′-phosphopantetheine cofactors, **4**, 335
purification, **4**, 327
structure
modular, **4**, 331
three-dimensional, **4**, 345
substrate activation, **4**, 323, 327
substrate specificity, **4**, 326
thioesterase domain, **4**, 344
thiolation sites, **4**, 336
peptide fragments, **4**, 336
thiotemplate sites, **4**, 335
structure, **4**, 336
gramicidin S synthetase 1 (GS1)
catalysis, **4**, 323
epimerization domain, **4**, 342
occurrence, **1**, 47
racemization domain, **4**, 342
structure, three-dimensional, **4**, 348
thiotemplate sites, **4**, 342
gramicidin S synthetase 2 (GS2)
catalysis, **4**, 323
mass spectra, **4**, 331
sequencing, **1**, 546
structure, **4**, 330
three-dimensional, **4**, 345
gramine
antifeedant activity, **8**, 336
occurrence, **8**, 336
Gramineae
ecdysteroids, lack of, **8**, 280
oxylipins, **1**, 229
phytoalexins, **8**, 190
Gram-negative bacteria, **7**, 575
activity against, **8**, 469
autoinducers, **8**, 392
occurrence, **8**, 392
capsule, **3**, 243
definition, **3**, 242
lipopolysaccharides, **3**, 288, 4
peptidoglycan layer, **3**, 242, 5
as symbionts, **8**, 392
Gram-positive bacteria
activity against, **8**, 469
antimicrobial, **8**, 601
kedarcidin, **7**, 575
capsule, **3**, 243
definition, **3**, 242
peptidoglycan layer, **3**, 242, 5
granary weevil *see Sitophilus granarius*
granaticin
biosynthesis, **1**, 478, **4**, 206
genetics, **3**, 354
grand fir *see Abies grandis*
grandisal, occurrence, **8**, 224
(1*S*,2*R*)-grandisal, occurrence, **8**, 224
(+)-grandisoic acid, occurrence, **8**, 224
grandisol, occurrence, **8**, 224

granule-bound starch synthases (GBSSs), **3**, 454
activity, deficiency, **3**, 466
conserved regions, **3**, 455
deficiency, **3**, 458
deficient mutants, **3**, 466
roles, in amylopectin synthesis, **3**, 467
waxy locus, **3**, 454
as structural gene, **3**, 455
Waxy proteins, **3**, 455
granule membrane protein *see* PADGEM protein
granulocytes, and endotoxin, **3**, 180
grapevine yellow speckle viroid-1 (GYSV-1), hosts, **6**, 171
grapevine yellow speckle viroid-2 (GYSV-2), hosts, **6**, 171
Grapholita molesta
mellein, **8**, 213
methyl jasmonate, **8**, 108, 215
epi-methyl jasmonate, **8**, 215
sex attractants, **1**, 134
grasses
lignins, **3**, 695
raphides, **8**, 149
grasshoppers
isophorones, **8**, 234
see also Romalea spp.
greater glider *see Petauroides volans*
green algae *see* Chlorophyta
green fluorescent protein (GFP)
Aequorea spp., cDNA, **8**, 454
chromophore
ESI spectra, **8**, 453
MALDI-PSD spectra, **8**, 453
MALDI-TOF spectra, **8**, 453
structure, **8**, 453
greening, effects of benzyladenine on, **8**, 59
green odor
biosynthesis, **1**, **83–115**
enzyme systems, **1**, 92
pathways, **1**, 87, 91
components, **1**, 84, 86, 91
early studies, **1**, 84
environmental stimuli, **1**, 107
enzymes producing, **1**, 92
distribution, **1**, 92
properties, **1**, 93
future research, **1**, 111
roles, **1**, 84
seasonal variations, **1**, 107
structure, **1**, 86
threshold values, **1**, 86
green pepper, fruits, chloroplasts, **3**, 464
green tea
epigallocatechin-3-gallate, **3**, 792
proanthocyanidins, **3**, 769
grey kangaroo *see Macropus fuliginosus*
grisan, structure, **1**, 437
griseofulvin
analogues, **1**, 459
antifungal activity, **4**, 198
biosynthesis, **1**, 437
griseusin, biosynthesis, **1**, 479
gris genes
cloning, **1**, 479
sequencing, **1**, 479
gRNA, insertion–deletion editing, **6**, 104
Grob fragmentation, in DNA damage, **7**, 394
Grocus bore, 10-homonerol oxide, **8**, 237
(±)-grossamide
antifeedant activity, **1**, 695
occurrence, **1**, 674
grossheimin, antifeedant activity, **8**, 308
grosshemin, antifeedant activity, **8**, 308
groundnut *see Arachis hypogaea*
growth inhibitors

azadirachtin, **8**, 322
lignans, **1**, 693
6α-senecioyloxychaparrinone, **8**, 322
growth retardants, prohexadione, **8**, 36
GRPs *see* glycine-rich proteins (GRPs)
grs genes
encoding, **4**, 209, 328
grsA
dissection, **4**, 335
identification, **4**, 328
products, **4**, 330
grsB
identification, **4**, 328
products, **4**, 330
grsT, identification, **4**, 328
Grs proteins
GrsA, **4**, 328
GrsB, **4**, 328
GrsT, **4**, 330
functions, **4**, 230
Gryllus bimaculatus, allatostatins, **8**, 301
GS *see* glutamate-ammonia ligase
GS1 *see* gramicidin S synthetase 1 (GS1)
GS2 *see* gramicidin S synthetase 2 (GS2)
GSA *see* glutamate 1-semialdehyde (GSA)
gsa genes, isolation, **4**, 70
GS-DCHQ *see* hydroquinone, dichloro-*S*-glutathionyl-
(GS-DCHQ)
GSK-3 *see* glycogen synthase kinase-3 (GSK-3)
GSK-5 *see* glycogen synthase kinase-5 (GSK-5)
GSL:GalTs *see* glycolipid:galactosyltransferases
(GSL:GalTs)
GSL:GLTs *see* glycolipid:glycosyltransferases
(GSL:GLTs)
GSLs *see* glycosphingolipids (GSLs)
gsp genes, localization, **4**, 329
Gsp proteins, identification, **4**, 329
GST *see* glutathione transferases
GS-TriCHQ *see* hydroquinone, 2,3,5-trichloro-6-*S*-
glutathionyl- (GS-TriCHQ)
gtc genes, localization, **4**, 330
Gtc proteins, GtcR, encoding, **4**, 330
GTI *see* flavonol 3-*O*-glucosyltransferase (FGT)
GTP *see* guanosine triphosphate (GTP)
GTPγS *see* guanosine 5′-γ-thiotriphosphate
GTX I *see* geographutoxin I (GTX I)
GTX II *see* geographutoxin II (GTX II)
guaiacol
in induced plant defense, **8**, 150
in plant–herbivore–predator interactions, **8**, 152
guaiac resin, early studies, **3**, 717
Guaiacum officinale, guaiaretic acid, **1**, 640, 676
guaiacyl, use of term, **3**, 620
guaiacylglycerol-β-guaiacyl ether, cleavage, **3**, 725
guaiacylglycerol-β-pinoresinol ether, as intermediate, **3**,
676
guaianolides, tricyclic, antifeedant activity, **8**, 308
guaiaretic acid
biosynthesis, **1**, 640, 676
occurrence, **1**, 640, 676
structure, **1**, 640
guaiaretic acid, 3′-*O*-methylnordihydro-, HIV studies, **1**,
703
guaiaretic acid, nordihydro- (NDGA)
allelopathic activity, **1**, 695
antibacterial activity, **1**, 692
antioxidant activity, **1**, 690
as lipoxygenase inhibitor, **1**, 123, 221, 243
nephrotoxicity, **1**, 691
α-guaiene, biosynthesis, **2**, 184
guanase *see* guanine deaminase
guanidines, antisense oligonucleotide linkages, **7**, 300
guanine, N^2-(anthracen-9-ylmethyl)-, in
oligodeoxynucleotides, **7**, 327
guanine, 9-(*p*-carbetoxyphenyl)-, binding, **5**, 86
guanine, N^7-cyanoborane-, in oligodeoxynucleotides, **7**,
329
guanine, 7-hydro-8-oxo-, in oligodeoxynucleotides, **7**, 328
guanine, N^2-imidazolylpropyl-, insertion, into
oligonucleotides, **7**, 214
guanine, C^6-*O*-methyl-, in oligodeoxynucleotides, **7**, 328
guanine, N^7-methyl-, dodecamer, synthesis, **7**, 329
guanine, C^8-oxo-7,8-dihydro-6-*O*-methyl-, in
oligodeoxynucleotides, **7**, 329
guanine aminase *see* guanine deaminase
guanine aminohydrolase *see* guanine deaminase
guanine arabinoside, biosynthesis, **5**, 74
guanine deaminase
biological functions, **5**, 86
inhibitors, **5**, 86
guanosine, 8-azido-, applications, photoaffinity labeling,
6, 229
guanosine, 3′-hydroxyl-, analogues, **7**, 279
guanosine, 2-methyl-, effects on dimethyl A loop, **6**, 195
guanosine, *N*-1-methyl-, hammerhead ribozyme
substitution, **6**, 225
guanosine, O^6-methyl-, use in hairpin ribozyme studies,
7, 277
guanosine, 9-*m*-phenylcarboxamido-, binding, **5**, 86
guanosine diphosphate mannose *see*
guanosinediphosphomannose (GDPMan)
guanosinediphosphomannose (GDPMan)
biosynthesis, **3**, 207
pathway, **3**, 207
roles
in galactomannan biosynthesis, **3**, 521
in pectin biosynthesis, **3**, 505
guanosine 5′-monophosphorothioate
applications, **6**, 219
binding, **6**, 128
guanosine nucleoside, reactions, with methanesulfonyl
chloride, **7**, 118
guanosine phosphorothioate, 5′-terminal,
posttranscriptional reactions, **6**, 230
guanosine(s)
binding sites, **6**, 163
depurination, **7**, 122
exogenous, **6**, 158
as molybdopterin precursors, **1**, 837
guanosine 5′-γ-thiotriphosphate
applications, **6**, 219
in oligonucleotide synthesis, **6**, 223
guanosine triphosphate (GTP)
allosteric inhibitor sites, **5**, 80
roles, in GPI anchor biosynthesis, **4**, 311
guar *see* Cyamopsis tetragonoloba
(*R*,*R*)-guattegaumerine, biosynthesis, **1**, 676
guibourtacidin, condensation rates, **3**, 753
guibourtacidin ions, mono-oxygenated moieties, **3**, 754
Guibourtia coleosperma
guibourtinidol-stilbene oligomers, **3**, 762
profisetinidins, **3**, 772
proguibourtinidins, **3**, 775
guibourtinidol, as profisetinidin precursor, **3**, 771
guibourtinidol-3′-*O*-4′-*ent*-epimopanone, biosynthesis, **3**,
777
guibourtinidol-(4α→6′)-fisetinidol, structure, **3**, 761
guide RNA *see* gRNA
guinea pig pancreas, lipase, **5**, 125
guineensine, occurrence, **8**, 304
G–U pairs
in RNA secondary structures, **6**, 29
in rRNA secondary structures, **6**, 192
G–U wobble pairs
conservation, **6**, 162
Group I introns, **6**, 155
in rRNA secondary structures, **6**, 192

gymnodimine
  occurrence, **8**, 515
  toxicity, **8**, 515
Gymnodinium breve
  brevetoxin, **8**, 511
  see also red tide
Gymnodinium cf. *mikimotoi*, gymnodimine, **8**, 515
Gymnospermae
  herbaceous, monoterpene synthases, **2**, 142
  lignans, **1**, 647
  lignins, **3**, 620
    cell wall deposition, **3**, 690
    evolution, **3**, 625

  heterogeneity, **3**, 691
  monoterpene synthases, **2**, 127
Gymnothorax javanicus, ciguatoxins, **8**, 501
gypsy moth *see Lymantria dispar*
gyrinal, occurrence, **8**, 234, 359
gyrinidal *see* gyrinal
gyrinidione, occurrence, **8**, 234, 359
gyrinidone
  occurrence, **8**, 234
  structure, **8**, 234
Gyrinus spp., gyrinal, **8**, 234
GYSV-1 *see* grapevine yellow speckle viroid-1 (GYSV-1)
GYSV-2 *see* grapevine yellow speckle viroid-2 (GYSV-2)

H

HA *see* homocitrate (HA); hyaluronan (HA)
Habronestes bradleyi, 6-methyl-5-hepten-2-one, **8**, 232
HADH *see* horse-liver alcohol dehydrogenase (HADH)
haedoxan A, occurrence, **1**, 687, 696
(+)-haedoxan A
  insecticidal activity, **1**, 693
  occurrence, **1**, 693
Haemophilus influenzae
  choline uptake, **3**, 229
  invasion capacity correlation, **3**, 229
  lipopolysaccharides, **3**, 180, 5
    biosynthesis, **3**, 228
  nrd genes, **3**, 345
  sequencing, **4**, 214
HAF *see* human amniotic fluid (HAF)
HAI-1
  mode of action, **8**, 396
  occurrence, **8**, 395
  properties, **8**, 395
  purification, **8**, 395
  structure, **8**, 395
  see also L-homoserine lactone, *N*-(3-*R*-
    hydroxybutyryl)-
HAI-2
  occurrence, **8**, 396
hairpin ribozymes, **7**, 274
  base residues, **6**, 226
  binding sites, **6**, 249
  catalysis
    early studies, **6**, 115
    metal ions in, **6**, 159, 251
  characteristics, **6**, 247
  classification, **6**, 236
  cleavage–ligation mediation, **6**, 251
  conformation, **6**, 229
  discovery, **6**, 236
  dissociation, **6**, 227
  functional residues, **6**, 120
  2′-hydroxyl group attack, **6**, 151
  kinetics, **6**, 250
  mechanisms, **6**, 250
  metal ion requirements, **6**, 252
  phosphorothioate linkages, **6**, 159
  purine residues, **6**, 249
  rate-limiting steps, **6**, 250
  RNA cleavage, **6**, 219, 250
  selection, **6**, 119
  sequencing, **6**, 248
  structure
    secondary, **6**, 119, 139, 154
    tertiary, **6**, 120, 249
  studies, **6**, 225
  substrate binding, **6**, 250
Halichoeres bleekeri, *Streptomyces hygroscopicus* in, **8**, 603
halicholactone, occurrence, **1**, 243
halichomycin
  cytotoxicity, **8**, 603
  occurrence, **8**, 603
  relative stereochemistry, **8**, 603
Halichondria okadai
  Alteromonas spp. in, **8**, 588
  halicholactone, **1**, 243
  neohalicholactone, **1**, 243
  okadaic acid, **8**, 490

Pseudomonas spp., **8**, 589
haliclamines, occurrence, **8**, 560
Haliclona spp.
  haliclamines, **8**, 560
  haliclonacyclamines, **8**, 566
  haliclonadiamine, **8**, 564
  halicyclamine A, **8**, 566
  manzamines, **8**, 553
  papuamine, **8**, 564
haliclonacyclamines
  occurrence, **8**, 566
  structure, **8**, 566
haliclonadiamine
  occurrence, **8**, 564
  structure, **8**, 564
halicyclamine A, occurrence, **8**, 566
halicyclamines, structure, **8**, 566
Haliotis spp.
  feeding, preferences, **8**, 418
  feeding deterrents against, **8**, 460
Haliotis discus, feeding, preferences, **8**, 419
Haliotis discus hannai, feeding deterrents, **8**, 459
Haliotis rufescens
  larval settlement induction, **8**, 433
  metamorphosis induction, **8**, 433
  prostaglandins, **1**, 244
haloacetate dehalogenase(s), use of term, **5**, 405
haloacetate halidohydrolase(s) *see* haloacetate
  dehalogenase(s)
haloacid dehalogenase(s)
  active sites, **5**, 406
  alkyl-enzyme intermediates, mechanisms, **5**, 406
  catalysis, **5**, 407
  classification, **5**, 405
  crystal structure, **5**, 406
  mechanisms, **5**, 406
  mutagenesis, site-directed, **5**, 406
  sequence homology, **5**, 406
  stereochemistry, **5**, 405
  studies, **5**, 405
  use of term, **5**, 405
haloalcohol dehalogenase(s)
  catalysis, **5**, 408
  occurrence, **5**, 408
haloalkane dehalogenase(s), **5**, 54, 57
  active sites, **5**, 405
  alkyl-enzyme intermediates, mechanisms, **5**, 404
  chloride binding sites, **5**, 405
  crystal structure, **5**, 403
  kinetic studies, **5**, 404
  mechanisms, **5**, 403
  mutagenesis, site-directed, **5**, 404
  nucleophiles, **5**, 53
  occurrence, **5**, 112, 403
  purification, **5**, 403
  sequences, **5**, 56
  substrate specificity, **5**, 405
1-haloalkane halidohydrolase *see* haloalkane
  dehalogenase(s)
haloalkanoate dehalogenase(s), occurrence, **5**, 405
Haloarcula marismortui, 50S rRNA, **6**, 201
halobacillin
  cytotoxicity, **8**, 594
  occurrence, **8**, 594
2-halobenzoate dioxygenase, occurrence, **5**, 417

Halocynthia spp.
  celluloses
    NMR spectra, **3**, 565
    Raman spectra, **3**, 558
Halocynthia roretzi, metamorphosis induction, **8**, 442
Haloferax volcanii, hydroxymethylglutaryl-CoA
    reductases, **2**, 27
halogenated aliphatic compounds, applications, **5**, 403
halohydrin hydrogen-halide lyases *see* haloalcohol
    dehalogenase(s)
haloperoxidases
  catalysis, **1**, 8
  in marine algae, **2**, 107
halophiles, hydroxymethylglutaryl-CoA reductase
    encoding, **2**, 23
halymecins
  antimicroalgal activity, **8**, 601
  occurrence, **8**, 601
Halymenia dilatata, *Fusarium* spp. in, **8**, 601
Haminoea navicula, haminols, **8**, 465
hammerhead ribozymes, **6**, 150, **7**, 274
  altered stems, **6**, 140
  applications, therapeutic, **6**, 237
  catalysis, **6**, 222, 224
    for chemical cleavage, **6**, 242
    double-metal-ion mechanism, **6**, 236, 243, 247
    early studies, **6**, 115
    magnesium in, **6**, 134
    metal ions in, **6**, 159
    single-metal-ion mechanism, **6**, 246
  characteristics, **6**, 237
  cholesterol attachment, **6**, 226
  cleavage
    kinetics, **6**, 164
    mechanisms, **6**, 91
  conformation, **6**, 229, 239
  conjugation, **6**, 118
  discovery, **6**, 236
  dissociation rate constants, **6**, 164
  disulfide bond formation, **6**, 89
  fraying model, **6**, 241
  FRET studies, **6**, 227
  2′-hydroxyl function, **6**, 88
  2′-hydroxyl group attack, **6**, 151
  inhibition, **6**, 225
  inhibitor complexes, **6**, 55
  kinetics, **6**, 164, 240
  mechanisms, **6**, 240
    two-metal ion, **6**, 159
  metal ion-binding sites, **6**, 159, 239, 247
  models, **6**, 227
  NUX rule, **6**, 237
  occurrence, **6**, 53
  phosphorothioate diastereomers, **6**, 222
  randomization, **6**, 121
  rate-limiting steps, **6**, 246
  RNA cleavage, **6**, 219
  roles, in base catalysis mediation, **6**, 236
  selection, **6**, 119
  sequencing, **6**, 237
    wild-type, **6**, 140
  structure, **6**, 110, **7**, 274
    secondary, **6**, 153
    studies, **6**, 89, 121
    tertiary, **6**, 156, 239
    three-dimensional, **6**, 55, 76
  studies, **6**, 225
  substrate binding, **6**, 240
  synthesis, **6**, 94
  6-thioguanosine incorporation, **6**, 93
  trans-acting, **6**, 237
  transition states, **6**, 56, 242
  use of term, **6**, 237

  in viroids, **6**, 180
  x-ray crystal structure, **6**, 239
Hammett correlations, in electrophilic reaction studies, **5**,
    317
Hammett plots, glycosidases, **5**, 288
Hammond postulate, intermediates, **5**, 11
hamsters
  hydroxymethylglutaryl-CoA reductases, **2**, 24
  tannin toxicity, **8**, 142
handelin, occurrence, **1**, 375
hapalosin, structure, **8**, 610
HAP complex
  roles, **4**, 178
  in *Saccharomyces cerevisiae*, **4**, 177
hap genes, *hapC*, cloning, **4**, 177
haplophytine
  insecticidal activity, **8**, 345
  occurrence, **8**, 345
Haplophyton cimicidum, haplophytine, **8**, 345
hapten phosphoramidites, synthesis, **7**, 175
haptens
  binding sites, **5**, 423
  design, **5**, 423
Haptophyceae
  hymenosulfate, **8**, 618
  red tide organisms, **8**, 518
harderoporphyrinogen, isolation, **4**, 95
hard tick *see Dermacentor variabilis*
Harrisina spp., (*S*)-2-butyl (*Z*)-7-tetradecenoate, **8**, 209
Harrisonia abyssinica, harrisonin, **8**, 321
harrisonin
  antifeedant activity, **8**, 321
  occurrence, **8**, 321
HAS *see* hyaluronan synthase (HAS)
HAS genes
  *HAS*1, expression, **3**, 174
  *HAS*2, expression, **3**, 174
  *HAS*3, expression, **3**, 174
  occurrence, **3**, 174
hatching factor, in barnacles, **1**, 247
hateramine, isolation, **8**, 431
haustorium, induction, **8**, 175
hawkmoths, roles, in pollination, **8**, 158
HBV *see* hepatitis B virus (HBV)
HC-toxin, peptide bonds, **4**, 226
HDV *see* hepatitis delta virus (HDV)
headspace analysis, and floral volatiles, **8**, 161
heart attack *see* heart infarction
heart disease
  and low-density lipoprotein cholesterol, **2**, 25
  red wine benefits, **3**, 792
heart infarction, superoxide free radical ion production,
    5, 80
heart muscle, glycogen synthase (mammalian), **3**, 479
heartwood
  formation, **1**, 696
    mechanisms, **1**, 697
    metabolites, **1**, 697
heartworm *see Dirofilaria immitis*
heavy metals, porphobilinogen synthase inhibition, **4**, 76
hedamycin, applications, antibiotics, **7**, 509
Hedera helix, α-hederin, **8**, 323
α-hederin
  applications, antifungal agents, **8**, 183
  occurrence, **8**, 323
β-hederin, applications, antifungal agents, **8**, 183
Hedyotis lawsoniae, hedyotol C, **1**, 688
hedyotol C, occurrence, **1**, 688
helenalin, **7**, 503
helenin, antifeedant activity, **8**, 308
Helianthus annuus, phenylalanine ammonia-lyase, **3**, 659
Helianthus tuberosus
    trans-cinnamate 4-monooxygenase, **1**, 720, **3**, 637

localization, **3**, 669
tuberization, **1**, 127
α-helices
    in the DNA major groove, **7**, 477
    helix-turn-helix peptides, **7**, 477
Helichrysum bracteatum, 6′-hydroxychalcones, **1**, 736
Helichrysum chionosphaerum
    ent-abieta-7,13-diene, **2**, 230, 238
    ent-atisir-16-ene, **2**, 238
    helifulvanic acid, **2**, 238
    ent-kaur-16-ene, **2**, 238
Helicobacter pylori
    2-dehydro-3-deoxyphosphogluconate aldolase, **3**, 421
    sequencing, **4**, 214
    type II dehydroquinase, **1**, 588
helicobasidin, biosynthesis, **2**, 163
Heliconius pachinus, (1*R*)-(9*Z*,11*E*)-9,11-octadecadien-
        13-olide, **8**, 218
Helicoverpa spp., pheromone biosynthesis activating
        neuropeptide, **8**, 300
Helicoverpa armigera, antifeedant studies, **8**, 332
Helicoverpa virescens see Heliothis virescens
Helicoverpa zea
    antifeedant activity against, **8**, 321
    growth inhibition, **8**, 321, 338, 346
    (*Z*)-9-hexadecenal acetates, **8**, 205
    (*Z*)-11-hexadecenal acetates, **8**, 205
    rutin toxicity, **8**, 338
helifulvanic acid, occurrence, **2**, 238
heliocides H$_1$, occurrence, **1**, 377
heliocides H$_4$, occurrence, **1**, 377
Heliopsis longipes, spilanthol, **8**, 303
Heliothis virescens
    activity against, **8**, 312
        insecticidal, **8**, 322
    antifeedant studies, **8**, 332
    feeding, **8**, 302
    growth inhibition, **8**, 321
        studies, **8**, 322
    20-hydroxyecdysone 22-palmitate, **8**, 283
    nicotine excretion, **8**, 348
    resistance to, **8**, 150
    rhodojaponin III resistance, **8**, 313
    rotenone activity, **8**, 341
    rutin toxicity, **8**, 338
Heliothis zea see Helicoverpa zea
heliotridane, biosynthesis, **4**, 31
Heliotropium bovei, 7-acetyleuropine, **4**, 31
helix-turn-helix motifs
    ArpA protein, **8**, 382
    barA genes, **8**, 387
    Cro protein, **7**, 478
    Hin recombinase, **7**, 478
    homeodomain, **7**, 479
    homology, **8**, 446
    peptide truncation, **7**, 480
    reviews, **7**, 478
    see also EF-hand proteins
helix-turn-helix peptides
    in α-helical DNA binding proteins, **7**, 478
    see also basic-helix-loop-helix peptides
cis,*trans*-helminthogermacradienyl cation, as
        intermediate, **2**, 187
Helminthosporium carbonum
    HC-toxin, **1**, 546
    peptide synthetase genes, **1**, 542
Helminthosporium maydis see Cochliobolus heterostrophus
helminthosporoside A, structure, **8**, 179
helper viruses, and viroids, **6**, 177
heme
    biosynthesis, **4**, 2, **61–107**
        future research, **4**, 103
        pathways, **4**, 62

from, uroporphyrinogen-III, **4**, 90
    protection against, **2**, 326
    roles, in prostaglandin-endoperoxide synthase activity,
        1, 257
hem genes
    encoding, **4**, 95
    hemA, **4**, 140
    hemB, encoding, **4**, 141
    hemF, **4**, 95, 98
    hemL, **4**, 140
        isolation, **4**, 70
    hemN, **4**, 95, 98
hemibrevetoxin B, structure, **8**, 511
hemicelluloses
    biochemistry, **3**, **599–615**
    biosynthesis, **3**, 2, 8
        extracellular signals, **3**, 608
        gene identification, **3**, 610
        polysaccharide turnover, **3**, 609
        regulatory mechanisms, **3**, 607
        sites, **3**, 602
    definitions, **3**, 599
    differential screening, **3**, 611
    enzymology, **3**, 603
    expressed sequence tag databases, **3**, 611
    families, **3**, 600
    immunolocalization, **3**, 603
    importance of, **3**, 599
    localization, **3**, 601
    manipulation, **3**, 612
    mutational analysis, **3**, 611
    primary wall, **3**, 600
    reverse genetics, **3**, 612
    secondary wall, **3**, 601
    structure, **3**, 9
    subcellular fractionation, **3**, 602
Hemileuca oliviae, zanthophylline toxicity, **8**, 344
Hemimetabola
    juvenile hormones, **8**, 265
    lifecycle, **8**, 265
Hemiptera, venoms, **8**, 360
hemiterpenes
    biosynthesis, **8**, 220
    in terpenoid pathway, **2**, 100
Hemizonia congesta, encecalin, **8**, 337
hemlock *see Tsuga heterophylla*
hemolysins
    bioactive properties, **4**, 197
    biosynthesis, **3**, 227
HEMPAS *see* hereditary erythroblastic multinuclearity
        with a positive acidified serum (HEMPAS)
hen egg white lysozyme (HEWL)
    glycosidases, **5**, 296
    mechanisms, acetamido participation, **5**, 298
(6*Z*,8*E*)-6,8-henicosadien-11-one, occurrence, **8**, 208
henicosane, occurrence, **8**, 218
(3*Z*,6*Z*,9*Z*)-1,3,6,9-henicosatetraene, occurrence, **8**, 207
(3*Z*,6*Z*,9*Z*)-3,6,9-henicosatriene, occurrence, **8**, 207
(*Z*)-7-henicosene, occurrence, **8**, 218
(*Z*)-9-henicosene, occurrence, **8**, 218
(*Z*)-10-henicosene, occurrence, **8**, 218
(*Z*)-6-henicosen-11-one, occurrence, **8**, 208
(9*Z*,19*Z*)-9,19-hentriacontadiene, occurrence, **8**, 219
(*Z*)-9-hentriacontene, occurrence, **8**, 219
(*Z*)-11-hentriacontene, occurrence, **8**, 219
heparan sulfate (HS)
    binding, **3**, 4
    biosynthesis, **3**, 2, 172
    substitution, **3**, 161
heparan sulfate proteoglycans (HSPGs), fate of, **3**, 172
heparin
    binding, **3**, 4
    biosynthesis, **3**, 2, 172

interactions, with sterol esterase, **5**, 128
substitution, **3**, 161
Hepaticae
evolution, **1**, 645
labeling studies, **2**, 63
lignans, **1**, 645, 673
and lignin evolution, **3**, 624
oxylipins, **1**, 228
stilbenoids, **1**, 763
see also Monoclea forsteri; Pellia epiphylla; Scapania undulata
hepatitis B virus (HBV), and hepatitis delta virus, **6**, 252
hepatitis delta virus (HDV)
and hepatitis B virus, **6**, 252
RNA, **5**, 87
editing, **6**, 103
topology, **7**, 344
hepatitis delta virus (HDV) ribozyme, **6**, 222
characteristics, **6**, 252
cleavage mediation, **6**, 253
discovery, **6**, 236
2'-hydroxyl group attack, **6**, 151
properties, **6**, 253
replication, rolling circle mechanism, **6**, 252
RNA cleavage mediation, **6**, 254
structure, **6**, 252
secondary, **6**, 154
structure–function relationships, **6**, 253
hepatocytes, lipopolysaccharide biosynthesis, **3**, 181
hepatomas
fucosyltransferases, **3**, 116
and β-1,4-N-mannosyl-glycoprotein β-1,4-N-acetylglucosaminyltransferase levels, **3**, 53
hepatotoxicity, prevention, lignans, **1**, 702
8R-HEPE *see* eicosapentaenoic acid, 8R-hydroxy- (8R-HEPE)
11R-HEPE *see* eicosapentaenoic acid, 11R-hydroxy- (11R-HEPE)
12R-HEPE *see* eicosapentaenoic acid, 12R-hydroxy- (12R-HEPE)
12S-HEPE *see* eicosapentaenoic acid, 12S-hydroxy- (12S-HEPE)
HepG2 cells, luciferase chimeric reporter gene, **2**, 261
hepialone, occurrence, **8**, 211
Hepialus spp., pheromones, **8**, 211
Hepialus californicus, hepialone, **8**, 211
Hepialus hecta
(2R)-6-ethyl-2-methyl-4H-2,3-dihydropyran-4-one, **8**, 211
pheromones, **8**, 244
Hepialus humuli, (E,E)-α-farnesene, **8**, 227
hepoxilin A$_3$
biosynthesis, **1**, 267
occurrence, **1**, 245
hepoxilin B$_3$
biosynthesis, **1**, 267
occurrence, **1**, 219
hepoxilins, biosynthesis, **1**, 267
HepPP synthases *see* heptaprenyl diphosphate synthases
(7Z,11Z)-7,11-heptacosadiene, occurrence, **8**, 219
(7Z,13Z)-7,13-heptacosadiene, occurrence, **8**, 219
heptacosan-2-one, 3,7-dimethyl-, occurrence, **8**, 247
heptacosan-2-one, 3,7,15-trimethyl-, occurrence, **8**, 247
(Z)-9-heptacosene, occurrence, **8**, 219
(Z)-13-heptacosene, occurrence, **8**, 219
(6Z,9Z)-6,9-heptadecadiene, occurrence, **8**, 217
heptadecane, occurrence, **8**, 217
heptadecane, (S)-2,5-dimethyl-
biosynthesis, **8**, 249
occurrence, **8**, 248
heptadecane, 3,13-dimethyl-, occurrence, **8**, 248
heptadecane, 5,9-dimethyl-, occurrence, **8**, 247
heptadecane, (5R,11S)-5,11-dimethyl-, occurrence, **8**, 248

heptadecane, 7,11-dimethyl-, occurrence, **8**, 247
heptadecane, 2-methyl-, occurrence, **8**, 240, 249
heptadecane, 7-methyl-, occurrence, **8**, 247
heptadecane, (S)-7-methyl-, occurrence, **8**, 248
1-heptadecene, occurrence, **8**, 217
(Z)-10-heptadecen-2-one, occurrence, **8**, 217
1,5-heptadiene, (R)-3-acetoxy-2,6-dimethyl-, occurrence, **8**, 234
2,5-heptadiene, (Z)-2-(3',4'-epoxy-4'-methylcyclohexyl)-6-methyl- *see* (Z)-α-bisabolene oxide
2,4-heptadiene-1,7-dioate, 2-hydroxy-, isolation, **5**, 35
2,4-heptadienoate, 1-methylethyl (2E,4E)-2,4-dimethyl-, occurrence, **8**, 241
3,5-heptadien-2-one, 6-methyl-, occurrence, **8**, 233
heptaketides, biosynthesis, **1**, 417, 560, **7**, 554
2,6-heptanedione, occurrence, **8**, 211
heptanoate, ethyl 4-methyl-, occurrence, **8**, 241
heptanoic acid, 7-mercapto-, conversion, **1**, 834
n-heptanoic acid δ-lactone, (2S,3S,4S,5R)-2,4-dimethyl-3,5-dihydroxy-, biosynthesis, **1**, 357
n-heptanoic acid triketide lactones, (2S,3S,4S,5R)-2,4-dimethyl-3,5-dihydroxy-, biosynthesis, **1**, 361
heptanoids, diaryl-
biosynthesis, **1**, 686
occurrence, **1**, 766
1-heptanol, occurrence, **8**, 211
2-heptanol, occurrence, **8**, 211
(R)-2-heptanol, occurrence, **8**, 208, 211
3-heptanol, (3R,4S)-4-methyl-, occurrence, **8**, 242
3-heptanol, (3S,4S)-4-methyl-, occurrence, **8**, 242
4-heptanol, 2-methyl-, occurrence, **8**, 245, 246
2-heptanone, occurrence, **8**, 161, 211
heptan-2-one, 6,7-epoxy-6-methyl-, in frontalin biosynthesis, **8**, 233
3-heptanone, (4S,5R)-5-hydroxy-4-methyl- *see* sitophilure
3-heptanone, 5-hydroxy-4-methyl-, as pheromone, **8**, 210
4-heptanone, occurrence, **8**, 211
heptanoyl-CoA, as substrate, **4**, 262
heptaprenyl diphosphate synthases
heteromeric components, **2**, 90
two dissociable components, **2**, 89
(9Z,19Z)-9,19-heptatriacontadiene, occurrence, **8**, 219
heptatriacontane, 13,25-dimethyl-, branching, **8**, 249
(Z)-1,2,4-heptatriene-6-yne, cycloaromatization via α,3-dehydrotoluene biradical, **7**, 556
3-heptene-1,7-dioate, 2-oxo-, isolation, **5**, 35
4-heptene-1,7-dioate, 2-oxo-, isolation, **5**, 35
(4Z,2R)-4-hepten-2-ol, occurrence, **8**, 208
2-hepten-4-ol, 4S,2E-methyl- *see* rhynchophorol
5-hepten-1-ol, 2,6-dimethyl-, occurrence, **8**, 233
5-hepten-1-ol, 2,3,6-trimethyl- *see* lasiol
5-hepten-2-ol, 6-methyl- *see* sulcatol
6-hepten-1-ol, 2,6-dimethyl-, occurrence, **8**, 233
3-hepten-2-one, (E)-3,5-dimethyl- *see* normanicone
5-hepten-2-one, 6-methyl-
occurrence, **8**, 232
oxygenation, **8**, 232
6-hepten-2-one, 6-methyl-, occurrence, **8**, 233
(Z)-4-hepten-2-one, occurrence, **8**, 208
heptitol, 2,6-diamino-2,6-imino-7-O-(β-D-glucopyranosyl)-D-glycero-L-gulo- (MDL), as glucosidase inhibitor, **3**, 153
D,L-$glycero$-D-$manno$-heptitol, 2,5-dideoxy-2,5-imino- (homoDMDP)
structure, **3**, 130
toxicity, **3**, 140
Heptophylla picea, (4R,7Z)-7,15-hexadecadien-4-olide, **8**, 217
L-$glycero$-D-$manno$-heptose, structure, **3**, 187
heptosyltransferase I, catalysis, **3**, 224
heptosyltransferase II, encoding, **3**, 224
hept-2-ynyl sulfide, 2-(acetoxyphenyl)-, prostaglandin-endoperoxide synthase inhibition, **5**, 253

Heracleum lanatum, coumarins, **1**, 625
herbicides
　bleaching, **2**, 338
　development, and aromatic amino acid biosynthesis, **4**, 9
　2,4-dichlorophenoxyacetic acid, **8**, 34
　phenoxyacetic acids, **8**, 34
　resistance, **2**, 347
herbivores
　defenses against, monoterpene role in, **2**, 101
　defensive agents, phenolics, **8**, 139
　effects of plant toxins on, **8**, 138
　feeding, and volatiles, **1**, 132
　grazing, and cyanogenesis, **1**, 883
　plant defense mechanisms against, **1**, 131
herculin, occurrence, **8**, 303
hereditary erythroblastic multinuclearity with a positive acidified serum (HEMPAS)
　etiology, **3**, 27, 150
　lysis test, **3**, 59
hermonionic acid, biosynthesis, **1**, 765
(6*S*,1′*S*)-hernandulcin, bioactivity, **8**, 10
herpentol, structure, **1**, 690
Herpetospermum caudigerum, herpentol, **1**, 690
hesperetin, occurrence, **8**, 338
hesperetin 7-rutinoside, antifeedant activity, **8**, 338
Hesperophylax occidentalis, 6-methylnonan-3-one, **8**, 243
HETCOR *see* heteronuclear correlation experiment (HETCOR)
5-HETE *see* eicosatetraenoic acid, 5-hydroxy- (5-HETE)
8*R*-HETE *see* eicosatetraenoic acid, 8*R*-hydroxy- (8*R*-HETE)
9-HETE *see* eicosatetraenoic acid, 9-hydroxy- (9-HETE)
9*S*-HETE *see* eicosatetraenoic acid, 9*S*-hydroxy- (9*S*-HETE)
11-HETE *see* eicosatetraenoic acid, 11-hydroxy- (11-HETE)
11*R*-HETE *see* eicosatetraenoic acid, 11*R*-hydroxy- (11*R*-HETE)
12-HETE *see* eicosatetraenoic acid, 12-hydroxy- (12-HETE)
12*R*-HETE *see* eicosatetraenoic acid, 12*R*-hydroxy- (12*R*-HETE)
12*S*-HETE *see* eicosatetraenoic acid, 12*S*-hydroxy- (12*S*-HETE)
15-HETE *see* eicosatetraenoic acid, 15-hydroxy- (15-HETE)
hetero auxin
　isolation, **8**, 24
　structure, **8**, 24
　see also indole-3-acetic acid (IAA)
Heterocampa manteo, formic acid, **8**, 356
Heteroconium spp., bulgarein, **7**, 600
heterocyclic compounds, diaryl-, prostaglandin-endoperoxide synthase inhibition, **5**, 252
heterocyclic compounds, eight-membered, biosynthesis, **1**, 320
heterocyclic *N*-oxides, DNA damage induction, **7**, 532
heteromeric components, heptaprenyl diphosphate synthases, **2**, 90
heteronuclear correlation experiment (HETCOR), improvements, **7**, 71
heteropeptides, in penicillin biosynthesis, **4**, 252
heteroscyphic acid A, labeling, **2**, 226
Heteroscyphus planus
　(+)-epicubenol, **2**, 189
　labeling studies, **2**, 63
　(1*S*)-7-methoxy-1,2-dihydrocadalenene, **2**, 188
Heterotropa talai M
　heterotropatrione, **1**, 379
　isoheterotropatrione, **1**, 379
heterotropatrione, occurrence, **1**, 379
heteroyohimbine alkaloids, biosynthesis, **4**, 113, 125

hevamine, mechanisms, **5**, 297
Hevea brasiliensis
　blight, **1**, 884
　cinnamyl-alcohol dehydrogenases, **3**, 655
　geranyl*trans*transferase, **2**, 82
HEWL *see* hen egg white lysozyme (HEWL)
(10*E*,12*Z*)-10,12-hexadecadienoic acid, occurrence, **8**, 205
(10*E*,12*Z*)-10,12-hexadecadien-1-ol *see* bombykol
(4*R*,7*Z*)-7,15-hexadecadien-4-olide, occurrence, **8**, 217
hexadecane, occurrence, **8**, 217
hexadecanoic acid, 8*S*-hydroxy-, occurrence, **1**, 228
hexadecanol, biosynthesis, **8**, 204
hexadecanolide, structure, **8**, 230
5-hexadecanolide, (5*R*,6*S*)-6-acetoxy-, occurrence, **8**, 217
(*R*)-5-hexadecanolide, occurrence, **8**, 217
hexadecanoyl-CoA, reduction, **8**, 204
8-hexadecenal, 14-methyl- *see* trogodermal
(*Z*)-9-hexadecenal, occurrence, **8**, 217
1-hexadecene, occurrence, **8**, 217
(*Z*)-9-hexadecenoate, 1-methylethyl, occurrence, **8**, 217
(*E*)-11-hexadecenoic acid, occurrence, **8**, 205
(*Z*)-11-hexadecenoic acid
　as intermediate, **8**, 205
　α-oxidation, **8**, 207
1,5-hexadienes, oxy-Cope rearrangement, **5**, 426
3,5-hexadienoic acid, 4-methyl-, occurrence, **8**, 236
hexahydroxybiphenyldicarbonyloxy groups, chirality, **3**, 783
hexahydroxydiphenoyl groups, chirality, **3**, 783
3,4,5,3′,4′,5′-hexahydroxydiphenoyl residues, **3**, 800
hexaketide, as intermediate, **7**, 554
hexaloops, in 23S rRNA, **6**, 195
hexanal, occurrence, **8**, 210
hexane, 1-chloro-, haloalkane dehalogenase catalysis, **5**, 405
1,6-hexanedioate, 2-oxo-, as substrate, **5**, 44
(2*R*,3*R*)-2,3-hexanediol, occurrence, **8**, 210
(2*S*,3*R*)-2,3-hexanediol, occurrence, **8**, 210
hexanenitrile, [1-¹³C]-5-methyl-, coupling, **1**, 142
hexanoate, ethyl, occurrence, **8**, 210
hexanoate, farnesyl, occurrence, **8**, 227
hexanoate, geranyl, occurrence, **8**, 223
hexanoate, methyl, occurrence, **8**, 210
hexanoic acid, occurrence, **8**, 210
1-hexanol, occurrence, **8**, 210
3-hexanol, 4-methyl-, occurrence, **8**, 242
hexanolide, *cis*-2-methyl-, occurrence, **8**, 240
2-hexanone, (*R*)-3-hydroxy-, occurrence, **8**, 210, 211
hexanoyl-CoA, as substrate, **4**, 262
hexanoyl-CoA, 2-methyl-3-oxo-, biosynthesis, **1**, 544
hexaploid wheat *see Triticum aestivum*
hexaprenyl diphosphate synthases
　motifs, **2**, 339
　purification, **2**, 89
　two dissociable components, **2**, 89
trans-hexaprenyl*trans*transferase, occurrence, **2**, 88
7*Z*,10*Z*,13*Z*-hexatrienoic acid, occurrence, **1**, 231
8*Z*,11*Z*,14*Z*-hexatrienoic acid, occurrence, **1**, 231
2-hexenal
　coupling, **8**, 215
　DNA adduct formation by, **7**, 502
　isolation, **1**, 84
2-hexenal, (*E*)-4-oxo-, occurrence, **8**, 210
(*E*)-2-hexenal
　early studies, **1**, 84
　isolation, **1**, 84
　isomers
　　occurrence, **1**, 84
　　synthesis, **1**, 85
　occurrence, **1**, 84, 91, **8**, 210
　in plant–herbivore–predator interactions, **8**, 152
　structure, **1**, 84
　synthesis, **1**, 85

industrial, **1**, 84
(*E*)-3-hexenal, odor, **1**, 86
(*n*)-hexenal, occurrence, **1**, 84
(*Z*)-3-hexenal
 biosynthesis, **1**, 85
 occurrence, **1**, 84, 91
 odor, **1**, 86
2-hexenals, odor, threshold values, **1**, 86
4-hexenals, odor, **1**, 86
5-hexenals, odor, **1**, 86
n-hexenals
 biosynthesis, **1**, 85
 green odor, structure, **1**, 86
 odor, threshold values, **1**, 86
 taste, threshold values, **1**, 86
3-hexenedioate, 5-carboxymethyl-2-oxo-, equilibria, **5**, 34
3-hexenedioate, 2-oxo-
 biosynthesis, **5**, 41
 equilibria, **5**, 34
4-hexenedioate, 5-carboxymethyl-2-oxo-, equilibria, **5**, 34
4-hexenedioate, 2-oxo-, equilibria, **5**, 34
(*E*)-2-hexenoate, (*E*)-2-hexenyl, occurrence, **8**, 210
(*Z*)-3-hexenoate, (*E*)-2-hexenyl, occurrence, **8**, 210
4(*E*)-hexenoic acid, 3-oxo-, as intermediate, **1**, 545
trans-3-hexenoic acid, in penicillins, **4**, 262
3-hexenol, isolation, **1**, 84
(*E*)-2-hexen-1-ol, in plant–herbivore–predator
  interactions, **8**, 152
(*Z*)-3-hexenol
 aromatization, **1**, 87
 early studies, **1**, 84
 isomers
  occurrence, **1**, 84
  synthesis, **1**, 85
 occurrence, **1**, 84, 87
 odor, **1**, 86
 structure, **1**, 84
 synthesis, **1**, 85
  industrial, **1**, 84
2-hexenols, odor, threshold values, **1**, 86
5-hexenols, odor, **1**, 86
n-hexenols
 green odor, structure, **1**, 86
 odor, threshold values, **1**, 86
 taste, threshold values, **1**, 86
trans-3-hexenoyl-CoA, as substrate, **4**, 262
hexosaminidase(s) *see* β-*N*-acetylhexosaminidase(s)
hexosaminoglycans, in *Escherichia coli*, **3**, 185
L-*arabino*-hexose, 4,*O*-isobutyryl-2,6-dideoxy-3-*C*-
   methyl- *see* L-olivomycose E
L-*arabino*-hexose, 2,3,6-trideoxy-3-*C*-methyl-4-*O*-methyl-
   3-nitro- *see* L-evernitrose
hexose chains, lipopolysaccharides, **3**, 226
hexose monophosphates, as energy source, **3**, 463
hexose-1-phosphate nucleotidyltransferases, roles, in 6-
   deoxyhexose biosynthesis, **3**, 333
hexose phosphates, translocation, **3**, 464
hexose-1-phosphate uridylyltransferase *see* UDPglucose-
   hexose-1-phosphate uridylyltransferase
hexoses
 in cellulose studies, **3**, 544
 in *Serratia marcescens*, **3**, 190
HexPP synthases *see* hexaprenyl diphosphate synthases
D-*arabino*-3-hexulose-6-phosphate, biosynthesis, **3**, 413
3-hexulose phosphate synthase, biochemistry, **3**, 413
HGA *see* homogalacturonan (HGA)
HGA methyltransferase (HGA-MT)
 activity, **3**, 519
 occurrence, **3**, 519
 roles, in pectin biosynthesis, **3**, 518
HGA-MT *see* HGA methyltransferase (HGA-MT)
HGL *see* human gastric lipase (HGL)
H glycolipid, synthesis, **3**, 115

HH16 ribozyme
 association rates, **6**, 164
 studies, **6**, 164
hide beetle
 pheromones, **8**, 209
 sex pheromones, **8**, 215
 see also Dermestes maculatus
high-density lipoprotein (HDL), lipopolysaccharide
   attenuation, **3**, 181
high performance liquid chromatography (HPLC)
 applications, **8**, 6
 in gibberellin purification, **8**, 44
himgravin, occurrence, **1**, 371
Hinc-repeats, in *rfb* gene clusters, **3**, 218
cis-hinokiresinol, phosphodiesterase inhibitory activity,
   1, 704
Hin recombinase, helix-turn-helix motifs, **7**, 478
hippodamine, occurrence, **8**, 351
*HIS*3 mRNA, stabilization, **6**, 209
His 57, pK_a, **5**, 25
His 95
 as electrophile, **5**, 12
 hydrogen-bonded, **5**, 12
 imidazole groups, **5**, 13
 neutral imidazole side chains, **5**, 36
 roles, in TIM-catalyzed reactions, **5**, 12
His motif
 in acyltransferases, **4**, 227
 roles, **4**, 231
hispidin, biosynthesis, **1**, 761, **3**, 624
histamine
 occurrence, **8**, 360
 in venoms, **8**, 354
  honeybee, **8**, 355
  wasp, **8**, 356
histidase *see* histidine ammonia-lyase
histidinase *see* histidine ammonia-lyase
histidine ammonia-lyase, active sites, **3**, 634
histidine α-deaminase *see* histidine ammonia-lyase
histidine kinase(s)
 functions, **4**, 295
 inhibition, **1**, 783
histidine phosphatases
 biochemistry, **5**, 154
 inhibitors, **5**, 154
histidine protein kinase, encoding, **8**, 402
histidine(s)
 catalytic, **4**, 227
 deamination, **3**, 632
 functionalities, **7**, 616
 in hydroxymethylglutaryl-CoA reductase catalysis, **2**,
   33
 pK, **7**, 616
 in sesquiterpene synthase, **2**, 193
 as starting material, for alkaloids, **4**, 54
histone H1, **7**, 582
HIV *see* human immunodeficiency virus (HIV)
HIV-1 reverse transcriptase (HIV-1 RT)
 binding, **7**, 626
 cross-linking, **6**, 228
 inhibitors, **1**, 703, **5**, 88
  calanolide A, **1**, 624
 photoaffinity labeling studies, **7**, 217
 RNA structural probing, **6**, 75
HLAL *see* human lysosomal acid lipase (HLAL)
6HM *see* mellein, 6-hydroxy- (6HM)
HMB *see* hydroxymethylbilane (HMB)
HMG-CoA *see* hydroxymethylglutaryl-CoA
HMG-CoA lyase(s) *see* hydroxymethylglutaryl-CoA
   lyase(s)
HMG-CoA reductase inhibitors *see*
   hydroxymethylglutaryl-CoA reductase
   inhibitors

HMG-CoA reductase(s) *see* hydroxymethylglutaryl-CoA
  reductase(s)
HMG-CoA synthase(s) *see* hydroxymethylglutaryl-CoA
  synthase(s)
hmg genes, upregulation, **1**, 236
6HM synthase *see* 6-hydroxymellein synthase
HNK-1 epitope, roles, **3**, 122
9-HOD *see* 10*E*,12*Z*-octadecadienoic acid, 9-hydroxy- (9-
  HOD)
9*S*-HOD *see* 10*E*,12*Z*-octadecadienoic acid, 9*S*-hydroxy-
  (9*S*-HOD)
13-HOD *see* 9*Z*,11*E*-octadecadienoic acid, 13-hydroxy-
  (13-HOD)
Hoechst 33258, applications, groove binding agents, **7**,
  595
Hoechst 33342, applications, groove binding agents, **7**,
  595
Hogness box *see* TATA box
Holcopasites calliopsidis, mandibular gland secretions, **8**,
  234
holly *see Ilex opaca*
Holomelinea spp., 2-methylheptadecane, **8**, 240
Holometabola
  lifecycle, **8**, 265
  metamorphosis, **8**, 265
holoprotein auromomycin, **7**, 578
Holotrichia parallela, L-isoleucine methyl ester, **8**, 223
homarine
  chemical defense studies, **8**, 465
  occurrence, **8**, 465
homeodomain
  engrailed, **7**, 479
  helix-turn-helix motifs, **7**, 479
homeodomain DNA binding, heterodimeric, **7**, 479
homo-γ-bisabolene, occurrence, **8**, 237
28-homobrassinolide, synthesis, **8**, 100
homocitrate (HA), as intermediate, **4**, 243
homocitrate synthase (HS), inhibition, **4**, 243
homodimers, in terpenoids, **1**, 377
homoDMDP *see* D,L-*glycero*-D-*manno*-heptitol, 2,5-
  dideoxy-2,5-imino- (homoDMDP)
homofarnesene, occurrence, **8**, 237
homofarnesol, conversion, **2**, 310
homoferreirin, occurrence, **1**, 808
homofuconojirimycin, inhibitory activity, **5**, 308
homogalacturonan (HGA)
  O-acetylation, **3**, 499
  biosynthesis, **3**, 8, 504, 510, 522
    models, **3**, 514
  in cell wall, **3**, 498, 503
  methylester distribution, **3**, 499
  methylesterification, **3**, 504, 518
  structure, **3**, 499
  substrates, **3**, 512
  xylosylation, **3**, 520
homogeraniol, conversion, **2**, 310
homology mapping, in cloning, **7**, 646
homology screening, developments, **3**, 58
homolysis, molecule-induced, and carbon–cobalt bond
  cleavage, **5**, 173
homomanicone, occurrence, **8**, 243
homomethionine, in sinigrin biosynthesis, **1**, 859
homomevalonate
  in juvenile hormones, **8**, 236
  roles, in ante-iso branching, **8**, 246
  structure, **8**, 237
  in terpene biosynthesis, **8**, 231
homomevalonic acid, synthesis, **8**, 272
10-homonerol oxide, occurrence, **8**, 237
α-homonojirimycin (HNJ), structure, **3**, 130
homoocimenes
  biosynthesis, **8**, 231
  occurrence, **8**, 236

L-homoserine
  occurrence, **3**, 249
  in peptidoglycan, **3**, 246
homoserine lactone, *N*-(3-oxohexanoyl)-
  structure, **8**, 393
  see also VAI-1
L-homoserine lactone, *N*-butyryl-
  structure, **8**, 398
  see also factor-2
L-homoserine lactone, *N*-(3-*R*-hydroxybutyryl)-
  structure, **8**, 395
  see also HAI-1
L-homoserine lactone, *N*-(3*R*-hydroxy-7*Z*-
    tetradecenoyl)-
  structure, **8**, 400
  see also small
L-homoserine lactone, *N*-octanoyl-
  structure, **8**, 395
  see also VAI-2
L-homoserine lactone, *N*-(3-oxododecanoyl)-
  structure, **8**, 398
  see also PAI-1
L-homoserine lactone, *N*-(3-oxooctanoyl)-
  structure, **8**, 399
  see also conjugation factor (CF)
homoserine lactones, *N*-acyl-, in autoinducers, **8**, 392
homoterpenes, as pheromones, **8**, 236
honeybees
  1,2-dioleyl-3-palmitylglycerol, **8**, 217
  (*E*,*E*)-farnesol, **8**, 227
  2-heptanone, **8**, 211
  (*E*)-9-hydroxy-2-decenoic acid, **8**, 213
  larvae, brood cell capping induction, **8**, 217
  3-methyl-1-butyl acetate, **8**, 220
  methyl palmitate, **8**, 217
  Nasonov pheromone, **8**, 223
  queen
    9-hydroxy-(*E*)-2-decenoic acid, **8**, 199
    methyl 4-hydroxybenzoate, **8**, 200
    9-oxo-(*E*)-2-decenoic acid secretion, **8**, 199
    'queen substance', **8**, 200
    9-oxo-(*E*)-2-decenoic acid, **8**, 213
  see also Apis mellifera
Hop *see Humulus lupulus*
hopanes, occurrence, **1**, 71
hopanoids
  bacterial, **2**, 308
    characterization, **2**, 47
    distribution, **2**, 47
    labeling, **2**, 48
    roles, **2**, 47
  bacterial triterpenoids, **2**, 47
  biosynthesis, operons for, **2**, 313
  occurrence, **2**, 308
  structure, **2**, 47
  in *Zymomonas mobilis*, **2**, 51
Hopea spp., hopanoids, **2**, 308
hopene cyclases, **2**, 307
  Alicyclobacillus acidocaldarius, **2**, 308
  Alicyclobacillus acidoterrestris, gene cloning, **2**, 313
  biochemistry, **2**, 308
  Bradyrhizobium japonicum, gene cloning, **2**, 313
  catalysis, **2**, 5
  CD measurements, **2**, 311
  future research, **2**, 316
  genetics, **2**, 313
    cloning strategies, **2**, 313
    common motifs, **2**, 315
    mutagenesis, **2**, 315
    sequence similarity, **2**, 313
  inhibitors, **2**, 311
  Methylococcus capsulatus, gene cloning, **2**, 313
  poisons, **2**, 311

product specificity, **2**, 310
purification, **2**, 308
purified, properties, **2**, 309
QW motif, **2**, 316
Rhodopseudomonas palustris, **2**, 308
gene cloning, **2**, 313
substrate specificity, **2**, 309
Synechocystis spp., gene cloning, **2**, 313
Zymomonas mobilis, **2**, 309
gene cloning, **2**, 313
hops, 2-methyl-3-buten-2-ol, **8**, 200
hop stunt viroid (HSV)
hosts, **6**, 186
pathogenicity, **6**, 185
sequencing, **6**, 175
hordenine
antifeedant activity, **8**, 336
occurrence, **8**, 336
Hordeum vulgare
2-*O*-[5-*O*-(*trans*-feruloyl)-β-L-arabinofuranosyl]-D-
xylopyranose, **3**, 697
gramine, **8**, 336
hordenine, **8**, 336
5-hydroxyferulic acid, **3**, 642
labeling studies, **2**, 61
leucoanthocyanidin 4-reductase, **1**, 730
lignins, **3**, 643
phenylalanine ammonia-lyase, **3**, 632
sequence homology, **1**, 654
tyrosine ammonia-lyase, **3**, 632
horhammerinine, biosynthesis, **4**, 121
hormones
adrenal cortical, cardiac glycosides, **3**, 328
definitions, **8**, 2, 21
overview, **8**, 2
roles, in insect growth, **8**, 265
stereochemistry, via optical rotatory dispersion, **8**, 6
see also antijuvenile hormones; diuretic hormones;
insect hormones; juvenile hormones; microbial
hormones; phytohormones; plant hormones
hormone-sensitive lipase (HSL), catalysis, **5**, 129
hormosirene, ^{13}C NMR spectra, **8**, 422
hormothamnin A
occurrence, **8**, 609
structure, **8**, 609
Hormothamnion enteromorphoides, hormothamnin A, **8**,
609
hornets, geranyl geranoate, **8**, 223
hornworts *see* Anthocerotae
horse-liver alcohol dehydrogenase (HADH), structure, **3**,
656
horseradishes *see* *Armoracia* spp.
horseshoe crabs *see* *Limulus polyphemus*
host factor, in symbiosis, **8**, 428
host–parasite chemical communication, plants, **8**, 175
host–parasite chemical transfer, mechanisms, **8**, 175
host-selective toxins, use of term, **8**, 178
host-specificity, definitions, **1**, 326
host–vector system, gene cluster expression, **1**, 484
9*R*-α-HOTE, occurrence, **1**, 242
9-HOTω6, biosynthesis, **1**, 223
13-HOTω6, biosynthesis, **1**, 223
houseflies *see* *Musca domestica*
house mouse *see* *Mus musculus*
9-HPEPE *see* eicosapentaenoic acid, 9-hydroperoxy- (9-
HPEPE); icosa-(5*Z*,7*E*,11*Z*,14*Z*,17*Z*)-
pentaenoic acid, 9-hydroperoxy- (9-HPEPE)
5-HPETE *see* eicosatetraenoic acid, 5-hydroperoxy- (5-
HPETE)
8*R*-HPETE *see* eicosatetraenoic acid, 8*R*-hydroperoxy-
(8*R*-HPETE)
11-HPETE *see* eicosatetraenoic acid, 11-hydroperoxy-
(11-HPETE)

12-HPETE *see* eicosatetraenoic acid, 12-hydroperoxy-
(12-HPETE)
12*S*-HPETE *see* eicosatetraenoic acid, 12*S*-hydroperoxy-
(12*S*-HPETE)
15-HPETE *see* eicosatetraenoic acid, 15-hydroperoxy-
(15-HPETE)
13-(*S*)-HPLA *see* linolenic acid, 13(*S*)-hydroperoxy-
HPLC *see* high performance liquid chromatography
(HPLC)
9*S*-HPOD *see* octadecadienoic acid, 9-hydroperoxy-
(9*S*-HPOD)
13*S*-HPOD *see* octadecadienoic acid, 13*S*-hydroperoxy-
(13*S*-HPOD)
HPO lyase *see* hydroperoxide lyase (HPO lyase)
HPOT *see* octadecatrienoic acid, 13*S*-hydroperoxy-
(HPOT)
9*R*-α-HPOTE, occurrence, **1**, 242
HS *see* heparan sulfate (HS); homocitrate synthase (HS)
HSL *see* hormone-sensitive lipase (HSL)
HSPGs *see* heparan sulfate proteoglycans (HSPGs)
HSS *see* human squalene synthase (HSS)
HSV *see* hop stunt viroid (HSV)
HTLV-1 *see* human T-cell leukemia virus type I (HTLV-
1)
HU *see* urea, hydroxy (HU)
human amniotic fluid (HAF), fucosyltransferases, **3**, 118
human colon carcinomas, galactosyltransferases, **3**, 112
human diseases, choroideremia, causes, **2**, 359
human gastric lipase (HGL)
sequences, **5**, 133
structure, **5**, 133
human genome
radiation damage, **5**, 372
sequencing, **6**, 21
human glycogen storage disease (type IV), etiology, **3**, 480
human immunodeficiency virus (HIV)
activity against, **3**, 143
complexation, RNA structural probing, **6**, 75
dumb-bell RNAs and, **7**, 362
HIV-1
inhibition, **1**, 690, 703
inhibitors, **7**, 187, 189
RNA studies, **6**, 76
sequences, **7**, 363
TAR RNA
cleavage, **7**, 562
intercalation, **7**, 469
human lysosomal acid lipase (HLAL)
mutants, **5**, 134
sequences, **5**, 133
structure, **5**, 133
human–plant relationships, future research, **1**, 111
humans
coproporphyrinogen oxidase, **4**, 95
geranyl*trans*transferase, **2**, 82
health, effects of isoflavonoids on, **1**, 782
hydroxymethylglutaryl-CoA reductases, **2**, 24
α-1,3-mannosyl-glycoprotein β-1,2-*N*-
acetylglucosaminyltransferase, genes, **3**, 50
human semen, prostaglandins, **1**, 160
human squalene synthase (HSS)
CCAAT box, **2**, 261
gene promoter structure, **2**, 261
NF-1 binding sites, **2**, 261
regulatory mechanisms, **2**, 259
Sp1 sites, **2**, 261
sterol regulatory element 1, **2**, 261
sterol regulatory element 3, **2**, 261
transcriptional regulation, **2**, 261
Y-Box sequences, **2**, 261
human squalene synthase (HSS) gene *see* *Fdft*1 gene
human T-cell leukemia virus type I (HTLV-1), expression,
3, 58

human thyroid stimulating hormone, functions, **6**, 226
Humicola insolens, endoglucanase V, **5**, 300
hummingbirds, roles, in pollination, **8**, 158
humulene, biosynthesis, **2**, 167
β-humulene, toxicity, **8**, 144
humulene synthase, occurrence, **2**, 167
humulone, isomerization, **1**, 760
Humulus lupulus, bitter acids, **1**, 760
Hyacinthaceae, 2,5-dihydroxymethyl-3,4-
        dihydroxypyrrolidine, **3**, 134
Hyacinthoides non-scripta, toxicity, **3**, 140
Hyalophora cecropia
    juvenile hormone I, **8**, 3
    juvenile hormones, **8**, 267, 272
hyaluronan (HA)
    attachment, **3**, 161
    binding, **3**, 4, 164
    biosynthesis, **3**, 174
    future research, **3**, 174
    roles, in cell proliferation, **3**, 174
hyaluronan synthase (HAS)
    catalysis, **3**, 174
    genes, **3**, 174
hyaluronidase
    catalysis, **8**, 355
    in honeybee venom, **8**, 355
hybridalactone, occurrence, **1**, 219
hydnocarpic acid, occurrence, **1**, 68
hydnocarpic acid, dihydro-, occurrence, **1**, 68
Hydnocarpus anthelmintica, fatty acids, **1**, 68
Hydnocarpus wightiana, hydnowightin, **1**, 685
hydnowightin, occurrence, **1**, 685
Hydractinia echinata
    eicosanoids, **1**, 242
    larval settlement induction, **8**, 432
Hydrangea macrophylla, phenylalanine ammonia-lyase,
        localization, **3**, 662
hydrangeic acid, biosynthesis, **1**, 765
Hydra vulgaris
    eicosanoids, **1**, 242
    phospholipase A₂, **1**, 242
hydrazines, **7**, 570
    superoxide production by, **7**, 540
hydrin, epichloro-, as substrate, **5**, 408
hydrocarbons
    cuticular, **8**, 247
    as pheromones, **8**, 247
hydrogen atoms
    abstraction, from DNA backbone, **7**, 493
    proR, **4**, 67
hydrogen bond donors, proton affinities, **5**, 19
hydrogen bonding
    reactive intermediate stabilization, in enzyme active
        sites, **5**, 5–29
    in substrate specificity determination, **5**, 6
hydrogen bonds
    normal, **5**, 13, 14, 16, 21
    roles, in reactive intermediate stabilization, **5**, 19
    short strong–low barrier, **5**, 21
        intermediate stabilization, **5**, 37
        measurement, **5**, 23
        physical organic models, **5**, 22
    strong, in intermediate stabilization, **5**, 24
    see also low barrier hydrogen bonds (LBHB)
hydrogen chloride, reactions, with methyl farnesoate, **8**,
        267
hydrogen cyanide, release, **1**, 20, 881
hydrogenobyrinic acid *a,c*-diamide synthase, roles, **4**, 146
hydrogenobyrinic acid (HBA)
    biosynthesis, **4**, 146
    from, aminolevulinic acid, **4**, 141
    as starting material, for cobalamin, **4**, 146
hydrogenobyrinic acid (HBA) synthase *see* precorrin 8
        mutase

hydrogen peroxide
    biosynthesis, **3**, 721
    DNA damage induction, **7**, 540
    extracellular, **3**, 720
    in laurediol studies, **1**, 304
    reactions, with hydroquinone, **8**, 364
    roles, in lignin biosynthesis, **3**, 720
hydrogen-peroxide:hydrogen-peroxide oxidoreductase
        see catalase
hydrogen transfer
    in lysine 2,3-aminomutase, **5**, 207
    mediation, **5**, 207, 208
α/β-hydrolase-fold superfamily, **1**, 893, **5**, 53
hydrolases, isolation, **7**, 632
hydrolysis
    esters, **5**, **101–137**
    sequential, **1**, 890
    simultaneous, **1**, 890
hydrolytic enzymes, **5**, 430
    effect of gibberellins on, **8**, 45
hydrolytic reactions, in antibody catalysis, **5**, 430
hydroperoxide, physiologic, as prostaglandin-
        endoperoxide synthase activator, **5**, 239
hydroperoxide cyclase, in jasmonic acid biosynthesis, **8**,
        115
hydroperoxide dehydratase
    catalysis, **1**, 232
    isolation, **1**, 232
    in jasmonic acid biosynthesis, **8**, 115
    in jasmonic acid biosynthetic pathway, **1**, 119
    in *Lemna* spp., **1**, 231
    nomenclature, **1**, 120
    purification, **1**, 120
hydroperoxide isomerase *see* hydroperoxide dehydratase
hydroperoxide lyase (HPO lyase)
    activity
        and chlorophyll content, **1**, 93
        in tomato plants, **1**, 92
    environmental stimuli, **1**, 108
    in green odor production, **1**, 92
    as heme protein, **1**, 95
    occurrence, **1**, 93, 95, 209
    product specificity, **1**, 102
    properties, **1**, 95
    purification, **1**, 95
    substrate specificity, **1**, 96, 102
    types, **1**, 95
hydroperoxides
    isomerization, **1**, 100
    reduction, **5**, 232, 234
9-hydroperoxides, biosynthesis, mediation, **1**, 92
13-hydroperoxides
    biosynthesis, **1**, 98
    as substrates, **1**, 102
hydroperoxy acids, cleavage, **8**, 204
hydroperoxyl radical, DNA cleavage by, **7**, 540
(9*Z*,11*E*,14*Z*)-(13*S*)-hydroperoxyoctadeca-(9,11,14)-
        trienoate 12,13-hydro-lyase *see* hydroperoxide
        dehydratase
hydroperoxy radical, **7**, 561
hydrophobic forces, in intercalation, **7**, 432
hydroprene
    applications, cockroach control, **8**, 275
    toxicity, **8**, 275
Hydropsyche angustipennis, pheromones, **8**, 212
hydroquinone, **7**, 575
    as allelopathic agent, **8**, 171
    applications, antifungal agents, **8**, 186
    oxidation, **3**, 711
    reactions, with hydrogen peroxide, **8**, 364
hydroquinone, dichloro-*S*-glutathionyl- (GS-DCHQ),
        biosynthesis, **5**, 415
hydroquinone, tetrachlorohydro- (TCHQ), biosynthesis,
        5, 418

hydroquinone, 2,3,5-trichloro-6-*S*-glutathionyl- (GS-TriCHQ), biosynthesis, **5**, 415
hydroquinone-*O*,*O*'-diacetic acid (QDA), **7**, 114
hydroxy acids, occurrence, **1**, 209, 219
3-hydroxyacyl-CoA, decarboxylation, **8**, 204
3-hydroxyacyl-CoA dehydrogenase
  activity, **1**, 51, 359
  catalysis, **1**, 348
  encoding, **1**, 356
(*S*)-3-hydroxyacyl-CoA:NAD⁺ oxidoreductase *see* 3-hydroxyacyl-CoA dehydrogenase
(*R*)-3-hydroxyacyl-CoA:NADP⁺ oxidoreductase(s) *see* acetoacetyl-CoA reductase(s)
β-hydroxyacyl-decanoyl-CoA dehydratase, catalysis, **1**, 359
β-hydroxyacyl dehydratase *see* 3-hydroxyacyl-CoA dehydrogenase
β-hydroxyacyl dehydrogenase *see* 3-hydroxyacyl-CoA dehydrogenase
S-(hydroxyalkyl)glutathione lyase(s) *see* glutathione transferase(s)
hydroxyalkyl-protein kinase(s) *see* protein kinase(s)
β-hydroxyamide, **7**, 580
3-hydroxyaspartate aldolase
  biochemistry, **3**, 403
  occurrence, **3**, 403
  substrate specificity, **3**, 404
erythro-3-hydroxy-L₅-aspartate glyoxylate-lyase *see* 3-hydroxyaspartate aldolase
p-hydroxybenzoate hydroxylase, catalysis, **5**, 418
3-hydroxybenzoyl-CoA, **1**, 759
2-hydroxybutane-1,2,4-tricarboxylate 2-oxoglutarate-lyase (CoA-acylating) *see* homocitrate synthase (HS)
(*R*)-3-hydroxybutanol-CoA, **8**, 209
hydroxycarboxylyl residues, detection, **1**, 298
hydroxycinnamate:CoA ligase *see* 4-coumarate-CoA ligase
hydroxycinnamic acid *O*-methyltransferase, localization, **3**, 672
hydroxycinnamoyl-CoA ligase *see* 4-coumarate-CoA ligase
hydroxycinnamoyl-CoA *O*-methyltransferase *see* caffeoyl-CoA *O*-methyltransferase
hydroxycinnamoyltransferases, occurrence, **1**, 741
hydroxycinnamyl *O*-methyltransferases
  cloning, **3**, 646
  early studies, **3**, 644
  genetics, **3**, 646
  localization, **3**, 671
  purification, **3**, 644
  roles, in monolignol biosynthesis, **3**, 643
2-hydroxy-1,2-diphenylethanone benzaldehyde-lyase *see* benzoin aldolase
4-hydroxy-3-hexanone propanal-lyase *see* propioin synthase
3-hydroxyisobutyryl-CoA hydrolase, active sites, **5**, 16
2-hydroxyisoflavanone dehydratase, purification, **1**, 793
2-hydroxyisoflavanone synthase, catalysis, **1**, 799
3-hydroxy-5-ketohexanoyl enzymes, as intermediate, **1**, 354
4-hydroxy-2-ketopimelate aldolase
  biochemistry, **3**, 413
  isolation, **3**, 413
  occurrence, **3**, 413
4-hydroxy-2-ketovalerate aldolase
  biochemistry, **3**, 384
  cloning, **3**, 385
  isolation, **3**, 384
  roles, **3**, 384
  stereospecificity, **3**, 385
hydroxykynureninase, detection, **3**, 397
3*R*-hydroxylacyl-CoA dehydrogenase, occurrence, **1**, 52
hydroxylamine, *O*-(2,3,4,5,6-pentafluorobenzyl)-, as trapping reagent, **1**, 632

hydroxylamine(s)
  applications, DNA structure probes, **7**, 93
  in hydroxymethylglutaryl-CoA reductase catalysis, **2**, 33
  palmitoylated protein treatment, **4**, 14
  superoxide production by, **7**, 540
hydroxylase
  in methane monooxygenase, **5**, 218
  purification, **1**, 843
2'-hydroxylase, catalysis, **1**, 800
3β-hydroxylase, in *Zea mays*, **2**, 236
17α-hydroxylase-17,20-lyase, *trans*-scission, **1**, 632
hydroxylation, cytochrome P450-dependent, **1**, 389, **3**, 637
2'-hydroxylation
  prerequisites, **1**, 795
  roles, in enzymatic reduction of isoflavones, **1**, 795
3'-hydroxylation, mechanism, **1**, 795
ω-hydroxylation, mechanisms, **1**, 268
(ω-1)-hydroxylation, mechanisms, **1**, 268
hydroxyl groups
  activation, via metal ions, **6**, 236
  deprotonation, **5**, 186
  interference analysis, **6**, 222
  loss, **5**, 188
  protection, **6**, 83, **7**, 126
hydroxyl radicals
  formation via Fenton reaction, **7**, 540
  from hydrogen peroxide, **7**, 540
  reactivity, **7**, 398
6-hydroxymellein synthase
  genetics, **1**, 416
  occurrence, **1**, 416
  purification, **1**, 416
hydroxymethylbilane (HMB), biosynthesis, **4**, 143
hydroxymethylbilane hydrolyase (cyclizing) *see* uroporphyrinogen-III synthase(s)
hydroxymethylbilane synthase(s)
  catalysis, **4**, 80
  conformational changes, during polymerization, **4**, 87
  inhibition, **4**, 85
  interactions, with dipyrromethane, **4**, 81
  mechanisms, **4**, 86
  occurrence, **4**, 80
  properties, **4**, 80
  roles, **4**, 143
  structure, **4**, 143
    x-ray crystal, **4**, 81
  substrate binding sites, **4**, 82
3-hydroxymethyl ceph-3-em *O*-carbamoyltransferase, catalysis, **4**, 172
hydroxymethylglutaryl-CoA
  binding, **2**, 32
  biosynthesis, **2**, 3
  from, acetyl-CoA, **2**, 22
  synthesis, **2**, 46
  thioester reductive deacylation, **2**, 22
(*S*)-3-hydroxy-3-methylglutaryl-CoA acetoacetate-lyase(s) *see* hydroxymethylglutaryl-CoA lyase(s)
(*S*)-3-hydroxy-3-methylglutaryl-CoA acetoacetyl-CoA-lyase(s) (CoA-acetylating) *see* hydroxymethylglutaryl-CoA synthase(s)
(*S*)-3-hydroxy-3-methylglutaryl-CoA hydro-lyase(s) *see* methylglutaconyl-CoA hydratase
hydroxymethylglutaryl-CoA lyase(s), **2**, 24
hydroxymethylglutaryl-CoA reductase inhibitors
  applications, hypocholesterolemic agents, **2**, 267
  fluvastatin, **2**, 246
  lovastatin, **2**, 246
  mevinolin, **2**, 355
  pravastatin, **2**, 246
  simvastatin, **2**, 246

hydroxymethylglutaryl-CoA reductase kinases *see* AMP-
    activated protein kinase (AMPK)
hydroxymethylglutaryl-CoA reductase phosphatases,
    purification, **2**, 39
hydroxymethylglutaryl-CoA reductase(s)
    active sites
        aspartate, **2**, 34, 36
        glutamate, **2**, 34, 36
        histidine, **2**, 33
        lysine, **2**, 34
    anchor domains, **2**, 27
        membrane, **2**, 38
    catalysis, **1**, 422, **2**, 17, 22
        and dephosphorylation, **2**, 39
        mechanisms, **2**, 34
        and phosphorylation, **2**, 39
        reductive stages, **2**, 30
    catalytic domains, **2**, 27
    characterization, **2**, 23
    degradation, **2**, 38
    domain structure, **2**, 24
    encoding, **2**, 37
    flap domain, **2**, 41
    genes, **1**, 236, **2**, 27
    helices, membrane-spanning, **2**, 24
    homology, **8**, 66
    inhibitors, **2**, 25, 33, 38, 378
    isozymes
        occurrence, **2**, 26
        regulatory mechanisms, **2**, 39
        stimulus responses, **2**, 26
        synthesis, **2**, 27
    minimum functional unit, **2**, 35
    molecular mass, **2**, 35
    NAD-dependent, **2**, 24
    occurrence, **2**, 23, 26
    post-transcriptional regulation, **2**, 38
    promoters, mutations, **2**, 37
    in *Pseudomonas mevalonii*, **2**, 24, 27, 41
        active site residues, **2**, 33
        binary complexes, **2**, 34
        dinucleotide binding fold, **2**, 29
        NADP specificity, **2**, 29
        structure, **2**, 28
        ternary complexes, **2**, 28
    purified, **2**, 27
    regulatory mechanisms, **2**, 3, 28, 36
    roles, in cholesterol homeostasis, **2**, 24
    site-directed mutagenesis, **2**, 35
    target serine, **2**, 39
    transcription, regulatory mechanisms, **2**, 37
    translation, regulatory mechanisms, **2**, 38
    x-ray crystal structure, **3**, 653
hydroxymethylglutaryl-CoA synthase(s)
    catalysis, **2**, 17, 19
    cloned, **2**, 21
    encoding, **2**, 37
    inhibitors, **2**, 22
    isozymes, **2**, 21
        ketogenic, **2**, 21
        physiologic functions, **2**, 26
    mutation, **2**, 22
    occurrence, **2**, 21
    substrate specificity, **2**, 19
4-hydroxy-4-methyl-2-oxoglutarate aldolase
    biochemistry, **3**, 385
    isolation, **3**, 385
    roles, **3**, 385
    substrate specificity, **3**, 386
4-hydroxy-4-methyl-2-oxoglutarate pyruvate-lyase *see* 4-
    hydroxy-4-methyl-2-oxoglutarate aldolase
3-hydroxy-2-methylpropanoyl-CoA hydrolase *see* 3-
    hydroxyisobutyryl-CoA hydrolase

R-3-hydroxymyristoyl-acyl carrier protein, as lipid A
    precursor, **3**, 220
R-3-hydroxymyristoyl-acyl carrier protein-dehydrase,
    localization, **3**, 221
hydroxyneurosporene, accumulation, **2**, 330
hydroxyneurosporene-*O*-methyltransferases, catalysis, **2**,
    343
hydroxyneurosporene synthases, homologues, **2**, 343
hydroxynitrile lyase *see* mandelonitrile lyase
α-hydroxynitrile lyases
    applications, **1**, 893
    biosynthesis, **1**, 893
    crystal structure, **1**, 893
    evolution, convergent, **1**, 893
    homologues, **1**, 893
    occurrence, **1**, 884
    properties, **1**, 893
4-hydroxy-2-oxoglutarate aldolase
    biochemistry, **3**, 381
    cloning, **3**, 382
    isolation, **3**, 381
    mechanisms, **3**, 402
    substrate specificity, **3**, 382
4-hydroxy-2-oxoglutarate glyoxylate-lyase *see* 4-hydroxy-
    2-oxoglutarate aldolase
β-hydroxyperoxide, base-catalyzed cleavage, **7**, 583
hydroxyphenylpyruvate synthase(s) *see* chorismate
    mutase(s); prephenate dehydrogenase(s)
4-hydroxyphenylserine aldolase, detection, **3**, 400
17α-hydroxyprogesterone acetaldehyde-lyase *see* 17α-
    hydroxyprogesterone aldolase
17α-hydroxyprogesterone aldolase
    biochemistry, **3**, 410
    inhibition, **3**, 411
    purification, **3**, 410
hydroxypropionyl groups, residues, **4**, 284
15-hydroxyprostaglandin dehydrogenase (NAD⁺),
    catalysis, **1**, 262
hydroxypyruvate reductase, transcription rate, **8**, 66
(hydroxystyryl)diisopropylsilyl (HSDIS), as
    photochemically removable protecting groups,
    7, 129
(hydroxystyryl)dimethylsilyl (HSDMS), as
    photochemically removable protecting groups, **7**, 129
hydroxytryptophan decarboxylase *see* aromatic-L-amino-
    acid decarboxylase
Hydrozoa
    eicosanoids, **1**, 242
    metamorphosis induction in, **8**, 431
hygrine
    occurrence, **4**, 30
    oxidation, **4**, 30
hygrinic acid, biosynthesis, **4**, 30
Hylobius abietis, female sex pheromones, **8**, 218
Hylotrupes bajulus
    (2*R*,3*R*)-2,3-hexanediol, **8**, 210
    (2*S*,3*R*)-2,3-hexanediol, **8**, 210
    (*R*)-3-hydroxy-2-hexanone, **8**, 210
hymatoxin A, phytotoxicity, **8**, 179
Hymenomonas spp., hymenosulfate, **8**, 618
Hymenoptera
    geranylgeraniol, **8**, 229
    venoms, **8**, 354
hymenoquinone, biosynthesis, **3**, 624
hymenosulfate
    Ca²⁺-releasing activity, in sarcoplasmic reticulum, **8**,
        618
    glycolipids in, **8**, 618
    occurrence, **8**, 618
hymenovin, mutagenesis, **7**, 503
hynapene A, biosynthesis, **1**, 370
hyodorilactone A, antifeedant activity, **8**, 308
hyoscyamine

isolation, **4**, 27
in nectars, **8**, 162
hyoscyamine, 6α-hydroxy-, epoxidation, **1**, 878
hyoscyamine 6S-hydroxylase, catalysis, **4**, 30
hyoscyamine 6α-hydroxylase, sequencing, **1**, 878
hyoscyamine 6β-hydroxylase *see* hyoscyamine 6S-
    hydroxylase
L-hyoscyamine,2-oxoglutarate:oxygen oxidoreductase
    ((6S)-hydroxylating) *see* hyoscyamine 6S-
    hydroxylase
Hyoscyamus muticus
    vetispiradiene, **2**, 183
    vetispiradiene synthases, **2**, 210
hyperalgesia, etiology, **5**, 226
Hypera postica, zanthophylline toxicity, **8**, 344
hypercholesterolemia
    risk factors, **2**, 24
    studies, **2**, 25
hyperglycemia, mechanisms, **3**, 444
hyperglycemic factors, release, **8**, 302
hypericin, insect sequestration, **8**, 152
hyperpolarization, plasma membranes, **8**, 31
hypertrehalosemic factors, existence, **8**, 299
hypertrehalosemic hormones, structure, **8**, 299
Hyphantria cunea, (3Z,6Z)-(9S,10R)-9,10-epoxy-3,6-
    henicosatriene, **8**, 207

Hyphomicrobium spp., dichloromethane dehalogenases,
    5, 407
hypocholesterolemic agents
    BMS-188494, **2**, 258
    hydroxymethylglutaryl-CoA reductase inhibitors, **2**,
        267
    lobastatin, **1**, 2
    pravastatin, **1**, 2
hypochromism
    induction, **7**, 452
    in RNA structural transition analyses, **6**, 23
Hypodamia spp.
    convergine, **8**, 351
    hippodamine, **8**, 351
hypoglycin, effects, on herbivores, **8**, 146
hypophyllanthin, cytotoxicity, **1**, 701
hypotrehalosemic factors, existence, **8**, 299
hypoxanthine oxidase *see* xanthine oxidase
hypoxanthine(s)
    applications, **6**, 225
    in oligodeoxynucleotides, **7**, 325
    oxidation, **5**, 80
hypoxilin, biosynthesis, **1**, 170
Hypsipyla grandella, antifeedant activity against, **8**, 321
Hyrtios altum, *Vibrio* spp. in, **8**, 588

I

IAA *see* indole-3-acetic acid (IAA)

I antigens, localization, **3**, 78

i antigens, localization, **3**, 78

IAT *see* acyl-CoA:isopenicillin N acyltransferase (IAT)

ibuprofen
    as jasmonic acid biosynthesis inhibitor, **1**, 131
    as lipoxygenase inhibitor, **1**, 123

I-cell disease *see* inclusion cell disease

ichthyotoxicity, Porifera, **8**, 466

icosanolide, occurrence, **8**, 218

icosa-(5Z,7E,11Z,14Z,17Z)-pentaenoic acid, 9-
    hydroperoxy- (9-HPEPE), biosynthesis, **8**, 423

(5Z,8Z,11Z,14Z)-icosa-5,8,11,14-tetraenoate,hydrogen-
    donor:oxygen oxidoreductase(s) *see*
    prostaglandin-endoperoxide synthase(s)

(Z)-11-icosen-1-ol, occurrence, **8**, 218

(Z)-7-icosen-11-one, occurrence, **8**, 208

Ictalusus punctatus, oxylipin studies, **1**, 238

idarubicin
    anticancer activity, **4**, 200
    cardiotoxicity, **7**, 605

Idea spp., pheromones, **8**, 215

Idea iasonia, dihydroactinidiolide, **8**, 234

Idea leuconoe
    geranyl methylsulfide, **8**, 222
    (4S,6S)-6-hydroxy-4-dodecanolide, **8**, 215

IDL *see* intermediate density lipoproteins (IDL)

IDP *see* isopentenyl diphosphate (IDP)

IEB E47, peptide, conformation, **7**, 481

IF3 *see* initiation factor 3 (IF3)

IFR, homologues, **1**, 817

IFR genes, transcription, **1**, 817

IGFII mRNA, degradation, **6**, 213

i β3-GlcNAc-T *see* N-acetyllactosaminide β-1,3-N-
    acetylglucosaminyltransferase

I β6-GlcNAc-T *see* UDP-N-
    acetylglucosamine:GlcNAcβ1-3 Gal (GlcNAc
    to Gal) β1,6-GlcNAc-transferase (I β6-GlcNAc-T)

IGS *see* internal guide sequence (IGS)

ikarugamycin, structure, **1**, 374

IL-1 *see* interleukin-1 (IL-1)

Ilex opaca, saponins, **8**, 144

ilicicolin H, biosynthesis, **1**, 370

Illicium religiosum, shikimic acid, **1**, 16, 574

illudins
    carcinogenicity, **7**, 508
    possible DNA damage induction, **7**, 507
    toxicity, **7**, 508

iloprost
    applications, **1**, 196
        pharmaceutical, **1**, 196
    biological activity, **1**, 190

IM, synthesis, **8**, 384

IM-2
    mode of action, **8**, 390
    occurrence, **1**, 140, **8**, 389

IM-2 receptor protein *see* Far proteins, FarA

imidazole
    in oligodeoxynucleotides, **7**, 334
    phosphate activation, **6**, 69

imidazole, 4,5-dichloro-, in oligonucleotide synthesis, **7**,
    133

imidazole, N-methyl-, in oligonucleotide synthesis, **7**, 108

imidazole alkaloids
    biosynthesis, **4**, 54

occurrence, **4**, 54

imidazole-4-carboxamide, 5-amino- (AICA), binding, **5**,
    86

imidazole hydrochloride, N-methyl-, as coupling reaction
    activator, **7**, 138

N²-3-imidazolepropionic acid, in oligodeoxynucleotides,
    7, 327

imidazole β-D-ribofuranoside, 5-amino, as intermediate,
    4, 150

imidazole riboside, 5-amino-, as intermediate, **1**, 838

imidazoles, nitro-
    in DNA damage, **7**, 583
    as DNA topoisomerase II inhibitors, **7**, 609
    one-electron reduction potential, **7**, 583
    Ro 15-0216, **7**, 609

imidazoles, 2-nitro-, reductive activation of, **7**, 521

imidazolium trifluoromethane sulfonate, N-methyl-, as
    coupling reaction activator, **7**, 138

imidazo[1,2-a]pyrazin-3-one, 3,7-dihydro-, in marine
    luminescent systems, **8**, 455

imines
    DNA damage induction, **7**, 495
    electrospray mass spectra, **1**, 586

imino protons
    exchange rates, **7**, 74
    exchange times, measurement, **7**, 75

imipenem *see* thienamycin, N-formidoyl-

immune system
    antibody catalysis, **5**, 423
    effects of endotoxins on, **3**, 198
    hyporesponsiveness, **3**, 183

immunization, reactive, **5**, 442

immunoassays
    in brassinolide, **8**, 100
    in castasterone, **8**, 100
    in plant hormone studies, **8**, 23

immunocytochemistry, probes, in lignin studies, **3**, 699

immunomycin, binding proteins, **1**, 541

immunosuppressive agents
    castanospermine, **3**, 143
    cyclosporin A, **1**, 16
    FK506, **1**, 518, **2**
    rapamycin, **1**, 2

incanin, antifeedant activity, **8**, 308

inclusion cell disease, etiology, **3**, 59

indacene, tetrahydro-
    deuterium incorporation, **7**, 560
    formation, **7**, 560

2,6-indacene biradical, formation, **7**, 560

indacen-12-ones, synthesis, mechanisms, **7**, 561

indan-4-carboxylic acid, 1-oxo-, conjugation, **1**, 135

indane, 1,3-dithiobenzyl-2,4,5,6-tetrahydroxy-,
    biosynthesis, **3**, 769

indane diastereomers, 1,3-dithiobenzyl-2,4,5,6-
    tetrahydroxy-, biosynthesis, **3**, 769

indanomycin, occurrence, **1**, 374

indans, biosynthesis, **3**, 767

Indian elephant *see* Elephas maximus

Indo-Chinese lacquer tree *see* Rhus succedanea

indole
    occurrence, **8**, 161
    odor, **8**, 161

indole, 4′,6-diamino-2-phenyl- (DAPI)
    fluorescence quantum yield, **7**, 459
    minor-groove binding, **7**, 457

sequence-dependent binding mode, **7**, 456
structure, **7**, 452
indoleacetaldehyde, as intermediate, **8**, 33
indole-3-acetaldehyde, occurrence, **8**, 26
indoleacetaldoxime, as intermediate, **8**, 34
indole-3-acetaldoxime, occurrence, **8**, 26
indoleacetamide, biosynthesis, **8**, 34
indole-3-acetic acid, 4-chloro-, occurrence, **8**, 26
indole-3-acetic acid, 5,6-dichloro-, auxin activity, **8**, 34
indole-3-acetic acid, 5-hydroxy-, occurrence, **8**, 26
indole-3-acetic acid (IAA)
    antibodies, **8**, 25
    from, tryptophan, **8**, 32
    occurrence, **8**, 26
    structure, **8**, 24
    see also hetero auxin
indole-3-acetoamide, occurrence, **8**, 26
indoleacetonitrile, in auxin biosynthesis, **8**, 34
indole-3-acetonitrile, occurrence, **8**, 26
indole-3-acetonitrile, 1-methoxy-, occurrence, **8**, 26
indole-3-acetonitrile, 4-methoxy-, occurrence, **8**, 26
indole-3-acetyl-L-aspartate acid, 4-chloro-, occurrence, **8**, 26
indole-3-acetyl-L-aspartic acid, occurrence, **8**, 26
indole-3-acrylic acid, occurrence, **8**, 26
indole aldehyde, as intermediate, **8**, 33
indole alkaloids
    applications, **4**, 110
    biosynthesis, reviews, **4**, 110
    classification
        Aspidosperma type, **4**, 110
        Corynanthé type, **4**, 110
        Iboga type, **4**, 110
    early studies, **4**, 110
    from, tryptamine, **4**, 109, 110
    insecticidal activity, **8**, 345
indole-3-butyric acid, occurrence, **8**, 26
3-(indole-3-)butyric acid, S-4,4,4-trifluoro- (TFIBA), structure, **8**, 34
indole-3-carboxaldehyde, occurrence, **8**, 26
indole-3-carboxylic acid, occurrence, **8**, 26
indole-3-ethanol, occurrence, **8**, 26
indoleglucosinolates
    in induced chemical defense, **8**, 151
    isolation, **8**, 26
    occurrence, **8**, 34
indole-3-glycerate, methyl 1-acetyl-, structure, **8**, 34
indole-3-isobutyric acid, 5,7-dichloro-, structure, **8**, 34
indole-3-methanesulfonic acid, structure, **8**, 34
indole phytoalexins, occurrence, **8**, 187
indole-3-propionic acid, occurrence, **8**, 26
indolepyruvic acid, as intermediate, **8**, 33
indolizidine alkaloids
    glycosidase inhibitory activity, **3**, 130
    occurrence, **3**, 134, **8**, 357
    structure, **3**, 132
indolmycin, structure, **1**, 150
indolocarbazoles, as DNA topoisomerase I inhibitors, **7**, 600
indomethacin
    as lipoxygenase inhibitor, **1**, 243
    prostaglandin-endoperoxide synthase inhibition, **5**, 252
γ-indomycinone, occurrence, **8**, 598
indospicine, effects, on herbivores, **8**, 146
Inducing Material (IM) *see* IM
Inducing Material-2 (IM-2) *see* IM-2
infectants, opportunistic, **8**, 392
infectivity, inhibition, **3**, 31
inflexin, occurrence, **8**, 312
influenza viruses
    exo-α-sialidases, **5**, 294
        mutagenesis studies, **5**, 296
    type A, activity against, **1**, 702

infochemicals, use of term, **8**, 199
infrared spectroscopy, and Raman spectroscopy compared, **3**, 543
ingenamines
    absolute configuration, **8**, 560
    occurrence, **8**, 560
ingenane, biosynthesis, **2**, 223
inhibitor binding, effects of reduced nicotinamide adenine dinucleotide phosphate on, **2**, 255
initiation factor 1 (IF1), binding, **6**, 202
initiation factor 2 (IF2), binding, **6**, 202
initiation factor 3 (IF3), cross-linking, **6**, 195
inosine
    aptamer-binding ability, **7**, 625
    biosynthesis, **5**, 73, **6**, 98
    use in hammerhead ribozyme studies, **7**, 276
inosine phosphorylase *see* purine-nucleoside phosphorylase
inosine-uridine nucleoside hydrolase, occurrence, **5**, 306
inositol
    biosynthesis, pathways, **1**, 154
    occurrence, **3**, 409
inositol, *N*-acetylglucosaminylphosphatidyl- (GlcNAc-PI), biosynthesis, **3**, 301, **4**, 306, 307
inositol, acylglucosaminylphosphatidyl- (GlcN-acyl PI), biosynthesis, **4**, 311
inositol, glucosaminylphosphatidyl- (GlcN-PI)
    biosynthesis, **3**, 300, **4**, 310
    elongation, **3**, 301
inositol monophosphatase, structure, **5**, 157
inositols, in cellulose studies, **3**, 544
inositols, glycosylphosphatidyl- (GPIs)
    analogues, **3**, 303
    biosynthesis, **3**, 6, **295–309**
    modification, **4**, 307, 316
    protein attachment, **4**, 315
    structure, **3**, 295, **4**, 305, 307
insect blood, detection, **8**, 271
insect chemical ecology, biochemistry, **8**, 263–375
insect control agents, neuropeptides, **8**, 302
insect hormones
    biochemistry, **8**, 263–375
    classification, **8**, 265
insecticides
    lignans, **1**, 693
    nicotine, **8**, 302
    sabadilla, **8**, 349
    solanine, **8**, 345
    tomatine, **8**, 345
insect juvenile hormones, **2**, 76
    bioassays, **8**, 266
    biochemistry, **8**, 265
    biosynthesis, **8**, 272
    chemical analysis, **8**, 271
    inactivation, **8**, 274
    isolation, **8**, 267
    structure, **8**, 267
    synthesis, **8**, 270
insect oviposition
    plant compounds
        deterrents, **8**, 156
        stimulants, **8**, 155
insects
    antifeedants, **8**, 303
    cholesterol, **8**, 290
    cuticle
        alkanes, **8**, 204
        alkenes, **8**, 204
        desaturases, **8**, 205
    evolution, **8**, 264
    glycosidase processing, **3**, 14
    growth, mechanism, **8**, 265
    herbivorous, cyanogenic, **1**, 883

α1,2-mannosidases, **3**, 24
monoterpenes, **2**, 101
neuropeptides, **8**, 294
occurrence, **8**, 264
oxylipins, reviews, **1**, 208, 248
pheromones, **8**, 204
plant defenses against, **8**, 303
plants toxic to, **8**, 302
predators, repellents, **8**, 350
sequestration of plant substances, **8**, 361
toxic, warning coloration, **8**, 152
toxins, **8**, 138
  biochemistry, **8**, 350
venoms, **8**, 354
see also social insects
insertion–deletion editing, **6**, 97, 104
  catalytic mechanisms, **6**, 105
    cleavage–ligation model, **6**, 105
    transesterification model, **6**, 105
  U-deletion, mechanisms, **6**, 105
  U-insertion, mechanisms, **6**, 105
insulin
  effects, on glycogen synthase, **3**, 487
  regulatory mechanisms, **3**, 444
  skeletal muscle stimulation, **3**, 487
insulin stimulated kinase (ISPK), activation, **3**, 487
integerrimine, structure, **4**, 33
intercalating agents
  acridine orange, applications, **7**, 428
  anilinoacridines, **7**, 606
  anthracenediones, **7**, 606
    modified, **7**, 606
  anthracenes, **7**, 606
  anthracyclines, **7**, 605
    applications, **7**, 428
  applications, **7**, 428
  association rate constants, **7**, 434
  benzoisoquinolinediones, **7**, 606
  benzophenazines, **7**, 606
  chemically switched, **7**, 461
  coupling, **7**, 226
  covalent, **7**, 470
  design of, major and minor grooves, **7**, 440
  discovery, **7**, 428
  DNA binding, **7**, 7
  as DNA topoisomerase II inhibitors, **7**, 604
  double-decker, **7**, 565
  ellipticines, **7**, 605
  ethidium bromide, applications, **7**, 428
  furamine, **7**, 458
  future research, **7**, 472
  incorporation, into oligonucleotides, **7**, 236
  minimal
    acridine-4-carboxamides, **7**, 607
    9-aminoacridine-4-carboxamide, **7**, 607
    as DNA topoisomerase II inhibitors, **7**, 607
  peptides, **7**, 487
  porphyrins, **7**, 441
  proflavine, **7**, 435
  pyrimidines S1-S3, **7**, 458
  quinacrine, applications, **7**, 428
  quinacrine mustard, **7**, 470
    applications, **7**, 428
  reactions, with DNA, **7**, 470
  self-assembly, **7**, 461
  simple systems, binding sites, **7**, 436
  threading, **7**, 437
    anthraquinone, **7**, 451
    nogalamycin, **7**, 437
    synthetic, **7**, 440
  triplex, naphthylquinoline, **7**, 468
  variations in, **7**, 435
  see also bisintercalators; DNA intercalators; RNA
    intercalators; trisintercalators

intercalating agents, multi-, **7**, 451, 461
intercalating agents, unfused aromatic, **7**, 452
intercalation
  barrier to, steric clash, **7**, 441
  dinucleotide binding sites, **7**, 436
  with distorted nucleic acid structures, **7**, 469
  and epoxide–DNA, **7**, 470
  inhibition, in multi-aromatic compounds, **7**, 451
  into distorted duplexes, **7**, 466
  into multistranded helices, **7**, 466
  models, Lerman's classical, **7**, 432, 433
  neighbor exclusion, **7**, 444
  NMR signal downfield shift, **7**, 441
  nonclassical, furamidine model, **7**, 459
  parallel, **7**, 437
  partial
    model systems, **7**, 463
    and protein–DNA recognition, **7**, 463
    of protein side chains, **7**, 465
    small aromatic systems, **7**, 463
  perpendicular, **7**, 437
  RNA and DNA duplexes compared, **7**, 433
  specificity, **7**, 436
  tetraplex, **7**, 469
  threading
    intercalation geometry, **7**, 441
    substituent position, **7**, 441
  triplex, **7**, 466
intercalation binding mode, **7**, 428
intercalation sites
  backbone torsional angles, **7**, 435
  essential features, **7**, 439
  formation, **7**, 434
  for nogalamycin, **7**, 438
  structural details, **7**, 435
  sugar conformation, **7**, 435
  variations in, **7**, 435
intercalation unwinding angle, **7**, 432
  and closed circular superhelical DNA, **7**, 433
intercalative binding model, in esperamicin A$_1$, **7**, 574
intercellular communications, microorganisms, **8**, 378
interconvertible forms
  of geranylgeranyl diphosphate synthase, **2**, 87
  of geranyl*trans*transferase, **2**, 74
    Cys residue oxidation, **2**, 85
interleukin, biosynthesis, **3**, 182
interleukin-1 (IL-1), effects, on proteoglycan mRNA, **3**, 167
intermediate density lipoproteins (IDL), components, **5**, 94
intermediates
  dienolic, **5**, 32, 39
    stability, **5**, 39
  Hammond postulate, **5**, 11
  physicochemical properties, equalization, **5**, 11
  proton affinities, **5**, 12
  reactive, stabilization, **5**, 5–29
  short strong–low barrier types, **5**, 14, 16, 19
  stabilization
    via electrostatic interactions, **5**, 27
    via strong hydrogen bonds, **5**, 24
  and transition states, **5**, 10
  see also acyl-enzyme intermediates; alkyl-enzyme
    intermediates; carbocationic intermediates;
    enolate intermediates; Meisenheimer
    intermediates; phosphoenzyme intermediates;
    tetrahedral intermediates
internal guide sequence (IGS), introns, **6**, 151
International Union of Biochemistry and Molecular
  Biology (IUBMB), DNA structure
  nomenclature, **7**, 56
International Union of Pure and Applied Chemistry
  (IUPAC), DNA structure nomenclature, **7**, 56

Internet
ESTHER database, **5**, 112
see also World Wide Web (WWW)
interplant communication, defensive gene expression, **1**, 132
interpretation, of biochemical results, **7**, 265
intoplicine
applications, antineoplastic agents, **7**, 607
structure, **7**, 608
intracellular membranes, glycosphingolipids, **3**, 87
introns
binding sites, **6**, 152
folding, kinetics, **7**, 49
Group I
adenosine platforms, **6**, 154
A-rich bulges, **6**, 155
binding, **6**, 221
binding sites, **6**, 163
catalysis, **6**, 115, 221
discovery, **6**, 236
guanosine binding sites, **6**, 151
G–U wobble pairs, **6**, 155
intervening sequences, **6**, 160
kinetics, **6**, 160
mechanisms, **6**, 110
oligonucleotide tag binding, **6**, 118
phosphoester transfer mechanisms, **6**, 160
rate constants, **6**, 150
ribose zippers, **6**, 155
in RNA catalysis, **6**, 158
RNA splicing, **6**, 222, 254
selection, **6**, 119
self-splicing, **6**, 257
structure, **6**, 110
tetraloops, **6**, 124, 154
x-ray crystal structure, **6**, 154
Group II
activity, **6**, 110
branch point adenosine, **6**, 226
7-deazaadenosine incorporation studies, **6**, 225
self-splicing, **6**, 150, 221, 258
structure, **6**, 152
internal guide sequence, **6**, 151
L-21 ScaI, **6**, 158
minor groove triple helix, **6**, 156
nucleotide analogue interference mapping, **6**, 155
nucleotide analogue interference suppression, **6**, 156
pre-mRNA, **7**, 345
pre-rRNA, **6**, 149
self-splicing, P4-P6 domains, **6**, 56
structure
secondary, **6**, 151
tertiary, **6**, 154
unspliced, **6**, 210
invertebrates
oxylipins, reviews, **1**, 208
platelet-activating factor, **1**, 286
invictolide
biosynthesis, **8**, 240
structure, **8**, 241, 244
iodine cleavage, applications, **6**, 221
iodonin, DNA damage induction, **7**, 532
iodosuprofen, prostaglandin-endoperoxide synthase inhibition, **5**, 232
ion cofactors, divalent metal, in monoterpene synthases, **2**, 124
ionizing radiation, DNA damage induction, **7**, 397
β-ionone, occurrence, **8**, 234
ion transport, mechanisms, **4**, 323
ipA *see* purine, N^6-(γ,γ-dimethylallylamino)-
IPCP *see* diphosphonate, isopentenyl methylene (IPCP)
IPN *see* isopenicillin N (IPN)
ipnA gene *see* pcb genes, *pcbC*

IPNS *see* isopenicillin N synthase (IPNS)
ipomeamarone, occurrence, **2**, 191
Ipomoea spp.
calystegines, **3**, 134, 140
swainsonine, **3**, 134
Ipomoea batatas
p-coumaroyl-D-glucose hydroxylase, **3**, 641
ipomeamarone, **2**, 191
Ipomoea piurensis, peptide ergot alkaloids, **4**, 53
Ipomopsis aggregata, pollination, **8**, 158
IPP *see* isopentenyl diphosphate (IDP)
Ips spp.
aggregation pheromones, **8**, 223
amitinol, **8**, 224
myrcenol, **8**, 224
Ips avulsus, pheromones, **8**, 14
Ips calligraphus, pheromones, **8**, 14
Ips cembrae, 3-methyl-3-buten-1-ol, **8**, 220
Ips cribricollis
ipsdienone, **8**, 223
ipsenone, **8**, 223
ipsdienol
biosynthesis, **8**, 224
occurrence, **8**, 14, 223, 224
(+)-ipsdienol, from, myrcene, **2**, 101
ipsdienone
detection, **8**, 224
occurrence, **8**, 223
ipsenol
biosynthesis, **8**, 224
occurrence, **8**, 223
ipsenone, occurrence, **8**, 223
Ips paraconfusus
ipsdienol, **8**, 14
pheromones, **8**, 14
Ips pini
lanierone, **8**, 234
pheromones, **8**, 14
Ips sexdentatus
ipsdienone, **8**, 223
ipsenone, **8**, 223
m-methandienol, **8**, 224
Ips typographus
isophorones, **8**, 234
2-methyl-3-buten-2-ol, **8**, 200
biosynthesis, **8**, 220
(E)-3-methyl-7-methylene-1,3,8-nonatriene, **8**, 236
IPTG *see* isopropyl-β-thio-D-galactopyranoside (IPTG)
ipt genes
activity, **8**, 70
coding region, **8**, 63
transformations, **8**, 63, 66
ircinal A
occurrence, **1**, 380
reduction, **8**, 556
ircinal B
occurrence, **1**, 380
reduction, **8**, 557
ircinals
occurrence, **8**, 554
structure, **8**, 554
Ircinia spp.
ircinals, **8**, 554
ircinianin, **1**, 378
ircinianin, occurrence, **1**, 378
ircinol A, occurrence, **1**, 380
ircinol B, occurrence, **1**, 380
ircinols, structure, **8**, 556
irenotecan
characteristics, **7**, 599
structure, **7**, 599
iridane monoterpenes, characterization, **2**, 106
iridodial

biosynthesis, **2**, 106, **4**, 112
occurrence, **8**, 226
iridoids
biosynthesis, **2**, 106, **8**, 353
from, citral, **8**, 234
in nectars, **8**, 162
occurrence, **2**, 106, **8**, 226
structure, **8**, 353
use of term, **8**, 353
iridoid toxins, biosynthesis, **8**, 176
iridomyrmecin
insecticidal activity, **8**, 353
occurrence, **8**, 226, 307, 353
Iridomyrmex spp., pheromones, **8**, 217
Iridomyrmex humilis
(*Z*)-9-hexadecenal, **8**, 217
iridomyrmecin, **8**, 307, 353
Iridomyrmex purpureus, 6-methyl-5-hepten-2-one, **8**, 232
iridotrial, biosynthesis, **2**, 106, **4**, 112
iristectorone A, occurrence, **1**, 384
irnine, isolation, **4**, 30
iron–bleomycin complexes, DNA cleavage, mechanisms,
7, 537
iron centers, dinuclear, in ribonucleotide reductases, **3**,
329, 343
iron response element binding protein, inhibitory activity,
6, 214
iron–sulfur clusters
EPR spectra, **5**, 214
oxidation states, **5**, 215
reduction, **5**, 214
iron–sulfur proteins, pyridoxamine 5'-phosphate-
dependent, **3**, 337
iron superoxide dismutase, gene homology, **8**, 66
irradiation, use in deprotection, **7**, 129
isoacanthodoral, occurrence, **2**, 192
3-isoadenine, in DNA hexamer, **7**, 324
isoamylase
identity, **3**, 468
oligosaccharide chain removal, **3**, 480
isoaucuparin, as phytoalexin, **8**, 187
isobavachalcone, occurrence, **1**, 130
isoboldine, antifeedant activity, **8**, 345
isoborneol, structure, **2**, 104
isoborreverine, biosynthesis, **1**, 369
isobutylamides
insecticidal activity, **8**, 303
occurrence, **8**, 303
isobutyric acid, occurrence, **8**, 220
isobutyric acid, 4-chlorophenoxy-, structure, **8**, 34
isobutyric acid, α-(2-naphthylmethylsulfido)-, structure,
8, 34
isobutyroin, biosynthesis, **3**, 394
isobutyryl-CoA, as starter unit, **1**, 760
4-isocaranol, biosynthesis, **2**, 135
isocaranone, biosynthesis, **2**, 135
isocarbacyclin, biological activity, **1**, 190
isochamigrene, biosynthesis, **2**, 162
isochorismatase(s), encoding, **1**, 616
isochorismate hydroxymutase(s) *see* isochorismate
synthase(s)
isochorismate pyruvate-hydrolase(s) *see*
isochorismatase(s)
isochorismate synthase(s)
encoding, **1**, 610, 613, 616
occurrence, **1**, 611, 618
regulatory mechanisms, **5**, 344
isochorismic acid
biosynthesis, **1**, 612
enzyme studies, **1**, 611
tracer studies, **1**, 610
via metabolic pathway engineering, **1**, 619
discovery, **1**, 609

from, chorismic acid, **1**, 619
metabolism
in bacteria, **1**, 612
in higher plants, **1**, 617
occurrence, **1**, 610
roles, in metabolism, **1**, **609–622**
as starting material
for menaquinones, **1**, 610
for siderophores, **1**, 610
structure, **1**, 609
isochromene, hydroxy-, formation, **7**, 566
Isochrysis spp., furan fatty acids, **1**, 226
isochrysohermidine, DNA cross-linking by, **7**, 503
(+)-isocotylocrebine, as oviposition stimulant, **8**, 156
isocoumarin, 3,4-dihydro-, occurrence, **8**, 241
isocoumarin, 6,8-dihydroxy-3-methyl-, isolation, **1**, 415
isocoumarin, 3-methyl-3,4-dihydro-8-hydroxy- *see*
mellein
isocoumarins
classification, biosynthetic, **1**, 625
occurrence, **1**, 14
phytotoxicity, **8**, 180
structure, **1**, 623
isocularines, biosynthesis, **4**, 40
isoculmorin, occurrence, **8**, 601
isocyanates, aliphatic, **6**, 227
isodactylyne, occurrence, **1**, 303
Isodictya setifera, *Pseudomonas aeruginosa* in, **8**, 590
isodomedin, occurrence, **8**, 312
Isodon inflexus, inflexin, **8**, 312
Isodon shikokianus
isodomedin, **8**, 312
shikodonin, **8**, 312
isoeudistomin U, occurrence, **8**, 528
isoeugenol
biosynthesis, **3**, 677
as floral volatile, **8**, 161
oxidation, **3**, 703
stereoselective coupling, **1**, 680
isofagaridine, occurrence, **7**, 601
isofagomine, binding, **5**, 302
isoferulic acid, biosynthesis, **3**, 624
isoflavan, biosynthesis, **1**, 812
isoflavan, 2'-hydroxy-, biosynthesis, **1**, 814
isoflavanol, 7,2'-dihydroxy-4'-methoxy- (DMI), as
intermediate, **1**, 797
isoflavanone reductase, roles, in pterocarpan
biosynthesis, **1**, 797
isoflavanones
antifungal activity, **1**, 779
from, isoflavones, **1**, 795
as intermediates, **1**, 795
structure, **1**, 786
isoflavanone(s), 2-hydroxy-, dehydration, **1**, 791
isoflavanone(s), 2'-hydroxy-
biosynthesis, **1**, 786
dehydration, **1**, 19
ring closure, **1**, 797
as substrate, **1**, 797
isoflavans
antifungal activity, **1**, 779
biosynthesis, **1**, 786, 786
isoflav-3-ene, 7,2'-dihydroxy-4'-methoxy-, as coumestan
precursor, **1**, 810
isoflavenes, occurrence, **1**, 775
isoflav-3-enes, as intermediates, **1**, 786, 810
isoflav-3-en-2-one, 7,2'-dihydroxy-4'-methoxy-, as
coumestan precursor, **1**, 810
isoflavone, from, flavanone, **1**, 791
isoflavone, 5,4'-dihydroxy-7-methoxy- *see* prunetin
isoflavone, 2'-hydroxylase, catalysis, **1**, 795
isoflavone, 4'-hydroxy-7-methoxy- *see* isoformononetin
isoflavone, 7-hydroxy-2',4,5'-trimethoxy-, as starting
material, for amorphigenin, **8**, 342

isoflavone, 2′,4′,5,7-tetrahydroxy-8-(3,3-dimethylallyl)-
  see kievitone
isoflavone, 6,7,4′-trihydroxy-, antioxidant activity, **1**, 815
isoflavone dimers
  biosynthesis, **1**, 806
  occurrence, **1**, 806
isoflavone glucoside malonylesterase(s)
  catalysis, **1**, 809
  properties, **1**, 809
isoflavone glucoside malonyltransferase(s), catalysis, **1**, 809
isoflavone 7-*O*-glucosides, malonylation, **1**, 809
isoflavone glucosyltransferase(s), purification, **1**, 809
isoflavone glycosides
  biosynthesis, **1**, 806
  catabolism, **1**, 808
  efflux, **1**, 806
  vacuolar storage, **1**, 806
isoflavone 7-*O*-methyltransferase
  induction, **1**, 799
  purification, **1**, 799
isoflavone reductase (IFR)
  antibodies, **1**, 796
  catalysis, **1**, 681
  homologues, **1**, 681
  occurrence, **1**, 665
  purification, **1**, 796
  sequencing, **1**, 797
  substrate specificity, **1**, 796
isoflavones
  antifungal activity, **1**, 779
  biosynthesis, **1**, 717, 786, 790
  as DNA topoisomerase II inhibitors, **7**, 610
  genistein, **7**, 610
  haustoria-inducing activity, **8**, 175
  2′-hydroxylation, **1**, 786, 795
  3′-hydroxylation, **1**, 795
  metabolism, **1**, 815
  as nodulating gene expression inhibitors, **8**, 174
  occurrence, **1**, 774
  role in plant–fungi symbiosis, **8**, 174
  as starting materials, for isoflavanones, **1**, 795
  structure, **1**, 19, 715, **8**, 342
isoflavones, 5-methoxy-, accumulation, **1**, 800
isoflavone synthase (IFS)
  catalysis, **1**, 800
  occurrence, **1**, 774
  properties, **1**, 793
  reaction mechanisms, **1**, 791
  reaction pathways, **1**, 793
  roles, in isoflavonoid biosynthesis, **1**, 791
isoflavonoids
  accumulation, factors affecting, **1**, 784
  antiestrogenic activity, **1**, 782
  antifungal activity, **1**, 806, **8**, 183
  antimicrobial, vacuolar storage, **1**, 809
  antimicrobial activity, **1**, 817
  biochemistry, **1**, 773–823
  biological activity, **1**, 777
  biological functions, **1**, 773–823
  biosynthesis, **1**, 784
    integrated control, **1**, 816
    studies, **1**, 19
  biosynthetic pathways
    acetate–polymalonate, **1**, 784
    phenylpropanoid, **1**, 784
  biosynthetic studies
    elicitor-treated cell suspension cultures, **1**, 784
    experimental systems, **1**, 784
    radiotracer experiments, **1**, 786
  catabolism, **1**, 812
  classification, **1**, 774
  degradation, **1**, 812

dietary effects, **1**, 782
effects, health, **1**, 782
estrogenic activity, **1**, 782
evolution, **1**, 817
fungitoxicity, **1**, 779
gene promoters, **1**, 817
glyceollin tolerance induction, **1**, 782
insecticidal activity, **1**, 806
malonylation, **1**, 809
metabolism
  via animals, **1**, 815
  via bacteria, **1**, 814
O-methylation, **1**, 798
methylenedioxy bridge functions, **1**, 802
molecular biology, **1**, **773–823**
nod gene inducers, metabolism, **1**, 814
occurrence, **1**, 774
as phytoalexins, **8**, 188
phytotoxicity, **1**, 779
prenylation, **1**, 803
reduction, **1**, 682
roles
  in mycorrhizal interactions, **1**, 780
  in plant–microbial pathogen interactions, **1**, 777
  in *Rhizobium*–legume symbiosis, **1**, 780
stress-induced, **1**, 774
substitution, **1**, 798
taxonomic distribution, **1**, 774
as taxonomic markers, **1**, 777
transcriptional regulation, **1**, 817
urinary excretion, **1**, 783
isoflavonoids, 4′-amino-, occurrence, **1**, 775
isoflavonoids, 5-deoxy-, prevalence, **1**, 790
isoformononetin, biosynthesis, **1**, 799
isofucosterol, in brassinosteroid biosynthesis, **8**, 105
iso-G *see* adenine, 2-oxo- (iso-G)
cis-isogeraniol, occurrence, **8**, 222
isoginkgolide, 1,7-dihydroxy-, isolation, **2**, 398
isoharderoporphyrinogen, as substrate, **4**, 95
isohemipinic acid, biosynthesis, **3**, 703
isoheterotropatrione, occurrence, **1**, 379
isolated spin-pair approximation (ISPA)
  definition, **7**, 63
  limitations, **7**, 64
isolaureatin
  from, (3*Z*)-prelaureatin, **1**, 317
  intermediates for, **1**, 312
  occurrence, **1**, 303
[1-²H]-isolaureatin, synthesis, **1**, 314, 319
isolaurepinnacin, occurrence, **1**, 303
isoleucine, **8**, 236
  as cyanogenic glycoside precursor, **1**, 885
  labeling studies, **8**, 240
  occurrence, **1**, 128
  roles, in ante-iso branching, **8**, 246
  in thiostrepton biosynthesis, **1**, 853
D(−)-isoleucine, replacement, **4**, 253
L-isoleucine, occurrence, **8**, 221
(*S*)-isoleucine, *N*-((+)-jasmonoyl)- (JA-Ile)
  activity, **1**, 135
  structure, **1**, 135
L-isoleucine methyl esters, occurrence, **8**, 221, 223
isoleucyl tRNA synthases, properties, **7**, 628
isoliquiritigenin, as *nod* gene inducer, **1**, 781
isomelacacidin, occurrence, **3**, 776
isomenthone, insecticidal activity, **8**, 306
(+)-isomenthone, biosynthesis, **2**, 144
isomerases
  general acid–base catalysis studies, **5**, 32
  mechanisms, **5**, 42
  in monoterpene isomerization, **2**, 102
isomerization, electrophilic, **5**, **315–341**
isomontanolide, antifeedant activity, **8**, 308

isonicotinic acid, 2,6-dichloro-, applications, plant
    activator, **1**, 626
isonicotinic acids, 1,6-dihydroxy-2-oxo-, inhibitory
    activity, **1**, 592
isopenicillin N acyltransferase, activity, **4**, 259
isopenicillin N epimerase
    catalysis, **4**, 171
    purification, **1**, 843, **4**, 171
isopenicillin N (IPN)
    biosynthesis, **1**, 840, **4**, 169, 243
    deacylation, **4**, 170
    immunoelectron fluorescence microscopy, **4**, 244
isopenicillin N synthase (IPNS)
    L-α-aminoadipic acid moiety replacement, **4**, 252
    catalysis, **1**, 842, **4**, 169
        mechanisms, **4**, 170
    characteristics, **4**, 250
    L-cysteinyl moiety substitution, **4**, 252
    mechanistic studies, **4**, 250
    mutagenesis, site-directed, **4**, 250
    occurrence, **1**, 842, **4**, 250
    purification, **1**, 842, **4**, 169
    ring formation, **4**, 169
    sequencing, **4**, 243
    substrate specificity, **4**, 170, 250
    D-valine moiety substitution, **4**, 253
isopentenyladenine ribotide
    biosynthesis, **8**, 69
    deribosylation, **8**, 70
isopentenyl diphosphate (IDP)
    binding, **4**, 199
    biosynthesis, **2**, 3, 46, 372, **5**, 318
        via acetate–mevalonate pathway, **2**, 46, 112
        via acetate pathway, **2**, 377
        via deoxyxylulose pathway, **2**, 377
        via glyceraldehyde phosphate–pyruvate pathway, **2**,
            3
    in carotenoid biosynthesis, **2**, 331
    condensation, **2**, 98, 340
    early studies, **2**, 70
    from
        glyceraldehyde 3-phosphate, **2**, 54
        mevalonic acid, **2**, 3
        pyruvate, **2**, 54
    homologues, **2**, 77
    isolation, early studies, **2**, 3
    isomerization, **2**, 5
    metabolism, **2**, 4
    mevalonate-independent route, **2**, **45–67**
        distribution, **2**, 57, 58
        future research, **2**, 62
        hypothetical biogenetic scheme, **2**, 55
        starting materials, **2**, 54
    occurrence, **2**, 46
    roles, **2**, 46
        in farnesyl diphosphate, **5**, 318
    as substrate, **5**, 321
isopentenyl-diphosphate Δ-isomerase, catalysis, **5**, 334
isopentenyl diphosphate isomerase(s), **2**, **69–96**
    activation, **2**, 71
    active site residues, identification, **5**, 336
    amino acid sequence alignments, **2**, 73
    analogues, synthesis, **2**, 70
    biotechnology, **2**, 72
    catalysis, **2**, 5
    enzymology, **2**, 70, **5**, 336
    gene cloning, **2**, 72
    inhibitors, **2**, 71, 72
        irreversible, **5**, 335
        mechanism-based, **5**, 335
    mechanisms, **2**, 72
    mechanistic studies, **5**, 334
    mutagenesis, site-directed, **2**, 73, **5**, 336

occurrence
    avian liver, **2**, 71
    baker's yeast, **2**, 71
    daffodil chromoplasts, **2**, 71
    pig liver, **2**, 71
    pumpkin fruit, **2**, 71
    rubber latex, **2**, 71
protein purification, **5**, 336
protonation–deprotonation mechanisms, **5**, 334
purification, **2**, 71
reactions, with substrate homologues, **2**, 71
silkworms, substrate specificities, **2**, 76
stereochemistry, **2**, 71
substrate homologues, **2**, 72
isopentenyl diphosphate synthases, motifs, **2**, 339
isopentenyl-diphosphate:tRNA isopentenyltransferase
    see tRNA isopentenyltransferase
isopentenyl pyrophosphate (IPP) *see* isopentenyl
    diphosphate (IDP)
isopentenyl transferase genes *see ipt* genes
isopentyl diphosphate (IDP)
    biosynthesis, **8**, 305
    as intermediate, **8**, 272
isopentyl diphosphate isomerase, roles, in homoterpene
    biosynthesis, **8**, 236
isopentyl diphosphate–magnesium complexes, in
    dimethylallyl*trans*transferase reaction, chain length
    distribution, **2**, 91
isoperiplanone-A, structure, **8**, 4
isophorone, occurrence, **8**, 234
isophorone, oxo-, occurrence, **8**, 234
isophthalic acid, 5-nitro-, in phosphoramidite synthesis,
    7, 158
isopimaric acid, biosynthesis, **2**, 228
isopimpinellin
    accumulation, **1**, 634
    biosynthesis, **1**, 634
    occurrence, **8**, 338
    toxicity, **8**, 338
(−)-*trans*-isopiperitenol, biosynthesis, **2**, 144
(+)-isopiperitenone, occurrence, **8**, 224
(−)-isopiperitenone, biosynthesis, **2**, 144
isoprene
    biosynthesis, **2**, 62
    in terpenoid pathway, **2**, 100
    as universal terpenoid building block, **2**, 98
isoprene cyclases
    enzymology, **5**, 330
    mechanistic studies, **5**, 325
    protein production, **5**, 330
isoprene rule *see* biogenetic isoprene rule
isoprenes, biosynthesis, **8**, 220, 305
isoprenoid-alcohol kinase(s) *see* undecaprenol kinase(s)
isoprenoid diphosphate(s)
    alkylation, **2**, 10
    chain coupling, **2**, 9
    chain elongation, **2**, 7
    cyclization, **2**, 8
    hydrogen transfers, **5**, 316
    isomerization, **2**, 8
    radiolabeled, **2**, 333
isoprenoids
    applications, **2**, 1
    biochemistry, early studies, **2**, 3
    biogenesis, **2**, 21
    biological Diels–Alder adducts, **1**, 374
    biosynthesis, **2**, 16, 69, **8**, 202, 219
        compartmentation, **2**, 62
        early studies, **2**, 11
        farnesyl-diphosphate farnesyltransferase in, **2**, 246
        future research, **2**, 64
        multidisciplinary approaches, **2**, 11
        overview, **2**, **1–13**

pathways, **5**, 316
protein-mediated, **2**, 12
via nonmevalonate pathway, **8**, 47
characteristics, **2**, 46
in chemical communication, **8**, 219
[13]C-labeled glucose studies, **2**, 52
cyclization, **2**, 5
degradation, **8**, 246
early development, **2**, 300
enzymes, **5**, 318
from
acetyl-CoA, **2**, 46
1-deoxy-D-xylulose 5-phosphate, **2**, 64
(*R*)-mevalonate, **2**, 22, 24
mevalonic acid, **2**, 3
functions, **2**, 1
genes, cloning, **2**, 12
glucose incorporation, **2**, 50
historical background, **2**, 70
occurrence, **2**, 1
overview, **2**, 45
role, **2**, 300
structure
crystal, **2**, 12
early studies, **2**, 3
isopropanolamine, occurrence, **4**, 148
isoprostanes, use of term, **1**, 171
isopsoralen, toxicity, **8**, 141
isopulegone, insecticidal activity, **8**, 306
isoquinocyclines, trioxacarcinose B, **3**, 322
isoquinoline alkaloids
antifeedant activity, **8**, 345
biosynthesis, **4**, 40
occurrence, **4**, 40
isorenieratene, accumulation, **2**, 336
β-isorenieratene, accumulation, **2**, 336
isoreserpiline, strictosidine studies, **4**, 118
isoretronecanol, biosynthesis, **4**, 31
isorhamnetin, in pollen, **8**, 163
isorhapontin, as allelopathic agent, **8**, 169

isosalipurposide, roles, in ultraviolet patterning, **8**, 160
isosegoline A, occurrence, **1**, 381
isoshonanin, biosynthesis, **3**, 731
isosteres, nonpolar, in synthetic oligodeoxynucleotides, **7**, 332
isothamnosin A, occurrence, **1**, 380
isothamnosin B, occurrence, **1**, 380
isotheaflavic acids, structure, **3**, 782
isotheoflavin, biosynthesis, **3**, 782
isothermal titration calorimetry (ITC), in RNA structural transition analyses, **6**, 26
isothiocyanate, allyl-
insect sequestration, **8**, 363
as oviposition stimulant, **8**, 156
toxicity, **8**, 363
(−)-3-isothujone, oxidation, **2**, 146
isotrichermol, biosynthesis, **2**, 164
isotrichodermin, biosynthesis, **2**, 164
isotrichodiol, biosynthesis, **2**, 164
isotrichotriol, biosynthesis, **2**, 164
isovalerate, as bacterial aromatic polyketide synthase primer, **1**, 475
isovaleric acid, occurrence, **8**, 220, 221
isovaleryl-CoA, as starter unit, **1**, 760
isovepaol, isolation, **8**, 327
isovincoside *see* strictosidine
isovitexin, biosynthesis, **1**, 738
isoxazole-4-propionate, *α*-amino-3-hydroxyl-5-methyl- (AMPA), receptors, **6**, 103
isozonarone, isolation, **8**, 460
isozymes, catalysis, **2**, 21
ISPA *see* isolated spin-pair approximation (ISPA)
ISPK *see* insulin stimulated kinase (ISPK)
Israeli pine scale, (2*E*,5*R*,6*E*,8*E*)-5,7-dimethyl-2,6,8-decatrien-4-one, **8**, 244
ITC *see* isothermal titration calorimetry (ITC)
Ithomiidae, isophorones, **8**, 234
IUBMB *see* International Union of Biochemistry and Molecular Biology (IUBMB)
IUPAC *see* International Union of Pure and Applied Chemistry (IUPAC)

J

jacaranone, larval settlement induction, **8**, 435
jack beans *see Canavalia ensiformis*
Jackiella javanica
   (−)-licarin A, **1**, 679
   lignans, **1**, 645
jack pine *see Pinus banksiana*
jacpaniculines, occurrence, **1**, 685
Jacquemontia paniculata, jacpaniculines, **1**, 685
jad genes
   cloning, **1**, 482
   sequencing, **1**, 482
jadomycin, biosynthesis, **1**, 482
JA-Ile *see* (*S*)-isoleucine, *N*-((+)-jasmonoyl)- (JA-Ile)
JA-Me *see* (−)-jasmonic acid methylester (JA-Me)
Jamesoniella autumnalis, lignans, **1**, 645
Janua brasiliensis, larval settlement induction, **8**, 432
Japan, diarrhetic shellfish poisoning (1976), **8**, 489
Japanese beetle *see Popillia japonica*
Japanese black pine *see Pinus thunbergii*
Japanese lacquer mushroom *see Psalliota campestris*
Japanese lacquer tree *see Rhus vernicifera*
Japanese pilchards *see Sardinops melanosticta*
japonilure, occurrence, **8**, 12
jasmine absolute, cucurbic acid from, **1**, 118
Jasminum grandiflorum
   cis-jasmone, **8**, 108
   (−)-jasmonic acid methylester, **1**, 117
jasmolin I
   isolation, **8**, 333
   synthesis, **8**, 333
jasmolin II, isolation, **8**, 333
jasmonate, methyl
   applications, **8**, 108
   as elicitor, **1**, 611
   occurrence, **1**, 117, **8**, 108, 215
   signaling activity, **8**, 150
   tomato leaf studies, **8**, 118
jasmonate, *epi*-methyl, occurrence, **8**, 215
(−)-jasmonate, methyl, occurrence, **1**, 134
jasmonate-induced proteins (JIPs)
   and gene expression, **1**, 129
   and signal transduction, **8**, 118
   use of term, **1**, 129
jasmonate-inducible glycosyltransferase (JIGT),
     characterization, **1**, 129
jasmonates
   and abscissic acid, compared, **1**, 127
   biosynthesis
     inducers, **1**, 134
     initiation, **1**, 134
   effects, in plants, **1**, 125
   external applications, and wound response, **1**, 131
   functions, **1**, 125
   interactions
     with abscissic acid, **1**, 133
     with ethylene, **1**, 133
     with plant hormones, **1**, 133
   and osmotic stress, **1**, 131
   responses, to environmental factors, **1**, 129
   role in pollen germination, **1**, 128
   secondary metabolite induction, **1**, 130
   and signal transduction, **1**, 129
   use of term, **1**, 118, **8**, 108
cis-jasmone, occurrence, **8**, 108
jasmonic acid

accumulation, **1**, 124
biochemistry, **8**, 108
biosynthesis, **1**, 119, 2
conjugates, **1**, 128
   as specific transduction signals, **1**, 132
diastereomers, **1**, 134
distribution, **1**, 124
from, 12-oxo-*cis*-10,15-phytodienoic acid, **1**, 120
germination inhibition, **1**, 128
historical background, **8**, 108
in induced chemical defense, **8**, 151
metabolism, **1**, 124
occurrence, **1**, 117, 127, 128, 234, **8**, 108
precursors, **1**, 132, 134
roles, in tuber formation, **1**, 7
structure, **1**, 7, **8**, 108
transport, **1**, 124
jasmonic acid, dihydro-
   glucosylation, **1**, 125
   occurrence, **1**, 118
jasmonic acid, (+)-9,10-dihydro-, biotransformation, **1**,
   124
jasmonic acid, (−)-9,10-dihydro-11-hydroxy-,
   biosynthesis, **1**, 124
jasmonic acid, hydroxy-, occurrence, **1**, 118
(+)-jasmonic acid, isomerization, **8**, 111
(−)-jasmonic acid, occurrence, **1**, 117
7-*iso*-jasmonic acid, occurrence, **1**, 231
iso-jasmonic acid, structure, **1**, 241
(−)-jasmonic acid methylester (JA-Me)
   occurrence, **1**, 117, 128
   senescence inhibition, **1**, 133
jasmonic acid-related compounds
   bioassays, **8**, 114
   biochemistry, **8**, 108
   biosynthesis, pathways, **8**, 115
   chemical structure, **8**, 108
   chemical synthesis, **8**, 112
   chromatography, **8**, 113
   extraction, **8**, 113
   (−)-form of, **8**, 111
   GC-MS, **8**, 113
   HPLC, **8**, 113
   identification, **8**, 113
   immunoassays, **8**, 113
   isolation, **8**, 113
   metabolism, **8**, 115
   metabolites, detection, **8**, 116
   mode of action, at molecular levels, **8**, 118
   multiple physiological effects, **8**, 117
   potato tuber-inducing activity, **8**, 114
   roles, in plant life cycles, **8**, 118
   stress factors, **8**, 117
   structure–activity relationships, **8**, 114
   use of term, **8**, 108
   wound signal transduction, **8**, 119
(−)-jasmonoid glucoside, occurrence, **8**, 112
jasmonoids
   biosynthesis, **1**, **117–138**
   biosynthetic pathways, evolution, **1**, 122
   functions, **1**, **117–138**
   structure–activity relationship, **1**, 134
   use of term, **1**, 118
Jaspis spp., narains, **8**, 442
Jaspis aff. *johnstoni*, fungus in, chloriolins, **8**, 601

Jasus lalandei, 20-hydroxyecdysone, **8**, 283
jatrophane, biosynthesis, **2**, 223
J-coupling, mechanisms, **6**, 5
jellyfish
    bioluminescence, **8**, 446
    see also Aequorea aequorea; *Aequorea victoria*
Jerusalem artichoke *see Helianthus tuberosus*
JHB₃ *see* juvenile hormone III bisepoxide (JHB₃)
JIGT *see* jasmonate-inducible glycosyltransferase (JIGT)
JIPs *see* jasmonate-induced proteins (JIPs)
jodrellin A, antifeedant index, **8**, 315
jodrellin B, antifeedant index, **8**, 315
jodrellins, occurrence, **8**, 315
josamycin, antibacterial activity, **4**, 198
Juglans nigra, juglone, **8**, 339
Juglans regia, juglone, **8**, 170, 339
juglone, occurrence, **8**, 170, 339
Julbernardia globiflora
    profisetinidins, **3**, 772
    proguibourtinidins, **3**, 775
*jun*B mRNA, AU rich elements, **6**, 208
Justicia procumbens
    justicidin A, **8**, 339
    justicidin B, **1**, 704, **8**, 339
    lignans, **8**, 339
    neojusticin A, **1**, 704
    taiwanin E, **1**, 704
Justicia procumbens var. *hayatai*, justicidins, **1**, 694
Justicia prostrata
    carpacin, **8**, 336
    prostalidins, **1**, 705
justicidin A
    occurrence, **8**, 339
    toxicity, **1**, 694
justicidin B
    antiinflammatory activity, **1**, 704
    occurrence, **8**, 339
    toxicity, **1**, 694
juvabione, occurrence, **8**, 276
(+)-juvabione, synthesis, **8**, 276

juvabiones, biochemistry, **8**, 276
juvenile hormone 0
    isolation, **8**, 269
    occurrence, **8**, 270
juvenile hormone I
    bioactivity, **8**, 10
    enantiomers, synthesis, **8**, 270
    isolation, **8**, 268
    occurrence, **8**, 3, 270
juvenile hormone I, 4-methyl
    configuration, **2**, 78
    enzymatic synthesis, **2**, 78
juvenile hormone II
    enantiomers, synthesis, **8**, 270
    isolation, **8**, 268
juvenile hormone III
    bioactivity, **8**, 10
    from, dimethylcyclohexanedione, **8**, 270
    isolation, **8**, 268
    metabolism, **8**, 274
    occurrence, **8**, 270, 276
(2*E*,6*S*,7*S*,10*R*)-juvenile hormone III bisepoxide,
    structure, **8**, 269
juvenile hormone III bisepoxide (JHB₃)
    from, geraniol, **8**, 271
    occurrence, **8**, 269
juvenile hormone binding proteins, binding, **8**, 272
juvenile hormones
    and ecdysis, **8**, 265
    effects, on insect development, **8**, 275
    homomevalonate in, **8**, 236
    mimics, **8**, 275, 303
    NMR spectra, **8**, 268
    radioimmunoassay, **8**, 271
    relative potency, **8**, 270
    transport, **8**, 272
    use of term, **8**, 265
    see also insect juvenile hormones
juvocimene-1, occurrence, **8**, 277
juvocimene-2, occurrence, **8**, 277

K

K1 killer toxin, resistance, **3**, 18
K-26
   biosynthesis, **1**, 869
   isolation, **1**, 865
KA *see* kainate (KA)
Kabat *see* methoprene
Kacser–Burns control analysis, enzyme studies, **3**, 472
Kadsura interior, schisantherin D, **1**, 703
kadsurenone, antiinflammatory activity, **1**, 704
kaempferol, in pollen, **8**, 163
kaempferol 7-glucoside, 8-prenyldihydro-, as oviposition
      deterrent, **8**, 156
kainate (KA), receptors, **6**, 103
kairomones
   definition, **8**, 2
   development, **2**, 101
   roles, **8**, 198
kakelokelose, occurrence, **8**, 544
kaladasterone, IR spectra, **8**, 285
kalafungin, biosynthesis, **1**, 478
kalihinenes, occurrence, **8**, 437
kalihinol A, occurrence, **8**, 437
Kallichroma tethys, isoculmorin, **8**, 601
kanamycin
   discovery, **4**, 200
   resistance, **6**, 194
K antigens, acidic polymers from, **3**, 190
kapakahines
   cytotoxicity, **8**, 583
   occurrence, **8**, 583
   structure, **8**, 583
kapurimycin A3
   applications, antibiotics, **7**, 510
   DNA damage induction, **7**, 510
   possible alkoxyl radicals from, **7**, 510
karahana lactone, enantiomeric purity, **8**, 7
Karplus equation
   in DNA structure determination, **7**, 64
   nucleic acids, **7**, 72
KAS *see* β-ketoacyl synthase (KAS)
kasugamycin, resistance, **6**, 195
(+)-kaur-16-ene, occurrence, **8**, 7
(−)-kaur-16-ene, occurrence, **8**, 7
ent-kaurene
   biosynthesis, **8**, 47
   in gibberellin A_{12}-aldehyde biosynthesis, **8**, 47
   subcellular localization, **8**, 50
ent-kaur-16-ene
   biosynthesis, **2**, 230
   from, *ent*-copalyl diphosphate, **2**, 231
   oxidative metabolism, **2**, 232
ent-kaurene oxidase, dwarf mutants, **8**, 50
ent-kaurene synthase
   catalysis, **8**, 47
   functions, **2**, 217
   occurrence, **8**, 47
ent-kaur-16-ene synthase, occurrence, **2**, 231
kaurene synthase A, occurrence, **2**, 211
kaurene synthase(s), **2**, 315
   cloning, **8**, 41
   DDTA motif, **2**, 315
kaurenoic acid, effects, on herbivores, **8**, 142
kaurenoic acid, *ent*-7-hydroxy-, ring condensation, **1**, 793
ent-kaur-16-en-19-oic acid, **2**, 232
ent-kaur-16-en-19-oic acid, 7α-hydroxy-, **2**, 232

oxidation, **2**, 232
ent-kaurenoic acid 7β-hydroxylase, and cytochromes
     P450, **8**, 50
kaurenolides, biosynthesis, **2**, 232
KDO *see* 3-deoxy-D-*manno*-octulosonate (KDO)
KDO-8P synthase *see* 2-dehydro-3-
     deoxyphosphooctonate aldolase
KDO aldolase *see* 3-deoxy-D-*manno*-octulosonate (KDO)
     aldolase
KDO transferase *see* 3-deoxy-D-*manno*-octulosonate
     (KDO) transferase
KDPG aldolase *see* 2-dehydro-3-deoxyphosphogluconate
     aldolase
kds genes
   kdsA, coding, **3**, 221
   kdsB, coding, **3**, 221
kedarcidin
   acidity, **7**, 575
   activation, **7**, 577
   activity against Gram-positive bacteria, **7**, 575
   applications, antibiotics, **7**, 554, 575
   classification, **1**, 557
   DNA damage, **7**, 577
   histone cleavage, **7**, 577
   occurrence, **7**, 575
   siderophore chelation, **7**, 577
   structure, **7**, 554, 575
kedarosamine, structure, **7**, 575
Keiferia lycopersicella, (*E*)-4-tetradecenyl acetate, **8**, 207
keramamide A, isolation, **8**, 573
keramamides
   absolute configuration, **8**, 572
   occurrence, **8**, 572
   structure, **8**, 572
keramamine C, isolation, **8**, 558
keramamines, occurrence, **8**, 553
keramaphidin B
   enantiomers, **8**, 557
   structure, **8**, 555
(+)-keramaphidin B, reduction, **8**, 555
keramaphidin C, isolation, **8**, 558
keramaphidins, occurrence, **1**, 380, **8**, 554
keratan sulfate (KS)
   binding, **3**, 4
   biosynthesis, **3**, 173
   substitution, **3**, 161
keratan sulfate proteoglycans (KSPGs)
   biosynthesis, **3**, 174
   types of, **3**, 173
keratinocytes, growth factor, **6**, 226
kerriamycin A, D-kerriose, **3**, 313
D-kerriose, occurrence, **3**, 312, 313
ketal groups, in 2′-hydroxyl group protection, **6**, 84
ketals, configuration, **1**, 596
12-KETE, occurrence, **1**, 245
ketene acetal, DNA binding, **7**, 562
ketenes, early studies, **1**, 2
kethoxal, applications, RNA structural probes, **6**, 68
ketoacid dehydrogenase, branched-chain, functions, **8**,
   407
4-keto acids, porphobilinogen synthase inhibition, **4**, 76
β-keto acids, decarboxylation, **5**, 440
β-ketoacyl-CoA, roles, in virginiae butanolide A
     biosynthesis, **1**, 147
3-ketoacyl-CoA thiolase(s) *see* acetyl-CoA *C*-
     acyltransferase(s)

β-ketoacyl reductase
  catalysis, **1**, 348
  disruption, **1**, 504
  encoding, **1**, 356
  sequencing, **1**, 412
β-ketoacyl synthase (KAS)
  catalysis, **1**, 348
  encoding, **1**, 356
  in fatty acid studies, **1**, 500
  genetics, **1**, 11
  homologues, **1**, 332
  roles, in fatty acid biosynthesis, **1**, 3
  sequencing, **1**, 412
  Type II, structure, **1**, 362
β-ketoacylsynthase thiols, reactions, with 1,3-
    dibromopropan-2-one, **1**, 351
2-keto-3-deoxy-ʟ-arabonate aldolase *see* 2-dehydro-3-
    deoxy-ʟ-pentonate aldolase
2-keto-3-deoxyglucarate aldolase *see* 2-dehydro-3-
    deoxyglucarate aldolase
2-keto-3-deoxy-6-phosphogalactonate aldolase *see* 2-
    dehydro-3-deoxy-6-phosphogalactonate
    aldolase
2-keto-3-deoxy-6-phosphogluconate aldolase *see* 2-
    dehydro-3-deoxyphosphogluconate aldolase
2-keto-3-deoxy-ᴅ-xylonate aldolase *see* 2-dehydro-3-
    deoxy-ᴅ-pentonate aldolase
keto–enol tautomerism
  in enzymatic reactions, **5**, 31–50
  future research, **5**, 48
  in solution, **5**, 32
  stereoelectronic control, **5**, 32
β-keto esters
  cyclization, **1**, 147
  synthesis, **1**, 144
ketols, dienone–phenol rearrangement, **2**, 396
3-keto-4-methylene steroids, occurrence, **1**, 379
ketone bodies, effects, on platelet-activating factor, **1**, 294
ketones
  occurrence, **8**, 230, 242
  pK_a, **5**, 33
  reduction, **5**, 198
ketones, 2-amino, biosynthesis, **4**, 67
ketones, *t*-butyl, in DNA damage studies, **7**, 393
ketones, diazo, DNA damage induction, **7**, 542
ketones, ethyl, biosynthesis, **8**, 242
ketones, methyl, biosynthesis, **8**, 242
ketones, vinyl, occurrence, **8**, 204
ketonization, stereospecific, **5**, 38
ketopantoaldolase
  activity, **3**, 409
  biochemistry, **3**, 409
  catalysis, **3**, 409
  purification, **3**, 409
  substrate specificity, **3**, 409
β-keto-reductase *see* 3-hydroxyacyl-CoA dehydrogenase
ketoreductases (KRs)
  in bacterial aromatic polyketide synthases, **1**, 475
  combinatorial analysis, **1**, 489
  in fatty acid studies, **1**, 500
  genetics, **1**, 11
  roles, in fatty acid biosynthesis, **1**, 3
ketosteroid isomerase, catalysis, **5**, 25
Δ⁵-3-ketosteroid isomerase (KSI) *see* 3-oxo-Δ⁵-steroid
    isomerase
ketotetrose-phosphate aldolase
  biochemistry, **3**, 408
  catalysis, **3**, 408
  isolation, **3**, 409
  substrate specificity, **3**, 409
β-ketothiolase(s) *see* acetyl-CoA *C*-acyltransferase(s)
khapra beetles *see Trogoderma* spp.
Kheper spp., nerolidol, **8**, 227

Kibdelosporangium aridum, ardacin biosynthesis, **1**, 483
kidney, glycogen synthase (mammalian), **3**, 479
kidney bean plants *see Phaseolus vulgaris*
kidney blood flow, effects of prostaglandins on, **1**, 174
kievitone
  as chalcone isomerase inhibitor, **1**, 722
  detoxification, **1**, 814
  as phytoalexin, **8**, 189
kifunensine
  as α-mannosidase inhibitor, **3**, 155
  as α1,2-mannosidase inhibitor, **3**, 25
  α1,2-mannosidase resistance, **3**, 22
  structure, **3**, 133
  as yeast α1,2-mannosidase inhibitor, **3**, 21
Kiggelaria africana, larvae, cyanogenic plant feeding, **1**,
    883
kijanimicins, structure, **1**, 370
killer virus, mRNA overexpression, **6**, 213
kinamycins
  applications, antibiotics, **7**, 541
  possible DNA damage induction, **7**, 541
kinetin, discovery, **8**, 57
kinoprene, applications, aphid control, **8**, 275
Kitasatosporia kifunense, kifunensine, **3**, 155
Klebsiella spp.
  cobalamin, **5**, 263
  diol dehydrase, **5**, 274
Klebsiella oxytoca, diol dehydrase, **5**, 274
Klebsiella pneumoniae
  chorismate mutase, **1**, 367, **5**, 345, 352
  5-dehydro-2-deoxyphosphogluconate aldolase, **3**, 409
  deoxysugar biosynthesis, genetics, **3**, 345
  fatty acids, **1**, 74
  galactan I, **3**, 188
  galactan II, **3**, 189
  4-α-glucanotransferase induction, **3**, 445
  glucose-1-phosphate adenylyltransferase, **3**, 469
  ketopantoaldolase, **3**, 409
  lipopolysaccharides, **3**, 188
  occurrence, **3**, 188
  phosphate groups, lack of, **3**, 189
  tagatose-1,6-diphosphate aldolase, **3**, 430
  see also Enterobacter aerogenes
Klebsiella pneumoniae 62-1
  p-aminobenzoic acid biosynthesis, **1**, 612
  isochorismate synthases, **1**, 611
  isochorismic acid, **1**, 610
Kluyveromyces van der Walt, ketopantoaldolase, **3**, 409
Klyne–Prelog notation, nucleic acid structure, **7**, 56
Knautia spp., verbenone, **8**, 224
knockout mice
  colon cancer studies, **1**, 258
  prostaglandin-enderoperoxide synthase studies, **1**, 258
(+)-kobusin, occurrence, **1**, 661
(+)-kobusinols, occurrence, **1**, 661
kolavenol, occurrence, **8**, 317
konbamide
  occurrence, **8**, 573
  structure, **8**, 573
9-KOTE, occurrence, **1**, 242
Kovats indices, in brassinosteroid studies, **8**, 100
krill fluorescent substance F, isolation, **8**, 457
KRs *see* ketoreductases (KRs)
KS *see* keratan sulfate (KS)
KSI *see* 3-oxo-Δ⁵-steroid isomerase
KSPGs *see* keratan sulfate proteoglycans (KSPGs)
kuanoniamine D, occurrence, **8**, 540
kudzuisoflavones, occurrence, **1**, 806
Kudzu vine *see Pueraria lobata*
Kuelpinia spp., cichoriin, **8**, 337
kumausallene, occurrence, **1**, 303
kumausynes, occurrence, **1**, 303
kumausynes, deacetyl, occurrence, **1**, 303

L

L-kynurenine, cleavage, **3**, 395
L-kynurenine hydrolase *see* kynureninase
L-19 ribozyme, nomenclature, **6**, 161
L-21 G414 ribozyme, construction, **6**, 161
L-21 ScaI ribozyme
  construction, **6**, 158
  nomenclature, **6**, 161
L-745,337, prostaglandin-endoperoxide synthase
    inhibition, **5**, 252
labdadienyl-PP *see* copalyl diphosphate
labdanes, biosynthesis, **2**, 62, 225
ent-labdanes, biosynthesis, **2**, 225
labdenediol, biosynthesis, **2**, 225
Labiatae
  anthocyanidins, **8**, 158
  feeding bioassays, **8**, 316
Labidus praedator
  homoocimenes, **8**, 236
  (*E*)-*β*-ocimene, **8**, 236
laccase(s)
  catalysis, mechanisms, **3**, 714
  homology, **1**, 435
  occurrence, **3**, 709, 711
  purification, **3**, 711
  roles
    in *o*-diquinone biosynthesis, **3**, 709
    in lignification, **3**, 713
    in lignin biosynthesis, **3**, 711
  substrate specificity, **3**, 714
LacCer *see* lactosylceramide (LacCer)
lac genes
  in cloning, **7**, 647
  lacZ
    in cloning, **7**, 646
    encoding, **7**, 650
    occurrence, **5**, 289
    translational fusion, **3**, 478
lacinilene C
  biosynthesis, **2**, 188
  occurrence, **2**, 186
α-lactalbumin
  in lactose biosynthesis, **3**, 112
  roles, **3**, 43
L-lactaldehyde, biosynthesis, **3**, 424
β-lactam antibiotics
  biosynthesis, **1**, 840
  chemical synthesis, **4**, 240
  classification, **4**, 240
  discovery, **4**, 160, 200
  industrial production, issues, **4**, 178
  occurrence, **4**, 240
  transpeptidase inhibition, **3**, 283
β-lactamase(s)
  detection, **5**, 145
  inhibition, **4**, 182
  mechanisms, **3**, 267
  roles, in peptidoglycan biosynthesis, **3**, 267
β-lactam biosynthesis, **4**, **159–193**, 196
  applications, **4**, 180
    gene expression increase, **4**, 180
    genetic engineering, **4**, 180
    novel compounds, **4**, 181
  evolution, **4**, 181
  gene clusters, **4**, 173
  horizontal gene transfer, **4**, 181

production strains
    expression increase, **4**, 179
    gene amplification, **4**, 179
    regulation, **4**, 178
  regulation, **4**, 173
    amino acids, **4**, 176
    carbon source, **4**, 174
    CCAAT box, **4**, 177
    nitrogen source, **4**, 176
    PACC, **4**, 175
    PENR1, **4**, 177
    pH, **4**, 175
    posttranscriptional, **4**, 174
    trans-acting mutations, **4**, 178
β-lactamhydrolase(s) *see* *β*-lactamase(s)
β-lactam ring, structure, **4**, 160
β-lactams
  biochemistry, **4**, 160
  early studies, **4**, 160
  industrial production, strategies, **4**, 180
  structure, classification, **4**, 160
β-lactams, monocyclic, biosynthesis, **4**, 187
γ-lactams, in antibiotics, **4**, 252
Lactarius piperatus, laccase, **3**, 711
lactase *see* *β*-galactosidase(s)
lactate, formation, during exercise, **3**, 444
D-lactate
  incorporation, into peptidoglycan, **3**, 272
  localization, **3**, 273
  occurrence, **3**, 247
lactic acid, neutralization, **5**, 80
lactic acid, 3-phosphono-, biosynthesis, **1**, 869
D-lactic acid, as substrate, **3**, 272
lacticin 481
  activity, **4**, 282
  gene clusters, **4**, 292
  structure, **4**, 279
lactobacillic acid, occurrence, **1**, 62
Lactobacillus leichmannii
  ribonucleoside-triphosphate reductase, **5**, 171
    catalysis, **5**, 195
  ribonucleotide reductases, **3**, 330, **5**, 166, 170
    mechanistic studies, **5**, 176
Lactobacillus plantarum
  cyclopropanation in, **1**, 64
  di-trans,*poly-cis*-decaprenyl*cis*transferase(s), **2**, 92
  fatty acid biomethylation, **1**, 65
  isopentenyl diphosphate, **2**, 46
  rhamnulose-1-phosphate aldolase, **3**, 426
lactocin S
  operons, **4**, 292
  residues, **4**, 284
  structure, **4**, 279
lactocin S lantibiotics
  characterization, **4**, 279
  gene clusters, **4**, 292
  modifying enzymes, **4**, 293
  peptidase functions, **4**, 294
  prepeptides, **4**, 293
  structure, **4**, 277
  transport functions, **4**, 294
Lactococcus cremoris, tagatose-1,6-diphosphate aldolase,
    3, 431
Lactococcus lactis
  lantibiotics, **4**, 276

220

nrd genes, **3**, 345
    phospho-β-galactosidase, **3**, 687
    tagatose-1,6-diphosphate aldolase, **3**, 431
1,4-lactone, 2,*C*-butyl-2,5-dideoxy-3-*O*-(3-
        methylbutanoyl)-L-arabinono- *see*
        blastmycinone
1,5-lactone, 4-*C*-acetyl-6-deoxy-2,3-*O*-methylene-D-
        galactono-, occurrence, **3**, 312
1,5-lactone, 4-*C*-[1-(*S*)-methoxyethyl]-2,3-*O*-methylene-
        L-arabinono-, occurrence, **3**, 312
lacto-*N*-neotetraose, sequential transfer, **3**, 228
lactones
    biosynthesis, **1**, 645
    occurrence, **8**, 226
lactones, triacetic, biosynthesis, **1**, 412
lactones, triketide, biosynthesis, **1**, 357
lactones, α,β-unsaturated, possible DNA damage
        induction, **7**, 503
δ-lactones, biosynthesis, **1**, 511
lactone toxins, in fungal pathogens, **8**, 179
δ-lactone triketides, biosynthesis, **1**, 515
lactoperoxidase (LPO)
    characterization, **1**, 307
    in cyclic bromoether biosynthesis, **1**, 307
lactosamine, poly-*N*-acetyl-, antennae termination, **3**, 40
lactose
    biosynthesis, **3**, 112
    as carbon source, in penicillin production, **4**, 174
lactose synthase, biosynthesis, **3**, 43
lactosylceramide (LacCer)
    biosynthesis, **3**, 94
    excess, **3**, 101
lactosylceramide synthase *see* galactosyltransferases
        (GalTs), GalT-2
lactoyl-CoA dehydratase, occurrence, **1**, 601
lactoyl-CoA hydro-lyase *see* lactoyl-CoA dehydratase
S-(D-lactoyl)glutathione, **5**, 67
Lactuca sativa
    germination inhibition, **1**, 695
    lettucenin A, **1**, 130
    root inhibition, **3**, 141
    seeds, germination, **8**, 69
lactucin, effects, on herbivores, **8**, 142
LAD II *see* leukocyte adhesion deficiency type II (LAD
        II)
lady beetle *see* Coleomegilla maculata
ladybirds *see* Coccinellidae
Laetisaria arvalis
    dioxygenase, **1**, 211
    laetisaric acid, **1**, 212
    oxylipins, as allelopathic agents, **1**, 209
laetisaric acid, occurrence, **1**, 212
laevopimaric acid, biosynthesis, **2**, 228
Lagascea rigida, encecalin, **8**, 337
Lagenidium callinectes, invective activity, **8**, 429
Lagenidium giganteum, oxylipins, roles, **1**, 209
Lagodon rhomboides, polyhydroxysterols, **8**, 471
lagopodin, biosynthesis, **2**, 163
lagunapyrones
    cytotoxicity, **8**, 597
    occurrence, **8**, 596
    structure, **8**, 596
LAH *see* lipolytic acyl hydrolase (LAH)
LALS programs *see* Linked Atom Least Squares (LALS)
        programs
Lambdina athasaria
    7,11-dimethylheptadecane, **8**, 247
    7-methylheptadecane, **8**, 247
Lambdina fiscellaria, (5*R*,11*S*)-5,11-
        dimethylheptadecane, **8**, 248
Lambdina pellucidaria, pheromones, **8**, 247
lamb liver
    threonine aldolase, **3**, 399

UTP-glucose-1-phosphate uridylyltransferase, **3**, 478
lamellarian gastropod *see* Marseniopsis mollis
Laminariales
    gametophytes, **8**, 421
    lamoxirene, **8**, 422
Laminaria sinclairii, neohalicholactone, **1**, 244
lamin B
    all-*trans*-2,6,10-trimethyldodecatriene, **2**, 355
    structure, **2**, 354
lamoxirene, occurrence, **8**, 422
Lampyridae
    defensive sterols, **8**, 361
    lucibufagins, **8**, 354
Lan *see* lanthionine (Lan)
Lan enzymes
    as ABC-transport proteins, **4**, 296
    LanB, in lantibiotics, **4**, 284, 288
    LanC, in lantibiotics, **4**, 284, 288
    LanD, in lantibiotics, **4**, 289
    LanE, functions, **4**, 284
    LanF, functions, **4**, 284
    LanG, functions, **4**, 284
    LanH, functions, **4**, 284
    LanI, functions, **4**, 284
    LanK, functions, **4**, 284, 295
    LanM, in lantibiotics, **4**, 284, 293
    LanP
        functions, **4**, 284
        in lantibiotics, **4**, 284
    LanR, functions, **4**, 284, 295
    LanT, in lantibiotics, **4**, 284, 290
lan genes
    lanA, encoding, **4**, 287
    lanB, encoding, **4**, 284, 288
    lanC, encoding, **4**, 284
    lanI, encoding, **4**, 296
    lanM, encoding, **4**, 284
    lanP, encoding, **4**, 291
    lanT, functions, **4**, 290
    occurrence, **4**, 284
lanierone, occurrence, **8**, 234
lankamycin
    L-arcanose, **3**, 322
    4,6-dideoxy-3-*O*-methyl-D-*xylo*-hexose, **3**, 321
lanosterol
    analogues, **2**, 286, 287
    biosynthesis, **2**, 6
    enantiomeric purity, **8**, 7
lanosterol cyclases, DCTA motif, **2**, 315
lanosterol synthase
    Asp-456, **2**, 6
    occurrence, **2**, 282
meso-lanthionine, as substrate, **3**, 259
lanthionine (Lan)
    in lantibiotics, **4**, 275
    occurrence, **3**, 246
    residues, **4**, 283
lanthionine (MeLan), methyl-
    in lantibiotics, **4**, 275
    residues, **4**, 283
lanthiopeptin *see* cinnamycin
lantibiotics
    activity, **4**, 280
    amino acids in, **4**, 275
    antibacterial activity, **4**, 300
    applications, food preservatives, **4**, 276
    biosynthesis
        genetics of, **4**, **275–304**
        pathways, **4**, 283
        regulatory mechanisms, **4**, 295
    derivation of term, **4**, 275
    early studies, **4**, 283
    expression systems, **4**, 298

future research, **4**, 300
genetic engineering, **4**, 298
modification, posttranslational, **4**, 283
modified residues, functions, **4**, 282
mutagenesis, site-directed, **4**, 298
non-proteinogenic amino acids, introduction, **4**, 299
optimization, **4**, 299
overview, **4**, 275
pore formation, **4**, 281
producer self-protection, **4**, 296
properties, **4**, 276
chemical, **4**, 299
physical, **4**, 299
structure, **4**, 276
subgroups, **4**, 276
see also lactocin S lantibiotics; nisin lantibiotics; streptococcin A-FF22; Type A-lantibiotics; Type B-lantibiotics
β-lapachone, applications, direct protein binding agents, **7**, 595
lappaol E, 7′-hydroxy-, occurrence, **1**, 688
lappaols, occurrence, **1**, 688
LAR *see* leucoanthocyanidin 4-reductase (LAR)
larch bark beetle *see Ips cembrae*
Lardoglyphus konoi, lardolure, **8**, 13, 244
lardolure, occurrence, **8**, 13, 209, 244
(+)-lariciresinol
biosynthesis, **1**, 662, 670
occurrence, **1**, 647
reduction, **1**, 682
(−)-lariciresinol, biosynthesis, **1**, 670
lariciresinol 9-*O*-*β*-D-glucoside, occurrence, **3**, 625
Larix europaea, coniferin, **3**, 683
larixinol, structure, **3**, 780
Larix leptolepis, xylem differentiation, **3**, 690
Larrea tridentata, nordihydroguaiaretic acid, **1**, 690
larval settlement, induction, **8**, 430
Las enzymes, LasT, functions, **4**, 295
laserolide, antifeedant activity, **8**, 308
las genes
lasA, sequencing, **4**, 293
lasM, encoding, **4**, 293
lasP, encoding, **4**, 294
occurrence, **8**, 398
Lasioderma spp., communication systems, **8**, 244
Lasioderma serricorne
feeding, **8**, 302
nicotine metabolism, **8**, 348
pheromones, **8**, 13
serricornin, **8**, 13, 244
Lasiodiplodia theobromae
β-glucosidase, **5**, 289
jasmonic acid, **8**, 108
(−)-jasmonic acid, **1**, 117
jasmonoids, **1**, 121
Lasioglossum malachurum, Dufour's gland secretions, **8**, 220
Lasioglossum zephyrum, macrolides, **8**, 218
lasiol, occurrence, **8**, 234
Lasius spp.
dendrolasin, **8**, 229
3,4-dihydroisocoumarin, **8**, 241
geranylcitronellal, **8**, 229
geranylgeranial, **8**, 229
Lasius fuliginosus
hexanoic acid, **8**, 210
mellein, **8**, 213, 241
Lasius meridionalis, lasiol, **8**, 234
Lasius niger
2,6-dimethyl-6-hepten-1-ol, **8**, 233
mellein, **8**, 241
Laspeyresia pomonella, (*Z,E*)-α-farnesene, **8**, 227
Las proteins

LasA, occurrence, **8**, 398
LasB
autoinduction, **8**, 398
occurrence, **8**, 398
LasI, encoding, **8**, 398
LasR, occurrence, **8**, 398
LAT *see* lysine *ε*-aminotransferase (LAT)
latanoprost, applications, in ophthalmology, **1**, 196
latex, effects, on herbivores, **8**, 148
latex vessels, linamarase, **1**, 885
lat genes, encoding, **4**, 165
latherane, biosynthesis, **2**, 223
lathodoratin, as phytoalexin, **8**, 189
Latrunculia magnifica, ichthyotoxicity, **8**, 466
latrunculins, ichthyotoxicity, **8**, 466
laurallene
from, (3*E*)-prelaureatin, **1**, 317
occurrence, **1**, 303
x-ray crystal structure, **1**, 321
laurate, attachment, **3**, 221
Laurea spp., cichoriin, **8**, 337
laureatin
from, (3*Z*)-prelaureatin, **1**, 317
occurrence, **1**, 303
synthesis, **1**, 312
[1-²H]-laureatin, synthesis, **1**, 314, 319
(*E*)-laureatin, synthesis, **1**, 316
laurediol, eight-membered ether ring formation, **1**, 322
(3*E*,6*R*,7*R*)-laurediol
from, laurencin, **1**, 310
as starting material, for deacetyllaurencin, **1**, 310
structure, **1**, 320, 321
as substrate, **1**, 319
(3*E*,6*S*,7*S*)-laurediol
cyclization, **1**, 316
structure, **1**, 320, 321
(3*Z*,6*S*,7*S*)-laurediol
cyclization, **1**, 312
as substrate, **1**, 319
laurediols
enzymatic reaction, **1**, 304
isolation, **1**, 304
laureepoxide
configuration, **1**, 310
occurrence, **1**, 303
laurefucin
occurrence, **1**, 303
synthesis, **1**, 312, 319
laurenan compounds
biosynthesis, **1**, 312
conformation, **1**, 321
nomenclature, **1**, 303, 310
laurencenynes, occurrence, **1**, 304
Laurencia spp., cyclic bromoethers, **1**, 303
Laurencia glandulifera, laurencin, **1**, 303
Laurencia hybrida, 12*S*-hydroxyeicosatetraenoic acid, **1**, 219
Laurencia nipponica
chloroperoxidase, **1**, 323
deacetylkumausynes, **1**, 303
deacetyllaurencin, **1**, 303
isolaureatin, **1**, 303
kumausallene, **1**, 303
kumausynes, **1**, 303
laurallene, **1**, 303
laureatin, **1**, 303
laurediols, **1**, 304
laureepoxide, **1**, 303
laurefucin, **1**, 303
laureoxanyne, **1**, 303
laureoxolane, **1**, 303
prelaureatin, **1**, 303
Laurencia obtusa, obtusin, **1**, 303

Laurencia okamurai
laurencenynes, **1**, 304
neolaurencenynes, **1**, 304
Laurencia pinnata
isolaurepinnacin, **1**, 303
pinnasterols, **8**, 280
Laurencia spectabilis, 12*S*-hydroxyeicosatetraenoic acid, **1**, 219
laurencin
biosynthesis, **1**, 8, 304, 310
hydrolysis, **1**, 310
isolation, **1**, 303
as starting material, for (3*E*,6*R*,7*R*)-laurediol, **1**, 310
structure, **1**, 304
x-ray crystal structure, **1**, 320
laurencin, deacetyl-
from, (3*E*,6*R*,7*R*)-laurediol, **1**, 310
metabolism, with lactoperoxidase, **1**, 312
occurrence, **1**, 303
synthesis, **1**, 310, 319
laurencin, deacetyloctahydro-, biosynthesis, **1**, 308
laureoxanyne
occurrence, **1**, 303
synthesis, **1**, 312, 319
laureoxolane, occurrence, **1**, 303
lauroyl-acyl carrier protein, as lipid A precursor, **3**, 220
lauroyltransferase
discovery, **3**, 221
encoding, **3**, 223
lauthisan compounds
biosynthesis, **1**, 310
conformation, **1**, 320
nomenclature, **1**, 303
lavandulol
biosynthesis, **2**, 108
occurrence, **8**, 234
LBHB *see* low barrier hydrogen bonds (LBHB)
LBP *see* lipopolysaccharide binding protein (LBP)
LCAA *see* long-chain alkylamine (LCAA)
LCADH *see* long-chain-acyl-CoA dehydrogenase (LCADH)
LCOs *see* lipo-chitin oligosaccharides (LCOs)
Lct enzymes
LctM, functions, **4**, 293
LctT, functions, **4**, 294
LDL *see* low-density lipoproteins (LDL)
LDL-receptors
encoding, **2**, 37
upregulation, **2**, 267
Le^a *see* Lewis A
Le^b *see* Lewis B
Le^x *see* Lewis X
Le^y *see* Lewis Y
lead ions, as cofactors, **7**, 632
leadzymes, identification, **6**, 165
leaf abscission
and ethylene, **8**, 91
role of jasmonates on, **1**, 127
leaf alcohol *see* (*Z*)-3-hexenol
leaf alcohol reaction, mechanism, **1**, 87
leaf aldehyde *see* (*E*)-2-hexenal
leaf beetles
lactones, **8**, 226
see also Chrysomela spp.
leaf-cutting ants
citral, **8**, 223
(*E*,*E*)-farnesol, **8**, 227
methyl-4-methylpyrrole-2-carboxylate, **8**, 221
see also Acromyrmex octospinosus; *Atta cepholotes*; *Atta texana*
leaf miner moths
sex pheromones, **8**, 247
see also Lyonetia clerkella; *Lyonetia prunifoliella*; *Stigmella malella*

leaves
cytosolic phosphoglucose isomerase, **3**, 473
phenolic content, **8**, 139
senescence, **1**, 133
Lec 23
leukoagglutinin resistance, **3**, 18
role of α-glucosidases in, **3**, 31
lecithinase A *see* phospholipase A$_2$
lecithinase B *see* lysophospholipase
lecithinase C *see* phospholipase C
lecithin liposomes, interactions, with gramicidin S, **4**, 322
lectin
galactose-specific, **3**, 48
homology, **8**, 66
Ledum palustre, amitinol, **8**, 224
leeches, exo-α-sialidases, **5**, 294
leek moth *see Acrolepiopsis assectella*
Legionella pneumophila
5-acetamidino-7-acetamido-8-*O*-acetyl-3,5,7,9-tetradeoxy-L-*glycero*-D-*galacto*-nonulosonic acid, **3**, 192
acetamidoyl groups, **3**, 192
N-acetyl groups, **3**, 192
lipid A, structure, **3**, 196
lipopolysaccharides, **3**, 192
Legionnaires' disease
etiology, **3**, 192
treatment, **1**, 497
Leguminosae
alkaloids, **8**, 146
applications, fertilizers, **1**, 7
chalcone synthase, genetics, **1**, 789
2,5-dihydroxymethyl-3,4-dihydroxypyrrolidine, **3**, 134
flavonoids, **1**, 19
indole alkaloid studies, **4**, 119
indolizidine alkaloids, **3**, 134
isoflavonoid biosynthesis, **1**, 19
isoflavonoids, **8**, 188
oxylipins, **1**, 232
phytoalexins, **1**, 778
pyrrolizidine alkaloids, **3**, 134
quinolizidine alkaloids, **4**, 34
symbiosis, with *Rhizobium* spp., **1**, 326
leinamycin
enzyme inactivation by, **7**, 526
occurrence, **7**, 522
reactions, with thiols, **7**, 523
thiol-activated DNA damage induction, **7**, 522
leiobunone, occurrence, **8**, 242
Leiobunum spp., leiobunone, **8**, 242
Leishmania spp.
glycolipids, **3**, 295
glycosylphosphatidylinositols, **3**, 306
GPI anchors, biosynthesis, **3**, 304
Leishmania mayor, lipophosphoglycans, **3**, 307
Leishmania tarentolae, DNA minicircles, **7**, 630
Leloir, Luis Federico (1906–87),
uridinediphosphoglucose studies, **3**, 444
LeLoir pathway, in enterobacteria, **3**, 203
Lemaceae, oxylipins, **1**, 231
Lemna spp.
7*Z*,10*Z*,13*Z*-hexatrienoic acid, **1**, 231
8*Z*,11*Z*,14*Z*-hexatrienoic acid, **1**, 231
hydroperoxide dehydratase, **1**, 231
Lemna gibba, labeling studies, **2**, 61
Lemna minor
apiosyltransferases, **3**, 517
8*Z*,11*Z*,14*Z*-hexatrienoic acid, **1**, 231
UDPapiose/UDPxylose synthase, **3**, 508
Lemna trisulca, 8*Z*,11*Z*,14*Z*-hexatrienoic acid, **1**, 231
Lens culinaris, amine oxidases, **3**, 721
lentiginosine, structure, **3**, 132
Lentinus lepideus

isoferulic acid, **3**, 624
    methyl *p*-methoxycinnamate, **3**, 624
L enzyme
    gene, encoding, **3**, 76
    N-glycosylation, **3**, 76
lepadiformine, occurrence, **8**, 547
Leperisinus varius
    (5*R*,7*S*)-7-methyl-1,6-dioxaspiro[4.5]decane, **8**, 212
    2-nonanone, **8**, 212
Lepidium sativum, desulfobenzylglucosinolate sulfation,
    1, 859
Lepidoptera
    ecdysis inhibition, **1**, 149
    feeding, flavonoid sensitivity, **8**, 141
    feeding preferences, restricted, **8**, 138
    ovipostion deterrents in, **8**, 156
    sex pheromones, **8**, 205
        (*Z*)-11-tetradecenyl acetate, **8**, 205
    Sf9 cells, **3**, 24
        cDNA, **3**, 26
    venoms, **8**, 360
    see also butterflies; *Idea* spp.; moths
Leptinotarsa decemlineata
    activity against, **8**, 308
        antifeedant, **8**, 321
        insecticidal, **8**, 346
    allatotrophins, **8**, 301
    juvenile hormone production, **8**, 301
Leptocorisa chinensis
    1-octanol, **8**, 211
    (*E*)-2-octenyl acetate, **8**, 211
Leptocorisa oratorius
    (*E*)-2-octenal, **8**, 211
    octyl acetate, **8**, 211
Leptogenys diminuta
    cis-isogeraniol, **8**, 222
    (3*R*,4*S*)-4-methyl-3-heptanol, **8**, 242
Leptoglossus zonatus, hexanoic acid derivatives, **8**, 210
leptosins
    antitumor activity, **8**, 603
    applications
        antibiotics, **7**, 527
        antitumor agents, **8**, 603
    cytotoxicity, **8**, 603
    occurrence, **8**, 603
    possible DNA damage induction, **7**, 527
    reactions, with thiol, **7**, 527
    structure, **8**, 603
Leptosphaeria spp., leptosins, **8**, 603
Leptospira interrogans, gene organization, **3**, 208
Lerix leptolepis callus, α-cedrene, **2**, 191
Lerman, classical intercalation model, **7**, 432
lesser grain borer *see Rhyzopertha dominica*
Lestrimelitta limao
    cephalic secretions, **8**, 232
    citral, **8**, 223
lettuce
    lipoxygenase activity, **1**, 93
    see also Lactuca sativa
lettucenin A, occurrence, **1**, 130
Leucania separata, pheromone biosynthesis activating
    neuropeptide, **8**, 300
leucine
    activation, **4**, 209
    biosynthesis, **2**, 376
    as cyanogenic glycoside precursor, **1**, 885, 886
    incorporation, **8**, 247
    metabolism, **2**, 49
    as methyl branch donor, **8**, 240
    in terminal branching, **8**, 239
leucineamino mutase, reactions, **5**, 264
leucine-responsive regulatory protein (Lrp) *see* Lrp
leucine-zipper, structure, **5**, 95

leucoanthocyanidin 4-reductase (LAR)
    biochemistry, **1**, 729
    genetics, **1**, 730
    molecular biology, **1**, 730
    occurrence, **1**, 729
    phosphorylation, **5**, 156
leucoanthocyanidins *see* flavan-3,4-diols
leucocyanidin(s)
    biosynthesis, **3**, 750
    instability, **3**, 753
    substitution, **3**, 755
leucocyanidins, oligomeric, occurrence, **3**, 757
leucodelphinidins, instability, **3**, 753
Leucoma salicis, (3*Z*)-*cis*-6,7-*cis*-9,10-
    diepoxyhenicosadiene, **8**, 207
Leuconostoc mesenteroides
    ligase enzymes, **3**, 261
    phosphoketolase, **3**, 392
cis-3,4-leucopelargonidin:NADP$^+$ 4-oxidoreductase *see*
    dihydrokaempferol 4-reductase
leucopelargonidins, instability, **3**, 753
leucopeptin *see* duramycin
Leucoptera malifoliella
    5,9-dimethylheptadecane, **8**, 247
    5,9-dimethyloctadecane, **8**, 247
leucorobinetinidin, semi-synthesis, **3**, 753
leucorobinetinidin carbocations, pyrogallol functionality,
    3, 754
leukemia
    β-1,3-galactosyl-*O*-glycosyl-glycoprotein β-1,6-*N*-
        acetylglucosaminyltransferase activity, **3**, 76
    and β-1,4-mannosyl-glycoprotein β-1,4-*N*-
        acetylglucosaminyltransferase levels, **3**, 53
    see also adult T-cell leukemia (ATL); human T-cell
        leukemia virus type I (HTLV-1)
leukoagglutinin, resistance, **3**, 18
leukocyte adhesion deficiency type II (LAD II)
    and Bombay phenotype, **3**, 55
    characterization, **3**, 58
    etiology, **3**, 59
leukocyte elastase, SELEX studies, **7**, 626
leukocytes, inflammation-activated homing, to
    endothelium cells, **3**, 57
leukosulfakinins, structure, **8**, 300
5,6-leukotriene A$_4$, occurrence, **1**, 236
leukotriene A$_4$
    acid-catalyzed hydrolysis, **5**, 52
    biosynthesis, **1**, 267
    conversion, to leukotriene B$_4$, **5**, 59
    as intermediate, **1**, 168
    receptors, **1**, 199
leukotriene-A$_4$ hydrolase, **5**, 53, 54
    arginine aminopeptidase activity, **5**, 54
    catalysis, **1**, 267, 279
    inactivation, **5**, 61
    inhibitors, **5**, 61
    mechanisms, **5**, 59
        catalytic, **5**, 59, 63
    resemblance to Zn^{2+}-dependent metalloproteinases, **5**,
        59
    structure, **5**, 59
leukotriene A$_4$ synthase *see* arachidonate 5-lipoxygenase
leukotriene B$_4$, **5**, 61
    agonists, **1**, 191
    antagonists, **1**, 191
    biological activity, **1**, 176
    biosynthesis, **1**, 267
    conversion, from leukotriene A$_4$, **5**, 59
    formation, **5**, 54
    leukocyte chemotactic properties, **5**, 61
    occurrence, **1**, 237, 238, 248, 249
    as proinflammatory mediator, **5**, 61
    synthesis, **1**, 184, 185

leukotriene B$_5$, occurrence, **1**, 237, 238
leukotriene C$_4$
    activity, **1**, 268
    applications, bronchoconstrictors, **1**, 197
    structure, **1**, 168, 168
    synthesis, **1**, 184
leukotriene C$_4$ synthase, **5**, 61, 62
    catalysis, **1**, 268, 280
    molecular phylogeny, **1**, 280
leukotriene D$_4$
    activity, **1**, 268
    agonists, **1**, 191
    antagonists, **1**, 191
    applications, bronchoconstrictors, **1**, 197
    biosynthesis, **1**, 168
    occurrence, **1**, 249
leukotriene E$_4$, applications, bronchoconstrictors, **1**, 197
leukotrienes
    applications
        antiasthmatic agents, **1**, 197
        bronchoconstrictors, **1**, 176, 197
        in respiratory system, **1**, 197
    biological activity, **1**, 255, 176
    biosynthesis, **1**, 263
    early studies, **1**, 160
    from, arachidonic acid, **1**, 10
    receptors, **1**, 10
    synthesis, **1**, 184
    see also slow reacting substance of anaphylaxis (SRS-
        A)
leupeptin, release, **2**, 27
levuglandin D$_2$, biosynthesis, **1**, 165
levuglandin E$_2$, biosynthesis, **1**, 165
levulinic acid, 5-amino-
    biosynthesis, **4**, 62, 70, **8**, 62
        via C$_5$ pathway, **4**, 67
    as starting material, for uroporphyrinogen-III, **4**, 72
levulinic acid, δ-amino-, biosynthesis, **2**, 64
levulinic acid, amino- (ALA)
    biosynthesis, **4**, 140
        via C$_5$ pathway, **4**, 140
        via Shemin pathway, **4**, 140
    as starting material, for hydrogenobyrinic acid, **4**, 141
levulinic acid, 3-chloro-, Cys-234 modification, **4**, 76
levulinyl, applications, 5′-hydroxyl group protection, **7**,
    127
Lewis A, biosynthesis, **3**, 57
Lewis acids, in trityl group removal, **7**, 126
Lewis B, biosynthesis, **3**, 57
Lewis X
    biosynthesis, **3**, 57, **5**, 308
    roles, **3**, 120
Lewis X, sialyl-
    biosynthesis, **5**, 308
    roles, **3**, 120
Lewis Y, biosynthesis, **3**, 57
lgt genes, poly-G tracts, **3**, 228
Licaria chrysophylla, monosaccharides, **1**, 684
(−)-licarin A
    antibacterial activity, **1**, 692
    enantiomeric purity, **1**, 679
    growth inhibitory activity, **1**, 693
    occurrence, **1**, 645, 679
    optical activity, **1**, 680
    structure, **1**, 681
licarin B, insecticidal activity, **1**, 693
lic genes, multiple tandem repeats, **3**, 229
licodione, accumulation, **1**, 794
licodione synthase, catalysis, **1**, 794
life, origin of, 'RNA World' hypothesis, **7**, 630
ligand–DNA binding, affinity cleavage, **7**, 253
ligands, unwinding angle, **7**, 433
ligases, isolation, **7**, 632, 633

ligation
    blunt-end, **7**, 661
    in cloning, **7**, 661
    cohesive-end, **7**, 661
    enzymatic method, **7**, 366
    mechanisms, **7**, 661
    nonenzymatic methods, **7**, 366
    selection scheme, **6**, 124
ligballinol
    isolation, **1**, 672
    occurrence, **1**, 672
    structure, **1**, 672
light, and cytokinins, **8**, 65
light-harvesting chlorophyll *a*/*b* proteins, occurrence, **8**,
    66
8-*O*-4′-lignan, Δ8′-hydroxy-3,3′-dimethoxy-7-oxo-,
    conversion, **1**, 692
lignanamides, occurrence, **1**, 673, 676, 685
lignans
    accumulation, **1**, 696
    acylation, **1**, 684
    allelopathy, **1**, 695
    allylic 7–8′ bond reduction, **1**, 682
    antiasthmatic activity, **1**, 704
    antidepressant activity, **1**, 704, 705
    antifungal activity, **1**, 691
    antiinflammatory activity, **1**, 704
    antimicrobial activity, **1**, 691
    antineoplastic activity, **1**, 698
    antioxidant activity, **1**, 690, 817
    antiviral activity, **1**, 702
    applications
        antiasthmatic agents, **1**, 704
        antifeedants, **1**, 694
        antiinflammatory agents, **1**, 704
        antineoplastic agents, **1**, 698
        antitumor agents, **1**, 701
        growth inhibitors, **1**, 693
        insecticides, **1**, 693
        nematocides, **1**, 694
    biological activity, **1**, 690
    biosynthesis, **1**, 2, 18, **639–712**
        regulatory mechanisms, **1**, 696
    biosynthetic pathways, evolution, **1**, 642
    cardiovascular activity, **1**, 705
    cytokinin-like activity, **1**, 695
    definitions, **1**, 640
    O-demethylation, **1**, 683
    deposition, **1**, 696
    Diels–Alder type, **1**, 379
    dietary, **1**, 698
    effects, on timber quality, **1**, 690
    enantiomers, separation, **1**, 649
    functions, **1**, **639–712**
    glucosides, **3**, 684
    growth inhibitory activity, **1**, 693
    hepatotoxicity prevention, **1**, 702
    localization, **1**, 645
    metabolism, **1**, 658
    nomenclature, **1**, 640
    occurrence, **1**, 645, **8**, 339
        Angiospermae, **1**, 647
        early land plants, **1**, 645
        Gymnospermae, **1**, 647
    optical activity, **1**, 647
    optical purity, **1**, 651
    physiological roles, in plants, **1**, 640, 690
    roles
        in human health, **1**, 698
        in lignin biosynthesis, **1**, 687
    8–8′ stereoselective coupling, **1**, 652
        mechanisms, **1**, 657
        sequence homology, **1**, 654

structure, diversity, **1**, 645
toxicity, **8**, 339
lignans, 8–*O*–4′ linked
  biosynthesis, **1**, 680
  diastereomers, **1**, 680
  metabolism, **1**, 680
  occurrence, **1**, 678
  optical activity, **1**, 679
  structure, **1**, 679
lignans, 8–5′ linked
  biosynthesis, **1**, 680
  enantiomeric purity, **1**, 679
  metabolism, **1**, 680
  occurrence, **1**, 678
  optical activity, **1**, 679
  structure, **1**, 679, 681
lignans, 8–8′ linked
  occurrence, **1**, 642
  reduction, **1**, 682
nor-lignans, use of term, **1**, 640
lignification
  in grasses, **3**, 695
  in herbaceous plants, **3**, 695
  initiation sites, **3**, 732
  intermediates, **1**, 690
  mechanisms, **1**, 687, **3**, 622, 680, 690
    stages, **3**, 692
  monolignols in, **3**, 703
  plant components, **3**, 659
  in trees, **3**, 712
lignin–carbohydrate complexes, occurrence, **3**, 725
lignins
  'abnormal', **1**, 697
  applications, cellulose extraction, **3**, 612
  biochemistry, **3**, **617–745**
  biosynthesis, **1**, 2, 18, 687, **3**, 2, 9
    enzymology, **3**, 708
    template polymerization, **3**, 730
    via phenylpropanoid pathway, **3**, 622
  'Brauns native', **1**, 697
  in cell walls, **3**, 687
    deposition, **3**, 690
    heterogeneity, **3**, 691
  condensed, **3**, 700
  dibenzodioxocin structures, **3**, 725
  early studies, **3**, 632
  ester–ether linkages, **3**, 696
  evolution, **3**, 618
  and fossil records, **3**, 622
  from, monolignols, **3**, 618
  heterogeneity, immunocytochemical probes, **3**, 699
  inter-unit linkages, **3**, 724
    biosynthetic mechanisms, **3**, 724
    probes, **3**, 699
    5–5′ structures, **3**, 725
    8–1′ structures, **3**, 726
    8–6′ structures, **3**, 728
    8–8′ structures, **3**, 728
  macromolecule formation
    in vitro, **3**, 703
    in vivo, **3**, 703
  macromolecules, structure, **3**, 727
  methyl groups in, **3**, 643
  modification, **3**, 626
  monomer compositions, **3**, 696
  occurrence, **3**, 620
    grasses, **3**, 695
    herbaceous plants, **3**, 695
    mistletoes, **3**, 700
    plant tissues, **3**, 687
  Raman spectra, **3**, 728
  roles, in carbon cycle, **3**, 621
  'stress', use of term, **1**, 698

structures
  early studies, **3**, 620
  origins, **3**, 731
  primary *in vivo*, **3**, 723
  secondary, **3**, 728
  toxicity, **8**, 339
lignins, guaiacyl–syringyl
  biosynthesis, **3**, 700
  occurrence, **3**, 702
lignins, syringyl, biosynthesis, **3**, 671
lignoceroyl-CoA synthase *see* long-chain-fatty-acid-CoA
    ligase
ligulatin B, antifeedant activity, **8**, 308
Ligumia subrostrata
  hydroxyeicosatetraenoic acid, **1**, 244
  prostaglandin E₂, **1**, 244
Ligusticum scotinum, dillapiole, **8**, 336
Lilium longiflorum, UDPglucose 6-dehydrogenase, **3**, 506
lima bean *see Phaseolus lunatus*
limaprost
  applications, **1**, 196
    pharmaceutical, **1**, 196
limatulone
  enantiomeric purity, **8**, 7
  occurrence, **8**, 7
limit dextrinase *see* α-dextrin endo-1,6-α-glucosidase
limonene
  applications, **2**, 102
  biosynthesis, **2**, 128
    regiochemistry, **2**, 134
  effects, on herbivores, **8**, 142
  insecticidal activity, **8**, 306
  occurrence, **8**, 222, 225
  optical purity, **2**, 132
  structure, **2**, 103
  toxicity, **8**, 143
(−)-limonene, conversion, to (−)-carvone, **2**, 144
limonene synthases
  activity, **2**, 110
  and casbene synthases compared, **2**, 183
  DNA sequences, **2**, 141
  labeling, **5**, 328
  occurrence, **2**, 209
  purification, **2**, 125
  regulatory mechanisms, **2**, 113
limonin
  antifeedant activity, **8**, 321
  isolation, **8**, 321
Limonius californicus, pentanoic acid, **8**, 210
Limonius canus, hexanoic acid, **8**, 210
limonoids
  biosynthesis, **8**, 328
  insecticidal activity, **8**, 321
  occurrence, **8**, 321
Limulus polyphemus
  endotoxin-neutralizing protein, **3**, 181
  8-hydroxyeicosatetraenoic acid, **1**, 247
Linaceae, oxylipins, **1**, 231
linalool
  antifeedant activity, **8**, 306
  biosynthesis, **2**, 102
  cyclization, **2**, 122
  in induced plant defense, **8**, 150
  insecticidal activity, **8**, 306
  occurrence, **8**, 161, 222, 223
  in plant–herbivore–predator interactions, **8**, 152
  in plant odor, **8**, 156
  structure, **8**, 233
(*R*)-(−)-linalool, in sex pheromones, **8**, 223
linalool, geranyl-, occurrence, **8**, 229
linalool, 8-hydroxy-, occurrence, **8**, 225
linalool oxides
  analogues, **8**, 229

biosynthesis, **8**, 225
structure, **8**, 233, 234
linalools, occurrence, **8**, 235
linalool synthases, isolation, **2**, 102
linalyl compounds, solvolysis, **2**, 122
linalyl diphosphate
biosynthesis, **2**, 99
homoallylic analogue, biosynthesis, **2**, 138
as intermediate, **2**, 8
isomerization, **5**, 325
as substrate, **2**, 99
linalyl diphosphate, 2-fluoro-, as substrate, **2**, 126, **5**, 327
linalyl *p*-nitrobenzoate, cyclization, **2**, 123
linamarase
localization, **1**, 885
nomenclature, **1**, 890
linamarin
decomposition, **8**, 144
insect sequestration, **8**, 152
occurrence, **1**, 882, 885
protective activity, **8**, 183
roles, defensive, **8**, 144
lindane
degradation, **5**, 403
dehalogenase induction, **5**, 409
linear free energy correlations, in electrophilic reaction
studies, **5**, 317
lineatin, as aggregation pheromone, **8**, 224
O-linkages, carbohydrate chains, **3**, 70
Linked Atom Least Squares (LALS) programs, in
cellulose studies, **3**, 570
linoleate:oxygen 13-oxidoreductase(s) *see* lipoxygenase(s)
linoleic acid, 7*S*,8*S*-dihydroxy-, biosynthesis, **1**, 212
linoleic acid, 13-hydroperoxy-
enzymatic cleavage, **1**, 106
isolation, **1**, 84
linoleic acid, 8*R*-hydroxy-, biosynthesis, **1**, 212
linoleic acid, 15*R*-hydroxy-, occurrence, **1**, 230
linoleic acid(s)
biosynthesis, **1**, 85, 92
chain elongation, **1**, 34
decarboxylation, **8**, 217
enzymatic peroxygenation, **1**, 105
isomerization, **1**, 98
metabolism pathways, **1**, 230
occurrence, **8**, 211
peroxidation, **1**, 7
as substrates, **1**, 98
and tea leaf blending, **1**, 87
linolenic acid
decarboxylation, **8**, 207
in galactolipids, **1**, 119
in phospholipids, **1**, 119
as proteinase inhibitor inducer, **1**, 132
roles
in pheromone biosynthesis, **8**, 207
in prostaglandin biosynthesis, **1**, 2
linolenic acid, 12,13(*S*)-epoxy-, biosynthesis, **1**, 119
linolenic acid, 13(*S*)-hydroperoxy-
biosynthesis, **1**, 119
incubation, **1**, 119
as proteinase inhibitor inducer, **1**, 132
α-linolenic acid(s)
biosynthesis, **1**, 85, 92
chromatography, **1**, 89
in jasmonic acid biosynthetic pathway, **1**, 119
occurrence, **1**, 84, 128, 214
as starting material, for 12-oxo-*cis*-10,15-phytodienoic
acid, **1**, 119
as substrates, **1**, 98
and tea leaf blending, **1**, 87
γ-linolenic acid(s)
carbocyclization, **1**, 215

as substrates, **1**, 102
linoleoyl-CoA desaturase, purification, **1**, 36
linoleoyl-CoA,hydrogen-donor:oxygen oxidoreductase
see linoleoyl-CoA desaturase
Linossier, Georges, peroxidase studies, **3**, 717
Linsmaier and Skook medium, in cell growth cultures, **4**,
128
Linum album, 5-methoxypodophyllotoxin, **1**, 696
Linum flavum
lignans, **1**, 645
podophyllotoxins, **1**, 671
Linum usitatissimum
dirigent proteins, **1**, 654
galactosyltransferases, **3**, 515
glucosides, **1**, 882
HGA methyltransferase, **3**, 519
13*S*-hydroperoxy-9*Z*,12*Z*,15*Z*-octadecatrienoic acid,
1, 232
lignans, **1**, 645
oxylipins, **1**, 231
pectin methyltransferase, **3**, 519
phytodienoic acid, **1**, 231
(−)-pinoresinol/(−)-lariciresinol reductase, **1**, 668
(+)-secoisolariciresinol glucosyltransferases, **1**, 668
substrate specificity, **1**, 119
seeds
applications, **1**, 668
chemoprotective activity, **1**, 700
linustatin
isolation, **1**, 884
levels, **1**, 884
Linyphia tenuipalpis
(3*R*)-3-hydroxybutanoic acid, **8**, 209
(3*R*,3*R*)-3-(3-hydroxybutanoyloxy)butanoic acid, **8**,
209
Linyphia triangularis
(3*R*)-3-hydroxybutanoic acid, **8**, 209
(3*R*,3*R*)-3-(3-hydroxybutanoyloxy)butanoic acid, **8**,
209
Liomys salvini, feeding problems, **8**, 141
lipase–colipase complexes, structure, **5**, 129
lipase(s) *see* triacylglycerol lipase(s)
lip genes
lipA, roles, **1**, 832
lipB, roles, **1**, 832
mutants, **1**, 832
lipid A
backbone, **3**, 195
biological activity, **3**, 200
biosynthesis, **3**, 202, 220, 5
attachment of Kdo, **3**, 221
completion of inner core, **3**, 224
heptosylation, **3**, 224
late acylation reactions, **3**, 221
regulatory mechanisms, **3**, 220
chemical synthesis, **3**, 197
conformation, endotoxic, **3**, 200
definition, **3**, 183
fluidity, **3**, 198, 201
isolation, **3**, 195
occurrence, **3**, 288
phosphate-free structure, **3**, 197
phosphate groups, **3**, 197
precursor Ia, biosynthesis, **3**, 220, 221
structure, **3**, 183
supramolecular structures
cubic, **3**, 199
hexagonal, **3**, 199
lamellar, **3**, 199
synchroton small-angle x-ray diffraction spectra, **3**,
199
lipid-A-disaccharide synthase, roles, **3**, 221
lipidation, proteins, **4**, 13

lipid bilayers, ion transport, brevetoxin-induced, **8**, 512
lipid bodies, roles, in nectars, **8**, 162
lipid carriers, polyisoprenoid, **3**, 288
lipid intermediate I *see* undecaprenyl-diphospho-
    MurNAc-pentapeptide:UDPGlc*N*Ac Glc*N*Ac
    transferase (translocase II)
lipid intermediate II, transglycosylation, **3**, 266
lipid mediators, biosynthesis, **1**, 291
lipid monomers, molecular recognition, **5**, 128
lipid–phosphorothioate oligonucleotides, HIV-1
    replication inhibition, **7**, 187
lipids
  bioactive, biosynthesis, **1**, **285–302**
  migration, **3**, 682
lipids, platelet-activating factor-like, biosynthesis, **1**, 297
lipid transfer proteins, lipopolysaccharides, **3**, 201
lipid X, biosynthesis, **3**, 221
lipid Y, biosynthesis, **3**, 221
lipiferolide, antifeedant activity, **8**, 308
Lipmann, Fritz Albert (1899–1986)
  metabolism studies, **4**, 222
  polyenzyme studies, **4**, 320
  thiotemplate model, **4**, 221
lipoamide reductase (NADH) *see* dihydrolipoamide
    dehydrogenase
lipocalins
  classification, **1**, 274
  molecular phylogeny, **1**, 274
lipo-chitin, biosynthesis, **1**, 7
lipo-chitin oligosaccharides (LCOs)
  biosynthesis, **1**, **325–344**, **3**, 2
  carbamoyl groups, **1**, 332
  fatty acids, **1**, 326
    biosynthesis, **1**, 337
    unusual, **1**, 332
  function, **1**, 326
  N-methylation, **1**, 332
  modification, **1**, 331
  secretion, **1**, 329
  structure, **1**, 329
Lipodex *see* cyclodextrins
lipogrammistin-A, ichthyotoxicity, **8**, 475
lipoic acid
  biosynthesis, **1**, 832
  from, octanoic acid, **1**, 832
  occurrence, **1**, 832
lipolytic acyl hydrolase (LAH), in green odor production,
  1, 92
lipooligosaccharides, biosynthesis, **1**, 7
lipopeptide(s), biosynthesis, **1**, **533–555**, **4**, 199
lipophosphodiesterase I *see* phospholipase C
lipopolysaccharide binding protein (LBP)
  biological activity, **3**, 181
  properties, **3**, 181
lipopolysaccharide receptors, CD14, **3**, 181
lipopolysaccharides (LPS)
  O-antigen, **3**, 322
  applications, **3**, 180
  biochemistry, **3**, 4, **179–239**
  biological activity, **3**, 5, 322
  biology, **3**, 180
  biosynthesis, **3**, 2, 202
    and central metabolism, **3**, 203
    reviews, **3**, 203
    wecA-dependent pathways, **3**, 214
    wecA-independent pathways, **3**, 214
  cell membrane interactions, **3**, 201
  cellular targets, **3**, 182
  chemistry, **3**, 183
  conformation, **3**, 198
  core oligosaccharides, **3**, 183, 185
  core types, **3**, 187
  critical aggregate concentration, **3**, 198

3-deoxy-D-*manno*-octulosonate in, **3**, 185
  deoxysugars, **3**, 312
  endotoxicity, **3**, 180, 5
  epitopes, phase-variable, **3**, 229
  future research, **3**, 229
  gel state, **3**, 199
  Gram-negative bacteria, **3**, 288, 4
  hexose chains, **3**, 226
  humoral, targets, **3**, 181
  hydrophobic interactions, **3**, 201
  as immunostimulators, **3**, 180
  inner core, biosynthesis, **3**, 220
  lipid A component, **3**, 195
    acylation, **3**, 195
  liquid crystalline state, **3**, 199
  localization, **3**, 242
  membrane fluidity alterations, **3**, 198
  monomers, **3**, 201
  non-carbohydrate substituents, **3**, 185
  occurrence, **3**, 321
  outer core
    antigenic variation, **3**, 228
    assembly in enteric bacteria, **3**, 226
    assembly in non-enteric bacteria, **3**, 228
    biosynthesis, **3**, 226
    phase variation, **3**, 228
  phase state, **3**, 198
  phase transition temperature, **3**, 199
  phosphoryl, **3**, 227
  physicochemistry, **3**, 198
  O-polysaccharide, repeating units, **3**, 183
  pyrophosphorylethanolamine substituents, **3**, 227
  roles, in bacterial virulence, **3**, 180
  rough, **3**, 183
  semirough, **3**, 183
  sialylation, **3**, 229
  smooth, **3**, 183
  O-specific chain, **3**, 183, 185
  structure, **3**, 5, 183
    aggregate, **3**, 198
    supramolecular, **3**, 199
  studies, **3**, 180
  see also endotoxins
lipoprotein lipase, mechanisms, **5**, 127
lipoproteins
  metabolism, **5**, 94, 113
  overproduction, **5**, 94
liposidomycin B, enzyme inhibitory activity, **3**, 280
liposidomycins, enzyme inhibitory activity, **3**, 280
lipoxidase(s) *see* lipoxygenase(s)
lipoxin A, occurrence, **1**, 236
lipoxin A₄
  biosynthesis, **1**, 267
  occurrence, **1**, 237, 238
lipoxin A₄, 11-*trans*-, occurrence, **1**, 237, 238
lipoxin B, occurrence, **1**, 236
lipoxin B₄, biosynthesis, **1**, 267
lipoxin(s)
  biosynthesis, **1**, 170, 267
  occurrence, **1**, 237, 238
  receptors, molecular phylogeny, **1**, 281
8*R*-lipoxygenase, occurrence, **1**, 278
9-lipoxygenase, not found, **1**, 169
12-lipoxygenase
  early studies, **1**, 169
  pathways, **1**, 169
15-lipoxygenase, occurrence, **1**, 169
lipoxygenase-1 (LOX-1)
  activity, **1**, 99
  purification, **1**, 99, 100
5-lipoxygenase activating protein (FLAP)
  molecular phylogeny, **1**, 280
  roles, in arachidonate metabolism, **1**, 264

sequence similarity, **5**, 62
sequencing, **1**, 280
lipoxygenase(s)
  arachidonic acid oxygenation, **1**, 255
  biological activity, **1**, 176
  catalysis, **1**, 263
  environmental stimuli, **1**, 108
  in green odor production, **1**, 92
  in induced plant defense, **8**, 150
  inhibitors, **1**, 123, 243
  iron removal, **1**, 111
  localization, **1**, 129
  mammalian, **1**, 278
  mechanisms, **1**, 161
  molecular phylogeny, **1**, 278
  occurrence, **1**, 93, 210, 232, 263, **8**, 211
  oxidation, **1**, 161
  product specificity, **1**, 96
  properties, **1**, 93
  regiospecificity, **1**, 119
  regulatory mechanisms, **1**, 291
  reviews, **1**, 232
  roles
    in eicosanoid biosynthesis, **1**, 160
    in fatty acid oxidation, **8**, 204
    in slow reacting substance of anaphylaxis
      biosynthesis, **1**, 168
  substrate specificity, **1**, 96, 99
  suicide inactivation, **1**, 263
lipoyl dehydrogenase *see* dihydrolipoamide
      dehydrogenase
Lippia asperifolia, ipsdienone, **8**, 224
liquiritigenin
  biosynthesis, **1**, 790
  reduction, **3**, 777
2(*S*)-liquiritigenin, conversion, to daidzein, **1**, 791
(−)-lirioresinol A, occurrence, **1**, 647
(−)-lirioresinol B, occurrence, **1**, 647
lissoclinotoxin A
  applications, antibiotics, **7**, 527
  chirality, **8**, 541
  isolation, **8**, 541
  possible DNA damage induction, **7**, 527
  reactions, with thiol, **7**, 527
lissoclinotoxin C, isolation, **8**, 541
lissoclinotoxin D, isolation, **8**, 541
lissoclinotoxins, occurrence, **8**, 541
lissoclins, occurrence, **8**, 541
Lissoclinum spp.
  lissoclinotoxins, **8**, 541
  lissoclins, **8**, 541
Lissoclinum bistratum, nairaiamides, **8**, 535
Lissoclinum fragile, eudistomin U, **8**, 528
Lissoclinum japonicum, metabolites, **8**, 541
Lissoclinum vareau, varacin, **8**, 541
Lithospermum spp., 4-hydroxybenzoic acid biosynthesis,
      3, 804
Lithospermum erythrorhizon
  4-coumarate-CoA ligase, **3**, 674
  p-coumaroyl-CoA hydroxylases, **3**, 641
  geranyl diphosphate synthases, **2**, 88, 121
Lithothamnion corallioides
  5*Z*,8*Z*,10*E*,12*E*,14*Z*-eicosapentaenoic acid, **1**, 223
  13-hydroxyarachidonic acid, **1**, 222
  13-hydroxyeicosapentaenoic acid, **1**, 222
  8-hydroxy13-keto-5*Z*,9*E*,11*E*,14*E*-eicosatetraenoate,
      1, 222
  oxylipins, **1**, 222
liver
  glycogen, **3**, 443
  glycogen synthase (mammalian), **3**, 479
    phosphorylation, **3**, 485
  UTP-glucose-1-phosphate uridylyltransferase, **3**, 478

liver cancer, chemoprotection, **1**, 702
liver damage, mediation, **1**, 702
liverworts *see* Hepaticae
lobastatin, applications, hypocholesterolemic agents, **1**, 2
Lobesia botrana, egg dispersion pheromones, **8**, 217
loblolly pine *see* Pinus taeda
Locusta spp.
  antifeedant activity against, **8**, 316
  diuretic hormone, **8**, 300
  salivation-stimulating peptides, **8**, 302
locust adipokinetic hormone, discovery, **8**, 295
Locusta migratoria
  adipokinetic hormone, **8**, 299
  antifeedant activity against, **3**, 141, **8**, 342, 345
  bruceine B toxicity, **8**, 322
  ecdysone 22-phosphate, **8**, 283
  feeding, **8**, 331
locusts
  feeding tests, **8**, 326
  monoterpenoid toxicity, **8**, 143
  repellents, **8**, 324
  see also Locusta migratoria; Schistocerca gregaria
lodgepole pine *see* Pinus contorta
Loganiaceae
  indole alkaloid studies, **4**, 113
  strychnos alkaloids, **4**, 49
loganic acid, methylation, **2**, 106
loganic acid methyltransferase, studies, **4**, 112
loganin
  biosynthesis, **4**, 110
  from
    geraniol, **4**, 110
    nerol, **4**, 110
  occurrence, **8**, 307
  structure, **4**, 109
lolitrem B
  applications, tremorgenic agents, **8**, 177
  occurrence, **8**, 177
Lolium spp., infection, **8**, 177
Lolium multiflorum, 2-*O*-[5-*O*-(*trans*-feruloyl)-β-L-
      arabinofuranosyl]-D-xylopyranose, **3**, 697
Lolium perenne, infection, and insect resistance, **8**, 177
Lolium rigidum
  corynetoxins, **8**, 177
  infection, and insect resistance, **8**, 177
loloatin B
  methicillin-resistant *Staphylococcus aureus* inhibition,
      8, 595
  occurrence, **8**, 595
  penicillin-resistant *Streptococcus pneumoniae*
      inhibition, **8**, 595
  vancomycin-resistant *Enterococcus* inhibition, **8**, 595
Lonchocarpus spp.
  rotenone, **8**, 340
  toxicity, **8**, 141
Lonchocarpus nicou, rotenone, **8**, 340
Lonchocarpus sericeus, 2,5-dihydroxymethyl-3,4-
      dihydroxypyrrolidine, **8**, 342
Lonchocarpus uruca, rotenone, **8**, 341
Lonchocarpus utilis, rotenone, **8**, 341
long-chain-acyl-CoA:(acceptor) 2,3-oxidoreductase *see*
      long-chain-acyl-CoA dehydrogenase
      (LCADH)
long-chain-acyl-CoA dehydrogenase (LCADH), residues,
      1, 51
long-chain alkylamine (LCAA), in controlled-pore glass,
      7, 112
long-chain-fatty-acid-CoA ligase
  catalysis, **1**, 47
  occurrence, **1**, 47
  sequencing, **1**, 47
long-chain molecules, early studies, **3**, 535
longestin, biosynthesis, **2**, 59

longhorn beetles
  rose oxide, **8**, 225
  see also Migdolus fryans
longithorone, occurrence, **1**, 377
longithorone A
  occurrence, **8**, 532
  structure, **8**, 532
Lophocolea heterophylla, labeling studies, **2**, 63
lophyrotomin, occurrence, **4**, 202
Loranthacae, lignins, **3**, 700
lotaustralin
  insect sequestration, **8**, 154
  occurrence, **1**, 882, 885
  roles, defensive, **8**, 144
Lotus corniculatus, cyanogenic polymorphism, **1**, 882
lovastatin
  applications, clinical, **2**, 246
  biosynthesis, via Diels–Alder reaction, **1**, 422
  in human squalene synthase regulation, **2**, 259
  structure, **1**, 410, 422
lovastatin synthase, catalysis, **1**, 422
low barrier hydrogen bonds (LBHB)
  in catalysis, **5**, 40
  in α-chymotrypsin, **5**, 119
  roles, in catalysis, **5**, 40
  solvent kinetic isotope effects, **5**, 78
low-density lipoprotein cholesterol
  and heart disease, **2**, 25
  reduction, **2**, 246
low-density lipoprotein receptors
  regulatory mechanisms, **2**, 25
  upregulation, **2**, 246
low-density lipoproteins (LDL)
  accumulation, **1**, 298
  components, **5**, 94
  oxidation, inhibition, **3**, 792
LOX *see* lipoxygenase(s)
Loxodonta africana
  frontalin, **8**, 233
  pheromones, **8**, 227
L-PAPA *see* L-phenylalanine, *p*-amino- (L-PAPA)
LPGs *see* glycans, lipophospho- (LPGs)
LPO *see* lactoperoxidase (LPO)
LPP *see* linalyl diphosphate
lpx genes
  lpxA, encoding, **3**, 220
  lpxB, localization, **3**, 221
  lpxC, encoding, **3**, 220
  lpxD, encoding, **3**, 221
Lrp, SELEX studies, **7**, 628
Ls locus, pea, **8**, 47
LTSV *see* lucerne transient streak virus (LTSV)
lubimin
  biosynthesis, **2**, 183, 184
  occurrence, **2**, 183
lubimin, hydroxy-, occurrence, **2**, 183
Lubrol PX, applications, **5**, 339
lucerne transient streak virus (LTSV)
  characterization, **6**, 180
  cleavage, **6**, 237
  replication, rolling circle mechanism, **6**, 183
  satellite RNA, cDNA clones, **6**, 182
lucibufagins, occurrence, **8**, 354
luciferase
  occurrence, **8**, 393
    fireflies, **4**, 331, 348
    Vargula spp., cDNA sequencing, **8**, 445
luciferase chimeric reporter gene, transfection into HepG2
    cells, **2**, 261
luciferin
  occurrence, **8**, 444
  reversibly oxidized, and bioluminescence, **8**, 444
luciferin–luciferase (L–L) reaction, mechanisms, **8**, 444

Luffariella variabilis, manoalide, **8**, 521
Luidia clathrata, feeding deterrents, **8**, 471
lumican, localization, **3**, 164
luminous squid, bioluminescence, **8**, 454
lung cancer, research, **7**, 4
lunularic acid
  biosynthesis, **1**, 765
  structure, **8**, 73
lunularin, biosynthesis, **1**, 765
lupanine, host–parasite chemical transfer, **8**, 176
lupeol cyclase, genetics, **2**, 307
lupinic acid
  occurrence, **8**, 61
  synthesis, **8**, 62
lupinine
  biosynthesis, **4**, 34
  occurrence, **8**, 344
lupins
  isoflavone glycosides, **1**, 807
  5-methoxyisoflavones, **1**, 800
Lupinus spp.
  isoflavonoids, **1**, 784
  quinolizidine alkaloids, **4**, 33
Lupinus albus, peroxidases, **3**, 718
Lupinus angustifolia, lupinic acid, **8**, 61
Lupinus luteus, lupinine, **8**, 344
lutein
  biosynthesis, **2**, 342
  labeling studies, **2**, 61
luteolin
  coupling, **1**, 685
  roles, in legume–*Rhizobium* symbiosis, **8**, 173
luteolin 7-malonylglucoside, as oviposition stimulant, **8**,
    156
luteolin 7-(6″-malonylglucoside), as insect attractant, **8**,
    156
luteone
  antifungal activity, **8**, 183
  metabolism, **1**, 815
luteone, 7-methyl, incubation, **1**, 815
lutetium(III)–texaphyrin complexes, conjugation, **7**, 164
Lutzomyia longipalpis, 9-methylgermacrene B, **8**, 237
lux genes
  functions, **8**, 394
  luxC, encoding, **8**, 394
  luxD, encoding, **8**, 394
  luxE, encoding, **8**, 394
  luxG, localization, **8**, 394
  luxI, functions, **8**, 394
  luxL, encoding, **8**, 396
  luxM, encoding, **8**, 396
  luxN, encoding, **8**, 396
  luxO, encoding, **8**, 396
  luxP, encoding, **8**, 396
  luxQ, encoding, **8**, 396
  luxR
    activator domain, **8**, 394
    regulator domain, **8**, 394
Lux proteins
  LuxI, functions, **8**, 398
  LuxN, transphosphorylation, **8**, 397
  LuxR-LuxI family, autoinducers, **8**, 397
LY191145, antivancomycin-resistance activity, **3**, 283
LY264826, biological activity, **3**, 327
Lycaenidae, cadinol, **8**, 228
lycopene
  biosynthesis, **2**, 334, 336, 338
  cyclization, **2**, 342
    inhibition, **2**, 338
    inhibitors, **2**, 343
    ORF 6 gene, **2**, 343
  in fruit pigment, **8**, 164
  protonation, **2**, 5

structure, **2**, 324
lycopene, 7,8,11,12-tetrahydro-
   as intermediate, **2**, 331
   isomerization, **2**, 324
all-*trans*-lycopene, biosynthesis, **2**, 341
lycopene cyclases
   in carotenoid biosynthesis, **2**, 342
   catalysis, **2**, 5
   classification, **2**, 342
   CrtL-type, **2**, 342, 348
   CrtY-type, **2**, 342, 348
Lycopersicon spp., tomatine, **8**, 346
Lycopersicon esculentum
   lateral bud growth stimulation, **8**, 68
   solanine, **8**, 345
   tomatine, **8**, 346
   viroid infection studies, **6**, 175
Lycopodium clavatum, nicotine, **8**, 347
Lycoriella mali, heptadecane, **8**, 217
lycorine, biosynthesis, **4**, 43
lydicamycin, biosynthesis, **1**, 370
Lygaeidae, cardiac glycosides, **8**, 360
Lygodium spp., antheridiogens, **8**, 56, 57
Lygodium circinnatum, gibberellin A$_{73}$ methyl ester
      biosynthesis, **8**, 57
Lygodium japonicum
   antheridiogens, **8**, 57
   8*S*-hydroxyhexadecanoic acid, **1**, 228
Lymantria dispar
   disparlure, **8**, 4
   (*Z*)-2-methyl-7-octadecene, **8**, 241
   osmeterial gland, **8**, 347
   pheromones, **8**, 4, 12
Lymantria monacha, pheromones, **8**, 12
Lymantriidae
   pheromones, **8**, 207
   sex pheromones, **8**, 207, 247
Lymnaea stagnalis, DNA library screening, **3**, 58
lymphoma cells, mutations, BW5147PHA^{R}2.7, **3**, 19
Lyngbya majuscula
   antillatoxin, **8**, 608
   barbaramide, **8**, 608
   curacin A, **8**, 606
   debromoaplysiatoxin, **8**, 603
   lyngbyatoxin, **8**, 603
   majusculamides, **8**, 603
   malyngamides, **8**, 603
   malyngic acid, **1**, 209, **8**, 603
   malyngolide, **8**, 603
   pukeleimides, **8**, 603
   ypaoamide, **8**, 608
lyngbyatoxin, occurrence, **8**, 603
Lyonetia clerkella, 14-methyl-1-octadecene, **8**, 247
Lyonetia prunifoliella, 10,14-dimethyl-1-octadecene, **8**,
      247
Lys-195
   localization, **4**, 77
   roles, in porphobilinogen synthase biosynthesis, **4**, 79
Lys-247
   isolation, **4**, 74
   localization, **4**, 77
   roles, in porphobilinogen synthase biosynthesis, **4**, 79
Lys-252, isolation, **4**, 74
Lys-313, identification, **4**, 67
lysergic acid
   biosynthesis, **4**, 52
   from, chanoclavine, **4**, 52
lysergol, as feeding deterrent, **8**, 148
lysidine, biosynthesis, **5**, 96
lysine, hydroxy-, occurrence, **3**, 246
[2-^{2}H]lysine
   EPR spectra, **5**, 211
   as substrate, **5**, 211

[2-^{2}H,2-^{15}N]lysine, EPR spectra, **5**, 211
[2-^{13}C]lysine, as substrate, **5**, 211
D-lysine, occurrence, **3**, 249
L-lysine
   biosynthesis, pathways, **4**, 243
   cross-links, **3**, 248
   interconversion, **5**, 206
   pK_a, **5**, 206
L-β-lysine
   biosynthesis, **5**, 206
   interconversion, **5**, 206
   pK_a, **5**, 206
S-[3-^{2}H$_2$]lysine, reactions, **5**, 208
S-β-[2-^{2}H$_1$]lysine, biosynthesis, **5**, 208
S-β-[2-^{2}H$_1$,3-^{2}H$_1$]lysine, biosynthesis, **5**, 208
S-β-[3-^{2}H$_1$]lysine, biosynthesis, **5**, 208
β-[3-^{3}H]lysine, tritium transfer, **5**, 208
L-lysine adding enzyme, purification, **3**, 259
lysine 2,3-aminomutase
   catalysis, **5**, 206
   components, **5**, 207
   EPR spectra, **5**, 211
   ESEEM spectra, **5**, 211
   hydrogen transfer mediation, **5**, 207
   iron–sulfur clusters, **5**, 214
   isotopic labeling, EPR spectra, **5**, 211
   lysine radical intermediates, spectroscopic
         characterization, **5**, 211
   occurrence, **5**, 206
   properties
      catalytic, **5**, 206
      molecular, **5**, 206
   purification, **5**, 206
   radical reactions, **5**, **205–223**
   stereochemistry, **5**, 207
   substrates, **5**, 213
   UV-vis spectra, **5**, 213
L-lysine 2,3-aminomutase *see* lysine 2,3-aminomutase
R-lysine 5,6-aminomutase, catalysis, **5**, 207
β-lysine 5,6-aminomutase, catalysis, **5**, 207
lysine ε-aminotransferase (LAT), discovery, **4**, 165
D-lysine mutase, reactions, **5**, 264
L-lysine mutase, reactions, **5**, 264
β-lysine mutase *see* β-lysine 5,6-aminomutase
lysine(s)
   degradation, **4**, 165
   effects on penicillin biosynthesis, **4**, 176
   residues, binding, **3**, 333
   as starting material(s), for alkaloids, **4**, 33
lysinoalanine, structure, **4**, 280
lysis, nisin-induced, **4**, 281
Lysobacter lactamgenus
   ACV synthetase, encoding, **1**, 840
   cefD gene encoding, **4**, 171
lysolecithinase *see* lysophospholipase
lysoPAF *see* glycerophosphocholine, 1-alkyl-
lysophosphatidic acid *see* 3-phosphate, 1-acyl-*sn*-glycero-
2-lysophosphatidylcholine acylhydrolase *see*
         lysophospholipase
lysophospholipase, in honeybee venom, **8**, 355
lysophospholipase D *see*
         alkylglycerophosphoethanolamine
         phosphodiesterase
lysophospholipids, acetyltransferase inhibition, **1**, 293
lysosomal α-*N*-acetylglucosaminidase *see* *N*-
         acetylglucosamine-1-phosphodiester α-*N*-
         acetylglucosaminidase
lysosomal acid phosphatase
   phosphohistidine in, **5**, 144
   structure, **5**, 152
lysosomal degradation
   of sphingolipids, **3**, 102
   topology, **3**, 98

M

Maackia amurensis, maackoline, **1**, 685
maackiain
  fungal degradation, **1**, 803
  hydroxylation, **1**, 803
  metabolism, **8**, 192
  occurrence, **1**, 808
maackiain, (+)-6a-hydroxy-
  O-methylation, **1**, 786, 800
  as substrate, **1**, 803
(+)-maackiain, stereochemistry, **1**, 797
(−)-maackiain
  biosynthesis, **1**, 795
  catabolism, **1**, 814
  stereochemistry, **1**, 797
maackoline, occurrence, **1**, 685
(−)-machilusin, growth inhibitory activity, **1**, 693
Machilus japonica, lignans, **1**, 693
Macrocentrus grandii
  (9Z,13Z)-9,13-alkadienes, **8**, 219
  pheromones, **8**, 240
  4-tridecenal, **8**, 219
macrocycles
  as probes of nucleic acid dynamics, **7**, 449
  synthesis, **7**, 449
macrocyclic compounds, bisintercalation, **7**, 449
macrocyclic lactones, occurrence, **8**, 215
macrolactins
  ¹³C-acetonide analysis, **8**, 590
  occurrence, **8**, 590
  structure, **8**, 590
macrolides
  biosynthesis, **1**, 495–532
  occurrence, **8**, 218
macrolites, biosynthesis, **4**, 201
macrophage migration inhibitory factor (MIF)
  catalysis, **5**, 47
  crystal structure, **5**, 47
  formation, **3**, 183
  identification, **5**, 47
macrophages
  1-alkyl-2-acylglycerophosphocholine, **1**, 291
  endotoxin exposure, **3**, 182
  lipopolysaccharide activation, **3**, 182
Macrophoma commelinae, macrophomic acid, **1**, 401
macrophomic acid
  biosynthesis, **1**, 368, 401
  from, 5-acetyl-4-methoxy-6-methyl-2-pyrone, **1**, 401
macrophomic acid synthase, catalysis, **1**, 404
Macropus fuliginosus, effects of fluoroacetate on, **8**, 148
madangamine A
  biogenesis, **8**, 566
  occurrence, **8**, 566
maduralide, occurrence, **8**, 591
maduropeptin
  activation, **7**, 580
  applications, **7**, 580
    antibiotics, **7**, 554, 580
  classification, **1**, 557
  DNA damage, **7**, 580
  occurrence, **7**, 580
  structure, **7**, 554, 580
madurosamine, structure, **7**, 580
Magicada spp., adipokinetic hormone, **8**, 299
magic bullets, Erhlich's hypothesis, **7**, 428
Magnaporthe grisea, melanin, **1**, 427

magnesidin A, isolation, **8**, 598
magnesidins, occurrence, **8**, 598
magnesium, in hammerhead ribozyme catalysis, **6**, 134
magnesium–adenosine–triphosphate complexes,
  nucleophilic attack, **4**, 324
Magnolia biondii
  (±)-eudesmins, **1**, 704
  fargesin, **1**, 704
Magnolia denudata, (+)-denudatin B, **1**, 677
Magnolia fargesii, (+)-epimagnolin A, **1**, 693
Magnolia kobus
  lignans, **1**, 661
  O-methyltransferases, **1**, 661
  pinoresinol, **1**, 661
  pinoresinol monomethyl ethers, **1**, 661
Magnolia salicifolia
  magnosalin, **1**, 705
  magnoshinin, **1**, 705
Magnolia virginiana, magnolol, **1**, 693
(+)-magnolin
  demethylation, **1**, 692
  occurrence, **1**, 661
magnolol
  antibacterial activity, **1**, 692
  antifungal activity, **1**, 691
  effects, on herbivores, **8**, 139
  occurrence, **1**, 693
  toxicity, **8**, 140
magnosalin, antiinflammatory activity, **1**, 705
magnoshinin, antiinflammatory activity, **1**, 705
maitotoxin (MTX)
  activity, **8**, 508
  ciguatera induction, **8**, 501
  collisionally activated dissociation MS/MS
    experiments, **8**, 506
  3D NMR, **8**, 506
  3D pulsed field gradient NOESY–HMQC spectra, **8**,
    506
  isolation, **8**, 506
  occurrence, **8**, 501, 504
  relative stereochemistry, **8**, 507
  structural studies, **8**, 506
maize
  amylose extender alleles, **3**, 461
  An-1 gene, **8**, 47
  Bt 2 genes, **3**, 447
  Dwarf-3 gene, **8**, 50
  Dwarf-8, **8**, 54
  glucose-1-phosphate adenylyltransferase, **3**, 447
  Sh 2 genes, **3**, 447
  soluble starch synthases, **3**, 455
  see also Zea mays
maize endosperm
  amyloplasts, **3**, 464
  branching enzyme isoforms, **3**, 459
  enzyme subunits, **3**, 451
  glucose-1-phosphate adenylyltransferase, **3**, 465
  mutants, **3**, 461
  plastids, **3**, 464
  starch synthase I, **3**, 454
  sugary 1 mutation, **3**, 468
maize kernel
  branching enzymes, cDNA clones, **3**, 462
  soluble starch synthase I, **3**, 457
maize seedlings, threonine aldolase, **3**, 401

maize weevil *see Sitophilus zeamais*
majusculamides, occurrence, **8**, 603
makaluvamine F
    applications, antibiotics, **7**, 501
    DNA reactions, **7**, 501
    occurrence, **7**, 501
MAK genes, *MAK1*, localization, **1**, 814
makisterone A
    moulting hormone activity, **8**, 293
    occurrence, **8**, 279
makisterone C *see* podecdysone B
malabathrins, structure, **3**, 783
malaccol, occurrence, **8**, 341
Malacosoma spp., caterpillars, 5β-cholestan-3-one, **8**, 230
Malanorrhea usitata, laccase, **3**, 711
malaria, pathology, **3**, 297
maleic acids, *cis-trans* equilibria, **5**, 23
maleic hydrazide
    applications, **8**, 34
    structure, **8**, 34
maleimide, *N*-ethyl-
    binding, **5**, 429
    hydroxymethylbilane synthase alkylation, **4**, 87
    as inhibitor, **2**, 283
        of patchouli synthase, **2**, 185
    in monoterpene synthase studies, **2**, 139
maleimide, *N*-(1-pyrene)-, reactions, with dithymidylyl
        phosphorothioate, **7**, 240
maleimides, *N*-alkyl-, cycloaddition, with
        tetrachlorothiophene dioxide, **5**, 429
maleimides, *N*-(carboxyalkyl)-, effects, on prostaglandin-
        endoperoxide synthases, **5**, 250
maleylacetate *enol*-lactonase *see*
        carboxymethylenebutenolidase
malic acid, (*R*)-phosphinomethyl-, isolation, **1**, 871
malonamide, as bacterial aromatic polyketide synthase
        primer, **1**, 475
malonate, as bacterial aromatic polyketide synthase
        primer, **1**, 475
malonate, diethyloxo-, trityl group removal, **7**, 126
malonates, replacement, **8**, 237
malonate semialdehyde, biosynthesis, **3**, 409, **5**, 410
malondialdehyde
    DNA adducts of, **7**, 502
    in oligodeoxynucleotides, **7**, 334
malonyl acyltransferase, sequencing, **1**, 412
malonylation, localization, **1**, 809
malonyl-CoA
    biosynthesis, **1**, 716, **5**, 87
    catalysis, **1**, 789
    chalcone biosynthesis, **1**, 750
    in fatty acid biosynthesis, **8**, 209
    pathways, **1**, 716
    roles
        in acetogenin biosynthesis, **8**, 203
        in isoflavonoid biosynthesis, **1**, 784
        in polyketide biosynthesis, **1**, 3
    as starting material, for 6-methylsalicylic acid, **1**, 411
    as substrate, **1**, 349
malonyl-CoA:[acyl-carrier-protein] transferase (MCAT),
        NodF activity, **1**, 336
malonyl-CoA carboxy-lyase *see* malonyl-CoA
        decarboxylase
malonyl-CoA:4-coumaroyl-CoA malonyltransferase
        (cyclizing) *see* chalcone synthase
malonyl-CoA decarboxylase, activity, of 6-methylsalicylic
        acid synthase, **1**, 361
malonyl-CoA:3-hydroxybenzoyl-CoA
        malonyltransferase *see* benzophenone synthase
malonyl glucosides, accumulation, **1**, 808
malonyl transacylase, catalysis, **1**, 27
malonyltransferase(s)
    characterization, **1**, 741

encoding, **1**, 356
malseccin
    occurrence, **8**, 181
    phytotoxicity, **8**, 181
maltase-glucoamylase(s) *see* a-glucosidase(s)
maltase(s) *see* α-glucosidase(s)
maltodextrin phosphorylase
    induction, **3**, 445
    occurrence, **5**, 305
maltose, as starting material, for glucans, **3**, 444
maltose binding protein (MBP), applications, in
        expression systems, **7**, 652
Malus domestica, jasmonic acid, **1**, 124
malvalic acid, occurrence, **1**, 62
malvalic acid, dihydro-, occurrence, **1**, 62
malvidin, in fruit pigment, **8**, 164
malvidin glycosides, in flower pigment, **8**, 158
malyngamide H
    absolute stereochemistry, **8**, 606
    ichthyotoxicity, **8**, 606
malyngamides, occurrence, **8**, 603
malyngic acid, occurrence, **1**, 209, **8**, 603
malyngolide, occurrence, **8**, 603
Mamestra brassicae, sex pheromones, **8**, 200
Mamestra suasa, sex pheromones, **8**, 200
mammalian cells
    cytosol, α-mannosidase activity, **3**, 27
    endo α-mannosidase, **3**, 20
    selenoproteins in, **4**, 371
mammalian enzymes
    farnesyl-diphosphate farnesyltransferase, regulatory
        mechanisms, **2**, 259
    sequences, **2**, 250
mammalian liver, threonine aldolase, **3**, 397
mammalian tissues
    α-glucosidase I, **3**, 18
    α-glucosidase II, **3**, 19
mammals
    acetyltransferases, **1**, 293
    5-aminolevulinate synthase, **4**, 65
    apolipoproteins, **6**, 99
    eicosanoids, **1**, **159–206**
        biological activity, **1**, 172
    glutamate receptors, mRNA, **6**, 103
    glycogen biosynthesis, **3**, **441–495**
    glycosidase inhibitors, toxicity, **3**, 140
    GPI anchors, biosynthesis, **3**, 306
    hydroxymethylglutaryl-CoA reductase, **2**, 17
    α1,2-mannosidase inhibitors, **3**, 25
    α-mannosidases, **3**, 28
    6-methyl-5-hepten-2-one, **8**, 232
    odor marks, **8**, 220
    polyunsaturated fatty acids, **1**, 161
    SELB homologues, **4**, 370
mammary glands
    lactating
        β-*N*-acetylglucosaminylglycopeptide β-1,4-
            galactosyltransferase expression, **3**, 44
        gene expression, **3**, 55
mammary tumors, and soy-rich diets, **1**, 783
Mammea africana, Mammea insecticide X, **8**, 337
Mammea americana, Mammea insecticide X, **8**, 337
Mammea insecticide X, occurrence, **8**, 337
Mammea longifolia, surangin B, **8**, 337
Manchurian ash *see Fraxinus mandschurica*
mandelate racemase
    active sites, **5**, 27
    catalysis, **5**, 16
        mechanisms, **5**, 16
mandelic acid
    from, phenylacetic acid, **1**, 78
    racemization, **5**, 33
mandelonitrile, *p*-hydroxy-, as intermediate, **1**, 889

mandelonitrile, (*S*)-*p*-hydroxy-, biosynthesis, **1**, 889
mandelonitrile benzaldehyde-lyase *see* mandelonitrile lyase
mandelonitrile lyase
  catalysis, **1**, 599
  in cyanogenic glycoside degradation, **1**, 881
Manduca spp.
  allatotrophins, **8**, 301
  diuretic hormone, **8**, 300
  juvenile hormone production, **8**, 301
Manduca sexta
  adipokinetic hormone, **8**, 299
  cocaine toxicity, **8**, 344
  corpora allata, **8**, 272
  dexamethasone inhibition of PLA$_2$, **1**, 248
  ecdysis-triggering hormone, **8**, 301
  eclosion hormone, **8**, 301
  effects of canavanine on, **8**, 146
  feeding, **8**, 302
    techniques, **8**, 151
  free acids, epoxidization, **8**, 272
  juvenile hormones, **8**, 268
    juvenile hormone 0, **8**, 269
    juvenile hormone III, **8**, 274
  nicotine excretion, **8**, 348
  prothoracicotropic hormone, **8**, 295
manganese centers, oxygen-linked, **3**, 345
manganese ions, EPR spectra, **5**, 67
manganese porphyrins, DNA damage induction, **7**, 373
Manica spp., manicone, **8**, 242
Manica rubida, manicones, **8**, 243
manicone, occurrence, **8**, 242
manicone, dihydro-, occurrence, **8**, 244
Manihot esculenta
  branching enzymes, cDNA clones, **3**, 462
  cyanogenic glucoside, **1**, 882
  waxy locus, DNA sequence, **3**, 454
Manα1-6(Manα1-3)Manβ1-4GlcNAcβ1-4GlcNAc-Asn-X, structure, **3**, 40
mannans
  biosynthesis, **3**, 606
  cellulose studies, **3**, 585
β-D-mannans, biosynthesis, **3**, 521
D-mannitol, 1,4-dideoxy-1,4-imino- (DIM), as α-mannosidase inhibitor, **3**, 154
mannosamine, as GPI anchor biosynthesis inhibitor, **3**, 303
mannosamine, 4-deoxy-*N*-acetyl-, *N*-acylneuraminate-9-phosphate synthase inhibition, **3**, 391
D-mannosamine, *N*-acetyl-
  reactions
    with phospho*enol*pyruvate, **3**, 390
    with pyruvate, **3**, 378
mannose, donors, **3**, 301
mannose glucosaminyl(acyl)phosphatidylinositols, biosynthesis, **4**, 311, 313
mannose-6-phosphate, receptors, **3**, 29
D-mannose 1,6-phosphomutase *see* phosphomannomutase
α1,2-mannosidase IA
  functions, **3**, 148
  murine, sequences, **3**, 23
α-mannosidase IA, isolation, **3**, 22
α1,2-mannosidase IB
  encoding, **3**, 23
  gene, **3**, 23
α-mannosidase IB, isolation, **3**, 22
α-mannosidase II
  activity, **3**, 42, 150
  cDNA, **3**, 25
    homologue, **3**, 27
    human, **3**, 25
  genes, mapping, **3**, 25

in Golgi apparatus, **3**, 17, 25
hereditary erythroblastic multinuclearity with a positive acidified serum induction, **3**, 27
inhibitors, **3**, 153
α-mannosidase II^x
  genes
    mapping, **3**, 25
    roles, **3**, 27
    specificity, **3**, 25
mannosidase inhibitors
  biochemistry, **3**, 153
  structure, **3**, 138
α-mannosidase(s)
  acrosomal, **3**, 29
  broad-specificity, **3**, 28
  Class 1
    and baculoviruses, **3**, 24
    characteristics, **3**, 23
    characterization, **3**, 21
    occurrence, **3**, 24
    properties, **3**, 22
    role in fly nervous system development, **3**, 24
    sequences, **3**, 24
    see also α1,2-mannosidase(s)
  Class 2
    characterization, **3**, 21
    comparisons, **3**, 29
    roles, **3**, 25
  classification, **3**, 21
  cytosolic, **3**, 25, 27
  in endoplasmic reticulum, **3**, 27
  in endoplasmic reticulum, kifunensine-insensitive, **3**, 27
  inhibitors, **3**, 153
  lysosomal, **3**, 21, 25, 27
    and mannosidosis, **3**, 28
    occurrence, **3**, 28
  mammals, **3**, 28
  occurrence, **3**, 26
  processing, **3**, 42
  recombinant, **3**, 22
  roles, in biosynthetic pathways, **3**, 14
  vacuolar, **3**, 21
  yeasts, **3**, 28
α1,2-mannosidase(s)
  cDNA, cloning from Sf9 cells, **3**, 24
  in endoplasmic reticulum, **3**, 17
  functions, **3**, 148
  insects, **3**, 24
  kifunensine-resistant, **3**, 22
  mammalian, specificity, **3**, 23
  occurrence, **3**, 24
  properties, **3**, 148
  roles, **3**, 21
  yeast processing, **3**, 23
    sequences, **3**, 23
  see also α-mannosidase(s), Class 1
α1,6-mannosidase(s), lysosomal, **3**, 28
mannoside, α-methyl-, in thrombin studies, **7**, 627
α-D-mannoside mannohydrolase(s) *see* α-mannosidase(s)
mannosidosis, etiology, **3**, 28
mannostatin A
  α-mannosidase II inhibition, **3**, 27, 156
  structure, **3**, 133
mannosylamine, cytosolic α-mannosidase stabilization, **3**, 27
α-1,3-mannosyl-glycoprotein β-1,2-*N*-acetylglucosaminyltransferase
  genes
    cloning, **3**, 50
    organization, **3**, 50
    roles, in *N*-glycan synthesis, **3**, 50
α-1,3-mannosyl-glycoprotein β-1,4-*N*-acetylglucosaminyltransferase

purification, **3**, 54
roles, in *N*-glycan synthesis, **3**, 54
α-1,6-mannosyl-glycoprotein *β*-1,2-*N*-
        acetylglucosaminyltransferase
    genes
        cloning, **3**, 52
        organization, **3**, 52
    roles
        in carbohydrate-deficient glycoprotein syndrome, **3**,
            52
        in *N*-glycan synthesis, **3**, 52
α-1,3(6)-mannosyl-glycoprotein *β*-1,6-*N*-
        acetylglucosaminyltransferase
    activity, **3**, 54
    genes, organization, **3**, 55
    roles, in *N*-glycan synthesis, **3**, 54
β-1,4-mannosyl-glycoprotein *β*-1,4-*N*-
        acetylglucosaminyltransferase
    expression, variations, **3**, 53
    genes
        organization, **3**, 53
        transfection, **3**, 53
    overexpression, **3**, 54
    roles, in *N*-glycan synthesis, **3**, 53
mannosyltransferase(s)
    catalysis, **3**, 212
    in Golgi apparatus, **3**, 17
    occurrence, **3**, 521
manoalide
    antiinflammatory activity, **8**, 521
    applications, antiinflammatory agents, **8**, 521
    occurrence, **8**, 521
    phospholipase A_2 inactivation, **8**, 521
Manskaya, lignification studies, **3**, 717
Manta *see* methoprene
manzamenones, occurrence, **1**, 384
manzamine A
    occurrence, **1**, 380
    structure, **8**, 553
manzamine B, occurrence, **1**, 380
manzamines
    biogenetic pathways, **8**, 557
    biosynthesis, pathways, **8**, 554
    future research, **8**, 566
    isolation, **8**, 557
    occurrence, **8**, 553
    structure, **8**, 553
MAPK *see* mitogen activated protein kinase (MAPK)
MAPKK *see* mitogen-activated protein kinase kinase
        (MAPKK)
Marah macrocarpus
    copalyl diphosphate synthase, **8**, 47
    gibberellin 20-oxidases, **2**, 236
    ent-kaurene synthase, **8**, 47
    ent-kaur-16-ene synthase, **2**, 231
Marasmius alliaceus, alliacolide, **2**, 176
Marcus formalism
    applications, **5**, 8
    parameters, **5**, 9
marein, roles, in ultraviolet patterning, **8**, 160
marine algae
    fatty acids, **8**, 422
    halogenated monoterpenes, **2**, 106
    haloperoxidases, **2**, 107
marine alkaloids, discovery, **1**, 380
marine animals
    feeding attractants, **8**, 417
    feeding stimulants, **8**, 417
    pheromones, **8**, 420
marine bacteria
    desaturation in, **1**, 38
    macrolactins, **8**, 590
marine chemical ecology, **8**, **415–649**

field of study, **8**, 416
marine crayfish *see Jasus lalandei*
marine invertebrates
    and microalgae, symbiosis, **8**, 426
    sesquiterpenes, **2**, 191
marine natural products, **8**, **415–649**
    bioactive, **8**, 521
        drug candidates, **8**, 521
        microbial metabolites, **8**, 587
        Porifera metabolites, **8**, 553
        Urochordata, **8**, 521, 525
    chemistry, reviews, **8**, 416
    Diels–Alder [4+2]-adducts, **1**, 378
    historical background, **8**, 416
marine organisms
    antifeedant activity, **8**, 459
    bioluminescence, **8**, 444
    chemical defense, **8**, 459
        anatomical distribution, **8**, 462
        predator-induced defenses, **8**, 462
marine sponges *see* Porifera
marine toxins
    brevetoxin, **8**, 511
    ciguatera, **8**, 501
    ciguatoxins, **8**, 501
    cone shells, **8**, 476
    gambieric acid, **8**, 508
    gymnodimine, **8**, 515
    maitotoxin, **8**, 504
    palytoxin, **8**, 509
    pinnatoxins, **8**, 518
    polycavernosides, **8**, 515
    prymnesin, **8**, 518
    saxitoxins, **8**, 485
    surugatoxin, **8**, 515
    tetrodotoxins, **8**, 480
marine worms, as cone shell food, **8**, 476
maritime pine scale *see Matsucoccus feytaudi*
markers, isotropic, nucleobase conjugation, **7**, 219
Markovnikov addition, in pinane synthesis, **2**, 104
Markovnikov's rules, and cyclization, **2**, 11
marmesin, (+)-3′-hydroxy-, intermediate, **1**, 633
(+)-marmesin
    biosynthesis, **1**, 628
    as starting material, for psoralen, **1**, 19, 631
(±)-marmesin, deuteration, **1**, 632
marrangin
    antifeedant activity, **8**, 332
    occurrence, **8**, 330
Marseniopsis mollis, homarine, **8**, 465
martrine, occurrence, **4**, 33
Marubium vulgare, labdane biosynthesis, **2**, 62
mas genes
    encoding, **4**, 233
    mas-1, encoding, **3**, 24
    mas-1*a*, encoding, **3**, 24
    mas-1*b*, encoding, **3**, 24
mass spectrometry, in carbohydrate studies, **3**, 1
mastoparans, purification, **8**, 356
Mastophora cornigera, (*Z*)-9-tetradecenyl acetate, **8**, 199
Mastotermes darwiniensis, adipokinetic hormone, **8**, 299
matairesinol
    antineoplastic activity, **1**, 698
    biosynthesis, **1**, 688
    occurrence, **3**, 676
matairesinol, 7′-hydroxy-
    biosynthesis, **1**, 668
    induction, **1**, 691
    occurrence, **1**, 668, 697
(+)-matairesinol, occurrence, **1**, 647
(−)-matairesinol
    biosynthesis, **1**, 662, 665
    growth inhibitory activity, **1**, 694

induction, **1**, 691
  occurrence, **1**, 662
  optical purity, **1**, 652
  phosphodiesterase inhibitory activity, **1**, 704
matairesinol *O*-methyltransferase, catalysis, **1**, 667
matricaria acid, (8*Z*)-dihydro-, occurrence, **8**, 351
Matsucoccus spp.
  matsuone, **8**, 244
  pheromones, **8**, 244
Matsucoccus feytaudi
  pheromones, **8**, 14
  (3*S*,7*R*,8*E*,10*E*)-3,7,9-trimethyl-8,10-dodecadien-6-
    one, **8**, 244
matsuone, occurrence, **8**, 244
Matthiola incana
  acyltransferases, **1**, 741
  anthocyanidin synthase, **1**, 730
  dihydrokaempferol 4-reductase, **1**, 727
  flavonol 3-*O*-glucosyltransferase, **1**, 731
  flavonol synthase, **1**, 727
  naringenin 3-dioxygenase, **1**, 725
  xylosyltransferases, **1**, 738
*MAT*α1 mRNA
  cis-acting sequences, **6**, 208
  codons, **6**, 208
  degradation, **6**, 209
*MAT*α1 transcripts, accumulation, **6**, 209
Maxam–Gilbert marker, **7**, 583
Maxam–Gilbert method (DNA sequencing) *see* chemical
    cleavage method
maximowicziol, occurrence, **1**, 686
Mayetiola destructor, (1*S*,9*E*)-1-methyl-9-dodecenyl
    acetate, **8**, 215
maytenone, occurrence, **1**, 377
Maytenus chuchuhuasca, xuxuarine Aα, **1**, 377
Maytenus mossambicensis, celabenzine, **8**, 344
MBED *see* eudistomin D, 9-methyl-7-bromo- (MBED)
MBOA *see* 2-benzoxazolinone, 6-methoxy- (MBOA)
MBP *see* maltose binding protein (MBP)
MBP-1 peptide, interaction, **7**, 484
MCADH *see* medium-chain acyl-CoA dehydrogenase
    (MCADH)
MCAT *see* malonyl-CoA:[acyl-carrier-protein]
    transferase (MCAT)
mcb genes
  mcbA, encoding, **1**, 850
  mcbB, roles, **1**, 850
  mcbC, roles, **1**, 850
  mcbD, roles, **1**, 850
  mcbE, encoding, **1**, 850
  mcbF, encoding, **1**, 850
mCD14
  as lipopolysaccharide receptor, **3**, 181
  and monocyte activation, **3**, 182
mcmU *see* uridine, 5-methylcarboxymethyl- (mcmU)
mcmUm *see* uridine-2′-*O*-methylribose, 5-
    methylcarboxymethyl- (mcmUm)
m-DAP adding enzyme, overexpression, **3**, 259
MDL 25,637 *see* heptitol, 2,6-diamino-2,6-imino-7-*O*-(β-
    D-glucopyranosyl)-D-glycero-L-gulo- (MDL)
meadow vole *see* Microtus pennsylvanicus
mealworm *see* Tenebrio molitor
mealy bugs *see* Planococcus citri
meat ant *see* Iridomyrmex purpureus
mec genes, determinants, **3**, 274
MeCoM *see* S-methyl coenzyme M (MeCoM)
Medicago sativa
  chalcone 2′-*O*-methyltransferases, **1**, 740
  chalcone synthase, genetics, **1**, 789
  trans-cinnamate 4-monooxygenase, **3**, 637
    localization, **3**, 669
  formononetin 7-*O*-glucoside-6″-*O*-malonate, **1**, 806
  hydroxycinnamyl *O*-methyltransferases, **3**, 646

isoflavone 7-*O*-methyltransferase, **1**, 799
  isoflavone reductase, **1**, 797
  isoflavonoids, **1**, 774
  licodione, **1**, 794
  phenylalanine ammonia-lyase, **3**, 659
  pterocarpan synthase, **1**, 797
  root inhibition, **3**, 141
  vestitone reductase, **1**, 797
Medicago truncatula, isoflavonoid studies, **1**, 817
medicarpin
  biosynthesis, **1**, 808
  interconvertibility, **1**, 786
  occurrence, **1**, 774, 780, 809
  precursors, **1**, 799
(−)-medicarpin, stereochemistry, **1**, 797
(6a*R*,11a*R*)-medicarpin, biosynthesis, **1**, 797
[³H]-medicarpin–glutathione conjugates, vacuolar
    uptake, **1**, 809
medicine, and DNA chemistry, **7**, 4
medioresinol
  biosynthesis, **1**, 673, 688
  occurrence, **1**, 673
Mediterranean fruit fly *see* Ceratitis capitata
medium-chain-acyl-CoA dehydrogenase (MCADH),
    characterization, **1**, 50
Megaceros flagellaris, (+)-megacerotonic acid, **1**, 645, 686
(+)-megacerotonic acid, occurrence, **1**, 645, 686
Megalomyrmex foreli
  pyrrolidine alkaloids, **8**, 357
  pyrroline alkaloids, **8**, 357
Megalophanes viciella, 1-methylethyl octanoate, **8**, 209,
    211
(−)-megaphone
  biosynthesis, **1**, 678
  occurrence, **1**, 677
Megoura viciae
  nepetalactone, **8**, 226
  (+)-nepetalactone, **8**, 11
Meisenheimer complexes
  as intermediates, **5**, 73
  stabilization, **5**, 14
Meisenheimer intermediates, biosynthesis, **5**, 72, 14
melacacidin
  isolation, **3**, 753
  occurrence, **3**, 776
melampodin A, antifeedant activity, **8**, 308
melampodinin, antifeedant activity, **8**, 308
Melampodium divaricatum, kolavenol, **8**, 317
MeLan *see* methyllanthionine (MeLan)
melanin
  biosynthesis, **1**, 414, 427
    gene clustering, **1**, 429
Melanoplus sanguinipes, zanthophylline toxicity, **8**, 344
Melia azadirachta see Azadirachta indica
Melia azedarach
  meliacarpins, **8**, 327, 330
  neem triterpenoids, **8**, 330
meliacarpins
  occurrence, **8**, 327, 330
  structure, **8**, 327
Meliaceae
  isoflavonoids, **1**, 774
  limonoids, **8**, 321
meliantriol, antifeedant activity, **8**, 325
Melia toosendan, toosendanin, **8**, 330
Melia volkensii, volkensin, **8**, 330
melittin, occurrence, honeybee venom, **8**, 355
melittin F
  occurrence, honeybee venom, **8**, 355
  structure, **8**, 355
mellein
  biosynthesis, **1**, 416
  occurrence, **8**, 210, 213, 241

mellein, 6-hydroxy- (6HM), biosynthesis, **1**, 416
(*R*)-(−)-mellein, occurrence, **1**, 134
Meloe proscarabeus, cantharidin, **8**, 350
melting temperature, determination, **6**, 23
menadione *see* quinone, 2-methyl-1,4-naphtho-
menaquinone, dihydro-, biosynthesis, **2**, 59
menaquinones
    biosynthesis, **1**, 611, 613, 618, 620, **5**, 344
    in *Escherichia coli*, **2**, 54
    from
        isochorismic acid, **1**, 610
        o-succinylbenzoic acid, **1**, 617
    overproduction, **1**, 611
Mendel, Gregor Johann (1822–84), laws of inheritance,
        1, 715
men genes
    menB, sequencing, **1**, 615
    menF
        discovery, **1**, 611
        regulatory mechanisms, **1**, 611
Menispermaceae, erythrina alkaloids, **4**, 42
menogaril, **7**, 606
    quinone methide, UV-vis spectra, **7**, 529
menstrual cycle, and soy-rich diets, **1**, 783
Mentha pulegium, pulegone biosynthesis, **2**, 62
Mentha spicata
    cytochrome P450 oxygenases, **2**, 116
    monoterpenes, **2**, 102
    oil gland secretory cells, **2**, 112
Mentha x piperita, deoxyxylulose phosphate synthase,
        encoding, **2**, 377
1-*p*-menthene-8-thiol, as odor principle, **8**, 165
p-menthenyl cations, deprotonation, **2**, 103
menthofuran
    as allelopathic agent, **8**, 171
    in peppermint, suppression, **2**, 148
    structure, **8**, 226
menthol
    biosynthesis, **2**, 114
    fumigant activity, **8**, 306
    insecticidal activity, **8**, 306
(−)-menthol, biosynthesis, **2**, 144
menthone
    biosynthesis, **2**, 62
    catabolism, **2**, 114
    insecticidal activity, **8**, 306
    ovicidal activity, **8**, 306
(−)-menthone, biosynthesis, **2**, 144
3,4-menthone lactone, biosynthesis, **2**, 114
menthyl acetate, biosynthesis, **2**, 114
M-enzyme, use of term, **3**, 77
merbarone, binding, **7**, 596
Mercuralis annua, sex determination, **8**, 71
mercuribenzenesulfonic acid, *p*-chloro-, as inhibitor, **2**,
        283
mercuribenzoate, *p*-chloro-, as tetrahymanol cyclase
        poison, **2**, 312
mercuribenzoate, *p*-hydroxyl-, in monoterpene synthase
        studies, **2**, 139
mercury-2′-deoxyuridine, 5-chloro-, reactions, with
        methyl acrylate, **7**, 197
mercury gels, oligonucleotide separation, **6**, 223
meristematic zones, formation, **8**, 67
mersacidin
    antibiotic activity, **4**, 276
    biosynthesis, **4**, 280
    cell wall biosynthesis inhibition, **4**, 282
    inhibitory activity, **3**, 281
    structure, **4**, 280
Mesembryanthemum crystallinum, caffeoyl-CoA *O*-
        methyltransferase, **3**, 671
mesifuranone, as odor principle, **8**, 165
mesitylene sulfonyl chloride (MS-Cl), in oligonucleotide
        synthesis, **7**, 107

mesoporphyrin IX, *N*-methyl- (NMM), in porphyrin
        metallation, **6**, 137, **7**, 634
mesoporphyrin IX (MPIX)
    in porphyrin metallation, **7**, 634
    as substrate, **6**, 137
mesquitol
    nucleophilicity, **3**, 760
    oxidative coupling, **3**, 783
mesquitol-(4α→8)-catechin, occurrence, **3**, 783
mesquitol-(5→8)-catechin, occurrence, **3**, 783
messagenin, as allelopathic agent, **8**, 171
messenger RNA *see* mRNA
messenger RNP *see* mRNP
Messor spp.
    anabaseine, **8**, 347
    venoms, **8**, 358
Messor capitatus, anabasine, **8**, 358
Messor ebeninus
    anabaseine, **8**, 358
    anabasine, **8**, 358
Messor mediorubra
    anabasine, **8**, 358
    N-methylanabasine, **8**, 358
metabolism
    and cyanogenesis, **1**, 884
    high energy bonds in, **4**, 222
metabolites
    antagonistic activity, **4**, 199
    biosynthesis, **4**, 196
        physiological roles, **4**, 196
    in chemical defense, **8**, 465
    C-prenylation, **1**, 742
    occurrence, **8**, 529
    Porifera, **8**, 553
    primary vs. secondary, **1**, 1
    see also microbial metabolites; secondary metabolites
metal complexes, applications, DNA structure probes, **7**,
        85
metal hydroxides, as bases, **6**, 157
metal ion catalysts, discovery, **6**, 236
metal ion cleavage, in RNA studies, **6**, 157
metal ions
    aqueous, in DNA structure probing, **7**, 86
    binding
        monovalent, **6**, 157
        site-specific, **6**, 157
    coordination
        inner-sphere, **6**, 157
        outer-sphere, **6**, 157
    divalent
        effects on glycosyltransferase activity, **3**, 73
        in ribozymes, **6**, 157
    and DNA damage, **7**, 417
    hard vs. soft, **6**, 221
    3′-hydroxyl group activation, **6**, 236
    as Lewis acids, **6**, 236
    and RNA folding, **6**, 157
    roles
        in Group I ribozyme catalysis, **6**, 257
        in hairpin ribozyme catalysis, **6**, 159, 251
        in hammerhead ribozyme catalysis, **6**, 159
        in ribonuclease P catalysis, **6**, 260
        in RNA catalysis, **6**, 150, 157
metalloenzymes
    evolution, **6**, 141
    ribozymes as, **6**, 157
    superfamily, **5**, 68
metalloglutathione transferases, **5**, 62
metallophosphatases
    biochemistry, **5**, 157
    characterization, **5**, 154
metalloporphyrins
    applications, DNA structure probes, **7**, 89

in DMA damage, **7**, 379
metalloproteinases, Zn^{2+}-dependent, **5**, 59
metalloribozymes
    artificial, **6**, 134
    catalysis, **6**, 134
    evolution, **6**, 141
metal rescue, in RNA studies, **6**, 157
metals
    in catalysis, selection studies, **6**, 141
    in ribozyme catalysis, **6**, 141
    as substrates, **6**, 137
    thiophilic, **6**, 158
Metamasius hemipterus
    ferruginol, **8**, 245
    2-methyl-4-heptanol, **8**, 246
    5-nonanol, **8**, 212
metamorphosis, larval, promoters, **8**, 441
metaphosphates, as intermediates, **5**, 142
Metarhizium anisopliae
    destruxin synthetase, **1**, 540
    swainsonine, **3**, 134
metastasis
    inhibition, **3**, 142
    ST6Gal I expression, **3**, 46
m-methandienol, occurrence, **8**, 224
methane, dichloro-, hydrolysis, **5**, 407
methane, hydroxyglutathionyl-, decomposition, **5**, 408
methane, tetranitro-, effects, on P-protein, **5**, 353
methane, tris(hydroxymethyl)amino- (Tris), applications,
    in RNA structural probing, **6**, 69
methaneboronic acid, in brassinosteroid studies, **8**, 100
methane hydroxylase *see* methane monooxygenase
methane monooxygenase, **3**, 338
    occurrence, **5**, 219
    oxygenation catalysis, mechanisms, **5**, 218
    properties
        catalytic, **5**, 218
        molecular, **5**, 218
    radical trap substrates, **5**, 219
    rebound mechanisms, **5**, 219
    soluble, **5**, 218
        components, **5**, 218
    stereochemical probes, **5**, 221
methane,NAD(P)H:oxygen oxidoreductase
    (hydroxylating) *see* methane monooxygenase
methanes, divinyl, in polyunsaturated fatty acids, **1**, 161
methanesulfon-*m*-anisidine, 4′-(9-acridinylamino)- *see*
    amsacrine
methanesulfonyl chloride, reactions, with guanosine
    nucleoside, **7**, 118
methanethiol, phenyl-, applications, **3**, 758
methanethiolsulfonate, methyl, as inhibitor of patchouli
    synthase, **2**, 185
Methanobacterium formicicum, coenzyme M, **1**, 833
Methanobacterium thermoautotrophicum
    geranylgeranyl diphosphate synthase
        gene cloning, **2**, 87
        purification, **2**, 87
    geranyl*trans*transferases, **5**, 324
Methanobacterium thermoformicicum, geranylgeranyl
    diphosphate synthase, purification, **2**, 87
Methanococcus jannaschii
    cbi genes, **4**, 153
    cyanocobalamin biosynthesis, **4**, 150
Methanococcus volta, *N*-(7-mercaptoheptanoyl)threonine
    phosphate biosynthesis, **1**, 834
methanol
    occurrence, **8**, 209
    as source of hydrogen, **7**, 560
methanol, methylazoxy-, insect sequestration, **8**, 362
Methanosarcina spp., coenzyme M, **1**, 833
Methanosarcina thermophila, 7-mercaptoheptanoic acid,
    1, 834

Methanothrix soehngenii, acetate-CoA ligase, **1**, 47
methicillin, biosynthesis, **3**, 283
methicillin-resistant *Staphylococcus aureus* (MRSA)
    antibiotic resistance, **3**, 5, **4**, 197
    inhibition, **8**, 594
    peptidoglycan enzymes, **3**, 274
methidiumpropylethylenediamine tetraacetate–iron(II)
    complex (MPE-EDTA/Fe^{II}, applications,
    DNA structure probes, **7**, 86
D,L-methionine, effects on cephalosporin C production,
    4, 176
D,L-[^{14}C]methionine, as lignin precursor, **3**, 643
L-methionine
    as esperamicin A$_1$ precursor, **7**, 554
    radiolabeled, **2**, 369
    as sparsomycin precursor, **1**, 847
    as substrate, **8**, 93
methionine cascade, precursors, **8**, 458
methionine cycle, in ethylene biosynthesis, **8**, 95
methionine repressor *see* MetJ
methionine(s)
    biosynthesis, **4**, 354, **5**, 185, 209, 217
    codon, AUG, **4**, 358
    in cyclopropanation studies, **1**, 65
    early studies, **3**, 643
    labeling studies, **8**, 240
    as starting material(s)
        for enediyne antibiotics, **7**, 554
        for gonyauline, **8**, 458
methionine synthase *see* *O*-acetylhomoserine (thiol)-lyase
methoprene
    applications, mosquito larvae control, **8**, 275
    toxicity, **8**, 275
methoxylamine, applications, DNA structure probes, **7**,
    93
methoxyneurosporene desaturases
    definition, **2**, 340
    homologues, **2**, 343
m-methoxyphenylacetyl-CoA, structure, **4**, 264
p-methoxyphenylacetyl-CoA, structure, **4**, 264
methyl, as phosphate protecting groups, **7**, 130
N-methylanthraniloyl-CoA, in acridone biosynthesis, **1**,
    759
L-*threo*-3-methylaspartate carboxy-aminomethylmutase
    see methylaspartate mutase
methylaspartate mutase
    catalysis, **5**, 272
    EPR spectra, **5**, 272
    histidine side chains, **5**, 268
    occurrence, **5**, 272
    reactions, **5**, 264
P-methylation
    mediation, **1**, 868
    substrates, **1**, 871
trans-methylation, animal studies, **3**, 643
S-methyl coenzyme M (MeCoM), biosynthesis, **1**, 833
methylenedioxy rings, biosynthesis, **1**, 802
2-methyleneglutarate carboxy-methylenemethylmutase
    see 2-methyleneglutarate mutase
2-methyleneglutarate mutase, reactions, **5**, 264
α-*exo*-methylene-γ-lactone, as dienophile, **1**, 374
methylenes, polyketo-, as intermediates, **1**, 2, 3
methylenes, poly-β-keto-
    chain length, **1**, 417
    chains, in polyketides, **1**, 411
    extender units, **1**, 411
    folding pattern variations, **1**, 417
    starter units, **1**, 411
5,10-methylenetetrahydrofolate:glycine
    hydroxymethyltransferase *see* threonine aldolase
methylenetetronate, cyclohexane ring formation, **1**, 370
methylglutaconyl-CoA hydratase, **2**, 17
methyl groups

in esperamicin A₁, biosynthetic origin, **1**, 566
in lignins, **3**, 643
methyl isosartortuoate, occurrence, **1**, 378
methylmalonyl-CoA
    biosynthesis, **8**, 240
    as substrate, **1**, 357
methylmalonyl-CoA mutase
    catalysis, **5**, 271
        mechanisms, **5**, 272
    EPR studies, **5**, 175, 269
    histidine side chains, **5**, 268
    occurrence, **5**, 271
    reactions, **5**, 264
    structure, **5**, 175, 272
methyl neosartortuoate, occurrence, **1**, 378
Methylobacterium spp., glucose metabolism, **2**, 50
Methylobacterium extorquens, threonine aldolase,
        cloning, **3**, 401
Methylobacterium fujisawaense
    hopanoids
        biosynthesis, **2**, 49
        labeling studies, **2**, 53
    isoprenoids
        biosynthesis, **2**, 377
        labelingstudies, **2**, 51
Methylobacterium organophilum
    hopanoids
        biosynthesis, **2**, 49
        labeling studies, **2**, 53
Methylococcus capsulatus
    cDNA cloning, **2**, 250
    hopene cyclase, gene cloning, **2**, 313
    hopene cyclase gene, upstream, **2**, 313
    methane monooxygenase, **5**, 219
Methylosinus trichosporium, methane monooxygenase, **5**,
        219
(*R*)-2-methyl-3-oxopropanoyl-CoA CoA-
        carbonylmutase *see* methylmalonyl-CoA
        mutase
m-methylphenylacetyl-CoA, structure, **4**, 264
p-methylphenylacetyl-CoA, structure, **4**, 264
6-methylsalicylic acid synthase (MSAS)
    assays, **1**, 349
    catalysis, **1**, 346, 361
        steric control, **1**, 359
    cDNA, **1**, 356
    characterization, **1**, 3
    cleavage sites, **1**, 350
    dehydratase reactions, **1**, 412
    gene cloning, **1**, 412
    inactivation, **1**, 357
    isolation, **1**, 349
    keto reductase reactions, **1**, 412
    limited proteolytic digestion studies, **1**, 350
    malonyl-CoA decarboxylase activity, **1**, 361
    mass spectra, **1**, 349
    mechanisms, **1**, 359
    nucleotide sequence, **1**, 355
    occurrence, **1**, 349
    properties, **1**, 349
    protein crosslinking studies, **1**, 351
    purification, **1**, 349, 410, 411
    relationship, to mammalian type I enzymes, **1**, 356
    sequencing, **1**, 348
    stereochemistry, **1**, 358
    structure, **1**, 350
        head-to-head model, **1**, 351
        head-to-tail model, **1**, 351
        three-dimensional, **1**, 362
    substrate specificity, **1**, 347, 356
    triacetic acid lactone biosynthesis, **1**, 357
    in vitro studies, **1**, 358
methyl sarcophytoate, occurrence, **1**, 378

P-methyltransferase, detection, **1**, 874
methyltransferases
    base-flipping mechanisms, **6**, 101
    catalysis, **3**, 519, 8
    identification, **1**, 423
    inhibition, **1**, 739
    prenyl protein-specific, **2**, 359
        steady-state kinetic analysis, **2**, 359
    roles, in pectin biosynthesis, **3**, 518
3′-*O*-methyltransferases, occurrence, **1**, 739, 800
4′-*O*-methyltransferases, occurrence, **1**, 739, 799
O-methyltransferases, occurrence, **1**, 625, 661, 739, **3**,
        644
O-methyltransferases, *S*-adenosylmethionine-dependent,
        characterization, **1**, 458
MetJ, SELEX studies, **7**, 628
metyrapone
    as inhibitor, **1**, 393
    in prochaetoglobosin studies, **1**, 393
mevaldehyde
    as intermediate, **2**, 32
    oxidation, **2**, 32
    reduction, **2**, 33
mevaldyl-CoA
    as intermediate, **2**, 32
    oxidation, **2**, 32
(±)-mevalolactones (MVL)
    incorporation, rates, **2**, 381
    labeled, as ginkgolide precursors, **2**, 371, 379
mevalonate
    biosynthesis, **2**, 33
    in hydroxymethylglutaryl-CoA reductase degradation
        studies, **2**, 38
    incorporation, **2**, 377
    roles
        in isoprenoid biosynthesis, **2**, 53, **8**, 219
        as monoterpene precursor, **2**, 106
mevalonate, 5-pyrophospho-, as intermediate, **2**, 3
(*R*)-mevalonate
    from, acetyl-CoA, **2**, 16
    as starting material, for isoprenoids, **2**, 22, 24
(*S*)-mevalonate:NAD⁺ oxidoreductase (CoA-acylating)
        see hydroxymethylglutaryl-CoA reductase(s)
(*R*)-mevalonate:NADP⁺ oxidoreductase (CoA-
        acylating) *see* hydroxymethylglutaryl-CoA
        reductase(s)
mevalonic acid
    from, acetyl-CoA, **2**, **15–44**
    incorporation, **2**, 378
        into abscisic acid, **8**, 84
    inhibitors, **2**, 353
    radiolabeled, studies, **2**, 353
    as starting material
        for isopentenyl diphosphate, **2**, 3
        for isoprenoids, **2**, 3
mevalonic acids, labeled, feeding experiments, **8**, 84
mevastatin, discovery, **2**, 25
mevinolin
    as hydroxymethylglutaryl-CoA reductase inhibitor, **2**,
        378
    in protein farnesyl group analysis, **2**, 355
    stable-isotope labeled precursors, incorporation, **1**, 384
    as sterol inhibitor, **2**, 60
Mexican fruit flies, sex pheromones, **8**, 236
mexicanin F, occurrence, **1**, 375
MFA2 mRNA
    deadenylation, **6**, 207
        rates, **6**, 206, 208
    degradation, **6**, 212
    mutations, *cis*-acting, **6**, 206
    stabilization, **6**, 209
    3′ UTR, **6**, 208
MFA2 transcripts

decapped, **6**, 209
decay, **6**, 207
studies, **6**, 206
*MF*α1 transcripts, accumulation, **6**, 209
*MGAT*1 gene, localization, **3**, 50
*MGAT*2 gene
　　CCAAT box, **3**, 52
　　localization, **3**, 52
MGDG *see* glycerol, monogalactosyldiacyl- (MGDG)
Micale cecilia, *Trichoderma harzianum* in, **8**, 600
mice
　　acetylcholinesterase, **5**, 122
　　β-*N*-acetylglucosaminylglycopeptide β-1,4-
　　　　galactosyltransferase studies, **3**, 44
　　albumin mRNA, **6**, 214
　　chromosomes
　　　　3F2, **3**, 23
　　　　4A13, **3**, 23
　　3,4-dehydro-*exo*-brevicomin, **8**, 213
　　(*E,E*)-α-farnesene, **8**, 227
　　(*E*)-β-farnesene, **8**, 227
　　*Fdft*1 genes, mapping, **2**, 262
　　immune responses, **7**, 632
　　mammary gland proliferation stimulation, **1**, 782
　　α-1,3-mannosyl-glycoprotein β-1,2-*N*-
　　　　acetylglucosaminyltransferase, genes, **3**, 50
　　2-(2′-methylbutyl)-4,5-dihydrothiazole, **8**, 220
　　pheromones, **8**, 213
　　squalene epoxidase, **2**, 270
　　see also knockout mice; *Mus musculus*; transgenic mice
micelles
　　fringed, concept of, **3**, 539
　　organization, concept of, **3**, 538
　　use of term, **3**, 538
Michaelis complexes, biosynthesis, **5**, 74
Michaelis–Menten complexes, formation, **6**, 240, 250
Michaelis–Menten equation, **5**, 103
Michaelis–Menten mechanism, **5**, 103
miconidin, effects, on herbivores, **8**, 139
microalgae
　　bioluminescence, **8**, 457
　　　　circadian rhythm studies, **8**, 457
　　and marine invertebrates, symbiosis, **8**, 426
　　studies, **8**, 619
microbial chemical ecology, and microbial hormones, **8**,
　　377–413
microbial dehalogenases
　　biochemistry, **5**, **401–422**
　　evolutionary origin, **5**, 402
　　future research, **5**, 420
　　mechanisms, diversity, **5**, 419
microbial hormones
　　and microbial chemical ecology, **8**, **377–413**
　　use of term, **8**, 378, 380
　　see also pheromones
microbial metabolites
　　bacteria, **8**, 587
　　blue-green algae, **8**, 603
　　fungi, **8**, 599
microbial resistance, mechanisms, **4**, 197
microcin B17, biosynthesis, **1**, 850
microcins, biosynthesis, **4**, 202
Micrococcus spp.
　　diketopiperazines, **8**, 587
　　isopentenyl diphosphate, **2**, 46
　　in *Tedania ignis*, **8**, 587
Micrococcus denitrificans, 3-hydroxyaspartate aldolase, **3**,
　　403
Micrococcus luteus
　　base excision repair pathway, **5**, 393
　　DNA polymerases, **7**, 220
　　geranylgeranyl diphosphate synthase, **2**, 86
　　glucose-1-phosphate adenylyltransferase, **3**, 469

glycitein, demethylation, **1**, 815
hexaprenyl diphosphate synthases, gene cloning, **2**, 90
trans-octaprenyl*trans*transferases, **2**, 91
Micrococcus luteus B-P 26, hexaprenyl diphosphate
　　synthases, **2**, 88
Micrococcus lysodeikticus, geranyl diphosphate
　　synthases, **2**, 121
Micrococcus varians
　　var genes, **4**, 292
　　variacin excretion, **4**, 279
microcybin, occurrence, **1**, 380
microcystin LR, occurrence, **8**, 610
microcystin(s)
　　biosynthesis, **4**, 203
　　hepatotoxicity, **4**, 200
　　protein phosphatases inhibition, **8**, 610
　　tumor promoters, **8**, 610
microfibrils, cellulose studies, **3**, 566, 587
microgravity, compression wood formation studies, **3**, 694
microheterogeneity, concept of, **3**, 41
Micromonospora chersina, dynemicin, **7**, 574
Micromonospora chersina M956-1, dynemicin A, **1**, 559
Micromonospora echinospora ssp. *calichensis*,
　　calicheamicin, **7**, 568
Micromonospora globosa, deoxydynemicin, **7**, 574
Micromonospora viridifaciens, exo-α-sialidase, **5**, 294
microorganisms
　　anaerobic, dehalogenation, **5**, 420
　　eicosanoids, **1**, 208
　　intercellular communications, **8**, 378
　　non-fungal, prenylation, **2**, 363
　　pathogenic, and plant defense, **1**, 131
microsomal epoxide hydrolase (mEH)
　　active site residues, **5**, 56
　　alkyl-enzyme intermediates, **5**, 55
　　and endoplasmic reticulum, **5**, 54
　　mechanisms, catalytic, **5**, 55
　　structure, **5**, 54
microsomal glutathione *S*-transferase-II, sequencing, **1**,
　　280
microsomal glutathione transferases, in xenobiotic
　　metabolism, **5**, 62
Microsporum canis, activity against, **1**, 691
microtubules
　　assembly inhibition, **8**, 606
　　disruption, **1**, 127
Microtus pennsylvanicus, feeding, phenolic toxicity
　　reduction, **8**, 139
MIF *see* macrophage migration inhibitory factor (MIF)
Migdolus fryans, L-isoleucine, **8**, 221
migration inhibition factor (MIF) *see* macrophage
　　migration inhibitory factor (MIF)
migratory locusts *see* *Locusta migratoria*
milk, bovine, galactosyltransferase studies, **3**, 113
milkweed bug *see* *Oncopeltus fasciatus*
millipedes *see* *Polyzonium rosalbum*
mimosine, effects, on herbivores, **8**, 146
minimycin, isolation, **8**, 390
minizymes
　　activity, **6**, 238
　　use of term, **6**, 238
minor-major groove binding model, in esperamicin A₁, **7**,
　　574
mint, monoterpene metabolism, **2**, 116
mirabilene isonitrile A, structure, **8**, 610
Mirabilis jalaba, ocimene, **8**, 161
mirabimide E, structure, **8**, 610
mirror carp *see* *Cyprinus carpio*
misonidazole
　　as dioxygen substitute, **7**, 583
　　　　DNA damage sensitization, **7**, 417
misoprostol, biological activity, **1**, 196
missense mutations, human, **5**, 79

mistletoes
  lignins, **3**, 700
  see also Phoradendron spp.; *Viscum* spp.
mites
  citral, **8**, 223
  6-methylsalicylic aldehyde, **8**, 211
  sex pheromones, **8**, 214
  see also Acarina; *Caloglyphus rodriguezi; Tetranychus
    urticae; Tortonia* spp.; *Tyrophagus* spp.
mithramycin
  biological activity, **3**, 323
  biosynthesis, **1**, 480
  2,6-dideoxy-D-*arabino*-hexose, **3**, 313
  structure, **3**, 324
mitochondria, isopentenyl diphosphate incorporation, **2**,
    377
mitochondrial matrix, acyl-CoA transport, **1**, 49
mitogen-activated protein kinase kinase (MAPKK),
    inhibition, **3**, 168
mitogen activated protein kinase (MAPK)
  isolation, **1**, 134
  phospholipase A$_2$ activation, **1**, 134
  and Ras proteins, **2**, 360
mitomycin C
  acidic activation, **7**, 516
  applications
    antibiotics, **7**, 529
    antineoplastic agents, **7**, 514
  conjugation, to oligonucleotides, **7**, 159
  DNA damage, redox-dependent, **7**, 529
  mechanism of DNA reactions, **7**, 515
  monofunctional vs. bifunctional activation, **7**, 516
  oxygen radical production by, **7**, 517
  reductive activation of, **7**, 515
  sequence specificity of cross-linking, **7**, 516
mitomycins, DNA damage induction, **7**, 514
mitonafide, inhibition, **7**, 606
mitoxantrone
  DNA binding, **7**, 606
  as DNA topoisomerase II inhibitor, **7**, 603
mixed lymphocyte reaction (MLR) assays, didemnin
    studies, **8**, 530
MM46115, structure, **1**, 370
MMO *see* methane monooxygenase
M motif *see* His motif
MMTr group, as 5'-hydroxyl protecting group, **7**, 126
Mn^{3+}-PGH synthase, reactions, with hydroperoxides, **5**,
    236
MNS genes
  *MNS*1
    cloning, **3**, 21
    and α1,2-mannosidase activity, **3**, 21
    overexpression, **3**, 21
MNU *see* urea, *N*-methyl-*N*-nitroso- (MNU)
moa genes
  moaD, encoding, **1**, 836
  moaE, encoding, **1**, 836
Modiolus demissus, prostaglandins, **1**, 244
moe genes
  moeB, **1**, 835
    roles, **1**, 836
moenomycin A, isolation, **3**, 281
moiramide B, methicillin-resistant *Staphylococcus aureus*
    inhibition, **8**, 594
molecular biology
  addressing problems, **7**, 619
  and chemistry, relevance, **7**, 6
  DNA, overview, **7**, 1–13
  techniques, **7**, 6, 8
molecular cloning
  techniques, **7**, 620
  vectors, **7**, 620
molecular dynamics simulations, DNA conformation, **7**,
    76

molecular electrostatic potential surfaces, preparation, **5**,
    92
molecularity
  in nucleic acid transition curves, **7**, 23
  pseudomonomolecular behavior, **7**, 32
molecular mimicry, concept of, **6**, 202
molecular modeling, enediyne antibiotics, **7**, 557
molecular probes
  design, **1**, 462, **7**, 451
  of DNA structure, **7**, **81–103**
molecular recognition, applications, **7**, 355
molecules
  outer membrane-associated, **3**, 228
  resonance in, **6**, 5
    and J-coupling, **6**, 5
mollisacacidin, condensation rates, **3**, 753
mollisacacidin analogues, pyrocatechol functionality, **3**,
    754
mollisin, biosynthesis, **1**, 3
Mollusca
  chemical defense, **8**, 462
  feeding attractants, **8**, 418
  feeding stimulants, **8**, 418
  larval settlement induction, **8**, 432
  prostaglandins, **1**, 244
  *see also Cyerce cristallina; Haminoea navicula; Tethys
    fimbria*
molybdate, phosphatase inhibition, **5**, 158
molybdopterin
  precursors, **1**, 837
  in pterin molybdenum cofactor biosynthesis, **1**, 835
momilactone A, biosynthesis, **1**, 131
momililactones, biosynthesis, **2**, 230
monachalure, occurrence, **8**, 207
monarch butterflies
  male pheromones, **8**, 225
  see also Danaus plexippus
Monascus ruber, compactin, **1**, 422
monensin
  biosynthesis, **1**, 483
  cellular transport inhibition, **3**, 88
  effects, on trans Golgi network, **3**, 96
  isolation, **4**, 200
mon genes
  cloning, **1**, 483
  sequencing, **1**, 483
monoaic acid, occurrence, **1**, 68
monobactamic acid, 3-amino-, acylation, **4**, 262
monobactams
  biosynthesis, **4**, 188
  characterization, **4**, 240
  occurrence, **4**, 187
monocarboxylic acids, detection, **1**, 297
monocarboxylyl residues, detection, **1**, 298
Monoclea forsteri, ene–yne metabolites, **1**, 228
monoclonal antibodies, **7**, 570
Monocotyledoneae, cell walls, **3**, 498
monocrotaline
  biosynthesis, **4**, 32
  insect sequestration, **8**, 361
  properties, **7**, 518
monocyclofarnesyl diphosphate, as intermediate, **2**, 192
monocytes
  activation, **3**, 182
  lipopolysaccharide activation, **3**, 182
monoepoxylignanolides, applications, germination
    inhibitors, **1**, 695
monoglucosidase, apoplastic, resistance, **1**, 884
monoglucosides, occurrence, **1**, 882
monoglucosides, cyanogenic, translocation, **1**, 884
monolactams
  biochemistry, **4**, 187
  biosynthesis, **4**, 188

monolignols
  biochemical fate, **3**, 677
  biosynthesis, **3**, 626
    control points, **3**, 629
    factors affecting, **3**, 626
    genetics, **3**, 631
    metabolic pool sizes, **3**, 627
    nitrogen availability, **3**, 626
  biosynthetic enzymes, **3**, 631
    localization, **3**, 658
  biosynthetic pathways
    multi-site modulation vs. rate-limiting steps, **3**, 630
    phenylpropanoid, **3**, 626
  coupling, **1**, 678, 685, **3**, 703
  dehydrogenation, early *in vitro* studies, **3**, 703
  dehydrogenative coupling, enzymes and proteins in, **3**, 708
  dimerization, **3**, 732
  from, phenylalanine, **3**, 677
  gene expression, **3**, 658
  intracellular transport, mechanisms, **3**, 680
  metabolism, **1**, 678
  partitioning, **3**, 677
  roles, in lignification, **3**, 703
  as starting materials, for lignins, **3**, 618
  transport, **1**, 687
Monomorium spp.
  cembrene A, **8**, 230
  indolizidine alkaloids, **8**, 357
  pyrrolizidine alkaloids, **8**, 357
Monomorium pharaonis
  control, **8**, 275
  faranal, **8**, 237
  trail pheromones, **8**, 215
monooxygenase(s)
  internal, **1**, 431
  occurrence, **5**, 418
  in oxidative degradation of polycyclic aromatic hydrocarbons, **5**, 53
monooxygenases, cytochrome P450-dependent
  cloning, **1**, 627
  dehydroabietane processing, **2**, 395
monophosphorothioates, properties, **6**, 138
Mono Q, high resolution anion exchange fast liquid chromatography, **4**, 327
monorden, occurrence, **1**, 534
monosaccharides
  activated, biosynthesis, **3**, 203
  biosynthesis, inhibition, **3**, 275
  conjugation, **1**, 683
  early studies, **3**, 530, 533
  ^{13}C NMR spectra, **3**, 560
  nucleotide-linked, biosynthesis, **3**, 249
monoterpene cyclases
  irreversible inhibitors, **5**, 328
  mechanistic studies, **5**, 325
  use of term, **2**, 122
monoterpenes
  applications
    flavorants, **2**, 101
    industrial, **2**, 101
    medicinal, **2**, 101
    perfumes, **2**, 101
  biosynthesis, **2**, 8, 60, 62, **97–153**
    chromatography, **2**, 119
    enzyme assays, **2**, 118
    enzyme enrichment, **2**, 118
    enzyme isolation, **2**, 117
    enzymology, **2**, 124
    experimental methods, **2**, 116
    future research, **2**, 147
    genetics, **2**, 115
    immunoblotting, **2**, 114

in vivo feeding experiments, **2**, 117
    Northern blot analysis, **2**, 114
    plastid isolation, **2**, 118
    in specialized structures, **2**, 110
    via cyclization, **2**, 122
  catabolism, **2**, 114
  classification, **2**, 102
  distribution, **2**, 100
  and geranyl diphosphate synthase, **2**, 88
  historical background, **2**, 98
  insecticidal activity, **8**, 306
  irregular, **2**, 102, 107
  loss from leaf litter, **8**, 173
  metabolism, **2**, 110
    regulatory mechanisms, **2**, 113
  modifications, secondary, **2**, 143
  natural functions, **2**, 101
  occurrence, **2**, 100, **8**, 221, 353
    in bark beetles, **8**, 223
    commercial, **2**, 102
    subcellular, **2**, 112
  production
    bioengineering, **2**, 148
    metabolic costs, **2**, 115
  redox, **2**, 146
  regular, **2**, 102
  roles, in chemical communication, **8**, 199
  as secondary metabolites, **2**, 101
  specificity studies, cell-free extracts, **2**, 98
  in terpenoid pathway, **2**, 100
  tritrophic interactions, **2**, 101
  water solubility, **8**, 173
monoterpenes, acyclic, characterization, **2**, 102
monoterpenes, cyclic, from, geranyl diphosphate, **2**, 99
monoterpenes, halogenated, from marine algae, **2**, 106
monoterpenes, menthane
  biosynthesis, **5**, 322
  metabolism, **2**, 146
monoterpenes, *p*-menthane, characterization, **2**, 103
monoterpene synthases
  branching, isotopically sensitive, **2**, 139, 140
  catalysis, **2**, 125
  cDNA encoding, **2**, 141
  characterization, **2**, 125
    immunochemical, **2**, 125
  chemical modification, **2**, 126
  cloning, **2**, 120, 141
  DDXXD motifs, **2**, 143
  expression, **2**, 141
  from herbaceous angiosperms, **2**, 127
  in fungi, unproven, **2**, 202
  GC-MS analysis, **2**, 211
  inhibitors, **2**, 126
  kinetic isotope effect
    induced, **2**, 139
    intrinsic, **2**, 140
    secondary, **2**, 140
  mechanisms, **2**, 125
  multiple products, **2**, 139
  purification, **2**, 124
  stereochemistry, **2**, 127
  use of term, **2**, 122
monoterpenoid indole alkaloids
  biosynthesis, **4**, 46, **109–138**
  from, vincoside, **4**, 113
monoterpenoids
  structural diversity, **5**, 325
  toxicity, to insects, **8**, 143
  see also monoterpenes
montanin B
  antifeedant activity, **8**, 319
  occurrence, **8**, 319
Monte Carlo simulation, in Claisen rearrangement studies, **5**, 351

montelukast, applications, antiasthmatic agents, **1**, 197
mopanane-(4β→6)-fisetinidol, occurrence, **3**, 777
mopanol, condensation, **3**, 754
Moraceae
    calystegines, **3**, 134
    coumarins, **1**, 623
moracin C, as oviposition stimulant, **8**, 156
moray eels *see Gymnothorax javanicus*
More–O'Ferrall–Jencks diagrams, applications, **5**, 142
morphine alkaloids
    biosynthesis, **4**, 35
        stages, **4**, 36
    occurrence, **4**, 35
morphogens, abscisic acid, **8**, 83
morphological differentiation, in prokaryotes, regulatory
        mechanisms, **8**, 400
Mortierella alpina, arachidonic acid, **1**, 209
Morus spp., calystegines, **3**, 134
Morus alba, chalcomoracin, **2**, 64
Morus bombycis, polyprenyl diphosphate synthase, **2**, 92
mosesin-1, activity, **8**, 474
mosquitoes
    control, **1**, 534
    prostaglandin F₂ₐ, **1**, 248
    see also Aedes aegypti; *Culex* spp.
mosses *see* Musci
moths
    Δ¹¹-desaturases, **8**, 205
    pheromones, biosynthetic pathways, **8**, 204
    sex pheromones, **8**, 198
    see also Acrolepiopsis assectella; *Adoxophyes* spp.;
        Aphomia gularis; Arctiidae; *Argyrotaenia velutinana*;
        Corcyra cephalonica; *Eriocrania cicatricella*;
        Estigmene acrea; *Grapholita molesta*; hawkmoths;
        Hepialus spp.; leaf miner moths; *Lobesia botrana*;
        Pectinophora gossypiella; *Phragmatobia*
        fuliginosa; Pyralidae; rice moths; *Stigmella*
        malella; *Thaumetopoea* spp.; wax moths
motuporin
    occurrence, **8**, 576
    structure, **8**, 576
moulting *see* ecdysis
mouse embryo, null mutations, **3**, 59
mouse liver, albumin mRNA, **6**, 214
mouse skeletal muscle, glycogen synthase,
        overexpression, **3**, 489
Mox *see* xanthen-9-yl, 9-*p*-methoxyphenyl- (Mox)
MPE-EDTA/Feᴵᴵ *see* methidiumpropylethylenediamine
        tetraacetate–iron(II) complex (MPE-EDTA/Feᴵᴵ)
MPIX *see* mesoporphyrin IX (MPIX)
MPTA *see* triethylamine, 2-(4-methylphenoxy)- (MPTA)
mRNA
    aberrant, turnover, **6**, 210
    antisense, expression, **2**, 212, **3**, 457
    binding, with antisense oligonucleotides, **7**, 286
    cap structure, **6**, 209
    cross-linking, **6**, 202
    deadenylation
        acceleration, **6**, 207
        cis-acting sequences, **6**, 208
        rates, **6**, 207
    decapping
        deadenylation-independent, **6**, 210
        hypotheses, **6**, 212
        regulatory mechanisms, **6**, 211
    decay, **6**, 205
        products, **6**, 207
    degradation, pathways, **6**, 205
    electroporation, **6**, 213
    mitochondrial, editing, **5**, 95, 96
    RNA editing, **6**, 105
        apolipoprotein B, **6**, 98
    self-splicing, **6**, 110

turnover, in gene expression, **6**, 205
viral, **6**, 213
see also eukaryotic mRNA; pre-mRNA
mRNA cytidine deaminase
    mammalian, biological functions, **5**, 94
    plant mitochondrial, biological functions, **5**, 95
mRNA surveillance
    mechanisms, **6**, 210
    roles, **6**, 210
mRNP, roles, in deadenylation, **6**, 208
MRSA *see* methicillin-resistant *Staphylococcus aureus*
        (MRSA)
mrs genes, *mrsA*, cloning, **4**, 295
MRT genes
    *MRT*1, functions, **6**, 211
    *MRT*3, functions, **6**, 211
*MRTri*5 gene, isolation, **2**, 203
6MSA *see* salicylic acid, 6-methyl- (6MSA)
MSAS *see* 6-methylsalicylic acid synthase (MSAS)
msb genes, *msbA*, encoding, **3**, 223
MSNT *see* 1,2,4-triazole, 1-(mesitylene-2-sulfonyl)-3-
        nitro- (MSNT)
MSP proteins
    MSP1, biosynthesis, **3**, 304
    MSP2, biosynthesis, **3**, 304
mtm genes, isolation, **1**, 480
MTX *see* maitotoxin (MTX)
mucins
    O-glycans on, **3**, 3, 70
        core structures, **3**, 71
    structure
        core 1, **3**, 71
        core 2, **3**, 71
    sulfated chains, **3**, 80
muconate, 5-carboxymethyl-2-hydroxy-, synthesis, **5**, 34
muconate, 2-hydroxy-
    isolation, **5**, 32
    ketonization, **5**, 41
    synthesis, **5**, 34
cis,cis muconate, NMR studies, **5**, 44
mucopolysaccharides, precipitation, **3**, 791
mucus glycoprotein, palmitoylation, **4**, 15
mulberry leaves, lipoxygenase activity, **1**, 93
Multiple-Carrier Thiotemplate Model *see* thiotemplate
        mechanism
α-multistriatin
    occurrence, **8**, 244
    structure, **8**, 244
Mundulea spp., rotenone, **8**, 340
Mundulea serica, munduserone, **8**, 341
munduserone, occurrence, **8**, 341
mung bean *see Vigna radiata*
muramic acid, *N*-acetyl- (Mur*N*Ac), in peptidoglycan, **3**,
        244
muramic acid, 1,6-anhydro-, biosynthesis, **3**, 269
muramic acid, *N*-glycolyl-, structure, **3**, 244
muramidase(s) *see* lysozyme(s)
mureidomycin A, inhibitory activity, **3**, 280
mureidomycins, antipseudomonal activity, **3**, 280
murein *see* peptidoglycan
mur genes
    encoding, **3**, 258
    murI, localization, **3**, 255
Mur*N*Ac *see* muramic acid, *N*-acetyl- (Mur*N*Ac)
muropeptides, fragments, **3**, 245
Murraya koenigii, carbazole alkaloids, **4**, 54
Murraya paniculata, yuehchukene, **1**, 369
Murrayella periclados
    hepoxillin B₃, **1**, 219
    12*S*-hydroxyeicosatetraenoic acid, **1**, 219
Musca spp., ecdysteroids, **8**, 280
Musca domestica
    activity against, **1**, 693, **8**, 303

(Z,E)-α-bishomofarnesene, **8**, 237
  farnesene, **8**, 269
Myrmicaria spp., indolizidine alkaloids, **8**, 358
Myrmicaria eumenoides
  indolizidine alkaloids, **8**, 358
  limonenes, **8**, 222
Myrmicaria opaciventris, pyrroloindolizidines, **8**, 358
Myrmicaria striata, decacyclic alkaloids, **8**, 358
Myrmica rubra, 3-octanol, **8**, 211
Myrmica scabrinodis
  3-octanol, **8**, 211
  pheromones, **8**, 15
myrocin C
  antitumor properties, **7**, 506
  applications
    antibiotics, **7**, 506
    antineoplastic agents, **7**, 506
    antitumor agents, **7**, 506
  possible DNA reactions of, **7**, 506
myrosinase(s) *see* thioglucosidase(s)
Myrothecium roridum, trichodiene synthase gene,
    sequence, **2**, 203
Myrrha spp., myrrhine, **8**, 351
myrrhine, occurrence, **8**, 351
Myrtaceae, casuarine, **3**, 134
myrtenal, biosynthesis, **8**, 224
myrtenol
  as allelopathic agent, **8**, 171
  occurrence, **8**, 224
Mytilus edulis
  diarrhetic shellfish poisoning, **8**, 489
  dinophysistoxin 1, **8**, 490
  prostaglandins, **1**, 244
  spirolides, **8**, 520

myxin
  applications, antiinfective agents, **7**, 532
  DNA damage induction, **7**, 532
myxobactin
  biosynthesis, **2**, 333, 334
  fatty acid esters, **2**, 346
myxobactone
  biosynthesis, **2**, 333
  fatty acid esters, **2**, 346
Myxococcus xanthus
  A-signal, **8**, 406
  B-signal, **8**, 406
  car nomenclature, **2**, 327
  carotenoid biosynthesis, **2**, 333
    regulatory mechanisms, **2**, 345
  crt genes, **2**, 334, 346
  C-signal, **8**, 406
  developmental signals, **8**, 404
  D-signal, **8**, 407
  E-signal, **8**, 407
  fruiting bodies, **8**, 404
  life cycle, **8**, 404
  morphological differentiation, **8**, 404
    regulatory mechanisms, **8**, 406
  myxospores, **8**, 404
  phosphorelays, **8**, 406
  pigmentation mutants, **2**, 334
  saframycin secretion, **4**, 198
  transcriptional factors, **8**, 406
myxospores, occurrence, **8**, 404
myxoxanthophyll, accumulation, **2**, 337
Myzus persicae
  activity against, **8**, 308
    antifeedant, **8**, 338
    azadirachtin resistance, **8**, 333

N

NAC *see* cysteamine, *N*-acetyl- (NAC)
N-AcO-AAF *see* fluorene, 2-*N*,*N*-acetoxyacetylamino-
 (N-AcO-AAF)
NAD⁺ *see* oxidized nicotinamide–adenine dinucleotide
NADH-cytochrome b₅ oxidoreductase, catalysis, **1**, 35
NADPH *see* reduced nicotinamide adenine dinucleotide
 phosphate (NADPH)
NADPH:acyldihydroxyacetone phosphate
 oxidoreductase, catalysis, **1**, 286
NADPH:adrenodoxin oxidoreductase *see* ferredoxin-
 NADP⁺ reductase
NADPH:alkyldihydroxyacetone phosphate
 oxidoreductase, catalysis, **1**, 288
NADPH-cytochrome-*c* reductases, early studies, **3**, 638
NADPH-cytochrome P450 reductase (P450R), **1**, 889
 purification, **1**, 802, **3**, 639
 x-ray crystal studies, **2**, 269
NADPH-dependent reductase, roles, in monolignol
 biosynthesis, **3**, 638
NADPH:dTDP-6-deoxy-L-*lyxo*-4-hexulose 4-reductase,
 catalysis, **3**, 208
NADPH reductase, occurrence, **1**, 817
naftifine, applications, antifungal agents, **2**, 247, 276
nagilactone D, occurrence, **8**, 312
nagstatin, structure, **3**, 133
NAG-thiazoline, *β*-*N*-acetylhexosaminidase inhibition, **5**,
 297
NAIM *see* nucleotide analogue interference mapping
 (NAIM)
nairaiamides
 occurrence, **8**, 535
 structure, **8**, 535
NAIS *see* nucleotide analogue interference suppression
 (NAIS)
Naja naja atra, venom, phospholipase A₂, **5**, 105, 107, 111
nakienone A
 cytotoxicity, **8**, 609
 occurrence, **8**, 609
namenamicin
 activation, **7**, 581
 applications, **7**, 581
 antibiotics, **7**, 554, 581
 cytotoxicity, **7**, 581
 occurrence, **7**, 581, **8**, 544
 structure, **7**, 554, 581
nanaimoal, occurrence, **2**, 192
nanoprobes, in carbohydrate studies, **3**, 1
naphterpin, biosynthesis, **2**, 59
naphthacenequinones, as DNA topoisomerase I
 inhibitors, **7**, 600
naphthalene
 cyclization, **1**, 414
 degradation, **3**, 375, 384
naphthalene, 1-chloro-, decomposition, **3**, 377
naphthalene, 2-chloro-, decomposition, **3**, 377
naphthalene, 1,8-dihydroxy-, occurrence, **1**, 415
naphthalene, 2,6-dimethyl-, metabolization, **3**, 377
naphthalene, tetrahydroxy-, as intermediate, **1**, 4
naphthalene, 1,3,6,8-tetrahydroxy- (T4HN), structure, **1**,
 414
naphthalene, 1,3,8-trihydroxy- (T3HN), as intermediate,
 1, 427
1(2*H*)-naphthalene, 3,4-dihydro-4,8-dihydroxy- (DDN),
 biosynthesis, **1**, 429
naphthaleneacetic acid, applications, **8**, 34

naphthalene diimides
 DNA dynamics, **7**, 441
 kinetics of association, **7**, 441
 use in the synthesis of threading intercalating agents, **7**,
 440
naphthalenes, aryl-, phosphodiesterase inhibitory
 activity, **1**, 704
1-naphthoate, 2-hydroxy-5-methyl-7-methoxy-, **7**, 558
naphthoate synthase(s), extraction, **1**, 615
1-naphthoic acid, 1,4-dihydro-, structure, **8**, 34
2-naphthoic acid, 1,4-dihydroxy-
 biosynthesis, **1**, 615, 617
 from, *o*-succinylbenzoic acid, **1**, 615
 occurrence, **1**, 613
2-naphthoic acid, 1-hydroxy-, cleavage, **3**, 375
1-naphthol, biosynthesis, **3**, 377
naphthoyl, deoxyadenosine protection, **7**, 123
2-naphthoyl, 3-hydroxy-6-isopropoxy-7,8-dimethoxy-,
 structure, **7**, 575
naphthyridinomycin
 applications, antibiotics, **7**, 499
 covalent DNA adducts with, **7**, 499
 occurrence, **7**, 499
 reduction-dependent DNA reaction, **7**, 499
napyradiomycins, **2**, 59
narains, occurrence, **8**, 442
narbosines, L-rhodinose, **3**, 321
Narcissus pseudonarcissus, geranyl diphosphate synthases,
 2, 122
narcotine, biosynthesis, **4**, 40
nargenicin A
 biosynthesis, **1**, 528
 occurrence, **1**, 528
nargenicin A₁
 biosynthesis, **1**, 370, 374
 feeding experiments, **1**, 384
naringenin, biosynthesis, **1**, 790
naringenin, 2-hydroxy-, as substrate, **1**, 738
naringenin, 6-isopentenyl-, antifungal activity, **8**, 181
naringenin chalcone
 biosynthesis, **1**, 786, 789
 isomerization, **1**, 790
naringenin-chalcone synthase *see* chalcone synthase
 (CHS)
naringenin 3-dioxygenase
 activity, **1**, 726
 biochemistry, **1**, 725
 cDNA clones, isolation, **1**, 726
 genetics, **1**, 726
 molecular biology, **1**, 726
 occurrence, **1**, 725
naringenin,2-oxoglutarate:oxygen oxidoreductase (3-
 hydroxylating) *see* naringenin 3-dioxygenase
narirutin, as oviposition stimulant, **8**, 156
Nasonov pheromone, honeybees, **8**, 223
Nasturtium officinale, phenylalanine ammonia-lyase,
 localization, **3**, 662
Nasutitermes spp., cembrene A, **8**, 230
Nasutitermes princeps, (+)-*α*-pinene, **8**, 222
National Center for Biological Information (NCBI),
 databases, **7**, 646
Natronobacterium pharaonis, geranylfarnesyl diphosphate
 synthase, **2**, 88
natural killer (NK) cells, toxicity suppression, **3**, 53
natural products

biosynthesis
oxygen metabolism, **1**, 448
via shikimate pathway, **1**, 16
carbonyl-containing, **7**, 502
covalent DNA modification, **7**, **491–552**
cyclic carbonate functionality, **1**, 208
Diels–Alder type, **1**, 368
biosynthesis, **1**, 370
biosynthetic studies, **1**, 384
lignans, **1**, 379
DNA damage induction, **7**, 492, 495
classification, **7**, 492
enantiomeric purity, **8**, 7
fungal, production factors, **2**, 207
interactions, with DNA, **7**, 5, 9
oxazolidine-containing, **7**, 499
structural diversity, **1**, 2
structure, developments, **7**, 644
sulfur-containing, biosynthesis, **1**, **825–863**
see also bioactive natural products; marine natural products
natural selection, and enzyme efficiency, **5**, 442
Nauphoeta cinerea, recognition pheromones, **8**, 219
nauphoetin, occurrence, **8**, 219
nazumamide A
occurrence, **8**, 576
structure, **8**, 576
total synthesis, **8**, 576
NC-190, inhibition, **7**, 606
N-CAM *see* nerve cell adhesion molecule (N-CAM)
NCBI *see* National Center for Biological Information (NCBI)
NCS *see* neocarzinostatin (NCS)
NCS-chrom *see* neocarzinostatin chromophore (NCS-chrom)
NDGA *see* guaiaretic acid, nordihydro- (NDGA)
NDP-6-deoxy-4-hexulose-3,5-epimerases, roles, in 6-deoxyhexose biosynthesis, **3**, 334
NDP-6-deoxy-4-hexulose-4-reductases, roles, in 6-deoxyhexose biosynthesis, **3**, 335
NDP-4-keto-6-deoxyhexoses, biosynthesis, **3**, 334
NDP-sugar phoshorylases *see* nucleotidyltransferases
NDP-sugars *see* nucleoside diphosphate sugars (NDP-sugars)
NDP-sugar synthases *see* nucleotidyltransferases
neamine, interactions, with RNA, **6**, 194
nearest-neighbor model, Watson–Crick base pairs, **6**, 29
Nebria brevicollis, effects of pyridopyrazines on, **8**, 361
necic acids, biosynthesis, **4**, 33
necine bases, biosynthesis, **4**, 31
necines, biosynthesis, **4**, 31
Necrodes surinamensis, defense compounds, **8**, 234
α-necrodol, occurrence, **8**, 234
β-necrodol, occurrence, **8**, 234
necrotic lesions phytotoxin-induced, **8**, 178
nectars, constituents, **8**, 162
Nectria haematococca
biochanin A, degradation, **1**, 813
isoflavonoids, **1**, 779
PDA genes, **1**, 813
pisatin, detoxification, **1**, 813
nectriapyrone B, occurrence, **8**, 600
nectrisine, structure, **3**, 130
neem tree *see Azadirachta indica*
neem triterpenoids
applications, in developing nations, **8**, 333
bioassays, **8**, 326
biosynthesis, **8**, 328
insecticidal activity, **8**, 324
prospects, **8**, 332
isolation, **8**, 324
mass spectra, **8**, 328
nomenclature, **8**, 327

properties
chemical, **8**, 328
physiological, **8**, 331
storage problems, **8**, 333
structure, **8**, 327
structure–activity relationships, **8**, 332
world markets, **8**, 333
negative point charges, in oxidosqualene cyclase mechanisms, **2**, 281
neighbor exclusion principle, **7**, 448
in intercalation, **7**, 444
negative cooperation, **7**, 446
Neisseria spp., amylosucrase, **3**, 445
Neisseria gonorrhoeae
gal genes, **3**, 204
lipopolysaccharide biosynthesis, **3**, 228
lipopolysaccharides, **3**, 185
Neisseria meningitidis
N-acetylneuraminate synthase, **3**, 390
aminoethanolphosphate, **3**, 197
gal genes, **3**, 204
lipopolysaccharides, **3**, 5, 185
biosynthesis, **3**, 228
mutants, **3**, 390
3-phosphoglyceric acid, **3**, 390
nematocides, lignans, **1**, 694
Nematoda, arachidonic acid metabolism, **1**, 249
neocarzinostatin
applications, antibiotics, **7**, 554
biosynthesis, studies, **1**, 559
^{13}C-labeled acetate incorporation, **1**, 567
occurrence, **1**, 567
neocarzinostatin, holo-, activation by 2-mercaptoethanol, **7**, 565
neocarzinostatin chromophore (NCS-chrom), **1**, 557
absolute stereochemistry, **7**, 559
activation
acid-induced, **7**, 561
apo-neocarzinostatin-directed, **7**, 565
base-catalyzed, **7**, 562
by nucleophiles, **7**, 559
by radicals, **7**, 559
by sodium borohydride, **7**, 559
by [2-^{2}H$_2$]-thioglycolate, **7**, 560
light-induced, **7**, 561
mechanisms, **7**, 559
thiol-induced, **7**, 559, 560
aerobic treatment, **7**, 561
antibiotic activity, **1**, 14
biosynthesis, **1**, 567
studies, **7**, 554
and bulged DNA cleavage, **7**, 562
cofactors
borohydride, **7**, 558
thiol, **7**, 558
DNA binding, **7**, 567
DNA damage, **7**, 560
activity, **7**, 554
as probe of DNA microheterogeneity, **7**, 567
reactions, with 4-hydroxy thiophenol, **7**, 561
structure, **7**, 558
neocarzinostatin (NCS)
applications, DNA structure probes, **7**, 98
bioconjugation, **7**, 558
biosynthesis, **7**, 558
cofactors
borohydride, **7**, 558
thiol, **7**, 558
crystal structure, **7**, 560
DNA/RNA hybrid damage, **7**, 566
DNA damage, **7**, 566
induction, **7**, 373, 380, 385, 394
DNA strand breakage induction, **7**, 421

occurrence, **7**, 554
oxygen radical production by, **7**, 540
proteolytic activity, **7**, 559
toxicity, **7**, 558
(*E,E,E*)-neocembrene *see* cembrene A
Neocosmospora spp.
cyclosporins, **1**, 534, 534
monorden, **1**, 534
Neocosmospora vasinfecta, cyclosporin C, **1**, 537
Neodiprion pinetum, pheromones, **8**, 14
Neodiprion sertifer
(1*S*,2*S*,6*S*)-diprionylacetate, **8**, 247
pheromones, **8**, 247
neohalicholactone, occurrence, **1**, 243, 244
neoherculin *see* echinacein
neojusticin A, antiinflammatory activity, **1**, 704
neolaurencenynes, occurrence, **1**, 304
neolignans, use of term, **1**, 640
neolinustatin, occurrence, **1**, 885
neomenthol, biosynthesis, **2**, 114
neomycin
applications, antibiotics, **7**, 433
interactions, with RNA, **6**, 194
nonintercalation, **7**, 433
neoplatyphylline, structure, **4**, 33
Neopyrochroa flabellata, cantharidin, **8**, 363
neoquassin, occurrence, **8**, 322
neosaxitoxin, structure, **8**, 485
Neosiphonia superstes, superstolide A, **1**, 371
Neostylopyga rhombifolia, antifeedant activity against, **8**, 338
9′-(*Z*)-neoxanthin, cleavage, **8**, 87
nepetalactone, **8**, 234
occurrence, **8**, 226
(+)-nepetalactone
bioactivity, **8**, 11
occurrence, **8**, 11
neplanocin A, as substrate, **5**, 74
2-*F*-neplanocin A, adenosine deaminase resistance, **5**, 74
Nepytia freemani, 3,13-dimethylheptadecane, **8**, 248
neral, occurrence, **8**, 223, 232
Nerium oleander
cardiac glycosides, **8**, 363
oleandrin, **8**, 363
nerol
biosynthesis, **2**, 102
occurrence, **8**, 222
as starting material
for loganin, **4**, 110
for monoterpenes, **2**, 98
nerolic acid, occurrence, **8**, 222, 223
nerolidol
occurrence, **8**, 227
oxidative cleavage, **8**, 231
nerolidyl diphosphate
conformation, **2**, 8
cyclization, to bisabolyl cation, **2**, 158
from, farnesyl diphosphate, **2**, 156
as intermediate, **2**, 187
isomerization, **5**, 329
role in cyclization, **2**, 191
single turnover reactions, **2**, 193
as substrate, **5**, 329
(3*R*)-nerolidyl diphosphate
steady-state kinetic parameters, **2**, 159
as substrate for trichodiene synthase, **2**, 159
nerolidyl pyrophosphate (NPP) *see* nerolidyl diphosphate
nerol oxide, occurrence, **8**, 225
nerve cell adhesion molecule (N-CAM)
polysialylation, **3**, 49
regulatory mechanisms, **3**, 50
nerve growth factor (NGF)
phosphorylation, **3**, 53

synthesis, stimulation, **8**, 600
neryl compounds, solvolysis, **2**, 122
netropsin
minor groove DNA binding, **7**, 456, 460, 486, 567
molecular comparisons, **7**, 457
torsional flexibility, **7**, 452
NeuAc *see* neuraminate, *N*-acetyl- (NeuAc)
NeuAc9P synthase *see* *N*-acylneuraminate-9-phosphate
synthase
neural factors, release, **8**, 299
neural networks
computational, **5**, 92
transition state prediction, **5**, 93
neuraminate, *N*-acetyl- (NeuAc)
biosynthesis, **3**, 378
occurrence, **3**, 378
neuraminic acid, *N*-acetyl-, K_m, **3**, 381
neuraminic acid, *N*-acetyl-4-*O*-acetyl-, as substrate, **3**, 378
neuraminic acid, 2,7-anhydro-*N*-acetyl-, biosynthesis, **5**, 295
neuraminic acid, 2-deoxy-2,3-dihydro-*N*-acetyl-(DANA), binding, **5**, 295
neuraminic acid, glycolyl-, as substrate, **3**, 378
neuraminic acid, *N*-glycolyl-, K_m, **3**, 381
neuraminidase(s) *see* exo-α-sialidase(s)
neurite promotion, mechanisms, **3**, 50
neuroblastoma cells, glutamate receptor subunits, **5**, 87
neuroblastomas
fucosyltransferases, **3**, 117
galactosyltransferases, **3**, 112
neurocan
binding, **3**, 164
promoters, **3**, 167
neurohaemal organs, localization, **8**, 294
neurohormones, biochemistry, **8**, 302
neuropeptides
applications, insect control agents, **8**, 302
functions, **8**, 294
identification, **8**, 294
insects, **8**, 294
isolation, **8**, 294
release, **8**, 302
roles, in insect development, **8**, 302
Neuroptera, venoms, **8**, 354
neurosecretory cells, distribution, **8**, 294
Neurospora spp., VS RNA, structure, **6**, 154
Neurospora crassa
activity against, **1**, 534
arom gene cluster, **1**, 589
cyclophilins, **1**, 541
dehydroquinases, **1**, 586, 589, 591
2-enoyl-CoA hydratase, **1**, 52
geranylgeranyl diphosphate synthase, gene cloning, **2**, 87
3*R*-hydroxylacyl-CoA dehydrogenase, **1**, 52
qa gene cluster, **1**, 589
quinate dehydrogenase, **1**, 590
shikimate kinase, **1**, 592
shikimate pathway, **1**, 575
type II dehydroquinase, **1**, 588
neurosporene, biosynthesis, **2**, 324, 331, 334
neurosporene, methoxy-, accumulation, **2**, 330
all-*trans*-neurosporene, biosynthesis, **2**, 341
neutrophil elastase *see* leukocyte elastase
neutrophils
activation, **1**, 298
1-alkyl-2-acylglycerophosphocholine, **1**, 291
Nezara spp., (*Z*)-α-bisabolene oxide, **8**, 228
Nezara viridula
(*Z*)-α-bisabolene oxide, **8**, 229
(*E*)-4-oxo-2-decenal, **8**, 213
nezukone, biosynthesis, **2**, 107
NF-1 binding sites, in human squalene synthase, **2**, 261

NF-E1 *see* GATA-1
NFX-2, isolation, **1**, 147
NFX-4, isolation, **1**, 147
NG2, localization, **3**, 164
NGF *see* nerve growth factor (NGF)
nickel, occurrence, **8**, 149
nickel complexes, applications, DNA structure probes, **7**, 89
Nicotiana spp.
 N-acylnornicotines, **8**, 302
 cytokinin-resistant mutants, **8**, 65
 feeders, *Manduca sexta*, **8**, 302
 nicotine, **8**, 347
 toxicity, to *Manduca sexta*, **8**, 302
Nicotiana benthamiana, cDNA cloning, **2**, 250
Nicotiana rustica, nicotine, **3**, 643, **8**, 347
Nicotiana sylvestris
 alkaloids, **8**, 151
 jasmonic acid, **1**, 124
 translocation, **1**, 124
Nicotiana tabacum
 blue mould disease resistance, **8**, 181
 caffeoyl-CoA *O*-methyltransferase, **3**, 671
 capsidiol, **2**, 181
 cell division stimulation, **1**, 695
 cinnamyl-alcohol dehydrogenases, **3**, 656
 cytokinin habituated clones, **8**, 65
 cytokinins, **8**, 57
 flavonoid 3′-*O*-methyltransferase, **1**, 739
 glycosyltransferase, **1**, 129
 HGA methyltransferase, **3**, 519
 hydroxycinnamyl *O*-methyltransferases, **3**, 646
 inhibition, **2**, 251
 in labdane biosynthesis, **2**, 225
 nicotine, **8**, 347
 peroxidases, **3**, 718
 phenylalanine ammonia-lyase, **3**, 659
 gene promoter expression, **3**, 667
 polygalacturonate 4-α-galacturonosyltransferase, **3**, 513
 putrescine *N*-methyltransferase activity, **4**, 27
nicotine
 applications, insecticides, **8**, 302
 contact toxicity, **8**, 348
 isolation, historical background, **8**, 347
 metabolism, **8**, 348
 occurrence, **3**, 643, **8**, 151, 347
 and rotenone compared, **8**, 348
 stability, **8**, 320
 toxicity, **8**, 302
nicotine alkaloids, in induced plant defense, **8**, 150
nicotinic acetylcholine receptors *see* nicotinic receptors
nicotinic acid, as cyanogenic glycoside precursor, **1**, 885, 887
nicotinic acid hydroxylase, catalysis, **4**, 375
nicotinic receptors, peptide ligands for, occurrence, **8**, 480
nicotyrine, occurrence, **8**, 347
niddamycin
 biosynthesis, **1**, 525
 occurrence, **1**, 525
nidurufin, studies, **1**, 455
nif genes, occurrence, **8**, 400
nigakilactone G *see* picrasin A
nigakilactone I *see* picrasin B
Nigrospora oryzae, activity against, **1**, 691
nikkomycins, chitin synthase inhibition, **3**, 286
nimbin
 isolation, **8**, 329
 occurrence, **8**, 330
nis genes
 nisA, nomenclature, **4**, 284
 nisE, encoding, **4**, 297
 nisG, encoding, **4**, 297

nisI, expression, **4**, 299
nisin
 antibacterial activity, **4**, 278, 300
 biosynthesis, **4**, 199, 202
 cell death induction, **4**, 280
 disadvantages, **4**, 299
 early studies, **4**, 278
 expression system, **4**, 298
 gene clusters, localization, **4**, 285
 gene fusion, **4**, 288
 lysis induction, **4**, 281
 mutagenesis, random, **4**, 300
 occurrence, **4**, 276, 278
 producer strains, **4**, 297
 as signal, **4**, 296
 spore germination inhibition, **4**, 281
 structure, **4**, 278
nisin A *see* nisin
nisin lantibiotics
 gene clusters, **4**, 284
 modifying enzymes, **4**, 288
 prepeptides, **4**, 287
 conserved motifs, **4**, 287
 protease LanP, **4**, 291
 structure, **4**, 277
nisin peptides, expression, **4**, 299
nisin Z, properties, **4**, 278
Nis proteins
 NisB
 encoding, **4**, 288
 expression, **4**, 296
 NisC, encoding, **4**, 288
 NisI, structure, **4**, 297
 NisK, structure, **4**, 295
 NisP, **4**, 291
 NisR, structure, **4**, 295
Nitella spp., evolution, **3**, 622
nitidine, occurrence, **7**, 601
Nitidulidae
 pheromones, **8**, 240
 biosynthesis, **8**, 242
 see also Carpophilus spp.
nitrate, (*Z*)-8-tetradecenyl, occurrence, **8**, 207
nitrate, (*Z*)-9-tetradecenyl, occurrence, **8**, 207
nitric oxide
 biosynthesis, **3**, 182
 and prostaglandin biosynthesis, **5**, 239
 reactions, with tyrosyl radicals, **5**, 244
nitrilase, cloning, **8**, 34
nitriles, α-hydroxy-
 biosynthesis, **1**, 887
 glucosylation, **1**, 887
 properties, **1**, 885
 see also cyanohydrin
nitrogen, and glycogen accumulation, **3**, 443
nitrogen fixation, and symbiosis, **8**, 428
nitrogen fixation gene *see nif* genes
nitrogen mustards, applications, DNA structure probes, **7**, 96
nitrogen regulatory protein, binding, **4**, 245
nitrophenol, occurrence, **8**, 212
nitrosamines
 DNA damage induction, **7**, 521
 metabolic activation, **7**, 521
N-nitroso compounds, DNA damage induction, **7**, 520
nitroxide, nucleobase conjugation, **7**, 219
nitroxides, DNA damage sensitization, **7**, 417
Nitzschia alba, ceramide-1-sulfonic acids, **8**, 598
Nitzschia pungens
 and amnesic shellfish poisoning, **1**, 227
 bacillariolides, **1**, 227
NK cells *see* natural killer (NK) cells
NMDA *see* D-aspartate, *N*-methyl- (NMDA)

NMM *see* mesoporphyrin IX, *N*-methyl- (NMM)
NMR *see* nuclear magnetic resonance (NMR)
Nocardia argentinesis, nargenicin A, **1**, 528
Nocardia lactamdurans
  ACV synthetase, encoding, **1**, 840
  cefD gene encoding, **4**, 171
  isopenicillin N epimerase, **1**, 843
  lysine ε-aminotransferase activity, **4**, 165
nocardicins
  applications, **4**, 188
  biosynthesis, **4**, 188
  characterization, **4**, 240
Noctuidae, pheromones, **8**, 207
NodC protein, properties, **1**, 340
NodF protein
  as acyl carrier protein homologue, **1**, 335
  function, compared with acyl carrier protein, **1**, 337
  in nodulation factor acylation, **4**, 206
  properties, **1**, 337
  roles, in fatty acid biosynthesis, **1**, 335
  structure, **1**, 336
nod genes
  APS kinase activity, **1**, 331
  ATP sulfurylase activity, **1**, 331
  homology, **1**, 7
  inducers, **1**, 814
  nodA, **1**, 329
    occurrence, **1**, 340
  nodB, **1**, 329
  nodC, **1**, 329
  nodD, **1**, 328, 780
  nodE, functions, **1**, 7, 332
  nodF, functions, **1**, 7, 332
  nodI, **1**, 329
  nodJ, **1**, 329
  nodT, mutation, **1**, 329
  nodZ, **1**, 331
  occurrence, **1**, 328
  transcription factors, **1**, 328
NodL protein, structure, **4**, 227
Nodularia spumigena, motuporin, **8**, 576
nodulation
  determinants, **1**, 326
  genes, **1**, 328
  mechanisms, **1**, 326
nodule meristems, formation, **1**, 328
nodules
  causes, **8**, 400
  formation, **1**, 7
NOEs *see* nuclear Overhauser effects (NOEs)
nogalamycin
  applications
    antibiotics, **7**, 351, 433, 437
    intercalating agents, **7**, 437
  biosynthesis, **1**, 482
    genetics, **3**, 349, 351
  intercalation sites, **7**, 438
  L-nogalose, **3**, 321
  structure, **7**, 351
L-nogalose, occurrence, **3**, 312, 321
nojirimycin B, structure, **3**, 130
nojirimycin(s)
  antimicrobial activity, **3**, 142
  plant growth inhibition, **3**, 141
  structure, **3**, 130
nojirimycin tetrazole, glycogen phosphorylase inhibition, **5**, 304
Nomada spp., nomadone, **8**, 227
nomadone, occurrence, **8**, 227
nomenclature
  DNA structure, **7**, 56
  proteoglycans, **3**, 163
nomilin, antifeedant activity, **8**, 321

(9*Z*,19*Z*)-9,19-nonacosadiene, occurrence, **8**, 219
nonacosan-2-one, 3,11-dimethyl-, occurrence, **8**, 240
nonacosan-2-one, 3,11-dimethyl-29-hydroxy-
  occurrence, **8**, 247
  structure, **8**, 240
(*Z*)-13-nonacosene, occurrence, **8**, 219
(*Z*)-14-nonacosene, occurrence, **8**, 219
nonactin, acetoacetate incorporation, **1**, 451
(6*Z*,9*Z*)-6,9-nonadecadien-3-one, occurrence, **8**, 208
nonadecane, occurrence, **8**, 218
nonadecane, 3,7-dimethyl-, occurrence, **8**, 249
(3*Z*,6*Z*,9*Z*,11*E*)-1,3,6,9-nonadecatetraene, occurrence, **8**, 207
(3*Z*,6*Z*,9*Z*,11*Z*)-1,3,6,9-nonadecatetraene, occurrence, **8**, 207
3*Z*,6*Z*,9*Z*,18-nonadecatetraene, occurrence, **1**, 218
(3*Z*,6*Z*,9*Z*)-1,3,6,9-nonadecatetraene, occurrence, **8**, 207
(3*Z*,6*Z*,9*Z*)-3,6,9-nonadecatriene, occurrence, **8**, 207, 208
(3*Z*,6*Z*,9*Z*)-1,3,6,9-nonadecatriene, occurrence, **8**, 207
6*Z*,9*Z*,18-nonadecatriene, occurrence, **1**, 218
(*Z*)-10-nonadecenal, occurrence, **8**, 219
(*Z*)-7-nonadecen-11-one, occurrence, **8**, 208
(2*S*)-6,8-nonadien-2-ol, occurrence, **8**, 212
(3*Z*,6*Z*)-3,6-nonadien-1-ol, occurrence, **8**, 212
6,8-nonadien-2-ol, occurrence, **8**, 209
(*E*)-2-(*Z*)-6-nonadienol, biosynthesis, **1**, 84
(2*Z*,6*Z*)-2,6-nonadien-4-olide, as moth aphrodisiac, **8**, 212
(*E*)-6,8-nonadien-2-one, 5-(1-methylethyl)-8-methyl- *see* solanone
nonadrides, as farnesyl-diphosphate farnesyltransferase inhibitors, **2**, 257
nonaketides, biosynthesis, **1**, 417
nonanal, occurrence, **8**, 212
nonanoic acid, occurrence, **8**, 209, 212
nonanoic acid, 4-acetyl-, inhibition, **8**, 114
nonanoic acid, 9-oxo-, occurrence, **1**, 235
nonanol, occurrence, **8**, 212
1-nonanol, (*R*)-4-methyl-, occurrence, **8**, 241
2-nonanol, occurrence, **8**, 212
5-nonanol, occurrence, **8**, 212
5-nonanol, (4*S*,5*S*)-4-methyl- *see* ferruginol
2-nonanone, occurrence, **8**, 212
3-nonanone, (4*S*,6*S*)-4,6-dimethyl-, structure, **8**, 244
3-nonanone, (4*S*,6*S*,7*S*)-7-hydroxy-4,6-dimethyl- *see* serricornin
nonan-3-one, 6-methyl-, occurrence, **8**, 243
5-nonanone, 3-hydroxy-4-methyl-, occurrence, **8**, 245
nonanoyl-CoA, as substrate, **4**, 262
nonaprenyl diphosphate synthases, occurrence, **2**, 92
all-trans-nonaprenyl-diphosphate synthase(s) *see* *trans*-octaprenyl*trans*transferase(s)
nonatriacontane, 13,17-dimethyl-, occurrence, **8**, 249
1,3,7-nonatriene, 4,8-dimethyl-
  in induced plant defense, **8**, 150
  in plant–herbivore–predator interactions, **8**, 152
1,3,7-nonatriene, (*E*)-4,8-dimethyl-, biosynthesis, **8**, 231
1,3,8-nonatriene, (*E*)-3-methyl-7-methylene-, occurrence, **8**, 236
2,4,6-nonatriene, (2*E*,4*E*,6*E*)-5-ethyl-3-methyl-, occurrence, **8**, 240
noncalorimetric methods, **7**, 21
noncoding strand, **7**, 466
non-cytochrome P450 enzyme, squalene epoxidase as, **2**, 267
2*E*-nonenal, 4-hydroperoxy-, occurrence, **1**, 235
2*E*-nonenal, 4-hydroxy-, occurrence, **1**, 234
3*Z*-nonenal, occurrence, **1**, 235
(*E*)-2-nonenal, occurrence, **8**, 212
6-nonene, (2*R*,6*E*)-3-acetoxy-7-methyl- *see* quadrilure
(2*S*,6*Z*)-6-nonen-2-ol, occurrence, **8**, 213
(*E*)-2-nonen-1-ol, occurrence, **8**, 212

(Z)-3-nonen-1-ol, occurrence, **8**, 212
nonenols, as sex pheromones, **8**, 209
nonen-3-one, (4S,6S)-4,6-dimethyl-, occurrence, **8**, 244
4-nonen-3-one, (E)-4,6-dimethyl-, occurrence, **8**, 243
(Z)-6-nonen-2-one, occurrence, **8**, 212, 213
non-proanthocyanidins, biochemistry, **3**, 780
nonsense codons, **6**, 210
    early, localization, **6**, 210
    frameshifting, **6**, 196
non-specific cholinesterase *see* cholinesterase
nonsteroid antiinflammatory agents
    classification, **5**, 247
    effects
        on colon cancer mediation, **5**, 226
        on thromboxane A₂ biosynthesis, **5**, 226
    prostaglandin-endoperoxide synthase inhibition, **1**,
        257, **5**, 247
    side effects, **5**, 226
nonterpenoid C15 compounds, biosynthesis, **1**, 303
(+)-nootkatone, as odor principle, **8**, 165
nopaline, in crown galls, **8**, 399
nor-1 genes
    cloning, **1**, 462
    disruption, **1**, 462
    identification, **1**, 462
noradrenaline, in honeybee venom, **8**, 355
norA genes
    identification, **1**, 462
    translation, **1**, 464
norbelladine, methylation, **4**, 43
norcoclaurine, biosynthesis, **4**, 39
(S)-norcoclaurine, biosynthesis, **4**, 41
norfloxacin, **7**, 462
    applications, antiinfective agents, **7**, 462
norflurazon
    CrtI enzyme sensitivity, **2**, 341
    resistance, **2**, 347
normanicone, occurrence, **8**, 243
nornicotine, occurrence, **8**, 151, 347
nornicotines, N-acyl-, occurrence, **8**, 302
Norrish type II photocyclization, **2**, 390
norsesquiterpenes
    fish toxicity, **8**, 234
    from, farnesal, **8**, 234
norsolorinic acid
    biosynthesis, **1**, 421
    determination, **1**, 446
    folding patterns, **1**, 448
    as intermediate, **1**, 420
    roles
        in aflatoxin biosynthesis, **1**, 16
        in penicillic acid biosynthesis, **1**, 2
    synthesis, **1**, 450
norsolorinic acid reductases, purification, **1**, 464
19-nortestosterone, spectral characteristics, **5**, 40
(−)-nortracheloside, occurrence, **1**, 647
norvaline, occurrence, **1**, 538
D-norvaline, replacement, **4**, 253
Norway spruce *see Picea abies*
nosiheptide, biosynthesis, **1**, 852
Nostoc spp., cryptophycin-1, **8**, 611
Notheia anomala, oxylipins, **1**, 217
notonesomycin A, trideoxysugars, **3**, 321
Notothylas temperata, (+)-megacerotonic acid, **1**, 645
Notropis atherinoides
    1,5Z-octadien-3-ol, **1**, 239
    oxylipins, **1**, 239
L-noviose
    occurrence, **3**, 312, 321
    tracer studies, **3**, 342
novobiocin
    applications, direct protein binding agents, **7**, 596
    L-noviose, **3**, 321

npe genes, *npe*E1, studies, **4**, 178
NPN43C9, structure, **5**, 430
NPP *see* nerolidyl diphosphate
p-NPP *see* phosphate, p-nitrophenyl (p-NPP)
nrd genes
    in deoxyribonucleotide biosynthesis, **3**, 342
    nrdAB, isolation, **3**, 343
    nrdD, encoding, **3**, 345
    nrdDG, occurrence, **3**, 345
    nrdE, isolation, **3**, 343
    nrdF, isolation, **3**, 343
    nrdG, encoding, **3**, 345
nre genes, cloning, **4**, 176
NSAIDs *see* nonsteroid antiinflammatory agents
nuclear factor A, binding, **4**, 245
nuclear magnetic resonance (NMR)
    applications, **7**, 72
    in carbohydrate studies, **3**, 1
    chemical shifts, **6**, 5
    DNA structure determination, **7**, 55–80
        advantages, **7**, 55
        interpretation, **6**, 12
    isotopic labeling, **6**, 7
    J-coupling, **6**, 5
    linewidths, **7**, 75
    multidimensional, **6**, 8
    in natural products chemistry, **2**, 11
    nuclear Overhauser effects, **6**, 6
    relaxation times
        spin–lattice, **6**, 6
        spin–spin, **6**, 6
    RNA structure determination, **6**, 4
    spectrometer, **6**, 4
    techniques, **6**, 4
nuclear Overhauser effects (NOEs)
    intensity, **6**, 10
    studies, **6**, 6
nucleases
    chemical, **6**, 69
    resistance to, **6**, 226
    in RNA structural probing, **6**, 67
nucleic acids
    antisense, **6**, 88
    Arrhenius activation energy, **7**, 41
    association, mononucleotide, **7**, 42
    backbone, torsion angles, **7**, 56, 434
    backbone atoms, thermal motions, **7**, 434
    base pairs
        dynamics, **7**, 74
        opening, **7**, 45
    bases, thermal motions, **7**, 434
    catalysis, **7**, 616
        metals in, **6**, 136
    conformation
        backbone, **7**, 72
        endo, **7**, 57
        envelope, **7**, 56
        exo, **7**, 57
        twist, **7**, 56
    counterion condensation effect, **7**, 20
    coupling constants, **7**, 64
        $J_{P-H3'}$, **7**, 72
        vicinal, **7**, 64, 68
    cross-linking, **6**, 227
    cross-relaxation rates, **7**, 62
    dihedral angles, **7**, 72
    distorted, intercalation, **7**, 469
    double helices
        dissociation, **7**, 44
        formation, **7**, 43
    duplexes, **7**, 33
        non-radioactive probes for, **7**, 448
        unusual, **7**, 36

equilibrium melting profiles, analysis, **7**, 21
exchange formalism, **7**, 74
extrathermodynamic parameters, **7**, 18
    cooperative unit size, **7**, 19
    equilibrium constants, **7**, 20
    free energy, **7**, 20
    thermal melting temperature, **7**, 18
Eyring transition state enthalpy, **7**, 41
folding
    kinetics, **7**, 36
    thermodynamics, **7**, 16
functions, nucleobase roles in, **6**, 91
hairpin helices, formation, **7**, 44
helical parameters, pictorial definition, **7**, 59
hybridization, **7**, 16
    calorimetry, **7**, 21
    probe, **7**, 35
hydrogen bonding, **7**, 270
ID spectra, **7**, 66
imino proton exchange rates, **7**, 74
interactions, with proteins, **7**, 266
intercalation sites, formation, **7**, 434
Karplus equation, **7**, 72
kinetics, **7**, **15–53**
    Biacore system, **7**, 40
    determination, **7**, 37
    interpretation, **7**, 41
    manual mixing, **7**, 41
    mixing, **7**, 39
    NMR, **7**, 39
    rate-limiting steps, **7**, 41
    steady-state, **7**, 41
    stopped flow, **7**, 40
    temperature jump, **7**, 38
loop–loop complexes, association rates, **7**, 46
monomeric units, **7**, 56
nearest neighbor thermodynamic data, **7**, 34
^{13}C NMR spectra, **7**, 73
^{1}H NMR spectra, **7**, 59
^{15}N NMR spectra, **7**, 72
^{31}P NMR spectra, **7**, 69
NOESY spectra, **7**, 62
photocross-linking, **6**, 228
polymer properties, **7**, 617
probing, **6**, 63
process rates, **7**, 42
proton exchange, **7**, 45
protons
    exchangeable, **7**, 66
    non-exchangeable, **7**, 64
    stereospecific assignment, **7**, 66
pseudorotation angles, **7**, 68
reaction rate
    laws, **7**, 41
    temperature dependence, **7**, 41
reactions, diffusion-controlled, **7**, 42
secondary structures, dynamic motions, **7**, 434
sequencing, **6**, 21
stacking, rates, **7**, 42
structure, **3**, 38
    inter-proton distances, **7**, 62
    Klyne–Prelog notation, **7**, 56
    phylogenetic analyses, **6**, 139
    pseudorotation angles, **7**, 57
sugar moieties, **7**, 287
synthesis
    chemical, **6**, 116
    historical background, **7**, 106
tertiary structures, dynamic motions, **7**, 434
thermodynamic parameters, **7**, 16
    adiabatic compressibility, **7**, 18
    common reference states, **7**, 18
    enthalpy change, **7**, 17, 29

entropy change, **7**, 17
experimental determination, **7**, 21
free energy change, **7**, 16
from transition curves, **7**, 22
heat capacity, **7**, 28
heat capacity change, **7**, 17, 29
interpretation, **7**, 32
standard states, **7**, 18
van't Hoff enthalpy, **7**, 21, 30
via calorimetry, **7**, 30
via differential scanning calorimetry, **7**, 28
via isothermal titration calorimetry, **7**, 31
via UV spectra, **7**, 22
thermodynamics, **7**, **15–53**
    importance of, **7**, 16
torsion angles, **7**, 64, 72
    glycosidic, **7**, 57
triplexes, **7**, 36
    intermolecular, **7**, 46
    kinetics, **7**, 46
    stability, **7**, 47
volumetric properties, **7**, 18
    apparent molar adiabatic compressibility, **7**, 32
    apparent molar volume, **7**, 32
    densitometry, **7**, 31
    measurement, **7**, 31
    molar sound velocity increment, **7**, 32
    ultrasonic velocimetry, **7**, 31
nucleic acids, single-stranded, **7**, 32
    structures, **7**, 33
nucleobases
    boronated, **7**, 221
    conjugation, **7**, 219
    cross-links, **6**, 228
    functionalization, **7**, 191
    modification, **6**, 224
    probing, **6**, 63
    pyrrole-containing, copolymerization, **7**, 216
    reactivity, **7**, 397
    roles, in nucleic acid functions, **6**, 91
nucleophiles
    neocarzinostatin chromophore activation, **7**, 559
    preassociation, **5**, 142
    in ribozyme reaction mechanisms, **6**, 236
nucleophilic aromatic substitution (S$_N$Ar)
    enzyme-catalyzed, **5**, 79
    mechanisms, **5**, 72
    rates, **5**, 414
nucleophilic catalysis, mechanisms, **5**, 436
nucleophilic substitution
    and aromatic substitution compared, **5**, 72
    carbonyl compounds, **5**, 7
5′-nucleoside aldehyde, formation, **7**, 567
nucleoside analogues
    acyclic carbohydrate linkers, **7**, 257
    with altered base residues, **7**, 271
    with altered carbohydrate residues, **7**, 273
    with altered phosphate linkages, **7**, 273
    base-modified, **7**, 276
        in protein–DNA probing, **7**, 266
        related group, **7**, 255
    carbohydrate structure and functionality, alterations,
        7, 256
    containing acyclic linkers, **7**, 273
    C-protonated, **7**, 273
    design, **7**, 253
    glycolysis, **7**, 260
    hydrogen bonding alteration, **7**, 253
    hydrophobic functionality alteration, **7**, 253
    impact, on pyrimidine–purine–pyrimidine DNA triplex
        stability, **7**, 271
    incorporation into DNA sequence, synthetic
        procedures, **7**, 259

phosphate linkage alteration, **7**, 258
phosphate-modified, in protein–nucleic acid probing,
   7, 268
as probes, for biochemical processes, **7**, **251–284**
in RNA catalysis, **7**, 274
site-specific placing
   in DNA sequences, **7**, 252
   in RNA sequences, **7**, 252
studies
   Eco RI restriction endonuclease, **7**, 266
   TBP-TATA box complex, **7**, 266
   trp repressor-operator, **7**, 266
sugar-modified, **7**, 144
   in protein–nucleic acid probing, **7**, 268
use in conjunction with affinity cleavage, **7**, 253
use in conjunction with footprinting, **7**, 252
nucleoside analogues, 2′-*O*-allyl, **7**, 256
nucleoside analogues, 2′-deoxy-2′-fluoro, **7**, 256
nucleoside analogues, 2′-*O*-methyl, **7**, 256
nucleoside antibiotics
   deoxysugars, **3**, 313
   minimycin, **8**, 390
   showdomycin, **8**, 390
nucleoside 2′,3′-cyclic phosphorothioates, synthesis, **6**,
   219
nucleoside diphosphate sugars (NDP-sugars)
   biosynthesis, **3**, 505
     sites, **3**, 603
   high energy, biosynthesis, **3**, 203
   interconversion, catalysis, **3**, 509
   metabolism, **3**, 510
   as substrates, **3**, 505
   translocation, **3**, 510
nucleoside *H*-phosphonates, for the synthesis of
   polynucleotides, **7**, 139
nucleoside phosphoramidites, cholesteryl, synthesis, **7**,
   189
3′-nucleoside radicals, as intermediates, **5**, 194
C2′-nucleoside radicals
   reactivity
     under aerobic conditions, **7**, 382
     under anaerobic conditions, **7**, 381
nucleosides
   C–N bond scission, **5**, 73
   deamination, **5**, **71–100**
   modification, **7**, 259, 264
     carbohydrate portions, **7**, 226
   probing, **6**, 63
   protecting groups, photochemically removable, **7**, 270
   protonation, **7**, 122
   synthesis, **7**, 259
nucleosides, arabinosyl, **7**, 257
nucleosides, 7-deazapurine, use in hammerhead ribozyme
   studies, **7**, 276

nucleosides, 2′-halo-, ribonucleotide reductase inhibition,
   5, 194
nucleosides, α-(ribo)-, **7**, 257
nucleosides, 2′-substituted, elimination, **5**, 192
C-nucleosides, synthesis, **7**, 262
nucleoside α-thiotriphosphates
   polymerization, **6**, 219
   as substrates, **6**, 218
nucleoside-triphosphate:RNA nucleotidyltransferase
   (DNA-directed) *see* DNA-directed RNA
   polymerase(s)
5′-nucleotidase, interconversions, **8**, 70
nucleotide analogue interference mapping (NAIM)
   applications, **6**, 221
   introns, **6**, 155
nucleotide analogue interference suppression (NAIS),
   introns, **6**, 156
nucleotide excision repair, pathways, **5**, 392
nucleotide 'mooring' sequence, **5**, 95
nucleotide phosphate-using transferases, roles, **5**, 280
nucleotides
   activated, **7**, 619
   conversion, to deoxynucleotides, **5**, 164
   deamination, **5**, **71–100**
   incorporation, in RNA, **6**, 82
   misincorporation, **7**, 621
   modified, applications, **6**, 75
   probing, **6**, 63
   reduction
     chain length studies, **5**, 177
     mechanisms, **5**, 166, 186
   selection, for cloning, **7**, 645
   structure, **7**, 56
nucleotides, 2′-*O*-alkyl-, synthesis, **6**, 88
nucleotides, 2′-amino-, reactions, with 2-pyridyl 3-
   isothiocyanatobenzyl disulfide, **6**, 227
nucleotides, 2′-*O*-methyl-, use in hairpin ribozyme studies,
   7, 279
nucleotide sugars *see* nucleoside diphosphate sugars
   (NDP-sugars)
nucleotidyl diphosphohexose-4,6-dehydratases, roles, in
   6-deoxyhexose biosynthesis, **3**, 334
nucleotidyltransferases
   homology, **3**, 336
   mechanisms, **3**, 333
nudibranchs
   antifouling agents, **8**, 438
   chemical defense, **8**, 462
   prostanoids, **1**, 245
   symbiosis, **8**, 426
   see also Tethys fimbria
N₃UDP *see* 2′-deoxyuridine diphosphate, 2′-azido-
   (N₃UDP)
nun moth *see Lymantria monacha*
Nuphar japonica, (−)-7-*epi*-deoxynupharidine, **8**, 344
NUX rule, hammerhead ribozymes, **6**, 237

O

oak galls, applications, **3**, 799
OAS *see* orsellinic acid synthase
oats *see* *Avena sativa*
oblongolide, biosynthesis, **1**, 370
obtusin, occurrence, **1**, 303
Ochrosia spp., ellipticine, **7**, 605
(*E*)-ochtodenol, occurrence, **8**, 224
(*Z*)-ochtodenol, occurrence, **8**, 224
ochtodenols, occurrence, **8**, 224
ocimene, occurrence, **8**, 161, 222
(*E*)-β-ocimene, occurrence, **8**, 236
trans-ocimene, as floral volatile, **8**, 161
β-ocimene, in plant–herbivore–predator interactions, **8**, 152
ocimenes, biosynthesis, **2**, 102, 132
Ocimum basilicum
  juvocimene-1, **8**, 277
  juvocimene-2, **8**, 277
Ocotea duckei, yangambin A, **1**, 704
Oct-1, binding, **4**, 368
Oct-2, binding, **4**, 368
octacosanoic acid, 27-hydroxy-, in *Legionella* lipid A, **3**, 196
(9*Z*,12*Z*)-9,12-octadecadienal, occurrence, **8**, 207
octadecadienoic acid, 9*S*-hydroperoxy- (9*S*-HPOD)
  occurrence, **1**, 209, 214, 233
  as substrate, **1**, 235
octadecadienoic acid, 13*S*-hydroperoxy- (13*S*-HPOD),
  occurrence, **1**, 209, 214, 233, 234
octadecadienoic acid, 13-hydroxy- (13-HOD),
  occurrence, **1**, 214
8*E*,12*Z*-octadecadienoic acid, 10*S*-hydroperoxy-, as substrate, **1**, 211
9*Z*,11*E*-octadecadienoic acid, 13-hydroxy- (13-HOD)
  biosynthesis, **1**, 223
  occurrence, **1**, 234
9*Z*,12*Z*-octadecadienoic acid, 11*R*-hydroxy-,
  biosynthesis, **1**, 223
9*Z*,12*Z*-octadecadienoic acid, 11-keto-, biosynthesis, **1**, 223
10*E*,12*Z*-octadecadienoic acid, 9-hydroxy- (9-HOD),
  biosynthesis, **1**, 223
10*E*,12*Z*-octadecadienoic acid, 9*R*-hydroxy, occurrence, **1**, 209
10*E*,12*Z*-octadecadienoic acid, 9*S*-hydroxy- (9*S*-HOD),
  occurrence, **1**, 243
10*E*,15*Z*-octadecadienoic acid, 12*S*,13*S*-epoxy-9*S*-hydroxy-, as intermediate, **1**, 209
10*E*,15*Z*-octadecadienoic acid, 9*S*,12*R*,13*S*-trihydroxy-, *see* malyngic acid
(*Z*)-9-(*E*)-11-octadecadienoic acid, 13-hydroperoxy-, substrate specificity, **1**, 102
(*Z*)-9-(*E*)-11-octadecadienoic acid, 13*S*-hydroperoxy-, biosynthesis, **1**, 105
(3*E*,13*Z*)-3,13-octadecadien-1-ol, occurrence, **8**, 207
(1*R*)-(9*Z*,11*E*)-9,11-octadecadien-13-olide, occurrence, **8**, 218
octadecane, 5,9-dimethyl-, occurrence, **8**, 247
octadecanoic acid, 17-methyl-, decarboxylation, **8**, 240
octadecanoic acid, *cis*-11,12-methylene- *see* lactobacillic acid
cis-9-octadecanoic acid *see* oleic acid
cis-11-octadecanoic acid *see* *cis*-vaccenic acid
octadecanoid pathway
  enzymes, **1**, 131

inhibitors, **1**, 123
mechanisms, **1**, 134
roles, **1**, 132
use of term, **1**, 119
octadecanoids, β-oxidization, **1**, 135
octadecanolide, occurrence, **8**, 218
6*Z*,8*E*,10*E*,12*Z*-octadecatetraenoic acid, biosynthesis, **1**, 223
(9*Z*,12*Z*,15*Z*)-9,12,15-octadecatrienal, occurrence, **8**, 207
octadecatrienoic acid, 13*S*-hydroperoxy- (HPOT),
  occurrence, **1**, 230
6*Z*,9*Z*,12*Z*-octadecatrienoic acid *see* γ-linolenic acid
9*Z*,11*E*,15*Z*-octadecatrienoic acid, 13*S*-hydroperoxy-, rearrangement, **1**, 209
9*Z*,12*Z*,15*Z*-octadecatrienoic acid, 13*S*-hydroperoxy-, occurrence, **1**, 232
10*E*,12*E*,14*E*-octadecatrienoic acid, 9*S*,16(*R*,*S*)-dihydroxy-, occurrence, **1**, 236
10*E*,12*Z*,14*E*-octadecatrienoic acid, 9*S*,16(*R*,*S*)-dihydroxy-, occurrence, **1**, 236
10*E*,12*Z*,15*Z*-octadecatrienoic acid, 9*R*-hydroxy-, occurrence, **1**, 209
cis-9,15-*trans*-11-octadecatrienoic acid, 13*S*-hydroperoxy- *see* linolenic acid, 13(*S*)-hydroperoxy-
(*Z*)-6-(*Z*)-9-(*E*)-11-octadecatrienoic acid, 13-hydroperoxy-, substrate specificity, **1**, 102
octadecene, (7*R*,8*S*)-7,8-epoxy-2-methyl-, occurrence, **8**, 241
1-octadecene, 10,14-dimethyl-, occurrence, **8**, 247
1-octadecene, 14-methyl-, occurrence, **8**, 247
7-octadecene, (*Z*)-2-methyl-, occurrence, **8**, 241
octadecenolide, occurrence, **8**, 218
10*E*,15*Z*-octadienoic acid, 12,13-*trans*-epoxy-9-oxo-, occurrence, **1**, 214
(*E*,*E*)-2,6-octadienoic acid, 4(*R*)-methyl-, biosynthesis, **1**, 543
1,5*Z*-octadien-3-ol, occurrence, **1**, 239
1,5*Z*-octadien-3*R*-ol, biosynthesis, **1**, 211
1,5*Z*-octadien-3*S*-ol, occurrence, **1**, 211
2,7-octadien-1-ol, (*E*)-3,7-dimethyl-, occurrence, **8**, 222
2,7-octadien-1-ol, (*Z*)-3,7-dimethyl-, occurrence, **8**, 222
octaketides, **7**, 554
  biosynthesis, **1**, 417
  as precursor, **1**, 562
octalactins
  cytotoxicity, **8**, 590
  occurrence, **8**, 590
  structure, **8**, 590
(2*S*,3*S*)-2,3-octanediol, occurrence, **8**, 211
octanoate, ethyl 4-methyl, occurrence, **8**, 241
octanoate, 1-methylethyl, occurrence, **8**, 209, 211
octanoic acid
  occurrence, **8**, 209
  as starting material, for lipoic acid, **1**, 832
octanoic acid, 8-[2-(*cis*-pent-2′-enyl)-3-oxo-*cis*-cyclopent-4-enyl]- *see* *cis*-10,15-phytodienoic acid, 12-oxo-
1-octanol, occurrence, **8**, 161, 211
3-octanol, occurrence, **8**, 211
(*S*)-3-octanol, occurrence, **8**, 211
4-octanol, 2-methyl-, occurrence, **8**, 245
4-octanol, (3*S*,4*S*)-3-methyl- *see* phoenicol
4-octanol, (4*S*,5*S*)-5-methyl- *see* cruentol
2-octanone, occurrence, **8**, 212
2-octanone, (*R*)-3-hydroxy-, occurrence, **8**, 211
3-octanone

in induced plant defense, **8**, 150
occurrence, **8**, 211
in plant–herbivore–predator interactions, **8**, 152
octan-3-one, (4*S*,6*S*)-4,6-dimethyl-, occurrence, **8**, 242
3-octanone, 4,6-dimethyl- *see* manicone, dihydro-
3-octanone, (*S*)-2-hydroxy-, occurrence, **8**, 211
3-octanone, 6-methyl-, occurrence, **8**, 244
octanoyl-CoA
    biosynthesis, **1**, 544
    as substrate, **4**, 262
octaprenyl diphosphate synthases
    in *Escherichia coli*, gene cloning, **2**, 92
    occurrence, **2**, 91
trans-octaprenyl*trans*transferase(s)
    chain-length specificity, **2**, 91
    occurrence, **2**, 91
    polyprenyl carrier protein, **2**, 91
2,4,6-octatriene, (2*E*,4*E*,6*E*)-3,5-dimethyl-, occurrence, **8**, 240
(*E*)-2-octenal, occurrence, **8**, 211
6(*E*)-octenoate, 3(*R*)-hydroxy-4(*R*)-methyl, as intermediate, **1**, 543
(*E*)-3-octenoate, ethyl, occurrence, **8**, 211
6(*E*)-octenoic acid, 3(*R*)-hydroxy-4(*R*)-methyl-, biosynthesis, **1**, 543
6(*E*)-octenoic acid, 4(*R*)-methyl-, biosynthesis, **1**, 543
7-octen-1-ol, 7-methyl-3-methylene-, occurrence, **8**, 222
(*R*)-1-octen-3-ol, occurrence, **8**, 211
6-octen-4-olide, (3*S*,4*R*)-3,7-dimethyl- *see* eldanolide
4-octen-3-one, (4*E*)-4,6-dimethyl- *see* manicone
6-octen-3-one, (6*E*)-4,6-dimethyl- *see* leiobunone
trans-3-octenoyl-CoA, as substrate, **4**, 262
octocorals, antifeedant activity, **8**, 470
octopine, in crown galls, **8**, 399
γ-octose, occurrence, **3**, 312, 322
ODNs *see* oligodeoxynucleotides (ODNs)
odor marks, mammals, **8**, 220
odorous compounds, in fish, **1**, 239
odors, fruits, **8**, 165
Oechalia schellenbergii, pheromones, **8**, 225
Oecophylla longinoda
    hexanal, **8**, 210
    1-hexanol, **8**, 210
    3-undecanone, **8**, 214
oestrone, occurrence, **8**, 361
Oiketicus kirbyi
    decanoic acid, **8**, 209
    dodecanoic acid, **8**, 209
    nonanoic acid, **8**, 209
    octanoic acid, **8**, 209
    (*R*)-2-pentanol, **8**, 209
oilseed rape embryos, adenosinediphosphoglucose, **3**, 463
okadaic acid
    biosynthesis, **8**, 492
    Favorski-type rearrangement, **8**, 496
    as inhibitor of protein phosphatases 1 and 2A, **8**, 490
    occurrence, **8**, 490
    structure–activity relationship, **8**, 491
        summary, **8**, 492
    as tumor promoter, **8**, 491
okadaxanthin
    occurrence, **8**, 589
    structure, **8**, 589
okilactomycin, isolation, **1**, 370
olean, occurrence, **8**, 15
oleandomycin, antibacterial activity, **4**, 198
oleandrin, insect sequestration, **8**, 363
D-oleandrose
    isolation, **3**, 313
    occurrence, **3**, 312
L-oleandrose
    in avermectins, **3**, 355
    isolation, **3**, 313

occurrence, **3**, 312
oleate, cholesteryl, occurrence, **8**, 230
olefins *see* alkenes
ole genes
    *OLE*1, **1**, 39
        expression, **1**, 46
        mutation, **1**, 44
    ole 1 mutant, **1**, 39
oleic acid
    cyclopropanation, **1**, 64
    epoxidization, **1**, 210
oleoresin
    in bark beetle defense mechanisms, **2**, 111
    composition, **2**, 101
    inducible, **2**, 111
olepupuane, 7-deacetoxy-, localization, **8**, 462
oligo(A) tails, production, **6**, 207
oligodendrocytes, galactosylceramide biosynthesis, **3**, 92
oligodeoxynucleotide duplexes
    ^{31}P NMR spectra, **7**, 69
    structure, determination, **7**, 56
oligodeoxynucleotides (ODNs)
    N^4-alkylcytosine in, **7**, 320
    2-aminoadenine in, **7**, 323
    N^2-(anthracen-9-ylmethyl)guanine in, **7**, 327
    6-azacytosine in, **7**, 322
    6-azathymine in, **7**, 319
    8-bromoadenine in, **7**, 325
    5-bromouracil in, **7**, 316
    N^7-cyanoboraneguanine in, **7**, 329
    7-deazaadenine in, **7**, 330
    7-deaza-8-azapurines in, **7**, 331
    3-deazaguanine in, **7**, 330
    2'-deoxy-3-deazaadenosine in, **7**, 329
    N-3 ethylthymine in, **7**, 315
    O^2-ethylthymine in, **7**, 314
    5-fluorouracil in, **7**, 316
    7-hydro-8-oxoguanine in, **7**, 328
    hypoxanthines in, **7**, 325
    imidazole in, **7**, 334
    N^2-3-imidazolepropionic acid in, **7**, 327
    5-iodouracil in, **7**, 316
    malondialdehyde in, **7**, 334
    N^4-methoxycytosine in, **7**, 321
    N^6-methoxyladenine in, **7**, 324
    C^6-*O*-methylguanine in, **7**, 328
    2'-*O*-methylpseudoisocytidine in, **7**, 332
    C^4-*O*-methylthymine in, **7**, 315
    O^2-methylthymine in, **7**, 314
    3-nitropyrrole in, **7**, 333
    C^8-oxo-7,8-dihydro-6-*O*-methylguanine in, **7**, 329
    phenothiazine in, **7**, 334
    phenoxazine in, **7**, 334
    C^5-propynylcytosine in, **7**, 322
    C^5-propynylpyrimidines in, **7**, 317
    C^5-propynyluracil in, **7**, 317
    spermine in, **7**, 322
    C^5-substituted pyrimidines, hybridization properties, **7**, 315
    synthetic, nonpolar isosteres, **7**, 332
    thiazoleuracil in, **7**, 318
    C^5-thiazoleuracil in, **7**, 318
    C^6-thiopurine, synthesis, **7**, 327
    2-thiothymine in, **7**, 314
    4-thiothymine in, **7**, 315
    2-thiouracil in, **7**, 314
    4-thiouracil in, **7**, 315
    zwitterionic oligomers, **7**, 318
oligodeoxyribonucleoside methylphosphonates, synthesis, **7**, 160
oligodeoxyribonucleotide-5'-phosphorothioate, nucleophilicity, **7**, 169
oligodeoxyribonucleotides

aminoalkylation, **7**, 154
biotinylation, **7**, 199
reactions
  with *p*-azidotetrafluorobenzoic acid esters, **7**, 161
  with 1,1′-carbonyldiimidazole, **7**, 162
oligodeoxyribonucleotides, 5′-aminoalkylated
applications, **7**, 159
conjugation, **7**, 159
oligodeoxyribonucleotides, 5′-thiolated, **7**, 234
oligoflavanoids
absolute configuration, at C-4 position, **3**, 763
precursor selection, **3**, 757
semi-synthesis, **3**, 757
oligoketides, incorporation, **1**, 384
oligolignols, linkages, **3**, 724
oligomannose *N*-glycans, structure, **3**, 40
oligomers
biotinylation, **7**, 170
fluorescent, as probes, **7**, 234
radioiodination, **7**, 170
zwitterionic, **7**, 318
oligonucleoside phosphorothioates, antihuman
      cytomegalovirus activity, **7**, 239
oligonucleotide–peptide conjugates, synthesis, **7**, 114
oligonucleotides
aminoalkylation, phosphoramidites for, **7**, 155
analogues, synthesis, **6**, 88
antisense, **6**, 88
as antisense nucleic acids, **6**, 88
applications, **7**, 144
  therapeutic, **7**, 142
biotinylation, **6**, 118, **7**, 166, 171
  by nick translation, **7**, 206
5′-biotinylation, **7**, 170
bulk production, via polymerase chain reaction, **7**, 652
carboxylation, **7**, 157
chemical synthesis, **7**, 154
cross-linking efficiency, **7**, 159
deprotection, **7**, 192
depurination, **7**, 122
derivatization, **7**, 233
deuterium-labeled, **7**, 560
digoxigenin labeling, **7**, 209
esterification, **6**, 128
functionalization
  labeling, **7**, 154
  solid supports, **7**, 114
  at 3′-terminus, **7**, 190
  at 5′ terminus, **7**, 154
labeling, **7**, 185
mercaptoalkylation, phosphoramidites for, **7**, 167
with modified internucleotide linkages, **7**, 265
NMR studies, **6**, 13
with non-bridging phosphate–oxygen atom, properties,
      7, 291
purification, **7**, 144
  by reversed-phase HPLC, **7**, 127
radiolabeling, **7**, 135
random-sequence, **7**, 619
retrosynthesis, **7**, 106
self-complementary, synthesis, **7**, 32
synthesis, **6**, 22, **7**, **105–152**
  automated, **7**, 112, 144
  capping, **7**, 143
  coupling, **7**, 143
  detritylation, **7**, 143
  dichlorophenylphosphate in, **7**, 106
  diphenylchlorophosphate in, **7**, 106
  exocyclic amino function protection, **7**, 119
  historical background, **7**, 106
  5′-hydroxy group protection, **7**, 126
  imide and lactam functions protection, **7**, 117
  methods, **6**, 82

mixed-sequence probes, **7**, 126
no protection option, **7**, 123, 136
oxidation, **7**, 143
phosphate protection, **7**, 130
phosphodiester approach, **6**, 82, **7**, 107
H-phosphonate approach, **6**, 82, **6**, 87, **7**, 109, 144,
      237
phosphoramidite approach, **6**, 82, **7**, 108, 142
phosphotriester approach, **6**, 82, **7**, 107
protecting groups in, **7**, 117
purine bases, protection, **7**, 121
solid-phase, **7**, 142, 195, 237
solid supports for, **7**, 110
'spacer arm', **7**, 112
using acyl protecting groups, **7**, 124
washing, **7**, 143
triplex-forming, **7**, 159
see also antisense oligonucleotides
oligonucleotides, aminoalkylated
reactions, with fluorescein isothiocyanate, **7**, 193
synthesis, **7**, 229
oligonucleotides, 5′-aminoalkylated
condensation, **7**, 159
reactions
  with Denny–Jaffe reagents, **7**, 160
  with dithiobis(*N*-succinimidyl)propionate, **7**, 168
oligonucleotides, bicyclic, **7**, 360
affinity, **7**, 360
disulfide, **7**, 360
specificity, **7**, 360
oligonucleotides, branched, triplexes, **7**, 355
oligonucleotides, circular, **7**, 356
DNA-binding properties, studies, **7**, 357
sequence specificity, **7**, 359
oligonucleotides, dansylated, as fluorescent labeled
      compounds, **7**, 316
oligonucleotides, europium(III)-labeled, synthesis, **7**, 211
oligonucleotides, lariat-shaped, triplexes, **7**, 359
oligonucleotides, 5′-mercaptoalkylated
reactions, with fullerenes, **7**, 167
synthesis, **7**, 167
oligonucleotides, phosphotyrosinyl, detection, **7**, 174
oligonucleotides, stem-loop, **7**, 356, 359
oligonucleotides, 5′-thiolated, synthesis, **7**, 167
oligonucleotides, topologically-modified, molecular
      recognition, **7**, 355
Oligonychus ilicis, feeding, effect of saponins on, **8**, 144
oligopeptide permease, encoding, **8**, 402
oligoribonucleotides
biotinylation, **6**, 226
convertible nucleoside approach, **6**, 227
fluorescent labels, **6**, 227
hydrolysis, **7**, 164
ligation, **6**, 218
metal derivatives, **6**, 230
synthesis, **6**, 50, 81
  chemical, **6**, 218
  template-directed, **6**, 218
oligoribonucleotides, 2′-*O*-alkyl-, as biochemical probes,
      6, 88
oligoribonucleotides, aminoalkylated, reactions, with
      ethylene diaminetetraacetic anhydride, **7**, 201
oligoribonucleotides, 2′-*O*-methyl, modification, **6**, 230
oligosaccharide amino group, in calicheamicins, **7**, 570
oligosaccharide processing pathway, asparagine-linked,
      glycosidases of, **3**, **13–35**
oligosaccharides, **7**, 571
as antiauxins, **8**, 26
biosynthesis, **3**, 38, 145, 3
  and peptidoglycan biosynthesis, **3**, 286
bisected, **3**, 43
in calicheamicin γ_1^1, **7**, 569
chains, minimal size, **3**, 480

complex, **3**, 17
effects of glycosidase inhibitors on, **3**, 143
expression, **3**, 5, 187
glucosidase processing of, **3**, 42
modification, **3**, 38
monoglucosylated, **3**, 31
monoglucosylated high mannose, **3**, 31
processing, **3**, 146
as starting material, for *N*-glycans, **3**, 15
structure, **3**, 38, 143
see also lipo-chitin oligosaccharides (LCOs)
oligosaccharyltransferase (OST)
activity, **3**, 41
catalysis, **3**, 15
purification, **3**, 41
subunits, **3**, 41
D-oliose, occurrence, **3**, 312
olivanic acids, occurrence, **4**, 186
olive fly *see Dacus oleae*
olive fruit fly *see Bactrocera oleae*
olivil, biosynthesis, **1**, 688
D-olivomose, occurrence, **3**, 312, 313
olivomycins
biological activity, **3**, 323
2,6-dideoxy-D-*arabino*-hexose, **3**, 313
D-olivomose, **3**, 313
L-olivomycose E, occurrence, **3**, 312, 321
D-olivose *see* 2,6-dideoxy-D-*arabino*-hexose
omega hydroxylase, occurrence, **1**, 211
Omphalea diandra, 2,5-dihydroxymethyl-3,4-
dihydroxypyrrolidine, **3**, 141
Omphalius pfeifferi, feeding stimulants, **8**, 420
omt-1 genes *see omtA* genes
omtA genes
identification, **1**, 462
transcription, **1**, 463
oncogenes, ST6Gal I expression, **3**, 46
Oncopeltus spp., makisterone A, **8**, 279
Oncopeltus fasciatus
in echinolone studies, **8**, 277
metamorphosis, **8**, 278
inhibition, **1**, 693
oncoprotein, human, ETS1, DNA major groove
recognition, **7**, 465
Oncorhynchus mykiss, prostaglandins, **1**, 236
oncorhyncolide
occurrence, **8**, 596
structure, **8**, 596
onnamide A
antiviral activity, **8**, 581
cytotoxicity, **8**, 581
occurrence, **8**, 581
α-onocerin, synthesis, **2**, 301
onopordopicrin, antifeedant activity, **8**, 308
Ooencyrtus nezarae, kairomone, **8**, 210
oolongtheanin, biosynthesis, **3**, 782
Oospora sulphrea-ochracea, (−)-bisdechlorogeodin, **1**,
437
opal codon *see* UGA
operons
regulation, **3**, 228
transcriptional regulation, **3**, 228
Operophtera spp., (3*Z*,6*Z*,9*Z*)-1,3,6,9-nonadecatetraene,
8, 207
Ophrys spp., pseudocopulation, **8**, 161
Ophrys lutea
decyl acetate, **8**, 161
linalool, **8**, 161
1-octanol, **8**, 161
ophthalmology, prostaglandin applications in, **1**, 196
Opiliones
ketones, **8**, 242
see also Leiobunum spp.

opine, in crown galls, **8**, 399
opisthobranch mollusk *see Tethys fimbria*
optical rotatory dispersion (ORD), applications, **8**, 6
orbiculamide A
occurrence, **8**, 570
structure, **8**, 570
orchids
ipsdienol, **8**, 224
pollination, **8**, 161
ord-1 genes, identification, **1**, 466
ord-2 genes, identification, **1**, 466
Oreana spp., sequestration, **8**, 362
Oreochromis niloticus, leukotrienes, **1**, 238
orf genes
occurrence, **1**, 878
orfA, localization, **1**, 878
orfB, localization, **1**, 878
organelles
biogenesis, and fatty acid desaturation defects, **1**, 44
fractionation studies, **3**, 662
organic chemistry, developments, **3**, 534
organic synthesis, use of enzymes in, **5**, 59
organoaluminum reagents, applications, in Claisen
rearrangements, **5**, 350
organotins, applications, antifouling agents, **8**, 431
organs, formation, cytokinin-induced, **8**, 59
Orgyia spp., (*Z*)-6-henicosen-11-one, **8**, 208
Orgyia pseudotsugata
(6*Z*,8*E*)-6,8-henicosadien-11-one, **8**, 208
(*Z*)-6-henicosen-11-one, **8**, 208
Oricia renieri, vepridimerines, **1**, 383
ent-oritin-(4*β*→5)-epioritin-4*β*-ol, isolation, **3**, 776
ent-oritin-(4*β*→7,5→6)-epioritin-4*α*-ol, isolation, **3**, 776
Orixa japonica
isopimpinellin, **8**, 338
xanthotoxin, **8**, 338
ornativolide A, occurrence, **1**, 375
ornithine
activation, **4**, 209
residues, **4**, 322
as starting material
for alkaloids, **4**, 26
for pyrrolidine alkaloids, **4**, 30
D-ornithine 4,5-aminomutase, catalysis, **5**, 207
ornithine mutase, reactions, **5**, 264
ornoprostil, biological activity, **1**, 196
orsellinic acid
biosynthesis, **1**, 346
occurrence, **1**, 412, 3
roles, in aflatoxin B$_1$ biosynthesis, **1**, 2
structure, **1**, 410
orsellinic acid, methyl-, as intermediate, **1**, 3
orsellinic acid synthase
mass spectra, **1**, 349
mechanisms, **1**, 360
occurrence, **1**, 360
purification, **1**, 349, 412
Orthodon formosanus, dillapiole, **8**, 336
orthophosphoric-monoester phosphohydrolase (acid
optimum) *see* acid phosphatase
orthophosphoric-monoester phosphohydrolase (alkaline
optimum) *see* alkaline phosphatase
orthosomycin antibiotics
branched-chain deoxysugars, **3**, 321
D-curacose, **3**, 313
Oryctes monocerus, pheromones, **8**, 241
Oryctes rhinoceros, ethyl 4-methyloctanoate, **8**, 241
Oryzaephilus spp., (*R*)-1-octen-3-ol, **8**, 211
Oryzaephilus mercator, (11*R*,3*Z*,6*Z*)-3,6-dodecadien-11-
olide, **8**, 215
Oryzaephilus surinamensis
(3*Z*,6*Z*)-3,6-dodecadien-12-olide, **8**, 215
(11*R*,3*Z*,6*Z*)-3,6-dodecadien-11-olide, **8**, 215

pheromones, **8**, 216
oryzalexins, biosynthesis, **2**, 230
oryzalexin *S*, biosynthesis, **2**, 238
Oryza sativa
    gibberellin deficiency, **8**, 45
    β-1,4-linkage formation, **3**, 581
    oxylipins, **1**, 229
    phenylalanine ammonia-lyase, **3**, 659
Oryzias latipes, activity against, **1**, 694
OSB *see* benzoic acid, *o*-succinyl- (OSB)
OSC *see* oxidosqualene cyclase (OSC)
oscillariolide
    occurrence, **8**, 610
    structure, **8**, 610
Oscillatoria spp.
    hydroperoxide lyase, **1**, 209
    oscillariolide, **8**, 610
Oscillatoria rosea, (2*S*)-1-*O*-palmitoyl-3-*O*-*β*-D-
        galactopyranosylglycerol, **8**, 610
OSLC *see* oxidosqualene:lanosterol cyclase (OSLC)
osmium tetroxide, applications, DNA structure probes,
    7, 92
osmotic stress
    and abscisic acid, **8**, 83
    and jasmonates, **1**, 131
OST *see* oligosaccharyltransferase (OST)
ostereocins
    electrospray ionization mass spectrometry, **8**, 510
    occurrence, **8**, 510
Ostereopsis siamensis, ostereocins, **8**, 510
osthenol, as starting material, for (−)-columbianetin, **1**,
    628
Ostrinia nubilalis, parasites, **8**, 249
4-OT *see* 4-oxalocrotonate tautomerase
oteromycin, biosynthesis, **1**, 370
ouabain, insect sequestration, **8**, 361
ovalicin
    applications, antibiotics, **2**, 165
    biosynthesis, **2**, 165, 167
    occurrence, **2**, 165
ovary, ST3Gal IV expression, **3**, 49
7-oxabicyclo[4.3.0]non-9-en-8-one, 2,6-dimethyl-2-vinyl-
        see anastrephin
oxadicarbocyanine, 3,3′-diethyl- (DODC), applications,
    DNA structure probes, **7**, 85
4-oxalocrotonate tautomerase
    catalysis, **5**, 41
    evolutionary relationships, **5**, 46
    isozymes, **5**, 42
    ketonization, **5**, 43
    kinetic barriers, **5**, 35
    mutants, **5**, 46
3-oxalomalate glyoxylate-lyase *see* oxalomalate lyase
oxalomalate lyase
    biochemistry, **3**, 413
    catalysis, **3**, 413
20-oxa-2,3-oxidosqualene, cyclization, **2**, 280
oxathiaphospholanes, as reagents, **7**, 133
oxazole pharmacophores, inhibitory activity, **5**, 160
oxazoline rings, in clavams, **4**, 182
oxazolines, biosynthesis, **5**, 286
oxazolinium ions, biosynthesis, **5**, 286, 297
oxetane, cleavage, **5**, 387
oxidases
    copper-containing, in lignin biosynthesis, **3**, 709
    non-heme iron-dependent, **4**, 250
    roles, in lignin biosynthesis, **3**, 716
oxidation
    hydroperoxide-dependent, **5**, 238
    two-electron, **1**, 304
α-oxidation, in pheromone biosynthesis, **8**, 207
β-oxidation
    cinnamoyl-CoA-dependent, **3**, 803

in fatty acid degradation, **1**, 47
oxidized nicotinamide-adenine dinucleotide, in
        dehydroquinate biosynthesis, **1**, 582
oxidizing agents, DNA damage induction, **7**, 384
4,6-oxidoreductases *see* nucleotidyl diphosphohexose-
    4,6-dehydratases
oxidosqualene cyclase (OSC)
    hydrophilic region, **2**, 283
    inhibitor, **2**, 273
    irreversible inactivator, **2**, 282
    occurrence, **2**, 282
    purification, **2**, 282
oxidosqualene-cycloartenol cyclases (OSCC), occurrence,
    2, 282
oxidosqualene:lanosterol cyclase (OSLC)
    Δ^{18} double bonds, **2**, 286
    as catalyst, for polyene cyclization, **2**, 267
    cDNA, **2**, 282
    in cholesterol biosynthesis, **2**, **267–298**
    enzymology, **2**, 282
    future research, **2**, 293
    inhibition studies, **2**, 284
    inhibitors, **2**, 283
        mechanisms, **2**, 293
    mechanisms, **2**, 279
    molecular biology, **2**, 282
    studies, **2**, 268
    substrate specificity, **2**, 284
    vertebrate
        inhibition kinetics, **2**, 291
        mechanism-based irreversible inhibitor, **2**, 287
    yeast, site-directed mutagenesis, **2**, 289
oxidosqualene(s)
    cyclization, anti-Markovnikov addition in, **2**, 280
    internal, **2**, 275
    transition state analogues, **2**, 304
oximes, as intermediates, **1**, 887
oxirane, 2-pyridyl-
    nucleophilic additions, **5**, 52
    transition metal-catalyzed opening, **5**, 53
oxirane rings, chemistry, **5**, 51
2-oxoacid dehydrogenase, His motif, **4**, 227
3-oxoacyl-CoA
    biosynthesis, **8**, 204
    decarboxylation, **8**, 204
3-oxoacyl-CoA thiolase, activity, **1**, 51
oxobutyryl groups
    biosynthesis, **4**, 278
    residues, **4**, 284
oxocarbenium ions
    azide selectivity, **5**, 291
    ground states, inhibition, **5**, 294
    lifetimes, **5**, 284
    transition states, **5**, 284
        inhibition, **5**, 294
oxocarbonium ions, transition states, **5**, 316
2-oxoglutarate dehydrogenases, catalysis, **1**, 614
3-oxohexanoyl acyl-carrier protein, as intermediate, **8**,
    394
3-oxo-7-methyloctanoyl-CoA, as intermediate, **8**, 385
12-oxo-PDA *see* phytodienoic acid, 12-oxo- (12-oxo-
    PDA)
8-[(1*R*,2*R*)-3-oxo-2-{(*Z*)-pent-2-
        enyl}cyclopentyl]octanoate:NADP$^+$ 4-
        oxidoreductase *see* 12-oxophytodienoate
        reductase
12-oxophytodienoate reductase
    catalysis, **1**, 120
    in jasmonic acid biosynthesis, **8**, 115
    purification, **1**, 120
    sequencing, **1**, 121
oxopropionyl groups
    biosynthesis, **4**, 278

residues, **4**, 284
3-oxo-Δ^5-steroid isomerase
  catalysis, **5**, 39
    mechanisms, **5**, 33
oxyanion holes
  homologues, **5**, 16
  mutagenesis, **5**, 25
  proton studies, **5**, 25
  structure, **5**, 19
oxy-Cope rearrangement
  in antibody catalysis, **5**, 426
  catalysis, **5**, 427
oxygen, effects on β-lactam production, **4**, 177
β-C-4-oxygenase, in xanthophyll biosynthesis, **2**, 344
oxygenases
  mechanisms, **1**, 11
  non-heme iron-dependent, **4**, 250
  roles, in arachidonic acid metabolism, **5**, 226
oxygenation, via methane monooxygenase, **5**, 218
oxygen metabolism, in natural product biosynthesis, **1**, 448
oxygen radicals
  from
    anthramycin, **7**, 497
    3*H*-1,2-benzodithiol-3-one 1-oxide, **7**, 524
    leinamycin, **7**, 524
    mitomycin C, **7**, 517
    phenazine *N*-oxides, **7**, 533
    polysulfides, **7**, 524
    quinones, **7**, 528
    renieramycins, **7**, 499

    resorcinols, **7**, 535
    safracins, **7**, 499
    saframycins, **7**, 499
    sibiromycin, **7**, 497
  production via reduction of molecular oxygen, **7**, 540
oxylipins
  metabolism, **1**, 209
    future research, **1**, 250
  occurrence, **1**, 216, 249
    algae, **1**, 213
    Amphibia, **1**, 248
    Annelida, **1**, 249
    ferns, **1**, 228
    fish, **1**, 236
    fungi, **1**, 209
    Hepaticae, **1**, 228
    insects, **1**, 208, 248
    invertebrates, **1**, 208
    Musci, **1**, 228
    non-mammalian animals, **1**, 236
  use of term, **1**, 207
oxyluciferin, occurrence, **8**, 444
Oxyporus spp., 2-*O*-[5-*O*-(*trans*-feruloyl)-β-L-arabinofuranosyl]-D-xylopyranose, **3**, 697
oxysterols, from, dioxidosqualene, **2**, 270
oxytetracycline
  biosynthesis, **1**, 475, **4**, 206
  cloning, **1**, 11
Oxytropis spp., swainsonine, **3**, 140
oysters
  prostaglandins, **1**, 244
  see also Crassostrea gigas

P

P1 helix, docking, **6**, 151, 162
p53, roles, cell regulation, **1**, 444
P450 family, in eicosanoid metabolism, **1**, 277
P450oxy, occurrence, **1**, 211
P450R *see* NADPH-cytochrome P450 reductase (P450R)
PA-46101A, structure, **1**, 370
Pab1p *see* poly(A) binding protein (Pab1p)
pab genes
  *PAB*1, **6**, 211
    deletion, **6**, 207
  *pab*1 mutants, **6**, 207, 211
  *pab*1Δ mutants, **6**, 207
PACC
  gene regulation, **4**, 177
  in β-lactam biosynthesis regulation, **4**, 175
pac genes, *pacC*, encoding, **4**, 175
Pachipellina spp., manzamines, **8**, 558
Pachlioptera aristolochiae, sequestration, **8**, 363
pachypostaudin A, structure, **1**, 640
Pacific yew *see* Taxus brevifolia
Pacifigorgia spp., *Streptomyces* spp. in, **8**, 590
pactamycin
  biosynthesis, **1**, 153
  structure, **1**, 152
PADGEM protein, PSGL-1 recognition, **3**, 72
2′-PADPR, SG14 activation, **3**, 476
Paecilomyces spp.
  saintopin, **7**, 600, 608
  UCE1022, **7**, 600
Paederus fuscipes, pederine, **8**, 351
Paederus sabalus, pederine, **8**, 351
Paeonia albiflora, tannins, **3**, 800
Paeonia lactiflora, gallotannins, **3**, 813
PAF *see* platelet-activating factor (PAF)
PAF antagonists *see* platelet-activating factor (PAF)
    antagonists
PAGE *see* polyacrylamide gel electrophoresis (PAGE)
pah genes, cloning, **4**, 183
PAI-1
  activity, with LasR, **8**, 398
  autoinduction, of LasB, **8**, 398
  occurrence, **8**, 398
  structure, **8**, 398
  see also L-homoserine lactone, *N*-(3-oxododecanoyl)-
PAL *see* phenylalanine ammonia-lyase
Palaemon macrodactylus, symbiosis, **8**, 429
PAL genes
  mutations, **4**, 175
  transcription, **1**, 817
palmetto weevil *see* Rhynchophorus cruentatus
palmitate, methyl, occurrence, **8**, 217
palmitic acid, **8**, 203
  biosynthesis, **1**, 29
  metabolism, **1**, 24
  occurrence, **8**, 205
  β-oxidation, **8**, 205
palmitoylation, proteins, **4**, **13–24**
palmitoyl-CoA
  as acyl donor, **4**, 20
  as protein palmitoyl group donor, **4**, 15
palmitoyl-CoA synthase *see* long-chain-fatty-acid-CoA
    ligase
palmitoyl protein thioesterase(s), purification, **4**, 20
palmitoyl transacylase, catalysis, **1**, 29
palustric acid, biosynthesis, **2**, 228

Palythoa toxica, palytoxin, **8**, 509
palytoxin
  effects
    biochemical, **8**, 511
    pharmacological, **8**, 511
  occurrence, **8**, 509
  sequestration, in crustaceans, **8**, 510
  stereochemistry, **8**, 509
pampas grass *see* Cortaderia selloana
pancreas, triacylglycerol lipase, **5**, 129
pancreatic DNase *see* deoxyribonuclease I (DNase I)
Pandaros acanthifolium, acanthifolicin, **8**, 491
Panicum miliaceum, root inhibition, **3**, 141
Panolis flammea
  α-pinene, **8**, 221
  β-pinene, **8**, 221
PANs *see* poly(A) nucleases (PANs)
pantothenic acid, detection, **4**, 168
Panurginus spp., (*E*)-8-oxocitronellyl acetate, **8**, 225
Papaver somniferum
  morphine alkaloids, **4**, 35
  sanguinarine, **1**, 131
paper manufacture
  cellulose applications, **3**, 533
  fiber quality, **3**, 612
Papilio spp., diuretic hormone, **8**, 300
Papilio memnon, caryophyllene oxide, **8**, 228
Papilio polyxenes
  feeding, effects of sinigrin on, **8**, 145
  xanthotoxin metabolism, **8**, 338
  xanthotoxin tolerance, **8**, 141
Papilio protenor, insect oviposition stimulants, **8**, 156
Papilio xuthus, insect oviposition stimulants, **8**, 156
PAPS *see* 3′-phosphoadenosine 5′-phosphosulfate
    (PAPS)
papuamine
  occurrence, **8**, 564
  structure, **8**, 564
papyriferic acid, effects, on herbivores, **8**, 142
Parabenzoin praecox
  (+)-epieudesmin, **1**, 694
  (+)-eudesmin, **1**, 694
Paracoccus denitrificans
  decaprenyl diphosphate synthase, **2**, 91
  nonaprenyl diphosphate synthase, **2**, 92
S-(−)-paraconic acid, as starting material, for A-factor,
    8, 381
paralytic shellfish poison (PSP), saxitoxins as, **8**, 485
Paraponera clavata
  poneratoxin, **8**, 359
  venom, **8**, 354
parasites, host–parasite chemical transfer, **8**, 175
parasitic wasps
  sex pheromones, **8**, 223
  see also Macrocentrus grandii; *Rhyssa persuasoria*
parasitic witchweed *see* Striga asiatica
parasitism, definition, **8**, 426
parasperone A, occurrence, **1**, 417
paratose
  in O-antigen, **3**, 345
  expression, **3**, 187
  occurrence, **3**, 312, 313
  substitution, **3**, 323
Paravespula pennsylvanica, venom, **8**, 354
Pardachirus spp., chemical defense, **8**, 473

Pardachirus pavoninus, surfactant peptides, **8**, 473
pardaxin P-2, structure, **8**, 474
pardaxins, occurrence, **8**, 473
Park–Johnson method, in branching enzyme assays, **3**, 458
Parnassius phoebus, sequestration, **8**, 362
paromomycin
    applications, antibiotics, **6**, 193
    binding, **6**, 193
    complexation, **6**, 193
paroxysmal nocturnal hemoglobinuria (PNH)
    etiology, **4**, 308
    PIG-A genes, **4**, 306
    somatic mutation, **4**, 306
PARP *see* procyclin
parsley *see Petroselinum crispum*
parsnip, boar-taint steroid, **8**, 230
parthenin, effects, on herbivores, **8**, 142
β-particles, in muscle, **3**, 442
partition function, in RNA structural transition analyses, **6**, 26
PAs *see* pyrrolizidine alkaloids (PAs)
Passiflora morifolia, glycoside biosynthesis, **1**, 70
Pasteurella pseudotuberculosis, glycogen synthase, **3**, 452
Pastinaca sativa
    coumarins, **1**, 625
    in induced chemical defense, **8**, 151
    seed predation, inhibition, **8**, 168
α-patchoulene, biosynthesis, **2**, 184
β-patchoulene, biosynthesis, **2**, 184
γ-patchoulene, biosynthesis, **2**, 184
patchouli synthases
    inhibitors
        diethylpyrocarbonate, **2**, 185
        N-ethylmaleimide, **2**, 185
        methyl methanethiolsulfonate, **2**, 185
    purification, **2**, 185
patchoulol
    biosynthesis, **2**, 184
    occurrence, **2**, 184
patchoulol synthase, purification, **5**, 330
pathogens
    defenses against, monoterpene role in, **2**, 101
    RNA enzymes as, **6**, 110
pathotoxins, use of term, **8**, 178
pathway gene expression, transcription factors, **2**, 205
Patinopecten yessoensis
    pectenotoxins, **8**, 497
    prostaglandins, **1**, 244
    yessotoxins, **8**, 499
patuletin 7-glycosides, roles, in ultraviolet patterning, **8**, 160
patulin
    antibiotic activity, **1**, 346
    antifungal activity, **1**, 2
    biosynthesis, **1**, 346, 427
    possible DNA damage, **7**, 503
    structure, **1**, 411
patuolide, biosynthesis, **1**, 410
patuolide A, structure, **1**, 410
pavetannins, occurrence, **3**, 779
Pavetta owariensis, pavetannins, **3**, 779
Payen, Anselme (1795–1871), cellulose studies, **3**, 530, 532, 533
PBAN *see* pheromone biosynthesis activating neuropeptide (PBAN)
PBDs *see* pyrrolo[1,4]benzodiazepines (PBDs)
PBG *see* porphobilinogen (PBG)
PBG deaminase(s) *see* hydroxymethylbilane synthase(s)
pBluescript phagemid, as expression vector, **7**, 650
PBPs *see* penicillin-binding proteins (PBPs)
pBR322, cloning, **3**, 477
PCA *see* principal components analysis (PCA)

pcb genes
    pcbAB
        chromosomal location, **4**, 245
        encoding, **4**, 168, 244
        expression, **4**, 173
        genetic manipulation, **4**, 253
        repression, **4**, 174
    pcbC
        chromosomal location, **4**, 245
        cloning, **4**, 168, 250
        encoding, **4**, 170, 244
        expression, **4**, 173
        occurrence, **4**, 245
        repression, **4**, 174
        transcription, **4**, 179
PCBs *see* polychlorinated biphenyls (PCBs)
PCGs *see* prochaetoglobosins (PCGs)
pch genes, *pchA*, isochorismate synthase encoding, **1**, 613
PCP *see* peptidyl carrier protein (PCP); phenol, pentachloro- (PCP)
PCR *see* polymerase chain reaction (PCR)
PCs *see* phosphatidylcholine(s) (PCs)
PCV *see* D-valine, phenylacetylcysteinyl- (PCV)
PD116740, biosynthesis, **1**, 483
PDA genes
    occurrence, **1**, 813
    PDA1, induction, **1**, 813
    PDA9, induction, **1**, 813
PDGF *see* platelet-derived growth factor (PDGF)
PE *see* phosphatidylethanolamine (PE)
peach latent mosaic viroid (PLMV)
    hammerhead self-cleavage structure, **6**, 180
    hosts, **6**, 182, 186
    localization, **6**, 178
pea embryo
    adenosinediphosphoglucose, **3**, 463
    starch synthase II, **3**, 454
pea isozymes, *waxy* locus, DNA sequence, **3**, 454
peas
    lhi (*lh-2*) mutation, **8**, 50
    Ls locus, **8**, 47
    (+)-pisatin, **1**, 800
    soluble starch synthases, **3**, 455
    wrinkled, starch levels, **3**, 462
    see also Pisum sativum
pea seedlings
    trans-cinnamate 4-monooxygenase, **3**, 635
    isoflavone reductase, **1**, 796
    3-phosphoshikimate 1-carboxyvinyltransferase, **1**, 593
pea seeds
    peroxygenase, **1**, 230
    r locus, **3**, 462
pea weevil *see Sitona lineatus*
pecan weevil, grandisol, **8**, 224
pectate lyase, occurrence, **8**, 398
pectate transeliminase *see* pectate lyase
Pecten maximus, larval settlement induction, **8**, 435
pectenotoxin 1 (PTX1)
    structure, **8**, 497
    studies, **8**, 499
pectenotoxin 2 (PTX2), cytotoxicity, **8**, 499
pectenotoxins (PTX)
    occurrence, **8**, 497
    structure, **8**, 497
pectinase *see* polygalacturonase
pectin demethoxylase *see* pectinesterase
pectin depolymerase *see* polygalacturonase
pectinesterase, activity, **3**, 518
pectin lyase, occurrence, **8**, 398
pectin methoxylase *see* pectinesterase
pectin methylesterase (PME) *see* pectinesterase

pectin methyltransferase (PMT)
  activity, **3**, 518
  occurrence, **3**, 519
  solubilization, **3**, 519
Pectinophora gossypiella
  gossyplure, **8**, 4
  7,11-hexadecadienyl acetates, **8**, 205
  pheromones, **8**, 4
pectin pectylhydrolase *see* pectinesterase
pectin(s)
  biosynthesis, **3**, 2, 8, **497–527**
    future research, **3**, 522
    regulatory mechanisms, **3**, 520
  biosynthetic enzymes, subcellular localization, **3**, 504
  in cell walls, **3**, 498
  methylesterification, **3**, 518
  structure, **3**, 499
pederine
  biosynthesis, **8**, 351
  insecticidal activity, **8**, 351
  occurrence, **8**, 351
pederone, structure, **8**, 351
pedunculagin, chemical synthesis, **3**, 817
PEG *see* polyethylene glycol (PEG)
peganine, 7-hydroxy- *see* vasicinol
Peganum harmala, vasicinone, **8**, 342
pelargonic acid, 8-amino-7-oxo-
  biosynthesis, **1**, 826
  as intermediate, **1**, 826
pelargonic acid, 7,8-diamino-, as intermediate, **1**, 826
pelargonidin, in bird pollinated plants, **8**, 158
Pelargonium spp., gallic acid biosynthesis, **3**, 804
Pelargonium graveolens
  geraniol biosynthesis, **2**, 62
  geranyl diphosphate synthases, **2**, 121
Pelargonium x hortorum, fatty acids, **1**, 42
Pellia epiphylla, lignans, **1**, 645, 673
Pellina spp., manzamines, **8**, 553
pellitorine, occurrence, **1**, 333, **8**, 303
(−)-α-peltatin, antiviral activity, **1**, 702
peltogynane-(4β→6)-fisetinidol, biosynthesis, **3**, 777
peltogynol, condensation, **3**, 754
pen genes
  penDE
    chromosomal location, **4**, 245
    cloning, **4**, 170, 245
    encoding, **4**, 244
    identification, **4**, 259
    introns, **4**, 181, 245
    repression, **4**, 174
penicillanic acid, 6-amino- (6-APA)
  analogues, **4**, 261
  biosynthesis, **3**, 283, **4**, 170, 240
  industrial production, **4**, 240
penicillic acid
  antifungal activity, **1**, 2
  biosynthesis, **1**, 427
  structure, **1**, 411
penicillin V
  biosynthesis, **4**, 254, 264
  side chains, **4**, 254
penicillin amidase, in 6-aminopenicillanic acid
    biosynthesis, **4**, 240
penicillin amidohydrolase *see* penicillin amidase
penicillinase(s) *see* β-lactamase(s)
penicillin-binding proteins (PBPs)
  classification, **3**, 266
  expression, **3**, 6
  PBP 1A
    characterization, **3**, 266
    purification, **3**, 266
  PBP 1B
    characterization, **3**, 266

purification, **3**, 266
properties, **3**, 266
use of term, **3**, 283
penicillin G
  biosynthesis, **4**, 240, 244, 254, 264
    pathways, **4**, 243
  biosynthetic enzymes, **4**, 246
  hydrolysis, **3**, 283
  side chains, **4**, 254
penicillin G, *m*-carboxy-, biosynthesis, **4**, 252
penicillin H, biosynthesis, **4**, 262
penicillin K, biosynthesis, **4**, 262, 264
penicillin N, biosynthesis, **1**, 840, **4**, 171
penicillins
  acylation, **3**, 267
  antibacterial activity, **4**, 240
  antimicrobial activity, **4**, 199
  bioactive properties, **4**, 197
  biochemistry, **4**, 160
  biosynthesis, **1**, 840, **4**, 344
    enzyme compartmentation, **4**, 182
    genetics, **4**, 173
    inhibition, **4**, 176
    overview, **4**, 162
  biosynthetic enzymes, localization, **4**, 244
  chemical synthesis, **4**, 268
  classification, **4**, 240, 242
  discovery, **1**, 10, **4**, 200, 319
  enzymatic synthesis, **4**, **239–274**
    biotechnological approach, **4**, 268
    coupled systems, **4**, 266
    future research, **4**, 269
    genetics, **4**, 244
    idiophase, **4**, 268
    trophophase, **4**, 268
  from, amino acids, **4**, 165
  genetic engineering, **4**, 240
  hydrophilic, **4**, 242
  hydrophobic, **4**, 242
    biosynthesis, **4**, 253
    specific enzymes, **4**, 253
  industrial production, **4**, 173, 179
    yield improvements, **4**, 180
  properties, **4**, 240
  resistance, **8**, 595
  semisynthetic, **4**, 240
  solubility, **4**, 240
  structure, **4**, 160, 240
Penicillium spp.
  communesins, **8**, 601
  penochalasins, **8**, 603
  penostatins, **8**, 603
  polyketides, **1**, 410
Penicillium brevicompactum, lovastatins, **1**, 424
Penicillium chrysogenum
  acetate-CoA ligase, **4**, 256
  ACV synthetase, **1**, 47
    encoding, **1**, 840
  isopenicillin N synthase, **4**, 169
  β-lactam biosynthesis, gene clusters, **4**, 173
  lysine degradation, **4**, 165
  mutations, **4**, 178
  nitrogen regulatory protein, **4**, 245
  nre genes, cloning, **4**, 176
  pcb genes, expression, **4**, 173
  penDE genes, **4**, 170
  penicillin biosynthesis, **4**, 267
    inhibition, **4**, 176
  penicillins, **4**, 199
    industrial production, **4**, 173, 179
  phenylacetyl-CoA ligase, expression, **4**, 268
  structural genes, amplification, **4**, 179
  ultrastructural studies, **4**, 244

Penicillium citrinum
  α1,2-mannosidases, **3**, 24
  pravastatin, **1**, 422
Penicillium cyclopium
  orsellinic acid, **1**, 412
  orsellinic acid synthase, **1**, 349, 360
Penicillium digitatum, ethylene, **8**, 93
Penicillium expansum, activity against, **1**, 691
Penicillium fellutanum, fellutamides, **8**, 599
Penicillium frequentans
  (+)-bisdechlorogeodin, **1**, 437
  dihydrogeodin oxidase, **1**, 435
Penicillium islandicum, emodin deoxygenase activity, **1**, 431
Penicillium notatum, early studies, **4**, 160, 319
Penicillium oxalicum, emodin deoxygenase activity, **1**, 431
Penicillium patulum
  methyl 6-methylsalicylate, **8**, 211
  6-methylsalicylic acid, **1**, 354
  6-methylsalicylic acid synthase, **1**, 349, 410
  polyketide pathway, **1**, 410
Penicillium roqueforti
  aristolochene synthase genes, isolation, **2**, 206
  aristolochene synthases, **2**, 177
  PR-toxin, **2**, 205
Penicillium stipitatum
  orsellinic acid, **1**, 3
  tetraacetic acid lactones, **1**, 3
Penicillium urticae, 6-methylsalicylic acid synthase, **1**, 411
penochalasins
  cytotoxicity, **8**, 603
  occurrence, **8**, 603
  stereostructure, **8**, 603
penostatins
  cytotoxicity, **8**, 603
  occurrence, **8**, 603
  stereostructure, **8**, 603
PENR1
  binding, **4**, 178
  chemical analysis, **4**, 177
  in β-lactam biosynthesis, **4**, 177
pentachlorophenol hydroxylase
  mechanisms, **5**, 418
  occurrence, **5**, 418
(Z)-9-pentacosene, occurrence, **8**, 219
(Z)-11-pentacosene, occurrence, **8**, 219
pentadecane, occurrence, **8**, 216
pentadecane, 5,9-dimethyl-, occurrence, **8**, 247
2-pentadecanone, occurrence, **8**, 216
2-pentadecanone, (6R,10R)-6,12-dimethyl-, occurrence, **8**, 244
pentadecan-2-one, 6,10,14-trimethyl- *see* acetone, hexahydrofarnesyl-
5,9,13-pentadecan-2-one, 6,10,14-trimethyl-, occurrence, **8**, 232
1-pentadecene, occurrence, **8**, 216, 217
(6Z)-pentadecene, occurrence, **8**, 216
(7Z)-pentadecene, occurrence, **8**, 216
(6R,7R,12E)-12-pentadecene-6,7-diol, as substrate, **1**, 308
(6S,7S,9E)-9-pentadecene-6,7-diol, as substrate, **1**, 307, 318
10-pentadecenoic acids, as intermediates, **8**, 207
(Z)-1-(Z)-4-pentadienes, in substrates, **1**, 98, 99
2,4-pentadienoate, 2-hydroxy-
  isolation, **5**, 35
  properties, **5**, 43
pentaketides
  intermediates, **1**, 414
  structure, **1**, 411
pentaketide synthases, catalysis, **1**, 414
pentalenenes
  conversion, to pentalenolactone, **2**, 171
  from, farnesyl diphosphate, **2**, 168

isolation, **2**, 169
  synthesis, mechanisms, **2**, 169
pentalenene synthase(s)
  crystal structure, **2**, 196
  occurrence, **2**, 210
  protein structure, **2**, 195
  RYR motif, **2**, 206
pentalene synthase
  cloning, **5**, 330
  purification, **5**, 330
pentalenic acid, biosynthesis, **2**, 168
pentalenolactones
  biosynthesis, **2**, 51, 171, 373, 377
  occurrence, **2**, 168
  synthesis, **2**, 168
pentanoate, (R)-3,5-dihydroxy-3-methyl *see* mevalonate
pentanoate, 1-ethylpropyl (2S,3R)-2-methyl-3-hydroxy-, occurrence, **8**, 241
pentanoic acid, as sex pheromone, **8**, 210
1-pentanol, occurrence, **1**, 209
(R)-2-pentanol, occurrence, **8**, 209
3-pentanone, occurrence, **8**, 210
pentasaccharides
  core structure, **3**, 40
  synthesis, **3**, 1
(9Z,19Z)-9,19-pentatriacontadiene, occurrence, **8**, 219
pentatriacontane, 15,23-dimethyl-, bioactivity, **8**, 249
8-pentatriacontene, (Z)-21-methyl-, occurrence, **8**, 249
cis-2-pentene, occurrence, **1**, 214
2-pentenoate, (S)-1-methylbutyl (2E)-2,4-dimethyl *see* dominicalure 2
3-pentenoate, 2-oxo-, isolation, **5**, 35
4-pentenoate, 2-oxo-, isolation, **5**, 35
N-pent-4-enoyl (PNT), as protecting group, **7**, 121
2-pentenyl diphosphate, (E)-3-methyl-, isomerization, **2**, 72
2-pentenyl diphosphate, (Z)-3-methyl-, **2**, 76
3-pentenyl diphosphate, (E)-3-methyl-, as substrate homologues, for isopentenyl diphosphate isomerase, **2**, 72
3-pentenyl diphosphate, (Z)-3-methyl-, isomerization, **2**, 72
pentitols, in cellulose studies, **3**, 544
pentitols, 1,5-anhydro-, in cellulose studies, **3**, 544
pentoses
  in cellulose studies, **3**, 544
  in *Serratia marcescens*, **3**, 190
3-pentynoate, 2-oxo-, synthesis, **5**, 45
PEP *see* phospho*enol*pyruvate (PEP)
Pep5
  gene clusters, localization, **4**, 286
  localization, **4**, 299
  properties, **4**, 279
  ring structures, **4**, 282
Pep enzymes
  PepB 967, encoding, **4**, 288
  PepC 398, encoding, **4**, 288
  PepP, inactivation, **4**, 291
  PepT, **4**, 290
pep genes
  pepC, inactivation, **4**, 289
  pepI, encoding, **4**, 296
peppermint
  cytochrome P450 oxygenases, **2**, 116
  enzymes, **2**, 147
  monoterpenes, **2**, 102, 110
    biosynthesis, **2**, 62
  see also Mentha x piperita
Pepsis formosa pattoni, venom, **8**, 354
peptide 401
  biological activity, **8**, 355
  in honeybee venom, **8**, 355
peptide 636-662, phosphorylation, **3**, 484

peptide antibiotics
  biosynthesis
    commercial, **4**, 211
    idiophase, **4**, 323
    non-ribosomal, **4**, 202
    ribosomal, **4**, 202
    tropophase, **4**, 323
    types of, **4**, 201
    via multifunctional peptide synthetases, **4, 195–220**
  diversity, **4**, 200
  from *Bacillus brevis*, **4**, 321
  future research, **4**, 217
  recombination techniques, **4**, 211
peptide ergot alkaloids
  biosynthesis, **4**, 53
  occurrence, **4**, 53
peptide ligands, receptors, molecular phylogeny, **1**, 281
peptide minor groove binders, A,T-hook, **7**, 486
peptide nucleic acids (PNAs)
  antisense oligonucleotide linkages, **7**, 306
  hybridization properties, **7**, 306
  synthesis, **6**, 95, **7**, 306
peptides
  applications, intercalating agents, **7**, 487
  bioactive, occurrence, **8**, 592
  bioactive products, **4**, 199
  bioactivity, **4**, 320
  biosynthesis
    combinatorial, **4**, 213, 349
    genetics, **4**, 321
    molecular biology, **4**, 321
    non-ribosomal, **4**, 232, 320
    overview, **4, 1–11**
    pathways, **4**, 206
    thiotemplate mechanism, **4**, 221, 344
    via peptide synthetases, **4**, 221
  cyclization, **4**, 230
  design strategies, **4**, 211
  disulfide-linked, synthesis, **7**, 483
  DNA binding, **7**, 352, **477–490**
  elongation, **4**, 230
  immunity, **4**, 296
  length, and peptide synthetase structure, **4**, 234
  minor groove binders, **7**, 486
    distamycin-based, **7**, 486
    netropsin-based, **7**, 486
  monomeric, synthesis, **7**, 483
  myotropic, **8**, 302
  non-ribosomal, biosynthesis, **4**, 344
  products, characteristics, **4**, 201
  random sequences, studies, **7**, 637
  salivation-stimulating, **8**, 302
  sequences, **4**, 221
  structure, **4**, 201
  synthesis, termination, **4**, 230
  synthetic, CD spectra, **8**, 474
  transit, **2**, 112
  zinc finger motif, **7**, 484
peptides, cyanobacterial, as protease inhibitors, studies,
  8, 610
peptides, cyclic, occurrence, **8**, 567
peptide substrates, glycosylation, **3**, 73
peptide synthetase(s)
  biosynthetic modules, **4**, 331
  catalysis, in acyl transfer reactions, **4**, 222
  channeling, **4**, 234
  domains
    acyltransferase, **4**, 222
    condensation, **4**, 227
    epimerization, **4**, 235
    thioesterase, **4**, 222
  early studies, **4**, 321
  epimerization mechanisms, **4**, 235

genes encoding, **4**, 213
genetic engineering, **4**, 181
identification, **4**, 214
isolation, **4**, 321
modular arrangements, **4**, 205
modular construction, **1**, 547
motif M, **4**, 342
multifunctional, for peptide antibiotic biosynthesis, **4**,
  195–220
occurrence, **1**, 542
organization, **4**, 246
recombinant, future research, **4**, 349
roles, **4**, 201
  in bond formation, **4, 221–238**
sequenced, **4**, 213
structure
  and peptide length, **4**, 234
  three-dimensional, **4**, 345
thioester activation, **4**, 222
thioester binding, **4**, 335
peptide toxins, from cone shells, **8**, 476
peptidoglycan
  D-amino acid biosynthesis in, **3**, 254
  carbohydrate structure, **3**, 243
  enzymes, occurrence, **3**, 274
  inhibition, **3**, 5, **241–294**
  interstrand cross-links, **3**, 247
  isolation, **3**, 243
  D-lactate incorporation, **3**, 272
  pentapeptide side chain
    structure, **3**, 245
    variations, **3**, 246
  permeability, **4**, 197
  precursors, **3**, 206
  processing, **3**, 269
  recycling, **3**, 271
  structure, **3**, 242
  synthesis, inhibition, **4**, 240
peptidoglycan *N*-acetylmuramoylhydrolase(s) *see*
  lysozyme(s)
peptidoglycan biosynthesis, **3**, 2, 5, **241–294**
  antibacterial agent development, **3**, 274
  in antibiotic-resistant bacteria, **3**, 271
  extracellular steps, **3**, 265
    inhibition, **3**, 281
  and fungal cell wall biosynthesis, **3**, 286
  and glycoprotein biosynthesis, **3**, 286
  inhibition, **3**, 274, 281
  intramembrane steps, **3**, 262
    inhibition, **3**, 279
  and oligosaccharide pathways, **3**, 286
peptidoglycan hydrolases, use of term, **3**, 269
peptidoglycan layer
  functions, **3**, 243
  Gram-negative bacteria, **3**, 242
  Gram-positive bacteria, **3**, 242
  structure, **3**, 242
peptidolactones, biosynthesis, **4**, 199
peptidyl carrier protein (PCP)
  conversion, **4**, 206
  in gramicidin S synthetase, **4**, 331, 340
peptidyltransferase
  23S rRNA, **6**, 200
  defects, **6**, 196
peptidyl transference, rRNA, **6**, 112
peptidyl-tRNA:aminoacyl-tRNA *N*-peptidyltransferase
  see peptidyltransferase
peramine, occurrence, **8**, 177
perdeuterolysine, EPR spectra, **5**, 211
Peganum harmala, serotonin biosynthesis, **4**, 54
Peribatodes rhomboidaria
  (6*Z*,9*Z*)-6,9-nonadecadien-3-one, **8**, 208
  (3*Z*,6*Z*,9*Z*)-3,6,9-nonadecatriene, **8**, 208

pericyclic processes
    in antibody catalysis, **5**, 424
    definition, **5**, 349
pericyclic reactions, mechanisms, **1**, 367
Peridroma saucia, rocaglamide toxicity, **8**, 340
Perileucoptera coffeella, 5,9-dimethylpentadecane, **8**, 247
Perilla frutescens, β-bisabolene, **2**, 164
perillenal, occurrence, **8**, 226
perillene
    analogues, **8**, 229
    occurrence, **8**, 226
perimycin, biosynthesis, **1**, 612
period shortening substances, occurrence, **8**, 457
periplanene-Br, occurrence, **8**, 227
Periplaneta spp., sex pheromones, **8**, 227
Periplaneta americana
    antifeedant activity against, **8**, 338
    hypertrehalosemic factor sensitivity, **8**, 299
    periplanone-B, **8**, 3, 4
    pheromones, **8**, 4
    sex pheromones, **8**, 227
Periplaneta brunnea, periplanene-Br, **8**, 227
Periplaneta fuliginosa, periplanone-D, **8**, 227
Periplaneta japonica, nauphoetin, **8**, 219
periplanetins, structure, **8**, 300
periplanone-A
    occurrence, **8**, 227
    specific rotation, **8**, 6
    structure, **8**, 4, 227
periplanone-B
    occurrence, **8**, 3, 4, 227
    structure, **8**, 227
periplanone-D, occurrence, **8**, 227
periplogenin, occurrence, **8**, 361
perlecan, localization, **3**, 164
permease(s)
    in penicillin G biosynthesis, **4**, 244
    qut genes, **1**, 590
    tripeptide uptake, **3**, 271
Perna canaliculus, brevetoxin B$_3$, **8**, 514
perosamine
    occurrence, **3**, 186
    in *Vibrio cholerae*, **3**, 195
Perovskia abrotanoides, perovskone, **1**, 377
perovskone, occurrence, **1**, 377
peroxidase(s)
    activation, **5**, 236
    catalysis, **1**, 274
        mechanisms, **3**, 718
    Class I, characterization, **3**, 718
    Class II, characterization, **3**, 718
    Class III
        characterization, **3**, 718
        structure, **3**, 719
    detection, **3**, 717
    in induced plant defense, **8**, 150
    mechanisms, **5**, 234
    molecular phylogeny, **1**, 274
    rate coefficients, **5**, 235
    roles
        in hydroperoxide reduction, **5**, 232
        in lignin biosynthesis, **3**, 716
peroxisomes
    acyl-CoA oxidase proteins, **1**, 51
    animal, **1**, 51
    phenylalanine ammonia-lyase, **3**, 662
peroxygenase, occurrence, **1**, 230
peroxyl radicals
    reactivity, **7**, 402
    reduction, **7**, 395
    synthesis, **7**, 402
peroxynitrite, as physiologic hydroperoxide activator, **5**, 239

peroxynitrous acid, prostaglandin-endoperoxide synthase activation, **5**, 235
persimmon *see Diospyros kaki*
perthamide B
    occurrence, **8**, 577
    structure, **8**, 577
Pestalotiopsis microspora, torreyanic acid, **1**, 377
Petauroides volans, feeding, effect of terpenes on, **8**, 144
Petroselinum crispum
    apiole, **8**, 336
    bergapten, **1**, 634
    cell enzymes, elicitor-induced, **8**, 97
    chalcone ketide reductase, **1**, 732
    chalcone synthase, **1**, 721, 752, 753
        genes, **1**, 755
    4-coumarate-CoA ligase, **1**, 47, 721
    coumarins, **1**, 625
    flavone synthases, **1**, 724
    flavonoid 3′-O-methyltransferase, **1**, 739
    flavonoid 3′-monooxygenase, **1**, 735
    flavonoid studies, **1**, 715
    flavonol synthase, **1**, 726
    hydroxycinnamyl O-methyltransferases, **3**, 646
    phenylalanine ammonia-lyase, **1**, 719, **3**, 634, 659
        mRNA, **3**, 663
    pyranocoumarins, **1**, 628
    xanthotoxin, **1**, 634
Petrosia serita, petrosins, **8**, 560
petrosins
    biogenetic path, **8**, 560
    occurrence, **8**, 560
    structure, **8**, 560
Petunia spp.
    flavonol 3-O-glucosyltransferase, **1**, 737
    naringenin 3-dioxygenase, **1**, 725
Petunia hybrida
    anthocyanidin synthase, **1**, 730
    chalcone isomerases, **1**, 723
    chalcone synthase, gene families, **1**, 755
    4-coumarate-CoA ligase, **3**, 650
    flavonol 3-O-glucosyltransferase, **1**, 731
    flavonol synthase, **1**, 727
    3-phosphoshikimate 1-carboxyvinyltransferase
        inhibitor, **1**, 595
        site-directed mutagenesis, **1**, 596
    tyramine, **1**, 128
petunidin, in fruit pigment, **8**, 164
petunidin glycosides, in flower pigment, **8**, 158
pEVP11 vector, in strictosidine synthase expression, **4**, 133
PF1052, biosynthesis, **1**, 370
PFL *see* formate *C*-acetyltransferase
PFL-AE *see* pyruvate formate lyase activating enzyme (PFL-AE)
PFT *see* protein farnesyltransferase (PFT)
Pfu DNA polymerase, applications, in polymerase chain reaction, **7**, 658
2-PGA *see* glycerate, 2-phospho- (2-PGA)
3-PGA, in starch synthesis, **3**, 464
PGA-GalAT *see* polygalacturonate 4-α-galacturonosyltransferase
PGD synthase *see* prostaglandin D synthase
PGE synthase *see* prostaglandin E synthase
PGF synthase *see* prostaglandin F synthase
PGGT-I *see* protein geranylgeranyltransferase-I (PGGT-I)
PGGT-II *see* protein geranylgeranyltransferase-II (PGGT-II)
PGH synthase(s) *see* prostaglandin-endoperoxide synthase(s)
PGI synthase *see* prostaglandin I synthase
*PGK*1 mRNA
    deadenylation, **6**, 207

rates, **6**, 206
decapping, **6**, 209
degradation, **6**, 212
shortened, **6**, 212
5′-UTR, translation inhibition, **6**, 208
*PGK*1 transcripts
accumulation, **6**, 209
decapped, **6**, 209
decay, **6**, 207
stabilization, **6**, 209
studies, **6**, 206
transcriptional pulse chase studies, **6**, 210
PHA$^{R\,2.7}$, role of α-glucosidases in, **3**, 31
PhAc *see* acetic acid, phenyl- (PhAc)
PhAc-CoA *see* phenylacetyl-CoA (PhAc-CoA)
PhAcCoAL *see* phenylacetyl-CoA ligase (PhAcCoAL)
PhAcTS *see* phenylacetic acid transport systems
(PhAcTS)
Phaedon cochleariae, pyrethrin toxicity, **8**, 335
Phaeoceros laevis, (+)-megacerotonic acid, **1**, 645
Phaeodactylum tricornutum, furan fatty acids, **1**, 226
Phaeophyta
lignins, **3**, 622
oxylipins, **1**, 216
see also Ecklonia stolonifera; Ectocarpus siliculosus;
Egregia menziesii; Giffordia mitchellae;
Notheia anomala
Phaeosphaeria spp.
gibberellin A$_1$, **8**, 41
gibberellin A$_4$, **8**, 41
kaurene synthase, **8**, 41
phage display, in random peptide studies, **7**, 637
phage display library, **7**, 485
phage receptors, lysogenic conversion, **3**, 216
phages
in cloning, **7**, 647
see also bacteriophages
Phalaenopsis spp., stilbene synthases, **1**, 753
Phalaris arundinacea
gramine, **8**, 336
hordenine, **8**, 336
Phalaris canariensis, auxin studies, **8**, 23
phalimide, *N*-(1-carboxypropyl)-, structure, **8**, 34
Phanerochaete chrysosporium
cellobiohydrolase studies, **3**, 593
peroxidases, **3**, 718
veratric acid, **3**, 624
Pharaoh's ants
trails, faranal, **2**, 78
see also Monomorium pharaonis
Pharorid *see* methoprene
phaseic acid
activity, **8**, 81
1′-*O*-β-D-glucosides, occurrence, **8**, 90
1-*O*-β-D-glucosyl esters, conversion, **8**, 90
isomerization, **8**, 89
phaseic acid, dihydro-
biosynthesis, **8**, 89
4′-*O*-β-D-glucosides, occurrence, **8**, 90
phaseic acid, *epi*-dihydro-
biosynthesis, **8**, 89
IR spectra, **8**, 75
phaseic acid, dihydro-, methyl ester, IR spectra, **8**, 75
phaseic acid, methyl ester, IR spectra, **8**, 75
phaseolin
accumulation, **1**, 785
metabolism, **1**, 814
phaseollidin
biosynthesis, **1**, 803
detoxification, **1**, 814
phaseolotoxin, occurrence, **4**, 203
Phaseolus spp., phenylalanine ammonia-lyase, **1**, 719
Phaseolus lunatus

isoflavonoids, **1**, 774
volatiles emission, **1**, 135
Phaseolus vulgaris
C$_6$-aldehydes, **1**, 110
arabinosyltransferases, **3**, 515
brassinosteroids, **8**, 100
chalcone isomerases, **1**, 722
chalcone synthase, genetics, **1**, 789
cinnamyl-alcohol dehydrogenases, **3**, 655
coumestrol release, **1**, 781
GDP-L-fucose, **3**, 509
genistin release, **1**, 781
gibberellin 2β-dioxygenases, **8**, 53
hydroperoxide lyase activity, **1**, 93
leukoagglutinin, **3**, 18
phenylalanine ammonia-lyase, **3**, 634, 659
prenylation studies, **1**, 803
proteins, **3**, 602
UDPglucose 6-dehydrogenase, **3**, 506
xylosyltransferases, **3**, 517
phebalin, occurrence, **1**, 380
(−)-α-phellandrene, biosynthesis, **2**, 140
(−)-β-phellandrene, biosynthesis, **2**, 140
α-phellandrene, structure, **2**, 103
β-phellandrene, structure, **2**, 103
(−)-β-phellandrene synthases, studies, **2**, 136
phenalenones, phenyl-, occurrence, **1**, 766
phenanthrene, degradation, **3**, 375
phenanthrene, (9*S*,10*S*)-9-(*S*-glutathionyl)-10-hydroxy-
9,10-dihydro-, biosynthesis, **5**, 63
phenanthrene alkaloids
biosynthesis, **4**, 40
occurrence, **4**, 35
phenanthrene 9,10-oxide, and epoxide ring opening, **5**, 62
1,10-phenanthroline–cuprous ion complexes
applications
DNA structure probes, **7**, 86
in rRNA studies, **6**, 200
phenazathionium chloride, 3-*N*-(4-
carboxybutyl)methylamino-7-dimethylamino-,
esters, **7**, 159
phenazine-di-*N*-oxide-oligonucleotide, DNA cleavage, **7**,
533
phenazine *N*-oxides
DNA damage induction, **7**, 532
oxygen radicals from, **7**, 533
phenazines, occurrence, **8**, 591
phenol
degradation, **3**, 384
roles, in L-tyrosine biosynthesis, **3**, 405
phenol, 3-azido-, reactions, with pyruvate, **3**, 408
phenol, 2,6-dibromo-, structure, **8**, 34
phenol, 3,5-dibromo-2-(3′,5′-dibromo-2′-
methoxyphenoxy)-, occurrence, **8**, 588
phenol, pentachloro- (PCP), monooxygenation, **5**, 418
phenolase(s) *see* catechol oxidase(s)
phenolic compounds, from, polyacetates, **1**, 2
phenolics
as allelopathic agents, **8**, 169
antimicrobial properties, **8**, 181
applications, herbivore defensive agents, **8**, 139
catechin-like, **8**, 186
classification, **8**, 139
effects, in soil, **8**, 173
loss from leaf litter, **8**, 173
occurrence
parasites, **8**, 175
plants, **8**, 139
phenol oxidative coupling, in (+)-geodin biosynthesis, **1**,
435
phenolphthiocerol, acyl transfer reactions, **4**, 234
phenols, alkyl-, biosynthesis, **3**, 677
phenols, allyl-

coupling, **1**, 678
metabolism, **1**, 678
phenols, bromo-, antifeedant activity, **8**, 461
phenols, di-*t*-butyl-, prostaglandin-endoperoxide
    synthase inhibition, **5**, 252
phenols, *o*-dihydroxy-, roles, in seed longevity, **8**, 169
phenothiazine, in oligodeoxynucleotides, **7**, 334
phenoxazine, in oligodeoxynucleotides, **7**, 334
phenoxyacetic acid, 2,4-dichloro-, structure, **8**, 34
phenoxyacetic acid (PhOAc), as penicillin side chain, **4**,
    254
phenoxyacetyl, in oligonucleotide synthesis, **7**, 123
phenoxyacetyl, *t*-butyl- as protecting group, **7**, 120
t-phenoxyacetyl, deoxyadenosine protection, **7**, 123
phenoxyl radicals, roles, **3**, 340
8–8′ phenoxy radical coupling, dirigent proteins in, **1**, 672
phenoxy radicals, thiyl radical biosynthesis, **5**, 183
phenyl, *p*-chloro-, as phosphate protecting groups, **7**, 130
phenyl, *p*-hydroxy-, use of term, **3**, 620
phenylacetaldoxime, occurrence, **1**, 130
phenylacetic acid transport systems (PhAcTS)
    activation, **4**, 254
    characterization, **4**, 244, 255
    properties, **4**, 254
    regulatory mechanisms, **4**, 255
    roles, in penicillin biosynthesis, **4**, 254
phenylacetyl-CoA ligase (PhAcCoAL)
    catalysis, **4**, 256
    comparative studies, **4**, 256
    expression, **4**, 268
    genes, characterization, **4**, 268
    in penicillin biosynthesis, **4**, 170, 268
    roles, in phenylacetic acid activation, **4**, 244
phenylacetyl-CoA (PhAc-CoA)
    analogues, **4**, 262
    biosynthesis, **4**, 244
phenylalanine
    analogues, **5**, 353
    binding, **6**, 128
    biosynthesis, **4**, 2, **5**, **5**, 344
        via shikimate–arogenate pathway, **1**, 719
        via shikimate–chorismate pathway, **3**, 626
        via shikimate pathway, **1**, 574
    as cyanogenic glycoside precursor, **1**, 885, 886
    deamination, **3**, 622, 631
    in gallic acid biosynthetic pathway, **3**, 804
    as intermediate, **3**, 626
    metabolic pool size, **3**, 627
    metabolism, **3**, 658
    as precursor, **1**, 2
    racemization, **4**, 342
    as starting material
        for alkaloids, **4**, 35
        for monolignols, **3**, 677
    in thiotropocin biosynthesis, **1**, 850
phenylalanine, *N*-(acetyl)jasmonyl-, occurrence, **1**, 118
phenylalanine, *m*-carboxy-, biosynthesis, **1**, 619
phenylalanine, *S*-dihydro-, phytotoxicity, **8**, 178
phenylalanine, L-3,4-dihydroxy- (L-DOPA)
    effects, on herbivores, **8**, 146
    larval settlement induction, **8**, 432
    synthesis, **3**, 408
L-phenylalanine, biosynthesis, **1**, 345
L-phenylalanine, *p*-amino- (L-PAPA), biosynthesis, **5**, 347
phenylalanine ammonia-lyase
    activity, **1**, 719
    biochemistry, **1**, 719
    catalysis, **1**, 2, 18, **3**, 622
    cloning, **3**, 634
    early studies, **3**, 631
    encoding, **1**, 785
    as flavonoid precursor, **1**, 719
    gene promoter expression, **3**, 667

genetics, **1**, 719, **3**, 659
induction, **1**, 130
inhibitors, **3**, 627, 634
K_m, **3**, 658
localization, **3**, 659
molecular biology, **1**, 719
mRNA localization, **3**, 662
occurrence, **3**, 622
organelle fractionation studies, **3**, 662
protein localization, **3**, 662
purification, **3**, 632
roles
    in hydroxycinnamic acid esters, **1**, 786
    in isoflavonoid biosynthesis, **1**, 784
    in monolignol biosynthesis, **3**, 631
L-phenylalanine ammonia-lyase *see* phenylalanine
    ammonia-lyase
phenylalanine racemase, classification, **4**, 325
phenylalanine–tyrosine pathways, overview, **4**, 5
phenylbutyryl-CoA, non-recognition, **4**, 264
p-phenylenediamine, oxidation, **3**, 711
phenylpropionyl-CoA, non-recognition, **4**, 264
phenylpyruvate *keto–enol*-isomerase *see* phenylpyruvate
    tautomerase
phenylpyruvate tautomerase
    identification, **5**, 47
    substrates, **5**, 47
phenyl radicals, carbon-centered, **7**, 543
phenylserine aldolase
    biochemistry, **3**, 397
    detection, **3**, 399
L-*threo*-3-phenylserine benzaldehyde-lyase *see*
    phenylserine aldolase
pheromone biosynthesis activating neuropeptide
    (PBAN), **8**, 205
    biochemistry, **8**, 300
pheromones
    acetogenins, **8**, 203
    in algae, **8**, 420
        biosynthesis, **8**, 425
    as attractants, **8**, 198
    behavior mediation, **8**, 201
    biochemistry, **8**, **197–261**
    classifications, **8**, 198
    definition, **8**, 2
    diterpenes, **8**, 229
    in *Enterococcus faecalis*
        inhibitors, **8**, 408
        structure, **8**, 408
    in fresh water diatoms, **8**, 425
    from, propanoates, **8**, 241
    hydrocarbons, **8**, 247
    identification, techniques, **8**, 201
    inhibition, **8**, 12
    isolation, techniques, **8**, 201
    marine animals, **8**, 420
    pattern recognition, and caste-specificity, **8**, 205
    primer, **8**, 198
    production, **8**, 163
    properties, synthetic v. natural product, **8**, 6
    releaser, **8**, 198
    sesquiterpenes, **8**, 227
    social insects, **8**, 205
    stereochemistry, via optical rotatory dispersion, **8**, 6
    stereochemistry–bioactivity relationship, **8**, 11
    steroids, **8**, 230
    in Teleostei, **8**, 426
    use of term, **8**, 378, 380
    see also aggregation pheromones; microbial hormones;
        sex pheromones; trail pheromones
philanthotoxin-433, occurrence, **8**, 356
Philanthus triangulum
    (*Z*)-11-icosen-1-ol, **8**, 218

venoms, **8**, 356
phleomycin, applications, antibiotics, **7**, 539
phlobatannins
    applications, **3**, 775
    structure, **3**, 773
phloretin, occurrence, **8**, 338
phloridzin, occurrence, **8**, 338
phloroglucinol
    antifeedant activity, **8**, 460
    biosynthesis, **1**, 814, 2
    roles, in flavan-3-ol biosynthesis, **3**, 755
phloroglucinol, monoacetyl-, biosynthesis, **1**, 763
phloroglucinol carboxylic acid, biosynthesis, **1**, 814
phloroisobutyrophenone (PIBPS), biosynthesis, **1**, 760
phloroisovalerophenone (PIVPS), biosynthesis, **1**, 760
phn genes, occurrence, **1**, 878
phoenicol, occurrence, **8**, 245
Phoma betae, betaenones, **1**, 388
phomactins
    occurrence, **8**, 599
    structure, **8**, 599
    as thrombocyte activating factor antagonist, **8**, 599
Phoma tracheiophila, malseccin, **8**, 181
phomazin, phytotoxicity, **8**, 179
phomenone, phytotoxicity, **8**, 179
phomodiol, occurrence, **1**, 370
phomopsichalasin, occurrence, **1**, 374
Phomopsis spp., phomopsichalasin, **1**, 374
Phoracantha synonyma, phoracantholide I, **8**, 213
phoracantholide I, occurrence, **8**, 213
Phoradendron spp., lignins, **3**, 700
Phorbas spp., phorboxazoles, **8**, 583
phorboxazoles
    cytostasis, **8**, 583
    occurrence, **8**, 583
    structure, **8**, 583
Phormia regina, juvenile hormones, **8**, 269
phosalacine, isolation, **1**, 865
phosphapyrimidine nucleosides, cytidine deaminase
        inhibition, **5**, 89
phosphatase inhibitors, **5**, 158
    affinity reagents, **5**, 160
    competitive, **5**, 158
    design, **5**, 141
    mechanism-based, **5**, 160
phosphatases
    activity, **5**, 330
    biochemistry, **5**, **139–162**
    catalysis, covalent intermediates, **5**, 143
    chemical labeling studies, **5**, 152
    classification, **5**, 140, 152
    in cytokinin chemistry, **8**, 60
    enzymology, **5**, **139–162**
    future research, **5**, 161
    isotope effects, **5**, 141
    mechanisms, **5**, 141
    mutagenesis studies, **5**, 152
    nonspecific, **5**, 152
    roles
        in biochemistry, **5**, 140
        in phosphate monoester hydrolysis, **5**, 139
    small molecule specific, **5**, 157
    transition states, **5**, 141
phosphate, acetyl
    biosynthesis, **3**, 393
    reactions, with D-glyceraldehyde-3-phosphate, **3**, 392
phosphate, aminoethanol, occurrence, **3**, 197
phosphate, carboxyallenyl, 3-phosphoshikimate 1-
        carboxyvinyltransferase inhibition, **1**, 598
phosphate, *O,O*-diethyl-4-nitrophenyl, structure, **5**, 150
phosphate, dimethyl 2,2-dichlorovinyl, effects on
        aflatoxin production, **1**, 447
phosphate, *p*-nitrophenyl (*p*-NPP)

hydrolysis, **5**, 149
    as substrate, **5**, 150
3-phosphate, 1-acyl-*sn*-glycero-, biosynthesis, **1**, 286
3-phosphate, 1-alkyl-2-acyl-*sn*-glycero-, biosynthesis, **1**,
        288
3-phosphate, 1-alkyl-*sn*-glycero-
    activity, **1**, 288
    acylation, **1**, 288
    biosynthesis, **1**, 288
    dephosphorylation, **1**, 288
3′-phosphate, formation, **7**, 571
phosphate diesters
    elimination, rate constants, **7**, 390
    reactivity, **6**, 221
phosphate ester hydrolysis
    enzyme-catalyzed, **5**, 143
    isotope effects, **5**, 148
        determination, **5**, 148
        primary, **5**, 148
        remote labeling, **5**, 148
        secondary, **5**, 148
    isotope ratio mass spectra, **5**, 148
    mechanisms, **5**, 139
    nonenzymatic, **5**, 141
phosphate esters
    cleavage, **5**, 142
    roles
        in biochemistry, **5**, 140
        in signal transduction, **5**, 140
phosphate esters, chiral, synthesis, **5**, 146
phosphate hydrolysis, enzymatic, **7**, 372
phosphate mapping, studies, **7**, 270
phosphate–metal ion coordination, probing, **6**, 221
phosphate monoesters, hydrolysis, **5**, 139
phosphate protecting groups, in oligonucleotide
        synthesis, **7**, 130
phosphate–protein interactions, interference analysis, **6**,
        222
phosphate(s)
    activation, **6**, 69
    dissociation, **1**, 602
    effects on cephalosporin C production, **4**, 177
    and glycogen accumulation, **3**, 443
    modification, **6**, 89
phosphates, acyl, as intermediates, **5**, 144
phosphates, cyclic, biosynthesis, **6**, 151
phosphates, phenyl chloro-, as coupling reaction
        activator, **7**, 139
phosphatidase *see* phospholipase A₂
phosphatidolipase *see* phospholipase A₂
phosphatidylcholine, short-chain fatty acid-containing
    biological activity, **1**, 298
    biosynthesis, **1**, 286, 298
phosphatidylcholine 2-acylhydrolase *see* phospholipase
        A₂
phosphatidylcholine cholinephosphohydrolase *see*
        phospholipase C
phosphatidylcholine(s) (PCs)
    fatty acids in, **1**, 35
    ω-hydroxylate moieties, **1**, 298
    oxidatively fragmented, **1**, 298
    semialdehyde moieties, **1**, 298
phosphatidylethanolamine (PE)
    binding, **4**, 282
    fatty acids in, **1**, 35
phosphatidylinositol kinases, regulatory mechanisms, **3**,
        488
phosphatidylinositol-specific phospholipase C (PI-PLC)
    functions, **4**, 307
    roles, in VSG protein release, **3**, 296
phosphinates, synthesis, **7**, 297, 298
phosphinates, aminoalkyl-, synthesis, **3**, 277, 278
phosphine, tributyl-, use in phosphate protection, **7**, 130

phosphinomethylmalic acid synthase, isolation, **1**, 872
phosphinothricin
    biosynthesis, **1**, 869
    biosynthetic pathway, **1**, 866
    carbon skeleton, origin of, **1**, 867
    as glutamine synthetase inhibitor, **2**, 257
    P-methyl group, origin of, **1**, 867
phosphinothricin, *N*-acetyl-, radioactivity incorporation,
        1, 871
phosphite, bisacyl-, synthesis, **7**, 139
phosphite, tristriazolyl-, in *H*-phosphonate synthesis, **7**,
        139
phosphites, bistriazolyl-, in phosphoramidite synthesis, **7**,
        132
phosphitylation reagents
    2-cyano-1,1-dimethylethyl phosphorodichloridite, **7**,
        130
    2,2,2-trichloro-1,1-dimethylethyl
        phosphorodichloridite, **7**, 130
3′-phosphoadenosine 5′-phosphosulfate (PAPS),
        biosynthesis, **1**, 331, **3**, 171
phosphoarginine, as intermediate, **5**, 144
3-phosphocholine, 1-*O*-alkyl-2-acetyl-*sn*-glycero- *see*
        platelet-activating factor (PAF)
phosphocysteine, as intermediate, **5**, 144
phosphodiesterases, lead-dependent, **7**, 622
phosphodiester bonds
    conformation, **7**, 76
    rearrangement, **6**, 115
phosphodiester hydrolases, discovery, **7**, 616
phosphodiester linkages, in antisense oligonucleotides, **7**,
        287
phosphodiesters
    in oligonucleotide synthesis, **6**, 82, **7**, 107
    transesterification, **7**, 630
phosphodiesters, internucleotide, in protein–DNA
        complexes, **7**, 268
phospho*enol*pyruvate, 3-fluoro-, proton addition, **1**, 595
phospho*enol*pyruvate, (*E*)-3-fluoro-, as pseudosubstrate,
        1, 594
phospho*enol*pyruvate, (*Z*)-3-fluoro-
    3-phosphoshikimate 1-carboxyvinyltransferase
        inhibition, **1**, 598
    as pseudosubstrate, **1**, 594
phospho*enol*pyruvate carboxylase, zeatin-induced, **8**, 66
phospho*enol*pyruvate kinase *see* pyruvate kinase
phospho*enol*pyruvate (PEP)
    addition, **1**, 833
    analogues, as substrate, **1**, 595
    binding, **1**, 593
    catalysis, **1**, 575
    energy, **5**, 33
    intramolecular rearrangement, to phosphonopyruvic
        acid, **1**, 868
    as precursor, **1**, 867
    reactions
        with *N*-acetyl-D-mannosamine, **3**, 390
        with arabinose 5-phosphate, **1**, 580, **3**, 387
        with 4,5-dideoxyshikimate 3-phosphate, **1**, 595
        with erythrose-4-phosphate, **1**, 575, **4**, 2
        with D-erythrose-4-phosphate, **3**, 386
        with shikimate 3-phosphate, **1**, 593
    as starting material, for chorismate, **1**, 574
phospho*enol*pyruvate (PEP) phosphomutase
    catalysis, **1**, 868, 875
    genetics, **1**, 874, 877
    purification, **1**, 869
phospho*enol*pyruvate:3-phosphoshikimate 5-*O*-(1-
        carboxyvinyl)-transferase *see* 3-phosphoshikimate 1-
        carboxyvinyltransferase
phospho*enol* transphosphorylase *see* pyruvate kinase
phosphoenzyme intermediates
    burst kinetics, **5**, 147

characteristics, **5**, 144
    detection, **5**, 144
    direct observation, **5**, 145
    electrophoresis, **5**, 145
    kinetic studies, **5**, 147
    mass spectra, **5**, 145
    NMR spectra, **5**, 145
    stereochemistry, **5**, 145
phosphoester bonds, cleavage, **6**, 109
phospho-*β*-galactosidases, occurrence, **3**, 687
phosphoglucomutase, mutants, **3**, 204
6-phosphogluconate-dehydrogenase, coding, **3**, 217
phosphoglucosamine mutase, activity, **3**, 206
phosphoglucose isomerase
    cytosolic, in leaves, **3**, 473
    mutants, **3**, 204
phosphoglycaldehydes, structure, **7**, 384
3-phospho-D-glycerate carboxy-lyase (dimerizing) *see*
        ribulose-bisphosphate carboxylase
2-phosphoglycerate dehydratase *see* phosphopyruvate
        hydratase
2-phospho-D-glycerate hydro-lyase *see* phosphopyruvate
        hydratase
3-phosphoglycol, (*R*)-1-octyl-2-(*N*-dodecanoylamino)-2-
        deoxyglycero-, binding, **5**, 110
3′-phosphoglycolate, and DNA damage, **7**, 403, 583
phosphoglycolohydroxamate, structure, **5**, 36
phosphoheptose isomerase, catalysis, **3**, 224
phosphoheptose mutase, catalysis, **3**, 224
phosphohistidine, as intermediate, **5**, 144
phosphohydrolases, activity, **1**, 296, **2**, 98
6-phospho-5-keto-2-deoxygluconate aldolase *see* 5-
        dehydro-2-deoxyphosphogluconate aldolase
phosphoketolase
    biochemistry, **3**, 392
    catalysis, **3**, 392
    purification, **3**, 392
    studies, **3**, 393
phosphoketotetrose aldolase *see* ketotetrose-phosphate
        aldolase
phospholipase A
    bioactive properties, **4**, 197
    inhibition, **4**, 282
phospholipase A₂
    absorption, **5**, 109
    activation, **1**, 134
    catalysis, **1**, 255
        mechanisms, **5**, 105
        Michaelis–Menten equation, **5**, 108
    classes, **5**, 110
    cytosolic, **1**, 256
    effects of auxins on, **8**, 32
    inactivation, **8**, 521
    inhibition, **1**, 248
    interfacial kinetics, **5**, 106
    molecular recognition
        of lipid interfaces, **5**, 109
        of phospholipid monomers, **5**, 111
    mutagenesis, site-specific, **5**, 112
    occurrence, **1**, 242, 249, **5**, 105, **8**, 479
        honeybee venom, **8**, 355
    regulatory mechanisms, **1**, 256
    roles
        in ester hydrolysis, **5**, 103, 105
        in platelet-activating factor biosynthesis, **1**, 289, 291
        in polyunsaturated fatty acid biosynthesis, **1**, 161
    scooting mode kinetics, **5**, 106, 108
    secretory, **1**, 256
    structure, **5**, 105, **8**, 355
    structure–function relationships, **5**, 106
    surface dilution kinetics, **5**, 106
phospholipase A₂ inhibitor, in octadecanoid pathway, **1**,
        123

phospholipase B *see* lysophospholipase
phospholipase C, effects of auxins on, **8**, 32
phospholipids
    fatty acids in, **1**, 24, 35
    linolenic acid in, **1**, 119
phospholipids, alkenyl ether-linked, biosynthesis, **1**, 289
phospholipids, ether-linked, biosynthesis, **1**, 286
phospholysine, as intermediate, **5**, 144
phosphomannomutase
    catalysis, **3**, 207
    defects, **3**, 59
phosphomonoesterase *see* acid phosphatase; alkaline
    phosphatase
phospho-Mur*N*Ac-pentapeptide translocase (translocase
    I)
    activity, **3**, 263
    catalysis, **3**, 263
    genes, encoding, **3**, 263
    inhibition, **3**, 279
    substrate specificity, **3**, 263
phosphonamidates, applications, hydrolytic enzyme
    inhibitors, **5**, 430
phosphonamidites, methyl-, synthesis, **7**, 161
phosphonate, α-difluoro-, activity, **5**, 304
phosphonate esters, applications, hydrolytic enzyme
    inhibitors, **5**, 430
phosphonates
    activity, **5**, 304
    as farnesyl-diphosphate farnesyltransferase inhibitors,
    2, 258
phosphonates, aminoalkyl-, synthesis, **7**, 294
phosphonates, α-halo-, applications, affinity reagents, **5**,
    160
phosphonates, α-keto-, applications, affinity reagents, **5**,
    160
phosphonates, methyl-
    linkage, **7**, 259
    in oligonucleotides, **7**, 619
    synthesis, **7**, 240, 287, 294
H-phosphonates
    in oligonucleotide synthesis, **6**, 82, 87, **7**, 109
    overactivation, **7**, 139
    synthesis, **7**, 139
phosphonic acid, reduction, to phosphinic acid, **1**, 867,
    869
phosphonic acid, 2-aminoethyl- (AEP)
    biosynthesis, pathways, **1**, 867
    conversion, to fosfomycin, **1**, 875
    occurrence, **1**, 865
phosphonic acid, (1*R*,2*S*)-1,2-epoxypropyl-
    structure, **5**, 62
    see also fosfomycin (FM)
phosphonic acid, 2-hydroxyethyl-
    conversion, to fosfomycin, **1**, 875
    as metabolite, **1**, 869
phosphonic acid, hydroxymethyl-, as metabolite, **1**, 869
phosphonic acid, 2-hydroxypropyl-
    dehydrogenation, **1**, 876
    as intermediate, **1**, 876
phosphonic acid, *cis*-propenyl-, as intermediate, **1**, 876
phosphonopyruvic acid decarboxylase, genetics, **1**, 877
α-phosphonosulfonates, as farnesyl-diphosphate
    farnesyltransferase inhibitors, **2**, 256, 258
4′-phosphopantetheine (4′PPan)
    attachment sites, **4**, 168
    binding, **1**, 423, **4**, 325
    in fatty acid biosynthesis, **1**, 27
    in peptide biosynthesis, **4**, 321
    residues, **1**, 16
    thiotemplate site representation, **4**, 335
phosphopantetheine transferases, superfamily, **4**, 329
4′-phosphopantetheine transferases, identification, **4**, 206
4′-phosphopantetheinyl groups, condensation, **4**, 206

3′-phosphopentenaldehyde, and DNA damage, **7**, 583
phosphoprotein phosphatase(s)
    biochemistry, **5**, 155
    calcium-modulated, **8**, 82
    inactivation, **3**, 487
    inhibition, by okadaic acid, **8**, 490
    synthesis, *de novo*, **1**, 134
phosphoprotein phosphohydrolases *see* phosphoprotein
    phosphatase(s)
3′-phosphopyridazine, and DNA damage, **7**, 583
phosphopyruvate hydratase
    active sites, **5**, 27
    catalysis, **5**, 16
        mechanisms, **5**, 18
    structure, **5**, 18
phosphoramidates, synthesis, **7**, 294, 295, 296, 297
phosphoramidates, *N*,*N*-diisopropyl-, **7**, 131
phosphoramidimidates, synthesis, **7**, 295
phosphoramidites
    O-allyl-protected, **7**, 135
    applications, **7**, 154
    O-aryl-protected, **7**, 135
    availability, **7**, 620
    biotinylation, **7**, 171
    mercaptoalkylation, **7**, 167
    for oligonucleotide aminoalkylation, **7**, 155
    for oligonucleotide mercaptoalkylation, **7**, 167
    in oligonucleotide synthesis, **6**, 82, **7**, 108, 142
    reporter and conjugate group attachment, **7**, 154
    support-bound, **7**, 137
    synthesis, **7**, 156
    universal base, **7**, 621
phosphoramidites, acridinyl, synthesis, **7**, 181
phosphoramidites, adamantylethyl, synthesis, **7**, 187
phosphoramidites, adenosine, insertion, into
    oligonucleotides, **7**, 229
phosphoramidites, aminoalkylated, synthesis, **7**, 191
phosphoramidites, anthracenyl deoxyguanosine,
    synthesis, **7**, 222
phosphoramidites, anthraquinone, synthesis, **7**, 183
phosphoramidites, bipyridinyl, synthesis, **7**, 185
phosphoramidites, carbocyclic, synthesis, **7**, 235
phosphoramidites, cholesteryl, synthesis, **7**, 187
phosphoramidites, β-cyanoethyl, in oligonucleotide
    synthesis, **7**, 132
phosphoramidites, dansyl, synthesis, **7**, 178
phosphoramidites, dichloro-, in phosphoramidite
    synthesis, **7**, 132
phosphoramidites, *N*,*N*-diisopropyl-, structure, **7**, 131
phosphoramidites, fluoresceinyl, synthesis, **7**, 177
phosphoramidites, methoxy, in oligonucleotide synthesis,
    7, 132
phosphoramidites, phosphotyrosinyl, synthesis, **7**, 174
phosphoramidites, polyalkyl, synthesis, **7**, 187
phosphoramidites, pyrenyl, synthesis, **7**, 178, 224
phosphoranes, as intermediates, **5**, 142
phosphorelays, functions, **8**, 406
phosphoribosylanthranilate isomerase(s)
    occurrence, **4**, 7
    structure, **4**, 7
phosphorodichloridate, 2,2,2-trichloro-1,1-dimethylethyl
    (TCDME), development, **7**, 130
phosphorodichloridite, 2-cyano-1,1-dimethylethyl, as
    phosphitylation reagent, **7**, 130
phosphorodichloridite, 2,2,2-trichloroethyl, in
    oligonucleotide synthesis, **7**, 108
phosphorodithioates, synthesis, **7**, 293
phosphorofluoridates, synthesis, **7**, 293
3′-phosphoroimidazoles, in SELEX studies, **7**, 633
phosphoroselenoates, synthesis, **7**, 293
phosphorotetrazolides, synthesis, **7**, 137
phosphorothioate(s)
    analogues, synthesis, **7**, 265

antisense mechanisms, **7**, 292
applications, **6**, 223, **7**, 280
 in ribonucleotide studies, **6**, 217
 in ribozyme cleavage, **7**, 280
 in stereochemical analysis, **6**, 219
chirality, **7**, 306
cleavage, iodine-mediated, **6**, 221
clinical trials, **7**, 290
diastereomers, **6**, 219
footprinting, **6**, 222
interactions
 with fluorescent dyes, **6**, 223
 with photoaffinity labels, **6**, 223
interference studies, **6**, 157, 221, 222
linkages
 configuration, **6**, 219
 in hairpin ribozymes, **6**, 159
 in RNA, **6**, 90, 157, 219
in oligonucleotides, **7**, 619
reactivity, **6**, 221
stereochemistry, **6**, 219
studies, **7**, 258
as substrates, **6**, 160
synthesis, **7**, 287, 291, 296, 298
terminal, **6**, 223
x-ray crystal structure, **6**, 222
phosphorothioate(s), 3'-bridging, **7**, 281
phosphorothioic acid(s) *see* phosphorothioate(s)
3'-*S*-phosphorothiolate, in substrates, **6**, 224
phosphorothiolate(s), *S*-bridging, **6**, 224
5'-*S*-phosphorothiolates, in hammerhead ribozyme
 studies, **6**, 224
phosphorus–oxygen–phosphorus bonds, in
 dimethylallyl*trans*transferase reaction, **2**, 81
phosphoryl, in lipopolysaccharides, **3**, 227
phosphorylase kinase, subunits, **3**, 487, **5**, 157
phosphorylase(s)
 in branching enzyme assays, **3**, 458
 degradative mechanisms, **3**, 442
 occurrence, **5**, 306
 in polyglucan synthesis, **3**, 442
phosphorylation, mechanisms, **1**, 294, **3**, 445
phosphorylcholine, lipopolysaccharide incorporation, **3**,
 229
phosphorylcholine-glyceride transferase *see*
 diacylglycerol cholinephosphotransferase
phosphoryl transfer, heavy atom isotope effects, **5**, 143
phosphoserine
 as intermediate, **5**, 144
 structure, **4**, 354
phosphoseryl-tRNA, as intermediate, **4**, 355
3-phosphoshikimate 1-carboxyvinyltransferase, **1**, 719
 active site residues, **1**, 596
 catalysis, **1**, 593
 complexation, **1**, 597
 inhibition, **4**, 9
 inhibitors, **1**, 598
  glyphosate, **1**, 596
 kinetics, **1**, 593
 mechanisms, **1**, 577, 593
 mutagenesis, **1**, 596
 NMR spectra, **1**, 596, 597
 occurrence, **1**, 593
 purification, **1**, 593
 roles, in aromatic amino acid biosynthesis, **4**, 4
 stereochemistry, **1**, 594
 structure, three-dimensional, **1**, 593
 substrates, **1**, 598
 tetrahedral intermediates, **1**, 594
  fluorinated, **1**, 594
  stereochemistry, **1**, 596
phosphosphingolipids, biosynthesis, **3**, 97
phosphotidylinositol-3-kinase (PI3K), p85 subunits, **7**,
 668

Sm-6-phosphotransferase, expression, **8**, 382
phosphotriesters
 in oligonucleotide synthesis, **6**, 82, **7**, 107
 synthesis, **7**, 107, 295
phosphotriose isomerase *see* triose-phosphate isomerase
 (TIM)
phosphotyrosine phosphatases *see* protein-tyrosine-
 phosphatase(s)
Photinus pyralis, luciferase, **4**, 348
photoactivation, of neocarzinostatin chromophore, **7**, 562
photoadducts, covalent, formation, **7**, 545
photoaffinity labeling, in aequorin structural analysis, **8**,
 453
photoaffinity labels, interactions, with
 phosphorothioates, **6**, 223
photoaffinity ligands, for vertebrate squalene epoxidase,
 2, 279
photochemically-activated agents
 DNA adduct formation, **7**, 544
 DNA damage, **7**, 544
photodehydroginkgolide A, **2**, 390
 biosynthesis, **2**, 394
photolabile supports, in oligonucleotide synthesis, **7**, 115
photolesions
 excision rates, **5**, 393
 mechanisms, **5**, **371–399**
 premutagenic, **5**, 372
(6-4) photoproduct
 formation, **5**, 386
  mechanisms, **5**, 386
 mutagenesis induction, **5**, 394
 repair pathways, **5**, 372
(6-4) photoproduct photolyase
 action spectra, **5**, 386, 388
 competing oxidation, **5**, 388
 mechanisms, **5**, 386
 occurrence, **5**, 386
photoproteins, purification, **8**, 447
photoreactivating enzyme *see* deoxyribodipyrimidine
 photo-lyase(s)
photoreactivation
 cyclobutane pyrimidine photodimers, **5**, 375
 type III, **5**, 389
photosynthesis
 anoxygenic, **2**, 327
 carbon fixation, **3**, 443
 oxygenic, **2**, 348
phototrityl group, **7**, 129
phototropism
 Cholodony–Went theory of, **8**, 26
 early studies, **8**, 23
pHPB *see* butan-2-one, 4-hydroxyphenyl- (pHPB)
Phragmatobia fuliginosa
 (3*Z*,6*Z*,9*Z*)-3,6,9-henicosatriene, **8**, 207
 linolenic acid, **8**, 207
Phramatopoma californica, larval settlement induction, **8**,
 432
Phryma leptostachya
 haedoxan A, **1**, 687, 696
 (+)-haedoxan A, **1**, 693
phthalideisoquinoline alkaloids, biosynthesis, **4**, 40
phthalimide, *N*-ethyl-, binding, **5**, 429
Phycomyces blakesleeanus
 car studies, **2**, 327
 gallic acid studies, **3**, 805
phyllamycin B, HIV-1 reverse transcriptase inhibition, **1**,
 703
phyllanthin, cytotoxicity, **1**, 701
phyllanthurinolactone
 occurrence, **8**, 7, 26
 structure, **8**, 7
Phyllanthus amarus
 hypophyllanthin, **1**, 701

phyllanthin, **1**, 701
Phyllanthus myrtifolius, retrojusticidin B, **1**, 703
Phyllanthus urinaria, phyllanthurinolactone, **8**, 7
Phyllidiidae, antifouling agents, **8**, 438
(+)-phylligenin, occurrence, **1**, 662
(+)-phyllirin, occurrence, **1**, 662
phyllocladene, biosynthesis, **2**, 237
Phyllophaga anxia, pheromones, **8**, 221
phylloquinone
    biosynthesis, **1**, 617, 620
    from, *o*-succinylbenzoic acid, **1**, 617
Phyllostachys spp., laccases, **3**, 709
Phyllostachys edulis, gibberellin A$_{19}$, **8**, 43
Phyllostachys heterocycla, laccases, **3**, 709
Phyllostachys nigra, laccases, **3**, 709
Phyllostachys rediculata, laccases, **3**, 709
Phyllostica maydis, PM-toxins, **1**, 424
Phyllotetra cruciferae, feeding, effects of sinalbin on, **8**, 145
phylogenetic tree, construction, neighbor joining method, **1**, 274
Physarum polycephalum
    Ras proteins, **2**, 360
    RNA editing, **6**, 98
Physcomitrella spp., cytokinin-resistant mutants, **8**, 65
Physcomitrella patens
    cytokinin-resistant mutants, **8**, 65
    dehydroquinases, **1**, 586
    shikimate 5-dehydrogenase, **1**, 591
physostigmines, bromo-, tunicate larval settlement induction, **8**, 440
phytoalexin hypothesis, bases, **1**, 779
phytoalexins
    accumulation, **1**, 812
    acetophenone-based, occurrence, **8**, 190
    biosynthesis, **1**, 626
    classification, **1**, 777
    definitions, **1**, 132
    elicitors, **1**, 132
    gene transcription, signal transduction, **1**, 817
    induction, **8**, 192
        in Compositae, **8**, 189
        in Cruciferae, **8**, 187
        in Gramineae, **8**, 190
    mechanisms, **8**, 186
        disease resistance, **8**, 192
    metabolism, **8**, 192
    O-methylation, **1**, 798
    occurrence, **1**, 774, **8**, 189
    origin studies, **2**, 183
    production rate, **1**, 784
    reviews, **8**, 186
    stilbenes, **1**, 750
    synthesis, elicitor-induced, **1**, 132
phytoalexins, isoflavonoid, biosynthetic pathways, evolution, **1**, 817
phytoanticipins, classification, **1**, 777
phytochrome A
    mRNA, degradation, **6**, 212
    regulatory mechanisms, **8**, 55
phytochrome B, regulatory mechanisms, **8**, 55
phytodienoic acid
    occurrence, **1**, 231
    as proteinase inhibitor inducer, **1**, 132
phytodienoic acid, 9*S*,13*S*-12-oxo-, occurrence, **1**, 231
phytodienoic acid, 12-oxo- (12-oxo-PDA)
    occurrence, **1**, 229, 234
    structure, **1**, 241
cis-10,15-phytodienoic acid, 12-oxo-
    cis configuration, **1**, 119
    from, α-linolenic acid, **1**, 119
    β-oxidation, **1**, 121
    as starting material, for jasmonic acid, **1**, 120

stereochemistry, **1**, 121
phytoecdysteroids
    moulting hormone activity, **8**, 293
    occurrence, **8**, 280, 284
    radioimmunoassay, **8**, 284
phytoene
    biosynthesis, **2**, 10, 324, 331, **5**, 336
    desaturation, **2**, 338
    from, geranylgeranyl diphosphate, **2**, 108
    structure, **2**, 323
15,15'-*cis*-phytoene
    desaturation, **2**, 324
    isomerization, **2**, 341
phytoene desaturases
    in carotenoid biosynthesis, **2**, 340
    CrtP-type, **2**, 348
    definition, **2**, 340
    encoding, **2**, 338
    structural conservation, **2**, 339
phytoene synthases
    ammonium ion analogues, **5**, 337
    in carotenoid biosynthesis, **2**, 340
    enzymology, **5**, 339
    homology, **2**, 250
    mechanistic studies, **5**, 336
    motifs, **2**, 340
    product studies, **5**, 338
    as rate-limiting enzymes, **2**, 338
    structural conservation, **2**, 339
phytohormones
    sugar-conjugation, **1**, 129
    see also plant hormones
phytojuvenoids
    biochemistry, **8**, 276, 277
    use of term, **8**, 276
phytol
    degradation, **8**, 234
    labeling studies, **2**, 61
(*E*)-phytol, occurrence, **8**, 230
phytonoic acid, structure, **1**, 119
Phytophthora megasperma
    effects on parsley seedlings, **3**, 665
    effects on soybean roots, **1**, 781
    elicitors, **1**, 804
    resistance to, **1**, 779
Phytophthora sojae
    soybean infection, **1**, 807
    zoospores, **1**, 780
Phytoseiulus persimilis, plant–herbivore–predator interactions, **8**, 152
phytosterols
    biosynthesis, inhibition, **1**, 626
    labeling studies, **2**, 61
    occurrence, **2**, 368
phytotoxins
    macromolecular toxins, **8**, 181
    monocyclic, **8**, 181
    necrotic lesion induction, **8**, 178
    nitrogen-based, cyclic and linear peptides, **8**, 180
    phenolic, **8**, 179
    research, objectives, **1**, 367
    terpenoid, **2**, 212
    use of term, **8**, 178
phytotoxins, polyketide
    biosynthesis
        via biological Diels–Alder reaction, **1**, 388
        via Diels–Alder reaction, **1**, **367–408**
PI3K *see* phosphotidylinositol-3-kinase (PI3K)
PI-201, occurrence, **1**, 370
PIBPS *see* phloroisobutyrophenone (PIBPS)
Picea abies
    cambium cells, **3**, 676
    cinnamoyl-CoA reductase, **3**, 652

cinnamyl-alcohol dehydrogenases, **3**, 655
α-conidendrin, induction, **1**, 691
coniferin, **3**, 683
4-coumarate-CoA ligase, **1**, 721, **3**, 650
flavonol 3-*O*-glucosides, **1**, 741
β-glucosidases, **3**, 686
7′-hydroxymatairesinol, induction, **1**, 691
lignin–carbohydrate complexes, **3**, 725
(−)-matairesinol, induction, **1**, 691
monosaccharides, **1**, 684
phenylalanine ammonia-lyase, localization, **3**, 662
α-pinene, **8**, 7
polysaccharides, **3**, 688
Picea excelsa, stilbene synthase, **1**, 753
Picea glauca, phenolic toxicity, **8**, 139
Picea mariana
    lignification, **3**, 691
    lignins, structure, **3**, 728
Picea sitchensis, histochemical staining, **3**, 709
Pichia pastoris, glycoproteins, **3**, 22
piclavines, occurrence, **8**, 546
picrasin A, nomenclature, **8**, 322
picrasin B, nomenclature, **8**, 322
picrasins
    mass spectra, **8**, 322
    nomenclature, **8**, 322
    occurrence, **8**, 322
Picrasma ailanthoides, picrasins, **8**, 322
Picrasma excelsa
    picrasins, **8**, 322
    quassin, **8**, 322
Picrasma quassioides, picrasin B, **8**, 322
picropodophyllone, antifungal activity, **1**, 691
pictamine, occurrence, **8**, 546
3-pi-5-deoxyenterocin, occurrence, **8**, 597
PIE *see* pipecolate-incorporating enzyme (PIE)
Pieridae, pheromones, **8**, 210
Pieris spp.
    citral, **8**, 223
    diuretic hormone, **8**, 300
    monoterpenes, **8**, 222
Pieris brassicae
    antifeedant activity against, **8**, 342
    feeding inhibition, **8**, 346
    pilocarpine toxicity, **8**, 342
PIG genes
    PIG-A
        cloning, **4**, 307
        encoding, **4**, 308
        expression, **4**, 310
        in GPI anchor biosynthesis, **4**, 306
        homologues, **4**, 309
        homology, **3**, 301
        localization, **4**, 308, 310
        mutations, **4**, 308
    PIG-B
        cloning, **3**, 301
        encoding, **4**, 313
        localization, **4**, 307
    PIG-C
        characterization, **4**, 309
        cloning, **4**, 307, 309
        homology, **3**, 301
    PIG-F, cloning, **3**, 302, **4**, 315
    PIG-H
        characterization, **4**, 309
        cloning, **4**, 307, 309
        expression, **4**, 310
        localization, **4**, 310
    PIG-L, cloning, **4**, 310
pig kidney, *N*-acetylneuraminate lyase, **3**, 378
pig liver
    dimethylallyl*trans*transferase, **8**, 272

farnesyl diphosphate isomerase, cloning, **2**, 74
isopentenyl diphosphate isomerase, **2**, 71
    purification, **2**, 71
threonine aldolase, **3**, 399
pigments
    flowers, **8**, 157
    in fruits, **8**, 164
pig pancreas
    α-amylase, **5**, 298
    phospholipase A$_2$, **5**, 110
pigs, 5α-androst-16-en-3-ol, **8**, 230
PIIF *see* proteinase inhibitor inducing factor (PIIF)
Pikonema alaskensis, female sex pheromones, **8**, 219
pillaromycin A, trideoxysugars, **3**, 322
L-pillarose
    occurrence, **3**, 312
    structure, **3**, 322
pilocarpine, occurrence, **4**, 54, **8**, 342
Pilocarpus spp., imidazole alkaloids, **4**, 54
Pilocarpus jaborandi, pilocarpine, **8**, 342
pimaradiene, as intermediate, **2**, 382
9β-pimara-7,15-diene, biosynthesis, **2**, 229
pimara-8,15-diene, biosynthesis, **2**, 226
pimara-8(14),15-diene, biosynthesis, **2**, 226
pimaranes, as intermediates, **2**, 381
ent-pimarenone cation, as intermediate, **2**, 368
pimarenyl cation, biosynthesis, **2**, 382
pimelate, *meso*-diamino-, cross-links, **3**, 248
pimelate, α-keto-
    chain elongation, **1**, 69
    as intermediate, **1**, 834
pimelic acid, *meso*-diamino-
    biosynthesis, **3**, 256
    localization, **3**, 246
    in pentapeptides, **3**, 245
    transpeptidation, **3**, 267
pimelic acid, 2,6-diamino-3-hydroxy-, occurrence, **3**, 246
pimeloyl-CoA, in biotin biosynthesis, **1**, 826
Pinaceae, isoflavonoids, **1**, 774
pinanes, characterization, **2**, 104
pine bark beetle *see Dendroctonus brevicomis*
pine beauty moth *see Panolis flammea*
(+)-α-pinene, occurrence, **8**, 222
α-pinene
    applications, **2**, 102
    biosynthesis, **2**, 140
    enantiomeric composition, **8**, 7
    mass spectra, **2**, 134
    occurrence, **8**, 7, 143, 221, 225
    oxidation, **8**, 224
β-pinene
    applications, **2**, 102
    biosynthesis, **2**, 140
    kinetic isotope effect, intrinsic, **2**, 140
    occurrence, **8**, 143, 221
    oxygenation, **8**, 224
α-pinene cyclase, substrate studies, **5**, 327
(+)-pinene synthases
    biosynthesis, **2**, 131
    studies, **2**, 130
(−)-pinene synthases, **2**, 125
    biosynthesis, **2**, 131
    studies, **2**, 130
pines, turpentine gum, cembrenes, **2**, 220
pine sawflies *see* Diprionidae
pinfish *see Lagodon rhomboides*
pinguisone, antifeedant activity, **8**, 308
pinidinol, host–parasite chemical transfer, **8**, 176
pink bollworm moth *see Pectinophora gossypiella*
Pinna attenuata, pinnatoxins, **8**, 518
Pinna muricata, pinnatoxins, **8**, 520
pinnasterols, occurrence, **8**, 280
pinnatoxin A, occurrence, **1**, 384

pinnatoxins
  as Ca²⁺channel activators, **8**, 518
  isolation, **8**, 520
  occurrence, **8**, 518
  structure, **8**, 520
  toxicity, **8**, 520
trans-pinocarveol, biosynthesis, **8**, 224
pinocarvone, biosynthesis, **8**, 224
pinocembrin, antifungal activity, **8**, 181
pinolidoxin, phytotoxicity, **8**, 181
pinoresinol, biosynthesis, **1**, 18, 692, **3**, 710, 714
(+)-pinoresinol
  biosynthesis, **1**, 652, 657, 662, 706
  occurrence, **1**, 645
  optical purity, **1**, 652
  phosphodiesterase inhibitory activity, **1**, 704
(+)-pinoresinol, 8–8′ linked, **3**, 722
(−)-pinoresinol
  biosynthesis, **1**, 706
  occurrence, **1**, 645
(+)-pinoresinol/(+)-lariciresinol reductase
  catalysis, **1**, 663
  encoding, **1**, 665
  purification, **1**, 663
  sequence homology, **1**, 665
(−)-pinoresinol/(−)-lariciresinol reductase, occurrence,
    1, 668
pinoresinol/lariciresinol reductase(s)
  catalysis, **1**, 681
  occurrence, **1**, 668
pinoresinol 4′,4″-di-*O*-β-D-glucopyranoside, (+)-
    hydroxy-, phosphodiesterase inhibitory activity, **1**,
    704
pinoresinol monomethyl ethers
  biosynthesis, **1**, 692
  occurrence, **1**, 661
pinoresinol(s)
  biosynthesis, **1**, 640, 652
  enantiomers, **1**, 651
  as intermediates, **1**, 658
  metabolism, **1**, 658
  occurrence, **1**, 661
  reduction, **1**, 682
  as substrates, **1**, 661
(±)-pinoresinols, biosynthesis, **3**, 704
pinosylvin, effects, on herbivores, **8**, 139
Pinus banksiana
  phenylalanine ammonia-lyase, genetics, **3**, 659
  xylem cells, **3**, 683
Pinus cembra, coniferin, **3**, 683
Pinus contorta
  abietadiene synthase, **2**, 228
  β-glucosidases, **3**, 686
  (−)-β-phellandrene synthases, **2**, 136
Pinus mugo, isoleucine, **1**, 128
Pinus pinaster
  caffeoyl-CoA *O*-methyltransferase, **3**, 672
  compression wood formation, **3**, 694
  diterpene cyclases, **2**, 384
Pinus radiata
  compression wood formation, **3**, 694
  lignification, **3**, 690
  lignins, structure, **3**, 728
Pinus strobus
  coniferin, **3**, 683
  coniferyl alcohol oxidase, **3**, 709
  coniferyl alcohol studies, **3**, 649
  feeding barriers, **8**, 139
  stilbene synthase, **1**, 759
  xylem cells, **3**, 683
Pinus sylvestris
  chalcone synthase, **1**, 734
  flavonol 3-*O*-glucosides, **1**, 741

  mistletoe lignin studies, **3**, 702
  monosaccharides, **1**, 684
  polysaccharides, **3**, 688
  stilbene synthase, **1**, 752
Pinus taeda
  cDNA libraries, **1**, 681
  cinnamyl-alcohol dehydrogenases, **3**, 656
  compression wood formation, **3**, 694
  coniferyl alcohol, **3**, 627
  p-coumaryl alcohol, **3**, 627
  dehydrodiconiferyl alcohol, **1**, 680, 698
  guaiacylglycerol 8-*O*-4′-coniferyl alcohol ether, **1**, 680
  hydroxycinnamyl *O*-methyltransferases, **3**, 646
  laccase, **3**, 713
  lignification, **3**, 690
  lignins, **3**, 708
  phenylalanine ammonia-lyase, genetics, **3**, 659
  phenylalanine metabolism, **3**, 658
  UDPglucose:glucosyltransferases, **3**, 683
Pinus thunbergii
  cinnamyl-alcohol dehydrogenases, **3**, 655
  hydroxycinnamyl *O*-methyltransferases, **3**, 645, 646
  monolignols, **3**, 691
pinyl cations, deprotonation, **2**, 104
pipecolate-incorporating enzyme (PIE), characterization,
    1, 520
Piper aduneum, dillapiole, **8**, 336
Piper angustifolia, apiole, **8**, 336
piperazinedione, D-phenylalanyl-L-prolyl-, biosynthesis,
    4, 326
piperazinediones, occurrence, **1**, 546
piperazines, diketo-, occurrence, **8**, 587, 590
piperazines, dioxo-, binding, **7**, 596
pipercide, occurrence, **8**, 304
(−)-piperenone, antifeedant activity, **1**, 694
Piper futokadsura
  antifeedant activity, **1**, 694
  kadsurenone, **1**, 704
Piper guineense, guineensine, **8**, 304
piperidine, *N*-alkylhydroxy-, monocyclic, as inhibitor of
    cycloartenol cyclase, **2**, 304
piperidine alkaloids, structure, **3**, 130
1-piperidine carboxylate, (isopropyl-5-methyl-4-
    trimethylammonium chloride)phenyl- *see*
    AMO 1618
piperidines, *N*-alkyl-3,3′-dimethyl-4-hydroxy-, as
    inhibitors, **2**, 291
piperidines, 2-alkyl-6-methyl-, in ant venoms, **8**, 357
piperidines, *N*-methyl-, in ant venoms, **8**, 357
piperidin-4-yl, 1-[(2-chloro-4-methyl)phenyl]-4′-
    methoxy- (Ctmp), applications, 2′-hydroxyl
    group protection, **7**, 144
piperidin-4-yl, 1-[(2-fluoro)phenyl]-4-methoxy- (Fpmp),
    applications, 2′-hydroxyl group protection, **6**, 84
2-piperidone, 3-amino-, biosynthesis, **4**, 326
piperine
  insecticidal activity, **8**, 337
  occurrence, **8**, 304
(+)-piperitol
  biosynthesis, **1**, 658
  occurrence, **1**, 658
(+)-piperitol synthase, occurrence, **1**, 658
Piper nigrum
  isobutylamides, **8**, 303
  pellitorine, **1**, 333
  pipercide, **8**, 304
  piperine, **8**, 304
Piper novae-hollandae, dillapiole, **8**, 336
PI-PLC *see* phosphatidylinositol-specific phospholipase
    C (PI-PLC)
Piricularia oryzae, rice-blast disease induction, **1**, 228
Piromonas communis, tetrahymanol, **2**, 308
pisatin

biosynthesis, **1**, 786, 803
6a-hydroxylation, **1**, 802
metabolism, **8**, 192
as phytoalexin, **8**, 189
pisatin, anhydro-, occurrence, **1**, 775
pisatin, (+)-2-hydroxy-
allelochemical activity, **1**, 775
occurrence, **1**, 775
(+)-pisatin
biosynthesis, **1**, 665, 800
occurrence, **1**, 774, 786
stereochemistry, **1**, 797
(−)-pisatin, occurrence, **1**, 775
Piscidia erythrina, 4′-aminoisoflavonoids, **1**, 775
pisiferic acid, antifungal activity, **8**, 181
Pissodes spp., aggregation pheromones, **8**, 224
Pissodes nemorensis, (1*S*,2*R*)-grandisal, **8**, 224
Pissodes strobi, (1*S*,2*R*)-grandisal, **8**, 224
Pisum sativum
aromatic acid transferases, **1**, 741
trans-cinnamate 4-monooxygenase, localization, **3**, 669
dehydroquinases, **1**, 586
fucosyltransferases, **3**, 516
gibberellin 2*β*-dioxygenases, **8**, 53
gibberellin 20-oxidases, **2**, 236
glucosyltransferases, **1**, 738
isoflavone reductase, **1**, 665
3′-*O*-methyltransferase, **1**, 800
phenylalanine ammonia-lyase, **3**, 659
polygalacturonate 4-α-galacturonosyltransferase, **3**, 513
shikimate 5-dehydrogenase, **1**, 591
UDPase, **3**, 510
pitch pine looper *see Lambdina pellucidaria*
Pithecolobium lobatum, djenkolic acid, **1**, 848
Pittosporum crassifolia, ferulic acid biosynthesis, **3**, 644
pittosporumxanthin A$_1$, occurrence, **1**, 384
Pituranthos triradiata, furanocoumarins, **8**, 141
Pityogenes spp.
aggregation pheromones, **8**, 224
ipsdienol, **8**, 223
ipsenol, **8**, 223
Pityogenes chalcographus
(2*S*,5*R*)-2-ethyl-1,6-dioxaspiro[4.4]nonane, **8**, 212, 213
2-ethyl-1,6-dioxaspiro[4.4]nonane, **8**, 199
methyl (2*E*,4*Z*)-2,4-decadienoate, **8**, 199, 213
Pityogenes quadridens, γ-geraniol, **8**, 222
pityol
biosynthesis, **8**, 232
structure, **8**, 233
(2*R*,5*S*)-pityol, occurrence, **8**, 233
cis-pityol, occurrence, **8**, 233
trans-pityol, occurrence, **8**, 233
Pityophthorus spp., **8**, 212
Pityophthorus pityographus, *trans*-pityol, **8**, 233
pivaloyl chloride, as coupling reaction activators, **7**, 139
PIVPS *see* phloroisovalerophenone (PIVPS)
5′-pixyl groups, as protecting groups, **7**, 126
5′-*S*-pixyl groups, as protecting groups, **7**, 126
pJUB5 vector, in strictosidine synthase expression, **4**, 133
PKR *see* polyketide reductase (PKR)
PKS *see* polyketide synthase (PKS)
PKS genes
CH-*PKS*1, **1**, 424
targeted disruption, **1**, 424
homology, **1**, 7
*PKS*1
expression, **1**, 414
sequencing, **1**, 414
pksA, disruption, **1**, 465
pksST, homologues, **1**, 465
*pksL*1 genes *see PKS* genes, *pksA*
pKSS1 expression vector, construction, **4**, 130

PLA2 *see* phospholipase A$_2$
placenta, ST3Gal IV expression, **3**, 49
Placopecten magellanicus, spirolides, **8**, 520
Plagiochila moritziana
plagiospirolide A, **1**, 375
plagiospirolide E, **1**, 375
plagiospirolide A, occurrence, **1**, 375
plagiospirolide E, occurrence, **1**, 375
plaice *see Pleuronectes platessa*
Plakortis spp., manzamenones, **1**, 384
plakotenin, occurrence, **1**, 384
Planche, Louis Antoine, guaiac resin studies, **3**, 717
Planobispora rosea, peptide synthetases, **4**, 214
Planococcus citri, (1*R*-*cis*)-(+)-1-acetoxymethyl-2,2-
dimethyl-3-(1-methylvinyl)cyclobutane, **8**, 224
Plantago lanceolata, catalpol, **8**, 307
plant–animal interactions, cyanogenesis, **1**, 882
plant cell cultures, applications, **2**, 370
plant chemical ecology, **8**, **137–196**
antimicrobial defense, constitutive, **8**, 181
chemical defense
constitutive, **8**, 137
induced, **8**, 149
historical background, **8**, 137
reviews, **8**, 138
symbiotic associations, biochemistry, **8**, 173
plant chemistry, and seed dispersal, **8**, 163
plant defensins, use of term, **8**, 186
plant enzymes
isolation, **2**, 117
sequences, **2**, 250
plant growth
allelopathy, **8**, 169
autotoxicity, **8**, 169
inhibition, **1**, 126, **3**, 141
plant–herbivore–predator interactions, mechanisms, **8**, 151
plant hormones, **8**, **19–136**
abscisic acid, **8**, 72
analysis, improved methodologies, **8**, 23
auxins, **8**, 23
brassinosteroids, **2**, 303, **8**, 99
characteristics, **8**, 21
classification, **8**, 22
cytokinins, **8**, 57
definitions, **8**, 21
ethylene, **8**, 91
GC-MS, **8**, 23
gibberellins, **8**, 35
historical background, **8**, 21
immunoassays, **8**, 23
interactions, in ethylene biosynthesis, **8**, 96
jasmonic acids, **8**, 108
synthetic mimetics, **8**, 23
see also phytohormones
plant–human relationships *see* human–plant relationships
plant–microbe interactions, cyanogenesis, **1**, 882
plant odor, and insect oviposition, **8**, 156
plants
acid growth, **8**, 26
alkaloids, **4**, 26
ecological significance, **8**, 146
allelopathy, **8**, 169
antifungal agents in, **8**, 181
apical dormancy, effects of auxins on, **8**, 30
applications, **3**, 799
branching enzymes, **3**, 458
calcium release, **8**, 32
cell wall loosening, effects of auxins on, **8**, 30
chalcone synthase, **1**, 750
chemicals, role in insect oviposition, **8**, 155
components, lignification, **3**, 659
coumarins, **1**, 623

factors affecting accumulation, **1**, 625
cyanogenesis, **8**, 145
cyanogenic, **1**, 882
    altitude factors, **1**, 882
defenses, **1**, 130, 131
    against insects, **8**, 303
    antimicrobial, **8**, 181
    future research, **2**, 212
    induced, **8**, 150
    mechanisms, **8**, 303
    and pathogenic microorganisms, **1**, 131
defensive barriers, phenolics, **8**, 139
Δ^{12}-desaturases, **1**, 40
ω^3-desaturases, **1**, 41
ω^6-desaturases, **1**, 40
desaturation in, **1**, 36
differentiated, strictosidine, **4**, 113
differentiation, polar transport auxin, **8**, 30
disease resistance, **1**, 132
early land-based, lignans, **1**, 645
ecdysteroids, biosynthesis, **8**, 291
effects of jasmonates on, **1**, 125
eicosanoids, **1**, 209
embryogenic cells, effects of auxins on, **8**, 30
fatty acid biosynthesis, **1**, 29
flower buds, effects of auxins on, **8**, 30
fossils, **1**, 645
gibberellins, **8**, 42
glucose-1-phosphate adenylyltransferase, regulatory
    mechanisms, **3**, 472
α-glucosidase I, **3**, 18
α-glucosidase II, **3**, 19
glycosidase processing, **3**, 14
guard cells
    calcium ion increase, **8**, 82
    effect of abscisic acid on, **8**, 82
herbaceous, lignins, **3**, 695
host–parasite chemical communication, **8**, 175
host–parasite chemical transfer, **8**, 175
hydroxymethylglutaryl-CoA reductase isozymes, **2**, 26,
    26
hypersensitive reaction, **1**, 133
insect deterrents, **8**, 302
insect toxicity, **8**, 302
isoflavonoids, **1**, 774
isoprenoid biosynthesis, mevalonate-independent
    pathway, **2**, 60
jasmonic acid, reviews, **1**, 228
leaf abscission, **8**, 91
leaves, effects of auxins on, **8**, 28
lignans, **1**, 640, 645
    physiological roles, **1**, 640, 690
lignins, **3**, 687
low temperature tolerance, **8**, 83
α1,2-mannosidase inhibitors, **3**, 25
metabolism, **1**, 812
    role of isochorismic acid in, **1**, **609–622**
metal requirements, **4**, 75
mitochondrial mRNA editing, **5**, 96
moth-pollinated species, **8**, 161
nectars, toxins in, **8**, 162
oxylipin, reviews, **1**, 228
pathogens, **1**, 884
petioles, effects of auxins on, **8**, 28
pigmentation, **8**, 160
pollination
    by bees, **8**, 158
    by birds, **8**, 158
    chemistry, **8**, 157
pollinators, color preferences, **8**, 157
prenylation, **2**, 363
RNA editing, **6**, 98
RNA enzymes, **6**, 110

root growth
    effects of abscisic acid on, **8**, 83
    effects of auxins on, **8**, 29
secondary metabolites in, roles, **8**, 138
selenium accumulation, **4**, 357
senescence, **1**, 126
    effect of kinetin on, **8**, 58
sexual reproduction, effect of auxins on, **8**, 30
shikimate pathway, **1**, 2
shoot elongation, effects of gibberellins on, **8**, 45
somatic embryo, effect of auxins on, **8**, 30
as sources of monoterpenes, **2**, 100
as sources of terpenoids, **2**, 209
starch biosynthesis, **3**, **441–495**
stearoyl-CoA desaturases, **1**, 40
stem growth, effect of auxins on, **8**, 26
stomata closure, effect of abscisic acid on, **8**, 82
tannases, **3**, 820
tannins, **8**, 142
terpene synthases, expression, **2**, 211
α,β-unsaturated fatty acids, **1**, 333
vascular, evolution, **1**, 645, **3**, 622, 626
vascular bundle, differentiation, **8**, 30
viroids, **6**, 171
wounding, **1**, 131, 133
see also flowers; fruits; grasses; leaves; seeds;
        transgenic plants; trees; wood
    seeds and buds, effects of auxins on, **8**, 30
plant substances, sequestration, **8**, 361
plant toxins, sequestration, by insects, **8**, 152
plasmalogens *see* phospholipids, alkenyl ether-linked
plasma membranes
    glycosphingolipids, **3**, 87
    hyperpolarization, **8**, 31
    lipid migration, **3**, 682
plasmids, in O-antigen biosynthesis, **3**, 216
plasmid transfer, in *Enterococcus faecalis*, **8**, 408
plasmid vectors
    applications, in cloning, **7**, 650
    characteristics, **7**, 650
    families, **7**, 650
        His-Patch ThioFusion, **7**, 652
        pET, **7**, 652
        pGEX, **7**, 650
        pMAL, **7**, 652
plasmodesmata, definitions, **2**, 110
Plasmodium falciparum
    adhesion prevention, **3**, 143
    GPI anchors, **3**, 297
        biosynthesis, **3**, 304
    surface antigens, **3**, 302
plastids
    branching enzymes, localization, **3**, 468
    definitions, **2**, 112
    fatty acid biosynthesis, **1**, 37
    isolation, **2**, 118
    isopentenyl diphosphate biosynthesis, **2**, 60
    metabolism, **3**, 463
    monoterpene biosynthesis, **2**, 112
    as starch biosynthesis site, **3**, 463
plastoquinone(s)
    biosynthesis, **5**, 344
    labeling studies, **2**, 61
platelet-activating factor (PAF)
    binding, **1**, 281
    biological activity, **1**, 286
    biosynthesis, **1**, **285–302**
        reduction, **1**, 291
    biosynthetic pathways, **1**, 289
        de novo, **1**, 296
        remodeling, **1**, 296
    discovery, **1**, 285
    early studies, **1**, 285

future research, **1**, 299
localization, **1**, 286
molecular phylogeny, **1**, 281
occurrence, **1**, 286
regulatory mechanisms, **1**, 286, 299
roles, pathophysiological, **1**, 298
structure, **1**, 10, 285
platelet-activating factor (PAF) antagonists
ginkgolides, **2**, 367
occurrence, **8**, 599
platelet activation-dependent granule-external membrane
protein *see* PADGEM protein
platelet-derived growth factor (PDGF), roles, in
proteoglycan biosynthesis, **3**, 168
platelets, aggregation inhibitors, **1**, 10, 174, 175
platenolides, replacement, **1**, 526
platomycins, applications, antibiotics, **7**, 539
platynecine, biosynthesis, **4**, 31
platyphylline, structure, **4**, 33
platyphylloside
applications, feeding inhibitors, **8**, 139
effects, on herbivores, **8**, 139
Platypus flavicornis, 1-hexanol, **8**, 210
Platysiphonia miniata
hepoxilin B₃, **1**, 219
12S-hydroxyeicosatetraenoic acid, **1**, 219
Plautia stali
juvenile hormone III, **8**, 269
methyl (2E,4E,6Z)-2,4,6-decatrienoate, **8**, 213
pleiocarpamine, 11-hydroxy-, biosynthesis, **4**, 121
pleuromutilin, biosynthesis, **2**, 228
Pleuronectes platessa, prostaglandin E₂, **1**, 237
Pleurotus mutilus, pleuromutilin, **2**, 228
Pleurotus ostreatus, activity against, **1**, 691
Plexaura homomalla
allene oxide pathway, **1**, 232
8R-lipoxygenase, **1**, 278
methyl 15R-acetoxy-prostaglandin A₂, **1**, 239
15R-prostaglandin A₂, **1**, 239
prostaglandin biosynthesis, **1**, 240
plicatic acid
biosynthesis, **1**, 668
occurrence, **1**, 668, 697
plicatin, occurrence, **1**, 697
PLMV *see* peach latent mosaic viroid (PLMV)
Plocamium spp., halogenated monoterpenes, **2**, 106
P loops, in 23S rRNA, **6**, 196
PLP *see* pyridoxal 5′-phosphate (PLP)
plumbemycin
biosynthesis, **1**, 869
isolation, **1**, 865
Plumeria acutifolia, plumieride, **8**, 307
Plumeria lancifolia, plumieride, **8**, 307
Plumeria rubra, plumieride, **8**, 307
plumieride, occurrence, **8**, 307
pluramycin A, possible alkoxyl radicals from, **7**, 510
pluramycinones
DNA adducts of, **7**, 508
DNA binding by, **7**, 508
pluramycins
applications
antibiotics, **7**, 471, 508
antiinfective agents, **7**, 508
antineoplastic agents, **7**, 508
DNA adducts of, **7**, 508
DNA binding by, **7**, 508
occurrence, **7**, 508
Plutella xylostella, activity against, **8**, 344
PME *see* pectinesterase
PMP *see* pyridoxamine 5′-phosphate (PMP)
pmr genes, *pmrA*, mutations, **3**, 225
PMSF *see* sulfonyl fluoride, *p*-methylphenyl- (PMSF)
PMT *see* pectin methyltransferase (PMT)

PM-toxins, occurrence, **1**, 424
PNAs *see* peptide nucleic acids (PNAs)
pneumocandin, biosynthesis, **4**, 203
pneumonia, atypical, etiology, **3**, 195
PNH *see* paroxysmal nocturnal hemoglobinuria (PNH)
Poaceae, cyclobutane lignans, **1**, 686
Pocillopora damicornis, host factor, **8**, 428
podecdysone B, moulting hormone activity, **8**, 293
Podisus spp., (E)-2-hexenal, **8**, 210
Podisus maculiventris, α-terpineol, **8**, 224
Podocarpus elatus, 20-hydroxyecdysone, **8**, 283
Podocarpus ferrugineus, (+)-kaur-16-ene, **8**, 7
Podocarpus gracilior, nagilactone D, **8**, 312
Podocarpus nagi, nagilactone D, **8**, 312
Podocarpus nakaii, ponasterone A, **8**, 283
Podocarpus neriifolius, podolactone C, **8**, 312
podolactone C, occurrence, **8**, 312
podophyllotoxin, 5-methoxy-, occurrence, **1**, 696
(−)-podophyllotoxin, occurrence, **1**, 671
podophyllotoxin(s)
antifungal activity, **1**, 691
antitumor activity, **1**, 701
antiviral activity, **1**, 702
biosynthesis, **1**, 672
occurrence, **1**, 671
as topoisomerase II inhibitor, **7**, 609
toxicity, **1**, 701
Podophyllum hexandrum
lignans, **1**, 691
picropodophyllone, **1**, 691
podophyllotoxins, **1**, 671, 701
Podophyllum peltatum, podophyllotoxins, **1**, 701
Poekiloceris spp., cardenolide disgorgement, **8**, 363
Pogestemon cablin, patchoulol, **2**, 184
Pogonomyrmex maricopa, venom, **8**, 354
poisoning, swainsonine-induced, **3**, 140
Pol III *see* DNA-directed RNA polymerase(s)
Polemoniaceae, anthocyanidins, **8**, 158
polhovolide, antifeedant activity, **8**, 308
pollen, germination, role of jasmonates in, **1**, 128
pollens, constituents, **8**, 162
pollination, nectar chemistry, simple sugars, **8**, 162
poly(A) binding protein (Pab1p)
binding, **6**, 207
cloning, **6**, 207
mRNA decapping inhibition, **6**, 208
polyacetate hypothesis, development, **1**, 410
polyacetates, as starting materials, for phenolic
compounds, **1**, 2
1,4-β-poly-N-acetylglucosaminidase(s) *see* chitinase(s)
poly(1,4-(N-acetyl-β-D-glucosaminide))
glycanohydrolase(s) *see* chitinase(s)
polyacrylamide gel electrophoresis (PAGE)
in DNA damage analysis, **7**, 385
in oligonucleotide purification, **7**, 144
in RNA structural probing, limitations, **6**, 65
polyadenylation, alternative, **5**, 228
polyamides, solid supports derived from, **7**, 110
polyamines, biosynthesis, **8**, 96
poly(A) mRNA
electroporation, **6**, 213
functional stability, **6**, 213
poly(A) nucleases (PANs)
mutants
PAN2, **6**, 207
PAN3, **6**, 207
purification, **6**, 207
3′-poly(A) tails
binding, **6**, 207
exonucleolytic decay protectivity, **6**, 207
shortening, **6**, 206
regulatory mechanisms, **6**, 208
Polycarpa aurata, polycarpine, **8**, 542

Polycarpa clavata, polycarpine, **8**, 542
polycarpine
    cytotoxicity, **8**, 542
    occurrence, **8**, 542
polycations, RNA major-groove binding, **7**, 428
Polycavernosa tsudai, polycavernosides, **8**, 515
polycavernoside A
    structure, **8**, 515
    synthesis, partial, **8**, 517
polycavernoside B, structure, **8**, 515
polycavernosides, occurrence, **8**, 515
Polychaeta
    as cone shell food, **8**, 476
    larval settlement induction, **8**, 432
polychlorinated biphenyls (PCBs), as environmental
        pollutants, **5**, 410
polycitone A
    occurrence, **8**, 539
    structure, **8**, 539
Polycitor spp.
    polycitone A, **8**, 539
    polycitrins, **8**, 539
polycitrins
    occurrence, **8**, 539
    structure, **8**, 539
polyclinal, occurrence, **8**, 473
Polyclinum planum, polyclinal, **8**, 473
polycyclic aromatic hydrocarbons (PAH)
    arene oxides, in xenobiotic metabolism, **5**, 58
    carcinogenicity, **7**, 222
    cell transformation, mechanisms, **7**, 223
    and diol epoxide derivatives, **7**, 470
    metabolism, **5**, 53
    reactions, with DNA, **7**, 470
polyd(A-T)$_2$, comparative binding studies, **7**, 455
polyd(G-C)$_2$, comparative binding studies, **7**, 455
poly(deoxyribonucleotide):poly(deoxyribonucleotide)
        ligase (AMP-forming) *see* DNA ligase (ATP)
polydeoxyribonucleotide synthase (ATP) *see* DNA ligase
        (ATP)
polyene cyclization, oxidosqualene:lanosterol cyclase as
        catalyst for, **2**, 267
polyenones, cross-conjugated, occurrence, **8**, 359
polyenzymes, early studies, **4**, 320
polyether macrolides, isolation, **8**, 613
polyethers, biosynthesis, **4**, 201
polyether toxins, occurrence, **8**, 497
polyethylene glycol–oligonucleotide conjugates,
        synthesis, **7**, 190
polyethylene glycol (PEG), roles, in cellular processes, **7**,
        190
polyethylene glycol phosphoramidites, synthesis, **7**, 190
polyethylene glycol–polystyrene (PEG–PS), in
        oligonucleotide synthesis, **7**, 113
Polygalaceae, isoflavonoids, **1**, 774
polygalacturonase, occurrence, **8**, 398
polygalacturonate 4-α-galacturonosyltransferase
    catalysis, **3**, 512
    solubilization, **3**, 513, 520
poly(1,4-α-D-galacturonide) glycanohydrolase *see*
        polygalacturonase
poly(1,4-α-D-galacturonide) lyase *see* pectate lyase
polyglucans, synthesis, *in vitro*, **3**, 442
α-1,4-polyglucans, biosynthesis, **3**, 442
poly-β-glucosaminidase(s) *see* chitinase(s)
polyglutamates, 5,10-methenyltetrahydrofolyl-, as
        cofactor, **5**, 375
polygodial
    antifeedant activity, **8**, 308, 462, 466
    hot taste, **8**, 467
    occurrence, **8**, 308
Polygonum hydropiper, polygodial, **8**, 308
Polygraphus poligraphus, α-terpineol, **8**, 224

poly(G) tracts
    insertion, **6**, 210
    slippage mechanisms, **3**, 228
    structure, **6**, 209
polyhydroxy alkaloids
    antimicrobial activity, **3**, 142
    antiviral activity, **3**, 142
    plant growth inhibition, **3**, 141
    synthetic, **3**, 139
    therapeutic activity, **3**, 142
poly(β-hydroxybutyrate), biosynthesis, **2**, 18, 19
polyketide pathway, early studies, **1**, 410
polyketide reductase (PKR)
    biosynthesis, **1**, 763
    nomenclature, **1**, 763
polyketides
    aldol-type condensation, **1**, 411
    applications, **1**, 2
        mycotoxins, **1**, 2
    biochemistry, **1**, 1–22
    biological activity, **1**, 474
    biosynthesis, **1**, 1, 2, 10, 75, 346, 474, **4**, 196, 344, **8**, 202
        early studies, **1**, 3
        and fatty acid biosynthesis, **1**, 500
        in filamentous fungi, **1**, **409–441**
        in fungi, **1**, 14
        pathways, **4**, 206
        via Diels–Alder reaction, **1**, **367–408**
    categorization, **1**, 474
    cyclization, **8**, 203
    degradation, **8**, 246
    Diels–Alder adducts, **1**, 370
    early studies, **1**, 3
    feeding experiments, **1**, 410
    future research, **1**, 437
    gene clusters, cloning, **1**, 11
    as intermediates, **1**, 346, 763
    intermolecular [4 + 2]-adducts, **1**, 374
    macrocyclic, **1**, 371
    nomenclature, **1**, 474
    Northern blot analysis, **1**, 414
    occurrence, **8**, 211
    roles, in okadaic acid biosynthesis, **8**, 493
    Southern blot analysis, **1**, 412
    structural diversity, **1**, 3
    structure, **1**, 496, **4**, 201
    with unbranched carbon skeletons, **8**, 204
    use of term, **1**, 1, 410
polyketides, non-fatty acid, as secondary metabolites, **1**,
        1
polyketides, reduced anthracycline, structure, **1**, 481
polyketides, reduced tetracycline, structure, **1**, 481
polyketide synthases (PKSs)
    acyl carrier protein, **4**, 340
    in aflatoxin biosynthesis, **1**, 420
    aldol-type condensation, **1**, 426
    aromatic, catalysis, **1**, 11, 411
    biosynthesis, **1**, 464
    catalysis, **1**, 19, 410
    categorization, **1**, 474
    in coumarin biosynthesis, **1**, 625
    definitions, **1**, 750
    evolution, **1**, 762
    fatty acid synthase models for, **1**, 347
    fungal, structure, **1**, 424
    genes, structure, **1**, 410
    higher aromatic, catalysis, **1**, 417
    hybrids, **1**, 526
        Type I, **1**, 508
    inactivation, **1**, 357
    mechanisms, **1**, 426
    minimal
        chain-length specificity, **1**, 488

combinatorial analysis, **1**, 487
modular, **1**, 503
non-aromatic, catalysis, **1**, 422
plant-specific, **1**, 750
primers, **1**, 450
products, biosynthetic reactions on, **1**, 426
roles, in cyclosporin biosynthesis, **1**, 543
sequence alignment, **1**, 421
sequencing, **1**, 363
substrate specificity, **1**, 347
type I, **1**, 424
    encoding, **1**, 414
    occurrence, **1**, 14
type II, **1**, 424
    occurrence, **1**, 10
see also bacterial aromatic polyketide synthases;
        erythromycin polyketide synthase
polymerase chain reaction (PCR), **7**, 346
advantages, **7**, 653
applications
    in oligonucleotide bulk production, **7**, 652
    in peptide antibiotic biosynthesis, **4**, 211
asymmetric, **7**, 620
development, **7**, 617
evaluation, **7**, 658
expression cassette strategy, **7**, 668
historical background, **7**, 652
mechanisms, **7**, 620
mutagenesis, **6**, 116, **7**, 620
polymerases, choice of, **7**, 658
primer-binding sites, **7**, 624
primers, **7**, 154
    availability, **7**, 658
    choice of, **7**, 655
processes, **7**, 652
products, purification, **7**, 660
templates, choice of, **7**, 654
total gene synthesis method, **7**, 658
troubleshooting, **7**, 659
polymerases, choice of, for polymerase chain reaction, **7**,
        658
polymerization
models, **3**, 212
of *O*-polysaccharide repeating units, **3**, 211
polymers, primordial, **7**, 639
poly(methoxy-L-galacturonide) lyase *see* pectin lyase
polymorphism, cyanogenic, **1**, 882
polymorphonuclear leukocytes (PMN),
        lipopolysaccharide recognition, **3**, 182
polymorphonuclear lysosomal elastase *see* leukocyte
        elastase
polymyxin
antibacterial activity, **4**, 199
discovery, **4**, 200
polymyxin B, resistance, **3**, 225
Polyneura latissima, polyneuric acid, **1**, 221
polyneuric acid, occurrence, **1**, 221
polynucleotide ligase *see* DNA ligase (ATP)
polynucleotides, nucleoside *H*-phosphonates, **7**, 139
polyoma virus, α-1,3(6)-mannosyl-glycoprotein β-1,6-*N*-
        acetylglucosaminyltransferase activity, **3**, 54
polyoxins, chitin synthase inhibition, **3**, 286
polypeptide *N*-acetylgalactosaminyltransferase
catalysis, **3**, 73
gene knockout, **3**, 75
genes, encoding, **3**, 75
and *O*-glycosylation mediation, **3**, 75
glycosylation sites, **3**, 75
in vitro studies, **3**, 74
localization, **3**, 73
purification, **3**, 74
roles, in *O*-glycan synthesis, **3**, 73
polypeptides

biosynthesis, **4**, 196
    in fungi, **1**, 14
in cloning, **7**, 645
farnesylated, structures, **2**, 355
purification, **7**, 667
structure, **4**, 201
polypeptin, applications, **4**, 199
polyphenol oxidase(s) *see* catechol oxidase(s)
polyphenols
applications, **3**, 799, 10
hydrophobic bonding, with proteins, **3**, 802
molecular weight, and tanning capacity, **3**, 802
roles, as chemopreventers, **3**, 791
polyphosphorylase *see* glycogen phosphorylase;
        maltodextrin phosphorylase; phosphorylase(s)
polypodine B
biological activity, **8**, 293
biosynthesis, **8**, 291
hydroxylation, **8**, 291
occurrence, **8**, 280
Polypodium vulgare, 7-dehydrocholesterol, **8**, 291
Polyporus spp., tannin degradation, **3**, 819
Polyporus hispidus
cell wall polymers, **3**, 624
4-coumarate-CoA ligase, **3**, 650
polyporusterones, occurrence, **8**, 280
Polyporus umbellatus, polyporusterones, **8**, 280
polyprenols, **3**, 15
polyprenyl carrier protein (PCP), *trans*-
        octaprenyl*trans*transferase(s), **2**, 91
polyprenyl diphosphate
binding sites, **2**, 250
aspartate-rich motif in, **2**, 250
polyprenyl diphosphate synthases, occurrence, **2**, 92
(*Z*)-polyprenyl diphosphate synthases *see*
        prenyltransferase IV
polyprenyl phosphate, chelation, **3**, 281
polypurines, cleavage, **7**, 410
polysaccharides
biodegradation, **3**, 592
biosynthesis, **3**, 8
    in cell walls, **3**, 510
    enzyme distribution, **3**, 602
    reviews, **3**, 203
    sites, **3**, 602
    subcellular localization, **3**, 504
in cell wall, **3**, 498
characterization, **3**, 600
early studies, **3**, 530
esterification, **3**, 502
heterogeneity, **3**, 688
occurrence, **3**, 688
reserves, **3**, 442
turnover, in hemicellulose biosynthesis, **3**, 609
water-soluble, **3**, 458
O-polysaccharides
O-acetylation, **3**, 215
assembly
    synthase-dependent pathway, **3**, 217
    Wzy-independent mechanism, **3**, 212
biosynthesis, **3**, 5
    plasmid-encoded determinants, **3**, 216
    as transmembrane process, **3**, 210
chain modification, **3**, 215
dissemination, **3**, 217
genetic polymorphism, **3**, 217
glucosylation, **3**, 215
O-chain length, bimodal distribution, **3**, 214
polymerization, regulatory mechanisms, **3**, 214
repeating units
    assembly, **3**, 209
    polymerization, **3**, 209
    Wzy-dependent polymerization, **3**, 211

rfb regions, clonal diversity, **3**, 220
  structure, variability, **3**, 217
  translocation, **3**, 210
polysaccharide synthases
  characterization, **3**, 603
  sugar donors, **3**, 603
polysialic acid
  chain extension, **3**, 49
  roles, nerve cell adhesion molecule regulation, **3**, 50
polysialyltransferases, **3**, 49
polystyrene, solid supports derived from, **7**, 110
poly(styrene-co-maleic acid)–neocarzinostatin conjugate
    (SMANCS), **7**, 558
polysulfide/thiol mixtures, superoxide production by, **7**,
    540
polysulfides
  DNA damage induction, **7**, 524
  formed by leinamycin, **7**, 526
  oxygen radicals from, **7**, 524
Polysyncraton lithostrotum, namenamicin, **7**, 581, **8**, 544
polytheonamide B, conformation, **8**, 579
polytheonamides
  cytotoxicity, **8**, 577
  occurrence, **8**, 577
  structure, **8**, 577
polyzonimine, occurrence, **8**, 226
Polyzonium rosalbum, polyzonimine, **8**, 226
Pompe's disease, etiology, **3**, 140
ponasterone A
  activity, **8**, 293
  occurrence, **8**, 279, 283, 291
  synthesis, **8**, 288
poneratoxin, occurrence, **8**, 359
ponerine ants *see Ectatomma ruidum*
'popcorn copolymer', in oligonucleotide synthesis, **7**, 110
Popillia japonica
  female sex attractant, **8**, 199
  japonilure, **8**, 12
  pheromones, **8**, 12
  tetradecan-4-olide, **8**, 216
  (*R*)-5-tetradecen-4-olide, **8**, 216
Populus spp.
  hydroxycinnamyl *O*-methyltransferases, **3**, 646
  salicortin, **8**, 139
Populus balsamifera, caffeoyl-CoA *O*-methyltransferase,
    3, 671
Populus deltoides
  laccase studies, **3**, 712
  phenylalanine ammonia-lyase, **3**, 659
Populus euramericana, cinnamoyl-CoA reductase, **3**, 652
Populus kitakamiensis
  caffeoyl-CoA *O*-methyltransferase, **3**, 671
  trans-cinnamate 4-monooxygenase, localization, **3**, 669
  phenylalanine ammonia-lyase, **3**, 659
    localization, **3**, 662
Populus nigra, labeling studies, **2**, 62
Populus tremuloides
  caffeoyl-CoA *O*-methyltransferase, **3**, 671
  cinnamyl-alcohol dehydrogenases, **3**, 676
  4-coumarate-CoA ligase, **1**, 721
  dirigent proteins, genes, **1**, 656
  hydroxycinnamic acid *O*-methyltransferase, **3**, 672
  hydroxycinnamyl *O*-methyltransferases, **3**, 646
  laccase studies, **3**, 712
Populus trichocarpa, phenylalanine ammonia-lyase, **3**,
    659
Populus x euramericana
  4-coumarate-CoA ligase, **1**, 720
  ferulate 5-hydroxylase, **3**, 642
Porcelia macrocarpa, tyramines, **1**, 673
pore formation, lantibiotic-induced, **4**, 281
Poria spp., tannin degradation, **3**, 819
Porifera

aqueous ethanol, **8**, 470
  biotransformation products, **8**, 468
  bromotyrosine, **8**, 468
  carotenoids, **8**, 589
  chemical defense, **8**, 465
  on coral reefs, **8**, 465
  discorhabdin A, **7**, 501
  epinardin D, **7**, 501
  ichthyotoxicity, **8**, 466
  makaluvamine F, **7**, 501
  with manzamine-related alkaloids, taxonomy, **8**, 566
  metabolites, **8**, 553
  oxylipins, **1**, 243
  renieramycins, **7**, 497
  symbiosis, **8**, 426
  see also Halichondria okadai; Luffariella variabilis;
      Pellina spp.
porphin–iron(III) complexes, in psoralen synthesis, **1**, 632
porphobilinogen deaminase(s) *see* hydroxymethylbilane
    synthase(s)
porphobilinogen (PBG), biosynthesis, **4**, 141
porphobilinogen synthase(s)
  acylation, **4**, 76
  bovine, **4**, 75
  catalysis, **4**, 73
  cysteine reactivity, **4**, 75
  inhibition, studies, **4**, 76
  mechanisms, **4**, 77
  metal binding regions, **4**, 75
  metal dependency
    magnesium, **4**, 75
    zinc, **4**, 75
  properties, **4**, 74
  roles, **4**, 141
  Schiff base linkage, **4**, 74
  structure, **4**, 75
  substrate binding, sites, **4**, 73
  x-ray crystal structure, **4**, 76
porphyrin, tetraphenyl-, ring current–chemical shift map,
    7, 443
porphyrin-13,17-dipropionic acid iron(II) coordination
    complex, 2,7,12,18-tetramethyl-3,8-divinyl- *see*
    heme
porphyrin metallases, derivation, **7**, 622
porphyrins
  applications, intercalating agents, **7**, 441
  biosynthesis, overview, **4**, 1–11
  destabilization, **7**, 444
  metallation, **6**, 137, 143, **7**, 627, 634
  stabilization, **7**, 444
porphyrins, cationic, interactions with DNA, **7**, 441
porphyrins, metallotris(methylpyridinium)-, activated, **7**,
    162
poststerone
  activity, **8**, 293
  biosynthesis, **8**, 291
potassium chelidonate, occurrence, **8**, 26
potassium ion channel, in larval settlement induction, **8**,
    434
potassium oxalate, toxicity, **8**, 148
potassium permanganate, applications, DNA structure
    probes, **7**, 92
potassium tetrathionate, effects, on P-protein, **5**, 353
potatoes
  amyloplasts, **3**, 464
  antisense RNA, **3**, 455
  5,12-dihydroxyeicosatetraenoic acid, **1**, 236
  9*S*,16(*R*,*S*)-dihydroxy-10*E*,12*E*,14*E*-octadecatrienoic
      acid, **1**, 236
  9*S*,16(*R*,*S*)-dihydroxy-10*E*,12*Z*,14*E*-octadecatrienoic
      acid, **1**, 236
  5,6-leukotriene A$_4$, **1**, 236
  lipoxin A, **1**, 236

sesquiterpenoid phytoalexins, **2**, 212
waxy locus, DNA sequence, **3**, 454
see also Solanum spp.
potato plants
  stolons, tuberization, **1**, 127
  tuberization, **1**, 127
  tuberonic acid, **1**, 125
potato spindle tuber viroid (PSTV)
  characterization, **6**, 171
  hosts, **6**, 171, 186
  localization, **6**, 178
  pathogenicity, **6**, 185
  replication, rolling circle mechanism, **6**, 183
  replication inhibition, **6**, 178
  sequence homology, **6**, 175
  sequencing, **6**, 175
potato tuber
  branching enzymes, **3**, 460
    cDNA clones, **3**, 462
  enzyme subunits, **3**, 451
  glucose-1-phosphate adenylyltransferase, **3**, 451
  heterotetrameric enzymes, **3**, 451
  proplastid membranes, **3**, 463
  small subunits, **3**, 451
  soluble starch synthases, **3**, 455
  starch synthases, **3**, 457
4′PPan *see* 4′-phosphopantetheine (4′PPan)
P-pant groups *see* 4′-phosphopantetheinyl groups
PPOs *see* catechol oxidase(s)
P-protein
  chemical modifications, **5**, 353
  feedback inhibition, **5**, 345
PPS *see* peptide synthetase(s)
ppsR genes, in *Rhodobacter* spp., **2**, 344
PPT *see* phenylpyruvate tautomerase
PRA *see* anthranilate, phosphoribosyl- (PRA)
PRA isomerase(s) *see* phosphoribosylanthranilate
    isomerase(s)
pranlukast, applications, antiasthmatic agents, **1**, 197
pratensin
  biosynthesis, **1**, 795
  5-hydroxylation, **1**, 802
pravastatin
  applications
    clinical, **2**, 246
    hypocholesterolemic agents, **1**, 2
  structure, **1**, 422
preclavulone-A, structure, **1**, 241
precoccinelline, occurrence, **8**, 351
precocene I, occurrence, **8**, 278
precocene II, occurrence, **8**, 278
precocenes
  biochemistry, **8**, 278
  biosynthesis, **8**, 278
  effects, on corpora allata, **8**, 278
Precor *see* methoprene
precorrin 1, biosynthesis, **4**, 143
precorrin 2, biosynthesis, **4**, 143
precorrin 2 methyltransferase, roles, **4**, 143
precorrin 2 synthase *see* uroporphyrinogen-III
    methyltransferase(s)
precorrin 3, biosynthesis, **4**, 143
precorrin 3 hydroxylactone, biosynthesis, **4**, 143
precorrin 3 hydroxylactone methyltransferase, roles, **4**,
    144
precorrin 3 hydroxylactone synthase *see* precorrin 3
    oxidase
precorrin 3 oxidase, roles, **4**, 143
precorrin 3 synthase *see* precorrin 2 methyltransferase
precorrin 4 methyltransferase, roles, **4**, 144
precorrin 4 synthase *see* precorrin 3 hydroxylactone
    methyltransferase
precorrin 5, biosynthesis, **4**, 144

precorrin 5 methyltransferase, roles, **4**, 145
precorrin 5 synthase *see* precorrin 4 methyltransferase
precorrin 6, biosynthesis, **4**, 145
precorrin 6, dihydro-, biosynthesis, **4**, 145
precorrin 6 reductase, roles, **4**, 145
precorrin 6 synthase *see* precorrin 5 methyltransferase
precorrin 8, biosynthesis, **4**, 146
precorrin 8 mutase, roles, **4**, 146
precorrin 8 synthase *see* dihydroprecorrin 6
    methyltransferase
precursor Z
  oxidation, **1**, 835
  structure, **1**, 835
predator-induced defenses
  and autotoxicity, **8**, 462
  in marine organisms, **8**, 462
predatory mite *see Phytoseiulus persimilis*
4-pregnen-21-ol-3,20-dione *see* cortexone
4-pregnen-3-one, 17α,20β-dihydroxy-
  occurrence, **8**, 230
  as sex pheromone, **8**, 426
prelaureatin
  occurrence, **1**, 303
  synthesis, **1**, 312, 319
[1-^{2}H]-prelaureatin
  enzymatic reactions, **1**, 319
  synthesis, **1**, 314
(3*E*)-prelaureatin
  enzymatic reaction, **1**, 316
  as starting material, for laurallene, **1**, 317
  synthesis, **1**, 316
(3*Z*)-prelaureatin
  as starting material
    for isolaureatin, **1**, 317
    for laureatin, **1**, 317
pre-mRNA
  7-deazaadenosine incorporation studies, **6**, 225
  introns, **7**, 345
  splicing, **6**, 221
prenylation
  early studies, **2**, 353
  isoflavonoids, **1**, 803
  proteins, **2**, 353–366
prenylcoumarins, biosynthesis, **1**, 628
prenyl diphosphate synthases, medium-chain *see*
    prenyltransferase II
prenyl diphosphate synthases, short-chain *see*
    prenyltransferase I
(*E*)-prenyl diphosphate synthases, long-chain *see*
    prenyltransferase III
prenyl protein-specific protease
  homogeneity, **2**, 359
  inhibitors, **2**, 359
prenyltransferase I, **2**, 74
prenyltransferase II
  enzymatic properties, **2**, 88
  gene cloning, **2**, 90
  mechanisms, **2**, 88
prenyltransferase III
  enzymology, **2**, 91
  expression, **2**, 92
  gene cloning, **2**, 92
prenyltransferase IV
  enzymology, **2**, 92
  reaction stereochemistry, **2**, 93
prenyltransferase(s) *see* dimethylallyl*trans*transferase(s)
prenyl transfer reactions, studies, **5**, 317
7-*O*-prenylumbelliferone, metabolism, **1**, 630
prepeptides
  encoding, **4**, 283
  isolation, **4**, 287
  lactocin S lantibiotics, **4**, 293
  nisin lantibiotics, **4**, 287

streptococcin lantibiotics, **4**, 293
type B-lantibiotics, **4**, 295
prephenate
  biosynthesis, **5**, 424
  from, (−)-chorismate, **1**, 367
prephenate dehydratase(s)
  catalysis, **5**, 344
  occurrence, **4**, 5
  substrates, **4**, 5
prephenate dehydrogenase(s), catalysis, **5**, 344
prephenate hydro-lyase (decarboxylating) *see* prephenate
    dehydratase(s)
prephenate:NAD⁺ oxidoreductase (decarboxylating) *see*
    prephenate dehydrogenase(s)
prephenic acid, biosynthesis, **1**, 619
prephytoene diphosphate, biosynthesis, **5**, 336
prephytoene-diphosphate synthase *see* geranylgeranyl-
    diphosphate geranylgeranyltransferase
prepro-α-factor, yeasts, **3**, 31
pre-rRNA
  5.8S, as substrate, **6**, 213
  introns, **6**, 149
  self-splicing, **6**, 254
presqualene diphosphate (PSDP)
  biosynthesis, **2**, 9, **5**, 336
  conversion, to squalene, **2**, 253
  as intermediate, **2**, 246
presqualene-diphosphate synthase *see* farnesyl-
    diphosphate farnesyltransferase
presteady-state kinetics, of glycidyl-4-nitrobenzoate
    enantiomers, **5**, 55
pre-tRNA
  cleavage, **6**, 260
  transcripts, **6**, 222
preuroporphyrinogen
  chemical synthesis, **4**, 87
  cyclization, **4**, 72
  stability, **4**, 87
preuroporphyrinogen synthase(s) *see*
    hydroxymethylbilane synthase(s)
prg genes, studies, **4**, 178
primaquine, transport inhibition, **3**, 92
primer elongation techniques, in RNA structural probing,
    6, 65
primers, roles, **8**, 198
primin, effects, on herbivores, **8**, 139
'primitive life', theories, **7**, 617
Primula praenitens, flavonol synthase, **1**, 727
principal components analysis (PCA), in cellulose studies,
    3, 564
Pristhesancus plagipennis, (*Z*)-3-hexenyl (*R*)-2-hydroxy-
    3-methylbutanoate, **8**, 221
pristinamycin I
  amide bonds, **4**, 226
  ester bonds, **4**, 226
  see also virginiamycin
Pro-1
  as general base catalyst, **5**, 46, 47
  mutants, construction, **5**, 45
  pK_a, **5**, 44, 46
  replacement, with sarcosine, **5**, 46
  roles, **5**, 44
  structure, **5**, 47
pro-amylopectin, debranching, **3**, 467
proanthocyanidin A-2 *see* epicatechin-(2β→7,4β→8)-
    epicatechin
proanthocyanidins, **3**, 800, **8**, 142
  A-type
    characterization, **3**, 778
    NMR spectra, **3**, 778
    occurrence, **3**, 779
    regiochemistry, **3**, 778
  biochemistry, **3**, **747–797**

biosynthesis, **1**, 717, 727, 729, **3**, 10
  B-type, characterization, **3**, 757
  conformation, **3**, 786
    boat, **3**, 786
  conformational isomerism, **3**, 786
  as feeding barriers, **8**, 142
  nomenclature, **3**, 748
  pyrogallol-type A-rings, **3**, 776
  strain effects, **3**, 787
  structure, **1**, 715
  use of term, **3**, 800
proanthocyanidins, dimeric, biosynthesis, **3**, 819
proanthocyanidins, oligomeric
  as antioxidants, in human diet, **3**, 748
  applications, **3**, 748
  astringency, **3**, 791
  biosynthesis, **3**, 819
  bonding positions, at nucleophilic centers, **3**, 761
  characterization, **3**, 757
  COSY studies, **3**, 761
  definitions, **3**, 748
  HETCOR studies, **3**, 761
  NOE difference spectra, **3**, 761
  occurrence, **3**, 757
  solvent shift studies, **3**, 761
proanthocyanidins, polymeric
  applications, **3**, 767
    industrial, **3**, 767
2,3-*cis*-proanthocyanidins synthesis, **3**, 750
probes
  chemical
    of RNA structure, **6**, **63–80**
    temperature-dependent, **6**, 73
  enzymatic, of RNA structure, **6**, **63–80**
  fluorine, in electrophilic reaction studies, **5**, 317
  hybridization, nucleic acids, **7**, 35
  immunocytochemical, lignin heterogeneity studies, **3**,
    699
  mixed-sequence, in oligonucleotide synthesis, **7**, 126
  non-radioactive, for nucleic acid duplexes, **7**, 448
  nucleic acid, design, **7**, 161
  nucleoside analogues, **7**, **251–284**
  polybiotinylated, **7**, 204
  for specific distorted conformations, in DNA and
    RNA, **7**, 444
  structural, historical background, **6**, 63
  synthetic methods, **7**, 451
  tethered, **6**, 68
  see also molecular probes; nanoprobes
probetaenone I, structure, **1**, 389
procaine, solubility, **4**, 240
procamine A, in honeybee venom, **8**, 355
procamine B, in honeybee venom, **8**, 355
Procaria capensis syriaca, furanocoumarin toxicity, **8**, 141
procaryotic organisms, effects, on squalene, **2**, 250
procassinidins, biosynthesis, **3**, 777
procentrolide, occurrence, **1**, 384
prochaetoglobosins (PCGs)
  biosynthetic pathway, **1**, 395
  isolation, **1**, 393
  transition states, **1**, 393
Prochloron spp., symbiosis, **8**, 428
proclavaminic acid, biosynthesis, **4**, 185
proclavaminic acid amidino hydrolase, discovery, **4**, 183
proctolin
  bioassays, **8**, 295
  biochemistry, **8**, 295
  discovery, **8**, 295
  identification, **8**, 295
  structure, **8**, 302
procyanidin B₁
  base-catalyzed cleavage, **3**, 767
  structure, **3**, 758

procyanidin B₃, occurrence, **3**, 756
procyanidin B₄
  occurrence, **3**, 756
  structure, **3**, 758
procyanidin B₅, semi-synthesis, **3**, 779
procyanidin B₇, nomenclature, **3**, 748
procyanidin–prodelphinidin trimers, mixed, **3**, 769
procyanidin–propelargonidin oligomers, mixed, **3**, 769
procyanidins
  antioxidant activity, **3**, 792
  cleavage, **3**, 767
  and feeding behavior, **8**, 142
  fluorescence, **3**, 789
  occurrence, **3**, 764
  rearrangement, base-catalyzed, **3**, 765
procyanidins, oligomeric, semi-synthesis, **3**, 765
procyanidins, polymeric, base-catalyzed reactions, **3**, 767
procyanidin trimers, branched, synthesis, **3**, 765
procyclin
  GPI anchors, **3**, 297
  occurrence, **4**, 307
prodelphinidins
  acid-catalyzed thiolytic cleavage, **3**, 769
  mixed oligomers, **3**, 769
  occurrence, **3**, 769
Prodenia litura, antifeedant activity against, **8**, 342
prodistenidins, biosynthesis, **3**, 777
prodrug, enediyne as, **7**, 557
profisetinidins
  applications, **3**, 770
  fluorescence, **3**, 789
  occurrence, **3**, 769, 772
  reductive cleavage, **3**, 771
  semi-synthesis, **3**, 770
profisetinidins, (4α→6)-linked, isomerization, **3**, 774
profisetinidins, (4α→8)-linked, structure, **3**, 761
profisetinidins, oligomeric
  base-catalyzed pyran ring rearrangement, **3**, 772
  semi-synthesis, **3**, 758
proflavine, **7**, 457
  applications, intercalating agents, **7**, 435
progesterone, 17-hydroxy-, hydroxylation, **3**, 637
proglycogen, isolation, **3**, 446
proguibourtinidins, occurrence, **3**, 775
prohexadione
  applications, growth retardant, **8**, 36
  gibberellin inhibition, **8**, 53
prokaryotes
  isoprenoid biosynthesis, **2**, 57
  morphological differentiation, regulatory mechanisms,
    8, 400
  porphobilinogen synthase, **4**, 76
  selenocysteine metabolism, **4**, 354
  shikimate pathway, **4**, 2
  two-component system, **8**, 406
proline
  activation, **4**, 209
  degradation, **8**, 210
  mutations, **5**, 45
D-proline, as substrate, **1**, 546
proline-rich proteins (PRPs)
  occurrence, cell walls, **3**, 732
  roles
    in digestive tract, **3**, 10
    in lignification, **3**, 732
promelacacinidin(s)
  biochemistry, **3**, 776
  occurrence, **3**, 776, 783
  structure, **3**, 761
promopanidins, biosynthesis, **3**, 777
promoter P_C, roles, **3**, 46
promoter P_K, roles, **3**, 46
promoter P_L, roles, **3**, 46

promoters
  constitutive 'house-keeping', **3**, 44
  germ cell-specific, **3**, 45
  regulatable, mRNA decay studies, **6**, 206
propanal
  reactions, with propioin synthase, **3**, 394
  as substrate, **3**, 373
propane, 1,2-diaryl-, in lignins, **3**, 726
propane, 1,3-dichloro-, as substrate, **5**, 408
propane-1,3-diols, 1,2-diaryl-, in lignins, **3**, 727
propanes, 1,2-diphenyl-, characterization, **1**, 774
propanes, 1,3-diphenyl-
  characterization, **1**, 774
  co-occurrence, with flavans, **3**, 752
propanoate, 1,7-dimethylnonyl, occurrence, **8**, 246
propanoate, (*R*)-10,14-dimethylpentadecyl 2-methyl,
  occurrence, **8**, 241
propanoate, (7*Z*,13*Z*,16*Z*,19*Z*)-7,13,16,19-
  docosatetraenyl 2-methyl, occurrence, **8**, 207
propanoate, (*Z*)-7-dodecenyl, occurrence, **8**, 207
propanoate, (*Z*)-16-methyl-9-heptadecenyl 2-methyl,
  occurrence, **8**, 241
propanoate, myristyl 2-methyl, occurrence, **8**, 210
propanoate, 2-oxo- *see* pyruvate
propanoate, tetradecyl, occurrence, **8**, 209, 216
propanoates
  in branched chain formation, **8**, 237
  occurrence, **8**, 209, 234
  as starting materials, for pheromones, **8**, 241
propanogenins, biosynthesis, **8**, 202, 237
propanoic acid, occurrence, **8**, 241
propanoic acid, β-aminooxy- (AOP), as phenylalanine
  ammonia-lyase inhibitor, **3**, 634
propanoic acid, L-2-aminooxy-3-phenyl- (AOPP)
  as glutamate-ammonia ligase inhibitor, **3**, 627
  inhibitory activity, **3**, 804
  as phenylalanine ammonia-lyase inhibitor, **3**, 634
propanoic acid, 2-methyl-, occurrence, **8**, 221
propanoic acid, 3-(methylthio)-, phytotoxicity, **8**, 178
propanoic acid, 2-nitroso-3-(*p*-hydroxyphenyl)-, as
  intermediate, **1**, 889
propanoic acid esters, occurrence, **8**, 241
propanoids, diaryl-, precursors, **1**, 716
propanoids, phenyl-
  biosynthetic pathways, **1**, 18
    in chalcone biosynthesis, **1**, 750
    evolution, **1**, 642
    initiation, **3**, 622
    in lignin biosynthesis, **3**, 622
    in monolignol biosynthesis, **3**, 626
  coupling reactions, **1**, 640
  dimerization, **1**, 18
  early studies, **1**, 715
  insecticidal activity, **8**, 336
  metabolism, **3**, 622, 626
  occurrence, **8**, 140
  random free radical coupling, **1**, 647
propan-2-ol, occurrence, **8**, 209
propan-2-ol, (*R*)-1-amino-, attachment, to ado-cobyric
  acid, **4**, 148
propan-2-ol, 1,3-bisbenzylthio-, **3**, 767
propan-2-ol, 1,3-diaryl-, biosynthesis, **3**, 771
propan-2-ol, 1,1,1,3,3,3-hexafluoro-, trityl group
  removal, **7**, 126
propan-2-one, 1,3-dibromo-
  in protein cross-linking studies, **1**, 351
  reactions, with β-ketoacylsynthase thiols, **1**, 351
propan-2-ones, biosynthesis, **3**, 767
propanoyl-CoA, roles, in fatty acid biosynthesis, **8**, 203,
  204
propelargonidins
  in A-type proanthocyanidins, **3**, 769
  occurrence, **3**, 769

propeltogynidins, biosynthesis, **3**, 777
propeptide, encoding, **4**, 283
prophages, gene mapping, **3**, 215
propidium iodide, applications, DNA structure probes, **7**, 85
propioin synthase
    biochemistry, **3**, 394
    inhibition, **3**, 394
    purification, **3**, 394
    reactions, with propanal, **3**, 394
propion, biosynthesis, **3**, 394
propionate
    biosynthesis, **8**, 272
    in erythromycin biosynthesis, **1**, 14
propionate, D,L-2-chloro-, as substrate, **5**, 405
propionate, 2,2-dichloro-, as substrate, **5**, 405
propionate, dithiobis(*N*-succinimidyl)-, reactions, with 5′-aminoalkylated oligonucleotides, **7**, 168
propionates, as bacterial aromatic polyketide synthase primers, **1**, 475
Propionibacterium pentosaceum, ketotetrose-phosphate aldolase, **3**, 409
Propionibacterium shermanii
    cbi genes, **4**, 141
    cob genes, **4**, 141
    cyanocobalamin biosynthesis, **4**, 140, 150
    hem genes, **4**, 141
    methylmalonyl-CoA mutase, **5**, 271
propionic acid, β-amino- *see* β-alanine
propionic acid, α-amino-β-oxalylamino-, effects, on herbivores, **8**, 146
propionic acid, L-α-aminooxy-β-phenyl-, effects, on medicarpin biosynthesis, **1**, 808
propionic acid, benzoyl-, **1**, 615
propionic acid, 2-(3-chloro-4-methylphenoxy)-, structure, **8**, 34
propionic acid, 3-(2,4-dichlorophenoxy)-, structure, **8**, 34
propionic acid, α-(2-naphthoxy)-, structure, **8**, 34
propionyl-CoA, activity, **1**, 293
Propylaea spp., propyleine, **8**, 351
propyleine, occurrence, **8**, 351
prorobinetinidins
    occurrence, **3**, 775
    semi-synthesis, **3**, 775
prorocentrolide
    ¹³C labeling patterns, **8**, 497
    occurrence, **8**, 496
Prorocentrum lima
    diol esters, **8**, 490
    okadaic acid, **8**, 490
    prorocentrolide, **8**, 496
Prorocentrum masculosum, diol esters, **8**, 490
pro-R_p phosphoryl oxygen, binding, **6**, 158
prosaposin
    encoding, **3**, 102
    roles, in ischemic damage, **3**, 102
prosolanapyrones
    enantioselectivity, **1**, 399
    enzymatic activity, *exo–endo* ratio, **1**, 399
    labeling, **1**, 397
    reactivity, **1**, 398
Prosopis glandulosa, promelacacinidins, **3**, 776, 783
prostacyclin *see* prostaglandin I₂
prostacyclin synthase *see* prostaglandin I synthase
prostaglandin A
    biosynthesis, **1**, 232
    vasodilatory activity, **1**, 172
15*R*-prostaglandin A₂, occurrence, **1**, 239
prostaglandin A₁, isomers, **1**, 161
prostaglandin A₂, biosynthetic pathways, proposed, **1**, 240
prostaglandin A₂, methyl 15*R*-acetoxy-, occurrence, **1**, 239

prostaglandin A₂-1,15-lactone, occurrence, **1**, 245
prostaglandin A₃-1,15-lactone, occurrence, **1**, 245
prostaglandin B, UV spectra, **1**, 162
prostaglandin B₁, isomers, **1**, 161
15*R*-prostaglandin B₂, occurrence, **1**, 239
15*S*-prostaglandin B₂, occurrence, **1**, 239
prostaglandin C, structure, **1**, 162
prostaglandin D, structure, **1**, 162
prostaglandin D₁, platelet aggregation inhibition, **1**, 174
prostaglandin D₂
    occurrence, **1**, 242, 249
    stability, **1**, 163, 193
prostaglandin D₂ 11-reductase *see* prostaglandin F synthase
prostaglandin D synthase
    brain-type, **1**, 260
    catalysis, **1**, 260
    hematopoietic-type, **1**, 260
    lipocalin-type, **1**, 260
    localization, **1**, 260
    spleen-type, **1**, 260
prostaglandin D₂ synthase
    brain-type, molecular phylogeny, **1**, 274
    catalysis, **1**, 274
    hematopoietic, **1**, 275
prostaglandin E
    stability, **1**, 162
    vasodilatory activity, **1**, 172
prostaglandin E₁
    applications, bronchodilators, **1**, 174
    early studies, **1**, 160
    isolation, **1**, 161
    platelet aggregation inhibition, **1**, 174
    structure, **1**, 161
prostaglandin E₁, 13,14-dihydro-, synthesis, **1**, 161
prostaglandin E₁α
    isolation, **1**, 161
    structure, **1**, 161
prostaglandin E₂
    applications, **1**, 194
        bronchodilators, **1**, 174
    biosynthesis, **1**, 237
    effects, on kidney blood flow, **1**, 174
    occurrence, **1**, 236, 242, 244, 245, 246, 248, 249
        in inflammatory diseases, **1**, 174
    pyretic activity, **1**, 174
    uterus contraction–relaxation effects, **1**, 174
prostaglandin E₃, occurrence, **1**, 245
prostaglandin E₃-1,15-lactone, occurrence, **1**, 245
prostaglandin E₃-1,15-lactone-11-acetate, occurrence, **1**, 245
prostaglandin-endoperoxide synthase-1
    arachidonic acid oxygenation, **5**, 243
    biochemistry, **5**, 226
    biological activity, **1**, 257
    crystal structure, **5**, 230
    future research, **5**, 256
    gene, mapping, **5**, 228
    localization, **1**, 257
    primary sequences, **5**, 230
    x-ray crystal structure, **1**, 258
prostaglandin-endoperoxide synthase-1–bromoacetylsalicylic acid complexes, structure, **5**, 247
prostaglandin-endoperoxide synthase-1-(*S*)-flurbiprofen complexes, structure, **5**, 247
prostaglandin-endoperoxide synthase-1 knockout mice, development, **5**, 227
prostaglandin-endoperoxide synthase-1–nonsteroid antiinflammatory agent complexes, structure, **5**, 248
prostaglandin-endoperoxide synthase-2
    arachidonic acid oxygenation, **5**, 243

biochemistry, **5**, 226
biological activity, **1**, 257
crystal structure, **5**, 230
future research, **5**, 256
gene expression, **5**, 226
   regulatory mechanisms, **5**, 229
inhibition, **1**, 10, 257
   steroid, **5**, 256
   structural bases, **5**, 253
inhibitors, development, **5**, 250
localization, **5**, 228
primary sequences, **5**, 230
substrate binding channel, **5**, 231
x-ray crystal structure, **1**, 258
prostaglandin-endoperoxide synthase-2 knockout mice,
      development, **5**, 227
prostaglandin-endoperoxide synthase(s)
activation
      hydroperoxide-dependent, **5**, 238, 239
      peroxidase, **5**, 238
active sites, **5**, 231, 232
arachidonic acid oxygenation, **1**, 255
biological activity, **1**, 257
catalysis, **1**, 256, 274, **5**, 233
      models, **5**, 240
catalytic domain, **5**, 231
Compound I, **5**, 236
cyclooxygenase–peroxidase integration, **5**, 244
epidermal growth factor domain, **5**, 230
functions, **5**, **225–261**
genes
      deletion, **5**, 227
      structure, **5**, 228
heme-binding sites, **5**, 232
inhibition, **1**, 10, 257, **5**, **225–261**
      competitive, **5**, 248
      covalent, **5**, 249
      nonsteroid antiinflammatory agent-induced, **5**, 247
      slow, tight-binding, **5**, 248
inhibitors, **1**, 10, 123
isoforms, **5**, 226
mechanisms, **1**, 161
      alternate, **5**, 246
      branched-chain, **5**, 244
      tightly coupled, **5**, 245
membrane association, **5**, 230
membrane binding domain, **5**, 230
peroxidase active sites, **5**, 232
proteins, structure, **5**, 229
roles, in eicosanoid biosynthesis, **1**, 160
structural homology, **5**, 233
structure, **5**, **225–261**
prostaglandin E synthase, catalysis, **1**, 260
prostaglandin F, stability, **1**, 162
prostaglandin F$_{1\alpha}$
biosynthesis, **1**, 163
early studies, **1**, 160
occurrence, **1**, 236
prostaglandin F$_{1\alpha}$, 6-keto-
biosynthesis, **1**, 166
oxidation, **1**, 167
prostaglandin F$_2$, occurrence, **1**, 246
prostaglandin F$_{2\alpha}$
applications, **1**, 194
      in ophthalmology, **1**, 196
bronchospasm induction, **1**, 174
occurrence, **1**, 236, 242, 245, 248, 249
vasodilatory activity, **1**, 172
prostaglandin F$_{2\alpha}$, 15-keto-
excretion, **1**, 237
occurrence, **1**, 242
prostaglandin F synthase
catalysis, **1**, 261

homology, **1**, 261
prostaglandin F$_{2\alpha}$ synthase, catalysis, **1**, 276
prostaglandin G$_2$
biosynthesis, **1**, 163, 256
      stereochemistry, **5**, 247
occurrence, **1**, 242
reduction, **5**, 226
synthesis, **1**, 182
prostaglandin H$_2$
analogues, synthesis, **1**, 188
biosynthesis, **1**, 256, 163
occurrence, **1**, 242
stability, **1**, 163
synthesis, **1**, 182
prostaglandin H$_2$ D-isomerase *see* prostaglandin D
      synthase
prostaglandin H$_2$ E-isomerase *see* prostaglandin E
      synthase
prostaglandin hydroperoxidase, biological activity, **1**, 257
prostaglandin I$_2$
analogues, synthesis, **1**, 189
biological activity, **1**, 175
biosynthesis, **1**, 166
early studies, **1**, 10
occurrence, **1**, 249
platelet aggregation inhibition, **1**, 175
synthesis, **1**, 181
prostaglandin I synthase
catalysis, **1**, 261
cDNA, cloning, **1**, 261
P450 nature of, **1**, 261
prostaglandin I$_2$ synthase
catalysis, **1**, 277
molecular phylogeny, **1**, 277
prostaglandin J$_2$, biosynthesis, **1**, 163
prostaglandins
analogues, synthesis, **1**, 186
applications
      in cytoprotectivity, **1**, 196
      gynecological, **1**, 194
      obstetric, **1**, 194
      in ophthalmology, **1**, 196
      peripheral circulation dysfunction treatments, **1**, 196
biological activity, **1**, 255, 172
biosynthesis, **1**, 2, 7, 163, 171, **5**, 226
      inhibition, **5**, 247
      and nitric oxide biosynthesis, **5**, 239
early studies, **1**, 8, 160
in fish reproduction, **1**, 237
localization, **1**, 160
metabolism, **1**, 262
nomenclature, **1**, 161
occurrence, **1**, 177
      aquatic organisms, **1**, 208
      fish, **1**, 236
as pheromones, **8**, 426
platelet aggregation inhibition, **1**, 174
primary, **1**, 163
receptors, **1**, 10, 192
      molecular phylogeny, **1**, 281
structure, **1**, 161
synthesis, **1**, 177
      via 1,4-addition, **1**, 178
      via Corey's lactone, **1**, 177
use of term, **1**, 160
uterus contraction–relaxation effects, **1**, 160, 174
vasodilatory activity, **1**, 172
prostaglandin synthase(s) *see* prostaglandin-
      endoperoxide synthase(s)
prostaglandin transporter
cDNAs, **1**, 282
molecular phylogeny, **1**, 283
prostalidins, antidepressant activity, **1**, 705

prostanoids, use of term, **1**, 160
prostate cancer
  etiology, **5**, 155
  protective agents, lignans, **1**, 698
  and soy-rich diets, **1**, 782
prostatic acid phosphatase
  phosphohistidine in, **5**, 144
  regulatory mechanisms, **5**, 155
  structure, **5**, 152
Prostephanus truncatus, dominicalure 1, **8**, 241
protease inhibitors, studies, **8**, 610
protease LanP, in nisin lantibiotics, **4**, 291
protecting groups, in RNA synthesis, **6**, 83
protein A, **2**, 211
protein amino acids, in nectars, **8**, 162
protein antenna complexes, light-harvesting, **2**, 326, 345
proteinase, activity, effects of cytokinins on, **8**, 59
proteinase inhibitor inducing factor (PIIF)
  induction, **8**, 150
  mechanisms, **8**, 149
proteinase inhibitors
  in induced plant defense, **8**, 150
  synthesis, **8**, 149
    inhibition, **8**, 119
  Theonella spp., **8**, 568
  wound-induced, **1**, 131, 133
Protein Data Bank
  DNA structures, **7**, 55
  RNA structures, **6**, 4
protein dimethylallyl*trans*transferase(s)
  catalysis, **2**, 358
  metal cofactors, **2**, 7
protein-DNA
  interactions, analysis, **7**, 669
  recognition
    and partial intercalation, **7**, 463
    topological variations, **7**, 349
protein–DNA binding, sequence determination, **7**, 628
protein–DNA complexes, probing, **7**, 266
protein enzymes
  evolution, **6**, 127
  and ribozymes compared, **6**, 115, 137, 139, 143
  studies, **6**, 109
protein farnesyltransferase (PFT)
  catalysis, **5**, 332
  enzymology, **5**, 333
  inhibitors, studies, **2**, 363
  linear free energy studies, **5**, 332
  mechanistic studies, **5**, 332
  mutagenesis, site-directed, **5**, 334
  prenyl group transfer, **2**, 358
  protein production, **5**, 333
  purification, **5**, 334
  recombinant, **5**, 334
  specificity, **2**, 358
  structure, **2**, 358
  substrates, **5**, 332
  transition state analogues, **5**, 333
  x-ray crystal structure, **5**, 334
protein geranylgeranyltransferase-I (PGGT-I)
  prenyl group transfer, **2**, 358
  specificity, **2**, 358
  structure, **2**, 358
  substrates, **5**, 332
protein geranylgeranyltransferase-II (PGGT-II)
  Rab Escort Protein in, **2**, 358
  structure, **2**, 358
  yeast homologues, **2**, 359
protein kinase A, regulatory mechanisms, **3**, 168
protein kinase C
  activation, via TPA-type promoters, **8**, 491
  calmodulin-dependent, **3**, 483
  inhibition, **3**, 168

roles, in phosphorylation, **1**, 294
  subunits, **1**, 295
protein kinase(s)
  calcium–calmodulin-dependent, **1**, 294
  cAMP-dependent, **3**, 482
  desensitization, **1**, 134
  occurrence, **1**, 134
  palmitoylation, **4**, 20
  proline-directed, **3**, 486
  regulatory mechanisms, **1**, 132
protein–nucleic acid complexes, probing, **7**, 268
protein palmitoyltransferases, purification, **4**, 20, 21
protein phosphatase(s) *see* phosphoprotein
        phosphatase(s)
protein phosphorylation, modulation, **8**, 470
protein radicals
  biosynthesis, **5**, 240
  prostaglandin-endoperoxide synthase-derived, **5**, 240
proteins
  alpha helices, **7**, 616
  amino acids in, **4**, 354
  amino acid side chains, **7**, 616
  amino-terminal labeling, **7**, 646
  anchoring, **3**, 297
  beta sheets, **7**, 616
  binding, **7**, 616
  binding pockets, **7**, 638
  biosynthesis
    RNA role in, **6**, 3
    tRNA role in, **6**, 52
  blue copper, **1**, 435
  bulk production, in *Escherichia coli*, **7**, 665
  carotenoid-binding, **2**, 326
  catalysis, **7**, 616
  chloroplast-localized, **8**, 50
  expression, SDS-polyacrylamide gel electrophoresis
      analysis, **7**, 665
  farnesylated
    methylation, **2**, 355
    structure, **2**, 354
    synthesis, **2**, 247
  farnesylation, **2**, 354
  fatty acid modification, **1**, 24
  folding studies, **7**, 645
  full length, cloning, **7**, 645
  geranylgeranylated
    mass spectrometry, **2**, 358
    structure, **2**, 358
  glycosylation, **4**, 13
  N-glycosylation, **3**, 14
  heterologously expressed, **2**, 104
  historical perceptions, **7**, 615
  hydrophobic bonding, with polyphenols, **3**, 802
  interactions, with nucleic acids, **7**, 266
  lipidation, **4**, 13
  malfolded, degradation, **3**, 31
  membrane, GPI anchoring, **3**, 295
  multicopper blue, **1**, 435
  multifunctional, **1**, 51
    purification, **1**, 52
  palmitoylated, **4**, 13–24
    data, **4**, 14
    fatty acids, **4**, 15
    fatty acyl chains, **4**, 15
    future research, **4**, 21
    structure, **4**, 14
  palmitoyl groups
    attachment, **4**, 15
    functions, **4**, 20
  pathogenesis-related, **1**, 133
    reviews, **8**, 186
  phosphorylation, **1**, 132, **4**, 13
  posttranslational modification, protein
      farnesyltransferase catalysis, **5**, 332

precipitation, **3**, 791
prenylated, **2**, **353–366**
  examples, **2**, 360
  future research, **2**, 363
  interactions with non-prenylated proteins, **2**, 363
  methylation, **2**, 361
  proteolysis, **2**, 359
  radiolabeled studies, **2**, 363
  reviews, **2**, 354
prenylation, **2**, 10, **5**, 332
prenyl groups, chemical structures, **2**, 354
proline-rich, **8**, 142
  cell wall, **1**, 130
proteolysis, **2**, 354
pyridine nucleotide binding sites, **1**, 426
recombinant, genetics, **1**, 654
recombinant sources, **5**, 339
redox properties, **5**, 385
roles, in RNA enzyme activity, **6**, 110
selenocysteine incorporation, **4**, 369
soluble, localization, **1**, 120
structure, **3**, 38
  inter-proton distances, **7**, 62
  secondary, **6**, 139
tertiary structure, encoding, **7**, 645
see also activator proteins; auxin binding proteins;
  chromoproteins; cytokinin-binding proteins;
  dirigent proteins; DNA binding proteins;
  fosfomycin resistance proteins; fusion proteins;
  jasmonate-induced proteins (JIPs); lipoproteins;
  penicillin-binding proteins (PBPs); selenoproteins;
  vegetative storage proteins (VSPs)
protein serine/threonine phosphatases, classification, **5**,
  140
protein thiotemplate mechanism *see* thiotemplate
  mechanism
protein-tyrosine-phosphatase(s)
  biochemistry, **5**, 156
  classification, **5**, 140
  inhibitors, **5**, 159
protein-tyrosine-phosphate phosphohydrolase(s) *see*
  protein-tyrosine-phosphatase(s)
protein venoms, ants, **8**, 359
proteoglycans
  biosynthesis, **3**, 2, 5, **161–177**
    future research, **3**, 175
    pathways, **3**, 163
    stages, **3**, 162
  carbohydrate chains, **3**, 4
  classifications, **3**, 4, 163
  core protein, biosynthesis, **3**, 164
  genes
    families, **3**, 164
    structural characteristics, **3**, 164
  nomenclature, **3**, 163
  TATA box, **3**, 167
proteolipids, occurrence, **4**, 13
proteolysis, promotion, **3**, 31
proteolytic cleavage, enzymes for, **7**, 648
proteracacinidins, biochemistry, **3**, 776
proteracacinidins, dimeric, occurrence, **3**, 776
prothoracic glands
  activation, **8**, 295
  activity, **8**, 290
  azadirachtin studies, **8**, 331
  stimulation, **8**, 279
prothoracicotropic hormone (PTTH)
  azadirachtin studies, **8**, 331
  biochemistry, **8**, 295
  characterization, **8**, 295
  prothoracic gland stimulation, **8**, 265
  roles, **8**, 290
  secretion, **8**, 279

see also brain hormone
protocatechuate
  biosynthesis, **1**, 589
  degradation, **3**, 385
  from, quinate, **1**, 585
protocatechuic acid
  biosynthesis, **3**, 804
  in gallic acid biosynthetic pathway, **3**, 803
protoheme ferro-lyase(s) *see* ferrochelatase(s)
protolimonoids, biosynthesis, **8**, 328
protonation
  of nucleosides, **7**, 122
  steric hindrance, **5**, 33
proton bridges, solvation catalytic, **5**, 119
proton elimination, in *Alicyclobacillus acidocaldarius*
  cyclase, **2**, 310
proto-oncogenes, α-1,3(6)-mannosyl-glycoprotein β-1,6-
  N-acetylglucosaminyltransferase activity, **3**, 55
protopine, occurrence, **3**, 643
protoplasts, applications, in auxin assays, **8**, 31
protoporphyrin IX
  accumulation, **2**, 333, 346
  binding, **4**, 103
  protection against, **2**, 326
protoporphyrin IX monomethyl ester oxidative cyclase,
  homology, **1**, 874
protoporphyrinogen oxidase(s)
  catalysis, **4**, 98
  mechanisms, **4**, 98
  occurrence, **4**, 100
  properties, **4**, 98
protoporphyrinogen-IX:oxygen oxidoreductase *see*
  protoporphyrinogen oxidase(s)
protosta-17(20)[16,21-*cis*],24-diene, 3β-hydroxy-,
  occurrence, **2**, 281
protosterol cation, as intermediate, **2**, 280
protosteryl cation, conformation, **2**, 302
protoveratrine A
  insecticidal activity, **8**, 349
  occurrence, **8**, 349
protoxin, insect growth inhibition, **3**, 821
Protozoa
  arachidonic acid metabolism, **1**, 249
  GPI anchors, biosynthesis, **3**, 304
  parasitic, glycosylphosphatidylinositol biosynthesis, **3**,
    295–309
  pathogenicity, **3**, 297
  surface antigens, **3**, 302
protozoans, DNA minicircles, **7**, 630
provitamin A *see* β-carotene
proximal sequence element (PSE)
  localization, **4**, 362
  sequences, **4**, 364
  transcription start points, **4**, 364
proxiphomin, occurrence, **1**, 393
PRPs *see* proline-rich proteins (PRPs)
PR-toxin
  occurrence, **2**, 177, 202, 205
  roles, in mycotoxicoses, **2**, 205
prunasin, hydrolysis, **1**, 890
(*R*)-prunasin, occurrence, **1**, 885, 886
prunasin hydrolase, **1**, 890
prunetin
  biosynthesis, **1**, 799
  as zoospore attractant, **8**, 174
Prunus dulcis, 5-hydroxyferulic acid, **3**, 671
Prunus jamasakura, dihydrobuddlenol B, **1**, 688
Prunus serotina
  cyanogenesis, **1**, 885
  glucosides, **1**, 882
prymnesin
  occurrence, **8**, 518
  structure, **8**, 518

Prymnesium parvum, prymnesin, **8**, 518
Psacothea hilaris, (*Z*)-21-methyl-8-pentatriacontene, **8**, 249
Psalliota bispora
  1,5*Z*-octadien-3*R*-ol, **1**, 211
  10-oxo-8*E*-decenoic acid, **1**, 211
Psalliota campestris, laccases, **3**, 709, 711
PSDP *see* presqualene diphosphate (PSDP)
PSE *see* proximal sequence element (PSE)
P-selectin *see* PADGEM protein
Pseudacanthotermes spiniger, (3*Z*,6*Z*,8*E*)-3,6,8-dodecatrien-1-ol, **8**, 214
pseudaminic acid
  in *Pseudomonas aeruginosa*, **3**, 193
  in *Shigella boidii*, **3**, 190
Pseudeurotium ovalis, ovalicin, **2**, 165
pseudobaptigenin, biosynthesis, **1**, 802
pseudobaptigenin, hydroxy-, reduction, **1**, 682
pseudobaptigenin, 2′-hydroxy-, as substrate, **1**, 795
pseudobaptigenin, 5′-hydroxy-, biosynthesis, **1**, 802
pseudocholinesterase *see* cholinesterase
Pseudococcus comstocki, (*R*)-3-acetoxy-2,6-dimethyl-1,5-heptadiene, **8**, 234
Pseudodistoma arborescens, arborescidines, **8**, 528
Pseudodistoma crucigaster, crucigasterins, **8**, 545
Pseudodistoma kanoko, pseudodistomins, **8**, 547
Pseudodistoma novaezelandae, long-chain amines, **8**, 545
pseudodistomin A, structure, **8**, 550
pseudodistomin A acetate, synthesis, **8**, 550
pseudodistomin B acetate
  NMR spectra, **8**, 550
  synthesis, **8**, 550
pseudodistomin C, synthesis, **8**, 550, 551
pseudodistomin C acetate, NMR spectra, **8**, 550
pseudodistomins
  absolute stereochemistry, exciton chirality method, **8**, 548
  antispasmodic activity, **8**, 547
  CD spectra, Cotton effect, **8**, 548
  chiral HPLC analysis, **8**, 551
  occurrence, **8**, 547
  structure, **8**, 547
  synthesis, **8**, 549
pseudoguaianolides, antifeedant activity, **8**, 308
pseudoisocytidine, 2′-*O*-methyl-
  from, pseudouridine, **7**, 262
  in oligodeoxynucleotides, **7**, 332
pseudoisocytosine, **7**, 255
Pseudolabrus japonicus, *Aspergillus fumigatus* in, **8**, 603
Pseudomonas spp.
  carotenoid biosynthesis, **2**, 323
  4-chlorobenzoate degradation, **5**, 411
  chlorobenzoyl CoA dehalogenase, **5**, 411
  2-dehydro-3-deoxy-L-pentonate aldolase, **3**, 425
  haloacid dehalogenases, **5**, 406
  haloalcohol dehalogenases, **5**, 408
  4-hydroxy-2-ketovalerate aldolase, **3**, 384
  kynureninase, **3**, 395
  metabolite biosynthesis, **4**, 197
  okadaxanthin, **8**, 589
  4-oxalocrotonate tautomerase, **5**, 42
  3-phosphoshikimate 1-carboxyvinyltransferase, glyphosate tolerance, **1**, 598
  thiotropocin, **1**, 849
Pseudomonas aeruginosa
  alg genes, **3**, 204
  autoinducers, **8**, 398
  carbamoyl substitution, **3**, 194
  core oligosaccharide, structure, **3**, 194
  diketopiperazines, **8**, 590
  isoprenoid biosynthesis, mevalonate-independent pathway, **2**, 58

lipopolysaccharides, **3**, 193
  A-band, **3**, 194
  aminosugars in, **3**, 193
  B-band, **3**, 194
  pseudaminic acid in, **3**, 193
as opportunistic infectants, **8**, 392
salicylic acid biosynthesis, **1**, 613
virulence factors, **8**, 398
Pseudomonas aeruginosa PAO1, O-side chain, **3**, 194
Pseudomonas amygdali, (*E*)-zeatin-2′-deoxyriboside, **8**, 61
Pseudomonas spp. B13, carboxymethylenebutenolidase, **5**, 112, 130
Pseudomonas cepacia, triacylglycerol lipases, **5**, 128
Pseudomonas denitrificans
  cobaltochelatase, **4**, 148
  cob genes, **4**, 143, 148
  cyanocobalamin biosynthesis, **4**, 140
  hem genes, **4**, 141
Pseudomonas fluorescens
  andrimid, **8**, 594
  benzoin aldolase, **3**, 394
  carbamoyl substitution, **3**, 194
  2-dehydro-3-deoxyphosphogluconate aldolase, **3**, 421
  isoprenoid biosynthesis, mevalonate-independent pathway, **2**, 58
  peptide synthetases, **4**, 214
  pigment production, **1**, 763
Pseudomonas fragi
  fao genes, **1**, 53
  HDT activity, **1**, 53
  long-chain-fatty-acid-CoA ligase, **1**, 49
  multifunctional proteins, **1**, 53
  penicillin biosynthesis, **4**, 267
Pseudomonas gladioli, phospho*enol*pyruvate phosphomutase, **1**, 869
Pseudomonas glumae, triacylglycerol lipases, **5**, 133
Pseudomonas halosaccharolytica, cyclopropane fatty acids, **1**, 63
Pseudomonas magnesiorubra, magnesidins, **8**, 598
Pseudomonas mevalonii
  hydroxymethylglutaryl-CoA reductases, **2**, 24, 27, 41
    active site residues, **2**, 33
    binary complexes, **2**, 34
    dinucleotide binding fold, **2**, 29
    NADP specificity, **2**, 29
    structure, **2**, 28
    ternary complexes, **2**, 28
Pseudomonas oleovarans, *alkK* gene, **1**, 47
Pseudomonas paucimobilis
  dehalogenases, **5**, 409
  lindane degradation, **5**, 403
Pseudomonas putida
  carbamoyl substitution, **3**, 194
  4-(2-carboxyphenyl)-2-oxobut-3-enoate aldolase, **3**, 376
  4-hydroxy-4-methyl-2-oxoglutarate aldolase, **3**, 385
Pseudomonas putida U
  penicillin biosynthesis, **4**, 267
  phenylacetyl-CoA ligase, **4**, 246
  expression, **4**, 268
Pseudomonas saccharophila, 2-dehydro-3-deoxy-6-phosphogalactonate aldolase, **3**, 429
Pseudomonas stutzeri, 4-α-glucanotransferase induction, **3**, 445
Pseudomonas syringae
  carbamoyl substitution, **3**, 194
  ethylene, **8**, 93
  ethylene-forming enzyme, **8**, 94
  fosfomycin, **1**, 875
  syringolide, **1**, 147
Pseudomonas tabaci, toxic mechanisms, **8**, 59
Pseudomonas vesicularis, 4-(2-carboxyphenyl)-2-oxobut-3-enoate aldolase, **3**, 376

Pseudomonas viridiflava, fosfomycin, **1**, 875
Pseudomyrmex mexicanus, venom, **8**, 354
pseudonidurufin, studies, **1**, 455
pseudopederine, structure, **8**, 351
Pseudoplexaura porosa, prostaglandin biosynthesis, **1**, 240
Pseudoplusia includens
    (*Z*)-7-dodecenyl propanoate, **8**, 207
    plant–herbivore–predator interactions, **8**, 152
Pseudopterogorgia elisabethae, pseudopterosin C, **8**, 521
pseudopterosin C
    antiinflammatory activity, **8**, 521
    applications, antiinflammatory agents, **8**, 521
    occurrence, **8**, 521
pseudorotaxanes, structure, **7**, 361
pseudotropine, as starting material, for calystegines, **4**, 29
Pseudotsuga menziesii
    compression wood formation, **3**, 694
    dihydrokaempferol 4-reductase, **1**, 727
    dihydroquercetin, **1**, 685
    pseudotsuganol, **1**, 685
pseudotsuganol, occurrence, **1**, 685
pseudouridine
    in Sec tRNA, **4**, 360
    as starting material, for 2′-*O*-methyl pseudoisocytidine, **7**, 262
PSGL-1
    expression, **3**, 76
    recognition, **3**, 72
psicothymidines, protection, **7**, 227
psiguavin, biosynthesis, **3**, 784
psilotins, biosynthesis, **1**, 765
Psilotum spp., psilotins, **1**, 765
Psithyrus spp., geranylcitronellol, **8**, 229
psoralen
    biosynthesis, **1**, 631
    from, (+)-marmesin, **1**, 19, 631
    hydroxylation, **1**, 633
    levels, seasonal, **1**, 625
    occurrence, **8**, 338
    phototoxicity, **8**, 338
psoralen, (±)-2′-acetyl-2′,3′-dihydro-, deuteration, **1**, 632
psoralen, 4′-[(3-carboxyproprionamido)methyl]-4,5,8-trimethyl-, synthesis, **7**, 161
psoralen, 5,8-dihydroxy-, biosynthesis, **1**, 633
psoralen, 5,8-dimethoxy- *see* isopimpinellin
psoralen, 8-hydroxy- *see* xanthoxol
psoralen, 4,5′,8-trimethyl-, applications, DNA structure probes, **7**, 96
psoralen–oligonucleotide conjugates, synthesis, **7**, 169
psoralen phosphoramidites, synthesis, **7**, 184
psoralens
    applications, DNA structure probes, **7**, 96
    light-dependent DNA reactions, **7**, 545
    toxicity, **1**, 623
psoralens, oxygenated, biosynthesis, **1**, 633
psoralen synthase
    catalysis, **1**, 632
    in psoralen biosynthesis, **1**, 632
psorospermin, DNA damage induction, **7**, 511
PSP *see* paralytic shellfish poison (PSP)
PSPP *see* presqualene diphosphate (PSDP)
PSTV *see* potato spindle tuber viroid (PSTV)
Psychidae
    pheromones, **8**, 215
    sex pheromones, **8**, 209
pTAex3 expression vector, in 6-methylsalicylic acid synthase studies, **1**, 14, 414
ptaquiloside, DNA adducts of, **7**, 507
Pteleobius vittatus, *cis*-pityol, **8**, 233
pteridine, hydration, **5**, 77
pteridine, 4-amino-, deamination, **5**, 77
pteridine hydrate, dehydration, **5**, 77
pteridines, biosynthesis, **1**, 837

Pteridium aquilinum, antheridiogens, **8**, 55
Pteridophyta
    lignans, **1**, 647
    lignins, **3**, 620
        evolution, **3**, 625
    oxylipins, **1**, 228
pterin molybdenum cofactors, biosynthesis, **1**, 835
Pteriomorphia
    prostaglandins, **1**, 244
    see also mussels; *Mytilus edulis*; oysters; scallops
Pteris podophylla, lignans, **3**, 625
Pteris vittata
    aglycones, **1**, 679
    dihydrodehydrodiconiferyl alcohol 9-*O*-β-D-glucoside, **3**, 625
    lariciresinol 9-*O*-β-D-glucoside, **3**, 625
    lignans, **1**, 647
pterocarpan, (6a*R*,11a*R*)-3,9-dihydroxy-, biosynthesis, **1**, 797
pterocarpan, 3,9-dihydroxy-
    6a-hydroxylation, **1**, 802
    prenylation, **1**, 803
    stereochemistry, **1**, 797
pterocarpan, 3,9-dihydroxy-10-dimethylallyl *see* phaseollidin
pterocarpan, 3,6a,9-trihydroxy-
    biosynthesis, **1**, 802
    prenyl group addition, **1**, 803
pterocarpan aglycones, accumulation, **1**, 808
pterocarpanoids, early studies, **1**, 784
pterocarpans
    antifungal activity, **1**, 779
    biosynthesis, **1**, 777, 786, 797
        in vitro, **1**, 797
    characterization, **8**, 186
    6a-hydroxylation, **1**, 774, 786, 802
    occurrence, **1**, 774
    ring-opening, **1**, 812
    structure, **1**, 786
pterocarpans, trihydroxy-, half-life, **1**, 812
(+)-pterocarpans, biosynthesis, mechanisms, **1**, 803
pterocarpan synthase, catalysis, **1**, 797
pterocarp-1,4-dien-3-ones, 1a-hydroxy-, biosynthesis, **1**, 814
pterocarp-6a-enes, as intermediates, **1**, 810
PTF *see* SNAP
ptilodene, occurrence, **1**, 224
Ptilota filicina
    5*Z*,7*E*,9*E*,14*Z*,17*Z*-eicosapentaenoic acid, **1**, 224
    ptilodene, **1**, 224
PTMT *see* benzoyl, 2-(isopropylthiomethoxymethyl)- (PTMT)
PTP1, isotope effects, **5**, 151
PTP1B, structure, **5**, 156
PTTH *see* prothoracicotropic hormone (PTTH)
PTX *see* pectenotoxins (PTX)
PTX1 *see* pectenotoxin 1 (PTX1)
PTX2 *see* pectenotoxin 2 (PTX2)
Puccia framinis tritici, epoxides, **1**, 210
puc genes, **2**, 330
Pueraria lobata
    chalcone reductase, **1**, 790
    chalcone synthase, **1**, 732
        genetics, **1**, 789
    isoflavone glycosides, **1**, 807
    isoflavone synthase, **1**, 793
    isoflavonoids, **1**, 784
    kudzuisoflavones, **1**, 806
puffer fish
    food poisoning caused by, **8**, 480
    sodium channels, **8**, 488
    see also *Fugu rubripes*
pukeleimides, occurrence, **8**, 603

pulegone
  biosynthesis, **2**, 62
  effects, on herbivores, **8**, 142
  insecticidal activity, **8**, 306
  structure, **2**, 101, 103
(+)-pulegone, biosynthesis, **2**, 144
pullulanase *see* α-dextrin endo-1,6-α-glucosidase
pulo'upone, occurrence, **1**, 374
pulp, consumption, in paper industry, **3**, 612
pummeloquinone, occurrence, **1**, 384
pumpkins
  fruit
    farnesyl diphosphate isomerase cloning, **2**, 74
    geranylgeranyl diphosphate synthase, **2**, 86
    isopentenyl diphosphate isomerase, **2**, 71
  gibberellin 20-oxidase, cDNA cloning, **8**, 51
  see also Cucurbita maxima
punaglandins, cytotoxicity, **1**, 242
pungiolide A, occurrence, **1**, 375
pur genes
  in deoxysugar biosynthesis, **3**, 342
  purF, encoding, **1**, 838
purine, 2-amino-, **7**, 254
  applications, **6**, 225, 227
purine, 6-benzylamino-9-[*O*-glucopyranosyl-(1-3)-
    ribofuranosyl]-, identification, **8**, 71
purine, *N*⁶-(γ,γ-dimethylallylamino)-
    hydroxylation, **8**, 70
  occurrence, **8**, 59
  roles, **8**, 59
purine, *N*⁶-methylamino-, occurrence, **8**, 59
purine arabinoside, 2-amino-6-methoxy-, conversion, **5**,
    74
purine bases, protection, **7**, 121
purine deaminase(s), early studies, **5**, 77
purine-2′-deoxyriboside, 2-amino-, **7**, 259
purine-2′-deoxyriboside, 2,6-diamino-, **7**, 259
purine-nucleoside:orthophosphate ribosyltransferase *see*
    purine-nucleoside phosphorylase
purine-nucleoside phosphorylase, catalysis, **5**, 73
purine nucleotides, hydroxy radical adducts, **7**, 409
purine–pyrimidine–purine triplexes, kinetics, **7**, 47
purine radicals, reactivity, **7**, 408
purine ribonucleoside(s), 6-hydroxymethyl-5,6-dihydro-
    adenosine deaminase inhibition, **5**, 76
  binding, **5**, 77
purine ribose 5′-phosphate, 6-hydroxy-6-amino-, lifetime,
    5, 82
purine riboside, binding, **5**, 76
6-*Br*-purine riboside, k_{cat} ratios, **5**, 77
6-*Cl*-purine riboside, k_{cat} ratios, **5**, 77
6-*I*-purine riboside, k_{cat} ratios, **5**, 77
purine riboside hydrate, transition state structure, **5**, 79
purine riboside 1,6-hydrate, binding, **5**, 76
purine(s)
  alkene cation radicals, **7**, 410
  aminoalkylation, **7**, 191
  applications, hammerhead ribozyme studies, **7**, 276
  biosynthesis, **5**, 80
  deamination, **5**, 73
    overview, **5**, 72
  effects, on DNA, **7**, 410
  incorporation studies, **6**, 225
  modified, **6**, 93
purines, 8-oxo-
  in DNA damage, **7**, 410
  synthesis, **7**, 409
Purkinje cells, vacuolation, **3**, 140
puromycin
  discovery, **4**, 200
  as protein synthesis inhibitor, **4**, 204
purple acid phosphatase
  biochemistry, **5**, 154

  catalysis, **5**, 141
  characterization, **5**, 154
Purves, C. B., on organic chemistry, **3**, 534
putaminoxin, phytotoxicity, **8**, 181
putidaredoxin, iron centers, **3**, 337
putrescine
  biosynthesis, **4**, 27
  in DNA damage, **7**, 570
  in hornet venom, **8**, 356
putrescine, *N*-methyl-, biosynthesis, **4**, 30
putrescine *N*-methyltransferase, activity, **4**, 27
Px *see* xanthen-9-yl, 9-phenyl- (Px)
pyochelin, **1**, 613
pyoverdin, occurrence, **4**, 203
Pyralidae
  pheromones, **8**, 207
  *see also Achroia innotata; Chilo auricilius; Ephestia
    elutella*
pyran, 2,2,6-trimethyl-3-hydroxytetrahydro- *see* vittatol
pyrano[2,3-*f*]chromenes, tetrahydro-
  biosynthesis, **3**, 774
  from, fisetinidol-(4→8)-catechin profisetinidins, **3**, 773
pyrano[2,3-*h*]chromenes, tetrahydro-, biosynthesis, **3**, 774
pyrano[3,2-*g*]chromenes, tetrahydro-, biosynthesis, **3**, 774
pyranocoumarins, occurrence, **1**, 628
2*H*-pyran-2-one, 3,5-dimethyl-6-(1′-
    methylbutyl)tetrahydro- *see* invictolide
2*H*-pyran-2-one, (3*S*,5*R*,6*S*)-3,5-dimethyl-6-(1-
    methylethyl)3,4,5,6-tetrahydro-, occurrence, **8**,
    240
pyran-4-one, (2*R*)-6-ethyl-2-methyl-4*H*-2,3-dihydro-,
    occurrence, **8**, 211
pyran-4-one, (*R*)-2-ethyl-6-methyl-4*H*-2,3-dihydro- *see*
    hepialone
4*H*-pyran-4-one, (2*S*,3*S*,1′*R*)-2,3-dihydro-2-ethyl-3,5-
    dimethyl-6-(1′-methyl-2′-oxobytyl)- *see* β-
    serricorone
4*H*-pyran-4-one, (2*S*,3*R*,1′*S*,2′*S*)-2,3-dihydro-2,3,5-
    trimethyl-6-(2′-hydroxy-1′-methylbytyl)- *see*
    stegobiol
pyrans, 2,3-dihydro-, occurrence, **8**, 211
pyranyl, tetrahydro-, applications, 2′-hydroxyl group
    protection, **6**, 84
pyran-4-yl, 4-methoxytetrahydro-
  applications
    2′-hydroxyl group protection, **6**, 84
    5′-hydroxyl group protection, **6**, 83
pyrazinc, 3-isopropyl-2-methoxy-, insect sequestration, **8**,
    152
pyrazine C-nucleoside, **7**, 255
pyrazines, in insects, bird predation protection, **8**, 154
pyrazines, imidazo-, chemiluminescence, **8**, 452
pyrazinones, imidazo-, in bioluminescent systems, **8**, 456
8*H*-pyrazolo[5,1-*a*]isoindole-8-one, 2-(4-
    methoxyphenyl)-3,3a-dihydro-, structure, **8**, 34
pyrazolo[4,3-*d*]pyrimidines, 3-methyl-, structure, **8**, 67
Pyrenochaeta terrestris
  dihydroemodin, **1**, 430
  pyrenochaetic acids, **1**, 401
  pyrenocines, **1**, 401
pyrenochaetic acid A
  from, α-pyrones, **1**, 401
  occurrence, **1**, 401
pyrenochaetic acid B, occurrence, **1**, 401
pyrenochaetic acid C, occurrence, **1**, 401
pyrenocine A, synthesis, **1**, 401
pyrenocine B, synthesis, **1**, 401
pyrethrin, stability, **8**, 320
pyrethrin I
  hydrolysis, **8**, 335
  insecticidal activity, **8**, 335
  isolation, **8**, 333
  total synthesis, **8**, 333

pyrethrin II
  hydrolysis, **8**, 335
  insecticidal activity, **8**, 335
  isolation, **8**, 333
pyrethrins
  biological activity, **8**, 335
  biosynthesis, **8**, 335
  detoxification, **8**, 335
  insecticidal activity, **8**, 333
  isolation, **8**, 333
  metabolism, **8**, 335
  model compounds, **8**, 336
  properties, **8**, 333
  stereochemistry, **8**, 333
  synergists, **8**, 335
pyrethroids
  as insect neurotoxins, **2**, 101
  use of term, **8**, 336
pyridazin-3(2*H*)one, 4-chloro-5-methylamino-2-(3-
    trifluoromethylphenyl)-, applications, herbicide, **2**,
    338
pyridine, bisdihydro-, Diels–Alder reaction, **1**, 380
pyridine *N*-oxides, in oligonucleotide synthesis, **7**, 108
pyridines, tetrahydro-, in ant venoms, **8**, 357
pyridoacridine alkaloids, occurrence, **8**, 540, 541
pyridoacridines, occurrence, **8**, 540
pyridone–2-aminopurine duplex, CD spectra, **7**, 332
2-pyridone C-nucleoside, **7**, 254
pyridopyrazines, occurrence, **8**, 361
pyridoxal
  in aldol reaction, **3**, 371
  oxidation, **3**, 371
pyridoxal phosphate
  binding sites, **3**, 449
  as cofactor, **1**, 545, 826
  glucose-1-phosphate adenylyltransferase activation, **3**,
    469
pyridoxal 5′-phosphate (PLP)
  in 5-aminolevulinate synthase, **4**, 65
  as cofactor, **3**, 254, **8**, 95
  in glucose-1-phosphate adenylyltransferase studies, **3**,
    448
  in lysine 2,3-aminomutase, **5**, 207
  roles, **5**, 304, 209
pyridoxamine 5′-phosphate (PMP), cofactors, **3**, 337
pyridoxine, from, 1-deoxy-D-xylulose, **2**, 376
pyridoxine–peptide–oligonucleotide conjugates,
    synthesis, **7**, 159
pyrimidine alkene cation radicals
  reactivity, **7**, 405
  synthesis, **7**, 405
pyrimidine hydroxyl radicals, intranucleotidyl hydrogen
    atom abstraction, **7**, 400
pyrimidine photodimers, cleavage, mechanisms, **5**, 385
pyrimidine–purine–pyrimidine triplexes, kinetics, **7**, 46,
    48
pyrimidine radicals, synthesis, **7**, 398
pyrimidine(s)
  aminoalkylation, **7**, 191
  applications, intercalating agents, **7**, 458
  biosynthesis, **1**, 838
  [2 + 2] cycloaddition, **5**, 372
  deamination, **5**, 87
    overview, **5**, 72
  effects, on DNA, **7**, 407
  incorporation, **6**, 91
pyrimidines, formamido-, in DNA damage, **7**, 410
pyrimidines, 5-halo-
  applications, radiosensitizers, **7**, 411
  DNA damage induction, **7**, 382
  DNA damage sensitization, **7**, 417
  triplexes, **7**, 316
pyrimidines, 4-keto-, binding, **5**, 92

pyrimidines, C^5-propynyl-, in oligodeoxynucleotides, **7**,
    317
pyrimidines, 2-substituted, synthesis, **6**, 93
pyrimidines, 4-substituted, synthesis, **6**, 93
pyrimidines, 5-substituted, synthesis, **6**, 91
2-pyrimidinone, applications, **6**, 225
4-pyrimidinone, **7**, 254
2,6-[1*H*,3*H*]-pyrimidinone, 4-amino-1-(*β*-D-
    ribofuranosyl)-, x-ray crystal analysis, **7**, 272
2-pyrimidinone-2′-deoxyribosides, synthesis, **7**, 259
pyrimidin-2-one ribonucleoside, 3,4-dihydro-, cytidine
    deaminase inhibition, **5**, 91
pyrimidin-2-one ribonucleoside, 5-fluoro-, binding, **5**, 90
pyrimidin-2-one ribonucleosides, cytidine deaminase
    inhibition, **5**, 90
pyrindamycin A, occurrence, **7**, 505
pyrindamycin B, occurrence, **7**, 505
pyriproxyfen, applications, *Chironomus fusciceps*
    inhibition, **8**, 275
Pyrobombus spp., geranylcitronellol, **8**, 229
pyrocarbonate, diethyl (DEPC), **2**, 19
  applications
    DNA structural probes, **7**, 94
    RNA structural probes, **6**, 64, 67, 68
  in branching enzyme studies, **3**, 463
  dehydroquinase inhibition, **1**, 588
  hydroxymethylglutaryl-CoA reductase inhibition, **2**, 33
  as inhibitor of patchouli synthase, **2**, 185
  as tetrahymanol cyclase poison, **2**, 312
Pyrococcus furiosus, polymerases, **7**, 658
Pyrocystis lunula, dinoflagellate luciferin, **8**, 457
pyroglutamic acid, structure, **8**, 299
L-pyroglutamic acid, biosynthesis, **4**, 30
2-pyrone, 5-acetyl-4-methoxy-6-methyl-, as starting
    material, for macrophomic acid, **1**, 401
α-pyrones
  occurrence, **8**, 600
  stability, **1**, 11
  as starting materials, for pyrenochaetic acid A, **1**, 401
pyron-2-one, (6*E*)-((1*E*)-pentenyl)-, occurrence, **8**, 213
Pyrophorus noctiluca, bioluminescence, **8**, 444
pyrophosphate *see* diphosphate
pyrophosphorylethanolamine substituents, in
    lipopolysaccharides, **3**, 227
1-pyrophosphorylribose-5-phosphate, SG14 activation,
    3, 476
Pyrrhidium sanguineum
  (2*R*,3*R*)-2,3-hexanediol, **8**, 210
  (2*S*,3*R*)-2,3-hexanediol, **8**, 210
  (*R*)-3-hydroxy-2-hexanone, **8**, 210
Pyrrhocoris apterus
  juvabione sensitivity, **8**, 277
  mutants, **8**, 276
2*H*-pyrrol, 3,4-dihydro-, occurrence, **8**, 210
pyrrole, 3-nitro-, in oligodeoxynucleotides, **7**, 333
pyrrole-2-carboxylate, methyl 4-methyl-, structure, **8**, 221
pyrrole-2-carboxylic acid, occurrence, **8**, 221
pyrroles, bromo-
  antifouling activity, **8**, 440
  occurrence, **1**, 381, **8**, 437
pyrrolidine, 2,5-dihydroxymethyl-3,4-dihydroxy-
    (DMDP)
  as glucosidase inhibitor, **3**, 151, 152
  insecticidal activity, **3**, 141
  occurrence, **3**, 134, 141, **8**, 342
  structure, **3**, 130
  toxicity, **3**, 140
pyrrolidine, *N*-hydroxyethyl-2-hydroxymethyl-3-
    hydroxy-, structure, **3**, 130
pyrrolidine, 2-hydroxymethyl-3-hydroxy- (CYB3),
    structure, **3**, 130
pyrrolidine alkaloids, **8**, 357
  biosynthesis, **4**, 30

from, ornithine, **4**, 30
host–parasite chemical transfer, **8**, 176
occurrence, **4**, 30
structure, **3**, 130
1-pyrroline, 3,4-dihydroxy-5-hydroxymethyl- *see*
    nectrisine
pyrroline alkaloids, occurrence, **8**, 357
pyrrolinium salts, *N*-methyl-, as intermediate, **4**, 30
pyrrolizidine alkaloids (PAs)
    biosynthesis, **4**, 31
    DNA damage by, **7**, 518
    host–parasite chemical transfer, **8**, 176
    insect sequestration, **8**, 154, 361, 362, 363
    as male insect pheromone, **8**, 154, 163
    NMR spectra, **4**, 33
    occurrence, **3**, 134, **4**, 31, **8**, 357
    oxidative activation, **7**, 518
    structure, **3**, 131
    toxicity, **8**, 147, 345
pyrrolo[1,4]benzodiazepines (PBDs)
    covalent adduct with DNA, **7**, 495
    DNA damage induction, **7**, 495
    oxygen radical production by, **7**, 497
    sequence selectivity, **7**, 497
    stability of DNA adducts, **7**, 497
    structure–function analysis, **7**, 495
pyrroloiminoquinones, possible DNA adduct formation
    by, **7**, 501
pyrroloindolizidines, occurrence, **8**, 358
pyrrolo[2,3-*d*]pyrimidines, 2-methyl-, structure, **8**, 67
pyruvate
    activation, **3**, 469, 369
    biosynthesis, **1**, 596, **2**, 52, 376, **3**, 381
    as carbon source, **2**, 54
    coupling reactions, **2**, 4
    decarboxylation, **2**, 376
    as esperamicin A₁ precursor, **7**, 554
    glucose-1-phosphate adenylyltransferase activation, **3**,
        470
    reactions
        with *N*-acetyl-D-mannosamine, **3**, 378
        with D-arabinose, **3**, 373
        with 3-azidophenol, **3**, 408
        with D-glyceraldehyde-3-phosphate, **3**, 421

with tartronate semialdehyde, **3**, 402
    roles, in L-tyrosine biosynthesis, **3**, 405
    as starting material
        for glyceraldehyde 3-phosphate, **2**, 50
        for isopentenyl diphosphate, **2**, 54
pyruvate, benzal-, biosynthesis, **3**, 377
pyruvate, 3-bromo-
    inhibitory activity, **1**, 579
    as substrate, **5**, 44
pyruvate, 2′-carboxybenzal-, as intermediate, **3**, 375
pyruvate, 2′,4′-dihydroxybenzal-, retroaldol addition, **3**,
    376
pyruvate, 2′,6′-dihydroxybenzal-, retroaldol addition, **3**,
    376
pyruvate, (diiodohydroxyphenyl)-, as substrate, **5**, 47
pyruvate, enol-
    isolation, **5**, 32
    ketonization, **5**, 39
    stability, **5**, 33
pyruvate, 2′-hydroxybenzal-
    metabolism, **3**, 377
    retroaldol addition, **3**, 376
pyruvate, (*p*-hydroxyphenyl)-
    biosynthesis, **5**, 344
    ketonization, **5**, 47
    as substrate, **5**, 47
pyruvate, phenyl-
    biosynthesis, **5**, 344
    enolization, **5**, 47
    as substrate, **5**, 47
pyruvate, phosphino-, analogues, **1**, 868
pyruvate, phosphono-, biosynthesis, **1**, 867
pyruvate dehydrogenase multienzyme complex, in
    Azotobacter vinelandii, **4**, 342
pyruvate formate lyase activating enzyme (PFL-AE),
    catalysis, **5**, 217
pyruvate formate-lyase (PFL) *see* formate *C*-
    acetyltransferase
pyruvate kinase, catalysis, **5**, 38
pyruvic acid, *m*-carboxyphenyl-, synthesis, **1**, 610
pyruvic acid, phenyl-
    biosynthesis, **4**, 5
    as intermediate, **1**, 850
pyruvic acid, phosphono-, decarboxylation, **1**, 876
Pythium aphanidermatum, **1**, 611

Q

Q/R editing, **5**, 87
  sites, **6**, 103
qa genes
  encoding, **1**, 590
  occurrence, **1**, 589
  qa-1F, encoding, **1**, 590
  qa-1S
    encoding, **1**, 590
    sequencing, **1**, 590
    transcription, **1**, 590
QAs *see* quinolizidine alkaloids (QAs)
Quadraspidiotus perniciosus, sex pheromones, **8**, 222, 234
quadrilure, occurrence, **8**, 246
quadrone
  biosynthesis, **2**, 174
  ^{13}C NMR spectra, **2**, 175
  occurrence, **2**, 174
quails, population control, **1**, 782
quaking aspen *see Populus tremuloides*
quality control, glycosidase processing, **3**, 31
quartromicin A$_1$, occurrence, **1**, 374
Quassia africana
  picrasin B, **8**, 322
  simalikalactone D, **8**, 322
Quassia amara
  neoquassin, **8**, 322
  quassin, **8**, 322
quassin
  occurrence, **8**, 322
  properties, **8**, 322
quassinoids
  biological activity, **8**, 322
  biosynthesis, **8**, 323
  cytotoxicity, **8**, 322
  insecticidal activity, **8**, 322
quercetagetin
  biosynthesis, **1**, 733
  roles, in ultraviolet patterning, **8**, 160
quercetin, antioxidant activity, **3**, 792
quercetin, dihydro-
  occurrence, **1**, 685
  reduction, **3**, 760
quercetin, (2*R*,3*R*)-dihydro-, reduction, **3**, 750
quercetin, (2*R*,3*S*)-*cis*-dihydro-, 3-*O*-β-D-xylosides,
    occurrence, **3**, 750
quercetin, (2*S*,3*R*)-*cis*-dihydro-, 3-*O*-β-D-xylosides,
    occurrence, **3**, 750
quercetin 3,7-disulfate, occurrence, **1**, 740
quercetin 3-*O*-β-D-glucopyranoside, (2*R*,3*S*)-2,3-*cis*-
    dihydro-, occurrence, **3**, 750
quercetin glycosides, roles, in ultraviolet patterning, **8**,
    160
quercetin-3-rutinoside *see* rutin
quercetin 3-sulfate, as substrate, **1**, 740
quercetin 3-(2^G-xylosylrutinoside), as insect deterrent, **8**,
    157
Quercus spp., flavonol glucosides, **1**, 741
Quercus ilex, flavonol 3-*O*-glucosides, **1**, 741
Quercus infectoria, Turkish gallotannin, **3**, 800, 813
Quercus robur
  esterases, **3**, 820
  β-glucogallin *O*-galloyltransferase, **3**, 808
questin
  biosynthesis, **1**, 433
  ring cleavage, **1**, 435

questin oxygenase
  catalysis, **1**, 433
  as monooxygenase, **1**, 434
quinacrine
  as antimalarial agent, **7**, 428
  applications, intercalating agents, **7**, 428
  binding, **7**, 457
  as phospholipase A$_2$ inhibitor, **1**, 123
  use in cytogenetic map preparation, **7**, 428
  use in pyrimidine triplex stabilization, **7**, 467
quinacrine mustard
  applications, intercalating agents, **7**, 470
  in DNA binding, **7**, 470
  use in cytogenetic map preparation, **7**, 428
quinate
  as carbon source, **1**, 589
  as starting material, for protocatechuate, **1**, 585
quinate dehydrogenase
  catalysis, **1**, 589
  genetics, **1**, 590
  occurrence, **1**, 590
  qut genes, **1**, 590
  substrate specificity, **1**, 590
quinate pathways, mechanisms, **1**, 585
quinic acid pathway
  mechanism, **1**, 589
  and shikimate pathway, flux between, **1**, 591
quinine, antifeedant activity, **8**, 342
quinobenzoxazines
  antineoplastic activity, **7**, 462
  applications, antineoplastic agents, **7**, 462
  self-assembly, **7**, 463
quinocarcin
  applications
    antibiotics, **7**, 500
    antineoplastic agents, **7**, 500
  disproportionation of, **7**, 541
  DNA damage, **7**, 500
  occurrence, **7**, 499
  superoxide production by, **7**, 541
quinocyclines
  γ-octose, **3**, 322
  tracer studies, **3**, 342
quinoid compounds, redox cycling, **7**, 528
quinoline, naphthyl-, triplex intercalator, **7**, 468
quinoline, 2-phenyl-, **7**, 468
quinolines
  CP-115,953, **7**, 609
  as DNA topoisomerase II inhibitors, **7**, 609
quinolinic acid, biosynthesis, **3**, 395
quinolizidine alkaloid esters, occurrence, **4**, 33
quinolizidine alkaloids (QAs)
  biosynthesis, **4**, 33
  occurrence, **4**, 33
  synthetic, **3**, 139
  toxicity, **8**, 147
quinolones
  antibacterial activity, **7**, 462
  applications, antiinfective agents, **7**, 462
  CP-67,804, **7**, 603
  CP-115,953, **7**, 603
  norfloxacin, **7**, 462
  Ro 15-0216, **7**, 603
quinone, biosynthesis, **8**, 364
quinone, 2,6-dichlorohydro- (DCHQ), biosynthesis, **5**,
    414

quinone, 1,4-dihydroxy-2-methylnaphtho-, occurrence, **8**, 339

quinone, 2-methyl-1,4-naphtho-, irradiation, **7**, 375

quinone, tetramethoxyazo-*p*-methylene, applications, **3**, 712

quinone, trichlorohydro- (TriCHQ), biosynthesis, **5**, 414

quinone methide(s)

    A-ring, **3**, 758

    C-4 carbocation, **3**, 758

    DNA alkylation by, **7**, 529

    from, flavans, **3**, 752

    roles, in base-catalyzed reactions of polymeric procyanidins, **3**, 767

    stabilization, **3**, 754

    tautomers, **7**, 575

o-quinone methides, as intermediates, **3**, 771

quinones

    chemical reduction of, **7**, 528

    DNA alkylation by, **7**, 531

    DNA damage induction, **7**, 527

    enzymatic reduction of, **7**, 528

    formation of quinone methides from, **7**, 529

    as pheromones, **8**, 202

    redox cycling, **7**, 528

quinones, naphtho-, biosynthesis, **1**, 617

D-quinovose, occurrence, **3**, 312, 313

quinoxaline antibiotics

    echinomycin, **7**, 444

    intercalation, **7**, 487

    triostin, **7**, 444

quinoxaline di-*N*-oxide, 2-carboxy, possible DNA damage induction, **7**, 533

quinoxaline *N*-oxides

    DNA damage induction, **7**, 533

    hydroxyl radical from, **7**, 533

    oxygen radicals from, **7**, 533

quinuclidines, 3-substituted, as farnesyl-diphosphate farnesyltransferase inhibitors, **2**, 258

quorum sensing factors *see* autoinducers

qut genes

    mutations

        *qut*E, **1**, 591

        *qut*R, **1**, 591

    occurrence, **1**, 589

    *qut*A, **1**, 590

    *qut*B, **1**, 590

    *qut*C, **1**, 590

    *qut*D, **1**, 590

    *qut*E, **1**, 590

    *qut*G, **1**, 590

    *qut*R, **1**, 590

    transcription, **1**, 590

Qut proteins

    QutA, sequencing, **1**, 590

    QutR, **1**, 590

QW motif, **2**, 315, 316

    hopene cyclases, **2**, 316

    in oxidosqualene cyclase mechanisms, **2**, 281

    in sequence comparisons, **2**, 282

    triterpene cyclases

        function, **2**, 316

        structural changes, **2**, 317

R

R/G editing, sites, **6**, 103
rabbit bone marrow, galactosyltransferases, **3**, 112
rabbit liver
    threonine aldolase, **3**, 398
    UTP-glucose-1-phosphate uridylyltransferase, **3**, 478
rabbit lung, platelet-activating factor, **1**, 297
rabbit muscle
    glycogen debranching enzyme, **5**, 306
    glycogenin glucosyltransferase, **3**, 446
        sequences, **3**, 480
    glycogen phosphorylase, **5**, 303
    glycogen synthase, **3**, 462, 477, 479
        regulatory mechanisms, **3**, 486
rabbits
    glycogen, **3**, 454
    α-1,3-mannosyl-glycoprotein β-1,2-N-
        acetylglucosaminyltransferase, genes, **3**, 50
    trans-methylation studies, **3**, 643
    stearoyl-CoA desaturases, **1**, 39
rabbit skeletal muscle
    branching enzymes, **3**, 479
    glycogen synthase, **3**, 482
        amino acid sequence, **3**, 484
        overexpression, **3**, 489
        phosphorylation sites, **3**, 483
Rabdosia japonica, β-amyrin cyclase, **2**, 305
Rab Escort Protein 1 (REP1), identification, **2**, 358
Rab Escort Protein 2 (REP2), identification, **2**, 359
rab geranylgeranyltransferase *see* protein
        geranylgeranyltransferase-II (PGGT-II)
Rab proteins
    methylation, **2**, 359
    prenylation, **2**, 363
RACE *see* rapid amplification of cDNA ends (RACE)
Radianthus kuekenthali, symbiosis, **8**, 429
radicals
    neocarzinostatin chromophore activation, **7**, 559
    reactions, with DNA, **7**, 493
radical trapping, substrates, **5**, 219
radiolabeling, of oligonucleotides, **7**, 135
radiosensitization, DNA damage studies, **7**, 583
radiosensitizers, 5-halopyrimidines, **7**, 411
radiotracer experiments, in isoflavonoid biosynthetic
        studies, **1**, 786
radishes
    acetyl-CoA *C*-acetyltransferases, **2**, 18
    hydroxymethylglutaryl-CoA reductases, **2**, 24
raffinose, in nectars, **8**, 162
ragged sea hare *see Bursatella leachii*
rainbow trout *see Salmo gairdneri*
Ralstonia pickettii, isoprenoid biosynthesis, mevalonate-
        independent pathway, **2**, 58
Raman spectroscopy
    development, **3**, 541
    and infrared spectroscopy compared, **3**, 543
ramoplanin, peptidoglycan biosynthesis inhibition, **3**, 280
Rana catesbiana, leukotriene D₄, **1**, 249
random coupling hypothesis, **1**, 687
    limitations, **1**, 647
Raney nickel, use in the analysis of lamin B, **2**, 355
Rangifer tarandus tarandus
    isobutyric acid, **8**, 220
    isovaleric acid, **8**, 220
rapamycin
    analogues, mutasynthesis, **1**, 520

applications, immunosuppressive agents, **1**, 2
binding proteins, **1**, 541
biosynthesis, **1**, 1, 75, 518
    chain termination in, **1**, 520
    genetics, **1**, 520
genetics, **1**, 14
immunosuppressant activity, **1**, 518
occurrence, **1**, 519
precursor studies, **1**, 519
sequencing, **4**, 231
structure, **1**, 497
rap genes
    rapL, mutation, **1**, 520
    rapP, encoding, **1**, 520
raphanatin, occurrence, **8**, 61
raphanusanin, occurrence, **8**, 26
raphanusol A, occurrence, **8**, 26
raphanusol B, occurrence, **8**, 26
Raphanus sativus, fucosyltransferases, **3**, 517
raphides, effects, on herbivores, **8**, 149
rapiculine, biosynthesis, **1**, 370
rapid amplification of cDNA ends (RACE), α-1,6-
        mannosyl-glycoprotein β-1,2-N-
        acetylglucosaminyltransferase studies, **3**, 52
rapid mix–freeze quench EPR, applications, **5**, 212
RAPS cassettes, structure, **1**, 520
raspberry ketone *see* butan-2-one, 4-hydroxyphenyl-
        (pHPB)
Ras proteins
    complexes, structure, **5**, 151
    farnesylation, **5**, 332
    function, **2**, 360
    from
        Dictyostelium discoideum, **2**, 360
        Drosophila melanogaster, **2**, 360
        Physarum polycephalum, **2**, 360
    geranylgeranylated, **2**, 360
    GTP-binding
        differentiation, **2**, 360
        signal transduction, **2**, 360
    H-Ras
        biosynthesis, **4**, 14
        palmitoylation, **4**, 21
    and mitogen activated protein kinase, **2**, 360
    N-Ras, biosynthesis, **4**, 14
    palmitoylation, **4**, 20, 21
    prenylation, function, **2**, 360
    RAS2, palmitoylation, **4**, 21
rat bone marrow, fucosyltransferases, **3**, 116
rat brain
    galactosyltransferases, **3**, 111
    α-mannosidases, **3**, 28
    ST8Sia II expression, **3**, 49
rat kidney, platelet-activating factor biosynthesis, **1**, 296
rat lingual lipase (RLL), structure, **5**, 133
rat liver
    branching enzymes, **3**, 479
    endoplasmic reticulum, cytosolic enzyme, **3**, 28
    glycogen synthase (mammalian), **3**, 479
    mitochondria, **2**, 381
rat muscle, AMP deaminase, **5**, 81
rats
    diabetic, β-1,3-galactosyl-*O*-glycosyl-glycoprotein β-
        1,6-N-acetylglucosaminyltransferase activity,
        3, 76

fatty acid synthase, **1**, 348
α-1,3-mannosyl-glycoprotein β-1,2-*N*-
    acetylglucosaminyltransferase, genes, **3**, 50
selenium deficient, **4**, 362
squalene epoxidase, **2**, 270
see also Sprague–Dawley rats
rat squalene synthase (RSS)
    localization to endoplasmic reticulum, **2**, 263
    regulatory mechanisms, **2**, 259
    subcellular localization, **2**, 263
    transcriptional regulation, **2**, 259
raucaffricine, occurrence, **1**, 130
Rauwolfia spp., hybridization, **4**, 134
Rauwolfia alkaloids, **4**, 110
    biosynthesis, **4**, 46
    occurrence, **4**, 46
Rauwolfia canescens, raucaffricine, **1**, 130
Rauwolfia serpentina
    cDNA library, **4**, 130
    cell suspension cultures, **4**, 113, 128
    Rauwolfia alkaloids, **4**, 46
    strictosidine synthase biosynthesis, **4**, 128
Rauwolfia vomitoria, alkaloid biosynthesis studies, **4**, 118
ravidomycin, applications, antibiotics, **7**, 545
RDPR *see* ribonucleoside-diphosphate reductase
reaction wood
    lignins, **3**, 693
    use of term, **3**, 693
Reactive Blue 4, in SELEX processes, **7**, 624
Reactive Red 120, in SELEX processes, **7**, 624
reagents
    base-specific, as DNA structure probes, **7**, 91
    chemical, in RNA structural probing, **6**, 65
rearrangements, electrophilic, **5**, **315–341**
recombinant DNA technology, advantages, **7**, 621
red abalone *see* Haliotis rufescens
red algae *see* Rhodophyta
redbanded leafroller *see* Argyrotaenia velutinana
red bean *see* Vigna angularis
red flour beetle *see* Tribolium castaneum
red foxes
    geranylacetone, **8**, 234
    2-hydroxy-2,6,6-trimethylcyclohexanone, **8**, 234
    3-methyl-3-butenyl methyl sulfide, **8**, 220
    6-methyl-5-hepten-2-one, **8**, 234
redox chemistry, protonation states, **5**, 199
redox cycling
    with nitro compounds, **7**, 521
    of quinones and quinoid compounds, **7**, 528
redox shuttles, **3**, 330
red squirrel, seed predation, inhibition, **8**, 168
red tide
    causes of, **8**, 511, 518
    see also Gymnodinium breve
reduced nicotinamide adenine dinucleotide phosphate
    (NADPH)
    binding, **2**, 32
    binding sites, **2**, 250
    biosynthesis, **1**, 582
    in dynemicin activation, **7**, 575
    effects, on inhibitor binding, **2**, 254, 255
    K_m, **2**, 252
    roles, in shikimate biosynthesis, **1**, 591
    SG14 activation, **3**, 476
    specificity, **2**, 29
        in fatty acids, **1**, 28
    use in the synthesis of (*R*)-mevalonate, **2**, 16
reductant/*N*-oxide systems, superoxide production by, **7**,
    540
reductive activation, of 2-nitroimidazoles, **7**, 521
red wine
    antioxidant activity, **3**, 792
    heart disease mediation, **3**, 792

Regnellidium diphyllum, ethylene biosynthesis, **8**, 94
regulatory systems, two-component, **3**, 226
reindeer *see* Rangifer tarandus tarandus
renieramycins
    applications, antibiotics, **7**, 497
    DNA adduct formation by, **7**, 497
    DNA damage, redox-activated, **7**, 497
    imines formed from, **7**, 497
    occurrence, **7**, 497
Reniera sarai, sarains, **8**, 562
renillafoulins, occurrence, **8**, 436
Renilla reniformis, renillafoulins, **8**, 436
R enzymes, identity, **3**, 468
REP1 *see* Rab Escort Protein 1 (REP1)
REP2 *see* Rab Escort Protein 2 (REP2)
replicon, blockage, **7**, 558
reporter groups, attachment to DNA, **7**, **153–249**
rescinnamine, biosynthesis, **4**, 46
reserpiline, strictosidine studies, **4**, 118
reserpine
    antipsychotic activity, **4**, 110
    biosynthesis, **4**, 46
resinol, *p*-coumaryl- *see* ligballinol
resorcinol
    biosynthesis, **1**, 2
    roles, in flavan-3-ol biosynthesis, **3**, 755
resorcinol, 5-pentadecyl-, antifungal activity, **8**, 181
resorcinol–copper mixtures, superoxide production by, **7**,
    540
resorcinols
    DNA binding by, **7**, 536
    DNA damage induction, **7**, 535
    oxygen radicals from, **7**, 535
resorcinols, 5-alkenyl, DNA cleavage, **7**, 535
resorcinols, alkyl-, DNA binding by, **7**, 536
resorcinols, 5-alkyl, DNA cleavage, **7**, 535
respiratory system, leukotriene applications in, **1**, 197
restriction digests, applications, in cloning, **7**, 660
restriction endonucleases
    applications, in cloning, **7**, 660
    DNA cleavage protection, **7**, 629
    Eco RI
        nucleoside analogue probing, **7**, 266
        studies, **7**, 270
        x-ray crystal structure, **7**, 266
restriction enzyme mediated integration (REMI), process,
    1, 424
resveratrol
    antioxidant activity, **3**, 792
    biosynthesis, **1**, 752
    as phytoalexin, **8**, 190
reticuline, biosynthesis, **4**, 39
(*S*)-reticuline, biosynthesis, **4**, 41
reticuline oxidase, cDNA, isolation, **4**, 41
(*S*)-reticuline:oxygen oxidoreductase (methylene-bridge-
    forming) *see* reticuline oxidase
Reticulitermes spp., (3*Z*,6*Z*,8*E*)-3,6,8-dodecatrien-1-ol, **8**,
    214
Reticulitermes flavipes, tetradecyl propanoate, **8**, 216
Reticulitermes speratus
    antifeedant activity against, **1**, 695
    antifeedant studies, **8**, 317
retinal, precursors, **2**, 327
retinol, deficiency, **2**, 347
retro-aldol reaction, stereospecificity, **3**, 396
retrojusticidin B, HIV-1 reverse transcriptase inhibition,
    1, 703
retronecine
    biosynthesis, **4**, 31
    insect sequestration, **8**, 152
retrorsine
    biosynthesis, **4**, 32
    properties, **7**, 518

retroviruses, activity against, **3**, 143

reversed-phase HPLC, in oligonucleotide purification, **7**, 127, 144

reverse genetics, procedures, **1**, 462

Rev-response element (RRE)
  cross-linking, **6**, 93
  synthesis, **6**, 91, 93

rfa genes, clusters, **3**, 226

rfb genes
  clusters, **3**, 206
    Hinc-repeats, **3**, 218
  coding, **3**, 207, 208
  in 3,6-deoxysugar biosynthesis, **3**, 342, 347
  in dTDP-6-deoxy-L-altrose biosynthesis, **3**, 342
  in dTDP-rhamnose biosynthesis, **3**, 342
  G+C content, **3**, 349
  genetic organization, **3**, 347
  intergeneric lateral transfer, **3**, 217
  recombination, **3**, 217

RG-I *see* rhamnogalacturonan I (RG-I)

RG-II *see* rhamnogalacturonan II (RG-II)

rhlI, in *Pseudomonas aeruginosa*, **8**, 398

Rhacophytales, evolution, **3**, 625

Rhadinoceraea nodicornis, sequestration, **8**, 362

Rhagoletis cerasi, oviposition deterring pheromones, **8**, 217

RHAMM, as hyaluronan receptor, **3**, 174

rhamnogalacturonan I (RG-I)
  acceptors, **3**, 519
  O-acetylation, **3**, 499
  arabinans in, **3**, 502
  in cell walls, **3**, 498, 503
  galactans in, **3**, 502
  occurrence, **3**, 502
  side chains, **3**, 520
  structure, **3**, 8, 499

rhamnogalacturonan II (RG-II)
  acceptors, **3**, 519
  in cell walls, **3**, 498, 503
  methyletherification, **3**, 519
  side chains, **3**, 520
  structure, **3**, 8, 499, 502

rhamnolipids
  autoinduction, **8**, 398
  as biosurfactants, **8**, 398

α-L-rhamnopyranoside, 3-*O*-methyl-, in calicheamicin γ_1^{1}, **7**, 569

rhamnose, 3,5-epimerases, **3**, 350

D-rhamnose, occurrence, **3**, 312, 313

L-rhamnose, occurrence, **3**, 312

rhamnosyltransferase(s)
  characterization, **3**, 515
  roles, in pectin biosynthesis, **3**, 511

rhamnosyltransferase-V, roles, in pectin biosynthesis, **3**, 511

rhamnulose-1-phosphate aldolase
  biochemistry, **3**, 426
  genes, localization, **3**, 426
  inhibition, **3**, 426
  isolation, **3**, 426
  substrate specificity, **3**, 428

Rhazya spp., indole alkaloid studies, **4**, 113

Rhazya orientalis, strictosidine studies, **4**, 117

Rhazya stricta
  glucoalkaloids, **4**, 113
  strictosidine studies, **4**, 117

Rheum officinale, β-glucogallin, **3**, 805

Rheum rhaponticum, stilbene synthase, **1**, 752

rhi genes
  occurrence, **8**, 400
  rhiABC operon, **8**, 400
  rhiR, transcription, **8**, 400

rhinacanthin E, antiviral activity, **1**, 702

rhinacanthin F, antiviral activity, **1**, 702

Rhinacanthus nasutus, rhinacanthins, **1**, 702

Rhithropanopeus harrisii, prostaglandins, **1**, 246

Rhizobium spp.
  2-dehydro-3-deoxy-L-pentonate aldolase, **3**, 425
  lipo-chitin oligosaccharides, **3**, 2
  nod genes, **1**, 780
  roles, in nodule formation, **1**, 7
  symbiosis, with leguminous plants, **1**, 326

Rhizobium–legume symbiosis, isoflavonoids in, **1**, 780

Rhizobium leguminosarum
  bacteroids, **8**, 400
  fatty acids, **1**, 332
    biosynthesis, **1**, 337
  nif genes, **8**, 400
  nodA genes, **1**, 340
  nodT genes, **1**, 329
  nodulation, **1**, 326
  nodule formation, **8**, 400
  rhi genes, **8**, 400
  symbiotic plasmids, **8**, 400

Rhizobium leguminosarum autoinducer (RLAI), **8**, 400
  occurrence, **8**, 400
  structure, **8**, 400

Rhizobium meliloti
  calystegines, **3**, 134, 142
  nod genes, **1**, 328

Rhizoclonium heiroglyphicum, cellulose hydrolysis studies, **3**, 554

Rhizoctonia leguminicola, swainsonine, **3**, 134

Rhizoma rhei, 1,6-di-*O*-galloyl-β-D-glucose, **3**, 822

Rhizomucor miehei, triacylglycerol lipases, **5**, 125, 128

Rhizophagus grandis, bark beetle larvae predation, **8**, 224

Rhizopus spp., indole-3-acetic acid, **8**, 24

rhizosphere-expressed genes *see rhi* genes

rhodanese, cyanide detoxification, **8**, 144

D-rhodinose, occurrence, **3**, 312, 321

L-rhodinose, occurrence, **3**, 312, 321

rhodium(II)–porphyrin complexes, methane addition, **5**, 174

rhodium complexes, DNA damage induction, **7**, 383

Rhodnius spp., diuretic hormone, **8**, 300

Rhodnius prolixus, juvenile hormones, **8**, 266

Rhodobacter spp.
  bch genes, **2**, 344
  carotenoid biosynthesis, **2**, 327
    regulatory mechanisms, **2**, 344
  glucose-1-phosphate adenylyltransferase, **3**, 469
  ppsR genes, **2**, 344
  tspO genes, **2**, 344
  xanthophyll biosynthesis enzymes, **2**, 343

Rhodobacter acidophila see Rhodopseudomonas acidophila

Rhodobacter capsulatus
  carotenoid biosynthesis, **2**, 327
  carotenoid biosynthesis gene, **2**, 87
  crt genes, **2**, 330
  crt studies, **2**, 327
  glucose-1-phosphate adenylyltransferase, **3**, 469
  isopentenyl diphosphate isomerases, **5**, 336
    cDNA cloning, **2**, 73
  lipid A, structure, **3**, 200

Rhodobacter gelatinosa, glucose-1-phosphate adenylyltransferase, **3**, 447, 470

Rhodobacter globiformis, glucose-1-phosphate adenylyltransferase, **3**, 447, 470

Rhodobacter palustris see Rhodopseudomonas palustris

Rhodobacter sphaeroides
  5-aminolevulinate synthase, **4**, 65
  carotenoid biosynthesis, **2**, 327
  coproporphyrinogen oxidase, **4**, 95, 98
  crt genes, **2**, 330
  glucose-1-phosphate adenylyltransferase, **3**, 447, 470
  3-oxotetradecanoic acid, **3**, 196

pigmentation mutants, **2**, 327
pigment–protein complexes, light-harvesting, **2**, 348
porphobilinogen synthase studies, **4**, 74
uroporphyrinogen decarboxylase, **4**, 92
Rhodobacter viridis
  glucose-1-phosphate adenylyltransferase, **3**, 447, 469
  lipid A, structure, **3**, 200
Rhodococcus spp., haloalkane dehalogenases, **5**, 403
Rhodocyclus gelatinosus, lipid A, structure, **3**, 200
Rhodocyclus purpureus, glucose-1-phosphate
  adenylyltransferase, **3**, 470
Rhododendron molle, rhodojaponin III, **8**, 313
rhodojaponin III, occurrence, **8**, 313
Rhodomela spp., bromophenols, **8**, 461
Rhodomelaceae, cyclic bromoethers, **1**, 303
Rhodomicrobium vannielii, glucose-1-phosphate
  adenylyltransferase, **3**, 469
rhodomycin
  biosynthesis, genetics, **3**, 351
  discovery, **4**, 200
  D-olivomose, **3**, 313
Rhodophyta
  cyclic bromoethers, **1**, **303–324**
  epoxyhydroxyacids, **1**, 219
  feeding deterrents, **8**, 461
  halogenated monoterpenes, **2**, 106
  hydroxyacids, **1**, 219
  oxylipins, **1**, 219
  see also Laurencia spp.; *Polycavernosa tsudai*;
    Rhodomela spp.
Rhodopseudomonas acidophila
  adenosylhopane, **2**, 47
  glucose-1-phosphate adenylyltransferase, **3**, 447, 469
  hopanoids
    biosynthesis, **2**, 49
    labeling studies, **2**, 53
Rhodopseudomonas palustris
  glucose-1-phosphate adenylyltransferase, **3**, 469
  hopanoids
    biosynthesis, **2**, 49
    labeling studies, **2**, 53
  hopene cyclase
    gene cloning, **2**, 313
    purification, **2**, 308
*Rhodopseudomonas sphaeroides see Rhodobacter
    sphaeroides*
Rhodopseudomonas viridis see Rhodobacter viridis
rhodopsin
  activation of transducin, **2**, 360
  mass spectra, **4**, 14
Rhodospiridium toruloides
  S-farnesyl-cysteine methyl ester, **2**, 353
  mating pheromone, **2**, 362
Rhodospirillaceae, hopanoids, **2**, 308
Rhodospirillum fulvum
  glucose-1-phosphate adenylyltransferase, **3**, 447, 470
  lipid A, structure, **3**, 200
Rhodospirillum molischianum, glucose-1-phosphate
  adenylyltransferase, **3**, 447, 470
Rhodospirillum photometricum, glucose-1-phosphate
  adenylyltransferase, **3**, 470
Rhodospirillum rubrum
  glucose-1-phosphate adenylyltransferase, **3**, 447, 470
    reaction mechanism, **3**, 448
  isopentenyl diphosphate, **2**, 46
Rhodospirillum tenue, glucose-1-phosphate
  adenylyltransferase, **3**, 447, 470, 471
Rhodotorucine A, structure, **2**, 353
Rhodotorula glutinis, phenylalanine ammonia-lyase, **3**,
  632
Rhopalosiphum padi, 6-methyl-5-hepten-2-one, **8**, 232
Rhs elements, Hinc-repeats, **3**, 218
rhubarb *see Rheum rhaponticum*

Rhus spp., profisetinidins, **3**, 770
Rhus semialata, Chinese gallotannin, **3**, 800, 813
Rhus succedanea, laccase, **3**, 711
Rhus typhina
  gallic acid, studies, **3**, 805
  gallotannins, **3**, 813
  [U-^{14}C]pentagalloylglucose biosynthesis, **3**, 817
Rhus vernicifera
  laccases, **3**, 711, 714
    blue, **3**, 712
Rhyacophila fasciata
  (*R*)-2-heptanol, **8**, 211
  2-heptanone, **8**, 211
  2-nonanol, **8**, 212
  2-nonanone, **8**, 212
rhynchophorol
  occurrence, **8**, 245
  structure, **8**, 246
Rhynchophorus spp., pheromones, **8**, 245
Rhynchophorus cruentatus, cruentol, **8**, 245
Rhynchophorus ferrugineus, ferruginol, **8**, 245
Rhynchophorus palmarum, rhynchophorol, **8**, 245
Rhynchophorus phoenicis, phoenicol, **8**, 245
Rhyssa persuasoria, 3-hydroxy-3-methylbutan-2-one, **8**,
  220
Rhyzopertha dominica
  dominicalure 1, **8**, 14, 241
  dominicalure 2, **8**, 14
  pheromones, **8**, 14
α-ribazole, in cyanocobalamin biosynthesis, **4**, 149
D-ribitol, 1,4-dideoxy-1,4-imino-, structure, **3**, 130
riboamidrazone, *p*-nitrophenyl-, nucleoside hydrolase
  inhibition, **5**, 307
riboflavin-5′-phosphate, as 5,6-dimethylbenzimidazole
  precursor, **4**, 150
ribonuclease A, crystal structure, **6**, 69
ribonuclease H, reactions, **6**, 88
ribonuclease L, activation, **6**, 214
ribonuclease P
  catalysis, **6**, 115, **6**, 260, **7**, 617
  characteristics, **6**, 259
  cleavage, **6**, 110, 112
  discovery, **6**, 149, **7**, 616
  functions, **6**, 151
  kinetics, multiple-turnover, **6**, 151
  protein component, roles, **6**, 260
  ribozymes, **6**, 236
  RNA
    discovery, **6**, 236
    phosphate groups, **6**, 222
    rate constants, **6**, 151
    tRNA binding, **6**, 222
  selection, **6**, 119
  structure, secondary, **6**, 153
ribonuclease(s)
  activity, effects of cytokinins on, **8**, 59
  early studies, **6**, 109
  probing, **6**, 64
  RNAse H, activity, **7**, 287, 292
  studies, **7**, 645
ribonucleoproteins *see* RNA–protein complexes
ribonucleoside, 2-aminopurine, in hairpin ribozyme
    studies, **7**, 277
ribonucleoside-diphosphate reductase
  inactivation studies, **5**, 182
  reactions, with mechanism-based inhibitors, **5**, 192
ribonucleosides, arabinosyl-, synthesis, **7**, 264
ribonucleosides, carbohydrate analogues, synthesis, **7**,
  264
ribonucleosides, xylo-, synthesis, **7**, 264
ribonucleoside-triphosphate reductase
  catalysis, **5**, 171, 176
    mechanisms, **5**, 172

cloning, **5**, 171
labeling studies, **5**, 171
occurrence, **5**, 170
overexpression, **5**, 171
structure, **5**, 175
ribonucleotide analogues
    applications, **6**, **217–233**
    ribose modification, **6**, 226
    and ribozyme mechanisms, **6**, 217
5′-ribonucleotide phosphohydrolase *see* 5′-nucleotidase
ribonucleotide reductases (RNRs)
    catalysis, **3**, 328, **5**, 164
    characterization, **5**, 164
    Class I, **3**, 329
        genetics, **3**, 343
        subunits, **3**, 329, **5**, 164, 165
    Class II, **3**, 330
        adenosylcobalamin cofactors, **5**, 165
        cysteines, **5**, 166
        genetics, **3**, 343
    Class III, **3**, 332
        genetics, **3**, 345
        subunits, **5**, 165
    Class IV, subunits, **5**, 166
    cysteine residues, **5**, 164
    diferric cofactors, **5**, 164
    future research, **5**, 199
    genetics, **3**, 343
    2′-hydroxyl group loss, **5**, 188
    inactivators
        mechanism-based, **3**, 331
        time-dependent, **3**, 330
    inhibition, **5**, 73
        by 2′-halonucleosides, **5**, 194
    kinetic isotope effects, **5**, 187
    mechanistic investigations, **5**, **163–203**
    metallocofactors, **5**, 165
    protein radical generation, **5**, 206
    R1 subunit
        electron transfer, **5**, 166
        structure, **5**, 164, 177
        thiyl radical biosynthesis, **5**, 166
    R2 subunit
        diferric cofactors, **5**, 166, 177
        electron transfer, **5**, 166
        structure, **5**, 164, 177
    reactions
        with 2′-deoxynucleotides, **5**, 172
        with 2′-fluoromethylene cytidine 5′-diphosphates, **5**,
            172
        with 2′-fluoromethylene cytidine 5′-triphosphates, **5**,
            172
    roles
        in cell cycle regulation, **5**, 164
        in nucleotide metabolism, **5**, 164
    structure, **3**, 329
    see also ribonucleoside-diphosphate reductase;
        ribonucleoside-triphosphate reductase
ribonucleotides
    hydrolysis, **7**, 632
    incorporation, into DNA, **7**, 619
    modification, **6**, 77, 218
ribonucleotide triphosphates, reduction, **3**, 330
ribophorin I, as oligosaccharyltransferase subunit, **3**, 41
ribophorin II, as oligosaccharyltransferase subunit, **3**, 41
ribopyranoside, 4-*N*-amino-4-deoxy-3-*C*-methyl-, in
        maduropeptin, **7**, 580
ribose, binding, **5**, 74
3′-ribose hydroxyls, in SELEX studies, **7**, 633
ribose-5-phosphate, isomerization, **3**, 387
D-ribose-5-phosphate, K_m, **3**, 416
ribose zippers, **6**, 56
    formation, **6**, 155

ribosomal proteins, binding sites, **6**, 195
ribosomal RNA *see* rRNA
ribosomes *see* rRNA
ribostamycin
    discovery, **4**, 200
    interactions, with RNA, **6**, 194
N-ribosyl hydrolases, occurrence, **5**, 306
ribozyme ligases
    catalysis, studies, **6**, 129
    Class I, **6**, 129
        conversion, **6**, 133
        evolution, **6**, 130
        pseudoknots, **6**, 142
        size factors, **6**, 145
    Class II, **6**, 129
    Class III, **6**, 129
        randomization, **6**, 130
        size factors, **6**, 145
        Watson–Crick pairing, **6**, 142
    pseudoknots, **6**, 130
    size, and catalytic activity, **6**, 145
ribozymes
    activities, selection, **6**, 118
    in amide bond synthesis, **6**, 128
    amplification, **6**, 118
    applications
        biomedical, **7**, 632
        therapeutic, **7**, 142
    association, with substrates, **7**, 45
    carbon center catalysis, **6**, 165
    catalysis, **6**, 219, **7**, 190, 616, 617
        improvements, **6**, 124
        mechanisms, **6**, 143
        metals in, **6**, 141
    for the catalysis of ligations, **7**, 367
    characteristics, **6**, 143
    chemical augmentation, **6**, 142
    cleavage, **6**, 244, **7**, 280
    discovery, **7**, 616
    DNA cleavage, **6**, 126
    enzymology, **6**, 129, **149–168**
    evolution, **6**, 115, 127, 146
    functional, **6**, 117
    future research, **6**, 263
    Group I
        catalysis, **6**, 115, 257
        characteristics, **6**, 254
        chemical specificity, **6**, 125
        disulfide cross-links, **6**, 227
        RNA cleavage, **6**, 257
        selection, **6**, 122
        structure, **6**, 123, 254
    Group II
        characteristics, **6**, 258
        tertiary interactions, **6**, 258
    historical background, **6**, 115
    2′-hydroxyl function, studies, **6**, 226
    interference analysis, **6**, 221
    kinetic properties, **6**, 129
    'leadzymes', **7**, 632
    mechanisms, **6**, **235–268**, **7**, 274
        and ribonucleotide analogues, **6**, 217
        two-metal ion, **6**, 158
    metal binding properties, **6**, 134
    as metalloenzymes, **6**, 157
    metal specificity, **6**, 134
    modification, **6**, 137, 142
    natural, selection, **6**, 140
    origins, **6**, 237
    and protein enzymes compared, **6**, 115, 137, 139, 143
    RNA cleavage, **6**, 126
    RNA targeting, **6**, 43
    roles, in translation, **6**, 127

selection, **6**, **115–148**
  evolution, **6**, 140
  in vitro, **6**, 116, 225
  randomized, **6**, 117
sequences, **7**, 363
  functional, **6**, 119
size
  factors, **6**, 144
  and functional complexity, **6**, 145
structure, **6**, **235–268**
  determination, **6**, 139
substrate specificity, **7**, 616
in *Tetrahymena* spp., **7**, 616, 617
  catalysis, **7**, 279
  kinetic studies, **7**, 277
unnatural
  catalysis, **6**, 141
  modification, **6**, 142
  selection, **6**, 141
use of term, **6**, 109
x-ray crystal structure, **6**, 256
see also deoxyribozymes; hairpin ribozymes;
    hammerhead ribozymes; hepatitis delta virus
    (HDV) ribozyme
ribozymes, 2′-fluoro-substituted, **7**, 278
ribulose-1,5-bisphosphate, oxidation, **3**, 397
ribulose-bisphosphate carboxylase, degradation, **1**, 126
Ric[15], in hybrid *N*-glycans, **3**, 27
Ric[19], in hybrid *N*-glycans, **3**, 27
Riccardia multifida, lignans, **1**, 645
rice
  ae mutants, **3**, 467
  amylose extender mutants, **3**, 462
  endosperm, branching enzymes, **3**, 461
  mutations, **8**, 50
  seedlings, infection, **8**, 2
  soluble starch synthases, **3**, 455
  waxy locus, DNA sequence, **3**, 454
  Waxy protein, **3**, 457
  see also Oryza sativa
rice-blast disease, etiology, **1**, 228
rice bug *see Leptocorisa chinensis*
rice moths
  (*E,E*)-farnesal, **8**, 227
  see also Corcyra cephalonica
rice seeds
  branching enzymes, cDNA clones, **3**, 462
  enzyme subunits, **3**, 451
  immature seed library, starch synthase studies, **3**, 457
rice weevil *see Sitophilus* spp.
ricinine, occurrence, **3**, 643
Ricinus communis
  casbene synthases, **2**, 219
  dienoic acid biosynthesis, **1**, 39
  geranyl*trans*transferase, **2**, 74
    cloning, **2**, 74
  phenylalanine ammonia-lyase, localization, **3**, 662
  ricinine, **3**, 643
  stearoyl-ACP desaturase, **1**, 42
Rickettsia prowazekii, dCTP deaminase, **5**, 94
Riella helicophylla, ethylene biosynthesis, **8**, 94
rifamycin
  analogues, mutasynthesis, **1**, 528
  biosynthesis, **1**, 527
    genetics, **1**, 527
  occurrence, **1**, 527
  precursor studies, **1**, 527
rif genes
  rifA, encoding, **1**, 527
  rifB, encoding, **1**, 527
  rifC, encoding, **1**, 527
  rifD, encoding, **1**, 527
  rifE, encoding, **1**, 527

rifF, encoding, **1**, 527
rifJ, localization, **1**, 528
rifK, encoding, **1**, 528
rillingol
  biosynthesis, **5**, 339
  synthesis, **2**, 254
Riptortus clavatus
  (*E*)-2-hexenyl (*E*)-2-hexenoate, **8**, 210
  (*E*)-2-hexenyl (*Z*)-3-hexenoate, **8**, 210
  myristyl 2-methylpropanoate, **8**, 210
rishitin, biosynthesis, **2**, 183
(−)-rishitin
  biosynthesis, **2**, 184
  occurrence, **2**, 183
ritterazine A, occurrence, **8**, 532
ritterazines
  cytotoxicity, **8**, 533
  structure, **8**, 532
  structure–activity relationship, **8**, 533
ritterazine T, cytotoxicity, **8**, 534
Ritterella sigillinoides, eudistomin K, **8**, 527
Ritterella tokioka, ritterazine A, **8**, 532
RLAI *see Rhizobium leguminosarum* autoinducer (RLAI)
RLL *see* rat lingual lipase (RLL)
r locus, occurrence, **3**, 462
RNA
  5S, **4**, 362
  binding pockets, **7**, 617
  biological activity, and RNA tertiary structures, **6**, 65
  chemical limitations, **7**, 617
  classification, **6**, 13
  crystallization, **6**, 50
    sparse matrix approaches, **6**, 51
  double helices, formation, **7**, 43
  early studies, **6**, 109
  electron density maps, **6**, 11
  enzymatic activity, **6**, 21
  evolution, **6**, 115, 146
  fluorescent markers, **6**, 76
  fluorophore insertion, **6**, 76
  footprinting studies, **6**, 64, 74
  groove shape, DNA compared, **7**, 452
  heterocyclic bases, **7**, 616
  historical perceptions, **7**, 615
  hydration, **6**, 52
  hydrolysis, **7**, 163, 211
  hypermutation, **6**, 103
  intercalation structures, **7**, 433
  interference studies, **6**, 75
  kinetics, relaxation, **7**, 37
  loops, **6**, 32
  metal binding sites, **6**, 157
  modification, **6**, 98
    natural, **6**, 77
    post-synthetic, **6**, 93
    site-selected, **6**, 76
  mutants, structural analyses, **6**, 71
  NMR spectra, **6**, 4
    assignments, **6**, 8
  non-coding functional, **8**, 66
  nucleotide incorporation, **6**, 82
  organization, **6**, 14
  packing, and hydration, **6**, 52
  phosphorothioate linkages, **6**, 90
  posttranscriptional regulation, **5**, 73
  probes, biotinylation, **7**, 197
  processing, **6**, 97
  purification, **6**, 50
  rearrangement, in viroid evolution, **6**, 175
  roles, **6**, 21, 149
    in protein biosynthesis, **6**, 3
  selection, *in vitro*, **7**, 617
  SELEX studies, **7**, 617

self-alkylating, **7**, 632
self-cleaving, **7**, 632
as tapes, **7**, 615
targeting, with ribozymes, **6**, 43
topological variants, **7**, 344
triplexes, stability, **7**, 47
UV spectra, **6**, 23
see also antisense RNA; circular RNA; dsRNA;
  dumb-bell RNA; gRNA; mRNA; rRNA;
  tRNA; VS RNA
RNA adenosine deaminase, double-stranded, **5**, 86
RNA adenylate deaminase(s), biological functions, **5**, 86
RNA–antibiotic complexes, structural probing, **6**, 75
RNA catalysis, **6**, 109
  discovery, **6**, 115
  field of study, **6**, 237
  metal ions in, **6**, 150, 157
  stereochemistry, **6**, 160
  types of, **6**, 150
  use of nucleoside analogues in, **7**, 274
  via hydrolysis, **6**, 151
  via internal 2′-hydroxyl group attack, **6**, 151
  via nucleophilic attack, **6**, 150
RNA catalysts, primordial, **7**, 630
RNA cleavage
  hepatitis delta virus ribozyme-mediated, **6**, 254
  mechanisms, **6**, 69
  primary, **6**, 67
  ribozyme-catalyzed, **6**, 126, 257
  secondary, **6**, 67
  sites, detection, **6**, 70
  stereochemistry, **6**, 219
  via deoxyribozymes, **6**, 137
  via hairpin ribozymes, **6**, 219, 250
RNA crystals, heavy atom derivatives, **6**, 51
RNA damage
  chemistry, **7**, 582
  mechanisms, **7**, 582
RNA–DNA hybrids, cleavage, bleomycin-mediated, **7**,
  539
RNA duplexes
  A-form, **6**, 51, **7**, 460
  metal ion interactions, **6**, 51
RNA editing, **6**, **97–108**
  future research, **6**, 107
  mechanisms, **6**, 107
  use of term, **6**, 97
  via adenosine deamination, **6**, 98, 100
  via base modification, **6**, 98
  see also insertion–deletion editing
RNA endonuclease, activity, **6**, 105
RNA enzymes
  activity, protein roles in, **6**, 110
  applications, **6**, 112
    in biotechnology, **6**, 112
  biological functions, **6**, 109
  classification, **6**, 109, 113
  discovery, **6**, 149
  and evolution, **6**, 113
  mechanisms, **6**, 150
  occurrence, **6**, 110
  overview, **6**, **109–113**
  as pathogens, **6**, 110
  SELEX studies, **6**, 113
  structures, **6**, 151
    three-dimensional, **6**, 154
  substrates, **6**, 112
  transesterification, two-step, **6**, 150
  see also ribonuclease(s); ribozymes; RNA catalysis
RNA–ethidium complex, intercalation sites, **7**, 435
RNA folding
  complex, **7**, 617
  kinetics, **7**, 48

and metal ions, **6**, 157
RNA grooves, groove-binding compounds, **7**, 435
RNA instability sequence, localization, **5**, 229
RNA intercalators, **7**, **427–476**
RNA ligases
  activity, **6**, 105
  applications, in oligoribonucleotide synthesis, **6**, 218
  isolation, **6**, 165
RNA ligations, ribozymes as catalyst, **7**, 367
RNA nucleotidyltransferase (DNA-directed) *see* DNA-
  directed RNA polymerase(s)
RNA polymerase I *see* DNA-directed RNA
  polymerase(s)
RNA polymerase II *see* DNA-directed RNA
  polymerase(s)
RNA polymerase III *see* DNA-directed RNA
  polymerase(s)
RNA polymerase(s) *see* DNA-directed RNA
  polymerase(s)
RNA–protein complexes
  conformation, **6**, 227
  cross-linking, **6**, 228
  enzymatic activity, **6**, 112
  structural probing, **6**, 73
RNA–protein interactions, phosphate groups in, **6**, 222
RNA replication, rolling circles, **7**, 346
RNA–RNA complexes, structural probing, **6**, 75
RNA–RNA duplexes
  conformation, **6**, 227
  in hammerhead ribozymes, **6**, 242
  Tm values, **7**, 288
RNA secondary structures
  bulge loops, **6**, 36
  coaxial stacks, **6**, 40
  dangling ends, **6**, 31
  duplex formation, **6**, 25
  future research, **6**, 43
  GU pairs, **6**, 29
  hairpin loops, **6**, 33
  hairpin ribozymes, **6**, 154
  hammerhead ribozymes, **6**, 153
  hepatitis delta virus ribozyme, **6**, 154
  internal loops, **6**, 16, 36
    asymmetric, **6**, 40
    asymmetrical motifs, **6**, 17
    large, **6**, 40
    single mismatches, **6**, 37
    symmetrical motifs, **6**, 16
    tandem mismatches, **6**, 37
  introns, **6**, 151
  junctions, **6**, 40
  lariats, **7**, 345
  ministem loops, **6**, 227
  multibranch loops, **6**, 40
  prediction, **6**, 22, 43
  pseudoknots, **6**, 18, 70, 122, **7**, 345
    double-nested, **6**, 154
  ribonuclease P, **6**, 153
  stem-loops, **6**, 14
  terminal loops, **6**, 14, 16
  terminal mismatches, **6**, 31
  tetraloops, **6**, 15, 33, 154
  thermodynamics, **6**, **21–47**
    applications, **6**, 42
    environmental effects on, **6**, 42
  U-turns, **6**, 14
RNAse H *see* ribonuclease H
RNAse L *see* ribonuclease L
RNAse P *see* ribonuclease P
RNAses *see* ribonuclease(s)
RNA structural motifs, **6**, **3–20**
RNA structural probing, **6**, **63–80**
  applications, **6**, 65

buffers, **6**, 69
chemical, **6**, 65
future research, **6**, 77
historical background, **6**, 63
methods, **6**, 69
   biochemical, **6**, 72
   biophysical, **6**, 72
with nucleases, **6**, 67
probes, **6**, 68
targets, **6**, 68
three-dimensional structures, **6**, 70
two-dimensional structures, **6**, 70
validation, **6**, 65
RNA structures
calculations, **6**, 10
cross-linking studies, **6**, 89
determination, **6**, 22
   COSY studies, **6**, 8
   early studies, **6**, 4, 64
   NOESY studies, **6**, 8, 10
   samples, **6**, 7
   via NMR spectroscopy, **6**, 4
   via x-ray crystallography, **6**, 4, **49–61**
distance estimation, **6**, 10
future research, **6**, 59
helices, **6**, 9
plasticity, detection, **6**, 72
solution and crystal compared, **6**, 11, 12
spectroscopy, **6**, **3–20**
three-dimensional, **6**, 22, 70
torsion angles, **6**, 9
transitions
   statistical analyses, **6**, 26
   thermodynamic analyses, **6**, 23
   two-state model, **6**, 23, 26
   zipper model, **6**, 27
two-dimensional, **6**, 70
Watson–Crick base pairs, **6**, 28
   alignments, **6**, 14
see also RNA secondary structures; RNA tertiary
   structures; tRNA structures
RNA synthesis, **7**, 144
automated, **7**, 617
chemical, **6**, 50, 76, **81–96**
   large scale production, **6**, 81
enzymatic, **6**, 81
inhibition, **8**, 97
protecting groups, **6**, 83
solid-phase, **6**, 82
solution-phase, **6**, 82
via *in vitro* transcription, **6**, 50
via randomization, **6**, 116
RNA tertiary structures, **6**, 150
hammerhead ribozymes, **6**, 156
interactions, **6**, 42
introns, Group I, **6**, 154
modeling, **6**, 43
and RNA biological activity, **6**, 65
RNA transcription, developments, **5**, 73
RNA uridylyltransferase, **6**, 105
'RNA World'
duration, **6**, 146
hypothesis, **6**, 146, **7**, 617, 630
RNA Z, parasitic activity, **6**, 131, 143
RNR genes
in deoxyribonucleotide biosynthesis, **3**, 342
isolation, **3**, 343
RNRs *see* ribonucleotide reductases (RNRs)
Ro 09-0198 *see* cinnamycin
Ro 15-0216, as DNA topoisomerase II inhibitor, **7**, 609
robber bee *see* Lestrimelitta limao
robinetinidol
nucleophilicity, **3**, 760

as profisetinidin precursor, **3**, 771
robinetinidol-4α-ol *see* leucorobinetinidin
Robinia pseudacacia
flavones, **3**, 761
4′-*O*-methyltransferases, **1**, 739
Robinson, Robert, *The Structural Relationships of
   Natural Products* (1955), **1**, 2
rocaglamides, occurrence, **8**, 340
rock hyrax *see* Procaria capensis syriaca
rol genes, *rolC*, occurrence, **8**, 72
Rollinia spp., squamosin, **8**, 305
Rollinia sylvatica, asimicin, **8**, 305
Romalea spp.
cardenolide disgorgement, **8**, 363
ketones, **8**, 234
Romalea microptera, romallenone, **8**, 363
romallenone, secretion, **8**, 363
root rot, etiology, **1**, 534
root worms, propanoic acid esters, **8**, 241
roridin E, structure, **2**, 202
Rosaceae
isoflavonoids, **1**, 774
leaves, bound toxins, **8**, 186
rosaprostol, biological activity, **1**, 196
rose furan, occurrence, **8**, 226
rosenonolactone
biosynthesis, **2**, 228
occurrence, **2**, 228
rose oxide, occurrence, **8**, 225
Rosidae, lignins, **3**, 700
rosmarinic acid, occurrence, **1**, 686
rosmarinine, biosynthesis, **4**, 32
Rossmann consensus, **3**, 337
rot-2′-enoic acid, ring closure, **1**, 804
rotenoids
biological activity, **8**, 341
biosynthesis, **1**, 810, **8**, 342
characterization, **1**, 810
structure, **8**, 342
toxicity, **8**, 141
   mammalian, **8**, 341
rotenone
insecticidal activity, **8**, 340
isolation, **8**, 340
and nicotine compared, **8**, 348
occurrence, **1**, 810, **8**, 340, 341
oxidative metabolites, **8**, 342
structure, **8**, 340
toxicity, fish, **8**, 340
rotenone, 12α-hydroxy-, isolation, **8**, 341
rotenones, absolute configuration, **8**, 340
rothrockanes, biosynthesis, **2**, 108
Roundup *see* glyphosate
Rous sarcoma oncovirus, α-1,3(6)-mannosyl-glycoprotein
   β-1,6-*N*-acetylglucosaminyltransferase activity,
   3, 54
rove beetles
iridoids, **8**, 226
(*E*)-8-oxocitronellyl acetate, **8**, 225
RP51A transcripts, accumulation, **6**, 209
RRE *see* Rev-response element (RRE)
rRNA
5S
   E loop motif, **6**, 192
   structure, **6**, 58, 72
16S
   antibiotic interactions, **6**, 75
   conformation, **6**, 201
   conformational switches, **6**, 201
   decoding region, **6**, 193
   dimethyl A loop, **6**, 195
   domains, **6**, 190
   methylation, **6**, 194

pseudoknots, **6**, 199
structural studies, **6**, 190
23S
  antibiotic interactions, **6**, 75
  discovery, **6**, 110
  domains, **6**, 190
  E loop motif, **6**, 196
  hexaloop, **6**, 195
  long-range base pairings, **6**, 199
  long-range tertiary interactions, **6**, 197
  peptidyltransferase, **6**, 200
  P loop, **6**, 196
  pseudoknots, **6**, 199
  sarcin–ricin loop, **6**, 196
  structural studies, **6**, 190
  uridine turns, **6**, 195
conformational complexity, **7**, 616
conformational switches, **6**, 201
decoding region, **6**, 193
discovery, **7**, 616
early studies, **6**, 109
electron microscopy, **6**, 201
methylation, **4**, 198
peptidyltransference, **6**, 112
phylogeny, **6**, 190
processing, **8**, 213
protection, **6**, 200
secondary structures
  central loops, **6**, 200
  comparative sequence analysis, **6**, 190, 192
  covariance analysis, **6**, 190
  domain II, **6**, 200
  domain IV, **6**, 200
  E loop motif, **6**, 192
  G–U pairs, **6**, 192
  G–U wobble pairs, **6**, 192
  motifs, **6**, 192, 199
  noncanonical pairing, **6**, 190
  protein recognition sites, **6**, 192
  reverse Hoogsteen pairs, **6**, 192
  S loops, **6**, 192
  terminal loops, **6**, 200
  tertiary interaction sites, **6**, 199
  tetraloops, **6**, 192, 200
  type II base pairing, **6**, 192
self-splicing, **6**, 110
site-directed mutagenesis, **6**, 201
structural elements, **6**, **189–204**
structure, **6**, 13
  high resolution, **6**, 193
  Watson–Crick base pairs, **6**, 190
subunits, **6**, 189
tertiary interactions, **6**, 199
tertiary structures, **6**, 197
  base triples, **6**, 195, 198, 199
  chemical footprinting studies, **6**, 200
  cleavage studies, **6**, 200
  crosslinking studies, **6**, 200
  functional studies, **6**, 200
  lone pairs, **6**, 198
  pseudoknots, **6**, 198
translation, hybrid transition states, **6**, 202
x-ray crystal structure, **6**, 201
see also pre-rRNA
RRP proteins
exoribonuclease activity, **6**, 213
RRP4, homologues, **6**, 212
RRP41, homologues, **6**, 212
RRP42, sequencing, **6**, 213

RRP43, sequencing, **6**, 213
RSS *see* rat squalene synthase (RSS)
RTPR *see* ribonucleoside-triphosphate reductase
rubber, isoprenoids in, **2**, 7
rubber latex, isopentenyl diphosphate isomerase, **2**, 71
rubber tree *see Hevea brasiliensis*
Rubiaceae, indole alkaloid studies, **4**, 113
rubiadin, occurrence, **1**, 130
Rubia tinctorum, rubiadin, **1**, 130
rubiflavin A, possible alkoxyl radicals from, **7**, 510
rubisco *see* ribulose-bisphosphate carboxylase
rubradirin, trideoxysugars, **3**, 322
L-rubranitrose
occurrence, **3**, 312
structure, **3**, 322
rubrofusarin
feeding studies, **1**, 420
occurrence, **1**, 419
rubrosterone
activity, **8**, 293
biosynthesis, **8**, 291
synthesis, **8**, 288
rudd *see Scardinius erythrophthalmus*
rugulosin
biosynthesis, **1**, 431
phototoxicity, **8**, 176
ruspolinone, biosynthesis, **4**, 30
rusty grain beetle *see Cryptolestes ferrugineus*
Rutaceae
coumarins, **1**, 623
limonoids, **8**, 321
Ruta chalepensis, rutacridone, **1**, 130
rutacridone, occurrence, **1**, 130
Ruta graveolens
acridones, **1**, 759
bergapten, **1**, 634
coumarins, **1**, 625
furanocoumarins, accumulation, **1**, 625
O-methyltransferases, **3**, 647
xanthotoxin, **1**, 634
ruthenium(IV) complexes, oxo-, DNA damage induction, **7**, 374
ruthenium complexes, luminescence, **7**, 165
ruthenium–oligonucleotide conjugates, in ssDNA detection, **7**, 166
rutin
occurrence, **8**, 338
as oviposition stimulant, **8**, 156
Ruzicka's Isoprene Rule *see* biogenetic isoprene rule
RX:glutathione R-transferase(s) *see* glutathione transferase(s)
ryania, stability, **8**, 320
Ryania spp., occurrence, **8**, 319
Ryania acuminata, ryanodine, **8**, 319
Ryania sagotiana, ryanodine, **8**, 319
Ryania speciosa
ryanodine, **8**, 319
ryanodol, **8**, 319
Ryania subuliflora, ryanodine, **8**, 319
Ryania tomentosa, ryanodine, **8**, 319
ryanodine
insecticidal activity, **8**, 319
isolation, **8**, 319
occurrence, **8**, 319
structure–activity relationships, **8**, 320
ryanodol
biosynthesis, **8**, 320
pyrrolecarboxylic ester, **8**, 319
ryegrass *see Lolium* spp.

S

S5 protein, roles, in rRNA structure, **6**, 201
S12 protein, roles, in rRNA structure, **6**, 201
sabadilla
  applications, insecticides, **8**, 349
  insecticidal activity, **8**, 349
  occurrence, **8**, 349
sabinane monoterpenes, biosynthesis, **5**, 322
sabinene, biosynthesis, **2**, 104
(+)-sabinene, allylic hydroxylation, **2**, 145
cis-sabinene hydrate, biosynthesis, **2**, 104
(+)-*cis*-sabinene hydrate, biosynthesis, **2**, 136
trans-sabinene hydrate, biosynthesis, **2**, 104
(+)-sabinene-3-hydroxylases, occurrence, **2**, 145
(+)-sabinene synthases, occurrence, **2**, 136
sabinol, biosynthesis, **2**, 104
(+)-*cis*-sabinol
  biosynthesis, **2**, 145
  oxidation, **2**, 146
(+)-sabinone, oxidation, **2**, 146
saccharogen amylase *see* β-amylase
Saccharomyces cerevisiae
  adenine deaminase, **5**, 85
  aminotransferases, **4**, 5
  aromatic amino acid biosynthesis, **4**, 2
    regulatory mechanisms, **4**, 7, 9
  arom pentafunctional protein, **1**, 598
  base excision repair pathway, **5**, 393
  carboxypeptidase Y mutants, **3**, 31
  chorismate mutase, **4**, 5, **5**, 346, 363
  in complementation studies, **3**, 480
  cytochrome P450 reductases, **3**, 670
  dehydroquinases, **1**, 586
  2-enoyl-CoA hydratase, **1**, 52
  FAA genes, **1**, 47
  α and a factors, reviews, **8**, 408
  farnesyl-diphosphate farnesyltransferase, purification, **2**, 248, **5**, 339
  fatty acid synthase, **1**, 33
  gene cloning, **2**, 70
  genome, sequencing, **4**, 360
  geranylgeranyl diphosphate synthase, gene cloning, **2**, 87
  geranyl*trans*transferase, **5**, 323
    gene cloning, **2**, 74
  glg genes, **3**, 481
  α-glucosidase I, **3**, 18, 147
  α-glucosidase II, activity, **3**, 19
  glycoproteins, **3**, 22
  glycosidase processing, **3**, 14
  GPI anchors, **3**, 299
    biosynthesis, **3**, 306
  HAP complex, **4**, 177
  3*R*-hydroxyacyl-CoA dehydrogenase, **1**, 52
  isopentenyl diphosphate isomerase, **5**, 336
  isoprenoid pathways, **5**, 318
  β-ketothiolase, **2**, 19
  lanosterol synthase, **2**, 282
  long-chain-fatty-acid-CoA ligase, **1**, 48
  α1,2-mannosidases, **3**, 21, 21
    in endoplasmic reticulum, **3**, 21
  mannosyltransferases in Golgi complex, **3**, 17
  mutants, lacking α-glucosidase I, **3**, 18
  *OLE*1 gene
    expression, **1**, 46
    mutation, **1**, 44

  overexpression, **1**, 464
  pEVP11 vector, **4**, 133
  phosphoribosylanthranilate isomerase, **4**, 7
  3-phosphoshikimate 1-carboxyvinyltransferase, **4**, 4
  RNR genes, **3**, 343
  shikimate 5-dehydrogenase, **1**, 591
  shikimate kinase, **1**, 592
  shikimate pathway, **1**, 575
  squalene epoxidase, **2**, 270
  ST6Gal I expression, **3**, 48
  stearoyl-CoA desaturase, **1**, 39
  STE 14 gene, **2**, 362
  threonine aldolase, **3**, 400
  transketolase, **3**, 416
  Tremerogen A-10, **2**, 353
  tryptophan synthase, **4**, 7
saccharopine, biosynthesis, **4**, 243
saccharopine dehydrogenase (SD), catalysis, **4**, 243
Saccharopolyspora erythraea
  acyltransferase domain swapping studies, **1**, 508
  DEBS1 1-TE protein, **1**, 507
  6-deoxyerythronolide B synthase, **1**, 348, 425
  erythromycin A, **1**, 497
Saccharopolyspora hirsuta, gene cloning, **1**, 483
Saccharothrix spp., phosphonothrixin, **1**, 865
Saccharum officinarum, *p*-coumaric acid, **3**, 696
safflowers *see Cartharmus tinctorius*
safracins
  applications, antibiotics, **7**, 497
  DNA adduct formation by, **7**, 497
  DNA damage, redox-activated, **7**, 497
  imines formed from, **7**, 497
  occurrence, **7**, 497
saframycin A
  applications, antibiotics, **7**, 529
  DNA damage, redox-dependent, **7**, 529
saframycin(s)
  applications, antibiotics, **7**, 497
  DNA adduct formation by, **7**, 497
  DNA damage, redox-activated, **7**, 497
  imines formed from, **7**, 497
  occurrence, **7**, 497
  oxygen radical protection by, **7**, 499
  redox cycling by, **7**, 499
  secretion, **4**, 198
safrole
  carcinogenic action, **7**, 519
  DNA damage induction, **7**, 519
saintopin
  applications, antineoplastic agents, **7**, 607
  occurrence, **7**, 600, 608
sakuranetin
  accumulation, **1**, 131
  antifungal activity, **8**, 181
  as phytoalexins, **8**, 189
sakurasosaponin, applications, antifungal agents, **8**, 183
salA genes, cloning, **4**, 292
salannin
  antifeedant activity, **8**, 330
  isolation, **8**, 329
  occurrence, **8**, 330
  structure–activity relationships, **8**, 332
salicin
  insect sequestration, **8**, 152
  occurrence, **8**, 337

305

salicortin
  effects, on herbivores, **8**, 139
  occurrence, **8**, 139
salicylaldehyde
  effects, on herbivores, **8**, 139
  as substrate, **3**, 377
salicylate, acetyl-CoA : 1-alkylglycerophosphocholine
      acetyltransferase inhibition, **1**, 293
salicylate, methyl-
  in induced plant defense, **8**, 150
  occurrence, **8**, 212
  in plant–herbivore–predator interactions, **8**, 152
  in plant odor, **8**, 156
salicylate, methyl 6-methyl-
  biosynthetic pathway, **8**, 211
  occurrence, **8**, 211
salicylates, Brønsted relationships, **5**, 22
salicylhydroxamic acid, as lipoxygenase inhibitor, **1**, 123
salicylic acid
  as allelopathic agent, **8**, 171
  biosynthesis, **1**, 612
  and disease resistance, **1**, 779
  roles, **1**, 613
  in systemic acquired resistance, **1**, 133
  in wound signal transduction, **8**, 119
salicylic acid, 6-methyl- (6MSA)
  in acetate hypothesis studies, **1**, 3
  biosynthesis, **1**, **345–365**
      mechanisms, **1**, 359
  biosynthetic pathways, **1**, 354
  from
      acetyl-CoA, **1**, 411
      malonyl-CoA, **1**, 411
  inactivation, **1**, 357
  inhibition studies, **1**, 354
  mass spectra, **1**, 358
  roles, in patulin biosynthesis, **1**, 2
  structure, **1**, 14, 410
salicylic acid, *o*-pentadecenyl-, effects, on herbivores, **8**,
      139
salicylic acids, 6-alkyl-, biosynthesis, **1**, 356, 362
salicylic aldehyde, 6-methyl-, occurrence, **8**, 211
salinamides
  absolute stereochemistry, via chiral GC analysis, **8**, 593
  antiinflammatory activity, **8**, 593
  occurrence, **8**, 593
  x-ray crystal structure, **8**, 593
salivaricin A
  isolation, **4**, 279
  salA genes, **4**, 292
Salix spp., chlorogenic acid, **8**, 337
Salix alba, cinnamyl-alcohol dehydrogenases, **3**, 655
Salix viminalis, labeling studies, **2**, 62
Salmo gairdneri, oxylipins, **1**, 239
salmon *see Salmo salar*
Salmonella spp.
  cobalamin, **5**, 263
  diol dehydrase, **5**, 274
  diversity, **3**, 187
  phosphatases, **5**, 140
Salmonella enterica
  abequose expression, **3**, 187
  aminoethanol, **3**, 197
  deoxysugar biosynthesis, genetics, **3**, 345
  3,6-dideoxyhexoses, **3**, 187
  lipid A, structure, **3**, 200
  lipopolysaccharide biosynthesis, **3**, 202
  lipopolysaccharides, **3**, 187
  nrd genes, **3**, 343
  oligosaccharide expression, **3**, 187
  paratose expression, **3**, 187
  rfb gene clusters, **3**, 206
  serovars, **3**, 187

  tyvelose expression, **3**, 187
  Wzy-dependent pathway, **3**, 210
Salmonella enteritidis, glucose-1-phosphate
      adenylyltransferase, **3**, 469
Salmonella newington, isopentenyl diphosphate, **2**, 46
Salmonella typhi
  aro genes, **1**, 599
  dehydroquinases, **1**, 586
  shikimate kinase, **1**, 592
Salmonella typhimurium
  cbi genes, **4**, 141, 153
  cob genes, **4**, 141
  coproporphyrinogen oxidase, **4**, 95
  cyanocobalamin biosynthesis, **4**, 140, 150
  cys genes, **4**, 141
  dCTP deaminase, **5**, 94
  diol dehydrase, **5**, 274
  ethanolamine ammonia-lyase, **5**, 273
  glg genes, **3**, 449, 453
  1,4-α-glucan branching enzyme, **3**, 444
  glucose-1-phosphate adenylyltransferase, **3**, 447, 469
      mutants, **3**, 474
  hem genes, **4**, 141
  isoprenoid biosynthesis, mevalonate-independent
      pathway, **2**, 58
  mutants, **3**, 445, 473
      2-dehydro-3-deoxyphosphooctonate aldolase, **3**, 389
  pur genes, **1**, 838
  pyrimidine biosynthesis, **1**, 838
Salmonella typhimurium LT-2
  exo-α-sialidase, **5**, 294
  mutants, **3**, 473
Salmo salar
  lipoxins, **1**, 238
  prostaglandins, **1**, 237
salonitenolide, antifeedant activity, **8**, 308
salsolidine, isolation, **4**, 40
Salvelinus fontinalis, prostaglandins, **1**, 237
Salvia spp., clerodanes, **8**, 316
Salvia miltiorrhiza
  deoxyxylulose pathway, **2**, 377
  ferruginol, **2**, 379
  isopentenyl diphosphate biosynthesis, **2**, 381
  labdane biosynthesis, **2**, 62
Salvia officinalis
  (+)-(1*R*,4*R*)-bornyl diphosphate synthases, **2**, 128
  and β-caryophyllene synthase, **2**, 167
  geranyl diphosphate synthases, **2**, 121
  humulene synthase, **2**, 167
  leaves, geranyl diphosphate synthase, **2**, 88
  (+)-pinene synthases, **2**, 130, 131
  (−)-pinene synthases, **2**, 130, 131
  (+)-sabinene-3-hydroxylases, **2**, 145
SAM *see S*-adenosyl-L-methionine (SAM)
Samaderia indica, samaderin A, **8**, 322
samaderin A, occurrence, **8**, 322
samarangenin A, occurrence, **3**, 776
samarangenin B, occurrence, **3**, 776
sambucinol
  biosynthesis, **2**, 164
  occurrence, **2**, 203
(*S*)-sambunigrin, occurrence, **1**, 885, 886
Samia cynthia ricini, prothoracicotropic hormone, **8**, 295
sandaracopimaradiene, biosynthesis, **2**, 226
ent-sandaracopimaradiene, biosynthesis, **2**, 229
sandaracopimarenyl cation, biosynthesis, **2**, 382
sand fly *see Lutzomyia longipalpis*
Sanger's method (DNA sequencing) *see* chain-
      termination method
sanguiin H-5, chemical synthesis, **3**, 817
sanguinarine, occurrence, **1**, 131
sanguinine, biosynthesis, **4**, 43
sanguisorbic acid, linkages, **3**, 801

San José scale *see Quadraspidiotus perniciosus*
α-sanshool *see* echinacein
Santales, lignins, **3**, 700
santarubin dyes, occurrence, **1**, 775
santolinatriene, biosynthesis, **2**, 108
α-santonin, antifeedant activity, **8**, 308
saponins
    as antifungal agents, in plants, **8**, 183
    effects
       on insect herbivory, **8**, 144
       on seed dispersal, **8**, 167
    insecticidal activity, **8**, 323
    occurrence, **3**, 313
    toxicity, **8**, 323
saponins, hemolytic, and steroid glycosides compared, **8**, 474
saposins *see* sphingolipid activator proteins (SAPs)
SAP-precursor protein *see* prosaposin
Saprolegnia parasitica
    arachidonic acid, **1**, 209, 212
    eicosapentaenoic acid, **1**, 212
SAPs *see* sphingolipid activator proteins (SAPs)
SAR *see* systemic acquired resistance (SAR)
S_NAr *see* nucleophilic aromatic substitution (S_NAr)
sarains
    occurrence, **8**, 562
    structure, **8**, 562
Sarcina spp., carotenoid biosynthesis, **2**, 323
Sarcina lutea, antimicrobial activity against, **8**, 532
sarcin–ricin loop (SRL)
    in 23S rRNA, **6**, 196
    conformation, **6**, 202
    interactions, with elongation factors, **6**, 196
    RNA studies, **6**, 13
Sarcophaga spp., ecdysteroids, **8**, 280
Sarcophaga bullata, hexanal, **8**, 210
Sarcophyton spp., *Symbiodinium* spp. in, **8**, 617
Sarcophyton glaucum
    furan fatty acids, **1**, 226
    methyl sarcophytoate, **1**, 378
sarcoplasmic reticulum (SR)
    Ca^{2+}-ATPase activators, symbioramide, **8**, 617
    calcium release, **8**, 526
sarcosine, replacement, **5**, 46
sardine *see Sardinops melanosticta*
Sardinops melanosticta, oxylipins, **1**, 239
Sargassum thunbergii, larval metamorphosis promoters, **8**, 441
Sargassum tortile
    Leptosphaeria spp. in, **8**, 603
    δ-tocotrienol epoxides, **8**, 431
sarmentogenin, occurrence, **8**, 361
D-sarmentose, occurrence, **3**, 312, 313
L-sarmentose, occurrence, **3**, 312, 313
sarmentosin, insect sequestration, **8**, 362
sarpagine, strictosidine studies, **4**, 118
sarubicin A
    biosynthesis, **1**, 616, 620
    from, 6-hydroxyanthranilic acid, **1**, 617
satellite RNAs
    discovery, **6**, 236
    hammerhead ribozymes, **6**, 237
    see also Varkud satellite RNA
sativan, occurrence, **1**, 774
SATs *see* sialyltransferases (SATs)
satutaridine, biosynthesis, **4**, 39
sawflies
    perillenal, **8**, 226
    pheromones, **8**, 247
    propanoates, **8**, 209
    see also Pikonema alaskensis; pine sawflies; *Rhadinoceraea nodicornis*
saxitoxins (STX)

biosynthesis, **8**, 486
    feeding experiments, **8**, 486
    occurrence, **8**, 485
    sodium channel blocking, **8**, 486
sayasapogenol A, haustoria-inducing activity, **8**, 175
SC-558, prostaglandin-endoperoxide synthase inhibition, **5**, 254
SCADH *see* short-chain-acyl-CoA dehydrogenase (SCADH)
scalaradials
    antifeedant activity, **8**, 467
    isolation, **8**, 467
scale insects *see* Coccidae
scallops
    polyether toxins, **8**, 497
    prostaglandins, **1**, 244
    see also Patinopecten yessoensis; *Pecten maximus*
Scapania undulata, lignans, **1**, 645
scarab beetles
    pheromones, **8**, 212
    see also Anomala albopilosa; *Anomala cuprea*; *Anomala orientalis*; *Heptophylla picea*; *Holotrichia parallela*; *Phyllophaga anxia*
Scardinius erythrophthalmus, oxylipin studies, **1**, 238
sCD14
    lipopolysaccharide attenuation, **3**, 181
    types of, **3**, 182
SCD genes
    encoding, **1**, 46
    expression, **1**, 44
Scenedesmus obliquus
    glucose-1-phosphate adenylyltransferase, **3**, 470
    isoprenoid biosynthesis, mevalonate-independent pathway, **2**, 60
sceptrin, occurrence, **1**, 381
Sch37137, as glucosamine-6-phosphate synthase inhibitor, **3**, 275
sch genes, cloning, **1**, 480
Schiff bases
    in aldol reaction, **3**, 369
    formation, **3**, 338
Schinopsis spp., profisetinidins, **3**, 770
Schinus molle, laccase, **3**, 712
schisantherin D, HIV replication inhibition, **1**, 703
Schistocerca spp., diuretic hormone, **8**, 300
Schistocerca americana, antifeedant studies, **8**, 331
Schistocerca gregaria
    activity against
       antifeedant, **3**, 141, **8**, 331, 342
       insecticidal, **8**, 324
    antifeedant studies, **8**, 315
    ecdysone 22-phosphate, **8**, 283
    ecdysteroids, **8**, 290
    nonanal, **8**, 212
    nonanoic acid, **8**, 212
    pheromones, **8**, 247
Schistosoma mansoni
    5-hydroxyeicosatetraenoic acid, **1**, 249
    leukotriene B_4, **1**, 249
    oxylipins, **1**, 249
    prenylation, **2**, 363
Schizaeaceae, antheridiogens, **8**, 55
Schizandra spp., lignans, **1**, 703
Schizandra chinensis
    applications, **1**, 702
    (+)-gomisin A, **1**, 676, 702
    lignans, **1**, 702
Schizaphis graminum
    antifeedant activity against, **8**, 338
    growth inhibition, **8**, 337
Schizophyllum commune, fruiting-inducing cerebroside, **8**, 408
Schizosaccharomyces pombe

farnesyl-diphosphate farnesyltransferase, **5**, 339
   inhibition, **8**, 597
   isopentenyl diphosphate isomerases, **5**, 336
      cDNA cloning, **2**, 73
   lanosterol synthase, **2**, 282
schizostatin, as farnesyl-diphosphate farnesyltransferase
   inhibitor, **2**, 257
Schizura concinna, formic acid, **8**, 356
schkuhrin I, antifeedant activity, **8**, 308
schkuhrin II, antifeedant activity, **8**, 308
Schmidt's deaminase *see* adenosine 5′-phosphate
   deaminase
Schoenocaulon officinale, sabadilla, **8**, 349
Schönbein, Christian Friedrich (1799–1868), guaiac resin
   studies, **3**, 717
Schulte–Frohlinde fragmentation, in DNA damage, **7**,
   394
Schulze, cellulose studies, **3**, 533
Sciaridae, control, **8**, 275
SCID *see* severe combined immunodeficiency disease
   (SCID)
Scirtothrips citri
   cevadine toxicity, **8**, 349
   veratridine toxicity, **8**, 349
sclarene, occurrence, **2**, 225
ent-sclarene, occurrence, **2**, 225
sclareol
   applications, antifungal agents, **8**, 181
   biosynthesis, **2**, 225
sclerosporin, occurrence, **8**, 408
Sclerotinia fruticola, sclerosporin, **8**, 408
scn genes, *scnA*, cloning, **4**, 292
Scolytus spp.
   (3*S*,4*S*)-4-methyl-3-heptanol, **8**, 242
   α-multistriatin, **8**, 244
Scolytus multistriatus, antifeedant activity against, **8**, 336,
   339
scopadulcic acid B, occurrence, **2**, 239
scopadulcic acids, biosynthesis, **2**, 239
scopadulin, biosynthesis, **2**, 239
Scoparia dulcis, scopadulcic acid B, **2**, 239
Scophthalmus maximus, prostaglandins, **1**, 237
scopolamine, biosynthesis, **1**, 876, **4**, 27
scopoletin
   accumulation, **1**, 625
   biosynthesis, **1**, 628
   occurrence, **1**, 626
scots pine *see Pinus sylvestris*
scratch-faced ambrosia beetle *see Gnathotrichus sulcatus*
Scutellaria galericulata, jodrellins, **8**, 315
Scutellaria woronowii, jodrellins, **8**, 315
scytalone
   double labeled acetate incorporation, **1**, 4
   structure, **1**, 414
scytalone dehydratase
   catalysis, **1**, 428
   purification, **1**, 428
scytalone 7,8-hydro-lyase *see* scytalone dehydratase
scytalone:NADP$^+$ Δ^5-oxidoreductase *see*
   tetrahydroxynaphthalene reductase
Scytonema pseudohofmanni, scytophycin C, **8**, 579
scytophycin C
   cytotoxicity, **8**, 579
   occurrence, **8**, 579
   structure, **8**, 579
Scytosiphonales, sexual reproduction, **8**, 422
SD *see* saccharopine dehydrogenase (SD)
SDP synthases *see trans*-octaprenyl*trans*transferase(s)
SDS-PAGE *see* SDS-polyacrylamide gel electrophoresis
SDS-polyacrylamide gel electrophoresis
   processes, **7**, 665
   protein expression analysis, **7**, 665
SDZ 214-103 synthetase

molecular weight, **1**, 546
   substrate specificity, **1**, 550
SE *see* squalene epoxidase (SE)
sea anemones
   symbiosis, **8**, 429
   see also Aiptasia pulchella; *Radianthus kuekenthali*;
      Stoichactis kenti
sea cucumbers, platelet-activating factor, **1**, 297
sea fireflies *see Vargula hilgendorfii*
sea hares
   feeding stimulants, **8**, 419
   oxylipins, **1**, 244
   see also Aplysia spp.; *Bursatella leachii*; *Stylocheilus*
      longicauda
sealase *see* DNA ligase (ATP)
sea pansies *see Renilla reniformis*
sea squirts *see* Ascidiacea
sea urchins
   eicosatetraenoic acid, **1**, 247
   oxylipins, **1**, 248
   see also Strongylocentrotus nudus
sea whips *see Pseudopterogorgia elisabethae*
Sec *see* selenocysteine (Sec)
Secale cereale
   glucuronosyltransferases, **1**, 738
   7-*O*-glucuronosyltransferases, **1**, 737
secapin
   in honeybee venom, **8**, 355
   physiological activity, **8**, 355
Sec insertion sequence elements, roles, **4**, 369
SECIS elements *see* Sec insertion sequence elements
seco-anthraquinones, occurrence, **1**, 431
14,15-secocurvularin
   occurrence, **8**, 601
   structure, **8**, 601
secoguaianolides, antifeedant activity, **8**, 308
(+)-secoisolariciresinol
   biosynthesis, **1**, 670
   isolation, **1**, 671
(−)-secoisolariciresinol, biosynthesis, **1**, 662, 670
(−)-secoisolariciresinol dehydrogenase
   catalysis, **1**, 665
   encoding, **1**, 665
   purification, **1**, 665
secoisolariciresinol diglucoside
   antineoplastic activity, **1**, 668
   biosynthesis, pathways, **1**, 668
   metabolism, **1**, 698
   occurrence, **1**, 668
(+)-secoisolariciresinol glucosyltransferase(s),
   occurrence, **1**, 668
secoisolariciresinol(s)
   antineoplastic activity, **1**, 698
   biosynthesis, **1**, 688
   enantiomers, **1**, 651
secologanin, biosynthesis, **4**, 109, 110, 136
secondary metabolites
   from fungi, **1**, 409
   induction, **1**, 130
   occurrence, **8**, 378
   phenolics, **8**, 139
   roles
      animal attractants, **8**, 138
      defensive agents, **8**, 138
secretory cavities
   formation, **2**, 110
   monoterpenes in, **2**, 110
secretory ducts
   formation, **2**, 110
   monoterpenes in, **2**, 110
Sec tRNA$^{[Ser]Sec}$
   acceptor stems, base pairings, **4**, 360
   biochemistry, **4**, 360

enrichment, **4**, 362
genes
  intragenic promoters, **4**, 363
  occurrence, **4**, 361
  sequencing, **4**, 363
gene transcription, **4**, 362
  A and B boxes, **4**, 366
  nucleosomal repression, **4**, 366
  promoters, **4**, 362
isoacceptors, distribution, **4**, 362
primary sequences, **4**, 360
roles, **4**, 360
selenocysteylation, **4**, 355
species, primary transcript modification, **4**, 361
TATA box, **4**, 364
use of term, **4**, 355
sedanin, occurrence, **8**, 321
sedges
  oxylipins, **1**, 229
  see also Eleocharis microcarpa
sedoheptulose-1,7-diphosphate, as electrophile, **3**, 390
sedoheptulose-7-phosphate, as ADP-L-*glycero*-D-*manno*-
    heptose precursor, **3**, 224
  dihydroxyacetone phosphate transfer, **3**, 417
D-sedoheptulose-7-phosphate, biosynthesis, **3**, 414
sedoheptulose-7-phosphate:D-glyceraldehyde-3-
    phosphate glyceronetransferase *see*
    transaldolase
sedoheptulose-7-phosphate:D-glyceraldehyde-3-
    phosphate glycolaldehydetransferase *see*
    transketolase
Sedum stenopetalum, sarmentosin, **8**, 362
seeds
  defensive chemistry of, **8**, 167
  dispersal
    mechanisms, **8**, 167
    and plant chemistry, **8**, 163
  dormancy, effects of cytokinins on, **8**, 58
  dormant, **1**, 133
  germination
    effects of cytokinins on, **8**, 58
    gibberellin-induced, **8**, 46
    inhibition, **8**, 83
    role of jasmonates in, **1**, 128, 133, 135
    and starch degradation, **3**, 443
  longevity, **8**, 169
  starch granules, **3**, 454
  toxicity, **8**, 163, 167
Seeman laboratory, DNA research, **7**, 353
segoline A, occurrence, **1**, 381
segoline B, occurrence, **1**, 381
Seiractia echo, sequestration, **8**, 362
Selaginella doederleinii, lignans, **1**, 647
SELB
  homologues, in mammals, **4**, 370
  Sec tRNA[Ser]Sec homologue, **4**, 370
  use of term, **4**, 369
selectins
  ligands, **3**, 120
  synthesis, **3**, 58
selectivity
  loci-, **7**, 582
  microstructure, **7**, 582
selenium
  dietary problems, **4**, 375
  properties, **4**, 375
  toxicity, **4**, 357
selenium deficiency, rat studies, **4**, 362
selenocysteine, *Se*-methyl-
  accumulation, **4**, 357
  effects, on herbivores, **8**, 146
selenocysteine (Sec)
  aminoacylation, discriminator base, **4**, 355

applications, in nature, **4**, 374
biosynthesis, **4**, **353–380**
  pathways, **4**, 354
codon, UGA, **4**, 354, 357
from, serine, **4**, 354
importance of, issues, **4**, 360
incorporation
  into protein, **4**, 369
  non-specific, **4**, 357
isoacceptors, **4**, 362
metabolism, **4**, 354
structure, **4**, 354
tRNA, **4**, 354
  UGA decoding, **4**, 358
  see also Sec tRNA[Ser]Sec
selenocysteine synthase, catalysis, **4**, 355
selenocysteyl-tRNA synthetase, **4**, 354
selenoenzymes, structure-based catalytic mechanism, **4**,
  375
selenols, ionized, **4**, 375
selenomethionine, tRNA attachment, **4**, 354
selenophosphate, biosynthesis, **4**, 355
selenophosphate synthetase (SPS)
  biochemistry, **4**, 373
  in selenophosphate biosynthesis, **4**, 355
selenoprotein P (SelP)
  stem-loop structures, **4**, 369
  UGA codons, **4**, 369
selenoproteins
  biochemistry, **4**, 371
  identification, **4**, 371
  mammalian 15kDa, **4**, 371
    biochemistry, **4**, 374
  occurrence, **4**, 354
selenoprotein W (SelW), termination codons, **4**, 371
selenothioredoxin, biosynthesis, **4**, 357
SELEX
  binder selection, **7**, 624
  blended, **7**, 635
  definitions, **7**, 617
  development, **7**, 617
  DNA vs. RNA, **7**, 638
  future research, **7**, 639
  goals, **7**, 619
  libraries
    'blanket', **7**, 622
    classes, **7**, 621
    encoded, **7**, 636
    'focused', **7**, 623
    randomness, **7**, 622
    'shotgun', **7**, 622
  limitations, **7**, 637
  optimization, **7**, 623
  REPSA procedures, **7**, 629
  RNA enzyme studies, **6**, 113
  scope, **7**, 637
  strategies, **7**, 621
    focused, **7**, 621
  techniques, **7**, 617, 619
  utility, **7**, 624
self-assembly, of quinobenzoxazines, **7**, 463
sel genes
  selA, identification, **4**, 355
  selB, identification, **4**, 355
  selC, identification, **4**, 355
  selD, identification, **4**, 355
β-selinene
  biosynthesis, **2**, 185
  occurrence, **2**, 185
β-selinene synthases, purification, **2**, 185
SelP *see* selenoprotein P (SelP)
SelW *see* selenoprotein W (SelW)
seminal vesicle, prostaglandins, **1**, 160

semiochemicals
  biogenetic analysis, **8**, 202
  biosynthesis, **8**, 204
  classification, **8**, 198, 202
  definition, **8**, 2
  GC, **8**, 201
  identification, NMR techniques, **8**, 201
  isolation
    electroantennographic methods, **8**, 201
    GC/FT-IR, **8**, 201
    GC/MS, **8**, 201
    GC-GC/MS-MS, **8**, 201
  overview, **8**, 2
  receiver alertness, **8**, 201
  receiver attention, **8**, 201
  solid phase microextraction, **8**, 201
  structure, **8**, 201
  structure–activity relationship, **8**, 202
  see also chemical signals
Semliki Forest virus transmembrane protein E1, peptide
    isolation, **4**, 14
Senecio spp., pyrrolizidine alkaloids, **8**, 361
Senecio jacobaea, seneciphylline, **8**, 361
senecionine
  biosynthesis, **4**, 33
  detection, **4**, 33
  host–parasite chemical transfer, **8**, 176
  insect sequestration, **8**, 361
  occurrence, **8**, 345
Senecio vulgaris, senecionine, **8**, 345, 361
6α-senecioyloxychaparrinone, applications, growth
    inhibitors, **8**, 322
seneciphylline, insect sequestration, **8**, 361
senescence
  acceleration, **1**, 135
  bioassay, **1**, 126
  in flowers, **1**, 133
  in leaves, **1**, 133
  retardation, effects of cytokinins on, **8**, 58
senkirkine
  insect sequestration, **8**, 361
  occurrence, **8**, 345
Senna occidentalis, galactomannan biosynthesis, **3**, 521
sense suppression techniques, in terpenoid function
    studies, **2**, 212
Sephadex G200, gel filtration processes, **4**, 327
Sepharose, covalent attachment, **7**, 168
Sepharose, 4-aminobutyl-, glycogen synthase absorption,
    3, 452
Sepharose 4B, in gramicidin S synthetase purification, **4**,
    327
Sepharose 6B, cystamine, coupling, **4**, 327
septic shock
  endotoxin-induced, pathways, **3**, 183
  mediation, **1**, 286
Septoria nodorum, isoflavan biosynthesis, **1**, 812
Septrin, applications, **5**, 349
sequencing
  end-labeling, **6**, 64
  historical background, **6**, 64
sequestration, of plant substances, **8**, 361
Sequoia sempervirens, compression wood formation, **3**,
    693
sequons, glycosylation, **3**, 41
sequoyitol, as oviposition stimulant, **8**, 156
SER-1 *see* sterol regulatory element 1 (SRE-1)
SER-3 *see* sterol regulatory element 3 (SRE-3)
seratrodast, applications, antiasthmatic agents, **1**, 198
serglycin, localization, **3**, 164
serine
  conversion, **1**, 847
  as starting material, for selenocysteine, **4**, 354
  structure, **4**, 354

serine, L-*threo*-dihydroxyphenyl-, K_m, **3**, 400
serine, L-*O*-methyl-, in penicillin biosynthesis, **4**, 250
D-serine
  in cyclosporin studies, **1**, 538
  localization, **3**, 273
  occurrence, **3**, 246, 247
L-serine, replacement, **4**, 252
serine/threonine-GalNAc *O*-glycans, synthesis,
    glycosyltransferases in, **3**, **69–85**
serine carboxypeptidases, homologues, **1**, 893
serine-dependent hydrolases, superfamily, **4**, 227
serine enzymes, bond lengths, **5**, 119
L-serine hydro-lyase (adding indoleglycerol-phosphate)
    see tryptophan synthase(s)
serine phosphatase(s)
  biochemistry, **5**, 157
  structure, **5**, 157
serine proteases
  bond lengths, **5**, 119
  subtilisin-like, **4**, 291
serine-tRNA ligase, encoding, **4**, 354
L-serine:tRNA^{Ser} ligase (AMP-forming) *see* serine-tRNA
    ligase
serotonin
  biosynthesis, **4**, 54
  in wasp venom, **8**, 356
serpentine, biosynthesis, **4**, 46
Serratia liquefaciens, glucose-1-phosphate
    adenylyltransferase, **3**, 470
Serratia marcescens
  β-*N*-acetylhexosaminidases, **5**, 297
  glucose-1-phosphate adenylyltransferase, **3**, 447
  K antigens, **3**, 190
  lipopolysaccharides, **3**, 190
  monosaccharides, **3**, 190
Serratia rubidaea, chorismate mutases, **5**, 346
serricornin, occurrence, **8**, 13, 244
serricorole, occurrence, **8**, 244
serricorone, structure, **8**, 244
α-serricorone, occurrence, **8**, 244
β-serricorone, occurrence, **8**, 244
serum, fucosyltransferases, **3**, 115
seryl-tRNA synthetase *see* serine-tRNA ligase
sesame *see* *Sesamum indicum*
sesamin
  antineoplastic activity, **1**, 698
  antioxidant activity, **1**, 690
  germination inhibitory activity, **1**, 695
  occurrence, **8**, 277
(+)-sesamin
  biosynthesis, **1**, 659
  growth inhibitory activity, **1**, 693
  occurrence, **1**, 658
sesamolin
  antioxidant activity, **1**, 690
  juvenile hormone activity, **8**, 277
(+)-sesamolin
  biosynthesis, **1**, 659
  growth inhibitory activity, **1**, 693
sesamolinol, antioxidant activity, **1**, 690
(+)-sesamolinol synthases, occurrence, **1**, 658
Sesamum indicum
  dirigent proteins, **1**, 654
  (+)-piperitol, **1**, 658
  seed pods, development, **1**, 658
  sesamin, **8**, 277
  (+)-sesamin, **1**, 658
  (+)-sesamolinol synthases, **1**, 658
Sesiidae, sex pheromones, **8**, 207
sesquilignans
  roles, in lignin biosynthesis, **1**, 687
  structure, **1**, 690
sesquiterpene cyclase(s) *see* trichodiene synthase(s)

sesquiterpene isocyanides, antifouling activity, **8**, 438
sesquiterpene lactones
    antifeedant activity, **8**, 308
    as phytoalexins, **8**, 189
sesquiterpenes
    in abscisic acid, **8**, 84
    acyclic precursor, farnesyl diphosphate, **2**, 156
    antifeedant activity, **8**, 308
    biosynthesis
        cyclization mechanisms, **2**, **155–200**
        farnesyl diphosphate folding, **2**, 157
        pathways, **2**, 158
        reviews, **2**, 156
    eremophilene, **2**, 177
        biogenesis, **2**, 178
        biogenetic isoprene rule in, **2**, 178
    from
        farnesol, **2**, 156
        marine invertebrates, **2**, 191
    insecticidal activity, **8**, 308
    occurrence, **8**, 466, 601
    as pheromones, **8**, 227
    physiological properties, **2**, 156
    stereochemical theory of formation, **2**, 157
sesquiterpene synthase genes, plant, isolation, **2**, 210
sesquiterpene synthases
    aspartate-rich motif, **2**, 193
    cysteine in, **2**, 193
    histidine in, **2**, 193
    presteady-state kinetics, **2**, 193
    protein chemistry, **2**, 192
    protein structure, **2**, 195
    purification, **2**, 206
    role of cyclase in, **2**, 157
sesquiterpenoid mycotoxin
    biosynthesis
        from aristolochene, **2**, 202
        from trichodiene, **2**, 202
sesquiterpenoid phytoalexins
    elicitors, cellulase, **2**, 212
    occurrence, **2**, 212
sesquiterpenoids, fungal, mycotoxins, **2**, 202
sessile organisms
    chemical defense, **8**, 430
    larval settlement induction, **8**, 430
sesterterpenes, occurrence, **8**, 467
sesterterpenoids, occurrence, **8**, 467
Setaria anceps cv *Nandi*, dihydroxytruxillic acids, **1**, 647
seudenol, occurrence, **8**, 211
seudenone, occurrence, **8**, 211
severe combined immunodeficiency disease (SCID)
    etiology, **5**, 73
    treatment, **5**, 73
sex attractants, algae, **8**, 420
sex hormone binding globulin (SHBG), studies, **1**, 699
sex pheromones
    Ectocarpus siliculosus, identification, **8**, 421
    in *Enterococcus faecalis*, **8**, 407
    Lepidoptera, **8**, 205
    moths, **8**, 198
Sf9 cells
    and baculovirus, **3**, 24
    α1,2-mannosidase cDNA cloning, **3**, 24
sfp genes, encoding, **4**, 208
Sfp proteins, functions, **4**, 329
SfrT proteins, functions, **4**, 230
Sh 2 genes
    coding, **3**, 451
    mutation, **3**, 447
SH3 domain
    cloning, **7**, 668
    identification, **7**, 668
shamixanthone, biosynthesis, **1**, 434

SHBG *see* sex hormone binding globulin (SHBG)
SHCHC *see* 2,4-cyclohexadiene-1-carboxylate, 2-
        succinyl-6-hydroxy- (SHCHC)
sheep, infertility, **1**, 782
β-sheet peptides, in DNA major groove, **7**, 486
shellfish, as cone shell food, **8**, 476
shermilamine B, occurrence, **8**, 540
shermilamine C, occurrence, **8**, 540
Shewanella spp.
    eicosapentaenoic acid, **1**, 38
    fatty acid biosynthesis, **1**, 38
Shewanella putrefaciens, 2-dehydro-3-
        deoxyphosphogluconate aldolase, **3**, 422
Shigella spp., lipopolysaccharides, **3**, 190
Shigella boidii
    lipopolysaccharides, **3**, 190
    pseudaminic acid, **3**, 190
Shigella dysenteriae
    glucose-1-phosphate adenylyltransferase, **3**, 469
    lipopolysaccharides, **3**, 190
Shigella flexneri
    drug resistance, **3**, 142
    lipopolysaccharides, **3**, 190
Shigella sonnei
    2,4-diamino-2,4,6-trideoxy-D-galactose, **3**, 190
    lipopolysaccharides, **3**, 190
shihunine, biosynthesis, **1**, 618
shikimate
    biosynthesis, **1**, 345, 591
    as intermediate, **1**, 345, 719
    K_m, **1**, 592
shikimate, 5-amino-, phosphorylation, **1**, 593
shikimate, E-5-O-(4-coumaroyl)-, conversion, **3**, 640
shikimate, 6-fluoro-
    from
        (6R)-6-fluorodehydroshikimate, **1**, 592
        (6S)-6-fluorodehydroshikimate, **1**, 592
shikimate, (6R)-6-fluoro-, as substrate, **1**, 593
shikimate, (6S)-6-fluoro-, as substrate, **1**, 593
shikimate–arogenate pathway, phenylalanine
        biosynthesis, **1**, 719
shikimate 5-dehydrogenase
    catalysis, **1**, 591
    K_m, **1**, 591
    occurrence, **1**, 590, 591
    pH, **1**, 591
    substrate specificity, **1**, 592
shikimate kinase(s)
    assays, **1**, 592
    catalysis, **1**, 592
    isoenzymes, **1**, 592
    occurrence, **1**, 590
    purification, **1**, 592
    roles, in aromatic amino acid biosynthesis, **4**, 4
    substrate specificity, **1**, 593
shikimate pathway
    aromatic amino acid biosynthesis, **1**, 345, **4**, 2
    chorismate mutase in, **5**, 344
    early studies, **1**, 16
    enzyme-catalyzed reactions, **4**, 2
    enzyme organisation, **1**, 575
    enzymology, **1**, 16, **573–607**
    future research, **1**, 602
    molecular biology, **1**, 16, **573–607**
    in natural product biosynthesis, **1**, 16
    overview, **1**, 574
    in plants, **1**, 2
    and quinic acid pathway, flux between, **1**, 591
shikimate 3-phosphate
    binding, **1**, 593
    biosynthesis, **1**, 592, 596
    complexation, **1**, 597
    NMR spectra, **1**, 597

reaction, with phospho*enol*pyruvate, **1**, 593
shikimic acid
  aromatization, **3**, 803
  biosynthesis, **1**, 645
    pathways, **1**, 154
  deuteration, **1**, 72
  as intermediate, **1**, 16
  isolation, **1**, 574
  pathways, **1**, 609
  as starting material
    for cyclohexanecarboxylic acids, **1**, 72
    for dihydrocyclohexanes, **1**, 75
shikiminoku *see Illicium religiosum*
shikodonin, occurrence, **8**, 312
shikonin, biosynthesis, **4**, 48
shimofuridin A
  cytotoxicity, **8**, 532
  occurrence, **8**, 532
  structure, **8**, 532
Shine–Dalgarno sequence, **6**, 202
ships, biofouling of, **8**, 431
shirimodiol 8-acetate, antifeedant activity, **8**, 308
shirimodiol diacetate, antifeedant activity, **8**, 308
shizukaol A, occurrence, **1**, 377
SHMT *see* threonine aldolase
shonanin, biosynthesis, **3**, 731
short-chain-acyl-CoA dehydrogenase (SCADH),
    residues, **1**, 50
showdomycin, isolation, **8**, 390
sialic acid(s)
  occurrence, **3**, 119
  residues, **3**, 3
    on *O*-glycans, **3**, 79
  studies, **3**, 379
  synthesis, **3**, 380
sialidase(s) *see* exo-α-sialidase(s)
sialoadhesins, occurrence, **3**, 79
sialo-fucosyl glycosphingolipids, expression, **3**, 114
sialoglycoconjugates, occurrence, **3**, 120
sialoglycolipids, regulatory mechanisms, **3**, 120
sialoglycoproteins, regulatory mechanisms, **3**, 120
sialosyl cations, biosynthesis, **5**, 294
sialylation, lipopolysaccharides, **3**, 229
sialylmotif
  roles, **3**, 79
  use of term, **3**, 48
α3-sialyl-T *see* β-galactoside α-2,3-sialyltransferase
sialyl-Tn antigen, localization, **3**, 80
α-2,3-sialyltransferases, encoding, **3**, 229
sialyltransferases (SATs), **3**, 112
  activity, **3**, 79
  assays, **3**, 39
  catalysis, **3**, 119
  cloning, **3**, 95
  in Colo 205 cells, **3**, 120
  roles, in *N*-glycan synthesis, **3**, 46
  SAT-1, catalysis, **3**, 120
  SAT-2, catalysis, **3**, 120
  SAT-3
    catalysis, **3**, 120
    characterization, **3**, 121
    occurrence, **3**, 120
  SAT-4
    catalysis, **3**, 120
    characterization, **3**, 121
  SAT-6
    catalysis, **3**, 121
    mutations, **3**, 124
  substrate specificity, **3**, 95
Siberian ginseng *see Eleutherococcus senticosus*
sibiromycin
  applications, antibiotics, **7**, 497
  cardiotoxicity, **7**, 497

siderophores
  applications, **4**, 199
  from, isochorismic acid, **1**, 610
  occurrence, **8**, 592
Siegel, Sandy, peroxidase studies, **3**, 717
[3,3]-sigmatropic reactions, early studies, **5**, 349
signaling
  chemical
    applications, **8**, 198
    evolution, **8**, 198
signal molecules
  isolation, **1**, 140
  structure, **1**, 141
signals, extracellular, **3**, 608
signal transduction
  in *Aplysia californica*, studies, **1**, 245
  and ceramide, **3**, 3
  GPI anchors in, **3**, 6, 297
  G proteins in, **4**, 20
  and jasmonates, **1**, 129
  and jasmonic acid-related compounds-induced
      proteins, **8**, 118
  neurochemical, **1**, 245
  pathways, studies, **7**, 668
  and sphingosine, **3**, 3, 88
  wounds, **8**, 119
silane, 3-aminopropyl triethoxy-, use in solid supports, **7**,
    111
Silene dioica
  chalcone synthase, **1**, 734
  flavin adenine dinucleotide-dependent enzymes, **3**, 640
  glycosylation, **1**, 738
Silene latifolia
  glucosyltransferases, **1**, 737
  glycosylation, **1**, 738
  3′-*O*-methyltransferases, **1**, 739
  xylosyltransferases, **1**, 738
Silene nutans, ecdysteroids, **8**, 290
Silene otites, ecdysteroids, **8**, 290
silkworms
  farnesyl diphosphate isomerase
    cloning, **2**, 74
    substrate specificities, **2**, 76
  feeding, and toxin tolerance, **8**, 140
  isopentenyl diphosphate isomerase, substrate
      specificities, **2**, 76
  see also Bombyx mori; Callosamia spp.
silphinyl-2α-yl mesylate, use in the synthesis of α-
    terrecyclene, **2**, 175
Silurian, fossil plants, **1**, 645
silver nitrate, in RNA synthesis, **6**, 86
silver tree fern *see Cyathea dealbata*
silyl groups, 2′-*t*-butyldimethyl- (TBDMS), in 2′-hydroxyl
    group protection, **6**, 86, **7**, 144
Simaba multiflora, quassinoids, **8**, 322
simalikalactone B, nomenclature, **8**, 322
simalikalactone D, occurrence, **8**, 322
sim genes
  simA
    disruption, **1**, 542
    functions, **1**, 539
simple sugars, in nectars, **8**, 162
simvastatin, applications, clinical, **2**, 246
sinaiticin, occurrence, **1**, 685
sinalbin, as feeding deterrent, **8**, 145
sinapate, as starting material, for flavonoids, **1**, 733
sinapic acid
  biosynthesis, **3**, 644
  insecticidal activity, **8**, 337
  occurrence, **3**, 620
Sinapis alba
  enzymes, **1**, 858
  sinalbin, **8**, 145

thioglucosidases, **3**, 687
sinapyl *p*-coumarate, linking, **3**, 698
Singapore, breast cancer studies, **1**, 782
single-stranded DNA *see* ssDNA
singlet oxygen, reactions, with DNA, **7**, 544
sinigrase(s) *see* thioglucosidase(s)
sinigrin
    insect sequestration, **8**, 152, 363
    occurrence, **1**, 859
    as oviposition stimulant, **8**, 156
    toxicity, **8**, 145
sinigrinase(s) *see* thioglucosidase(s)
Siphonochalina tabernacula, cyanobacteria, **8**, 428
siphonodin, insect sequestration, **8**, 152
sirodesmins
    applications, antibiotics, **7**, 527
    possible DNA damage induction, **7**, 527
    reactions, with thiol, **7**, 527
siroheme, biosynthesis, **4**, 72, 90
sirosterol, occurrence, **1**, 379
Sitona lineatus, diketones, **8**, 242
sitophilure, biosynthesis, **8**, 242
Sitophilus spp., 3-pentanone, **8**, 210
Sitophilus granarius
    antifeedant activity against, **1**, 694
    1-ethylpropyl (2*S*,3*R*)-2-methyl-3-hydroxypentanoate, **8**, 241
Sitophilus oryzae, sitophilure, **8**, 242
Sitophilus zeamais, antifeedants, **8**, 140
sitosterol
    biosynthesis, **2**, 368
    in brassinosteroid biosynthesis, **8**, 105
    incorporation rates, **2**, 371, 381
    labeling patterns, **2**, 387
    labeling studies, **2**, 64
    ^{13}C NMR spectra, **2**, 371, 374
    ^{1}H NMR spectra, **2**, 371
    occurrence, **8**, 230
7SK, promoters, **4**, 362
skatole, odor, **8**, 161
skeletal muscle
    glycogen, **3**, 443
    glycogen synthase (mammalian), **3**, 479
    stimulation, insulin-induced, **3**, 487
SKI genes
    SKI2, products, **6**, 213
    SKI3, products, **6**, 213
    SKI8, products, **6**, 213
skin cancer, ultraviolet radiation-induced, **5**, 372
SKI proteins
    SKI2, homologues, **6**, 212
    Ski2p, models, **6**, 213
    SKI6, homologues, **6**, 212
SLE *see* systemic lupus erythematosus (SLE)
sliding clamp, DNA polymerase III, **7**, 350
slow reacting substance of anaphylaxis (SRS-A)
    antagonists, **1**, 191
    biological activity, **1**, 176
    biosynthesis, **1**, 168
    early studies, **1**, 10, 160
    receptors, **1**, 199
    release, **1**, 168
    see also leukotrienes
slugs
    acetyltransferases, **1**, 293
    platelet-activating factor, **1**, 286
SM *see* sphingomyelin (SM)
small (bacteriocin)
    structure, **8**, 400
    see also L-homoserine lactone, *N*-(3*R*-hydroxy-7*Z*-
        tetradecenoyl)-
smaller tea tortrix moth *see Adoxophyes* spp.
SMG genes, mutations, **6**, 210

smoky brown cockroach *see Periplaneta fuliginosa*
snails
    N-acetyllactosaminide β-1,6-*N*-
        acetylglucosaminyltransferases, **3**, 43
    see also Ligumia subrostrata; *Lymnaea stagnalis*
SNAP, subunits, **4**, 368
sno genes, encoding, **1**, 482
snowshoe hares, feeding preferences, **8**, 142
social insects
    caste-specificity, **8**, 205
    pheromones, **8**, 205
    see also ants; bees; bumblebees; honeybees; termites;
        wasps
sodium borohydride, neocarzinostatin chromophore
    activation, **7**, 559
sodium bromide, in cyclic bromoether studies, **1**, 307, 310
sodium channel
    in pufferfish, **8**, 481
    single point mutation, **8**, 486
    structure deduction from cDNA, **8**, 486
sodium cyanoboranuide, applications, **3**, 771
sodium diethyldithiocarbamate, as prostaglandin-
    endoperoxide synthase inhibitor, **1**, 123
sodium [1-^{13}C]isovalerate, in virginiae butanolide A
    studies, **1**, 141
sodium–potassium ATPase *see* adenosine triphosphatase
    (potassium sodium)
soft rot, causes, **8**, 398
softwood
    lignins, **3**, 725
    structure, **3**, 727
soil, effect of phenolics in, **8**, 173
Solanaceae
    calystegines, **3**, 134, 140
    eicosanoids, **1**, 235
    indole alkaloid studies, **4**, 119
    lignanamides, **1**, 673
solanapyrone A
    isolation, **1**, 395
    synthesis, **1**, 396
solanapyrone B, isolation, **1**, 395
solanapyrone C, isolation, **1**, 395
solanapyrone D
    isolation, **1**, 395
    synthesis, **1**, 396
solanapyrone E, isolation, **1**, 395
solanapyrones
    biosynthesis, **1**, 368
    biosynthetic studies, **1**, 396
    occurrence, **1**, 395
    structure, **1**, 396
solanapyrone synthase
    catalysis, **1**, 404
    kinetic parameters, **1**, 399
    substrate specificity, **1**, 400
solanesyl diphosphate synthase(s) *see trans*-
    octaprenyl*trans*transferase(s)
solanine
    applications, insecticides, **8**, 345
    occurrence, **8**, 345
solanone, occurrence, **8**, 235
Solanum spp., tomatine, **8**, 346
Solanum nigrum, solanine, **8**, 345
Solanum tuberosum
    colneleic acid, **1**, 235
    colnelenic acid, **1**, 235
    flavonol synthase, **1**, 727
    phenylalanine ammonia-lyase, **3**, 632
    localization, **3**, 662
    (−)-rishitin, **2**, 183
    solanine, **8**, 345
    threonine aldolase, cloning, **3**, 401
solenolide D, bisdeacetyl-, isolation, **8**, 431

Solenopsis spp.
dialkylpyrrolidines, **8**, 357
dialkylpyrrolines, **8**, 357
indolizidine alkaloids, **8**, 357
pyrrolizidine alkaloids, **8**, 357
venoms, **8**, 357
Solenopsis geminata, venoms, **8**, 357
Solenopsis invicta
dihydroactinidiolide, **8**, 234
(*Z*,*E*)-α-farnesene, **8**, 227
homofarnesene, **8**, 237
invictolide, **8**, 240
(6*E*)-((1*E*)-pentenyl)-pyron-2-one, **8**, 213
venoms, **8**, 357
Solenopsis xyloni, venoms, **8**, 357
soles *see Pardachirus* spp.
solid phase microextraction (SPME), semiochemicals, **8**, 201
solid supports
for functionalized oligonucleotide synthesis, **7**, 114
for oligonucleotide synthesis, overview, **7**, 110
tentacle support, **7**, 113
universal, **7**, 113
Solieriaceae, fatty acids, **1**, 70
soluble epoxide hydrolase (sEH), **5**, 54
active site residues, **5**, 56
alkyl-enzyme intermediates, **5**, 55
mechanisms, catalytic, **5**, 55
structure, **5**, 54
soluble starch synthases (SSS), **3**, 454
characterization, **3**, 455
isoforms, **3**, 457
occurrence, **3**, 455
SSSI
activity, **3**, 457
elution, **3**, 455
molecular mass, **3**, 457
occurrence, **3**, 454
purification, **3**, 457
SSSII
activity, **3**, 457
deficiency, **3**, 458
deficient mutants, **3**, 466
elution, **3**, 455
molecular mass, **3**, 457
occurrence, **3**, 454
solution structures
and crystal structures compared, **6**, 11, 12
properties, **6**, 11
solvating agents, chiral, **8**, 270
solvent kinetic isotope effects, in low barrier hydrogen bonds, **5**, 78
solvents, secretion, **8**, 200
Sonchus spp., cichoriin, **8**, 337
Sophora spp., ammodendrine, **8**, 344
(−)-sophorol
biosynthesis, **1**, 795
CD spectra, **1**, 797
(3*R*)-sophorol, biosynthesis, **1**, 665
3-sophorosides, in pollen, **8**, 163
Sordaria araneosa, cycloaraneosene, **1**, 378
sordaricin, occurrence, **1**, 378
sordidin, occurrence, **8**, 7
sorghum, soluble starch synthases, **3**, 455
Sorghum bicolor
cyanogenesis, **1**, 883
dhurrin biosynthesis, **1**, 858
microsomal preparations, **1**, 889
phenylalanine ammonia-lyase, **1**, 719
sorgolactone, characterization, **8**, 175
Soulamea pacheri, picrasin B, **8**, 322
Soulamea soulameoides, quassinoids, **8**, 322
Soulamea tomentosum, isobruceine A, **8**, 322

southern corn rootworm *see Diabrotica* spp.
southern pine beetle *see Dendroctonus frontalis*
southern puffer *see Arothron nigropunctatus*
Southern red mite *see Oligonychus ilicis*
Soviet gramicidin *see* gramicidin S
soybean *see Glycine max*
soy-rich diets
and breast cancer, **1**, 782
effects, on menstrual cycle, **1**, 783
isoflavonoid concentration, **1**, 782
and mammary tumors, **1**, 783
and prostate cancer, **1**, 782
spa genes
occurrence, **4**, 284
spaA, nomenclature, **4**, 284
spaT, replacement, **4**, 290
spaN gene *see nis* genes, *nisA*
Spanish fly *see Lytta vesicatoria*
Spa proteins
SpaB
encoding, **4**, 288
expression, **4**, 296
SpaC, encoding, **4**, 288
SpaF, structure, **4**, 297
SpaG, structure, **4**, 297
SpaI
disruption, **4**, 297
structure, **4**, 297
SpaR, structure, **4**, 295
sparsomycin
biosynthesis, **1**, 845
pathways, **1**, 849
precursors, **1**, 847
sparteine, occurrence, **4**, 33
spaS gene *see spa* genes, *spaA*
SP-C protein, palmitoylated cysteinyl unit, **4**, 14
spearmint *see Mentha spicata*
speciociliatine, strictosidine studies, **4**, 118
spectinomycin, discovery, **4**, 200
spectroscopy, RNA structures, **6**, 3–20
spermidine
in hornet venom, **8**, 356
roles, in hairpin ribozyme folding, **6**, 252
spermine
in hornet venom, **8**, 356
in oligodeoxynucleotides, **7**, 322
Sphaceloma manihoticola, gibberellin A$_4$, **8**, 41
sphagnum acid, occurrence, **3**, 624
spheroidene
in bacteria, **2**, 327
conversion, to spheroidenone, **2**, 345
spheroidenone
in bacteria, **2**, 327
biosynthesis, **2**, 345
sphinganine
acylation, **3**, 101
signaling inactivity, **3**, 90
D-*erythro*-sphinganine, biosynthesis, **3**, 89
sphinganine-1-phosphate, 4-D-hydroxy-, as substrate, **3**, 403
sphinganine-1-phosphate aldolase
biochemistry, **3**, 402
K_m, **3**, 403
occurrence, **3**, 402
substrate specificity, **3**, 403
sphinganine-1-phosphate palmitaldehyde-lyase *see* sphinganine-1-phosphate aldolase
sphinganine-1-phosphonate, 1-desoxy-, as substrate, **3**, 403
sphingolipid activator proteins (SAPs)
encoding, **3**, 102
roles, **3**, 102
SAP-B, discovery, **3**, 102

SAP-C, deficiency, **3**, 102
SAP-D, ceramide degradation stimulation, **3**, 102
sphingolipids
   degradation, **3**, 2
   DNA polymerase α inhibition, **8**, 598
   glycosylation, **3**, 91
   lysosomal degradation, activator proteins in, **3**, 102
   metabolism
      organization and topology, **3**, **87–106**
      pathways, **3**, 104
   transport, **3**, 2
      pathways, **3**, 98
sphingolipid storage diseases, **3**, 100
   etiology, **3**, 102
Sphingomonas chlorophenolica
   2,6-dichlorohydroquinone dehalogenase, **5**, 414
   pentachlorophenol degradation, **5**, 418
   pentachlorophenol hydroxylase, **5**, 418
   tetrachlorohydroquinone dehalogenase, **5**, 414
sphingomyelin, dihydro-, desaturation, **3**, 90
sphingomyelin (SM)
   biosynthesis, **3**, 97
   hydrolysis, **3**, 88
   occurrence, **3**, 97
sphingomyelin synthase, activity, **3**, 97
sphingosine
   acylation, **3**, 101
   glucuronyltransferase inhibition, **3**, 122
   occurrence, **8**, 545
   residues, **3**, 3
   roles, in signal transduction, **3**, 88, 3
sphingosine-1-phosphate (SPP), roles, in signaling, **3**, 88
SPH motif, Sec tRNA$^{[Ser]Sec}$ expression, **4**, 368
spider mite *see Tetranychus urticae*
spiders
   pheromones, **8**, 209
   see also Habronestes bradleyi; Linyphia tenuipalpis;
      Linyphia triangularis
Spilanthes mauritiana, isobutylamides, **8**, 303
Spilanthes oleraceae, spilanthol, **8**, 303
spilanthol, occurrence, **8**, 303
spinach
   shikimate kinase, **1**, 592
   see also Spinacia oleracea
spinach beet *see Beta vulgaris*
spinach leaf
   antibodies, **3**, 451
   glucose-1-phosphate adenylyltransferase, **3**, 447
   soluble starch synthases, **3**, 455
Spinacia oleracea
   acetoacetyl-ACP synthase, **1**, 29
   3-*O*-(3-*O*-feruloyl-α-L-arabinofuranosyl)-L-arabinose,
      3, 697
   4-*O*-(6-*O*-feruloyl-β-D-galactopyranosyl)-D-galactose,
      3, 697
   gibberellin 20-oxidases, **2**, 236
   oxidases, **3**, 721
   phenylalanine ammonia-lyase, localization, **3**, 662
   polysaccharides, esterification, **3**, 502
spined citrus bug *see Biprorulus bibax*
spined soldier bug *see Podisus maculiventris*
spin labels, **7**, 238
spin–lattice relaxation, times, **6**, 6
spin–spin relaxation
   mechanisms, **6**, 6
   molecular weight limitations, **6**, 7
   times, **6**, 6
spiramycin
   antirickettsial activity, **4**, 200
   biosynthesis, **1**, 525
   occurrence, **1**, 525
Spirastrella vagabunda, fungus in, 14,15-secocurvularin,
   8, 601

spiroacetals
   activity, **8**, 199
   occurrence, **8**, 212, 213, 214
spirobrassinin, as phytoalexin, **8**, 187
Spirodela polyrrhiza, apiosyltransferases, **3**, 517
spirodienones, analogues, **1**, 459
Spirogyra spp., evolution, **3**, 622
spirolactone
   cyclic, formation, **7**, 562
   as double-decker intercalator, **7**, 565
spirolactone biradical, **7**, 562
spirolactone cumulene, formation, via Michael addition,
   7, 562
spirolides, occurrence, **8**, 520
spleen, fucosyltransferases, **3**, 115
spliceosomal assembly, mechanisms, **6**, 226
spliceosome, functions, **7**, 345
Spl sites, in human squalene synthase, **2**, 261
SPME *see* solid phase microextraction (SPME)
Spodoptera eridania
   antifeedant activity against, **8**, 322
   feeding inhibition, **8**, 322
   growth inhibition, **8**, 321
Spodoptera exempta
   activity against, **8**, 308
      antifeedant, **8**, 336, 342
   antifeedant studies, **8**, 315
Spodoptera exigua, plant–herbivore–predator
   interactions, **8**, 152
Spodoptera frugiperda
   AcMNPV vector, **4**, 133
   antifeedant activity against, **8**, 318, 321
   antifeedant studies, **8**, 316, 332
   Class 1 α1,2-mannosidases, **3**, 24
      and baculovirus, **3**, 24
   cytochrome P450 reductases, **3**, 670
   dirigent proteins, **1**, 654
   feeding stimulation, **8**, 319
   growth inhibition, **8**, 321
      studies, **8**, 322
   rhodojaponin III toxicity, **8**, 313
Spodoptera littoralis
   activity against, **8**, 306, 308
      antifeedant, **3**, 141, **8**, 315, 318, 342
   antifeedant studies, **8**, 315, 316, 332
   resistance to, **8**, 312
Spodoptera litura
   antifeedant activity against, **1**, 694, **8**, 314, 345
   antifeedant studies, **8**, 314, 315
   azadirachtin resistance, **8**, 333
   clerodin studies, **8**, 318
   growth inhibitors, **1**, 693, **8**, 140
spo genes, *spoO*, occurrence, **8**, 402
sponges *see* Porifera
Spo proteins
   SpoOA, **4**, 330
      encoding, **8**, 402
   SpoOB, **4**, 330
   SpoOR, **4**, 330
spore photoproduct
   formation, **5**, 389
   repair pathways, **5**, 372, 392
spore photoproduct lyase, mechanisms, **5**, 392
spores
   bacterial, germination inhibition, **4**, 281
   ultraviolet irradiation, **5**, 389
sporochnols, isolation, **8**, 461
Sporochnus bolleanus, sporochnols, **8**, 461
sporogen, occurrence, **8**, 402
sporogen-AO 1, occurrence, **8**, 408
sporulation
   genetics, **8**, 402
   tyrothricin-induced, **4**, 323

sporulation factor (SF), in *Bacillus subtilis*, **8**, 402
Sporumosa ovata, methanol metabolism, **4**, 150
SPP *see* sphingosine-1-phosphate (SPP)
SPP synthase(s) *see trans*-octaprenyl*trans*transferase(s)
Sprague–Dawley rats, tumor studies, **1**, 700
spreading factors, secretion, **8**, 200
springbok antelopes
    α-farnesene, **8**, 227
    β-farnesene, **8**, 227
    geranylacetone, **8**, 234
    6-methyl-3,5-heptadien-2-one, **8**, 233
    6-methyl-5-hepten-2-one, **8**, 234
    springene, **8**, 230
springene, occurrence, **8**, 230
(3*E*,6*E*,10*E*)-α-springene, occurrence, **8**, 230
β-springene, occurrence, **8**, 230
spring hemlock looper *see Lambdina athasaria*
springtails *see* Collembola
sprouting, and starch degradation, **3**, 443
spruce budworm *see Choristoneura fumiferana*
SPS *see* styrylpyrone synthase (SPS)
sps genes
    Sps1, **4**, 355
    Sps2, **4**, 355
        TGA codon, **4**, 355
SPT14 gene
    isolation, **4**, 309
    as *PIG-A* homologue, **3**, 301, **4**, 309
SQDG *see* glycerol, sulfoquinobosyldiacyl- (SQDG)
squalamine
    antibiotic properties, **8**, 475
    as host-defense agent, **8**, 474
    occurrence, **8**, 474
    synthesis, **8**, 475
squalene
    cyclization, **2**, 5, 47
    from, farnesyl diphosphate, **2**, 108
squalene, 2-aza-2,3-dihydro-
    as inhibitor
        of cycloartenol cyclase, **2**, 304
        of oxidosqualene cyclase, **2**, 273
squalene, 24,30-bisnor-2,3-oxido-, cyclization, **2**, 305
squalene, 10,15-didesmethyl-2,3-oxido-, conversion, **2**, 286
squalene, 2,3-dihydro-
    as starting material, for euph-7-ene, **2**, 312
    as substrate, for hopene cyclase, **2**, 310
squalene, 2,3-dihydro-2,3-imino-, as inhibitor, **2**, 311
squalene, dioxido-, as starting material, for oxysterols, **2**, 270
squalene, 2,3:18,19-dioxido-, synthesis, **2**, 291
squalene, 2,3:22,23-dioxido-, **2**, 284
squalene, 2,3-imino-
    as inhibitor, **2**, 290
    as tetrahymanol cyclase inhibitor, **2**, 312
squalene, 27-methylidene-2,3-oxido-, conversion, **2**, 286
squalene, 29-methylidene-2,3-oxido-
    as oxidosqualene cyclase irreversible inactivator, **2**, 282
    as oxidosqualene:lanosterol cyclase irreversible inactivator, **2**, 287
squalene, [³H]29-methylidene-2,3-oxido-, affinity labeling, **2**, 287
squalene, 2,3-oxido-
    analogues, cyclization, **2**, 6
    bicyclic analogue, cyclization, **2**, 305
    as starting material, for terpenes, **2**, 6
    sulfur-containing analogues, synthesis, **2**, 291
squalene, all-*trans* (*S*)-2,3-oxido-, as starting material, for cycloartenol, **2**, 303
squalene biosynthesis, **2**, 9, **5**, 336
    stereochemistry, reviews, **2**, 70
squalene cyclase inhibitors, enzyme studies, **2**, 38
squalene epoxidase (SE)

cDNA encoding, **2**, 270
in cholesterol biosynthesis, **2**, **267–298**
enzymology, **2**, 270
epoxidation, equation, **2**, 269
future research, **2**, 293
gene cloning, **2**, 270
inhibition studies, **2**, 273
inhibitors, **2**, 270, **2**, 273, 276, 277
    SAR studies, **2**, 277
mechanisms, **2**, 268
molecular biology, **2**, 270
non-cytochrome P450 enzyme, **2**, 267
occurrence, **2**, 270
regulation, **2**, 270
slow tight-binding inhibitors, **2**, 270
studies, **2**, 268
substrate specificity, **2**, 273
vertebrates, **2**, 271
    inhibitor, **2**, 273
    inhibitor studies, **2**, 277
    photoaffinity ligands for, **2**, 279
yeast, allylamine-resistant, **2**, 270
squalene epoxides, internal, IC$_{50}$ values, **2**, 275
squalene monooxygenase *see* squalene epoxidase (SE)
squalene oxide *see* squalene, 2,3-oxido-
squalene synthase *see* farnesyl-diphosphate farnesyltransferase
squalenol, biosynthesis, **5**, 338
squalestatins
    as farnesyl-diphosphate farnesyltransferase inhibitors, **2**, 256
    structure, **2**, 257
Squalus acanthias, squalamine, **8**, 474
squamosin, occurrence, **8**, 305
square necked grain beetle *see Cathartus quadricollis*
squash beetles *see Epilachna borealis*
squid *see Watasenia scintillan*
squirting cucumber *see Ecballium elaterium*
Src homology 3 domain *see* SH3 domain
SREBPs *see* sterol regulatory element binding proteins (SREBPs)
srf genes, encoding, **4**, 208, 330
Srf proteins, SrfAD, **4**, 330
SRL *see* sarcin–ricin loop (SRL)
srm genes, expression, **1**, 526
SRS-A *see* slow reacting substance of anaphylaxis (SRS-A)
ssDNA
    detection, **7**, 165
    labeling, **7**, 198
    selective cleavage, **7**, 164
SSS *see* soluble starch synthases (SSS)
ST3Gal I *see* β-galactoside α-2,3-sialyltransferase
ST3Gal III *see N*-acetyllactosaminide α-2,3-sialyltransferase (ST3Gal III)
ST3Gal IV *see* CMP-sialic acid:Galβ1-4GlcNAc-R/Galβ1-3GalNAc-R α2-3-sialyltransferase (ST3Gal IV)
ST3N I *see N*-acetyllactosaminide α-2,3-sialyltransferase (ST3Gal III)
ST3N II *see* CMP-sialic acid:Galβ1-3/4GlcNAc-R α2-3-sialyltransferase II (ST3N II)
ST6Gal I *see* β-galactoside α-2,6-sialyltransferase (ST6Gal I)
ST6GalNAc I *see* α-*N*-acetylgalactosaminide α-2,6-sialyltransferase
ST8Sia II *see* CMP-sialic acid:[sialylα2-8]$_n$sialylα2-3Galβ1-3/4GlcNAc-R α2-8-sialyltransferase (ST8Sia II)
ST8Sia III *see* CMP-sialic acid:sialylα2-3Galβ1-4GlcNAc-R α2-8-sialyltransferase (ST8Sia III)
ST8Sia IV *see* CMP-sialic acid:[sialylα2-8]$_n$sialylα2-3Galβ1-3/4GlcNAc-R α2-8-sialyltransferase (ST8Sia IV)

stable flies *see Stomoxys* spp.
Stachybotrys atra, β-glucosidase, **5**, 289
Stachybotrys chartarum, cyclosporins, **1**, 534
Staf, isolation, **4**, 368
staggers, ryegrass-induced, **8**, 177
Stains-All *see* thiacarbocyanine bromide, 4,5:4′,5′-
        dibenzo-3,3′-diethyl-9-methyl-
staphylococcin 1580, structure, **4**, 279
Staphylococcus spp., carotenoid biosynthesis, **2**, 323
Staphylococcus aureus
    activity against, nargenicin A, **1**, 528
    aro genes, **1**, 593, 599
    carotenoid biosynthesis, **2**, 337
    crt genes, **2**, 337
    early studies, **4**, 160
    fem genes, **3**, 264
    inhibition, **1**, 692
    2-*C*-methyl-D-erythritol, **2**, 56
    phospho-MurNAc-pentapeptide translocase, **3**, 263
    3-phosphoshikimate 1-carboxyvinyltransferase, **1**, 593
    tagatose-1,6-diphosphate aldolase, **3**, 430
    see also methicillin-resistant *Staphylococcus aureus*
        (MRSA)
Staphylococcus epidermidis
    epidermin biosynthesis, **4**, 279
    epilancin K7 biosynthesis, **4**, 279
    Pep5 excretion, **4**, 279, 296
    ultraviolet irradiation, **5**, 389
Staphylococcus gallinarum, gallidermin biosynthesis, **4**,
        279
starch
    bacterial, biosynthesis, **3**, 444
    biosynthesis, **3**, 2, 7
        in algae, **3**, 445
        enzyme properties, **3**, 447
        initiation, **3**, 463
        in plants, **3**, **441–495**
        problems, **3**, 454
        regulatory mechanisms, **3**, 468, 472
        sites, **3**, 463
    degradation, **3**, 443
    granules, **3**, 454
    hexose incorporation, **3**, 466
    insolubility, **3**, 454
    roles, **3**, 443
        in plants, **3**, 443
    structure, **3**, 442
    synthesis, Kacser–Burns control analysis, **3**, 472
starch synthase(s)
    activity, measurement, **3**, 454
    catalysis, **3**, 445
    isoforms, **3**, 454
    occurrence, **3**, 457
    see also glycogen(starch) synthase; glycogen synthase
        (bacterial); glycogen synthase (mammalian);
        granule-bound starch synthases (GBSSs); soluble
        starch synthases (SSS)
starfish
    chemical defense, **8**, 471
    eicosatetraenoic acid, **1**, 247
    saponins, **3**, 313
    see also Evasterias troschelii; Luidia clathrata
statin drugs, structure, **2**, 25
stawamycin, occurrence, **1**, 374
stc genes
    stcP, disruptions, **1**, 463
    stcS
        functions, **1**, 462
        sequencing, **1**, 462
    stcU, functions, **1**, 462
*STE*2 mRNA, stabilization, **6**, 209
stearate, desaturation, **1**, 38
stearic acid, **8**, 203

β-oxidation, **8**, 205, 213
stearic acid, (+)-*threo*-9,10-dihydroxy-, biosynthesis, **1**,
        210
stearidonic acid, occurrence, **1**, 214
stearoyl-ACP desaturase
    catalysis, **1**, 42
    occurrence, **1**, 42
stearoyl-CoA desaturase(s)
    genetics, **1**, 39
    occurrence, **1**, 39
    purification, **1**, 35, 43
stearoyl-CoA,hydrogen-donor:oxygen oxidoreductase(s)
        see stearoyl-CoA desaturase(s)
(−)-steganacin
    antineoplastic activity, **1**, 701
    biosynthesis, **1**, 676
    occurrence, **1**, 676
(−)-steganangin, antineoplastic activity, **1**, 701
steganoate B, antitumor activity, **1**, 701
Steganotaenia araliacea
    steganacin, **1**, 676
    (−)-steganangin, **1**, 701
STE 14 genes, mutant, *Saccharomyces cerevisiae*, **2**, 362
stegobinone, occurrence, **8**, 13, 244
stegobiol, occurrence, **8**, 244
Stegobium paniceum
    pheromones, **8**, 13
    stegobinone, **8**, 13
    stegobiol, **8**, 244
Stellaria longipes, caffeoyl-CoA *O*-methyltransferase, **3**,
        671
Stelletta spp., stellettadine, **8**, 442
stellettadine, occurrence, **8**, 442
Stelletta maxima, cyclostellettamines, **8**, 560
stemar-16-ene, formation, **2**, 238
ent-stemarenes, occurrence, **2**, 241
stemarin, occurrence, **2**, 238
stemodanes, occurrence, **2**, 238
Stemodia chiensis, stemodanes, **2**, 238
Stemodia maritima, stemarin, **2**, 238
stemodin, biosynthesis, **2**, 238
stemodinone, biosynthesis, **2**, 238
Stemphylium botryosum, stemphyloxin I, **1**, 388
stemphyloxin I, occurrence, **1**, 388
sterculic acid, dihydro-, occurrence, **1**, 62
sterculic acid, 2-dihydro-, occurrence, **1**, 62
sterculynic acid, occurrence, **1**, 62
stereochemistry–bioactivity relationship, pheromones, **8**,
        11
Stereum purpureum, sterpurene, **2**, 172
steric clash, barrier to intercalation, **7**, 441
sterigmatocystin
    biosynthesis, **1**, 449, 458
        molecular biological approaches, **1**, 461
    DNA damage induction, **7**, 511
    folding patterns, **1**, 448
    as intermediate, **1**, 16
    isolation, **1**, 445
    labeling, **1**, 445
    occurrence, **1**, 421
sterigmatocystin, demethyl-
    accumulation, **1**, 463
    as starting material, for versicolorin A, **1**, 462
    synthesis, **1**, 458
sterigmatocystin, 10-hydroxy-*O*-methyl-, synthesis, **1**, 459
sterigmatocystin, *O*-methyl-
    conversion, **1**, 462
    as starting material, for aflatoxin B₁, **1**, 459
steroids
    as pheromones, **8**, 230, 426
    prostaglandin-endoperoxide synthase-2 inhibition, **5**,
        256
steroids, polyhydroxy-, antifeedant activity, **8**, 471

sterol biosynthesis inhibitor, compactin as, **2**, 257
sterol esterase
  binding, **5**, 127
  interactions, with heparin, **5**, 128
  structure, **5**, 125
sterol regulatory element 1 (SRE-1)
  in human squalene synthase, **2**, 261
  identification, **2**, 37
sterol regulatory element 3 (SRE-3), in human squalene
    synthase, **2**, 261
sterol regulatory element binding proteins (SREBPs),
    encoding, **2**, 37
sterols
  biosynthesis, **2**, 377
  defensive, **8**, 361
  in hydroxymethylglutaryl-CoA reductase degradation
      studies, **2**, 38
  in hydroxymethylglutaryl-CoA reductase regulation, **2**,
      36
  labeling, **2**, 60
  synthesis, **2**, 26, 247
sterpurenes, occurrence, **2**, 172
steryl-ester acylhydrolase *see* sterol esterase
Stevia rebaudiana, stevioside, **8**, 166
stevioside, occurrence, **8**, 166
STFI *see* Swedish Forest Products Laboratory (STFI)
Stigmella malella
  (2*S*)-6,8-nonadien-2-ol, **8**, 212
  6,8-nonadien-2-ol, **8**, 209
stilbene, dihydro-, haustoria-inducing activity, **8**, 175
stilbene, 3,4,3′,5′-tetrahydroxy- *see* resveratrol
stilbenecarboxylic acids, biosynthesis, **1**, 765
stilbenes
  biosynthesis, **1**, 750
  occurrence, **1**, 750
  roles, **1**, 750
  structure, **1**, 2
stilbenes, hydroxy-, as phytoalexins, **8**, 190
stilbenes, reduced, biosynthesis, **1**, 765
stilbene synthase (STS), **1**, **749–771**
  activity
    after heterologous expression, **1**, 754
    studies, **1**, 758
  and chalcone synthase compared, **1**, 754
  condensation, **1**, 756
  consensus sequences, **1**, 754, 756
  cysteine
    active site environment, **1**, 756
    conserved, **1**, 756
  definitions, **1**, 750
  dimers, **1**, 752
  evolution, **1**, 762
  from chalcone synthase, via mutagenesis, **1**, 758
  function, **1**, 756
  future research, **1**, 765
  intron, conserved, **1**, 753
  mutant proteins, **1**, 756, 758
  pathway channeling, **1**, 752
  properties, **1**, 752
  reactions, **1**, 750
  relationship tree, **1**, 753
  ring folding, **1**, 751
  roles, **1**, 750
  sequencing, **1**, 753
  structure, **1**, 756
  subgroups, occurrence, **1**, 753
  substrate specificity, **1**, 752
  subunit interactions, **1**, 757
  superfamily, **1**, 759
stilbenoids
  with carboxyl group, **1**, 750
  occurrence, **1**, 763
stilbenolignans, occurrence, **1**, 685

stink bugs
  (*E*)-2-hexenal, **8**, 210
  see also Campyloma verbasci; Euschistus spp.;
      Leptoglossus zonatus; *Nezara* spp.; *Plautia stali*;
      Stiretrus anchorago
stipitatonic acid, biosynthesis, **1**, 3
Stiretrus anchorago, 6,10,13-trimethyltetradecan-1-ol, **8**,
    241
Stoichactis kenti, symbiosis, **8**, 430
stomach, acid lipases, **5**, 133
stomach cancer, inhibition, **1**, 783
Stomoxys spp., female contact pheromones, **8**, 249
Stomoxys calcitrans, sex stimulants, **8**, 249
stored product beetle *see* Lasioderma serricorne
str 1 gene
  characterization, **4**, 134
  chemotaxonomic issues, **4**, 134
  isolation, **4**, 134
stratification
  induction, **1**, 128
  jasmonic acid accumulation, **1**, 124
strawberries *see* Fragraria ananassa Duch
streptavidin, interactions, with biotin, **7**, 154
streptococcin A-FF22
  activity, **4**, 282
  biosynthesis, **4**, 279
  characterization, **4**, 279
  gene clusters, **4**, 292
  modifying enzymes, **4**, 293
  peptidase functions, **4**, 294
  prepeptides, **4**, 293
    conserved motifs, **4**, 293
  scn genes, **4**, 292
  structure, **4**, 277, 279
  transport functions, **4**, 294
Streptococcus spp., carotenoid biosynthesis, **2**, 323
Streptococcus faecalis see Enterococcus faecalis
Streptococcus mitis
  1,4-α-glucan branching enzyme, **3**, 444
  4-α-glucanotransferase induction, **3**, 445
  glycogen, **3**, 443
Streptococcus mutans
  4-α-glucanotransferase induction, **3**, 445
  inhibition, **1**, 692
  mutacin II biosynthesis, **4**, 282
Streptococcus oralis, sialic acid studies, **3**, 379
Streptococcus pneumoniae, *sul* genes, **3**, 374
Streptococcus pneumoniae, penicillin-resistant, inhibition,
    8, 595
Streptococcus pyogenes, streptococcin A-FF22
    biosynthesis, **4**, 279
Streptomyces spp.
  antibiotic production, **1**, 8
  autoinducers, **8**, 378
  autoregulators, **1**, 140
  azinomycin B, **7**, 513
  bacterial aromatic polyketides, **1**, 474
  bioactive compounds, **1**, 140
  bioxalomycins, **7**, 499
  butyrolactones, **8**, 378
  carotenogenesis in, **2**, 346
  carzinophilin, **7**, 513
  CC-1065, **7**, 504
  cinnamycin lantibiotics biosynthesis, **4**, 280
  cyanocyclines, **7**, 499
  daunomycin, **7**, 605
  5-deoxyenterocin, **8**, 597
  dephostatin, **7**, 521
  2,5-dihydroxymethyl-3,4-dihydroxypyrrolidine, **3**, 134
  doxorubicin, **7**, 605
  enterocins, **8**, 543, 597
  fatty acids, **1**, 71
  fosfomycin, **5**, 66

future research, **8**, 392
γ-indomycinone, **8**, 598
isoprenoid biosynthesis, **2**, 63
leinamycin, **7**, 522
lysine 2,3-aminomutase, **5**, 207
metabolite biosynthesis, **4**, 197
naphthyridinomycin, **7**, 499
neocarzinostatin, **1**, 567
octalactins, **8**, 590
pentalenolactones, **2**, 168
phenazines, **8**, 591
3-pi-5-deoxyenterocin, **8**, 597
pluramycins, **7**, 508
quinocarcin, **7**, 499
safracins, **7**, 497
saframycins, **7**, 497
secondary metabolites, **8**, 378
signal molecules, **1**, 140
spore pigments, **1**, 480
teleocidins, **8**, 603
tetrazomine, **7**, 499
urauchimycins, **8**, 589
virginiae butanolide A biosynthesis, **1**, 140
wailupemycins, **8**, 597
Streptomyces actuosus, nosiheptide biosynthesis, **1**, 852
Streptomyces aeriouvifer, isoprenoid biosynthesis,
    mevalonate-independent pathway, **2**, 59
Streptomyces spp. AJ 9463
    allosamidins, **1**, 151
        studies, **1**, 150
Streptomyces amakusaensis, 4-hydroxyphenylserine
    aldolase, **3**, 400
Streptomyces ambofaciens
    polyketide synthase studies, **1**, 511
    spiramycin, **1**, 525
Streptomyces aminophilus
    p-aminobenzoic acid biosynthesis, **1**, 612
    perimycin, **1**, 612
Streptomyces antibioticus
    erythromycins, **1**, 510
    fatty acids, **1**, 71
    proclavaminic acid biosynthesis, **4**, 185
    virginiae butanolide A
        biosynthesis, **1**, 141
        biosynthetic pathways, **1**, 147
    virginiae butanolides
        biosynthesis, **8**, 385
        mode of action, **8**, 387
Streptomyces argenteolus, longestin, **2**, 59
Streptomyces argillaceus, mithramycin biosynthesis, **1**,
    480
Streptomyces aureofaciens, 1,4-α-glucan branching
    enzyme, **3**, 444
Streptomyces avermitilis
    avermectins, **1**, 522
    feeding studies, **1**, 524
Streptomyces azureus, thiostrepton biosynthesis, **1**, 852
Streptomyces bambergiensis, moenomycin A, **3**, 281
Streptomyces bikiniensis
    afs genes, **8**, 382
    autoregulators, **1**, 140, **8**, 391
Streptomyces caelestis, niddamycin, **1**, 525
Streptomyces carzinostaticus, neocarzinostatin, **1**, 567, **7**,
    554, 558
Streptomyces cinnamonensis, *mon* genes, **1**, 483
Streptomyces clavuligerus
    ACV synthetase, **1**, 840
    cephamycin biosynthesis, regulation, **4**, 179
    cephamycin C biosynthesis, **4**, 164
    clavulanic acid biosynthesis, gene clusters, **4**, 185
    isopenicillin N epimerase, **1**, 843
        characterization, **4**, 171
    lysine ε-aminotransferase activity, **4**, 165

pcb genes, transcription, **4**, 179
Streptomyces coelicolor
    act genes, **1**, 484
    actinorhodin biosynthesis, **1**, 476, 10
    acyl carrier protein, **1**, 363
    p-aminobenzoic acid biosynthesis, **1**, 612
    candicidin, **1**, 612
    dehydroquinase, site-directed mutagenesis, **1**, 588
    β-lactam biosynthesis, gene clusters, **4**, 173
    nodulation, **1**, 337
    spore pigments, **1**, 480
    studies, **8**, 379
    type II dehydroquinase, **1**, 588
    ultraviolet irradiation, **5**, 389
Streptomyces coelicolor CH999
    erythromycin polyketide synthase, **1**, 507
    δ-lactone biosynthesis, **1**, 511
Streptomyces collinus
    1-cyclohexenylcarbonyl-CoA reductase, **1**, 74
    fatty acids, **1**, 71
Streptomyces cuspidosporus, sparsomycin biosynthesis, **1**,
    845
Streptomyces cyaneofuscatus, autoregulators, **1**, 140, **8**,
    391
Streptomyces exfoliatus, carquinostatin B, **2**, 59
Streptomyces fradiae
    fosfomycin, **1**, 876
    polyketide synthase studies, **1**, 511
    tylosin, **1**, 525
    urdamycin biosynthesis, **1**, 483
Streptomyces spp. FRI-5
    D-cycloserine, **8**, 389
    effects of FarA in, **8**, 390
    FarA, purification, **8**, 389
    IM-2
        activity, **1**, 140
        mode of action, **8**, 390
        structure, **8**, 389
Streptomyces galilaeus, aklavinone biosynthesis, **1**, 482,
    11
Streptomyces glaucescens, tetracenomycin biosynthesis, **1**,
    479, 11
Streptomyces globisporus, C-1027, **7**, 578
Streptomyces griseus
    A-factor, **1**, 140, **8**, 380
        biosynthesis, **1**, 147
        diphenylcarbanilates, **8**, 380
        mode of action, **8**, 382
        structure, **8**, 379
    afs genes, **8**, 382
    ArpA protein, **8**, 382
    carotenoid biosynthesis, **2**, 336
    crt genes, **2**, 336
    griseusin biosynthesis, **1**, 479
    mutants, **2**, 336, **8**, 380
    physiologically active compounds, **8**, 378
    pigment production, **1**, 763
    tetrahydrofolic acid, **1**, 612
    ultraviolet irradiation, **5**, 375, 389
Streptomyces halstedii
    sch genes, **1**, 480
    spore pigments, **1**, 480
Streptomyces hygroscopicus
    bialaphos, **1**, 866
    halichomycin, **8**, 603
    phosphoeno*l*pyruvate phosphomutase, **1**, 869
    polyketide synthase, sequencing, **1**, 508
    rapamycin, **1**, 519
Streptomyces laurentii, thiostrepton biosynthesis, **1**, 852
Streptomyces lipmanii
    cefD gene encoding, **4**, 171
    pcb genes, transcription, **4**, 179
Streptomyces lividans, studies, **8**, 379

Streptomyces spp. LL-B7, (+)-epicubenol, **2**, 189
Streptomyces nogalater, nogalamycin biosynthesis, **1**, 482
Streptomyces olivaceus, elloramycin biosynthesis, **1**, 480
Streptomyces peuceticus, daunomycin biosynthesis, **1**, 481
Streptomyces refuineus, anthramycin, **1**, 566
Streptomyces rimosus
    oxytetracycline biosynthesis, **1**, 11
    PD116740 biosynthesis, **1**, 483
    tetracycline biosynthesis, **1**, 482
Streptomyces roseofulvus, frenolicin biosynthesis, **1**, 478, 11
Streptomyces scabies, triacylglycerol lipases, **5**, 133
Streptomyces setonii, carotenoid biosynthesis, regulatory
    mechanisms, **2**, 346
Streptomyces sparsogenes, sparsomycin biosynthesis, **1**, 845
Streptomyces tanashiensis, kalafungin biosynthesis, **1**, 478
Streptomyces toyoycaensis, gabaculine biosynthesis, **1**, 616
Streptomyces tsukabaensis, FK506, **1**, 520
Streptomyces UC5319
    isopentenyl diphosphate biosynthesis, **2**, 373
    pentalenene synthase genes, isolation, **2**, 210
    pentalenolactones, **2**, 51, 373, 377
Streptomyces venezuelae
    jadomycin biosynthesis, **1**, 482
    polyketide synthase, sequencing, **1**, 508
Streptomyces violaceoruber, granaticin biosynthesis, **1**, 478
Streptomyces virginiae
    autoregulators, **8**, 384
    virginiae butanolide receptor proteins, **8**, 387
    virginiae butanolides, **8**, 384
    virginiamycin, **1**, 140
Streptomyces viridochromogenes
    acn genes, **1**, 872
    autoregulators, **8**, 391
    factor-1, **1**, 140
Streptomyces viridochromogenes Tü57, avilamycin, **1**, 414
Streptomyces wedmorensis, fosfomycin, **1**, 874
Streptomyces WP4669, tetrangulol biosynthesis, **1**, 483
streptomycetes
    autoregulators
        future research, **8**, 392
        structure, **8**, 391
    immunosuppressant activity, **1**, 75
    polyketide biosynthesis, **1**, 10, 410
    salinamides, **8**, 593
streptomycin
    applications, antibiotics, **7**, 433
    biosynthesis, **3**, 6
        genetics, **3**, 353
        regulatory mechanisms, **8**, 383
    discovery, **4**, 200
    3,5-epimerases, **3**, 350
    nonintercalation, **7**, 433
streptomycin sugars, biosynthesis, genetics, **3**, 342
streptonigrin, **7**, 528, 536
    applications, antibiotics, **7**, 528
L-streptose
    occurrence, **3**, 312, 321
    precursors, **3**, 353
Streptoverticillium spp., cinnamycin lantibiotics
    biosynthesis, **4**, 280
Streptoverticillium verticillus, mannostatin, **3**, 156
streptozocin, DNA damage induction, **7**, 520
stress
    effects
        on ethylene biosynthesis, **8**, 96
        on jasmonate accumulation, **1**, 124
        on jasmonic acid biosynthesis, **8**, 117
    isoflavonoid biosynthesis, **1**, 774
str genes, in streptomycin sugar biosynthesis, **3**, 342

striatoxin (StTX)
    as cardiotonic agent, **8**, 478
    occurrence, **8**, 478
strictosamide, as starting material. for camptothecin, **4**, 117
strictosidine
    applications, for biomimetic synthesis, **4**, 125
    biochemistry, **4**, **109–138**
    biomimetic transformations, **4**, 125
    biosynthesis, **4**, 46
        cell-free, **4**, 113
        preparative, **4**, 125
    chemical synthesis, **4**, 127
    classification, **4**, 109
    functions, **4**, 109
        biosynthetic, **4**, 117
    occurrence, **4**, 110, 118
        in differentiated plants, **4**, 113
    roles, in monoterpenoid indole alkaloid biosynthesis,
        4, 117, 134
    significance, **4**, 117
        ecological, **4**, 118
    structure, **4**, 116
strictosidine, 5-carboxy-, indole alkaloid biosynthesis
    studies, **4**, 118
strictosidine, 9-hydroxy-, biosynthesis, **4**, 121
strictosidine glucosidase, localization, **4**, 124
strictosidine lactam, identification, **4**, 116
strictosidine synthase
    activity, **4**, 125
        distribution, **4**, 119
    in alkaloid biosynthesis, **4**, 134
    antibodies, **4**, 120
    cDNA, **4**, 134
    expression, heterologous, **4**, 130
    from, *Rauwolfia serpentina* cultures, **4**, 128
    future research, **4**, 124
    genetic analyses, **4**, 130
    identification, **4**, 116
    immobilization, **4**, 126
    isoforms, **4**, 120
    isolation, **4**, 128
    localization, **4**, 124
    nomenclature, **4**, 118
    purification, **4**, 118
        of isoforms, **4**, 123
    regulatory mechanisms, **4**, 135
    substrate specificity, **4**, 121
strictosidine synthase gene
    chemotaxonomic issues, **4**, 134
    cloning, **4**, 130
3-α(*S*)-strictosidine tryptamine-lyase *see* strictosidine
    synthase
Striga asiatica, seed germination, **8**, 175
strigol, characterization, **8**, 175
Strongylocentrotus nudus, feeding deterrents, **8**, 459
strophanthidin glycosides, as oviposition deterrents, **8**, 156
Strophanthus spp., cardenolides, **8**, 361
Str proteins, StrR, occurrence, **8**, 383
structural biology
    developments, **7**, 644
    scope, **7**, 6
structure–activity relationships
    ecdysteroids, **8**, 280, 292
    glycosidase inhibitors, **3**, 138
    neem triterpenoids, **8**, 332
    okadaic acid, **8**, 491
    ritterazines, **8**, 533
structure–function relationships, in bioluminescence, **8**, 447
Struthiopteris amabilis, lignans, **1**, 647
Struthiopteris niponica, lignans, **1**, 647

strychnine
  antifeedant activity, **8**, 342
  biosynthesis, **4**, 49
  studies, **4**, 110
Strychnos spp., insect toxicity, **8**, 342
strychnos alkaloids
  biosynthesis, **4**, 49
  occurrence, **4**, 49
  reviews, **4**, 49
Strychnos nux-vomica, loganin, **8**, 307
Stryphnodendron adstringens, prorobinetinidins, **3**, 775
STS *see* stilbene synthase (STS)
StTX *see* striatoxin (StTX)
STX *see* saxitoxins (STX)
stylocheilamide
  occurrence, **8**, 606
  structure revision, **8**, 606
Stylocheilus longicauda, stylocheilamide, **8**, 606
Stylotella spp.
  fungus in
    demethyl nectriapyrone A, **8**, 600
    nectriapyrone B, **8**, 600
styrylpyrones
  biosynthesis, **3**, 624
  occurrence, **1**, 761
  triketide intermediates, **1**, 761
styrylpyrone synthase (SPS)
  condensation, **1**, 761
  evolution, **1**, 762
su 1 gene, products, **3**, 468
suberate, α-keto-, biosynthesis, **1**, 834
suberins, biosynthesis, **3**, 9
suberosin, demethyl-, cyclization, **1**, 628, 630
substitution, mechanisms, **5**, 6
substrate analogues, binding characteristics, **2**, 126
substrate homologues
  reactions
    with geranyl*trans*transferase, **2**, 76
    with isopentenyl diphosphate isomerases, **2**, 71
substrates
  association, with ribozymes, **7**, 45
  binding, two-step model, **6**, 162
  folded, topological model, **2**, 126
  gramicidin S synthetase-activated, **4**, 323, 327
  as 'radical clocks', **5**, 219
  specificity, determination, **5**, 6
  transpeptidation, **4**, 325
subterranean clover *see Trifolium subterraneum*
subtilin
  antibacterial activity, **4**, 279
  applications, **4**, 300
  biosynthesis, **4**, 202
  expression system, **4**, 299
  gene clusters, localization, **4**, 286
  gene fusion, **4**, 288
  producer strains, **4**, 297
  spore germination inhibition, **4**, 281
subtilisin
  biosynthesis, **4**, 202
  catalytic efficiency, **5**, 437
  oxyanion holes, **5**, 126
  substitution, **4**, 357
Subulitermes spp., cadinol, **8**, 228
succinate, in amphidinolide J biosynthesis, **8**, 632
succinates, chiral, in coproporphyrinogen oxidase studies, **4**, 96
succinic acid(s), methyl-
  glyoxylic acid cycle inhibition, **4**, 255
  structure, **1**, 679
succinoglycan, biosynthesis, **3**, 288
succinsemialdehyde
  from, 2-oxoglutarate, **1**, 614
  thiamine diphosphate adduct, **1**, 614

O-succinylbenzoate synthases
  catalysis, **1**, 617
  purification, **1**, 614
O-succinylbenzoyl-CoA 1,4-dihydroxy-2-naphthoate-
    lyase (cyclizing) *see* naphthoate synthase(s)
succinyl-CoA
  conversion, **1**, 834
  reactions, with glycine, **4**, 65
succinyl-CoA:glycine *C*-succinyltransferase
    (decarboxylating) *see* 5-aminolevulinate
    synthase
N-succinyl-L,L-diaminopimelic acid aminotransferase,
    inhibition, **3**, 277
succinyl linkers, in oligonucleotide synthesis, **7**, 142
sucrose
  biosynthesis, **3**, 443
  effects, on gene expression, **3**, 608
  as starting material, for glucans, **3**, 444
  seed importation, **3**, 463
sucrose-glucan glucosyltransferase *see* amylosucrase
sucrose:1,4-α-D-glucan 4-α-D-glucosyltransferase *see*
    amylosucrase
sugar-cane *see Saccharum officinarum*
sugar-cane borer *see Eldana saccharina*
sugar cane weevil *see Metamasius hemipterus*
sugar-conjugation, of phytohormones, **1**, 129
sugar maple *see Acer saccharum*
sugar nucleotides, glycosyl transfer, **3**, 444
sugar oxyradicals, formation, **7**, 583
sugar peroxyradicals
  DNA damage, **7**, 582
  formation, **7**, 583
sugar puckers
  in A-form DNA structure, **7**, 76
  in B-form DNA structure, **7**, 76
  in RNA structures, **6**, 9
  use of term, **7**, 56
  in Z-form DNA structure, **7**, 77
sugar radicals, **7**, 582
sugars
  conformation, **7**, 64, 67
  coupling constants, **7**, 68
  proton distances, **7**, 68
  pseudorotation angles, **7**, 68
sugars, *N*-acetylamino-, in *Serratia marcescens*, **3**, 190
sugars, acidic diamino-, in *Pseudomonas aeruginosa*, **3**,
    193
sugars, acidic monoamino-, in *Pseudomonas aeruginosa*,
    3, 193
sugars, amino-, in *Pseudomonas aeruginosa*, **3**, 193
sugars, O-specific, precursors, biosynthesis, **3**, 206
sugary 1 mutation, occurrence, **3**, 468
sugiresinol, hydroxy-, structure, **1**, 640
Suidasia medanensis, (*E,E*)-farnesal, **8**, 227
sulcatol
  occurrence, **8**, 3, 14, 232
  structure, **8**, 233
sulfamethoxazole, applications, in bacterial treatments, **5**,
    349
sulfanilamide, applications, in bacterial treatments, **5**, 349
sulfasalazine, acetyl-CoA:1-alkylglycerophosphocholine
    acetyltransferase inhibition, **1**, 293
sulfate, accumulation, in ascidians, **8**, 524
sulfate, dimethyl (DMS)
  applications
    DNA structural probes, **7**, 95
    RNA structural probes, **6**, 64, 67, 68
sulfate, *N*-methyl-(*S*)-4-([1′-²H]neryloxy)pyridinium
    methyl, in monoterpene studies, **2**, 123
sulfate adenylyltransferase, activity, **1**, 331
sulfatides, synthesis, **3**, 113
sulfazecin, biosynthesis, **4**, 187
sulfhydryl, **3**, 25

residues, **3**, 453
sulfide, geranyl methyl, occurrence, **8**, 222
sulfide, 3-methyl-3-butenyl methyl, occurrence, **8**, 220
sulfides, antisense oligonucleotide linkages, **7**, 304
sulfoacetaldehyde, biosynthesis, **1**, 833
sulfobactin A, occurrence, **8**, 598
sulfogucuronyl glycolipids, expression, **3**, 123
Sulfolobus spp., caldariellaquinone biosynthesis, **1**, 856
Sulfolobus acidocaldarius
    caldariellaquinone biosynthesis, **1**, 856
    geranylgeranyl diphosphate synthase, gene cloning, **2**, 87
    geranylgeranyl diphosphate synthases, random mutation, **2**, 88
Sulfolobus solfataricus, hydroxymethylglutaryl-CoA reductases, **2**, 27
sulfonamide, acyl-, prostaglandin-endoperoxide synthase inhibition, **5**, 254
sulfonamides
    antisense oligonucleotide linkages, **7**, 304
    prostaglandin-endoperoxide synthase inhibition, **5**, 252
sulfonate, *p*-methoxy-, nucleophilic rate constants, **5**, 332
sulfonates, antisense oligonucleotide linkages, **7**, 304
sulfones, antisense oligonucleotide linkages, **7**, 304
sulfonium ions, analogues, **5**, 328
sulfonyl, *o*-nitrophenyl-, as protecting groups, **7**, 123
sulfonyl chloride, 2,4,6-triisopropylbenzene (TPS-CL), in oligonucleotide synthesis, **7**, 107
sulfonyl fluoride, *p*-methylphenyl- (PMSF)
    binding, **1**, 516
    as GPI anchor biosynthesis inhibitor, **3**, 303
sulfopyruvate, biosynthesis, **1**, 833
3-*O*-sulfotransferase, isozymes, sulfation, **3**, 172
sulfotransferases
    roles
        in *O*-glycan sulfation, **3**, 80
        in proteoglycan biosynthesis, **3**, 162
7-*O*-sulfotransferases, purification, **1**, 740
sulfur
    and glycogen accumulation, **3**, 443
    natural products containing, biosynthesis, **1**, 20, **825–863**
sulfur atoms, in esperamicin A$_1$, biosynthetic origin, **1**, 565
sulfurylase *see* sulfate adenylyltransferase
sul genes, occurrence, **3**, 374
sulochrin, biosynthesis, **1**, 435
sulochrin oxidase, catalysis, **1**, 437
sulphurein, roles, in ultraviolet patterning, **8**, 160
sumatrol, isolation, **8**, 341
sumatrolic acid, as starting material, for α-toxicarol, **1**, 812
sunflowers *see Helianthus annuus*
sunY ribozyme, structural probing, **6**, 73
Supella longipalpa, supellapyrone, **8**, 241
supellapyrone, occurrence, **8**, 241
superoxide
    cellular protection from, **7**, 541
    DNA damage due to, **7**, 540
    hydroxyl radical formation from, **7**, 540
    production, **7**, 378
superoxide free radical ions, production, during heart infarction, **5**, 80
superstolide A, occurrence, **1**, 371
supramolecular aggregates, structure, **3**, 198
surangin B, occurrence, **8**, 337
SURF, techniques, **7**, 636
surfactant peptides, **8**, 473
surfactants, secretion, **8**, 200
surfactin
    amide bonds, **4**, 226
    applications, **4**, 199
    biosynthesis, **4**, 202, 208, 321

ester bonds, **4**, 226
    secretion, **4**, 198
surfactin synthetase, mutagenesis, site-directed, **4**, 342
surugatoxin, occurrence, **8**, 515
suspensolide, occurrence, **8**, 236
SW15 peptide, binding, **7**, 484
Swainsona spp., swainsonine, **3**, 140
swainsonine
    antimetastatic activity, **3**, 142
    biological activity, **3**, 140, 141
    and Class 1 α1,2-mannosidases, **3**, 24
    and Class 2 α-mannosidases, **3**, 25
    cytosolic α-mannosidase inhibition, **3**, 27
    discovery, **3**, 130
    inhibitory activity, **3**, 138
    insecticidal activity, **3**, 141
    lysosomal α-mannosidase inhibition, **3**, 28
    α-mannosidase II inhibition, **3**, 27
    α-mannosidase inhibition, **3**, 24, 153, 155
        broad-specificity, **3**, 28
    occurrence, **3**, 134
    structure, **3**, 132
    structure–activity relationships, **3**, 138
    toxicity, **3**, 140
swallowtail butterflies
    (−)-germacrene A, **8**, 227
    see also Papilio memnon
Swedish Forest Products Laboratory (STFI), cellulose studies, **3**, 564
sweet potatoes *see Ipomoea batatas*
sweet proteins, occurrence, **8**, 166
swift moth *see Hepialus hecta*
swinholide A
    occurrence, **8**, 579
    x-ray crystal structure, **8**, 579
sycamore *see Acer pseudoplatanus*
sycamore maple, buds, dormancy, **8**, 72
Symbiobacterium thermophilium, tyrosine phenol-lyase, **3**, 405
Symbiodinium spp.
    16-deoxysarcophine, **8**, 617
    symbioramide, **8**, 617
    zooxanthellatoxins, **8**, 614
symbionts, Gram-negative bacteria as, **8**, 392
symbioramide
    occurrence, **8**, 617
    as sarcoplasmic reticulum Ca^{2+}-ATPase activator, **8**, 617
    structure, **8**, 617
symbiosis
    between marine invertebrates and microalgae, **8**, 426
    biochemistry, **8**, 173
    host factor, **8**, 428
    legume–*Rhizobium*, **8**, 173
    and nitrogen fixation, **8**, 428
    types of, **8**, 426
symbiotic plasmids, occurrence, **8**, 400
Symplectoteuthis oualaniensis, bioluminescence studies, **8**, 454
syndecans, localization, **3**, 164
Synechococcus spp.
    branching enzymes, **3**, 480
    carotenoid biosynthesis, **2**, 337
    crt genes, **2**, 337
    glutamate 1-semialdehyde aminotransferase, **4**, 70
Synechococcus PCC7002, desaturases, **1**, 45
Synechococcus PCC7942, desaturases, **1**, 41
Synechocystis spp.
    carotenoid biosynthesis, **2**, 337
    glucose-1-phosphate adenylyltransferase, **3**, 450
    hopene cyclase, gene cloning, **2**, 313
    nakienone A, **8**, 609
Synechocystis PCC6714, isoprenoid biosynthesis, mevalonate-independent pathway, **2**, 58

Synechocystis PCC6803
  desaturases, **1**, 40, 45
  fatty acids, desaturation, **1**, 38
synomones
  definition, **8**, 2
  roles, **8**, 198
synthases, native, N-terminal sequencing problems, **2**, 125
synthetic urandomization of randomized fragments
      (SURF) *see* SURF
syringaldazine, applications, histochemical staining
      reagents, **3**, 712
syringaldehyde, occurrence, **3**, 696
(−)-syringaresinol *see* (−)-lirioresinol B
(+)-syringaresinol di-*O*-β-D-glucopyranoside,
      phosphodiesterase inhibitory activity, **1**, 704
(+)-syringaresinol di-*O*-β-D-glucoside, cardiovascular
      activity, **1**, 705
syringaresinol(s)
  biosynthesis, **1**, 673, **3**, 717
  enantiomers, **1**, 651
  occurrence, **1**, 673
  optical rotation, **1**, 649

syringic acid, occurrence, **3**, 696
syringin
  biosynthesis, **3**, 676
  hydrolysis, **3**, 686
  occurrence, **3**, 677
(*E*)-syringin, as substrate, **3**, 686
syringolide, occurrence, **1**, 147
syringotoxin, occurrence, **4**, 203
syringyl
  residues, **3**, 692
  use of term, **3**, 620
Systematic Evolution of Ligands by Exponential
      Enrichment (SELEX) *see* SELEX
systemic acquired resistance (SAR), in plants, **1**, 133
systemic lupus erythematosus (SLE), treatment, **7**, 168
systemin
  activity, **8**, 150
  ethylene induction, **1**, 133
  in jasmonic acid studies, **1**, 133
  occurrence, **1**, 132
  roles, in octadecanoid pathway, **1**, 134

T

T3HN reductase *see* 1,3,8-trihydroxynaphthalene
    reductase
T4HN reductase *see* 1,3,6,8-tetrahydroxynaphthalene
    reductase
T4HN synthase *see* 1,3,6,8-tetrahydroxynaphthalene
    synthase
T4L *see* T4 lysozyme (T4L)
T4 lysozyme (T4L), as inverter, **5**, 298
Tabernaemontana divaricata, strictosidine synthase, **4**, 124
tabersonine, 11-hydroxy-, biosynthesis, **4**, 121
tabersonine, 11-methoxy-, biosynthesis, **4**, 121
taboxinine-β-lactam, as glutamine synthetase inhibitor, **2**,
    257
tafricanin A, antifeedant activity, **8**, 316
tafricanin B, antifeedant activity, **8**, 316
tafricanins, occurrence, **8**, 316
tagatose-1,6-diphosphate aldolase
    activity, **3**, 430
    biochemistry, **3**, 430
    isolation, **3**, 431
    occurrence, **3**, 430
    substrate specificity, **3**, 431
D-tagatose-6-phosphate, biosynthesis, **3**, 430
Tagetes patula, flavonol hydroxylation, **1**, 733
Taiwan cobra *see Naja naja atra*
taiwanin E, antiinflammatory activity, **1**, 704
tajixanthone, biosynthesis, **1**, 434
Takakiophyta, and lignin evolution, **3**, 624
TAL *see* triacetic acid lactone (TAL); tyrosine ammonia-
    lyase
tallysomycin, applications, antibiotics, **7**, 539
D-talomethylose, occurrence, **3**, 312, 313
L-talomethylose, occurrence, **3**, 312, 313
D-talooctonate, 2,6-anhydro-3-deoxy-2β-
        phosphonylmethyl-8-phosphate-D-glycero-,
        properties, **3**, 389
tamynine, isolation, **4**, 40
Tanacetum sibiricum, antifeedants, **8**, 338
Tanacetum vulgare
    ($-$)-(1*S*,4*S*)-bornyl diphosphate synthases, **2**, 128
    ($+$)-sabinene-3-hydroxylases, **2**, 145
tannase
    applications, industrial, **3**, 820
    catalysis, **3**, 819
    depsidase activity, **3**, 819
    ecological significance, **3**, 821
    esterase activity, **3**, 819
    fungal, **3**, 813
        properties, **3**, 820
    in plants, **3**, 820
    roles, **3**, 821
    substrate specificity, **3**, 820
tannic acid, DNA damage, **7**, 536
tannin acylhydrolase *see* tannase
tanning, capacity, **3**, 802
tannins
    and aphid resistance, **8**, 142
    applications, **3**, 799
    biosynthesis, **3**, 2, 10
    complex, use of term, **3**, 783
    dietary factors, **3**, 791
    and fruit astringency, **8**, 167
    and fruit rejection, **8**, 167
    hydrolyzable
        biogenetic relationships, **3**, 802

    biosynthesis, **3**, 10, **799–826**
    characterization, **3**, 800
    classification, **3**, 800
    enzymatic degradation, **3**, 819
    structure, **3**, 800
    plants, as feeding barriers, **8**, 142
    see also camelliatannins; ellagitannins; gallotannin(s);
        pavetannins; phlobatannins
tannins, condensed *see* proanthocyanidins
tannin–tannase system, chemical defense, in plants, **3**, 821
tantazole B, structure, **8**, 610
T antigen, in mucins, **3**, 71
Tapes japonicus, feeding attractants and stimulants, **8**, 417
Taphrorychus bicolor, bicolorin, **8**, 234
Tapinoma spp., pheromones, **8**, 246
Taq DNA polymerase(s)
    applications, in polymerase chain reaction, **7**, 658
    mutagenesis, **7**, 621
Taraktogenos kurzii, fatty acids, **1**, 68
L-($+$)-tartrate, histidine phosphatase inhibition, **5**, 154
tartronate semialdehyde, reactions, with pyruvate, **3**, 402
tartronate semialdehyde carboxylase *see* tartronate-
    semialdehyde synthase
tartronate-semialdehyde synthase, catalysis, **1**, 599
TASV *see* tomato apical stunt viroid (TASV)
TATA-binding protein (TBP)
    mutation, **4**, 368
    roles, **4**, 364
    structural studies, **7**, 465
TATA box
    class III genes, **4**, 366
    localization, **4**, 362
    proteoglycans, **3**, 167
    Sec tRNA$^{[Ser]Sec}$, **4**, 364
tau *see* transcription factor IIIC (TFIIIC)
tautomerases, encoding, **3**, 351
taxa-4,11-diene, biosynthesis, **2**, 220
taxadiene synthases
    functions, **2**, 217
    isolation, **2**, 209
taxanes
    biosynthesis, **2**, 62
    occurrence, **2**, 220
Taxillus kaempferi, (2*R*,3*S*)-2,3-*cis*-dihydroquercetin 3-
    O-β-D-glucopyranoside, **3**, 750
(*R*)-taxiphyllin, structure, **1**, 887
taxol
    applications, antineoplastic agents, **2**, 220
    studies, **2**, 220
    terpenoid pharmaceutical, **2**, 212
Taxus brevifolia, taxol, **2**, 220
Taxus chinensis, taxane biosynthesis, **2**, 62
taxuyunnanine C, biosynthesis, **2**, 222
Tayassu tajacu, dorsal gland secretions, **8**, 230
Tay–Sachs disease, GalT-3 levels, **3**, 111
TBDMS *see* silyl groups, 2′-*t*-butyldimethyl- (TBDMS)
TBP *see* TATA-binding protein (TBP)
TBP eukaryotic transcription factor, studies, **7**, 268
TC cyclobutane photodimers, hydrolysis, **5**, 396
T-cell receptors *see* T-lymphocyte receptors
T-cells *see* T-lymphocytes
TCHQ *see* hydroquinone, tetrachlorohydro- (TCHQ)
tcm genes
    biochemical analysis, **1**, 490
    cloning, **1**, 479

combinatorial analysis, **1**, 487
deletion analysis, **1**, 486
encoding, **1**, 479
sequencing, **1**, 479
tcmH, homologues, **1**, 481
T-DNA
occurrence, **1**, 41
transfers, **8**, 399
TDP *see* thiamine diphosphate (TDP)
tea leaves
C_6-aldehyde biosynthesis, **1**, 89
blending, **1**, 87
green odor, **1**, 84
seasonal variations, **1**, 107
hydroperoxide lyase activity, **1**, 95
lipoxygenase activity, **1**, 94
see also black tea; *Camellia japonica*; *Thea sinensis*
teasterone, synthesis, **8**, 105
tea tortrix moths *see Adoxophyes* spp.
Tectona grandis
deoxylapachol, **8**, 339
1,4-dihydroxy-2-methylnaphthoquinone, **8**, 339
tectoquinone, **8**, 339
tectoquinone, occurrence, **8**, 339
Tedania charcoti, aqueous ethanol, **8**, 470
Tedania ignis, *Micrococcus* spp. in, **8**, 587
teichoic acids
in bacterial cell walls, **3**, 242
in peptidoglycan layer, **3**, 243
teicoplanin
binding, **3**, 283
effects, on Gram-positive bacteria, **3**, 281
teleocidins, occurrence, **8**, 603
Teleostei, pheromonal attractants, **8**, 426
Tellima grandiflora, ellagic acid biosynthesis, **3**, 817
tellimagrandin I, chemical synthesis, **3**, 817
tellimagrandin II, biosynthesis, **3**, 800
tellimagrandin II, permethyl, chemical synthesis, **3**, 817
tellurium, role in squalene epoxidase inhibition, **2**, 276
telomerase, reviews, **7**, 8
telomeres, **7**, 469
development, **7**, 346
T_4 endonuclease V, catalysis, **5**, 393
tendrils
coiling
bioassays, **1**, 128
induction, **1**, 128
Tenebrio spp. assay, development, **8**, 266
Tenebrio molitor
activity against, **8**, 303
diuretic hormone, **8**, 300
in echinolone studies, **8**, 277
(*R*)-4-methyl-1-nonanol, **8**, 241
Tenebrionidae, monoterpenes, **8**, 222
teniposide
applications, pharmaceutical, **1**, 701
as DNA topoisomerase II inhibitor, **7**, 603, 609
tension wood, formation, **3**, 693, 695
tent caterpillars *see Malacosoma* spp.
tenulin, antifeedant activity, **8**, 308
teosinte seeds, soluble starch synthases, **3**, 455
Tephrosia spp., rotenone, **8**, 340
Tephrosia vogelii
deguelin, **1**, 812
iron proteins, **1**, 804
tephrosin, isolation, **8**, 341
teracacidin, occurrence, **3**, 776
(2*R*,3*R*)-2,3-*cis*-3,4-*cis*-teracacidin, carbocation
generation, **3**, 755
terbinafine
applications, antifungal agents, **2**, 247
binding, **2**, 277
as squalene epoxidase inhibitor, **2**, 270

studies, **2**, 277
terephthalate, metabolism, **3**, 385
termilignan
antifungal activity, **1**, 691
structure, **1**, 672
Terminalia bellerica
termilignan, **1**, 672, 691
thannilignan, **1**, 672, 691
terminal mismatches, definition, **6**, 31
terminal uridylyl transferase *see* RNA uridylyltransferase
termination codons, UGA, **4**, 357
termites
α-bisabolene, **8**, 228
δ-cadinene, **8**, 228
diterpenes, **8**, 230
(*E*,*E*)-farnesal, **8**, 227
geranyllinalool, **8**, 229
(−)-germacrene A, **8**, 227
3-ketoaldehydes, **8**, 204
monoterpenes, **8**, 222
sex pheromones, **8**, 214
trail pheromones, **8**, 214
vinyl ketones, **8**, 204
see also Amitermes spp.; *Ancistrotermes* spp.;
Cubitermes umbratus; *Nasutitermes* spp.;
Pseudacanthotermes spiniger; *Reticulitermes* spp.;
Subulitermes spp.; *Trinervitermes bettonianus*
ternary complex
drug–DNA-enzyme, **7**, 594
formation, **7**, 603
terpenes
biosynthesis, **3**, 10, **8**, 305
via hydride shifts, **2**, 98
via Wagner–Meerwein rearrangement, **2**, 98
from, 2,3-oxidosqualene, **2**, 6
insecticidal activity, **8**, 305
isolation, early studies, **2**, 3
rearrangement, **8**, 231
terpene synthase deficient mutants, disease interactions
virulence reduction, **2**, 212
terpene synthase genes
cloning, **2**, **201–215**
expression, **2**, **201–215**
heterologous, **2**, 202, 210
future research, **2**, 212
isolation, **2**, 202, 207
plant, identification problems, **2**, 211
terpene synthase(s)
applications, **2**, 212
commercial, **2**, 213
heterologous expression in plants, **2**, 211
historical background, **2**, 201
microbial, **2**, 210
kinetic parameters, **2**, 210
plants, **2**, 211
expression, **2**, 211
purification, **2**, 209
purification, culture growth conditions, **2**, 207
terpenoid cyclases
anomalous substrates for, **2**, 160
aspartate in, **2**, 162
terpenoid cyclization, intermediates for, **2**, 160
terpenoid function, sense suppression techniques, **2**, 212
terpenoids
as allelopathic agents, **8**, 169
antifeedant activity, herbivores, **8**, 142
antimicrobial properties, **8**, 181
applications, **2**, 212
flavorings, **2**, 212
fragrances, **2**, 212
pharmaceuticals, **2**, 212
biosynthesis, **2**, 98
occurrence, **2**, 201

historical background, **2**, 98
homodimers, **1**, 377
leaf, as allelopathic agents, **8**, 171
metabolism, **2**, 98
occurrence, **8**, 235
  plants, **2**, 209
  in parasites, **8**, 175
production traits, stability, **2**, 206
terpenoid synthases, mechanism-based inhibitors,
    development, **2**, 180
terpentecins, **2**, 59
α-terpinene
  conversion, to ascaridole, **2**, 146
  structure, **2**, 103
γ-terpinene, structure, **2**, 103
α-terpinene synthases, studies, **2**, 136
γ-terpinene synthases
  purification, **2**, 125
  studies, **2**, 136
terpinen-4-ol, biosynthesis, **2**, 103
terpinen-4-yl cations, biosynthesis, **2**, 136
terpineol, ovicidal activity, **8**, 306
α-terpineol
  biosynthesis, **2**, 122
  occurrence, **8**, 224
  structure, **2**, 103
terpinolene
  biosynthesis, **2**, 122
  structure, **2**, 103
terramycin, discovery, **4**, 200
α-terrecyclene, synthesis, **2**, 175
terrecyclic acid
  biosynthesis, **2**, 174
  ¹³C NMR spectra, **2**, 175
  occurrence, **2**, 174
terrecyclic acid, dihydro-
  ¹³C NMR spectra, **2**, 175
  ²H NMR spectra, **2**, 175
terreic acid, structure, **1**, 411
terrestrol *see* farnesol, (*S*)-2,3-dihydro-
tertiapin
  in honeybee venom, **8**, 355
  structure, **8**, 355
tessulatoxin (TsTX), occurrence, **8**, 479
testis, ST3Gal IV expression, **3**, 49
testosterone
  occurrence, **8**, 361
  in pheromones, **8**, 230
Tethys fimbria
  autotomy, **8**, 464
  lactones, **1**, 245
  prostaglandin E₂, **1**, 245
  prostaglandin E₃, **1**, 245
tetraacetic acid lactones, occurrence, **1**, 3
tetraacetic anhydride, ethylene diamine-, reactions, with
    aminoalkylated oligoribonucleotides, **7**, 201
4-17-tetrabenzo[*a,c,g,i*]fluorenylmethyl, **7**, 127
tetra-*n*-butylammonium fluoride (TBAF), in
    oligonucleotide synthesis, **7**, 114
tetracenomycins
  biochemical analysis, **1**, 490
  biosynthesis, **1**, 479
  cloning, **1**, 11
  coding, **1**, 432
  deletion analysis, **1**, 486
tetrachloroethene dehalogenase, occurrence, **5**, 420
tetrachlorohydroquinone dehalogenase
  catalysis, **5**, 414, 416
  mechanisms, **5**, 415
  occurrence, **5**, 414
  oxidative damage, **5**, 415
  thiol disulfide exchange, **5**, 416
tetracosanolide, occurrence, **8**, 218

(*Z*)-9-tetracosenoate, octadecyl *see* nauphoetin
tetracycline
  applications, antibiotics, **1**, 2
  biosynthesis, **4**, 196
  discovery, **4**, 200
  isolation, **4**, 200
tetracyclines
  biosynthesis, **1**, 482
  photochemical DNA damage, **7**, 544
(9*E*,11*E*)-9,11-tetradecadienoic acid, as intermediate, **8**,
    205
(*E,Z*)-3,5-tetradecadienoic acid, occurrence, **8**, 216
(*Z,Z*)-3,5-tetradecadienoic acid, occurrence, **8**, 216
(13*R*)-(5*Z*,8*Z*)-5,8-tetradecadien-13-olide, occurrence, **8**,
    216
(13*S*)-(5*Z*,8*Z*)-5,8-tetradecadien-13-olide, occurrence, **8**,
    216
tetradecane, occurrence, **8**, 216
tetradecanoic acid, 3-oxo-, occurrence, **3**, 196
tetradecan-1-ol, 6,10,13-trimethyl-, occurrence, **8**, 241
tetradecan-4-olide, occurrence, **8**, 216
(*R,2E*)-2,4,5-tetradecatrienoate, methyl, occurrence, **8**,
    216
(*Z*)-5-tetradecenoate, methyl, occurrence, **8**, 216
(*Z*)-7-tetradecenoate, (*S*)-2-butyl, occurrence, **8**, 209
(9*Z*)-tetradecenoic acid, 1-methylethyl esters, occurrence,
    8, 216
11-tetradecenoic acid, chain-shortening, **8**, 205
Δ-7-tetradecenoic acid, lipopolysaccharide-antagonizing
    activity, **3**, 196
tetradecenoic acids
  biosynthesis, **8**, 205
  chain-shortening, **8**, 205
  occurrence, **8**, 216
9-tetradecenoic acids, as intermediates, **8**, 207
(*E*)-11-tetradecenoic acids, biosynthesis, **8**, 205
(*Z*)-11-tetradecenoic acids, biosynthesis, **8**, 205
(*Z*)-5-tetradecen-1-ol, occurrence, **8**, 219
(*R*)-5-tetradecen-4-olide, occurrence, **8**, 216
(*S*)-5-tetradecen-4-olide, occurrence, **8**, 216
(*Z*)-5-tetradecen-13-olide, occurrence, **8**, 216
3,5,7,9-tetradeoxy-L-*glycero*-D-*galacto*-nonulosonic acid,
    5-acetamidino-7-acetamido-8-*O*-acetyl-,
    occurrence, **3**, 192
Tetragonisca angustula, alarm detection, **8**, 232
tetrahedral intermediates
  anionic, generation, **5**, 6
  generation, **5**, 16
  neutral, pK_a, **5**, 8
  stabilization, **5**, 18
tetrahydroprotoberberine synthase *see* reticuline oxidase
tetrahydroxynaphthalene reductase, catalysis, **1**, 427
1,3,6,8-tetrahydroxynaphthalene reductase, encoding, **1**,
    428
1,3,6,8-tetrahydroxynaphthalene synthase, coding, **1**, 414
tetrahymanol
  bacterial, **2**, 308
  occurrence, **2**, 308
tetrahymanol cyclases, **2**, 307
  biochemistry, **2**, 312
  inactivators, **2**, 312
  inhibitors, **2**, 312
  poisons, **2**, 312
  purification, **2**, 312
  substrate specificity, **2**, 312
Tetrahymena spp.
  desaturases, **1**, 45
  Group I introns, **6**, 154
    domains, **6**, 151
    kinetics, **6**, 160
    rate constants, **6**, 150
    in RNA catalysis, **6**, 158
  ribozymes, **6**, 236, **7**, 277, 279, 616, 617

randomization, **6**, 125
  RNA cleavage, **6**, 257
  structure, **6**, 256
RNA studies, **6**, 13
rRNA, **6**, 110
tetrahymanol, **2**, 308
Tetrahymena pyriformis
  2-aminoethylphosphonic acid, **1**, 865, 868, 874
  platelet-activating factor, **1**, 286, 297
Tetrahymena thermophila
  desaturases, **1**, 45
  introns, **6**, 56
  pre-rRNA, **6**, 149, 254
tetraketides
  as intermediates, **1**, 750
  occurrence, **1**, 410
  structure, **1**, 411
tetraketide synthases, catalysis, **1**, 411
tetralin, synthesis, **7**, 557
tetraloops, in rRNA, **6**, 192
tetramic acid, acyl-, structure, **1**, 370
tetraneurin A, antifeedant activity, **8**, 308
tetrangulol, biosynthesis, **1**, 483
Tetranychus urticae
  citronellol, **8**, 222
  nerolidol, **8**, 227
  plant–herbivore–predator interactions, **8**, 151
tetrapeptides, NMR spectra, **5**, 332
tetraphylline, biosynthesis, **4**, 121
tetraplexes
  conformation, **7**, 469
  intercalation, **7**, 469
Tetraponera spp., tetraponerines, **8**, 358
tetraponerines, occurrence, **8**, 358
tetrapyrroles
  biosynthesis, **4**, 68, 72
    reviews, **4**, 103
  roles, **4**, 62
tetraterpenoids, structure, **2**, 323
tetrazole, in oligonucleotide synthesis, **6**, 82
tetrazole, nitrophenyl-, as coupling reaction activator, **7**, 138
tetrazole, thioethyl-, as coupling reaction activator, **7**, 138
1*H*-tetrazole, as coupling reaction activator, **7**, 138
1*H*-tetrazole, 5-trifluoromethyl-, as coupling reaction activator, **7**, 138
tetrazolides, diisopropyl-, in oligonucleotide synthesis, **7**, 133
tetrazomine
  applications
    antibiotics, **7**, 500
    antineoplastic agents, **7**, 500
  disproportionation of, **7**, 541
  DNA damage, **7**, 500
  occurrence, **7**, 499
  superoxide production by, **7**, 541
tetrocarcins, structure, **1**, 370
tetrodecamycin, occurrence, **1**, 370
Tetrodontophora bielanensis, pyridopyrazines, **8**, 361
tetrodotoxins (TTX)
  analogues, isolation, **8**, 481
  biosynthesis, **8**, 482
  competitive binding assays, **8**, 484, 488
  enzyme immunoassay, with monoclonal antibodies, **8**, 481
  identification
    by FABMS, **8**, 481
    by fluorometric HPLC, **8**, 481
  neurotoxicity, **8**, 480
  ^{1}H NMR spectra, **8**, 484
  photoaffinity labeling, **8**, 485
  site-directed mutagenesis, **8**, 485
  sodium channel binding, **8**, 483

  sodium channel blocking, **8**, 486
tetronic acid, acyl-, structure, **1**, 370
tetronothiodin, isolation, **1**, 370
Teucrium spp.
  antifeedant studies, **8**, 316
  clerodanes, **8**, 316
Teucrium africanum, tafricanins, **8**, 316
Teucrium flavum
  antifeedant activity studies, **8**, 319
  teuflavoside, **8**, 319
Teucrium marum, dolichodial, **8**, 226
Teucrium montanum, montanin B, **8**, 319
Teucrium polium, antifeedant activity, **8**, 316
teucvin, antifeedant activity, **8**, 318
teuflavoside
  as feeding stimulant, **8**, 319
  occurrence, **8**, 319
teumarin, antifeedant activity, **8**, 319
teumassilin, antifeedant activity, **8**, 319
teumassilin, 16,19-diacetyl-, antifeedant activity, **8**, 319
textile industry, cellulose applications, **3**, 533
TFIBA *see* 3-(indole-3-)butyric acid, *S*-4,4,4-trifluoro-(TFIBA)
TFIID *see* transcription factor IID (TFIID)
TFIIIA *see* transcription factor IIIA (TFIIIA)
TFIIIB *see* transcription factor IIIB (TFIIIB)
TFIIIC *see* transcription factor IIIC (TFIIIC)
TGA codon, in formate dehydrogenase H, **4**, 357
TGF-β_1 *see* transforming growth factor-β_1 (TGF-β_1)
TGN *see* trans Golgi network (TGN)
thamnosin, occurrence, **1**, 380
Thamnosma montana
  bergapten, **8**, 338
  psoralen, **8**, 338
  xanthotoxin, **8**, 338
thannilignan
  antifungal activity, **1**, 691
  structure, **1**, 672
Thaumatococcus daniellii, sweet proteins, **8**, 166
Thaumetopoea spp., (*Z*)-13-hexadecen-11-yn-1-yl acetate, **8**, 207
theaflavic acids, structure, **3**, 782
theaflavin(s)
  biosynthesis, **3**, 782
  occurrence, **3**, 782
  structure, **3**, 782
theaflavonin, biosynthesis, **3**, 782
theaflavonin, desgalloyl, biosynthesis, **3**, 782
thearubigins, occurrence, **3**, 782
theasinensins, isolation, **3**, 782
Thea sinensis see Camellia sinensis
Theobroma cacao
  oligomeric leucocyanidins, **3**, 757
  proanthocyanidins, **3**, 779
theobromine, occurrence, **8**, 147
theogallinin, biosynthesis, **3**, 782
theoneberine
  antimicrobial activity, **8**, 581
  cytotoxicity, **8**, 581
  occurrence, **8**, 581
theonegramide
  antifungal activity, **8**, 576
  occurrence, **8**, 576
Theonella spp.
  aurantosides, **8**, 580
  cyclic peptides, **8**, 567
  cyclotheonamides, **8**, 568
  keramamides, **8**, 572
  konbamide, **8**, 573
  metabolites, **8**, 567
  nazumamide A, **8**, 576
  onnamide A, **8**, 581
  orbiculamide A, **8**, 570

perthamide B, **8**, 577
proteinase inhibition, **8**, 568
theoneberine, **8**, 581
theonellamides, **8**, 575
theonezolides, **8**, 581
theopederins, **8**, 581
theonellamides
  Marfey analysis, **8**, 576
  occurrence, **8**, 575
  structure, **8**, 575
theonellapeptolides
  occurrence, **8**, 573
  structure, **8**, 573
theonellasterone, occurrence, **1**, 379
Theonella swinhoei
  bioactive cyclic peptides, from symbiotic
    cyanobacteria, **8**, 580
  bistheonellasterone, **1**, 379
  conicasterone, **1**, 379
  cyanobacteria, **8**, 428
  cyclotheonamides, **8**, 568
  genetics, **1**, 540
  motuporin, **8**, 576
  polytheonamides, **8**, 577
  swinholide A, **8**, 579
  theonegramide, **8**, 576
  theonellapeptolides, **8**, 573
  theonellasterone, **1**, 379
theonezolide A
  isolation, **8**, 581
  platelet shape change, **8**, 581
theonezolides
  cytotoxicity, **8**, 581
  occurrence, **8**, 581
  structure, **8**, 581
theopederins
  antitumor activity, **8**, 581
  applications, antitumor agents, **8**, 581
  cytotoxicity, **8**, 581
  occurrence, **8**, 581
Theorell, Axel Hugo Teodor (1903–82), peroxidase
  studies, **3**, 717
therapeutics, oligonucleotide-based, future research, **7**,
  335
Therioaphis maculata, (−)-germacrene A, **8**, 227
Thermomonospora fusca, endocellulase E2, **5**, 300
thermophiles, hydroxymethylglutaryl-CoA reductase
  encoding, **2**, 23
Thermus spp., carotene biosynthesis, **2**, 335
Thermus aquaticus, polymerases, **7**, 658
Thermus caldophilus, glycogen biosynthetic enzymes, **3**,
  445
Thermus flavus, 5S rRNA, **6**, 72
Thermus thermophilus
  carotenoid biosynthesis, **2**, 335
  crt genes, **2**, 335
  tRNA^{Phe}, **6**, 222
D-thevetose, occurrence, **3**, 312, 313
THF *see* folic acid, tetrahydro- (THF)
THF-OOH *see* furan, 2-hydroperoxytetrahydro- (THF-
  OOH)
thiacarbocyanine bromide, 4,5:4′,5′-dibenzo-3,3′-diethyl-
  9-methyl-, applications, DNA structure probes,
  7, 85
4-thia-L-lysine, as substrate, **5**, 213
4-thia-L-[3-^{2}H$_2$]lysine, EPR spectra, **5**, 213
4-thia-L-[3-^{13}C]lysine, EPR spectra, **5**, 213
4-thia-L-[5,6-^{2}H$_4$]lysine, substitution, **5**, 213
thiamine
  biosynthesis, **1**, 837
  from, 1-deoxy-D-xylulose, **2**, 376
thiamine diphosphate, 2-hydroxyethyl-, biosynthesis, **3**,
  370

thiamine diphosphate glucose
  glycogen synthase activity, **3**, 452
  pyrophosphorolysis, **3**, 478
thiamine diphosphate (TDP), **1**, 614
  in aldol reaction, **3**, 370
  catalysis, **2**, 376, **3**, 342
thiamine pyrophosphate (TPP) *see* thiamine diphosphate
  (TDP)
thiazines, dihydro-, biosynthesis, **4**, 164
thiazole, 2-(2′-methylbutyl)-4,5-dihydro-, occurrence, **8**,
  220
1,3-thiazole, 2-isobutyl-, occurrence, **8**, 220
thiazolidines
  ring-opening, **4**, 164
  structure, **4**, 240
thidiazuron, cytokinin oxidase inhibition, **8**, 71
thienamycin, *N*-formidoyl-, applications, **4**, 186
thienamycins
  biological activity, **3**, 285
  biosynthesis, **4**, 187
  occurrence, **4**, 186
thietane, 2,2-dimethyl-, occurrence, **8**, 220
thietane, 2,3-dimethyl-, occurrence, **8**, 220
thi genes
  thiC roles, **1**, 839
  thiE, roles, **1**, 839
  thiF, roles, **1**, 839
  thiG, roles, **1**, 839
  thiH, roles, **1**, 839
thioadenosine, 5′-methyl- (MTA), biosynthesis, **8**, 95
thioates, synthesis, **7**, 109
thiobenzoate, iodo-, in calicheamicin $\gamma_1{}^1$, **7**, 569
thiobenzoate, 2,3-methoxy-4-oxy-5-iodo-6-
  methylbenzoyl iodo-, in calicheamicin $\gamma_1{}^1$, **7**, 569
thiobutyrate, 2-oxo-4-methyl-, in ethylene biosynthesis,
  8, 94
thiocarbamide, imidazolyl-, applications, guanine
  deaminase inhibitors, **5**, 86
6,8-thioctic acid *see* lipoic acid
4-thiodeoxyriconucleosides, aminoalkylation, **7**, 205
4-thio-2′-deoxyuridine phosphoramidite, incorporation,
  into oligonucleotides, **7**, 202
thioesterase(s)
  absence, in 6-methylsalicylic acid synthase, **1**, 412
  catalysis, **1**, 348, **5**, 130
  domains
    of peptide synthetases, **4**, 227
    substrate specificity, **1**, 516
  homologues, **4**, 330
  occurrence, **1**, 14, **5**, 130
thioesters, activation, **4**, 222
β-thio-D-galactopyranoside, isopropyl- (IPTG),
  applications, in protein expression, **7**, 647
thioglucosidase(s)
  catalysis, **1**, 130
  mechanisms, **5**, 290
  occurrence, **3**, 687
  role in plant defense, **1**, 130
thioglucoside glucohydrolase(s) *see* thioglucosidase(s)
thioglucosides, roles, **1**, 130
thioglycolate, methyl (MTG), DNA damage, **7**, 560
[2-^{2}H$_2$]-thioglycolate, neocarzinostatin chromophore
  activation, **7**, 560
6-thioguanine, applications, **6**, 225
C^6-thioguanine, phosphoramidite monomer, **7**, 327
6-thioguanosine
  photocross-linking, **6**, 228
  synthesis, **6**, 93
thiohydroximate β-D-glucosyltransferase, purification, **1**,
  859
6-thioinosine, applications, photoaffinity probes, **6**, 229
thiol
  as cofactor, **7**, 558

1,5-hydrogen shift, **7**, 560
thiolate salts, aminoalkyl-, reactions, with 8-
    bromodeoxyadenosine, **7**, 198
thiol–neocarzinostatin chromophore adduct, formation,
    yield-determining step, **7**, 560
thiols
  basicity, **7**, 560
  hexose, **7**, 566
  nucleophilicity, **7**, 560
thiophene, dihydro-, formation, **7**, 570
thiophene dioxide, tetrachloro- (TCTD), cycloaddition,
    with *N*-alkylmaleimides, **5**, 429
thiophenol, 4-hydroxy- (HTP), reactions, with
    neocarzinostatin chromophore, **7**, 561
thiophenoxyacetyl-CoA, replacement, **4**, 264
thiophile, activation of allylic trisulfide, **7**, 570
thiophosphate esters, hydrolysis, **5**, 148
C^6-thiopurine, in oligodeoxynucleotides, **7**, 327
6-thiopurines, synthesis, **7**, 260
thiopyrido[2,3-*d*]pyrimidines, 2-methyl-, structure, **8**, 67
2-thiopyrimidines, synthesis, **7**, 260
4-thiopyrimidines, synthesis, **7**, 260
thioredoxin reductase, **4**, 357
  biochemistry, **4**, 371
  homologues, **4**, 373
  identification, **4**, 371
  selenocysteine residues, **4**, 373
thioredoxin (trxA)
  encoding, **7**, 652
  in *Escherichia coli*, **3**, 330, **4**, 357
  superfamily, **5**, 62
4'-thioribonucleosides, synthesis, **7**, 264
5'-thioribonucleotides, synthesis, **6**, 90
thioribose, 5'-methyl- (MTR), biosynthesis, **8**, 95
thiostrepton, biosynthesis, **1**, 852
thiosugar, **7**, 554
thiosulfenic acid, formation, **7**, 570
thiotemplate mechanism
  concept of, **4**, 344
  historical background, **4**, 321
  in peptide biosynthesis, **4**, 221, 344
4-thiothymidine, photocross-linking, **6**, 228
2-thiothymine, in oligodeoxynucleotides, **7**, 314
4-thiothymine
  hydrogen abstraction, **5**, 391
  in oligodeoxynucleotides, **7**, 315
thiotropocin
  biosynthesis, **1**, 77, 849
  occurrence, **1**, 849
2-thiouracil, in oligodeoxynucleotides, **7**, 314
4-thiouracil, in oligodeoxynucleotides, **7**, 315
2-thiouridine, synthesis, **6**, 93
2-thiouridine, 5-methylaminomethyl-, occurrence, **4**, 68
4-thiouridine
  applications, **6**, 225
    photoaffinity probes, **6**, 229
    probes, **6**, 93
  photocross-linking, **6**, 228
thiyl radicals
  biosynthesis, **3**, 332
    kinetics, **5**, 184
    mechanisms, **5**, 166
    thermodynamics, **5**, 184
    tyrosyl radicals in, **5**, 177
    via adenosylcobalamin bond cleavage, **5**, 170
  evidence for, **5**, 170
  from
    glycyl radicals, **5**, 185
    tyrosyl radicals, **5**, 183
  hydrogen atom abstraction, **3**, 330
    evidence for, **5**, 187
    kinetics, **5**, 186
    thermodynamics, **5**, 186

reactivity, **5**, 185
regeneration, **5**, 199
Thlaspi arvense
  gibberellin studies, **8**, 55
  shoots, cold treatment, **8**, 55
Thlaspi montanum, nickel accumulation, **8**, 149
Thr-327, as general acid catalyst, **5**, 39
three-phase tests, metaphosphate studies, **5**, 142
threonine, cleavage, **3**, 397
D-threonine, metabolism, **1**, 538
L-threonine, (4*R*)-4-[(*E*)-2-butenyl]-4-methyl-
  accumulation, **1**, 542
  biosynthesis, **1**, 543
  as starting material, for cyclosporins, **1**, 543
L-threonine acetaldehyde-lyase *see* threonine aldolase
threonine aldolase
  bacterial sources, **3**, 400
  biochemistry, **3**, 397
  cloning, **3**, 400
  cytosolic, **3**, 399
  eukaryotic sources, **3**, 400
  isolation, **3**, 397
  in mammalian liver, **3**, 397
  mechanisms, **3**, 401
  mitochondrial, **3**, 399
  plant sources, **3**, 401
  reviews, **3**, 397
  roles, **3**, 397
D-threonine dehydratase, induction, **1**, 538
threonine phosphatase(s)
  biochemistry, **5**, 157
  structure, **5**, 157
threonine phosphate, *N*-(7-mercaptoheptanoyl)-
  biosynthesis, **1**, 834
  in coenzyme M biosynthesis, **1**, 833
THR genes, *THR*1, **1**, 429
thrips
  pheromones, **8**, 213, 214
  see also Frankliniella occidentalis
thrixin, phosphono-, occurrence, **1**, 865
thrombin
  applications, proteolytic cleavage, **7**, 648
  aptamers
    anticoagulant activity, **7**, 627
      5-(propynyl)-2'-deoxyuridine incorporation, **6**, 225
    structure, **7**, 627
  inhibition, **8**, 568
  in SELEX studies, **7**, 626
thrombocyte-activating factor *see* platelet-activating
    factor (PAF)
thrombocyte-activating factor antagonists *see* platelet-
    activating factor antagonists
thrombotic phenomena, inhibition, **3**, 792
thromboxane-A synthase
  catalysis, **1**, 261, 277
  cDNA, cloning, **1**, 262
  molecular phylogeny, **1**, 277
  purification, **1**, 262
  ulcerogenicity, **1**, 176
thromboxane A$_2$ (TxA$_2$)
  agonists, **1**, 188
  analogues, synthesis, **1**, 188
  antagonists, **1**, 189
  applications, contractile agents, **1**, 176
  biological activity, **1**, 176
  biosynthesis, **5**, 226
  bronchoconstrictor activity, **1**, 198
  characterization, **1**, 161
  platelet coagulation induction, **1**, 10
  structure, **1**, 167
  synthesis, **1**, 183
thromboxane B$_2$ (TxB$_2$), occurrence, **1**, 246
thromboxanes

biological activity, **1**, 255
early studies, **1**, 10, 167
nomenclature, **1**, 167
receptors
  molecular phylogeny, **1**, 281
  structure, **1**, 198
stability, **1**, 167
thromboxane synthase *see* thromboxane-A synthase
thujane monoterpenes
biosynthesis, **2**, 104, 136
characterization, **2**, 104
metabolism, **2**, 146
Thuja orientalis, *O*-methyltransferases, **3**, 645
Thuja plicata
cDNA libraries, **1**, 656
cinnamyl-alcohol dehydrogenases, **3**, 676
lignans, **1**, 645, 668
pinoresinol/lariciresinol reductases, **1**, 668
plicatic acid, **1**, 697
plicatin, **1**, 697
γ-thujaplicin, biosynthesis, **2**, 107
α-thujene
biosynthesis, **2**, 104
in plant odor, **8**, 156
(+)-3-thujone, oxidation, **2**, 146
α-thujone, as seed toxin, **8**, 168
Thujopsis dolabrata
(2*R*,3*S*)-*cis*-dihydroquercetin 3-*O*-β-D-xylosides, **3**, 750
(2*S*,3*R*)-*cis*-dihydroquercetin 3-*O*-β-D-xylosides, **3**, 750
Thunbergia alata, fatty acids, **1**, 42
thunder-god vine *see Tripterygium wilfordii*
Thy-1, expression, **4**, 307
thymidine, 6-amino-, synthesis, **7**, 261
thymidine, 5,6-dihydro-, synthesis, **7**, 407
thymidine, 5,6-dihydro-5,6-dihydroxy-, synthesis, **7**, 407
thymidine, 5,6-dihydro-5-hydroxy-, synthesis, **7**, 407
thymidine glycol, polymerase blocking activity, **7**, 407
thymidine phosphoramidites, synthesis, **7**, 231
thymidine phosphoramidites, trifluoro-, incorporation,
  into oligonucleotides, **7**, 221
thymid-5-yl, 5,6-dihydro-
DNA strand breakage induction, **7**, 401
reactivity, **7**, 403
synthesis, **7**, 401
thymine, Norrish type II hydrogen atom abstraction, **5**, 390
thymine, N^3-ethyl-, in oligodeoxynucleotides, **7**, 315
thymine, O^2-ethyl-, in oligodeoxynucleotides, **7**, 314
thymine, C^4-*O*-methyl-, in oligodeoxynucleotides, **7**, 315
thymine, O^2-methyl-, in oligodeoxynucleotides, **7**, 314
thymine cyclobutane photodimer radical anions,
  fragmentation, **5**, 382
thymine cyclobutane photodimers, dimethyl-,
  thermodynamics, **5**, 382
thymine dimers
enzymatic reaction mechanisms, **5**, 382
formation, **5**, 372
mutagenesis induction, **5**, 394
photochemistry, **5**, **371–399**
thymine dimers, *cis-syn* 1,3-dimethyl-, crystal structure,
  5, 375
thymine photodimers
cleavage, **5**, 376
formation, **5**, 375
fragmentation reactions, **5**, 376
oxidation, **5**, 376
reduction, **5**, 376
thymine(s)
adjacent, **5**, 372
triplet states, **5**, 372
ultraviolet irradiation, **5**, 373
thymocytes, β-1,3-galactosyl-*O*-glycosyl-glycoprotein β-
  1,6-*N*-acetylglucosaminyltransferase activity,
  3, 76

thymol
biosynthesis, **2**, 62, 103
fumigant activity, **8**, 306
as odor principle, **8**, 165
thymoma cells, mutant, **3**, 299
thymonuclease *see* deoxyribonuclease I (DNase I)
Thymus vulgaris
γ-terpinene synthases, **2**, 136
α-thujene, **2**, 104
thymol biosynthesis, **2**, 62
thymyl trifluoroacetate, fumigant activity, **8**, 306
thyroxine, biosynthesis, **5**, 47
thyrsiflorins
biosynthesis, **2**, 239
occurrence, **2**, 239
TIBA *see* benzoic acid, 2,3,5-triiodo- (TIBA)
ticarcillin, chemical synthesis, **4**, 268
ticks
pheromones, **8**, 230
phospholipase A_2, **1**, 249
prostaglandins, **1**, 249
see also Amblyomma variegatum; *Dermacentor
    variabilis*
tigliane, biosynthesis, **2**, 223
13α-tigloyloxylupanine, (−)-3β-hydroxy-, isolation, **4**, 35
O-tigloyltransferase, purification, **4**, 35
Tilapia spp., leukotrienes, **1**, 238
TIM *see* triose-phosphate isomerase (TIM)
TIM barrels, in adenosine deaminase, **5**, 77
Tinospora cordifolia, furano–clerodanes, **2**, 226
Tiostrea chilensis, gymnodimine, **8**, 515
Ti plasmids
in auxin biosynthesis, **8**, 34
conjugal transfer, **8**, 399
occurrence, **8**, 399
Tipulidae, ketones, **8**, 242
tissue development, and fatty acid desaturation defects,
  1, 44
T-lymphocyte receptors, **3**, 31
TCRα, degradation, **3**, 31
TCRβ, degradation, **3**, 31
T-lymphocytes
CD45 adhesion, **3**, 46
development, **5**, 73
β-1,3-galactosyl-*O*-glycosyl-glycoprotein β-1,6-*N*-
  acetylglucosaminyltransferase activity, **3**, 76
lipopolysaccharide activation, **3**, 182
T-lymphomas, galactosyltransferase studies, **3**, 112
TMPyP(4)
imino proton NMR signals, **7**, 441
intercalation, **7**, 441
selectivity, **7**, 443
TMTFA *see* acetophenone, *m*-(*N*,*N*,*N*-
  trimethylammonio)trifluoro- (TMTFA)
TNF-α *see* tumor necrosis factor-α (TNF-α)
TNSA *see* alcohol, trisnorsqualene (TNSA)
tobacco
cytokinin-binding proteins, **8**, 64
fatty acids, **1**, 42
IFR homologues, **1**, 818
sesquiterpene synthase expression in, **2**, 213
solanone, **8**, 235
wildfire disease, **8**, 59
see also Nicotiana spp.
tobacco alkaloids
biological activity, **8**, 348
biosynthesis, **8**, 348
insecticidal activity, **8**, 347
metabolism, **8**, 348
occurrence, **8**, 358
tobacco armyworm *see Spodoptera litura*
tobacco budworms
antifeedant studies, **8**, 332

see also Heliothis virescens
tobacco cutworm *see Spodoptera litura*
tobacco hornworm *see Manduca sexta*
tobacco leaves, cembrenes, **2**, 220
tobacco plants
  norflurazon-resistant, **2**, 347
  L-phenylalanine ammonia-lyase studies, **1**, 786
tobacco ringspot virus (TRSV)
  RNA, **6**, 183
  satellite RNA
    catalytic site, **6**, 248
    hammerhead ribozyme, **6**, 247
tobacco wireworm *see Conoderus vespertinus*
D,L-α-tocopherol phosphoramidites, synthesis, **7**, 189
δ-tocotrienol epoxides, larval settlement induction, **8**, 431
toddacoumalone, occurrence, **1**, 380
Toddalia asiatica, toddacoumalone, **1**, 380
toddasin, occurrence, **1**, 380
toluene, degradation, **3**, 384
p-toluene sulfonate, 1-cyclohexyl-3-(2-
    morpholinoethyl)carbodiimide methyl- (CMCT),
    applications, RNA structural probes, **6**, 68
toluene-α-thiol *see* methanethiol, phenyl-
toluquinone, 4-methoxy-, structure, **1**, 411
p-tolylmethyl, as trityl protecting groups, **7**, 126
tolypin
  detection, **1**, 534
  insecticidal activity, **1**, 535
Tolypocladium cylindrosporum, identification, **1**, 543
Tolypocladium extinguens, identification, **1**, 543
Tolypocladium inflatum
  cyclosporins, **1**, 534
  ergocornine C, **1**, 534
Tolypocladium niveum
  cyclophilins, **1**, 541
  cyclosporin A secretion, **4**, 198
  cyclosporins, **1**, 536
  simA gene, **1**, 542
Tolypocladium niveum YP582, characterization, **1**, 542
tolyporphin, structure, **8**, 610
tolytoxin, structure, **8**, 610
tomatine
  applications, insecticides, **8**, 345
  occurrence, **8**, 346
tomato apical stunt viroid (TASV), sequence homology,
  6, 175
tomatoes
  ACC synthase studies, **8**, 97
  ACS genes, **8**, 97
  enzymes, wound-induced, **8**, 97
  genetic engineering, **8**, 98
  sesquiterpenoid phytoalexins, **2**, 212
  as viroid hosts, **6**, 171
  see also Lycopersicon spp.
tomato fruit
  chloroplasts, **3**, 464
  chromoplasts, **3**, 464
  green, alkaloids, **8**, 164
tomato leaves
  methyl jasomonate studies, **8**, 118
  systemin, **1**, 132
tomato pinworm *see Keiferia lycopersicella*
tomato planta macho viroid (TPMV), hosts, **6**, 171
tomato plants
  enzyme activity, leaves vs. fruit, **1**, 92
  hydroperoxide lyase activity, **1**, 92
  lypoxygenase activity, **1**, 109
tomosamine, occurrence, **3**, 186
tongue, acid lipases, **5**, 133
Toona ciliata
  6-acetyltoonacilin, **8**, 321
  toonacilin, **8**, 321
toonacilin, occurrence, **8**, 321

toonacilin, 6-acetyl-, occurrence, **8**, 321
toosendanin
  insecticidal activity, **8**, 330
  occurrence, **8**, 330
topoisomerase I *see* DNA topoisomerase I
topoisomerase II *see* DNA topoisomerase II
topoisomerase-directed agents, future developments, **7**,
  597
topotecan
  characteristics, **7**, 599
  structure, **7**, 599
Torpedo californica
  acetylcholinesterase, **5**, 112
  structure, **5**, 114
torreyanic acid, occurrence, **1**, 377
Tortonia spp.
  (6Z,9Z)-6,9-heptadecadiene, **8**, 217
  pheromones, **8**, 217
total gene synthesis, method, **7**, 658
TOTO
  DNA binding
    fluorescence enhancement, **7**, 448
    sequence selectivity, **7**, 448
  from thiazole orange, binding, **7**, 448
  specificity, **7**, 448
toucans, seed predation, toxins, **8**, 168
tox genes, *Tox*1, **1**, 424
toxicarol, isolation, **8**, 341
α-toxicarol, from, sumatrolic acid, **1**, 812
toxins
  bound, **8**, 183
  host-selective use of term, **8**, 178
  macromolecular, **8**, 181
  in seeds, **8**, 167
  see also aflatoxins; aplysiatoxins; brevetoxins (BTX);
    ciguatoxins (CTX); conotoxins; endotoxins;
    epipodophyllotoxins; iridoid toxins; lactone
    toxins; lissoclinotoxins; marine toxins; mycotoxins;
    myotoxins; pathotoxins; pectenotoxins (PTX);
    peptide toxins; phytotoxins; pinnatoxins;
    plant toxins; PM-toxins; polyether toxins;
    saxitoxins (STX); tetrodotoxins (TTX); T-
    toxins; yessotoxins (YTX); zooxanthellatoxins
Toxoplasma gondii, GPI anchors, biosynthesis, **3**, 305
TPMV *see* tomato planta macho viroid (TPMV)
TPP *see* thiamine diphosphate
TPS-CL *see* sulfonyl chloride, 2,4,6-triisopropylbenzene
  (TPS-CL)
trachelanthamidine, biosynthesis, **4**, 31
(+)-*nor*-trachelogenin *see* (+)-wikstromol
(−)-trachelogenin
  HIV-1 virus inhibition, **1**, 690, 703
  structure, **1**, 640
nor-trachelogenin, structure, **1**, 640
ent-trachylobane, biosynthesis, **2**, 230
trachylobanic acids, effects, on herbivores, **8**, 142
tra genes, *tra*I, localization, **8**, 399
trail pheromones, ants, **8**, 198
Trametes spp., tannin degradation, **3**, 819
Tramtrack, cocrystal structure, **7**, 484
transaldolase
  biochemistry, **3**, 417
  catalysis, **3**, 417
  cloning, **3**, 419
  isozymes, **3**, 417
  mechanisms, **3**, 419
  occurrence, **3**, 417
  purification, **3**, 419
transaminase(s), identification, **4**, 5
transamination, mechanisms, **4**, 70
transcriptional pulse-chase
  mRNA studies, **6**, 206
  yeasts, **6**, 206, 210

transcriptional regulation
  of isoflavonoids, **1**, 817
  of rat squalene synthase gene, **2**, 259
transcription factor IID (TFIID), binding, **4**, 367
transcription factor IIIA (TFIIIA), binding, **4**, 366
transcription factor IIIB (TFIIIB), complexes, **4**, 367
transcription factor IIIC (TFIIIC)
  binding, **4**, 366
  interactions, **4**, 367
  TFIIIC1, structure, **4**, 367
  TFIIIC2, structure, **4**, 367
  in yeast, **4**, 367
transcription factors
  expression, patterns, **3**, 46
  for *nod* genes, **1**, 328
  occurrence, **8**, 406
  Sp1, promoter control, **3**, 44
transducin
  activation, **2**, 360
  binding, **2**, 361
  crystal structure, **2**, 361
  farnesylation, **2**, 361
  functions, **2**, 360
  studies, **2**, 361
transesterification
  endonucleolytic
    hairpin ribozyme-catalyzed, **6**, 251
    hammerhead ribozyme-catalyzed, **6**, 242
transfer DNA *see* T-DNA
transfer factor *see* EF-Tu
transferrin receptors
  acylation, **4**, 14
  apoII mRNA, degradation, **6**, 213
  3′ UTR, **6**, 214
transfer RNA *see* tRNA
transfer RNA synthetase *see* tRNA synthetases
transformation
  mechanisms, **7**, 662
  requirements, **7**, 662
transforming growth factor-β_1 (TGF-β_1), effects, on
    aggrecan mRNA, **3**, 167
transgenic mice, β-1,4-mannosyl-glycoprotein β-1,4-*N*-
    acetylglucosaminyltransferase overexpression,
    3, 54
transgenic plants, **2**, 347
  increased cytokinin levels, **8**, 63
  terpene synthase gene expression in, **2**, 211
transglycosylase
  inhibition, **3**, 281
  soluble lytic, **5**, 297
trans Golgi network (TGN)
  ganglioside biosynthesis, **3**, 96
  glycosphingolipids, **3**, 87
transient absorption spectroscopy,
    deoxyribodipyrimidine photo-lyase in, **5**, 384
transition metal complexes, RNA cleavage, **6**, 69
transition metals, applications, DNA structure probes, **7**,
    85
transition state analogues (TSAs)
  binding, **5**, 76, **7**, 632
  in catalytic antibody synthesis, **6**, 95
transition states
  flanking, **5**, 6
  inhibition, **5**, 74
  and intermediates, **5**, 10
  stabilization, **5**, 76, **6**, 158
    electrostatic, **5**, 78
transition state theory, predictions, for AMP deaminase,
    5, 84
transketolase
  biochemistry, **3**, 414
  catalysis, **3**, 414
  cloning, **3**, 416
  mechanisms, **3**, 416
  occurrence, **3**, 416
  roles, **3**, 416
  structure, **3**, 416
  substrate specificity, **3**, 417
translation, evolution, **6**, 127
translation initiation factors, interactions, **6**, 212
translation initiation rates, factors affecting, **6**, 212
translocase *see* EF-G
translocase I *see* phospho-Mur*N*Ac-pentapeptide
    translocase (translocase I)
translocase II *see* undecaprenyl-diphospho-Mur*N*Ac-
    pentapeptide:UDPGlc*N*Ac Glc*N*Ac transferase
    (translocase II)
transmembrane, flipping, **3**, 265
transpeptidases
  acylation, **4**, 240
  catalysis, **3**, 5
  inhibition, via β-lactam antibiotics, **3**, 283
  mechanisms, **3**, 267
D,D-transpeptidases, roles, in peptidoglycan biosynthesis,
    3, 267
transpeptidation
  mechanisms, **4**, 344
  substrates, **4**, 325
transphosphoribosidase *see* adenine
    phosphoribosyltransferase
transpiration, cytokinin-stimulated, **8**, 59
transplantation, allograft rejection, **1**, 540
transport proteins, identification, **2**, 205
transposons, mutagenesis, **4**, 216
transposon tagging, maize *D3* gene, **8**, 50
transversadiene, as intermediate, **2**, 222
transversial
  biosynthesis, **2**, 222
  occurrence, **2**, 222
tree cotton *see* *Gossypium arboreum*
tree locust *see* *Anacridium melanorhoda*
trees
  lignification, **3**, 712
  see also wood
trehalose, levels, **8**, 299
trehazolin
  as glucosidase inhibitor, **3**, 153
  structure, **1**, 152, **3**, 133
Trematoda
  arachidonic acid metabolism, **1**, 249
  see also *Schistosoma mansoni*
Tremerogen A-10, source of, **2**, 353
tremorgenic agents, lolitrem B, **8**, 177
tremulacin, effects, on herbivores, **8**, 139
triacetic acid lactone (TAL)
  biosynthesis, **1**, 357
  release, **1**, 3
triacontane, 17,21-dimethyl-, bioactivity, **8**, 249
triacylglycerol acylhydrolase *see* triacylglycerol lipase(s)
triacylglycerol lipase(s)
  catalysis, **5**, 124
    mechanisms, **5**, 125
  future research, **5**, 134
  interfacial recognition, **5**, 126
  occurrence, **5**, 112, 125
  structure, **5**, 125
s-triazine, 2-chloro-4-cyclohexylamino-6-ethylamino-,
    flowering induction, **8**, 69
triazine di-*N*-oxides
  DNA damage induction, **7**, 534
  as hypoxia-selective redox-activated cytotoxin, **7**, 534
1,2,4-triazole, 1-(mesitylene-2-sulfonyl)-3-nitro-
    (MSNT), in oligonucleotide synthesis, **6**, 82, **7**,
    117
Tribolium spp.
  4,8-dimethyldecanal, **8**, 217

1-pentadecene, **8**, 216
pheromones, **8**, 217
Tribolium castaneum
  1-alkenes, **8**, 204
  (4*R*,8*R*)-4,8-dimethyldecanal, **8**, 236
  pheromones, **8**, 15
  tribolure, **8**, 15, 246
Tribolium confusum
  antifeedant activity against, **1**, 694
  sex pheromones, **8**, 217
tribolure, occurrence, **8**, 15, 246
2,2,2-tribromoethyl, as phosphate protecting groups, **7**,
  130
tributyrase(s) *see* triacylglycerol lipase(s)
tricarboxylic acid cycles, in acetate metabolism, **2**, 52, 58
Trichilia roka, trichilin A, **8**, 321
trichilin A, occurrence, **8**, 321
Trichoderma harzianum, trichoharzin, **8**, 600
Trichoderma reesei
  cellobiohydrolase II, **5**, 300
  cellobiohydrolases, **3**, 593
  endoglucanases, **3**, 593
trichodermin, early studies, **2**, 158
trichodiene
  biosynthesis, **2**, 162, **2**, 162, **5**, 329
  early studies, **2**, 158
  from, farnesyl diphosphate, **2**, 158
  metabolism, **2**, 163
trichodiene, 15-hydroxy-, and capsidiol levels, compared,
  2, 212
trichodiene-derived mycotoxins, trichothecenes, **2**, 202
trichodiene synthase genes, isolation, **2**, 203
trichodiene synthase(s)
  active site, **2**, 160
  amino acid sequences, alignment, **5**, 331
  aza analogues, **5**, 330
  biosynthesis, **2**, 158
  catalysis, **5**, 329
  cloning, **5**, 330
  conformation, **2**, 161
  cyclization mechanism, site-directed mutants in, **2**, 162
  gene cloning, **2**, 161, 202
  inhibition, **5**, 333
  isolation, **2**, 158
  mechanistic studies, **5**, 329
  occurrence, **2**, 158, 203
  presteady-state kinetics, **2**, 193
  purification, **2**, 203, **5**, 330
  rate-limiting steps, **2**, 193
  recombinant, **5**, 330
  sequences, **5**, 322
  use in the cyclization of farnesyl diphosphate, **2**, 158
Trichogramma nubilale, 13,17-dimethylnonatriacontane,
  8, 249
trichoharzin
  absolute stereochemistry, **8**, 600
  biosynthesis, **1**, 370
  occurrence, **8**, 600
Trichophyton mentagrophytes
  activity against, **1**, 691
  antimicrobial activity against, **8**, 532
Trichoplusia ni, antifeedant activity against, **8**, 321
trichothecanes
  antibiotics, **2**, 158
  biosynthesis, **2**, 158, 163
  farnesyl diphosphate incorporation, **2**, 158
  mycotoxins, **2**, 158
trichothecene pathway genes, macrocyclic, **2**, 205
trichothecenes
  as fungal terpenoid pathway gene cluster, **2**, 205
  macrocyclic, roridin E, **2**, 202
  production, **2**, 212
  source, **2**, 202

structure, core, **2**, 202
trichothecin, early studies, **2**, 158
Trichothecium spp., trichodiene synthase, **2**, 203
Trichothecium roseum, rosenonolactone, **2**, 228
trichothecolone, biosynthesis, **2**, 164
TriCHQ *see* quinone, trichlorohydro- (TriCHQ)
tricin, as allelopathic agent, **8**, 169
(*Z*)-5-tricosene, occurrence, **8**, 219
(*Z*)-7-tricosene, occurrence, **8**, 218, 219
(*Z*)-9-tricosene, occurrence, **8**, 200, 219
(*Z*)-14-tricosen-10-one, occurrence, **8**, 219
2,6-tridecadienoate, methyl (*E*,*Z*)-10,11-epoxy-3,11-
  dimethyl-7-ethyl-, structure, **8**, 267
9*E*,11*E*-tridecadienoic acid, 13-oxo-, occurrence, **1**, 214
9,11-tridecadienoic acid, 13-oxo-, occurrence, **1**, 209
2,4-tridecadien-7-one, (2*E*,4*E*,6*R*,10*R*)-4,6,10,12-
  tetramethyl- *see* matsuone
tridecane, occurrence, **8**, 214
tridecanoate, methyl 2,6,10-trimethyl-, occurrence, **8**, 241
tridecanoic acid, ω-cyclohexyl-, occurrence, **1**, 71
2-tridecanone, occurrence, **8**, 215
2-tridecanone, (*R*)-10-methyl-, occurrence, **8**, 244
4-tridecenal, occurrence, **8**, 219
(*Z*)-4-tridecenal, occurrence, **8**, 240
(*Z*)-4-tridecene, occurrence, **8**, 214
(*Z*)-5-tridecene, occurrence, **8**, 216
8-tridecenoic acids, as intermediates, **8**, 207
tridec-5-en-2-ol, (*R*)-(*E*)-1-amino-
  occurrence, **8**, 545
  structure, **8**, 545
2,3,6-trideoxy-4-*C*-glycolyl-L-*threo*-hexose *see* L-pillarose
2,3,6-trideoxy-D-*erythro*-hexose *see* D-amicetose
2,3,6-trideoxy-D-*threo*-hexose *see* D-rhodinose
2,3,6-trideoxy-L-*erythro*-hexose *see* L-amicetose
2,3,6-trideoxy-L-*threo*-hexose *see* L-rhodinose
2,3,6-trideoxy-L-*glycero*-hexos-2-en-4-ulose *see* L-aculose
2,3,6-trideoxy-D-*glycero*-hexos-4-ulose *see* D-cinerulose A
2,3,6-trideoxy-L-*glycero*-hexos-4-ulose *see* L-cinerulose A
2,3,6-trideoxy-4-*O*-methyl-D-*erythro*-hexose, occurrence,
  3, 312
2,3,6-trideoxy-3-*C*-methyl-4-*O*-methyl-3-nitro-L-*xylo*-
  hexose *see* L-rubranitrose
2,3,6-trideoxy-3-*C*-methyl-3-nitro-L-*ribo*-hexose *see* L-
  decilonitrose
trideoxysugars, occurrence, **3**, 322
Trididemnum solidum
  didemnin B, **8**, 521
  didemnins, **8**, 529
trienes
  Diels–Alder reaction, **1**, 389
  as sex pheromones, **8**, 207
triesters, synthesis, **7**, 109
triethylamine, 2-(4-chlorophenylthio)- (CPTA), lycopene
  cyclization inhibition, **2**, 338
triethylamine, 2-(4-methylphenoxy)- (MPTA), lycopene
  cyclization inhibition, **2**, 338
triflavonoids
  angular, biosynthesis, **3**, 758
  definitions, **3**, 748
Trifolium spp., cyanogenesis, **1**, 882
Trifolium repens
  cyanogenic β-glucosidase, **3**, 687
  cyanogenic polymorphism, **1**, 882
Trifolium subterraneum, mutants, **1**, 799
Triglochin maritima, microsomes, **1**, 889
triglyceride lipase(s) *see* triacylglycerol lipase(s)
triglycosylceramides, characterization, **3**, 122
Trigona mellicolor, formic acid, **8**, 359
Trigonella foenum-graecum
  galactomannan biosynthesis, **3**, 521
  mannosyltransferase, **3**, 521
trigonelline, occurrence, **8**, 26
1,3,8-trihydroxynaphthalene reductase

catalysis, **1**, 428
encoding, **1**, 428
(5Z,13E)-(15S)-9α,11α:15-trihydroxyprosta-5,13-
  dienoate:NADP$^+$ 11-oxidoreductase *see*
  prostaglandin F synthase
triketides, as intermediates, **1**, 761
trilobalide, antifeedant activity, **8**, 308
trimethylamine, as starting material, for formaldehyde, **3**,
  411
trimethylamine-oxide aldolase
  biochemistry, **3**, 411
  purification, **3**, 412
Trimyema compressum, tetrahymanol, **2**, 308
trinervitanes, occurrence, **8**, 230
Trinervitermes bettonianus, cembrene A, **8**, 230
Trinervitermes trinertoides, adipokinetic hormone, **8**, 299
triose-phosphate isomerase (TIM)
  active sites, structure, **5**, 12
  Albery–Knowles analysis, **5**, 8
  catalysis, **5**, 36
    mechanisms, **5**, 13
  mobile ten-residue loops, deletion, **5**, 37
  NMR spectra, **5**, 36
  and starch carbon flow, **3**, 463
  stereoelectronic control, **5**, 36
  structure, **5**, 12
  triose interconversion, **2**, 374
triosephosphate mutase *see* triose-phosphate isomerase
  (TIM)
triostin
  applications, quinoxaline antibiotics, **7**, 444
  bisintercalation, with neighbor exclusion, **7**, 446
  specificity, **7**, 448
  x-ray crystal structure, **7**, 444
triostin A
  bisintercalation, **7**, 488
  structure, **7**, 352
trioxacarcinose B, occurrence, **3**, 312, 322
trioxilin A$_4$, occurrence, **1**, 247
trioxilin(s)
  biosynthesis, **1**, 170
  occurrence, **1**, 237
triphenic acids, nonahydroxy-, interconnections, **3**, 801
triphenylmethyl, as protecting groups, **7**, 126
5′-triphosphates, in SELEX studies, **7**, 633
triphyllin A, stereochemistry, **3**, 756
triphyllin B, stereochemistry, **3**, 756
Tripterygium wilfordii
  celabenzine, **8**, 344
  wilfordine alkaloids, **8**, 344
Tris *see* methane, tris(hydroxymethyl)amino- (Tris)
trisaccharide, **7**, 571
tris(4,7-diphenylphenanthroline)ruthenium(II),
  applications, DNA structure probes, **7**, 88
trisindoline
  antibiotic activity, **8**, 588
  occurrence, **8**, 588
  structure, **8**, 588
trisintercalators
  and anthraquinone threading intercalating agents, **7**,
    451
  threading, **7**, 452
trisnorsqualene cyclopropylamine (TNS-CPA), as
  inhibitor, **2**, 273
trisnorsqualene difluoromethylidene (TNS-DFM),
  inhibition, time-dependent, **2**, 275
tris(phenanthroline)–metal complexes, applications,
  DNA structure probes, **7**, 88
tris(1,10-phenanthroline)ruthenium(II), applications,
  DNA structure probes, **7**, 88
tris(1,10-phenanthroline)zinc(II), applications, DNA
  structure probes, **7**, 88
trisporic acid, occurrence, **8**, 408

trisulfide, allylic, nucleophilic attack by thiophile, **7**, 570
triterpene cyclases, **2**, **299–319**
  amino acids, **2**, 315
    aromatic, **2**, 316
  catalytic versatility, **2**, 300
  cloned, data, **2**, 313
  common phylogenetic origin, hypothesis, **2**, 315
  evolution hypothesis, **2**, 316
  future research, **2**, 316
  inhibitors, reviews, **2**, 303
  mechanisms, **2**, 300
  QW motif, function, **2**, 316
  reviews, **2**, 303
  similarity, **2**, 313
  substrates, **2**, 301
  synthesis, **2**, 305
  x-ray structure, future research, **2**, 317
triterpenes
  insecticidal activity, **8**, 320
  occurrence, **2**, 300
triterpenes, cyclic, **2**, 301
triterpenes, pentacyclic, **2**, 301
  see also hopanes
triterpenes, tetracyclic, **2**, 301
triterpenoids, structure, **2**, 323
triterpenol esterase *see* sterol esterase
Triticum aestivum
  branching enzymes, **3**, 461
  cinnamyl-alcohol dehydrogenases, **3**, 656
  coniferyl alcohol studies, **3**, 649
  immunocytochemical labeling, **3**, 700
  sequence homology, **1**, 654
Triton X100, applications, **3**, 121
(5Z,27Z)-5,27-tritriacontadiene, occurrence, **8**, 219
(9Z,19Z)-9,19-tritriacontadiene, occurrence, **8**, 219
tritriacontane, 15,19-dimethyl-, occurrence, **8**, 249
tritriacontane, 15-methyl-, occurrence, **8**, 249
(Z)-9-tritriacontene, occurrence, **8**, 219
(Z)-11-tritriacontene, occurrence, **8**, 219
(Z)-13-tritriacontene, occurrence, **8**, 219
Tritrichomonas foetus, adenine deaminase, **5**, 86
trityl, 4-decyloxy-, as 5′-hydroxyl protecting group, **7**, 127
trityl, dimethoxy- (DMTr), applications, 5′-hydroxyl
  group protection, **6**, 83, **7**, 126
trityl, 4-hexadecyloxy-, as 5′-hydroxyl protecting group,
  7, 127
trityl, trisbenzoyloxy-, as protecting groups, **7**, 123
trityl, 4,4′,4′-trisbenzoyloxy-, as 5′-hydroxyl protecting
  groups, **7**, 126
trityl, 4,4′,4′-tris-(4,5-dichlorophthalimido)-, as 5′-
  hydroxyl protecting groups, **7**, 126
trityl, 4,4′,4′-tris-levulinyloxy-, as 5′-hydroxyl protecting
  groups, **7**, 126
tRNA
  as 'adapter', **7**, 616
  association, with anticodon loops, **7**, 46
  base triples, **6**, 199
  CCA terminus, **6**, 200
  conformational complexity, **7**, 616
  early studies, **6**, 109
  folding, kinetics, **7**, 48
  mass spectra, **6**, 53
  nucleotide studies, **6**, 76
  probing, **6**, 64
  roles, in protein biosynthesis, **6**, 52
  rRNA affinity, **6**, 202
  synthesis
    chemical, **6**, 53
    in vitro, **6**, 52
  see also pre-tRNA
tRNA^{Asp}
  occurrence, **6**, 222
  structural probing, **6**, 72, 73

structural studies, **6**, 223
tRNA^Glu
    as cofactor, in 5-aminolevulinic acid biosynthesis, **4**, 67
    encoding, **4**, 68
tRNA^Lys, structural probing, **6**, 72
tRNA^Phe
    cleavage, **6**, 69
    disulfide cross-links, **6**, 227
    irradiation, **6**, 228
    occurrence, **6**, 222
    structural probing, **6**, 65
tRNA^Ser, interactions, with aminoacyl synthetase, **6**, 222
tRNA^Val, irradiation, **6**, 228
tRNA crystals, heavy atom derivatives, **6**, 51
tRNA isopentenyltransferase, mutation, **8**, 70
tRNA ligases, catalysis, **4**, 324
tRNA structures
    determination
        via probing, **6**, 64
        via x-ray crystallography, **6**, 52
    solution and crystal compared, **6**, 12
    three-dimensional, **7**, 616
tRNA synthetases
    reactions, **6**, 88
    SELEX studies, **7**, 628
Trogoderma spp.
    hexanoic acid, **8**, 210
    pheromones, **8**, 210
    trogodermal, **8**, 247
trogodermal, occurrence, **8**, 247
Tropaeolum majus, phenylacetaldoxime, **1**, 130
tropane alkaloids
    biosynthesis, **4**, 26
        pathways, **4**, 27
    in induced plant defense, **8**, 150, 151
    isolation, **4**, 26
    in nectars, **8**, 162
    occurrence, **4**, 26
*nor*tropane alkaloids
    occurrence, **3**, 132
    structure, **3**, 132
trout *see Oncorhynchus mykiss*; *Salmo gairdneri*;
        Salvelinus fontinalis
D-Trp *see* D-tryptophan
L-Trp *see* L-tryptophan
trp genes, *trpC*, **1**, 541
trp repressors
    binding affinity, **7**, 268
    x-ray crystal structure, **7**, 268
TRSV *see* tobacco ringspot virus (TRSV)
true cholinesterase *see* acetylcholinesterase
truxillic acids, dihydroxy-, occurrence, **1**, 647
trxA *see* thioredoxin (trxA)
Trypanosoma brucei brucei
    glycolipids, **3**, 295
    GPI anchors, biosynthesis, **3**, 304
    surface antigens, **3**, 302
Trypanosoma congolense, GPI anchors, **3**, 297
Trypanosoma cruzi
    Chagas' disease induction, **3**, 143
    glycosylphosphatidylinositols, **3**, 306
    swainsonine studies, **3**, 156
trypanosomes
    GPI anchors, **3**, 300
        biosynthesis, **3**, 304
    insertion–deletion editing, **6**, 104
    pathways, **3**, 20
    RNA editing, **6**, 97
Trypodendron spp., lineatin, **8**, 224
Trypodendron lineatum, 3-hydroxy-3-methylbutan-2-one,
        8, 220
trypsin
    applications, **4**, 336

branching enzyme proteolysis, **3**, 460
    inhibitory activity, **3**, 791
    6-methylsalicylic acid synthase inactivation, **1**, 350
tryptamine
    in auxin biosynthesis, **8**, 33
    as starting material, for indole alkaloids, **4**, 109, 110
tryptamine, hydroxy-, in hornet venom, **8**, 356
tryptamine, 5-hydroxy-, in venoms, **8**, 354
tryptic peptides, isolation, **4**, 130
tryptophan, **8**, 32
    binding, **7**, 638
    biosynthesis, **4**, 2, 5
        via shikimate pathway, **1**, 574
    labeling, **1**, 846
    methylation, **1**, 855
    as starting material
        for alkaloids, **4**, 46
        for indole-3-acetic acid, **8**, 32
    structure, **4**, 109
    in thiostrepton biosynthesis, **1**, 853
tryptophan, *N*-acetyl-, in cyclobutane pyrimidine
        photodimer radical anion cleavage, **5**, 379
tryptophan, dimethylallyl- (DMAT)
    in ergolene biosynthesis, **4**, 52
    N-methylation, **4**, 52
D-tryptophan, in auxin biosynthesis, **8**, 33
L-tryptophan
    alkylation, **5**, 331
    in auxin biosynthesis, **8**, 33
    biosynthesis, **1**, 345
    7-substituted analogues, **5**, 331
L-tryptophan, 4-[(*E*)-4′-hydroxy-3′-methylbut-2′-enyl]-
        (E-HODMAT), isolation, **4**, 52
(*S*)-tryptophan, *N*-[(+)-cucurbinoyl]-, occurrence, **1**, 128
(*S*)-tryptophan, *N*-[(−)-jasmonoyl]-, occurrence, **1**, 128
tryptophan decarboxylase *see* aromatic-L-amino-acid
        decarboxylase
tryptophan desmolase(s) *see* tryptophan synthase(s)
tryptophan radicals, in cofactor assembly, **3**, 329
tryptophan synthase(s)
    occurrence, **4**, 7
    roles, in tryptophan biosynthesis, **4**, 7
tryptophol, phytotoxicity, **8**, 178
TSAs *see* transition state analogues (TSAs)
tsetse flies
    pheromones, **8**, 214
    see also Glossina spp.
tspO genes, in *Rhodobacter* spp., **2**, 344
TsTX *see* tessulatoxin (TsTX)
Tsuga heterophylla
    cDNA libraries, **1**, 656
    α-conidendrin, **1**, 697
    7′-hydroxylappaol B, **1**, 688
    7′-hydroxymatairesinol, **1**, 697
    lignans, **1**, 668
    pinoresinol/lariciresinol reductases, **1**, 668
T-2 toxin, source, **2**, 203
T-toxins
    occurrence, **1**, 424
    structure, **1**, 424
T-toxin synthase, catalysis, **1**, 424
TTX *see* tetrodotoxins (TTX)
tuberculatin, antiinflammatory activity, **1**, 705
tuberization, bioassay, **1**, 127
tuberonic acid
    glucoside, occurrence, **1**, 127
    β-D-glucoside, occurrence, **1**, 125
    occurrence, **1**, 118
tuberonic acid glucoside
    metabolism, **8**, 117
    structure, **8**, 108
tubers, starch granules, **3**, 454
tube worms

Bacillus spp. in, **8**, 595
see also Phramatopoma californica
tubifolines, biosynthesis, **4**, 50
tubotoxin *see* rotenone
Tulipa spp.
    flavonoid 3'-O-methyltransferase, **1**, 739
    phenylalanine ammonia-lyase, **1**, 719
epi-tulipinolide diepoxide, antifeedant activity, **8**, 308
tumor cells, mammalian, metabolic suicide, **5**, 93
tumor necrosis factor-α (TNF-α)
    effects, on proteoglycans, **3**, 167
    and malaria, **3**, 297
tumor progression, ST6Gal I expression, **3**, 46
tumor promoters, okadaic acid, **8**, 491
tumors
    boron neutron capture therapy, **7**, 221
    chemoprotection, **1**, 700
tungstate
    binding, **5**, 156
    phosphatase inhibition, **5**, 158
tunicamycin, inhibitory activity, **3**, 41, 279
tunicates *see* Urochordata
Turbo cornutus, feeding stimulants, **8**, 420
turbot *see Scophthalmus maximus*
turkey X disease, aflatoxin-induced, **1**, 444
Turnera ulmifolia, cyanogenic glucoside, **1**, 882
turnip yellow mosaic virus (TYMV), RNA, **6**, 70
TUTase *see* RNA uridylyltransferase
Tween 80, as tetrahymanol cyclase inactivator, **2**, 312
twist (conformation), definition, **7**, 56
two-spotted spider mites *see Tetranychus urticae*
TxA₂ *see* thromboxane A₂ (TxA₂)
TXA synthase *see* thromboxane-A synthase
TxB₂ *see* thromboxane B₂ (TxB₂)
TycA synthetase, roles, **4**, 208
TycB synthetase, roles, **4**, 208
tyc genes
    tycA
        dissection, **4**, 335
        encoding, **4**, 330
    tycB, encoding, **4**, 330
    tycC, encoding, **4**, 330
    tycTE, encoding, **4**, 330
tyc operons, expression, **4**, 330
Tyc proteins
    TycA, structure, **4**, 330
    TycB, structure, **4**, 330
tylactones, incorporation, **1**, 526
tyl genes, in mycaminose biosynthesis, **3**, 342
tylosin
    antibacterial activity, **1**, 496
    biosynthesis, **1**, 525, **4**, 196
        genetics, **3**, 352
    occurrence, **1**, 525
TYMV *see* turnip yellow mosaic virus (TYMV)
Type A-lantibiotics, structure, **4**, 276
Type B-lantibiotics
    gene clusters, **4**, 295
    prepeptides, **4**, 295
    structure, **4**, 276
    subgroups, **4**, 280
typhasterol, synthesis, **8**, 105
typhasterol, 6-deoxo-, isomerization, **8**, 105
Tyr14, as general acid catalyst, **5**, 39
Tyr122 radical
    electron transfer, long-range, **3**, 329
    identification, **3**, 329
Tyr355
    localization, **5**, 248
    roles, in arachidonic acid binding, **5**, 247
Tyr385
    localization, **5**, 233, 243
    mutagenesis, **5**, 243

tyramine, bromo-, antifouling activity, **8**, 440
(*S*)-tyramine, *N*-[(−)-jasmonoyl]-, occurrence, **1**, 128
tyramines
    occurrence, **1**, 673
        wasp venom, **8**, 356
tyr genes, *tyrB*, expression, **4**, 5
Tyria jacobaeae, (3*Z*,6*Z*,9*Z*)-1,3,6,9-henicosatetraene, **8**, 207
tyrocidine
    biosynthesis, **4**, 196, 202, 208, 323, 325
        genetics, **4**, 327, 330
    occurrence, **4**, 322
    structure, **4**, 320
tyrocidine synthases, amino terminus, **1**, 616
tyrocidine synthetase 1
    catalysis, **4**, 325
    sequencing, **4**, 321
    Tyc proteins, **4**, 330
tyrocidine synthetase 2
    catalysis, **4**, 325
    Tyc proteins, **4**, 330
tyrocidine synthetase 3, catalysis, **4**, 325
Tyrophagus spp., pheromones, **8**, 216
Tyrophagus neiswanderi, alarm pheromones, **8**, 216
Tyrophagus perniciosus, 2*S*,3*S*-epoxyneral, **8**, 225
Tyrophagus putrescentiae, neryl formate, **8**, 222
Tyrophagus similis, (+)-isopiperitenone, **8**, 224
β-tyrosinase *see* tyrosine phenol-lyase
tyrosinase(s) *see* catechol oxidase(s)
tyrosine, bromo-
    biotransformation products, antibiotic activity, **8**, 469
    in Porifera, **8**, 468
tyrosine, *m*-carboxy-, biosynthesis, **1**, 619
tyrosine, *N*-hydroxy-, as intermediate, **1**, 889
tyrosine, nitro-, biosynthesis, **5**, 244
L-tyrosine
    biosynthesis, **1**, 345, **3**, 405
    characterization, **1**, 838
    conversion, **1**, 858
L-tyrosine, 2-azido-, biosynthesis, **3**, 408
tyrosine/DOPA decarboxylase, induction, **1**, 131
(*S*)-tyrosine, *N*-[(−)-jasmonoyl]-, occurrence, **1**, 128
β-tyrosine, 3'-chloro-5'-hydroxy-, in C-1027
        chromophore, **7**, 578
tyrosine ammonia-lyase (TAL)
    catalysis, **3**, 622
    early studies, **3**, 631
    roles, in monolignol biosynthesis, **3**, 631
tyrosine esters, ribosyl 3' *O*-phospho-, **7**, 599
L-tyrosine *N*-hydroxylase, inhibition, **1**, 889
tyrosine kinase, inhibition, **1**, 783
tyrosine phenol-lyase
    active sites, **3**, 406
    biochemistry, **3**, 405
    catalysis, **3**, 405
    inhibitors, **3**, 405
    mechanisms, **3**, 405
    occurrence, **3**, 405
    purification, **3**, 405
    structure, **3**, 405
    substrate specificity, **3**, 407
tyrosine residues, glycosylation, **3**, 446
tyrosine(s), **7**, 578
    biosynthesis, **4**, 2, 5, **5**, 344
        via shikimate–chorismate pathway, **3**, 626
        via shikimate pathway, **1**, 574
    as cyanogenic glycoside precursor, **1**, 885, 887
    deamination, **3**, 622, 631
    as intermediates, **3**, 626
    mutagenesis, **5**, 243
    oxidation, **5**, 178
    oxidized, identification, **5**, 243
    roles, in prostaglandin-endoperoxide synthase
        catalysis, **5**, 243

as starting material, for alkaloids, **4**, 35
tyrosine-tRNA ligase, interactions, **6**, 222
ʟ-tyrosine-tRNA^{Tyr} ligase (AMP-forming) *see* tyrosine-
　　tRNA ligase
tyrosyl radicals
　biosynthesis
　　kinetics, **5**, 178
　　thermodynamics, **5**, 178
　detection, **5**, 240
　electron transfer
　　indirect evidence, **5**, 181
　　R1–R2, **5**, 181
　hydrogen bonding, spectroscopy, **5**, 178
　magnetic interactions, **3**, 329
　R2, thermodynamic and kinetic studies, **5**, 180
　reactions, with nitric oxide, **5**, 244
　in ribonucleotide reductases, **3**, 329, 343
　roles

　in active site thiyl radical biosynthesis, **5**, 177
　　in catalysis, **5**, 177
　scavengers, **3**, 330
　signaling, **5**, 240
　thiyl radical biosynthesis, **5**, 183
　time-dependent changes, **5**, 240
　see also Tyr122 radical
tyrosyl-tRNA synthetase *see* tyrosine-tRNA ligase
tyrothricin
　early studies, **4**, 320
　sporulation induction, **4**, 323
TyrR protein, functions, **4**, 5, 9
tyvelose
　in O-antigen, **3**, 345
　expression, **3**, 187
　occurrence, **3**, 312, 313
　substitution, **3**, 323

U

U6 snRNA, promoters, **4**, 362
U18666A *see* androst-5-en-17-one, 3β-[2-
  (diethylamino)ethoxy]-
U-46619, applications, thromboxane agonists, **1**, 188
ubiquinone(s)
  biosynthesis, **2**, 377, **5**, 344
  in *Escherichia coli*, **2**, 51
  isopentenyl diphosphate units, **2**, 376
  mass spectra, **2**, 376
  synthesis, **2**, 26, 247
ubiquinones, polyprenylated, toxicity, **8**, 436
UCE6, occurrence, **7**, 600
UCE1022, occurrence, **7**, 600
UDP *see* undecaprenyl diphosphate (UDP)
UDP-*N*-acetyl-D-galactosamine:polypeptide *N*-
  acetylgalactosaminyltransferase *see* polypeptide *N*-
  acetylgalactosaminyltransferase
UDP-*N*-acetylglucosamine
  biosynthesis, **3**, 206, 249
  complexation, **1**, 593
  as glycosyl donor, **3**, 203
  roles, **3**, 206
    in peptidoglycan biosynthesis, **3**, 249
UDP-*N*-acetylglucosamine *O*-acyltransferase
  biosynthesis, **4**, 227
  catalysis, **3**, 220
UDP-*N*-acetyl-D-glucosamine:chitin 4-β-*N*-
  acetylglucosaminyltransferase(s) *see* chitin
  synthase(s)
UDP-*N*-acetylglucosamine enolpyruvyl transferase
  catalysis, **3**, 251
  mechanisms, **1**, 577
  structure, **1**, 593
  substrates, **1**, 595
UDP-*N*-acetylglucosamine-2-epimerase, coding, **3**,
  17
UDP-*N*-acetyl-D-glucosamine:β-D-galactosyl-1,4-*N*-
  acetyl-D-glucosamine β-1,3-acetyl-D-
  glucosaminyltransferase *see* *N*-
  acetyllactosaminide β-1,3-*N*-
  acetylglucosaminyltransferase
UDP-*N*-acetyl-D-glucosamine:β-D-galactosyl-1,4-*N*-
  acetyl-D-glucosaminide β-1,6-*N*-acetyl-D-
  glucosaminyltransferase *see* *N*-
  acetyllactosaminide β-1,6-*N*-
  acetylglucosaminyltransferase(s)
UDP-*N*-acetylglucosamine:Gal β1-3GalNAc-R (GlcNAc
  to GalNAc) β1,6-GlcNAc-transferase *see* β-1,3-
  galactosyl-*O*-glycosyl-glycoprotein β-1,6-*N*-
  acetylglucosaminyltransferase
UDP-*N*-acetylglucosamine:Galβ1-3 (R1-6) GalNAc-R
  (GlcNAc to Gal) β1,3-GlcNAc-transferase *see*
  β-1,3-galactosyl-*O*-glycosyl-glycoprotein β-1,3-*N*-
  acetylglucosaminyltransferase
UDP-*N*-acetylglucosamine:GlcNAcβ1-3 Gal (GlcNAc to
  Gal) β1,6-GlcNAc-transferase (I β6-GlcNAc-T)
  roles, in *O*-glycan synthesis, **3**, 78
  transfection, **3**, 78
UDP-*N*-acetylglucosamine:GlcNAcβ1-3GalNAc-R
  (GlcNAc to GalNAc) β1,6-GlcNAc-transferase
  see acetylgalactosaminyl-*O*-glycosyl-glycoprotein
  β-1,6-*N*-acetylglucosaminyltransferase
UDP-*N*-acetyl-D-glucosamine:glycoprotein (*N*-acetyl-D-
  glucosamine to α-D-mannosyl-1,3-(R₁)-β-D-
  mannosyl-R₂) β-1,2-*N*-acetyl-D-

glucosaminyltransferase *see* α-1,3-mannosyl-
  glycoprotein β-1,2-*N*-
  acetylglucosaminyltransferase
UDP-*N*-acetyl-D-glucosamine:glycoprotein (*N*-acetyl-D-
  glucosamine to α-D-mannosyl-1,6-(R₁)-β-D-
  mannosyl-R₂) β-1,2-*N*-acetyl-D-
  glucosaminyltransferase *see* α-1,6-mannosyl-
  glycoprotein β-1,2-*N*-
  acetylglucosaminyltransferase
UDP-*N*-acetyl-D-glucosamine:*O*-glycosyl-glycoprotein
  (*N*-acetyl-D-glucosamine to *N*-acetyl-D-
  galactosaminyl-R) β-1,3-*N*-acetyl-D-
  glucosaminyltransferase *see* acetylgalactosaminyl-*O*-
  glycosyl-glycoprotein β-1,3-*N*-
  acetylglucosaminyltransferase
UDP-*N*-acetylglucosamine:Manα1-3R[GlcNAc to
  Manα1-3] β-1,2-*N*-acetylglucosaminyltransferase,
  activity, **3**, 42
UDP-*N*-acetylglucosamine:Manα1-3R[GlcNAc to
  Manα1-3] β-1,2-*N*-
  acetylglucosaminyltransferase I (GnT I) *see* α-1,3-
  mannosyl-glycoprotein β-1,2-*N*-
  acetylglucosaminyltransferase
UDP-*N*-acetylglucosamine:Manα1-6R[GlcNAc to
  Manα1-6] β-1,2-*N*-acetylglucosaminyltransferase II
  (GnT II) *see* α-1,6-mannosyl-glycoprotein β-1,2-
  N-acetylglucosaminyltransferase
UDP-*N*-acetylglucosamine:R₁-Manα1-6R[GlcNAcβ1-
  2Manα1-3]Manβ1-4R₂[GlcNAc to Manβ1-4] β-
  1,4-*N*-acetylglucosaminyltransferase III (GnT III)
  see β-1,4-mannosyl-glycoprotein β-1,4-*N*-
  acetylglucosaminyltransferase
UDP-*N*-acetylglucosamine:R₁-Manα1-3R₂[GlcNAc to
  Manα1-3] β-1,4-*N*-
  acetylglucosaminyltransferase IV (GnT IV) *see* α-
  1,3-mannosyl-glycoprotein β-1,4-*N*-
  acetylglucosaminyltransferase
UDP-*N*-acetylglucosamine:R₁-Manα1-6R₂[GlcNAc to
  Manα1-6] β-1,6-*N*-
  acetylglucosaminyltransferase V (GnT V) *see* α-
  1,3(6)-mannosyl-glycoprotein β-1,6-*N*-
  acetylglucosaminyltransferase
UDP-*N*-acetylglucosamine:R₁(R₂)Manα1-6R₃[GlcNAc
  to Manα1-6] β-1,4-*N*-acetylglucosaminyltransferase
  VI, occurrence, **3**, 55
UDP-*N*-acetylmuramate–alanine ligase, purification, **3**,
  259
UDP-*N*-acetylmuramic acid, biosynthesis, **3**, 251, 252
UDP-*N*-acetylmuramic acid-pentapeptide, assembly, **3**,
  258
UDP-*N*-acetylmuramic acid-tripeptide, assembly, **3**, 258
UDP-*N*-acetylmuramoyl-L-alanine, activity, **3**, 255
UDP-*N*-acetylmuramoyl-L-alanyl-γ-D-glutamyl-*m*-
  diaminopimelate, catalysis, **3**, 261
UDP-*N*-acetylmuramoyl-L-alanyl-D-glutamyl-*m*-
  diaminopimelate-D-alanyl-D-alanine, assembly, **3**,
  258
UDP-*N*-acetylmuramoyl-L-alanyl-γ-D-glutamyl-*m*-
  diaminopimelate-D-alanyl-D-alanine, biosynthesis, **3**,
  261
UDP-*N*-acetyl*enol*pyruvylglucosamine, biosynthesis, **1**,
  593
UDP-D-apiose
  biosynthesis, **3**, 508
  purification, **3**, 508

UDPapiose/UDPxylose synthase
  catalysis, **3**, 508
  purification, **3**, 508
UDP-L-arabinose, biosynthesis, **3**, 507
UDParabinose 4-epimerase
  catalysis, **3**, 507
  localization, **3**, 509
UDPase, localization, **3**, 510
UDP-2,3-diacyl-GlcN, biosynthesis, **3**, 220
UDP-Gal *see* uridinediphosphogalactose (UDPGal)
UDP-GalA *see* UDP-D-galacturonic acid (UDP-GalA)
UDP-D-galactopyranose furanomutase(s) *see*
      UDPgalactopyranose mutase(s)
UDPgalactopyranose mutase(s), encoding, **3**, 209
UDPgalactose *see* uridinediphosphogalactose (UDPGal)
UDPgalactose: *N*-acetyl-*β*-D-glucosaminylglycopeptide
      β-1,4-galactosyltransferase *see* *β*-*N*-
      acetylglucosaminylglycopeptide *β*-1,4-
      galactosyltransferase
UDPgalactose 4-epimerase *see* UDPglucose 4-epimerase
UDPgalactose: Gal-R α1,3-Gal-transferase
  gene, encoding, **3**, 81
  structure, **3**, 81
UDPgalactose: GlcNAc-R *β*-1,3-galactosyltransferase
      (*β*3-GalT)
  activity, **3**, 78
  characterization, **3**, 78
UDPgalactose: GlcNAc-R *β*-1,4-galactosyltransferase
      (*β*4-Gal-T) *see* *β*-*N*-acetylglucosaminylglycopeptide
      β-1,4-galactosyltransferase
UDPgalactose-glucose galactosyltransferase *see* lactose
      synthase
UDPgalactose: D-glucose 4-*β*-D-galactotransferase *see*
      lactose synthase
UDPgalactose: glycoprotein-*N*-acetyl-D-galactosamine 3-
      β-D-galactosyltransferase *see* glycoprotein-*N*-
      acetylgalactosamine
UDPgalactose-glycoprotein galactosyltransferase *see* *β*-
      N-acetylglucosaminylglycopeptide *β*-1,4-
      galactosyltransferase
UDP-D-galacturonate: 1,4-α-poly-D-galacturonate 4-α-D-
      galacturonosyltransferase *see*
      polygalacturonate 4-α-galacturonosyltransferase
UDP-D-galacturonic acid (UDP-GalA)
  biosynthesis, **3**, 507
  as substrate, **3**, 512
UDP-Glc *see* uridinediphosphoglucose (UDPGlc)
UDP-GlcA *see* UDP-D-glucuronic acid (UDP-GlcA)
UDP-GlcNAc *see* UDP-*N*-acetylglucosamine
UDPGlc PPase *see* UTP-glucose-1-phosphate
      uridylyltransferase
UDPglucose *see* uridinediphosphoglucose (UDPGlc)
UDPglucose: glycogenin glucosyltransferase *see*
      glycogenin glucosyltransferase
UDPglucose: coniferyl-alcohol 4'-*β*-D-
      glucosyltransferase *see* coniferyl-alcohol
      glucosyltransferase
UDPglucose 4,6-dehydratase, catalysis, **3**, 508
UDPglucose 6-dehydrogenase
  catalysis, **3**, 506
  cDNA cloning, **3**, 506
  occurrence, **3**, 506
  purification, **3**, 506
UDPglucose: DNA *β*-D-glucosyltransferase *see* DNA *β*-
      glucosyltransferase
UDPglucose 4-epimerase
  catalysis, **3**, 508
  genetic encoding, **3**, 508
  occurrence, **3**, 508
  reactions, **1**, 154
UDPglucose: flavonol 3-*O*-D-glucosyltransferase *see*
      flavonol 3-*O*-glucosyltransferase (FGT)
UDPglucose: α-D-galactose-1-phosphate
      uridylyltransferase *see* UDPglucose-hexose-1-
      phosphate uridylyltransferase
UDPglucose: 1,3-*β*-D-glucan glucosyltransferase *see* 1,3-
      β-glucan synthase
UDPglucose: glucosyltransferase(s)
  biosynthesis, **1**, 890
  catalysis, **3**, 683
  α-hydroxynitrile glucosylation, **1**, 887
  occurrence, **1**, 890
  purification, **3**, 683
  roles, in monolignol partitioning, **3**, 683
  x-ray crystal structure, **3**, 684
UDPglucose: glycogen 4-α-D-glucosyltransferase *see*
      glycogen(starch) synthase
UDPglucose: glycoprotein glucosyltransferase,
      substrates, **3**, 31
UDPglucose-hexose-1-phosphate uridylyltransferase,
      activity, **6**, 105
UDPglucose pyrophosphorylase *see* UTP-glucose-1-
      phosphate uridylyltransferase
UDPglucose: thiohydroximate *S*-*β*-D-glucosyltransferase
      see thiohydroximate *β*-D-glucosyltransferase
UDPglucuronate carboxylase, localization, **3**, 509
UDPglucuronate 4-epimerase
  catalysis, **3**, 507
  purification, **3**, 507
UDPglucuronate *β*-D-glucuronosyltransferase (acceptor-
      unspecific) *see* glucuronosyltransferase(s)
UDP-D-glucuronic acid carboxylase
  purification, **3**, 507
  regulatory mechanisms, **3**, 507
UDP-D-glucuronic acid (UDP-GlcA)
  biosynthesis, **3**, 506
  decarboxylation, **3**, 507
UDP-3-*O*-(*R*-3-hydroxymyristoyl)-*N*-acetylglucosamine-
      deacetylase, encoding, **3**, 220
UDP-3-*O*-(*R*-3-hydroxymyristoyl)-glucosamine-*N*-
      acyltransferase, encoding, **3**, 221
UDPmannose, pyrophosphorolysis, **3**, 478
UDP-MurNAc *see* UDP-*N*-acetylmuramic acid
UDPrhamnose, isolation, **3**, 515
UDP-L-rhamnose, biosynthesis, **3**, 508
UDP synthase(s) *see* di-*trans*,poly-*cis*-
      decaprenyl*cis*transferase(s)
UDP-Xyl *see* UDP-D-xylose (UDP-Xyl)
UDP-D-xylose (UDP-Xyl)
  biosynthesis, **3**, 507
  inhibitory activity, **3**, 506
  pyrophosphorolysis, **3**, 478
  transporters, **3**, 510
UDP-D-xylose: zeatin *O*-*β*-D-xylosyltransferase(s) *see*
      zeatin *O*-*β*-D-xylosyltransferase(s)
UGA
  evolution, **4**, 357
  roles
    multiple, **4**, 369
    selenocysteine codon, **4**, 354, 357
    suppressor codon, **4**, 369
    termination codon, **4**, 357
    in universal genetic code, **4**, 357
ugandensidial *see* cinnamodial
ultrafast, DNA synthesis, **7**, 120
ultraviolet melting curves, **6**, 23, 73
ultraviolet patterning, in flowers, **8**, 160
ultraviolet radiation
  DNA, thymine dimer formation, **5**, 372
  DNA damage, **7**, 561
  lesions, **5**, 372
Umbelliferae, coumarins, **1**, 628
umbelliferone
  biosynthesis, **1**, 19, 626
  insect sequestration, **8**, 152
  prenylation, **1**, 628

Umbellularia californica, terpene, **8**, 173
umi botaru see Vargula hilgendorfii
Uncaria gambir, strictosidine studies, **4**, 117
undecanal, occurrence, **8**, 212
undecane
    biosynthesis, **8**, 204
    occurrence, **8**, 214
1-undecane, occurrence, **1**, 91
undecanoate, ω-cycloheptyl-, occurrence, **1**, 75
undecanoic acid, ω-cyclohexyl-, occurrence, **1**, 71
2-undecanol, occurrence, **8**, 214
2-undecanone, occurrence, **8**, 214
3-undecanone, occurrence, **8**, 214
undecaprenol kinase(s), identification, **3**, 262, 281
undecaprenyl diphosphate, 2′-deoxy-3′-keto-,
    biosynthesis, **5**, 195
undecaprenyl diphosphate synthase(s) *see di-trans,poly-
    cis*-decaprenyl*cis*transferase(s)
undecaprenyl diphosphate (UDP)
    complexation, **3**, 280
    dephosphorylation, **3**, 262
undecaprenyl-diphospho-Mur*N*Ac-
        pentapeptide:UDPGlc*N*Ac Glc*N*Ac
        transferase (translocase II)
    catalysis, **3**, 264
    inhibition, **3**, 280
undecaprenyl phosphate
    biosynthesis, **3**, 262
    complexation, **3**, 281
    as lipid carrier, **3**, 288
undecaprenyl pyrophosphate *see* undecaprenyl
    diphosphate (UDP)
2,4,6,8-undecatetraene, (2*E*,4*E*,6*E*,8*E*)-5,7-diethyl-3-
    methyl-, biosynthesis, **8**, 240
2,4,6,8-undecatetraene, (2*E*,4*E*,6*E*)-7-ethyl-3,5-
    dimethyl-, biosynthesis, **8**, 240
2,4,6,8-undecatetraene, (2*E*,4*E*,6*E*,8*E*)-3,5,7-trimethyl-,
    biosynthesis, **8**, 240
3,5,7-undecatriene, (3*E*,5*E*,7*E*)-5-ethyl-7-methyl-,
    biosynthesis, **8**, 240
(*E*)-5-undecenoic acid, occurrence, **8**, 214
(*E*)-10-undecenoic acid, 11-formyl-, detection, **1**, 89
(*Z*)-5-undecenoic acid, occurrence, **8**, 214
(*Z*)-9-undecenoic acid, 11-formyl-, detection, **1**, 89
uniconazole, as brassinosteroid biosynthesis inhibitor, **8**,
    107
unoprostone, applications, in ophthalmology, **1**, 196
3′ untranslated regions
    extended, **6**, 210
    roles, in deadenylation, **6**, 208
    sequencing, **6**, 206
5′ untranslated regions, hairpin insertion, **6**, 208
UPF genes
    *UPF*1, products, **6**, 211
    *UPF*2, products, **6**, 211
    *UPF*3, products, **6**, 211
upland cotton *see Gossypium hirsutum*
UPP *see* undecaprenyl diphosphate (UDP)
uracil, biosynthesis, **5**, 87, 391
uracil, 5-bromo-, in oligodeoxynucleotides, **7**, 316
uracil, (*E*)-5-(2-bromovinyl)-, in dodecanucleotides, **7**,
    317
uracil, 5-*t*-butyl-, ultraviolet irradiation, **5**, 391
uracil, carboranyl-, localization, **7**, 319
uracil, 5-fluoro-
    from, 5-fluorocytosine, **5**, 93
    in oligodeoxynucleotides, **7**, 316
uracil, 5-iodo-, in oligodeoxynucleotides, **7**, 316
uracil, C5-propynyl-, in oligodeoxynucleotides, **7**, 317
uracil, thiazole-, in oligodeoxynucleotides, **7**, 318
uracil, *C*⁵-thiazole-, in oligodeoxynucleotides, **7**, 318
uracil-5-yl, DNA damage induction, **7**, 413
uracil-5-yl radicals, synthesis, **7**, 413

Urania fulgens
    2,5-dihydroxymethyl-3,4-dihydroxypyrrolidine, **3**, 134
        accumulation, **3**, 141
urauchimycins, occurrence, **8**, 589
urdamycin, biosynthesis, **1**, 483
urd genes
    cloning, **1**, 483
    sequencing, **1**, 483
urea, diphenyl-, structure, **8**, 61
urea, *N*-ethyl-*N*-nitroso- (ENU), applications, RNA
        structural probes, **6**, 64, 67, 68
urea, hydroxy (HU), in ribonucleotide reductase studies,
        5, 180
urea, *N*-methyl-*N*-nitroso- (MNU)
    decomposition, **7**, 520
    DNA methylation by, **7**, 520
    tumor studies, **1**, 783
urea, phenyl-, cytokinin activity, **8**, 57
urea(s)
    antisense oligonucleotide linkages, **7**, 301
    soluble, **5**, 350
uric acid
    biosynthesis, **5**, 86
    overproduction, **5**, 80
uridine, biosynthesis, **6**, 98
uridine, 5-azido-, applications, photoaffinity labeling, **6**,
        229
uridine, 5-bromo-
    applications, photoaffinity labeling, **6**, 229
    complexation, **6**, 91
    photocross-linking, **6**, 228
uridine, 2′-chloro-2′-deoxy-6′-nitrohomo-, in
        ribonucleotide reductase studies, **5**, 193
uridine, 3,4-dihydro-, cytidine deaminase inhibition, **5**,
        90, 91
uridine, 5,6-dihydro-, deamination, **5**, 88
uridine, 5-fluoro-3,4-dihydro-, binding, **5**, 90
uridine, 5-imidazole, modified, **6**, 138
uridine, 5-imidazolylmethyl-, incorporation, **6**, 225
uridine, 5-iodo-
    applications, photoaffinity labels, **6**, 229
    photocross-linking, **6**, 228
uridine, 5-methylcarboxymethyl- (mcmU), occurrence, **4**,
        360
uridine, 5-pyridylmethyl-, incorporation, **6**, 225
uridine, 5-pyridylmethylcarboxamide-, modified, **6**, 139
uridine, 3,4,5,6-tetrahydro-, cytidine deaminase
        inhibition, **5**, 88, 89
uridine, 5-thiocyanato-, synthesis, **6**, 91
uridine-*N*-acetylglucosamine, as substrate, **5**, 66
uridine 5′-diphosphate-*N*-acetylglucosamine-3-
        enolpyruvyltransferase, in fosfomycin activation, **5**,
        66
uridinediphosphogalactose (UDPGal)
    biosynthesis, **3**, 508
    as glycosyl donor, **3**, 203
    K_m, **3**, 515
    pyrophosphorolysis, **3**, 478
    roles
        in galactomannan biosynthesis, **3**, 521
        in proteoglycan biosynthesis, **3**, 173
    transporters, **3**, 510
uridinediphospho-α-D-glucose, structure, **5**, 280
uridinediphosphoglucose (UDPGlc)
    biosynthesis, **3**, 468, 506
    in cellulose biosynthesis, **3**, 581
    discovery, **3**, 444
    in glycogen synthesis, **3**, 468
    as glycosyl donor, **3**, 203
    inhibitory activity, **3**, 478
    occurrence, **3**, 478
    reactions, with gallic acid, **3**, 805
    roles, in pectin biosynthesis, **3**, 505

starch synthase activity, **3**, 445
uridine-2′-*O*-methylribose, 5-methylcarboxymethyl-
　　(mcmUm), occurrence, **4**, 360
uridine phosphoramidites
　insertion, into oligomers, **7**, 229
　synthesis, **7**, 202
uridine phosphoramidites, 5-(thioalkyl)-, synthesis, **7**, 203
uridine triphosphate, 5-methyleneamino-, photocross-
　　linking studies, **6**, 229
uridine triphosphate, 5-sulfhydryl-, incorporation, **6**, 230
uridine-5′-triphosphate, 5-[(4-azidophenacyl)thio]-,
　　synthesis, **7**, 216
uridylyl transferase *see* UDPglucose-hexose-1-phosphate
　　uridylyltransferase
urishi (lacquer), laccase, **3**, 711
urishiol oxidase *see* laccase(s)
urochordamines, isolation, **8**, 440
Urochordata
　β-carbolines, **8**, 525
　eudistomins, **8**, 525
　larval settlement induction, **8**, 440
　metabolites, **8**, 529
　oxylipins, **1**, 243
　symbiosis, **8**, 428
　vanadium accumulation, **8**, 521
　see also Lissoclinum spp.; *Trididemnum solidum*
uronic acid, D-galactosyl-
　occurrence, **3**, 503
　structure, **3**, 499
uronic acids, in *Serratia marcescens*, **3**, 190
Urophora stylata, 4-methyl-3,5-hexadienoic acid, **8**, 236
uroporphyrinogen-I, biosynthesis, **4**, 72
uroporphyrinogen-III
　from, 5-aminolevulinic acid, **4**, 72
　as starting material, for heme, **4**, 90
uroporphyrinogen-III carboxy-lyase(s) *see*
　　uroporphyrinogen decarboxylase(s)
uroporphyrinogen-III methyltransferase, roles, **4**, 143
uroporphyrinogen-III synthase(s)
　catalysis, **4**, 87

genetic encoding, **4**, 88
inhibition, studies, **4**, 89
as intermediates, **4**, 90
spiro-mechanism, **4**, 89
properties, **4**, 87
rearrangement, **4**, 88
roles, **4**, 143
substrate specificity, **4**, 88
uroporphyrinogen decarboxylase(s)
　acetic acid side chain recognition, **4**, 92
　active sites, **4**, 94
　mechanisms, **4**, 91, 92
　occurrence, **4**, 91
　properties, **4**, 91
　stereochemical analysis, **4**, 92
　substrate specificity, **4**, 90
　x-ray crystal structure, **4**, 92
ursolic acid, as allelopathic agent, **8**, 173
urushiol, DNA damage, **7**, 536
usaramine, structure, **4**, 33
USF, peptide, conformation, **7**, 482
Ustilago hordei, phenylalanine ammonia-lyase, **3**, 632
UT-1 cells, α-mannosidase studies, **3**, 154
uterus, prostaglandin-induced contraction–relaxation
　　effects, **1**, 160, 174
Utethesia bella, 3,3-dimethylacryloylcholine, **8**, 353
UTP-glucose-1-phosphate uridylyltransferase
　catalysis, **3**, 446
　inhibition, **3**, 478
　occurrence, **3**, 203, 478
　overexpression, **3**, 486
　properties, **3**, 478
　reaction mechanisms, **3**, 478
UTP:RNA uridylyltransferase *see* RNA
　　uridylyltransferase
3′ UTRs *see* 3′ untranslated regions
5′ UTRs *see* 5′ untranslated regions
UV melting curves *see* ultraviolet melting curves
UvrABC endonuclease, catalysis, **5**, 392
UV radiation *see* ultraviolet radiation

V

cis-vaccenic acid, cyclopropanation, **1**, 64
vaccinia viruses, phosphatases, **5**, 140
vacuoles, δ-(L-α-aminoadipyl)-L-cysteinyl-D-valine in, **4**, 244
VAI-1
  biosynthesis, **8**, 394
  mode of action, **8**, 394
  occurrence, **8**, 393
  properties, **8**, 393
  structure, **8**, 393
  see also homoserine lactone, *N*-(3-oxohexanoyl)-;
    Vibrio fischeri, autoinducers
VAI-2
  isolation, **8**, 395
  structure, **8**, 395
  see also L-homoserine lactone, *N*-octanoyl-; *Vibrio*
    fischeri, autoinducers
valeric acid, 4-amino-5-hydroxy-, as transaminating
    substrate, **4**, 70
valeric acid, 4,5-diamino-, biosynthesis, **4**, 70
valeric acid, (3*R*)-3,5-dihydroxy-3-methyl- *see* mevalonic
    acid
valeryl-CoA, as substrate, **4**, 262
valine
  activation, **4**, 209
  binding, **7**, 638
  biosynthesis, **2**, 376, **4**, 165
  as cyanogenic glycoside precursor, **1**, 885
  labeling studies, **8**, 240
D-valine, δ-(L-α-aminoadipyl)-L-cysteinyl- (ACV)
  assays, **4**, 246
  biosynthesis, **4**, 167, 321
  as intermediate, **4**, 243
  localization, **4**, 244
  peptide bonds, **4**, 226
  structure, **4**, 178
D-valine, L-cysteinyl-
  cyclization, **4**, 243
  isolation, **4**, 250
D-valine, *N*-hydroxy-, replacement, **4**, 253
D-valine, phenylacetylcysteinyl- (PCV), in penicillin
    biosynthesis, **4**, 252
L-valine
  biosynthesis, **2**, 54, 58
  condensation, **1**, 840
  in cyclosporin studies, **1**, 538
  epimerization, **4**, 249
  in penicillin biosynthesis, **4**, 162, 165
valinomycin, bioactive properties, **4**, 197
Vallesia glabra
  alkaloid biosynthesis studies, **4**, 118
  strictosidine studies, **4**, 117
valoneic acid, linkages, **3**, 801
Valonia spp., celluloses, NMR spectra, **3**, 565
Valonia macrophysa
  celluloses, **3**, 587
    NMR spectra, **3**, 561
    Raman spectra, **3**, 558
  microfibrils, **3**, 566
Valonia ventricosa
  celluloses, **3**, 536
    cellulose I, **3**, 552
    Raman spectra, **3**, 558
valyl-AMP, hydrolysis, **7**, 628
VAM association *see* vesicular arbuscular mycorrhizal
    (VAM) association

vanadate, phosphatase inhibition, **5**, 151, 158
vanadium, accumulation, by ascidians, **8**, 521
vanadocytes, in ascidians, **8**, 523
vancomycin
  and antibiotic resistance, **3**, 5, 272, **4**, 197
  biological activity, **3**, 327
  complexation, **3**, 272
  effects, on Gram-positive bacteria, **3**, 281
vancomycin-resistant *Enterococcus* (VRE) *see*
    Enterococcus spp., vancomycin resistance
vancosamine, in vancomycin, **3**, 327
van der Waals
  interactions, in intercalation, **7**, 432
  ranges, **7**, 560
van genes, occurrence, **3**, 272
vanillic acid, occurrence, **3**, 696
vanillin
  biosynthesis, **3**, 622
  occurrence, **3**, 696
Van proteins
  VanR, phosphorylation, **3**, 272
  VanS, **3**, 272
van't Hoff enthalpy
  determination, **7**, 21
    from transition curves, **7**, 23
varacin
  antifungal activity, **8**, 541
  applications
    antibiotics, **7**, 527
    antineoplastic agents, **7**, 527
  chirality, **8**, 541
  cytotoxicity, **8**, 541
  occurrence, **8**, 541
  possible DNA damage induction, **7**, 527
  reactions, with thiol, **7**, 527
var genes, *varA*, occurrence, **4**, 292
Vargula hilgendorfii
  bioluminescence, **8**, 444
  luciferin, **8**, 444
variacin
  isolation, **4**, 279
  var genes, **4**, 292
variamycin, D-cymarose, **3**, 313
variola viruses, phosphatases, **5**, 140
D-variose *see* D-cymarose
Varkud satellite RNA
  2′-hydroxyl group attack, **6**, 151
  structure, secondary, **6**, 154
vasicine, 7-hydroxy- *see* vasicinol
vasicinol, occurrence, **8**, 342
vasicinone, occurrence, **8**, 342
vasopressin, effects, on phosphorylation, **3**, 485
VB *see* virginiae butanolides
VB A *see* virginiae butanolide A (VB A)
VB receptor A *see* Vbr proteins, VbrA
Vbr proteins, VbrA, **8**, 387
VBS *see* versicolorin B synthase (VBS)
vbs genes, identification, **1**, 462
vegetative storage proteins (VSPs), accumulation, **1**, 129
venoms
  insects, **8**, 354
    ants, **8**, 356
    bees, **8**, 355
    cockroaches, **8**, 360
    Hemiptera, **8**, 360

Lepidoptera, **8**, 360
wasps, **8**, 356
vepaol, isolation, **8**, 327
vepridimerines, occurrence, **1**, 383
Vepris louisii, vepridimerines, **1**, 383
ver-1 genes, cloning, **1**, 462
veracevine, toxicity, **8**, 349
veracevine, 3,5-dimethoxybenzoyl esters, insecticidal
activity, **8**, 349
verA genes *see stc* genes, *stcU*
(+)-veraguensin, demethylation, **1**, 692
veratric acid, biosynthesis, **3**, 624, 703
veratridine, toxicity, **8**, 349
Veratrum album
ceveratrine alkaloids, **8**, 362
protoveratrine A, **8**, 349
Veratrum sabadilla, sabadilla, **8**, 349
Verbascum sinaiticum, sinaiticin, **1**, 685
Verbascum thapsus, rotenone, **8**, 341
Verbena spp., naringenin 3-dioxygenase, **1**, 725
Verbena hybrida
chalcone synthase, **1**, 734
flavonoid 3′,5′-hydroxylase, **1**, 735
verbenalin, occurrence, **8**, 307
Verbena officinalis, verbenalin, **8**, 307
verbenene, biosynthesis, **8**, 224
(4*S*)-*cis*-verbenol, biosynthesis, **8**, 224
(4*S*)-*trans*-verbenol, biosynthesis, **8**, 224
cis-verbenol
as aggregation pheromone, **8**, 224
occurrence, **8**, 224
trans-verbenol
as aggregation pheromone, **8**, 224
biosynthesis, **2**, 101
occurrence, **8**, 224
verbenone
biosynthesis, **8**, 224
inhibitory activity, **8**, 224
verB genes *see stc* genes, *stcS*
vermelone, structure, **1**, 414
vermisporin, biosynthesis, **1**, 370
vernamycin B, rRNA protection, **6**, 200
vernodalin, antifeedant activity, **8**, 308
vernodalol, antifeedant activity, **8**, 308
Verongia aerophoba, chemical defense, **8**, 468
versican
binding, **3**, 164
isoforms, **3**, 164
localization, **3**, 164
promoters, **3**, 167
versicolorin A
determination, **1**, 446
folding patterns, **1**, 448
as starting material, for demethylsterigmatocystin, **1**,
462
synthesis, **1**, 457
versicolorin B, synthesis, **1**, 457
versicolorin B synthase (VBS), purification, **1**, 458, 463
versicolorins, DNA damage induction, **7**, 511
versicolorone, 6,8-di-*O*-methylhydroxy-, synthesis, **1**, 455
versicolorone, 1′-hydroxy-
isolation, **1**, 454
synthesis, **1**, 454, 457
versiconal acetate
characterization, **1**, 457
folding patterns, **1**, 448
synthesis, **1**, 455, 456
versiol, biosynthesis, **1**, 370
vertebrates, platelet-activating factor, **1**, 286
1*S*-verticillene, biosynthesis, **2**, 221
Verticillium dahliae, melanin, **1**, 427
very long-chain-acyl-CoA dehydrogenase (VLCADH),
residues, **1**, 51

very low-density lipoproteins (VLDL), components, **5**, 94
vesicular arbuscular mycorrhizal (VAM) association, of
fungi, **1**, 780
vesicular stomatitis virus, glycoprotein, **4**, 14
Vespa spp., pheromones, **8**, 200
Vespa crabro
hydroxytryptamine, **8**, 356
2-methyl-3-buten-2-ol, **8**, 200, 220
3-methyl-2-butenyl 3-methyl-2-butenoate, **8**, 220
Vespa orientalis, (*R*)-5-hexadecanolide, **8**, 217
Vespula spp., venom, **8**, 354
Vespula maculifrons, attractants, **8**, 224
vestitol
interconvertibility, **1**, 786
occurrence, **1**, 774, 775
vestitone, biosynthesis, **1**, 795
(3*R*)-vestitone, biosynthesis, **1**, 797
vestitone reductase, catalysis, **1**, 797
vetispiradiene
biosynthesis, **2**, 183
from, farnesyl diphosphate, **2**, 183
vetispiradiene synthase(s)
biosynthesis, **2**, 183
genes
cloning, **2**, 183, **5**, 330
occurrence, **2**, 210
occurrence, **2**, 183
presteady-state kinetics, **2**, 194
VFCDP *see* 2′-deoxycytidine 5′-diphosphate, 2′-
vinylfluoro- (VFCDP)
VHR, isotope effects, **5**, 151
Vibrio spp.
brominated diphenyl ethers, **8**, 588
trisindoline, **8**, 588
Vibrio cholerae
core oligosaccharides, structure, **3**, 195
exo-α-sialidase, **5**, 294
lipopolysaccharides, **3**, 195
O-forms
Inaba, **3**, 195
Ogawa, **3**, 195
Vibrio fischeri
luciferase, **8**, 393
as symbionts, **8**, 392
see also VAI-1; VAI-2
Vibrio gazogenes, magnesidin A, **8**, 598
Vibrio harveyi
bioluminescence, possible regulatory systems, **8**, 397
as symbionts, **8**, 392
thioesterases, **5**, 130
see also HAI-1; HAI-2
vicenin-2, as oviposition stimulant, **8**, 156
Vicia spp., nodulation, **1**, 337
Vicia faba
4-hydroxy-2*E*-nonenal, **1**, 234
jasmonic acid, **1**, 234
jasmonic acid conjugates, **1**, 128
12-oxophytodienoic acid, **1**, 234
proanthocyanidins, **3**, 791
UDPglucose 4-epimerase, **3**, 508
victomycin, applications, antibiotics, **7**, 539
victorin C, phytotoxicity, **8**, 180
Vigna angularis, ligballinol, **1**, 672
Vigna radiata
trans-cinnamate 4-monooxygenase, **3**, 637
gallic acid biosynthesis, **3**, 804
gene expression, **8**, 97
α-mannosidase II, **3**, 26
medicarpin, **1**, 809
shikimate kinase, **1**, 592
villanovanes, occurrence, **2**, 238
Villanova titicaensis, villanovanes, **2**, 238
Vinca alkaloids, and P-glycoprotein, **8**, 613

vincaleucoblastine, applications, in chemotherapy, **4**, 110
Vinca minor, hybridization, **4**, 134
vincaminoridine, biosynthesis, **4**, 121
vincanidine, biosynthesis, **4**, 121
Vinca rosea
  reclassification, **4**, 113
  trans-zeatin, **8**, 69
  see also Catharanthus roseus
vincine, biosynthesis, **4**, 121
vincoside
  as starting material, for monoterpenoid indole
      alkaloids, **4**, 113
  structure, **4**, 116
vincoside, 5-carboxy-, indole alkaloid biosynthesis
    studies, **4**, 118
3β-vincoside, as starting material, for ajmalicine, **4**, 116
vincoside lactam, differentiation, **4**, 116
vincristine, applications, in chemotherapy, **4**, 110
vindoline, biosynthesis, **4**, 48, 121
L-vinelose
  occurrence, **3**, 312
  tracer studies, **3**, 342
vinyl ether, allyl (AVE), rearrangement, **5**, 348
vinyl ether, 6-methoxyallyl, Claisen rearrangement, **5**, 350
Violales, metabolites, **1**, 70
violaxanthin
  as starting material, for abscisic acid, **8**, 72
  stereochemistry, **8**, 72
viosamine, occurrence, **3**, 186
virenamides
  occurrence, **8**, 538
  structure, **8**, 538
virenomycin, D-virenose, **3**, 321
D-virenose, occurrence, **3**, 312, 321
L-virenose
  localization, **3**, 323
  occurrence, **3**, 312
virescene, biosynthesis, **2**, 226
virescenol B, NMR spectra, **2**, 226
virginiae butanolide A (VB A)
  biological activity, **1**, 139
  biosynthesis, **1**, 140
  biosynthetic pathways, **1**, 147
    in vitro studies, **1**, 144
    in vivo studies, **1**, 142
  carbon atoms, **1**, 141
  structure, **1**, 141
virginiae butanolides
  biosynthesis, **8**, 385
  isolation, **1**, 140
  receptor proteins, **8**, 387
  structure, **8**, 384
virginiamycin
  occurrence, **1**, 140
  synthesis, **8**, 384
    suppression, **8**, 389
  see also pristinamycin I
viridiofungins, as farnesyl-diphosphate
    farnesyltransferase inhibitors, **2**, 257
viridogrisein, biosynthesis, **1**, 546
viridopentaoses, D-quinovose, **3**, 313
viroids
  ASBV group, **6**, 171
    structural models, **6**, 172
  biochemistry, **6**, **169–187**
  cDNA clones, **6**, 172, 174
  central conserved regions, **6**, 184

  characterization, **6**, 169
  classification, **6**, 171
  diseases, **6**, 169
  evolution, via RNA rearrangement, **6**, 175
  hammerhead self-cleavage structure, **6**, 180
    determination, **6**, 181
  historical background, **6**, 171
  hosts, determinants, **6**, 186
  isolation, **6**, 171
  occurrence, **6**, 169
  pathogenicity, **6**, 185
  PSTV group, **6**, 171
    central conserved regions, **6**, 184
    domain model, **6**, 172
    sequencing, **6**, 175
  purification, **6**, 172
  replication, **6**, 171
    localization, **6**, 178
    rolling circle mechanism, **6**, 177, 183, 236
    via host enzymes, **6**, 178
  RNA synthesis, **6**, 178
  sequencing, **6**, 172, 174
    purine and pyrimidine tracts, **6**, 177
  size, **6**, 171
  topology, **7**, 344
virulence, bacterial, role of lipopolysaccharides in, **3**, 180
virulence factors
  in *Erwinia carotovora*, **8**, 398
  in *Pseudomonas aeruginosa*, **8**, 398
viruses, assembly, inhibition, **3**, 31
virusoids *see* satellite RNAs
Viscaceae, lignins, **3**, 700
viscometric titration, **7**, 433
Viscum spp., lignins, **3**, 700
Viscum album
  guaiacyl–syringyl lignins, **3**, 702
  lignins, **3**, 702
vitamin A *see* retinol
vitamin B$_1$ *see* thiamine
vitamin B$_6$ *see* pyridoxine
vitamin B$_{12}$ *see* cobalamin, cyano-
vitamin K, isopentenyl diphosphate units, **2**, 376
vitamins, definition, **8**, 2
vitexin, biosynthesis, **1**, 738
Vitis vinifera
  caffeoyl-CoA *O*-methyltransferase, **3**, 671
  geranyl diphosphate synthases, **2**, 122
  phenylalanine ammonia-lyase, **3**, 659
vittatol
  biosynthesis, **8**, 232
  structure, **8**, 233, 234
VLCADH *see* very long-chain-acyl-CoA dehydrogenase
    (VLCADH)
VLDL *see* very low-density lipoproteins (VLDL)
Voacanga africana, alkaloid biosynthesis studies, **4**, 118
volatiles
  occurrence, **8**, 421
  in plant defense, **1**, 132
volkensin
  antifeedant activity, **8**, 330
  occurrence, **8**, 330
vomifoliol, metabolism, **8**, 88
VRE *see Enterococcus* spp., vancomycin resistance
VSG protein
  occurrence, **3**, 295
  release, **3**, 296
VSPs *see* vegetative storage proteins (VSPs)
VS RNA *see* Varkud satellite RNA

W

waa genes
  waaM
    encoding, **3**, 223
    multicopy suppressors, **3**, 223
Waa proteins, WaaA, **3**, 222
wA gene
  cloning, **1**, 417
  encoding, **1**, 14
  expression, **1**, 419
  occurrence, **1**, 417
  open reading frame, **1**, 417
wailupemycins, occurrence, **8**, 597
Waksman, Selman Abraham (1888–1973), antibiotic
    studies, **4**, 200
warburganal
  antifeedant activity, **8**, 308
  occurrence, **8**, 308
Warburgia salutaris
  cinnamodial, **8**, 308
  muzigadial, **8**, 308
  warburganal, **8**, 308
Warburgia stuhlmannii, polygodial, **8**, 308
wasps
  geranyl geranoate, **8**, 223
  venoms, **8**, 356
  see also Bembix spp.; Mutillidae; parasitic wasps;
    Trichogramma nubilale; *Vespa* spp.
Watasenia scintillan, bioluminescence, **8**, 454
water, zinc-activated, **5**, 77
water beetles
  pheromones, **8**, 230
  see also Dineutes spp.; Dytiscidae; *Gyrinus* spp.
watercress *see Nasturtium officinale*
Watson, James Dewey (1928–), DNA structure studies,
    7, 81
Watson–Crick base pairs
  alignments
    DNA structure, **7**, 58, 66
    RNA structures, **6**, 14
  canonical, formation, **7**, 20
  nearest-neighbor model, **6**, 29
  noncanonical, **6**, 52
  ribozyme ligases, **6**, 142
  in RNA structures, **6**, 28, 116
  in rRNA structures, **6**, 190
Watson–Crick duplexes *see* Watson–Crick base pairs
Watson–Crick nucleotides, editing, **6**, 103
wax moths
  pheromones, **8**, 212
  see also Aphomia sociella; *Galleria melonella*
waxy locus
  DNA sequence, **3**, 454
  in granule-bound starch synthases, **3**, 454
  as starch synthase structural gene, **3**, 455
waxy mutants, **3**, 445
  amylose, lack of, **3**, 454
Waxy proteins
  expression, **3**, 455
  occurrence, **3**, 455, 457
wbp genes, roles, **3**, 209
weevils
  pheromones, **8**, 245
  see also boll weevils; *Callosobruchus chinensis*;
    Cosmopolites sordidus; pecan weevil; *Rhynchophorus*
    spp.; *Sitona lineatus*; *Sitophilus* spp.

welwitindolinone A isonitrile, structure, **8**, 610
western corn rootworm *see Diabrotica vergifera*
western hemlock *see Tsuga heterophylla*
western pine beetle *see Dendroctonus brevicomis*
western red cedar *see Thuja plicata*
wheat
  waxy locus, DNA sequence, **3**, 454
  xylem cell studies, **3**, 681
  see also Triticum aestivum
wheat endosperm
  adenosinediphosphoglucose, **3**, 463
  amyloplasts, **3**, 464
  soluble starch synthases, **3**, 455
whiE genes
  deletion analysis, **1**, 487
  encoding, **1**, 480
  homologues, **1**, 480
whirligig beetles
  gyrinidione, **8**, 234
  gyrinidone, **8**, 234
white birch *see Betula papyrifera*
white lupin
  geranylgeranyl diphosphate synthase, gene cloning, **2**,
    87
  geranyl*trans*transferase, **2**, 82
white peach scale, pheromones, **8**, 234
white pine sawfly *see Neodiprion pinetum*
wighteone, antifungal activity, **8**, 183
Wikstroemia foetida, (+)-wikstromol, **1**, 701
Wikstroemia indica, (+)-arctigenin, **1**, 645
wikstrol A, biosynthesis, **3**, 780
wikstrol B, biosynthesis, **3**, 780
wikstrols, biochemistry, **3**, 780
(+)-wikstromol
  antineoplastic activity, **1**, 701
  occurrence, **1**, 647
wild cotton *see Gossypium hirsutum*
wildfire disease, tobacco, **8**, 59
wild parsnip *see Pastinaca sativa*
wilfordine alkaloids, insect toxicity, **8**, 344
wilforine
  occurrence, **8**, 344
  structure, **8**, 312
winter squash *see Cucurbita maxima*
WIPK *see* wound-induced protein kinase (WIPK)
wobble–wobble receptor interactions, **6**, 162
wood
  celluloses, NMR spectra, **3**, 530
  delignification, **3**, 725
  lignans, **1**, 696
  see also heartwood; softwood
woodinine, occurrence, **8**, 527
wood roach *see Cryptocercus punctulatus*
Woodwardia orientalis, lignans, **1**, 647
Woodwardia prolifera, lignans, **1**, 647
World Wide Web (WWW), glycosyltransferase resource,
    3, 38
wound-induced protein kinase (WIPK), occurrence, **1**,
    134
wounding, in plants, **1**, 133
wounds
  effects on ethylene biosynthesis, **8**, 96
  responses, and xylogenesis, **3**, 609
  signal transduction, role of jasmonic acid-related
    compounds in, **8**, 119

X

xan genes, *xanA*, **3**, 207

xanthenyl, as protecting groups, **7**, 126

xanthen-9-yl, 9-*p*-methoxyphenyl- (Mox), applications, 5′-hydroxyl group protection, **6**, 83, **7**, 126

xanthen-9-yl, 9(4-octadecyloxyphenyl)-, applications, 5′-hydroxyl group protection, **7**, 127

xanthen-9-yl, 9-phenyl- (Px), applications, 5′-hydroxyl group protection, **6**, 83, **7**, 126

xanthine
oxidation, **5**, 86
as universal base, **7**, 326

xanthine oxidase, functions, **5**, 86

xanthine:oxygen oxidoreductase *see* xanthine oxidase

xanthipungolide, biosynthesis, **1**, 375

Xanthium pungens
pungiolide A, **1**, 375
xanthipungolide, **1**, 375

Xanthobacter autotrophicus
carboxypeptidase II, **5**, 112
haloalkane dehalogenases, **5**, 112, 130, 403
thioesterases, **5**, 130

Xanthomonas campestris
gene organization, **3**, 208
lipopolysaccharide biosynthesis, **3**, 207

xanthones
biosynthesis, **1**, 434, 759
as intermediates, **1**, 16
properties, **1**, 759

xanthophyll cycle, mechanism, **2**, 327

xanthophylls
in bacteria, **2**, 327, 333
biosynthesis, **2**, 344
evolutionary conservation, **2**, 348
in carotenoid biosynthesis, **2**, 343
use of term, **2**, 323

xanthosine, synthesis, **7**, 260

xanthotoxin
accumulation, **1**, 634
levels, seasonal, **1**, 625
occurrence, **8**, 338
as oviposition stimulant, **8**, 156
phototoxicity, **8**, 338
as seed toxin, **8**, 168
toxicity, **8**, 141

xanthotoxin, 5-hydroxy-, as intermediate, **1**, 633

xanthoxin
as intermediate, **8**, 72
as starting material, for abscisic acid, **8**, 86

xanthoxin acid, metabolism, **8**, 86

xanthoxol, biosynthesis, **1**, 633

xanthumin, antifeedant activity, **8**, 308

xenobiotic esters, detoxification, **5**, 113

xenobiotics
metabolism, **5**, 58
vacuolar uptake, **1**, 809

xenognosin A, haustoria-inducing activity, **8**, 175

xenognosin B, haustoria-inducing activity, **8**, 175

Xenopus spp.
α-mannosidase II, **3**, 26
Sec tRNA[Ser]Sec, **4**, 355
enrichment, **4**, 362
gene, **4**, 361

Xenopus laevis
ADARs, **6**, 101, 103
12-hydroxyeicosatetraenoic acid, **1**, 248

leukotriene B$_4$, **1**, 248
(6-4) photoproduct lyase, **5**, 386

(±)-xenovenine, biosynthesis, **4**, 31

xerantholide, antifeedant activity, **8**, 308

xestocyclamines
occurrence, **8**, 560
structure, **8**, 560

Xestospongia spp.
manzamines, **8**, 558
xestocyclamines, **8**, 560

Xestospongia exigua, xestospongins, **8**, 560

Xestospongia ingens
ingenamines, **8**, 560
madangamine A, **8**, 566

xestospongins
biogenetic path, **8**, 560
occurrence, **8**, 560

Xlhbox2B mRNA, degradation, **6**, 213

x-ray crystallography
in carbohydrate studies, **3**, 1
DNA structure determination, **7**, 55
RNA structure determination, **6**, 4, **49–61**
tRNA structure determination, **6**, 52

*XRN*1 genes
deletion, **6**, 212
encoding, **6**, 209
exonuclease, **6**, 207
*xrn*1Δ strains, **6**, 209
decapped transcripts, **6**, 209
nonsense codons, **6**, 210

XRN1 proteins, homologues, **6**, 212

xuxuarine Aα, occurrence, **1**, 377

xylanase *see* xylan endo-1,3-β-xylosidase

xylan endo-1,3-β-xylosidase, occurrence, **5**, 290, 292

xylans
biosynthesis, regulatory mechanisms, **3**, 607
cellulose studies, **3**, 585
characterization, **3**, 601
occurrence, **3**, 601

xylan synthases
activity, **3**, 605
characterization, **3**, 605

xylem cells
cell walls, **3**, 733
deposition, **3**, 681
formation, **3**, 688
lignins, **3**, 620

Xylocleptes spp.
ipsdienol, **8**, 223
ipsenol, **8**, 223

Xylocopa hirsutissima, *cis*-2-methylhexanolide, **8**, 240

xylogalacturonans, occurrence, **3**, 499

xylogenesis
studies, **3**, 607
and wounding responses, **3**, 609

xyloglucan endotransglycosidase, roles, **8**, 30

xyloglucan endotransglycosylases, effects, on xyloglucans, **3**, 609

xyloglucan glucosyltransferase, occurrence, **3**, 604

xyloglucans
biosynthesis, **3**, 8
regulatory mechanisms, **3**, 607
cellulose studies, **3**, 585
characterization, **3**, 600
effects of auxins on, **8**, 30

occurrence, **3**, 604
xyloglucan synthases, characterization, **3**, 604
Xylopia aethiopica, lignanamides, **1**, 673, 695
Xylopia aromatica, asimicin, **8**, 305
(1→4)-D-xylopyranose, *O*-(5-*O*-feruloyl-α-L-
    arabinofuranosyl)-(1→3)-*O*-β-D-xylopyranosyl-,
    isolation, **3**, 697
D-xylopyranose, 2-*O*-[5-*O*-(*trans*-feruloyl)-β-L-
    arabinofuranosyl]-, occurrence, **3**, 697
xylose, 2-*O*-methyl, biosynthesis, **3**, 519
D-xylose
    fermentation, **3**, 393
    oxidation, **3**, 429
D-xylose-5-phosphate
    biosynthesis, **3**, 392

K_m, **3**, 416
xylosyltransferase(s)
    characterization, **3**, 604, 605, 517
    inhibition, **3**, 515
    occurrence, **1**, 738
    roles
        in glycosaminoglycan biosynthesis, **3**, 169
        in pectin biosynthesis, **3**, 511
Xylotrechus spp.
    (*S*)-2-hydroxy-3-octanone, **8**, 211
    (2*S*,3*S*)-2,3-octanediol, **8**, 211
D-xylulose-5-phosphate D-glyceraldehyde-3-phosphate-
    lyase (phosphate-acetylating) *see*
    phosphoketolase

Y

YA-56, applications, antibiotics, **7**, 539
YAC *see* yeast artificial chromosome (YAC)
(+)-yamataimine, biosynthesis, **4**, 33
yams *see Dioscorea* spp.
(+)-yangambin, **1**, 692
  occurrence, **1**, 661
yangambin A, antiinflammatory activity, **1**, 704
(−)-yatein, antifeedant activity, **1**, 694
Y-Box sequences, in human squalene synthase, **2**, 261
yDPM1 gene, roles, mammalian class E deficiency
    restoration, **4**, 307
yeast artificial chromosome (YAC), DNA, in human
    squalene synthase gene mapping, **2**, 262
yeast enzymes
  sequences, **2**, 250
  steady-state kinetic analysis, **2**, 256
yeast(s)
  AMP deaminase, **5**, 81
  B-related factor, **4**, 367
  cell wall elicitors, **1**, 124
  chitinases, **1**, 149
  coproporphyrinogen oxidase, **4**, 95
  cyclomaltodextrin glucanotransferases, **5**, 299
  cytidine deaminase, **5**, 87
  dolichyl-phosphate *β*-D-mannosyltransferase, genes, **4**,
    307
  farnesyl-diphosphate farnesyltransferase,
    hydrophobicity, **5**, 339
  fatty acid synthases, **1**, 30
    molecular weights, **1**, 32
  geranyl*trans*transferase, **2**, 82
  α-glucosidase I, **3**, 18
  α-glucosidase II, **3**, 19
  α-glucosidases, **5**, 298
  glycosylphosphatidylinositol biosynthesis, **3**, **295–309**
  GPI anchors, biosynthesis, **3**, 306
  hydroxymethylglutaryl-CoA reductase
    isozymes, **2**, 27
    regulatory mechanisms, **2**, 38, 39
  α1,2-mannosidase inhibitors, **3**, 25
  α1,2-mannosidases, **3**, 21
    disulfide bonds, **3**, 22
    as inverting glycosidase, **3**, 22
    *MNS*1 gene, **3**, 21
    sulfhydryl group, **3**, 22
    x-ray crystal structure, **3**, 22
  methylotrophic, glycoproteins, **3**, 22
  mRNA
    oligo(A) tails, **6**, 207
    poly(A) tail shortening, **6**, 206, 207
  mutants, **3**, 20
  platelet-activating factor, **1**, 286
  porphobilinogen synthase, x-ray crystal structure, **4**, 76
  prepro-α-factor, **3**, 31
  protein farnesyltransferase, **5**, 332
  tannin degradation, **3**, 819
  transcriptional pulse-chase studies, **6**, 206, 210
  transcription factor IIIC, **4**, 367
  tRNA^Asp, **6**, 72, 222
  tRNA^Phe, **6**, 65, 69

  tRNA^Val, **6**, 228
  UTP-glucose-1-phosphate uridylyltransferase, **3**, 478
    see also Rhodotorula glutinis; *Saccharomyces cerevisiae*
yellow compound (YC)
  isolation, **8**, 450
  structure, **8**, 451
yellowjackets
  acetamides, **8**, 220
  see also Vespula maculifrons
yellow scale *see Aonidiella citrina*
yellow-spotted longhorn beetle *see Psacothea hilaris*
Yersinia spp., lipopolysaccharides, **3**, 192
Yersinia enterocolitica
  core, biosynthesis, **3**, 228
  6-deoxy-*β*-L-altropyranose, **3**, 192
  4,6-dideoxy-4-formamido-α-D-mannose, **3**, 192
  lipopolysaccharides, **3**, 192
  Yop51, **5**, 156
Yersinia pestis
  lipopolysaccharides, **3**, 192
  phosphatases, **5**, 140
Yersinia pseudotuberculosis
  ascarylose, **3**, 192
  CDP-D-glucose-4,6-dehydratase, **3**, 334
  6-deoxy-D-*manno*-heptose, **3**, 192
  deoxysugar biosynthesis, genetics, **3**, 345
  lipopolysaccharides, **3**, 192
  yersiniose, **3**, 192
yersiniose A, occurrence, **3**, 192, 312, 322
yersiniose B, occurrence, **3**, 312, 322
yessotoxins (YTX)
  absolute configuration, via modified Mosher's method,
    8, 500
  NMR spectra, **8**, 499
  occurrence, **8**, 499
  structure, ladder-shape polycyclic skeleton, **8**, 499
yohimbine
  biosynthesis, **4**, 46
  pharmacological activity, **4**, 110
Yop51
  catalysis, **5**, 156
  isotope effects, **5**, 151
  mutagenesis studies, **5**, 156
  occurrence, **5**, 156
  structure, **5**, 156
YOYO
  DNA binding, fluorescence enhancement, **7**, 448
  from thiazole orange, binding, **7**, 448
ypaoamide
  occurrence, **8**, 608
  structure, **8**, 608
YTX *see* yessotoxins (YTX)
yuehchukene
  biomimetic synthesis, **1**, 369
  biosynthesis, **1**, 369
YW3548, as GPI anchor biosynthesis inhibitor, **3**, 304
YWA1
  biosynthesis, via Claisen-type condensation, **1**, 420
  feeding studies, **1**, 420
  structure, **1**, 419

Z

zafirlukast, applications, antiasthmatic agents, **1**, 197
zanthophylline, occurrence, **8**, 344
Zanthoxylum spp., toxicity, **8**, 344
Zanthoxylum ailanthoides, lignans, **1**, 651
Zanthoxylum clava-herculis
  echinacein, **8**, 303
  herculin, **8**, 303
Zanthoxylum macrophylla, fagaramide, **8**, 304
Zanthoxylum monophyllum, zanthophylline, **8**, 344
Zanthoxylum nitidum
  chelerythrine, **7**, 601
  isofagaridine, **7**, 601
  nitidine, **7**, 601
Zanthoxylum piperitum, echinacein, **8**, 303
Zanthoxylum procerum
  culantraramine, **1**, 369
  culantraraminol, **1**, 369
Zanthoxylum senegalense
  fagaramide, **8**, 304
  fagaridine, **7**, 601
  fagaronine chloride, **7**, 182
Zanthoxylum zanthoxyloides see Zanthoxylum senegalense
λ-ZAP, as expression vector, **7**, 649
zaragozic acid A, as farnesyl-diphosphate
  farnesyltransferase inhibitor, **2**, 255
zaragozic acid C
  inhibition, **2**, 251
  as inhibitor, **2**, 255
zaragozic acids
  as farnesyl-diphosphate farnesyltransferase inhibitors,
    2, 256
  structure, **2**, 257
  studies, reviews, **2**, 255
z-DNA *see* DNA structure, Z-form
β-zeacarotene, as substrate, **2**, 341
Zea mays
  allen oxide pathway, **1**, 232
  amine oxidases, **3**, 721
  auxin binding protein 1, **8**, 32
  CCR genes, **3**, 676
  cinnamoyl-CoA:NADP(H)-dependent
    oxidoreductases, **3**, 6245
  O-(5-*O*-feruloyl-α-L-arabinofuranosyl)-(1→3)-*O*-β-D-
    xylopyranosyl-(1→4)-D-xylopyranose, **3**, 697
  flavanone 4-reductase, **1**, 728
  flavonol 3-*O*-glucosyltransferase, **1**, 731
  fucosyltransferases, **3**, 516
  gibberellin deficiency, **8**, 45
  glutathione transferases, **1**, 742
  13*S*-hydroperoxyoctadecatrienoic acid, **1**, 230
  p-hydroxybenzaldehyde, **3**, 696
  hydroxycinnamic acid *O*-methyltransferase, **3**, 673
  5-hydroxyferulic acid, **3**, 642
  3β-hydroxylase, **2**, 236
  oxylipins, **1**, 229
  3-phosphoshikimate 1-carboxyvinyltransferase, **1**, 593
  plant–herbivore–predator interactions, **8**, 152
  syringaldehyde, **3**, 696
  vanillin, **3**, 696
  waxy locus, **3**, 454
zeatin, discovery, **8**, 57
zeatin, dihydro-, structure, **8**, 61
zeatin, 9-β-D-glucopyranosyl-, synthesis, **8**, 62
zeatin, *O*-β-D-glucopyranosyl-, synthesis, **8**, 62
zeatin, 7-β-D-glucosyl-, synthesis, **8**, 62

zeatin, *O*-glucosyl-, isolation, **8**, 61
(*E*)-zeatin, structure, **8**, 61
trans-zeatin
  occurrence, **8**, 69
  and sex determination, **8**, 71
(*Z*)-zeatin, structure, **8**, 61
(*Z*)-zeatin, 9-ribosyl-, occurrence, **8**, 61
(*E*)-zeatin-2′-deoxyriboside, isolation, **8**, 61
zeatin *O*-glucosyltransferases, purification, **8**, 71
cis-trans zeatin isomerase, purification, **8**, 69
zeatin reductase, purification, **8**, 71
zeatin *O*-β-D-xylosyl transferase(s), purification, **8**, 71
zeaxanthin
  accumulation, **2**, 347
  binding proteins, **2**, 325
  biosynthesis, **2**, 332
    in *Escherichia coli*, **2**, 337
  occurrence, **8**, 469
  as substrate, **2**, 344
zeaxanthin diglucoside, biosynthesis, **2**, 332, 344
zeaxanthin glucosides
  biosynthesis, **2**, 333
  fatty acid esters, **2**, 336
zeaxanthin glucosyltransferases, characterization, **2**, 344
zeaxanthin monoglucoside, biosynthesis, **2**, 332, 344
Z-form (DNA) *see* DNA structure, Z-form
zinc
  in adenosine deaminase, **5**, 77
  in aldol reaction, **3**, 369
  enzyme-bound, **5**, 79
zinc cluster motifs, in fungal regulatory proteins, **1**, 467
zinc finger(s), **7**, 484
  applications, **7**, 669
  double, **7**, 484
  encoding, **4**, 368
  research, **7**, 671
  single, **7**, 484
  triple, **7**, 485
zinc–histidine bridges, formation, **5**, 74
zinc–oxygen bonds, in adenosine deaminase, **5**, 77
zinc proteases, structure, **5**, 79
Zingiber cassumunar, cassumunarin A, **1**, 385
zingiberene, effects, on herbivores, **8**, 142
Zinnia spp., peroxidases, **3**, 718
Zinnia elegans
  anabasine, **8**, 347
  caffeoyl-CoA *O*-methyltransferase, **3**, 671, 672
  trans-cinnamate 4-monooxygenase, localization, **3**, 669
  cinnamyl-alcohol dehydrogenases, **3**, 676
  hydroxycinnamic acid *O*-methyltransferase, **3**, 672
  hydroxycinnamyl *O*-methyltransferases, **3**, 646
  5-hydroxyferulic acid, **3**, 671
  lignins, **3**, 708
  malonyltransferases, **1**, 741
  phenylalanine ammonia-lyase, localization, **3**, 662
  xylogenesis studies, **3**, 607
zipper model, in RNA structural transition analyses, **6**,
  27
zomepirac, prostaglandin-endoperoxide synthase
  inhibition, **5**, 252
zonarol, isolation, **8**, 460
zonarone, isolation, **8**, 460
zooecdysteroids, occurrence, **8**, 279, 280, 283
Zoogloea ramigera, acetyl-CoA *C*-acetyltransferases, **2**,
  18

zooxanthellae
  isolation, **1**, 240
  zooxanthellatoxins, **8**, 614
zooxanthellatoxin-A
  Ca^{2+}-influx, **8**, 615
  structure, **8**, 614
  vasoconstrictive activity, **8**, 614
zooxanthellatoxins, occurrence, **8**, 614
zorbamycin, applications, antibiotics, **7**, 539
zorbonamycins, applications, antibiotics, **7**, 539
zucchini isogenes, expression, **8**, 97
zygadenine, 3-acetyl-, insect sequestration, **8**, 152
Zygaena spp., cyanogenic glucoside biosynthesis, **1**, 883
Zygaena trifolii, cyanogenic glycosides, **8**, 154
Zygaenidae

attractants, **8**, 224
  pheromones, **8**, 209, 215
Zymomonas mobilis
  2-dehydro-3-deoxyphosphogluconate aldolase, **3**, 422
  glucose metabolism, **2**, 50
  hopanoids, **2**, 51, 56
    biosynthesis, **2**, 48
  hopene cyclase, purification, **2**, 309
  hopene cyclase gene, **2**, 313
    cloning, **2**, 313
  isopentenyl diphosphate, **2**, 46
  isoprenoids, biosynthesis, **2**, 377
zymosan, opsonized, effects, on acetyl-CoA:1-
    alkylglycerophosphocholine acetyltransferase,
    1, 294

WITHDRAWAL